Practice, Engage, and Assess

- **Enhanced eText**—The Pearson eText gives students access to their textbook anytime, anywhere. In addition to note-taking, highlighting, and bookmarking, the Pearson eText offers interactive and sharing features. Students actively read and learn, through embedded and auto-graded practice, real-time data-graphs, animations, author videos, and more. Instructors can share comments or highlights, and students can add their own, for a tight community of learners in any class.

- **Practice**—Algorithmically generated homework and study plan exercises with instant feedback ensure varied and productive practice, helping students improve their understanding and prepare for quizzes and tests. Draw-graph exercises encourage students to practice the language of economics.

- **Learning Resources**—Personalized learning aids such as Help Me Solve This problem walkthroughs, Teach Me explanations of the underlying concept, and figure Animations provide on-demand help when students need it most.

- **Adaptive Study Plan**—Monitors each student's progress and offers a continuously personalized study plan based on his or her own homework, quiz, and test results. Includes unlimited practice exercises and the opportunity to prove mastery through quizzes based on recommended learning objectives.

- **Dynamic Study Modules**—With a focus on key topics, these modules work by continuously assessing student performance and activity in real time and, using data and analytics, provide personalized content to reinforce concepts that target each student's particular strengths and weaknesses.

- **Digital Interactives**—Focused on a single core topic and organized in progressive levels, each interactive immerses students in an assignable and auto-graded activity. Digital Interactives are also engaging lecture tools for traditional, online, and hybrid courses, many incorporating real-time data, data displays, and analysis tools for rich classroom discussions.

with MyEconLab®

- **Learning Catalytics**—Generates classroom discussion, guides lectures, and promotes peer-to-peer learning with real-time analytics. Students can use any device to interact in the classroom, engage with content, and even draw and share graphs.

- **Real-Time Data Analysis Exercises**—Using current macro data to help students understand the impact of changes in economic variables, Real-Time Data Analysis Exercises communicate directly with the Federal Reserve Bank of St. Louis's FRED® site and update as new data are available.

- **Current News Exercises**—Every week, current microeconomic and macroeconomic news stories, with accompanying exercises, are posted to MyEconLab. Assignable and auto-graded, these multi-part exercises ask students to recognize and apply economic concepts to real-world events.

- **Experiments**—Flexible, easy-to-assign, auto-graded, and available in Single and Multiplayer versions, Experiments in MyEconLab make learning fun and engaging.

- **Reporting Dashboard**—View, analyze, and report learning outcomes clearly and easily. Available via the Gradebook and fully mobile-ready, the Reporting Dashboard presents student performance data at the class, section, and program levels in an accessible, visual manner.

- **LMS Integration**—Link from any LMS platform to access assignments, rosters, and resources, and synchronize MyLab grades with your LMS gradebook. For students, new direct, single sign-on provides access to all the personalized learning MyLab resources that make studying more efficient and effective.

- **Mobile Ready**—Students and instructors can access multimedia resources and complete assessments right at their fingertips, on any mobile device.

PEARSON

Macroeconomics

Sixth Edition

R. Glenn Hubbard
Columbia University

Anthony Patrick O'Brien
Lehigh University

PEARSON

Boston   Columbus   Indianapolis   New York   San Francisco
Amsterdam   Cape Town   Dubai   London   Madrid   Milan   Munich   Paris   Montréal   Toronto
Delhi   Mexico City   São Paulo   Sydney   Hong Kong   Seoul   Singapore   Taipei   Tokyo

Vice President, Business Publishing: Donna Battista
Executive Editor: David Alexander
Executive Development Editor: Lena Buonanno
Editorial Assistant: Michelle Zeng
Vice President, Product Marketing: Maggie Moylan
Director of Marketing, Digital Services and Products: Jeanette Koskinas
Senior Product Marketing Manager: Alison Haskins
Field Marketing Manager: Ramona Elmer
Product Marketing Assistant: Jessica Quazza
Team Lead, Program Management: Ashley Santora
Program Manager: Lindsey Sloan
Team Lead, Project Management: Jeff Holcomb
Project Manager: Carla Thompson
Operations Specialist: Carol Melville
Creative Director: Blair Brown
Art Director: Jon Boylan
Vice President, Director of Digital Strategy and Assessment: Paul Gentile

Manager of Learning Applications: Paul DeLuca
Digital Editor: Denise Clinton
Director, Digital Studio: Sacha Laustsen
Digital Studio Manager: Diane Lombardo
Digital Studio Project Manager: Melissa Honig
Digital Studio Project Manager: Robin Lazrus
Digital Content Team Lead: Noel Lotz
Digital Content Project Lead: Courtney Kamauf
Full-Service Project Management and Composition: Cenveo® Publisher Services
Interior Designer: Cenveo Publisher Services
Cover Designer: Jon Boylan
Cover Art: © Oleksiy Mark/Fotolia
Printer/Binder: RR Donnelley / Willard
Cover Printer: Phoenix Color / Hagerstown

Library of Congress Cataloging-in-Publication Data

Names: Hubbard, R. Glenn, author. | O'Brien, Anthony Patrick, author.
Title: Macroeconomics / R. Glenn Hubbard, Columbia University, Anthony Patrick O'Brien, Lehigh University.
Description: Sixth Edition. | Boston : Pearson Education, [2017] | Includes index.
Identifiers: LCCN 2015044127 | ISBN 9780134106229 | ISBN 0134106229
Subjects: LCSH: Macroeconomics.
Classification: LCC HB172.5 .H86 2017 | DDC 339—dc23
LC record available at http://lccn.loc.gov/2015044127

10 9 8 7 6 5 4 3 2 1

ISBN 10: 0-13-410622-9
ISBN 13: 978-0-13-410622-9

For Constance, Raph, and Will
—*R. Glenn Hubbard*

For Cindy, Matthew, Andrew, and Daniel
—*Anthony Patrick O'Brien*

Glenn Hubbard, policymaker, professor, and researcher.
R. Glenn Hubbard is the dean and Russell L. Carson Professor of Finance and Economics in the Graduate School of Business at Columbia University and professor of economics in Columbia's Faculty of Arts and Sciences. He is also a research associate of the National Bureau of Economic Research and a director of Automatic Data Processing, Black Rock Closed-End Funds, and MetLife. He received his Ph.D. in economics from Harvard University in 1983. From 2001 to 2003, he served as chairman of the White House Council of Economic Advisers and chairman of the OECD Economic Policy Committee, and from 1991 to 1993, he was deputy assistant secretary of the U.S. Treasury Department. He currently serves as co-chair of the nonpartisan Committee on Capital Markets Regulation. Hubbard's fields of specialization are public economics, financial markets and institutions, corporate finance, macroeconomics, industrial organization, and public policy. He is the author of more than 100 articles in leading journals, including *American Economic Review, Brookings Papers on Economic Activity, Journal of Finance, Journal of Financial Economics, Journal of Money, Credit, and Banking, Journal of Political Economy, Journal of Public Economics, Quarterly Journal of Economics, RAND Journal of Economics,* and *Review of Economics and Statistics*. His research has been supported by grants from the National Science Foundation, the National Bureau of Economic Research, and numerous private foundations.

Tony O'Brien, award-winning professor and researcher.
Anthony Patrick O'Brien is a professor of economics at Lehigh University. He received his Ph.D. from the University of California, Berkeley, in 1987. He has taught principles of economics for more than 20 years, in both large sections and small honors classes. He received the Lehigh University Award for Distinguished Teaching. He was formerly the director of the Diamond Center for Economic Education and was named a Dana Foundation Faculty Fellow and Lehigh Class of 1961 Professor of Economics. He has been a visiting professor at the University of California, Santa Barbara, and the Graduate School of Industrial Administration at Carnegie Mellon University. O'Brien's research has dealt with issues such as the evolution of the U.S. automobile industry, the sources of U.S. economic competitiveness, the development of U.S. trade policy, the causes of the Great Depression, and the causes of black–white income differences. His research has been published in leading journals, including *American Economic Review, Quarterly Journal of Economics, Journal of Money, Credit, and Banking, Industrial Relations, Journal of Economic History,* and *Explorations in Economic History*. His research has been supported by grants from government agencies and private foundations.

BRIEF CONTENTS

CONTENTS

*These end-of-chapter resource materials repeat in all chapters. Select chapters also include Real-Time Data Exercises.

The following chart helps you organize your syllabus based on your teaching preferences and objectives:

Core	Optional	Policy
Chapter 1: Economics: Foundations and Models	**Chapter 1 Appendix:** Using Graphs and Formulas	
Chapter 2: Trade-offs, Comparative Advantage, and the Market System		
Chapter 3: Where Prices Come From: The Interaction of Demand and Supply		
	Chapter 4 Appendix: Quantitative Demand and Supply Analysis	**Chapter 4:** Economic Efficiency, Government Price Setting, and Taxes
		Chapter 5: The Economics of Health Care
	Chapter 6: Firms, the Stock Market, and Corporate Governance	
	Chapter 6 Appendix: Tools to Analyze Firms' Financial Information	
Chapter 7: Comparative Advantage and the Gains from International Trade		
Chapter 8: GDP: Measuring Total Production and Income		
Chapter 9: Unemployment and Inflation		
Chapter 10: Economic Growth, the Financial System, and Business Cycles		
Chapter 11: Long-Run Economic Growth: Sources and Policies		

Core	Optional	Policy
	Chapter 12: Aggregate Expenditure and Output in the Short Run	
	Chapter 12 Appendix: The Algebra of Macroeconomic Equilibrium	
Chapter 13: Aggregate Demand and Aggregate Supply Analysis		
	Chapter 13 Appendix: Macroeconomic Schools of Thought	
Chapter 14: Money, Banks, and the Federal Reserve System		
		Chapter 15: Monetary Policy
	Chapter 16 Appendix: A Closer Look at the Multiplier	**Chapter 16:** Fiscal Policy
		Chapter 17: Inflation, Unemployment, and Federal Reserve Policy
	Chapter 18: Macroeconomics in an Open Economy	
	Chapter 19: The International Financial System	
	Chapter 19 Appendix: The Gold Standard and the Bretton Woods System	

Our approach in this new edition remains what it was in the first edition, published more than 10 years ago: To provide students and instructors with an economics text that delivers complete economics coverage with many real-world business examples. Our goal has been to teach economics in a "widget-free" way by using real-world business and policy examples. We are gratified by the enthusiastic response from students and instructors who have used the first five editions of this book and who have made it one of the best-selling economics textbooks on the market.

Much has happened in the U.S. and world economies since we prepared the previous edition. We have incorporated many of these developments in the new real-world examples in this edition and also in the digital resources.

Digital Resources

While our basic approach of placing applications in the forefront of the discussion remains the same, this new edition has been thoroughly revised. We have a wide array of digital resources for students and instructors to use with either the eText version of the book or the MyEconLab supplement to the printed text. Below is an overview. Please see Preface pages 13–15 for more details.

Digital Features Located in MyEconLab

MyEconLab is a unique online course management, testing, and tutorial resource. It is included with the eText version of the book or as a supplement to the print book. Students and instructors will find the following online resources to accompany the sixth edition:

- **Videos.** There are 58 *Making the Connection* features in the book that provide real-world reinforcement of key concepts. Each feature is accompanied by a two- or three-minute video of the author explaining the key point of that *Making the Connection*. Related assessment is included with each video, so students can test their understanding. The goal of these videos is to summarize key content and bring the applications to life. In our experience, many students benefit from this type of online learning and assessment.

- **Concept Checks.** Each section of each learning objective concludes with an online Concept Check that contains one or two multiple-choice, true/false, or fill-in questions. These checks act as "speed bumps" that encourage students to stop and check their understanding of fundamental terms and concepts before moving on to the next section. The goal of this digital resource is to help students assess their progress on a section-by-section basis, so they can be better prepared for homework, quizzes, and exams.

- **Animations.** Graphs are the backbone of introductory economics, but many students struggle to understand and work with them. Each of the 166 numbered figures in the text has a supporting animated version online. The goal of this digital resource is to help students understand shifts in curves, movements along curves, and changes in equilibrium values. Having an animated version of a graph helps students who have difficulty interpreting the static version in the printed text. Graded practice exercises are included with the animations. In our experience, many students benefit from this type of online learning.

- **Interactive *Solved Problems*.** Many students have difficulty applying economic concepts to solving problems. The goal of this digital resource is to help students overcome this hurdle by giving them a model of how to solve an economic problem by breaking it down step by step. Each of the 35 *Solved Problems* in the printed text is accompanied by a similar problem online, so students can have more practice and build their problem-solving skills. These interactive tutorials help students learn to think like economists and apply basic problem-solving skills to homework, quizzes, and exams. The goal is for students to build skills they can use to analyze real-world economic issues they hear and read about in the news. Each *Solved Problem* in MyEconLab and the digital eText also includes at least one additional graded practice exercise for students.

- **Graphs Updated with Real-Time Data from FRED.** Approximately 25 graphs are continuously updated online with the latest available data from FRED (Federal Reserve Economic Data), which is a comprehensive, up-to-date data set maintained by the Federal Reserve Bank of St. Louis. Students can display a pop-up graph that shows new data plotted in the graph. The goal of this digital feature is to help students work with data and to see including new data affects graphs.
- **Interactive Problems and Exercises Updated with Real-Time Data from FRED.** The end-of-chapter problems in select chapters include *Real-Time Data Exercises* that use the latest data from FRED. The book contains more than 50 of these exercises. The goals of this digital feature are to help students become familiar with this key data source, learn how to locate data, and develop skills in interpreting data.

New to the Sixth Edition Chapters

- All companies in the chapter openers have been either replaced with new companies or updated with current information.
- Chapters 1–4 include new *An Inside Look* news articles and analyses to help students apply economic thinking to current events and policy debates. Additional news articles and analyses are updated weekly on MyEconLab.
- There are 9 new *Making the Connection* features to help students tie economic concepts to current events and policy issues.
- There are 9 new *Solved Problems*. This feature helps students break down and answer economic problems step by step.

New Chapter Openers, *Making the Connections*, *Solved Problems*, and *Inside Looks*

Here are the new or heavily revised chapter-opening business cases and accompanying *Inside Look* news articles. The business or issue introduced in the chapter opener is revisited within the chapter in either a *Making the Connection* or a *Solved Problem*. The following are new to this edition. Please see the detailed table of contents for the list of features for all chapters.

Chapter 1, "Economics: Foundations and Models," opens with a new discussion of whether smart devices will revolutionize health care and closes with *An Inside Look* newspaper article and analysis of how Google is adding to its growing list of technological innovations by partnering with Swiss pharmaceutical company Novartis to develop smart contact lenses to help patients manage diabetes. New *Solved Problem 1.1* examines how managers at medical technology firm OraSure use marginal analysis to make an advertising decision. A new *Making the Connection* examines how opportunity costs can help us understand why many students have stopped attending college football games.

Chapter 2, "Trade-offs, Comparative Advantage, and the Market System," opens with a new discussion of the manufacturing decisions managers at Tesla Motors face and closes with *An Inside Look* that discusses the resources Apple has assembled to meet an aggressive plan to develop and produce an electric vehicle as early as 2020. A new *Making the Connection* uses Sir Arthur Conan Doyle's legendary character Sherlock Holmes to illustrate copyright laws for books and movies.

Chapter 3, "Where Prices Come From: The Interaction of Demand and Supply," opens with a new discussion of the market for smartwatches and closes with *An Inside Look* that examines how the Apple smartwatch is inspiring the development of other wearable devices. There are three new *Making the Connections*: "Are Smartwatches Substitutes for Smartphones?"; "Tough Times for Big Macs and Golf"; and "Demand and Supply Trashes Plastic Recycling."

Chapter 4, "Economic Efficiency, Government Price Setting, and Taxes," opens with an updated discussion of how Airbnb and the sharing economy affects rent control policy in San Francisco and closes with *An Inside Look* that examines why government officials in Malibu, California, imposed a tax on short-term rentals of apartments booked through Airbnb. A new *Making the Connection* examines why investors expect Uber to be very profitable.

Chapter 5, "The Economics of Health Care," opens with a new discussion of how the Patient Protection and Affordable Care Act of 2010 could affect the health care plan at T. Cain Grocery, which operates five Piggly Wiggly supermarkets in Alabama and Florida. New *Solved Problem 5.4* shows students how to use the demand and supply model to explain changes in health care spending. A new *Making the Connection* discusses the increasing importance of health care in the U.S. economy.

Chapter 6, "Firms, the Stock Market, and Corporate Governance," opens with a new discussion of Twitter and the benefits and costs of becoming a publicly owned firm. New *Solved Problem 6.2* analyzes why Warren Buffett likes mutual funds, and new *Solved Problem 6.4* discusses whether Dodd-Frank will improve corporate governance. There are two new *Making the Connections*: "Why Are Fewer Young People Starting Businesses?" and "Why Are Many People Poor Stock Market Investors?"

Chapter 7, "Comparative Advantage and the Gains from International Trade," opens with a new discussion of President Obama, Nike, and the Trans-Pacific Partnership (TPP). There are three new *Making the Connections*: "Would New Balance Be Helped or Hurt By the Trans-Pacific Partnership?"; "Smoot-Hawley, the Politics of Tariffs, and Protecting a Vanishing Industry"; and "Protecting Consumer Health or Protecting U.S. Firms from Competition?"

Chapter 8, "GDP: Measuring Total Production and Income," opens with updated coverage of how the business cycle affects Ford Motor Company and includes a new *Making the Connection* about how calculating GDP changes the way the standard of living in Nigeria is measured.

Chapter 9, "Unemployment and Inflation," opens with a new discussion of JPMorgan's 2015 decision to lay off workers. There are two new *Making the Connections*: "Eight Million Workers Are Missing!" and "How Should We Categorize Unemployment at JPMorgan Chase?" New *Solved Problem 9.5* shows students how to use data to calculate real hourly wages.

Chapter 10, "Economic Growth, the Financial System, and Business Cycles," opens with a new discussion of how Corning has experienced long-run growth while experiencing the ups and downs of the business cycle. New *Solved Problem 10.1* focuses on the connection between productivity and prosperity, and new *Solved Problem 10.2* shows students how to apply the loanable funds model to analyze the effect of budget deficits. Chapter 10 also includes a new section that discusses why firms like Corning are particularly vulnerable to fluctuations in demand during the business cycle.

Chapter 11, "Long-Run Economic Growth: Sources and Policies," opens with a new discussion of whether economic reforms will help to increase Mexico's growth rate and includes a new *Making the Connection* that compares economic growth in Mexico and China.

Chapter 12, "Aggregate Expenditure and Output in the Short Run," opens with an updated opener on the effects of fluctuations in aggregate expenditure on Intel and includes a new *Making the Connection* about the link between student loans and the number of young people purchasing homes.

Chapter 13, "Aggregate Demand and Aggregate Supply Analysis," opens with a new discussion of the effect of the business cycle on Delta Airlines and includes a new *Making the Connection* that discusses how unusually long it took following the 2007–2009 recession for real GDP and employment to return to the levels achieved at the business cycle peak.

Chapter 14, "Money, Banks, and the Federal Reserve System," opens with a new discussion of the 2015 banking crisis in Greece and includes a new *Making the Connection* on peer-to-peer lending.

Chapter 15 "Monetary Policy," opens with a new discussion of the connection between monetary policy and borrowers in Europe paying negative nominal interest rates on bank loans. Two new *Making the Connections* examine the connection between central bank policies of quantitative easing and negative interest rates, and why the Federal Reserve usually ignores fluctuations in food and energy prices. Chapter 15 includes new Table 15.3, "Treasury and Fed Actions at the Beginning of the Financial Crisis."

Chapter 16, "Fiscal Policy," opens with a new discussion of the effects of federal government spending to rebuild a highway leading to the Golden Gate Bridge. A new *Making the Connection* discusses whether macroeconomic policy is too dependent on the Federal Reserve. New *Solved Problem 16.6* analyzes the effects of the Greek government attempting to balance its budget during a recession.

Chapter 17, "Inflation, Unemployment, and Federal Reserve Policy," opens with a new discussion of why a company like Goodyear is concerned about monetary policy. A new *Making the Connection* examines whether it is important for the Fed to provide the public with accurate guidance on the future of monetary policy. Chapter also includes 17 includes a new final section that covers the debate over the future of the Fed.

Chapter 18, "Macroeconomics in an Open Economy," opens with a new discussion on how fluctuations in the exchange rate affect IBM's profits. A new *Making the Connection* examines whether a strong dollar is a good for the U.S. economy. New *Solved Problem 18.2* analyzes how Subaru is affected by fluctuations in the value of the yen.

Chapter 19, "The International Financial System," opens with a new discussion about how Bayer deals with fluctuating exchange rates. There are two new *Making the Connections*: "Greece and Germany: Diverse Economies, Common Currency" and "The Chinese Yuan: The World's Most Controversial Currency."

Other Changes to Chapters

- To make room for the new content described earlier, we have cut approximately 23 *Making the Connections* and 9 *Solved Problems* from the previous edition and transferred some of them to the book's *Instructor's Manual*, where they are available for instructors who wish to continue using them.

- Figures and tables have been updated with the latest data available.

- Many of the end-of-chapter problems have been either replaced or updated. To most chapters, we have added one or two new problems that include graphs for students to analyze. Select chapters have a category called *Real-Time Data Exercises*. Some of these exercises have been updated for this new edition.

- Finally, we have gone over the text literally line by line, tightening the discussion, rewriting unclear points, and making many small changes. We are grateful to the many instructors and students who made suggestions for improvements in the previous edition. We have done our best to incorporate as many of those suggestions as possible.

The Foundation:
Contextual Learning and Modern Organization

Students come to study macroeconomics with a strong interest in understanding events and developments in the economy. We try to capture that interest and develop students' economic intuition and understanding. We present macroeconomics in a way that is modern and based in the real world of business and economic policy. And we believe we achieve this presentation without making the analysis more difficult. We avoid the recent trend of using simplified versions of intermediate models, which are often more detailed and complex than what students need to understand the basic macroeconomic issues. Instead, we use a more realistic version of the familiar aggregate demand and aggregate supply model to analyze short-run fluctuations and monetary and fiscal policy. We also avoid the "dueling schools of thought" approach often used to teach macroeconomics at the principles level. We emphasize the many areas of macroeconomics where most economists agree. And we present throughout real business and policy situations to develop students' intuition. Here are a few highlights of our approach to macroeconomics:

- **A broad discussion of macro statistics.** Many students pay at least some attention to the financial news and know that the release of statistics by federal agencies can cause movements in stock and bond prices. A background in macroeconomic statistics helps clarify some of the policy issues encountered in later chapters. In Chapter 8, "GDP: Measuring Total Production and Income," and Chapter 9, "Unemployment and Inflation," we provide students with an understanding of the uses and potential shortcomings of the key macroeconomic statistics, without getting bogged down in the minutiae of how the statistics are constructed. So, for instance, we discuss the important differences between the payroll survey and the household survey for understanding conditions in the labor market. We explain why financial markets react more strongly to news from the payroll survey. We provide a discussion of the employment–population ratio, which is not covered in some other books but which many economists regard as a key measure of labor market performance. Chapter 15, "Monetary Policy," discusses why the Federal Reserve prefers to measure inflation using the core personal consumption expenditures price index rather than the consumer price index.

- **Early coverage of long-run topics.** We place key macroeconomic issues in their long-run context in Chapter 10, "Economic Growth, the Financial System, and Business Cycles," and Chapter 11 "Long-Run Economic Growth: Sources and Policies." Chapter 10 puts the business cycle in the context of underlying long-run growth and discusses what actually happens during the phases of the business cycle. We believe this material is important if students are to have the understanding of business cycles they will need to interpret economic events; this material is often discussed only briefly or omitted entirely in other books. We know that many instructors prefer to have a short-run orientation to their macro courses, with a strong emphasis on policy. Accordingly, we have structured Chapter 10 so that its discussion of long-run growth is sufficient for instructors who want to move quickly to short-run analysis. Chapter 11 uses a simple neoclassical growth model to explain important growth issues. We apply the model to topics such as the decline of the Soviet economy, the long-run prospects for growth in China, the implications of the slowdown in productivity growth for the U.S. economy, and the failure of many developing countries to sustain high growth rates. *And* we challenge students with the discussion "Why Isn't the Whole World Rich?"

- **A dynamic model of aggregate demand and aggregate supply.** We take a fresh approach to the standard aggregate demand and aggregate supply (*AD–AS*) model. We realize there is no good, simple alternative to using the *AD–AS* model when explaining movements in the price level and in real GDP. But we know that more instructors are dissatisfied with the *AD–AS* model than with any other aspect of the macro principles

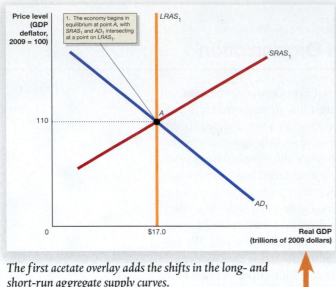

The first acetate overlay adds the shifts in the long- and short-run aggregate supply curves.

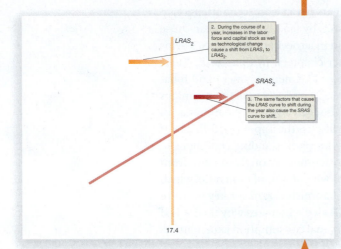

The second acetate overlay adds the shifts in the aggregate demand curve to complete the dynamic model.

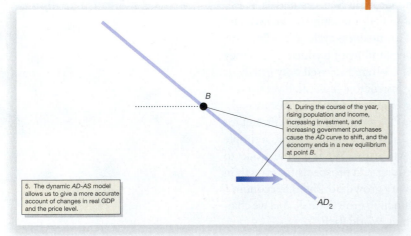

course. The key problem, of course, is that *AD–AS* is a static model that attempts to account for dynamic changes in real GDP and the price level. Our approach retains the basics of the *AD–AS* model but makes it more accurate and useful by making it more dynamic. We emphasize two points: (1) Changes in the position of the short-run (upward-sloping) aggregate supply curve depend mainly on the state of expectations of the inflation rate and (2) the existence of growth in the economy means that the long-run (vertical) aggregate supply curve shifts to the right every year. This "dynamic" *AD–AS* model provides students with a more accurate understanding of the causes and consequences of fluctuations in real GDP and the price level. Chapter 13, "Aggregate Demand and Aggregate Supply Analysis," includes a three-layer, full-color acetate for the key introductory dynamic *AD–AS* graph (Figure 13.8, "A Dynamic Aggregate Demand and Aggregate Supply Model," on page 456 and reproduced on the left). We created this acetate to help students see how the graph builds step by step and to help make the graph easier for instructors to present. The acetate will help instructors who want to use dynamic *AD–AS* in class but believe the model needs to be developed carefully. We introduce this model in Chapter 13 and use it to discuss monetary policy in Chapter 15, "Monetary Policy," and fiscal policy in Chapter 16, "Fiscal Policy." The material on dynamic *AD–AS* is presented in self-contained sections in Chapters 13, 15, and 16, so instructors may safely omit the sections on the dynamic *AD–AS* model without any loss in continuity to the discussion of macroeconomic theory and policy.

- **Extensive coverage of monetary policy.** Because of the central role monetary policy plays in the economy and in students' curiosity about business and financial news, we devote two chapters—Chapter 15, "Monetary Policy," and Chapter 17, "Inflation, Unemployment, and Federal Reserve Policy"—to the topic. We emphasize the issues involved in the Fed's choice of monetary policy targets, and we include coverage of the Taylor rule. We also cover the debate over the Fed's policies, including recent proposals in Congress to reduce the Fed's independence.

- **Coverage of both the demand-side and supply-side effects of fiscal policy.** Our discussion of fiscal policy in Chapter 16, "Fiscal Policy," carefully distinguishes between automatic stabilizers and discretionary fiscal policy. We also provide significant coverage of the supply-side effects of fiscal policy.

- **A self-contained but thorough discussion of the Keynesian income–expenditure approach.** The Keynesian income–expenditure approach (the "45°-line diagram," or "Keynesian cross") is useful for introducing students to the short-run relationship between spending and production. Many instructors, however, prefer to omit this material.

Therefore, we use the 45°-line diagram only in Chapter 12, "Aggregate Expenditure and Output in the Short Run." The discussions of monetary and fiscal policy in Chapter 15, "Monetary Policy," and Chapter 16, "Fiscal Policy," respectively, uses only the *AD–AS* model, making it possible to omit Chapter 12.

- **Extensive international coverage.** We include three chapters devoted to international topics: Chapter 7, "Comparative Advantage and the Gains from International Trade," Chapter 18, "Macroeconomics in an Open Economy," and Chapter 19, "The International Financial System." Having a good understanding of the international trading and financial systems is essential to understanding the macroeconomy and to satisfying students' curiosity about the economic world around them. In addition to the material in our three international chapters, we weave international comparisons into the narratives of several other chapters, including our discussion of labor market policies in Chapter 17, "Inflation, Unemployment, and Federal Reserve Policy," and central banking in Chapter 14, "Money, Banks, and the Federal Reserve System."

- **Flexible chapter organization.** Because we realize that there are a variety of approaches to teaching principles of macroeconomics, we have structured our chapters for maximum flexibility. For example, our discussion of long-run economic growth in Chapter 10, "Economic Growth, the Financial System, and Business Cycles," makes it possible for instructors to omit the more thorough discussion of these issues in Chapter 11, "Long-Run Economic Growth: Sources and Policies." Our discussion of the Keynesian 45°-line diagram is confined to Chapter 12, "Aggregate Expenditure and Output in the Short Run," so that instructors who do not use this approach can proceed directly to aggregate demand and aggregate supply analysis in Chapter 13, "Aggregate Demand and Aggregate Supply Analysis." While we devote two chapters to monetary policy, the first of these—Chapter 15, "Monetary Policy"—is a self-contained discussion, so instructors may safely omit the material in Chapter 17, "Inflation, Unemployment, and Federal Reserve Policy," if they choose to. Finally, instructors may choose to omit all three of the international chapters (Chapter 7, "Comparative Advantage and the Gains from International Trade," Chapter 18, "Macroeconomics in an Open Economy," and Chapter 19, "The International Financial System"), cover just Chapter 7 on international trade, cover just Chapter 18, or cover Chapters 18 and 19 while omitting Chapter 7. Please refer to the flexibility chart on Preface pages xv–xvi to help select the chapters and order best suited to your classroom needs.

Special Features:
A Real-World, Hands-on Approach to Learning Economics

Business Cases and *An Inside Look* News Articles

Each chapter-opening case provides a real-world context for learning, sparks students' interest in economics, and helps unify the chapter. The case describes an actual company facing a real situation. The company is integrated in the narrative, graphs, and pedagogical features of the chapter. Some of the chapter openers focus on the role of entrepreneurs in developing new products and bringing them to market. For example, Chapter 1 discusses Walter De Brouwer, the founder of Scanadu, which develops smart devices for health care; Chapter 2 discusses Elon Musk of Tesla Motors; and Chapter 13 discusses the founders of what became Delta Airlines.. Here are a few examples of companies we discuss in the chapter openers:

- Tesla Motors (Chapter 2, "Trade-offs, Comparative Advantage, and the Market System")
- Apple (Chapter 3, "Where Prices Come From: The Interaction of Demand and Supply")
- Twitter (Chapter 6, "Firms, the Stock Market, and Corporate Governance")
- Delta Airlines (Chapter 13, "Aggregate Demand and Aggregate Supply Analysis")

An Inside Look is a two-page feature that shows students how to apply the concepts from the chapter to the analysis of a news article. The feature appears at the end of Chapters 1–4. *An Inside Look* feature presents an excerpt from an article, analysis of the article, a graph(s), and critical thinking questions. Additional articles are located on MyEconLab, where they are continuously updated.

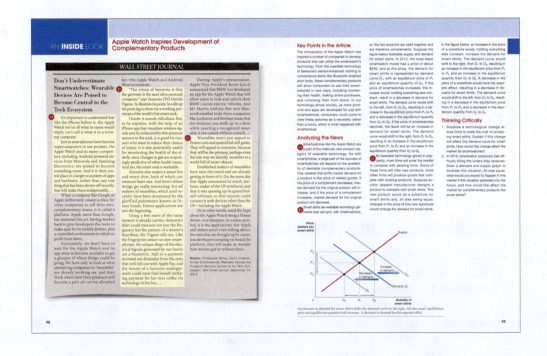

Economics in Your Life

After the chapter-opening real-world business case, we have added a personal dimension to the chapter opener with a feature titled *Economics in Your Life*, which asks students to consider how economics affects their lives. The feature piques the interest of students and emphasizes the connection between the material they are learning and their experiences.

Economics in Your Life

Will You Buy a Smartphone or a Smartwatch?

You use your smartphone mainly to text, read e-mail, and keep track of your appointments. Your smartphone is old, though, and you are thinking of buying a new one ... or should you buy a smartwatch? What factors are most important in your decision: the features of a smartwatch versus a smartphone, or the relative prices of these products? If you know that you are soon going to get a raise at your job, would you be more likely to buy a smartwatch? As you read this chapter, try to answer these questions. You can check your answers against those we provide on **page 97** at the end of this chapter.

At the end of the chapter, we use the chapter concepts to answer the questions asked at the beginning of the chapter.

Continued from page 73

Economics in Your Life

Will You Buy a Smartphone or a Smartwatch?

At the beginning of this chapter, we asked you to consider how you might choose between buying a smartwatch and buying a smartphone. There are certain activities, such as watching YouTube or Netflix, that you can do on a smartphone but not on a smartwatch. There are other activities, such as tracking calories burned during a workout, that are probably easier to do on a smartwatch. If you can engage in the activities you like most on either device, then you probably consider the two devices to be close substitutes, and you are likely to buy the one with the lower price. Suppose that you are currently leaning toward buying a smartphone because its price is lower than the price of a comparable smartwatch. If an increase in your income would cause you to change your decision and buy the smartwatch, then the smartphone is an inferior good for you.

The following are examples of the topics we cover in the *Economics in Your Life* feature:

- Will you buy a smartphone or a smartwatch? (Chapter 3, "Where Prices Come From: The Interaction of Demand and Supply")
- Is your take-home pay affected by what your employer spends on your health insurance? (Chapter 5, "The Economics of Health Care")
- Is an employer likely to cut your pay during a recession? (Chapter 13, "Aggregate Demand and Aggregate Supply Analysis")

Solved Problems

Many students have great difficulty handling applied economics problems. We help students overcome this hurdle by including in each chapter two or three worked-out problems tied to select chapter-opening learning objectives. Our goals are to keep students focused on the main ideas of each chapter and give them a model of how to solve an economic problem by breaking it down step by step. Additional exercises in the end-of-chapter *Problems and Applications* section are tied to every *Solved Problem*. Additional *Solved Problems* appear in the *Instructor's Manual*. In addition, the Test Item Files include problems tied to the *Solved Problems* in the main book.

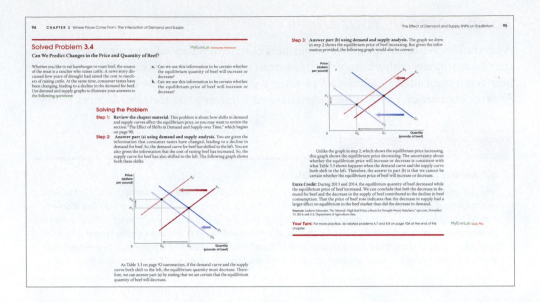

Don't Let This Happen to You

We know from many years of teaching which concepts students find most difficult. Each chapter contains a box feature called *Don't Let This Happen to You* that alerts students to the most common pitfalls in that chapter's material. We follow up with a related question in the end-of-chapter *Problems and Applications* section.

Don't Let This Happen to You

Remember: A Change in a Good's Price Does *Not* Cause the Demand or Supply Curve to Shift

Suppose a student is asked to draw a demand and supply graph to illustrate how an increase in the price of oranges would affect the market for apples, with other variables being constant. He draws the graph on the left and explains it as follows: "Because apples and oranges are substitutes, an increase in the price of oranges will cause an initial shift to the right in the demand curve for apples, from D_1 to D_2. However, because this initial shift in the demand curve for apples results in a higher price for apples, P_2, consumers will find apples less desirable, and the demand curve will shift to the left, from D_2 to D_3, resulting in a final equilibrium price of P_3." Do you agree or disagree with the student's analysis?

MyEconLab Study Plan

You should disagree. The student has correctly understood that an increase in the price of oranges will cause the demand curve for apples to shift to the right. But, the second demand curve shift the student describes,

from D_2 to D_3, will not take place. Changes in the price of a product do not result in shifts in the product's demand curve. Changes in the price of a product result only in movements along a demand curve.

The graph on the right shows the correct analysis. The increase in the price of oranges causes the demand curve for apples to increase from D_1 to D_2. At the original price, P_1, the increase in demand initially results in a shortage of apples equal to $Q_3 - Q_1$. But, as we have seen, a shortage causes the price to increase until the shortage is eliminated. In this case, the price will rise to P_2, where both the quantity demanded and the quantity supplied are equal to Q_2. Notice that the increase in price causes a decrease in the *quantity demanded*, from Q_3 to Q_2, but does *not* cause a decrease in demand.

Your Turn: Test your understanding by doing related problems 4.13 and 4.14 on page 105 at the end of this chapter.

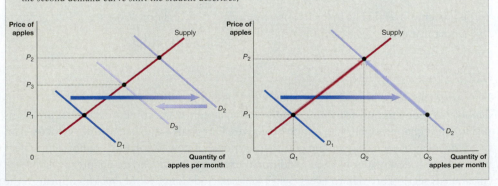

Making the Connection

Each chapter includes two to four *Making the Connection* features that provide real-world reinforcement of key concepts and help students learn how to interpret what they read on the Web and in newspapers. Most *Making the Connection* features use relevant, stimulating, and provocative news stories focused on businesses and policy issues. One-third of them are new to this edition, and most others have been updated. Several discuss health care, which remains a pressing policy issue. Each *Making the Connection* has at least one supporting end-of-chapter problem to allow students to test their understanding of the topic discussed.

Making the Connection

MyEconLab Video

Are Smartwatches Substitutes for Smartphones?

Two products are rarely perfect substitutes because consumers may find them more or less useful for some purposes. As Apple and other firms began selling smartwatches, a key question they needed to answer was whether consumers considered smartwatches close substitutes for smartphones. You can use either a smartwatch or a smartphone to check the time, send a text, keep a list of appointments, or use a GPS map. But you need a smartphone if you want to surf the Web or watch a movie, while you are better off buying a smartwatch if you want to monitor your heartbeat or keep track of how many calories you are burning while exercising.

Is the smartwatch a hot new must-have gadget, even for people who already own a smartphone?

So smartwatches and smartphones are substitutes—but they aren't *perfect* substitutes. To correctly forecast sales and produce the correct quantity of smartwatches, firms that sell them need to evaluate how close substitutes consumers consider smartwatches and smartphones to be. Many people who might consider buying a smartwatch already own a smartphone. So the closer consumers consider the two products to be as substitutes, the less likely they are to buy a smartwatch in addition to a smartphone.

When Apple introduced the Apple Watch in 2015, sales were initially very strong, which would seem to indicate that many consumers believed that the unique features of the smartwatch made it worth buying, even if they owned a smartphone. Some analysts, though, wondered how large future sales would be after people who buy each new electronic device soon after it hits the market—early adopters—had made their purchases. One early reviewer of the Apple Watch noted that he was unsure "that I need this thing on my wrist every day." Similarly, the *Economist* magazine offered the opinion, "Apple seems unlikely to turn its watch into the next big must-have gadget. ... People are unlikely to want to shell out ... $350 ... for something with so few extra functions."

Other industry observers were more optimistic about the size of the market for smartwatches. Writing in the *Wall Street Journal*, one analyst argued that smartwatches performed several functions faster or more conveniently than smartphones. He concluded, "Billions of consumers who own a smartphone are likely to consider purchasing a smartwatch." Given these different evaluations, it wasn't surprising that forecasts of sales of the Apple Watch during its first year varied widely from 8 million to 41 million.

In the end, as with most new products, the success of smartwatches depends on whether consumers see them as filling a need that other products don't meet. In other words, the less close a substitute consumers believe smartwatches to be for smartphones, the more likely they are to buy a smartwatch.

Sources: Joshua Topolsky, "Apple Watch Review: You'll Want One, but You Don't Need One," bloomberg.com, April 8, 2015; "The Time Machine," *Economist*, March 9, 2015; and Daniel Matte and Kevin McCullagh, "Will Smartwatches Be a Hit?" *Wall Street Journal*, May 10, 2015.

Your Turn: Test your understanding by doing related problem 1.12 on page 101 at the end of this chapter.   MyEconLab Study Plan

---

Graphs and Summary Tables

Graphs are an indispensable part of a principles of economics course but are a major stumbling block for many students. Every chapter except Chapter 1 includes end-of-chapter problems that require students to draw, read, and interpret graphs. Interactive graphing exercises appear on the book's supporting Web site. We use four devices to help students read and interpret graphs:

1. Detailed captions
2. Boxed notes
3. Color-coded curves
4. Summary tables with graphs (see pages 80, 85, and 440 for examples)

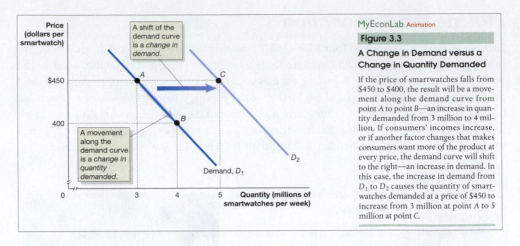

MyEconLab Animation

Figure 3.3

A Change in Demand versus a Change in Quantity Demanded

If the price of smartwatches falls from $450 to $400, the result will be a movement along the demand curve from point A to point B—an increase in quantity demanded from 3 million to 4 million. If consumers' incomes increase, or if another factor changes that makes consumers want more of the product at every price, the demand curve will shift to the right—an increase in demand. In this case, the increase in demand from D_1 to D_2 causes the quantity of smartwatches demanded at a price of $450 to increase from 3 million at point A to 5 million at point C.

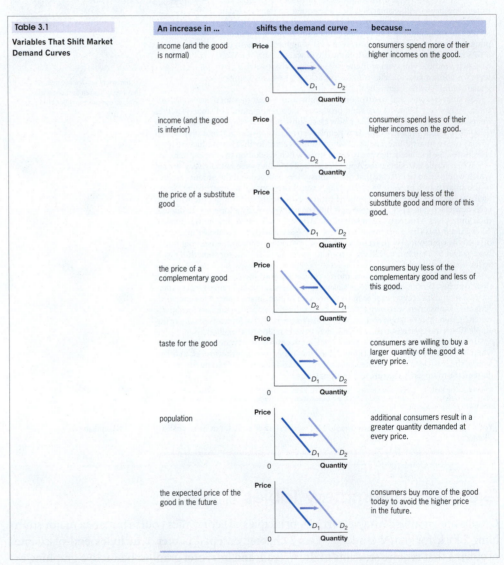

Table 3.1	An increase in ...	shifts the demand curve ...	because ...
Variables That Shift Market Demand Curves	income (and the good is normal)		consumers spend more of their higher incomes on the good.
	income (and the good is inferior)		consumers spend less of their higher incomes on the good.
	the price of a substitute good		consumers buy less of the substitute good and more of this good.
	the price of a complementary good		consumers buy less of the complementary good and less of this good.
	taste for the good		consumers are willing to buy a larger quantity of the good at every price.
	population		additional consumers result in a greater quantity demanded at every price.
	the expected price of the good in the future		consumers buy more of the good today to avoid the higher price in the future.

Review Questions and *Problems and Applications*—
Grouped by Learning Objective to Improve Assessment

All end-of-chapter material—*Summary*, *Review Questions*, and *Problems and Applications*—is grouped under learning objectives. The goals of this organization are to make it easier for instructors to assign problems based on learning objectives, both in the book and in MyEconLab, and to help students efficiently review material that they find difficult. If students have difficulty with a particular learning objective, an instructor can easily identify which end-of-chapter questions and problems support that objective and assign them as homework or discuss them in class. Every exercise in a chapter's *Problems and Applications* section is available in MyEconLab. Using MyEconLab, students can complete these and many other exercises online, get tutorial help, and receive instant feedback and assistance on exercises they answer incorrectly. Also, student learning will be enhanced by having the summary material and problems grouped together by learning objective, which will allow them to focus on the parts of the chapter they find most challenging. Each major section of the chapter, paired with a learning objective, has at least two review questions and three problems.

As in the previous editions, we include one or more end-of-chapter problems that test students' understanding of the content presented in the *Solved Problem*, *Making the Connection*, and *Don't Let This Happen to You* special features in the chapter. Instructors can cover a feature in class and assign the corresponding problem for homework. The Test Item Files also include test questions that pertain to these special features.

Real-Time Data Exercises

Select chapters end with at least two *Real-Time Data Exercises* that help students become familiar with a key data source, learn how to locate data, and develop skills in interpreting data. *Real-Time Data Analysis (RTDA) Exercises*, marked with 🔴, allow students and instructors to use the very latest data from FRED.

Integrated Supplements

The authors and Pearson Education/Prentice Hall have worked together to integrate the text, print, and media resources to make teaching and learning easier.

MyEconLab

MyEconLab is a unique online course management, testing, and tutorial resource.

For the Instructor

Instructors can choose how much or how little time to spend setting up and using MyEconLab. Here is a snapshot of what instructors are saying about MyEconLab:

> MyEconLab offers [students] a way to practice every week. They receive immediate feedback and a feeling of personal attention. As a result, my teaching has become more targeted and efficient.—Kelly Blanchard, Purdue University

> Students tell me that offering them MyEconLab is almost like offering them individual tutors.—Jefferson Edwards, Cypress Fairbanks College

> MyEconLab's eText is great—particularly in that it helps offset the skyrocketing cost of textbooks. Naturally, students love that.—Doug Gehrke, Moraine Valley Community College

Each chapter contains two preloaded exercise sets that can be used to build an individualized study plan for each student. These study plan exercises contain tutorial resources, including instant feedback, links to the appropriate learning objective in the eText, pop-up definitions from the text, and step-by-step guided solutions, where appropriate. After the initial setup of the course by the instructor, student use of these materials requires no further instructor setup. The online grade book records each student's performance and time spent on the tests and study plan and generates reports by student or chapter.

Alternatively, instructors can fully customize MyEconLab to match their course exactly, including reading assignments, homework assignments, video assignments, current news assignments, and quizzes and tests. Assignable resources include:

- Preloaded exercise assignments sets for each chapter include the student tutorial resources mentioned earlier.
- Preloaded quizzes for each chapter are unique to the text and not repeated in the study plan or homework exercise sets.
- Study plan problems are similar to the end-of-chapter problems and numbered exactly as in the book to make assigning homework easier.
- *Real-Time Data Analysis Exercises*, marked with , allow students and instructors to use the very latest data from FRED. By completing the exercises, students become familiar with a key data source, learn how to locate data, and develop skills in interpreting data. In the eText available in MyEconLab, select figures labeled MyEconLab Real-time Data allow students to display a pop-up graph updated with real-time data from FRED.
- *Current News Exercises* provide a turnkey way to assign gradable news-based exercises in MyEconLab. Each week, Pearson scours the news, finds a current microeconomics article and a current macroeconomics article, creates exercises around these news articles, and adds them to MyEconLab. Assigning and grading current news-based exercises that deal with the latest micro and macro events and policy issues has never been more convenient.
- *Experiments in MyEconLab* provide a fun and engaging way to promote active learning and mastery of important economic concepts. Pearson's Experiments program is flexible, easy-to-assign, auto-graded, and available in Single and Multiplayer versions. Single-player experiments allow your students to play against virtual players from anywhere at any time, as long as they have an Internet connection. Multiplayer experiments allow you to assign and manage a real-time experiment with your class. Pre- and postquestions for each experiment are available for assignment in MyEconLab. For a complete list of available experiments, visit **www.myeconlab.com**.
- Test Item File questions allow you to assign quizzes or homework that look just like your exams.
- *Econ Exercise Builder* allows you to build customized exercises. Exercises include multiple-choice, graph drawing, and free-response items, many of which are generated algorithmically so that each time a student works them, a different variation is presented. MyEconLab grades every problem type except essays—even problems with graphs. When working homework exercises, students receive immediate feedback, with links to additional learning tools.

Customization and Communication

MyEconLab in MyLab/Mastering provides additional optional customization and communication tools. Instructors who teach distance-learning courses or very large lecture sections find the MyLab/Mastering format useful because they can upload course documents and assignments, customize the order of chapters, and use communication features such as Document Sharing, Chat, ClassLive, and Discussion Board.

For the Student

MyEconLab puts students in control of their learning through a collection of testing, practice, and study tools tied to the online, interactive version of the textbook and other media resources. Here is a snapshot of what students are saying about MyEconLab:

> It was very useful because it had EVERYTHING, from practice exams to exercises to reading. Very helpful.—student, Northern Illinois University

> I would recommend taking the quizzes on MyEconLab because it gives you a true account of whether or not you understand the material.—student, Montana Tech

> It made me look through the book to find answers, so I did more reading.—student, Northern Illinois University

Students can study on their own or can complete assignments created by their instructor. In MyEconLab's structured environment, students practice what they learn, test their understanding, and pursue a personalized study plan generated from their performance on sample tests and from quizzes created by their instructors. In Homework or Study Plan mode, students have access to a wealth of tutorial features, including:

- Instant feedback on exercises that helps students understand and apply the concepts
- Links to the eText to promote reading of the text just when the student needs to revisit a concept or an explanation
- Step-by-step guided solutions that force students to break down a problem in much the same way an instructor would do during office hours
- Pop-up key term definitions from the eText to help students master the vocabulary of economics
- A graphing tool that is integrated into the various exercises to enable students to build and manipulate graphs to better understand how concepts, numbers, and graphs connect

Additional MyEconLab Tools

MyEconLab includes the following additional features:

- **Enhanced eText.** Students actively read and learn, and with more engagement than ever before, through embedded and auto-graded practice, real-time data-graph updates, animations, author videos, and more.
- **Print upgrade.** For students who wish to complete assignments in MyEconLab but read in print, Pearson offers registered MyEconLab users a loose-leaf version of the print text at a significant discount.
- **Glossary flashcards.** Every key term is available as a flashcard, allowing students to quiz themselves on vocabulary from one or more chapters at a time.

MyEconLab content has been created through the efforts of Chris Annala, State University of New York–Geneseo; Charles Baum, Middle Tennessee State University; Peggy Dalton, Frostburg State University; Carol Dole, Jacksonville University; David Foti, Lone Star College; Sarah Ghosh, University of Scranton; Satyajit Ghosh, University of Scranton; Melissa Honig, Pearson Education; Woo Jung, University of Colorado; Courtney Kamauf, Pearson Education; Chris Kauffman, University of Tennessee–Knoxville; Russell Kellogg, University of Colorado–Denver; Noel Lotz, Pearson Education; Katherine McCann, University of Delaware; Daniel Mizak, Frostburg State University; Christine Polek, University of Massachusetts–Boston; Mark Scanlan, Stephen F. Austin State University; Leonie L. Stone, State University of New York–Geneseo; and Bert G. Wheeler, Cedarville University.

Other Resources for the Instructor

Instructor's Manual

Edward Scahill of the University of Scranton prepared the *Instructor's Manual* I, which includes chapter-by-chapter summaries, learning objectives, extended examples and class exercises, teaching outlines incorporating key terms and definitions, teaching tips, topics for class discussion, new *Solved Problems*, new *Making the Connection* features, and solutions to all review questions, problems, and real-time-data exercises in the book. The *Instructor's Manual* is available in print and for download from the Instructor's Resource Center (**www. pearsonhighered.com/hubbard**). The solutions to the end-of-chapter review questions and problems were prepared by the authors and Edward Scahill of the University of Scranton.

Test Item File

Randy Methenitis of Richland College prepared Test Item Files, which includes 4,000 multiple-choice, true/false, short-answer, and graphing questions. There are questions to support each key feature in the book. The Test Item File is available in print and for download from the Instructor's Resource Center (**www.pearsonhighered.com/hubbard**). Test questions are annotated with the following information:

- **Difficulty**—1 for straight recall, 2 for some analysis, 3 for complex analysis
- **Type**—multiple-choice, true/false, short-answer, essay
- **Topic**—the term or concept the question supports
- **Learning outcome**
- **AACSB** (see the description that follows)
- **Page number** in the text
- **Special feature in the main book**—chapter-opening business example, *Economics in Your Life*, *Solved Problem*, *Making the Connection*, and *Don't Let This Happen to You*

The Association to Advance Collegiate Schools of Business (AACSB)

The Test Item File author has connected select questions to the general knowledge and skill guidelines found in the AACSB Assurance of Learning Standards.

What Is the AACSB?

The AACSB is a not-for-profit corporation of educational institutions, corporations, and other organizations devoted to the promotion and improvement of higher education in business administration and accounting. A collegiate institution offering degrees in business administration or accounting may volunteer for AACSB accreditation review. The AACSB makes initial accreditation decisions and conducts periodic reviews to promote continuous quality improvement in management education. Pearson Education is a proud member of the AACSB and is pleased to provide advice to help you apply AACSB Assurance of Learning Standards.

What Are AACSB Assurance of Learning Standards?

One of the criteria for AACSB accreditation is the quality of curricula. Although no specific courses are required, the AACSB expects a curriculum to include learning experiences in the following categories of Assurance of Learning Standards:

- Written and Oral Communication
- Ethical Understanding and Reasoning
- Analytical Thinking Skills
- Information Technology
- Diverse and Multicultural Work
- Reflective Thinking
- Application of Knowledge

Questions that test skills relevant to these standards are tagged with the appropriate standard. For example, a question testing the moral questions associated with externalities would receive the Ethical Understanding and Reasoning tag.

How Can Instructors Use the AACSB Tags?

Tagged questions help you measure whether students are grasping the course content that aligns with the AACSB guidelines noted earlier. This in turn may suggest enrichment activities or other educational experiences to help students achieve these skills.

TestGen

The computerized TestGen package allows instructors to customize, save, and generate classroom tests. The test program permits instructors to edit, add, or delete questions from the Test Item Files; analyze test results; and organize a database of tests and student results. This software allows for extensive flexibility and ease of use. It provides many options for organizing and displaying tests, along with search and sort features. The software and the Test Item Files can be downloaded from the Instructor's Resource Center (www. pearsonhighered.com/hubbard).

PowerPoint Lecture Presentation

Three sets of PowerPoint slides, prepared by Paul Holmes of Ashland University, are available:

1. A comprehensive set of PowerPoint slides can be used by instructors for class presentations or by students for lecture preview or review. These slides include all the graphs, tables, and equations in the textbook. Two versions are available—step-by-step mode, in which you can build graphs as you would on a blackboard, and automated mode, in which you use a single click per slide.

2. A comprehensive set of PowerPoint slides have Classroom Response Systems (CRS) questions built in so that instructors can incorporate CRS "clickers" into their classroom lectures. Instructors can download these PowerPoint presentations from the Instructor's Resource Center (www.pearsonhighered.com/hubbard).

3. A student version of the PowerPoint slides is available as .pdf files. This version allows students to print the slides and bring them to class for note taking. Instructors can download these PowerPoint presentations from the Instructor's Resource Center (www.pearsonhighered.com/hubbard).

Learning Catalytics

Learning Catalytics is a "bring your own device" Web-based student engagement, assessment, and classroom intelligence system. This system generates classroom discussion, guides lectures, and promotes peer-to-peer learning with real-time analytics. Students can use any device to interact in the classroom, engage with content, and even draw and share graphs.

To learn more, ask your local Pearson representative or visit www.learningcatalytics. com.

Digital Interactives

Focused on a single core topic and organized in progressive levels, each interactive immerses students in an assignable and auto-graded activity. Digital Interactives are also engaging lecture tools for traditional, online, and hybrid courses, many incorporating real-time data, data displays, and analysis tools for rich classroom discussions.

Other Resources for the Student

In addition to MyEconLab, Pearson provides the following resources.

Dynamic Study Modules

With a focus on key topics, these modules work by continuously assessing student performance and activity in real time and, using data and analytics, provide personalized content to reinforce concepts that target each student's particular strengths and weaknesses.

PowerPoint Slides

For student use as a study aid or note-taking guide, PowerPoint slides, prepared by Paul Holmes of Ashland University, can be downloaded from MyEconLab or the Instructor's Resource Center and made available to students. The slides include:

- All graphs, tables, and equations in the text
- Figures in step-by-step mode and automated modes, using a single click per graph curve
- End-of-chapter key terms with hyperlinks to relevant slides

Accuracy Review Board and Reviewers

The guidance and recommendations of the following instructors helped us develop the revision plans for the sixth edition and the supplements package. While we could not incorporate every suggestion from every consultant board member, reviewer, or accuracy checker, we do thank each and every one of you and acknowledge that your feedback was indispensable in developing this text. We greatly appreciate your assistance in making this the best text it could be; you have helped teach a whole new generation of students about the exciting world of economics.

Accuracy Review Board

Our accuracy checkers did a particularly painstaking and thorough job of helping us proof the graphs, equations, and features of the text and supplements. We are grateful for their time and commitment:

Fatma Abdel-Raouf, Goldey-Beacom College
Clare Battista, California Polytechnic State University
Doris Bennett, Jacksonville State University
Harry Ellis, University of North Texas
Robert Gillette, University of Kentucky
Edward T. Gullason, formerly, Dowling College
Anthony Gyapong, Pennsylvania State University— Abington
Randy Methenitis, Richland College
Brian Rosario, University of California–Davis
Edward Scahill, University of Scranton

Reviewers

The guidance and thoughtful recommendations of many instructors helped us develop and implement a revision plan that improved the book's content, enhanced the figures, and strengthened the assessment features. We extend special thanks to Edward Scahill of the University of Scranton for helping us revise the chapter openers and the solutions to the end-of-chapter questions and problems, to Randy Methenitis of Richland College for helping us revise the *An Inside Look* feature in Chapters 1–4, and to Fernando Quijano for creating all the figures in the book and supplements. We are grateful for the comments and many helpful suggestions received from the following reviewers:

Sindy Abadie, Southwest Tennessee Community College
Olugbenga Ajilore, The University of Toledo
Robert Berman, American University
Benjamin Blair, Columbus State University
William Browning, Florida Gulf Coast University
Eliane P. Catilina, Graduate School USA
Lisa Citron, Cascadia College
Erik Craft, University of Richmond
Eva Dziadula, University of Notre Dame
Christi Esquivel, Navarro College
Mary Flannery, University of Notre Dame
Alan S. Fudge, Linn-Benton Community College
Ward Hooker, Central Community College
Michael Jones, University of Cincinnati
Janice Kinghorn, Miami University
Tom Lehman, Indiana Wesleyan University

Svitlana Maksymenko, University of Pittsburgh

Robin S. McCutcheon, Marshall University College of Business

Charles Meyrick, Housatonic Community College

Victoria Willis-Miller, Piedmont Technical College

Fola Odebunmi, Cypress College

Sheri Perez, College of Southern Nevada

Mehul Rangwala, University of Phoenix

Nicole L. Cornell Sadowski, York College of Pennsylvania

Edward Scahill, University of Scranton

Richard Lee Slotkin, Pasadena City College

Ralph Sonenshine, American University

Laura Storino, Rowan University

John Tommasi, University of Massachusetts–Lowell

Christopher Westley, Jacksonville State University

Mark Witte, Northwestern University

Previous Edition Class Testers, Accuracy Reviewers, and Consultants

Class Testers

We are grateful to both the instructors who class-tested manuscript of the first edition and their students for providing useful recommendations on how to make chapters more interesting, relevant, and comprehensive:

Charles A. Bennett, Gannon University

Anne E. Bresnock, University of California–Los Angeles, and California State Polytechnic University–Pomona

Linda Childs-Leatherbury, Lincoln University, Pennsylvania

John Eastwood, Northern Arizona University

David Eaton, Murray State University

Paul Elgatian, St. Ambrose University

Patricia A. Freeman, Jackson State University

Robert Godby, University of Wyoming

Frank Gunter, Lehigh University

Ahmed Ispahani, University of LaVerne

Brendan Kennelly, Lehigh University and National University of Ireland–Galway

Ernest Massie, Franklin University

Carol McDonough, University of Massachusetts–Lowell

Shah Mehrabi, Montgomery College

Sharon Ryan, University of Missouri–Columbia

Bruce G. Webb, Gordon College

Madelyn Young, Converse College

Susan Zumas, Lehigh University

Accuracy Review Boards

We are grateful to the following accuracy checkers of the previous editions for their hard work on the book and supplements:

Fatma Abdel-Raouf, Goldey-Beacom College

Anne Alexander, University of Wyoming

Mohammad Bajwa, Northampton Community College

Cynthia Bansak, St. Lawrence University

Hamid Bastin, Shippensburg University

Kelly Hunt Blanchard, Purdue University

Don Bumpass, Sam Houston State University

Charles Callahan III, State University of New York–Brockport

Mark S. Chester, Reading Area Community College

Kenny Christianson, Binghamton University

Ishita Edwards, Oxnard College

Harold Elder, University of Alabama

Harry Ellis, University of North Texas

Can Erbil, Brandeis University

Marc Fusaro, Arkansas Tech University

Sarah Ghosh, University of Scranton

Robert Gillette, University of Kentucky

Maria Giuili, Diablo Valley College

Mark Gius, Quinnipiac University

Robert Godby, University of Wyoming

William L. Goffe, Pennsylvania State University

Anthony Gyapong, Pennsylvania State University—Abington

Travis Hayes, University of Tennessee–Chattanooga

Carol Hogan, University of Michigan–Dearborn

Anisul M. Islam, University of Houston–Downtown

Aaron Jackson, Bentley College

Nancy Jianakoplos, Colorado State University

Thomas C. Kinnaman, Bucknell University

Mary K. Knudson, University of Iowa

Faik A. Koray, Louisiana State University

Stephan Kroll, California State University–Sacramento

Tony Lima, California State University–East Bay

Randy Methenitis, Richland College

Normal C. Miller, Miami University

David Mitch, University of Maryland–Baltimore County

James A. Moreno, Blinn College

Michael Potepan, San Francisco State University

Mary L. Pranzo, California State University–Fresno

Fernando Quijano, Dickinson State University

Matthew Rafferty, Quinnipiac University

Ratha Ramoo, Diablo Valley College

Jeff Reynolds, Northern Illinois University

Brian Rosario, University of California–Davis

Joseph M. Santos, South Dakota State University
Edward Scahill, University of Scranton
Mark V. Siegler, California State University–Sacramento
Rachel Small, University of Colorado–Boulder
Stephen Smith, Bakersfield College
Rajeev Sooreea, Pennsylvania State University–Altoona
Rebecca Stein, University of Pennsylvania
Ed Steinberg, New York University
Michael Stone, Quinnipiac University
Arlena Sullivan, Jones County Junior College
Wendine Thompson–Dawson, University of Utah
Julianne Treme, University of North Carolina–
   Wilmington
Robert Whaples, Wake Forest University

Consultant Boards

We received guidance from a dedicated consultant board during the development of the previous editions at several critical junctures. We relied on the board for input on content, figure treatment, and design:

Kate Antonovics, University of California–San Diego
Robert Beekman, University of Tampa
Valerie Bencivenga, University of Texas–Austin
Kelly Blanchard, Purdue University
Susan Dadres, Southern Methodist University
Harry Ellis, Jr., University of North Texas
Sherman T. Folland, Oakland University
Robert Gillette, University of Kentucky
Robert Godby, University of Wyoming
William L. Goffe, Pennsylvania State University
Jane S. Himarios, University of Texas–Arlington
Donn M. Johnson, Quinnipiac University
Mark Karscig, Central Missouri State University
Jenny Minier, University of Kentucky
David Mitch, University of Maryland–Baltimore County
Nicholas Noble, Miami University
Michael Potepan, San Francisco State University
Matthew Rafferty, Quinnipiac University
Helen Roberts, University of Illinois–Chicago
Robert Rosenman, Washington State University
Joseph M. Santos, South Dakota State University
Stephen Snyder, University of Pittsburgh
Martin C. Spechler, Indiana University–Purdue
   University Indianapolis
Robert Whaples, Wake Forest University
Jonathan B. Wight, University of Richmond

Reviewers

The guidance and recommendations of the following instructors helped us shape the previous editions.

ALABAMA

William P. Aldridge, University of Alabama
Doris Bennett, Jacksonville State University

Harold W. Elder, University of Alabama–Tuscaloosa
Wanda Hudson, Alabama Southern Community College
Keith D. Malone, University of North Alabama
Edward Merkel, Troy University
James L. Swofford, University of Southern Alabama

ARIZONA

Doug Conway, Mesa Community College
John Eastwood, Northern Arizona University
Price Fishback, University of Arizona
Anne Williams, Gateway Community College

ARKANSAS

Jerry Crawford, Arkansas State University
Marc Fusaro, Arkansas Tech University
Randall Kesselring, Arkansas State University
Dan Marburger, Arkansas State University

CALIFORNIA

Shawn Abbott, College of the Siskiyous
Renatte Adler, San Diego State University
Ercument Aksoy, Los Angeles Valley College
Maneeza Aminy, Golden Gate University
Kate Antonovics, University of California–San Diego
Becca Arnold, Mesa College
Asatar Bair, City College of San Francisco
Diana Bajrami, College of Alameda
Robert Bise, Orange Coast Community College
Victor Brajer, California State University–Fullerton
Anne E. Bresnock, University of California–Los Angeles,
   and California State Polytechnic University–Pomona
David Brownstone, University of California–Irvine
Maureen Burton, California State Polytechnic
   University–Pomona
Annette Chamberlin, National College
Anoshua Chaudhuri, San Francisco State University
James G. Devine, Loyola Marymount University
Jose Esteban, Palomar College
Roger Frantz, San Diego State University
Craig Gallet, California State University–Sacramento
Andrew Gill, California State University–Fullerton
Maria Giuili, Diablo Valley College
Julie Gonzalez, University of California–Santa Cruz
Lisa Grobar, California State University–Long Beach
Steve Hamilton, California State University–Fullerton
Dewey Heinsma, Mt. San Jacinto Community College
Jessica Howell, California State University–Sacramento
Greg Hunter, California State University–Pomona
John Ifcher, Santa Clara University
Ahmed Ispahani, University of LaVerne
George A. Jouganatos, California State University–
   Sacramento
Jonathan Kaplan, California State University–Sacramento
Leland Kempe, California State University–Fresno
Philip King, San Francisco State University
Lori Kletzer, University of California, Santa Cruz
Stephan Kroll, California State University–Sacramento

David Lang, California State University–Sacramento

Carsten Lange, California State Polytechnic University–Pomona

Don Leet, California State University–Fresno

Rose LeMont, Modesto Junior College

Tony Lima, California State University–East Bay

Solina Lindahl, California Polytechnic State University–San Luis Obispo

Roger Mack, DeAnza College

Michael Marlow, California Polytechnic State University

Kristen Monaco, California State University–Long Beach

W. Douglas Morgan, University of California, Santa Barbara

Nivedita Mukherji, Oakland University

Solomon Namala, Cerritos College

Andrew Narwold, University of San Diego

Hanna Paulson, West Los Angeles College

Joseph M. Pogodzinksi, San Jose State University

Michael J. Potepan, San Francisco State University

Mary L. Pranzo, California State University–Fresno

Sasha Radisich, Glendale Community College

Ratha Ramoo, Diablo Valley College

Scott J. Sambucci, California State University–East Bay

Ariane Schauer, Marymount College

Frederica Shockley, California State University–Chico

Mark Siegler, California State University–Sacramento

Jonathan Silberman, Oakland University

Lisa Simon, California Polytechnic State University–San Louis Obispo

Stephen Smith, Bakersfield College

Rodney B. Swanson, University of California–Los Angeles

Martha Stuffler, Irvine Valley College

Lea Templer, College of the Canyons

Kristin A. Van Gaasbeck, California State University–Sacramento

Va Nee Van Vleck, California State University–Fresno

Michael Visser, Sonoma State University

Steven Yamarik, California State University–Long Beach

Guy Yamashiro, California State University–Long Beach

Kevin Young, Diablo Valley College

Anthony Zambelli, Cuyamaca College

COLORADO

Mohammed Akacem, Metropolitan State College of Denver

Rhonda Corman, University of Northern Colorado

Dale DeBoer, University of Colorado–Colorado Springs

Debbie Evercloud, University of Colorado–Denver

Karen Gebhardt, Colorado State University

Scott Houser, Colorado School of Mines

Murat Iyigun, University of Colorado at Boulder

Nancy Jianakoplos, Colorado State University

Jay Kaplan, University of Colorado–Boulder

William G. Mertens, University of Colorado–Boulder

Rachael Small, University of Colorado–Boulder

Stephen Weiler, Colorado State University

CONNECTICUT

Christopher P. Ball, Quinnipiac University

Mark Gius, Quinnipiac University

Mark Jablonowski, University of Hartford

Donn M. Johnson, Quinnipiac University

Robert Martel, University of Connecticut

Judith Mills, Southern Connecticut State University

Matthew Rafferty, Quinnipiac University

Christian Zimmermann, University of Connecticut

DELAWARE

Fatma Abdel-Raouf, Goldey-Beacom College

Ali Ataiifar, Delaware County Community College

Andrew T. Hill, University of Delaware

FLORIDA

Frank Albritton, Seminole State College

Herman Baine, Broward Community College

Robert L. Beekman, University of Tampa

Eric P. Chiang, Florida Atlantic University

Martine Duchatelet, Barry University

Hadley Hartman, Santa Fe Community College

Richard Hawkins, University of West Florida

Brad Kamp, University of South Florida

Brian Kench, University of Tampa

Carrie B. Kerekes, Florida Gulf Coast University

Thomas McCaleb, Florida State University

Barbara A. Moore, University of Central Florida

Augustine Nelson, University of Miami

Jamie Ortiz, Florida Atlantic University

Deborah Paige, Santa Fe Community College

Robert Pennington, University of Central Florida

Bob Potter, University of Central Florida

Jerry Schwartz, Broward Community College–North

William Stronge, Florida Atlantic University

Nora Underwood, University of Central Florida

Zhiguang Wang, Florida International University

Joan Wiggenhorn, Barry University

GEORGIA

Greg Brock, Georgia Southern University

Donna Fisher, Georgia Southern University

Shelby Frost, Georgia State University

John King, Georgia Southern University

Constantin Ogloblin, Georgia Southern University

Dr. Greg Okoro, Georgia Perimeter College–Clarkston

Michael Reksulak, Georgia Southern University

Bill Yang, Georgia Southern University

IDAHO

Cynthia Hill, Idaho State University

Don Holley, Boise State University

Tesa Stegner, Idaho State University

ILLINOIS

Teshome Abebe, Eastern Illinois University

Ali Akarca, University of Illinois–Chicago

Zsolt Becsi, Southern Illinois University–Carbondale

James Bruehler, Eastern Illinois University

Louis Cain, Loyola University and Northwestern University

Rosa Lea Danielson, College of DuPage

Kevin Dunagan, Oakton Community College

Scott Gilbert, Southern Illinois University

Rajeev K. Goel, Illinois State University

David Gordon, Illinois Valley Community College

Alan Grant, Eastern Illinois University

Rik Hafer, Southern Illinois University–Edwardsville

Alice Melkumian, Western Illinois University

Christopher Mushrush, Illinois State University

Jeff Reynolds, Northern Illinois University

Helen Roberts, University of Illinois–Chicago

Thomas R. Sadler, Western Illinois University

Eric Schulz, Northwestern University

Dennis Shannon, Southwestern Illinois College

Charles Sicotte, Rock Valley Community College

Neil T. Skaggs, Illinois State University

Kevin Sylwester, Southern Illinois University–Carbondale

Wendine Thompson-Dawson, Monmouth College

Tara Westerhold, Western Illinois University

Mark Witte, Northwestern University

Laurie Wolff, Southern Illinois University–Carbondale

Paula Worthington, Northwestern University

INDIANA

Kelly Blanchard, Purdue University

Cecil Bohanon, Ball State University

Kirk Doran, University of Notre Dame

Thomas Gresik, University of Notre Dame

Robert B. Harris, Indiana University–Purdue University Indianapolis

Fred Herschede, Indiana University–South Bend

Abraham Mathew, Indiana University–Purdue University Indianapolis

John Pomery, Purdue University

Curtis Price, University of Southern Indiana

Rob Rude, Ivy Tech Community College

James K. Self, Indiana University–Bloomington

Esther-Mirjam Sent, University of Notre Dame

Virginia Shingleton, Valparaiso University

Martin C. Spechler, Indiana University–Purdue University Indianapolis

Arun K. Srinivasan, Indiana University–Southeast Campus

Geetha Suresh, Purdue University

IOWA

Terry Alexander, Iowa State University

Paul Elgatian, St. Ambrose University

Jennifer Fuhrman, University of Iowa

Ken McCormick, University of Northern Iowa

Andy Schuchart, Iowa Central Community College

John Solow, University of Iowa

Jonathan Warner, Dordt College

KANSAS

Guatam Bhattacharya, University of Kansas

Amanda Freeman, Kansas State University

Dipak Ghosh, Emporia State University

Alan Grant, Baker University

Wayne Oberle, St. Ambrose University

Jodi Messer Pelkowski, Wichita State University

Martin Perline, Wichita State University

Joel Potter, Kansas State University

Joshua Rosenbloom, University of Kansas

Shane Sanders, Kansas State University

Dosse Toulaboe, Fort Hays State University

Bhavneet Walia, Kansas State University

KENTUCKY

Tom Cate, Northern Kentucky University

Nan-Ting Chou, University of Louisville

David Eaton, Murray State University

Ann Eike, University of Kentucky

Robert Gillette, University of Kentucky

Barry Haworth, University of Louisville

Gail Hoyt, University of Kentucky

Donna Ingram, Eastern Kentucky University

Waithaka Iraki, Kentucky State University

Hak Youn Kim, Western Kentucky University

Martin Milkman, Murray State University

Jenny Minier, University of Kentucky

David Shideler, Murray State University

John Vahaly, University of Louisville

LOUISIANA

Lara Gardner, Southeastern Louisiana University

Jay Johnson, Southeastern Louisiana University

Faik Koray, Louisiana State University

Paul Nelson, University of Louisiana–Monroe

Sung Chul No, Southern University and A&M College

Tammy Parker, University of Louisiana–Monroe

Wesley A. Payne, Delgado Community College

Nancy Rumore, University of Louisiana at Lafayette

MARYLAND

Carey Borkoski, Anne Arundel Community College

Kathleen A. Carroll, University of Maryland–Baltimore County

Jill Caviglia-Harris, Salisbury University

Dustin Chambers, Salisbury University

Karl Einolf, Mount Saint Mary's University

Marsha Goldfarb, University of Maryland–Baltimore City

Bruce Madariaga, Montgomery College

Shah Mehrabi, Montgomery College

Gretchen Mester, Anne Arundel Community College

David Mitch, University of Maryland–Baltimore County

John Neri, University of Maryland

Henry Terrell, University of Maryland

MASSACHUSETTS

William L. Casey, Jr., Babson College
Arthur Schiller Casimir, Western New England College
Michael Enz, Western New England College
Can Erbil, Brandeis University
Lou Foglia, Suffolk University
Gerald Friedman, University of Massachusetts
Todd Idson, Boston University
Aaron Jackson, Bentley College
Russell A. Janis, University of Massachusetts–Amherst
Anthony Laramie, Merrimack College
Carol McDonough, University of Massachusetts–Lowell
William O'Brien, Worcester State College
Ahmad Saranjam, Bridgewater State College
Howard Shore, Bentley College
Janet Thomas, Bentley College
Gregory H. Wassall, Northeastern University
Bruce G. Webb, Gordon College
Gilbert Wolpe, Newbury College
Jay Zagorsky, Boston University

MICHIGAN

Eric Beckman, Delta College
Jared Boyd, Henry Ford Community College
Victor Claar, Hope College
Dr. Sonia Dalmia, Grand Valley State University
Daniel Giedeman, Grand Valley State University
Allen C. Goodman, Wayne State University
Steven Hayworth, Eastern Michigan University
Gregg Heidebrink, Washtenaw Community College
Carol Hogan, University of Michigan–Dearborn
Marek Kolar, Delta College
Susan J. Linz, Michigan State University
James Luke, Lansing Community College
Ilir Miteza, University of Michigan–Dearborn
John Nader, Grand Valley State University
Norman P. Obst, Michigan State University
Laudo M. Ogura, Grand Valley State University
Robert J. Rossana, Wayne State University
Michael J. Ryan, Western Michigan University
Charles A. Stull, Kalamazoo College
Michael J. Twomey, University of Michigan–Dearborn
Mark Wheeler, Western Michigan University
Wendy Wysocki, Monroe County Community College

MINNESOTA

Mary Edwards, Saint Cloud State University
Phillip J. Grossman, Saint Cloud State University
Monica Hartman, University of St. Thomas
Matthew Hyle, Winona State University
David J. O'Hara, Metropolitan State University–Minneapolis
Kwang Woo (Ken) Park, Minnesota State University–Mankato
Artatrana Ratha, Saint Cloud State University

Ken Rebeck, Saint Cloud State University
Katherine Schmeiser, University of Minnesota

MISSISSIPPI

Becky Campbell, Mississippi State University
Randall Campbell, Mississippi State University
Patricia A. Freeman, Jackson State University
Arlena Sullivan, Jones County Junior College

MISSOURI

Chris Azevedo, University of Central Missouri
Ariel Belasen, Saint Louis University
Catherine Chambers, University of Central Missouri
Paul Chambers, University of Central Missouri
Kermit Clay, Ozarks Technical Community College
Ben Collier, Northwest Missouri State University
John R. Crooker, University of Central Missouri
Jo Durr, Southwest Missouri State University
Julie H. Gallaway, Southwest Missouri State University
Terrel Gallaway, Southwest Missouri State University
Mark Karscig, Central Missouri State University
Nicholas D. Peppes, Saint Louis Community College–Forest Park
Steven T. Petty, College of the Ozarks
Sharon Ryan, University of Missouri–Columbia
Ben Young, University of Missouri–Kansas City

MONTANA

Agnieszka Bielinska-Kwapisz, Montana State University–Bozeman
Jeff Bookwalter, University of Montana–Missoula

NEBRASKA

John Dogbey, University of Nebraska–Omaha
Allan Jenkins, University of Nebraska–Kearney
James Knudsen, Creighton University
Craig MacPhee, University of Nebraska–Lincoln
Kim Sosin, University of Nebraska–Omaha
Mark E. Wohar, University of Nebraska–Omaha

NEVADA

Michael H. Lampert, Truckee Meadows Community College
Bernard Malamud, University of Nevada–Las Vegas
Bill Robinson, University of Nevada–Las Vegas

NEW HAMPSHIRE

Evelyn Gick, Dartmouth College
Neil Niman, University of New Hampshire

NEW JERSEY

Len Anyanwu, Union County College
Maharuk Bhiladwalla, Rutgers University–New Brunswick
Giuliana Campanelli-Andreopoulos, William Paterson University
Gary Gigliotti, Rutgers University–New Brunswick
John Graham, Rutgers University–Newark
Berch Haroian, William Paterson University
Paul Harris, Camden County College
Jeff Rubin, Rutgers University

Henry Ryder, Gloucester County College
Donna Thompson, Brookdale Community College

NEW MEXICO

Donald Coes, University of New Mexico
Kate Krause, University of New Mexico
Curt Shepherd, University of New Mexico

NEW YORK

Seemi Ahmad, Dutchess Community College
Chris Annala, State University of New York–Geneseo
Erol Balkan, Hamilton College
John Bockino, Suffolk County Community College–Ammerman
Charles Callahan III, State University of New York–Brockport
Michael Carew, Baruch College
Sean Corcoran, New York University
Ranjit S. Dighe, City University of New York–Bronx Community College
Debra Dwyer, Stony Brook University
Glenn Gerstner, Saint John's University–Queens
Susan Glanz, Saint John's University–Queens
Wayne A. Grove, LeMoyne College
Nancy Howe, Hudson Valley Community College
Christopher Inya, Monroe Community College
Ghassan Karam, Pace University
Clifford Kern, State University of New York–Binghamton
Mary Lesser, Iona College
Anna Musatti, Columbia University
Theodore Muzio, St. John's University, New York
Emre Ozsoz, Fashion Institute of Technology
Howard Ross, Baruch College
Ed Steinberg, New York University
Leonie Stone, State University of New York–Geneseo
Ganti Subrahmanyam, University of Buffalo
Jogindar S. Uppal, State University of New York–Albany
Susan Wolcott, Binghamton University

NORTH CAROLINA

Rita Balaban, University of North Carolina
Otilia Boldea, North Carolina State University
Robert Burrus, University of North Carolina–Wilmington
Lee A. Craig, North Carolina State University
Alexander Deshkovski, North Carolina Central University
Kathleen Dorsainvil, Winston–Salem State University
Lydia Gan, School of Business, University of North Carolina–Pembroke
Michael Goode, Central Piedmont Community College
Salih Hakeem, North Carolina Central University
Melissa Hendrickson, North Carolina State University
Haiyong Liu, East Carolina University
Kosmas Marinakis, North Carolina State University
Todd McFall, Wake Forest University

Shahriar Mostashari, Campbell University
Jonathan Phillips, North Carolina State University
Bobby Puryear, North Carolina State University
Jeff Sarbaum, University of North Carolina–Greensboro
Peter Schuhmann, University of North Carolina–Wilmington
Robert Shoffner, Central Piedmont Community College
Catherine Skura, Sandhills Community College
Carol Stivender, University of North Carolina–Charlotte
Vera Tabakova, East Carolina University
Eric Taylor, Central Piedmont Community College
Julianne Treme, University of North Carolina–Wilmington
Hui-Kuan Tseng, University of North Carolina at Charlotte
Robert Whaples, Wake Forest University
John Whitehead, Appalachian State University
Gary W. Zinn, East Carolina University
Rick Zuber, University of North Carolina at Charlotte

OHIO

John P. Blair, Wright State University
Bolong Cao, Ohio University–Athens
Kyongwook Choi, Ohio University
James D'Angelo, University of Cincinnati
Darlene DeVera, Miami University
Rudy Fichtenbaum, Wright State University
Tim Fuerst, Bowling Green University
Harley Gill, Ohio State University
Leroy Gill, Ohio State University
Steven Heubeck, Ohio State University
Daniel Horton, Cleveland State University
Kristen Keith, University of Toledo
Jean Kujawa, Lourdes College
Ernest Massie, Franklin University
Ida A. Mirzaie, Ohio State University
Jay Mutter, University of Akron
Mike Nelson, University of Akron
Nicholas Noble, Miami University
Dennis C. O'Neill, University of Cincinnati
Joseph Palardy, Youngstown State University
Charles Reichheld, Cuyahoga Community College
Teresa Riley, Youngstown State University
Rochelle Ruffer, Youngstown State University
Kate Sheppard, University of Akron
Richard Stratton, University of Akron
Albert Sumell, Youngstown State University
Steve Szheghi, Wilmington College
Melissa Thomasson, Miami University
Yaqin Wang, Youngstown State University
Bert Wheeler, Cedarville University
Kathryn Wilson, Kent State University
Sourushe Zandvakili, University of Cincinnati

OKLAHOMA

David Hudgins, University of Oklahoma
Bill McLean, Oklahoma State University
Denny Myers, Oklahoma City Community College
Ed Price, Oklahoma State University
Abdulhamid Sukar, Cameron University
Zhen Zhu, University of Central Oklahoma

OREGON

Bill Burrows, Lane Community College
Tom Carroll, Central Oregon Community College
Tim Duy, University of Oregon
B. Starr McMullen, Oregon State University
Ted Scheinman, Mount Hood Community College
Larry Singell, University of Oregon
Ayca Tekin-Koru, Oregon State University

PENNSYLVANIA

Bradley Andrew, Juniata College
Mohammad Bajwa, Northampton Community College
Gustavo Barboza, Mercyhurst College
Charles A. Bennett, Gannon University
Cynthia Benzing, West Chester University
Howard Bodenhorn, Lafayette College
Milica Bookman, St. Joseph's University
Robert Brooker, Gannon University
Eric Brucker, Widener University
Shirley Cassing, University of Pittsburgh
Linda Childs-Leatherbury, Lincoln University
Scott J. Dressler, Villanova University
Satyajit Ghosh, University of Scranton
William L. Goffe, Pennsylvania State University
Anthony Gyapong, Pennsylvania State University–
   Abington
Mehdi Haririan, Bloomsburg University
Andrew Hill, Federal Reserve Bank of Philadelphia
Steven Husted, University of Pittsburgh
James Jozefowicz, Indiana University of Pennsylvania
Stephanie Jozefowicz, Indiana University of Pennsylvania
Nicholas Karatjas, Indiana University of Pennsylvania
Mary Kelly, Villanova University
Brendan Kennelly, Lehigh University
Thomas C. Kinnaman, Bucknell University
Christopher Magee, Bucknell University
Katherine McCann, Penn State
Judy McDonald, Lehigh University
Ranganath Murthy, Bucknell University
Hong V. Nguyen, University of Scranton
Cristian Pardo, Saint Joseph's University
Iordanis Petsas, University of Scranton
Denis Raihall, West Chester University
Adam Renhoff, Drexel University
Nicole Sadowski, York College of Pennsylvania
Edward Scahill, University of Scranton
Ken Slaysman, York College of Pennsylvania
Rajeev Sooreea, Pennsylvania State University–Altoona

Rebecca Stein, University of Pennsylvania
Sandra Trejos, Clarion University
Peter Zaleski, Villanova University
Ann Zech, Saint Joseph's University
Lei Zhu, West Chester University
Susan Zumas, Lehigh University

RHODE ISLAND

Jongsung Kim, Bryant University
Leonard Lardaro, University of Rhode Island
Nazma Latif-Zaman, Providence College

SOUTH CAROLINA

Calvin Blackwell, College of Charleston
Ward Hooker, Orangeburg–Calhoun Technical College
Woodrow W. Hughes, Jr., Converse College
John McArthur, Wofford College
Chad Turner, Clemson University
Madelyn Young, Converse College

SOUTH DAKOTA

Joseph M. Santos, South Dakota State University
Jason Zimmerman, South Dakota State University

TENNESSEE

Sindy Abadie, Southwest Tennessee Community College
Charles Baum, Middle Tennessee State University
John Brassel, Southwest Tennessee Community College
Bichaka Fayissa, Middle Tennessee State University
Michael J. Gootzeit, University of Memphis
Travis Hayes, University of Tennessee–Chattanooga
Christopher C. Klein, Middle Tennessee State University
Leila Pratt, University of Tennessee at Chattanooga
Millicent Sites, Carson-Newman College

TEXAS

Carlos Aguilar, El Paso Community College
Rashid Al-Hmoud, Texas Tech University
William Beaty, Tarleton State University
Klaus Becker, Texas Tech University
Alex Brown, Texas A&M University
Jack A. Bucco, Austin Community College–Northridge
   and Saint Edward's University
Don Bumpass, Sam Houston State University
Marilyn M. Butler, Sam Houston State University
Mike Cohick, Collin County Community College
Cesar Corredor, Texas A&M University
Steven Craig, University of Houston
Patrick Crowley, Texas A&M University–Corpus Christi
Richard Croxdale, Austin Community College
Susan Dadres, Southern Methodist University
David Davenport, McLennan Community College
Harry Ellis, Jr., University of North Texas
Paul Emberton, Texas State University
Diego Escobari, Texas A&M University
Nicholas Feltovich, University of Houston–Main
Charles Harold Fifield, Baylor University
Jamal G. Husein, Angelo State University
Mark Frank, Sam Houston State University

Alejandro Gelves, Midwestern State University

Edgar Ghossoub, University of Texas–San Antonio

Richard Gosselin, Houston Community College–Central

Sheila Amin Gutierrez de Pineres, University of Texas–Dallas

Tina J. Harvell, Blinn College–Bryan Campus

James W. Henderson, Baylor University

Jane S. Himarios, University of Texas–Arlington

James Holcomb, University of Texas–El Paso

Jamal Husein, Angelo State University

Ansul Islam, University of Houston–Downtown

Karen Johnson, Baylor University

Kathy Kelly, University of Texas–Arlington

Thomas Kemp, Tarrant County College–Northwest

Jim Lee, Texas A&M University–Corpus Christi

Ronnie W. Liggett, University of Texas–Arlington

Akbar Marvasti, University of Houston–Downtown

James Mbata, Houston Community College

Kimberly Mencken, Baylor University

Randy Methenitis, Richland College

Carl Montano, Lamar University

James Moreno, Blinn College

Camille Nelson, Texas A&M University

Michael Nelson, Texas A&M University

Charles Newton, Houston Community College–Southwest College

John Pisciotta, Baylor University

Shofiqur Rahman, University of Texas–El Paso

Sara Saderion, Houston Community College–Southwest College

George E. Samuels, Sam Houston State University

David Schutte, Mountain View College

Ivan Tasic, Texas A&M University

David Torres, University of Texas–El Paso

Ross vanWassenhove, University of Houston

Roger Wehr, University of Texas–Arlington

Jim Wollscheid, Texas A&M University–Kingsville

J. Christopher Wreh, North Central Texas College

David W. Yoskowitz, Texas A&M University–Corpus Christi

Inske Zandvliet, Brookhaven College

UTAH

Chris Fawson, Utah State University

Lowell Glenn, Utah Valley State College

Aric Krause, Westminster College

Arden Pope, Brigham Young University

VERMONT

Nancy Brooks, University of Vermont

VIRGINIA

Lee Badgett, Virginia Military Institute

Lee A. Coppock, University of Virginia

Janelle Davenport, Hampton University

Philip Heap, James Madison University

George E. Hoffer, Virginia Commonwealth University

Oleg Korenok, Virginia Commonwealth University

Larry Landrum, Virginia Western Community College

Frances Lea, Germanna Community College

Carrie Meyer, George Mason University

John Min, Northern Virginia Community College

Eugene Bempong Nyantakyi, West Virginia University

James Roberts, Tidewater Community College–Virginia Beach

Robert Rycroft, University of Mary Washington

Araine A. Schauer, Mary Mount College

Sarah Stafford, The College of William & Mary

Bob Subrick, James Madison University

Susanne Toney, Hampton University

Michelle Vachris, Christopher Newport University

James Wetzel, Virginia Commonwealth University

George Zestos, Christopher Newport University

WASHINGTON

Genevieve Briand, Washington State University

Andrew Ewing, University of Washington

Stacey Jones, Seattle University

Dean Peterson, Seattle University

Robert Rosenman, Washington State University

WEST VIRGINIA

Jacqueline Agesa, Marshall University

Richard Agesa, Marshall University

WISCONSIN

Peng Huang, Ripon College

Marina Karabelas, Milwaukee Area Technical College

Elizabeth Sawyer Kelly, University of Wisconsin–Madison

Pascal Ngoboka, University of Wisconsin–River Falls

Kevin Quinn, St. Norbert College

John R. Stoll, University of Wisconsin–Green Bay

WYOMING

Robert Godby, University of Wyoming

DISTRICT OF COLUMBIA

Leon Battista, American Enterprise Institute

Michael Bradley, George Washington University

Colleen M. Callahan, American University

Robert Feinberg, American University

Walter Park, American University

INTERNATIONAL

Minh Quang Dao, Carleton University–Ottawa, Canada

A Word of Thanks

Once again, we benefited greatly from the dedication and professionalism of the Pearson Economics team. Executive Editor David Alexander's energy and support were indispensable. David helped mold the presentation and provided words of encouragement whenever our energy flagged. Executive Development Editor Lena Buonanno worked tirelessly to ensure that this text was as good as it could be and to coordinate the many moving parts involved in a project of this magnitude. This new edition posed particular challenges, and we remain astonished at the amount of time, energy, and unfailing good humor she brings to this project. As we worked on the first edition, former Director of Key Markets David Theisen provided invaluable insight into how best to structure a principles text. His advice helped shape nearly every chapter. Lindsey Sloan managed all aspects of the media resources and helped keep both them and the print book on schedule. Carla Thompson managed the entire production process, and Sarah Dumouchelle managed the extensive supplement package that accompanies the book. Carla Thompson and Jonathan Boylan turned our manuscript pages into a beautiful published book. Editorial Assistant Michelle Zeng assisted the team in completing several tasks to help produce both the media resources and the book. We received excellent research assistance on this and previous editions from Dante DeAntonio, Ed Timmons, Matthew Saboe, David Van Der Goes, and Jason Hockenberry. We thank Elisa Adams, Pam Smith, Elena Zeller, Jennifer Brailsford, Lindsay K. Clark, Debroah Crowell, Ellen Vandevort Wolf, and Cindy O'Brien for their careful proofreading of first- and second-round page proofs. Over all editions of our books, we received helpful feedback and recommendations from Lehigh University faculty colleagues Frank R. Gunter, Thomas J. Hyclak, and Robert J. Thornton.

As instructors, we recognize how important it is for students to view graphs that are clear and accessible. We are fortunate to have Fernando Quijano render all the figures in our books and also our supplements. Market feedback on the figures continues to be positive. We extend our thanks to Fernando not only for collaborating with us and creating the best figures possible but also for his patience with our demanding schedule.

This sixth edition has several media components, which required skilled and patient creators and developers. We extend special thanks to Andy Taylor of Hodja Media for preparing the video clips and to Paul Graf of the University of Indiana–Bloomington for preparing the graph animations. These videos and animations are an important part of our revision.

A good part of the burden of a project of this magnitude is borne by our families. We appreciate the patience, support, and encouragement of our wives and children.

Economics: Foundations and Models

Chapter Outline and Learning Objectives

Will Smart Devices Revolutionize Health Care?

If you get sick, your doctor may send you to a hospital or clinic for a series of tests. You'll need to schedule an appointment, travel to the clinic, and spend time in a waiting room. Depending on your medical insurance, you'll also need to pay for the tests. But what if you had an inexpensive smart device that would allow you to test yourself at home and send the results to your doctor? Walter De Brouwer is a Belgian-born entrepreneur who worked in various industries, including telecommunications and publishing. When his son was badly injured in a fall, De Brouwer was inspired to create such a smart device. His California-based firm, Scanadu, developed the Scout, a small disk that when pressed against the side of your head can record your blood pressure, heart rate, and temperature. According to the firm's advertising, the Scout allows you to "Check your health as easily as your e-mail." Some people have compared the Scout to the Tricorder medical device from the *Star Trek* TV series.

Scanadu is not alone in developing new consumer medical devices. The Apple Watch monitors your heart rate, as well as how much exercise you've performed and how many calories you've burned; OraSure sells a home HIV test; and Alivecor sells a device that can be attached to a smartphone and allows people with heart problems to perform their own electrocardiograms.

These firms are reacting to several trends: Many people have become more health conscious; as the population ages, more people are experiencing medical problems; and technological progress has made it possible for small electronic devices, including smartwatches and smartphones, to monitor blood pressure and perform other tasks. These firms are responding to changing *economic incentives*. As we will see, the *market system* provides firms with the incentive and the resources to both create new goods and services and improve existing goods and services. The result is an ever-increasing standard of living for the average person.

Over time, as technology, consumer demand, and government policies change, the market system enables the flow of resources out of some industries and into others. For instance, in the United States resources have been flowing out of the production of manufactured goods such as steel, shoes, and furniture and into the production of services, including medical services. In fact, health care has been the most rapidly expanding sector of the U.S. economy.

AN INSIDE LOOK on **page 20** explores how Google is adding to its growing list of technological innovations by developing smart contact lenses to help patients manage diabetes.

Sources: Timothy Hay, "Gadgets Bring Diagnostics into the Home," *Wall Street Journal*, April 27, 2015; Jacopo Prisco, "Scanadu: The Medical Tricorder from *Star Trek* Is Here," cnn.com, February 11, 2015; and Peter Andrey Smith, "Zombies, Workout Music and Baby Trackers: Health Tech for Everyone," *New York Times*, March 10, 2014.

Economics in Your Life

Will There Be Plenty of Jobs Available in the Health Care Industry?

The U.S. Health Resources and Services Administration (HRSA) forecasts that there will be 866,400 doctors in the United States in 2020. The HRSA also forecasts that by 2020 the country will need 922,000 doctors. In other words, this federal government agency forecasts that there will be a *shortage* of about 55,600 doctors in 2020. The U.S. Bureau of Labor Statistics forecasts that 13 of the 20 fastest-growing occupations over the next 10 years will be in the medical field. But the availability of these jobs depends on the reliability of the forecasts. What is the basis for these forecasts and how reliable are they? As you read this chapter, try to answer this question. You can check your answer against the one we provide on **page 19** at the end of this chapter.

In this book, we use economics to answer questions such as the following:

- What determines the prices of smartwatches?
- Why have health care costs risen so rapidly?
- Why do firms engage in international trade, and how do government policies affect international trade?
- Why does the government control the prices of some goods and services, and what are the effects of those controls?

Economists do not always agree on the answers to every question, and there are lively debates on some issues. Because new problems and issues are constantly arising, economists are always developing new methods to analyze economic questions.

All the topics we discuss in this book illustrate a basic fact of life: To attain our goals, we must make choices. We must make choices because we live in a world of **scarcity**, which means that although our wants are *unlimited*, the resources available to fulfill those wants are *limited*. You might want to own a BMW and spend each summer vacationing at five-star European hotels, but unless Bill Gates is a close and generous relative, you probably lack the funds to fulfill these wants. Every day, you make choices as you spend your limited income on the many goods and services available. The finite amount of time you have also limits your ability to attain your goals. If you spend an hour studying for your economics midterm, you have one hour less to study for your history midterm. Firms and the government are in the same situation as you: They must also attain their goals with limited resources. **Economics** is the study of the choices consumers, business managers, and government officials make to attain their goals, given their scarce resources.

We begin this chapter by discussing three important economic ideas that we will return to many times in the following chapters: *People are rational, people respond to economic incentives,* and *optimal decisions are made at the margin.* Then, we consider the three fundamental questions that any economy must answer: *What* goods and services will be produced? *How* will the goods and services be produced? and *Who* will receive the goods and services produced? Next, we consider the role of *economic models* in analyzing economic issues. **Economic models** are simplified versions of reality used to analyze real-world economic situations. We will explore why economists use models and how they construct them. Finally, we will discuss the difference between microeconomics and macroeconomics, and we will preview some important economic terms.

Scarcity A situation in which unlimited wants exceed the limited resources available to fulfill those wants.

Economics The study of the choices people make to attain their goals, given their scarce resources.

Economic model A simplified version of reality used to analyze real-world economic situations.

Market A group of buyers and sellers of a good or service and the institution or arrangement by which they come together to trade.

1.1 Three Key Economic Ideas

LEARNING OBJECTIVE: Explain these three key economic ideas: People are rational; people respond to economic incentives; and optimal decisions are made at the margin.

Whether your goal is to buy a smartwatch or find a part-time job, you will interact with other people in *markets*. A **market** is a group of buyers and sellers of a good or service and the institution or arrangement by which they come together to trade. Examples of markets are the markets for smartwatches, houses, haircuts, stocks and bonds, and labor. Most of economics involves analyzing how people make choices and interact in markets. Here are the three important ideas about markets that we'll return to frequently:

1. People are rational.
2. People respond to economic incentives.
3. Optimal decisions are made at the margin.

People Are Rational

Economists generally assume that people are rational. This assumption does *not* mean that economists believe everyone knows everything or always makes the "best" decision. It means that economists assume that consumers and firms use all available information as they act to achieve their goals. Rational individuals weigh the benefits and costs of each action, and they choose an action only if the benefits outweigh the costs. For example, if Apple charges a price of $349 for the basic model of its smartwatch, economists assume that the managers at Apple have estimated that this price will earn the company the most profit. Even though the managers may be wrong—maybe a price of $325 or $375 would be more profitable—economists assume that the managers at Apple have acted rationally, on the basis of the information available to them, in choosing the price of $349. Although not everyone behaves rationally all the time, the assumption of rational behavior is very useful in explaining most of the choices that people make.   MyEconLab Concept Check

People Respond to Economic Incentives

Human beings act from a variety of motives, including envy, compassion, and religious belief. While not ignoring other motives, economists emphasize that consumers and firms consistently respond to *economic incentives*. This point may seem obvious, but it is often overlooked. For example, according to an article in the *Wall Street Journal*, the FBI couldn't understand why banks were not taking steps to improve security in the face of an increase in robberies: "FBI officials suggest that banks place uniformed, armed guards outside their doors and install bullet-resistant plastic, known as a 'bandit barrier,' in front of teller windows." FBI officials were surprised that few banks took their advice. But the article also reported that installing bullet-resistant plastic costs $10,000 to $20,000, and a well-trained security guard receives $50,000 per year in salary and benefits. The average loss in a bank robbery is only about $1,200. The economic incentive to banks is clear: It is less costly to put up with bank robberies than to take additional security measures. FBI agents may be surprised by how banks respond to the threat of robberies—but economists are not.

In each chapter, the *Making the Connection* feature discusses a news story or another application related to the chapter material. Read this *Making the Connection* for a discussion of whether people respond to economic incentives even when deciding how much to eat and how much to exercise.   MyEconLab Concept Check

Does Health Insurance Give People an Incentive to Become Obese?

Obesity is a significant health problem in the United States. Body mass index (BMI) is a measurement of a person's weight relative to the person's height. The U.S. Centers for Disease Control and Prevention (CDC) defines *obesity* for an adult as having a body mass index (BMI) of 30 or greater. For example, a 5'4" adult with a BMI of 30 is 30 pounds overweight. Obesity is a factor in a variety of diseases, including heart disease, stroke, diabetes, and hypertension.

The two maps on the next page show the dramatic increase in obesity between 1994 and 2013. In 1994, in a majority of states, only between 10 percent and 14 percent of the adult population was obese, and in no state was more than 20 percent of the adult population obese. By 2013, in every state, at least 20 percent of the adult population was obese, and in 43 states, at least 25 percent of the adult population was obese.

Many people who suffer from obesity have underlying medical conditions. For these people, obesity is a medical problem that they cannot control. The fact that obesity has increased, though, indicates that for some people obesity is the result of

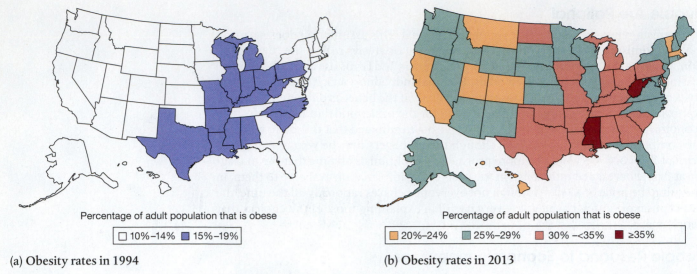

Percentage of adult population that is obese

□ 10%–14% ■ 15%–19%

(a) Obesity rates in 1994

Percentage of adult population that is obese

□ 20%–24% ■ 25%–29% ■ 30% –<35% ■ ≥35%

(b) Obesity rates in 2013

Source: Centers for Disease Control and Prevention, "Prevalence of Self-Reported Obesity among U.S. Adults."

diet and lifestyle choices. Potential explanations for the increase in obesity include greater intake of high-calorie fast foods, insufficient exercise, and a decline in the physical activity associated with many jobs. The CDC recommends that teenagers get a minimum of 60 minutes of aerobic exercise per day, a standard that only 15 percent of high school students meet. In 1960, 50 percent of jobs in the United States required at least moderate physical activity. Today, only 20 percent of jobs do. As a result, a typical worker today who may work at a computer is burning off about 130 *fewer* calories per workday than a worker in the 1960s who may have walked frequently in a manufacturing plant.

In addition to eating too much and not exercising enough, could having health insurance be a cause of obesity? Obese people tend to suffer more medical problems and so incur higher medical costs. Obese people with health insurance that will reimburse them for only part of their medical bills, or who have no health insurance, must pay some or all of these higher medical bills themselves. People with health insurance that covers most of their medical bills will not suffer as large a monetary cost from being obese. In other words, by reducing some of the costs of obesity, health insurance may give people an economic incentive to gain weight.

At first glance, this argument may seem implausible. Some people suffer from medical conditions that can make physical activity difficult or that can cause weight gain even with moderate eating, so they may become obese whether they have health insurance or not. Some people are obese because of poor eating habits or lack of exercise, and they probably don't consider health insurance when deciding whether to have another slice of chocolate cake or to watch Netflix instead of going to the gym. But if economists are correct about the importance of economic incentives, then we would expect that if we hold all other personal characteristics—such as age, gender, and income—constant, people with health insurance will be more likely to be overweight than people without health insurance.

Jay Bhattacharya and Kate Bundorf of Stanford University, Noemi Pace of the University of Venice, and Neeraj Sood of the University of Southern California, have analyzed the effects of health insurance on weight. Using a sample that followed nearly 80,000 people from 1989 to 2004, they found that after controlling for factors including age, gender, income, education, and race, people with health insurance were significantly more likely to be overweight than people without health insurance. Having private health insurance increased BMI by 1.3 points. Having public health insurance, such as Medicaid, which is a program under which the government provides health care to low-income people, increased BMI by 2.3 points. These findings suggest that people respond to economic incentives even when making decisions about what they eat and how much they exercise.

Note: The exact formula for the body mass index is BMI = (Weight in pounds/Height in inches^2) × 703.

Sources: Centers for Disease Control and Prevention, "Prevalence of Self-Reported Obesity among U.S. Adults," www.cdc.gov; Katherine M. Flegal, Margaret D. Caroll, Cynthia L. Ogden, and Lester R. Curtin, "Prevalence and Trends in Obesity among U.S. Adults, 1999–2008," *Journal of the American Medical Association,* Vol. 303, No. 3, January 20, 2010, pp. 235–241; Jay Bhattacharya, Kate Bundorf, Noemi Pace, and Neeraj Sood, "Does Health Insurance Make You Fat?" in Michael Grossman and Naci H. Mocan, eds., *Economic Aspects of Obesity,* Chicago: University of Chicago Press, 2011; and Tara Parker-Pope, "Less Active at Work, Americans Have Packed on Pounds," *New York Times,* May 25, 2011.

Your Turn: Test your understanding by doing related problems 1.7 and 1.8 on page 23 at the end of this chapter.

MyEconLab Study Plan

Optimal Decisions Are Made at the Margin

Some decisions are "all or nothing." For instance, when an entrepreneur decides whether to open a new restaurant, she starts the new restaurant or she doesn't. When you decide whether to attend graduate school, you either enter graduate school or you don't. But rather than being all or nothing, most decisions in life involve doing a little more or a little less. If you are trying to decrease your spending and increase your saving, the decision is not really between saving all the money you earn or spending it all. Rather, many small choices are involved, such as whether to buy a caffè mocha at Starbucks every day or just once a week.

Economists use the word *marginal* to mean "extra" or "additional." Should you watch another hour of television or spend that hour studying? The *marginal benefit* (MB) of watching more television is the additional enjoyment you receive. The *marginal cost* (MC) is the reduction in your test score from having studied a little less. Should Apple produce an additional 300,000 smartwatches? Firms receive *revenue* from selling goods. Apple's marginal benefit is the additional revenue it receives from selling 300,000 more smartwatches. Apple's marginal cost is the additional cost—for wages, parts, and so forth—of producing 300,000 more smartwatches. *Economists reason that the optimal decision is to continue any activity up to the point where the marginal benefit equals the marginal cost— that is, to the point where* MB = MC. Often we apply this rule without consciously thinking about it. Usually you will know whether the additional enjoyment from watching a television program is worth the additional cost you pay by not spending that hour studying, without giving the decision a lot of thought. In business situations, however, firms often have to make careful calculations to determine, for example, whether the additional revenue received from increasing production is greater or less than the additional cost of the production. Economists refer to analysis that involves comparing marginal benefits and marginal costs as **marginal analysis**.

In each chapter, you will see the feature *Solved Problem.* This feature will increase your understanding of the material by leading you through the steps of solving an applied economic problem. After reading the problem, test your understanding by doing the related problems that appear at the end of the chapter. You can also complete Solved Problems on **www.myeconlab.com** and receive tutorial help. MyEconLab Concept Check

Marginal analysis Analysis that involves comparing marginal benefits and marginal costs.

Solved Problem 1.1

MyEconLab Interactive Animation

OraSure Makes a Decision at the Margin

OraSure is a medical technology firm based in Pennsylvania that produces, among other products, a device that allows consumers to test for HIV (human immunodeficiency virus) at home. In 2015, OraSure decided to reduce advertising for this device. The firm's chief executive officer (CEO) stated that the advertising had not been as effective as he had hoped in increasing sales of the device. A news story quoted him as saying, "Consequently, we had to adjust our [spending on advertising to] make it more proportional to revenue." Assuming that reducing advertising will reduce OraSure's sales of the device, how should the firm determine by what amount to reduce its advertising? Is it possible that OraSure is making a mistake by reducing its advertising? Briefly explain.

Solving the Problem

Step 1: **Review the chapter material.** This problem is about making decisions, so you may want to review the section "Optimal Decisions Are Made at the Margin," which begins on page 7.

Step 2: **Explain how OraSure should determine by what amount to reduce its advertising.** We have seen that any activity should be continued to the point where the marginal benefit is equal to the marginal cost. In this case, OraSure apparently believes it is violating this rule because the additional cost from advertising is greater than the additional revenue it receives from the increased sales that result from the advertising. Therefore, OraSure will be better off reducing its advertising because the decline in cost will be greater than the decline in revenue. The company's goal should be to reduce advertising spending to the amount where the additional revenue resulting from the last dollar of advertising equals the additional cost of the advertising.

Step 3: **Explain whether it is possible that OraSure's decision to reduce advertising is a mistake.** OraSure's CEO was disappointed in the extent to which advertising was increasing sales of the device. But the firm might still be spending the optimal amount on advertising even though the CEO hoped the effect of the advertising would be greater than it was. If the marginal revenue from the last dollar of advertising were equal to its marginal cost, reducing advertising spending would make the firm worse off. The only way to ensure a correct decision is for the firm to analyze the effect of changes in advertising spending on the firm's revenues and costs.

Source: Scott Krause, "OraSure's Ebola Test Moving Forward in Africa," (Allentown, PA) *Morning Call*, May 6, 2015.

MyEconLab Study Plan

Your Turn: For more practice, do related problems 1.9 and 1.10 on page 23 at the end of this chapter.

1.2 The Economic Problem That Every Society Must Solve

LEARNING OBJECTIVE: Discuss how an economy answers these questions: What goods and services will be produced? How will the goods and services be produced? Who will receive the goods and services produced?

Because we live in a world of scarcity, any society faces the *economic problem* that it has only a limited amount of economic resources—such as workers, machines, and raw materials—and so can produce only a limited amount of goods and services. Therefore, every society faces **trade-offs**: Producing more of one good or service means producing less of another good or service. The best measure of the cost of producing a good or service is the value of what has to be given up to produce it. The **opportunity cost** of any activity—such as producing a good or service—is the highest-valued alternative that must be given up to engage in that activity. The concept of opportunity cost is very important in economics and applies to individuals, firms, and society as a whole. For instance, suppose that you earn a salary of $100,000 per year working for Scanadu, the medical technology firm discussed at the beginning of the chapter. You decide to open your own firm to create and sell medical devices. In this case, the opportunity cost of the services you supply to your own firm is the $100,000 you give up by not working for Scanadu, *even if you do not explicitly pay yourself a salary.* As in this example, opportunity costs often do not involve actual payments of money.

Trade-off The idea that, because of scarcity, producing more of one good or service means producing less of another good or service.

Opportunity cost The highest-valued alternative that must be given up to engage in an activity.

Making the Connection
MyEconLab Video

It's Saturday Afternoon; Why Aren't You at the Game?

For many students, attending college football games is an enjoyable way to spend Saturday afternoons in the fall. However, some colleges have experienced a decline in the number of students attending their games. In 2014, average attendance at the 127 larger schools that make up the Football Bowl Subdivision declined to the lowest level in 14 years. In the past few years, nearly 40 percent of the tickets allocated to students at the University of Georgia have gone unsold. Even coach Nick Saban, whose University of Alabama team has won several national championships in recent years, has publically voiced concern about low student attendance at the team's games.

What explains the decrease in the number of students willing to attend football games? In some schools, rising ticket prices help explain the decline. One student at the University of Michigan was quoted as saying: "People are looking to trim costs, and for a lot of folks, football is an easy thing to cut. It's not essential to going to college."

There are more empty seats at college football stadiums because the opportunity cost of attending games has increased.

Remember that the opportunity cost of engaging in an activity is the value of the best alternative that must be given up to engage in that activity. The opportunity cost of attending a college football game is *not* just the price of a ticket. If the price of a ticket to a game is $50, your opportunity cost is the ticket price *plus* the value you place on what else you could do if you don't attend the game. At one time, relatively few college football games were televised, but today multiple cable networks broadcast games. If you attend your college's games, you miss the opportunity to watch the games being broadcast at the same time—in high-definition with replays shown from multiple camera angles and expert commentary to clarify what is happening. When watching games in your room or at a sports restaurant, you can also post to Facebook, Instagram, or Twitter, read e-mail, surf the Web, and take or receive phone calls. Wi-Fi and cellular reception is often poor in college stadiums, making these activities difficult.

So the opportunity cost of attending college football games has increased in recent years, not just because ticket prices have risen but because the number of alternative activities that students value highly has also increased. We expect that when the opportunity cost of engaging in an activity increases, people will engage in that activity less, as we've seen with student attendance at college football games.

Colleges have responded to declining student attendance by reducing ticket prices, improving Wi-Fi and cellular service, and installing high-definition video boards that show replays as they appear on television. Whether these attempts to lower the opportunity cost of attending college football games will succeed remains to be seen.

Sources: Jon Solomon, "College Football Attendance: Home Crowds Drop to Lowest in 14 Years," cbssports.com, December 15, 2014; Adam Rittenberg, "Attendance Challenges Big Deal for B1G," espn.com, February 14, 2014; and Ben Cohen, "At College Football Games, Student Sections Likely to Have Empty Seats," *Wall Street Journal*, August 27, 2014.

Your Turn: Test your understanding by doing related problem 2.7 on page 24 at the end of this chapter.

Trade-offs force society to make choices when answering the following three fundamental questions:

1. *What* goods and services will be produced?
2. *How* will the goods and services be produced?
3. *Who* will receive the goods and services produced?

Throughout this book, we will return to these questions many times. For now, we briefly introduce each question.

What Goods and Services Will Be Produced?

How will society decide whether to produce more economics textbooks or more Blu-ray players? More daycare facilities or more football stadiums? Of course, "society" does not make decisions; only individuals make decisions. The answer to the question of what will be produced is determined by the choices that consumers and people working for firms or the government make. Every day, you help decide which goods and services firms will produce when you choose to buy an iPhone instead of a Samsung Galaxy or a caffè mocha rather than a chai tea. Similarly, managers at Apple must choose whether to devote the company's scarce resources to making more iPhones or more smartwatches. Members of Congress and the president must choose whether to spend more of the federal government's limited budget on breast cancer research or on repairing highways. In each case, consumers, managers of firms, and government policymakers face the problem of scarcity by trading off one good or service for another. And each choice made comes with an opportunity cost, measured by the value of the best alternative given up.   MyEconLab **Concept Check**

How Will the Goods and Services Be Produced?

Firms choose how to produce the goods and services they sell. In many cases, firms face a trade-off between using more workers or using more machines. For example, a local service station has to choose whether to provide car repair services using more diagnostic computers and fewer auto mechanics or fewer diagnostic computers and more auto mechanics. Similarly, movie studios have to choose whether to produce animated films using highly skilled animators to draw them by hand or fewer animators and more computers. In deciding whether to move production offshore to China, firms may need to choose between a production method in the United States that uses fewer workers and more machines and a production method in China that uses more workers and fewer machines.   MyEconLab **Concept Check**

Who Will Receive the Goods and Services Produced?

In the United States, who receives the goods and services produced depends largely on how income is distributed. The higher a person's income, the more goods and services he or she can buy. Often, people are willing to give up some of their income—and, therefore, some of their ability to purchase goods and services—by donating to charities to increase the incomes of poorer people. Each year, Americans donate more than $325 billion to charity, or an average donation of $2,800 for each household in the country. An important policy question, however, is whether the government should intervene to make the distribution of income more equal. Such intervention already occurs in the United States because people with higher incomes pay a larger fraction of their incomes in taxes and because the government makes payments to people with low incomes. There is disagreement over whether the current attempts to redistribute income are sufficient or whether there should be more or less redistribution.   MyEconLab **Concept Check**

Centrally Planned Economies versus Market Economies

Centrally planned economy An economy in which the government decides how economic resources will be allocated.

Market economy An economy in which the decisions of households and firms interacting in markets allocate economic resources.

To answer the three questions—what, how, and who—societies organize their economies in two main ways. A society can have a **centrally planned economy** in which the government decides how economic resources will be allocated. Or a society can have a **market economy** in which the decisions of households and firms interacting in markets allocate economic resources.

From 1917 to 1991, the most important centrally planned economy in the world was that of the Soviet Union, which was established when Vladimir Lenin and the Communist Party staged a revolution and took control of the Russian Empire. In the Soviet Union, the government decided what goods to produce, how the goods would be produced, and who would receive the goods. Government employees managed factories and stores. The objective of these managers was to follow the government's orders rather than to satisfy the wants of consumers.

Centrally planned economies like that of the Soviet Union have not been successful in producing low-cost, high-quality goods and services. As a result, the standard of living of the average person in a centrally planned economy tends to be low. All centrally planned economies have also been political dictatorships. Dissatisfaction with low living standards and political repression finally led to the collapse of the Soviet Union in 1991. Today, only North Korea still has a completely centrally planned economy.

All high-income democracies, including the United States, Canada, Japan, and the countries of Western Europe, have market economies. Market economies rely primarily on privately owned firms to produce goods and services and to decide how to produce them. Markets, rather than the government, determine who receives the goods and services produced. In a market economy, firms must produce goods and services that meet the wants of consumers, or the firms will go out of business. In that sense, it is ultimately consumers who decide what goods and services will be produced. Because firms in a market economy compete to offer the highest-quality products at the lowest price, they are under pressure to use the lowest-cost methods of production. For example, in the past 10 years, some U.S. firms have been under pressure to reduce their costs to meet competition from Chinese firms.

In a market economy, the income of an individual is determined by the payments he receives for what he has to sell. If you become a civil engineer, and firms are willing to pay a salary of $85,000 per year for someone with your training and skills, you will have this amount of income to purchase goods and services. If you also buy a house that you rent out, your income will be even higher. One of the attractive features of markets is that they reward hard work. Generally, the more extensive the training you have received and the longer the hours you work, the higher your income will be. Of course, luck—both good and bad—also plays a role here. Someone might have a high income because she won the state lottery, while someone else might have a low income because he has severe medical problems. We can conclude that market economies respond to the question, "Who receives the goods and services produced?" with the answer, "Those who are most willing and able to buy them."   MyEconLab Concept Check

The Modern "Mixed" Economy

In the 1800s and early 1900s, the U.S. government engaged in relatively little regulation of markets for goods and services. Beginning in the mid-1900s, government intervention in the economy dramatically increased in the United States and other market economies. This increase was primarily caused by the high rates of unemployment and business bankruptcies during the Great Depression of the 1930s. Some government intervention was also intended to raise the incomes of the elderly, the sick, and people with limited skills. For example, in the 1930s, the United States established the *Social Security system*, which provides government payments to retired and disabled workers, and minimum wage legislation, which sets a floor on the wages employers can pay workers in many occupations. In more recent years, government intervention in the economy has also expanded to meet goals such as protecting the environment, promoting civil rights, and providing medical care to low-income people and the elderly.

Some economists argue that the extent of government intervention makes it no longer accurate to refer to the economies of the United States, Canada, Japan, and Western Europe as pure market economies. Instead, they should be referred to as *mixed economies*. A **mixed economy** is still primarily a market economy because most economic decisions result from the interaction of buyers and sellers in markets. However, the government plays a significant role in the allocation of resources. As we will see in later chapters, economists continue to debate the role government should play in a market economy.

One of the most important developments in the international economy in recent years has been the movement of China from being a centrally planned economy to being a more mixed economy. The Chinese economy suffered decades of economic

Mixed economy An economy in which most economic decisions result from the interaction of buyers and sellers in markets but in which the government plays a significant role in the allocation of resources.

stagnation following the takeover of the government in 1949 by Mao Zedong and the Communist Party. Although China remains a political dictatorship, the production of most goods and services is now determined in the market rather than by the government. The result has been rapid economic growth that has lifted more than a billion people in China out of poverty.   MyEconLab **Concept Check**

Efficiency and Equity

Productive efficiency A situation in which a good or service is produced at the lowest possible cost.

Allocative efficiency A state of the economy in which production is in accordance with consumer preferences; in particular, every good or service is produced up to the point where the last unit provides a marginal benefit to society equal to the marginal cost of producing it.

Voluntary exchange A situation that occurs in markets when both the buyer and the seller of a product are made better off by the transaction.

Market economies tend to be more efficient than centrally planned economies. There are two types of efficiency. **Productive efficiency** occurs when a good or service is produced at the lowest possible cost. **Allocative efficiency** occurs when production is in accordance with consumer preferences. Markets tend to be efficient because they promote competition and facilitate voluntary exchange. With **voluntary exchange**, both the buyer and the seller of a product are made better off by the transaction. We know that they are both made better off because, otherwise, the buyer would not have agreed to buy the product or the seller would not have agreed to sell it. Productive efficiency is achieved when competition among firms forces them to produce goods and services at the lowest cost. Allocative efficiency is achieved when the combination of competition among firms and voluntary exchange between firms and consumers results in firms producing the mix of goods and services that consumers prefer the most. Competition will result in firms continuing to produce and sell goods and services as long as the additional benefit to consumers is greater than the additional cost of production. In this way, the mix of goods and services produced will match consumer preferences.

Although markets promote efficiency, they don't guarantee it. Inefficiency can arise from various sources. For instance, it may take some time for firms to learn how to efficiently produce a good or service. When Blu-ray players were introduced, firms did not instantly achieve productive efficiency because it took several years to discover the lowest-cost method of producing this good. As we will discuss in later chapters, inefficiency can also arise if governments interfere with voluntary exchange in markets. For example, many governments limit the imports of some goods from foreign countries. This limitation reduces efficiency by keeping goods from being produced at the lowest cost. The production of some goods damages the environment. In this case, government intervention can increase efficiency because without such intervention, firms may ignore the costs of environmental damage and thereby fail to produce the goods at the lowest possible cost.

Equity The fair distribution of economic benefits.

An economically efficient outcome is not necessarily desirable. Many people prefer economic outcomes that they consider fair or equitable, even if those outcomes are less efficient. **Equity** is harder to define than efficiency because there isn't an agreed-upon definition of fairness. For some people, equity means a more equal distribution of economic benefits than would result from an emphasis on efficiency alone. For example, some people support raising taxes on people with higher incomes to provide the funds for programs that aid the poor. Although governments may increase equity by reducing the incomes of high-income people and increasing the incomes of the poor, efficiency may be reduced. People have less incentive to open new businesses, work hard, and save if the government takes a significant amount of the income they earn from working or saving. The result is that fewer goods and services are produced, and less saving takes place. As this example illustrates, *there is often a trade-off between efficiency and equity*. Government policymakers frequently confront this trade-off.   MyEconLab **Concept Check**

MyEconLab **Study Plan**

Economic Models

1.3   LEARNING OBJECTIVE: Describe the role of models in economic analysis.

As mentioned at the start of the chapter, economic models are simplified versions of reality. Many professions rely on models: An engineer may use a computer model of a bridge to help test whether it will withstand high winds, or a biologist may make a physical model of a nucleic acid to better understand its properties. Economists rely on economic models, or theories, to analyze real-world issues ranging from the role of government in monitoring smart devices to whether a society should redistribute income. (This book uses the words *model* and *theory* interchangeably.) One purpose of economic models is to make economic ideas sufficiently explicit and concrete so that individuals, firms, or the government can use them to make decisions. For example, we will see in Chapter 3 that the model of demand and supply is a simplified version of how the prices of products are determined by the interactions among buyers and sellers in markets.

Economists use economic models to answer questions such as, "Will the United States have a sufficient number of doctors in 2020?" Economists at the U.S. Bureau of Labor Statistics (BLS) build models that allow them to forecast future employment in different occupations. These models enable the BLS to forecast how many doctors there are likely to be at a future date. Economists also use models to forecast the demand for medical services. By separately forecasting the number of doctors and the demand for medical services, these models provide a forecast of whether there will be a sufficient number of doctors in 2020. As mentioned at the beginning of the chapter, economists at the U.S. Health Resources and Services Administration (HRSA) have used models to forecast that there will be a shortage of 55,600 doctors in 2020.

Sometimes economists use an existing model to analyze a real-world problem or issue, but in other cases, they have to develop a new model. To develop a model, economists generally follow these steps:

1. Decide on the assumptions to use in developing the model.
2. Formulate a testable hypothesis.
3. Use economic data to test the hypothesis.
4. Revise the model if it fails to explain the economic data well.
5. Retain the revised model to help answer similar economic questions in the future.

The Role of Assumptions in Economic Models

Any model is based on making assumptions because models have to be simplified to be useful. For example, economic models make *behavioral assumptions* about the motives of consumers and firms. Economists assume that consumers will buy the goods and services that will maximize their well-being or their satisfaction. Similarly, economists assume that firms act to maximize their profits. These assumptions are simplifications because they do not describe the motives of every consumer and every firm. How can we know whether the assumptions in a model are too simplified or too limiting? We can determine the usefulness of assumptions by forming hypotheses based on the assumptions and then testing the hypotheses using real-world information.   MyEconLab Concept Check

Forming and Testing Hypotheses in Economic Models

An **economic variable** is something measurable that can have different values, such as the incomes of doctors. In an economic model, a hypothesis is a statement that may be either correct or incorrect about an economic variable. An example of a hypothesis in an economic model is the statement that the falling incomes earned by primary care physicians—often referred to as *family doctors*—will result in a decline in the number of physicians choosing to enter primary care in the United States in 2020. An economic hypothesis is usually about a *causal relationship*; in this case, the hypothesis states that lower incomes cause, or lead to, fewer doctors entering primary care.

Before we can accept a hypothesis, we have to test it by analyzing statistics on the relevant economic variables. In our example, we would gather statistics on the incomes of family doctors, the number of family doctors, and perhaps other variables. Testing a hypothesis can be tricky. For example, showing that the number of family doctors

Economic variable Something measurable that can have different values, such as the incomes of doctors.

declined at a time when the average income of these doctors declined would not be enough to demonstrate that the decline in income *caused* the decline in the number of family doctors. Just because two things are correlated—that is, they happen at the same time—does not mean that one caused the other. For example, before entering practice, a doctor spends time in a teaching hospital as a resident in his or her field. Teaching hospitals determine how many residencies they will offer in a particular field. Suppose that teaching hospitals decreased the number of residencies in primary care at the same time that the incomes of family doctors were declining. In that case, the declining number of residencies, rather than the declining incomes, might have caused the decline in the number of family doctors. Over a period of time, many economic variables change, which complicates the testing of hypotheses. In fact, when economists disagree about a hypothesis, such as the effect of falling incomes on the number of family doctors, it is often because of disagreements over interpreting the statistical analysis used to test the hypothesis.

Note that hypotheses must be statements that could, in principle, turn out to be incorrect. Statements such as "Increasing the number of family doctors is good" or "Increasing the number of family doctors is bad" are value judgments rather than hypotheses because it is not possible to disprove them.

Economists accept and use an economic model if it leads to hypotheses that are confirmed by statistical analysis. In many cases, the acceptance is tentative, however, pending the gathering of new data or further statistical analysis. In fact, economists often refer to a hypothesis having been "not rejected," rather than having been "accepted," by statistical analysis. But what if statistical analysis clearly rejects a hypothesis? For example, what if a model leads to a hypothesis that declining incomes of family doctors will cause a decline in the number of these doctors, but the data reject this hypothesis? In this case, the model must be reconsidered. It may be that an assumption used in the model was too simplified or too limiting. For example, perhaps the model ignored the fact that family doctors were moving from owning their own practices to becoming salaried employees of hospitals, where their incomes would be lower but they would be freed from the responsibilities involved in running their own businesses. This change in how primary care physicians are employed might explain why the data rejected the hypothesis.

The BLS has analyzed the accuracy of the projections it had made in 1996 of employment levels in 2006. Some projections were quite accurate, while others were less so. For instance, the BLS had projected that 677,917 physicians and surgeons would be employed in 2006, but actual employment was only 633,292, or about 7 percent less than projected. The error with respect to physician's assistants was much larger, with the projection being that 93,485 physician's assistants would be employed in 2006, but actual employment was only 65,628, or about 30 percent fewer than expected. Analyzing the errors in these projections helps the BLS to improve the models it uses to make projections of occupational employment.

The process of developing models, testing hypotheses, and revising models occurs not just in economics but also in disciplines such as physics, chemistry, and biology. This process is often referred to as the *scientific method*. Economics is a *social science* because it applies the scientific method to the study of the interactions among individuals.

MyEconLab Concept Check

Positive and Normative Analysis

Positive analysis Analysis concerned with what is.

Normative analysis Analysis concerned with what ought to be.

Throughout this book, as we build economic models and use them to answer questions, bear in mind the following important distinction: **Positive analysis** is concerned with *what is*, and **normative analysis** is concerned with *what ought to be*. Economics is about positive analysis, which measures the costs and benefits of different courses of action.

We can use the federal government's minimum wage law to compare positive and normative analysis. In 2015, under this law, it was illegal for an employer to hire a worker at a wage less than $7.25 per hour. Without the minimum wage law, some firms and workers would voluntarily agree to a lower wage. Because of the minimum wage law, some workers have difficulty finding jobs, and some firms end up paying more for labor than they otherwise would have. A positive analysis of the federal minimum wage law uses an economic model to estimate how many workers have lost their jobs because of the law, its effect on the costs and profits of businesses, and the gains to workers receiving the minimum wage. After economists complete this positive analysis, the decision as to whether the minimum wage law is a good or a bad idea is a normative one and depends on how people evaluate the trade-off involved. Supporters of the law believe that the losses to employers and workers who are unemployed as a result of the law are more than offset by the gains to workers who receive higher wages than they would without the law. Opponents of the law believe the losses are greater than the gains. The assessment by any individual depends, in part, on that person's values and political views. The positive analysis an economist provides would play a role in the decision but can't by itself decide the issue one way or the other.

In each chapter, you will see a *Don't Let This Happen to You* box like the one below. These boxes alert you to common pitfalls in thinking about economic ideas. After reading this box, test your understanding by working the related problem that appears at the end of the chapter. MyEconLab Concept Check

---

Don't Let This Happen to You

Don't Confuse Positive Analysis with Normative Analysis

"Economic analysis has shown that the minimum wage law is a bad idea because it causes unemployment." Is this statement accurate? As of 2015, the federal minimum wage law prevents employers from hiring workers at a wage of less than $7.25 per hour. This wage is higher than some employers are willing to pay some workers. If there were no minimum wage law, some workers who currently cannot find any firm willing to hire them at $7.25 per hour would be able to find employment at a lower wage. Therefore, positive economic analysis indicates that the minimum wage law causes unemployment. (In Chapter 4, we'll explore why economists disagree about *how much* unemployment the minimum wage law causes.) But, some workers who have

jobs benefit from the minimum wage law because they are paid a higher wage than they otherwise would be. In other words, the minimum wage law creates both losers—the workers who become unemployed and the firms that have to pay higher wages—and winners—the workers who receive higher wages.

Should we value the gains to the winners more than we value the losses to the losers? The answer involves normative analysis. Positive economic analysis can show the consequences of a particular policy, but it cannot tell us whether the policy is "good" or "bad." So, the statement at the beginning of this box is inaccurate.

MyEconLab Study Plan

Your Turn: Test your understanding by doing related problems 3.6 and 3.7 on page 25 at the end of this chapter.

Economics as a Social Science

Because economics studies the actions of individuals, it is a social science. Economics is therefore similar to other social science disciplines, such as psychology, political science, and sociology. As a social science, economics considers human behavior—particularly decision-making behavior—in every context, not just in the context of business. Economists have studied issues such as how families decide on the number of children to have, why people have difficulty losing weight or attaining other goals, and why people often ignore relevant information when making decisions. Economics also has much to contribute to questions of government policy. As we will see throughout this book, economists have played an important role in formulating government policies in areas such as the environment, health care, and poverty. MyEconLab Concept Check

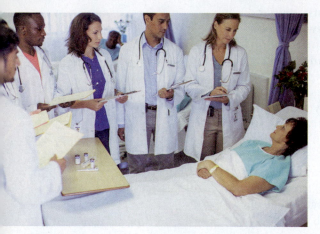

Should these medical students have to pay tuition?

Making the Connection
MyEconLab Video

Should Medical School Be Free?

The U.S. population continues to increase, which by itself would increase the demand for medical services. In addition, the average age of the population is rising, and older people need more medical care than do younger people. So, over time, the number of doctors needs to increase. As mentioned at the beginning of this chapter, the U.S. Health Resources and Services Administration (HRSA) estimates that the number of doctors needed to provide patient care will rise to 922,000 in 2020.

Can we be sure that these additional doctors will be available in 2020? The HRSA forecasts that, in fact, there will be a shortage of 55,600 doctors in 2020. The bulk of that shortage is likely to be in primary care physicians, or family doctors. As we will discuss in later chapters, ordinarily we expect that when consumers want more of a product, higher wages and salaries and more job openings will attract workers to that industry. For example, during the U.S. housing boom of the mid-2000s, the number of workers in the building trades—carpenters, plumbers, roofers, and others—increased rapidly. But producing more doctors is a long process. After completing an undergraduate education, a doctor spends four years in medical school and then three to five years at a teaching hospital, pursuing a residency in a particular field of medicine. Apparently convinced that hospitals will not train enough doctors unless they get help, Congress contributes $10 billion per year to teaching hospitals, based on the number of residents they train.

Peter Bach of the Sloan-Kettering Cancer Center and Robert Kocher of the Brookings Institution have proposed that medical schools should charge no tuition. They argue that nearly all students graduate from medical school owing money on student loans, with the average student owing more than $160,000. We might expect that these debts, although large, would *not* deter students from applying to medical school, because in 2015, the average income of physicians was more than $250,000 per year. Bach and Kocher argue, however, that the high cost of medical school has two bad outcomes: (1) Some good students do not apply because they either do not want to be saddled with such large debts or are unable to borrow sufficient money, and (2) many students avoid going into primary care—where average incomes are $190,000—in favor of specialties such as plastic surgery or anesthesiology—where average incomes are $325,000. Teaching hospitals pay doctors a salary of about $50,000 per year during their residencies. Bach and Kocher propose that hospitals continue to pay residents who pursue primary care but not pay residents who specialize. The money that hospitals would otherwise pay to these residents would be paid to medical schools instead to finance the free tuition. The plan would give residents an incentive to pursue primary care rather than to specialize. Critics of the Bach and Kocher proposal have questioned whether many students capable of being admitted to medical school actually are deterred by medical school tuition. They also question whether many residents who intend to specialize would choose primary care instead, even if specializing means they have to borrow to meet living expenses rather than pay for them with a hospital salary.

Like many other policy debates, the debate over whether changes should be made in how medical school is paid for has positive and normative elements. By gathering data and using economic models, we can assess some of the quantitative claims made by each side in the debate: What role does tuition play in a student's decision about whether to attend medical school? Have tuition increases had a large effect or a small effect on the number of applications to medical school? How do changes in expected future incomes affect the decisions of medical students about which specialty to choose? These are all positive questions, so it is possible to formulate quantitative answers. Ultimately, though, this debate also has a normative element. For instance, some doctors, economists, and policymakers argue that it is important that people living in low-income or rural areas have improved access to health care, so they are willing to support policies that would redirect medical students away from specialized fields and toward primary care. Other doctors, economists, and policymakers believe that medical students who enter specialized fields make a larger contribution to society than do students who enter primary care. A disagreement of this type is unlikely to be resolved by building models and analyzing data because the issue involved is essentially normative.

In 2010, President Obama and Congress enacted the Patient Protection and Affordable Care Act, which made major changes to the U.S. health care system. Most of the changes were in effect by 2015. Additional changes are likely as policymakers grapple with the increasing costs of health care. Whether Congress and the president will enact policies intended to increase the number of family doctors remains to be seen.

Sources: Uwe E. Reinhardt, "Producing More Primary-Care Doctors," *New York Times*, June 10, 2011; Uwe E. Reinhardt, "The Debt of Medical Students," *New York Times*, September 14, 2012; and Peter B. Bach and Robert Kocher, "Why Medical School Should Be Free," *New York Times*, May 28, 2011.

Your Turn: Test your understanding by doing related problem 3.8 on page 25 at the end of this chapter.

MyEconLab Study Plan

1.4 ## Microeconomics and Macroeconomics

LEARNING OBJECTIVE: Distinguish between microeconomics and macroeconomics.

Economic models can be used to analyze decision making in many areas. We group some of these areas together as *microeconomics* and others as *macroeconomics*. **Microeconomics** is the study of how households and firms make choices, how they interact in markets, and how the government attempts to influence their choices. **Macroeconomics** is the study of the economy as a whole, including topics such as inflation, unemployment, and economic growth. Table 1.1 gives examples of microeconomic and macroeconomic issues.

The division between microeconomics and macroeconomics is not a bright line. Many economic situations have *both* a microeconomic aspect and a macroeconomic aspect. For example, the level of total investment by firms in new machinery and equipment helps to determine how rapidly the economy grows—which is a macroeconomic issue. But to understand how much new machinery and equipment firms decide to purchase, we have to analyze the incentives individual firms face—which is a microeconomic issue.

MyEconLab Concept Check

Microeconomics The study of how households and firms make choices, how they interact in markets, and how the government attempts to influence their choices.

Macroeconomics The study of the economy as a whole, including topics such as inflation, unemployment, and economic growth.

MyEconLab Study Plan

Table 1.1

Issues in Microeconomics and Macroeconomics

Examples of microeconomic issues	Examples of macroeconomic issues
• How consumers react to changes in product prices • How firms decide what prices to charge for the products they sell • Which government policy would most efficiently reduce teenage smoking • What are the costs and benefits of approving the sale of a new prescription drug • What is the most efficient way to reduce air pollution	• Why economies experience periods of recession and increasing unemployment • Why, over the long run, some economies have grown much faster than others • What determines the inflation rate • What determines the value of the U.S. dollar • Whether government intervention can reduce the severity of recessions

---

1.5 ## A Preview of Important Economic Terms

LEARNING OBJECTIVE: Define important economic terms.

In the following chapters, you will encounter certain important terms again and again. Becoming familiar with these terms is a necessary step in learning economics. Here we provide only a brief introduction to some of these terms. We will discuss them all in greater depth in later chapters:

- *Firm, company, or business.* A *firm* is an organization that produces a good or service. Most firms produce goods or services to earn profits, but there are also nonprofit firms, such as universities and some hospitals. Economists use the terms *firm, company,* and *business* interchangeably.

- *Entrepreneur.* An *entrepreneur* is someone who operates a business. In a market system, entrepreneurs decide what goods and services to produce and how to produce them. An entrepreneur starting a new business puts his or her own funds at risk. If an entrepreneur is wrong about what consumers want or about the best way to produce goods and services, his or her funds can be lost. Losing money in a failed business is not unusual: In the United States, about half of new businesses close within four years. Without entrepreneurs willing to assume the risk of starting and operating businesses, economic progress would be impossible in a market system.

- *Innovation.* There is a distinction between an *invention* and an *innovation.* An *invention* is a new good or a new process for making a good. An *innovation* is the practical application of an invention. (*Innovation* may also be used more broadly to refer to any significant improvement in a good or in the means of producing a good.) Much time often passes between the appearance of a new idea and its development for widespread use. For example, the Wright brothers first achieved self-propelled flight at Kitty Hawk, North Carolina, in 1903, but the Wright brothers' plane was very crude, and it wasn't until the introduction of the DC-3 by Douglas Aircraft in 1936 that regularly scheduled intercity airline flights became common in the United States. Similarly, the first digital electronic computer—the ENIAC—was developed in 1945, but the first IBM personal computer was not introduced until 1981, and widespread use of computers did not have a significant effect on the productivity of U.S. business until the 1990s.

- *Technology.* A firm's *technology* is the processes it uses to produce goods and services. In the economic sense, a firm's technology depends on many factors, such as the skill of its managers, the training of its workers, and the speed and efficiency of its machinery and equipment.

- *Goods. Goods* are tangible merchandise, such as books, computers, or Blu-ray players.

- *Services. Services* are activities done for others, such as providing haircuts or investment advice.

- *Revenue.* A firm's *revenue* is the total amount received for selling a good or service. We calculate it by multiplying the price per unit by the number of units sold.

- *Profit.* A firm's *profit* is the difference between its revenue and its costs. Economists distinguish between *accounting profit* and *economic profit.* In calculating accounting profit, we exclude the costs of some economic resources that the firm does not pay for explicitly. In calculating economic profit, we include the opportunity costs of all resources used by the firm. When we refer to *profit* in this book, we mean economic profit. It is important not to confuse *profit* with *revenue.*

- *Household.* A *household* consists of all persons occupying a home. Households are suppliers of factors of production—particularly labor—used by firms to make goods and services. Households also demand goods and services produced by firms and governments.

- *Factors of production, economic resources, or inputs.* Firms use *factors of production* to produce goods and services. The main factors of production are labor, capital, natural resources—including land—and entrepreneurial ability. Households earn income by supplying the factors of production to firms. Economists use the terms *factors of production, economic resources,* and *inputs* interchangeably.

- *Capital.* In everyday speech, the word *capital* can refer to *financial capital* or to *physical capital.* Financial capital includes stocks and bonds issued by firms, bank accounts, and holdings of money. In economics, though, *capital* refers to physical capital, which includes manufactured goods that are used to produce other goods and services. Examples of physical capital are computers, factory buildings, machine tools, warehouses, and trucks. The total amount of physical capital available in a country is referred to as the country's *capital stock*.

- *Human capital. Human capital* refers to the accumulated training and skills that workers possess. For example, college-educated workers generally have more skills and are more productive than workers who have only high school degrees; therefore, college-educated workers have more human capital.   MyEconLab Concept Check   MyEconLab Study Plan

Continued from page 3

Economics in Your Life

Will There Be Plenty of Jobs Available in the Health Care Industry?

At the beginning of this chapter, we posed the question: "What is the basis for the forecasts on the availability of jobs in health care, and how reliable are the forecasts?" As the U.S. population increases and as the average age of the population rises, it seems likely that there will be an increase in the number of doctors, nurses, physician's assistants, and other health care workers. The U.S. Bureau of Labor Statistics (BLS) publishes the most widely used occupational forecasts. Economists at the BLS base these forecasts on economic models. The forecasts can be inaccurate, however. For example, in 1996, the BLS forecast that 93,485 physician's assistants would be employed in 2006, when in fact only 65,628 were. The BLS analyzes errors like these in attempting to improve its forecasts. So, it is likely that the BLS's forecasts will become more accurate over time, but it would be a mistake to expect the forecasts to be exact.

Conclusion

Economics is a group of useful ideas about how individuals make choices. Economists have put these ideas into practice by developing economic models. Consumers, business managers, and government policymakers use these models every day to help make choices. In this book, we explore many key economic models and give examples of how to apply them in the real world.

Reading the news is an important part of understanding the current business climate and learning how to apply economic concepts to a variety of real-world events. At the end of each of the first four chapters, you will see a two-page feature titled *An Inside Look*. This feature consists of an excerpt from an article that relates to the company or economic issue introduced at the start of the chapter and also to the concepts discussed in the chapter. A summary and an analysis with a supporting table or graph highlight the key economic points of the article. Read *An Inside Look* for a discussion of how technological change, such as the development of smart medical devices, affects the way doctors provide health care. Test your understanding by answering the *Thinking Critically* questions.

FORBES

Google Smart Contact Lens Focuses On Healthcare Billions

(a) Google is developing a smart contact lens, with pharmaceutical giant Novartis, to help patients manage diabetes—in one of a number of moves focused squarely on billions of dollars of potential revenue available across the total digital healthcare market.

As technology moves further into treatment with remote consultations, monitoring and operations, robotic treatments, and advanced digital diagnosis, Google has seen the opportunity to apply its own eyewear technology (up until now limited as glasses called Google Glass) to the healthcare field.

Google's 3D mobile technology and its offering around health record digitization form potential other strands of its expansion in the health market. Last month, it released the Google Fit platform to track exercise and sleep, among other health factors—but it is far from alone, as Apple and Samsung offer similar systems in that area.

(b) Today, under a new development and licensing deal between Google and the Alcon eyewear division at Novartis, the two companies said they will create a smart contact lens that contains a low power microchip and an almost invisible, hair-thin electronic circuit. The lens can measure diabetics' blood sugar levels directly from tear fluid on the surface of the eyeball. The system sends data to a mobile device to keep the individual informed.

Google co-founder Sergey Brin said the company wanted to use "the latest technology in 'minituarisation' of electronics" in order to improve people's "quality of life".

Novartis chief executive Joe Jimenez added that technology as a whole, starting with smart eyewear, could be used to "manage human diseases," and indicated that diseases will be mapped in the body using a range of other devices in the future—many of which are in development across universities and research laboratories.

An official timescale for the product's development and commercialization has not been made public, though Jimenez said in *Reuters* and *WSJ* interviews respectively that the company "would hope to be able to commercialize it within about five years", adding that it was expected to create a "large revenue stream".

(c) The combination of Google's technology background and Novartis' pharmaceutical knowledge would help meet "unmet medical needs," Jimenez claimed.

The pharmaceutical firm is also looking into how to enable the contact lens technology to assess long sighted people's vision and autofocus it on what they are looking at, working rather like an automatic camera lens when taking a picture. Such technology would help them avoid the need for glasses when reading or looking at other nearby objects.

The Google team involved in the contact lens development is called Google[x], and it focuses on "finding new solutions to big global problems" in healthcare and beyond, according to the companies.

The secretive Google[x] facility operates in Mountain View, California, and one of its most high profile projects has been a self driving car. It is also working closely on speech recognition, balloon powered internet access for rural areas, wind power, and technology for the Internet of Things—in which internet connected home, personal and city objects communicate with each other and take automatic action when different events take place.

Source: Leo King, "Google Smart Contact Lens Focuses On Healthcare Billions," *Forbes*, July 15, 2014.

Key Points in the Article

Google is adding to its growing list of technological innovations by partnering with Swiss pharmaceutical company Novartis to develop smart contact lenses to help patients manage diabetes. A microchip and electronic circuit in the contact lenses will measure blood sugar levels from tear fluids on the surface of the eye and transmit the data to a mobile device. Novartis is also exploring ways to incorporate autofocus technology in the contact lens, which could eliminate the need for reading glasses. The smart contact lens is just one of a growing number of products being developed in the multibillion-dollar, rapidly expanding digital health care market. Novartis chief executive Joe Jiminez hopes to see the smart contact lens available in the market within five years.

Analyzing the News

(a) Advances in technology are having a profound effect on many sectors of the economy, and one of the fastest-growing sectors is the digital health care market. Rapid improvements in smartphone technology have played a large role in expanding the use of smart medical devices. The future of health care may be greatly affected by partnerships between high-tech firms like Google and health industry firms like Novartis. These partnerships can lead to the development of smart devices designed to facilitate and improve medical diagnoses and conditions.

(b) According to the Centers for Disease Control and Prevention (CDC), diabetes ranks seventh among the leading causes of death in the United States, with more than 75,000 deaths in 2012 attributed to the disease. The total estimated cost of diabetes that year was $245 billion, which included the costs of direct medical care as well as the costs associated with disability, work loss, and premature death. In 2012, the CDC estimated that 28.9 million people in the United States age 20 or older had diabetes, and almost 28 percent of those cases were undiagnosed. The table below shows these data as well as data on the number of new, diagnosed cases of diabetes. Given the number of people suffering from diabetes, the development of the smart contact lens has the potential to help patients manage their disease. For example, being able to monitor blood sugar levels via the contact lens and a smartphone could be more convenient and less painful than the common finger-prick testing method and might therefore encourage more people to regularly monitor their diabetes. An effective and relatively inexpensive smart contact lens could end up saving not only time and money but also lives.

(c) The health care industry is growing as well as changing, and technology is fueling a large part of the change. Smart medical devices are still in their infancy, but rapid technological advancement has led many new firms to enter this industry, introducing innovative new products. As the average age of the U.S. population continues to increase, and as people spend more time and resources on maintaining good health, smart medical devices may revolutionize the way health care is administered. This revolution will benefit not only those companies involved with the development of new products but also health care professionals and their patients.

Thinking Critically

1. One key economic idea is that people respond to economic incentives. What economic incentives are Google and Novartis responding to?

2. Some diabetic patients need to monitor their condition by pricking their finger for blood to check blood sugar levels. If these patients could instead use the smart contact lens, it could improve the effectiveness of monitoring and, therefore, treatment. Develop an economic model to analyze the relationship between using the smart contact lens or the finger-prick method of monitoring blood sugar levels and the number of diabetes-related deaths in the United States. Use information from the article to explain the steps you would take to develop this model.

Total cases of diabetes (diagnosed and undiagnosed), and new cases of diagnosed diabetes among people aged 20 years or older, United States, 2012

	Total Number in Age Group with Diabetes	Percentage of Age Group with Diabetes	Number of New Diabetes Cases	Rate of New Diabetes Cases Per 1,000 People
20 years or older	28.9 million	12.3%	1,663,000	7.8
20–44	4.3 million	4.1	371,000	3.6
45–64	13.4 million	16.2	892,000	12.0
65 years or older	11.2 million	25.9	400,000	11.5

Sources: 2010–2012 National Health Interview Survey, 2009–2012 National Health and Nutrition Examination Survey; and 2012 U.S. Census data.

CHAPTER SUMMARY AND PROBLEMS

Key Terms

Allocative efficiency, p. 12

Centrally planned economy, p. 10

Economic model, p. 4

Economic variable, p. 13

Economics, p. 4

Equity, p. 12

Macroeconomics, p. 17

Marginal analysis, p. 7

Market, p. 4

Market economy, p. 10

Microeconomics, p. 17

Mixed economy, p. 11

Normative analysis, p. 14

Opportunity cost, p. 8

Positive analysis, p. 14

Productive efficiency, p. 12

Scarcity, p. 4

Trade-off, p. 8

Voluntary exchange, p. 12

1.1 Three Key Economic Ideas, pages 4–8

LEARNING OBJECTIVE: Explain these three key economic ideas: People are rational; people respond to economic incentives; and optimal decisions are made at the margin.

Summary

Economics is the study of the choices consumers, business managers, and government officials make to attain their goals, given their scarce resources. We must make choices because of **scarcity**, which means that although our wants are unlimited, the resources available to fulfill those wants are limited. Economists assume that people are rational in the sense that consumers and firms use all available information as they take actions intended to achieve their goals. Rational individuals weigh the benefits and costs of each action and choose an action only if the benefits outweigh the costs. Although people act from a variety of motives, ample evidence indicates that they respond to economic incentives. Economists use the word **marginal** to mean extra or additional. The optimal decision is to continue any activity up to the point where the marginal benefit equals the marginal cost.

 Visit **www.myeconlab.com** to complete these exercises online and get instant feedback.

Review Questions

1.1 Briefly discuss each of the following economic ideas: People are rational, people respond to economic incentives, and optimal decisions are made at the margin.

1.2 What is scarcity? Why is scarcity central to the study of economics?

Problems and Applications

1.3 Do you agree with the following statement: "The problem with economics is that it assumes that consumers and firms always make the correct decisions. But we know that everyone makes mistakes."

1.4 According to the FBI Bank Crime Statistics, there were nearly 4,000 bank robberies in the United States in 2014. The FBI claims that banks have made themselves easy targets by refusing to install clear acrylic partitions, called *bandit barriers*, that separate bank tellers from the public. According to a special agent with the FBI, "Bandit barriers are a great deterrent. We've talked to guys who rob banks, and as soon as they see a bandit barrier, they go find another bank." Despite this finding, many banks have been reluctant to install these barriers. Wouldn't banks have a strong incentive to install bandit barriers to deter robberies? Why, then, do so many banks not do so?

Sources: U.S. Department of Justice, Federal Bureau of Investigation, "Bank Crime Statistics (BCS) Federally Insured Financial Institutions, January 1, 2014–December 31, 2014," www.fbi.gov; and Richard Cowen, "FBI Says Banks Are to Blame for Rise in Robberies," NorthJersey.com, March 10, 2009.

1.5 The grading system plays an important role in student learning. In their book *Effective Grading: A Tool for Learning and Assessment in College*, Barbara Walvoord and Virginia Anderson state that "grading infuses everything that happens in the classroom." They also argue that grading "needs to be acknowledged and managed from the first moment that an instructor begins planning a class."

a. How could the grading system a teacher uses affect the incentives of students to learn the course material?

b. If teachers put too little weight in the grading scale on a certain part of the course, such as readings outside the textbook, how might students respond?

c. Teachers often wish that students came to class prepared, having read the upcoming material. How could a teacher design the grading system to motivate students to come to class prepared?

Source: Barbara E. Walvoord and Virginia Johnson Anderson, *Effective Grading: A Tool for Learning and Assessment in College*, 2nd ed., San Francisco: Jossey-Bass, 2010, p. 1.

1.6 The federal government subsidizes some loans to college students. Typically, the more students who participate in these programs and the more they borrow, the higher the cost to the federal government. In 2011, President Barack Obama convinced Congress to pass these changes to the federal student loan programs: (1) Payments were capped at 10 percent of a borrower's discretionary income; (2) any unpaid balances for people working for government or in the nonprofit sector were forgiven after 10 years; and (3) people working in the private sector had their loans forgiven after 20 years.

a. As a result of these changes in the federal student loan program, would you predict that the total amount that students borrowed under these programs increased or decreased? Briefly explain.

b. As part of his 2016 federal budget proposals, President Obama recommended significant changes to the federal student loan programs. Given your answer to part (a), do you think President Obama was likely to have recommended changes that would increase or changes that would decrease the payments that borrowers would have to make? Briefly explain.

   c. How might President Obama and his advisers have failed to correctly forecast the effects of the 2011 changes to the loan programs?

Sources: Allesandra Lanza, "What Obama's 2016 Budget Proposal Means for Student Borrowers," usnews.com, February 11, 2015; and Josh Mitchell, "Student-Debt Forgiveness Plans Skyrocket, Raising Fears over Costs, Higher Tuition," *Wall Street Journal*, April 22, 2014.

1.7 **(Related to the** Making the Connection **on page 5)** Many universities and corporations offer a health and wellness program that helps their employees improve or maintain their health and get paid (a relatively small amount) for doing so. The programs vary but typically consist of employees completing a health assessment, receiving a program for healthy living, and monitoring their monthly health activities.

   a. Why would universities and corporations pay employees to improve or maintain their health?

   b. How does health insurance affect the incentive of employees to improve or maintain their health?

   c. Would a wellness program increase or decrease the health insurance premiums that an insurance company would charge the university or corporation to provide insurance coverage? Briefly explain.

1.8 **(Related to the** Making the Connection **on page 5)** Jay Bhattacharya and Kate Bundorf of Stanford University have found evidence that people who are obese and who work for firms that provide health insurance receive lower wages than workers at those firms who are not obese. At firms that do not provide health insurance, obese workers do not receive lower wages than workers who are not obese.

   a. Why might firms that provide workers with health insurance pay a lower wage to obese workers than to workers who are not obese?

   b. Is Bhattacharya and Bundorf's finding relevant to the question of whether health insurance provides people with an incentive to become obese? Briefly explain.

Source: Jay Bhattacharya and M. Kate Bundorf, "The Incidence of the Health Care Costs of Obesity," *Journal of Health Economics*, Vol. 28, No. 3, May 2009, pp. 649–658.

1.9 **(Related to** Solved Problem 1.1 **on page 7)** McDonald's typically serves breakfast until only 10:30 A.M. on weekdays and 11:00 A.M. on weekends. In 2015, the company began to experiment with serving breakfast all day at various locations in San Diego. Several owners of McDonald's restaurants, however, point out that offering breakfast 24 hours a day presents two logistical problems: (1) Burgers and other meats need to be cooked at a higher temperature than eggs, so it would be difficult for employees to set the grill at the right temperature for both foods, and (2) scrambled eggs require employees to continually stir, while hamburgers don't require this attention. In addition, some customers might buy the cheaper breakfast rather than the more expensive lunch or dinner meals. If McDonald's made you responsible for making this decision, discuss how you would go about analyzing whether to serve breakfast all day. Would your decision have to be all or nothing—either serve breakfast up to 10:30 A.M. or serve breakfast all day? Would you have to serve the entire breakfast menu all day?

Sources: Associated Press, "McDonald's Gives All-Day Breakfast a Test Try," usatoday.com, March 30, 2015; and Susan Berfield and Leslie Patton, "What's So Hard About a 24/7 McMuffin?" *Bloomberg BusinessWeek*, May 6–12, 2013.

1.10 **(Related to** Solved Problem 1.1 **on page 7)** Late in the semester, a friend tells you, "I was going to drop my psychology course so I could concentrate on my other courses, but I had already put so much time into the course that I decided not to drop it." What do you think of your friend's reasoning? Would it make a difference to your answer if your friend has to pass the psychology course at some point to graduate? Briefly explain.

1.11 In a paper written by Bentley College economists Patricia M. Flynn and Michael A. Quinn, the authors state:

> We find evidence that Economics is a good choice of major for those aspiring to become a CEO [chief executive officer]. When adjusting for size of the pool of graduates, those with undergraduate degrees in Economics are shown to have had a greater likelihood of becoming an S&P 500 CEO than any other major.

A list of famous economics majors published by Marietta College includes business leaders Elon Musk, Warren Buffett, Donald Trump, David Rockefeller, Ted Turner, Bill Belichick, Diane von Furstenberg, and Sam Walton, as well as Presidents George H.W. Bush, Gerald Ford, and Ronald Reagan and Supreme Court Justice Sandra Day O'Connor. Why might studying economics be particularly good preparation for being the top manager of a corporation or a leader in government?

Sources: Patricia M. Flynn and Michael A. Quinn, "Economics: A Good Choice of Major for Future CEOs," *Social Science Research Network*, November 28, 2006; and *Famous Economics Majors*, Marietta College, Marietta, Ohio, November 21, 2014.

The Economic Problem That Every Society Must Solve, pages 8–12

LEARNING OBJECTIVE: Discuss how an economy answers these questions: What goods and services will be produced? How will the goods and services be produced? Who will receive the goods and services produced?

Summary

Society faces **trade-offs**: Producing more of one good or service means producing less of another good or service. The **opportunity cost** of any activity—such as producing a good or service—is the highest-valued alternative that must be given up to engage in that activity. The choices of consumers, firms, and governments determine what goods and services will be produced. Firms choose how to produce the goods and services they sell. In the United States, who receives the goods and services produced depends largely on how income is distributed in the marketplace. In a **centrally planned economy**, most economic decisions are made by the government. In a **market economy**, most economic decisions are made by consumers and firms. Most economies, including that of the United States, are **mixed economies** in which most economic decisions are made by consumers and firms but in which the government also plays a significant role. There are two types of efficiency: productive efficiency and allocative efficiency. **Productive efficiency** occurs when a good or service is produced at the lowest possible cost. **Allocative efficiency** occurs when production corresponds with consumer preferences. **Voluntary exchange** is a situation that occurs in markets when both the buyer and the seller of a product are made better off by the transaction. **Equity** is more difficult to define than efficiency, but it usually involves a fair distribution of economic benefits. Government policymakers often face a trade-off between equity and efficiency.

MyEconLab   Visit **www.myeconlab.com** to complete these exercises online and get instant feedback.

Review Questions

2.1 Why does scarcity imply that every society and every individual face trade-offs?

2.2 What are the three economic questions that every society must answer? Briefly discuss the differences in the way centrally planned, market, and mixed economies answer these questions?

2.3 What is the difference between productive efficiency and allocative efficiency?

2.4 What is the difference between efficiency and equity? Why do government policymakers often face a trade-off between efficiency and equity?

Problems and Applications

2.5 According to Forbes magazine, in 2015 Bill Gates was the world's richest person, with wealth of $79.2 billion. Does Bill Gates face scarcity? Does everyone? Are there any exceptions?
Source: "The World's Billionaires," forbes.com, March 2, 2015.

2.6 Consider an organization that exists to help the poor. The members of the organization are discussing alternative methods of aiding the poor, when a proponent of one particular method asserts, "If even one poor person is helped with this method, then all our time and money would have been worth it." If you were a member of the organization, how would you reply to this assertion?

2.7 **(Related to the** Making the Connection **on page 9)** An article on espn.com about declining attendance at college football games noted that schools in the central time zone had particular problems with attendance at games that started at 11 A.M. The athletic director at the University of Illinois was quoted as saying, "I'm a big fan of evening games." How would playing games in the late afternoon or evening rather than in the morning affect the opportunity cost of a student attending a game?
Source: Adam Rittenberg, "Attendance Challenges Big Deal for B1G," espn.com, February 14, 2014.

2.8 In a market economy, why does a firm have a strong incentive to be productively efficient and allocatively efficient? What does the firm earn if it is productively and allocatively efficient, and what happens if it is not?

2.9 Alberto Chong of the University of Ottawa and several colleagues conducted an experiment to test the efficiency of government postal services around the world. They mailed letters to nonexistent businesses in 159 countries and kept track of how many of the letters were returned. Was this test most relevant to evaluating the productive efficiency or the allocative efficiency of these postal services? Briefly explain.
Source: Alberto Chong, Rafael La Porta, Florencio Lopez-de-Silanes, and Andrei Shleifer, "Letter Grading Government Efficiency," *Journal of the European Economic Association*, Vol. 12, No. 2, April 2014, pp. 277–299.

2.10 The Food and Drug Administration (FDA) is part of the federal government's Department of Health and Human Services. Among its other functions, the FDA evaluates the safety and effectiveness of drugs and medical devices. FDA approval had to be granted before OraSure was allowed to market its home HIV test. In a centrally planned economy, the government decides how resources will be allocated. In a market economy, the decisions of households and firms interacting in markets allocate resources. Briefly explain which statement is more accurate: (a) The regulation of the production and sale of drugs and medical devices in the United States is an example of how resources are allocated in a centrally planned economy, or (b) the regulation of the production and sale of drugs and medical devices in the United States is an example of how resources are allocated in a market economy.

2.11 Would you expect a centrally planned economy to be better at productive efficiency or allocative efficiency? Be sure to define productive efficiency and allocative efficiency in your answer.

2.12 Leonard Fleck, a philosophy professor at Michigan State University, has written:

> When it comes to health care in America, we have limited resources for unlimited health care needs. We want everything contemporary medical technology can offer that will improve the length or quality of our lives as we age. But as presently healthy taxpayers, we want costs controlled.

Why is it necessary for all economic systems to limit services such as health care? How does a market system prevent people from getting as many goods and services as they want?
Source: Leonard Fleck, *Just Caring: Health Care Rationing and Democratic Deliberation*, New York: Oxford University Press, 2009.

2.13 Suppose that your college decides to give away 1,000 tickets to the football game against your school's biggest rival. The athletic department elects to distribute the tickets by giving them away to the first 1,000 students who show up at the department's office at 10 A.M. the following Monday.
  a. Which groups of students will be most likely to try to get the tickets? Think of specific examples and then generalize.
  b. What is the opportunity cost of distributing the tickets this way?
  c. Productive efficiency occurs when a good or service (such as the distribution of tickets) is produced at the lowest possible cost. Is this an efficient way to distribute the tickets? If possible, think of a more efficient method of distributing the tickets.
  d. Is this an equitable way to distribute the tickets? Briefly explain.

Economic Models, pages 12–17

1.3 LEARNING OBJECTIVE: Describe the role of models in economic analysis.

Summary

An **economic variable** is something measurable that can have different values, such as the wages of software programmers. Economists rely on economic models when they apply economic ideas to real-world problems. **Economic models** are simplified versions of reality used to analyze real-world economic situations. Economists accept and use an economic model if it leads to hypotheses that are confirmed by statistical analysis. In many cases, the acceptance is tentative, however, pending the gathering of new data or further statistical analysis. Economics is a *social science* because it applies the scientific method to the study of the interactions among individuals. Economics is concerned with positive analysis rather than normative analysis. **Positive analysis** is concerned with what is. **Normative analysis** is concerned with what ought to be. As a social science, economics considers human behavior in every context of decision making, not just in business.

MyEconLab   Visit **www.myeconlab.com** to complete these exercises online and get instant feedback.

Review Questions

3.1 Why do economists use models? How are economic data used to test models?

3.2 Describe the five steps economists follow to arrive at a useful economic model.

3.3 What is the difference between normative analysis and positive analysis? Is economics concerned mainly with normative analysis or positive analysis? Briefly explain.

Problems and Applications

3.4 Suppose an economist develops an economic model and finds that "it works great in theory, but it fails in practice." What should the economist do next?

3.5 Dr. Strangelove's theory is that the price of mushrooms is determined by the activity of subatomic particles that exist in another universe parallel to ours. When the subatomic particles are emitted in profusion, the price of mushrooms is high. When subatomic particle emissions are low, the price of mushrooms is also low. How would you go about testing Dr. Strangelove's theory? Discuss whether this theory is useful.

3.6 **(Related to the** Don't Let This Happen to You **on page 15)** Briefly explain which of the following statements represent positive analysis and which represent normative analysis.
a. A 50-cent-per-pack tax on cigarettes will lead to a 12 percent reduction in smoking by teenagers.
b. The federal government should spend more on AIDS research.
c. Rising wheat prices will increase bread prices.
d. The price of coffee at Starbucks is too high.

3.7 **(Related to the** Don't Let This Happen to You **on page 15)** Warren Buffet is the chief executive officer of the investment firm Berkshire Hathaway and one of the wealthiest people in the world. In an editorial in the *Wall Street Journal*, Buffet argued that economic policies in the United States should be designed so that people who are willing to work receive enough income to live a "decent lifestyle." He argued that an expansion of the Earned Income Tax Credit (EITC) would be superior to an increase in the minimum wage as a means to reach this goal. The EITC is a program under which the federal government makes payments to low-income workers. Is Buffet correct that it is the role of the federal government to make sure people who work will have enough income to live a "decent lifestyle"?
Source: Warren Buffet, "Better Than Raising the Minimum Wage," *Wall Street Journal*, May 21, 2015.

3.8 **(Related to the** Making the Connection **on page 16)** The *Making the Connection* feature explains that there are both positive and normative elements to the debate over whether medical schools should charge tuition and whether hospitals should continue to pay residents who pursue primary care but not residents who specialize. What economic statistics would be most useful in evaluating the positive elements in this debate? Assuming that these statistics are available or could be gathered, are they likely to resolve the normative issues in this debate?

3.9 **(Related to the** Chapter Opener **on page 3)** An article in the *Wall Street Journal* discussing Sanadu's prospects for successfully selling its home medical devices observes, "Another challenge will be getting doctors on board with the idea of patients bringing them information from home." What economic incentives do doctors have to accept this information? What economic incentives do they have not to accept it?
Source: Timothy Hay, "Gadgets Bring Diagnostics into the Home," *Wall Street Journal*, April 27, 2015.

3.10 Suppose you were building an economic model to forecast the number of physicians and physician's assistants likely to be needed in 2020. Should your model take into account the growth of the home medical device industry? Briefly explain.

3.11 To receive a medical license in the United States, a doctor must complete a residency program at a hospital. Hospitals are not free to expand their residency programs in a particular medical specialty without approval from a residency review committee (RRC), which is made up of physicians in that specialty. A hospital that does not abide by the rulings of the RRC runs the risk of losing its accreditation from the Accreditation Council for Graduate Medical Education (ACGME). The RRCs and ACGME argue that this system ensures that residency programs do not expand to the point where they are not providing residents with high-quality training.
a. How does this system help protect consumers?
b. How might this system protect the financial interests of doctors more than the well-being of consumers?
c. Briefly explain whether you consider this system to be good or bad. Is your conclusion an example of normative economics or of positive economics? Briefly explain.
Sources: Brian Palmer, "We Need More Doctors, Stat!" *Slate*, June 27, 2011; and Sean Nicholson, "Barriers to Entering Medical Specialties," Wharton School, September 2003.

1.4 Microeconomics and Macroeconomics, page 17

LEARNING OBJECTIVE: Distinguish between microeconomics and macroeconomics.

Summary

Microeconomics is the study of how households and firms make choices, how they interact in markets, and how the government attempts to influence their choices. **Macroeconomics** is the study of the economy as a whole, including topics such as inflation, unemployment, and economic growth.

MyEconLab   Visit **www.myeconlab.com** to complete these exercises online and get instant feedback.

Review Question

4.1 Briefly discuss the difference between microeconomics and macroeconomics.

4.2 Is every economic issue either strictly microeconomic or strictly macroeconomic? Briefly explain.

Problems and Applications

4.3 Briefly explain whether each of the following is primarily a microeconomic issue or a macroeconomic issue.
  a. The effect of higher cigarette taxes on the quantity of cigarettes sold
  b. The effect of higher income taxes on the total amount of consumer spending
  c. The reasons the economies of East Asian countries grow faster than the economies of sub-Saharan African countries
  d. The reasons for low rates of profit in the airline industry

4.4 Briefly explain whether you agree with the following assertion: "Microeconomics is concerned with things that happen in one particular place, such as the unemployment rate in one city. In contrast, macroeconomics is concerned with things that affect the country as a whole, such as how the rate of teenage smoking in the United States would be affected by an increase in the tax on cigarettes."

1.5 A Preview of Important Economic Terms, pages 17–19

LEARNING OBJECTIVE: Define important economic terms.

Summary

Becoming familiar with important terms is a necessary step in learning economics. These important economic terms include *capital, entrepreneur, factors of production, firm, goods, household, human capital, innovation, profit, revenue, services,* and *technology.*

Appendix

Using Graphs and Formulas

LEARNING OBJECTIVE: Use graphs and formulas to analyze economic situations.

Graphs are used to illustrate key economic ideas. Graphs appear not just in economics textbooks but also on Web sites and in newspaper and magazine articles that discuss events in business and economics. Graphs serve two useful purposes: (1) They simplify economic ideas, and (2) they make the ideas more concrete so they can be applied to real-world problems. Economic and business issues can be complicated, but a graph can help cut through complications and highlight the key relationships needed to understand the issue. In that sense, a graph can be like a street map.

Suppose you take a bus to New York City to see the Empire State Building. After arriving at the Port Authority Bus Terminal, you will probably use a map similar to this one to find your way to the Empire State Building.

Maps are simplified versions of reality. This map shows the streets in this part of New York City and some of the most important buildings. The map does not show stores, most buildings, or the names, addresses, and telephone numbers of the people who live and work in the area. In fact, the map shows almost nothing about the messy reality of life in this section of New York City, except how the streets are laid out, which is the essential information you need to get from the Port Authority Bus Terminal to the Empire State Building.

Street map of New York City. Copyright © 2011 City Maps Inc. Reprinted by permission.

Think about someone who says, "I know how to get around in the city, but I just can't figure out how to read a map." It certainly is possible to find your destination in a city without a map, but it's a lot easier with one. The same is true of using graphs in economics. It is possible to arrive at a solution to a real-world problem in economics and business without using graphs, but it is usually a lot easier if you use them.

With practice, you will become familiar with the graphs and formulas in this text, and you will know how to use them to analyze problems that would otherwise seem very difficult. What follows is a brief review of how graphs and formulas are used.

Graphs of One Variable

Figure 1A.1 displays values for *market shares* in the U.S. automobile market, using two common types of graphs. Market shares show the percentage of industry sales accounted for by different firms. In this case, the information is for groups of firms: the "Big Three"—Ford, General Motors, and Chrysler—as well as Japanese, European, and Korean firms. Panel (a) displays the information about market shares as a *bar graph*, where the market share of each group of firms is represented by the height of its bar. Panel (b) displays the same information as a *pie chart*, where the market share of each group of firms is represented by the size of its slice of the pie.

Information about an economic variable is also often displayed in a *time-series graph*, which shows on a coordinate grid how the values of a variable change over time. In a coordinate grid, we can measure the value of one variable along the vertical axis (or *y*-axis) and the value of another variable along the horizontal axis (or *x*-axis). The point where the vertical axis intersects the horizontal axis is called the *origin*. At the origin, the value of both variables is zero. The points on a coordinate grid represent values of the two variables.

In Figure 1A.2, we measure the number of automobiles and trucks sold worldwide by Ford Motor Company on the vertical axis, and we measure time on the horizontal axis. In time-series graphs, the height of the line at each date shows the value of the

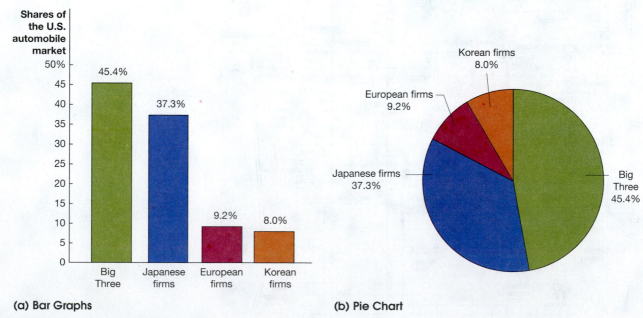

(a) Bar Graphs

(b) Pie Chart

Figure 1A.1   **Bar Graphs and Pie Charts**

Values for an economic variable are often displayed as a bar graph or a pie chart. In this case, panel (a) shows market share data for the U.S. automobile industry as a bar graph, where the market share of each group of firms is represented by the height of its bar. Panel (b) displays the same information as a pie chart, where the market share of each group of firms is represented by the size of its slice of the pie.

Source: "Auto Sales," *Wall Street Journal*, May 21, 2015.

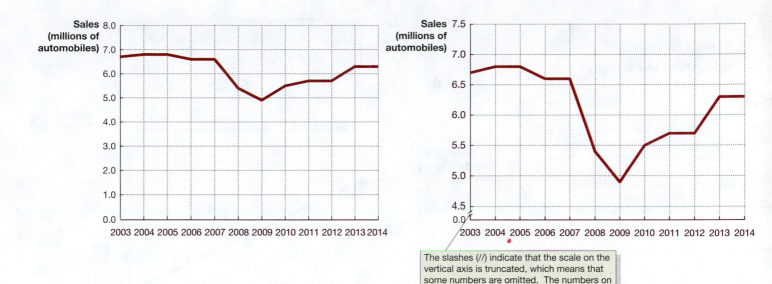

(a) Time-series graph where the scale is not truncated

(b) Time-series graph with truncated scale

The slashes (//) indicate that the scale on the vertical axis is truncated, which means that some numbers are omitted. The numbers on the vertical axis jump from 0 to 4.5.

MyEconLab Animation

Figure 1A.2   Time-Series Graphs

Both panels present time-series graphs of Ford Motor Company's worldwide sales during each year from 2003 to 2014. In panel (a), the vertical axis starts at 0, and the distance between each pair of values shown is the same. In panel (b), the scale on the vertical axis is truncated, which means that

although it starts at 0, it then jumps to 4.5 million. As a result, the fluctuations in Ford's sales appear smaller in panel (a) than in panel (b).

Source: Ford Motor Company, *Annual Report*, various years.

variable measured on the vertical axis. Both panels of Figure 1A.2 show Ford's worldwide sales during each year from 2003 to 2014. The difference between panel (a) and panel (b) illustrates the importance of the scale used in a time-series graph. In panel (a), the vertical axis starts at 0, and the distance between each pair of values shown is the same. In this panel, the decline in Ford's sales during 2008 and 2009 appears relatively small. In panel (b), the scale on the vertical axis is truncated, which means that although it starts at zero, it jumps to 4.5 million. As a result, the distance on the vertical axis from 0 to 4.5 million is much smaller than the distance from 4.5 million to 5.0 million. The slashes (//) near the bottom of the axis indicate that the scale is truncated. In panel (b), the decline in Ford's sales during 2008 and 2009 appears much larger than in panel (a). (Technically, the horizontal axis in both panels is also truncated because we start with 2003, not 0.)

MyEconLab Concept Check

Graphs of Two Variables

We often use graphs to show the relationship between two variables. Suppose you are interested in the relationship between the price of a cheese pizza and the quantity of pizzas sold per week in the town of Statesboro, Georgia. A graph showing the relationship between the price of a good and the quantity of the good demanded at each price is called a *demand curve*. (As we will discuss later, in drawing a demand curve for a good, we have to hold constant any variables other than price that might affect the willingness of consumers to buy the good.) Figure 1A.3 shows the data collected on price and quantity. The figure shows a two-dimensional grid on which we measure the price of pizza along the y-axis and the quantity of pizza sold per week along the x-axis. Each point on the grid represents one of the price and quantity combinations listed in the table. We can connect the points to form the demand curve for pizza in Statesboro, Georgia. Notice that the scales on both axes in the graph are truncated. In this case, truncating the axes allows the graph to illustrate more clearly the relationship between price and quantity by excluding low prices and quantities.

Figure 1A.3

Plotting Price and Quantity Points in a Graph

The figure shows a two-dimensional grid on which we measure the price of pizza along the vertical axis (or *y*-axis) and the quantity of pizza sold per week along the horizontal axis (or *x*-axis). Each point on the grid represents one of the price and quantity combinations listed in the table. By connecting the points with a line, we can better illustrate the relationship between the two variables.

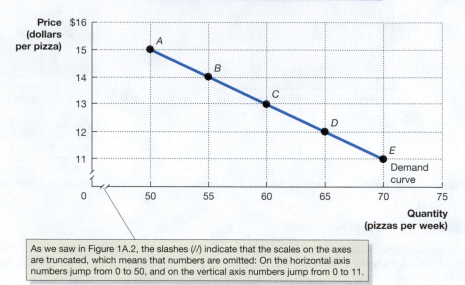

Price (dollars per pizza)	Quantity (pizzas per week)	Points
$15	50	A
14	55	B
13	60	C
12	65	D
11	70	E

As we saw in Figure 1A.2, the slashes (//) indicate that the scales on the axes are truncated, which means that numbers are omitted: On the horizontal axis numbers jump from 0 to 50, and on the vertical axis numbers jump from 0 to 11.

Slopes of Lines

Once you have plotted the data in Figure 1A.3, you may be interested in how much the quantity of pizza sold increases as the price decreases. The *slope* of a line tells us how much the variable we are measuring on the *y*-axis changes as the variable we are measuring on the *x*-axis changes. We can use the Greek letter delta (Δ) to stand for the change in a variable. The slope is sometimes referred to as the rise over the run. So, we have several ways of expressing slope:

$$\text{Slope} = \frac{\text{Change in value on the vertical axis}}{\text{Change in value on the horizontal axis}} = \frac{\Delta y}{\Delta x} = \frac{\text{Rise}}{\text{Run}}.$$

Figure 1A.4 reproduces the graph from Figure 1A.3. Because the slope of a straight line is the same at any point, we can use any two points in the figure to calculate the slope of the line. For example, when the price of pizza decreases from $14 to $12, the quantity of pizza sold increases from 55 per week to 65 per week. Therefore, the slope is:

$$\text{Slope} = \frac{\Delta \text{Price of pizza}}{\Delta \text{Quantity of pizza}} = \frac{(\$12 - \$14)}{(65 - 55)} = \frac{-2}{10} = -0.2.$$

The slope of this line shows us how responsive consumers in Statesboro, Georgia, are to changes in the price of pizza. The larger the value of the slope (ignoring the negative sign), the steeper the line will be, which indicates that not many additional pizzas are sold when the price falls. The smaller the value of the slope, the flatter the line will be, which indicates a greater increase in pizzas sold when the price falls.   MyEconLab Concept Check

Taking into Account More Than Two Variables on a Graph

The demand curve graph in Figure 1A.4 shows the relationship between the price of pizza and the quantity of pizza demanded, but we know that the quantity of any good demanded depends on more than just the price of the good. For example, the quantity of pizza demanded in a given week in Statesboro, Georgia, can be affected by other

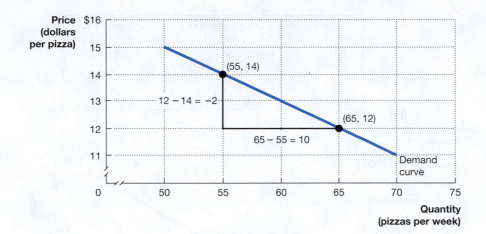

MyEconLab Animation

Figure 1A.4

Calculating the Slope of a Line

We can calculate the slope of a line as the change in the value of the variable on the *y*-axis divided by the change in the value of the variable on the *x*-axis. Because the slope of a straight line is constant, we can use any two points in the figure to calculate the slope of the line. For example, when the price of pizza decreases from $14 to $12, the quantity of pizza demanded increases from 55 per week to 65 per week. So, the slope of this line equals −2 divided by 10, or −0.2.

variables—the price of hamburgers, whether an advertising campaign by local pizza parlors has begun that week, and so on. Allowing the values of any other variables to change will cause the position of the demand curve in the graph to change.

Suppose that the demand curve in Figure 1A.4 were drawn holding the price of hamburgers constant, at $1.50. If the price of hamburgers rises to $2.00, some consumers will switch from buying hamburgers to buying pizza, and more pizzas will be demanded at every price. The result on the graph will be to shift the line representing the demand curve to the right. Similarly, if the price of hamburgers falls from $1.50 to $1.00, some consumers will switch from buying pizza to buying hamburgers, and fewer pizzas will be demanded at every price. The result on the graph will be to shift the line representing the demand curve to the left.

The table in Figure 1A.5 shows the effect of a change in the price of hamburgers on the quantity of pizza demanded. On the graph, suppose that at first we are on the line labeled Demand curve₁. If the price of pizza is $14 (point *A*), an increase in the price of

Price (dollars per pizza)	Quantity (pizzas per week)		
	When the Price of Hamburgers = $1.00	When the Price of Hamburgers = $1.50	When the Price of Hamburgers = $2.00
$15	45	50	55
14	50	55	60
13	55	60	65
12	60	65	70
11	65	70	75

MyEconLab Animation

Figure 1A.5

Showing Three Variables on a Graph

The demand curve for pizza shows the relationship between the price of pizzas and the quantity of pizzas demanded, *holding constant other factors that might affect the willingness of consumers to buy pizza.* If the price of pizza is $14 (point *A*), an increase in the price of hamburgers from $1.50 to $2.00 increases the quantity of pizzas demanded from 55 to 60 per week (point *B*) and shifts us to Demand curve₂. Or, if we start on Demand curve₁ and the price of pizza is $12 (point *C*), a decrease in the price of hamburgers from $1.50 to $1.00 decreases the quantity of pizza demanded from 65 to 60 per week (point *D*) and shifts us to Demand curve₃.

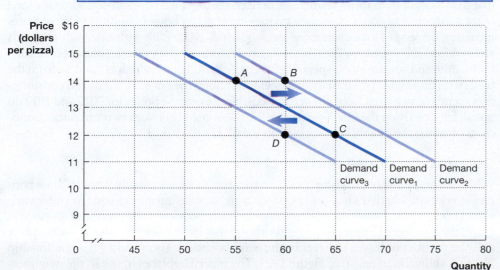

Figure 1A.6

Graphing the Positive Relationship between Income and Consumption

In a positive relationship between two economic variables, as one variable increases, the other variable also increases. This figure shows the positive relationship between disposable personal income and consumption spending. As disposable personal income in the United States has increased, so has consumption spending.

Source: U.S. Department of Commerce, Bureau of Economic Analysis.

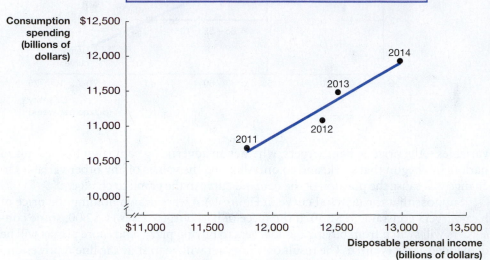

Year	Disposable Personal Income (billions of dollars)	Consumption Spending (billions of dollars)
2011	$11,801	$10,689
2012	12,384	11,083
2013	12,505	11,484
2014	12,986	11,930

hamburgers from $1.50 to $2.00 increases the quantity of pizzas demanded from 55 to 60 per week (point *B*) and shifts us to Demand curve₂. Or, if we start on Demand curve₁ and the price of pizza is $12 (point *C*), a decrease in the price of hamburgers from $1.50 to $1.00 decreases the quantity of pizzas demanded from 65 to 60 per week (point *D*) and shifts us to Demand curve₃. By shifting the demand curve, we have taken into account the effect of changes in the value of a third variable—the price of hamburgers. We will use this technique of shifting curves to allow for the effects of additional variables many times in this book.　　　　MyEconLab Concept Check

Positive and Negative Relationships

We can use graphs to show the relationships between any two variables. Sometimes the relationship between the variables is *negative*, meaning that as one variable increases in value, the other variable decreases in value. This was the case with the price of pizza and the quantity of pizzas demanded. The relationship between two variables can also be *positive*, meaning that the values of both variables increase or decrease together. For example, when the level of total income—or *disposable personal income*—received by households in the United States increases, the level of total *consumption spending*, which is spending by households on goods and services, also increases. The table in Figure 1A.6 shows the values (in billions of dollars) for income and consumption spending for 2011–2014. The graph plots the data from the table, with disposable personal income measured along the horizontal axis and consumption spending measured along the vertical axis. Notice that the points for 2012 and 2013 do not all fall exactly on the line. To examine the relationship between two variables, economists often use the straight line that best fits the data.　　　　MyEconLab Concept Check

Determining Cause and Effect

When we graph the relationship between two variables, we usually want to draw conclusions about whether changes in one variable are causing changes in the other variable. Doing so can, however, lead to mistakes. Suppose over the course of a year you graph the number of homes in a neighborhood that have a fire burning in the fireplace and the number of leaves on trees in the neighborhood. You would get a relationship like that shown in panel (a) of Figure 1A.7: The more fireplaces in use in the neighborhood, the fewer leaves the trees have. Can we draw the conclusion from this graph that

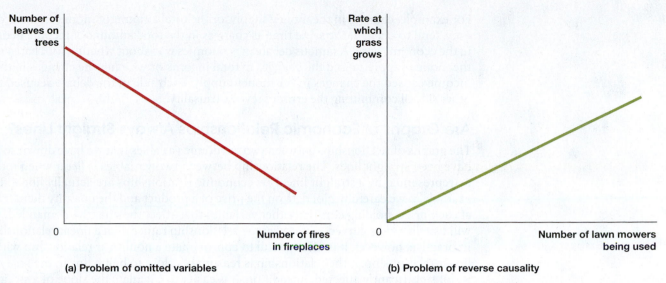

MyEconLab Animation

Figure 1A.7 **Determining Cause and Effect**

Using graphs to draw conclusions about cause and effect can be hazardous. In panel (a), we see that there are fewer leaves on the trees in a neighborhood when many homes have fires burning in their fireplaces. We cannot draw the conclusion that using fireplaces causes the leaves to fall because we have an *omitted variable*—the season of the year. In panel (b), we see that more lawn mowers are used in a neighborhood during times when the grass grows rapidly and fewer lawn mowers are used when the grass grows slowly. Concluding that using lawn mowers *causes* the grass to grow faster would be making the error of *reverse causality*.

using a fireplace causes trees to lose their leaves? We know, of course, that such a conclusion is incorrect. In spring and summer, there are relatively few fireplaces being used, and the trees are full of leaves. In the fall, as trees begin to lose their leaves, fireplaces are used more frequently. And in winter, many fireplaces are being used and many trees have lost all their leaves. The reason that the graph in Figure 1A.7 is misleading about cause and effect is that there is obviously an *omitted variable* in the analysis—the season of the year. An omitted variable is one that affects other variables, and its omission can lead to false conclusions about cause and effect.

Although in our example the omitted variable is obvious, there are many debates about cause and effect where the existence of an omitted variable has not been clear. For instance, it has been known for many years that people who smoke cigarettes suffer from higher rates of lung cancer than do nonsmokers. For some time, tobacco companies and some scientists argued that there was an omitted variable—perhaps failure to exercise or poor diet—that made some people more likely to smoke and more likely to develop lung cancer. If this omitted variable existed, then the finding that smokers were more likely to develop lung cancer would not have been evidence that smoking *caused* lung cancer. In this case, however, nearly all scientists eventually concluded that the omitted variable did not exist and that, in fact, smoking does cause lung cancer.

A related problem in determining cause and effect is known as *reverse causality*. The error of reverse causality occurs when we conclude that changes in variable X cause changes in variable Y when, in fact, it is actually changes in variable Y that cause changes in variable X. For example, panel (b) of Figure 1A.7 plots the number of lawn mowers being used in a neighborhood against the rate at which grass on lawns in the neighborhood is growing. We could conclude from this graph that using lawn mowers *causes* the grass to grow faster. We know, however, that in reality, the causality is in the other direction. Rapidly growing grass during the spring and summer causes the increased use of lawn mowers. Slowly growing grass in the fall or winter or during periods of low rainfall causes the decreased use of lawn mowers.

Once again, in our example, the potential error of reverse causality is obvious. In many economic debates, however, cause and effect can be more difficult to determine.

For example, changes in the money supply, or the total amount of money in the economy, tend to occur at the same time as changes in the total amount of income people in the economy earn. A famous debate in economics was about whether the changes in the money supply caused the changes in total income or whether the changes in total income caused the changes in the money supply. Each side in the debate accused the other side of committing the error of reverse causality.   MyEconLab Concept Check

Are Graphs of Economic Relationships Always Straight Lines?

The graphs of relationships between two economic variables that we have drawn so far have been straight lines. The relationship between two variables is *linear* when it can be represented by a straight line. Few economic relationships are actually linear. For example, if we carefully plot data on the price of a product and the quantity demanded at each price, holding constant other variables that affect the quantity demanded, we will usually find a curved—or *nonlinear*—relationship rather than a linear relationship. In practice, however, it is often useful to approximate a nonlinear relationship with a linear relationship. If the relationship is reasonably close to being linear, the analysis is not significantly affected. In addition, it is easier to calculate the slope of a straight line, and it is also easier to calculate the area under a straight line. So, in this textbook, we often assume that the relationship between two economic variables is linear, even when we know that this assumption is not precisely correct.   MyEconLab Concept Check

Slopes of Nonlinear Curves

In some situations, we need to take into account the nonlinear nature of an economic relationship. For example, panel (a) of Figure 1A.8 shows the hypothetical relationship between Apple's total cost of producing smartwatches and the quantity of smartwatches produced. The relationship is curved rather than linear. In this case, the cost of production is increasing at an increasing rate, which often happens in manufacturing. In other words, as we move up the curve, its slope becomes larger. (Remember that with a straight line, the slope is always constant.) To see why, first remember that we calculate the slope of a curve by dividing the change in the variable on the *y*-axis by the change in the variable on the *x*-axis. As we move from point A to point B, the quantity produced increases by 1 million smartwatches, while the total cost of production increases by $50 million. Farther up the curve, as we move from point C to point D, the change in quantity is the same—1 million smartwatches—but the change in the total cost of production is now much larger—$250 million. Because the change in the *y* variable has increased, while the change in the *x* variable has remained the same, we know that the slope has increased.

To measure the slope of a nonlinear curve at a particular point, we measure the slope of the line that is tangent to that curve at that point. This tangent line will touch the curve only at that point. We can measure the slope of the tangent line just as we would measure the slope of any other straight line. In panel (b), the tangent line at point B has a slope equal to:

$$\frac{\Delta \text{Cost}}{\Delta \text{Quantity}} = \frac{75}{1} = 75.$$

The tangent line at point C has a slope equal to:

$$\frac{\Delta \text{Cost}}{\Delta \text{Quantity}} = \frac{150}{1} = 150.$$

Once again, we see that the slope of the curve is larger at point C than at point B.   MyEconLab Concept Check

Formulas

We have just seen that graphs are an important economic tool. In this section, we will review several useful formulas and show how to use them to summarize data and calculate important relationships.

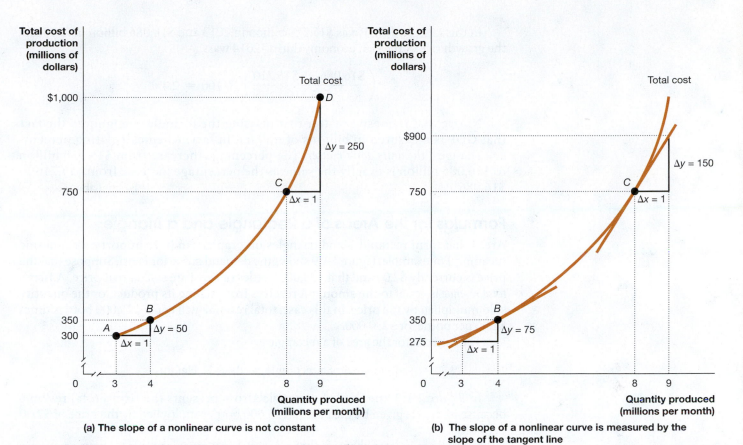

Figure 1A.8   The Slope of a Nonlinear Curve

The relationship between the quantity of Apple Watches produced and the total cost of production is curved rather than linear. In panel (a), when we move from point A to point B, the quantity produced increases by 1 million Apple Watches, while the total cost of production increases by $50 million. Farther up the curve, as we move from point C to point D, the change in quantity is the same—1 million Apple Watches—but the change in the total cost of production is now much larger—$250 million.

Because the change in the y variable has increased, while the change in the x variable has remained the same, we know that the slope has increased. In panel (b), we measure the slope of the curve at a particular point by calculating the slope of the tangent line at that point. The slope of the tangent line at point B is 75, and the slope of the tangent line at point C is 150.

Formula for a Percentage Change

The *percentage change* is the change in some economic variable, usually from one period to the next, expressed as a percentage. A key macroeconomic measure is the real gross domestic product (GDP). GDP is the value of all the final goods and services produced in a country during a year. "Real" GDP is corrected for the effects of inflation. When economists say that the U.S. economy grew 2.4 percent during 2014, they mean that real GDP was 2.4 percent higher in 2014 than it was in 2013. The formula for making this calculation is:

$$\left(\frac{GDP_{2014} - GDP_{2013}}{GDP_{2013}} \right) \times 100$$

or, more generally, for any two periods:

$$\text{Percentage change} = \left(\frac{\text{Value in the second period} - \text{Value in the first period}}{\text{Value in the first period}} \right) \times 100.$$

In this case, real GDP was $15,710 billion in 2013 and $16,086 billion in 2014. So, the growth rate of the U.S. economy during 2014 was:

$$\left(\frac{\$16{,}086 - \$15{,}710}{\$15{,}710}\right) \times 100 = 2.4\%.$$

Notice that it doesn't matter that in using the formula, we ignored the fact that GDP is measured in billions of dollars. In fact, when calculating percentage changes, *the units don't matter*. The percentage increase from $15,710 billion to $16,086 billion is exactly the same as the percentage increase from $15,710 to $16,086.   MyEconLab Concept Check

Formulas for the Areas of a Rectangle and a Triangle

Areas that form rectangles and triangles on graphs can have important economic meaning. For example, Figure 1A.9 shows the demand curve for Pepsi. Suppose that the price is currently $2.00 and that 125,000 bottles of Pepsi are sold at that price. A firm's *total revenue* is equal to the amount it receives from selling its product, or the quantity sold multiplied by the price. In this case, total revenue will equal 125,000 bottles times $2.00 per bottle, or $250,000.

The formula for the area of a rectangle is:

$$\text{Area of a rectangle} = \text{Base} \times \text{Height}.$$

In Figure 1A.9, the shaded rectangle also represents the firm's total revenue because its area is given by the base of 125,000 bottles multiplied by the price of $2.00 per bottle.

We will see in later chapters that areas that are triangles can also have economic significance. The formula for the area of a triangle is:

$$\text{Area of a triangle} = \frac{1}{2} \times \text{Base} \times \text{Height}.$$

The shaded area in Figure 1A.10 is a triangle. The base equals 150,000 − 125,000, or 25,000. Its height equals $2.00 − $1.50, or $0.50. Therefore, its area equals 1/2 × 25,000 × $0.50, or $6,250. Notice that the shaded area is a triangle only if the demand curve is a straight line, or linear. Not all demand curves are linear. However, the formula for the area of a triangle will usually still give a good approximation, even if the demand curve is not linear.   MyEconLab Concept Check

MyEconLab Study Plan

MyEconLab Animation

Figure 1A.9

Showing a Firm's Total Revenue on a Graph

The area of a rectangle is equal to its base multiplied by its height. Total revenue is equal to quantity multiplied by price. Here, total revenue is equal to the quantity of 125,000 bottles times the price of $2.00 per bottle, or $250,000. The area of the shaded rectangle shows the firm's total revenue.

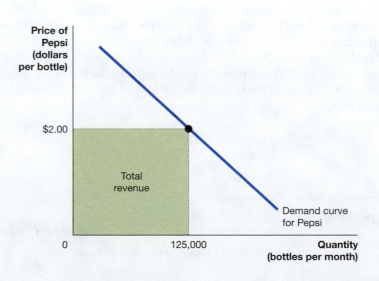

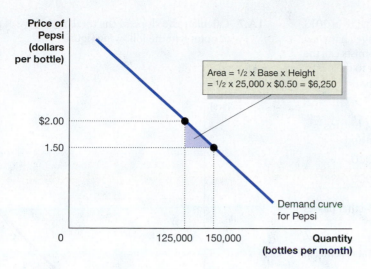

MyEconLab Animation

Figure 1A.10

The Area of a Triangle

The area of a triangle is equal to 1/2 multiplied by its base multiplied by its height. The area of the shaded triangle has a base equal to 150,000 − 125,000, or 25,000, and a height equal to $2.00 − $1.50, or $0.50. Therefore, its area is equal to 1/2 × 25,000 × $0.50, or $6,250.

Summary of Using Formulas

You will encounter several other formulas in this book. Whenever you use a formula, you should follow these steps:

1. Make sure you understand the economic concept the formula represents.
2. Make sure you are using the correct formula for the problem you are solving.
3. Make sure the number you calculate using the formula is economically reasonable. For example, if you are using a formula to calculate a firm's revenue and your answer is a negative number, you know you made a mistake somewhere.   MyEconLab Concept Check   MyEconLab Study Plan

 Using Graphs and Formulas, pages 27–37

LEARNING OBJECTIVE: Use graphs and formulas to analyze economic situations.

MyEconLab   Visit www.myeconlab.com to complete these exercises online and get instant feedback.

Problems and Applications

1A.1 The following table shows the relationship between the price of custard pies and the number of pies Jacob buys per week:

Price (dollars per pie)	Quantity of pies	Week
$3.00	6	July 2
2.00	7	July 9
5.00	4	July 16
6.00	3	July 23
1.00	8	July 30
4.00	5	August 6

a. Is the relationship between the price of pies and the number of pies Jacob buys a positive relationship or a negative relationship?
b. Plot the data from the table on a graph similar to Figure 1A.3 on page 30. Draw a straight line that best fits the points.
c. Calculate the slope of the line.

1A.2 The following table gives information about the quantity of glasses of lemonade demanded on sunny and overcast days:

Price (dollars per glass)	Quantity (glasses of lemonade per day)	Weather
$0.80	30	Sunny
0.80	10	Overcast
0.70	40	Sunny
0.70	20	Overcast
0.60	50	Sunny
0.60	30	Overcast
0.50	60	Sunny
0.50	40	Overcast

Plot the data from the table on a graph similar to Figure 1A.5 on page 31. Draw two straight lines representing the two demand curves—one for sunny days and one for overcast days.

1A.3 Using the information in Figure 1A.2 on page 29, calculate the percentage change in Ford's auto sales from one year to the next. During which year did sales fall at the highest rate?

1A.4 Real GDP in 2012 was $15,369 billion. Real GDP in 2013 was $15,710 billion. What was the percentage change in real GDP from 2012 to 2013? What do economists call the percentage change in real GDP from one year to the next?

1A.5 Assume that the demand curve for Pepsi passes through the following two points:

Price per bottle of Pepsi (in dollars)	Number of bottles demanded
$2.50	100,000
1.25	200,000

a. Draw a graph with a linear demand curve that passes through these two points.

b. Show on the graph the areas representing total revenue at each price. Give the value for total revenue at each price.

1A.6 What is the area of the triangle shown in the following figure?

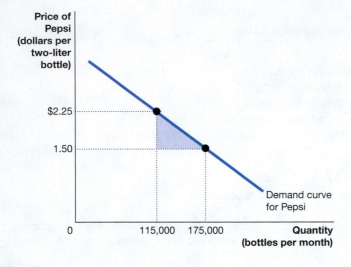

1A.7 Calculate the slope of the total cost curve at point A and at point B in the following figure.

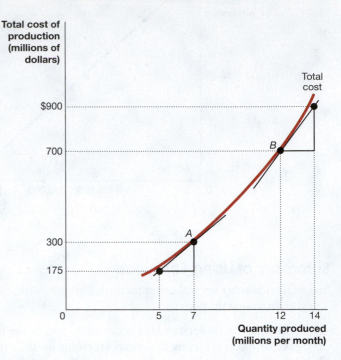

Trade-offs, Comparative Advantage, and the Market System

Chapter Outline and Learning Objectives

Managers at Tesla Motors Face Trade-offs

Are all-electric cars the wave of the future? If you're like most drivers, you probably like the idea of skipping the gas station in favor of powering up your car by plugging it into an electric outlet. Yet, all-electric cars have struggled to succeed in the marketplace for two key reasons: (1) The lithium batteries that power electric cars are costly, forcing up the prices of the cars, and (2) available batteries need to be recharged every 100 to 300 miles, making the cars impractical for long trips.

Tesla Motors is an American-based automobile manufacturer founded in 2003 by billionaire Elon Musk, who also started the online payment system PayPal and the private space firm SpaceX. Although in 2015 the firm held only a tiny 0.1 percent share of the U.S. car market, it had the goal of becoming the first firm to sell large numbers of all-electric cars. Tesla is building a nationwide network of fast-charging stations to make it easier for drivers to make longer trips. In 2015, its current models had high prices, but it intended to introduce a lower-priced model that would appeal to people who had been buying gasoline-powered cars such as the Toyota Camry or Honda Accord.

Tesla manufactures its cars in Fremont, California. To compete in the automobile market, Tesla's managers must make many strategic decisions, such as whether to introduce new car models. Tesla initially sold only the Model S sedan, with a base price of $75,000. In late 2015, Tesla introduced a second model, the Model X, a cross between a sport utility vehicle (SUV) and a minivan. The Model X was designed for families who would otherwise buy traditional gasoline-powered SUVs or minivans. But it also had a very high base price. Ultimately, Tesla's plan to gain a significant share of the automobile market required that it allocate resources to producing an all-electric car priced at about $35,000.

Tesla's managers must also decide how to sell and service its cars. Tesla has no dealerships. Instead, the company sells its cars only online and relies on company-owned service centers to provide maintenance and repair services. Some economists have questioned whether Tesla will be able to meet its future sales goals without selling cars through dealerships.

Managers also make smaller-scale decisions. For instance, in scheduling production at its Fremont plant, each month Tesla's managers must decide the quantity of Model S sedans and Model X SUVs to manufacture. Like other decisions managers make, this one involves a trade-off: Producing more of one of these two models means producing fewer of the other.

Apple is among a growing list of companies exploring the electric vehicle market. **AN INSIDE LOOK** on page 64 discusses the resources Apple has assembled to produce an electric vehicle as early as 2020.

Sources: Mike Ramsey and Anne Steele, "Tesla Loss Widens as Spending Jumps," *Wall Street Journal*, May 6, 2015; and Charles Fleming, "Tesla Introduces Lower Priced AWD Electric Model S," *Los Angeles Times*, April 8, 2015.

Economics in Your Life

The Trade-offs When You Buy a Car

When you buy a gasoline-powered car, you probably consider factors such as safety and fuel efficiency. To increase fuel efficiency, automobile manufacturers make some cars that are small and light. Large cars absorb more of the impact of an accident than do small cars, so people are usually safer driving large cars. What do these facts tell us about the relationship between safety and fuel efficiency? Under what circumstances would it be possible for automobile manufacturers to make cars that are both safer and more fuel efficient? As you read the chapter, try to answer these questions. You can check your answers against those provided on **page 62** at the end of this chapter.

Scarcity A situation in which unlimited wants exceed the limited resources available to fulfill those wants.

In a market system, managers are always making decisions like those made by Tesla's managers. These decisions reflect a key fact of economic life: *Scarcity requires trade-offs*. **Scarcity** exists because we have unlimited wants but only limited resources available to fulfill those wants. Goods and services are scarce. So, too, are the economic resources, or *factors of production*—workers, capital, natural resources, and entrepreneurial ability—used to make goods and services. Your time is scarce, which means you face trade-offs: If you spend an hour studying for an economics exam, you have one less hour to spend studying for a psychology exam or going to the movies. If your university decides to use some of its scarce budget to buy new computers for the computer labs, those funds will not be available to buy new books for the library or to resurface the student parking lots. If Tesla decides to devote some of the scarce workers and machinery in its Fremont assembly plant to producing more Model X SUVs, those resources will not be available to produce more Model S sedans.

Households and firms make many of their decisions in markets. Trade is a key activity that takes place in markets. Trade results from the decisions of millions of households and firms around the world. By engaging in trade, people can raise their incomes. In this chapter, we provide an overview of how the market system coordinates the independent decisions of these millions of households and firms. We begin our analysis of the economic consequences of scarcity and how a market system works by introducing an important economic model: the *production possibilities frontier*.

2.1 Production Possibilities Frontiers and Opportunity Costs

LEARNING OBJECTIVE: Use a production possibilities frontier to analyze opportunity costs and trade-offs.

As we saw in the chapter opener, Tesla operates an automobile factory in Fremont, California, where it assembles two car models. Because the firm's resources—workers, machinery, materials, and entrepreneurial ability—are limited, Tesla faces a trade-off: Resources devoted to producing one model are not available for producing the other model. Chapter 1 explained that economic models can be useful in analyzing many questions. We can use a simple model called the *production possibilities frontier* to analyze the trade-offs Tesla faces in its Fremont plant. A **production possibilities frontier (PPF)** is a curve showing the maximum attainable combinations of two goods that can be produced with available resources and current technology. In Tesla's case, the company produces only Model S sedans and Model X SUVs at the Fremont plant, using workers, materials, robots, and other machinery.

Production possibilities frontier (PPF) A curve showing the maximum attainable combinations of two goods that can be produced with available resources and current technology.

Graphing the Production Possibilities Frontier

Figure 2.1 uses a production possibilities frontier to illustrate the trade-offs that Tesla faces. The numbers from the table are plotted in the graph. The line in the graph represents Tesla's production possibilities frontier. If Tesla uses all its resources to produce Model S sedans, it can produce 80 per day—point A at one end of the production possibilities frontier. If Tesla uses all its resources to produce Model X SUVs, it can produce 80 per day—point E at the other end of the production possibilities frontier. If Tesla devotes resources to producing both vehicles, it could be at a point like B, where it produces 60 sedans and 20 SUVs.

All the combinations either on the frontier—like points A, B, C, D, and E—or inside the frontier—like point F—are *attainable* with the resources available. Combinations on the frontier are *efficient* because all available resources are being fully

MyEconLab Animation

Figure 2.1

Tesla's Production Possibilities Frontier

Tesla's Production Choices at Its Fremont Plant		
Choice	Quantity of Sedans Produced	Quantity of SUVs Produced
A	80	0
B	60	20
C	40	40
D	20	60
E	0	80

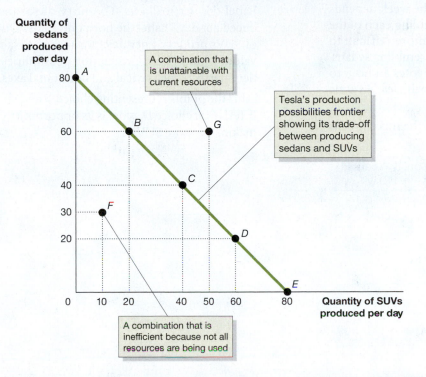

Tesla faces a trade-off: To build one more sedan, it must build one fewer SUV. The production possibilities frontier illustrates the trade-off Tesla faces. Combinations on the production possibilities frontier—like points A, B, C, D, and E—are *efficient* because the maximum output is being obtained from the available resources. Combinations inside the frontier—like point F—are *inefficient* because some resources are not being used. Combinations outside the frontier—like point G—are *unattainable* with current resources.

utilized, and the fewest possible resources are being used to produce a given amount of output. Combinations inside the frontier—like point *F*—are *inefficient* because maximum output is not being obtained from the available resources—perhaps because the assembly line is not operating at its capacity. Tesla might like to be beyond the frontier—at a point like *G*, where it would be producing 60 sedans and 50 SUVs per day—but points beyond the production possibilities frontier are *unattainable*, given the firm's current resources. To produce the combination at *G*, Tesla would need more machines and more workers.

Notice that if Tesla is producing efficiently and is on the production possibilities frontier, the only way to produce more of one vehicle is to produce fewer of the other vehicle. Recall from Chapter 1 that the **opportunity cost** of any activity is the highest-valued alternative that must be given up to engage in that activity. For Tesla, the opportunity cost of producing one more SUV is the number of sedans the company will not be able to produce because it has shifted those resources to producing the SUV. For example, if Tesla moves from point *B* to point *C*, the opportunity cost of producing 20 more SUVs per day is the 20 fewer sedans that it can produce.

What point on the production possibilities frontier is best? We can't tell without further information. If consumer demand for SUVs is greater than the demand for sedans, the company is likely to choose a point closer to *E*. If demand for sedans is greater than the demand for SUVs, the company is likely to choose a point closer to *A*.

Opportunity cost The highest-valued alternative that must be given up to engage in an activity.

MyEconLab Concept Check

Solved Problem 2.1

MyEconLab Interactive Animation

Drawing a Production Possibilities Frontier for Tesla Motors

Suppose, for simplicity, that during any given week, the machinery and number of workers at Tesla Motors's Fremont plant cannot be increased. So the number of sedans or SUVs the company can produce during the week depends on how many hours are devoted to assembling each of the different models. Assume that SUVs are more difficult to assemble, so if Tesla devotes an hour to assembling sedans, it will produce 15 vehicles, but if Tesla devotes an hour to producing SUVs, it will produce only 10 vehicles. Assume that the plant can run for 8 hours per day.

a. Use the information given to fill in the missing cells in the following table:

Choice	Hours Spent Making Sedans	Hours Spent Making SUVs	Quantity Produced per Day Sedans	Quantity Produced per Day SUVs
A	8	0		
B	7	1		
C	6	2		
D	5	3		
E	4	4		
F	3	5		
G	2	6		
H	1	7		
I	0	8		

b. Use the data in the table to draw a production possibilities frontier graph illustrating Tesla's trade-off between assembling sedans and assembling SUVs. Label the vertical axis "Quantity of sedans produced per day." Label the horizontal axis "Quantity of SUVs produced per day." Make sure to label the values where Tesla's production possibilities frontier intersects the vertical and horizontal axes.

c. Label the points representing choice D and choice E. If Tesla is at choice D, what is its opportunity cost of making 10 more SUVs?

Solving the Problem

Step 1: **Review the chapter material.** This problem is about using production possibilities frontiers to analyze trade-offs, so you may want to review the section "Graphing the Production Possibilities Frontier," which begins on page 42.

Step 2: **Answer part (a) by filling in the table.** If Tesla can assemble 15 sedans in 1 hour, then with choice A, it can assemble 120 sedans and 0 SUVs. Because Tesla can assemble 10 SUVs in 1 hour, with choice B, it will produce 105 sedans and 10 SUVs. Using similar reasoning, you can fill in the remaining cells in the table as follows:

Choice	Hours Spent Making Sedans	Hours Spent Making SUVs	Quantity Produced per Day Sedans	Quantity Produced per Day SUVs
A	8	0	120	0
B	7	1	105	10
C	6	2	90	20
D	5	3	75	30
E	4	4	60	40
F	3	5	45	50
G	2	6	30	60
H	1	7	15	70
I	0	8	0	80

Step 3: **Answer part (b) by drawing the production possibilities frontier graph.** Using the data in the table in step 2, you should draw a graph that looks like this:

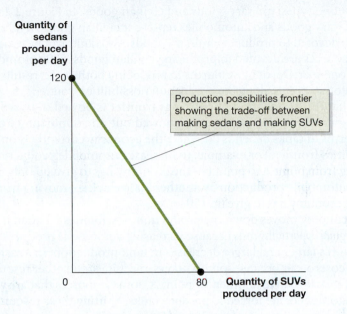

If Tesla devotes all 8 hours to assembling sedans, it will produce 120 sedans. Therefore, Tesla's production possibilities frontier will intersect the vertical axis at 120 sedans produced. If Tesla devotes all 8 hours to assembling SUVs, it will produce 80 SUVs. Therefore, Tesla's production possibilities frontier will intersect the horizontal axis at 80 SUVs produced.

Step 4: **Answer part (c) by labeling choices D and E on your graph.** The points for choices *D* and *E* can be plotted using the information from the table:

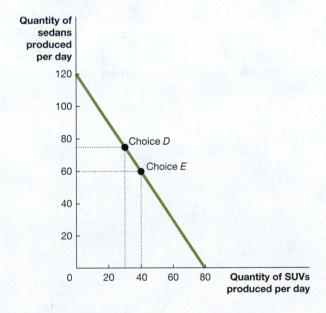

Moving from choice *D* to choice *E* increases Tesla's production of SUVs by 10 but lowers its production of sedans by 15. Therefore, Tesla's opportunity cost of producing 10 more SUVs is making 15 fewer sedans.

Your Turn: For more practice, do related problem 1.10 on page 67 at the end of this chapter.   MyEconLab Study Plan

Increasing Marginal Opportunity Costs

We can use the production possibilities frontier to explore issues concerning the economy as a whole. Suppose we divide all the goods and services produced in the economy into just two types: military goods and civilian goods. In Figure 2.2, we let tanks represent military goods and automobiles represent civilian goods. If all the country's resources are devoted to producing military goods, 400 tanks can be produced in one year. If all resources are devoted to producing civilian goods, 500 automobiles can be produced in one year. Devoting resources to producing both goods results in the economy being at other points along the production possibilities frontier.

Notice that this production possibilities frontier is bowed outward rather than being a straight line. Because the curve is bowed out, the opportunity cost of automobiles in terms of tanks depends on where the economy currently is on the production possibilities frontier. For example, to increase automobile production from 0 to 200—moving from point *A* to point *B*—the economy has to give up only 50 tanks. But to increase automobile production by another 200 vehicles—moving from point *B* to point *C*—the economy has to give up 150 tanks.

As the economy moves down the production possibilities frontier, it experiences *increasing marginal opportunity costs* because increasing automobile production by a given quantity requires larger and larger decreases in tank production. Increasing marginal opportunity costs occur because some workers, machines, and other resources are better suited to one use than to another. At point *A*, some resources that are well suited to producing automobiles are forced to produce tanks. Shifting these resources into producing automobiles by moving from point *A* to point *B* allows a substantial increase in automobile production, without much loss of tank production. But as the economy moves down the production possibilities frontier, more and more resources that are better suited to tank production are switched to automobile production. As a result, the increases in automobile production become increasingly smaller, while the decreases in tank production become increasingly larger. We would expect in most situations that production possibilities frontiers will be bowed outward rather than linear, as in the Tesla example discussed earlier.

The idea of increasing marginal opportunity costs illustrates an important economic concept: *The more resources already devoted to an activity, the smaller the payoff to devoting additional resources to that activity.* For example:

- The more hours you have already spent studying economics, the smaller the increase in your test grade from each additional hour you spend—and the greater the opportunity cost of using the hour in that way.

Figure 2.2

Increasing Marginal Opportunity Costs

As the economy moves down the production possibilities frontier, it experiences *increasing marginal opportunity costs* because increasing automobile production by a given quantity requires larger and larger decreases in tank production. For example, to increase automobile production from 0 to 200—moving from point *A* to point *B*—the economy has to give up only 50 tanks. But to increase automobile production by another 200 vehicles—moving from point *B* to point *C*—the economy has to give up 150 tanks.

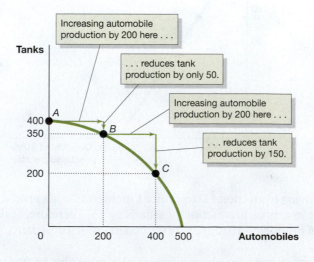

- The more funds a firm has devoted to research and development during a given year, the smaller the amount of useful knowledge it receives from each additional dollar spent—and the greater the opportunity cost of using the funds in that way.

- The more funds the federal government spends cleaning up the environment during a given year, the smaller the reduction in pollution from each additional dollar spent—and, once again, the greater the opportunity cost of using the funds in that way.   MyEconLab Concept Check

Economic Growth

At any given time, the total resources available to any economy are fixed. So, for example, if the United States produces more automobiles, it must produce less of something else—tanks in our example. The capital stock is the amount of machinery and other physical capital available in an economy. Over time, the resources available to an economy may increase because both the labor force and the capital stock increase. When the amount of resources increases, the economy's production possibilities frontier shifts outward, making it possible to produce both more automobiles and more tanks. Panel (a) of Figure 2.3 shows that over time the economy can move from point A to point B, producing more tanks and more automobiles.

Similarly, technological change makes it possible to produce more goods with the same number of workers and the same amount of machinery, which also shifts the production possibilities frontier outward. Technological change need not affect all sectors equally. Panel (b) of Figure 2.3 shows the results of technological change in the automobile industry that increases the quantity of automobiles workers can produce per year while leaving unchanged the quantity of tanks they can produce.

Outward shifts in the production possibilities frontier represent **economic growth** because they allow the economy to increase the production of goods and services, which ultimately raises the standard of living. In the United States and other high-income countries, the market system has aided the process of economic growth, which over the past 200 years has greatly increased the well-being of the average person.   MyEconLab Concept Check

Economic growth The ability of the economy to increase the production of goods and services.

MyEconLab Study Plan

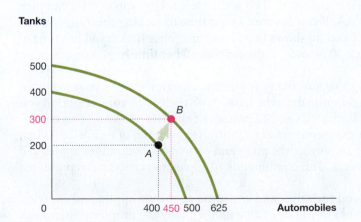

(a) Shifting out the production possibilities frontier

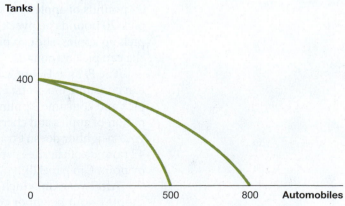

(b) Technological change in the automobile industry

MyEconLab Animation

Figure 2.3   Economic Growth

Panel (a) shows that as more economic resources become available and technological change occurs, the economy can move from point A to point B, producing more tanks and more automobiles. Panel (b) shows the results of technological change in the automobile industry that increases

the quantity of vehicles workers can produce per year while leaving unchanged the maximum quantity of tanks they can produce. Outward shifts in the production possibilities frontier represent *economic growth*.

2.2 Comparative Advantage and Trade

LEARNING OBJECTIVE: Describe comparative advantage and explain how it serves as the basis for trade.

Trade The act of buying and selling.

We can use the concepts of the production possibilities frontier and opportunity cost to understand the basic economic activity of *trade*. Markets are fundamentally about **trade**, which is the act of buying and selling. Sometimes we trade directly, as when children trade one baseball card for another baseball card. But often we trade indirectly: We sell our labor services as, say, an accountant, a salesperson, or a nurse for money, and then we use the money earned to buy goods and services. Although in these cases trade takes place indirectly, ultimately the accountant, salesperson, or nurse is trading his or her services for food, clothing, and other goods and services. One of the great benefits of trade is that it makes it possible for people to become better off by increasing both their production and their consumption.

Specialization and Gains from Trade

Consider the following situation: You and your neighbor both have fruit trees on your properties. Initially, suppose you have only apple trees and your neighbor has only cherry trees. In this situation, if you both like apples and cherries, there is an obvious opportunity for both of you to gain from trade: You trade some of your apples for some of your neighbor's cherries, making you both better off. But what if there are apple and cherry trees growing on both of your properties? In that case, there can still be gains from trade. For example, your neighbor might be very good at picking apples, and you might be very good at picking cherries. It would make sense for your neighbor to concentrate on picking apples and for you to concentrate on picking cherries. You can then trade some of the cherries you pick for some of the apples your neighbor picks. But what if your neighbor is actually better at picking both apples and cherries than you are?

We can use production possibilities frontiers (*PPFs*) to show how your neighbor can benefit from trading with you *even though she is better than you are at picking both apples and cherries*. (For simplicity, and because it will not have any effect on the conclusions we draw, we will assume that the *PPFs* in this example are straight lines.) The table in Figure 2.4 shows how many apples and how many cherries you and your neighbor can pick in one week. The graph in the figure uses the data from the table to construct *PPFs*. Panel (a) shows your *PPF*. If you devote all your time to picking apples, you can pick 20 pounds of apples per week. If you devote all your time to picking cherries, you can pick 20 pounds per week. Panel (b) shows that if your neighbor devotes all her time to picking apples, she can pick 30 pounds. If she devotes all her time to picking cherries, she can pick 60 pounds.

The *PPFs* in Figure 2.4 show how many apples and cherries you and your neighbor can consume *without trade*. Suppose that when you don't trade with your neighbor, you pick and consume 8 pounds of apples and 12 pounds of cherries per week. This combination of apples and cherries is represented by point *A* in panel (a) of Figure 2.5. When your neighbor doesn't trade with you, she picks and consumes 9 pounds of apples and 42 pounds of cherries per week. This combination of apples and cherries is represented by point *C* in panel (b).

After years in which you each pick and consume your own apples and cherries, suppose your neighbor comes to you one day with the following proposal: Next week she will trade you 15 pounds of her cherries for 10 pounds of your apples. Should you accept this proposal? As we can show in Figure 2.5, you should accept because you will end up with more apples and more cherries to consume. To take advantage of her proposal, you should specialize in picking only apples rather than splitting your time between picking apples and picking cherries. We know specializing will allow you to pick 20 pounds of apples. You can trade 10 pounds of apples to your neighbor for 15 pounds of her cherries. The result is that you will be able to consume 10 pounds of

	You		**Your Neighbor**	
	Apples	Cherries	Apples	Cherries
Devote all time to picking apples	20 pounds	0 pounds	30 pounds	0 pounds
Devote all time to picking cherries	0 pounds	20 pounds	0 pounds	60 pounds

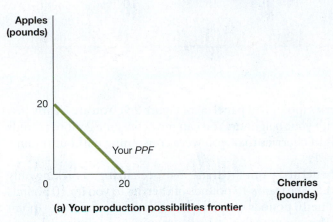

(a) Your production possibilities frontier

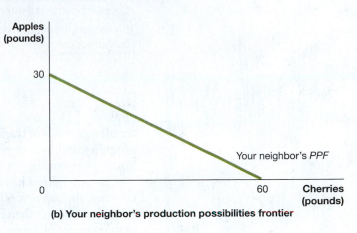

(b) Your neighbor's production possibilities frontier

MyEconLab Animation

Figure 2.4   Production Possibilities for You and Your Neighbor, without Trade

The table shows how many pounds of apples and how many pounds of cherries you and your neighbor can each pick in one week. The graphs use the data from the table to construct *PPF*s for you and your neighbor. Panel (a) shows your *PPF*. If you devote all your time to picking apples and none to picking cherries, you can pick 20 pounds. If you devote all your time to picking cherries, you can pick 20 pounds. Panel (b) shows that if your neighbor devotes all her time to picking apples, she can pick 30 pounds. If she devotes all her time to picking cherries, she can pick 60 pounds.

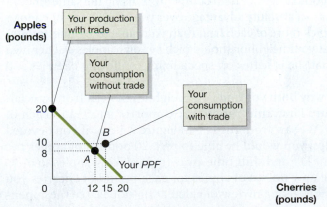

(a) Your production and consumption with trade

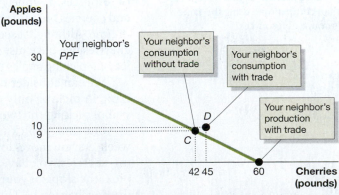

(b) Your neighbor's production and consumption with trade

MyEconLab Animation

Figure 2.5   Gains from Trade

When you don't trade with your neighbor, you pick and consume 8 pounds of apples and 12 pounds of cherries per week—point *A* in panel (a). When your neighbor doesn't trade with you, she picks and consumes 9 pounds of apples and 42 pounds of cherries per week—point *C* in panel (b). If you specialize in picking apples, you can pick 20 pounds. If your neighbor specializes in picking cherries, she can pick 60 pounds. If you trade 10 pounds of your apples for 15 pounds of your neighbor's cherries, you will be able to consume 10 pounds of apples and 15 pounds of cherries—point *B* in panel (a). Your neighbor can now consume 10 pounds of apples and 45 pounds of cherries—point *D* in panel (b). You and your neighbor are both better off as a result of the trade.

Table 2.1

A Summary of the Gains from Trade

	You		Your Neighbor	
	Apples (in pounds)	**Cherries (in pounds)**	**Apples (in pounds)**	**Cherries (in pounds)**
Production *and* consumption *without* trade	8	12	9	42
Production *with* trade	20	0	0	60
Consumption *with* trade	10	15	10	45
Gains from trade (increased consumption)	2	3	1	3

apples and 15 pounds of cherries (point *B* in panel (a) of Figure 2.5). You are clearly better off as a result of trading with your neighbor: You can now consume 2 more pounds of apples and 3 more pounds of cherries than you were consuming without trading. You have moved beyond your *PPF*!

Your neighbor has also benefited from the trade. By specializing in picking only cherries, she can pick 60 pounds. She trades 15 pounds of cherries to you for 10 pounds of apples. She can then consume 10 pounds of apples and 45 pounds of cherries (point *D* in panel (b) of Figure 2.5). This combination is 1 more pound of apples and 3 more pounds of cherries than she was consuming before trading with you. She also has moved beyond her *PPF*. Table 2.1 summarizes the changes in production and consumption that result from your trade with your neighbor. (In this example, we chose one specific rate of trading cherries for apples—15 pounds of cherries for 10 pounds of apples. There are, however, many other rates of trading cherries for apples that would also make you and your neighbor better off.)   MyEconLab **Concept Check**

Absolute Advantage versus Comparative Advantage

Perhaps the most remarkable aspect of the preceding example is that your neighbor benefits from trading with you even though she is better than you at picking both apples and cherries. **Absolute advantage** is the ability of an individual, a firm, or a country to produce more of a good or service than competitors, using the same amount of resources. Your neighbor has an absolute advantage over you in picking both apples and cherries because she can pick more of each fruit than you can in the same amount of time. Although it seems that your neighbor should pick her own apples *and* her own cherries, we have just seen that she is better off specializing in picking cherries and leaving picking apples to you.

We can consider further why both you and your neighbor benefit from specializing in picking only one fruit. First, think about the opportunity cost to each of you of picking the two fruits. We saw from the *PPF* in Figure 2.4 that if you devoted all your time to picking apples, you would be able to pick 20 pounds of apples per week. As you move down your *PPF* and shift time away from picking apples to picking cherries, you have to give up 1 pound of apples for each pound of cherries you pick (the slope of your *PPF* is −1). (For a review of calculating slopes, see the appendix to Chapter 1.) Therefore, your opportunity cost of picking 1 pound of cherries is 1 pound of apples. By the same reasoning, your opportunity cost of picking 1 pound of apples is 1 pound of cherries. Your neighbor's *PPF* has a different slope, so she faces a different trade-off: As she shifts time from picking apples to picking cherries, she has to give up 0.5 pound of apples for every 1 pound of cherries she picks (the slope of your neighbor's *PPF* is −0.5). As she shifts time from picking cherries to picking apples, she gives up 2 pounds of cherries for every 1 pound of apples she picks. Therefore, her opportunity cost of picking 1 pound of apples is 2 pounds of cherries, and her opportunity cost of picking 1 pound of cherries is 0.5 pound of apples.

Absolute advantage The ability of an individual, a firm, or a country to produce more of a good or service than competitors, using the same amount of resources.

MyEconLab Study Plan

Table 2.2

Opportunity Costs of Picking Apples and Cherries

	Opportunity Cost of Picking 1 Pound of Apples	Opportunity Cost of Picking 1 Pound of Cherries
You	1 pound of cherries	1 pound of apples
Your Neighbor	2 pounds of cherries	0.5 pound of apples

Table 2.2 summarizes the opportunity costs for you and your neighbor of picking apples and cherries. Note that even though your neighbor can pick more apples in a week than you can, the *opportunity cost* of picking apples is higher for her than for you because when she picks apples, she gives up more cherries than you do. So, even though she has an absolute advantage over you in picking apples, it is more costly for her to pick apples than it is for you. The table also shows that her opportunity cost of picking cherries is lower than yours. **Comparative advantage** is the ability of an individual, a firm, or a country to produce a good or service at a lower opportunity cost than competitors. In picking apples, your neighbor has an *absolute advantage* over you, while you have a *comparative advantage* over her. Your neighbor has both an absolute advantage and a comparative advantage over you in picking cherries. As we have seen, you are better off specializing in picking apples, and your neighbor is better off specializing in picking cherries.

Comparative advantage The ability of an individual, a firm, or a country to produce a good or service at a lower opportunity cost than competitors.

MyEconLab Concept Check

Comparative Advantage and the Gains from Trade

We have just arrived at an important economic principle: *The basis for trade is comparative advantage, not absolute advantage.* The fastest apple pickers do not necessarily do much apple picking. If the fastest apple pickers have a comparative advantage in some other activity—picking cherries, playing Major League Baseball, or being industrial engineers—they are better off specializing in that activity. Individuals, firms, and countries are better off if they specialize in producing goods and services for which they have a comparative advantage and obtain the other goods and services they need by trading. We will return to the important concept of comparative advantage in Chapter 9, which is devoted to the subject of international trade.

MyEconLab Concept Check

Don't Let This Happen to You

Don't Confuse Absolute Advantage and Comparative Advantage

First, make sure you know the definitions:

- **Absolute advantage.** The ability of an individual, a firm, or a country to produce more of a good or service than competitors, using the same amount of resources. In our example, your neighbor has an absolute advantage over you in both picking apples and picking cherries.
- **Comparative advantage.** The ability of an individual, a firm, or a country to produce a good or service at a lower opportunity cost than competitors. In our example, your neighbor has a comparative advantage in picking cherries, but you have a comparative advantage in picking apples.

Keep these two key points in mind:

1. It is possible to have an absolute advantage in producing a good or service without having a comparative advantage. This is the case with your neighbor picking apples.
2. It is possible to have a comparative advantage in producing a good or service without having an absolute advantage. This is the case with your picking apples.

MyEconLab Study Plan

Your Turn: Test your understanding by doing related problem 2.5 on page 68 at the end of this chapter.

Solved Problem 2.2

Comparative Advantage and the Gains from Trade

Suppose that Canada and the United States both produce maple syrup and honey, which are sold for the same price in both countries. These are the combinations of the two goods that each country can produce in one day, using the same amounts of capital and labor:

Canada		United States	
Honey (in tons)	Maple Syrup (in tons)	Honey (in tons)	Maple Syrup (in tons)
0	60	0	50
10	45	10	40
20	30	20	30
30	15	30	20
40	0	40	10
		50	0

a. Which country has a comparative advantage in producing maple syrup? Which country has a comparative advantage in producing honey?

b. Suppose that Canada is currently producing 30 tons of honey and 15 tons of maple syrup, and the United States is currently producing 10 tons of honey and 40 tons of maple syrup. Demonstrate that Canada and the United States can both be better off if they specialize in producing only one good and trade for the other.

c. Illustrate your answer to part (b) by drawing a *PPF* for the United States and a *PPF* for Canada. Show on your *PPFs* the combinations of honey and maple syrup produced and consumed in each country before and after trade.

Solving the Problem

Step 1: **Review the chapter material.** This problem is about comparative advantage, so you may want to review the section "Absolute Advantage versus Comparative Advantage," which begins on page 50.

Step 2: **Answer part (a) by calculating which country has a comparative advantage in each activity.** Remember that a country has a comparative advantage in producing a good if it can produce the good at the lowest opportunity cost. When Canada produces 1 more ton of honey, it produces 1.5 tons less of maple syrup. When the United States produces 1 more ton of honey, it produces 1 ton less of maple syrup. Therefore, for the United States, the opportunity cost of producing honey—1 ton of maple syrup—is lower than for Canada—1.5 tons of maple syrup. When Canada produces 1 more ton of maple syrup, it produces 0.67 ton less of honey. When the United States produces 1 more ton of maple syrup, it produces 1 ton less of honey. Therefore, Canada's opportunity cost of producing maple syrup—0.67 ton of honey—is lower than that of the United States—1 ton of honey. We can conclude that the United States has a comparative advantage in the production of honey and Canada has a comparative advantage in the production of maple syrup.

Step 3: **Answer part (b) by showing that specialization makes Canada and the United States better off.** We know that Canada and the United States should each specialize where it has a comparative advantage. If both countries specialize, Canada will produce 60 tons of maple syrup and 0 tons of honey, and the United States will produce 0 tons of maple syrup and 50 tons of honey. After both countries specialize, the United States could then trade 30 tons of honey to Canada for 40 tons of maple syrup. (Other mutually beneficial trades are possible as well.) We can summarize the results in a table:

	Before Trade		After Trade	
	Honey (in tons)	Maple Syrup (in tons)	Honey (in tons)	Maple Syrup (in tons)
Canada	30	15	30	20
United States	10	40	20	40

The United States is better off after trade because it can consume the same amount of maple syrup and 10 more tons of honey. Canada is better off after trade because it can consume the same amount of honey and 5 more tons of maple syrup.

Step 4: **Answer part (c) by drawing the PPFs.**

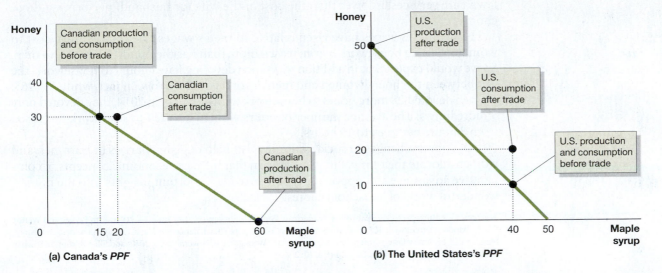

(a) Canada's *PPF*

(b) The United States's *PPF*

Your Turn: For more practice, do related problems 2.6 and 2.7 on pages 68–69 at the end of this chapter.

What's the most efficient way to divide up household chores?

Making the Connection
MyEconLab Video

Comparative Advantage, Opportunity Cost, and Housework

Among roommates, married couples, and other people living together, dividing up the household chores can be a source of stress. Traditionally among married couples, women did most of the housework, such as preparing meals, cleaning, and doing laundry. In 1965, married women with children averaged about 32 hours of housework per week, while married men averaged only 4 hours. Today, women average about 15 hours of housework, while men average about 10 hours.

Housework doesn't seem to be part of buying, selling, and the usual topics of business and economics. In fact, we can use basic economic concepts to analyze housework. Consider first the most efficient way to divide up household chores. Suppose Jack and Jill need to decide how they will get the cooking and laundry done. Assume that Jack has an absolute advantage over Jill in both chores, but he has a big advantage over Jill in cooking—he takes much less time to prepare very tasty meals—but is only a little faster than Jill in doing laundry. In other words, assuming that they have the same amount of time available to do housework, Jack has a comparative advantage in cooking, while Jill has a comparative advantage in doing laundry. So rather than Jack and Jill both doing some of the cooking and some of the laundry, they would be better off if Jack follows his comparative advantage and does all the cooking, while Jill follows her comparative advantage and does all the laundry.

Economics can also provide some insight into the decline in the number of hours spent on housework since the 1960s. Combined, men and women now spend more than 30 percent fewer hours on housework. This decline has been partly driven by technology, particularly improvements in household appliances, such as dishwashers and microwave ovens. The decline in the number of hours women devote to housework also reflects the greater job opportunities available to women today compared with the 1960s. The opportunity cost to a woman of spending time on housework and childcare is the wage she gives up by not spending that time in paid work. If a woman could work for an hour at a wage of $20 but spends that hour doing household chores, the opportunity cost of the time spent on chores is $20. As job opportunities for women and the wages those jobs pay have increased, so has the opportunity cost of doing housework. So in addition to taking advantage of improved appliances, many families have found that the cost of hiring specialists in household chores, such as cleaning services and lawn care services, is lower than the cost of the wife (or husband) performing those chores.

As women's wages have risen relative to men's wages, the opportunity cost to women of doing housework has increased more than has the opportunity cost to men. So we would expect that in addition to women devoting fewer hours to housework, the gap between the hours women and men devote would narrow. In fact, while in 1965, women devoted 28 more hours to housework than did men, in 2014, they devoted only 5 more hours. The average number of hours women devoted to paid work increased from 8 hours per week to 19 hours.

Of course, changes in social attitudes also help explain changes in how men and women allocate their time. But we have seen that the basic economic concepts of comparative advantage and opportunity cost provide important insights into the not-so-wonderful world of household chores.

Sources: U.S. Bureau of Labor Statistics, "American Time Use Survey—2014," June 24, 2015; Kim Parker and Wendy Wang, "Modern Parenthood: Roles of Moms and Dads Converge as They Balance Work and Family," pewsocialtrends.org, March 14, 2013; Emily Oster, "You're Dividing the Chores Wrong," *Slate*, November 21, 2012; and Ellen Byron, "A Truce in the Chore Wars," *New York Times*, December 4, 2012.

MyEconLab Study Plan

Your Turn: Test your understanding by doing related problems 2.14 and 2.15 on page 69 at the end of this chapter.

2.3 | The Market System

LEARNING OBJECTIVE: Explain the basics of how a market system works.

We have seen that households, firms, and the government face trade-offs and incur opportunity costs because resources are scarce. We have also seen that trade allows people to specialize according to their comparative advantage. By engaging in trade, people can raise their incomes and their standard of living. Of course, trade in the modern world is much more complex than the examples we have considered so far. Trade today involves the decisions of millions of people around the world. How are the decisions of these millions of people coordinated? In the United States and most other countries, trade is carried out in markets. Markets also determine the answers to the three fundamental questions discussed in Chapter 1:

1. What goods and services will be produced?
2. How will the goods and services be produced?
3. Who will receive the goods and services produced?

Market A group of buyers and sellers of a good or service and the institution or arrangement by which they come together to trade.

Recall that a **market** is a group of buyers and sellers of a good or service and the institution or arrangement by which they come together to trade. Markets take many forms: They can be physical places, such as the pizza parlors in your city or the New York Stock Exchange, or virtual places, such as eBay. In a market, the buyers are demanders of goods or services, and the sellers are suppliers of goods or services. Households and firms interact in two types of markets: *product markets* and *factor markets*. **Product markets** are markets for goods—such as computers—and services—such as medical treatment. In product markets, households are demanders and firms are suppliers. **Factor markets** are markets for the *factors of production*. **Factors of production** are the inputs used to make goods and services. Factors of production are divided into four broad categories:

Product market A market for goods—such as computers—or services—such as medical treatment.

Factor market A market for the factors of production, such as labor, capital, natural resources, and entrepreneurial ability.

Factors of production Labor, capital, natural resources, and other inputs used to make goods and services.

1. *Labor* includes all types of work, from the part-time labor of teenagers working at McDonald's to the work of senior managers in large corporations.
2. *Capital* refers to physical capital, such as computers and machine tools, that is used to produce other goods.
3. *Natural resources* include land, water, oil, iron ore, and other raw materials (or "gifts of nature") that are used in producing goods.

4. An *entrepreneur* is someone who operates a business. *Entrepreneurial ability* is the ability to bring together the other factors of production to successfully produce and sell goods and services.

The Circular Flow of Income

Two key groups participate in markets:

1. *Households* are all the individuals in a home. Households are suppliers of factors of production—particularly labor—employed by firms to make goods and services. Households use the income they receive from selling the factors of production to purchase the goods and services supplied by firms. We are familiar with households as suppliers of labor because most people earn most of their income by going to work, meaning they are selling their labor services to firms in the labor market. But households own the other factors of production as well, either directly or indirectly, by owning the firms that own these resources. All firms are owned by households. Small firms, like a neighborhood restaurant, might be owned by one person. Large firms, like Apple, are owned by millions of households that buy shares of stock in them. When firms pay profits to the people who own them, the firms are paying for using the capital and natural resources that are supplied to them by those owners. So, we can generalize by saying that in factor markets, households are suppliers and firms are demanders.
2. *Firms* are suppliers of goods and services. Firms use the funds they receive from selling goods and services to buy or hire the factors of production needed to make the goods and services.

We can use a simple economic model called the **circular-flow diagram** to see how participants in markets are linked. Figure 2.6 shows that in factor markets, households supply labor and other factors of production in exchange for wages and other

Circular-flow diagram A model that illustrates how participants in markets are linked.

MyEconLab Animation

Figure 2.6

The Circular-Flow Diagram

Households and firms are linked together in a circular flow of production, income, and spending. The blue arrows show the flow of the factors of production. In factor markets, households supply labor, entrepreneurial ability, and other factors of production to firms. Firms use these factors of production to make goods and services that they supply to households in product markets. The red arrows show the flow of goods and services from firms to households. The green arrows show the flow of funds. In factor markets, households receive wages and other payments from firms in exchange for supplying the factors of production. Households use these wages and other payments to purchase goods and services from firms in product markets. Firms sell goods and services to households in product markets, and they use the funds to purchase the factors of production from households in factor markets.

Households — Wages and other payments to the factors of production — Goods and services — Product markets — Factor markets — Spending on goods and services — Labor, capital, natural resources, and entrepreneurial ability — Firms payments from firms. In product markets, households use the payments they earn in factor markets to purchase the goods and services supplied by firms. Firms produce these goods and services using the factors of production supplied by households. In the figure, the blue arrows show the flow of factors of production from households through factor markets to firms. The red arrows show the flow of goods and services from firms through product markets to households. The green arrows show the flow of funds from firms through factor markets to households and the flow of spending from households through product markets to firms.

Like all economic models, the circular-flow diagram is a simplified version of reality. Figure 2.6 leaves out the important role of government in buying goods from firms and in making payments, such as Social Security or unemployment insurance payments, to households. The figure also leaves out the roles played by banks, the stock and bond markets, and other parts of the *financial system* in aiding the flow of funds from lenders to borrowers. Finally, the figure does not show that some goods and services purchased by domestic households are produced in foreign countries and some goods and services produced by domestic firms are sold to foreign households. (We explore the government, the financial system, and the international sector further in later chapters.) Despite these simplifications, the circular-flow diagram in Figure 2.6 is useful for seeing how product markets, factor markets, and their participants are linked together. One of the great wonders of the market system is that it manages to successfully coordinate the independent activities of so many households and firms. **MyEconLab** Concept Check

The Gains from Free Markets

Free market A market with few government restrictions on how a good or service can be produced or sold or on how a factor of production can be employed.

A **free market** exists when the government places few restrictions on how goods and services can be produced or sold or on how factors of production can be employed. Governments in all modern economies intervene more than is consistent with a fully free market. In that sense, we can think of the free market as being a benchmark against which we can judge actual economies. There are relatively few government restrictions on economic activities in the United States, Canada, Western Europe, Hong Kong, Singapore, and Estonia. So these countries come close to the free market benchmark. In countries such as Cuba and North Korea, the free market system has been rejected in favor of centrally planned economies with extensive government control over product and factor markets. Countries that come closest to the free market benchmark have been more successful than countries with centrally planned economies in providing their people with rising living standards.

The Scottish philosopher Adam Smith is considered the father of modern economics because his book, *An Inquiry into the Nature and Causes of the Wealth of Nations*, published in 1776, was an early and very influential argument for the free market system. Smith was writing at a time when extensive government restrictions on markets were common. In many parts of Europe, the *guild system* prevailed. Under this system, governments would give guilds, or organizations of producers, the authority to control the production of a good. For example, the shoemakers' guild controlled who was allowed to produce shoes, how many shoes they could produce, and what price they could charge. In France, the cloth makers' guild even dictated the number of threads in the weave of the cloth.

Smith argued that such restrictions reduced the income and wealth of a country and its people by restricting the quantity of goods produced. Some people at the time supported the restrictions of the guild system because it was in their financial interest to do so. If you were a member of a guild, the restrictions served to reduce the competition you faced. But other people sincerely believed that the alternative to the guild system was economic disorder. Smith argued that these people were wrong and that a country could enjoy a smoothly functioning economic system if firms were freed from guild restrictions. **MyEconLab** Concept Check

The Market Mechanism

In Smith's day, defenders of the guild system argued that if the shoemakers' guild did not control shoe production, either too many or too few shoes would be produced.

In contrast, Smith maintained that prices would do a better job of coordinating the activities of buyers and sellers than the guilds could. A key to understanding Smith's argument is the assumption that *individuals usually act in a rational, self-interested way*. In particular, individuals take those actions that are most likely to make themselves better off financially. This assumption of rational, self-interested behavior underlies nearly all economic analysis. In fact, economics can be distinguished from other disciplines that study human behavior—such as sociology and psychology—by its emphasis on the assumption of self-interested behavior. Adam Smith understood—as economists today understand—that people's motives can be complex. But when we analyze people in the act of buying and selling, the motivation of financial reward usually provides the best explanation for the actions people take.

For example, suppose that a significant number of consumers switch from buying regular gasoline-powered cars to buying gasoline/electric-powered hybrid cars, such as the Toyota Prius, or all-electric cars, such as the Tesla Model S. Firms will find that they can charge relatively higher prices for hybrid cars and electric cars than they can for gasoline-powered cars. The self-interest of these firms will lead them to respond to consumers' wishes by producing more hybrid and electric cars and fewer gasoline-powered cars. Or suppose that consumers decide that they want to eat less bread, pasta, and other foods that are high in carbohydrates. Then the prices firms can charge for bread and pasta will fall. The self-interest of firms will lead them to produce less bread and pasta, which, in fact, is what has happened over the past 10 years.

Note that for the market mechanism to work in response to changes in consumers' wants, *prices must be flexible*. The *relative price* is the price of one good or service relative to the prices of other goods or services. Changes in relative prices provide information, or a signal, to both consumers and firms. For example, consumers worldwide have increased their demand for cattle and poultry. Because corn is fed to cattle and poultry, prices for corn have increased relative to prices for other crops. Many farmers in the United States received this price signal and responded by increasing the amount of corn they planted and decreasing the amount of soybeans and wheat. One Kansas farmer was quoted as saying, "It seemed to me there was $100 to $150 per acre more money in the corn than there was in the beans. That's the kind of math that a lot of guys were using." In recent years, the United States has experienced record corn crops. Similarly, falling prices for DVDs and music CDs in the 2000s were a signal to movie studios and record companies to devote fewer resources to these products and more resources to making movies and music available online.

In the United States today, governments at the federal, state, and local levels set or regulate the prices of only about 10 to 20 percent of goods and services. The prices of other goods and services are free to change as consumer wants change and as costs of production change.

In the case where consumers want more of a product, and in the case where they want less of a product, the market system responds without a guild or the government giving orders about how much to produce or what price to charge. Economists have used Adam Smith's metaphor of the *invisible hand* to describe how the market leads firms to provide consumers with the goods they want. Firms respond *individually* to changes in prices by making decisions that *collectively* end up satisfying the wants of consumers.   MyEconLab Concept Check

Making the Connection

MyEconLab Video

A Story of the Market System in Action: How Do You Make an iPad?

Apple produces the iPad. Because Apple's headquarters is in Cupertino, California, it seems reasonable to assume that iPads are also manufactured in that state. A poll by the *New York Times* showed that, in fact, a majority of people interviewed believed that iPads were manufactured in the United States, if not specifically in California. Although engineers at Apple designed the iPad, the company produces none of the components of the iPad, nor does it assemble the

The market coordinates the activities of many people spread around the world who contribute to making an iPad.

components into a finished product. Far from being produced entirely by one company in one country, the iPad requires the coordinated activities of thousands of workers and dozens of firms spread around the world.

Foxconn, which is based in Taiwan, assembles the iPad in factories in Shenzhen and Chengdu, China, and Jundiai, São Paulo, Brazil, and ships them to Apple for sale in the United States. Although Foxconn does final assembly, it doesn't make any of the components and, in fact, charges Apple only about $6 for assembling each iPad.

The following table lists just some of the suppliers of iPad components.

Firm	Location of the firm	The iPad component the firm supplies
AKM	Japan	Motion sensor
AU Optronics	Taiwan	Display
Avago Technologies	United States (Pennsylvania)	Wireless technology
Bosch Sensortec	Germany	Accelerometer
Broadcom	United States (California)	Touchscreen controller and wireless chip
Cirrus Logic	United States (Texas)	Audio chip
Corning	United States (New York)	Glass screen cover
Dialog Semiconductor	Germany	Power management chip
Elpida	United States (Idaho)	System memory
Infineon Technologies	Germany	Semiconductors
LG Electronics	South Korea	Display
Quicomm	United Kingdom	Wireless section
Samsung	South Korea	Display, flash memory, and applications processor
Sharp	Japan	Display
SK Hynix	South Korea	Flash memory
Skyworks Solutions	United States (Massachusetts)	Wireless technology
STMicroelectronics	France/Italy	Motion sensors
Texas Instruments	United States (Texas)	Touchscreen controller
Toshiba	Japan	Flash memory
TriQuint Semiconductor	United States (Oregon)	Wireless technology

Each of these suppliers in turn relies on its own suppliers. For example, Broadcom designs the touchscreen controller for the iPad and supplies it to Apple, but it does not manufacture the components of the controller or assemble them. To manufacture the components, Broadcom relies on SilTerra, based in Malaysia; SMIC, based in mainland China; and Taiwan Semiconductor Manufacturing Corporation (TSMC) and UMC, based in Taiwan. TSMC's factories are for the most part not in Taiwan but in mainland China and Eastern Europe. To assemble the components, Broadcom uses several companies, including Amkor Technology, based in Chandler, Arizona, and STATS ChipPAC, based in Singapore.

All told, an iPad contains hundreds of parts that are designed, manufactured, and assembled by firms around the world. Many of these firms are not even aware of which other firms are also producing components for the iPad. Few of the managers of these firms have met managers of the other firms or shared knowledge of how their particular components are produced. In fact, no one person from Tim Cook, the chief executive officer of Apple, on down possesses the knowledge of how to produce all the components that are assembled into an iPad. Instead, the invisible hand of the market has led these firms to contribute their knowledge and resources to the process that ultimately results in an iPad available for sale in a store in the United States. Apple has so efficiently organized the process of producing the iPad that you can order a custom iPad with a personal engraving and have it delivered from an assembly plant in China or Brazil to your doorstep in the United States in as little as three days.

Sources: Marjorie Connelly, "Poll Finds Consumer Confusion on Where Apple Devices Are Made," *New York Times*, January 25, 2012; "New iPad Air Costs Less to Make Than Third-Generation iPad Model, IHS Teardown Reveals," technology.ihs.com, November 5, 2013; and Arik Hesseldahl, "iPad Air Has Spendier Display, Costs Less to Make Than Earlier Models," allthingsd.com, November 5, 2013.

Your Turn: Test your understanding by doing related problems 3.8 and 3.9 on page 70 at the end of this chapter.

MyEconLab Study Plan

The Role of the Entrepreneur in the Market System

Entrepreneurs are central to the working of the market system. An **entrepreneur** is someone who operates a business. Entrepreneurs first determine what goods and services they believe consumers want and then decide how to produce those goods and services most profitably, using the available factors of production—labor, capital, and natural resources. Successful entrepreneurs are able to search out opportunities to provide new goods and services. Frequently these opportunities are created by new technology. Consumers and existing businesses often do not at first realize that the new technology makes new products feasible. For example, even after the development of the internal combustion engine had made automobiles practicable, Henry Ford remarked, "If I had asked my customers what they wanted, they would have said a faster horse." Because consumers often cannot evaluate a new product before it exists, some of the most successful entrepreneurs, such as the late Steve Jobs of Apple, rarely use *focus groups*, or meetings with consumers in which the consumers are asked what new products they would like to see. Instead, entrepreneurs think of products that consumers may not even realize they need, such as, in Jobs's case, an MP3 player— the iPod— or a tablet computer— the iPad. Entrepreneurs are important to the economy because they are often responsible for making new products widely available to consumers, as Henry Ford did with the automobile and Steve Jobs did with the iPod.

The firms that entrepreneurs found are typically small at first, as Apple and Ford were. Table 2.3 lists some of the important products entrepreneurs at small firms introduced during the twentieth century.

Entrepreneurs put their own funds at risk when they start businesses. If they are wrong about what consumers want or about the best way to produce goods and services, they can lose those funds. In fact, it is not unusual for entrepreneurs who eventually achieve great success to fail at first. For instance, early in their careers, both Henry Ford and Sakichi Toyoda, who eventually founded the Toyota Motor Corporation, started companies that quickly failed. Research by Richard Freeman of Harvard University has shown that a typical entrepreneur earns less than an employee at a large firm who has the same education and other characteristics. Few entrepreneurs make the fortunes earned by Mark Zuckerberg (Facebook), Steve Jobs (Apple), or Bill Gates (Microsoft).

Entrepreneurs make a vital contribution to economic growth through their roles in responding to consumer demand and introducing new products. Government policies that encourage entrepreneurship are also likely to increase economic growth and raise the standard of living. In the next section, we consider the legal framework required for a successful market in which entrepreneurs can succeed.   MyEconLab Concept Check

Entrepreneur Someone who operates a business, bringing together the factors of production—labor, capital, and natural resources—to produce goods and services.

The Legal Basis of a Successful Market System

In a free market, government does not restrict how firms produce and sell goods and services or how they employ factors of production. But the absence of government intervention is not enough for the market system to work well. Government has to take active steps to provide a *legal environment* that will allow markets to operate efficiently.

Table 2.3

Important Products Introduced by Entrepreneurs at Small Firms

Product	Inventor
Air conditioning	William Haviland Carrier
Airplane	Orville and Wilbur Wright
Automobile, mass produced	Henry Ford
Automobile windshield wiper	Mary Anderson
Biomagnetic imaging	Raymond Damadian
Biosynthetic insulin	Herbert Boyer
Disposable diaper	Marion Donovan
DNA fingerprinting	Alec Jeffries
FM radio	Edwin Howard Armstrong
Helicopter	Igor Sikorsky
High-resolution CAT scanner	Robert Ledley
Hydraulic brake	Malcolm Lockheed
Integrated circuit	Jack Kilby
Microprocessor	Ted Hoff
Optical scanner	Everett Franklin Lindquist
Oral contraceptives	Carl Djerassi
Overnight delivery service	Fred Smith
Personal computer	Steve Jobs and Steve Wozniak
Quick-frozen foods	Clarence Birdseye
Safety razor	King Gillette
Soft contact lens	Kevin Tuohy
Solid fuel rocket engine	Robert Goddard
Supercomputer	Seymour Cray
Vacuum tube (television)	Philo Farnsworth
Zipper	Gideon Sundback

Sources: William J. Baumol, *The Microtheory of Innovative Entrepreneurship*, Princeton, NJ: Princeton University Press, 2010; Lemelson-MIT Program (http://lemelson.mit.edu); and various other sources. Note that historians sometimes dispute the identity of the person who first commercially developed a particular product.

Protection of Private Property For the market system to work well, individuals must be willing to take risks. Someone with $250,000 can be cautious and keep it safely in a bank—or even in cash, if the person doesn't trust banks. But the market system won't work unless a significant number of people are willing to risk their funds by investing them in businesses. Investing in businesses is risky in any country. Many businesses fail every year in the United States and other high-income countries. But in high-income countries, someone who starts a new business or invests in an existing business doesn't have to worry that the government, the military, or criminal gangs might decide to seize the business or demand payments for not destroying it. Unfortunately, in many poor countries, business owners are not well protected from having their businesses seized by the government or from having their profits taken by criminals. Where these problems exist, opening a business can be extremely risky. Cash can be concealed easily, but a business is difficult to conceal or move.

Property rights The rights individuals or firms have to the exclusive use of their property, including the right to buy or sell it.

Property rights are the rights individuals or firms have to the exclusive use of their property, including the right to buy or sell it. Property can be physical property, such as a store or factory. Property can also be intangible, such as the right to an idea. Two amendments to the U.S. Constitution guarantee property rights: The Fifth Amendment states that the federal government shall not deprive any person "of life, liberty, or property, without due process of law." The Fourteenth Amendment extends this guarantee to the actions of state governments: "No state . . . shall deprive any person of life, liberty, or property, without due process of law." Similar guarantees exist in every high-income country. Unfortunately, in many developing countries, such guarantees do not exist or are poorly enforced.

In any modern economy, *intellectual property rights* are very important. Intellectual property includes books, films, software, and ideas for new products or new ways of producing products. To protect intellectual property, the federal government grants a *patent* that gives an inventor—often a firm—the exclusive right to produce and sell a new product for a period of 20 years from the date the patent was filed. For instance, because Microsoft has a patent on the Windows operating system, other firms cannot sell their own versions of Windows. The government grants patents to encourage firms to spend money on the research and development necessary to create new products. If other companies could freely copy Windows, Microsoft would not have spent the funds necessary to develop it. Just as a new product or a new method of making a product receives patent protection, new books, films, and software receive *copyright* protection. Under U.S. law, the creator of a book, film, or piece of music has the exclusive right to use the creation during the creator's lifetime. The creator's heirs retain this exclusive right for 70 years after the death of the creator.

In providing copyright protection for only a limited time, Congress provides economic incentives to creators while eventually—after the period of copyright has ended—allowing the creators' works to be freely available to others. The longer the period of copyright, the longer the creator (or the creators' family) can restrict others from using the work.

Making the **Connection** MyEconLab Video	## An Elementary Case of Copyright

The U.S. Congress provides copyright protection to authors to give them an economic incentive to invest the time and effort required to write a book. While a book is under copyright, only the author—or whoever the author sells the copyright to—can legally publish a paper or digital copy of the book. Once the copyright expires, however, the book enters the *public domain*, and anyone is free to publish the book. Copies of classic books written in the 1800s, such as Mark Twain's *Huckleberry Finn* and Charles Dickens's *Oliver Twist*, are available from many publishers that do not have to pay a fee to the authors' heirs.

Arthur Conan Doyle was a doctor in England when he published his first story featuring the detective Sherlock Holmes in 1887. Anyone who wants to publish any of the Sherlock Holmes stories that Doyle wrote from 1887 through the end of 1922 is free do so. But the last 10 Sherlock Holmes stories that Doyle wrote from 1923 to 1927 remain under copyright protection. Doyle's heirs argue that because the author continued to develop the personalities of Sherlock Holmes and his companion Dr. John Watson in the 10 stories that remain under copyright protection, the characters cannot be used in new books, films, or television shows without payment. Doyle's heirs have asked anyone who wants to include Holmes in a new work to pay them a fee of $5,000 per use.

The producers of two recent Sherlock Holmes films starring Robert Downey, Jr., and the producers of the television series *Sherlock*, starring Benedict Cumberbatch, and *Elementary*, starring Jonny Lee Miller, agreed to pay the fee, as have most authors of books using Holmes as a character. In 2011, when Leslie S. Klinger published *A Study in Sherlock*, a collection of new stories involving Sherlock Holmes, his publisher insisted that he pay the usual fee to Doyle's descendants. But two years later, when Klinger decided to publish another collection, *In the Company of Sherlock Holmes*, he decided that rather than pay the fee he would sue Doyle's descendants, hoping the federal courts would rule against their copyright claims.

Federal Appeals Judge Richard Posner—who is also an economist—eventually ruled in favor of Klinger. He argued that copyright law did not allow authors or their heirs to require fees for the use of characters from stories in the public domain. He also noted that, "the longer the copyright term is, the less public-domain material there will be and so the greater will be the cost of authorship, because authors will have to obtain

Who owns the classic character Sherlock Holmes?

licenses from copyright holders for more material." As a result of this ruling, for the first time since 1887, anyone can use Sherlock Holmes as a character in a book, television show, or movie without having to pay a fee.

Sources: Jennifer Schuessler, "Appeals Court Affirms Sherlock Holmes Is in Public Domain," *New York Times*, June 17, 2014; Jennifer Schuessler, "Conan Doyle Estate Told to Pay Legal Fees," *New York Times*, August 5, 2014; Eriq Gardner, "Conan Doyle Estate Loses Appeal Over 'Sherlock Holmes' Rights," *Hollywood Reporter*, June 16, 2014; and *Leslie S. Kling v. Conan Doyle Estate, Ltd.* (7th Cir. 2014), media.ca7.uscourts.gov.

MyEconLab Study Plan

Your Turn: Test your understanding by doing related problems 3.15 and 3.16 on page 71 at the end of this chapter.

Enforcement of Contracts and Property Rights

Business activity often involves someone agreeing to carry out some action in the future. For example, you may borrow $20,000 to buy a car and promise the bank—by signing a loan contract—that you will pay back the money over the next five years. Or Facebook may sign a licensing agreement with a small technology company, agreeing to use that company's technology for a period of several years in return for a fee. Usually these agreements take the form of legal contracts. For the market system to work, businesses and individuals have to rely on these contracts being carried out. If one party to a legal contract does not fulfill its obligations—perhaps the small company had promised Facebook exclusive use of its technology but then begins licensing it to other companies—the other party can go to court to have the agreement enforced. Similarly, if you believe that the federal or state government has violated your property rights under the Fifth or Fourteenth Amendments, you can go to court to have your rights enforced.

But going to court to enforce a contract or property rights will be successful only if the court system is independent and judges are able to make impartial decisions on the basis of the law. In the United States and other high-income countries, the court systems have enough independence from other parts of the government and enough protection from intimidation by outside forces—such as criminal gangs—that they are able to make their decisions based on the law. In many developing countries, the court systems lack this independence and will not provide a remedy if the government violates property rights, or if a person with powerful political connections decides to violate a business contract.

If property rights are not well enforced, fewer goods and services will be produced. This reduces economic efficiency, leaving the economy inside its production possibilities frontier.

MyEconLab Study Plan

MyEconLab Concept Check

Continued from page 41

Economics in Your Life

The Trade-offs When You Buy a Car

At the beginning of the chapter, we asked you to think about two questions: What is the relationship between safety and fuel efficiency for gasoline-powered cars? and, Under what circumstances would it be possible for automobile manufacturers to make cars that are both safer and more fuel efficient? To answer the first question, you have to recognize that there is a trade-off between safety and fuel efficiency. With the technology available at any particular time, an automobile manufacturer can increase fuel efficiency by making a car smaller and lighter. But driving a lighter car increases your chances of being injured if you have an accident. The trade-off between safety and fuel efficiency would look much like the relationship in Figure 2.1 on page 43. To get more of both safety and gas mileage, automobile makers would have to discover new technologies that allow them to make cars lighter and safer at the same time. Such new technologies would make points like *G* in Figure 2.1 attainable.

Conclusion

We have seen that by trading in markets, people are able to specialize and pursue their comparative advantage. Trading on the basis of comparative advantage makes all participants in trade better off. The key role of markets is to facilitate trade. In fact, the market system is a very effective means of coordinating the decisions of millions of consumers, workers, and firms. At the center of the market system is the consumer. To be successful, firms must respond to the desires of consumers. These desires are communicated to firms through prices. To explore how markets work, we must study the behavior of consumers and firms. We continue this exploration of markets in Chapter 3, when we develop the model of demand and supply.

Before moving on to Chapter 3, read *An Inside Look* on the next page for a discussion of Apple's plans to produce an electric car.

You're Going to Need a MUCH Bigger Charging Station

BLOOMBERG

Apple Wants to Start Producing Cars as Soon as 2020

(a) Apple Inc., which has been working secretly on a car, is pushing its team to begin production of an electric vehicle as early as 2020, people with knowledge of the matter said.

The timeframe—automakers typically spend five to seven years developing a car—underscores the project's aggressive goals and could set the stage for a battle for customers with Tesla Motors Inc. and General Motors Co. Both automakers are targeting a 2017 release of an electric vehicle that can go more than 200 miles on a single charge and cost less than $40,000....

Apple, which posted record profit of $18 billion during the past quarter, has $178 billion in cash with few avenues to spend it. The Cupertino, California-based company's research and development costs were $6.04 billion in the past year, and Chief Executive Officer Tim Cook is facing increased pressure to return cash to shareholders....

Car Team

Tesla's success in creating a startup car company has shown that the traditional barriers of entry into the auto industry aren't as difficult to overcome as originally thought, said one person, who asked not to be identified because the matter is private. At the same time, automakers have struggled to bring technical leaps to car development, something that Silicon Valley is also seeking to accomplish. For example, Google Inc. has invested in developing an autonomous vehicle since 2010.

(b) "Apple would have some advantages as a new entrant to the auto industry," including its cash, ability to connect with its own devices and the infancy of the electric-vehicle market, Barclays analysts Ben Reitzes and Brian Johnson wrote in a note to investors. "Finally, Apple's brand—arguably the most important advantage—is a big attraction for the next generation of car customers."

Apple may decide to scrap its car effort or delay it if executives are unhappy with progress, as they've done before with other secret projects, the people said. The car team, which already has about 200 people, began ramping up hiring within the past couple of months as the company sought out experts in technologies for batteries and robotics, said one of the people.

Battery Lawsuit

An experienced automaker typically spends five to seven years developing a new vehicle before bringing it to market, according to Dennis Virag, president of Automotive Consulting Group.

"If you're starting from scratch, you're probably talking more like 10 years," Virag said. "A car is a very complex technological machine."

A lawsuit filed this month gives a window into Apple's efforts to create an automotive team for the project. Apple began around June an "aggressive campaign to poach" employees from A123 Systems LLC, the Waltham, Massachusetts-based battery maker said in the lawsuit.

Apple hired five people from A123 and has tried to hire battery experts from LG Chem Ltd., Samsung Electronics Co., Panasonic Corp., Toshiba Corp. and Johnson Controls Inc., according to the lawsuit....

Tesla CEO Elon Musk told Bloomberg Businessweek this month that Apple was seeking to hire away his workers, offering $250,000 signing bonuses and 60 percent salary increases.

Bricks and Mortar

(c) "Apple is good at developing technology but car making is, and will continue to be, a bricks-and-mortar proposition," Matt DeLorenzo, an analyst at Kelley Blue Book, wrote in an e-mail. "Apple will need a partner, perhaps a Chinese manufacturer, with an infrastructure if it's going to hit the five-year goal."

Some parts of the automotive industry seem unfazed by Silicon Valley's increasing interest in the market. Last month, before Apple's efforts were revealed, Volkswagen AG Chief Executive Officer Martin Winterkorn brushed off the increasing competition.

"We're not afraid of these new competitors," Winterkorn said at a reception outside Stuttgart, Germany, according to a transcript obtained by Bloomberg. "The opposite is true: they encourage us to look more intensively into the chances of the digital world."

Source: Tim Higgins, "Apple Wants to Start Producing Cars as Soon as 2020," *Bloomberg*, February 19, 2015.

Key Points in the Article

Apple is on a growing list of companies exploring the electric vehicle market and has assembled a team of managers to develop and produce an electric vehicle as early as 2020. To meet this aggressive five-year timeframe, Apple has been aggressive in hiring away experts from a number of companies, including Samsung, Panasonic, Toshiba, battery maker A123 Systems, and electric car manufacturer Tesla. By taking advantage of its available cash, communications technology, and extensive and loyal customer base, Apple has developed the potential to produce a successful product that can effectively compete with electric vehicles manufactured by companies like Tesla and General Motors.

Analyzing the News

(a) With $178 billion in cash, Apple tops the list of the world's most cash-rich companies. Apple has a history of developing innovative technology for its computers and smartphones, and it has the resources to continue developing these technological innovations while branching out into new markets. Apple also wants to keep the investors who bought its stock happy because they are the legal owners of the company. So Apple has to carefully choose new projects that help it remain successful and profitable. Once Apple decides which products to make, its managers must choose the quantities of these products to make. The managers face trade-offs when choosing which products to make and how to make them.

Suppose that Apple does begin selling electric cars in 2020; that it produces two models, a two-door convertible and a four-door sedan; and that it has the capability of producing a total of 100,000 vehicles per month. This capacity is represented by PPF_{2020} in the figure below. This curve shows that Apple would have to sacrifice production (and therefore sales) of one type of vehicle to produce more of the other. If these vehicles are successful and the market grows, Apple will need to produce a larger number of these electric automobiles, which is represented by PPF_{2025} in the figure.

(b) Not only do companies have decisions to make when choosing which projects to pursue, but once a decision is made, a company may choose to delay or even kill a project if it proves difficult to develop or if the market for the product changes. Apple has a brand and an image to protect, and moving forward with projects that may not be successful, even after the company has invested substantial funds in developing them, could harm its reputation. Not mentioned in the article is that Apple has had its share of failed products, from computers like the $10,000 Lisa in 1983 and the 16-pound Macintosh Portable in 1989 to the Pippin game console in 1995, which retailed for two to three times the price of the PlayStation and Nintendo consoles. In some instances, a failed product can do more damage to a company than scrapping the development of the product even after millions of dollars have been invested.

(c) Automobile manufacturing is not part of Apple's core consumer electronics business, so the company needs a completely different set of manufacturing, service, and distribution skills. With such a tight timeline to bring its car to market, Apple will face a trade-off when deciding on the production of its electric vehicle. As Kelly Blue Book's Matt DeLorenzo stated, "Apple will need a partner, perhaps a Chinese manufacturer, with an infrastructure if it's going to hit the five-year goal." Should Apple decide to work with an outside firm in the production of its automobile rather than attempt to build the vehicle completely in-house, it will give up some level of control in exchange for a greater chance at producing a successful product in a short period of time.

Thinking Critically

1. Suppose that from 2020 to 2025, the resources Apple uses to produce its automobiles remain constant, while improvements in technology in 2025 allow Apple to produce the additional quantity of two-door convertibles shown in the figure below, but no additional four-door sedans. Draw a graph that illustrates this technology change. Be sure to show both the 2020 and the new 2025 PPFs. What is the opportunity cost to Apple of producing one four-door sedan in 2020? Briefly explain whether the opportunity cost will be the same in 2025.

2. Assume that the figure below accurately represents Apple's PPFs for 2020 and 2025 and that in 2025 it has customer orders for 110,000 four-door sedans and 65,000 two-door convertibles. Explain whether Apple can fill all of these orders.

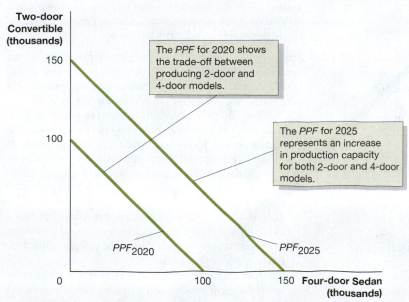

The *PPF* for 2020 shows the trade-off between producing 2-door and 4-door models.

The *PPF* for 2025 represents an increase in production capacity for both 2-door and 4-door models.

These *PPFs* show the trade-off Apple's managers face between producing different types of cars, and how that trade-off may change over time.

CHAPTER SUMMARY AND PROBLEMS

Key Terms

Absolute advantage, p. 50

Comparative advantage, p. 51

Economic growth, p. 47

Entrepreneur, p. 59

Factor market, p. 54

Factors of production, p. 54

Free market, p. 56

Market, p. 54

Opportunity cost, p. 43

Product market, p. 54

Production possibilities frontier (PPF), p. 42

Property rights, p. 60

Scarcity, p. 42

Trade, p. 48

2.1 **Production Possibilities Frontiers and Opportunity Costs, pages 42–47**

LEARNING OBJECTIVE: Use a production possibilities frontier to analyze opportunity costs and trade-offs.

Summary

The **production possibilities frontier (PPF)** is a curve that shows the maximum attainable combinations of two goods that can be produced with available resources. The PPF is used to illustrate the trade-offs that arise from **scarcity**. Points on the PPF are technically efficient. Points inside the PPF are inefficient, and points outside the PPF are unattainable. The **opportunity cost** of any activity is the highest-valued alternative that must be given up to engage in that activity. Because of increasing marginal opportunity costs, production possibilities frontiers are usually bowed out rather than straight lines. This illustrates the important economic concept that the more resources that are already devoted to any activity, the smaller the payoff from devoting additional resources to that activity is likely to be. **Economic growth** is illustrated by an outward shift in the production possibilities frontier.

 Visit **www.myeconlab.com** to complete these exercises online and get instant feedback.

Review Questions

1.1 What do economists mean by *scarcity*? Can you think of anything that is not scarce according to the economic definition?

1.2 What is a production possibilities frontier? How can we show efficiency on a production possibilities frontier? How can we show inefficiency? What causes a production possibilities frontier to shift outward?

1.3 What does increasing marginal opportunity costs mean? What are the implications of this idea for the shape of the production possibilities frontier?

Problems and Applications

1.4 Draw a production possibilities frontier that shows the trade-off between the production of cotton and the production of soybeans.
 a. Show the effect that a prolonged drought would have on the initial production possibilities frontier.
 b. Suppose that genetic modification makes soybeans resistant to insects, allowing yields to double. Show the effect of this technological change on the initial production possibilities frontier.

1.5 (Related to the Chapter Opener on page 41) One of the trade-offs Tesla faces is between safety and the maximum range someone can drive an all-electric car before having to recharge it. For example, adding steel to a car makes it safer but also heavier, which results in fewer miles between recharges. Draw a hypothetical production possibilities frontier that Tesla engineers face that shows this trade-off.

1.6 (Related to the Chapter Opener on page 41) In addition to making cars, Tesla planned to open a new factory in Nevada in 2016 to make batteries, including home storage battery packs. What is the opportunity cost to Tesla of investing in a battery factory?

Source: Mike Ramsey and Anne Steele, "Tesla Loss Widens as Spending Jumps," *Wall Street Journal*, May 6, 2015.

1.7 An economist remarks that "the cost of consuming a book is the combination of the retail price and the opportunity cost of the time spent reading." Isn't the cost of consuming a book just the price you pay to buy the book? Why include the cost of the time spent reading the book in the cost of consuming the book?

Source: Craig L. Garthwaite, "Demand Spillovers, Combative Advertising, and Celebrity Endorsements," *American Economic Journal: Applied Economics*, Vol. 6, No. 2, April 2014, p. 78.

1.8 Suppose we can divide all the goods produced by an economy into two types: consumption goods and capital goods. Capital goods, such as machinery, equipment, and computers, are goods used to produce other goods.
 a. Use a production possibilities frontier graph to illustrate the trade-off to an economy between producing consumption goods and producing capital goods. Is it likely that the production possibilities frontier in this situation will be a straight line (as in Figure 2.1 on page 43) or bowed out (as in Figure 2.2 on page 46)? Briefly explain.
 b. Suppose a technological change occurs that has a favorable effect on the production of capital goods but not consumption goods. Show the effect on the production possibilities frontier.
 c. Suppose that Lichtenstein and Luxembourg currently have identical production possibilities frontiers but that Lichtenstein devotes only 5 percent of its resources to producing capital goods over each of the

next 10 years, while Luxembourg devotes 30 percent. Which country is likely to experience more rapid economic growth in the future? Illustrate using a production possibilities frontier graph. Your graph should include production possibilities frontiers for Lichtenstein and Luxembourg today and in 10 years.

1.9 Use the following production possibilities frontier for a country to answer the questions.

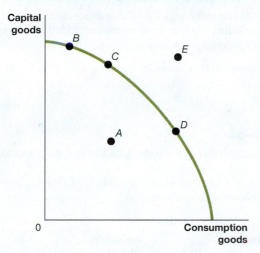

a. Which point or points are unattainable? Briefly explain why.

b. Which point or points are efficient? Briefly explain why.

c. Which point or points are inefficient? Briefly explain why.

d At which point is the country's future growth rate likely to be the highest? Briefly explain why.

1.10 **(Related to Solved Problem 2.1 on page 44)** You have exams in economics and chemistry coming up, and you have 5 hours available for studying. The following table shows the trade-offs you face in allocating the time you will spend studying each subject:

	Hours Spent Studying		Midterm Score	
Choice	Economics	Chemistry	Economics	Chemistry
A	5	0	95	70
B	4	1	93	78
C	3	2	90	84
D	2	3	86	88
E	1	4	81	90
F	0	5	75	91

a. Use the data in the table to draw a production possibilities frontier graph. Label the vertical axis "Score on economics exam," and label the horizontal axis "Score on chemistry exam." Make sure to label the values where your production possibilities frontier intersects the vertical and horizontal axes.

b. Label the points representing choice C and choice D. If you are at choice C, what is your opportunity cost of increasing your chemistry score by 4 points?

c. Under what circumstances would choice A be a sensible choice?

1.11 Suppose the U.S. president is attempting to decide whether the federal government should spend more on research to find a cure for heart disease. Imagine that you are the president's economic advisor and need to prepare a report discussing the relevant factors the president should consider. Use the concepts of opportunity cost and trade-offs to discuss some of the main issues you would deal with in your report.

1.12 State government Medicaid programs provide medical insurance to poor and disabled people. Under federal law, the programs must provide reimbursements to people who use any prescription drug that has been approved as effective by the U.S. Food and Drug Administration (FDA). In recent years, pharmaceutical firms have developed new prescription drugs that cost as much as $1,000 per pill to treat hepatitis C, a liver disease. A news story notes, "State Medicaid programs are particularly sensitive to annual cost increases . . . [because] coverage is paid for, in part, out of state budgets, which have to be balanced every year." What trade-offs do state governments face when new prescription drugs are introduced with much higher prices than existing drugs? Do you agree with the federal law requiring that Medicaid programs must cover every drug that has FDA approval? Briefly explain.

Sources: Joseph Walker, "Expensive Hepatitis C Medications Drive Prescription-Drug Spending," *Wall Street Journal*, March, 10, 2015; and Margot Sanger-Katz, "$1,000 Hepatitis Pill Shows Why Fixing Health Costs Is So Hard," *New York Times*, August 2, 2014.

1.13 Lawrence Summers served as secretary of the Treasury in the Clinton administration and as director of the National Economic Council in the Obama administration. He has been quoted as giving the following defense of the economic approach:

> There is nothing morally unattractive about saying: We need to analyze which way of spending money on health care will produce more benefit and which less, and using our money as efficiently as we can. I don't think there is anything immoral about seeking to achieve environmental benefits at the lowest possible costs.

Would it be more ethical to reduce pollution without worrying about the cost or by taking the cost into account? Briefly explain.

Source: David Wessel, "Precepts from Professor Summers," *Wall Street Journal*, October 17, 2002.

1.14 In *The Wonderful Wizard of Oz* and his other books about the Land of Oz, L. Frank Baum observed that if people's wants were limited enough, most goods would not be scarce. According to Baum, this was the case in Oz:

> There were no poor people in the Land of Oz, because there was no such thing as money. . . . Each person was given freely by his neighbors whatever he required for his use, which is as much as anyone may reasonably desire. Some tilled the lands and raised great crops of grain, which was divided equally among the whole population, so that

all had enough. There were many tailors and dressmakers and shoemakers and the like, who made things that any who desired them might wear. Likewise there were jewelers who made ornaments for the person, which pleased and beautified the people, and these ornaments also were free to those who asked for them. Each man and woman, no matter what he or she produced for the good of the community, was supplied by the neighbors with food and clothing and a house and furniture and ornaments and games. If by chance the supply ever ran short, more

was taken from the great storehouses of the Ruler, which were afterward filled up again when there was more of any article than people needed. . . .

You will know, by what I have told you here, that the Land of Oz was a remarkable country. I do not suppose such an arrangement would be practical with us.

Do you agree with Baum that the economic system in Oz wouldn't work in the contemporary United States? Briefly explain why or why not.

Source: L. Frank Baum, *The Emerald City of Oz*, 1910, pp. 30–31.

2.2 Comparative Advantage and Trade, pages 48–54

LEARNING OBJECTIVE: Describe comparative advantage and explain how it serves as the basis for trade.

Summary

Fundamentally, markets are about **trade**, which is the act of buying and selling. People trade on the basis of comparative advantage. An individual, a firm, or a country has a **comparative advantage** in producing a good or service if it can produce the good or service at the lowest opportunity cost. People are usually better off specializing in the activity for which they have a comparative advantage and trading for the other goods and services they need. It is important not to confuse comparative advantage with absolute advantage. An individual, a firm, or a country has an **absolute advantage** in producing a good or service if it can produce more of that good or service using the same amount of resources. It is possible to have an absolute advantage in producing a good or service without having a comparative advantage.

MyEconLab   Visit **www.myeconlab.com** to complete these exercises online and get instant feedback.

Review Questions

2.1 What is absolute advantage? What is comparative advantage? Is it possible for a country to have a comparative advantage in producing a good without also having an absolute advantage? Briefly explain.

2.2 What is the basis for trade: absolute advantage or comparative advantage? How can an individual or a country gain from specialization and trade?

Problems and Applications

2.3 Look again at the information in Figure 2.4 on page 49. Choose a rate of trading cherries for apples different from the rate used in the text (15 pounds of cherries for 10 pounds of apples) that will allow you and your neighbor to benefit from trading. Prepare a table like Table 2.1 on page 50 to illustrate your answer.

2.4 Using the same amount of resources, the United States and Canada can both produce lumberjack shirts and

lumberjack boots, as shown in the following production possibilities frontiers:

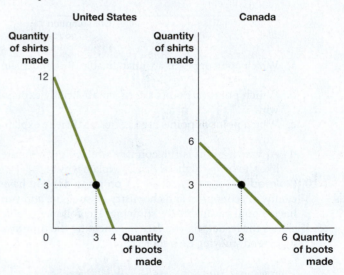

a. Who has a comparative advantage in producing lumberjack boots? Who has a comparative advantage in producing lumberjack shirts? Explain your reasoning.

b. Does either country have an absolute advantage in producing both goods? Briefly explain.

c. Suppose that both countries are currently producing three pairs of boots and three shirts. Show that both can be better off if they each specialize in producing one good and then trade for the other.

2.5 **(Related to the** Don't Let This Happen to You **on page 51)** In the 1950s, the economist Bela Balassa compared 28 manufacturing industries in the United States and Britain. In every one of the 28 industries, Balassa found that the United States had an absolute advantage. In these circumstances, would there have been any gain to the United States from importing any of these products from Britain? Explain.

2.6 **(Related to** Solved Problem 2.2 **on page 52)** Suppose the United Kingdom and Norway both produce oil and fish oil, which are sold for the same prices in both countries.

The following table shows the combinations of both goods that each country can produce in a day, measured in thousands of barrels, using the same amounts of capital and labor:

United Kingdom		Norway	
Oil	Fish oil	Oil	Fish Oil
0	8	0	4
2	6	1	3
4	4	2	2
6	2	3	1
8	0	4	0

a. Who has the comparative advantage in producing oil? Explain.

b. Can these two countries gain from trading oil and fish oil? Explain.

2.7 (Related to Solved Problem 2.2 on page 52) Suppose that France and Germany both produce schnitzel and wine. The following table shows combinations of the goods that each country can produce in a day:

France		Germany	
Wine (bottles)	Schnitzel (pounds)	Wine (bottles)	Schnitzel (pounds)
0	8	0	15
1	6	1	12
2	4	2	9
3	2	3	6
4	0	4	3
		5	0

a. Who has a comparative advantage in producing wine? Who has a comparative advantage in producing schnitzel?

b. Suppose that France is currently producing 1 bottle of wine and 6 pounds of schnitzel, and Germany is currently producing 3 bottles of wine and 6 pounds of schnitzel. Demonstrate that France and Germany can both be better off if they specialize in producing only one good and then trade for the other.

2.8 Can an individual or a country produce beyond its production possibilities frontier? Can an individual or a country consume beyond its production possibilities frontier? Explain.

2.9 If Nicaragua can produce with the same amount of resources twice as much coffee as Colombia, explain how Colombia could have a comparative advantage in producing coffee.

2.10 Imagine that the next time the Indianapolis Colts play the New England Patriots at Lucas Oil Stadium in Indianapolis, Colts star quarterback Andrew Luck has a temporary lack of judgment and plans to sell Colts memorabilia during the game because he realizes that he can sell five times more Colts products than any other player. Likewise, imagine that you are a creative and effective manager at work and that you tell your employees that during the next six months, you plan to clean the offices because you can clean five times better than the cleaning staff. What error in judgment are both you and Andrew making? Why shouldn't you and Andrew do what you are better than anyone else at doing?

2.11 After Russia seized what had formerly been the Ukrainian territory of Crimea in February 2014, the United States and many other countries imposed economic sanctions that reduced the ability of Russia to engage in international trade. A columnist writing in the *New York Times* noted, "If sanctions push Russia onto a path of greater self-reliance, its manufacturing and service industries will surely grow faster...." If the columnist is correct about the effect of the sanctions, are the sanctions likely to improve the economic well-being of the average Russian in the long run? Briefly explain.

Source: Anatole Kaletsky, "Reasons to Welcome a Ukraine Deal," *New York Times*, September 18, 2014.

2.12 In colonial America, the population was spread thinly over a large area, and transportation costs were very high because it was difficult to ship products by road for more than short distances. As a result, most of the free population lived on small farms, where they not only grew their own food but also usually made their own clothes and very rarely bought or sold anything for money. Explain why the incomes of these farmers were likely to rise as transportation costs fell. Use the concept of comparative advantage in your answer.

2.13 During the 1928 U.S. presidential election campaign, Herbert Hoover, the Republican candidate, argued that the United States should import only products that could not be produced here. Do you believe that this would be a good policy? Explain.

2.14 (Related to the Making the Connection on page 53) In discussing dividing up household chores, Emily Oster, an economist at the University of Chicago, advises, "No, you shouldn't always unload the dishwasher because you're better at it." If you are better at unloading the dishwasher, why shouldn't you be the one to unload it?

Source: Emily Oster, "You're Dividing the Chores Wrong," *Slate*, November 21, 2012.

2.15 (Related to the Making the Connection on page 53) The chapter mentions that in 1965, married women with children did an average of 32 hours of housework per week, while men did an average of only 4 hours of housework—a total of 36 hours of housework. In 2014, the estimated average weekly hours of housework for women declined to 15, while the hours worked by men increased to 10—a total of 25 hours of housework. Does the decrease in the total number of hours of housework—from 36 to 25—mean that families are willing to live in messier homes? Briefly explain.

Source: U.S. Bureau of Labor Statistics, "American Time Use—2014," June 24, 2015.

2.3 | **The Market System, pages 54–63**
LEARNING OBJECTIVE: Explain the basics of how a market system works.

Summary

A **market** is a group of buyers and sellers of a good or service and the institution or arrangement by which they come together to trade. **Product markets** are markets for goods and services, such as computers and medical treatment. **Factor markets** are markets for the **factors of production**, such as labor, capital, natural resources, and entrepreneurial ability. A **circular-flow diagram** shows how participants in product markets and factor markets are linked. Adam Smith argued in his 1776 book *The Wealth of Nations* that in a **free market**, where the government does not control the production of goods and services, changes in prices lead firms to produce the goods and services most desired by consumers. If consumers demand more of a good, its price will rise. Firms respond to rising prices by increasing production. If consumers demand less of a good, its price will fall. Firms respond to falling prices by producing less of a good. An **entrepreneur** is someone who operates a business. In the market system, entrepreneurs are responsible for organizing the production of goods and services. The market system will work well only if there is protection for **property rights**, which are the rights of individuals and firms to use their property.

MyEconLab   Visit **www.myeconlab.com** to complete these exercises online and get instant feedback.

Review Questions

3.1 What is a circular-flow diagram, and what does it demonstrate?

3.2 What are the two main categories of participants in markets? Which participants are of greatest importance in determining what goods and services are produced?

3.3 What is a free market? In what ways does a free market economy differ from a centrally planned economy?

3.4 What is an entrepreneur? Why do entrepreneurs play a key role in a market system?

3.5 Under what circumstances are firms likely to produce more of a good or service? Under what circumstances are firms likely to produce less of a good or service?

3.6 What are property rights? What role do they play in the working of a market system? Why are independent courts important for a well-functioning economy?

Problems and Applications

3.7 Identify whether each of the following transactions will take place in the factor market or in the product market and whether households or firms are supplying the good or service or demanding the good or service.
a. George buys a Tesla Model S.
b. Tesla increases employment at its Fremont plant.
c. George works 20 hours per week at McDonald's.
d. George sells the land he owns to McDonald's so that it can build a new restaurant.

3.8 **(Related to the** Making the Connection **on page 57)** Nobel Prize–winning economist Kenneth Arrow of Stanford University once wrote that the argument that the

outcomes in a market system "may be very different from, and even opposed to, intentions is surely the most important intellectual contribution that economic thought has made." Briefly explain how it is possible for the outcomes in a market system to be different from what firms and consumers intended them to be. Why is this idea such an important intellectual contribution?

Sources: Kenneth J. Arrow, "Economic Equilibrium," *Encyclopedia of the Social Sciences*, 1968; and Encyclopedia.com.

3.9 **(Related to the** Making the Connection **on page 57)** In a famous essay on the market system, the economist Leonard Read discussed how a pencil sold by the U.S. firm Eberhard Faber Pencil Company (now owned by Paper Mate) was made. He noted that logging companies in California and Oregon grew the cedar wood used in the pencil. The wood was milled into pencil-width slats at a factory in San Leandro, California. The graphite for the pencil was mined in Sri Lanka and mixed with clay purchased from a firm in Mississippi and wax from a firm in Mexico. The rubber was purchased from a firm in Indonesia. Was it necessary for the managers of all these firms to know how the components they produced were assembled into a pencil? Was it necessary for the chief executive officer (CEO) of the Eberhard Faber Company to know this information? Briefly explain.

Source: Leonard E. Read, *I, Pencil: My Family Tree as told to Leonard E. Read*, Irvington-on-Hudson, NY: The Foundation for Economic Education, Inc., December 1958.

3.10 Evaluate the following argument: "Adam Smith's analysis of the market system is based on a fundamental flaw: He assumes that people are motivated by self-interest. But this isn't true. I'm not selfish, and most people I know aren't selfish."

3.11 Writing in the *New York Times*, Michael Lewis argued that "a market economy is premised on a system of incentives designed to encourage an ignoble human trait: self-interest." Do you agree that self-interest is an "ignoble human trait"? What incentives does a market system provide to encourage self-interest?

Source: Michael Lewis, "In Defense of the Boom," *New York Times*, October 27, 2002.

3.12 Some economists have been puzzled that although entrepreneurs take on the risk of losing money by starting new businesses, on average their incomes are lower than those of people with similar characteristics who go to work at large firms. Economist William Baumol believes part of the explanation for this puzzle may be that entrepreneurs are like people who buy lottery tickets. On average, people who don't buy lottery tickets are left with more money than people who buy tickets because lotteries take in more money than they give out. Baumol argues that "the masses of purchasers who grab up the [lottery] tickets are not irrational if they receive an adequate payment in another currency: psychic rewards."
a. What are "psychic rewards"?
b. What psychic rewards might an entrepreneur receive?

c. Do you agree with Baumol that an entrepreneur is like someone buying a lottery ticket? Briefly explain.

Source: William J. Baumol, *The Microtheory of Innovative Entrepreneurship*, Princeton, NJ: Princeton University Press, 2010.

3.13 In a report on property rights around the world, Peruvian economist Hernando De Soto noted the increasing evidence of a strong relationship between "economic successes and countries that include protective policy measures over property rights." Why would the protection of property rights be likely to increase economic growth in a developing, or low-income, country?

Source: Hernando De Soto, "Introduction," *International Property Rights Index, 2014,* internationalpropertyrightsindex.org.

3.14 According to an article on Phillyburbs.com, some farmers in rural Pennsylvania are causing a "stink" by using pig manure for fertilizer. The farmers purchase the pig manure, which is an organic fertilizer, from a nearby pork processing plant and spread it across the fields where they grow corn and soybeans. The article asserts that the farmers switched to pig manure because of the skyrocketing price of chemical fertilizers. Some of the residents of the town of Milford, however, have complained about the smell, but the "farmers are likely protected under Pennsylvania's Right to Farm Act, which allows farmers to engage in practices that are common to agriculture."

a. What price signal did the farmers respond to in their switch to the organic pig manure fertilizer?

b. According to the Pennsylvania Right to Farm Act, do the farmers or the townspeople have the property right to the smell of the air around the farms? (Some of the residents did ask the township to urge the farmers to plow under the manure to reduce its stench.)

Source: Amanda Cregan, "Milford Farmers Switch to Pig Manure Causing a Stink for Neighbors," Phillyburbs.com, March 6, 2013.

3.15 **(Related to the** Making the Connection **on page 61)** The British historian Thomas Macaulay once remarked that copyrights are "a tax on readers." In what sense are copyrights a tax on readers? If copyrights are a tax on readers, why do governments enact them?

3.16 **(Related to the** Making the Connection **on page 61)** In the court case over whether anyone could use Conan Doyle's character Sherlock Holmes without paying a fee, Judge Posner argued that the first Sherlock Holmes story was written in 1887, so allowing the author's descendants to continue to claim a copyright to the character raised the possibility of "perpetual, or at least nearly perpetual, copyright." The judge also noted that the U.S. Constitution had given Congress the authority to grant copyright for only a limited time. What would be the disadvantages to the economy of allowing an author and his or her descendants to have a copyright forever on a book or character? Would there be any advantages? Briefly explain.

Source: *Leslie S. Kling v. Conan Doyle Estate, Ltd.* (7th Cir. 2014), media.ca7.uscourts.gov.

Where Prices Come From: The Interaction of Demand and Supply

Chapter Outline and **Learning Objectives**

How Smart Is Your Watch?

Fashions can change quickly. For many years, most people wore wristwatches. With the popularity of cellphones in the 2000s, many people stopped wearing wristwatches—which was bad news for the watch industry. Once a product falls out of fashion, its sales are unlikely to return to past levels. Will watches prove an exception?

Until recently attempts to have watches do more than tell the time have not been successful. For instance, during the 1980s Texas Instruments and several other firms added small calculators to watches, but sales were limited. In 2004, Microsoft introduced the SPOT watch, which enabled users to receive instant messages, weather reports, and news headlines. But few consumers purchased it so the company stopped production of the watch in 2008. By 2013, several firms had introduced "smartwatches" that enabled users to make phone calls, text, take photos or videos, monitor their heart rates, and calculate calories burned while exercising.

In 2015, Apple introduced the Apple Watch, which combined most of the capabilities of the smartwatches from competing firms with popular features from Apple's iPhone and iPad, such as access to the iTunes music store and Siri, the voice-activated personal assistant. The Apple Watch was immediately popular, with more than 2.5 million being sold during the first five weeks. These sales were higher than initial sales of Apple's previous products—the iPod, iPhone, or iPad. More than 25 other firms entered the smartwatch market, hoping to participate in the rapid growth of a hot product.

But there are no guarantees in a market system. Would the Apple Watch and its competitors succeed in bringing the wristwatch back into style, or would they fail like the Texas Instruments calculator watch and the Microsoft SPOT watch? Smartwatches have relatively high prices, are somewhat complicated to use, and have small screens that make it difficult to display photos or maps. Ultimately, the success of the smartwatch is likely to depend on whether consumers like the applications, or "apps," on these watches and are willing to wear wristwatches again.

The intense competition among firms selling smartwatches is a striking example of how the market responds to changes in technology and consumer tastes. Although competition is not always good news for firms trying to sell products, it is great news for consumers because it increases the available choice of products and lowers the prices consumers pay for those products.

AN INSIDE LOOK on **page 98** discusses how the Apple smartwatch is inspiring firms to develop other wearable devices.

Sources: Daniel Matte and Kevin McCullagh, "Will Smartwatches Be a Hit?" *Wall Street Journal*, May 10, 2015; and Mitchel Broussard, "Apple Watch Orders Estimated to Average 30,000 per Day in U.S. after Initial Surge," macrumors.com, May 22, 2015.

Economics in Your Life

Will You Buy a Smartphone or a Smartwatch?

You use your smartphone mainly to text, read e-mail, and keep track of your appointments. Your smartphone is old, though, and you are thinking of buying a new one … or should you buy a smartwatch? What factors are most important in your decision: the features of a smartwatch versus a smartphone, or the relative prices of these products? If you know that you are soon going to get a raise at your job, would you be more likely to buy a smartwatch? As you read this chapter, try to answer these questions. You can check your answers against those we provide on **page 97** at the end of this chapter.

I n Chapter 1, we explored how economists use models to predict human behavior. In Chapter 2, we used the production possibilities frontiers (*PPF*) model to analyze scarcity and trade-offs. In this chapter and the next, we explore the model of demand and supply, which is the most powerful tool in economics, and use the model to explain how prices are determined.

Economic models are simplified versions of reality that are based on assumptions. In some cases, the assumptions of a model may not describe exactly the economic situation we are analyzing. For example, the model of demand and supply assumes that we are analyzing a **perfectly competitive market**, which is a market where there are many buyers and sellers, all the products sold are identical, and there are no barriers to new firms entering the market. These assumptions are very restrictive and apply exactly to only a few markets, such as the markets for wheat and other agricultural products. Experience has shown, however, that the model of demand and supply can be very useful in analyzing markets where competition among sellers is intense, even if there are relatively few sellers and the products being sold are not identical. In fact, in recent studies, the model of demand and supply has been successful in analyzing markets with as few as four buyers and four sellers. As we will see in this chapter, this model is often successful in predicting changes in quantities and prices in many markets.

We begin studying the model of demand and supply by discussing consumers and the demand side of the market, and then we turn to firms and the supply side. Throughout this text, we will apply this model to understand business, the economy, and economic policy.

Perfectly competitive market A market that meets the conditions of having (1) many buyers and sellers, (2) all firms selling identical products, and (3) no barriers to new firms entering the market.

3.1 The Demand Side of the Market

LEARNING OBJECTIVE: List and describe the variables that influence demand.

We saw in Chapter 2 that in a market system, consumers ultimately determine which goods and services will be produced. The most successful businesses are the ones that respond best to consumer demand. But what determines consumer demand for a product? Certainly, many factors influence the willingness of consumers to buy a particular product. For example, consumers who are considering buying a smartwatch, such as an Apple Watch or a Samsung Gear S, will make their decisions based on, among other factors, the income they have available to spend and the effectiveness of the advertising campaigns of the companies that sell smartwatches. For most consumers, the primary factor in their buying decision is the price of the product. So, we focus on this factor first. As we discuss demand, keep in mind that we are considering not what a consumer *wants* to buy but what the consumer is both willing and *able* to buy.

Demand Schedules and Demand Curves

Demand schedule A table that shows the relationship between the price of a product and the quantity of the product demanded.

Quantity demanded The amount of a good or service that a consumer is willing and able to purchase at a given price.

Demand curve A curve that shows the relationship between the price of a product and the quantity of the product demanded.

Market demand The demand by all the consumers of a given good or service.

Tables that show the relationship between the price of a product and the quantity of the product demanded are called **demand schedules**. The table in Figure 3.1 shows the number of smartwatches consumers would be willing and able to buy over the course of a week at five different prices. The amount of a good or service that a consumer is willing and able to purchase at a given price is called the **quantity demanded**. The graph in Figure 3.1 plots the numbers from the table as a **demand curve**, which shows the relationship between the price of a product and the quantity of the product demanded. (Note that, for convenience, we made the demand curve in Figure 3.1 a straight line, or linear. There is no reason that all demand curves need to be straight lines.) The demand curve in Figure 3.1 shows the **market demand**, which is the demand by all the consumers of a given good or service. The market for a product, such as restaurant meals, that is sold locally would include all the consumers in a city or a relatively small area. The market for a product, such as smartwatches, that is sold internationally would include all the consumers in the world.

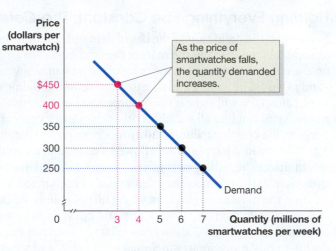

MyEconLab Animation

Figure 3.1

A Demand Schedule and Demand Curve

As the price changes, consumers change the quantity of smartwatches they are willing and able to buy. We can show this as a *demand schedule* in a table or as a *demand curve* on a graph. The table and graph both show that as the price of smartwatches falls, the quantity demanded increases. When the price of smartwatches is $450, consumers buy 3 million smartwatches per week. When the price falls to $400, consumers buy 4 million. Therefore, the demand curve for smartwatches is downward sloping.

The demand curve in Figure 3.1 slopes downward because consumers will buy more smartwatches as the price falls. When the price of smartwatches is $450, consumers buy 3 million smartwatches per week. When the price falls to $400, consumers buy 4 million. Buyers demand a larger quantity of a product as the price falls because the product becomes less expensive relative to other products and because they can afford to buy more at a lower price.   MyEconLab Concept Check

The Law of Demand

The inverse relationship between the price of a product and the quantity of the product demanded is called the **law of demand**: Holding everything else constant, when the price of a product falls, the quantity demanded of the product will increase, and when the price of a product rises, the quantity demanded of the product will decrease. The law of demand holds for any market demand curve. Economists have found only a very few exceptions to this law.   MyEconLab Concept Check

Law of demand A rule that states that, holding everything else constant, when the price of a product falls, the quantity demanded of the product will increase, and when the price of a product rises, the quantity demanded of the product will decrease.

What Explains the Law of Demand?

It makes sense that consumers will buy more of a good when its price falls and less of a good when its price rises, but let's look more closely at why this result holds. When the price of a product falls, consumers buy a larger quantity because of two effects, the *substitution effect* and the *income effect*:

1. The **substitution effect** refers to the change in the quantity demanded of a good that results because a change in price makes the good more or less expensive *relative* to other goods that are *substitutes*. When the price of smartwatches falls, people will substitute buying smartwatches for other goods, such as regular wristwatches or smartphones, such as the iPhone.

2. The **income effect** of a price change refers to the change in the quantity demanded of a good that results because a change in the good's price increases or decreases consumers' purchasing power. *Purchasing power* is the quantity of goods a consumer can buy with a fixed amount of income. When the price of a good falls, the increased purchasing power of consumers' incomes will usually lead them to purchase a larger quantity of the good. When the price of a good rises, the decreased purchasing power of consumers' incomes will usually lead them to purchase a smaller quantity of the good.

Substitution effect The change in the quantity demanded of a good that results from a change in price, making the good more or less expensive relative to other goods that are substitutes.

Income effect The change in the quantity demanded of a good that results from the effect of a change in the good's price on consumers' purchasing power.

Although we can analyze them separately, the substitution effect and the income effect occur simultaneously whenever a price changes. So, a fall in the price of smartwatches leads consumers to buy more smartwatches both because the smartwatches are now less expensive relative to substitute products and because the purchasing power of consumers' incomes has increased.   MyEconLab Concept Check

Holding Everything Else Constant: The *Ceteris Paribus* Condition

Notice that the definition of the law of demand contains the phrase *holding everything else constant*. In constructing the market demand curve for smartwatches, we focused only on the effect that changes in the price of smartwatches would have on the quantity consumers would be willing and able to buy. We were holding constant other variables that might affect the willingness of consumers to buy smartwatches. Economists refer to the necessity of holding all variables other than price constant in constructing a demand curve as the **ceteris paribus condition**. *Ceteris paribus* means "all else equal" in Latin.

What would happen if we allowed a change in a variable—other than price—that might affect the willingness of consumers to buy smartwatches? Consumers would then change the quantity they demanded at each price. We can illustrate this effect by shifting the market demand curve. A shift of a demand curve is *an increase or a decrease in demand*. A movement along a demand curve is *an increase or a decrease in the quantity demanded*. As Figure 3.2 shows, we shift the demand curve to the right if consumers decide to buy more smartwatches at each price, and we shift the demand curve to the left if consumers decide to buy less at each price.

Ceteris paribus ("all else equal") **condition** The requirement that when analyzing the relationship between two variables—such as price and quantity demanded—other variables must be held constant.

Variables That Shift Market Demand

Many variables other than price can influence market demand. These five are the most important:

- Income
- Prices of related goods
- Tastes
- Population and demographics
- Expected future prices

We next discuss how changes in each of these variables affect the market demand curve.

Income The income that consumers have available to spend affects their willingness and ability to buy a good. Suppose that the market demand curve in Figure 3.1 on page 75 represents the willingness of consumers to buy smartwatches when average household income is $50,000. If average household income rises to $52,000, the demand for smartwatches will increase, which we show by shifting the demand curve to the right. A good is a **normal good** when the demand for the good increases following a rise in income and decreases following a fall in income. Most goods are

Normal good A good for which the demand increases as income rises and decreases as income falls.

MyEconLab Animation

Figure 3.2

Shifting the Demand Curve

When consumers increase the quantity of a product they want to buy at a given price, the demand curve shifts to the right, from D_1 to D_2. When consumers decrease the quantity of a product they want to buy at a given price, the demand curve shifts to the left, from D_1 to D_3.

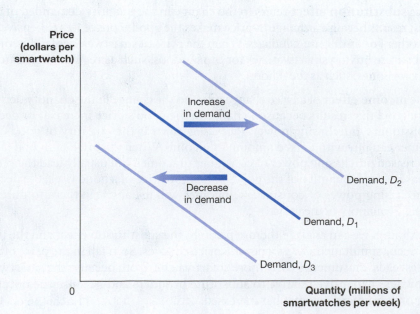

normal goods, but some goods are *inferior goods*. A good is an **inferior good** when the demand for it decreases following a rise income and increases following a fall in income. For instance, as your income rises, you might buy fewer cans of tuna or packages of instant noodles, and buy more shrimp or whole grain pasta. So, for you, canned tuna and instant noodles would be examples of inferior goods—not because they are of low quality but because you buy less of them as your income increases.

Inferior good A good for which the demand increases as income falls and decreases as income rises.

Prices of Related Goods The prices of other goods can also affect consumers' demand for a product. Consumers who would use a smartwatch primarily for checking the time, making phone calls, and keeping track of their appointments could use a smartphone instead. Goods and services that can be used for the same purpose are called **substitutes**. When two goods are substitutes, the more you buy of one, the less you will buy of the other. A decrease in the price of a substitute causes the demand curve for a good to shift to the left. An increase in the price of a substitute causes the demand curve for a good to shift to the right.

Substitutes Goods and services that can be used for the same purpose.

Suppose that the market demand curve in Figure 3.1 on page 75 represents the willingness and ability of consumers to buy smartwatches during a week when the average price of smartphones is $400. If the average price of smartphones falls to $300, consumers will demand fewer smartwatches at every price. We show this change by shifting the demand curve for smartwatches to the left.

Suppose that the market demand curve in Figure 3.1 on page 75 represents

Making the Connection

MyEconLab Video

Are Smartwatches Substitutes for Smartphones?

Two products are rarely perfect substitutes because consumers may find them more or less useful for some purposes. As Apple and other firms began selling smartwatches, a key question they needed to answer was whether consumers considered smartwatches close substitutes for smartphones. You can use either a smartwatch or a smartphone to check the time, send a text, keep a list of appointments, or use a GPS map. But you need a smartphone if you want to surf the Web or watch a movie, while you are better off buying a smartwatch if you want to monitor your heartbeat or keep track of how many calories you are burning while exercising.

Is the smartwatch a hot new must-have gadget, even for people who already own a smartphone?

So smartwatches and smartphones are substitutes—but they aren't *perfect* substitutes. To correctly forecast sales and produce the correct quantity of smartwatches, firms that sell them need to evaluate how close substitutes consumers consider smartwatches and smartphones to be. Many people who might consider buying a smartwatch already own a smartphone. So the closer consumers consider the two products to be as substitutes, the less likely they are to buy a smartwatch in addition to a smartphone.

When Apple introduced the Apple Watch in 2015, sales were initially very strong, which would seem to indicate that many consumers believed that the unique features of the smartwatch made it worth buying, even if they owned a smartphone. Some analysts, though, wondered how large future sales would be after people who buy each new electronic device soon after it hits the market—early adopters—had made their purchases. One early reviewer of the Apple Watch noted that he was unsure "that I need this thing on my wrist every day." Similarly, the *Economist* magazine offered the opinion, "Apple seems unlikely to turn its watch into the next big must-have gadget. … People are unlikely to want to shell out … $350 … for something with so few extra functions."

Other industry observers were more optimistic about the size of the market for smartwatches. Writing in the *Wall Street Journal*, one analyst argued that smartwatches performed several functions faster or more conveniently than smartphones. He concluded, "Billions of consumers who own a smartphone are likely to consider purchasing a smartwatch." Given these different evaluations, it wasn't surprising that forecasts of sales of the Apple Watch during its first year varied widely from 8 million to 41 million.

In the end, as with most new products, the success of smartwatches depends on whether consumers see them as filling a need that other products don't meet. In other words, the less close a substitute consumers believe smartwatches to be for smartphones, the more likely they are to buy a smartwatch.

Sources: Joshua Topolsky, "Apple Watch Review: You'll Want One, but You Don't Need One," bloomberg.com, April 8, 2015; "The Time Machine," *Economist*, March 9, 2015; and Daniel Matte and Kevin McCullagh, "Will Smartwatches Be a Hit?" *Wall Street Journal*, May 10, 2015.

MyEconLab Study Plan

Your Turn: Test your understanding by doing related problem 1.12 on page 101 at the end of this chapter.

Complements Goods and services that are used together.

Goods and services that are used together—such as hot dogs and hot dog buns—are called **complements**. When two goods are complements, the more consumers buy of one, the more they will buy of the other. A decrease in the price of a complement causes the demand curve for a good to shift to the right. An increase in the price of a complement causes the demand curve for a good to shift to the left.

People use applications, or "apps," on their smartwatches. So, smartwatches and apps are complements. Suppose the market demand curve in Figure 3.1 represents the willingness of consumers to buy smartwatches at a time when the average price of an app is $1.99. If the average price of apps falls to $0.99, consumers will buy more apps *and* more smartwatches, and the demand curve for smartwatches will shift to the right.

Tastes An advertising campaign for a product can influence consumer demand. If Apple, Samsung, LG, and other firms making smartwatches begin to advertise heavily, consumers are likely to buy more smartwatches at every price, and the demand curve will shift to the right. An economist would say that the advertising campaign has affected consumers' *taste* for smartwatches. Taste is a catchall category that refers to the many subjective elements that can enter into a consumer's decision to buy a product. A consumer's taste for a product can change for many reasons. Sometimes trends play a substantial role. For example, the popularity of low-carbohydrate diets caused a decline in demand for some goods, such as bread and donuts, and an increase in demand for fish. In general, when consumers' taste for a product increases, the demand curve will shift to the right, and when consumers' taste decreases, the demand curve will shift to the left.

Demographics The characteristics of a population with respect to age, race, and gender.

Population and Demographics

As the population of a country increases, the number of consumers and the demand for most products will increase. The **demographics** of a population refers to its characteristics, with respect to age, race, and gender. As the demographics of a country or region change, the demand for particular goods will increase or decrease because different categories of people tend to have different preferences for those goods. For instance, the U.S. Census Bureau forecasts that Hispanics will increase from 18 percent of the U.S. population in 2015 to 26 percent in 2050. This increase will expand demand for Spanish-language books, Web sites, and cable television channels, among other goods and services.

McDonalds introduced new products to appeal to millennials as sales of Big Macs declined.

Making the Connection

MyEconLab Video

Tough Times for Big Macs and Golf

Changing demographics can affect the demand for products. Clearly, the usefulness of products may vary with age. For example, when birth rates are high, the demand for formula, diapers, and other baby products increases. Similarly, when there are more older people, the demand for nursing homes increases. Some retail analysts believe, though, that tastes for products may also differ across generations, so that some products may remain popular with older generations while declining in popularity with younger generations. There are no exact definitions of generations, but the chart on the next page shows common labels.

Years Born	Generation Label	Age Range in 2015	Number of People in the Generation in 2015
1946–1964	Baby boom generation	51–69	79 million
1965–1984	Generation X	31–50	83 million
1985–2004	Millennials, or Generation Y	11–30	87 million

The millennials outnumber the two generations that preceded them, but the size of each generation doesn't tell the whole story for retailers. Market research indicates that consumers between the ages of 18 and 49 account for a large fraction of all retail sales. This fact helps explain why firms are willing to pay high prices to run commercials on television programs, such as NBC's *The Voice*, that this "prime demographic" watches. Note that the whole of the baby boom generation is now older than this age group. Members of generation X are also beginning to age out of this group, and over time millennials will begin to make up the bulk of this demographic.

Because of their importance as consumers, firms become concerned if millennials don't have a strong demand for their products. Consider problems that McDonald's and Dick's Sporting Goods were facing in 2015. Millennials were shifting from buying Big Macs to visiting "fast casual" restaurants, such as Chipotle Mexican Grill and Panera Bread. In 2014, the revenue and profits of McDonald's both declined for the first time in more than 30 years. McDonald's was suffering particular problems with college-age consumers. The number of consumers aged 19 to 21 who visit McDonald's at least once per month declined 15 percent between 2011 and 2015.

Dick's Sporting Goods faced a similar problem with demand for golf clubs and other golf equipment. The average age of people who regularly play golf has increased over time and was 56 in 2015. During the past five years, the number of people aged 18 to 34 who played at least one round of golf during the year has been continually declining. As fewer young people play golf, sales of golf equipment, rounds of golf at golf courses, and ratings of golf tournaments on television have all declined. Sales of golf equipment at Dick's declined by more than 15 percent between 2013 and 2015.

How should a business respond if the demand for its products is decreasing among younger consumers? The answer depends partly on whether offering different products or changing existing products might increase demand from these consumers. McDonald's tried this strategy by introducing McWrap sandwiches—tortillas stuffed with chicken or vegetables— and other new meals to appeal to millennials. It also planned to use healthier ingredients by, for example, reducing the use of chicken that had been fed antibiotics while being raised. Dick's decided that it probably could not revive demand for its golf equipment. The chain laid off most of the golf pros who had been working in its stores, and reduced the number of golf clubs and golf balls and the amount of golf clothing it offered for sale.

As firms make plans for the long run, they have to take into account how changing demographics may affect demand for their products.

Sources: Annie Gasparro, "McDonald's Puts Its Plan on Display," *Wall Street Journal*, May 3, 2015; Julie Jargon, "McDonald's Faces 'Millennial' Challenge," *Wall Street Journal*, August 24, 2014; Sara Germano, "A Game of Golf? Not for Many Millennials," *Wall Street Journal*, August 1, 2014; Lisa Beilfuss, "Dick's Sporting Goods Profit Falls 10%," *Wall Street Journal*, May 19, 2015; and "Dick's Sporting Goods Lays Off 478 PGA Golf Pros," Associated Press, July 24, 2014.

Your Turn: Test your understanding by doing related problem 1.13 on page 101 at the end of this chapter.

MyEconLab Study Plan

Expected Future Prices Consumers choose not only which products to buy but also when to buy them. For instance, if enough consumers become convinced that houses will be selling for lower prices in three months, the demand for houses will decrease now, as some consumers postpone their purchases to wait for the expected price decrease. Alternatively, if enough consumers become convinced that the price of houses will be higher in three months, the demand for houses will increase now, as some consumers try to beat the expected price increase.

Table 3.1 summarizes the most important variables that cause market demand curves to shift. Note that the table shows the shift in the demand curve that results from an *increase* in each of the variables. A *decrease* in these variables would cause the demand curve to shift in the opposite direction.　MyEconLab Concept Check

Table 3.1

Variables That Shift Market Demand Curves

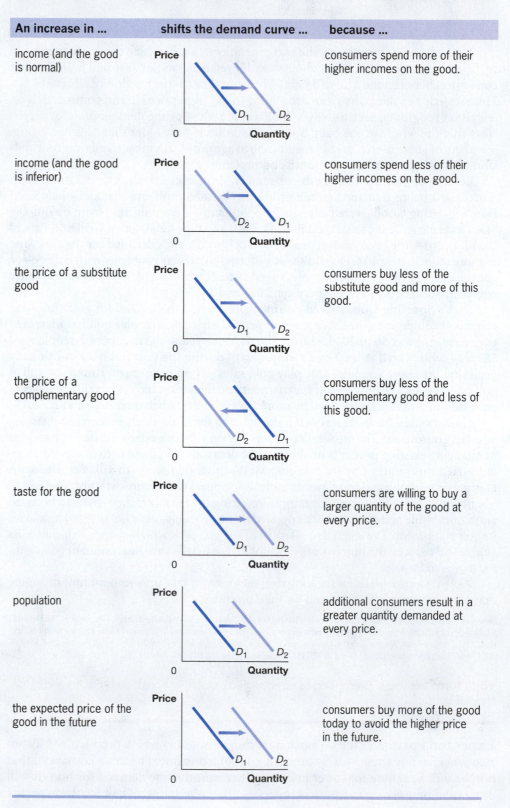

An increase in ...	shifts the demand curve ...	because ...
income (and the good is normal)		consumers spend more of their higher incomes on the good.
income (and the good is inferior)		consumers spend less of their higher incomes on the good.
the price of a substitute good		consumers buy less of the substitute good and more of this good.
the price of a complementary good		consumers buy less of the complementary good and less of this good.
taste for the good		consumers are willing to buy a larger quantity of the good at every price.
population		additional consumers result in a greater quantity demanded at every price.
the expected price of the good in the future		consumers buy more of the good today to avoid the higher price in the future.

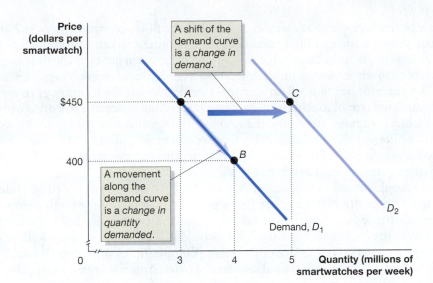

Price (dollars per smartwatch)

A shift of the demand curve is a *change in demand.*

A movement along the demand curve is a *change in quantity demanded.*

$450

400

A

B

C

D_2

Demand, D_1

0   3   4   5   Quantity (millions of smartwatches per week)

MyEconLab Animation

Figure 3.3

A Change in Demand versus a Change in Quantity Demanded

If the price of smartwatches falls from $450 to $400, the result will be a movement along the demand curve from point A to point B—an increase in quantity demanded from 3 million to 4 million. If consumers' incomes increase, or if another factor changes that makes consumers want more of the product at every price, the demand curve will shift to the right—an increase in demand. In this case, the increase in demand from D_1 to D_2 causes the quantity of smartwatches demanded at a price of $450 to increase from 3 million at point A to 5 million at point C.

A Change in Demand versus a Change in Quantity Demanded

It is important to understand the difference between a *change in demand* and a *change in quantity demanded.* A change in demand refers to a shift of the demand curve. A shift occurs if there is a change in one of the variables—*other than the price of the product*—that affects the willingness of consumers to buy the product. A change in quantity demanded refers to a movement along the demand curve as a result of a change in the product's price. Figure 3.3 illustrates this important distinction. If the price of smartwatches falls from $450 to $400, the result will be a movement along the demand curve from point A to point B—an increase in quantity demanded from 3 million to 4 million. If consumers' incomes increase, or if another factor changes that makes consumers want more of the product at every price, the demand curve will shift to the right—an increase in demand. In this case, the increase in demand from D_1 to D_2 causes the quantity of smartwatches demanded at a price of $450 to increase from 3 million at point A to 5 million at point C.

Making the Connection

MyEconLab Video

Forecasting the Demand for iPhones

One of the most important decisions that managers of any large firm face is choosing which new products to develop. A firm must devote people, time, and money to design a new product, negotiate with suppliers, create a marketing campaign, and perform many other tasks. But any firm has only limited resources and so faces a trade-off: Resources used to develop one product will not be available to develop another product. Ultimately, the products a firm chooses to develop will be those that it believes will be the most profitable. So, to decide which products to develop, firms need to forecast the demand for those products.

David Sobotta, who worked at Apple for 20 years and eventually became its national sales manager, has described discussions at Apple during 2002 about whether to develop a tablet computer. According to Sobotta, representatives of the U.S. National Institutes of Health urged Apple to develop a tablet computer, arguing that it would be particularly useful to doctors, nurses, and hospitals. In 2001, Bill Gates, chairman of Microsoft, had predicted that "within five years … [tablet PCs] will be the most popular form of PC sold in America." Apple's managers decided not to develop a tablet computer, however, because they believed the technology available at that time was too complex for an average computer user, and they also believed that the demand from doctors and nurses

Will demand for iPhones continue to grow despite increasing competition?

would be small. Apple's forecast was correct. Despite Bill Gates's prediction, in 2006, tablet computers made up only 1 percent of the computer market. According to Sobotta, "Apple executives had a theory that the route to success will not be through selling thousands of relatively expensive things, but millions of very inexpensive things like iPods."

Apple continued to work on smartphones, developing the technology to eliminate keyboards in favor of touchscreen displays. Rather than proceed immediately to building a tablet computer, Steve Jobs, then Apple's CEO, realized he could use this technology in a different way: "I thought 'My God we can build a phone out of this.'" From its introduction in 2007, the iPhone was an immediate success. By mid-2015, Apple had sold more than 600 million iPhones worldwide.

As Apple attempts to forecast demand for its iPhone, it needs to consider two factors: competition from other firms producing smartphones and competition from substitute goods, including tablets and smartwatches. By 2015, industry analysts were divided as to whether Apple would be able to maintain its share of the smartphone market in the face of increasing competition from other firms. The outlook for substitute goods was also mixed. Smartphones were an increasing share of the overall worldwide cellphone market, so there are relatively few consumers left to switch to smartphones from basic cellphones. The increasing availability of apps, including mobile payment apps like Apple Pay that can be used in place of credit cards, was increasing the usefulness of smartphones. But some consumers preferred to use tablets, with their larger screens, for checking e-mail and surfing the Web. With apps like FaceTime or Skype, a tablet can be used to make phone calls. Another unknown was the extent to which sales of smartwatches might eventually cut into smartphone sales.

As any firm does in forecasting demand, Apple faced a trade-off: If it was too cautious in expanding capacity or buying components for smartphones, other firms might seize a large share of the market. But, if Apple was too optimistic, it ran the risk of spending on capacity to produce more units than it could actually sell—an outcome that might turn potential profits into losses. Apple has spent billions of dollars buying large quantities of motion sensors, screens, and other components from suppliers. That will be money well spent ... if the forecast of demand turns out to be accurate. Time will tell whether the future demand for smartphones will be as large as Apple and other firms were forecasting.

Sources: Daisuke Wakabayashi, "Apple Earnings Surge 33% on iPhone Sales," *Wall Street Journal*, April 27, 2015; David Sobotta, "What Jobs Told Me on the iPhone," (London) *Guardian*, January 3, 2007; "Jobs Says iPad Idea Came before iPhone," Associated Press, January 2, 2010; and "More Smartphones Were Shipped in Q1 2013 Than Feature Phones, an Industry First According to IDC," www.idc.com, April 25, 2013.

 MyEconLab Study Plan   **Your Turn:** Test your understanding by doing related problem 1.17 on page 101 at the end of this chapter.

3.2 ## The Supply Side of the Market

LEARNING OBJECTIVE: List and describe the variables that influence supply.

Just as many variables influence the willingness and ability of consumers to buy a particular good or service, many variables influence the willingness and ability of firms to supply a good or service. The most important of these variables is price. The amount of a good or service that a firm is willing and able to supply at a given price is the **quantity supplied**. Holding other variables constant, when the price of a good rises, producing the good is more profitable, and the quantity supplied will increase. When the price of a good falls, selling the good is less profitable, and the quantity supplied will decrease. In addition, as we saw in Chapter 2, devoting more and more resources to the production of a good results in increasing marginal costs. For example, if Apple, Samsung, LG, and other firms increase production of smartwatches during a given time period, they are likely to find that the cost of producing additional smartwatches increases as their suppliers run existing factories for longer hours and pay higher prices for components

Quantity supplied The amount of a good or service that a firm is willing and able to supply at a given price.

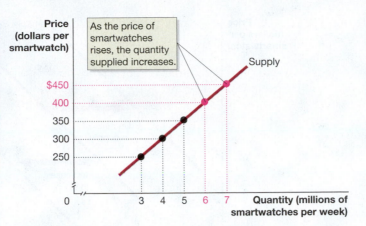

Supply Schedule	
Price (dollars per smartwatch)	Quantity (millions of smartwatches per week)
$450	7
400	6
350	5
300	4
250	3

As the price of smartwatches rises, the quantity supplied increases.

MyEconLab Animation

Figure 3.4

A Supply Schedule and Supply Curve

As the price changes, Apple, Samsung, LG, and other firms producing smartwatches change the quantity they are willing to supply. We can show this as a *supply schedule* in a table or as a *supply curve* on a graph. The supply schedule and supply curve both show that as the price of smartwatches rises, firms will increase the quantity they supply. At a price of $400 per smartwatch, firms will supply 6 million smartwatches per week. At a price of $450, firms will supply 7 million.

and higher wages for workers. With higher marginal costs, firms will supply a larger quantity only if the price is higher.

Supply Schedules and Supply Curves

A **supply schedule** is a table that shows the relationship between the price of a product and the quantity of the product supplied. The table in Figure 3.4 is a supply schedule showing the quantity of smartwatches that firms would be willing to supply per month at different prices. The graph in Figure 3.4 plots the numbers from the table as a **supply curve**, which shows the relationship between the price of a product and the quantity of the product supplied. The supply schedule and supply curve both show that as the price of smartwatches rises, firms will increase the quantity they supply. At a price of $400 per smartwatch, firms will supply 6 million smartwatches per week. At a higher price of $450, firms will supply 7 million. (Once again, we are assuming for convenience that the supply curve is a straight line, even though not all supply curves are actually straight lines.)   MyEconLab Concept Check

Supply schedule A table that shows the relationship between the price of a product and the quantity of the product supplied.

Supply curve A curve that shows the relationship between the price of a product and the quantity of the product supplied.

The Law of Supply

The *market supply curve* in Figure 3.4 is upward sloping. We expect most supply curves to be upward sloping, according to the **law of supply**, which states that, holding everything else constant, increases in price cause increases in the quantity supplied, and decreases in price cause decreases in the quantity supplied. Notice that the definition of the law of supply—like the definition of the law of demand—contains the phrase *holding everything else constant*. If only the price of the product changes, there is a movement along the supply curve, which is *an increase or a decrease in the quantity supplied*. As Figure 3.5 shows, if any other variable that affects the willingness of firms to supply a good changes, the supply curve will shift, which is *an increase or a decrease in supply*. When firms increase the quantity of a product they want to sell at a given price, the supply curve shifts to the right. The shift from S_1 to S_3 represents *an increase in supply*. When firms decrease the quantity of a product they want to sell at a given price, the supply curve shifts to the left. The shift from S_1 to S_2 represents *a decrease in supply*.   MyEconLab Concept Check

Law of supply A rule that states that, holding everything else constant, increases in price cause increases in the quantity supplied, and decreases in price cause decreases in the quantity supplied.

Variables That Shift Market Supply

The following are the five most important variables that shift market supply:

- Prices of inputs
- Technological change
- Prices of related goods in production
- Number of firms in the market
- Expected future prices

We next discuss how changes in each of these variables affect the market supply curve.

Figure 3.5

Shifting the Supply Curve

When firms increase the quantity of a product they want to sell at a given price, the supply curve shifts to the right. The shift from S_1 to S_3 represents an *increase in supply*. When firms decrease the quantity of a product they want to sell at a given price, the supply curve shifts to the left. The shift from S_1 to S_2 represents a *decrease in supply*.

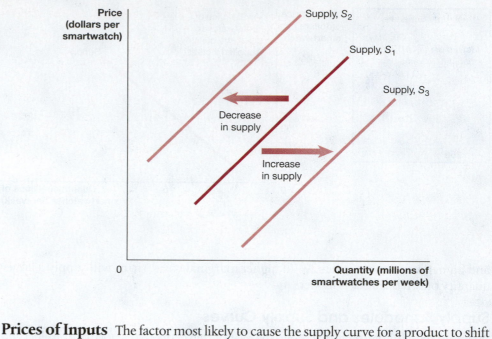

Technological change A positive or negative change in the ability of a firm to produce a given level of output with a given quantity of inputs.

Prices of Inputs The factor most likely to cause the supply curve for a product to shift is a change in the price of an *input*. An input is anything used in the production of a good or service. For instance, if the price of a component of smartwatches, such as memory chips, rises, the cost of producing smartwatches will increase, and smartwatches will be less profitable at every price. The supply of smartwatches will decline, and the market supply curve for smartwatches will shift to the left. Similarly, if the price of an input declines, the supply of smartwatches will increase, and the market supply curve will shift to the right.

Technological Change A second factor that causes a change in supply is **technological change**, which is a positive or negative change in the ability of a firm to produce a given level of output with a given quantity of inputs. Positive technological change occurs whenever a firm is able to produce more output using the same amount of inputs. In other words, the *productivity* of the firm's workers or machines has increased. If a firm can produce more output with the same amount of inputs, its costs will be lower, and the good will be more profitable to produce at any given price. As a result, when positive technological change occurs, the firm will increase the quantity supplied at every price, and its supply curve will shift to the right.

Negative technological change is relatively rare, although it could result from an earthquake or another natural disaster or from a war that reduces the ability of firms to supply as much output with a given amount of inputs. Negative technological change will raise firms' costs, and firms will earn lower profits from producing the good. Therefore, negative technological change will cause the market supply curve to shift to the left.

Prices of Related Goods in Production Firms often choose which good or service they will produce. Alternative goods that a firm could produce are called *substitutes in production*. Many of the firms that produce smartwatches also produce other consumer electronics. For example, Apple produces the iPhone and the iPad, and Samsung produces the Galaxy S smartphone and Galaxy Tab. These products typically use similar components and are often assembled in the same factories. If the price of smartphones increases relative to the price of smartwatches, smartphones will become more profitable, and Apple, Samsung, and other firms making smartwatches will shift some of their productive capacity away from smartwatches and toward smartphones. The firms will offer fewer smartwatches for sale at every price, so the supply curve for smartwatches will shift to the left.

Goods that are produced together are called *complements in production*. For example, the same geological formations that contain oil usually also contain natural gas. If the price of oil rises, oil companies that begin pumping more oil from these formations will also produce more natural gas. As a result, an increase in the price of oil will cause the supply curve for natural gas—a complement in production—to shift to the right.

Number of Firms in the Market A change in the number of firms in the market will change supply. When new firms *enter* a market, the supply curve shifts to the right, and when existing firms leave, or *exit*, a market, the supply curve shifts to the left. In 2015, for instance, Apple entered the market for smartwatches, which shifted the market supply curve to the right.

Expected Future Prices If a firm expects that the price of its product will be higher in the future, it has an incentive to decrease supply now and increase it in the future. For instance, if Apple believes that prices for smartwatches are temporarily low—perhaps because of a recession—it may store some of its production today to sell later on, when it expects prices to be higher.

Table 3.2 summarizes the most important variables that cause market supply curves to shift. Note that the table shows the shift in the supply curve that results from an *increase* in each of the variables. A *decrease* in these variables would cause the supply curve to shift in the opposite direction.   MyEconLab Concept Check

Table 3.2

Variables That Shift Market Supply Curves

An increase in ...	shifts the supply curve ...	because ...
the price of an input		the costs of producing the good rise.
productivity		the costs of producing the good fall.
the price of a substitute in production		more of the substitute is produced and less of the good is produced.
the price of a complement in production		more of the good and the complementary good are produced.
the number of firms in the market		additional firms result in a greater quantity supplied at every price.
the expected future price of the product		less of the good will be offered for sale today to take advantage of the higher price in the future.

Figure 3.6

A Change in Supply versus a Change in Quantity Supplied

If the price of smartwatches rises from $400 to $450, the result will be a movement up the supply curve from point *A* to point *B*—an increase in the quantity supplied by Apple, Samsung, Nokia, and other firms from 6 million to 7 million. If the price of an input decreases, or if another factor changes that causes sellers to supply more of the product at every price, the supply curve will shift to the right—an increase in supply. In this case, the increase in supply from S_1 to S_2 causes the quantity of smartwatches supplied at a price of $450 to increase from 7 million at point *B* to 9 million at point *C*.

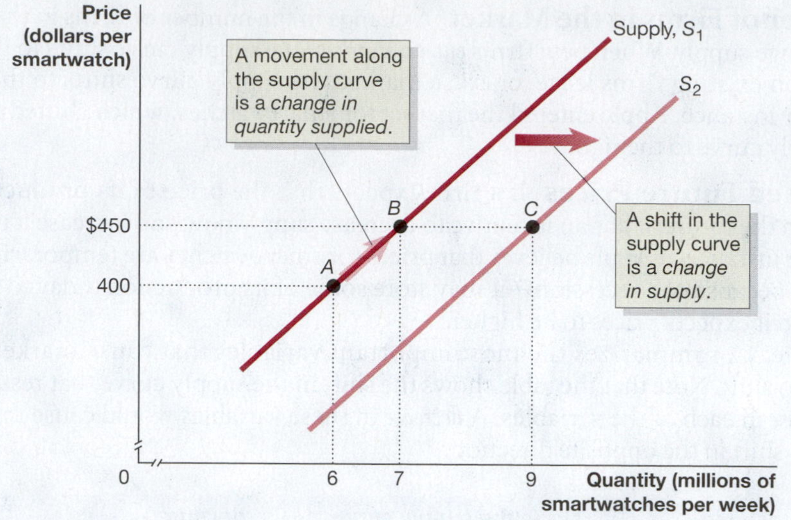

A Change in Supply versus a Change in Quantity Supplied

We noted earlier the important difference between a change in demand and a change in quantity demanded. There is a similar difference between a *change in supply* and a *change in quantity supplied*. A change in supply refers to a shift of the supply curve. The supply curve will shift when there is a change in one of the variables—*other than the price of the product*—that affects the willingness of suppliers to sell the product. A change in quantity supplied refers to a movement along the supply curve as a result of a change in the product's price. Figure 3.6 illustrates this important distinction. If the price of smartwatches rises from $400 to $450, the result will be a movement up the supply curve from point *A* to point *B*—an increase in quantity supplied from 6 million to 7 million. If the price of an input decreases, or if another factor changes that causes sellers to supply more of a product at every price, the supply curve will shift to the right—an increase in supply. In this case, the increase in supply from S_1 to S_2 causes the quantity of smartwatches supplied at a price of $450 to increase from 7 million at point *B* to 9 million at point *C*.

3.3 Market Equilibrium: Putting Demand and Supply Together

LEARNING OBJECTIVE: Use a graph to illustrate market equilibrium.

The purpose of markets is to bring buyers and sellers together. As we saw in Chapter 2, instead of being chaotic and disorderly, the interaction of buyers and sellers in markets ultimately results in firms being led to produce the goods and services that consumers want most. To understand this process, we first need to see how markets work to reconcile the plans of buyers and sellers.

In Figure 3.7, we bring together the market demand curve and the market supply curve for smartwatches. Notice that the demand curve crosses the supply curve at only one point. This point represents a price of $350 and a quantity of 5 million smartwatches per week. Only at this point of **market equilibrium** is the quantity of smartwatches consumers are willing and able to buy equal to the quantity of smartwatches firms are willing and able to sell. In this case, the *equilibrium price* is $350, and the *equilibrium quantity* is 5 million. As we noted at the beginning of the chapter, markets that have many buyers and sellers are competitive markets, and equilibrium in these markets is a **competitive market equilibrium**. In the market for smartwatches, there are many buyers but only about 25 firms. Whether 25 firms are enough for our model of demand and supply to apply to this market is a matter of judgment. In this chapter, we are assuming that the market for smartwatches has enough sellers to be competitive.

Market equilibrium A situation in which quantity demanded equals quantity supplied.

Competitive market equilibrium A market equilibrium with many buyers and sellers.

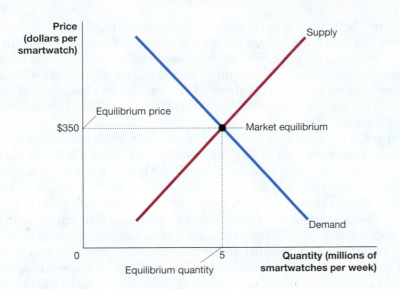

MyEconLab Animation

Figure 3.7

Market Equilibrium

Where the demand curve crosses the supply curve determines market equilibrium. In this case, the demand curve for smartwatches crosses the supply curve at a price of $350 and a quantity of 5 million smartwatches. Only at this point is the quantity of smartwatches consumers are willing to buy equal to the quantity that Apple, Samsung, LG, and other firms are willing to sell: The quantity demanded is equal to the quantity supplied.

How Markets Eliminate Surpluses and Shortages

A market that is not in equilibrium moves toward equilibrium. Once a market is in equilibrium, it remains in equilibrium. To see why, consider what happens if a market is not in equilibrium. Suppose that the price in the market for smartwatches was $400 rather than the equilibrium price of $350. As Figure 3.8 shows, at a price of $400, the quantity of smartwatches supplied would be 6 million, and the quantity of smartwatches demanded would be 4 million. When the quantity supplied is greater than the quantity demanded, there is a **surplus** in the market. In this case, the surplus is

Surplus A situation in which the quantity supplied is greater than the quantity demanded.

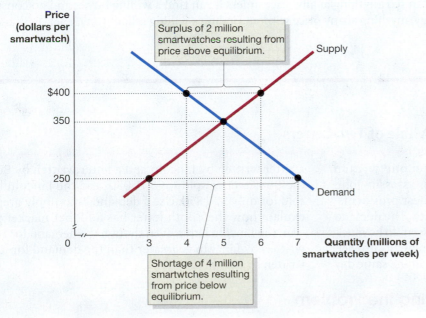

MyEconLab Animation

Figure 3.8   The Effect of Surpluses and Shortages on the Market Price

When the market price is above equilibrium, there will be a *surplus*. A price of $400 for smartwatches results in 6 million smartwatches being supplied but only 4 million being demanded, or a surplus of 2 million. As Apple, Nokia, LG, and other firms cut the price to dispose of the surplus, the price will fall to the equilibrium price of $350. When the market price is below equilibrium, there will be a *shortage*. A price of $250 results in 7 million smartwatches being demanded but only 3 million being supplied, or a shortage of 4 million. As firms find that consumers who are unable to find smartwatches available for sale are willing to pay higher prices to get them, the price will rise to the equilibrium price of $350.

equal to 2 million smartwatches (6 million – 4 million = 2 million). When there is a surplus, firms will have unsold goods piling up, which gives them an incentive to increase their sales by cutting the price. Cutting the price will simultaneously increase the quantity demanded and decrease the quantity supplied. This adjustment will reduce the surplus, but as long as the price is above $350, there will be a surplus, and downward pressure on the price will continue. Only when the price falls to $350 will the market be in equilibrium.

Shortage A situation in which the quantity demanded is greater than the quantity supplied.

If, however, the price were $250, the quantity demanded would be 7 million, and the quantity supplied would be 3 million, as shown in Figure 3.8. When the quantity demanded is greater than the quantity supplied, there is a **shortage** in the market. In this case, the shortage is equal to 4 million smartwatches (7 million – 3 million = 4 million). When a shortage occurs, some consumers will be unable to buy smartwatches at the current price. In this situation, firms will realize that they can raise the price without losing sales. A higher price will simultaneously increase the quantity supplied and decrease the quantity demanded. This adjustment will reduce the shortage, but as long as the price is below $350, there will be a shortage, and upward pressure on the price will continue. Only when the price rises to $350 will the market be in equilibrium.

At a competitive market equilibrium, all consumers willing to pay the market price will be able to buy as much of the product as they want, and all firms willing to accept the market price will be able to sell as much of the product as they want. As a result, there will be no reason for the price to change unless either the demand curve or the supply curve shifts. **MyEconLab** Concept Check

Demand and Supply Both Count

Keep in mind that the interaction of demand and supply determines the equilibrium price. Neither consumers nor firms can dictate what the equilibrium price will be. No firm can sell anything at any price unless it can find a willing buyer, and no consumer can buy anything at any price without finding a willing seller. **MyEconLab** Concept Check

---

Solved Problem 3.3

MyEconLab Interactive Animation

Demand and Supply Both Count: A Tale of Two Letters

Which letter is likely to be worth more: one written by Abraham Lincoln or one written by his assassin, John Wilkes Booth? Lincoln is one of the greatest presidents, and many people collect anything he wrote. The demand for letters written by Lincoln surely would seem to be much greater than the demand for letters written by Booth. Yet, when R.M. Smythe and Co. auctioned off on the same day a letter written by Lincoln and a letter written by Booth, the Booth letter sold for $31,050, and the Lincoln letter sold for only $21,850. Use a demand and supply graph to explain how the Booth letter has a higher market price than the Lincoln letter, even though the demand for letters written by Lincoln is greater than the demand for letters written by Booth.

Solving the Problem

Step 1: **Review the chapter material.** This problem is about prices being determined at market equilibrium, so you may want to review the section "Market Equilibrium: Putting Demand and Supply Together," which begins on page 86.

Step 2: **Draw demand curves that illustrate the greater demand for Lincoln's letters.** Begin by drawing two demand curves. Label one "Demand for Lincoln's letters" and the other "Demand for Booth's letters." Make sure that the Lincoln demand curve is much farther to the right than the Booth demand curve.

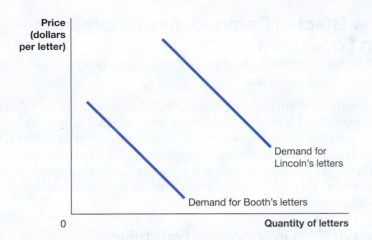

Step 3: **Draw supply curves that illustrate the equilibrium price of Booth's letters being higher than the equilibrium price of Lincoln's letters.** Based on the demand curves you have just drawn, think about how it might be possible for the market price of Lincoln's letters to be lower than the market price of Booth's letters. This outcome can occur only if the supply of Lincoln's letters is much greater than the supply of Booth's letters. Draw on your graph a supply curve for Lincoln's letters and a supply curve for Booth's letters that will result in an equilibrium price of Booth's letters of $31,050 and an equilibrium price of Lincoln's letters of $21,850. You have now solved the problem.

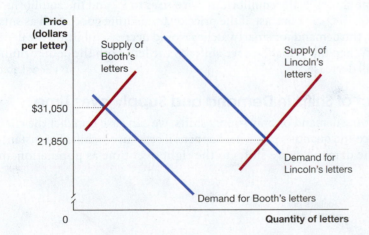

Extra Credit: The explanation for this puzzle is that both demand and supply count when determining market price. The demand for Lincoln's letters is much greater than the demand for Booth's letters, but the supply of Booth's letters is very small. Historians believe that only eight letters written by Booth exist today. (Note that the supply curves for letters written by Booth and by Lincoln are upward sloping, even though only a fixed number of each of these letters is available and, obviously, no more can be produced. The upward slope of the supply curves occurs because the higher the price, the larger the quantity of letters that will be offered for sale by people who currently own them.)

Your Turn: For more practice, do related problems 3.5, 3.6, and 3.7 on page 103 at the end of this chapter.

MyEconLab Study Plan

3.4 | The Effect of Demand and Supply Shifts on Equilibrium

LEARNING OBJECTIVE: Use demand and supply graphs to predict changes in prices and quantities.

We have seen that the interaction of demand and supply in markets determines the quantity of a good that is produced and the price at which it is sold. We have also seen that several variables cause demand curves to shift and other variables cause supply curves to shift. As a result, demand and supply curves in most markets are constantly shifting, and the prices and quantities that represent equilibrium are constantly changing. In this section, we look at how shifts in demand and supply curves affect equilibrium price and quantity.

The Effect of Shifts in Supply on Equilibrium

When Apple entered the market for smartwatches, the market supply curve for smartwatches shifted to the right. Figure 3.9 shows the supply curve shifting from S_1 to S_2. When the supply curve shifts to the right, there will be a surplus at the original equilibrium price, P_1. The surplus is eliminated as the equilibrium price falls to P_2 and the equilibrium quantity rises from Q_1 to Q_2. If an existing firm exits the market, the supply curve will shift to the left, causing the equilibrium price to rise and the equilibrium quantity to fall. **MyEconLab** Concept Check

The Effect of Shifts in Demand on Equilibrium

Because smartwatches are a normal good, when incomes increase, the market demand curve shifts to the right. Figure 3.10 shows the effect of a demand curve shifting to the right, from D_1 to D_2. This shift causes a shortage at the original equilibrium price, P_1. To eliminate the shortage, the equilibrium price rises to P_2, and the equilibrium quantity rises from Q_1 to Q_2. In contrast, if the price of a substitute good, such as smartphones, were to fall, the demand for smartwatches would decrease, shifting the demand curve to the left. When the demand curve shifts to the left, both the equilibrium price and quantity will decrease. **MyEconLab** Concept Check

The Effect of Shifts in Demand and Supply over Time

Whenever only demand or only supply shifts, we can easily predict the effect on equilibrium price and quantity. But, what happens if *both* curves shift? For instance, in many markets, the demand curve shifts to the right over time as population and income

MyEconLab Animation

Figure 3.9

The Effect of an Increase in Supply on Equilibrium

If a firm enters a market, as Apple entered the market for smartwatches, the equilibrium price will fall, and the equilibrium quantity will rise:

1. As Apple enters the market for smartwatches, a larger quantity of smartwatches will be supplied at every price, so the market supply curve shifts to the right, from S_1 to S_2, which causes a surplus of smartwatches at the original price, P_1.
2. The equilibrium price falls from P_1 to P_2.
3. The equilibrium quantity rises from Q_1 to Q_2.

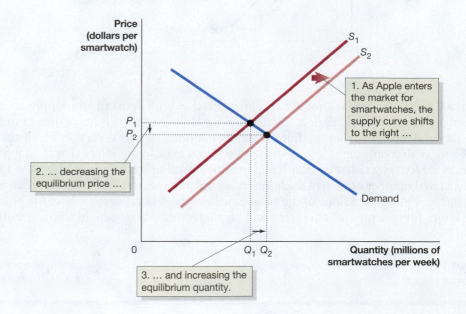

1. As Apple enters the market for smartwatches, the supply curve shifts to the right ...

2. ... decreasing the equilibrium price ...

3. ... and increasing the equilibrium quantity.

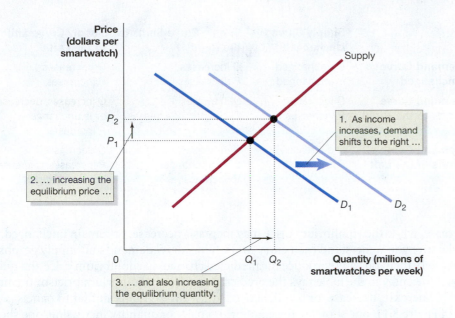

MyEconLab Animation

Figure 3.10

The Effect of an Increase in Demand on Equilibrium

Increases in income will cause the equilibrium price and quantity to rise:

1. Because smartwatches are a normal good, as income increases, the quantity demanded increases at every price, and the market demand curve shifts to the right, from D_1 to D_2, which causes a shortage of smartwatches at the original price, P_1.
2. The equilibrium price rises from P_1 to P_2.
3. The equilibrium quantity rises from Q_1 to Q_2.

increase. The supply curve also often shifts to the right as new firms enter the market and positive technological change occurs. Whether the equilibrium price in a market rises or falls over time depends on whether demand shifts to the right more than does supply. Panel (a) of Figure 3.11 shows that when demand shifts to the right more than supply, the equilibrium price rises, while panel (b) shows that when supply shifts to the right more than demand, the equilibrium price falls.

Table 3.3 on page 92 summarizes all possible combinations of shifts in demand and supply over time and the effects of the shifts on equilibrium price (*P*) and quantity (*Q*). For example, the entry in red in the table shows that if the demand curve shifts to the right and the supply curve also shifts to the right, the equilibrium quantity will

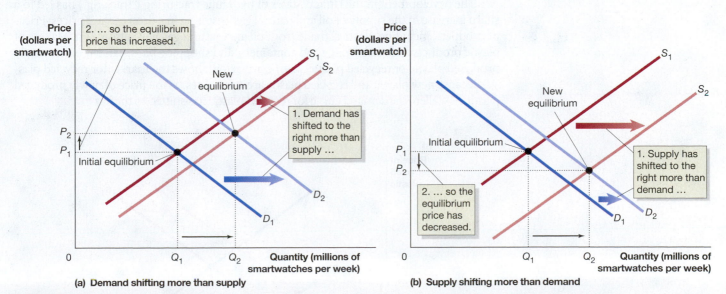

Figure 3.11   Shifts in Demand and Supply over Time

Whether the price of a product rises or falls over time depends on whether demand shifts to the right more than supply.

In panel (a), demand shifts to the right more than supply, and the equilibrium price rises:
1. Demand shifts to the right more than supply.
2. The equilibrium price rises from P_1 to P_2.

In panel (b), supply shifts to the right more than demand, and the equilibrium price falls:
1. Supply shifts to the right more than demand.
2. The equilibrium price falls from P_1 to P_2.

Table 3.3

How Shifts in Demand and Supply Affect Equilibrium Price (P) and Quantity (Q)
The entry in red shows that if the demand curve shifts to the right and the supply curve also shifts to the right, the equilibrium quantity will increase, while the equilibrium price may increase, decrease, or remain unchanged.

	Supply Curve Unchanged	Supply Curve Shifts to the Right	Supply Curve Shifts to the Left
Demand Curve Unchanged	Q unchanged P unchanged	Q increases P decreases	Q decreases P increases
Demand Curve Shifts to the Right	Q increases P increases	Q increases P increases, decreases, or is unchanged	Q increases, decreases, or is unchanged P increases
Demand Curve Shifts to the Left	Q decreases P decreases	Q increases, decreases, or is unchanged P decreases	Q decreases P increases, decreases, or is unchanged

increase, while the equilibrium price may increase, decrease, or remain unchanged. To make sure you understand each entry in the table, draw demand and supply graphs to check whether you can reproduce the predicted changes in equilibrium price and quantity. If the entry in the table says the predicted change in equilibrium price or quantity can be increase, decrease, or be unchanged, draw three graphs similar to panels (a) or (b) of Figure 3.11, one showing the equilibrium price or quantity increasing, one showing it decreasing, and one showing it unchanged.   MyEconLab Concept Check

Making the Connection
MyEconLab Video

Demand and Supply Trashes Plastic Recycling

Cities hire private firms to collect plastic bottles and containers for recycling. Until recently, recycling was profitable for these firms. The profits attracted thieves who would steal the used bottles and containers from recycling bins before the firms could pick them up. By 2015, though, firms no longer had to worry about thieves because they had bigger problems: Falling oil prices were decreasing the demand for recycled plastic at the same time that costs were rising as cities began requiring recycling firms to recycle many more types of plastic.

The development in the United States of hydraulic fracturing ("fracking") has led to a sharp increase in the supply of oil and natural gas, resulting in a drop in their prices. Prices of products, including plastics, made from oil and natural gas have also fallen. Makers of plastic products such as bottles, food containers, and shopping bags, can use either newly produced plastic or recycled plastic. The figure below shows the market for recycled plastic. Because new plastic and recycled plastic are substitutes, as the price of newly produced plastic has fallen, the demand curve for recycled plastic has shifted to the left.

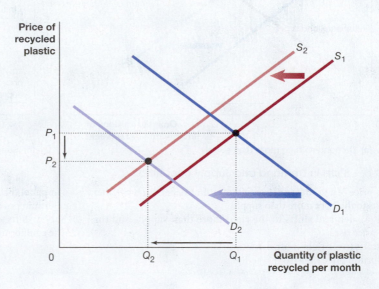

Many cities began plastic recycling by focusing on soda and milk bottles. But as recycling plans have become more ambitious, cities have required recycling firms to pick up nearly all plastics, including products like shopping bags and fast-food containers that are made of lower-quality plastic. It's costly for firms to separate different types of plastic before they can be processed and resold. This increase in cost shifts the supply curve for recycled plastic to the left. The figure shows that the equilibrium price of recycled plastic fell from P_1 to P_2, and the equilibrium quantity fell from Q_1 to Q_2. (Note that if the shift in the supply curve had been greater than the shift in the demand curve, the equilibrium price would have increased.)

As the quantity of recycled plastic declined, a number of recycling firms went out of business. Other firms stored plastic recyclables in the hopes that oil prices would eventually rise, increasing the demand for recyclable plastic.

The effects of these shifts in demand and supply were not good news for the recycling programs in many cities. Plastic recycling had been a steady source of revenue for local governments, but now they faced losing money by having to pay recycling companies to haul away some plastic the companies could no longer sell for a profit. Unless cities were willing to suffer losses or scale back their recycling programs, they would have to hope that higher oil prices might eventually increase the demand for recycled plastic.

Sources: Georgi Kantchev and Serena Ng, "Recycling Becomes a Tougher Sell as Oil Prices Drop," *Wall Street Journal*, April 5, 2015; Stacey Vanek Smith, "How the Price of Oil Caused a Downturn in the Recycling Business," npr.org, April 3, 2015; and Aaron Elstein, "City's Recycling Is Trashed as Cheap Oil Sinks Plastic," crainsnewyork.com, May 10, 2015.

Your Turn: Test your understanding by doing related problem 4.6 on page 104 at the end of this chapter.

The decline in demand for recycled plastic has left some recycling firms stuck with mountains of plastic bottles.

MyEconLab Study Plan

Solved Problem 3.4

MyEconLab Interactive Animation

Can We Predict Changes in the Price and Quantity of Beef?

Whether you like to eat hamburger or roast beef, the source of the meat is a rancher who raises cattle. A news story discussed how years of drought had raised the cost to ranchers of raising cattle. At the same time, consumer tastes have been changing, leading to a decline in the demand for beef. Use demand and supply graphs to illustrate your answers to the following questions:

a. Can we use this information to be certain whether the equilibrium quantity of beef will increase or decrease?

b. Can we use this information to be certain whether the equilibrium price of beef will increase or decrease?

Solving the Problem

Step 1: **Review the chapter material.** This problem is about how shifts in demand and supply curves affect the equilibrium price, so you may want to review the section "The Effect of Shifts in Demand and Supply over Time," which begins on page 90.

Step 2: **Answer part (a) using demand and supply analysis.** You are given the information that consumer tastes have changed, leading to a decline in demand for beef. So, the demand curve for beef has shifted to the left. You are also given the information that the cost of raising beef has increased. So, the supply curve for beef has also shifted to the left. The following graph shows both these shifts:

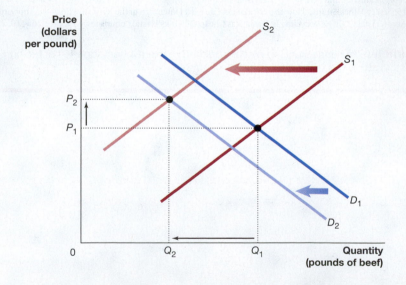

As Table 3.3 on page 92 summarizes, if the demand curve and the supply curve both shift to the left, the equilibrium quantity must decrease. Therefore, we can answer part (a) by stating that we are certain that the equilibrium quantity of beef will decrease.

Step 3: **Answer part (b) using demand and supply analysis.** The graph we drew in step 2 shows the equilibrium price of beef increasing. But given the information provided, the following graph would also be correct:

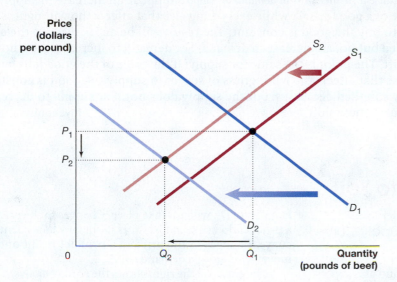

Unlike the graph in step 2, which shows the equilibrium price increasing, this graph shows the equilibrium price decreasing. The uncertainty about whether the equilibrium price will increase or decrease is consistent with what Table 3.3 shows happens when the demand curve and the supply curve both shift to the left. Therefore, the answer to part (b) is that we cannot be certain whether the equilibrium price of beef will increase or decrease.

Extra Credit: During 2013 and 2014, the equilibrium quantity of beef decreased while the equilibrium price of beef increased. We can conclude that *both* the decrease in demand for beef and the decrease in the supply of beef contributed to the decline in beef consumption. That the price of beef rose indicates that the decrease in supply had a larger effect on equilibrium in the beef market than did the decrease in demand.

Sources: Andrew Schneider, "No 'Misteak': High Beef Prices a Boon for Drought-Weary Ranchers," npr.com, November 19, 2014; and U.S. Department of Agriculture data.

Your Turn: For more practice, do related problems 4.7 and 4.8 on page 104 at the end of this chapter.

MyEconLab Study Plan

Shifts in a Curve versus Movements along a Curve

When analyzing markets using demand and supply curves, remember that *when a shift in a demand or supply curve causes a change in equilibrium price, the change in price does not cause a further shift in demand or supply*. Suppose an increase in supply causes the price of a good to fall, while everything else that affects the willingness of consumers to buy the good is constant. The result will be an increase in the quantity demanded but not an increase in demand. For demand to increase, the whole curve must shift. The point is the same for supply: If the price of the good falls but everything else that affects the willingness of sellers to supply the good is constant, the quantity supplied decreases, but the supply does not. For supply to decrease, the whole curve must shift.

MyEconLab Study Plan

MyEconLab Concept Check

Don't Let This Happen to You

Remember: A Change in a Good's Price Does *Not* Cause the Demand or Supply Curve to Shift

Suppose a student is asked to draw a demand and supply graph to illustrate how an increase in the price of oranges would affect the market for apples, with other variables being constant. He draws the graph on the left and explains it as follows: "Because apples and oranges are substitutes, an increase in the price of oranges will cause an initial shift to the right in the demand curve for apples, from D_1 to D_2. However, because this initial shift in the demand curve for apples results in a higher price for apples, P_2, consumers will find apples less desirable, and the demand curve will shift to the left, from D_2 to D_3, resulting in a final equilibrium price of P_3." Do you agree or disagree with the student's analysis?

MyEconLab Study Plan

You should disagree. The student has correctly understood that an increase in the price of oranges will cause the demand curve for apples to shift to the right. But, the second demand curve shift the student describes, from D_2 to D_3, will not take place. Changes in the price of a product do not result in shifts in the product's demand curve. Changes in the price of a product result only in movements along a demand curve.

The graph on the right shows the correct analysis. The increase in the price of oranges causes the demand curve for apples to increase from D_1 to D_2. At the original price, P_1, the increase in demand initially results in a shortage of apples equal to $Q_3 - Q_1$. But, as we have seen, a shortage causes the price to increase until the shortage is eliminated. In this case, the price will rise to P_2, where both the quantity demanded and the quantity supplied are equal to Q_2. Notice that the increase in price causes a decrease in the *quantity demanded*, from Q_3 to Q_2, but does *not* cause a decrease in demand.

Your Turn: Test your understanding by doing related problems 4.13 and 4.14 on page 105 at the end of this chapter.

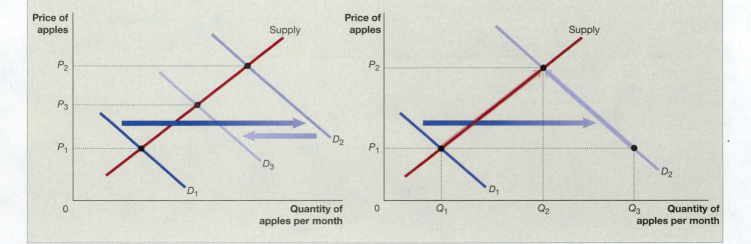

Continued from page 73

Economics in Your Life

Will You Buy a Smartphone or a Smartwatch?

At the beginning of this chapter, we asked you to consider how you might choose between buying a smartwatch and buying a smartphone. There are certain activities, such as watching YouTube or Netflix, that you can do on a smartphone but not on a smartwatch. There are other activities, such as tracking calories burned during a workout, that are probably easier to do on a smartwatch. If you can engage in the activities you like most on either device, then you probably consider the two devices to be close substitutes, and you are likely to buy the one with the lower price. Suppose that you are currently leaning toward buying a smartphone because its price is lower than the price of a comparable smartwatch. If an increase in your income would cause you to change your decision and buy the smartwatch, then the smartphone is an inferior good for you.

Conclusion

The interaction of demand and supply determines market equilibrium. The model of demand and supply is a powerful tool for predicting how changes in the actions of consumers and firms will cause changes in equilibrium prices and quantities. As we have seen in this chapter, we can use the model to analyze markets that do not meet all the requirements for being perfectly competitive. As long as there is intense competition among sellers, the model of demand and supply can often successfully predict changes in prices and quantities. We will use this model in the next chapter to analyze economic efficiency and the results of government-imposed price floors and price ceilings.

Before moving on to Chapter 4, read *An Inside Look* on the next page for a discussion of how the Apple watch has inspired companies to develop complementary products.

WALL STREET JOURNAL

Don't Underestimate Smartwatches: Wearable Devices Are Poised to Become Central to the Tech Ecosystem

(a) It's important to understand that like the iPhone before it, the Apple Watch isn't at all what its name would imply. Let's call it what it is: a wrist-top computer.

Just as smartphones have become supercomputers in our pockets, the Apple Watch and its many competitors, including Android-powered devices from Motorola and Samsung Electronics, are poised to become something more. And it is their central place in a larger ecosystem of apps and hardware, rather than any one thing that has been shown off recently, that will make them indispensable. ...

When a company like Google or Apple deliberately creates a place for other companies to sell their own, complementary wares, it is called a platform. Apple, more than Google, has mastered this art, having worked hard to give developers the tools to make apps for its mobile devices, plus a controlled environment in which to profit from them.

Fortunately, we don't have to wait for the Apple Watch and its app store to become available to get a glimpse of where things could be going. We have only to look at what pioneering companies in "wearables" are already working on, and then think about how their products will become a part of—or be absorbed

by—the Apple Watch and Android Wear ecosystems.

(b) "The vision of Sensoria is that the garment is the next ultra personal computer," says Sensoria CEO Davide Vigano. To illustrate his point, he rolls up his pants leg to show me a working prototype of the world's first smart sock.

I know, it sounds ridiculous. But, as he explains, with the help of an iPhone app that visualizes wireless signals sent by indiscernibly thin pressure sensors in the sock, it is good for runners who want to reduce their chance of injury. It is also potentially useful for monitoring the health of the elderly, since changes in gait are surprisingly predictive of other health issues. And yes, the smart sock is washable.

Sensoria also makes a smart bra and smart shirt, both of which can measure heart rate. And here's where things get really interesting: For all makers of wearables, which until recently have been dominated by the glorified pedometers known as fitness bands, fitness applications are just the beginning.

Using a few more of the same sensors it already carries, Sensoria's shirt could measure not just the frequency but the pattern of a wearer's heartbeat, Mr. Vigano tells me. Like the fingerprint sensor on new smartphones, the unique shape of the electrical signals generated by our hearts are a biometric. Add in a payment terminal not dissimilar from the ones that will roll out with Apple Pay, and the wearer of a Sensoria undergarment could soon find herself verifying payment for her next coffee via technology in her bra. ...

During Apple's presentation, Apple Vice President Kevin Lynch announced that BMW has developed an app for the Apple Watch that will allow users to lock and unlock their BMW i-series electric vehicles. And Mr. Martin told me that new bluetooth-enabled locks from companies like Lockitron and Kwikset mean that the moment you walk up to a door while sporting a recognized wearable, it can unlock without a touch. ...

(c) Wearables won't just appeal to fitness nuts and quantified-self geeks. They will appeal to everyone, because they will be the primary, perhaps even the sole way we identify ourselves to a world full of smart objects.

Established makers of wearables have seen this trend and are already getting in front of it. On the same day that Apple announced its watch, Jawbone, maker of the UP wristband, said that it was opening up its quantified-self software so that anyone could connect it with devices other than the UP—including the Apple Watch.

Or in other words, amid the hype about the Apple Watch being a fitness device, or a timepiece, or a status symbol, it is the applications that Apple and others aren't even talking about, the ones that are thought up by countless developers jumping on board the platform, that will make us wonder how we ever got by without them. ...

Source: Christopher Mims, "Don't Underestimate Smartwatches: Wearable Devices Are Poised to Become Central to the Tech Ecosystem," *Wall Street Journal*, September 14, 2014.

Key Points in the Article

The introduction of the Apple Watch has inspired a number of companies to develop products that can utilize the smartwatch's technology. From the wearable technology of Sensoria's sensor-enhanced clothing to convenience items like Bluetooth-enabled door locks, these complementary products will allow consumers to use their smartwatches in new ways, including monitoring their health, making online purchases, and unlocking their front doors. In our technology-driven society, as more products and apps are developed for use with smartwatches, consumers could come to view these watches as a necessity rather than a luxury, which is what happened with smartphones.

Analyzing the News

(a) Smartwatches like the Apple Watch are a part of the relatively new product category of wearable technology. As with smartphones, a large part of the success of smartwatches will depend on the availability of desirable complementary products. One variable that shifts market demand for a product is the price of related goods. If the price of a complement decreases, market demand for the original product will increase, and if the price of a complement increases, market demand for the original product will decrease.

(b) Smart shirts are wearable technology garments that will sync with smatrwatches,

so the two products are used together and are therefore complements. Suppose the figure below illustrates supply and demand for smart shirts. In 2015, the most basic smartwatch model had a price of about $350, and at this price, the demand for smart shirts is represented by demand curve D_1, with an equilibrium price of P_1 and an equilibrium quantity of Q_1. If the price of smartwatches increases, this increase would, holding everything else constant, result in a decrease in demand for smart shirts. The demand curve would shift to the left, from D_1 to D_3, resulting in a decrease in the equilibrium price from P_1 to P_3 and a decrease in the equilibrium quantity from Q_1 to Q_3. If the price of smartwatches declines, the result will be an increase in demand for smart shirts. The demand curve would shift to the right, from D_1 to D_2, resulting in an increase in the equilibrium price from P_1 to P_2 and an increase in the equilibrium quantity from Q_1 to Q_2.

(c) As wearable technology grows in popularity, more firms will enter the market to compete with existing firms. Some of these firms will offer new products, while other firms will produce goods that compete with existing products. Suppose another apparel manufacturer designs a product to compete with smart shirts. This new product would be a substitute for smart shirts and, all else being equal, changes in the price of this new substitute would change the demand for smart shirts.

In the figure below, an increase in the price of a substitute would, holding everything else constant, increase the demand for smart shirts. The demand curve would shift to the right, from D_1 to D_2, resulting in an increase in the equilibrium price from P_1 to P_2 and an increase in the equilibrium quantity from Q_1 to Q_2. A decrease in the price of a substitute would have the opposite effect, resulting in a decrease in demand for smart shirts. The demand curve would shift to the left, from D_1 to D_3, resulting in a decrease in the equilibrium price from P_1 to P_3 and a decrease in the equilibrium quantity from Q_1 to Q_3.

Thinking Critically

1. Suppose a technological change allows firms to lower the cost of producing smart shirts. Explain if this change will affect the demand curve for smart shirts. How would this change affect the market for smartwatches?

2. In 2015, smartwatch producers had difficulty filling the orders they received. Draw a demand and supply graph to illustrate this situation. All else equal, what would you expect to happen in this market if this situation persisted into the future, and how would this affect the market for complementary products like smart shirts?

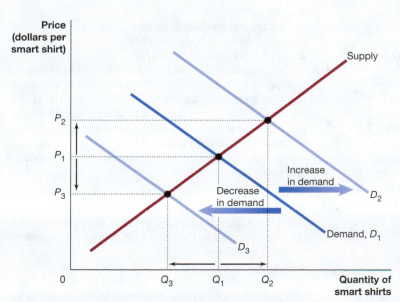

An increase in demand for smart shirts shifts the demand curve to the right. All else equal, equilibrium price and equilibrium quantity both increase. A decrease in demand has the opposite effect.

CHAPTER SUMMARY AND PROBLEMS

Key Terms

Ceteris paribus ("all else equal") condition, p. 76

Competitive market equilibrium, p. 87

Complements, p. 78

Demand curve, p. 74

Demand schedule, p. 74

Demographics, p. 78

Income effect, p. 75

Inferior good, p. 77

Law of demand, p. 75

Law of supply, p. 83

Market demand, p. 74

Market equilibrium, p. 86

Normal good, p. 76

Perfectly competitive market, p. 74

Quantity demanded, p. 74

Quantity supplied, p. 82

Shortage, p. 88

Substitutes, p. 77

Substitution effect, p. 75

Supply curve, p. 83

Supply schedule, p. 83

Surplus, p. 87

Technological change, p. 84

3.1 **The Demand Side of the Market, pages 74–82**

LEARNING OBJECTIVE: List and describe the variables that influence demand.

Summary

The model of demand and supply is the most powerful tool in economics. The model applies exactly only to **perfectly competitive markets**, where there are many buyers and sellers, all the products sold are identical, and there are no barriers to new sellers entering the market. But the model can also be useful in analyzing markets that don't meet all these requirements. The **quantity demanded** is the amount of a good or service that a consumer is willing and able to purchase at a given price. A **demand schedule** is a table that shows the relationship between the price of a product and the quantity of the product demanded. A **demand curve** is a graph that shows the relationship between the price of a product and the quantity of the product demanded. **Market demand** is the demand by all consumers of a given good or service. The **law of demand** states that *ceteris paribus*—holding everything else constant—the quantity of a product demanded increases when the price falls and decreases when the price rises. Demand curves slope downward because of the **substitution effect**, which is the change in quantity demanded that results from a price change making one good more or less expensive relative to another good, and the **income effect**, which is the change in quantity demanded of a good that results from the effect of a change in the good's price on consumer purchasing power. Changes in income, the prices of related goods, tastes, population and demographics, and expected future prices all cause the demand curve to shift. **Substitutes** are goods that can be used for the same purpose. **Complements** are goods that are used together. A **normal good** is a good for which demand increases as income increases. An **inferior good** is a good for which demand decreases as income increases. **Demographics** refers to the characteristics of a population with respect to age, race, and gender. A change in demand refers to a shift of the demand curve. A change in quantity demanded refers to a movement along the demand curve as a result of a change in the product's price.

 Visit **www.myeconlab.com** to complete these exercises online and get instant feedback.

Review Questions

1.1 What is a demand schedule? What is a demand curve?

1.2 What do economists mean when they use the Latin expression *ceteris paribus*?

1.3 What is the difference between a change in demand and a change in quantity demanded?

1.4 What is the law of demand? Use the substitution effect and the income effect to explain why an increase in the price of a product causes a decrease in the quantity demanded.

1.5 What are the main variables that will cause the demand curve to shift? Give an example of each.

Problems and Applications

1.6 For each of the following pairs of products, briefly explain which are complements, which are substitutes, and which are unrelated.
  a. New cars and used cars
  b. Houses and washing machines
  c. UGG boots and Apple Watches
  d. Apple Watches and Apple iPads

1.7 An article in the *Wall Street Journal* titled "Auto Sales Zoom, Helped by Low Prices at the Pump" includes a graphic showing increasing car and truck sales in one panel and decreasing gasoline prices in the other panel. Does the graphic assume that autos and gasoline are substitutes or complements? Briefly explain.

  Source: "Auto Sales Zoom, Helped by Low Prices at the Pump," *Wall Street Journal*, December 3, 2014.

1.8 **(Related to the Chapter Opener on page 73)** A number of industry analysts believe that smartphone prices will decline over the next few years. If these forecasts are correct, what will be the effect on the demand for smartwatches? Briefly explain.

  Sources: Phil Goldstein, "IDC: Smartphone Shipments to Hit 1.4B in 2015, and Prices Will Keep Falling," fiercewireless.com, December 2, 2014; and Rob van der Meulen, "Gartner Says Global Devices Shipments to Grow 2.8 Percent in 2015," gartner.com, March 19, 2015.

1.9 State whether each of the following events will result in a movement along the demand curve for McDonald's Big Mac hamburgers or whether it will cause the curve to shift. If the demand curve shifts, indicate whether it will shift to the left or to the right and draw a graph to illustrate the shift.

a. The price of Burger King's Whopper hamburger declines.

b. McDonald's distributes coupons for $1.00 off the purchase of a Big Mac.

c. Because of a shortage of potatoes, the price of French fries increases.

d. Fast-food restaurants post nutrition warning labels.

e. The U.S. economy enters a period of rapid growth in incomes.

1.10 Suppose that the following table shows the quantity demanded of UGG boots at five different prices in 2016 and 2017:

	Quantity Demanded (thousands of pairs of boots)	
Price	2016	2017
$160	5,000	4,000
170	4,500	3,500
180	4,000	3,000
190	3,500	2,500
200	3,000	2,000

Name two different variables that if their values were to change would cause the quantity demanded of UGG boots to change from 2016 to 2017, as indicated in the table.

1.11 Suppose that the curves in the following graph represent two demand curves for traditional chicken wings (basket of six) at Buffalo Wild Wings. What would cause a movement from point A to point B on D_1? Name two variables that if their values were to change would cause a movement from point A to point C.

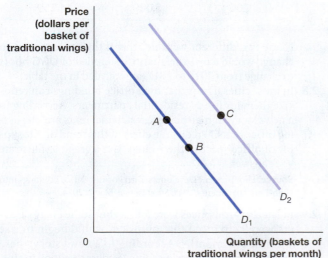

1.12 **(Related to the** Making the Connection **on page 77)** Both smartwatches and smartphones use applications, or "apps," which are software that consumers can download and use to play games, check stock market prices, and read news stories, among many other activities. Particularly useful apps are called "killer apps." One industry analyst remarked, "There is no one killer app for smartwatches." If the analyst's observation is correct, does it make smartwatches closer or less close substitutes for smartphones? Briefly explain.

Source: Daniel Matte and Kevin McCullagh, "Will Smartwatches Be a Hit?" *Wall Street Journal*, May 10, 2015

1.13 **(Related to the** Making the Connection **on page 78)** Since 1979, China has had a policy that allows couples to have only one child. This policy has caused a change in the demographics of China. Between 1980 and 2013, the share of the population under age 14 decreased from 36 percent to 18 percent. And, as parents attempt to ensure that the lone child is a son, the number of newborn males relative to females has increased. Choose three goods and explain how the demand for them has been affected by China's one-child policy.

Sources: World Bank, *World Development Indicators*, April 2015; and "China's Family Planning: Illegal Children Will Be Confiscated" and "China's Population: Only and Lonely," *Economist*, July 21, 2011.

1.14 Suppose the following table shows the price of a base model Toyota Prius hybrid and the quantity of Priuses sold for three years. Do these data indicate that the demand curve for Priuses is upward sloping? Briefly explain.

Year	Price	Quantity
2014	$31,880	35,265
2015	30,550	33,250
2016	33,250	36,466

1.15 An article in the *Wall Street Journal* noted that an "increase in the price of oil quickly reduces demand for oil." Do you agree with this statement? Briefly explain.

Source: Josh Zumbrun, "Oil's Plunge Could Help Send Its Price Back Up," *Wall Street Journal*, February 22, 2015.

1.16 A journalist wrote the following about the effects of falling gasoline prices: "With lower prices, demand rises and people consume more." Briefly explain whether you agree with the journalist's analysis.

Source: Jeff Sommer, "Cheaper Oil, Fatter Wallets and a National Opportunity," *New York Times*, December 20, 2014.

1.17 **(Related to the** Making the Connection **on page 81)** According to an article in the *Wall Street Journal* in 2015, "Apple Inc.'s surging smartphone sales in China may have busted a myth: that many Chinese consumers couldn't, or wouldn't, shell out for an iPhone." The article noted that iPhone sales were growing faster in China than in the United States, Europe, or other high-income countries.

a. Why would sales of iPhones be likely to be growing faster in China than in the United States and in other high-income countries?

b. Why were many industry analysts surprised by Apple's strong sales in China? Would forecasting sales in the United States be easier or harder than forecasting sales in countries such as China? Briefly explain.

Source: Juro Osawan, "China's Middle-Class Propels Apple's iPhone Sales," *Wall Street Journal*, April 28, 2015.

3.2 **The Supply Side of the Market, pages 82-86**

LEARNING OBJECTIVE: List and describe the variables that influence supply.

Summary

The **quantity supplied** is the amount of a good that a firm is willing and able to supply at a given price. A **supply schedule** is a table that shows the relationship between the price of a product and the quantity of the product supplied. A **supply curve** is a curve that shows the relationship between the price of a product and the quantity of the product supplied. When the price of a product rises, producing the product is more profitable, and a greater amount will be supplied. The **law of supply** states that, holding everything else constant, the quantity of a product supplied increases when the price rises and decreases when the price falls. Changes in the prices of inputs, technology, the prices of related goods in production, the number of firms in a market, and expected future prices all cause the supply curve to shift. **Technological change** is a positive or negative change in the ability of a firm to produce a given level of output with a given quantity of inputs. A change in supply refers to a shift of the supply curve. A change in quantity supplied refers to a movement along the supply curve as a result of a change in the product's price.

MyEconLab   Visit **www.myeconlab.com** to complete these exercises online and get instant feedback.

Review Questions

2.1 What is a supply schedule? What is a supply curve?

2.2 What is the difference between a change in supply and a change in the quantity supplied?

2.3 What is the law of supply? What are the main variables that cause a supply curve to shift? Give an example of each.

Problems and Applications

2.4 Briefly explain whether each of the following statements describes a change in supply or a change in quantity supplied.
   a. To take advantage of high prices for snow shovels during a snowy winter, Alexander Shovels, Inc., decides to increase output.
   b. The success of the Apple Watch leads more firms to begin producing smartwatches.
   c. In the six months following the Japanese earthquake and tsunami in 2011, production of automobiles in Japan declined by 20 percent.

2.5 According to a news story about the International Energy Agency, the agency forecast that "the current slide in [oil] prices won't [reduce] global supply." Would a decline in oil prices ever cause a reduction in the supply of oil? Briefly explain.
   Source: Sarah Kent, "Plunging Oil Prices Won't Dent Supply in Short Term," *Wall Street Journal*, December 12, 2014.

2.6 Suppose that the curves in the following graph represent two supply curves for traditional chicken wings (basket of six) at Buffalo Wild Wings. What would cause

a movement from point A to point B on S_1? Name two variables that if their values were to change would cause a movement from point A to point C.

2.7 Suppose that the following table shows the quantity supplied of UGG boots at five different prices in 2016 and 2017:

	Quantity Supplied (thousands of pairs of boots)	
Price	2016	2017
$160	3,000	2,000
170	3,500	2,500
180	4,000	3,000
190	4,500	3,500
200	5,000	4,500

Name two different variables that if their values were to change would cause the quantity supplied of UGG boots to change from 2016 to 2017, as indicated in the table.

2.8 In most cities, firms that own office buildings can renovate them for use as residential apartments. According to a news story, in many cities "residential rents are surpassing office rents." Predict the effect of this trend on the supply of office space in these cities. Use a graph to illustrate your answer.
   Source: Eliot Brown, "Developers Turn Former Office Buildings into High-End Apartments," *Wall Street Journal*, May 7, 2014.

2.9 In late 2014, oil prices were falling, but some energy traders were convinced that oil prices would begin to rise within a few months. According to a news story, these expectations were causing some "traders to put oil in storage while they wait for prices to rise." Predict the effect of this strategy for the supply of oil. Use a graph to illustrate your answer.
   Source: Nicole Friedman, "Saudi Arabia's Surprise Move Spurs Quirk for U.S. Oil Futures," *Wall Street Journal*, November 4, 2014.

3.3 Market Equilibrium: Putting Demand and Supply Together, pages 86–89
LEARNING OBJECTIVE: Use a graph to illustrate market equilibrium.

Summary

Market equilibrium occurs where the demand curve intersects the supply curve. A **competitive market equilibrium** has a market equilibrium with many buyers and sellers. Only at this point is the quantity demanded equal to the quantity supplied. Prices above equilibrium result in **surpluses**, with the quantity supplied being greater than the quantity demanded. Surpluses cause the market price to fall. Prices below equilibrium result in **shortages**, with the quantity demanded being greater than the quantity supplied. Shortages cause the market price to rise.

MyEconLab Visit www.myeconlab.com to complete these exercises online and get instant feedback.

Review Questions

3.1 What do economists mean by *market equilibrium*?

3.2 What do economists mean by *shortage*? By *surplus*?

3.3 What happens in a market if the current price is above the equilibrium price? What happens if the current price is below the equilibrium price?

Problems and Applications

3.4 Briefly explain whether you agree with the following statement: "When there is a shortage of a good, consumers eventually give up trying to buy it, so the demand for the good declines, and the price falls until the market is finally in equilibrium."

3.5 (Related to Solved Problem 3.3 on page 88) In *The Wealth of Nations*, Adam Smith discussed what has come to be known as the "diamond and water paradox":

> Nothing is more useful than water: but it will purchase scarce anything; scarce anything can be had in exchange for it. A diamond, on the contrary, has scarce any value in use; but a very great quantity of other goods may frequently be had in exchange for it.

Graph the market for diamonds and the market for water. Show how it is possible for the price of water to be much lower than the price of diamonds, even though the demand for water is much greater than the demand for diamonds.

Source: Adam Smith, *An Inquiry into the Nature and Causes of the Wealth of Nations*, Vol. I, Oxford, UK: Oxford University Press, 1976; original edition, 1776.

3.6 (Related to Solved Problem 3.3 on page 88) An article discusses the market for autographs by Mickey Mantle, the superstar center fielder for the New York Yankees during the 1950s and 1960s: "At card shows, golf outings, charity dinners, Mr. Mantle signed his name over and over." One expert on sport autographs is quoted as saying, "He was a real good signer. … He is not rare." Yet the article quotes another expert as saying, "Mr. Mantle's autograph ranks No. 3 of most-popular autographs, behind Babe Ruth and Muhammad Ali." A baseball signed by Mantle is likely to sell for the relatively high price of $250 to $400. By contrast, baseballs signed by Whitey Ford, a teammate of Mantle's on the Yankees, typically sell for less than $150. Use one graph to show both the demand and supply for autographs by Whitey Ford and the demand and supply for autographs by Mickey Mantle. Show how it is possible for the price of Mantle's autographs to be higher than the price of Ford's autographs, even though the supply of Mantle autographs is larger than the supply of Ford autographs.

Source: Beth DeCarbo, "Mantle Autographs Not Rare, but Collectors Don't Care," *Wall Street Journal*, August 4, 2008.

3.7 (Related to Solved Problem 3.3 on page 88) Comic book fans eagerly compete to buy copies of *Amazing Fantasy* No. 15, which contains the first appearance of the superhero Spider-Man. At the same time the publisher printed copies of the comic for the U.S. market, with the price printed on the cover in cents, it printed copies for the U.K. market, with the price printed on the cover in British pence. About 10 times as many U.S. copies of *Amazing Fantasy* No. 15 have survived as U.K. copies. Yet in auctions that occurred at about the same time, a U.S. copy sold for $29,000, while a U.K. copy in the same condition sold for only $10,755. Use a demand and supply graph to explain how the U.S. version of the comic has a higher price than the U.K. version, even though the supply of the U.S. version is so much greater than the supply of the U.K. version.

Source: Auction price data from *GPA Analysis for CGC Comics*, www.comics.gpanalysis.com.

3.8 If a market is in equilibrium, is it necessarily true that all buyers and sellers are satisfied with the market price? Briefly explain.

3.9 A news story from 2015 about the oil market stated, "the global glut of crude that has hit [oil] prices is starting to shrink."
   a. What does the article mean by a "glut"? What does a glut imply about the quantity demanded of oil relative to the quantity supplied?
   b. What would be the effect of the glut on oil prices?
   c. Briefly explain what would make the glut start to shrink.

Source: Christopher Harder, "Investors Take Closer Look at Output," *Wall Street Journal*, May 18, 2015.

3.4 **The Effect of Demand and Supply Shifts on Equilibrium, pages 90–96**

LEARNING OBJECTIVE: Use demand and supply graphs to predict changes in prices and quantities.

Summary

In most markets, demand and supply curves shift frequently, causing changes in equilibrium prices and quantities. Over time, if demand increases more than supply, equilibrium price will rise. If supply increases more than demand, equilibrium price will fall.

 MyEconLab   Visit **www.myeconlab.com** to complete these exercises online and get instant feedback.

Review Questions

4.1 Draw a demand and supply graph to show the effect on the equilibrium price in a market in the following situations.
  a. The demand curve shifts to the right.
  b. The supply curve shifts to the left.

4.2 If, over time, the demand curve for a product shifts to the right more than the supply curve does, what will happen to the equilibrium price? What will happen to the equilibrium price if the supply curve shifts to the right more than the demand curve? For each case, draw a demand and supply graph to illustrate your answer.

Problems and Applications

4.3 **(Related to the Chapter Opener on page 73)** Suppose the demand for smartwatches increases rapidly during 2016. At the same time, six more firms begin producing smartwatches. A student remarks that, because of these events, we can't know for certain whether the price of smartwatches will rise or fall. Briefly explain whether you agree. Be sure to include a demand and supply graph of the market for smartwatches to illustrate your answer.

4.4 According to an article in the *Wall Street Journal*, a decline in demand for ethanol, which is made from corn, has reduced the demand for corn. Many U.S. farmers can use the same acreage to grow either corn or soybeans. Use a demand and supply graph to analyze the effect on the equilibrium price of soybeans resulting from a fall in the demand for corn.

Source: Jesse Newman, "Soybeans and Corn Locked in Food Fight," *Wall Street Journal*, March 29, 2015.

4.5 According to an article in the *Wall Street Journal*, the demand for orange juice is declining in the United States "as newer entrants in the beverage aisle, including more-exotic fruit juices, such as pomegranate, energy drinks and ready-to-drink coffee, have grabbed a greater share of the market." At the same time, orange juice production has been declining as bacterial infections reduce the quantity of fruit that orange trees can produce. The article notes that despite the decline in the demand for orange juice, the price of orange juice might increase. Use a demand and supply graph of the orange juice market to illustrate how the price of orange juice might increase as a result of these events. Be sure that all curves on your graphs are properly labeled, that you show any shifts in those curves, and that you indicate the initial and final equilibrium points.

Source: Alexandra Wexler, "U.S. Orange-Juice Sales Fall to Record Low," *Wall Street Journal*, August 18, 2014.

4.6 **(Related to the Making the Connection on page 92)** Suppose that oil prices sharply increase, while more cities pass laws banning the use of plastic bags at stores. Use a demand and supply graph to illustrate your answers to the following questions.
  a. Can we use this information to be certain whether the equilibrium price of recycled plastic will increase or decrease?
  b. Can we use this information to be certain whether the equilibrium quantity of recycled plastic will increase or decrease?

4.7 **(Related to Solved Problem 3.4 on page 93)** The demand for watermelons is highest during summer and lowest during winter. Yet watermelon prices are normally lower in summer than in winter. Use a demand and supply graph to demonstrate how this is possible. Be sure to carefully label the curves in your graph and to clearly indicate the equilibrium summer price and the equilibrium winter price.

4.8 **(Related to Solved Problem 3.4 on page 93)** According to one observer of the lobster market: "After Labor Day, when the vacationers have gone home, the lobstermen usually have a month or more of good fishing conditions, except for the occasional hurricane." Use a demand and supply graph to explain whether lobster prices are likely to be higher or lower during the fall than during the summer.

Source: Jay Harlow, "Lobster: An Affordable Luxury," www.Sallybernstein.com.

4.9 Years ago, an apple producer argued that the United States should enact a tariff, or a tax, on imports of bananas. His reasoning was that "the enormous imports of cheap bananas into the United States tend to curtail the domestic consumption of fresh fruits produced in the United States."
  a. Was the apple producer assuming that apples and bananas are substitutes or complements? Briefly explain.
  b. If a tariff on bananas acts as an increase in the cost of supplying bananas in the United States, use two demand and supply graphs to show the effects of the apple producer's proposal. One graph should show the effect on the banana market in the United States, and the other graph should show the effect on the apple market in the United States. Be sure to label the change in equilibrium price and quantity in each market and any shifts in the demand and supply curves.

Source: Douglas A. Irwin, *Peddling Protectionism: Smoot-Hawley and the Great Depression*, Princeton, NJ: Princeton University Press, 2011, p. 22.

4.10 According to one news story, the cost of producing 4K televisions has been declining. According to a second story, many people have switched from watching programs on television sets to watching them on smartphones, tablets, or laptops. After reading these news stories, a student argues: "From this information, we know that the price of 4K televisions will fall, but we don't know whether the quantity of television sets sold will increase or decrease." Is the student's analysis correct? Illustrate your answer with a demand and supply graph.

Sources: Geoffrey A. Fowler, "Vizio Fixes Flaw in Cheap 4K TV … as Competition Heats Up," *Wall Street Journal*, January 13, 2015; and Suzanne Vranica and Shalini Ramachandran, "Streaming Services Hammer Cable TV Ratings," *Wall Street Journal*, March 10, 2015.

4.11 Historically, the production of many perishable foods, such as dairy products, was highly seasonal. As the supply of those products fluctuated, prices tended to fluctuate tremendously—typically by 25 to 50 percent or more—over the course of the year. One effect of mechanical refrigeration, which was commercialized on a large scale in the last decade of the nineteenth century, was that suppliers could store perishable foods from one season to the next. Economists have estimated that as a result of refrigerated storage, wholesale prices rose by roughly 10 percent during peak supply periods, while they fell by almost the same amount during the off season. Use a demand and supply graph for each season to illustrate how refrigeration affected the market for perishable food.

Source: Lee A. Craig, Barry Goodwin, and Thomas Grennes, "The Effect of Mechanical Refrigeration on Nutrition in the U.S.," *Social Science History*, Vol. 28, No. 2, Summer 2004, pp. 327–328.

4.12 If the equilibrium price and quantity of a product were $100 and 1,000 units per month in 2015 and $150 and 800 units per month in 2016, did this product experience a larger shift in its demand curve or in its supply curve from 2015 to 2016? Briefly explain.

4.13 (Related to the Don't Let This Happen to You on page 95) A student writes the following: "Increased production leads to a lower price, which in turn increases demand." Do you agree with his reasoning? Briefly explain.

4.14 (Related to the Don't Let This Happen to You on page 95) A student was asked to draw a demand and supply graph to illustrate the effect on the market for smartwatches of a fall in the price of displays used in smartwatches, holding everything else constant. She drew the following graph and explained it as follows:

> Displays are an input to smartwatches, so a fall in the price of displays will cause the supply curve for smartwatches to shift to the right

(from S_1 to S_2). Because this shift in the supply curve results in a lower price (P_2), consumers will want to buy more smartwatches, and the demand curve will shift to the right (from D_1 to D_2). We know that more smartwatches will be sold, but we can't be sure whether the price of smartwatches will rise or fall. That depends on whether the supply curve or the demand curve has shifted farther to the right. I assume that the effect on supply is greater than the effect on demand, so I show the final equilibrium price (P_3) as being lower than the initial equilibrium price (P_1).

Explain whether you agree with the student's analysis. Be careful to explain exactly what—if anything—you find wrong with her analysis.

4.15 The following four graphs represent four market scenarios, each of which would cause either a movement along the supply curve for Pepsi or a shift of the supply curve. Match each scenario with the appropriate graph.

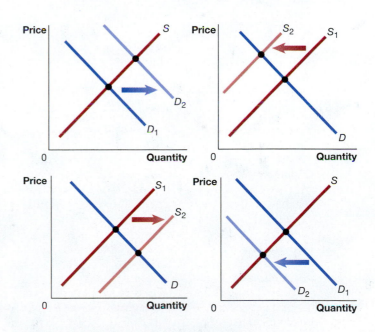

   a. A decrease in the supply of Coke
   b. A drop in the average household income in the United States from $52,000 to $50,000
   c. An improvement in soft drink bottling technology
   d. An increase in the prices of sugar and high-fructose corn syrup

4.16 Proposals have been made to increase government regulation of firms providing childcare services by, for instance, setting education requirements for childcare workers. Suppose that these regulations increase the quality of childcare and cause the demand for childcare services to increase. At the same time, assume that complying with the new government regulations increases the costs of firms providing childcare services. Draw a demand and supply graph to illustrate the effects of these changes in the market for childcare services. Briefly explain whether the total quantity of childcare services purchased will increase or decrease as a result of the regulations.

4.17 Which of the following graphs best represents what happens in the market for hotel rooms at a ski resort during the winter? Briefly explain. From the graph that you picked, what would be the result during the winter if hotel rates stayed at their summer level?

4.18 The following graphs show the supply and demand curves for two markets. One of the markets is for Tesla automobiles, and the other is for a cancer-fighting drug, without which lung cancer patients will die. Briefly explain which graph most likely represents which market.

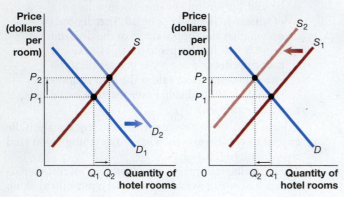

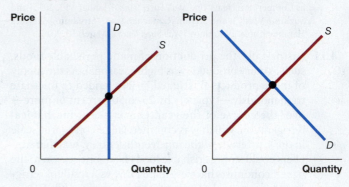

Economic Efficiency, Government Price Setting, and Taxes

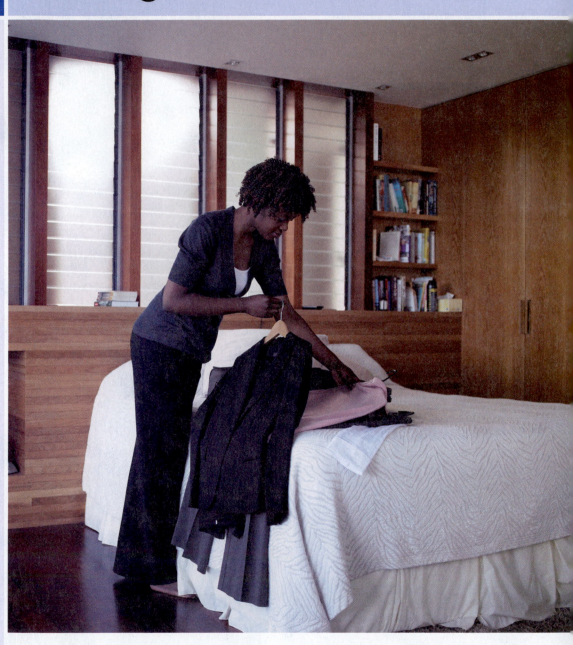

The Sharing Economy, Phone Apps, and Rent Control

The role of markets is to bring together buyers and sellers. A market can be a physical place, like a retail mall, or a virtual place, like eBay. What if you need to rent an apartment or a bicycle for only a day or a week? Internet startup companies have created rental markets for short-term use of products including apartments, cars, boats, and bicycles. For example, people who download the Airbnb app can search for short-term room rentals in 30,000 cities in 192 countries. The suppliers in this market are typically people who want to earn extra money by renting their house, apartment, or sometimes just a single room for a few days. The *Economist* magazine has referred to the rapid increase in the number of people using peer-to-peer rental sites as the rise of the "sharing economy."

More than 25 million people had rented rooms on Airbnb by 2015. Despite this success, Airbnb has run into problems, particularly in cities that have rent control regulations. In New York, San Francisco, Los Angeles, and nearly 200 smaller cities in the United States, apartments are subject to rent control by the local government. Rent control puts a legal limit on the rent that landlords can charge for an apartment. Supporters of rent control argue that it is necessary to preserve affordable apartments in cities where equilibrium market rents would be above what middle- and lower-income people are willing and able to pay. But, as we will see in this chapter, rent controls cause a shortage of apartments and give people an incentive to list their apartments on sites like Airbnb at rents far above the controlled rents. In San Francisco, landlords complain that some high-income renters have moved out of the city but have kept their rent-controlled apartments in order to rent them using the apartment-sharing sites. In New York, where it is against the law to rent a room in an apartment for less than 30 days, officials struggled with how to enforce the rules despite Airbnb's great popularity.

Some observers argue that the difficulty governments face regulating peer-to-peer rental sites will make it impossible to enforce rent control rules. In San Francisco, where an estimated 1,300 people a night were renting rooms through Airbnb, supporters and opponents were battling over attempts to further regulate the site, including imposing fines of $1,000 a day on anyone violating existing rental regulations.

AN INSIDE LOOK AT POLICY on **page 132** explores why government officials in Malibu, California, imposed a tax on short-term rentals of apartments booked through Airbnb.

Sources: "The Rise of the Sharing Economy," *Economist*, March 9, 2013; Ronda Kaysen, "What's Up Next in New York?" *New York Times*, December 26, 2014; Carolyn Said, "Airbnb Fights Back as Pending Laws Seek to Curtail Home Stays," sfgate.com, April 19, 2015; and C.W. Nevius, "Rent Control Sometimes Benefitting the Rich," *San Francisco Chronicle*, June 16, 2012.

Economics in Your Life

Does Rent Control Make It Easier for You to Find an Affordable Apartment?

Suppose you have job offers in two cities. One factor in deciding which job to accept is whether you can find an affordable apartment. If one city has rent control, are you more likely to find an affordable apartment in that city, or would you be better off looking for an apartment in a city without rent control? As you read the chapter, try to answer this question. You can check your answer against the one we provide on **page 131** at the end of this chapter.

I n a competitive market, the price adjusts to ensure that the quantity demanded equals the quantity supplied. Stated another way, in equilibrium, every consumer willing to pay the market price is able to buy as much of the product as the consumer wants, and every firm willing to accept the market price can sell as much as it wants. Consumers would naturally prefer to pay a lower price, and sellers would prefer to receive a higher price. Normally, consumers and firms have no choice but to accept the equilibrium price if they wish to participate in the market.

Occasionally, however, consumers or firms persuade the government to intervene to try to lower or raise the market price of a good or service:

Price ceiling A legally determined maximum price that sellers may charge.

- Consumers sometimes succeed in having the government impose a **price ceiling**, which is a legally determined maximum price that sellers may charge. Rent control is an example of a price ceiling.

Price floor A legally determined minimum price that sellers may receive.

- Firms sometimes succeed in having the government impose a **price floor**, which is a legally determined minimum price that sellers may receive. In markets for farm products such as milk, the government has been setting price floors that are above the equilibrium market price since the 1930s.

Another way the government intervenes in markets is by imposing taxes. The government relies on the revenue raised from taxes to finance its operations. But taxes also affect the decisions that consumers and firms make.

Each of these government interventions has predictable negative consequences for economic efficiency. Economists have developed the concepts of *consumer surplus, producer surplus,* and *deadweight loss* to help policymakers and voters analyze the economic effects of price ceilings, price floors, and taxes.

 4.1 ## Consumer Surplus and Producer Surplus
LEARNING OBJECTIVE: Distinguish between the concepts of consumer surplus and producer surplus.

Consumer surplus measures the dollar benefit consumers receive from buying goods or services in a particular market. Producer surplus measures the dollar benefit firms receive from selling goods or services in a particular market. Economic surplus in a market is the sum of consumer surplus and producer surplus. As we will see, *when the government imposes a price ceiling or a price floor, the amount of economic surplus in a market is reduced*; in other words, price ceilings and price floors reduce the total benefit to consumers and firms from buying and selling in a market. To understand why this is true, we need to understand how consumer surplus and producer surplus are determined.

Consumer Surplus

Consumer surplus The difference between the highest price a consumer is willing to pay for a good or service and the actual price the consumer pays.

Consumer surplus is the difference between the highest price a consumer is willing to pay for a good or service and the actual price the consumer pays. Suppose you are in Walmart, and you see a DVD of *Star Wars: The Force Awakens* on the shelf. The DVD doesn't have a price sticker, so you take it to the register to check the price. As you walk to the register, you think to yourself that $18 is the highest price you would be willing to pay. At the register, you find out that the price is actually $12, so you buy the DVD. Your consumer surplus in this example is $6: the difference between the $18 you were willing to pay and the $12 you actually paid.

Marginal benefit The additional benefit to a consumer from consuming one more unit of a good or service.

We can use the demand curve to measure the total consumer surplus in a market. Demand curves show the willingness of consumers to purchase a product at different prices. Consumers are willing to purchase a product up to the point where the marginal benefit of consuming a product is equal to its price. The **marginal benefit** is the additional benefit to a consumer from consuming one more unit of a good or service. As a simple example, suppose there are only four consumers in the market for chai tea: Theresa, Tom, Terri, and Tim. Because these four consumers have different tastes for

Consumer	Highest Price Willing to Pay
Theresa	$6
Tom	5
Terri	4
Tim	3

MyEconLab Animation

Figure 4.1

Deriving the Demand Curve for Chai Tea

With four consumers in the market for chai tea, the demand curve is determined by the highest price each consumer is willing to pay. At prices above $6, no tea is sold because $6 is the highest price any consumer is willing to pay. At prices of $3 and below, each of the four consumers is willing to buy a cup of tea.

tea and different incomes, the marginal benefit each of them receives from consuming a cup of tea will be different. Therefore, the highest price each is willing to pay for a cup of tea is also different. In Figure 4.1, the information from the table is used to construct a demand curve for chai. At prices above $6 per cup, no tea is sold because $6 is the highest price any of the consumers is willing to pay. At a price of $5, both Theresa and Tom are willing to buy tea, so two cups are sold. At prices of $3 and below, all four consumers are willing to buy tea, and four cups are sold.

Suppose the market price of tea is $3.50 per cup. As Figure 4.2 shows, the demand curve allows us to calculate the total consumer surplus in this market. Panel (a) shows

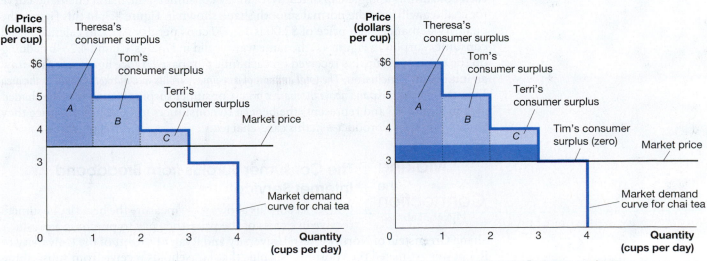

(a) Consumer surplus with a market price of $3.50

(b) Consumer surplus with a market price of $3.00

MyEconLab Animation

Figure 4.2 **Measuring Consumer Surplus**

Panel (a) shows the consumer surplus for Theresa, Tom, and Terri when the price of tea is $3.50 per cup. Theresa's consumer surplus is equal to the area of rectangle A and is the difference between the highest price she would pay—which is $6—and the market price of $3.50. Tom's consumer surplus is equal to the area of rectangle B, and Terri's consumer surplus is equal to the area of rectangle C. Total consumer surplus in this market is equal to the sum of the areas of rectangles A, B, and C, or the total area below the demand curve and above the market price. In panel (b), consumer surplus increases by the dark blue area as the market price declines from $3.50 to $3.00.

MyEconLab Animation

Figure 4.3

Total Consumer Surplus in the Market for Chai Tea

The demand curve shows that most buyers of chai tea would have been willing to pay more than the market price of $2.00. For each buyer, consumer surplus is equal to the difference between the highest price he or she is willing to pay and the market price actually paid. Therefore, the total amount of consumer surplus in the market for chai tea is equal to the area below the demand curve and above the market price. Consumer surplus represents the benefit to consumers in excess of the price they paid to purchase a product.

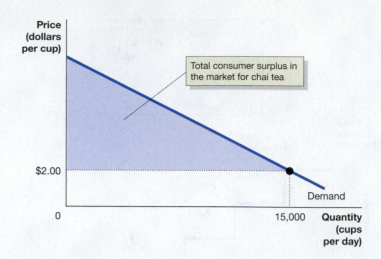

that the highest price Theresa is willing to pay is $6, but because she pays only $3.50, her consumer surplus is $2.50 (shown by the area of rectangle A). Similarly, Tom's consumer surplus is $1.50 (rectangle B), and Terri's consumer surplus is $0.50 (rectangle C). Tim is unwilling to buy a cup of tea at a price of $3.50, so he doesn't participate in this market and receives no consumer surplus. In this simple example, the total consumer surplus is equal to $2.50 + $1.50 + $0.50 = $4.50 (or the sum of the areas of rectangles A, B, and C). Panel (b) shows that a lower price will increase consumer surplus. If the price of tea falls from $3.50 per cup to $3.00, Theresa, Tom, and Terri each receive $0.50 more in consumer surplus (shown by the dark blue areas), so the total consumer surplus in the market rises to $6.00. Tim now buys a cup of tea but doesn't receive any consumer surplus because the price is equal to the highest price he is willing to pay. In fact, Tim is indifferent between buying the cup or not—his well-being is the same either way.

The market demand curves shown in Figures 4.1 and 4.2 do not look like the typical smooth demand curve because in this case we have only a small number of consumers, each consuming a single cup of tea. With many consumers, the market demand curve for chai tea will have the normal smooth shape shown in Figure 4.3. In this figure, the quantity demanded at a price of $2.00 is 15,000 cups per day. We can calculate total consumer surplus in Figure 4.3 the same way we did in Figures 4.1 and 4.2—by adding up the consumer surplus received on each unit purchased. Once again, we can draw an important conclusion: *The total amount of consumer surplus in a market is equal to the area below the demand curve and above the market price.* Consumer surplus is shown as the shaded area in Figure 4.3 and represents the benefit to consumers in excess of the price they paid to purchase a product—in this case, chai tea. MyEconLab Concept Check

Making the Connection
MyEconLab Video

The Consumer Surplus from Broadband Internet Service

Consumer surplus allows us to measure the benefit consumers receive in excess of the price they pay to purchase a product. Shane Greenstein of Northwestern University and Ryan McDevitt of the University of Rochester estimated the consumer surplus that households receive from subscribing to broadband Internet service. To carry out the analysis, they estimated the demand curve for broadband Internet service and then computed the shaded area shown in the following graph.

In the year they analyzed, 47 million consumers paid an average price of $36 per month to subscribe to a broadband Internet service. The demand curve shows the marginal benefit consumers receive from subscribing to a broadband Internet service rather than using dialup or doing without access to the Internet. The area below the demand curve and above the $36 price line represents the difference between the price consumers

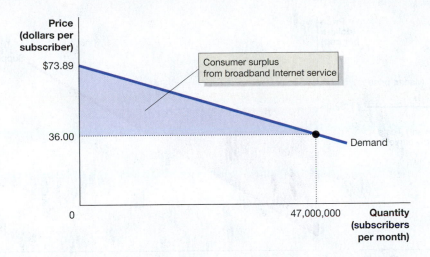

would have paid rather than do without broadband service and the $36 they did pay. The shaded area on the graph represents the total consumer surplus in the market for broadband Internet service. Greenstein and McDevitt estimate that the value of this area is $890.4 million. This value is one month's benefit to the consumers who subscribe to a broadband Internet service.

Sources: Shane Greenstein and Ryan C. McDevitt, "The Broadband Bonus: Estimating Broadband Internet's Economic Value," *Telecommunications Policy*, Vol. 35, No. 7, August 2011, pp. 617–632; and Shane Greenstein, "Measuring Consumer Surplus Online," *Economist*, March 11, 2013.

Your Turn: For more practice do related problem 1.13 on page 135 at the end of this chapter.   MyEconLab Study Plan

Producer Surplus

Just as demand curves show the willingness of consumers to buy a product at different prices, supply curves show the willingness of firms to supply a product at different prices. The willingness to supply a product depends on the cost of producing it. Firms will supply an additional unit of a product only if they receive a price equal to the additional cost of producing that unit. **Marginal cost** is the additional cost to a firm of producing one more cup of tea: In this case, the marginal cost includes the ingredients to make the tea and the wages paid to the worker preparing the tea. Often, the marginal cost of producing a good increases as more of the good is produced during a given period of time. Increasing marginal cost is the key reason that supply curves are upward sloping.

Marginal cost The additional cost to a firm of producing one more unit of a good or service.

Panel (a) of Figure 4.4 shows Heavenly Tea's producer surplus. For simplicity, we show Heavenly producing only a small quantity of tea. The figure shows that Heavenly's marginal cost of producing the first cup of tea is $1.25, its marginal cost of producing the second cup is $1.50, and so on. The marginal cost of each cup of tea is the lowest price Heavenly is willing to accept to supply that cup. The supply curve, then, is also a marginal cost curve. Suppose the market price of tea is $2.00 per cup. On the first cup of tea, the price is $0.75 higher than the lowest price that Heavenly is willing to accept. **Producer surplus** is the difference between the lowest price a firm would be willing to accept for a good or service and the price it actually receives. Therefore, Heavenly's producer surplus on the first cup is $0.75 (shown by the area of rectangle A), its producer surplus on the second cup is $0.50 (rectangle B), and its producer surplus on the third cup is $0.25 (rectangle C). Heavenly will not be willing to supply the fourth cup because the marginal cost of producing it is greater than the market price. Heavenly Tea's total producer surplus is equal to $0.75 + $0.50 + $0.25 = $1.50 (or the sum of the areas of rectangles A, B, and C). A higher price will increase producer surplus. For example, if the market price of chai tea rises from $2.00 to $2.25, Heavenly Tea's producer surplus

Producer surplus The difference between the lowest price a firm would be willing to accept for a good or service and the price it actually receives.

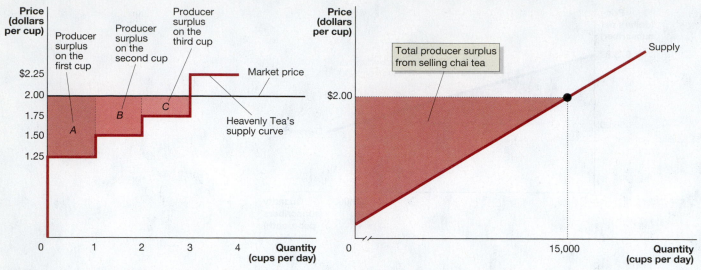

(a) Producer surplus for Heavenly Tea

(b) Total producer surplus in the market for chai tea

MyEconLab Animation

Figure 4.4 **Measuring Producer Surplus**

Panel (a) shows Heavenly Tea's producer surplus. The lowest price Heavenly Tea is willing to accept to supply a cup of tea is equal to its marginal cost of producing that cup. When the market price of tea is $2.00, Heavenly receives producer surplus of $0.75 on the first cup (the area of rectangle A), $0.50 on the second cup (rectangle B), and $0.25 on the third cup (rectangle C). In panel (b), the total amount of producer surplus tea sellers receive from selling chai tea can be calculated by adding up for the entire market the producer surplus received on each cup sold. In the figure, total producer surplus is equal to the shaded area above the supply curve and below the market price.

will increase from $1.50 to $2.25. (Make sure you understand how the new level of producer surplus was calculated.)

The supply curve shown in panel (a) of Figure 4.4 does not look like the typical smooth supply curve because we are looking at a single firm producing only a small quantity of tea. With many firms, the market supply curve for chai tea will have the normal smooth shape shown in panel (b) of Figure 4.4. In panel (b), the quantity supplied at a price of $2.00 is 15,000 cups per day. We can calculate total producer surplus in panel (b) the same way we did in panel (a): by adding up the producer surplus received on each cup sold. Therefore, *the total amount of producer surplus in a market is equal to the area above the market supply curve and below the market price.* The total producer surplus tea sellers receive from selling chai tea is shown as the shaded area in panel (b) of Figure 4.4.   MyEconLab Concept Check

What Consumer Surplus and Producer Surplus Measure

We have seen that consumer surplus measures the benefit to consumers from participating in a market, and producer surplus measures the benefit to producers from participating in a market. It is important to be clear about what these concepts are measuring. In a sense, consumer surplus measures the *net* benefit to consumers from participating in a market rather than the *total* benefit. That is, if the price of a product were zero, the consumer surplus in a market would be all of the area under the demand curve. When the price is not zero, consumer surplus is the area below the demand curve and above the market price. So, consumer surplus in a market is equal to the total benefit consumers receive minus the total amount they must pay to buy the good or service.

Similarly, producer surplus measures the *net* benefit received by producers from participating in a market. If producers could supply a good or service at zero cost, the producer surplus in a market would be all of the area below the market price. When cost is not zero, producer surplus is the area below the market price and above the supply curve. So, producer surplus in a market is equal to the total dollar amount firms receive from consumers minus the cost of producing the good or service.   MyEconLab Concept Check

MyEconLab Study Plan

4.2 The Efficiency of Competitive Markets

LEARNING OBJECTIVE: Explain the concept of economic efficiency.

Recall that a *competitive market* is a market with many buyers and many sellers. An important advantage of the market system is that it results in efficient economic outcomes. But what does *economic efficiency* mean? The concepts we have developed so far in this chapter give us two ways to think about the economic efficiency of competitive markets. We can think in terms of marginal benefit and marginal cost. We can also think in terms of consumer surplus and producer surplus. As we will see, these two approaches lead to the same outcome, but using both can increase our understanding of economic efficiency.

Marginal Benefit Equals Marginal Cost in Competitive Equilibrium

Figure 4.5 again shows the market for chai tea. Recall that the demand curve shows the marginal benefit received by consumers, and the supply curve shows the marginal cost of production. For this market to achieve economic efficiency, the marginal benefit from the last unit sold should equal the marginal cost of production. The figure shows that this equality occurs at competitive equilibrium where 15,000 cups per day are produced and marginal benefit and marginal cost are both equal to $2.00. This outcome is economically efficient because every cup of chai tea has been produced where the marginal benefit to buyers is greater than or equal to the marginal cost to producers.

To further understand why the level of output at competitive equilibrium is efficient, consider what the situation would be if output were at a different level. Suppose that output of chai tea were 14,000 cups per day. Figure 4.5 shows that at this level of output, the marginal benefit from the last cup sold is $2.20, while the marginal cost is only $1.80. This level of output is not efficient because 1,000 more cups could be produced for which the additional benefit to consumers would be greater than the additional cost of production. Consumers would willingly purchase those cups, and tea sellers would willingly supply them, making both consumers and sellers better off. Similarly, if the output of chai tea were 16,000 cups per day, the marginal cost of the 16,000th cup is $2.20, while the marginal benefit is only $1.80. Tea sellers would only be willing to supply this cup at a price of $2.20, which is $0.40 higher than consumers would be willing to pay. In fact, consumers would not be willing to pay the price tea sellers would need to receive for any cup beyond the 15,000th.

To summarize: *Equilibrium in a competitive market results in the economically efficient level of output, at which marginal benefit equals marginal cost.* MyEconLab Concept Check

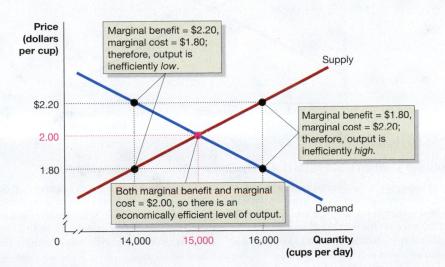

Price (dollars per cup)

Marginal benefit = $2.20, marginal cost = $1.80; therefore, output is inefficiently *low*.

Supply

Marginal benefit = $1.80, marginal cost = $2.20; therefore, output is inefficiently *high*.

Both marginal benefit and marginal cost = $2.00, so there is an economically efficient level of output.

Demand

$2.20 / 2.00 / 1.80

0   14,000   15,000   16,000   **Quantity (cups per day)**

MyEconLab Animation

Figure 4.5

Marginal Benefit Equals Marginal Cost Only at Competitive Equilibrium

In a competitive market, equilibrium occurs at a quantity of 15,000 cups and a price of $2.00 per cup, where marginal benefit equals marginal cost. This level of output is economically efficient because every cup has been produced for which the marginal benefit to buyers is greater than or equal to the marginal cost to producers.

Figure 4.6

Economic Surplus Equals the Sum of Consumer Surplus and Producer Surplus

The economic surplus in a market is the sum of the blue area, representing consumer surplus, and the red area, representing producer surplus.

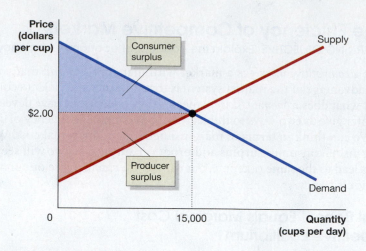

Economic Surplus

Economic surplus The sum of consumer surplus and producer surplus.

Economic surplus in a market is the sum of consumer surplus and producer surplus. In a competitive market, with many buyers and sellers and no government restrictions, economic surplus is at a maximum when the market is in equilibrium. To see this point, let's look at the market for chai tea shown again in Figure 4.6. The consumer surplus in this market is the blue area below the demand curve and above the line indicating the equilibrium price of $2.00. The producer surplus is the red area above the supply curve and below the price line.   MyEconLab Concept Check

Deadweight Loss

To show that economic surplus is maximized at equilibrium, consider a situation in which the price of chai tea is *above* the equilibrium price, as shown in Figure 4.7. At a

	At Competitive Equilibrium	At a Price of $2.20
Consumer Surplus	$A + B + C$	A
Producer Surplus	$D + E$	$B + D$
Deadweight Loss	None	$C + E$

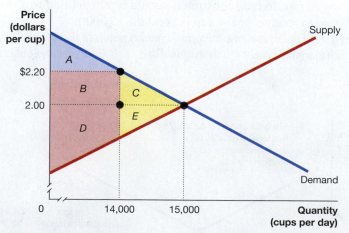

Figure 4.7 **When a Market Is Not in Equilibrium, There Is a Deadweight Loss**

Economic surplus is maximized when a market is in competitive equilibrium. When a market is not in equilibrium, there is a deadweight loss. For example, when the price of chai tea is $2.20 instead of $2.00, consumer surplus declines from an amount equal to the sum of areas A, B, and C to just area A. Producer surplus increases from the sum of areas D and E to the sum of areas B and D. At competitive equilibrium, there is no deadweight loss. At a price of $2.20, there is a deadweight loss equal to the sum of triangles C and E.

price of $2.20 per cup, the number of cups consumers are willing to buy per day falls from 15,000 to 14,000. At competitive equilibrium, consumer surplus is equal to the sum of areas *A*, *B*, and *C*. At a price of $2.20, fewer cups are sold at a higher price, so consumer surplus declines to just the area of *A*. At competitive equilibrium, producer surplus is equal to the sum of areas *D* and *E*. At the higher price of $2.20, producer surplus changes to be equal to the sum of areas *B* and *D*. The sum of consumer and producer surplus—economic surplus—has been reduced to the sum of areas *A*, *B*, and *D*. Notice that this sum is less than the original economic surplus by an amount equal to the sum of triangles *C* and *E*. Economic surplus has declined because at a price of $2.20, all the cups between the 14,000th and the 15,000th, which would have been produced in competitive equilibrium, are not being produced. These "missing" cups are not providing any consumer or producer surplus, so economic surplus has declined. The reduction in economic surplus resulting from a market not being in competitive equilibrium is called the **deadweight loss**. In the figure, deadweight loss is equal to the sum of the triangles *C* and *E*.   MyEconLab *Concept Check*

Deadweight loss The reduction in economic surplus resulting from a market not being in competitive equilibrium.

Economic Surplus and Economic Efficiency

Consumer surplus measures the benefit to consumers from buying a particular product, such as chai tea. Producer surplus measures the benefit to firms from selling a particular product. Therefore, economic surplus—which is the sum of the benefit to firms plus the benefit to consumers—is the best measure we have of the benefit to society from the production of a particular good or service. Economic surplus gives us a second way of characterizing the economic efficiency of a competitive market: *Equilibrium in a competitive market results in the greatest amount of economic surplus, or total net benefit to society, from the production of a good or service.* Anything that causes the market for a good or service not to be in competitive equilibrium reduces the total benefit to society from the production of that good or service.

Now we can give a more general definition of *economic efficiency* in terms of our two approaches: **Economic efficiency** is a market outcome in which the marginal benefit to consumers of the last unit produced is equal to its marginal cost of production and in which the sum of consumer surplus and producer surplus is at a maximum.   MyEconLab *Concept Check*

Economic efficiency A market outcome in which the marginal benefit to consumers of the last unit produced is equal to its marginal cost of production and in which the sum of consumer surplus and producer surplus is at a maximum.

4.3 # Government Intervention in the Market: Price Floors and Price Ceilings

LEARNING OBJECTIVE: Explain the economic effect of government-imposed price floors and price ceilings.

Notice that we have *not* concluded that every *individual* is better off if a market is at competitive equilibrium. We have concluded only that economic surplus, or the *total* net benefit to society, is greatest at competitive equilibrium. Any individual producer would rather receive a higher price, and any individual consumer would rather pay a lower price, but usually producers can sell and consumers can buy only at the competitive equilibrium price.

Producers or consumers who are dissatisfied with the competitive equilibrium price can lobby the government to legally require that a different price be charged. In the United States, the government only occasionally overrides the market outcome by setting prices. When the government does intervene, it can attempt to aid either sellers by requiring that a price be above equilibrium—a price floor—or buyers by requiring that a price be below equilibrium—a price ceiling. To affect the market outcome, the government must set a legal price floor that is above the equilibrium price or set a legal price ceiling that is below the equilibrium price. Otherwise, the price ceiling or price floor will not be *binding* on buyers and sellers. We can use the concepts of consumer surplus, producer surplus, and deadweight loss to understand more clearly why price floors and price ceilings reduce economic efficiency.

Price Floors: Government Policy in Agricultural Markets

The Great Depression of the 1930s was the worst economic disaster in U.S. history, affecting every sector of the economy. Many farmers could sell their products only at very low prices, so they convinced the federal government to set price floors for many agricultural products, such as wheat and corn. Government intervention in agriculture—often referred to as the *farm program*—has continued ever since. To understand how a price floor in an agricultural market works, suppose that the equilibrium price in the wheat market is $6.50 per bushel, but the government decides to set a price floor of $8.00 per bushel. As Figure 4.8 shows, the price of wheat rises from $6.50 to $8.00, and the quantity of wheat sold falls from 2.0 billion bushels per year to 1.8 billion. Initially, suppose that production of wheat also falls to 1.8 billion bushels.

The producer surplus received by wheat farmers increases by an amount equal to the area of rectangle A and decreases by an amount equal to the area of triangle C. (This is the same result we saw in the market for chai tea in Figure 4.7.) The area of rectangle A represents a transfer from consumer surplus to producer surplus. The total fall in consumer surplus is equal to the sum of the areas of rectangle A and triangle B. Wheat farmers benefit from this program, but consumers lose. There is also a deadweight loss equal to the areas of triangles B and C because economic efficiency declines as the price floor reduces the amount of economic surplus in the market for wheat. In other words, the price floor has caused the marginal benefit of the last bushel of wheat to be greater than the marginal cost of producing it. We can conclude that a price floor reduces economic efficiency.

We assumed initially that farmers reduce their production of wheat to the amount consumers are willing to buy. In fact, as Figure 4.8 shows, a price floor will cause the quantity of wheat that farmers want to supply to increase from 2.0 billion to 2.2 billion bushels. Because the higher price also reduces the amount of wheat consumers want to buy, the result is a surplus of 0.4 billion bushels of wheat (the 2.2 billion bushels supplied minus the 1.8 billion demanded).

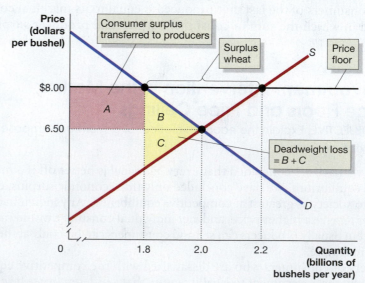

MyEconLab Animation

Figure 4.8 **The Economic Effect of a Price Floor in the Wheat Market**

If wheat farmers convince the government to impose a price floor of $8.00 per bushel, the amount of wheat sold will fall from 2.0 billion bushels per year to 1.8 billion. If we assume that farmers produce 1.8 billion bushels, producer surplus then increases by rectangle A—which is transferred from consumer surplus—and falls by triangle C.

Consumer surplus declines by rectangle A plus triangle B. There is a deadweight loss equal to triangles B and C, representing the decline in economic efficiency due to the price floor. In reality, a price floor of $8.00 per bushel will cause farmers to expand their production from 2.0 billion to 2.2 billion bushels, resulting in a surplus of wheat.

The federal government's farm programs have often resulted in large surpluses of wheat and other agricultural products. In response, the government has usually either bought the surplus food or paid farmers to restrict supply by taking some land out of cultivation. Because both of these options are expensive, Congress passed the Freedom to Farm Act of 1996. The intent of the act was to phase out price floors and government purchases of surpluses and return to a free market in agriculture. To allow farmers time to adjust, the federal government began paying farmers *subsidies*, or cash payments based on the number of acres planted. Although the subsidies were originally scheduled to be phased out, Congress has passed additional farm bills that have resulted in the continuation of subsidies requiring substantial federal government spending. In 2015, the Congressional Budget Office estimated that the farm program would result in federal spending of more than $145 billion over the following 10 years.   MyEconLab Concept Check

Making the Connection
MyEconLab Video

Price Floors in Labor Markets: The Debate over Minimum Wage Policy

The minimum wage may be the most controversial "price floor." Supporters see the minimum wage as a way of raising the incomes of low-skilled workers. Opponents argue that it results in fewer jobs and imposes large costs on small businesses.

Since 2009, the national minimum wage as set by Congress has been $7.25 per hour for most occupations. It is illegal for an employer to pay less than this wage in these occupations. Although only about 4 percent of workers in the United States earn the minimum wage or less, many people are concerned that workers who receive the minimum wage or a wage a little above the minimum are not earning a "living wage" that would allow them to escape from poverty. In 2015, President Barack Obama proposed raising the minimum wage in a series of steps to $10.10 per hour. Some members of Congress introduced legislation to raise it to $12 per hour. Several cities and states are increasing their minimum wage to as high as $15 per hour. Protests in a number of cities were intended to pressure fast-food restaurants and other employers to voluntarily raise the minimum wage they paid to $15 per hour.

For many workers, the legal minimum wage is irrelevant because it is well below the wage employers are voluntarily willing to pay them. But for some low-skilled workers—such as restaurant workers—the minimum wage is above the wage they would otherwise receive. The following figure shows the effect of the minimum wage on employment in the market for low-skilled labor.

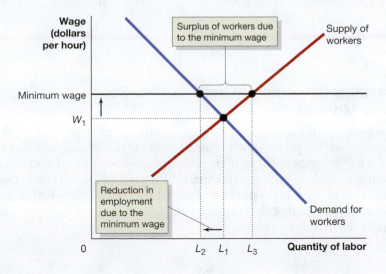

Without a minimum wage, the equilibrium wage would be W_1 and the number of workers hired would be L_1. With a minimum wage set above the equilibrium wage, the number of workers employers demand declines from L_1 to L_2, and the quantity of labor supplied increases to L_3, leading to a surplus of workers unable to find jobs equal to $L_3 - L_2$. The quantity of labor supplied increases because the higher wage attracts more people to work. For instance, some teenagers may decide that working after school is worthwhile at the minimum wage of $7.25 per hour but would not be worthwhile at a lower wage.

This analysis is very similar to our analysis of the wheat market in Figure 4.8. Just as a price floor in the wheat market leads to less wheat being consumed, a price floor in the labor market should lead to fewer workers being hired. Views differ sharply among economists, however, concerning how large a reduction in employment the minimum wage causes. The U.S. Congressional Budget Office (CBO) estimates that raising the minimum wage to $10.10 per hour would result in a decline in employment of 500,000 workers. Some economists believe that the effects of the minimum wage on employment are far smaller, however. For instance, David Card of the University of California, Berkeley, and Alan Krueger of Princeton University conducted a study of fast-food restaurants in New Jersey and Pennsylvania. Their study indicated that the effect of past minimum wage increases on employment has been very small. This study has been controversial, and other economists have examined similar data and come to the different conclusion that the minimum wage leads to a significant decrease in employment.

Whatever the extent of employment losses from the minimum wage, because it is a price floor, it will cause a deadweight loss, just as a price floor in the wheat market does. Therefore, many economists favor alternative policies for attaining the goal of raising the incomes of low-skilled workers. One policy many economists support is the *earned income tax credit*, which reduces the amount of tax that low-income wage earners would otherwise pay to the federal government. Workers with very low incomes who do not owe any tax receive a payment from the government. Unlike with the minimum wage, the earned income tax credit can increase the incomes of low-skilled workers without reducing employment. The earned income tax credit also places a lesser burden on the small businesses that employ many low-skilled workers and may cause a smaller loss of economic efficiency.

Sources: Noam Scheiber, "Democrats Are Rallying around $12 Minimum Wage," *New York Times*, April 22, 2015; U.S. Bureau of Labor Statistics, "Characteristics of Minimum Wage Workers, 2014," BLS Reports 1054, April 2015; U.S. Congressional Budget Office, "The Effects of a Minimum-Wage Increase on Employment and Family Income," February 2014; David Card and Alan B. Krueger, *Myth and Measurement: The New Economics of the Minimum Wage*, Princeton, NJ: Princeton University Press, 1995; and David Neumark and William Wascher, "Minimum Wages and Employment: A Case Study of the Fast-Food Industry in New Jersey and Pennsylvania: Comment," *American Economic Review*, Vol. 90, No. 5, December 2000, pp. 1362–1396.

MyEconLab Study Plan

Your Turn: Test your understanding by doing related problem 3.10 on page 138 at the end of this chapter.

Price Ceilings: Government Rent Control Policy in Housing Markets

Support for governments setting price floors typically comes from sellers, and support for governments setting price ceilings typically comes from consumers. For example, when there is a sharp increase in gasoline prices, proposals are often made for the government to impose a price ceiling on the market for gasoline. As we saw in the chapter opener, a number of cities impose rent control, which puts a ceiling on the maximum rent that landlords can charge for an apartment. Figure 4.9 shows the market for apartments in a city that has rent control.

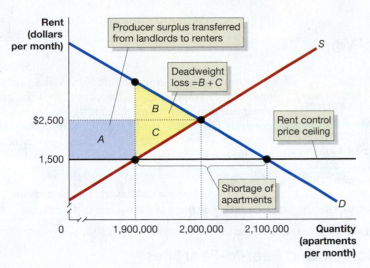

Figure 4.9   The Economic Effect of a Rent Ceiling

Without rent control, the equilibrium rent is $2,500 per month. At that price, 2,000,000 apartments would be rented. If the government imposes a rent ceiling of $1,500 per month, the quantity of apartments supplied decreases to 1,900,000, and the quantity of apartments demanded increases to 2,100,000, resulting in a shortage of 200,000 apartments. Producer surplus equal to the area of rectangle A is transferred from landlords to renters, and there is a deadweight loss equal to the areas of triangles B and C.

Without rent control, the equilibrium rent would be $2,500 per month, and 2,000,000 apartments would be rented. With a maximum legal rent of $1,500 per month, landlords reduce the quantity of apartments supplied to 1,900,000. The fall in the quantity of apartments supplied can be the result of landlords converting some apartments into offices, selling some off as condominiums, or converting some small apartment buildings into single-family homes. Over time, landlords may even abandon some apartment buildings. At one time in New York City, rent control resulted in landlords abandoning whole city blocks because they were unable to cover their costs with the rents the government allowed them to charge. In London, when rent controls were applied to rooms and apartments located in a landlord's own home, the quantity of these apartments supplied decreased by 75 percent.

In Figure 4.9, with the rent ceiling of $1,500 per month, the quantity of apartments demanded rises to 2,100,000, resulting in a shortage of 200,000 apartments. Consumer surplus increases by rectangle A and falls by triangle B. Rectangle A would have been part of producer surplus if rent control were not in place. With rent control, it is part of consumer surplus. Rent control causes the producer surplus landlords receive to fall by rectangle A plus triangle C. Triangles B and C represent the deadweight loss, which results from rent control reducing the amount of economic surplus in the market for apartments. Rent control has caused the marginal benefit of the last apartment rented to be greater than the marginal cost of supplying it. We can conclude that a price ceiling, such as rent control, reduces economic efficiency. The appendix to this chapter shows how we can make quantitative estimates of the deadweight loss and provides an example of the changes in consumer surplus and producer surplus that can result from rent control.

Renters as a group benefit from rent controls—total consumer surplus is larger—but landlords lose. Because of the deadweight loss, the total loss to landlords is greater than the gain to renters. Notice also that although renters as a group benefit, the number of renters is reduced, so some renters are made worse off by rent controls because they are unable to find an apartment at the legal rent.   MyEconLab Concept Check

Don't Let This Happen to You

Don't Confuse "Scarcity" with "Shortage"

At first glance, the following statement seems correct: "There is a shortage of every good that is scarce." In everyday conversation, we describe a good as "scarce" if we have trouble finding it. For instance, if you are looking for a gift for a child, you might call the latest hot toy "scarce" if you are willing to buy it at its listed price but can't find it online or in any store. But recall that economists have a broader definition of *scarce*. In the economic sense, almost everything—except undesirable things like garbage—is scarce. A shortage of a good occurs only if the quantity demanded is greater than the quantity supplied at the current price. Therefore, the preceding statement—"There is a shortage of every good that is scarce"—is incorrect. In fact, there is no shortage of most scarce goods.

MyEconLab Study Plan

Your Turn: Test your understanding by doing related problem 3.13 on page 138 at the end of this chapter.

Black Markets and Peer-to-Peer Sites

When governments regulate prices by enacting price ceilings or price floors, buyers and sellers often find a way around the regulations. As a result, renters may be worse off and landlords may be better off than Figure 4.9 makes it seem. We have assumed that renters and landlords actually abide by the price ceiling, but sometimes they don't. Because rent control leads to a shortage of apartments, renters who would otherwise not be able to find apartments have an incentive to offer landlords rents *above* the legal maximum. The result is a **black market** in which buying and selling take place at prices that violate government price regulations.

Black market A market in which buying and selling take place at prices that violate government price regulations.

Online peer-to-peer rental sites like Airbnb have provided landlords and tenants another way to avoid rent controls. Landlords can use these sites to convert a regular yearly rental into a series of short-term rentals for which they can charge above the legal maximum rent. Tenants can also use the sites to make a profit from rent controls. As we saw in the chapter opener, in San Francisco, some tenants moved out of the city but kept their rent-controlled apartments and rented them using peer-to-peer rental sites. Both San Francisco and New York have taken actions against peer-to-peer rental sites because some government officials believe the sites undermine rent control. Both cities have laws that prohibit landlords from renting apartments for less than 30 days. San Francisco also announced that anyone renting rooms through Airbnb and similar sites must pay the city's 14 percent hotel tax.

Some government officials in both cities, however, were reluctant to take actions that might limit the growth of the sharing economy of peer-to-peer rental sites. The sharing economy has the potential to improve economic efficiency and make available to consumers goods, such as cars, bikes, boats, and apartments, at lower prices. When cities have rent control laws, though, peer-to-peer sites perform a somewhat different function, making apartments available at rents higher than the legal price ceiling— apartments that renters might otherwise have difficulty finding because of the shortage caused by rent control. It remains to be seen whether local policymakers can resolve the conflict between putting legal ceilings on rents and encouraging peer-to-peer sites to operate in their cities.

MyEconLab Concept Check

Solved Problem 4.3

MyEconLab Interactive Animation

What's the Economic Effect of a Black Market in Renting Apartments?

In many cities that have rent controls, such as New York and San Francisco, the actual rents paid can be much higher than the legal maximum. Because rent controls cause a shortage of apartments, desperate tenants are often willing to pay landlords rents that are higher than the law allows, perhaps by writing a check for the legally allowed rent and paying an additional amount in cash. Look again at Figure 4.9 on page 121. Suppose that competition among tenants results in the black market rent rising to $3,500 per month. At this rent, tenants demand 1,900,000 apartments. Draw a graph showing the market for apartments and compare this situation with the one shown in Figure 4.9. Be sure to note any differences in consumer surplus, producer surplus, and deadweight loss.

Solving the Problem

Step 1:   Review the chapter material. This problem is about price controls in the market for apartments, so you may want to review the section "Price Ceilings: Government Rent Control Policy in Housing Markets," which begins on page 120.

Step 2:   Draw a graph similar to Figure 4.9, with the addition of the black market price.

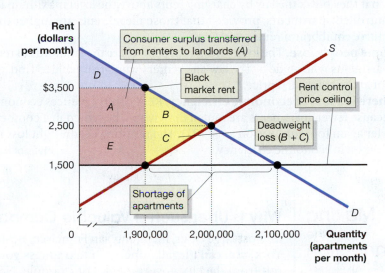

Step 3:   Analyze the changes from Figure 4.9. The black market rent is now $3,500 per month—even higher than the original competitive equilibrium rent shown in Figure 4.9. So, consumer surplus declines by an amount equal to the sum of the areas of rectangle A and rectangle E. The remaining consumer surplus is triangle D. Note that rectangle A, which would have been part of consumer surplus without rent control, represents a transfer from renters to landlords. Compared with the situation shown in Figure 4.9, producer surplus has increased by an amount equal to the sum of the areas of rectangles A and E, and consumer surplus has declined by the same amount. Deadweight loss is equal to the sum of the areas of triangles B and C, the same as in Figure 4.9.

Extra Credit: This analysis leads to a surprising result: With an active black market in apartments, rent control may leave renters as a group worse off—with less consumer surplus—than if there were no rent control. There is one more possibility to consider, however. If enough landlords become convinced that they can get away with charging rents above the legal ceiling, the quantity of apartments supplied will increase. Eventually, the market could even end up at the competitive equilibrium, with an equilibrium rent of $2,500 and equilibrium quantity of 2,000,000 apartments. In that case, the rent control price ceiling becomes nonbinding, not because it was set below the equilibrium price but because it was not legally enforced.

Your Turn: For more practice, do related problem 3.14 on page 138 at the end of this chapter.   MyEconLab Study Plan

---

Rent controls can also lead to an increase in racial and other types of discrimination. With rent controls, more renters are looking for apartments than there are apartments to rent. Landlords can afford to indulge their prejudices by refusing to rent to people from groups they don't like. In cities without rent controls, landlords face more competition, which makes it more difficult to reject tenants on the basis of irrelevant characteristics, such as race.

The Results of Government Price Controls: Winners, Losers, and Inefficiency

When the government imposes price floors or price ceilings, three important results occur:

1. **Some people win.** The winners from rent control are the people who are paying less for rent because they live in rent-controlled apartments. Landlords may also gain if they break the law by charging rents above the legal maximum for their rent-controlled apartments, provided that those illegal rents are higher than the competitive equilibrium rents would be.

2. **Some people lose.** The losers from rent control are the landlords of rent-controlled apartments who abide by the law and renters who are unable to find apartments to rent at the controlled price.

3. **There is a loss of economic efficiency.** Rent control reduces economic efficiency because fewer apartments are rented than would be rented in a competitive market (refer again to Figure 4.9, on page 121). The resulting deadweight loss measures the decrease in economic efficiency.   MyEconLab Concept Check

---

Making the Connection MyEconLab Video

Why Is Uber Such a Valuable Company?

In most large cities, including San Francisco, Boston, and New York, you can't legally operate a taxi unless you have a permit from the city government. For example, New York City requires taxi drivers to purchase a medallion issued by the city government. The number of medallions issued is limited, and in recent years, the price of a medallion has sometimes exceeded $1 *million*. Clearly, it is very expensive to enter the taxi business in most large cities. City governments also typically regulate the price of taxi rides. Because the price of taxi rides in these cities is usually above its equilibrium level, we know that there is a loss of consumer surplus.

Entrepreneur Travis Kalanick of California founded Uber Technologies in 2009 as an alternative to conventional taxis. The firm's slogan is "Choice is a beautiful thing." Uber is a mobile app that allows users to quickly summon a car—often a luxury car such as a BMW or Cadillac—owned by a driver who signs up with Uber and agrees to meet certain requirements. Anyone in a big city who wants to enter the business of offering rides would find it much easier to sign up with Uber than to obtain the permit necessary to operate a conventional taxi. Uber believes that local regulations governing taxis do not apply to its services.

Some people would rather use their smartphone to order a ride from Uber than use a taxi.

Uber claims to be adding as many as 20,000 new drivers per month worldwide. Taxi drivers in many cities have protested against Uber because they believe competition from Uber drivers will reduce the profitability of driving a taxi. In New York City, in 2015, the price of taxi medallions had fallen by more than 20 percent. Some New York City taxi drivers predicted that the industry would collapse unless the city government more closely regulated Uber.

Investors have estimated that Uber could have a value of $50 billion—or more than three times the values of auto rental firms Hertz and Avis combined. A much smaller rival ride-sharing service, Lyft, was valued at $2.5 billion. Investors expect that Uber and Lyft will be very profitable because they offer consumers lower-priced or more convenient car rides than are available from taxis. Uber and Lyft's high profits depend on the large gap between the regulated price of taxi rides and the equilibrium price.

In other words, the high profits show that government regulation of the taxi industry has greatly reduced consumer surplus.

Sources: Douglas MacMillan and Telis Demosu, "Uber Eyes $50 Billion Valuation in New Funding," *Wall Street Journal*, May 9, 2015; Douglas MacMillan, "Carl Icahn Takes $100 Million Stake in Lyft," *Wall Street Journal*, May 15, 2015; and Andrew J. Hawkins, "Taxi Interests Sue City, Predicting Collapse of Their Industry," crainsnewyork.com, May 27, 2015.

Your Turn: Test your understanding by doing related problem 3.15 on page 138 at the end of this chapter.

MyEconLab Study Plan

Positive and Normative Analysis of Price Ceilings and Price Floors

Are rent controls, government farm programs, and other price ceilings and price floors bad? As we saw in Chapter 1, questions of this type do not have right or wrong answers. Economists are generally skeptical of government attempts to interfere with competitive market equilibrium. Economists know the role competitive markets have played in raising the average person's standard of living. They also know that too much government intervention has the potential to reduce the ability of the market system to produce similar increases in living standards in the future.

But recall the difference between positive and normative analysis. Positive analysis is concerned with *what is*, and normative analysis is concerned with *what should be*. Our analysis of rent control and the federal farm programs in this chapter is positive analysis. We discussed the economic results of these programs. Whether these programs are desirable or undesirable is a normative question. Whether the gains to the winners more than make up for the losses to the losers and for the decline in economic efficiency is a matter of judgment and not strictly an economic question. Price ceilings and price floors continue to exist partly because people who understand their downside still believe they are good policies and therefore support them. The policies also persist because many people who support them do not understand the economic analysis in this chapter and so do not understand the drawbacks to these policies.   MyEconLab Concept Check

MyEconLab Study Plan

4.4 The Economic Effect of Taxes

LEARNING OBJECTIVE: Analyze the economic effect of taxes.

Supreme Court Justice Oliver Wendell Holmes once remarked: "Taxes are what we pay for a civilized society." When the government taxes a good or service, however, it affects the market equilibrium for that good or service. Just as with a price ceiling or price floor, one result of a tax is a decline in economic efficiency. Analyzing taxes is an important part of the field of economics known as *public finance*. In this section, we will use the model of demand and supply and the concepts of consumer surplus, producer surplus, and deadweight loss to analyze the economic effect of taxes.

The Effect of Taxes on Economic Efficiency

Whenever a government taxes a good or service, less of that good or service will be produced and consumed. For example, a tax on cigarettes will raise the cost of smoking and reduce the amount of smoking that takes place. We can use a demand and supply graph to illustrate this point. Figure 4.10 shows the market for cigarettes.

Without the tax, the equilibrium price of cigarettes would be $5.00 per pack, and 4 billion packs of cigarettes would be sold per year (point *A*). If the federal government requires sellers of cigarettes to pay a $1.00-per-pack tax, then their cost of selling cigarettes will increase by $1.00 per pack. This increase in cost causes the supply curve for cigarettes to shift up by $1.00 because sellers will now require a price that is $1.00 greater to supply the same quantity of cigarettes. In Figure 4.10, the supply curve shifts up by $1.00 to show the effect of the tax, and there is a new equilibrium price of $5.90 and a new equilibrium quantity of 3.7 billion packs (point *B*).

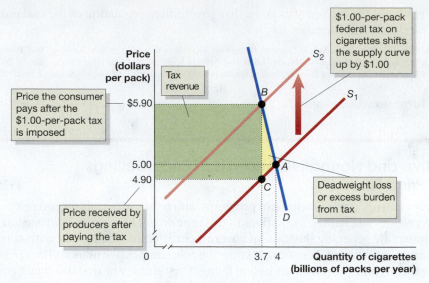

MyEconLab Animation

Figure 4.10   The Effect of a Tax on the Market for Cigarettes

Without the tax, market equilibrium occurs at point A. The equilibrium price of cigarettes is $5.00 per pack, and 4 billion packs of cigarettes are sold per year. A $1.00-per-pack tax on cigarettes will cause the supply curve for cigarettes to shift up by $1.00, from S_1 to S_2. The new equilibrium occurs at point B. The price of cigarettes will increase by $0.90, to $5.90 per pack, and the quantity sold will fall to 3.7 billion packs. The tax on cigarettes has increased the price paid by consumers from $5.00 to $5.90 per pack. Producers receive a price of $5.90 per pack (point B), but after paying the $1.00 tax, they are left with $4.90 (point C). The government will receive tax revenue equal to the green-shaded box. Some consumer surplus and some producer surplus will become tax revenue for the government, and some will become deadweight loss, shown by the yellow-shaded area.

The federal government will collect tax revenue equal to the tax per pack multiplied by the number of packs sold, or $3.7 billion. The area shaded in green in Figure 4.10 represents the government's tax revenue. Consumers will pay a higher price of $5.90 per pack. Although sellers appear to be receiving a higher price per pack, once they have paid the tax, the price they receive falls from $5.00 per pack to $4.90 per pack. There is a loss of consumer surplus because consumers are paying a higher price. The price producers receive falls, so there is also a loss of producer surplus. Therefore, the tax on cigarettes has reduced *both* consumer surplus and producer surplus. Some of the reduction in consumer and producer surplus becomes tax revenue for the government. The rest of the reduction in consumer and producer surplus is equal to the deadweight loss from the tax, shown by the yellow-shaded triangle in the figure.

We can conclude that the true burden of a tax is not just the amount consumers and producers pay the government but also includes the deadweight loss. The deadweight loss from a tax is referred to as the *excess burden* of the tax. *A tax is efficient if it imposes a small excess burden relative to the tax revenue it raises.* One contribution economists make to government tax policy is to advise policymakers on which taxes are most efficient.   MyEconLab Concept Check

Tax Incidence: Who Actually Pays a Tax?

The answer to the question "Who pays a tax?" seems obvious: Whoever is legally required to send a tax payment to the government pays the tax. But there can be an important difference between who is legally required to pay the tax and who actually *bears the burden* of the tax. The actual division of the burden of a tax between buyers and sellers is referred to as **tax incidence**. For example, the federal government currently levies an excise tax of 18.4 cents per gallon of gasoline sold. Gas station owners collect this tax and forward it to the federal government, but who actually bears the burden of the tax?

Tax incidence The actual division of the burden of a tax between buyers and sellers in a market.

MyEconLab **Animation**

Figure 4.11

The Incidence of a Tax on Gasoline

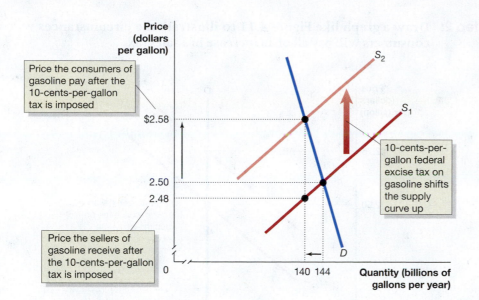

With no tax on gasoline, the price would be $2.50 per gallon, and 144 billion gallons of gasoline would be sold each year. A 10-cents-per-gallon excise tax shifts up the supply curve from S_1 to S_2, raises the price consumers pay from $2.50 to $2.58, and lowers the price sellers receive from $2.50 to $2.48. Therefore, consumers pay 8 cents of the 10-cents-per-gallon tax on gasoline, and sellers pay 2 cents.

Determining Tax Incidence on a Demand and Supply Graph

Suppose that currently the federal government does not impose a tax on gasoline. In Figure 4.11, equilibrium in the retail market for gasoline occurs at the intersection of the demand curve and supply curve, S_1. The equilibrium price is $2.50 per gallon, and the equilibrium quantity is 144 billion gallons per year. Now suppose that the federal government imposes a 10-cents-per-gallon tax. As a result of the tax, the supply curve for gasoline will shift up by 10 cents per gallon. At the new equilibrium, where the demand curve intersects the supply curve, S_2, the price has risen by 8 cents per gallon, from $2.50 to $2.58. Notice that only in the extremely unlikely case that demand is a vertical line will the market price rise by the full amount of the tax. Consumers are paying 8 cents more per gallon. Sellers of gasoline receive a new higher price of $2.58 per gallon, but after paying the 10-cents-per-gallon tax, they are left with $2.48 per gallon, or 2 cents less than they were receiving in the old equilibrium.

Although the sellers of gasoline are responsible for collecting the tax and sending the tax receipts to the government, they do not bear most of the burden of the tax. In this case, consumers pay 8 cents of the tax because the market price has risen by 8 cents, and sellers pay 2 cents of the tax because after sending the tax to the government, they are receiving 2 cents less per gallon of gasoline sold. Expressed in percentage terms, consumers pay 80 percent of the tax, and sellers pay 20 percent of the tax.

Solved Problem 4.4

MyEconLab **Interactive Animation**

When Do Consumers Pay All of a Sales Tax Increase?

A student makes the following statement: "If the federal government raises the sales tax on gasoline by $0.25, then the price of gasoline will rise by $0.25. Consumers can't get by without gasoline, so they have to pay the whole amount of any increase in the sales tax." Under what circumstances will the student's statement be true? Use a graph of the market for gasoline to illustrate your answer.

Solving the Problem

Step 1: **Review the chapter material.** This problem is about tax incidence, so you may want to review the section "Tax Incidence: Who Actually Pays a Tax?" which begins on page 126.

Step 2: **Draw a graph like Figure 4.11 to illustrate the circumstances when consumers will pay all of an increase in a sales tax.**

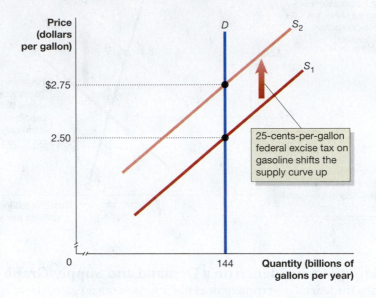

Step 3: **Use the graph to evaluate the statement.** The graph shows that consumers will pay all of an increase in a sales tax only if the demand curve is a vertical line. It is very unlikely that the demand for gasoline would look like this because we expect that for every good, an increase in price will cause a decrease in the quantity demanded. Because the demand curve for gasoline is not a vertical line, the statement is incorrect.

MyEconLab Study Plan

Your Turn: For more practice, do related problem 4.8 on page 140 at the end of the chapter.

Does It Make a Difference Whether the Government Collects a Tax from Buyers or Sellers? We have already seen the important distinction between who is legally required to pay a tax and who actually bears the burden of a tax. We can reinforce this point by noting explicitly that the incidence of a tax does *not* depend on whether the government collects a tax from the buyers of a good or from the sellers. Figure 4.12 illustrates this point by showing the effect on equilibrium in the market for gasoline if a 10-cents-per-gallon tax is imposed on buyers rather than on sellers. That is, we are now assuming that instead of sellers having to collect the 10-cents-per-gallon tax at the pump, buyers are responsible for keeping track of how many gallons of gasoline they purchase and sending the tax to the government. (Of course, it would be very difficult for buyers to keep track of their purchases or for the government to check whether they were paying all of the taxes they owe. That is why the government collects the tax on gasoline from sellers.)

Figure 4.12 is similar to Figure 4.11 except that it shows the gasoline tax being imposed on buyers rather than on sellers. In Figure 4.12, the supply curve does not shift because nothing has happened to change the quantity of gasoline sellers are willing to supply at any given price. The demand curve has shifted, however, because consumers now have to pay a 10-cent tax on every gallon of gasoline they buy. Therefore, at every quantity, they are willing to pay a price 10 cents lower than they would have without the tax. In the figure, we indicate the effect of the tax by shifting the demand curve down by 10 cents, from D_1 to D_2. Once the tax has been imposed and the demand curve has shifted down, the new equilibrium quantity of gasoline is 140 billion gallons, which is exactly the same as in Figure 4.11.

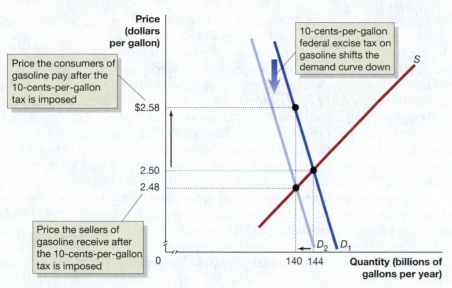

Price the consumers of gasoline pay after the 10-cents-per-gallon tax is imposed

10-cents-per-gallon federal excise tax on gasoline shifts the demand curve down

Price the sellers of gasoline receive after the 10-cents-per-gallon tax is imposed

MyEconLab Animation

Figure 4.12   The Incidence of a Tax on Gasoline Paid by Buyers

With no tax on gasoline, the demand curve is D_1. If a 10-cents-per-gallon tax is imposed that consumers are responsible for paying, the demand curve shifts down by the amount of the tax, from D_1 to D_2.

In the new equilibrium, consumers pay a price of $2.58 per gallon, including the tax. Producers receive $2.48 per gallon. The result is the same as when producers were responsible for paying the tax.

The new equilibrium price after the tax is imposed appears to be different in Figure 4.12 than in Figure 4.11, but if we include the tax, buyers will pay the same price and sellers will receive the same price in both figures. To see this point, notice that in Figure 4.11, buyers pay sellers a price of $2.58 per gallon. In Figure 4.12, they pay sellers only $2.48, but they must also pay the government a tax of 10 cents per gallon. So, the total price buyers pay remains $2.58 per gallon. In Figure 4.11, sellers receive $2.58 per gallon from buyers, but after they pay the tax of 10 cents per gallon, they are left with $2.48, which is the same amount they receive in Figure 4.12.   MyEconLab Concept Check

Making the Connection
MyEconLab Video

Is the Burden of the Social Security Tax Really Shared Equally between Workers and Firms?

Most people who receive paychecks have several different taxes withheld by their employers, who forward the taxes directly to the government. In fact, after getting their first job, many people are shocked when they discover the gap between their gross pay and their net pay after taxes have been deducted. The largest tax many people of low or moderate income pay is FICA, which stands for the Federal Insurance Contributions Act. FICA funds the Social Security and Medicare programs, which provide income and health care to the elderly and disabled. FICA is sometimes referred to as the *payroll tax*. When Congress passed the act, it wanted employers and workers to equally share the burden of the tax. Currently, FICA is 15.3 percent of wages, with workers paying 7.65 percent, which is withheld from their paychecks, and employers paying the other 7.65 percent.

But does requiring workers and employers to each pay half the tax mean that the burden of the tax is also shared equally? Our discussion in this chapter shows that the answer is "no." In the labor market, employers are buyers, and workers are sellers. As we saw in the example of the federal tax on gasoline, whether the tax is collected from buyers or from sellers does not affect the incidence of the tax. Most economists believe, in fact, that the burden of FICA falls almost entirely on workers. The following figure, which shows the market for labor, illustrates why.

In the market for labor, the demand curve represents the quantity of labor demanded by employers at various wages, and the supply curve represents the quantity of labor supplied by workers at various wages. The intersection of the demand curve and the supply curve determines the equilibrium wage. In both panels, the equilibrium wage without a Social Security payroll tax is $10 per hour. For simplicity, let's assume that the payroll tax equals $1 per hour of work. In panel (a), we assume that employers must pay the tax. The tax causes the demand for labor curve to shift down by $1 at every quantity of labor because firms must now pay a $1 tax for every hour of labor they hire. We have drawn the supply curve for labor as being very steep because most economists believe the quantity of labor supplied by workers does not change much as the wage rate changes. In panel (a), after the tax is imposed, the equilibrium wage declines from $10 per hour to $9.05 per hour. Firms are now paying a total of $10.05 for every hour of work they hire: $9.05 in wages to workers and $1 in tax to the government. In other words, workers have paid $0.95 of the $1 tax, and firms have paid only $0.05.

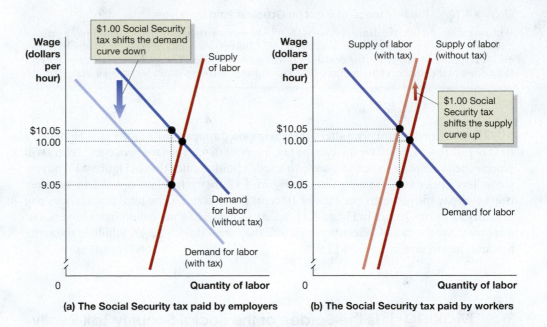

(a) The Social Security tax paid by employers   (b) The Social Security tax paid by workers

Panel (b) shows that this result is exactly the same when the tax is imposed on workers rather than on firms. In this case, the tax causes the supply curve for labor to shift up by $1 at every quantity of labor because workers must now pay a tax of $1 for every hour they work. After the tax is imposed, the equilibrium wage increases to $10.05 per hour. But workers receive only $9.05 after they have paid the $1.00 tax. Once again, workers have paid $0.95 of the $1 tax, and firms have paid only $0.05.

Although the figure presents a simplified analysis, it reflects the conclusion of most economists who have studied the incidence of FICA: Even though Congress requires employers to pay half the tax and workers to pay the other half, in fact, the burden of the tax falls almost entirely on workers. This conclusion would not be changed even if Congress revised the law to require either employers or workers to pay all of the tax. The forces of demand and supply working in the labor market, and not Congress, determine the incidence of the tax.

Your Turn: Test your understanding by doing related problems 4.9 and 4.10 on page 140 at the end of this chapter.

Continued from page 109

Economics in Your Life

Does Rent Control Make It Easier for You to Find an Affordable Apartment?

At the beginning of the chapter, we posed the following question: If you have job offers in two different cities, one with rent control and one without, are you more likely to find an affordable apartment in the city with rent control, or would you be better off looking for an apartment in a city without rent control? This chapter has shown that although rent control can keep rents lower than they might otherwise be, it can also lead to a permanent shortage of apartments. You may have to search for a long time to find a suitable apartment, and landlords may even ask you to give them additional payments in violation of the rent control law, which would make your actual rent higher than the controlled rent. Finding an apartment in a city without rent control should be much easier, although the rent may be higher.

Conclusion

Our discussion of the model of demand and supply shows that markets free from government intervention eliminate surpluses and shortages and do a good job of responding to the wants of consumers. We have seen that both consumers and firms sometimes try to use the government to change market outcomes in their favor. The concepts of consumer surplus, producer surplus, and deadweight loss allow us to measure the benefits consumers and producers receive from competitive market equilibrium. These concepts also allow us to measure the effects of government price floors and price ceilings and the economic effect of taxes.

Read *An Inside Look at Policy* on the next page for an example of regulatory and legal challenges that Airbnb faced in Malibu, California.

MALIBU TIMES

Airbnb to Begin Collecting Taxes for City: Nearly a Year after Subpoenas Were Sent, Airbnb and Malibu Have Come to an Agreement

Those who rent out their homes or guest houses during busy weekends or keep a rental property by the beach to make extra cash will soon be kicking a few bucks back to Malibu [California] since Airbnb, one of the last holdouts against Malibu's demand for taxes, has finally come to an agreement with the City.

City Council's May 2014 decision to subpoena vacation rental sites for info so they could collect transient occupancy "hotel" tax (TOT) from individuals leasing out private homes raised a few eyebrows around town, but nearly a year later, Airbnb has finally responded and, beginning on April 20, four out of the five sites they requested will now be handing the City its 12%.

"We are pleased to add Malibu to the growing list of cities where Airbnb is able to collect and remit occupancy taxes on behalf of our hosts, and where local rules embrace home sharing and the peer to peer economy," reads the official Airbnb announcement, authored by regional head of public policy David Owen.

City Attorney Christi Hogin explained that Airbnb is essentially agreeing to provide a service to those who rent out houses and apartments on its site, who are the ones legally responsible for collecting the tax.

"Airbnb is going to make it easy on the hosts by collecting the tax on their behalf and remitting it to the City, which the City is thrilled with," Hogin said.

"We think that Airbnb is totally doing the right thing here," Hogin added.

The story began 11 months ago, when Assistant City Manager Reva Feldman prepared a staff report for City Council suggesting they go after rental sites, including Airbnb, HomeAway (owners of VRBO and FlipKey) and YBYC.

According to Feldman, the City was missing out on hundreds of thousands of dollars in tax revenue.

Now, Feldman says, though numbers from Airbnb aren't finalized, the city expects a bump from TOT.

"I can tell you that we expect for this fiscal year to get $450,000," Feldman said, "That's what we expect [now]. But I don't know until Airbnb provides me with data, what we can expect."

Hogin added that the tax money goes back to renters and hosts. "The money that we can use from those taxes is basically used for police, fire, roads, clean water: all of those things that both the residents and visitors employ," Hogin said.

As for the other sites issued subpoenas, only HomeAway is holding out. According to Feldman, there doesn't seem to be much hope for the City to collect the TOT from them, since they are not under legal obligation.

Since HomeAway does not have an L.A. County office, the subpoena from the City does not put any pressure on them, and, in addition, unlike some of the other sites, VRBO and FlipKey do not collect rental fees themselves.

"They're just an advertising site; they don't collect revenue through the site," Feldman said. "Unless they willingly comply, there's nothing we can do further with that."

The City is making its money, but there has been little word about whether the tax will help cut down on vacation rentals, which was listed as a primary reason to issue the subpoenas in spring 2014.

"This is not a revenue-generating item. The reason we're doing this, the genesis of this, was we've been getting a tremendous amount of complaints from residents throughout all areas of the city," said Councilman Lou La Monte during a May 2014 council meeting.

Airbnb seems to have taken its agreement with the City to mean it's more welcome than ever to operate in Malibu neighborhoods.

"Our community in Malibu already brings significant economic and cultural benefits to the city, and this is another way we can make it even stronger," reads the Airbnb statement.

Source: Emily Sawicki, "Airbnb to Begin Collecting Taxes for City: Nearly a Year after Subpoenas Were Sent, Airbnb and Malibu Have Come to an Agreement," *Malibu Times*, April 8, 2015.

Key Points in the Article

The affluent beach community of Malibu, California, has reached an agreement with Airbnb that will require the company to collect hotel taxes on behalf of its customers who rent their homes through the Internet site. Beginning in April 2015, the city's 12 percent transient occupancy tax (TOT) will apply to anyone leasing out private homes via Airbnb. The city's initial estimate of first-year tax revenues collected from Airbnb was $450,000, which City Attorney David Hogin said will go toward services such as police and fire protection. While the collection of the TOT will generate revenue for the city, the primary motivation for collecting the tax was to cut down on vacation rentals in the community.

Analyzing the News

a Airbnb is an Internet site that matches homeowners who want to rent out rooms or their entire homes for a short period with travelers looking for short-term rentals. Since the company's inception in 2008, Airbnb has been criticized by hotel companies and some local government officials for not collecting local hotel taxes from its customers. Over the past few years, Airbnb has made an effort to appease the cities and hotel companies by agreeing to collect these taxes, as was demonstrated by the company's agreement with the city of Malibu to collect the 12 percent TOT. The figure below shows a

hypothetical example of the effect of this tax on the market for vacation rental homes in Malibu. Without the tax, the equilibrium rent is $1,000 per week, with a quantity of 400 homes being rented each month. With a 12 percent tax ($120), the supply curve shifts up by $120, increasing the price the consumer pays to $1,060, decreasing the price the homeowner receives to $940, and decreasing the quantity of homes being rented to 320. The tax revenue is equal to $38,400 per month ($120 per rental × 320 rentals).

b The imposition of the 12 percent tax on Airbnb rentals will generate revenue for the city of Malibu, but it will also affect economic efficiency by reducing consumer and producer surplus. The renters (consumers), will pay a higher price for their vacation home rentals, which reduces consumer surplus, and the homeowners, or suppliers, will receive a lower price for renting their homes, which reduces producer surplus. Some of the reduction in consumer and producer surplus will become tax revenue for the city of Malibu, which the assistant city manager estimates at $450,000 for the first fiscal year the tax is in effect, but the rest of the loss in consumer and producer surplus is deadweight loss from the tax, a result of the decrease in the number of rentals due to the imposition of the tax.

c Although the imposition of a tax does generate revenue for Malibu, additional revenue is not necessarily the reason

certain taxes are imposed. While the city pledged that the tax will be used to help pay for city services, the primary motivation for this tax is to discourage vacation home rentals. The city council cited complaints from residents about the number of homes in the community being used as short-term rental properties and proposed charging this tax as a way to reduce the number of rentals. As the figure below illustrates, when a tax is imposed, supply decreases, as does the equilibrium quantity of the product or service.

Thinking Critically about Policy

1. The figure below shows the market for vacation rental homes before and after the imposition of a 12 percent tax. How can we use the figure to measure the effect the tax has on economic efficiency? Redraw the graph and show the area representing the excess burden created by the implementation of the tax.

2. Airbnb has begun collecting hotel taxes in a number of cities. The figure below shows a hypothetical example of the effects of this tax on the market for vacation rental homes in Malibu. Redraw the graph to show what happens if renters, instead of Airbnb, were responsible for directly paying the tax to the city. Explain any differences in price, quantity, and tax incidence.

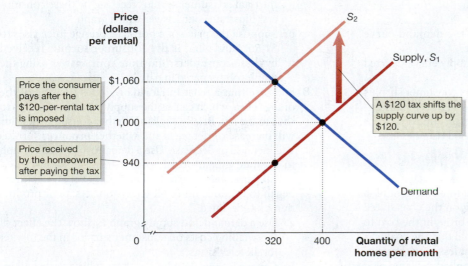

The market for vacation rental homes before and after the imposition of a 12 percent hotel tax shows that the tax shifts the supply curve up by $120, increasing the price paid by the consumer from $1,000 to $1,060 and decreasing the price received by the homeowner from $1,000 to $940.

Key Terms

4.1 Consumer Surplus and Producer Surplus, pages 110–114

LEARNING OBJECTIVE: Distinguish between the concepts of consumer surplus and producer surplus.

Summary

Although most prices are determined by demand and supply in markets, the government sometimes imposes *price ceilings* and *price floors*. A **price ceiling** is a legally determined maximum price that sellers may charge. A **price floor** is a legally determined minimum price that sellers may receive. Economists analyze the effects of price ceilings and price floors by using the concepts of *consumer surplus*, *producer surplus*, and *deadweight loss*. **Marginal benefit** is the additional benefit to a consumer from consuming one more unit of a good or service. The demand curve is also a marginal benefit curve. **Consumer surplus** is the difference between the highest price a consumer is willing to pay for a good or service and the actual price the consumer pays. The total amount of consumer surplus in a market is equal to the area below the demand curve and above the market price. **Marginal cost** is the additional cost to a firm of producing one more unit of a good or service. The supply curve is also a marginal cost curve. **Producer surplus** is the difference between the lowest price a firm is willing to accept for a good or service and the price it actually receives. The total amount of producer surplus in a market is equal to the area above the supply curve and below the market price.

 MyEconLab Visit www.myeconlab.com to complete these exercises online and get instant feedback.

Review Questions

1.1 What is marginal benefit? Why is the demand curve referred to as a marginal benefit curve?

1.2 What is marginal cost? Why is the supply curve referred to as a marginal cost curve?

1.3 What is consumer surplus? How does consumer surplus change as the equilibrium price of a good rises or falls?

1.4 What is producer surplus? How does producer surplus change as the equilibrium price of a good rises or falls?

Problems and Applications

1.5 On a shopping trip, Melanie decided to buy a light blue coat made from woven fabric. A tag on the coat stated that the price was $79.95. When she brought the coat to the store's sales clerk, Melanie was told that the coat was on sale, and she would pay 20 percent less than the price on the tag. After the discount was applied, Melanie paid $63.96, $15.99 less than the original price. Was the value of Melanie's consumer surplus from this purchase $79.95? $63.96? $15.99? Or some other amount? Briefly explain.

1.6 Uber is a company that offers people transportation by drivers who use their own cars for this purpose. Customers pay for their rides with their smartphone apps. Uber's prices fluctuate with the demand for the service. This "surge pricing" can result in different prices for the same distance traveled at different times of day or days of the week. Annie Lowrey, a writer for the *New York Times*, explained that she paid $13 for a 10 P.M. two-mile trip in downtown Washington, DC, on New Year's Eve. Three hours later she paid $47 for the return trip to her home. Did she receive negative consumer surplus on her return trip? Briefly explain.

Source: Annie Lowrey, "Is Uber's Surge-Pricing an Example of High Tech Gouging?" *New York Times*, January 10, 2014.

1.7 Consider the information given in the table on four consumers in the market for orange juice.

Consumer	Highest Price Willing to Pay
Jill	$4
Jose	3
Josh	2
Jordan	1

a. If the price of a bottle of orange juice is $0.75, what is the total consumer surplus received by these consumers? Illustrate your answer with a graph.

b. Suppose the price of a bottle of orange juice rises to $1.50. Now what is the consumer surplus received by these consumers? Illustrate your answer using the graph you prepared in part (a).

1.8 Suppose that a frost in Florida reduces the size of the orange crop, which causes the supply curve for oranges to shift to the left. Briefly explain whether consumer surplus will increase or decrease and whether producer surplus will increase or decrease. Use a demand and supply graph to illustrate your answers.

1.9 A *Wall Street Journal* article noted that as manufacturers began to produce more 4K television sets, their production costs declined.

a. Use a demand and supply graph to show the effect of these falling costs on consumer surplus in the marker for 4K televisions.

b. Can we be certain whether these falling costs will increase producer surplus? Briefly explain.

Source: Jack Wetherill and Brett Sappington, "Is Now the Time to Buy a 4K TV Set?" *Wall Street Journal*, May 11, 2014.

1.10 A student makes the following argument: "When a market is in equilibrium, there is no consumer surplus. We know this because in equilibrium, the market price is equal to the price consumers are willing to pay for the good." Briefly explain whether you agree with the student's argument.

1.11 In the following graph, is the consumer surplus larger with demand curve D_1 or demand curve D_2? Briefly explain. Compare the producer surplus with demand curve D_1 and with demand curve D_2.

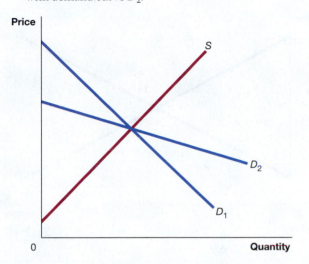

1.12 Assume that the following graph illustrates the market for a breast cancer–fighting drug, without which breast cancer patients cannot survive. What is the consumer surplus in this market? How does it differ from the consumer surplus in the markets you have studied up to this point?

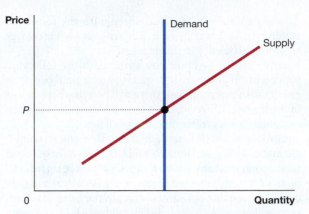

1.13 **(Related to the** Making the Connection **on page 112)** The *Making the Connection* states that the value of the area representing consumer surplus from broadband Internet service is $890.4 million. Use the information from the graph in the *Making the Connection* to show how this value was calculated. (For a review of how to calculate the area of a triangle, see the appendix to Chapter 1.)

1.14 The following graph shows the market for tickets to a concert that will be held in a local arena that seats 15,000 people. What is the producer surplus in this market? How does it differ from the producer surplus in the markets you have studied up to this point?

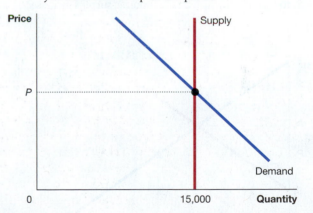

4.2 **The Efficiency of Competitive Markets, pages 115–117**
LEARNING OBJECTIVE: Explain the concept of economic efficiency.

Summary

Equilibrium in a competitive market is economically efficient. **Economic surplus** is the sum of consumer surplus and producer surplus. **Economic efficiency** is a market outcome in which the marginal benefit to consumers from the last unit produced is equal to the marginal cost of production and in which the sum of consumer surplus and producer surplus is at a maximum. When the market price is above or below the equilibrium price, there is a reduction in economic surplus. The reduction in economic surplus resulting from a market not being in competitive equilibrium is called the **deadweight loss**.

Review Questions

2.1 Define *economic surplus* and *deadweight loss*.

2.2 What is economic efficiency? Why do economists define efficiency in this way?

Problems and Applications

2.3 A *Wall Street Journal* article about a drought in California indicated that one result would be a smaller tomato crop. Use a demand and supply graph of the tomato market to illustrate the effect of the drought. Is economic efficiency affected? Briefly explain.

Source: Jim Carlton, "California Farmers Face Another Year without Federal Water," *Wall Street Journal*, February 27, 2015.

 MyEconLab   Visit **www.myeconlab.com** to complete these exercises online and get instant feedback.

2.4 Briefly explain whether you agree with the following statement: "A lower price in a market always increases economic efficiency in that market."

2.5 Briefly explain whether you agree with the following statement: "If at the current quantity, marginal benefit is greater than marginal cost, there will be a deadweight loss in the market. However, there is no deadweight loss when marginal cost is greater than marginal benefit."

2.6 According to a *Wall Street Journal* article, many restaurant chains, including McDonald's and Chick-fil-A, have begun serving only chickens that were raised without being fed antibiotics. Using this method of raising chickens increases their cost. Suppose that consumers react to the news of restaurants selling antibiotic-free chicken sandwiches by increasing their demand for the sandwiches. Can you tell whether economic surplus will increase in the market for chicken sandwiches? Use a graph of the market for chicken sandwiches to illustrate your answer.

Source: David Kesmodel, Jacob Bunge, and Annie Gasparro, "McDonald's to Curb Antibiotics in Chicken," *Wall Street Journal*, March 4, 2015.

2.7 Briefly explain whether you agree with the following statement: "If consumer surplus in a market increases, producer surplus must decrease."

2.8 Using the following graph, show the effects on consumer surplus and producer surplus of an increase in supply from S_1 to S_2. By how much does economic surplus increase?

2.9 A student argues: "Economic surplus is greatest at the level of output where the difference between marginal benefit and marginal cost is largest." Do you agree? Briefly explain.

2.10 Using the following graph, explain why economic surplus would be smaller if Q_1 or Q_3 were the quantity produced than if Q_2 is the quantity produced.

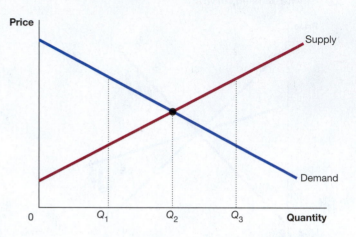

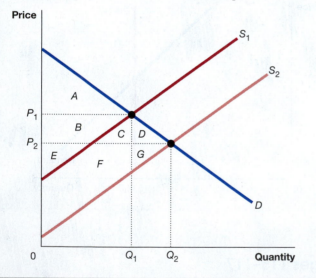

4.3 **Government Intervention in the Market: Price Floors and Price Ceilings, pages 117–125**

LEARNING OBJECTIVE: Explain the economic effect of government-imposed price floors and price ceilings.

Summary

Producers or consumers who are dissatisfied with the equilibrium in a market can attempt to convince the government to impose a price floor or a price ceiling. Price floors usually increase producer surplus, decrease consumer surplus, and cause a deadweight loss. Price ceilings usually increase consumer surplus, reduce producer surplus, and cause a deadweight loss. The results of the government imposing price ceilings and price floors are that some people win, some people lose, and a loss of economic efficiency occurs. Price ceilings and price floors can lead to a **black market**, in which buying and selling take place at prices that violate government price regulations. Positive analysis is concerned with *what is*, and normative analysis is concerned with *what should be*. Positive analysis shows that price ceilings and price floors cause deadweight losses. Whether these policies are desirable or undesirable, though, is a normative question.

MyEconLab   Visit **www.myeconlab.com** to complete these exercises online and get instant feedback.

Review Questions

3.1 Why do some consumers tend to favor price controls while others tend to oppose them?

3.2 Do producers tend to favor price floors or price ceilings? Briefly explain.

3.3 What is a black market? Under what circumstances do black markets arise?

3.4 Can economic analysis provide a final answer to the question of whether the government should intervene in markets by imposing price ceilings and price floors? Briefly explain.

Problems and Applications

3.5 The following graph shows the market for apples. Assume that the government has imposed a price floor of $10 per crate.

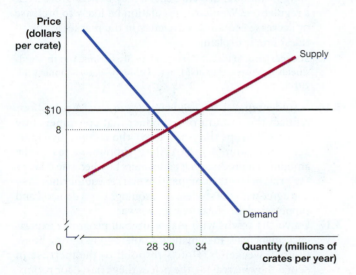

a. How many crates of apples will be sold to consumers after the price floor has been imposed?

b. Will there be a shortage or a surplus of apples? If there is a shortage or a surplus, how large will it be?

c. Will apple producers benefit from the price floor? If so, explain how they will benefit.

3.6 Use the information on the kumquat market in the table to answer the following questions:

Price (per Crate)	Quantity Demanded (Millions of Crates per Year)	Quantity Supplied (Millions of Crates per Year)
$10	120	20
15	110	60
20	100	100
25	90	140
30	80	180
35	70	220

a. What are the equilibrium price and quantity? How much revenue do kumquat producers receive when the market is in equilibrium? Draw a graph showing the market equilibrium and the area representing the revenue kumquat producers receive.

b. Suppose the federal government decides to impose a price floor of $30 per crate. Now how many crates of kumquats will consumers purchase? How much revenue will kumquat producers receive? Assume that the government does not purchase any surplus kumquats. On your graph from part (a), show the price floor, the change in the quantity of kumquats purchased, and the revenue kumquat producers receive after the price floor is imposed.

c. Suppose the government imposes a price floor of $30 per crate and purchases any surplus kumquats from producers. Now how much revenue will kumquat producers receive? How much will the government spend on purchasing surplus kumquats? On your graph from part (a), show the area representing the amount the government spends to purchase the surplus kumquats.

3.7 Suppose that the government sets a price floor for milk that is above the competitive equilibrium price and that the government does not purchase any surplus milk.

a. Draw a graph showing this situation. Be sure your graph shows the competitive equilibrium price, the price floor, the quantity that would be sold in competitive equilibrium, and the quantity that would be sold with the price floor.

b. Compare the economic surplus in this market when there is a price floor and when there is not.

3.8 In Allentown, Pennsylvania, in the summer of 2014, the average price of a gallon of gasoline was $3.68—a 22-cent increase from the year before. Many consumers were upset by the increase. One consumer was quoted in a local newspaper as saying, "It's crazy. The government should step in." Suppose the government had stepped in and imposed a price ceiling equal to the old price of $3.46 per gallon.

a. Draw a graph showing the effect of the price ceiling on the market for gasoline. Be sure that your graph shows:
   i. The price and quantity of gasoline before and after the price ceiling is imposed
   ii. The areas representing consumer surplus and producer surplus before and after the price ceiling is imposed
   iii. The area of deadweight loss

b. Will the consumer who was complaining about the increase in the price of gasoline definitely be made better off by the price ceiling? Briefly explain.

Source: Sam Kennedy, "Valley Feeling Pain at the Pump," (Allentown, PA) *Morning Call*, June 21, 2014.

3.9 According to a *New York Times* article, the Venezuelan government "imposes strict price controls that are intended to make a range of foods and other goods more affordable for the poor. They are often the very products that are the hardest to find."

a. Why would imposing price controls on goods make them hard to find?

b. One of the goods subject to price controls was toothpaste. Draw a graph to illustrate this situation. On your graph, be sure to indicate the areas representing consumer surplus, producer surplus, and deadweight loss.

Source: William Neuman, "With Venezuelan Cupboards Bare, Some Blame Price Controls," *New York Times*, April 20, 2012.

3.10 **(Related to the** Making the Connection **on page 119)** A *Wall Street Journal* article noted that a study by the U.S. Congressional Budget Office "estimated raising the minimum wage to $10.10 an hour would reduce U.S. employment by 500,000 but lift 900,000 Americans out of poverty." Why might raising the minimum wage reduce employment? How would it raise some people out of poverty? What effect might these estimates have on a *normative* analysis of the minimum wage?

Source: Julie Jargon and Eric Morath, "As Wage Debate Rages, Some Have Made the Shift," *Wall Street Journal*, April 8, 2014.

3.11 **(Related to the** Chapter Opener **on page 109)** If San Francisco were to repeal its rent control law, would the prices for short-term rentals in the city listed on Airbnb and other peer-to-peer sites be likely to rise or fall? Briefly explain.

3.12 **(Related to the** Chapter Opener **on page 109)** The competitive equilibrium rent in the city of Lowell is currently $1,000 per month. The government decides to enact rent control and establish a price ceiling of $750 per month for apartments. Briefly explain whether rent control is likely to make each of the following people better or worse off.
a. Someone currently renting an apartment in Lowell
b. Someone who will be moving to Lowell next year and who intends to rent an apartment
c. A landlord who intends to abide by the rent control law
d. A landlord who intends to ignore the law and illegally charge the highest rent possible for his apartments

3.13 **(Related to the** Don't Let This Happen to You **on page 121)** Briefly explain whether you agree with the following statement: "If there is a shortage of a good, it must be scarce, but there is not a shortage of every scarce good."

3.14 **(Related to** Solved Problem 4.3 **on page 122)** Use the information on the market for apartments in Bay City in the table to answer the following questions:

Rent	Quantity Demanded	Quantity Supplied
$500	375,000	225,000
600	350,000	250,000
700	325,000	275,000
800	300,000	300,000
900	275,000	325,000
1,000	250,000	350,000

a. In the absence of rent control, what is the equilibrium rent, and what is the equilibrium quantity of apartments rented? Draw a demand and supply graph of the market for apartments to illustrate your answer. In equilibrium, will there be any renters who are unable to find an apartment to rent or any landlords who are unable to find a renter for an apartment?
b. Suppose the government sets a ceiling of $600 per month on rents. What is the quantity of apartments demanded, and what is the quantity of apartments supplied?
c. Assume that all landlords abide by the law in part (b). Use a demand and supply graph to illustrate the effect of this price ceiling on the market for apartments. Be sure to indicate on your graph each of the following:

(i) the area representing consumer surplus after the price ceiling has been imposed, (ii) the area representing producer surplus after the price ceiling has been imposed, and (iii) the area representing the deadweight loss after the price ceiling has been imposed.
d. Assume that the quantity of apartments supplied is the same as you determined in (b), but now assume that landlords ignore the law and rent this quantity of apartments for the highest rent they can get. Briefly explain what this rent will be.

3.15 **(Related to the** Making the Connection **on page 124)** According to a news story, after taxi drivers in Paris protested against Uber, the government passed a new regulation "requiring a minimum 15-minute wait between the time a car is booked and the passenger is picked up." Why would taxi drivers believe they benefit from such a regulation? Would the regulation be likely to increase or decrease economic efficiency in the market for hired rides? Briefly explain.

Source: Carol Matlack, "Paris Cabbies Slash Tires, Smash Windshields in Protest Against Uber," *businessweek.com*, January 13, 2014.

3.16 A student makes the following argument: "A price floor reduces the amount of a product that consumers buy because it keeps the price above the competitive market equilibrium. A price ceiling, though, increases the amount of a product that consumers buy because it keeps the price below the competitive market equilibrium." Do you agree with the student's reasoning? Use a demand and supply graph to illustrate your answer.

3.17 University towns with major football programs experience an increase in demand for hotel rooms during home football weekends. Hotels respond to the increase in demand by increasing the prices they charge for rooms. Periodically, there is an outcry against the higher prices and accusations of "price gouging."
a. Draw a demand and supply graph of the market for hotel rooms in Boostertown for weekends with home football games and another graph for weekends without home football games. If the Boostertown city council passes a law stating that prices for rooms are not allowed to rise, what would happen to the market for hotel rooms during home football game weekends? Show your answer on your graph.
b. If the prices of hotel rooms are not allowed to increase, what will be the effect on out-of-town football fans?
c. How might the city council's law affect the supply of hotel rooms over time? Briefly explain.
d. University towns are not the only places that face peak and nonpeak "seasons." Can you think of other locations that face a large increase in demand for hotel rooms during particular times of the year? Why do we typically not see laws limiting the prices hotels can charge during peak seasons?

3.18 Suppose that initially the gasoline market is in equilibrium, at a price of $2.50 per gallon and a quantity of 45 million gallons per month. Then a war in the Middle East disrupts imports of oil into the United States, shifting the supply curve for gasoline from S_1 to S_2. The price of gasoline begins to rise, and consumers protest. The federal government responds by setting a price ceiling of $2.50 per gallon. Use the graph to answer the following questions.

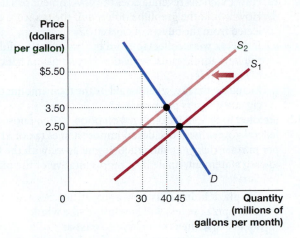

a. If there were no price ceiling, what would be the equilibrium price of gasoline, the quantity of gasoline demanded, and the quantity of gasoline supplied? Now assume that the price ceiling is imposed and that there is no black market in gasoline. What are the price of gasoline, the quantity of gasoline demanded, and the quantity of gasoline supplied? How large is the shortage of gasoline?

b. Assume that the price ceiling is imposed, and there is no black market in gasoline. Show on the graph the areas representing consumer surplus, producer surplus, and deadweight loss.

c. Now assume that there is a black market, and the price of gasoline rises to the maximum that consumers are willing to pay for the amount supplied by producers, at $2.50 per gallon. Show on the graph the areas representing producer surplus, consumer surplus, and deadweight loss.

d. Are consumers made better off with the price ceiling than without it? Briefly explain.

3.19 An editorial in the *Economist* magazine discusses the fact that in most countries—including the United States—it is illegal for individuals to buy or sell body parts, such as kidneys.

a. Draw a demand and supply graph for the market for kidneys. Show on your graph the legal maximum price of zero and indicate the quantity of kidneys supplied at this price. (*Hint:* Because we know that some kidneys are donated, the quantity supplied will not be zero.)

b. The editorial argues that buying and selling kidneys should be legalized:

> With proper regulation, a kidney market would be a big improvement over the current sorry state of affairs. Sellers could be checked for disease and drug use, and cared for after operations. … Buyers would get better kidneys, faster. Both sellers and buyers would do better than in the illegal market, where much of the money goes to middlemen.

Do you agree with this argument? Should the government treat kidneys like other goods and allow the market to determine the price?

Source: "Psst, Wanna Buy a Kidney?" *Economist*, November 18, 2006.

<table>
<tr><td>**4.4**</td><td>### The Economic Effect of Taxes, pages 125–130
LEARNING OBJECTIVE: Analyze the economic effect of taxes.</td></tr>
</table>

Summary

Most taxes result in a loss of consumer surplus, a loss of producer surplus, and a deadweight loss. The true burden of a tax is not just the amount consumers and producers pay to the government but also includes the deadweight loss. The deadweight loss from a tax is called the excess burden of the tax. **Tax incidence** is the actual division of the burden of a tax. In most cases, consumers and firms share the burden of a tax levied on a good or service.

  Visit **www.myeconlab.com** to complete these exercises online and get instant feedback.

Review Questions

4.1 What is meant by *tax incidence*?

4.2 What do economists mean by an *efficient tax*?

4.3 Does who is legally responsible for paying a tax—buyers or sellers—make a difference in the amount of tax each pays? Briefly explain.

4.4 As explained in the chapter, economic efficiency is a market outcome in which the marginal benefit to consumers of the last unit produced is equal to its marginal cost of production. Using this explanation of economic efficiency, explain why a tax creates a deadweight loss.

Problems and Applications

4.5 Suppose the current equilibrium price of a quarter-pound hamburger is $5, and 10 million quarter-pound hamburgers are sold per month. After the federal government imposes a tax of $0.50 per hamburger, the equilibrium price of hamburgers rises to $5.20, and the equilibrium quantity falls to 9 million. Illustrate this situation with a demand and supply graph. Be sure your graph shows the equilibrium price before and after the tax; the equilibrium quantity before and after the tax; and the areas representing consumer surplus after the tax, producer surplus after the tax, tax revenue collected by the government, and deadweight loss.

4.6 The following graph shows the effect of a tax imposed on soft drinks. Use this graph to answer the questions.

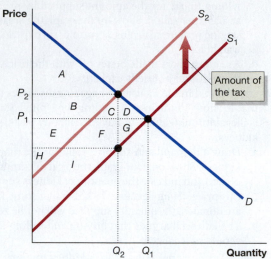

a. Which areas in the graph represent the excess burden (deadweight loss) of the tax?
b. Which areas represent the revenues collected by the government from the tax?
c. Would this tax on soft drinks be considered efficient? Briefly explain.

4.7 Use the following graph of the market for cigarettes to answer the questions.

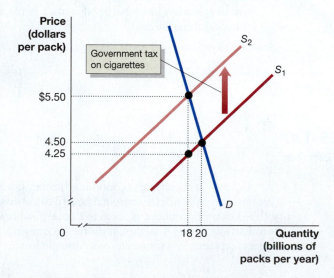

a. According to the graph, how much is the government tax on cigarettes?
b. What price do producers receive after paying the tax?
c. How much tax revenue does the government collect?
d. How would the graph be different if the tax were collected from the buyers of cigarettes?
e. If the tax were collected from buyers, what would be the new equilibrium price that buyers pay producers of cigarettes?
f. Including the tax, what would be the total amount that cigarette buyers pay per pack?

4.8 **(Related to** Solved Problem 4.4 **on page 127)** Suppose the federal government decides to impose a sales tax of $1.00 per pizza. Briefly explain whether you agree with the following statement, made by a representative of the pizza industry:

> The pizza industry is very competitive. As a result, pizza sellers will have to pay the whole tax because they are unable to pass any of it on to consumers in the form of higher prices. Therefore, a sales tax of $1.00 per pizza will result in pizza sellers receiving $1.00 less on each pizza sold, after paying the tax.

Illustrate your answer with a graph.

4.9 **(Related to the** Making the Connection **on page 129)** According to a news story, Pennsylvania's liquor tax is "paid by the seller—the restaurant or bar owner—when the seller buys liquor from state-run wine and spirit stores." Briefly explain the effect of how liquor taxes in Pennsylvania are collected has on the price of a glass of wine purchased by a consumer in a restaurant in the state.

Source: Matt Assad, "How Booze Brings Heady Development," (Allentown, PA) *Morning Call*, February 22, 2015.

4.10 **(Related to the** Making the Connection **on page 129)** Suppose the government imposes a payroll tax of $1 per hour of work and collects the tax from employers. Use a graph for the market for labor to show the effect of the payroll tax, assuming the special case of a vertical supply curve of labor. By how much does the new equilibrium wage that employers pay workers fall?

Appendix

Quantitative Demand and Supply Analysis

LEARNING OBJECTIVE: Use quantitative demand and supply analysis.

Graphs help us understand economic change *qualitatively*. For instance, a demand and supply graph can tell us that if household incomes rise, the demand curve for a normal good will shift to the right, and the price of the good will rise. Often, though, economists, business managers, and policymakers want to know more than the qualitative direction of change; they want a *quantitative estimate* of the size of the change.

In this chapter, we carried out a qualitative analysis of rent controls. We saw that imposing rent controls involves a trade-off: Renters as a group gain, but landlords lose, and the market for apartments becomes less efficient, as shown by the deadweight loss. To better evaluate rent controls, we need to know more than just that these gains and losses exist; we need to know how large they are. A quantitative analysis of rent controls will tell us how large the gains and losses are.

Demand and Supply Equations

The first step in a quantitative analysis is to supplement our use of demand and supply curves with demand and supply *equations*. Economists use data on prices, quantities, and other economic variables to statistically estimate equations for demand and supply curves. For example, suppose that economists have estimated that the demand for apartments in New York City is:

$$Q^D = 4,750,000 - 1,000P,$$

and the supply of apartments is:

$$Q^S = -1,000,000 + 1,300P.$$

We have used Q^D for the quantity of apartments demanded per month, Q^S for the quantity of apartments supplied per month, and P for the apartment rent, in dollars per month. In reality, both the quantity of apartments demanded and the quantity of apartments supplied will depend on more than just the rental price of apartments in New York City. The demand for apartments in New York City will also depend, for instance, on the average incomes of families in the New York area and on the rents of apartments in the surrounding cities. For simplicity, we will ignore these other factors.

With no government intervention, we know that at competitive market equilibrium, the quantity demanded must equal the quantity supplied, or:

$$Q^D = Q^S.$$

We can use this equation, which is called an *equilibrium condition*, to solve for the equilibrium monthly apartment rent by setting the quantity demanded from the demand equation equal to the quantity supplied from the supply equation:

$$4,750,000 - 1,000P = -1,000,000 + 1,300P$$

$$5,750,000 = 2,300P$$

$$P = \frac{5,750,000}{2,300} = \$2,500.$$

We can then substitute this price back into either the supply equation or the demand equation to find the equilibrium quantity of apartments rented:

$$Q^D = 4{,}750{,}000 - 1{,}000P = 4{,}750{,}000 - 1{,}000(2{,}500) = 2{,}250{,}000,$$

or:

$$Q^S = -1{,}000{,}000 + 1{,}300P = -1{,}000{,}000 + 1{,}300(2{,}500) = 2{,}250{,}000.$$

Figure 4A.1 illustrates the information from these equations in a graph. The figure shows the values for rent when both the quantity supplied and the quantity demanded are zero. These values can be calculated from the demand and supply equations by setting Q^D and Q^S equal to zero and solving for price:

$$Q^D = 0 = 4{,}750{,}000 - 1{,}000P$$

$$P = \frac{4{,}750{,}000}{1{,}000} = \$4{,}750$$

and:

$$Q^S = 0 = -1{,}000{,}000 + 1{,}300P$$

$$P = \frac{-1{,}000{,}000}{-1{,}300} = \$769.23.$$

MyEconLab Concept Check

Calculating Consumer Surplus and Producer Surplus

Figure 4A.1 shows consumer surplus and producer surplus in this market.

Recall that the sum of consumer surplus and producer surplus equals the net benefit that renters and landlords receive from participating in the market for apartments. We can use the values from the demand and supply equations to calculate the value of consumer surplus and producer surplus. Remember that consumer surplus is the area below the demand curve and above the line representing market price. Notice that this area forms a right triangle because the demand curve is a straight line—it is *linear*. As we noted in the appendix to Chapter 1, the area of a triangle is equal to ½ × Base × Height. In this case, the area is:

$$\frac{1}{2} \times (2{,}250{,}000) \times (4{,}750 - 2{,}500) = \$2{,}531{,}250{,}000.$$

So, this calculation tells us that the consumer surplus in the market for rental apartments in New York City is about $2.5 billion per month.

MyEconLab Animation

Figure 4A.1

Graphing Supply and Demand Equations

After statistically estimating supply and demand equations, we can use the equations to draw supply and demand curves. In this case, the equilibrium rent for apartments is $2,500 per month, and the equilibrium quantity of apartments rented is 2,250,000. The supply equation tells us that at a rent of $769, the quantity of apartments supplied will be zero. The demand equation tells us that at a rent of $4,750, the quantity of apartments demanded will be zero. The areas representing consumer surplus and producer surplus are also indicated on the graph.

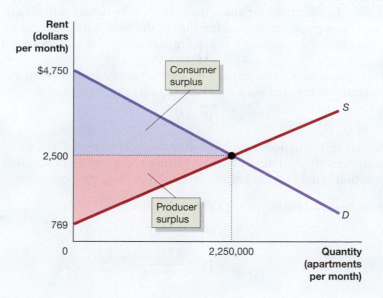

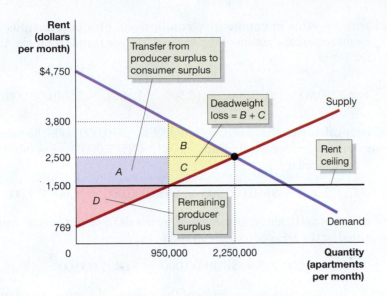

MyEconLab Animation

Figure 4A.2

Calculating the Economic Effect of Rent Controls

Once we have estimated equations for the demand and supply of rental housing, a diagram can guide our numerical estimates of the economic effects of rent control. Consumer surplus falls by an amount equal to the area of triangle *B* and increases by an amount equal to the area of rectangle *A*. Producer surplus falls by an amount equal to the sum of the areas of rectangle *A* and triangle *C*. The remaining producer surplus is equal to the area of triangle *D*. Deadweight loss is equal to the sum of the areas of triangles *B* and *C*.

We can calculate producer surplus in a similar way. Remember that producer surplus is the area above the supply curve and below the line representing market price. Because the supply curve is also a straight line, producer surplus in the figure is equal to the area of the triangle:

$$\frac{1}{2} \times 2{,}250{,}000 \times (2{,}500 - 769) = \$1{,}947{,}375{,}000.$$

This calculation tells us that the producer surplus in the market for rental apartments in New York City is about $1.9 billion per month.

We can use the same type of analysis to measure the effect of rent control on consumer surplus, producer surplus, and economic efficiency. For instance, suppose the city imposes a rent ceiling of $1,500 per month. Figure 4A.2 can help guide us as we measure the effect.

First, we can calculate the quantity of apartments that will actually be rented by substituting the rent ceiling of $1,500 into the supply equation:

$$Q^S = -1{,}000{,}000 + (1{,}300 \times 1{,}500) = 950{,}000.$$

We also need to know the price on the demand curve when the quantity of apartments is 950,000. We can do this by substituting 950,000 for quantity in the demand equation and solving for price:

$$950{,}000 = 4{,}750{,}000 - 1{,}000P$$

$$P = \frac{-3{,}8000{,}000}{-1{,}000} = \$3{,}800.$$

Compared with its value in competitive equilibrium, consumer surplus has been reduced by a value equal to the area of triangle *B* but increased by a value equal to the area of rectangle *A*. The area of triangle *B* is:

$$\frac{1}{2} \times (2{,}250{,}000 - 950{,}000) \times (3{,}800 - 2{,}500) = \$845{,}000{,}000,$$

and the area of rectangle *A* is Base × Height, or:

$$(\$2{,}500 - \$1{,}500) \times (950{,}000) = \$950{,}000{,}000.$$

The value of consumer surplus in competitive equilibrium was $2,531,250,000. As a result of the rent ceiling, it will be increased to:

$$(\$2{,}531{,}250{,}000 + 950{,}000{,}000) - \$845{,}000{,}000 = \$2{,}636{,}250{,}000.$$

Compared with its value in competitive equilibrium, producer surplus has been reduced by a value equal to the sum of the areas of triangle C and rectangle A. The area of triangle C is:

$$\frac{1}{2} \times (2{,}250{,}000 - 950{,}000) \times (2{,}500 - 1{,}500) = \$650{,}000{,}000.$$

We have already calculated the area of rectangle A as \$950,000,000. The value of producer surplus in competitive equilibrium was \$1,947,375,000. As a result of the rent ceiling, it will be reduced to:

$$\$1{,}947{,}375{,}000 - \$650{,}000{,}000 - \$950{,}000{,}000 = \$347{,}375{,}000.$$

The loss of economic efficiency, as measured by the deadweight loss, is equal to the value represented by the areas of triangles B and C, or:

$$\$845{,}000{,}000 + \$650{,}000{,}000 = \$1{,}495{,}000{,}000$$

The following table summarizes the results of the analysis (the values are in millions of dollars):

Consumer Surplus		Producer Surplus		Deadweight Loss	
Competitive Equilibrium	Rent Control	Competitive Equilibrium	Rent Control	Competitive Equilibrium	Rent Control
\$2,531	\$2,636	\$1,947	\$347	\$0	\$1,495

Qualitatively, we know that imposing rent control will make consumers better off, make landlords worse off, and decrease economic efficiency. The advantage of the analysis we have just gone through is that it puts dollar values on the qualitative results. We can now see how much consumers have gained, how much landlords have lost, and how great the decline in economic efficiency has been. Sometimes the quantitative results can be surprising. Notice, for instance, that after the imposition of rent control, the deadweight loss is actually much greater than the remaining producer surplus. Of course, these results are dependent on the numbers we chose for the demand and supply curve equations. Choosing different numbers would have changed the results.

Economists often study issues where the qualitative results of actions are apparent, even to non-economists. You don't have to be an economist to understand who wins and who loses from rent control or that if a company cuts the price of its product, its sales will increase. Business managers, policymakers, and the general public do, however, need economists to measure quantitatively the effects of different actions—including policies such as rent control—so that they can better assess the results of these actions.

MyEconLab Study Plan

Quantitative Demand and Supply Analysis, pages 141–144

LEARNING OBJECTIVE: Use quantitative demand and supply analysis.

MyEconLab   Visit **www.myeconlab.com** to complete these exercises online and get instant feedback.

Review Questions

4A.1 In a linear demand equation, what economic information is conveyed by the intercept on the price axis? Similarly, what economic information is conveyed by the intercept on the price axis in a linear supply equation?

4A.2 Suppose you were assigned the task of choosing a price that maximizes economic surplus in a market. What price would you choose? Why?

4A.3 Consumer surplus is used as a measure of a consumer's net benefit from purchasing a good or service. Explain why consumer surplus is a measure of net benefit.

4A.4 Why would economists use the term *deadweight loss* to describe the effect on consumer surplus and producer surplus from a price control?

Problems and Applications

4A.5 Suppose that you have been hired to analyze the effect on employment from the imposition of a minimum wage in the labor market. Further suppose that you estimate the demand and supply functions for labor, where L stands for the quantity of labor (measured in thousands of workers) and W stands for the wage rate (measured in dollars per hour):

$$\text{Demand: } L^D = 100 - 4W$$

$$\text{Supply: } L^S = 6W$$

First, calculate the free market equilibrium wage and quantity of labor. Now suppose the proposed minimum wage is $12. How large will the surplus of labor in this market be?

4A.6 The following graphs illustrate the markets for two different types of labor. Suppose an identical minimum wage is imposed in both markets. In which market will the minimum wage have the largest impact on employment? Why?

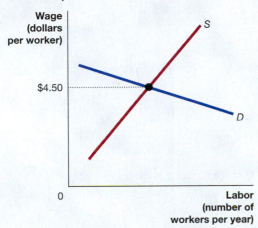

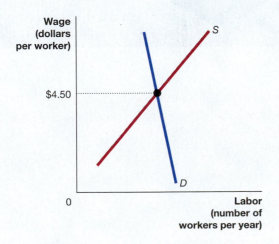

4A.7 Suppose that you are the vice president of operations of a manufacturing firm that sells an industrial lubricant in a competitive market. Further suppose that your economist gives you the following demand and supply functions:

$$\text{Demand: } Q^D = 45 - 2P$$

$$\text{Supply: } Q^S = -15 + P$$

What is the consumer surplus in this market? What is the producer surplus?

4A.8 The following graph shows a market in which a price floor of $3.00 per unit has been imposed. Calculate the values of each of the following.

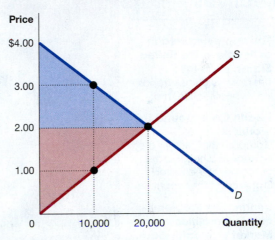

a. The deadweight loss
b. The transfer of producer surplus to consumers or the transfer of consumer surplus to producers
c. Producer surplus after the price floor is imposed
d. Consumer surplus after the price floor is imposed

4A.9 Construct a table like the one in this appendix on page 144 but assume that the rent ceiling is $2,000 rather than $1,500.

The Economics of Health Care

Chapter Outline and Learning Objectives

How Much Will You Pay for Health Insurance?

In 2010, President Barack Obama and Congress enacted the Patient Protection and Affordable Care Act (ACA), which made major changes to the U.S. health care system. If you are young and healthy, you may rarely go to the doctor and may not think much about health insurance. Under the ACA, however, you must have health insurance or pay a fine. In 2016, the fine was $695 or 2.5 percent of your income, whichever was higher.

Many people receive health insurance through their employers. If you take a full-time job, how much will you pay for health insurance? T. Cain Grocery operates five Piggly Wiggly supermarkets in Alabama and Florida. In 2015, Cain deducted $2,800 per year from each employee's paycheck in exchange for providing health insurance. The insurance would pay most of an employee's medical bills—but only *after* the employee had paid for the first $4,500 in bills. Some of the state and federal taxes withheld from the employee's paycheck would be used to support two federal programs: *Medicare*, which provides health insurance to people aged 65 and older, and *Medicaid*, which provides health insurance to low-income people. When they take their first job, many college students are surprised at the big bite that health care costs take out of their paychecks.

For many small firms like Cain's, providing health insurance for workers represents their most rapidly increasing cost. Included in the ACA was a provision that businesses with 50 or more full-time employees (those working 30 or more hours per week) must provide health insurance to all full-time employees or face fines. Under the act, states have also set up health insurance marketplaces with the goal of making health insurance less expensive for small businesses and individuals by allowing them to enter an insurance pool where both healthy and sick people will be in the same insurance plan and pay the same insurance premium.

The increasing health care costs faced by small businesses are reflected in trends in the overall economy. Health care spending increased from about 5 percent of gross domestic product (GDP) in 1960 to about 18 percent in 2015, an upward trend that is expected to continue.

It remains to be seen what the full effects of the ACA will be on health care spending and on health care outcomes.

Sources: Angus Loten, "Small Business Owners Scramble to Prepare for New Tax Form," *Wall Street Journal*, March 4, 2015; Sarah E. Needleman and Angus Loten, "Small Businesses Find Benefits, Costs as They Navigate Affordable Care Act," *Wall Street Journal*, April 23, 2014; U.S. Centers for Medicare & Medicaid Studies, "National Health Expenditure Data," www.cms.gov; and "Employment," cainspigglywiggly.com.

Economics in Your Life

Is Your Take-Home Pay Affected by What Your Employer Spends on Your Health Insurance?

If you work for a firm that offers you health insurance, the firm will withhold some amount from each of your paychecks to pay for the insurance. Typically, firms pay the majority of the cost of health insurance for their employees. In 2014, employees paid only 18 percent of the cost of coverage for themselves or 29 percent of the cost of coverage for their family. Your paycheck probably doesn't show the amount your employer pays on your behalf for health insurance, but does that amount affect your take-home pay? As you read this chapter, try to answer this question. You can check your answer against the one we provide on **page 173** at the end of this chapter.

Source: The Kaiser Family Foundation and Health Research and Educational Trust, *Employer Health Benefits, 2014 Annual Survey*, September 10, 2014.

Health care Goods and services, such as prescription drugs, consultations with a doctor, and surgeries, that are intended to maintain or improve a person's health.

Health care refers to goods and services, such as prescription drugs, consultations with a doctor, and surgeries, that are intended to maintain or improve a person's health. Health care makes up more than one-sixth of the U.S. economy—about the size of the entire economy of France. Improvements in health care are an important part of the tremendous increase in living standards people in the United States and other high-income countries have experienced over the past 100 years. Health care has seen rapid technological change with new products, such as MRI units and other diagnostic equipment; prescription drugs to treat cancer, high blood pressure, and AIDS; vaccinations for meningitis; and new surgical techniques, such as cardiac catheterizations for treatment of heart disease.

Health care is provided through markets, just as are most other goods and services, such as smartphones and haircuts. So, we can apply to health care the tools of economic analysis we used in previous chapters. But the market for health care is different from other markets. In the United States, doctors and hospitals that supply most health care are primarily private firms, but the government also provides some health care services directly through the Veterans Health Administration, which is part of the U.S. Department of Veterans Affairs, and indirectly through the Medicare and Medicaid programs.

In addition to having a large role for government, the market for health care differs from most markets in other ways. Most importantly, a typical consumer of health care doesn't pay full price for that care. Most people have private health insurance, either provided through their employers or purchased on the government-run health insurance marketplaces, or they are enrolled in the Medicare or Medicaid programs. Consumers who have insurance make different decisions about the quantity of health care they wish to consume than they would if they were paying the full cost of the services. So, to analyze the market for health care, we will need to use economic tools beyond those introduced in previous chapters. We begin our analysis of health care with an overview of health care around the world.

5.1 The Improving Health of People in the United States

LEARNING OBJECTIVE: Use data to discuss trends in U.S. health over time.

Two hundred years ago, the whole world was very poor by modern standards. Today, an average person in a high-income country has a standard of living well beyond what even the richest people in the past could have imagined. One aspect of this higher standard of living is the improved health the average person enjoys. For example, in the late 1700s, England had the highest level of income per person of any large country. But the average person in England had a short life span and many people suffered from diseases—such as cholera, yellow fever, dysentery, and smallpox—that have disappeared from high-income countries today. The average life expectancy at birth was only 38 years, and 30 percent of the population died before reaching age 30. Even people who survived to age 20 could expect to live only an average of 34 more years. Today, the average life expectancy at birth in the United Kingdom and other high-income countries is around 80 years. People in eighteenth-century England were also short by modern standards. The average height of an adult male was 5 feet, 5 inches compared with 5 feet, 9 inches today.

In this section, we discuss the health of people in the United States. In Section 5.2, we discuss health care in other countries.

Variable	1850	2015
Life expectancy at birth	38.3 years	79.6 years
Average height (adult males)	5'7"	5'9.5"
Infant mortality (death of a child aged 1 year or less)	228.9 per 1,000 live births	6.2 per 1,000 live births

Table 5.1

Health in the United States, 1850 and 2015

Note: The data on heights for 1850 include only native-born white and black male citizens. The data on height for 2015 were gathered in 2007–2010 and represent the median height of adult males 20 years and older.

Sources: Susan B. Carter et al., eds., *Historical Statistics of the United States: Millennium Edition*; U.S. National Center for Health Statistics, *Anthropometric Reference Data for Children and Adults: United States, 2007–2010*, October 2012; and U.S. Central Intelligence Agency, *World Factbook*.

Changes over Time in U.S. Health

When economists measure changes over time in the standard of living in a country, they usually look first at increases in income per person. However, changes in health are also important because health is an essential part of a person's well-being and, therefore, of his or her standard of living. The health of the average person in the United States improved significantly during the nineteenth and twentieth centuries, and by and large, it continues to improve today.

Table 5.1 compares three indicators of health in the United States in 1850 and 2015. Individuals in the United States today are taller, live much longer, and are much less likely to die in the first months of life than was true 165 years ago. Economists often use height as a measure of long-run changes in the average well-being of a population. A person's height depends partly on genetics—that is, tall parents tend to have tall children—but also on a person's *net nutritional status*. Net nutritional status depends on a person's food intake relative to the work the person has to perform, whether the person is able to remain warm in cold weather, and the diseases to which the person is exposed. Over time, people in the United States and other high-income countries have, on average, become taller, which is an indication that their nutritional status has improved.

MyEconLab Concept Check

Reasons for Long-Run Improvements in U.S. Health

For most of the country's history, the health of people in the United States has steadily improved, with life expectancies increasing and death rates decreasing. Panel (a) of Figure 5.1 shows for the years 1900–2013 the increase in life expectancy and the decline in the mortality rate, or death rate, measured as deaths per 100,000 people. Note that the mortality rate is "age adjusted," which means that it is not affected by changes in the number of people in each age group. Life expectancy at birth in the United States increased from 47.3 years in 1900 to 79.6 years in 2015. Panel (b) shows for recent years the change in the overall mortality rate of the U.S. population, measured as deaths per 100,000 people, and the age-adjusted mortality rates for several diseases. The overall mortality rate decreased by more than 25 percent between 1981 and 2013. Over this same period, deaths from cancer, cardiovascular disease, such as heart attacks and strokes, and diseases of the liver all declined significantly. For example, cancer deaths were 20 percent lower in 2013 than they were in 1981, while deaths from cardiovascular disease declined by more than half during this time. Deaths from diabetes and kidney disease both increased slightly during this period, largely due to the effects of increasing obesity. The overall decline in death rates in the United States since 1981 was due to changes in lifestyle, particularly a decline in smoking, and advances in new diagnostic equipment, prescription drugs, and surgical techniques.

What explains increases in life expectancy and declines in death rates in the years since 1850? Improvements in sanitation and in the distribution of food during the late 1800s and early 1900s led to better health during that period. More generally, the late Nobel Laureate Robert Fogel of the University of Chicago and Roderick Floud of Gresham College, along

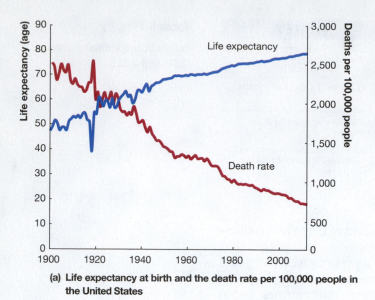

(a) Life expectancy at birth and the death rate per 100,000 people in the United States

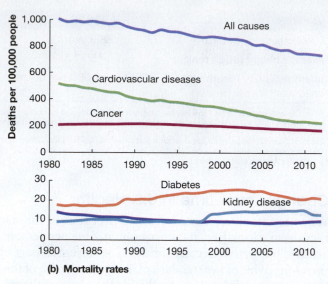

(b) Mortality rates

MyEconLab Animation

Figure 5.1 The Improving Health of the U.S. Population

Since 1900, life expectancy has increased and mortality rates have decreased in the United States. Since 1981, there have been significant decreases in rates of death due to cancer, cardiovascular diseases, and diseases of the liver. Rates of death due to kidney disease and diabetes increased slightly because of an increase in obesity. Note that in panel (a), the increase in mortality and decrease in life expectancy in 1918 are due to the severe influenza epidemic of that year.

Sources: For panel (a): Susan B. Carter et al., eds., *Historical Statistics of the United States: Millennium Edition*, Series Ab644; and Centers for Disease Control and Prevention, *National Vital Statistics Reports*, various issues; for panel (b): Centers for Disease Control and Prevention, National Center for Health Statistics, *National Vital Statistics Reports*, Vol. 63, No. 9: Deaths Final Data for 2012. (2015), http://www.cdc.gov/nchs/data/nvsr/nvsr63/nvsr63_09.pdf.

MyEconLab Study Plan

with coauthors, have described a process by which better health makes it possible for people to work harder as they become taller, stronger, and more resistant to disease. Working harder raises a country's total income, making it possible for the country to afford better sanitation, more food, and a better system for distributing the food. In effect, improving health shifts out a country's production possibilities frontier. Higher incomes also allow the country to devote more resources to research and development, including medical research. The United States has been a pioneer in the development of medical technology, new surgical techniques, and new pharmaceuticals, which have played important roles in lengthening life spans and reducing the death toll from diseases. MyEconLab Concept Check

5.2 Health Care around the World

LEARNING OBJECTIVE: Compare the health care systems and health care outcomes in the United States and other countries.

In the United States, private firms provide most health care, through either doctors' practices or hospitals. The main exception is the care the government provides through the network of hospitals operated by the federal government's Veterans Administration, although some cities also own and operate hospitals. Governments in most countries outside the United States have a more substantial direct role in paying for or providing health care. Policymakers and economists debate the effects of greater government involvement in the health care system on health outcomes such as life expectancy, infant mortality, and successful treatment of diseases.

The U.S. Health Care System

Health insurance A contract under which a buyer agrees to make payments, or *premiums*, in exchange for the provider's agreeing to pay some or all of the buyer's medical bills.

One important difference among health care systems in different countries is the way people pay for their health care. Most people in the United States have *health insurance* that helps them to pay their medical bills. **Health insurance** is a contract

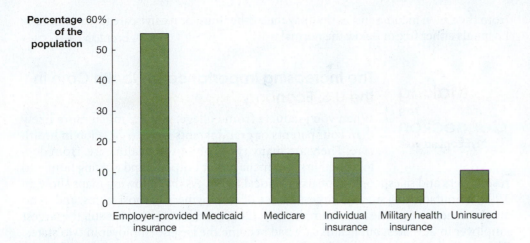

Figure 5.2

Sources of Health Insurance in the United States, 2014

In 2014, about 55 percent of people received health insurance through their employer and about 15 percent directly purchased an individual or family health insurance policy from an insurance company. About 36 percent of people received health insurance through a government program including Medicaid, Medicare, and the program run by the Department of Veteran Affairs. About 10 percent of people were uninsured.

Note: Because some people have more than one type of health insurance, the sum of the values for each category shown is greater than 100 percent.

Source: Jessica Smith and Carla Medalia, *Health Insurance Coverage in the United States: 2014*, U.S. Census Bureau, Current Population Reports, P60–253, Washington, DC: U.S. Government Printing Office, September 2015, Table 1.

under which a buyer agrees to make payments, or *premiums*, in exchange for the provider's agreeing to pay some or all of the buyer's medical bills. Figure 5.2 shows the sources of health insurance in the United States in 2014. Some people have insurance of more than one type by, for example, participating in a government insurance program such as Medicare as well as having a private insurance policy. About 55 percent of people received health insurance through their employer, and about 15 percent directly purchased an individual or family health insurance policy from an insurance company. About 36 percent of people received health insurance through a government program including Medicaid, Medicare, and the program run by the Department of Veterans Affairs.

Most people who have private health insurance receive it through their employer. In 2014, about 98 percent of firms employing more than 200 workers and about 54 percent of firms employing between 3 and 199 workers offered health insurance as a fringe benefit (that is, a type of non-wage compensation) to their employees. Private health insurance companies can be either not-for-profit firms, such as some of the Blue Cross and Blue Shield organizations, or for-profit firms, such as Aetna and John Hancock, which typically also sell other types of insurance. Private health insurance companies sell *group plans* to employers to cover all of their employees and individual plans directly to the public. Some health insurance plans reimburse doctors and hospitals on a **fee-for-service** basis, which means that doctors and hospitals receive a payment for each service they provide. Other health insurance plans are organized as *health maintenance organizations* (HMOs), which typically reimburse doctors mainly by paying a flat fee per patient rather than paying a fee for each individual office visit or other service provided.

About 10 percent of people were not covered by health insurance in 2014. This percentage was lower than in previous years, partly as a result of passage of the Affordable Care Act in 2010, but still represented millions of uninsured people. Many people lack health insurance because their incomes are low, and they believe they cannot afford to buy private health insurance even with government subsidies. Some low-income people either do not qualify for Medicaid or choose not to participate in that program. About 70 percent of uninsured people live in families in which at least one member has a job. These individuals either were not offered health insurance through their employers or chose not to purchase it. Some young people opt out of employer-provided health insurance because they are healthy and do not believe that the cost of the premium their employer charges for the insurance is worth the benefit of having the insurance. More than half the uninsured were younger than age 35. Although most large firms offer their employees health insurance, fewer than two-thirds accept it. The remaining employees are covered by a spouse's policy, are not eligible for coverage, or have decided to go uninsured because they do not want to pay the premium for the insurance. The uninsured must pay for their own medical bills *out of pocket*, with money

Fee-for-service A system under which doctors and hospitals receive a payment for each service they provide.

from their own income, just as they pay their other bills, or receive care from doctors or hospitals either free or below the normal price.   MyEconLab Concept Check

Making the Connection
MyEconLab Video

The Increasing Importance of Health Care in the U.S. Economy

When you graduate from college, you are much more likely than your parents or grandparents were to get a job in health care. There are many types of jobs in health care, from doctors and nurses to managers at hospitals and nursing homes to researchers and salespeople at pharmaceutical firms. As the following maps show, in 1990, manufacturing was the largest source of employment in most states, and in no state was health care the largest employer. By 2000, manufacturing was still the largest employer in 27 states, but health care had become the largest employer in two states. The results for 2014 are strikingly different, with manufacturing the largest employer in only 7 states and health care the largest employer in 34 states.

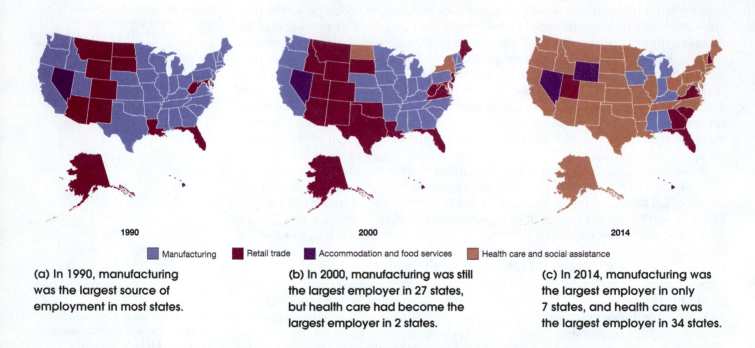

1990   2000   2014

■ Manufacturing   ■ Retail trade   ■ Accommodation and food services   ■ Health care and social assistance

(a) In 1990, manufacturing was the largest source of employment in most states.

(b) In 2000, manufacturing was still the largest employer in 27 states, but health care had become the largest employer in 2 states.

(c) In 2014, manufacturing was the largest employer in only 7 states, and health care was the largest employer in 34 states.

In 1990, almost twice as many people in the United States worked in manufacturing as worked in health care. Today, employment in health care has doubled, while employment in manufacturing has declined by more than 30 percent. And these trends are likely to continue. The U.S. Bureau of Labor Statistics forecasts that 13 of the 20 fastest-growing occupations over the next 10 years will be in health care.

What explains these trends? We discuss explanations for rising health care spending in the United States in Section 5.4. For now, note that the growth of employment in health care is similar to that in other service industries, such as retail stores and restaurants, and that the growth of employment in the health care and service industries is much faster than that in goods-producing industries, such as manufacturing. In addition, there is evidence that as people's incomes grow, their demand for health care grows faster than their demand for most other goods and services. The average age of the U.S. population is also increasing, and older people have a greater demand for health care. Finally, the Affordable Care Act has increased the demand for health care among low-income people in two ways: by providing subsidies to buy health insurance for people whose incomes fall below a certain level and by expanding the Medicaid system.

It seems likely that health care will continue to be a booming sector of the economy and an important source of new jobs in the coming decades.

Sources: U.S. Bureau of Labor Statistics; U.S. Census Bureau; Rani Molla, "How America's Top Industries Have Changed," *Wall Street Journal*, July 28, 2014; and "Why Nurses Are the New Auto Workers," *Economist*, July 25, 2014.

Your Turn: Test your understanding by doing related problem 2.9 on page 175 at the end of this chapter.

The Health Care Systems of Canada, Japan, and the United Kingdom

In many countries, such as Canada, Japan, and the United Kingdom, the government either supplies health care directly by operating hospitals and employing doctors and nurses or pays for most health care expenses, even if hospitals are not government owned and doctors are not government employees. In this section, we look briefly at the health care systems in three countries.

Canada Canada has a **single-payer health care system**, in which the government provides *national health insurance* to all Canadian residents. Each of the 10 Canadian provinces has its own system, although each system must meet the federal government's requirement of covering 100 percent of the cost of all medically necessary procedures. Individuals pay nothing for doctor's visits or hospital stays; instead, they pay for medical care indirectly through the taxes they pay to the provincial and federal governments. As in the United States, most doctors and hospitals are private businesses, but unlike in the United States, doctors and hospitals are required to accept the fees that are set by the government. Also as in the United States, doctors and hospitals are typically reimbursed on a fee-for-service basis.

Single-payer health care system A system, such as the one in Canada, in which the government provides health insurance to all of the country's residents.

Japan Japan has a system of *universal health insurance* under which every resident of the country is required to enroll either in one of the many nonprofit health insurance societies that are organized by industries or professions or in the health insurance program provided by the national government. The system is funded by a combination of premiums paid by employees and firms and a payroll tax similar to the tax that funds the Medicare program in the United States. Unlike the Canadian system, the Japanese system requires substantial *copayments*, under which patients pay as much as 30 percent of their medical bills, while health insurance pays for the rest. Japanese health insurance does not pay for most preventive care, such as annual physical exams, or for medical expenses connected with pregnancies, unless complications result. Health insurance in the United States and Canada typically does cover these expenses. As in the United States, most doctors in Japan do not work for the government, and there are many privately owned hospitals. The number of government-run hospitals, though, is greater than in the United States.

The United Kingdom In the United Kingdom, the government, through the National Health Service (NHS), owns nearly all hospitals and directly employs nearly all doctors. This system contrasts with those in the United States, Canada, and Japan, where the government employs relatively few doctors and owns relatively few hospitals. Because there are few private insurance plans and private hospitals in the United Kingdom, its health care system is often called **socialized medicine**. With 1.7 million employees, the NHS is the largest government-run health care system in the world. Apart from a small copayment for prescriptions, the NHS supplies health care services without charge to patients because it receives its funding from income taxes. The NHS concentrates on preventive care and care for acute conditions. Nonemergency care, also called elective care—such as hip replacements, knee surgery following a sports injury, or reconstructive surgery following a mastectomy—is a low priority. The NHS's goals result in waiting lists for elective procedures that can be very long, with patients sometimes waiting a year or more for a procedure that would be available in a few weeks or less in the United States. To avoid the waiting lists, more than 10 percent of the population also has private health insurance, frequently provided by employers, which the insured use to pay for elective procedures.

Socialized medicine A health care system under which the government owns most of the hospitals and employs most of the doctors.

The NHS essentially trades off broader coverage for longer waiting times and performing fewer procedures, particularly nonemergency surgeries.   MyEconLab Concept Check

Comparing Health Care Outcomes around the World

We have seen that the way health care systems are organized varies significantly across countries. Health care outcomes and the amounts countries spend on health care are also quite different. As Figure 5.3 shows, typically, the higher the level of income per person in a country, the higher the level of spending per person on health care. This result is not surprising because health care is a *normal good*. We know that as income increases, so does spending on normal goods (see Chapter 3, Section 3.1). The line in the figure shows the average relationship between income per person and health care spending per person. The dots for most countries are fairly close to the line, but note that the dot representing the United States is significantly above the line. Being well above the line indicates that health care spending per person in the United States is higher than in other countries, even taking into account the relatively high income levels in the United States. In Section 5.4, we will discuss explanations for the high level of health care spending in the United States.

Has the high level of health care spending in the United States resulted in better health outcomes? Are people in the United States healthier, and do they have their medical problems addressed more rapidly than do people in other countries? Table 5.2 compares several health outcomes for the countries that are members of the Organization for Economic Co-operation and Development (OECD), a group of 34 high-income countries. The table shows that the United States does relatively poorly with respect to infant mortality, while it does about average with respect to life expectancy. People in the United States are more likely to be obese than are people in other countries, which can lead to developing diabetes and other health problems.

The United States rates well in the availability of medical equipment that can be used in diagnosing and treating illness. Table 5.2 shows that the United States has nearly three times as many MRI units and over 50 percent more CT scanners than the average of European countries, although the United States has relatively fewer of these machines than does Japan. The United States also appears to do well in cancer treatment with a lower rate of cancer deaths and a relatively low mortality ratio from cancer. The mortality ratio measures the rate at which people die from cancer relative to the rate at which they are diagnosed with cancer. A low cancer mortality ratio indicates that the U.S. health care system does a relatively good job of reducing the death rate among people diagnosed with cancer.

MyEconLab Animation

Figure 5.3

Levels of Income per Person and Spending per Person on Health Care

The United States is well above the line showing the average relationship between income per person and health care spending per person, which indicates that the United States spends more on health care per person than do other countries, even taking into account the relatively high levels of income in the United States.

Note: Income per person is measured as real GDP per person.

Source: Organization for Economic Co-operation and Development, *OECD Health Data 2014,* November 2014.

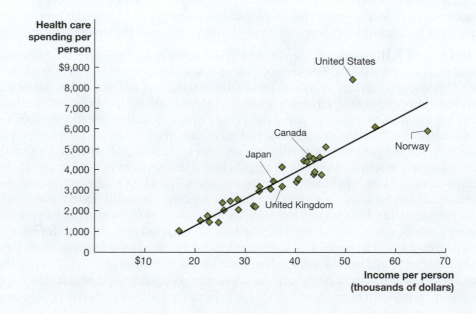

Table 5.2   Health Outcomes in High-Income Countries

Health Care Outcome	United States	Canada	Japan	United Kingdom	OECD Average
Life Expectancy					
Life expectancy at birth	79.6 years	81.0 years	82.7 years	81.1 years	80.1 years
Male life expectancy at age 65	17.8 years	18.8 years	18.9 years	18.5 years	17.6 years
Female life expectancy at age 65	20.4 years	21.7 years	23.8 years	20.9 years	20.9 years
Infant mortality (deaths per 1,000 live births)	6.1	4.9	2.3	4.3	4.1
Health Problems					
Obesity (percentage of the population with BMI > 30)	33.7%	28.0%	3.3%	28.1%	23.4%
Diagnostic Equipment					
MRI units per 1,000,000 population	34.5	8.8	46.9	6.8	12.3
CT scanners per 1,000,000 population	40.9	14.6	101.3	8.7	23.1
Cancer					
Deaths from cancer per 100,000 population	105.8	103.2	93.8	110.0	109.5
Risk of dying of cancer before age 75	11.2%	10.8%	9.3%	11.3%	11.5%
Mortality ratio for cancer	33.3%	34.9%	43.2%	40.3%	40.4%

Sources: Organization for Economic Co-operation and Development, *OECD Health Statistics,* most recent data available, typically 2012; World Health Organization, *Global Health Observatory Data Repository,* 2014; and World Health Organization, Agency for Research on Cancer, "Globocan 2012: Estimated Cancer Incidence, Mortality, and Prevalence Worldwide in 2012." For cancer data, the final column uses the average for European Union countries rather than for OECD countries.

How useful are cross-country comparisons of health outcomes in measuring the effectiveness of different health care systems? Health economists and other researchers disagree strongly about the answer to this question. Here are some factors that make cross-country comparisons in health outcomes difficult:

- **Data problems.** Countries do not always collect data on diseases and other health problems in the same way. So, there are not enough consistent data available to compare health outcomes for more than a few diseases.

- **Problems with measuring health care delivery.** The easiest outcomes to measure are deaths because a specific event has occurred. So, measures of life expectancy, infant mortality, and mortality rates from some diseases, such as cancer, are available across countries. But much of health care involves treatment for injuries, simple surgical procedures, writing of pharmaceutical prescriptions, and other activities for which outcomes are difficult to measure. For example, although the United Kingdom does well in many of the measures shown in Table 5.2, patients have long waiting times for elective surgical procedures that can be arranged much more quickly in some other countries, including the United States. Economists have difficulty measuring the cost to patients of these waiting times.

- **Problems with distinguishing health care effectiveness from lifestyle choices.** Health outcomes depend partly on the effectiveness of doctors and hospitals in delivering medical services. But they also depend on the choices of individuals. For example, in the United States, the high rates of obesity and hospitalizations for diabetes—which can be a complication of obesity—may be caused more by the decisions individuals make about diet and exercise than by the effectiveness of the U.S. health care system.

- **Problems with determining consumer preferences.** In most markets, we can assume that the quantities and prices we observe reflect the interactions of the preferences of consumers (demand) with the costs to firms of producing goods and services (supply). Given their incomes and preferences, consumers compare the prices of different goods and services when making their buying decisions. The prices firms charge represent the costs of providing the good or service. In the market for health care, however, the government plays the dominant role in supplying the service in most countries other than the United States, so the cost of the service is not fully represented in its price, which in some countries is zero. Even in countries where consumers must pay for medical services, the prices they pay usually do not represent the cost of providing the service. In the United States, for instance, consumers with private health insurance typically pay only 10 to 20 percent of the price as a copayment. For these reasons, it is difficult to determine whether some countries do a better job than others in providing health care services whose cost and effectiveness are consistent with consumer preferences.

MyEconLab Study Plan

MyEconLab Concept Check

5.3 Information Problems and Externalities in the Market for Health Care

LEARNING OBJECTIVE: Define information problems and externalities, and explain how they affect the market for health care.

Asymmetric information A situation in which one party to an economic transaction has less information than the other party.

The market for health care is significantly affected by the problem of **asymmetric information**, which occurs when one party to an economic transaction has less information than the other party. Understanding the concept of asymmetric information can help us analyze the actions of buyers and sellers of health care and health insurance and the actions of the government in the health care market. The consequences of asymmetric information may be easier to understand if we first consider its effect on the market for used automobiles, which is the market in which economists first began to carefully study this problem.

Adverse Selection and the Market for "Lemons"

Nobel Laureate George Akerlof of Georgetown University pointed out that the seller of a used car will always have more information on the true condition of the car than will potential buyers. For example, a car that has not had its oil changed regularly may have damage that even a trained mechanic may have difficulty detecting.

If potential buyers of used cars know that they will have difficulty distinguishing good used cars from bad used cars, or "lemons," they will take this into account in the prices they are willing to pay. Consider the following simple example: Suppose that half of the 2013 Volkswagen Jettas offered for sale have been well maintained and are good, reliable used cars. The other half have been poorly maintained and are lemons that will be unreliable. Suppose that potential buyers of 2013 Jettas would be willing to pay $10,000 for a reliable one but only $5,000 for an unreliable one. The sellers know how well they have maintained their cars and whether they are reliable, but the buyers do not have this information and so have no way of distinguishing the reliable used cars from the unreliable ones.

In this situation, buyers will generally offer a price somewhere between the price they would be willing to pay for a good car and the price they would be willing to pay for a lemon. With a 50–50 chance of buying a good car or a lemon, buyers might offer $7,500, which is halfway between the price they would pay if they knew for certain the car was a good one and the price they would pay if they knew it was a lemon.

Unfortunately for used car buyers, a major glitch arises at this point. From the buyers' perspective, given that they don't know whether any particular car offered for sale is a good car or a lemon, an offer of $7,500 seems reasonable. But the sellers do know whether the cars they are offering are good cars or lemons. To a seller of a good car, an offer of $7,500 is $2,500 below the true value of the car, and the seller will be reluctant to sell. But to a seller of a lemon, an offer of $7,500 is $2,500 above the true value of the car, and the seller will be quite happy to sell. As sellers of lemons take advantage of knowing more about the cars they are selling than buyers do, buyers in the used car market will fall victim to **adverse selection**: Most used cars offered for sale will be lemons. In other words, because of asymmetric information, the market has selected adversely the cars that will be offered for sale. Notice as well that the problem of adverse selection reduces the total quantity of used cars bought and sold in the market because few good cars are offered for sale. MyEconLab Concept Check

> **Adverse selection** The situation in which one party to a transaction takes advantage of knowing more than the other party to the transaction.

Asymmetric Information in the Market for Health Insurance

Asymmetric information problems are particularly severe in the markets for all types of insurance, including health insurance. To understand this point, first consider how insurance works. Insurance companies provide the service of *risk pooling* when they sell policies to households. For example, if you own a $150,000 house but do not have a fire insurance policy, a fire that destroys your house can be a financial catastrophe. But an insurance company can pool the financial risk of your house burning down by selling fire insurance policies to you and thousands of other homeowners. Homeowners are willing to accept the certain cost represented by the premium they pay for insurance in return for eliminating the uncertain—but potentially very large—cost should their house burn down.

Notice that for the insurance company to cover all of its costs, the total amount it receives in premiums must be greater than the amount it pays out in claims to policyholders. To survive, insurance companies have to predict accurately the amount they are likely to pay out to policyholders. For instance, if an insurance company predicts that the houses of only 2 percent of policyholders will burn down during a year when 5 percent of houses actually burn down, the company will suffer losses. However, if the company predicts that 8 percent of houses will burn down when only 5 percent actually do, the company will have charged premiums that are too high. A company that charges premiums that are too high will lose customers to other companies and may eventually be driven out of business.

Adverse Selection in the Market for Health Insurance   One obstacle to health insurance companies accurately predicting the number of claims policyholders will make is that buyers of health insurance policies always know more about the state of their health—and, therefore, how likely they are to submit medical bills for payment—than will the insurance companies. In other words, insurance companies face an adverse selection problem because sick people are more likely to want health insurance than are healthy people. If insurance companies have trouble determining who is healthy and who is sick, they are likely to sell policies to more sick people than they had expected, with the result that the premiums they charge will be too low to cover their costs.

An insurance company faces a financial problem if the premiums it is charging are too low to cover the costs of the claims being submitted. The company might try to increase the premiums it charges, but this may make the adverse selection problem worse. If premiums rise, then younger, healthier people who rarely visit the doctor may respond to the increase in premiums by dropping their insurance. The higher premiums have made the adverse selection problem worse for the insurance company because it will have fewer healthy policyholders than it had before the premium increase. The situation is similar to that facing a used car buyer who knows that adverse selection is a problem in the used car market and decides to compensate for it by lowering the price he is willing to pay for a car. The lower price will reduce the number of sellers of good cars willing to sell to him, making his adverse selection problem worse.

One way to deal with the problem of adverse selection is for the government to require every person to buy insurance. Most states require all drivers to buy automobile insurance so that both high-risk and low-risk drivers will carry insurance. The Patient Protection and Affordable Care Act (ACA) passed in 2010 requires that residents of the United States must buy health insurance or pay a fine. This provision of the law is known as the *individual mandate* and has been controversial. We discuss it further in Section 5.4.

Moral hazard The actions people take after they have entered into a transaction that make the other party to the transaction worse off.

Moral Hazard in the Market for Health Insurance The insurance market is subject to a second consequence of asymmetric information. **Moral hazard** refers to actions people take after they have entered into a transaction that make the other party to the transaction worse off. Moral hazard in the insurance market occurs when people change their behavior after becoming insured. For example, once a firm has taken out a fire insurance policy on a warehouse, its managers might be reluctant to install an expensive sprinkler system. Similarly, someone with health insurance may visit the doctor for treatment of a cold or other minor illness, which he would not do if he lacked insurance. Or someone with health insurance might engage in risky activities, such as riding a motorcycle, which she would not do if she lacked insurance.

One way to think about the basic moral hazard problem with insurance is to note that normally there are two parties to an economic transaction: the buyer and the seller. The insurance company becomes a third party to the purchase of medical services because the insurance company, rather than the patient, pays for some or all of the service. For this reason, economists refer to traditional health insurance as a *third-party payer* system. Because of this system, consumers of health care do not pay a price that reflects the full cost of providing the service. This lower price leads consumers to use more health care than they otherwise would.

Don't Let This Happen to You

Don't Confuse Adverse Selection with Moral Hazard

The two key consequences of asymmetric information are adverse selection and moral hazard. It is easy to mix up these concepts. One way to keep the concepts straight is to remember that adverse selection refers to what happens at the time of entering into a transaction. An example would be an insurance company selling a life insurance policy to a terminally ill person because the company lacks full information on the person's health. Moral hazard refers to what happens after entering into a transaction, such as a nonsmoker buying a life insurance policy and then starting to smoke four packs of cigarettes a day. (It may help to remember that *a* comes before *m* alphabetically, just as *a*dverse selection comes before *m*oral hazard.)

MyEconLab Study Plan

Your Turn: Test your understanding by doing related problems 3.9 and 3.10 on page 176 at the end of this chapter.

Principal–agent problem A problem caused by agents pursuing their own interests rather than the interests of the principals who hired them.

Third-party payer health insurance can also lead to another consequence of moral hazard, known as the *principal–agent problem*, because doctors may be led to take actions that are not necessarily in the best interests of their patients, such as increasing their incomes by prescribing unnecessary tests or other treatments for which the doctors receive payment. The **principal–agent problem** results from agents—in this case, doctors—pursuing their own interests rather than the interests of the principals—in this case, patients—who hired them. If patients had to pay the full price of lab tests, MRI scans, and other procedures, they would be more likely to question whether the procedures were really necessary. Because health insurance pays most of the bill for these procedures, patients are more likely to accept them. Note that the fee-for-service aspect of most health insurance in the United States can make the principal–agent problem worse because doctors and hospitals are paid for each service performed, whether or not the service was necessary or effective.

The number of medical procedures performed in the United States has been continually increasing. Many doctors argue that the increasing number of medical procedures is not the result of third-party payer health insurance. Instead, the increase is due to the improved effectiveness of the procedures in diagnosing illness and the tendency of some doctors to practice "defensive medicine" because they fear that if they fail to correctly diagnose an illness, a patient may file a malpractice lawsuit against them.

How Insurance Companies Deal with Adverse Selection and Moral Hazard Insurance companies can take steps to reduce adverse selection and moral hazard problems. For example, insurance companies can use deductibles and coinsurance (or copayments) to reduce moral hazard. A deductible requires the policyholder to pay a certain dollar amount before the insurance begins paying claims. With coinsurance, the insurance company pays only a percentage of any claim. Suppose you have a health insurance policy with a $200 deductible and 20 percent coinsurance, and you receive a medical bill for $1,000. You must pay the first $200 of the bill and 20 percent of the remaining $800. Deductibles and coinsurance make the policies less attractive to people who intend to file many claims, thereby reducing the adverse selection problem. Deductibles and coinsurance also provide policyholders with an incentive to avoid filing claims, thereby reducing the moral hazard problem. Notice, though, that deductibles and coinsurance reduce, but do not eliminate, adverse selection and moral hazard. People who anticipate having large medical bills will still have a greater incentive than healthy people to buy insurance, and people with health insurance are still more likely to visit the doctor even for a minor illness than are people without health insurance.

To reduce the problem of adverse selection, someone applying for an individual health insurance policy is usually required to submit his or her medical records to the insurance company. Insurance companies often also carry out their own medical examinations. Prior to the passage of the ACA in 2010, companies typically limited coverage of *preexisting conditions*, which are medical problems, such as heart disease or cancer, that the buyer already has before purchasing insurance. Health insurance companies typically would not cover preexisting conditions for a year or two after a consumer purchased insurance, and sometimes they would permanently decline to cover these conditions. Limits on coverage of preexisting conditions were very common in health insurance policies for individuals but were also sometimes included in *group policies*, such as the policy T. Cain Grocery purchased to cover its employees, as described in the chapter opener. Exclusions and limits on coverage of preexisting conditions have been controversial.

Critics argue that by excluding coverage of preexisting conditions, insurance companies were forcing people with serious illnesses to pay the entire amount of what might be very large medical bills or to go without medical care. Some people with chronic or terminal illnesses found it impossible to buy an individual health insurance policy. The insurance companies argued that if they did not exclude coverage of preexisting conditions, they might have been unable to offer any health insurance policies or might have been forced to charge premiums that were so high as to cause relatively healthy people to not renew their policies, which would have made adverse selection problems worse. To some extent, the debate over coverage of preexisting conditions is a normative one. Ordinarily, in a market system, people who cannot afford a good or service must do without it. However, many people do not want others to be without health insurance because they cannot afford it. As we will discuss in the next section, Congress included significant restrictions on the ability of insurance companies to limit coverage of preexisting conditions when it passed the ACA. MyEconLab Concept Check

Externalities in the Market for Health Care

For most goods and services, we assume that the consumer receives all the benefits from consuming the good and that the firm producing the good bears all of the costs of production. Some goods or services, though, involve an *externality*, which is a benefit or cost that affects someone who is not directly involved in the production or consumption of a good or service. For example, if a utility burns coal to produce electricity, the result will be air pollution, which causes a *negative externality* because people with asthma or other breathing problems may bear a cost even though they were not involved in buying or selling the electricity that caused the pollution. College education may result in a *positive externality* because college-educated people are less likely to commit crimes and, by being better-informed voters, more likely to contribute to better government policies. So, although you receive most of the benefits of your college education, other people also receive some of the benefits.

Externalities interfere with the economic efficiency of a market equilibrium. A competitive market achieves economic efficiency by maximizing the sum of consumer surplus and producer surplus (see Chapter 4, Section 4.1). But when there is a negative externality in production, as with air pollution, the market will produce more than the efficient quantity. When there is a positive externality in consumption, as with college educations, the market will produce less than the efficient quantity.

Many economists believe several aspects of health care involve externalities. For example, anyone vaccinated against a communicable disease not only protects herself or himself but also reduces the chances that people who have not been vaccinated will contract the disease. The positive externality from vaccinations causes a difference between the *private benefit* from being vaccinated and the *social benefit*. The *private benefit* is the benefit received by the consumer of a good or service. The *social benefit* is the total benefit from consuming a good or service, and it is equal to the private benefit plus any external benefit, such as the benefit to others from a reduced chance of getting a disease for which you have been vaccinated. Because of the positive externality, the social benefit of vaccinations is greater than the private benefit.

Figure 5.4 shows the market for vaccinations. If people receiving vaccinations could capture all the benefits, the demand curve would be D_2, which represents the marginal social benefit. The actual demand curve is D_1, however, which represents only the marginal private benefit received by people getting vaccinations. The efficient equilibrium would occur at price $P_{Efficient}$ and quantity $Q_{Efficient}$. At this equilibrium, economic surplus is maximized (see Chapter 4). The market equilibrium, at price P_{Market} and quantity Q_{Market}, will not be efficient because the demand curve is above the supply curve for production of the vaccinations between Q_{Market} and $Q_{Efficient}$. That is, the marginal benefit—including the external benefit—for producing these vaccinations is greater than the marginal cost. As a result, there is a deadweight loss equal to the area of the yellow triangle. Because of the positive externality, economic efficiency would be improved if more people were vaccinated.

Figure 5.4 assumes that the market for vaccinations is like the market for goods such as hamburgers, with consumers paying the full price of the vaccinations. In practice, people with health insurance pay a reduced price for vaccinations, and the government often provides further subsidies to the firms that produce vaccines. One reason for the government subsidies is to overcome the effects of the positive externality.

Externalities are important in health care markets, though economists and policymakers continue to debate the extent to which they require significant government involvement in health care. MyEconLab Concept Check

Figure 5.4

The Effect of a Positive Externality on the Market for Vaccinations

People who do not get vaccinated still benefit from other people being vaccinated. As a result, the marginal social benefit from vaccinations is greater than the marginal private benefit to people being vaccinated. Because only the marginal private benefit is represented in the market demand curve D_1, the quantity of vaccinations produced, Q_{Market}, is too low. If the market demand curve were D_2 instead of D_1, the level of vaccinations would be $Q_{Efficient}$, which is the efficient level. At the market equilibrium of Q_{Market}, there is a deadweight loss equal to the area of the yellow triangle.

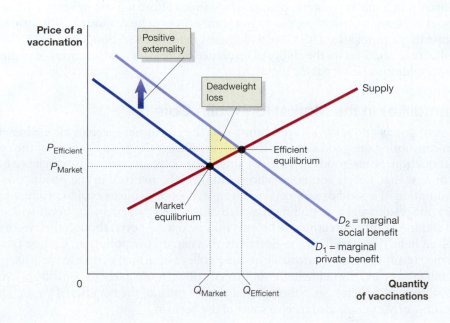

Should the Government Run the Health Care System?

Some members of Congress have proposed expanding the federal government's role in health care by adopting a system similar to the single-payer system used in Canada, under which the government would provide health care to all residents of the United States. What role the federal government should play in health care is a controversial public policy issue.

Economists categorize goods on the basis of whether they are *rival* and *excludable*. Rivalry occurs when one person consuming a unit of a good means no one else can consume it. If you consume a burrito from Chipotle Mexican Grill, for example, no one else can consume it. Excludability means that anyone who does not pay for a good cannot consume it. If you don't pay for a burrito, for example, Chipotle can exclude you from consuming it. A *public good* is both nonrival and nonexcludable. Public goods are often, although not always, supplied by a government rather than by private firms. The classic example of a public good is national defense. Your consuming national defense does not interfere with your neighbor consuming it, so consumption is nonrival. You also cannot be excluded from consuming it, whether you pay for it or not. No private firm would be willing to supply national defense because everyone can consume national defense without paying for it.

Is health care a public good that government should supply—or, at least, pay for? Is it a private good, like furniture, clothing, or computers, that private firms should supply and consumers should pay for without government aid? Should private firms supply most health care, subject to some government regulation? Economists differ in their answers to these questions because the delivery of health care involves a number of complex issues, but we can consider briefly some of the most important points. Because public goods must be both nonrival and nonexcludable, health care does not qualify as a public good under the usual definition. More than one person cannot simultaneously "consume" the same surgical operation performed by a particular doctor in a particular hospital. And someone who will not pay for an operation can be excluded from consuming it. (Most states require hospitals to treat patients who are too poor to pay for treatment, and many doctors will treat poor people at a reduced price. But health care does not fit the definition of a public good because there is nothing about health care that keeps people who do not pay for it from being excluded from consuming.)

However, there are aspects of the delivery of health care that have convinced some economists that government intervention is justified. For example, consuming certain types of health care generates positive externalities. Being vaccinated against a communicable disease, such as influenza or meningitis, reduces not only the chance that the person vaccinated will catch the disease but also the probability that an epidemic of the disease will occur. Therefore, the market may supply an inefficiently small quantity of vaccinations unless vaccinations receive a government subsidy.

Information problems can also be important in the market for private health insurance. Consumers who buy health insurance often know much more about the state of their health than do the companies selling health insurance. This information problem may raise costs to insurance companies when the pool of people being insured is small, making insurance companies less willing to offer health insurance to consumers the companies suspect may file too many claims. Economists debate how important information problems are in health care markets and whether government intervention is required to reduce them.

Many economists believe that market-based solutions are the best approach to improving the health care system. As we saw in Table 5.2 on page 155, the United States has a mixed record on health outcomes. The United States is, however, a world leader in innovation in medical technology and prescription drugs. The market-oriented approach to reforming health care starts with the goal of improving health care outcomes while preserving incentives for U.S. firms to continue with innovations in medical screening equipment, surgical procedures, and prescription drugs. Presently, markets are delivering inaccurate signals to consumers because when buying health care, unlike when buying most other goods and services, consumers pay a price well below the true cost of providing the service. Under current tax laws, people do not pay taxes on health insurance benefits they receive from their employers, and this benefit encourages them to want generous coverage that reduces incentives to control costs. As we will discuss later in the chapter, market-based approaches to health care reform attempt to address these issues.

It remains an open question whether the U.S. health care system will continue to move toward greater government intervention, which is the approach adopted in most other countries, or whether market-based reforms will be implemented. Because health care is so important to consumers and because health care is an increasingly large part of the U.S. economy, the role of the government in the health care system is likely to be the subject of intense debate for some time to come.   MyEconLab Concept Check

5.4 The Debate over Health Care Policy in the United States

LEARNING OBJECTIVE: Explain the major issues involved in the debate over health care policy in the United States.

Shortly after taking office in January 2009, President Barack Obama proposed far-reaching changes in the U.S. health care system. The result was the Patient Protection and Affordable Care Act (ACA), which Congress passed in March 2010. The act was controversial, with every Republican member of Congress and 34 Democratic members voting against it. Since passage of the ACA, economists have vigorously debated its effects on health care and the economy. Next we explore the issue of rising health care costs, which played an important role in the health care debate, before discussing the details of the ACA and the debate over the legislation's effect.

The Rising Cost of Health Care

Figure 5.5 illustrates a key fact underlying the debate over health care policy in the United States: Health care's share of gross domestic product (GDP), which is the total value of output in the economy, is increasing. Panel (a) shows that spending on health care was less than 6 percent of GDP in 1965 but had risen to nearly 18 percent in 2015 and is projected to continue rising in future years. In other words, an increasing percentage of total production in the United States is being devoted to health care. Panel (b) shows increases in health care spending per person in the United States and 10 other high-income countries. Spending on health care has grown faster in the United States than in other countries.

Does it matter that spending on health care is an increasing share of total spending and output in the U.S. economy? The shares of different products in total spending change frequently. For instance, in the United States, the shares of spending on smartphones or 4K televisions were much greater in 2015 than in 2010. Spending on food as a share of total spending has been declining for decades. Economists interpret these changes as reflecting in part consumers' preferences: Consumers choose to spend relatively more of their incomes on smartphones and relatively less on food. As we have seen, though, most people pay for health care by relying on third-party payers, such as employer-provided health insurance or government-provided Medicare or Medicaid. Out-of-pocket spending, spending on health care that consumers pay out of their own incomes rather than through health insurance, has been declining.

Figure 5.6 shows that out-of-pocket spending on health care as a percentage of all spending on health care has fallen steadily since 1960. In 1960, 48 percent of all health care spending was out of pocket, while today only about 12 percent is. As a result, in recent years, consumers of health care have been directly paying for only a small fraction of the true cost of providing health care, with third-party payers picking up the remainder. As average incomes rise, consumers might be expected to spend a rising share of the increase on health care. But because consumers do not pay the full cost of increases in health care spending, they may not be willing to buy as much health care as they currently receive if they had to pay the full price.

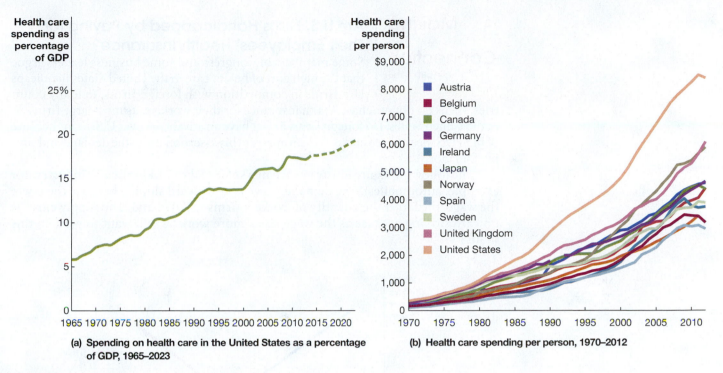

(a) Spending on health care in the United States as a percentage of GDP, 1965–2023

(b) Health care spending per person, 1970–2012

MyEconLab Real-time data

Figure 5.5   Spending on Health Care around the World

Panel (a) shows that health care spending has been a rising percentage of GDP in the United States. Health care spending rose from less than 6 percent of GDP in 1965 to nearly 18 percent in 2015, and it is projected to rise to further in future years. (The projected increases are shown by the dotted line.) Panel (b) shows that health care spending per person

has been growing faster in the United States than in other high-income countries.

Sources: For panel (a): U.S. Department of Health and Human Services, Centers for Medicare & Medicaid Services; for panel (b): Organization for Economic Co-operation and Development, *OECD Health Data 2014*, November 2014.

Because the federal and state governments in the United States pay for just over half of health care spending through Medicare, Medicaid, and other programs, increases in health care spending can cause problems for government budgets. The Medicare and Medicaid programs began in 1965. By 2015, spending on these programs had grown to 6 percent of GDP. That percentage is expected to double over the next 40 years unless health care costs begin to grow at a slower rate. Congress and the president have been struggling to find ways to pay for the projected increases in Medicare and Medicaid without severely cutting other federal spending or sharply raising taxes.   MyEconLab Concept Check

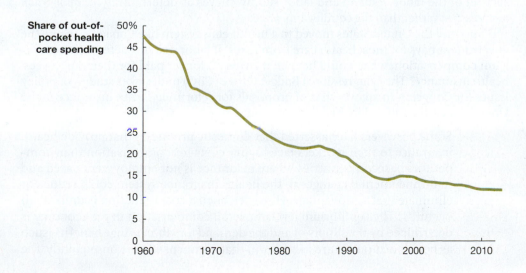

MyEconLab Animation

Figure 5.6

The Declining Share of U.S. Out-of-Pocket Health Care Spending

Out-of-pocket spending on health care has declined sharply as a fraction of all health care spending, while the fraction of spending accounted for by third-party payers, such as firms or the government, has increased.

Source: U.S. Department of Health and Human Services, Centers for Medicare & Medicaid Services.

Making the Connection
MyEconLab Video

Are U.S. Firms Handicapped by Paying for Their Employees' Health Insurance?

Some members of Congress and some business leaders argue that the high cost of health care in the United States handicaps U.S. firms in competition with foreign firms. In many countries, firms do not purchase health insurance for their workers, as most large firms do in the United States. Do foreign firms in fact have an advantage over U.S. firms because of high U.S. health care costs? We can analyze this assertion using the demand and supply for labor.

The following figure illustrates the market for labor in a particular industry (for example, automobiles). The demand curve is downward sloping because the lower the wage, the larger the quantity of workers firms will demand. The supply curve is upward sloping because as the wage rises, more workers will want to work in this industry.

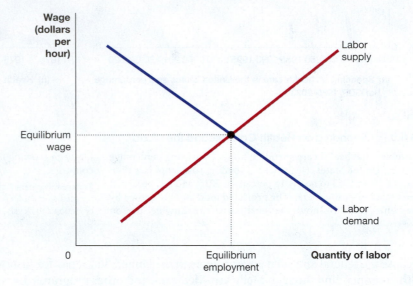

Equilibrium in this labor market occurs where the quantity of labor demanded equals the quantity of labor supplied. On the vertical axis, we measure the wage, so the graph shows the determination of the equilibrium wage. When choosing among jobs, however, workers don't just consider the wages firms offer; they also take into account *fringe benefits*, such as employer contributions to retirement accounts or employer-provided health insurance. It would therefore be more accurate to describe the intersection of the labor demand and labor supply curves as determining *the equilibrium compensation* rather than the equilibrium wage.

Suppose the United States moved to a health care system like Canada's, where the government pays for most health care from taxes. If labor markets determine equilibrium compensation, what would happen if firms no longer paid for their employees' health insurance? The Congressional Budget Office (CBO) undertakes studies of policy issues for Congress. In an overview of proposals for reforming health insurance in the United States, the CBO addressed this question:

> Some observers have asserted that domestic producers that provide health insurance to their workers face higher costs for compensation than competitors based in countries where insurance is not employment based and that fundamental changes to the health insurance system could reduce or eliminate that disadvantage. However, such a cost reduction is unlikely to occur. . . . The equilibrium level of overall compensation in the economy is determined by the supply of and the demand for labor. Fringe benefits (such as health insurance) are just part of that compensation. Consequently, the

costs of fringe benefits are borne by workers largely in the form of lower cash wages than they would receive if no such benefits were provided by their employer. Replacing employment-based health care with a government-run system could reduce employers' payments for their workers' insurance, but the amount that they would have to pay in overall compensation would remain essentially unchanged.

To give an example, suppose a firm was paying its workers $50,000 in wages and paying $10,000 per worker for health insurance, thereby providing total compensation of $60,000. If the government began paying all health care expenses, it might appear that the firm's labor costs would drop by $10,000 per worker. But if the firm offered its employees only $50,000 in wages as their total compensation, many would leave to work for other firms. The firm would have to pay its employees an additional $10,000 in wages so that the total compensation it offered would be at the equilibrium level of $60,000 for the industry. In other words, basic demand and supply analysis indicates that having firms rather than the government provide health insurance to workers changes the *composition* of the compensation the firms pay but does not change its level.

Source: Congressional Budget Office, "Key Issues in Analyzing Major Health Insurance Proposals," December 2008, p. 167.

Your Turn: Test your understanding by doing related problem 4.11 on page 178 at the end of this chapter.

MyEconLab Study Plan

Explaining Increases in Health Care Spending

In this section, we briefly discuss some explanations for why health care's share of the U.S. economy has been continually increasing. We start by reviewing explanations that are sometimes offered by policymakers and journalists but that are unlikely to account for most of the increases in health care costs.

Factors That Do *Not* Explain Sustained Increases in Health Care Spending

The two panels of Figure 5.5 on page 163 show that spending on health care has been growing faster than the economy as a whole for at least the past several decades. Explaining the rapid growth of health care spending requires identifying factors that have more than a one-time effect. For example, because the U.S. health care system relies on many independent hospitals, medical practices, and insurance companies, some observers argue that it generates more paperwork, duplication, and waste than systems in other countries. Even if this observation is correct, it cannot account for health care's rising share of GDP unless paperwork and waste are *increasing* year after year, which seems unlikely.

Unlike in most countries, it is relatively easy in the United States for patients who have been injured by medical errors to sue doctors and hospitals for damages. The Congressional Budget Office (CBO) estimates, though, that the payments to settle malpractice lawsuits plus the premiums doctors pay for malpractice insurance amount to less than 1 percent of health care costs. Other economists believe the CBO estimate is too low and that the costs of malpractice lawsuits, including the costs of unnecessary tests and procedures doctors order to avoid being sued, are as much as 7 percent of total health care costs. Still, these costs have not been significantly increasing over time.

Somewhere between 1 and 4 percent of health care costs are due to uninsured patients receiving treatments at hospital emergency rooms that could have been provided less expensively in doctors' offices. But once again, this cost has not been increasing rapidly enough to account for much of the increase in health care costs as a percentage of GDP.

"Cost Disease" in the Health Care Sector

Some economists argue that health care suffers from a problem often encountered in service industries. In the sectors of the economy that produce goods, such as the manufacturing sector, *productivity*, or the amount of output each worker can produce in a given period, increases steadily. These increases in productivity occur because over time firms provide workers with more machinery and equipment, including computers, with which to work, and because technological progress results in improvements in machinery and equipment and in other parts of the production process. As workers produce more goods, firms are able to pay them higher wages. In service-producing industries, increasing output per worker is more difficult. In medicine, MRI units, CT scanners, and other medical technology have improved diagnosis and treatment, but most medicine still requires a face-to-face meeting between a doctor and a patient. As wages rise in industries in which productivity is increasing rapidly, service industries in which productivity is increasing less rapidly must match these wage increases or lose workers. Because increases in wages are not offset by increases in productivity in service industries, the cost to firms of supplying services increases.

William Baumol of New York University has labeled the tendency for low productivity in service industries to lead to higher costs in those industries as "the cost disease of the service sector." There is good reason to think that health care suffers from this cost disease because growth in labor productivity in health care has been less than half as fast as labor productivity growth in the economy as a whole. This slow growth in productivity can help explain why the cost of health care has been rising rapidly, thereby increasing health care's share of total spending and output.

The Aging of the Population and Advances in Medical Technology As people age, they increase their spending on health care. Firms continue to develop new prescription drugs and medical equipment that typically have higher costs than the drugs and equipment they replace. The aging of the U.S. population and the introduction of higher-cost drugs and medical equipment interact to drive up spending on the federal government's Medicare program and on health care generally. Many newly introduced drugs and diagnostic tools are used disproportionately by people over age 65. Partly as a result, health care spending on people over age 65 is six times greater than spending on people aged 18 to 24 and four times greater than on people aged 25 to 44. In 2015, more than 54 million people were enrolled in Medicare, and that number is expected to grow to 74 million by 2025. As we have seen, even in the absence of the development of new drugs and other medical technology, low rates of productivity in the health care sector could be expected to drive up costs. In fact, as Figure 5.7 illustrates, the CBO estimates that most of the increase in federal spending on Medicare and Medicaid benefits will be due to increases in the cost of providing health care rather than to the aging of the population. In the figure, "effect of excess cost growth" refers to the extent to which health care costs

MyEconLab Animation

Figure 5.7

Reasons for Rising Federal Spending on Medicare and Medicaid

Although the aging of the U.S. population will increase federal government spending on the Medicare and Medicaid programs, increases in the cost of providing health care will have a larger effect on government spending on these programs.

Source: U.S. Congressional Budget Office.

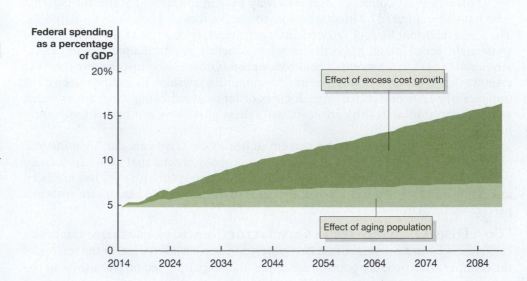

per person grow faster than GDP per person. An aging population and increases in the cost of providing health care are key reasons why health care spending is an increasing percentage of GDP.

Distorted Economic Incentives   As we noted earlier, some part of the increase in health care spending over the years represents consumers choosing to allocate more of their incomes to health care as their incomes rise. But as we have also seen, consumers usually pay less than the true cost of medical treatment because a third party—typically an insurance company or the government—often pays most of the bill. For example, consumers who have health insurance provided by their employers usually pay only a small amount—perhaps $20—for a visit to a doctor's office, when the true cost of the visit might be $80 or $90. The result is that consumers demand a larger quantity of health care services than they would if they paid a price that better represented the cost of providing the services.

Figure 5.8 illustrates this situation. If consumers paid the full price of medical services, their demand would be D_1. The marginal benefit to consumers from medical services would equal the marginal cost of producing the services, and the equilibrium quantity would be at the efficient level $Q_{Efficient}$. However, because consumers pay only a fraction of the true cost of medical services, their demand increases to D_2. In this equilibrium, the quantity of medical services produced increases to Q_{Market}, which is beyond the efficient level. The marginal cost of producing these additional units is greater than the marginal benefit consumers receive from them. As a result, there is a deadweight loss equal to the area of the yellow triangle. Doctors and other suppliers of medical services receive a price, P_{Market}, that is well above the price, P, paid by consumers. Note that the effect of a third-party payer is common to nearly all health care systems, whether the government provides health care directly, as is done in the United Kingdom, or whether many people have private health insurance, as in the United States.

In important ways, health insurance is different from other types of insurance. As we discussed earlier, the basic idea of insurance is that the financial risk of an unpredictable, high-cost event—a house fire or a serious car accident—is pooled among the many consumers who buy insurance. Health insurance, though, also typically covers many planned expenses, such as routine health checkups, annual physicals, and other low-cost events, such as treatment for minor illnesses. By disguising the true cost of these routine expenses, health insurance encourages overuse of health care services.

We discuss the role of economic incentives in health care further in the next section.

MyEconLab Concept Check

MyEconLab Animation

Figure 5.8

The Effect of the Third-Party Payer System on the Demand for Medical Services

If consumers paid the full price of medical services, their demand would be D_1, and the equilibrium quantity would be at the efficient level $Q_{Efficient}$. Because consumers pay only a fraction of the true cost of medical services, their demand is D_2, and the equilibrium quantity of medical services produced increases to Q_{Market}, which is beyond the efficient level. There is a deadweight loss equal to the yellow triangle. Doctors and other suppliers of medical services receive a price, P_{Market}, that is well above the price, P, paid by consumers.

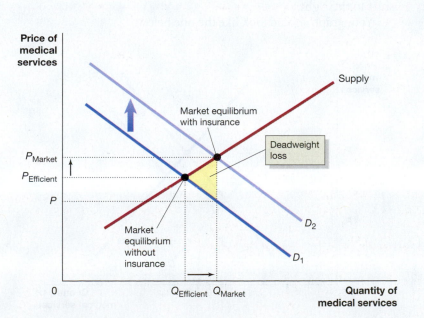

Solved Problem 5.4

Recent Trends in Health Care

An article in the *New York Times* about recent trends in health care mentioned several developments:

1. An increase in the size of deductibles in employer-provided health care plans. For instance, the health plan at T. Cain Grocery supermarket chain mentioned in the chapter opener changed from having a premium of $950 per month and a yearly deductible of $500 to having a premium of $400 per month and a yearly deductible of $4,500.
2. An increase in the availability of lower-cost generic drugs.
3. A decline in patients being readmitted to hospitals after the Patient Protection and Affordable Care Act (ACA)

imposed penalties on hospitals that readmit too many patients.

a. Use a graph of the market for medical services to show the effect of these trends. Be sure to explain any shifts in the demand curve or supply curve.
b. Assuming that these are the only changes happening in the market for medical services, can we be certain whether they will result in an increase or decrease in the equilibrium price of medical services? In the equilibrium quantity of medical services? Briefly explain.

Solving the Problem

Step 1: **Review the chapter material.** This problem is about explaining changes in health care spending, so you may want to review the section "Explaining Increases in Health Care Spending," which begins on page 165.

Step 2: **Answer part (a) by drawing a graph of the market for medical services that shows the effect of the three trends and by explaining shifts in the curves.** The first trend—higher deductibles—reduces moral hazard and adverse selection problems by increasing the quantity of medical services that employees purchase out-of-pocket. Employees are likely to visits doctors less frequently for minor illnesses such as colds. So, the demand curve for medical services will shift to the left. The second trend—greater availability of lower-cost drugs—reduces the cost of providing this type of medical service, which will shift the supply curve for medical services to the right. The third trend—a decline in the number of patients being readmitted to hospitals—should reduce the cost of hospitalizations because more patients are being successfully treated in a single stay. This trend will also cause the supply curve for medical services to shift to the right.

Your graph should look like the one below.

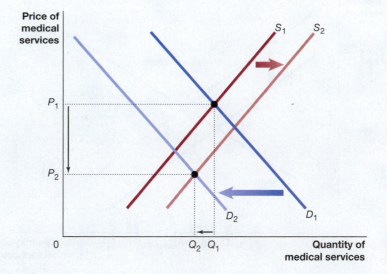

Step 3: **Answer part (b) by explaining whether these trends will increase or decrease the equilibrium price and quantity of medical services.** The graph in part (a) shows both the equilibrium price and the equilibrium quantity declining. We can be certain that the equilibrium price will decline because the shift of the demand curve to the left and the shift of the supply curve to the right both cause the equilibrium price to decline. However, we can't be certain that the equilibrium quantity will decline because the effect of the supply curve shifting to the right is to make the equilibrium quantity *increase*. Whether the equilibrium quantity declines depends on whether demand shifts more or less than supply shifts. Although two of the trends listed affect supply and only one affects demand, we do not know the size of the shift that results from any of the trends, so we can't tell with certainty what the effect will be on the equilibrium quantity.

Extra Credit: The cost of medical care has continued to increase. In 2015, however, economists were analyzing the reasons for a slowdown in the *rate* of that increase. The trends mentioned in this problem were among the likely factors. The quantity of medical services continued to increase, at least partly as a result of the effects of the Affordable Care Act. The act provides subsidies to buy health insurance for people whose incomes fall below a certain level and has expanded the Medicaid system, thereby increasing the demand for health care among low-income people.

Source: Margot Sanger-Katz, "Has the Law Contributed to a Slowdown in Health Care Spending?" *New York Times*, October 26, 2014.

Your Turn: For more practice, do related problems 4.12 on page 178 at the end of this chapter.

MyEconLab Study Plan

The Continuing Debate over Health Care Policy

As we have seen, the United States has been unusual among high-income countries in relying on private health insurance, usually purchased through employers or the new health insurance marketplaces, to provide health care coverage to the majority of the population. Most other high-income countries either provide health care directly, as the United Kingdom does, through government-owned hospitals and government-employed doctors, or provide health insurance to all residents, as Canada does, without directly employing doctors or owning hospitals. There have been several attempts to reorganize the U.S. health care system to make it more like the systems in other countries. In 1945, President Harry Truman proposed a plan for *national health insurance* under which anyone could purchase health insurance from the federal government. The health insurance would have covered treatment received from doctors and hospitals that agreed to enroll in the system. Congress declined to enact the plan. In 1993, President Bill Clinton proposed a health care plan intended to provide universal coverage. While somewhat complex, the plan was based on requiring most businesses to provide health insurance to their employees and new government-sponsored health alliances that would ensure coverage for anyone who otherwise would not have health insurance. After a prolonged political debate, Congress chose not to enact President Clinton's plan.

The Patient Protection and Affordable Care Act In 2009, President Barack Obama proposed health care legislation that after much debate and significant changes was signed into law as the **Patient Protection and Affordable Care Act (ACA)** in March 2010. The act was long and complex, taking up over 20,000 pages and touching nearly every aspect of health care in the United States. Here is a summary of only the main provisions of the act:

Patient Protection and Affordable Care Act (ACA) Health care reform legislation passed by Congress and signed by President Barack Obama in 2010.

- **Individual mandate.** The act requires that, with limited exceptions, every resident of the United States have health insurance that meets certain basic requirements. Individuals who do not acquire health insurance are subject to a fine. In 2016 the fine was $695 or 2.5 percent of income, whichever was greater. (The fine will rise with inflation in future years). For example, in 2016 an adult with an income of $40,000 per year paid a fine of $1,000 if he or she did not buy health insurance.

- **State health insurance marketplaces.** Each state must establish a marketplace called an Affordable Insurance Exchange. Separate marketplaces were established for individuals and small businesses with fewer than 50 employees. The marketplaces offer health insurance policies that meet certain specified requirements. Although the marketplaces were intended to be run by a state government agency or a nonprofit firm, a number of states decided to allow the federal government to run the marketplace in their state. Private insurance companies compete by offering policies on the marketplaces to individuals and small businesses. Low-income individuals and small businesses with 25 or fewer employees are eligible for tax credits to offset the costs of buying health insurance. The purpose of the marketplaces is to allow greater risk pooling and lower administrative costs than had existed in the market for health insurance policies sold to individuals or small businesses. If successful, greater risk pooling and lower administrative costs will make it possible for individuals and small businesses to buy polices with lower premiums than had been available.

- **Employer mandate.** Every firm with more than 200 full-time employees must offer health insurance to its employees and must automatically enroll them in the plan. Firms with 50 or more full-time employees must offer health insurance or pay a fee of $3,000 to the federal government for every employee who receives a tax credit from the federal government for obtaining health insurance through a health insurance marketplace. A worker is a full-time employee if he or she works at least 30 hours per week.

- **Regulation of health insurance.** Insurance companies are required to participate in a high-risk pool that will insure individuals with preexisting medical conditions who have been unable to buy health insurance for at least six months. All individual and group policies must provide coverage for dependent children up to age 26. Lifetime dollar maximums on coverage are prohibited. Limits are also placed on the size of deductibles and on the waiting period before coverage becomes effective.

- **Changes to Medicare and Medicaid.** Eligibility for Medicaid was originally expanded to persons with incomes up to 138 percent of the federal poverty line, although a 2012 Supreme Court decision resulted in the states being allowed to opt out of this requirement. In an attempt to control increases in health care costs, the Independent Payment Advisory Board (IPAB) was established and given the power to reduce Medicare payments for prescription drugs and the use of diagnostic equipment and other technology if Medicare spending exceeds certain levels. Some Medicare reimbursements to hospitals and doctors were reduced.

- **Taxes.** Several new taxes help fund the program. Workers earning more than $200,000 pay higher Medicare payroll taxes, and people who earn more than $200,000 pay a new 3.8 percent tax on their investment income. Beginning in 2018, a tax is scheduled to be imposed on employer-provided health insurance plans that have a value above $10,200 for an individual or $27,500 for a family—so-called Cadillac plans. Pharmaceutical firms, health insurance firms, and firms producing medical devices also pay new taxes.

The ACA is scheduled to be fully implemented by 2019, at which point more than 30 million additional individuals are expected to have health care coverage. The CBO estimates that the law will increase federal government spending by about $2.0 trillion over the period 2016 to 2025. Increases in taxes and fees will reduce the net increase in federal spending resulting from the act to about $1.4 trillion.

The Debate over the ACA Any law as far-reaching and complex as the ACA is bound to draw criticism. The congressional debate over the law was highly partisan, with every Republican ultimately voting against it and most Democrats voting in favor of it. Critics of the act can be divided into two broad groups: those who argue that health care reform should involve a greater movement toward a system similar to the British, Canadian, and Japanese systems and those who argue that health care reform should include more market-based changes.

As we discussed in the previous section, some economists and policymakers believe that information problems and externalities in the market for health care are sufficiently large that the government should either provide health care directly through government-owned hospitals and government-employed doctors or pay for health care through national health insurance, sometimes called a *single-payer system*. Although the ACA significantly increased the federal government's involvement in the health care system, it stopped short of the degree of government involvement that exists in Canada, Japan, or the United Kingdom. Those in favor of moving toward greater government involvement typically argue that doing so would reduce the paperwork and waste caused by the current system. They argue that the current Medicare system—which is essentially a single-payer system for people over age 65—has proved to have lower administrative costs than have private health insurance companies. Supporters of greater government involvement in the health care system have also argued that the Canadian and British systems have had lower levels of health care spending per person and lower rates of increase in total health care spending, while providing good health outcomes.

Market-based reforms involve changing the market for health care so that it becomes more like the markets for other goods and services. As in other markets, the prices consumers pay and suppliers receive would do a better job of conveying information on consumer demand and supplier costs. The expectation is that increased competition among doctors, hospitals, pharmaceutical companies, and other providers of health care would reduce costs and increase economic efficiency. Economists who support market-based reforms as the best way to improve the health care system were disappointed that the ACA did not adopt this approach. Currently, markets are delivering inaccurate signals to consumers because when buying health care, unlike when buying most other goods and services, consumers pay a price well below the true cost of providing the service.   MyEconLab Concept Check

Market-based reforms Changes in the market for health care that would make it more like the markets for other goods and services.

Making the Connection
MyEconLab Video

How Much Is That MRI Scan?

Magnetic resonance imaging (MRI) units play an important role in modern medicine. First introduced in the early 1980s, they allow doctors to see inside the body's soft tissues to identify tumors, torn muscles, and other medical problems. As we noted in Section 5.2, MRI units are more widely available in the United States than in most other countries. We would normally expect that when a product is widely available, competition among firms results in the price of the product being about the same everywhere. Customers would not buy a best-selling book from Amazon.com if the price was 50 percent higher there than on BarnesandNoble.com.

Does competition equalize the prices of medical services? The evidence indicates that it doesn't. The exact services each hospital or clinic offers are difficult to discover, which makes it difficult for consumers to compare prices. The data in the table below indicate that the prices of abdominal MRI scans vary widely. In most cities in the United States, the most expensive MRI scan has a price that is more than double the least expensive scan. And prices for MRI scans also vary widely across cities. Two reporters looking at prices for shoulder MRI scans in Pensacola, Florida, found that Sacred Heart Hospital was charging $800 for a shoulder MRI scan, while Pensacola Open MRI & Imaging, a private firm located less than one mile away, was charging $450 for the same scan. Pensacola Open MRI & Imaging was actually using newer MRI units that give higher-resolution images, so it was charging less for a better service.

City	Highest Price	Lowest Price	Difference
Houston, Texas	$4,800	$675	$4,125
Baton Rouge, Louisiana	4,400	600	3,800
Chicago, Illinois	4,200	450	3,750
Atlanta, Georgia	4,400	700	3,700
Omaha, Nebraska	4,100	600	3,500
Lexington, Kentucky	4,000	550	3,450
Charlotte, North Carolina	3,500	600	2,900
Orlando, Florida	2,475	650	1,825
San Francisco, California	2,400	650	1,750
New York, New York	2,175	800	1,375

How can some providers of medical services charge hundreds or thousands of dollars more than competitors and remain in business? The answer is that most patients are not concerned about prices because they either do not pay them or they pay only a small fraction of them. Patients typically rely on doctors to refer them to a facility for an MRI scan or other procedure and make little or no effort to determine the price the facility charges. A goal of market-based reforms of the health care system is to give patients an incentive to pay more attention to the prices of medical services.

Sources: Caitlin Kenney, "Shopping for an MRI," www.npr.org, November 6, 2009; MRI prices from newchoicehealth.com, June 3, 2015.

MyEconLab Study Plan   **Your Turn:** Test your understanding by doing related problem 4.13 on page 178 at the end of this chapter.

Supporters of market-based reforms note that employees have to pay federal income and payroll taxes on the wages their employers pay them, but in most circumstances they do not pay taxes on the value of the health insurance their employers provide them. This feature of the tax laws encourages employees to want generous health care coverage; in fact, if offered the choice between a $1,000 salary increase or increased health care coverage that was worth $1,000, many people would choose the increased health care coverage because it would be tax free (although someone who was young and healthy and did not expect to have medical bills would probably choose the increase in salary). The size of this tax break is quite substantial—more than $250 billion in 2015. But individuals typically get no tax break when buying an individual health insurance policy or when they spend money on health care out of pocket.[1]

Some economists have proposed making the tax treatment of employer-provided health insurance the same as the tax treatment of individually purchased health insurance and out-of-pocket health care spending. They argue that this change could, potentially, significantly reduce spending on health care without reducing the effectiveness of the health care received. Such tax law changes would make it more likely that employer-provided health insurance would focus on large medical bills—such as those resulting from hospitalizations—while consumers would pay prices closer to the costs of providing routine medical care. John Cogan of the Hoover Institution, Glenn Hubbard of Columbia University, and Daniel Kessler of Stanford University estimate that repealing the tax preference for employer-provided health insurance would reduce spending by people enrolled in these programs by 33 percent.

---

[1] Individuals receive a deduction on their federal income tax only if their medical expenses are greater than 10 percent of their income. Only a relatively small number of individuals have expenses high enough to use that deduction.

Currently, the U.S. health care system is a world leader in innovation in medical technology and prescription drugs. About two-thirds of pharmaceutical patents are issued to U.S. firms and about two-thirds of research on new medicines is carried out in the United States. One goal of market-based reforms would be to ensure that U.S. firms continue with innovations in medical screening equipment, surgical procedures, and prescription drugs. Executives of U.S. pharmaceutical firms have voiced concern over whether aspects of the ACA will affect their ability to profitably bring new prescription drugs to market. In particular, managers at these firms worry that the new Independent Payment Advisory Board (IPAB) might reduce the payments Medicare would make for new prescription drugs.

Both critics of the ACA who favor greater government involvement in health care and those who favor market reforms raise questions about the act's individual mandate. The individual mandate requires every U.S. resident to have health insurance. The mandate was considered necessary because otherwise healthy people might avoid buying insurance until they become ill. Because insurance companies would not be allowed to deny coverage for preexisting conditions, they would end up paying large medical bills for people who had not been paying premiums to support the system while they were healthy. People who do not buy insurance are subject to fines under the act, but there were questions about how effective the fines would be in pushing people to buy insurance. In 2015, several million people paid the fine rather than buy insurance.

MyEconLab Study Plan

Continued from page 147

Economics in Your Life

Is Your Take-Home Pay Affected by What Your Employer Spends on Your Health Insurance?

At the beginning of this chapter, we asked you to think about this question: Your paycheck doesn't show the amount your employer pays on your behalf for health insurance, but does that amount affect your take-home pay? The *Making the Connection* on page 164 shows that the equilibrium compensation that workers receive in labor markets is made up partly of wages and partly of fringe benefits such as health insurance. So, while the amount that a firm pays on your behalf for health insurance may not affect your total compensation, it will affect the amount of your take-home pay. For a given level of compensation, the more a firm pays for your health insurance, the less it will pay you in wages. A related question is why a firm would buy health insurance for you rather than increase your wages by the same amount and let you buy your own insurance. We have seen that there are two important reasons so many people receive health insurance from their employers: (1) The wage an employer pays you is taxable income to you, but the money an employer spends to buy health insurance for you is not taxable; and (2) insurance companies are typically willing to charge lower premiums for group insurance, particularly to large employers, because risk pooling is improved and adverse selection and moral hazard problems are lower than with individual policies.

Conclusion

In this chapter, we have seen that economic analysis can provide important insights into the market for health care. As with many other policy issues, though, economic analysis can help inform the debate but cannot resolve it. Because health care is so important to consumers and health care services are such a large part of the U.S. economy, the role of the government in the health care system is likely to be the subject of intense debate for years to come.

Visit MyEconLab for a news article and analysis related to the concepts in this chapter.

Key Terms

Adverse selection, p. 157

Asymmetric information, p. 156

Fee-for-service, p. 151

Health care, p. 148

Health insurance, p. 150

Market-based reforms, p. 171

Moral hazard, p. 158

Patient Protection and Affordable Care Act (ACA), p. 169

Principal–agent problem, p. 158

Single-payer health care system, p. 153

Socialized medicine, p. 153

5.1 | **The Improving Health of People in the United States, pages 148–150**

LEARNING OBJECTIVE: Discuss trends in U.S. health over time.

Summary

Health care refers to goods and services, such as prescription drugs and consultations with a doctor, that are intended to maintain or improve health. Over time, the health of people in most countries has improved. In the United States, as a result of improving health, life expectancy has increased, death rates have decreased, infant mortality has decreased, and the average person has become taller.

 Visit **www.myeconlab.com** to complete these exercises online and get instant feedback.

Review Questions

1.1 Briefly discuss the most important differences between the market for health care and the markets for other goods and services.

1.2 Briefly describe changes over time in the health of the average person in the United States.

1.3 How can improvements in health increase a country's total income? How can increases in a country's total income improve health?

Problems and Applications

1.4 In what sense have improvements in the health of the average American caused the U.S. production possibilities frontier to shift out? Panel (a) in Figure 5.1 on page 150 indicates that life expectancy in the United States declined in 1918. What effect did this decline in life expectancy likely have on the U.S. production possibilities frontier? Briefly explain.

1.5 The widespread realization in the late nineteenth century that bacteria causes diseases helped lead to a public health movement. This movement eventually brought sewers, clean drinking water, and garbage removal to all U.S. cities. What effect did the public health movement in the United States in the late nineteenth and early twentieth centuries have on the country's production possibilities frontier?

1.6 Between 1830 and 1890, the height of the average adult male in the United States declined by about 2 inches at the same time that average incomes more than tripled. Did the standard of living in the United States increase during this period? What insight into the health and well-being of the U.S. population might the decline in height provide? Briefly explain.

5.2 | **Health Care around the World, pages 150–156**

LEARNING OBJECTIVE: Compare the health care systems and health care outcomes in the United States and other countries.

Summary

Health insurance is a contract under which a buyer agrees to make payments, or premiums, in exchange for the provider agreeing to pay some or all of the buyer's medical bills. A majority of people in the United States live in households that have private health insurance, which they typically obtain through an employer. Other people have health insurance through the Veteran's Administration or the Medicare and Medicaid programs. In 2014, about 10 percent of people in the United States lacked health insurance. Many health insurance plans operate on a **fee-for-service** basis, under which doctors and hospitals receive a payment for each service they provide. Most countries outside the United States have greater government involvement in their health care systems. Canada has a **single-payer health care system**, in which the government provides national health insurance to all Canadian residents. In the United Kingdom, the government owns most hospitals and employs most doctors, so the health care system is referred to as **socialized medicine**. The United States spends more per person on health care than do other high-income countries. The United States has lower life expectancy, higher infant mortality, and a greater incidence of obesity than do other high-income countries. The United States has more medical technology per person and has lower mortality rates for people diagnosed with cancer than do other high-income countries. Data and other problems make it difficult to compare health care outcomes across countries.

 Visit **www.myeconlab.com** to complete these exercises online and get instant feedback.

Review Questions

2.1 Define the following terms:
  a. Health insurance
  b. Fee-for-service
  c. Single-payer health care system
  d. Socialized medicine

2.2 What are the main sources of health insurance in the United States?

2.3 Briefly compare the health care systems in Canada, Japan, and the United Kingdom with the health care system in the United States.

2.4 What is meant by the phrase "health outcome"? How do health outcomes in the United States compare with those of other high-income countries? What problems arise in attempting to compare health outcomes across countries?

Problems and Applications

2.5 According to an article in the *Economist* about the health care system in the United Kingdom: "A defining principle of the National Health Service is that it is 'free at the point of delivery.'" What does "free at the point of delivery" mean? Is health care actually free to residents of the United Kingdom? Briefly explain.
Source: "Free-for-All," *Economist*, June 1, 2013.

2.6 In an opinion column about improving the performance of doctors in the United States, a health economist observed that "it's very hard to measure the things we really care about, like quality of life and improvements in functioning." Why is it difficult to measure outcomes like these? Does the economist's observation have relevance to comparisons in health outcomes across countries? Briefly explain.
Source: Aaron E. Carroll, "The Problem With 'Pay for Performance' in Medicine," *New York Times*, July 28, 2014.

2.7 An article in the *Economist* on evaluating health outcomes is subtitled "To Improve Health Care, Governments Need to Use the Right Data." Among the data not currently being collected in most countries, the article mentions "how soon after surgery patients get back to work." Why don't governments currently collect such data? Why might such data be important in evaluating the effectiveness of a country's health care system?
Source: "Measuring Health Care," *Economist*, February 1, 2014.

2.8 Two health care analysts argue that in the United States, "we have arrived at a moment where we are making little headway in defeating various kinds of diseases. Instead, our main achievements today consist of devising ways to marginally extend the lives of the very sick."
  a. Should "marginally extend[ing] the lives of the very sick" be an important goal of a health care system? What other goals should have a higher priority? (*Note:* This question is basically a normative one without a definitive correct or incorrect answer. You are being asked to consider what the goals of a health care system *should be*.)
  b. Would it be possible to measure how successful the health care systems of different countries are in extending the lives of the very sick? If so, how might it be done?
Source: David Brooks, "Death and Budgets," *New York Times*, July 14, 2011.

2.9 (Related to the Making the Connection on page 152) An article in the *Economist* notes that about 10 percent of people in the United States work in health care and that "these workers have the crucial job of making American health care more efficient, probably the country's top domestic challenge."
  a. How might we measure the efficiency of a country's health care sector? Is there evidence that the U.S. health care sector is more or less efficient than the health care sectors in other countries? Briefly explain.
  b. If the efficiency of the U.S. health care sector improves, will it be likely to employ more workers or fewer workers than if its efficiency does not improve? Briefly explain.
Source: "Why Nurses Are the New Auto Workers," *Economist*, July 25, 2014.

5.3 **Information Problems and Externalities in the Market for Health Care, pages 156–162**
LEARNING OBJECTIVE: Discuss how information problems and externalities affect the market for health care.

Summary

The market for health care is affected by the problem of **asymmetric information**, which occurs when one party to an economic transaction has less information than the other party. **Adverse selection**, the situation in which one party to a transaction takes advantage of knowing more than the other party to the transaction, is a problem for firms selling health insurance policies because it results in people who are less healthy being more likely to buy insurance than people who are healthier. **Moral hazard**, actions people take after they have entered into a transaction that make the other party to the transaction worse off, is also a problem for insurance companies because once people have health insurance, they are likely to make more visits to their doctors and in other ways increase their use of medical services. Moral hazard can also involve a **principal–agent problem**, in which doctors may order more lab tests, MRI scans, and other procedures than they would if their patients lacked health insurance. Insurance companies use deductibles and copayments to reduce the problems of adverse selection and moral hazard. There may be externalities involved with medicine and health care because, for example, people who are vaccinated against influenza or other diseases may not receive all of the benefits from having been vaccinated, and people who become obese may not bear all of the costs from their obesity.

 MyEconLab   Visit **www.myeconlab.com** to complete these exercises online and get instant feedback.

Review Questions

3.1 Define the following terms:
  a. Asymmetric information
  b. Adverse selection
  c. Moral hazard
  d. Principal–agent problem

3.2 What are the asymmetric information problems in the market for health insurance?

3.3 How do health insurance companies deal with asymmetric information problems?

3.4 What is an externality? Are there externalities in the market for health care? Briefly explain.

Problems and Applications

3.5 Suppose you see a 2013 Volkswagen Jetta GLS Turbo Sedan advertised in the campus newspaper for $9,000. If you knew the car was reliable, you would be willing to pay $10,000 for it. If you knew the car was unreliable, you would be willing to pay $5,000 for it. Under what circumstances should you buy the car?

3.6 What is the *lemons problem*? Is there a lemons problem in the market for health insurance? Briefly explain.

3.7 Michael Kinsley, a political columnist, observes: "The idea of insurance is to share the risks of bad outcomes." In what sense does insurance involve sharing risks? How does the problem of adverse selection affect the ability of insurance to provide the benefit of sharing risk?

Source: Michael Kinsley, "Congress on Drugs," *Slate*, August 1, 2002.

3.8 Under the Social Security retirement system, the federal government collects a tax on most people's wage income and makes payments to retired workers above a certain age who are covered by the system. (The age to receive full Social Security retirement benefits varies based on the year the worker was born.) The Social Security retirement system is sometimes referred to as a program of social insurance. Is Social Security an insurance program in the same sense as a health insurance policy that a company provides to its workers? Briefly explain.

3.9 (Related to the Don't Let This Happen to You on page 158) Briefly explain whether you agree with the following statement: "The reluctance of healthy young adults to buy health insurance creates a moral hazard problem for insurance companies."

3.10 (Related to the Don't Let This Happen to You on page 158) While teaching the concepts of asymmetric information, a professor asked his students for examples of adverse selection or moral hazard in marriage. One of the students, who happened to be married, replied: "Your spouse doesn't bring you flowers anymore!" Would the student's reply be an example of adverse selection or moral hazard? Briefly explain.

3.11 A news story notes that some features of the U.S. health care system contribute "to the high cost of medical care by encouraging hospitals and doctors to perform tests and procedures regardless of the value to a patient." What features is the article referring to? Why would hospitals and doctors perform tests that may not be of any value to patients?

Source: Reed Abelson, "Industry Group to Back Results-Focused Care," *New York Times*, January 28, 2015.

3.12 An opinion column in the *Wall Street Journal* observes about "defensive medicine" that "many physicians maintain that fear of lawsuits significantly affects the practice of medicine, and that reform of the malpractice system is crucial for containing costs." Is there another economic explanation—apart from fear of lawsuits—for why doctors may end up ordering unnecessary tests and other medical procedures? Briefly explain.

Source: Amitabh Chandra, Anupam B. Jena, and Seth A. Seabury, "Defensive Medicine May Be Costlier Than It Seems," *Wall Street Journal*, February 7, 2013.

3.13 An article in the *Economist* argues that the real problem with health insurance is:

> The healthy people who decide not to buy insurance out of rational self-interest, and who turn out to be right. By not buying insurance, those (largely young) healthy people will be failing to subsidize the people insurance is meant for: the ones who end up getting sick.

  a. Why is it rational for healthy people not to buy health insurance?
  b. Do you agree that health insurance is meant for people who end up getting sick?
  c. Why is the situation described here a problem for a system of health insurance? If it is a problem, suggest possible solutions.

Source: "Romney on Health Care: To Boldly Go Where He Had Already Been Before," *Economist*, May 13, 2011.

3.14 An article in the *Los Angeles Times* describes a healthy 23-year-old woman who has decided not to buy health insurance as "exactly the type of person insurance plans, states and the federal government are counting on to make health reform work." Why are healthy 23-year-olds needed to make health reform work?

Source: Anna Gorman, "Affordable Care Act's Challenge: Getting Young Adults Enrolled," *Los Angeles Times*, June 2, 2013.

3.15 Explain whether you agree with the following statement:

> Providing health care is obviously a public good. If one person becomes ill and doesn't receive treatment, that person may infect many other people. If many people become ill, then the output of the economy will be negatively affected. Therefore, providing health care is a public good that should be supplied by the government.

5.4 ## The Debate over Health Care Policy in the United States, pages 162–173

LEARNING OBJECTIVE: Explain the major issues involved in the debate over health care policy in the United States.

Summary

In 2010, Congress passed the **Patient Protection and Affordable Care Act (ACA)**, which significantly reorganized the U.S. health care system. Spending on health care in the United States has been growing rapidly as a percentage of GDP, and spending per person on health care has been growing more rapidly than in other high-income countries. Third-party payers, such as employer-provided health insurance and the Medicare and Medicaid programs, have financed an increasing fraction of health care spending, while out-of-pocket payments have sharply declined as a fraction of total health care spending. Several explanations have been offered for the rapid increase in health care spending in the United States: Slow rates of growth of labor productivity in health care may be driving up costs, the U.S. population is becoming older, medical technology and new prescription drugs have higher costs, and the tax system and the reliance on third-party payers have distorted the economic incentives of consumers and suppliers of health care. The ACA has several important provisions: (1) an individual mandate that requires every resident of the United States to obtain health insurance or be fined; (2) the establishment of health exchanges that will be run by the state or federal governments and provide a means for individuals and small businesses to purchase health insurance; (3) an employer mandate that requires every firm with more than 200 employees to offer health insurance to them; (4) increased regulation of health insurance companies; (5) expansion of eligibility for Medicaid and the establishment of the Independent Payment Advisory Board (IPAB), which has the power to reduce Medicare payments for prescription drugs and for the use of diagnostic equipment and other technology if Medicare spending exceeds certain levels; and (6) increased taxes on people with incomes above $200,000. Some critics of the ACA argue that it does not go far enough in increasing government involvement in the health care system, while other critics argue that health care reform should rely more heavily on **market-based reforms**, which involve changing the market for health care so that it becomes more like the markets for other goods and services.

MyEconLab Visit **www.myeconlab.com** to complete these exercises online and get instant feedback.

Review Questions

4.1 What is the Patient Protection and Affordable Care Act (ACA)? Briefly list its major provisions.

4.2 In the United States, what has been the trend in health care spending as a percentage of GDP? Compare the increases in health care spending per person in the United States with the increases in health care spending per person in other high-income countries. What implications do current trends in health care spending have for the growth of federal government spending in the United States?

4.3 Briefly discuss how economists explain the rapid increases in health care spending.

4.4 What arguments do economists and policymakers who believe that the federal government should have a larger role in the health care system make in criticizing the ACA?

4.5 What arguments do economists and policymakers who believe that market-based reforms are the key to improving the health care system make in criticizing the ACA?

Problems and Applications

4.6 Figure 5.7 on page 166 shows that the Congressional Budget Office forecasts that only about 10 percent of future increases in spending on Medicare as a percentage of GDP will be due to the aging of the population. What factors explain the other 90 percent of the increase?

4.7 Improvements in technology usually result in lower costs of production or new and improved consumer goods and services. Assume that an improvement in medical technology results in an increase in life expectancy for people 65 years of age and older. How would this technological advance be likely to affect expenditures on health care?

4.8 Some economists and policymakers have argued that one way to control federal government spending on Medicare is to have a board of experts decide whether new medical technologies are worth their higher costs. If the board decides that they are *not* worth the costs, Medicare would not pay for them. Other economists and policymakers argue that the costs to beneficiaries should more closely represent the costs of providing medical services. This result might be attained by raising premiums, deductibles, and copayments or by "means testing," which would limit the Medicare benefits that high-income individuals receive. Political columnist David Brooks has summarized these two ways to restrain the growth of spending on Medicare: "From the top, a body of experts can be empowered to make rationing decisions. ... Alternatively, at the bottom, costs can be shifted to beneficiaries with premium supports to help them handle the burden."
   a. What are "rationing decisions"? How would these decisions restrain the growth of Medicare spending?
   b. How would shifting the costs of Medicare to beneficiaries restrain the growth of Medicare spending? What does Brooks mean by "premium supports"?
   c. Should Congress and the president be concerned about the growth of Medicare spending? If so, which of these approaches should they adopt, or is there a third approach that might be better? (*Note:* This last question is normative and has no definitive answer. It is intended to lead you to consider possible approaches to the Medicare program.)
   Source: David Brooks, "The Missing Fifth," *New York Times*, May 9, 2011.

4.9 The text refers to health care as a normal good. Briefly explain why. In the future, is it possible that health care in the United States could become an inferior good? Briefly explain how it would be possible to tell if this change had occurred.

4.10 The late Nobel Laureate Robert Fogel of the University of Chicago argued, "Expenditures on health care are driven by demand, which is spurred by income and by advances in biotechnology that make health interventions increasingly effective."

a. If Fogel was correct, should policymakers be concerned by projected increases in health care spending as a percentage of GDP?

b. What objections do some economists raise to Fogel's analysis of what is driving increases in spending on health care?

Source: Robert Fogel, "Forecasting the Cost of U.S. Healthcare," *The American*, September 3, 2009.

4.11 **(Related to the** Making the Connection **on page 164)** Employees in most circumstances do not pay taxes on the value of the health insurance provided by their employers. If employees were taxed on the value of the employer-provided health insurance, what would you expect to happen to the overall compensation employers pay employees? To the value of health insurance provided by employers? To the wages paid to employees? Briefly explain.

4.12 **(Related to** Solved Problem 5.4 **on page 168)** Suppose consumers pay less than the true cost of medical services because a third party, such as an insurance company or the government, pays most of the bill. In the following graph, D_1 represents the demand for medical services if consumers paid the full price of medical services; D_2 represents the demand for medical services when consumers pay only a fraction of the true cost of medical services; and S represents the supply of medical services. Use the graph to answer the following questions. Briefly explain your answers.

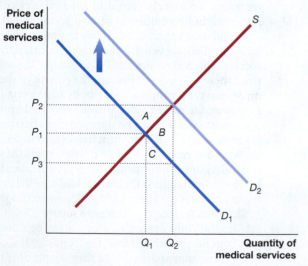

a. What is the equilibrium market price received by doctors and other suppliers of medical services?

b. What is the efficient quantity of medical services?

c. What is the price paid by consumers of medical services?

d. Which area represents the deadweight loss resulting from consumers not paying the full price of medical services?

4.13 **(Related to the** Making the Connection **on page 171)** A column in the *Wall Street Journal* observes, "Independent websites like Edmunds.com, AutoTrader.com and Kelley Blue Book publish detailed pricing information [on automobiles] for consumers and do so for free. Consumers want such information and businesses see opportunity in providing it, even for free, in order to attract eyeballs for advertising. … Such information doesn't exist in health care." Why aren't there Web sites that offer pricing data on health care and make a profit from selling advertisements?

Source: Holman W, Jenkins, Jr., "The Young Won't Buy ObamaCare," *Wall Street Journal*, June 18, 2013.

4.14 **(Related to the** Chapter Opener **on page 147)** We saw in the chapter opener that the T. Cain Grocery offers its employees a health care plan with a high deductible of $4,500 per year. What effect do high-deductible plans have on how often employees visit doctors or otherwise use health care services? If the federal government were to require that employer health care plans have deductibles that were no greater than $200 per year, would the employees in these plans be better off? Would the employers offering these plans be worse off? Briefly explain.

Firms, the Stock Market, and Corporate Governance

Is Twitter the Next Facebook?

Most people today have trouble imagining a world without Facebook, Twitter, Snapchat, and Instagram. All four of these social networking applications ("apps") are businesses that started small but have since grown rapidly. To finance that growth, they needed to raise funds. Some businesses raise funds by borrowing from banks. Once firms grow large enough, they can become *public firms* and sell stocks and bonds to investors in financial markets, such as the New York Stock Exchange. Firms that do not sell stock are called *private firms*. Both Facebook and Twitter have made the transition to being public firms. The founders of Snapchat, the mobile photo-sharing app, took a different approach: In 2012, they sold their company to Facebook for $1 billion. In the summer of 2015, Instagram, which allows people to share photos and 15-second videos, was still a private company. It was relying on investments from venture capital firms, which provide funds to private companies in exchange for part ownership.

A major decision for a successful social media startup is whether to remain a private firm, to become a public firm, or to sell itself to a larger firm as Snapchat did. Becoming a public firm provides access to greater financing but can also have drawbacks. From the time Mark Zuckerberg started Facebook in 2004 as a sophomore in college until the company went public in 2012, he was the unquestioned leader of the company. But buyers of Facebook's stock have partial ownership of the firm and a claim on its profits and can question Zuckerberg's decisions. Twitter became a public firm in 2013.

Stockholders want to invest in companies that can earn a profit. During its first year as a public company, Facebook struggled to meet the expectations of its investors. Eventually, Facebook was able to find a better way to target advertising on its app, and its stock more than doubled from its initial price in 2012 of $38 per share.

Twitter, however, found life as a public company to be more challenging. By 2015, it had more than 300 million active users and had become an important part of many people's lives. But advertisers who provided most of the company's revenue weren't convinced that advertising on the site was actually effective.

As we will see in this chapter, the ability of firms such as Twitter and Facebook to raise funds in financial markets is crucial to the health of the economy. Financial markets are also an important source of investment opportunities to households as they accumulate savings to buy houses, pay for college, and prepare for retirement.

Sources: Jack Marshall and Yoree Koh, "The Problem with Twitter Ads," *Wall Street Journal*, April 30, 2015; Douglas MacMillan, "Snapchat Raises Another $500 Million From Investors," *Wall Street Journal*, May 29, 2015; and Vindu Goel, "An Early Twitter Investor Calls for Change," *New York Times*, June 3, 2015.

Economics in Your Life

Would You Pay to Use Facebook or Twitter?

You can use Facebook or Twitter for free—or can you? Social media apps don't charge you directly; instead they earn their revenue primarily by displaying ads as you use the app. Most sites collect data about your Web searches and browsing habits and then display ads for products they think you might buy. But many people see targeted ads as an invasion of their privacy. Some of these people would be willing to pay to use these apps if they could do so without having to see advertisements. Would you be willing to pay to use social media apps? Do you think other users would be willing to pay enough that firms could rely on that source of revenue? As you read this chapter, try to answer these questions. You can check your answers against those we provide on **page 199** at the end of this chapter.

I n this chapter, we look at firms: how they are organized, how they raise funds, and the information they provide to investors. As we have discussed in earlier chapters, firms in a market system are responsible for organizing the factors of production to produce goods and services. Entrepreneurs start firms to earn a profit by offering a good or service. To succeed, entrepreneurs must meet consumers' wants by producing new or better goods and services or by finding ways to produce existing goods and services at a lower cost so that they can be sold at a lower price. Entrepreneurs also need access to sufficient funds, and they must be able to efficiently organize production. As the typical firm in many industries has become larger over the past 100 years, the task of efficiently organizing production has become more difficult. In the final section of this chapter, we look at problems of *corporate governance* that have occurred in recent years. We also look at the steps firms and the government have taken to avoid similar problems in the future.

6.1 Types of Firms

LEARNING OBJECTIVE: Categorize the major types of firms in the United States.

In studying a market economy, it is important to understand the basics of how firms operate. In the United States, there are three main categories of firms:

Sole proprietorship A firm owned by a single individual and not organized as a corporation.

Partnership A firm owned jointly by two or more persons and not organized as a corporation.

Corporation A legal form of business that provides owners with protection from losing more than their investment should the business fail.

1. A **sole proprietorship** is a firm owned by a single individual. Although most sole proprietorships are small, some employ many workers and earn large profits.
2. A **partnership** is a firm owned jointly by two or more—sometimes many— persons. Most law and accounting firms are partnerships. Some of them can be quite large. For instance, in 2015, the Baker & McKenzie law firm based in Chicago had 1,400 partners.
3. A **corporation** is a legal form of business that provides owners with protection from losing more than their investment in the firm should the business fail. Most large firms are organized as corporations.

Who Is Liable? Limited and Unlimited Liability

Asset Anything of value owned by a person or a firm.

A key distinction among the three types of firms is that the owners of sole proprietorships and partnerships have unlimited liability, which means that there is no legal distinction between the personal assets of the owners of the firm and the assets of the firm. An **asset** is anything of value owned by a person or a firm. If a sole proprietorship or a partnership owes a lot of money to the firm's suppliers or employees, the suppliers and employees have a legal right to sue the firm for payment, even if in order to pay their debts, the firm's owners have to sell some of their personal assets, such as stocks or bonds. In other words, with sole proprietorships and partnerships, the owners are not legally distinct from the firms they own.

It may only seem fair that the owners of a firm be responsible for the firm's debts. But in the early 1800s, many state legislatures in the United States realized that unlimited liability was a significant problem for any firm that was attempting to raise funds from large numbers of investors. An investor might be interested in making a relatively small investment in a firm but be unwilling to become a partner in the firm for fear of placing at risk all of his or her personal assets if the firm were to fail. To get around this problem, state legislatures began to pass *general incorporation laws*, which allowed firms to more easily be organized as corporations. Under the corporate form of business, the owners of a firm have **limited liability**, which means that if the firm fails, the owners can never lose more than the amount they have invested in the firm. The personal assets of the owners of the firm are not affected by the failure of the firm. In fact, in the eyes of the law, a corporation is a legal "person," separate from its owners. Limited liability has made it possible for corporations to raise funds by issuing shares of stock to large numbers of investors. For example, if you buy a share of Twitter stock, you are a part owner of the firm, but if Twitter were to go bankrupt, you would not be

Limited liability A legal provision that shields owners of a corporation from losing more than they have invested in the firm.

Table 6.1

Differences among Business Organizations

	Sole Proprietorship	Partnership	Corporation
Advantages	• Control by owner • No layers of management	• Ability to share work • Ability to share risks	• Limited personal liability • Greater ability to raise funds
Disadvantages	• Unlimited personal liability • Limited ability to raise funds	• Unlimited personal liability • Limited ability to raise funds	• Costly to organize • Possible double taxation of income

personally responsible for any of Twitter's debts. Therefore, you could not lose more than the amount you paid for the stock.

Organizing a firm as a corporation also has some disadvantages. In the United States, corporate profits are taxed twice—once at the corporate level and again when investors in the firm receive a share of the firm's profits. Corporations generally are larger than sole proprietorships and partnerships and are therefore more difficult to organize and run. Table 6.1 reviews the advantages and disadvantages of the three types of business organizations. **MyEconLab** Concept Check

Corporations Earn the Majority of Revenue and Profits

Figure 6.1 gives basic statistics on the three types of business organizations. Panel (a) shows that almost three-quarters of all firms are sole proprietorships. Panels (b) and (c) show that although only 18 percent of all firms are corporations, they account for a majority of the revenue and profits earned by all firms. *Profit* is the difference between revenue and the total cost to a firm of producing the goods and services it offers for sale.

There are more than 5.8 million corporations in the United States, but only 37,000 have annual revenues of more than $50 million. We can think of these 37,000 firms—including Apple, McDonald's, and Facebook—as representing "big business." These large firms earn more than 80 percent of the total profits of all corporations in the United States. **MyEconLab** Concept Check

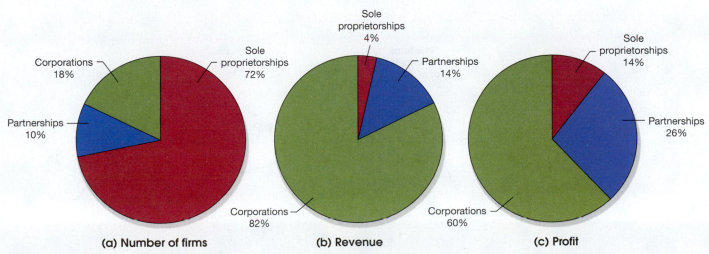

MyEconLab Animation

Figure 6.1   **Business Organizations: Sole Proprietorships, Partnerships, and Corporations**

The three types of firms in the United States are sole proprietorships, partnerships, and corporations. Panel (a) shows that only 18 percent of all firms are corporations. Yet, as panels (b) and (c) show, corporations account for a majority of the revenue and profit earned by all firms. **Source:** Internal Revenue Service, *Statistics on Income,* April 27, 2015.

Why Are Fewer Young People Starting Businesses?

We have seen that although a large majority of all firms are sole proprietorships, they account for only a small fraction of the total revenue and profit earned by all firms. In fact, more than 70 percent of people work at firms that have 50 or more employees. Does this mean that small businesses are not important to the U.S. economy?

On the contrary, most economists would argue that small businesses are vital to the health of the economy. Starting a small firm provides an entrepreneur with a vehicle for bringing a new product or process to market. During the late nineteenth and early twentieth centuries, Thomas Edison, Henry Ford, and the Wright Brothers were all responsible for introducing important products shortly after starting what were initially very small firms. In more recent years, Bill Gates, Steve Jobs, Michael Dell, and Mark Zuckerberg decided that the best way to develop their ideas was by founding Microsoft, Apple, Dell Computer, and Facebook rather than by choosing to work for large corporations.

In most years, more than 400,000 new firms open in the United States, and, of these, more than 95 percent employ fewer than 20 workers. In a typical year, new small firms create 3.3 million jobs. Forty percent of all new jobs are created by small firms, and in some years more than half are. Looking just at newly started firms, more than 85 percent of jobs created are created by small firms.

Because of the importance of small firms, some economists and policymakers have been concerned by a slowdown in recent years in the number of firms started. As the graph below shows, in the late 1970s, more than 15 percent of all firms were less than a year old. In recent years, only about 8 percent were. In absolute numbers, in recent years business startups have been running about 25 percent below the levels of just 10 years ago. The decline in starting new businesses is not concentrated in one industry or geographic area but has occurred across industries, including the information and high-tech sectors, and in most states and cities.

The decline in starting new firms has been particularly large among people under the age of 35. At first, this trend may seem surprising because of the publicity received by high-tech startups such as Twitter, Facebook, Uber, and Airbnb, all of which were started by young entrepreneurs. But while in the 1990s about one-third of all new firms were started by people younger than 35, today fewer than one-quarter are.

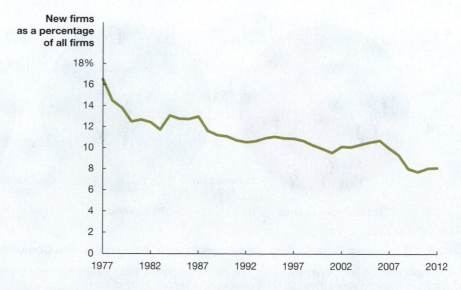

Source: U.S. Census Bureau, "Business Dynamics Statistics, Firm Characteristics Data Tables," June 2015.

Economists have not come to a consensus on the reasons for the decline in business startups. Some economists believe that despite the publicity received by innovative high-tech firms, the overall U.S. economy is experiencing a slowdown in technological progress. With fewer new technologies being introduced, there are fewer opportunities to start new firms selling new goods and services. Some economists believe that an increase in government regulations has raised the costs of starting and running a small business. For example, state and local governments have imposed licensing requirements on many occupations. According to one study, while at one time only 5 percent of workers were in an occupation that required a license, today more than 20 percent are. Slowing population growth may also have reduced the opportunities to start new businesses.

Whatever the explanation, many economists and policymakers worry that without an increase in young entrepreneurs starting new firms, the U.S. economy will become less dynamic and less able to sustain high rates of economic growth.

Sources: Asma Ghribi, "Why It's Worrying That U.S. Companies Are Getting Older," *Wall Street Journal*, August 4, 2014; Ian Hathaway and Robert E. Litan, "What's Driving the Decline in the Firm Formation Rate? A Partial Explanation," *Brookings Economic Studies*, November 20, 2014; Morris M. Kleiner and Alan B. Krueger, "Analyzing the Extent and Influence of Occupational Licensing on the Labor Market," *Journal of Labor Economics*, Vol. 31, No. 2, April 2013, pp. S173–S202; David Neumark, Brandon Wall, and Junfu Zhang, "Do Small Businesses Create More Jobs? New Evidence for the United States from the National Establishment Time Series," *Review of Economics and Statistics*, Vol. 93, No. 1, February 2011, pp. 16–29.

Your Turn: Test your understanding by doing related problems 1.10 and 1.11 on page 201 at the end of this chapter.

MyEconLab Study Plan

The Structure of Corporations and the Principal–Agent Problem

Large corporations account for a majority of sales and profits in the economy, so it is important to know how they are managed. Most large corporations have a similar management structure. The way in which a corporation is structured and the effect that structure has on the corporation's behavior is referred to as **corporate governance**.

Corporations are legally owned by their *shareholders*, the owners of the corporation's stock. Unlike with a sole proprietorship, a corporation's shareholders own the firm but don't directly manage it. Instead, they elect a *board of directors* to represent their interests. The board of directors appoints a *chief executive officer* (CEO) to run the day-to-day operations of the corporation. Sometimes the board of directors also appoints other members of *top management*, such as the *chief financial officer* (CFO). At other times, the CEO appoints other members of top management. Members of top management—sometimes called C-suite executives—including the CEO and CFO, often serve on the board of directors. They are called *inside directors*. Members of the board of directors who do not have a direct management role in the firm are called *outside directors*. The outside directors are intended to act as a check on the decisions of top managers.

Unlike the owners of family businesses, the top management of a large corporation does not generally own a large share of the firm's stock, so large corporations have a **separation of ownership from control**. Although the shareholders actually own the firm, the top management controls the firm's day-to-day operations. Because top managers own only a small percentage of the firm's stock, they may decrease the firm's profits by spending money to purchase private jets or schedule management meetings at luxurious resorts. Economists refer to the conflict between the interests of shareholders and the interests of the top management as a **principal–agent problem**.[1] This problem occurs when agents—in this case, a firm's top management—pursue their own interests rather than the interests of the principal who hired them—in this case, the shareholders of the corporation. Because the outside directors are not involved with the daily operations of the firm, they may have difficulty deciding whether the actions taken by

Corporate governance The way in which a corporation is structured and the effect that structure has on the corporation's behavior.

Separation of ownership from control A situation in a corporation in which the top management, rather than the shareholders, controls day-to-day operations.

Principal–agent problem A problem caused by an agent pursuing his own interests rather than the interests of the principal who hired him.

[1] In Chapter 5, we saw that the principal–agent problem arises from moral hazard that can occur because of asymmetric information. In this case, the asymmetric information involves top managers knowing more about how the firm is actually run than do the firm's shareholders.

top managers really are in the best interests of shareholders. To reduce the effect of the principal–agent problem, many boards of directors in the 1990s began to tie the salaries of top managers to the profits of the firm or to the price of the firm's stock. They hoped this step would give top managers an incentive to make the firm as profitable as possible, thereby benefiting its shareholders. Sometimes, though, top managers act in ways that increase the profits of the firm in the short run—and the salaries and bonuses of the top managers—but actually reduce the profits of the firm in the long run.

MyEconLab Concept Check

6.2 How Firms Raise Funds

LEARNING OBJECTIVE: Explain how firms raise the funds they need to operate and expand.

Owners and managers of firms try to earn a profit. To succeed, a firm must raise funds to pay for its operations, including paying its employees and buying or renting computers and other machinery and equipment. In fact, a central challenge for anyone running a firm, whether that person is a sole proprietor or a top manager of a large corporation, is raising the funds needed to operate and expand the business. Suppose you develop a new social networking app, and you decide to start a business using $100,000 you have saved in a bank. You use the $100,000 to rent an office for your firm, buy computers, and pay other startup expenses. Your firm is a great success, and you decide to expand it by moving to a larger office and buying more computers. As the owner of a small business, you can raise the funds for this expansion in three ways:

1. If you are making a profit, you could reinvest the profits back into your firm. Profits that are reinvested in a firm rather than taken out of the firm and paid to the firm's owners are called *retained earnings*.
2. You could raise funds by recruiting additional owners to invest in the firm. This arrangement would increase the firm's *financial capital*.
3. Finally, you could borrow the funds from relatives, friends, or a bank.

   The managers of a large public firm have some additional ways to raise funds, as we will see in the next section.

Sources of External Funds

Unless firms rely on retained earnings, they have to raise the *external funds* they need from those who have funds available to invest. It is the role of an economy's *financial system* to transfer funds from savers to borrowers.

Indirect finance A flow of funds from savers to borrowers through financial intermediaries such as banks. Intermediaries raise funds from savers to lend to firms (and other borrowers).

Most firms raise external funds in two ways. The first way, called **indirect finance**, relies on financial intermediaries such as banks. If you put $1,000 in a checking account or in a certificate of deposit (CD), the bank will loan most of those funds to borrowers. The bank will combine your funds with those of other depositors and, for example, make a $100,000 loan to a local business. Small businesses rely heavily on bank loans as their primary source of external funds.

Direct finance A flow of funds from savers to firms through financial markets, such as the New York Stock Exchange.

A second way for firms to acquire external funds is through *financial markets*. Raising funds in these markets, such as the New York Stock Exchange on Wall Street in New York City, is called **direct finance**. Direct finance usually takes the form of the borrower selling the lender a *financial security*. A financial security is a document—sometimes in electronic form—that states the terms under which the funds are passed from the buyer of the security (who is lending funds) to the borrower. *Bonds* and *stocks* are the two main types of financial securities. Typically, only large corporations are able to sell bonds and stocks on financial markets. Investors are generally unwilling to buy securities issued by small and medium-sized firms because the investors lack sufficient information on the financial health of smaller firms.

Bond A financial security that represents a promise to repay a fixed amount of funds.

Bonds **Bonds** are financial securities that represent promises to repay a fixed amount of funds. When Apple sells a bond to raise funds, it promises to pay the purchaser of the bond an interest payment each year for the term of the bond, as well as a payment of the loan amount, or the *principal*, at the end of the term. Apple may need to raise many millions of dollars to build new offices, but each individual bond has a principal, or *face value*, of $1,000, which is the amount each bond purchaser is lending Apple. So, Apple must sell many bonds to raise all the funds it needs. Suppose Apple promises it will pay interest of $40 per year to anyone who buys one of its bonds. The interest payments on a bond are called **coupon payments**. The **interest rate** is the cost of borrowing funds, usually expressed as a percentage of the amount borrowed. We can calculate the interest rate on the bond, called the *coupon rate*, by dividing the coupon by the face value of the bond. In this case, the coupon rate is:

$$\frac{\$40}{\$1,000} = 0.04, \text{ or } 4\%.$$

Many bonds that corporations issue have terms, or *maturities*, of 30 years. In this example, if you bought a bond from Apple, Apple would pay you $40 per year for 30 years, and at the end of the thirtieth year, Apple would repay the $1,000 principal to you.

The interest rate that a corporation selling a bond has to pay depends on how likely bond buyers—investors—think that the corporation is to default, or not make the promised coupon or principal payments. The higher the *default risk* on a bond, the higher the interest rate will be. For example, investors see the federal government as being very unlikely to default on its bonds, so federal government bonds pay a lower interest rate than do bonds of a firm such as Apple. In turn, Apple pays a lower interest rate on its bonds than does a corporation that investors believe is not as likely to make its bond payments.

Coupon payment An interest payment on a bond.

Interest rate The cost of borrowing funds, usually expressed as a percentage of the amount borrowed.

The Rating Game: Is the U.S. Treasury Likely to Default on Its Bonds?

Federal regulations require that before they can sell bonds to investors, firms and governments must first have bonds rated by one of the credit-rating agencies. The three largest rating agencies are Moody's Investors Service, Standard & Poor's Corporation, and Fitch Ratings. These private firms rate bonds by giving them letter grades—AAA or Aaa being the highest—that reflect the likelihood that the firm or government will be able to make the payments on the bond. The following table shows the ratings:

	Moody's Investors Service	Standard & Poor's (S&P)	Fitch Ratings	Meaning of the Ratings
Investment-grade bonds	Aaa	AAA	AAA	Highest credit quality
	Aa	AA	AA	Very high credit quality
	A	A	A	High credit quality
	Baa	BBB	BBB	Good credit quality
Non-investment-grade bonds	Ba	BB	BB	Speculative
	B	B	B	Highly speculative
	Caa	CCC	CCC	Substantial default risk
	Ca	CC	CC	Very high levels of default risk
	C	C	C	Exceptionally high levels of default risk
	—	D	D	Default

Note: The entries in the "Meaning of the Ratings" column are slightly modified from those that Fitch uses. The other two rating agencies have similar descriptions. For each rating from Aa to Caa, Moody's adds a numerical modifier of 1, 2, or 3. The rating Aa1 is higher than the rating Aa2, and the rating Aa2 is higher than the rating Aa3. Similarly, Standard & Poor's and Fitch Ratings add a plus (+) or minus (−) sign. The rating AA+ is higher than the rating AA, and the rating AA is higher than the rating AA-.

Source: *Money, Banking, and the Financial System*, 2nd edition, by R. Glenn Hubbard and Anthony P. O'Brien. Copyright © 2014 by Pearson Education, Inc. Reprinted and electronically reproduced by permission of Pearson Education, Inc., Upper Saddle River, New Jersey.

Investors can use the ratings in deciding how much risk they are willing to accept when buying a bond. Generally, the lower the rating, the higher the interest rate an investor will receive but also the higher the risk that the issuer of the bond will default.

The rating agencies charge firms and governments—rather than investors—for their services. This arrangement raises the question of whether rating agencies face a conflict of interest. Because firms issuing bonds can choose which of the agencies to hire to rate their bonds, the agencies may have an incentive to give higher ratings than might be justified in order to keep the firms' business. During the housing boom of the mid-2000s, some financial firms issued *mortgage-backed bonds*. These bonds were similar to regular corporate bonds except that the interest payments came from mortgage loans people had taken out to buy houses. The money from those mortgage payments was passed along to investors who had bought the mortgage-backed bonds. The rating agencies gave many of these bonds AAA ratings, even though when housing prices began to decline in 2006, many homeowners stopped making their mortgage payments and the value of the bonds declined sharply. Some economists and policymakers believe the rating agencies provided the high ratings primarily to ensure that the firms that issued the bonds would continue to hire them.

Some investors worry that the U.S. government might someday default on the bonds that it has sold. Over the past 15 years, the federal government has been spending more than it has been collecting in taxes. The result is a federal budget deficit, which forces the Treasury to sell bonds equal to the amount of the deficit. The budget deficit was particularly large during and immediately after the 2007–2009 recession, which resulted in sharp declines in tax receipts and increases in government spending. Forecasts from the U.S. Congressional Budget Office indicate that large budget deficits will continue indefinitely because spending on Social Security, Medicare, Medicaid, and other government programs is expected to increase faster than tax revenues.

In 2011, Standard & Poor's (S&P) decided that because of these continuing deficits, it would downgrade U.S. Treasury bonds from AAA to AA+. Never before had a rating agency given Treasury bonds less than an AAA rating.

Is it likely that the U.S. Treasury will default on its bonds? S&P argued that while a default is still unlikely, the continuing large deficits increased the chance that someday the Treasury might not make the interest payments on its bonds. Most investors, though, appear confident that the Treasury will not default and are willing to buy Treasury bonds despite the historically low interest rates on the bonds. Like the Ghost of Christmas Yet to Come in Charles Dickens's *A Christmas Carol*, S&P was giving a warning of something that might happen rather than something that necessarily must happen.

Sources: Mary Williams Walsh, "Credit Ratings Services Give Mixed Reviews to Tax Deal," *New York Times*, January 3, 2013; and Cyrus Sanati, "S.E.C. Urges Changes to Ratings-Agency Rules," *New York Times*, August 28, 2009.

MyEconLab Study Plan

Your Turn: Test your understanding by doing related problems 2.8 and 2.9 on page 202 at the end of this chapter.

Stock A financial security that represents partial ownership of a firm.

Stocks　When you buy a newly issued bond from a firm, you are lending funds to that firm. When you buy **stock** issued by a firm, you are actually buying part ownership of the firm. When a corporation sells stock, it is doing the same thing the owner of a small business does when he or she takes on a partner: The firm is increasing its financial capital by bringing additional owners into the firm. Any one shareholder usually owns only a small fraction of the total shares of stock issued by a corporation.

Many small investors buy shares of *mutual funds* rather than directly buying stocks issued by individual companies. Mutual funds, such as Fidelity Investment's Magellan Fund, sell shares to investors and use the funds to invest in a portfolio of financial assets, such as stocks and bonds. By buying shares in a mutual fund, small investors reduce the costs they would pay to buy many individual stocks and bonds. Small savers who have only enough money to buy a few individual stocks and bonds can use mutual funds to *diversify*, which lowers their investment risk because most mutual funds hold a large number of stocks and bonds. If a firm issuing a stock or bond declares bankruptcy, causing the stock or bond to lose all of its value, the effect on a mutual fund's portfolio is likely to be small. The effect might be devastating, though, to a small investor who invested most of his or her savings in the stock or bond. Because mutual funds are willing to buy back their shares at any time, they also provide savers with easy access to their money.

Exchange-traded funds (ETFs) are similar to mutual funds in that when you buy shares in an ETF, you are buying a claim to a portfolio of stocks or bonds. But mutual funds can only be bought from or sold back to the firm that issues them. ETFs can be bought and sold to other investors in financial markets, just as individual stocks or bonds can.

A shareholder is entitled to a portion of the corporation's profits, if there are any. Corporations generally keep some of their profits as retained earnings to finance future expansion. The remaining profits are paid to shareholders as **dividends**. If a firm uses its retained earnings to grow and earn economic profits, its share price rises, which provides a *capital gain* for investors. If a corporation is unable to make a profit, it usually does not pay a dividend. Under the law, corporations must make payments on any debt they have before making payments to their owners. That is, a corporation must make promised payments to bondholders before it can make any dividend payments to shareholders. Unlike bonds, stocks do not have a maturity date, so the firm is not obliged to return the investor's funds at any particular date.   MyEconLab Concept Check

Dividends Payments by a corporation to its shareholders.

Stock and Bond Markets Provide Capital—and Information

The original purchasers of stocks and bonds may resell them to other investors. In fact, most of the buying and selling of stocks and bonds that takes place each day involves investors reselling existing stocks and bonds to each other rather than corporations selling new stocks and bonds to investors. The buyers and sellers of stocks and bonds together make up the *stock and bond markets*. There is no single place where stocks and bonds are bought and sold. Some trading of stocks and bonds takes place in buildings known as *exchanges*, such as the New York Stock Exchange or the Tokyo Stock Exchange. In the United States, the stocks and bonds of the largest corporations are traded on the New York Stock Exchange. The development of computer technology has spread the trading of stocks and bonds outside exchanges to *securities dealers* linked by computers. These dealers comprise the *over-the-counter market*. The stocks of many high-technology firms—including Apple, Twitter, and Facebook—are traded in the most important of the over-the-counter markets, the *National Association of Securities Dealers Automated Quotations* system, which is referred to by its acronym, NASDAQ.

Shares of stock represent claims on the profits of the firms that issue them. Therefore, as the fortunes of the firms change and they earn more or less profit, the prices of the stock the firms have issued should also change. Similarly, bonds represent claims to receive coupon payments and one final payment of the principal. Therefore, a particular bond that was issued in the past may have its price go up or down, depending on whether the coupon payments being offered on newly issued bonds are higher or lower than those on existing bonds. If you hold a bond with a coupon of $30 per year, and similar newly issued bonds have coupons of $40 per year, the price of your bond will fall because it is less attractive to investors. The price of a bond will also be affected by changes in *default risk*, which reflects investors' expectations of the issuing firm's ability to make the coupon payments. For example, if investors begin to believe that a firm may soon go out of business and stop making coupon payments to its bondholders, the price of the firm's bonds will fall to very low levels.

Changes in the value of a firm's stocks and bonds provide important information for a firm's managers, as well as for investors. An increase in the stock price means that investors are more optimistic about the firm's profit prospects, and the firm's managers might want to expand the firm's operations as a result. By contrast, a decrease in the firm's stock price indicates that investors are less optimistic about the firm's profit prospects, so management may want to shrink the firm's operations. Similarly, changes in the value of the firm's bonds imply changes in the cost of external funds to finance the firm's investment in research and development or in new factories. A higher bond price indicates a lower cost of new external funds, while a lower bond price indicates a higher cost of new external funds.   MyEconLab Concept Check

Don't Let This Happen to You

When Twitter Shares Are Sold, Twitter Doesn't Get the Money

Twitter is a popular investment, with investors buying and selling shares often as their views about the value of the firm shift. That's great for Twitter, right? Think of Twitter collecting all that money as shares change hands and the stock price goes up. *Wrong.* Twitter raises funds in a primary market, but its shares trade in a secondary market. Those trades don't put money into Twitter's hands, but they do give important information to the firm's managers. Let's see why.

Primary markets are markets in which firms sell newly issued stocks and bonds to initial buyers. Businesses can raise funds in a primary financial market in two ways—by borrowing (selling bonds) or selling shares of stock—which result in different types of claims on the borrowing firm's future income. Although you may hear about the stock market fluctuations every day in news updates, bonds actually account for more of the funds raised by borrowers. The total value of bonds in the United States is typically about twice the value of stocks.

In *secondary markets*, stocks and bonds that have already been issued are sold by one investor to another.

If Twitter sells shares to the public, it is turning to a primary market for new funds. Once Twitter shares are issued, investors trade the shares in the secondary market. Twitter does not receive any new funds when its shares are traded. The initial seller of a stock or bond raises funds from an investor only in the primary market. Secondary markets convey information to firms' managers and investors by determining the price of stocks and bonds. For example, a major increase in Twitter's stock price conveys the market's optimism about the firm, and Twitter may decide to raise funds to expand. So, secondary markets are valuable sources of information for corporations that are considering raising funds.

Primary and secondary markets are both important, but they play different roles. As an investor, you principally trade stocks and bonds in a secondary market. As a corporate manager, you may help decide how to raise new funds to expand the firm where you work.

MyEconLab Study Plan

Your Turn: Test your understanding by doing related problem 2.11 on page 202 at the end of this chapter.

The Fluctuating Stock Market

The performance of the U.S. stock market is often measured using *stock market indexes*. Stock market indexes are averages of stock prices, with the value of the index set equal to 100 in a particular year, called the *base year*. Because the stock indexes are intended to show movements in prices from one year to the next, rather than the actual dollar values of the underlying stocks, the year chosen for the base year is unimportant. Figure 6.2 shows movements from January 1998 to June 2015 in the three most widely followed stock indexes (the shaded areas represent months in which the U.S. economy was in a business cycle recession when the production and profits of many firms are falling):

- The Dow Jones Industrial Average, which is an index of the stock prices of 30 large U.S. corporations.

- The S&P 500, which is an index prepared by Standard & Poor's Corporation and includes the stock prices of 500 large U.S. firms.

- The NASDAQ Composite Index, which includes the stock prices of more than 4,000 firms whose shares are traded in the NASDAQ stock market. NASDAQ is an over-the-counter market, meaning that buying and selling on NASDAQ is carried out between dealers who are linked together by computer. The listings on NASDAQ are dominated by high-tech firms such as Apple, Facebook, and Twitter.

As we have seen, ownership of a firm's stock represents a claim on the firm's profits. So, the larger the firm's profits are, the higher its stock price will be. When the overall economy is expanding, incomes, employment, and spending will all increase, as will corporate profits. When the economy is in a recession, incomes, employment, and spending will fall, as will corporate profits. Therefore, we would expect that stock prices will rise when the economy is expanding and fall when the economy is in recession. We see this pattern reflected in the three stock market indexes shown in Figure 6.2. All three

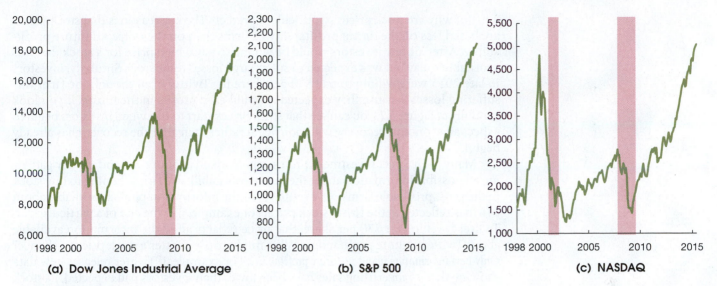

MyEconLab Real-time data

Figure 6.2   Movements in Stock Market Indexes, January 1998 to June 2015

The performance of the U.S. stock market is often measured by market indexes, which are averages of stock prices. The three most important indexes are the Dow Jones Industrial Average, the S&P 500, and the NAS-DAQ. During the period from 1998 to 2015, the three indexes followed similar patterns, rising when the U.S. economy was expanding and falling when the economy was in recession. Note that in all three panels, the vertical axis does not start at zero.

indexes follow a roughly similar pattern: increases in stock prices during the economic expansion of the late 1990s, declines after the "dot-com crash" of 2000 and the recession of 2001, increases from late 2001 to late 2007, declines as the U.S. economy entered a recession at the end of 2007, and then increases beginning in early 2009.

The stock prices of many early Internet companies soared in the late 1990s, as some analysts made what turned out to be overly optimistic predictions about how rapidly online retailing would grow. In 2000, when investors realized that many dot-coms would never be profitable, their stock prices crashed. Because the NASDAQ is dominated by high-tech stocks, it experienced greater swings during the dot-com boom and bust of the late 1990s and early 2000s than did the other two indexes. The sharp declines in all three indexes beginning in late 2007 reflected the severity of the recession that began in December of that year. The severity of the recession was due in part to problems with financial firms, which we will discuss in Section 6.4. By 2015, as recovery from the recession continued, all three indexes had reached their highest values ever.   MyEconLab Concept Check

Making the Connection
MyEconLab Video

Why Are Many People Poor Stock Market Investors?

You've probably heard this standard advice about investing: "Buy low and sell high." That is, you should buy shares of stocks and other financial assets when their prices are low and sell them when their prices are high. Unfortunately, many people do the opposite. For instance, many people bought shares of Apple stock when it was selling for more than $700 per share in September 2012 and sold when it was below $400 per share in April 2013.

Stock prices are difficult to predict, but many people convince themselves that a stock whose price has been rising will continue to rise and that a stock whose price has been falling will continual to fall. As a result, people end up buying high and selling low rather than the reverse. Studies have shown that individual investors consistently earn lower returns on their investments when they frequently buy and sell stock hoping to predict changes in stock prices.

New information about Twitter's future profitability would cause the price of its stock to change.

But why are stock prices so difficult to predict? The key reason is that stock prices are based less on the *current* profitability of firms than on their *expected* future profitability. After all, few investors would be willing to pay a high price for a stock that was profitable today but was expected to suffer large losses tomorrow. Similarly, investors in late 2015 were willing to pay $30 per share for Twitter even though the firm was suffering losses because they expected it would earn profits in the future. If you look carefully at Figure 6.2, you can see that stock prices start to rise when investors begin to expect an economic recovery will soon begin rather than after the recovery has already begun.

Many Wall Street investment professionals spend a lot of time and money gathering all possible information about the future profitability of firms, hoping to buy stock in the most profitable firms. As a result, all of the information publicly available about a firm is reflected in the firm's stock price. For example, if at the end of a particular day, Twitter is selling for $30 per share, that price reflects all of the information available about Twitter's future profitability. What might cause Twitter's stock price to change? *Only new information about its future profitability.* For example, if Twitter releases new data showing that its advertising sales have been lower than investors had expected, its stock price will fall.

Even highly paid professional investors cannot consistently predict stock prices. The managers of mutual funds who try to earn high returns by frequently buying and selling stocks are rarely able to beat the stock market averages, such as the S&P 500. One study found that, in a typical year, only one-third of mutual fund managers were able to earn their investors a higher return than a small investor could earn by investing in an index mutual that buys only the stocks in the S&P 500. Only 10 percent of mutual fund managers earned a higher return than an index fund for two consecutive years.

Whichever way you—or Wall Street professionals—predict stock prices will move in the future, you are as likely to be wrong as you are to be right.

Sources: Morgan Housel, "Three Mistakes Investors Keep Making Again and Again," *Wall Street Journal*, September 12, 2014; Joe Light, "How to Find a Fund Manager Who Can Beat the Market," *Wall Street Journal*, January 11, 2013; and Howard Gold, "Almost No One Can Beat the Market," marketwatch.com, October 25, 2013.

MyEconLab Study Plan   **Your Turn:** Test your understanding by doing related problem 2.12 on page 202 at the end of this chapter.

Solved Problem 6.2

MyEconLab Interactive Animation

Why Does Warren Buffett Like Mutual Funds?

Warren Buffett is considered one of the greatest investors who has ever lived. His ability to predict which firms' stocks are likely to rise in price helped make him one of the richest people in the world. Yet Buffett advises that individual investors not try to pick individual stocks but instead use 90 percent of their savings to buy shares in mutual funds that charge low fees, such as those offered by the Vanguard Group. Is it likely that anyone investing mostly in mutual funds will become as wealthy as Buffett? Why would Buffett give this advice?

Solving the Problem

Step 1: **Review the chapter material.** This problem is about investing in the stock market, so you may want to review the section "The Fluctuating Stock Market" on page 190 and the *Making the Connection*, "Why Are Many People Poor Stock Market Investors?" which begins on page 191.

Step 2: **Answer the first question by discussing whether investing in low-cost mutual funds is a way to become as wealthy as Warren Buffett.** Most investors who have become wealthy have done so by making large investments in just a few firms. Mutual funds typically hold large numbers of stocks and bonds, so even if one or two of the stocks do extremely well, the total investment return from the fund will be held back by the smaller increases (or losses) in the other stocks in the fund. By investing in mutual funds, you can accumulate significant amounts to pay for a house, a college education, or retirement. Many people who have earned only middle-class incomes have accumulated a million dollars or more by retirement age by investing in low-cost mutual funds. But no one is known to have become fabulously wealthy with this approach to saving.

Step 3: **Answer the second question by explaining why Warren Buffett would advise most people to put their savings in mutual funds, even though they are unlikely to become wealthy by doing so.** Mutual funds give individual investors a low-cost way to diversify. Although it's possible to earn a high return investing in the stocks of individual firms, it's also easy for a small investor to lose all of his or her money if those firms run into financial problems.

Extra Credit: Warren Buffett may have become a billionaire by being better than other investors at predicting the future profits of the firms he invests in. Or he may have become a billionaire because he was lucky that the firms he invested in did particularly well—in which case he may not be better at forecasting the future profitability of firms than are other investors. Given that nearly all other equally intelligent and hardworking professional investors have been unable to consistently "beat the market" by earning higher returns than those earned by the typical low-cost, well-diversified mutual fund, it is impossible to know with certainty the true reasons for Buffett's success.

Source: Warren Buffett, *Letter to Berkshire Shareholders*, March 1, 2014, p. 20.

Your Turn: For more practice, do related problem 2.13 on page 202 at the end of this chapter.   MyEconLab Study Plan

6.3 Using Financial Statements to Evaluate a Corporation

LEARNING OBJECTIVE: Understand the information corporations include in their financial statements.

To raise funds, a firm's managers must persuade potential lenders or investors that the firm will be profitable. Before a firm can sell new issues of stocks or bonds, it must first provide investors and financial regulators with information about its finances. To borrow from a bank, a firm must also provide the bank with financial information.

In most high-income countries, government agencies require firms to disclose specific financial information to the public before they are allowed to sell securities such as stocks or bonds in financial markets. In the United States, the Securities and Exchange Commission (SEC) requires publicly owned firms to report their performance in financial statements prepared using standard accounting methods, often referred to as *generally accepted accounting principles.* Such disclosure reduces the cost to investors of gathering information about firms, but it doesn't eliminate these costs—for two reasons. First, some firms may be too young to have much information for potential investors to evaluate. Second, managers may try to present the required information in the most favorable way so that investors will overvalue their securities.

Private firms also collect information on business borrowers and sell the information to lenders and investors. If the information-gathering firms do a good job, lenders and investors purchasing the information will be better able to judge the quality of borrowing firms. Some firms—including Moody's Investors Service, Standard & Poor's Corporation, Value Line, and Dun & Bradstreet—collect information from businesses and sell it to subscribers. Buyers include individual investors, libraries, and financial intermediaries. You can find some of these publications in your college library or through online information services.

What kind of information do investors and firm managers need? A firm must answer three basic questions: What to produce? How to produce it? What price to charge? To answer these questions, a firm's managers need two pieces of information: The first is the firm's revenues and costs, and the second is the value of the property and other assets the firm owns and the firm's debts, or other **liabilities**, that it owes to households and other firms. Potential investors in the firm also need this information to decide whether to buy the firm's stocks or bonds. The information can be found in the firm's *financial statements*, principally its income statement and balance sheet, which we discuss next.

MyEconLab Concept Check

Liability Anything owed by a person or a firm.

The Income Statement

Income statement A financial statement that shows a firm's revenues, costs, and profit over a period of time.

A firm's **income statement** shows its revenues, costs, and profit over a period of time. Corporations issue annual income statements, although the 12-month *fiscal year* covered may be different from the calendar year to better represent the seasonal pattern of the business. We explore income statements in greater detail in the appendix to this chapter.

Accounting profit A firm's net income, measured as revenue minus operating expenses and taxes paid.

Accounting Profit   An income statement shows a firm's revenue, costs, and profit for the firm's fiscal year. To determine profitability, the income statement starts with the firm's revenue and subtracts its operating expenses and taxes paid. The remainder, *net income*, is the **accounting profit** of the firm.

Economic Profit   Accounting profit provides information on a firm's current net income, measured according to accepted accounting standards. Accounting profit is not, however, the ideal measure of a firm's profits because it neglects some of the firm's costs. *Economic profit* provides a better indication than accounting profit of how successful a firm is because economic profit is calculated using all of a firm's costs. Firms making an economic profit will remain in business and may even expand. Firms making an *economic loss* are unlikely to remain in business in the long run. To understand how economic profit is calculated, remember that economists always measure cost as *opportunity cost*. The **opportunity cost** of any activity is the highest-valued alternative that must be given up to engage in that activity. Costs are either *explicit* or *implicit*. When a firm spends money, an **explicit cost** results. If a firm incurs an opportunity cost but does not spend money, an **implicit cost** results. For example, firms incur an explicit labor cost when they pay wages to employees. Firms have many other explicit costs as well, such as the cost of the electricity used to light their buildings or the costs of advertising or insurance.

Opportunity cost The highest-valued alternative that must be given up to engage in an activity.

Explicit cost A cost that involves spending money.

Implicit cost A nonmonetary opportunity cost.

Some costs are implicit, however. The most important of these is the opportunity cost to investors of the funds they have invested in the firm. Economists use the term *normal rate of return* to refer to the minimum amount that investors must earn on the funds they invest in a firm, expressed as a percentage of the amount invested. If a firm fails to provide investors with at least a normal rate of return, it will not be able to remain in business over the long run because investors will not continue to invest their funds in the firm. For example, Borders was once the second-largest bookstore chain in the United States and a very profitable firm, with stock that sold for more than $40 per share. By 2010, investors became convinced that the firm's difficulty competing with Amazon and other online booksellers and its loss of sales to e-books meant that the firm would never be able to provide investors with a normal rate of return. Many investors expected that the firm would eventually have to declare bankruptcy, and as a result, the price of Borders stock plummeted to less than $1 per share. Within a year, the firm declared bankruptcy, and its remaining assets were sold off. The return (in dollars) that investors require to continue investing in a firm is a true cost to the firm and should be subtracted from the firm's revenues to calculate its profits.

The rate of return that investors require to continue investing in a firm varies from firm to firm. If the investment is risky—as would be the case with a biotechnology startup—investors may require a high rate of return to compensate them for the risk. Investors in firms in more established industries, such as electric utilities, may require lower rates of return. The exact rate of return investors require to invest in any particular firm is difficult to calculate, which also makes it difficult for an accountant to include the return as a cost on an income statement. Firms have other implicit costs, besides the return investors require, that can also be difficult to calculate. As a result, the rules of accounting generally require that only explicit costs be included in the firm's financial records. *Economic costs* include both explicit costs *and* implicit costs. **Economic profit** is equal to a firm's revenues minus its economic costs. Because accounting profit excludes some implicit costs, it is larger than economic profit.   MyEconLab Concept Check

Economic profit A firm's revenues minus all of its implicit and explicit costs.

The Balance Sheet

A firm's **balance sheet** shows its financial position on a particular day, usually the end of a quarter or year. Recall that an asset is anything of value that a firm owns, and a liability is a debt or an obligation owed by a firm. Subtracting the value of a firm's liabilities from the value of its assets leaves its *net worth*. We can think of the net worth as what the firm's owners would be left with if the firm were closed, its assets were sold, and its liabilities were paid off. Investors can determine a firm's net worth by inspecting its balance sheet. We analyze a balance sheet in more detail in the appendix to this chapter.   MyEconLab Concept Check

Balance sheet A financial statement that sums up a firm's financial position on a particular day, usually the end of a quarter or year.

MyEconLab Study Plan

6.4 Corporate Governance Policy and the Financial Crisis of 2007–2009

LEARNING OBJECTIVE: Explain the role that corporate governance problems may have played in the financial crisis of 2007–2009.

Accurate and easy-to-understand financial statements help the firm's managers make decisions and provide information to investors who are considering buying the firm's stock or bonds. In fact, the information in financial statements helps guide resource allocation in the economy.

Firms disclose financial statements in periodic filings to the federal government and in *annual reports* to shareholders. An investor is more likely to buy a firm's stock if the firm's income statement shows a large after-tax profit and if its balance sheet shows a large net worth. The top management of a firm has at least two reasons to attract investors and keep the firm's stock price high. First, a higher stock price increases the funds the firm can raise when it sells a given amount of stock. Second, to reduce the principal–agent problem, boards of directors often tie the salaries of top managers to the firm's stock price or to the profitability of the firm.

Top managers clearly have an incentive to maximize the profits reported on the income statement and the net worth reported on the balance sheet. If top managers make good decisions, the firm's profits will be high, and the firm's assets will be large relative to its liabilities. Problems that surfaced during the early 2000s, however, revealed that some top managers have inflated profits and hidden liabilities that should have been listed on their balance sheets. At other firms, managers took on more risk than they disclosed to investors. We will explore problems with corporate governance and the government's reaction to these problems by discussing the accounting scandals of the early 2000s and problems that many financial firms encountered during 2007–2009.

The Accounting Scandals of the Early 2000s

In the early 2000s, the top managers of several well-known firms, including Enron, an energy trading firm, and WorldCom, a telecommunications firm, falsified their firms' financial statements in order to mislead investors about how profitable the firms actually were. Several top managers were sentenced to long prison terms, and some of the firms, including Enron, went out of business.

How was it possible for corporations such as Enron and WorldCom to falsify their financial statements? The federal government regulates how financial statements are prepared, but this regulation cannot by itself guarantee the accuracy of the statements. All firms that issue stock to the public have certified public accountants working for outside firms *audit* their financial statements. Unfortunately, as the Enron and WorldCom scandals revealed, top managers who are determined to deceive investors about the true financial condition of their firms can also deceive outside auditors.

To guard against future scandals, new federal legislation was enacted in 2002. The landmark *Sarbanes-Oxley Act* of 2002 requires that CEOs personally certify the accuracy of financial statements. The Sarbanes-Oxley Act also requires that financial analysts and auditors disclose whether any conflicts of interest might exist that would limit their independence in evaluating a firm's financial condition. On balance, most observers acknowledge that the Sarbanes-Oxley Act increased confidence in the U.S. corporate governance system. However, as we will discuss in the next section, problems during 2007–2009 at financial firms again raised questions about whether corporations were adequately disclosing information to investors.   MyEconLab Concept Check

The Financial Crisis of 2007–2009

Beginning in 2007 and lasting into 2009, the U.S. economy suffered the worst financial crisis since the Great Depression of the 1930s. At the heart of the crisis was a problem in the market for home mortgages. When people buy houses, they typically borrow the money by taking out a mortgage loan from a bank or another financial institution. The house they are buying is pledged as collateral for the loan, meaning that the bank can take possession of the house and sell it if the borrower defaults by failing to make the payments on the loan.

Securitizing Home Mortgages For many years, a bank or other financial institution granting a mortgage would keep the loan until the borrower had paid it off. Beginning in the 1970s, financial institutions began *securitizing* some mortgage loans, which means that groups of mortgages were bundled together and sold to investors. These *mortgage-backed securities* are very similar to bonds in that the investor who buys one receives regular interest payments, which in this case come from the payments being made on the original mortgage loans. At first, the securitization process was carried out by the Federal National Mortgage Association ("Fannie Mae") and the Federal Home Loan Mortgage Corporation ("Freddie Mac"), which Congress had established to help increase the volume of lending in the home mortgage market. Fannie Mae and Freddie Mac would buy mortgages granted to creditworthy borrowers and bundle them into securities that were then sold to investors.

Looser Lending Standards Fuel a Housing Bubble Beginning in the 1990s, private financial firms, primarily investment banks, started to securitize mortgages. By the early 2000s, banks and other financial institutions were loosening the standards for granting mortgages. Lenders began granting mortgages to "subprime" borrowers, whose credit histories included failing to pay all of their bills on time, and "Alt-A" borrowers, who failed to document that their incomes were high enough to afford their mortgage payments. The ease of obtaining a mortgage increased demand for housing, and caused prices to soar. This housing bubble began to deflate in mid-2006, with prices in many cities beginning a sharp downturn. By 2007, many borrowers—particularly subprime and Alt-A borrowers—began to default on their mortgages. These defaults were bad news for anyone owning mortgage-backed securities because the value of these securities depended on steady payments being made on the underlying mortgages. As prices of these securities plunged, the result was a financial crisis as many financial institutions suffered heavy losses, and some of the largest of them remained in business only because they received aid from the federal government. Some economists argue that the firms did a poor job of correctly assessing the risk of the investments they made in these securities. This failure may be an indication of poor corporate governance if top managers were unable to effectively monitor the employees who were deciding to invest in risky securities.

Government Regulation in Response to the Financial Crisis During the financial crisis, many investors complained that they weren't aware of the riskiness of some of the assets—particularly mortgage-backed securities—on the balance sheets of financial firms. Some observers believed that the managers of many financial firms had intentionally misled investors about the riskiness of these assets. Others argued that the managers themselves had not understood how risky the assets were. In the fall of 2008, Fannie Mae and Freddie Mac were brought under direct control of the government. As the crisis passed, in July 2010, Congress overhauled the regulation of the financial system with the passage of the **Wall Street Reform and Consumer Protection Act**, referred to as the **Dodd-Frank Act**. Among its provisions, the act created the Consumer Financial Protection Bureau, housed in the Federal Reserve— the central bank of the United States—to write rules intended to protect consumers in their borrowing and investing activities. The act also established the Financial Stability Oversight Council, which includes representatives from all the major federal financial regulatory bodies, including the SEC and the Federal Reserve. The council is intended to identify and act on risks to the financial system. Economists are divided in their opinions about whether the Dodd-Frank Act will significantly reduce the risk of future financial crises.

MyEconLab Concept Check

Wall Street Reform and Consumer Protection Act (Dodd-Frank Act) Legislation passed during 2010 that was intended to reform regulation of the financial system.

Did Principal–Agent Problems Help Cause the 2007–2009 Financial Crisis?

As we have seen, the process of securitizing mortgages played an important role in the financial crisis of 2007–2009. Beginning in the 1990s, private investment banks began to securitize mortgages. Unlike commercial banks, whose main activities are accepting deposits and making loans, investment banks had traditionally concentrated on providing advice to corporations on selling new stocks and bonds and on *underwriting* the issuance of stocks and bonds by guaranteeing a price to the firm selling them. Investment banking is considered riskier than commercial banking because investment banks can suffer substantial losses on underwriting. To address this greater risk, Congress passed the *Glass-Steagall Act* in 1933. The act prevented financial firms from being both commercial banks and investment banks.

Some economists and policymakers argued that Glass-Steagall reduced competition for investment banking services by prohibiting commercial banks from offering these services. Congress repealed the Glass-Steagall Act in 1999, after which some commercial banks began engaging in investment banking. Many of the largest, best-known investment banks, such as Lehman Brothers, Bear Stearns, Goldman Sachs, Merrill Lynch, and Morgan Stanley, remained exclusively investment banks. The mortgage-backed securities originated by the investment banks were mostly sold to investors, but some were retained as investments by these firms. As a result, when the prices of these securities declined beginning in 2007, the investment banks suffered heavy losses. Lehman Brothers was forced to declare bankruptcy; Merrill Lynch and Bear Stearns were sold to commercial banks in deals arranged by the U.S. government; and Goldman Sachs and Morgan Stanley became bank holding companies, which allowed them to engage in commercial banking activity.

Why did investment banks take on so much risk by originating securities backed by mortgages granted to borrowers who had a significant likelihood of defaulting on the loans? Michael Lewis, a financial journalist and former Wall Street bond salesman, has argued that a key reason was a change in how the investment banks were organized. Traditionally, large Wall Street investment banks had been organized as partnerships, but by 2000 they had all converted to being publicly traded corporations. As we have seen, in a partnership, the funds of the relatively small group of owners are put directly at risk, and the principal–agent problem is reduced because there is little separation of ownership from control. With a publicly traded corporation, on the other hand, the principal–agent problem can be severe. Lewis argues:

> No investment bank owned by its employees would have … bought and held $50 billion in [exotic mortgage-backed securities] … or even allow [these securities] to be sold to its customers. The hoped-for short-term gain would not have justified the long-term hit.

Issues of corporate governance will clearly continue to be a concern for economists, policymakers, and investors. MyEconLab Concept Check

---

Solved Problem 6.4

MyEconLab Interactive Animation

Will Dodd-Frank Improve Corporate Governance?

Commercial and investment banks, mutual funds, and brokerage firms are often called *financial service firms*. A review of the effects of the Dodd-Frank Act by an accountant included the opinion that, "Clearly, the drive for improved governance in financial services will continue for years to come." What does the author mean by "improved governance"? Why has improved governance at financial service firms been a significant policy issue?

Solving the Problem

Step 1: **Review the chapter material.** This problem is about whether government regulation can reduce the principal–agent problem in financial firms, so you may want to review the section "Government Regulation in Response to the Financial Crisis" and the section "Did Principal–Agent Problems Help Cause the 2007–2009 Financial Crisis?" which are both on page 197.

Step 2: **Answer the first question by explaining what "improved governance" means.** Some economists argue that one factor that caused the financial crisis of 2007–2009 was top managers of large financial services firms making riskier investments than were in the best interests of the firms' shareholders. Some economists also argue that financial service firms should have done a better job of assessing the risk involved in investing in mortgage-backed securities. Better governance in this context refers to improvements in aligning the actions of top managers with the preferences of shareholders and in improving the assessment and monitoring of investments.

Step 3: **Answer the second question by explaining why improved governance at financial service firms has become a political issue.** Policymakers recognize that poor corporate governance may have played a role in the financial crisis. Given its severity, they have been looking for ways to increase the stability of the financial system.

Extra Credit: Many economists and policymakers are hopeful that the Dodd-Frank Act has improved governance at financial service firms. Some economists, though, believe that the administrative costs the act imposes on firms may be greater than any benefits from improved governance. Some economists have also criticized other provisions of the act that restrict the monetary policy actions the Federal Reserve may take in a financial crisis.

Source: David Wright. "Dodd-Frank Four Years Later," *Wall Street Journal*, January 28, 2015.

MyEconLab Study Plan

Your Turn: Test your understanding by doing related problem 4.6 on page 203 at the end of this chapter.

Continued from page 181

Economics in Your Life

Would You Pay to Use Facebook or Twitter?

At the beginning of the chapter, we asked you to consider two questions: Would you be willing to pay to use social media apps such as Facebook and Twitter if the apps no longer targeted you with ads? and Do you think other users would be willing to pay enough that firms could rely on that source of revenue? The answer to the first question is likely to depend on what price the apps would charge, what your income is, and how annoyed you are by targeted ads. Of course, some people find the information in targeted ads useful and would prefer to see the ads rather than pay any fee.

In practice, people have become increasingly reluctant to pay anything to download and use an app. Some free apps are downloaded millions of times, while very similar apps that charge a small fee have significantly fewer downloads. In a given year, only about one-third of smartphone or tablet owners will pay for any apps. App developers have mostly adopted the business model of allowing their apps to be downloaded and used for free, while trying to still earn money from users. For instance, the popular games *Clash of Clans* and *Candy Crush Saga* can be downloaded and played for free. The developers earn a profit from people who pay to play the game faster, get extra turns, or otherwise receive benefits not available to those who play for free. The usefulness of social media apps increases as more people use them. If only a few people were on Facebook or used Twitter, these apps wouldn't be much fun. So, these apps can't afford the significant decline in users that would likely occur if they began to charge a fee. The remaining users who were paying would likely find the apps less fun because fewer people would be on them, and they might gradually stop using them.

So, whether you like targeted ads or hate them, it seems likely that you will have to continue putting up with them on social media apps.

Conclusion

In a market system, firms make independent decisions about which goods and services to produce, how to produce them, and what prices to charge. In modern high-income countries, such as the United States, large corporations account for a majority of the sales and profits earned by firms. Generally, the managers of these corporations do a good job of representing the interests of stockholders while providing the goods and services demanded by consumers. As the business scandals of the early 2000s and the problems with financial firms in 2007–2009 showed, however, the principal–agent problem can sometimes become severe. Economists debate the costs and benefits of regulations proposed to address these problems.

Visit MyEconLab for a news article and analysis related to the concepts in this chapter.

Key Terms

6.1 ## Types of Firms, pages 182–186

LEARNING OBJECTIVE: Categorize the major types of firms in the United States.

Summary

There are three types of firms: A **sole proprietorship** is a firm owned by a single individual and not organized as a corporation; a **partnership** is a firm owned jointly by two or more persons and not organized as a corporation; and a **corporation** is a legal form of business that provides its owners with limited liability. An **asset** is anything of value owned by a person or a firm. The owners of sole proprietorships and partnerships have unlimited liability, which means there is no legal distinction between the personal assets of the owners of the business and the assets of the business. The owners of corporations have **limited liability**, which means they can never lose more than their investment in the firm. Although only 18 percent of firms are corporations, they account for the majority of revenue and profits earned by all firms. **Corporate governance** refers to the way in which a corporation is structured and the effect a corporation's structure has on the firm's behavior. Most corporations have a similar management structure: The shareholders elect a board of directors that appoints the corporation's top managers, such as the chief executive officer (CEO). Because top managers often do not own a large fraction of the stock in the corporation, large corporations have a **separation of ownership from control**. When top managers have less incentive to increase the corporation's profits than to increase their own salaries and their own enjoyment, corporations can suffer from the **principal–agent problem**. The principal–agent problem exists when the principals—in this case, the shareholders of the corporation—have difficulty getting the agent—the corporation's top management—to carry out their wishes.

 MyEconLab Visit **www.myeconlab.com** to complete these exercises online and get instant feedback.

Review Questions

1.1 What are the three major types of firms in the United States? Briefly discuss the most important characteristics of each type.

1.2 What is limited liability? Why does the government grant limited liability to the owners of corporations?

1.3 Why is limited liability more important for firms trying to raise funds from a large number of investors than for firms trying to raise funds from a small number of investors?

1.4 What does it mean to say that there is a separation of ownership from control in large corporations?

1.5 How is the separation of ownership from control related to the principal–agent problem?

Problems and Applications

1.6 Suppose that shortly after graduating from college, you decide to start your own business. Will you be likely to organize the business as a sole proprietorship, a partnership, or a corporation? Explain your reasoning.

1.7 An article discussing the reasons that the Connecticut state legislature passed a general incorporation law observes that prior to the passage of the law, investors were afraid that large businesses "were not a safe bet for their money." Briefly explain the author's reasoning.

Source: Anne Rajotte, "Connecticut's General Incorporation Law Was the First of Its Kind," ctstatelibrary.org, June 10, 2014.

1.8 Evaluate the following argument:

I would like to invest in the stock market, but I think that buying shares of stock in a corporation is too risky. Suppose I buy $10,000 of Twitter stock, and the company ends up going bankrupt. Because as a stockholder I'm part owner of the company, I might be responsible for paying hundreds of thousands of dollars of the company's debts.

1.9 According to an article in the *Economist*, historian David Faure has argued that the Chinese economy failed to grow rapidly during the nineteenth century because "family-run companies ... could not raise sufficient capital to exploit the large-scale opportunities tied to the rise of the steam engine, notably railways and (with limited exceptions) global shipping and automated manufacturing." How did the United States solve the problem of firms raising enough funds to operate railroads and other large-scale businesses?

Source: "The PCCW Buy-Out in Court," *Economist*, April 21, 2009.

1.10 (Related to the Making the Connection on page 184) Two economists at the Brookings Institution argue that "new firms rather than existing ones have accounted for a disproportionate share of disruptive and thus highly productivity enhancing innovations in the past—the automobile, the airplane, the computer and personal computer, air conditioning, and Internet search, to name just a few."

   a. Why might new firms be more likely than older firms to introduce "disruptive" innovations?

   b. Assuming these economists are correct about the most important source of productivity enhancing innovations, what are the implications for the future of the U.S. economy of recent trends in the formation of new businesses?

Source: Ian Hathaway and Robert E. Litan, "What's Driving the Decline in the Firm Formation Rate? A Partial Explanation," *Brookings Economic Studies*, November 20, 2014.

1.11 (Related to the Making the Connection on page 184) An Associated Press article noted that some groups have filed law suits over what the groups describe as "overzealous licensing schemes, in occupations such as hair braiders, yoga teachers and casket makers."

   a. What effect might such government licensing requirements have on the rate of new businesses being formed?

   b. Given your answer to part (a), why might state and local governments pass such licensing requirements?

Source: Associated Press, "High Court Asked to Rule on Tour-Guide Licensing," *New York Times*, November 18, 2014.

1.12 The principal–agent problem arises almost everywhere in the business world, and it also crops up even closer to home. Discuss the principal–agent problem that exists in the college classroom. Who is the principal? Who is the agent? What potential conflicts in objectives exist between this principal and this agent?

1.13 In a public corporation, the principal–agent problem between ownership and top management results from asymmetric information. What information, if known, would prevent this principal–agent problem?

1.14 Salespeople, whether selling life insurance, automobiles, or pharmaceuticals, typically get paid on commission instead of a straight hourly wage. How does paying a commission help solve the principal–agent problem between the owners of a business and their salespeople?

1.15 Private equity firms, such as Blackstone and Kohlberg Kravis Roberts & Co., search for firms where the managers appear not to be maximizing profits. A private equity firm can buy stock in these firms and have its employees elected to the firms' boards of directors and may even acquire control of the targeted firm and replace the top management. Does the existence of private equity firms reduce any problems in corporate governance? Briefly explain.

6.2	**How Firms Raise Funds, pages 186–193**
	LEARNING OBJECTIVE: Explain how firms raise the funds they need to operate and expand.

Summary

Firms rely on retained earnings—which are profits kept by the firm and not paid out to the firm's owners—or on using the savings of households for the funds they need to operate and expand. With **direct finance**, the savings of households flow directly to businesses when investors buy **stocks** and **bonds** in financial markets. With **indirect finance**, savings flow indirectly to businesses when households deposit money in savings and checking accounts in banks and the banks lend these funds to businesses. Federal, state, and local governments also sell bonds in financial markets, and households also borrow funds from banks. When a firm sells a bond, it is borrowing money from the buyer of the bond. Firms make **coupon payments** to buyers of bonds. The **interest rate** is the cost of borrowing funds, usually expressed as a percentage of the amount borrowed. When a firm sells stock, it is selling part ownership of the firm to the buyer of the stock. **Dividends** are payments by a corporation to its shareholders. The original purchasers of stocks and bonds may resell them in stock and bond markets, such as the New York Stock Exchange. The performance of the U.S. stock market is often measured using stock market indexes. The three most widely followed stock indexes are the Dow Jones Industrial Average, the S&P 500, and the NASDAQ Composite Index.

Review Questions

2.1 What is the difference between direct finance and indirect finance? If you borrow money from a bank to buy a new car, are you using direct finance or indirect finance?

2.2 Why is a bond considered to be a loan but a share of stock is not? Why do corporations issue both bonds and shares of stock?

2.3 How do the stock and bond markets provide information to businesses? Why do stock and bond prices change over time?

Problems and Applications

2.4 Suppose that a firm in which you have invested is losing money. Would you rather own the firm's stock or the firm's bonds? Briefly explain.

2.5 Suppose you originally invested in a firm when it was small and unprofitable. Now the firm has grown to be large and profitable. Would you be better off if you had bought the firm's stock or the firm's bonds? Briefly explain.

2.6 If you deposit $20,000 in a savings account at a bank, you might earn 1 percent interest per year. Someone who borrows $20,000 from a bank to buy a new car might have to pay an interest rate of 6 percent per year on the loan. Knowing this, why don't you just lend your money directly to the car buyer and cut out the bank?

2.7 **(Related to the** Chapter Opener **on page 181)** Were the shares of stock issued as a result of Twitter's initial public offering (IPO) sold in a primary market or a secondary market? Was the IPO an example of direct finance or indirect finance?

2.8 **(Related to the** Making the Connection **on page 187)** According to an article in the *Wall Street Journal*, in May 2015, Moody's Investors Service cut its rating on McDonald's bonds from A3 to A2.

a. What is Moody's top bond rating? Under what circumstances would Moody's, or the other bond rating agencies, be likely to cut the rating on a firm's bonds?

b. What will be the likely result of this rating's cut for the interest rate McDonald's will have to pay when it sells new bonds? Briefly explain.

Source: Chelsey Dulaney, "Moody's Downgrades McDonald's, Following S&P and Fitch," *Wall Street Journal*, May 15, 2015.

2.9 **(Related to the** Making the Connection **on page 187)** Investors use the bond ratings from Moody's, S&P, and Fitch to determine which bonds they will buy and the prices they are willing to pay for them. The rating services charge the firms and governments that issue bonds, rather than investors, for their services. Critics argue that the rating agencies may give higher ratings than are justified in order to continue to sell their services to bond issuing firms. To avoid this impression, why don't Moody's, S&P, and Fitch sell their services directly to investors?

2.10 What effect would the following events be likely to have on the price of Google's stock?

a. A competitor launches a search engine that is better than Google's.

b. The corporate income tax is abolished.

c. Google's board of directors becomes dominated by close friends and relatives of its top management.

d. The price of wireless Internet connections in developing countries unexpectedly drops, so more and more people worldwide use the Internet.

e. Google announces a profit of $10 billion, but investors anticipated that Google would earn a profit of $11 billion.

2.11 **(Related to the** Don't Let This Happen to You **on page 190)** Briefly explain whether you agree with the following statement: "The total value of the shares of Microsoft stock traded on the NASDAQ last week was $250 million, so the firm actually received more revenue from stock sales than from selling software."

2.12 **(Related to the** Making the Connection **on page 191)** A column in the *Wall Street Journal* listed "trying to forecast what stocks will do next" as one of the three mistakes investors make repeatedly. Briefly explain why trying to forecast stock prices would be a mistake for the average investor.

Source: Morgan Housel, "Three Mistakes Investors Keep Making Again and Again," *Wall Street Journal*, September 12, 2014.

2.13 **(Related to** Solved Problem 6.2 **on page 192)** In a letter to his company's stockholders, Warren Buffett offered the following opinion: "Most investors, of course, have not made the study of business prospects a priority in their lives. . . . I have good news for these non-professionals: The typical investor doesn't need this skill." Briefly explain Buffett's reasoning.

Source: Warren Buffett, *Letter to Berkshire Shareholders*, March 1, 2014, p. 20.

6.3 | Using Financial Statements to Evaluate a Corporation, pages 193–195

LEARNING OBJECTIVE: Understand the information corporations include in their financial statements.

Summary

A firm's **income statement** shows its revenues, costs, and profit over a period of time. A firm's **balance sheet** shows its financial position on a particular day, usually the end of a quarter or year. A balance sheet records a firm's assets and liabilities. A **liability** is anything owed by a person or a firm. Firms report their **accounting profit** on their income statements. Accounting profit does not always include all of a firm's **opportunity cost**. **Explicit cost** is a cost that involves spending money. **Implicit cost** is a nonmonetary opportunity cost. Because accounting profit excludes some implicit costs, it is larger than **economic profit**.

 MyEconLab   Visit **www.myeconlab.com** to complete these exercises online and get instant feedback.

Review Questions

3.1 What is the difference between a firm's assets and its liabilities? Give an example of an asset and an example of a liability.

3.2 What is the difference between a firm's balance sheet and its income statement?

3.3 Distinguish between a firm's explicit costs and its implicit costs and between a firm's accounting profit and its economic profit.

3.4 Would a business be expected to survive in the long run if it earned a positive accounting profit but a negative economic profit? Briefly explain.

Problems and Applications

3.5 Paolo currently has $100,000 invested in bonds that earn him 10 percent interest per year. He wants to open a pizza restaurant and is considering either selling the bonds and using the $100,000 to start his restaurant or borrowing $100,000 from a bank, which would charge him an annual interest rate of 7 percent. He finally decides to sell the bonds and not take out the bank loan. He reasons, "Because I already have the $100,000 invested in the bonds, I don't have to pay anything to use the money. If I take out the bank loan, I have to pay interest, so my costs of producing pizza will be higher if I take out the loan than if I sell the bonds." Evaluate Paolo's reasoning.

3.6 Paolo and Alfredo are twins who both want to open pizza restaurants. Their parents have always liked Alfredo best, and they buy two pizza ovens and give both to him. Unfortunately, Paolo must buy his own pizza ovens. Does Alfredo have a lower cost of producing pizza than Paolo does because Alfredo received his pizza ovens as a gift, while Paolo had to pay for his? Briefly explain.

3.7 Dane decides to give up a job earning $200,000 per year as a corporate lawyer and converts the duplex that he owns into a UFO museum. (He had been renting out the duplex for $20,000 a year.) His explict costs are $75,000 per year paid to his assistants and $10,000 per year for utilities. Fans flock to the museum to see his collection of extraterrestrial paraphernalia, which he could easily sell on eBay for $1,000,000. Over the course of the year, the museum brings in revenues of $200,000.

a. How much is Dane's accounting profit for the year?
b. Is Dane earning an economic profit? Explain.

3.8 Twitter was founded in 2006, but it wasn't until 2013 that Twitter filed its first annual report with the Securities and Exchange Commission (SEC). Briefly explain why.

3.9 Jay Ritter, a professor at the University of Florida, was quoted in the *Wall Street Journal* as saying about Facebook: "It's entirely possible for a company to have solid growth prospects while its stock is overvalued."

a. What does it mean to say that a stock is "overvalued"?
b. Why might a firm's stock be overvalued despite the firm having "solid growth prospects"?

Source: Mark Hulbert, "A Year after Its Debut, Facebook Still Looks Overpriced," *Wall Street Journal*, May 17, 2013.

6.4 Corporate Governance Policy and the Financial Crisis of 2007–2009, pages 195–198

LEARNING OBJECTIVE: Explain the role that corporate governance problems may have played in the financial crisis of 2007–2009.

Summary

Because their compensation often rises with the profitability of the corporation that employs them, top managers have an incentive to overstate the profits reported on their firm's income statements. During the early 2000s, it became clear that the top managers of several large corporations had done this, even though intentionally falsifying financial statements is illegal. The *Sarbanes-Oxley Act* of 2002 took several steps intended to increase the accuracy of financial statements and increase the penalties for falsifying them. The financial crisis of 2007–2009 revealed that many financial firms held assets that were far riskier than investors had realized. Congress passed the **Wall Street Reform and Consumer Protection Act (Dodd-Frank Act)** in July 2010 to address some of the issues raised by the financial crisis of 2007–2009.

 Visit **www.myeconlab.com** to complete these exercises online and get instant feedback.

Review Questions

4.1 What is the Sarbanes-Oxley Act? Why was it passed?
4.2 What was the source of the problems encountered by many financial firms during the crisis of 2007–2009?

Problems and Applications

4.3 The following is from an article in *USA Today*:

> In what some call a worldwide corporate-governance movement, shareholders are pushing for stronger corporate-governance laws, teaming with investors from different countries and negotiating behind the scenes with businesses.

What is corporate governance? Why would shareholders push for stronger corporate governance laws?

Sources: Edward Iwata, "Corporate Governance Gets More Transparent Worldwide," *USA Today*, February 17, 2008.

4.4 According to an article in the *Wall Street Journal*, "Companies in Standard & Poor's 500 stock index elected the smallest number of new directors last year in 10 years." Is having members of boards of directors serve for longer periods likely to be good news or bad news for corporate governance? Briefly explain.

Source: Joann S. Lublin, "The 40-Year Club: America's Longest-Serving Directors," *Wall Street Journal*, July 16, 2013.

4.5 Michael Dell founded PCs Limited in 1984. The firm had an initial public offering (IPO) in 1988, under the name Dell Computer Corporation, which enabled the company to raise money it used for expansion. In 2013, Michael Dell and a private equity firm bought back ownership of the company from its shareholders. Dell is now a privately owned firm. What would motivate Michael Dell to make this change?

Source: Michael Dell, "Going Private Is Paying Off for Dell," *Wall Street Journal*, November 24, 2014.

4.6 (Related to Solved Problem 6.4 on page 198) An article on forbes.com about corporate fraud stated that "misleading accounting and disclosure practices weaken the integrity of capital markets." The article noted that using incentive contracts for top managers can create a "'perverse' incentive to manipulate stock prices because their (executive) total package is based on stock price appreciation."

a. Why do financial markets depend on accurate accounting and disclosure practices? Why can misleading accounting and disclosure practices weaken the integrity of financial markets?
b. Why do corporate boards of directors sometimes link top managers' compensation to the corporations' stock prices? Briefly explain how tying compensation too closely to stock prices might create an incentive for corporate fraud.

Source: John Wasik, "How Corporate Fraud Costs You Money: Four Red Flags," forbes.com, June 17, 2013.

Real-Time Data Exercises

D6.1 **(Exploring stock data)** On June 19, 2015 the closing price of a share of Facebook stock was $82.51. About 21.5 million shares of stock were traded on this date. Go to wsj.com for a recent trading day and use Facebook's stock symbol (FB) to find the following.
  a. The closing price of Facebook stock
  b. The market value of the shares traded
  c. The number of shares (volume) traded
  d. The total number of shares outstanding
  e. The number of shares traded relative to the number of shares outstanding

D6.2 **(The stock market and recessions)** Go to the Web site of the Federal Reserve Bank of St. Louis (FRED) (research.stlouisfed.org/fred2/) and download and graph the data series for the Nasdaq Composite Index from February 1971 until the most recent day available. Go to the Web site of the National Bureau of Economic Research (nber.org) and find the dates for business cycle peaks and troughs (the period between a business cycle peak and trough is a recession). Describe how stock prices move just before, during, and just after a recession. Is the pattern the same across recessions?

D6.3 **(Exploring dividends)** Go to wsj.com and find the dividend per share for each of the following firms.
  a. Microsoft
  b. Apple
  c. Coca-Cola
  d. Facebook
To find the dividend per share, enter the company's name in the search box on the home page. Which pays the highest dividend? Which has the highest dividend yield? Which does not pay a dividend? Why might a firm not pay a dividend? Why would investors buy the stock of a firm that does not pay a dividend?

D6.4 **(Using stock data)** The following table lists the closing stock prices for three financial firms—Morgan Stanley, Citigroup Inc. and PNC Bank—for Friday, June 19, 2015. The table also includes the most recent dividends paid to shareholders by these firms.

	Morgan Stanley	Citigroup Inc.	PNC
Stock symbol	MS	C	PNC
Closing price	$39.37	$56.23	$97.13
Latest dividend	$0.15	$0.05	$0.51
Number of shares	100	100	100
Value of shares			
Total dividend			
Stock price increase	5 percent	5 percent	5 percent
New stock price			
Value of shares			
Capital gain			

Fill in the blank cells in the table by computing (a) the value of 100 shares of each company's stock, (b) total dividend payments for 100 shares of stock, and (c) assuming that each company's stock price increases by 5 percent, the new stock prices, the value of shares, and the increase in the value of each company's stock (capital gains). How will the price increases affect the total amount of dividends paid for each company's stock?

Appendix

Tools to Analyze Firms' Financial Information

LEARNING OBJECTIVE: Understand the concept of present value and the information contained on a firm's income statement and balance sheet.

As we saw in the chapter, modern firms are not just "black boxes" transforming inputs into output. The majority of business revenues and profits are earned by large corporations. Unlike founder-dominated firms, the typical large corporation is run by managers who generally do not own a controlling interest in the firm. Large firms raise funds from outside investors, and outside investors seek information on firms and the assurance that the managers of firms will act in the interests of the investors.

This chapter shows how corporations raise funds by issuing stocks and bonds. This appendix provides more detail to support that discussion. We begin by analyzing *present value* as a key concept in determining the prices of financial securities. We then provide greater information on *financial statements* issued by corporations, using Twitter as an example.

Using Present Value to Make Investment Decisions

Firms raise funds by selling equity (stock) and debt (bonds and loans) to investors and lenders. If you own shares of stock or a bond, you will receive payments in the form of dividends or coupons over a number of years. Most people value funds they already have more highly than funds they will receive some time in the future. For example, you would probably not trade $1,000 you already have for $1,000 you will not receive for one year. The longer you have to wait to receive a payment, the less value it will have for you. One thousand dollars you will not receive for two years is worth less to you than $1,000 you will receive after one year. The value you give today to money you will receive in the future is called the future payment's **present value**. The present value of $1,000 you will receive in one year will be less than $1,000.

Present value The value in today's dollars of funds to be paid or received in the future.

Why is the $1,000 you will not receive for one year less valuable to you than the $1,000 you already have? The most important reason is that if you have $1,000 today, you can use that $1,000 today. You can buy goods and services with the money and receive enjoyment from them. The $1,000 you receive in one year does not have direct use to you now.

Also, prices will likely rise during the year you are waiting to receive your $1,000. So, when you finally do receive the $1,000 in one year, you will not be able to buy as much with it as you could with $1,000 today. Finally, there is some risk that you will not receive the $1,000 in one year. The risk may be very great if an unreliable friend borrows $1,000 from you and vaguely promises to pay you back in one year. The risk may be very small if you lend money to the federal government by buying a U.S. Treasury bond. In either case, though, there is at least some risk that you will not receive the funds promised.

When someone lends money, the lender expects to be paid back both the amount of the loan and some additional interest. Say you are willing to lend $1,000 today if you are paid back $1,100 one year from now. In this case, you are charging $100/$1,000 = 0.10, or 10 percent interest on the funds you have loaned. Economists would say that you value $1,000 today as equivalent to the $1,100 to be received one year in the future.

Notice that $1,100 can be written as $1,000(1 + 0.10). That is, the value of money received in the future is equal to the value of money in the present multiplied by 1 plus the interest rate, with the interest rate expressed as a decimal. Or:

$$\$1,100 = \$1,000(1 + 0.10).$$

Notice, also, that if we divide both sides by $(1 + 0.10)$, we can rewrite this formula as:

$$\$1,000 = \frac{\$1,100}{(1 + 0.10)}.$$

The rewritten formula states that the present value is equal to the future value to be received in one year divided by 1 plus the interest rate. This formula is important because you can use it to convert any amount to be received in one year into its present value. Writing the formula generally, we have:

$$\text{Present value} = \frac{\text{Future value}_1}{(1 + i)}.$$

The present value of funds to be received in one year—Future value$_1$—can be calculated by dividing the amount of those funds to be received by 1 plus the interest rate. With an interest rate of 10 percent, the present value of $\$1,000,000$ to be received one year from now is:

$$\frac{\$1,000,000}{(1 + 0.10)} = \$909,090.91.$$

This formula allows us to calculate the value today of funds that will be received in one year. But financial securities such as stocks and bonds involve promises to pay funds over many years. Therefore, it would be useful if we could expand this formula to calculate the present value of funds to be received more than one year in the future.

Go back to the original example, where we assumed you were willing to loan out your $\$1,000$ for one year, provided that you received 10 percent interest. Suppose you are asked to lend the funds for two years and that you are promised 10 percent interest per year for each year of the loan. That is, you are lending $\$1,000$, which at 10 percent interest will grow to $\$1,100$ after one year, and you are agreeing to loan that $\$1,100$ for a second year at 10 percent interest. So, after two years, you will be paid back $\$1,100(1 + 0.10)$, or $\$1,210$. Or:

$$\$1,210 = \$1,000(1 + 0.10)\,(1 + 0.10),$$

or:

$$\$1,210 = \$1,000(1 + 0.10)^2.$$

This formula can also be rewritten as:

$$\$1,000 = \frac{\$1.210}{(1 + 0.10)^2}.$$

To put this formula in words, the $\$1,210$ you receive two years from now has a present value equal to $\$1,210$ divided by the quantity 1 plus the interest rate squared. If you agree to lend out your $\$1,000$ for three years at 10 percent interest, you will receive:

$$\$1,331 = \$1,000(1 + 0.10)^3.$$

Notice, again, that:

$$\$1,000 = \frac{\$1,331}{(1 + 0.10)^3}.$$

You can probably see a pattern here. We can generalize the concept to say that the present value of funds to be received n years in the future—whether n is 1, 20, or 85 does not matter—equals the amount of the funds to be received divided by the quantity 1 plus the interest rate raised to the nth power. For instance, with an interest rate of 10 percent, the value of $\$1,000,000$ to be received 25 years in the future is:

$$\text{Present value} = \frac{\$1,000,000}{(1 + 0.10)^{25}} = \$92,296.$$

Or, more generally:

$$\text{Present value} = \frac{\text{Future value}_n}{(1 + i)^n},$$

where Future value$_n$ represents funds that will be received in n years.

Solved Problem 6A.1

MyEconLab Interactive Animation

How to Receive Your Contest Winnings

Suppose you win a contest and are given the choice of the following prizes:

Prize 1: $50,000 to be received right away, with four additional payments of $50,000 to be received each year for the next four years

Prize 2: $175,000 to be received right away

Explain which prize you would choose and the basis for your decision.

Solving the Problem

Step 1: Review the material. This problem involves applying the concept of present value, so you may want to review the section "Using Present Value to Make Investment Decisions," which begins on page 205.

Step 2: Explain the basis for choosing the prize. Unless you need cash immediately, you should choose the prize with the highest present value.

Step 3: Calculate the present value of each prize. Prize 2 consists of one payment of $175,000 received right away, so its present value is $175,000. Prize 1 consists of five payments spread out over time. To find the present value of the prize, we must find the present value of each of these payments and add them together. To calculate present value, we must use an interest rate. Let's assume an interest rate of 10 percent. In that case, the present value of Prize 1 is:

$$\$50,000 + \frac{\$50,000}{(1 + 0.10)} + \frac{\$50,000}{(1 + 0.10)^2} + \frac{\$50,000}{(1 + 0.10)^3} + \frac{\$50,000}{(1 + 0.10)^4}$$

$$= \$50,000 + \$45,454.55 + \$41,322.31 + \$37,565.74 + \$34,150.67$$

$$= \$208,493.27$$

Step 4: State your conclusion. Prize 1 has the greater present value, so you should choose it rather than Prize 2.

Your Turn: For more practice, do related problems 6A.6, 6A.7, 6A.8, and 6A.9 on page 212 at the end of this appendix.

MyEconLab Study Plan

Using Present Value to Calculate Bond Prices

Anyone who buys stocks or bonds is really buying a promise to receive certain payments—dividends in the case of stocks or coupons in the case of bonds. The price investors are willing to pay for a financial asset should be equal to the value of the payments they will receive as a result of owning the asset. Because most of the coupon or dividend payments will be received in the future, it is their present value that matters. We therefore have the following important idea: *The price of a financial asset should be equal to the present value of the payments to be received from owning that asset.*

Let's look at an example. Suppose that in 1988, General Electric issued a bond with an $80 coupon that will mature in 2018. It is now 2016, and that bond has been bought and sold by investors many times. You are considering buying it. If you buy the bond, you will receive two years of coupon payments plus a final payment of the bond's principal, or face value, of $1,000. Suppose, once again, that you need an interest rate of 10 percent to invest your funds. If the bond has a coupon of $80, the present value of the payments you receive from owning the bond—and, therefore, the present value of the bond—will be:

$$\text{Present value} = \frac{\$80}{(1 + 0.10)} + \frac{\$80}{(1 + 0.10)^2} + \frac{\$1,000}{(1 + 0.10)^2} = \$965.29.$$

That is, the present value of the bond will equal the present value of the three payments you will receive during the two years you own the bond. You should, therefore, be willing to pay $965.29 to own this bond and have the right to receive these payments from GE. This process of calculating present values of future payments is used to determine bond prices, with one qualification: The relevant interest rate used by investors in the bond market to calculate the present value and, therefore, the price of an existing bond is usually the coupon rate on comparable newly issued bonds. Therefore, the general formula for the price of a bond is:

$$\text{Bond price} = \frac{\text{Coupon}_1}{(1+i)} + \frac{\text{Coupon}_2}{(1+i)^2} + \cdots + \frac{\text{Coupon}_n}{(1+i)^n} + \frac{\text{Face value}}{(1+i)^n},$$

where:

- Coupon_1 is the coupon payment to be received after one year.
- Coupon_2 is the coupon payment to be received after two years.
- Coupon_n, is the coupon payment received in the year the bond matures.
- The ellipsis takes the place of the coupon payments—if any—received between the second year and the year when the bond matures.
- Face value is the amount that will be received when the bond matures.
- i is the interest rate on comparable newly issued bonds.   MyEconLab Concept Check

Using Present Value to Calculate Stock Prices

When you own a firm's stock, you are legally entitled to your share of the firm's profits. Remember that the profits a firm pays out to its shareholders are called *dividends*. The price of a share of stock should equal the present value of the dividends investors expect to receive as a result of owning that stock. Therefore, the general formula for the price of a stock is:

$$\text{Stock price} = \frac{\text{Dividend}_1}{(1 + i)} + \frac{\text{Dividend}_2}{(1 + i)^2} + \cdots$$

Notice that this formula looks very similar to the one we used to calculate the price of a bond, with a couple of important differences:

- First, unlike a bond, a share of stock has no maturity date, so we have to calculate the present value of an infinite number of dividend payments. It may seem that the stock's price must be infinite as well, but remember that dollars you don't receive for many years are worth very little today. For instance, a dividend payment of $10 that will be received 40 years in the future is worth only a little more than $0.20 today at a 10 percent interest rate.
- Second, you know with certainty the coupon payments you will receive from owning the bond because they are set when the bond is issued and cannot be changed. However, you don't know for sure what the dividend payments from owning a stock will be. How large a dividend payment you will receive depends on how profitable the company will be in the future.

Although it is possible to forecast the future profitability of a company, this cannot be done with perfect accuracy. To emphasize this point, some economists rewrite the basic stock price formula by adding a superscript e to each dividend term to emphasize that these are *expected* dividend payments. Because the future profitability of companies is often very difficult to forecast, it is not surprising that differences of opinion exist over what the price of a particular stock should be. Some investors will be optimistic about the future profitability of a company and will, therefore, believe that the company's stock should have a high price. Other investors might be pessimistic and believe that the company's stock should have a low price.   MyEconLab Concept Check

A Simple Formula for Calculating Stock Prices

It is possible to simplify the formula for determining the price of a stock. If we assume that dividends will grow at a constant rate, we get the following equation:

$$\text{Stock price} = \frac{\text{Dividend}}{(i \; - \; \text{Growth rate})}.$$

In this equation, Dividend is the dividend expected to be received one year from now, and Growth rate is the rate at which those dividends are expected to grow. If a company pays a dividend of $1 per share to be received one year from now and Growth rate is 10 percent, the company is expected to pay a dividend of $1.10 the following year, $1.21 the year after that, and so on.

Now suppose that IBM will pay a dividend of $5 per share at the end of year, the consensus of investors is that these dividends will increase at a rate of 5 percent per year for the indefinite future, and the interest rate is 10 percent. Then the price of IBM's stock should be:

$$\text{Stock price} = \frac{\$5.00}{(0.10 \; - \; 0.05)} = \$100.00.$$

In recent years, investors have debated whether the high prices of the stocks of many high-tech firms, including Twitter, were justified, given that many of these companies had not made any profit yet and so had not paid any dividends. Is there any way that a rational investor would pay a high price for the stock of a company currently not earning profits? The formula for determining stock prices shows that it is possible, provided that the investor's assumptions are optimistic enough! For example, during 2015, one stock analyst predicted that Twitter would soon be earning $1 per share of stock. That is, Twitter's total earnings divided by the number of shares of its stock outstanding would be $1. Suppose Twitter pays out that $1 in dividends and that the $1 will grow rapidly over the years, by, say, 7 percent per year. Then the formula indicates that the price of Twitter's stock should be:

$$\text{Stock price} = \frac{\$1.00}{(0.10 \; - \; 0.07)} = \$33.33.$$

If you are sufficiently optimistic about the future prospects of a company, a high stock price can be justified even if the company is not currently earning a profit. But investors in stocks must be careful. Suppose investors decide that growth prospects for Twitter are only 4 percent per year instead of 7 percent because the firm turns out not to be as profitable as initially believed. Then our formula indicates that the price of Twitter's stock should be:

$$\text{Stock price} = \frac{\$1.00}{(0.10 \; - \; 0.04)} = \$16.67.$$

This price is only half the price determined assuming a more optimistic growth rate. We can conclude that investors use information about a firm's profitability and growth prospects to determine what the firm is worth.   MyEconLab Concept Check

Going Deeper into Financial Statements

Corporations disclose substantial information about their business operations and financial position to actual and potential investors. Some of this information meets the demands of participants in financial markets and of information-collection agencies, such as Moody's Investors Service, which develops credit ratings that help investors judge how risky corporate bonds are. Other information meets the reporting requirements of the U.S. Securities and Exchange Commission.

Key sources of information about a corporation's profitability and financial position are its principal financial statements—the *income statement* and the *balance sheet*. These important information sources were first introduced in the chapter. In the following section we go into more detail, using recent data for Twitter as an example.

Analyzing Income Statements

As discussed in the chapter, a firm's income statement summarizes its revenues, costs, and profit over a period of time. Figure 6A.1 shows Twitter's income statement for 2014.

Twitter's income statement presents the results of the company's operations during the year. Listed first are the revenues it earned, largely from selling advertising on its app, from January 1, 2014, to December 31, 2014: $1,403 million. Listed next are Twitter's operating expenses, the most important of which is its *cost of revenue*—which is commonly known as *cost of sales* or *cost of goods sold*: $446 million. Cost of revenue is the direct cost of producing the products sold, including in this case the salaries of the computer programmers Twitter hires to write the software for its app. Twitter also has substantial costs for researching and developing its products ($692 million) and for advertising and marketing them ($614 million). General and administrative expenses ($190 million) include costs such as the salaries of top managers.

The difference between a firm's revenue and its costs is its *profit*. Profit shows up in several forms on an income statement. A firm's *operating income* is the difference between its revenue and its operating expenses. Most corporations, including Twitter, also have interest expenses and income from investments, such as government and corporate bonds. In this case, Twitter paid $39 million more in interest expenses than it earned on its investments. Because its costs were greater than its revenue, Twitter's *income before taxes* was a loss (a loss in financial statements is indicated by the use of parenthesis) of $578 million. The federal government taxes the profits of corporations, but because Twitter experienced a

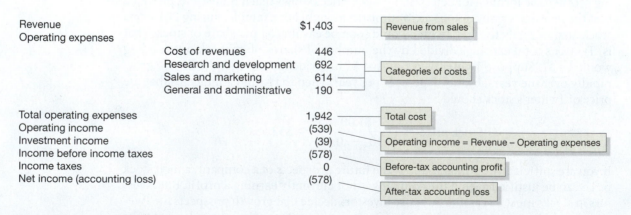

Note: All numbers are in millions of dollars.

Figure 6A.1 **Twitter's Income Statement for 2014**

Twitter's income statement shows the company's revenue, costs, and profit for 2014. The difference between its revenue ($1,403 million) and its operating expenses ($1,942 million) is its operating income (a loss of $539 million). Most corporations also have interest expenses and income from investments, such as government and corporate bonds. In this case, Twitter

paid $39 million more in interest expenses than it earned on its investments, so its *income before taxes* was a loss of $578 million. Twitter had a net loss, or accounting loss, of $578 million for the year.
Note: Negative values in the figure are shown in parentheses.
Source: Twitter, *Annual Report, 2014.*

loss in 2014, it paid no taxes. Therefore, Twitter's *net income* after taxes was also a loss of $578 million. The fact that Twitter could experience a loss while still having a high stock price is an indication that investors were expecting Twitter to earn significant profits in the future. The net income that firms report on their income statements is referred to as their after-tax *accounting profit*.

MyEconLab **Concept Check**

Analyzing Balance Sheets

As discussed in the chapter, while a firm's income statement reports the firm's activities for a period of time, a firm's balance sheet summarizes its financial position on a particular day, usually the end of a quarter or year. To understand how a balance sheet is organized, first recall that an asset is anything of value that the firm owns, and a liability is a debt or an obligation that the firm owes. Subtracting the value of a firm's liabilities from the value of its assets leaves its *net worth*. Because a corporation's stockholders are its owners, net worth is often listed as **stockholders' equity** on a balance sheet. Using these definitions, we can state the balance sheet equation (also called the basic accounting equation) as follows:

$$\text{Assets} - \text{Liabilities} = \text{Stockholders' Equity},$$

or:

$$\text{Assets} = \text{Liabilities} + \text{Stockholders' Equity}.$$

Stockholders' equity The difference between the value of a corporation's assets and the value of its liabilities; also known as *net worth*.

This equation tells us that the value of a firm's assets must equal the value of its liabilities plus the value of stockholders' equity. An important accounting convention dating back to the beginning of modern bookkeeping in fifteenth-century Italy holds that balance sheets should list assets on the left side and liabilities and net worth, or stockholders' equity, on the right side. Notice that this means that *the value of the left side of the balance sheet must always equal the value of the right side*. Figure 6A.2 shows Twitter's balance sheet as of December 31, 2014.

A couple of the entries on the asset side of the balance sheet may be unfamiliar: *Current assets* are assets that the firm could convert into cash quickly, such as the balance in its checking account or its accounts receivable, which is money currently owed to the firm for products that have been delivered but not yet paid for. *Goodwill* represents the difference between the purchase price of a company and the market value of its assets. It represents the ability of a business to earn an economic profit from its assets. For example, if you buy a restaurant that is located on a busy intersection and you employ a chef with a reputation for preparing delicious food, you may pay more than the market value of the tables, chairs, ovens, and other assets. This additional amount you pay will be entered on the asset side of your balance sheet as goodwill.

Current liabilities are short-term debts such as accounts payable, which is money owed to suppliers for goods received but not yet paid for, or bank loans that will be paid back in less than one year. Long-term bank loans, the value of outstanding corporate bonds, and other long-term debts are *long-term liabilities*.

MyEconLab **Study Plan**

Assets		Liabilities and Stockholders' Equity	
Current assets	$4,256	Current liabilities	$ 394
Property and equipment	557	Long-term liabilities	1,563
Goodwill	623	Total liabilities	1,957
Other assets	147	Stockholders' equity	3,626
Total assets	$5,583	Total liabilities and stockholders' equity	$5,583

Note: All values are in millions of dollars.

Figure 6A.2

Twitter's Balance Sheet as of December 31, 2014

Corporations list their assets on the left of their balance sheets and their liabilities on the right. The difference between the value of a firm's assets and the value of its liabilities equals the net worth of the firm, or stockholders' equity. Stockholders' equity is listed on the right side of the balance sheet. Therefore, the value of the left side of the balance sheet must always equal the value of the right side. **Source:** Twitter, *Annual Report, 2014*.

Key Terms

Present value, p. 205   Stockholders' equity, p. 211

Tools to Analyze Firms' Financial Information, pages 205–211

6A

LEARNING OBJECTIVE: Understand the concept of present value and the information contained on a firm's income statement and balance sheet.

MyEconLab   Visit **www.myeconlab.com** to complete these exercises online and get instant feedback.

Review Questions

6A.1 Why is money you receive at some future date worth less to you than money you receive today? If the interest rate rises, what effect does this have on the present value of payments you receive in the future?

6A.2 Give the formula for calculating the present value of a bond that will pay a coupon of $100 per year for 10 years and that has a face value of $1,000.

6A.3 Compare the formula for calculating the present value of the payments you will receive from owning a bond to the formula for calculating the present value of the payments you will receive from owning a stock. What are the key similarities? What are the key differences?

6A.4 How is operating income calculated? How does operating income differ from net income? How does net income differ from accounting profit?

6A.5 What is the key difference between a firm's income statement and its balance sheet? What is listed on the left side of a balance sheet? What is listed on the right side?

Problems and Applications

6A.6 (Related to Solved Problem 6A.1 on page 207) If the interest rate is 10 percent, what is the present value of a bond that matures in two years, pays $85 one year from now, and pays $1,085 two years from now?

6A.7 (Related to Solved Problem 6A.1 on page 207) Before the 2013 season, the Los Angeles Angels signed outfielder Josh Hamilton to a contract that would pay him an immediate $10 million signing bonus and the following amounts: $15 million for the 2013 season, $15 million for the 2014 season, $23 million for the 2015 season, $30 million for the 2016 season, and $30 million for the 2017 season. The contract also specified that $2 million would be given to a charity. Assume that Hamilton receives each of his five seasonal salaries as a lump-sum payment at the end of the season.
   a. Some newspaper reports described Hamilton as having signed a $125 million contract with the Angels. Do you agree that $125 million was the value of this contract? Briefly explain.
   b. What was the present value of Hamilton's contract at the time he signed it (assuming an interest rate of 10 percent)? For simplicity, you can ignore the $2 million given to charity.

   c. If you use an interest rate of 5 percent, what was the present value of Hamilton's contract?
   Source: Drew Silva, "Breaking Down Josh Hamilton's Five-Year, $125M Contract," hardballtalk.nbcsports.com, December 15, 2012.

6A.8 (Related to Solved Problem 6A.1 on page 207) A winner of the Pennsylvania Lottery was given the choice of receiving $18 million at once or $1,440,000 per year for 25 years.
   a. If the winner had opted for the 25 annual payments, how much in total would she have received?
   b. At an interest rate of 10 percent, what would be the present value of the 25 payments?
   c. At an interest rate of 5 percent, what would be the present value of the 25 payments?
   d. What interest rate would make the present value of the 25 payments equal to the one payment of $18 million? (This question is difficult and requires the use of a financial calculator or a spreadsheet. *Hint:* If you are familiar with the Excel spreadsheet program, use the RATE function. You can answer parts (b) and (c) by using the Excel PV [Present Value] function.)

6A.9 (Related to Solved Problem 6A.1 on page 207) Before the start of the 2000 baseball season, the New York Mets decided that they didn't want Bobby Bonilla playing for them any longer. But Bonilla had a contract with the Mets for the 2000 season that would have obliged the Mets to pay him $5.9 million. When the Mets released Bonilla, he agreed to take the following payments in lieu of the $5.9 million the Mets would have paid him in the year 2000: He would receive 25 equal payments of $1,193,248.20 each July 1 from 2011 to 2035. If you were Bobby Bonilla, which would you rather have had, the lump-sum $5.9 million in 2000 or the 25 payments beginning in 2011? Explain the basis for your decision.
   Source: Mike Sielski, "There's No Accounting for This," *Wall Street Journal*, July 1, 2010.

6A.10 Suppose that eLake, an online auction site, is paying a dividend of $2 per share. You expect this dividend to grow 2 percent per year, and the interest rate is 10 percent. What is the most you would be willing to pay for a share of stock in eLake? If the interest rate is 5 percent, what is the most you would be willing to pay? When interest rates in the economy decline, would you expect stock prices in general to rise or fall? Briefly explain.

6A.11 Suppose you buy the bond of a large corporation at a time when the inflation rate is very low. If the inflation rate increases during the time you hold the bond, what is likely to happen to the price of the bond?

6A.12 Use the information in the following table for calendar year 2014 to prepare an income statement for McDonald's Corporation. Be sure to include entries for operating income and net income.

Revenue from company restaurants	$18,169 million
Revenue from franchised restaurants	9,272 million
Cost of operating company-owned restaurants	15,288 million
Income taxes	2,614 million
Interest expense	577 million
General and administrative cost	2,507 million
Cost of restaurant leases	1,697 million

Source: McDonalds Corp., *Annual Report, 2014.*

6A.13 Use the information in the following table on the financial situation of Starbucks Corporation as of September 28, 2014 (the end of the firm's financial year), to prepare a balance sheet for the firm. Be sure to include an entry for stockholders' equity.

Current assets	$4,169 million
Current liabilities	3,039 million
Property and equipment	3,519 million
Long-term liabilities	2,441 million
Goodwill	856 million
Other assets	2,209 million

Source: Starbucks Corp., *Annual Report, 2014.*

6A.14 The *current ratio* is equal to a firm's current assets divided by its current liabilities. Use the information in Figure 6A.2 on page 211 to calculate Twitter's current ratio on December 31, 2014. Investors generally prefer that a firm's current ratio be greater than 1.5. What problems might a firm encounter if the value of its current assets is low relative to the value of its current liabilities?

Comparative Advantage and the Gains from International Trade

CHAPTER

7

President Obama, Nike, and Free Trade

Where were your shoes made? If you answer either China or Vietnam, you are likely to be correct. But if you lived in the United States during the 1930s, you would have answered "right here." At that time, there were nearly 2,000 shoe factories in the United States, employing more than 275,000 workers. Today, 99 percent of shoes sold in the United States are made overseas, and U.S. shoe factories employ fewer than 15,000 workers. Nike illustrates the evolution of today's U.S. shoe industry. Headquartered in Beaverton, Oregon, Nike employs about 26,000 people in the United States, but most work in administration, sales, and research and development. Nike has contracts with foreign shoe firms that employ nearly 1 million workers to manufacture Nike shoes in factories in China, Vietnam, and Indonesia.

Would U.S. consumers and workers be better off if the federal government banned imports of shoes, so all shoes bought in the United States were made here? President Barack Obama would answer "no." In 2015, he visited Nike's headquarters to push for Congressional passage of the *Trans-Pacific Partnership* (TPP), an agreement between the United States and 11 other countries, including Canada, Japan, Mexico, and Vietnam. The TPP is meant to reduce trade barriers among these countries. The Obama administration argued that the TPP will "unlock opportunities for American manufacturers, workers, service providers, farmers, and ranchers—to support job creation and wage growth."

Critics argued that the TPP will further expose U.S. firms and workers to competition from foreign firms where the average wage is less than $5 per day. Although the TPP includes provisions to enforce environmental standards in foreign factories, some environmentalists are skeptical that the provisions will be enforced. The AFL-CIO, a labor union organization, argued, "Unfortunately, it is becoming clear the TPP will not create jobs, protect the environment and ensure safe imports."

Does eliminating restrictions on international trade help workers and consumers in the United States, or does it hurt them? In this chapter, we will analyze this and other important questions related to international trade.

Sources: Peter Baker, "Obama Scolds Democrats on Trade Pact Stance," *Wall Street Journal*, May 8, 2015; Office of the United States Trade Representative, "TPP Issue-by-Issue Information Center," ustr.gov; "Trans-Pacific Partnership Free Trade Agreement (TPP)," aflcio.org; and U.S. Department of Commerce, Bureau of the Census, *Fifteenth Census of the United States, Manufactures: 1929*, Vol. III, Washington, DC: Government Printing Office, 1933.

Economics in Your Life

Did You Know There Is a Tariff on Running Shoes?

Politicians often support polices that restrict imports from foreign countries because they want to convince people to vote for them. The workers in the industries these restrictions protect are likely to vote for the politicians because they believe the restrictions will save their jobs. But most people do *not* work in industries that are protected from foreign competition by trade restrictions. The federal government imposes a tariff, or tax, on imports of most shoes into the United States. As a result, U.S. consumers pay higher prices for shoes. But very few people in the United States today are employed in shoe factories. Why, then, does the federal government have a tariff on shoes, and why are so few people aware that it exists? As you read this chapter, try to answer these questions. You can check your answers against those we provide on **page 239** at the end of this chapter.

Trade is simply the act of buying or selling. Is there a difference between trade that takes place within a country and international trade? Within the United States, domestic trade makes it possible for consumers in Ohio to eat salmon caught in Alaska and for consumers in Montana to drive cars built in Michigan or Kentucky. Similarly, international trade makes it possible for consumers in the United States to drink wine from France and use Blu-ray players from Japan. One significant difference between domestic trade and international trade is that international trade is more controversial. At one time, nearly all the televisions, shoes, clothing, and toys bought in the United States were also produced here. Today, firms in other countries produce most of these goods. This shift has benefited U.S. consumers because foreign-made goods have lower prices or higher quality than the U.S.-made goods they have replaced. At the same time, though, many U.S. firms that produced these goods have gone out of business, and their workers have had to find other jobs. Not surprisingly, opinion polls show that many Americans favor reducing international trade because they believe doing so will preserve jobs in the United States. But is this belief accurate?

We can use the tools of demand and supply to analyze markets for internationally traded goods and services. We have seen that trade in general—whether within a country or between countries—is based on the principle of comparative advantage (see Chapter 2). In this chapter, we look more closely at the role of comparative advantage in international trade. We also use the concepts of consumer surplus, producer surplus, and deadweight loss (see Chapter 4) to analyze government policies that interfere with trade. With this background, we can return to the political debate over whether the United States benefits from international trade. We begin by looking at how large a role international trade plays in the U.S. economy.

7.1 | The United States in the International Economy

LEARNING OBJECTIVE: Discuss the role of international trade in the U.S. economy.

International trade has grown tremendously over the past 50 years due primarily to these three factors: The decreasing costs of shipping products around the world, the spread of inexpensive and reliable communications, and changes in government policies. Firms can use large container ships to send their products across oceans at low cost. Businesspeople today can travel to Europe or Asia, using fast, inexpensive, and reliable air transportation. The Internet, cellphones, and text messaging allow managers to communicate instantaneously and at a very low cost with customers and suppliers around the world. These and other improvements in transportation and communication have created an integrated global marketplace that earlier generations of businesspeople could only dream of.

Tariff A tax imposed by a government on imports.

Imports Goods and services bought domestically but produced in other countries.

Exports Goods and services produced domestically but sold in other countries.

Over the past 50 years, many governments have changed policies to facilitate international trade. For example, tariff rates have fallen. A **tariff** is a tax imposed by a government on *imports* into a country. **Imports** are goods and services bought domestically but produced in other countries. In the 1930s, the United States charged an average tariff rate above 50 percent. Today, the rate is less than 1.5 percent. In North America, most tariffs between Canada, Mexico, and the United States were eliminated following the passage of the North American Free Trade Agreement (NAFTA) in 1994. In Europe, 29 countries have formed the European Union, which has eliminated all tariffs among member countries, greatly increasing both imports and **exports**, which are goods and services produced domestically but sold in other countries. In 2015, the Obama administration concluded negotiating the Trans-Pacific Partnership (TPP), which is an agreement between the United States and 11 other countries around the Pacific Ocean, including Canada, Japan, Mexico, and Vietnam. The TPP will eliminate most tariffs between these countries, which together account for nearly 40 percent of world production of goods and services.

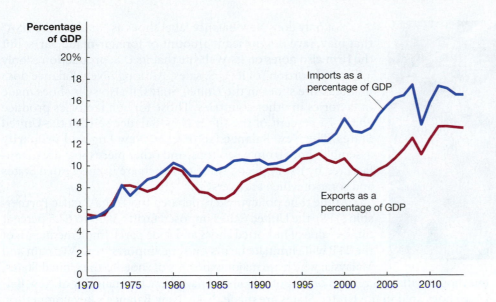

MyEconLab Real-time data

Figure 7.1

International Trade Is of Increasing Importance to the United States

Exports and imports of goods and services as a percentage of total production—measured by GDP—show the importance of international trade to an economy. Since 1970, both imports and exports have been steadily rising as a fraction of U.S. GDP.

Source: U.S. Department of Commerce, Bureau of Economic Analysis.

The Importance of Trade to the U.S. Economy

U.S. consumers buy increasing quantities of goods and services produced in other countries. At the same time, U.S. businesses sell increasing quantities of goods and services to consumers in other countries. Figure 7.1 shows that since 1970, with the exception of the period of the severe recession of 2007–2009, both exports and imports have been increasing as a fraction of U.S. gross domestic product (GDP). Recall that GDP is the value of all the final goods and services produced in a country during a year. In 1970, exports and imports were both less than 6 percent of U.S. GDP. In 2014, exports were about 13 percent of GDP, and imports were about 17 percent.

Not all sectors of the U.S. economy are affected equally by international trade. For example, although it's difficult to import or export some services, such as haircuts and appendectomies, a large percentage of U.S. agricultural production is exported. Each year, the United States exports about 50 percent of its wheat and rice crops and 20 percent of its corn crop.

Many U.S. manufacturing industries also depend on trade. About 20 percent of U.S. manufacturing jobs depend directly or indirectly on exports. In some industries, such as pharmaceutical drugs, the products are directly exported. In other industries, such as steel, the products are used to make other products, such as bulldozers or machine tools, that are then exported. In all, about two-thirds of U.S. manufacturing industries depend on exports for at least 10 percent of jobs. MyEconLab Concept Check

Making **the** **Connection**
MyEconLab Video

Would New Balance Be Helped or Hurt By the Trans-Pacific Partnership?

Founded in 1906, New Balance Athletic Shoe, which is headquartered in Boston, Massachusetts, seems to have bucked the long-run trend of shoe production leaving the United States. New Balance operates two factories in Massachusetts and three in Maine, employing about 1,400 workers to manufacture shoes. Many people think of New Balance as the "Made in America" shoe company, and it is the only company making significant quantities of shoes in the United States. It labels its shoes as "Made in the USA" when they contain at least 70 percent U.S.-made parts.

New Balance Athletic Shoe assembles more than 4 million pairs of athletic shoes a year in its Massachusetts and Maine factories.

Not only does New Balance label shoes as "Made in the USA" that may have a significant amount of foreign-made parts, but the firm also notes on its Web site that its U.S. production is only a "limited portion" of its U.S. sales. Although New Balance does manufacture shoes in the United States, it also sells shoes made in factories in other countries. Those foreign factories produce about 75 percent of the shoes New Balance sells in the United States. The New Balance factories in New England primarily assemble shoes from soles, tops, and other pieces that are manufactured by its suppliers, some of which are in the United States and some of which are overseas.

At the time policymakers debated the Trans-Pacific Partnership (TPP), the United States imposed tariffs of 25 to 67.5 percent on the value of imported shoes and shoe parts. Implementation of the TPP will eliminate tariffs on shoe imports from Vietnam and Malaysia, which are major exporters of shoes to the United States, but those tariffs will remain on imports from China, where the majority of New Balance shoes sold in the United States are made. Nike, New Balance's key competitor, imports the majority of its shoes from Vietnam, so it will receive a larger benefit from the passage of the TPP than New Balance will.

New Balance, then, was in a somewhat complicated situation as the debate over the TPP took place. Eliminating the tariff on shoes imported from TPP countries will hurt New Balance by lowering the prices on some of the imported shoes sold by other companies that compete with New Balance's U.S.-produced shoes. But New Balance will benefit because it will be able to sell the shoes it imports from TPP countries at a lower price, and because the cost of the shoe parts it imports from TPP countries for use in its U.S. factories will also decline. Not surprisingly, the company did not voice a strong position either for or against the TPP. A spokesperson for the company was quoted as saying, "We've had productive discussions with the Obama administration regarding TPP, and we're hopeful that the final agreement will reflect those discussions and will allow us to continue to thrive as a domestic producer."

Today, few U.S.-based manufacturing firms make their products exclusively in the United States out of entirely U.S.-made parts. As a result, the positions of these firms on reducing barriers to international trade can be difficult to predict.

Sources: William Mauldin and Sara Germano, "Obama Visits Importer Nike, Defends Pacific Trade Agreement," *Wall Street Journal*, May 8, 2015; Eric Bradner, "Obama Steps in with Outsourcer at Nike," cnn.com, May 8, 2015; and New Balance, *New Balance Responsible Leadership Report*, newbalance.com.

MyEconLab Study Plan   **Your Turn:** Test your understanding by doing related problem 1.7 on page 240 at the end of this chapter.

U.S. International Trade in a World Context

The United States is the second-largest exporter in the world, just behind China, as Figure 7.2 illustrates. Six of the other seven leading exporting countries are also high-income countries. Although China is still a relatively low-income country, the rapid growth of the Chinese economy over the past 35 years has resulted in its becoming the largest exporter. Three of the top exporting countries are in East Asia, four are in Western Europe, and one is in North America.

Figure 7.3 shows that international trade is less important to the United States than it is to many other countries, with imports and exports being lower percentages of GDP. In some smaller countries, such as Belgium and the Netherlands, imports and exports make up more than half of GDP. In the larger European economies, imports and exports make up one-quarter to one-half of GDP.

     MyEconLab Concept Check

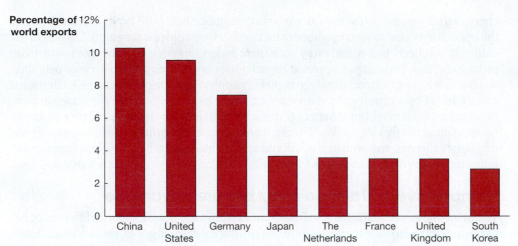

MyEconLab Animation

Figure 7.2

The Eight Leading Exporting Countries, 2014

China is the leading exporting country, accounting for 10.3 percent of total world exports. The United States is second, with a 9.6 percent share. The values are the shares of total world exports of merchandise and commercial services.

Source: World Trade Organization, *International Trade Statistics*, 2014.

7.2 Comparative Advantage in International Trade

LEARNING OBJECTIVE: Explain the difference between comparative advantage and absolute advantage in international trade.

Why have businesses around the world increasingly looked for markets in other countries? Why have consumers increasingly purchased goods and services made in other countries? People trade for one reason: Trade makes them better off. Whenever a buyer and seller agree to a sale, they must both believe they are better off; otherwise, there would be no sale. This outcome must hold whether the buyer and seller live in the same city or in different countries. As we will see, governments are more likely to interfere with international trade than they are with domestic trade, but the reasons for the interference are more political than economic.

A Brief Review of Comparative Advantage

Recall that **comparative advantage** is the ability of an individual, a firm, or a country to produce a good or service at a lower opportunity cost than competitors. **Opportunity cost** is the highest-valued alternative that must be given up to engage in an activity. People, firms, and countries specialize in economic activities in which they have a comparative advantage. In trading, we benefit from the comparative advantage of other people (or firms or countries), and they benefit from our comparative advantage.

A good way to think of comparative advantage is to recall the example of you and your neighbor picking fruit (see Chapter 2). Your neighbor is better at picking both apples and

Comparative advantage The ability of an individual, a firm, or a country to produce a good or service at a lower opportunity cost than competitors.

Opportunity cost The highest-valued alternative that must be given up to engage in an activity.

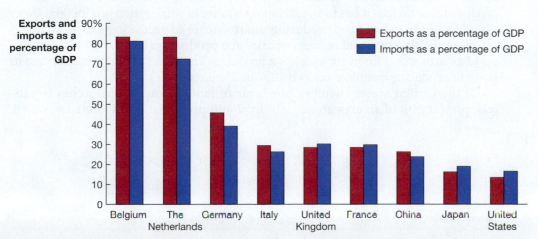

MyEconLab Real-time data

Figure 7.3

International Trade as a Percentage of GDP, 2014

International trade is still less important to the United States than it is to most other countries.

Source: Organization for Economic Co-operation and Development, *Country Statistical Profiles*.

cherries than you are. Why, then, doesn't your neighbor pick both types of fruit? Because the opportunity cost to your neighbor of picking her own apples is very high: She is a particularly skilled cherry picker, and every hour spent picking apples is an hour taken away from picking cherries. You can pick apples at a much lower opportunity cost than your neighbor, so you have a comparative advantage in picking apples. Your neighbor can pick cherries at a much lower opportunity cost than you can, so she has a comparative advantage in picking cherries. Your neighbor is better off specializing in picking cherries, and you are better off specializing in picking apples. You can then trade some of your apples for some of your neighbor's cherries, and both of you will end up with more of each fruit. (If you have trouble following the point here, refer back to Tables 2.1 and 2.2.) *MyEconLab* Concept Check

Comparative Advantage and Absolute Advantage

The principle of comparative advantage can explain why people pursue different occupations. It can also explain why countries produce different goods and services. International trade involves many countries importing and exporting many different goods and services. Countries are better off if they specialize in producing the goods for which they have a comparative advantage. They can then trade for the goods for which other countries have a comparative advantage.

We can illustrate why specializing on the basis of comparative advantage makes countries better off with a simple example involving just two countries and two products. Suppose the United States and Japan produce only smartwatches and tablet computers, like Apple's iPad or Samsung's Galaxy Tab. Assume that each country uses only labor to produce each good and that Japanese and U.S. smartwatches and tablets are exactly the same. Table 7.1 shows how much each country can produce of each good with one hour of labor.

Absolute advantage The ability to produce more of a good or service than competitors when using the same amount of resources.

Notice that Japanese workers are more productive than U.S. workers in making both goods. In one hour, Japanese workers can make six times as many smartwatches and one and one-half times as many tablets as U.S. workers. Japan has an *absolute advantage* over the United States in producing both goods. **Absolute advantage** is the ability to produce more of a good or service than competitors when using the same amount of resources. In this case, Japan can produce more of both goods using the same amount of labor as the United States.

It might seem at first that Japan has nothing to gain from trading with the United States because it has an absolute advantage in producing both goods. However, Japan should specialize and produce only smartwatches and obtain the tablets it needs by exporting smartwatches to the United States in exchange for tablets. The reason Japan benefits from trade is that although it has an *absolute advantage* in the production of both goods, it has a *comparative advantage* only in the production of smartwatches. The United States has a comparative advantage in the production of tablets.

If it seems contrary to common sense that Japan should import tablets from the United States even though Japan can produce more of them per hour of labor, think about the opportunity cost to each country of producing each good. If Japan wants to produce more tablets, it has to switch labor away from smartwatch production. Every hour of labor switched from producing smartwatches to producing tablets increases tablet production by 6 and reduces smartwatch production by 12. Japan has to give up 12 smartwatches for every 6 tablets it produces. Therefore, the opportunity cost to Japan of producing one more tablet is 12/6, or 2 smartwatches.

If the United States switches one hour of labor from smartwatches to tablets, production of smartwatches falls by 2 and production of tablets rises by 4.

Table 7.1

An Example of Japanese Workers Being More Productive Than American Workers

	Output per Hour of Work	
	Smartwatches	**Tablets**
Japan	12	6
United States	2	4

	Opportunity Costs	
	Smartwatches	**Tablets**
Japan	0.5 tablet	2 smartwatches
United States	2 tablets	0.5 smartwatch

Table 7.2

The Opportunity Costs of Producing Smartwatches and Tablets
The table shows the opportunity cost each country faces in producing smartwatches and tablets. For example, the entry in the first row and second column shows that Japan must give up 2 smartwatches for every tablet it produces.

Therefore, the opportunity cost to the United States of producing one more tablet is 2/4, or 0.5 smartwatch. The United States has a lower opportunity cost of producing tablets and, therefore, has a comparative advantage in making this product. By similar reasoning, we can see that Japan has a comparative advantage in producing smartwatches. Table 7.2 summarizes the opportunity cost each country faces in producing these goods.   MyEconLab Concept Check

7.3 How Countries Gain from International Trade

LEARNING OBJECTIVE: Explain how countries gain from international trade.

Can Japan really gain from producing only smartwatches and trading with the United States for tablets? To see that it can, assume at first that Japan and the United States do not trade with each other. A situation in which a country does not trade with other countries is called **autarky**. Assume that in autarky, each country has 1,000 hours of labor available to produce the two goods, and each country produces the quantities of the two goods shown in Table 7.3. Because there is no trade, these quantities also represent consumption of the two goods in each country.

Autarky A situation in which a country does not trade with other countries.

Increasing Consumption through Trade

Suppose now that Japan and the United States begin to trade with each other. The **terms of trade** is the ratio at which a country can trade its exports for imports from other countries. For simplicity, let's assume that the terms of trade end up with Japan and the United States being willing to trade one smartwatch for one tablet.

Terms of trade The ratio at which a country can trade its exports for imports from other countries.

Once trade has begun, the United States and Japan can exchange tablets for smartwatches or smartwatches for tablets. For example, if Japan specializes by using all 1,000 available hours of labor to produce smartwatches, it will be able to produce 12,000 smartwatches. It then could export 1,500 smartwatches to the United States in exchange for 1,500 tablets. (Remember that we are assuming the terms of trade are 1 smartwatch for 1 tablet.) Japan ends up with 10,500 smartwatches and 1,500 tablets. Compared with the situation before trade, Japan has the same number of tablets but 1,500 more smartwatches. If the United States specializes in producing tablets, it will be able to produce 4,000 tablets. It could then export 1,500 tablets to Japan in exchange for 1,500 smartwatches. The United States ends up with 2,500 tablets and 1,500 smartwatches. Compared with the situation before trade, the United States has the same number of smartwatches but 1,500 more tablets. Trade has allowed both countries to increase the quantities of goods consumed. Table 7.4 summarizes the gains from trade for the United States and Japan.

By trading, Japan and the United States are able to consume more than they could without trade. This outcome is possible because world production of both goods increases after trade. (In this example, our "world" consists of just the United States and Japan.)

Why does total production of smartwatches and tablets increase when the United States specializes in producing tablets and Japan specializes in producing smartwatches?

	Production and Consumption	
	Smartwatches	**Tablets**
Japan	9,000	1,500
United States	1,500	1,000

Table 7.3

Production without Trade

Table 7.4

Gains from Trade for Japan and the United States

Without Trade

	Production and Consumption	
	Smartwatches	Tablets
Japan	9,000	1,500
United States	1,500	1,000

With Trade

	Production with Trade		Trade		Consumption with Trade	
	Smartwatches	Tablets	Smartwatches	Tablets	Smartwatches	Tablets
Japan	12,000	0	Export 1,500	Import 1,500	10,500	1,500
United States	0	4,000	Import 1,500	Export 1,500	1,500	2,500

With trade, the United States and Japan specialize in the good they have a comparative advantage in producing . . .

. . . and export some of that good in exchange for the good the other country has a comparative advantage in producing.

Gains from Trade

	Increased Consumption
Japan	1,500 Smartwatches
United States	1,500 Tablets

The increased consumption made possible by trade represents the gains from trade.

A domestic analogy helps to answer this question: If a company shifts production from an old factory to a more efficient modern factory, its output will increase. The same thing happens in our example. Producing tablets in Japan and smartwatches in the United States is inefficient. Shifting production to the more efficient country—the one with the comparative advantage—increases total production. The key point is: *Countries gain from specializing in producing goods in which they have a comparative advantage and trading for goods in which other countries have a comparative advantage.*   MyEconLab Concept Check

---

Solved Problem 7.3

MyEconLab Interactive Animation

The Gains from Trade

The first discussion of comparative advantage appears in *On the Principles of Political Economy and Taxation*, a book written by the British economist David Ricardo in 1817. Ricardo provided a famous example of the gains from trade, using wine and cloth production in Portugal and England. The following table is adapted from Ricardo's example, with cloth measured in sheets and wine measured in kegs:

	Output per Year of Labor	
	Cloth	Wine
Portugal	100	150
England	90	60

a. Explain which country has an absolute advantage in the production of each good.

b. Explain which country has a comparative advantage in the production of each good.

c. Suppose that Portugal and England currently do not trade with each other. Each country has 1,000 workers, so each has 1,000 years of labor time to use in producing cloth and wine, and the countries are currently producing the amounts of each good shown in the following table:

	Cloth	Wine
Portugal	18,000	123,000
England	63,000	18,000

Show that Portugal and England can both gain from trade. Assume that the terms of trade are that one sheet of cloth can be traded for one keg of wine.

Solving the Problem

Step 1: **Review the chapter material.** This problem is about absolute and comparative advantage and the gains from trade, so you may want to review the sections "Comparative Advantage in International Trade," which begins on page 219, and "How Countries Gain from International Trade," which begins on page 221.

Step 2: **Answer part (a) by determining which country has an absolute advantage.** Remember that a country has an absolute advantage over another country when it can produce more of a good using the same resources. The first table in the problem shows that Portugal can produce more cloth *and* more wine with one year's worth of labor than can England. Therefore, Portugal has an absolute advantage in the production of both goods, and England does not have an absolute advantage in the production of either good.

Step 3: **Answer part (b) by determining which country has a comparative advantage.** A country has a comparative advantage when it can produce a good at a lower opportunity cost. To produce 100 sheets of cloth, Portugal must give up producing 150 kegs of wine. Therefore, Portugal's opportunity cost of producing 1 sheet of cloth is 150/100, or 1.5 kegs of wine. England has to give up producing 60 kegs of wine to produce 90 sheets of cloth, so its opportunity cost of producing 1 sheet of cloth is 60/90, or 0.67 keg of wine. The opportunity costs of producing wine can be calculated in the same way. The following table shows the opportunity cost to Portugal and England of producing each good.

	Opportunity Costs	
	Cloth	Wine
Portugal	1.5 kegs of wine	0.67 sheet of cloth
England	0.67 keg of wine	1.5 sheets of cloth

Portugal has a comparative advantage in wine because its opportunity cost is lower. England has a comparative advantage in cloth because its opportunity cost is lower.

Step 4: **Answer part (c) by showing that both countries can benefit from trade.** By now it should be clear that both countries will be better off if they specialize in producing the good for which they have a comparative advantage and trade for the other good. The following table is very similar to Table 7.4 and shows one example of trade making both countries better off. (To test your understanding, construct another example.)

Without Trade

	Production and Consumption	
	Cloth	Wine
Portugal	18,000	123,000
England	63,000	18,000

With Trade

	Production with Trade		Trade		Consumption with Trade	
	Cloth	Wine	Cloth	Wine	Cloth	Wine
Portugal	0	150,000	Import 18,000	Export 18,000	18,000	132,000
England	90,000	0	Export 18,000	Import 18,000	72,000	18,000

Gains from Trade	
	Increased Consumption
Portugal	9,000 wine
England	9,000 cloth

MyEconLab Study Plan   **Your Turn:** For more practice, do related problems 3.5 and 3.6 on page 242 at the end of this chapter.

Why Don't We See Complete Specialization?

In our example of two countries producing only two products, each country specializes in producing one of the goods. In the real world, many goods and services are produced in more than one country. For example, the United States, Japan, Germany, Canada, Mexico, India, China, and other countries produce automobiles. We do not see complete specialization in the real world for three main reasons:

- **Not all goods and services are traded internationally.** For example, even if Japan had a comparative advantage in the production of medical services, it would be difficult for Japan to specialize in producing medical services and then export them. There is no easy way for U.S. patients who need appendectomies to receive them from surgeons in Japan.

- **Production of most goods involves increasing opportunity costs.** Recall that production of most goods involves increasing opportunity costs (see Chapter 2). In our example, if the United States devotes more workers to producing tablets, the opportunity cost of producing more tablets will increase. At some point, the opportunity cost of producing tablets in the United States may rise to the level of the opportunity cost of producing tablets in Japan. When that happens, international trade will no longer push the United States further toward specialization. The same will be true of Japan: The increasing opportunity cost of producing smartwatches will cause Japan to stop short of complete specialization.

- **Tastes for products differ.** Most products are *differentiated*. Smartwatches, tablets, cars, and televisions—to name just a few products—come with a wide variety of features. When buying automobiles, some people look for reliability and fuel efficiency, others look for room to carry seven passengers, and still others want styling and high performance. So, some car buyers prefer Toyota Prius hybrids, and some prefer Chevy Suburbans, and others prefer BMWs. As a result, Japan, the United States, and Germany may each have a comparative advantage in producing different types of automobiles.   MyEconLab Concept Check

Does Anyone Lose as a Result of International Trade?

In our smartwatch and tablet example, consumption increases in both the United States and Japan as a result of trade. Everyone gains, and no one loses. Or do they? In our example, we referred repeatedly to "Japan" or the "United States" producing smartwatches or tablets. But countries do not produce goods—firms do. In a world without trade, there would be smartwatch and tablet firms in both Japan and the United States. In a world with trade, there would be only Japanese smartwatch firms and U.S. tablet firms. Japanese tablet firms and U.S. smartwatch firms would close. Overall, total employment would not change, and production would increase as a result of trade. Nevertheless, the owners of Japanese tablet firms, the owners of U.S. smartwatch firms, and the people who work for them are worse off as a result of trade. The losers from trade are likely to do their best to convince the Japanese and U.S. governments to interfere with trade by barring imports of the competing products from the other country or by imposing high tariffs on them.   MyEconLab Concept Check

Don't Let This Happen to You

Remember That Trade Creates Both Winners and Losers

The following statement is from a Federal Reserve publication: "Trade is a win–win situation for all countries that participate." People sometimes interpret statements like this to mean that there are no losers from international trade. But notice that the statement refers to *countries*, not individuals. When countries participate in trade, they make their consumers better off by increasing the quantity of goods and services available to them. As we have seen, however, expanding trade eliminates the jobs of workers employed at companies that are less efficient than foreign companies. Trade also creates new jobs at companies that export products to foreign markets. It may be difficult, though, for workers who lose their jobs because of trade

to easily find others. That is why in the United States the federal government uses the Trade Adjustment Assistance program to provide funds for workers who have lost their jobs due to international trade. Qualified unemployed workers can use these funds to pay for retraining, searching for new jobs, or relocating to areas where new jobs are available. This program—and similar programs in other countries—recognizes that there are losers from international trade as well as winners.

Source: Federal Reserve Bank of Dallas, "International Trade and the Economy," www.dallasfed.org/educate/everyday/ev7.html.

MyEconLab Study Plan

Your Turn: Test your understanding by doing related problem 3.12 on page 243 at the end of this chapter.

Where Does Comparative Advantage Come From?

Among the main sources of comparative advantage are the following:

- **Climate and natural resources.** This source of comparative advantage is the most obvious. Because of geology, Saudi Arabia has a comparative advantage in the production of oil. Because of climate and soil conditions, Costa Rica has a comparative advantage in the production of bananas, and the United States has a comparative advantage in the production of wheat.

- **Relative abundance of labor and capital.** Some countries, such as the United States, have many highly skilled workers and a great deal of machinery. Other countries, such as China, have many unskilled workers and relatively little machinery. As a result, the United States has a comparative advantage in the production of goods that require highly skilled workers or sophisticated machinery, such as aircraft and computer software. China has a comparative advantage in the production of goods, such as tools, clothing, and children's toys, that require unskilled workers and small amounts of simple machinery.

- **Technology.** Broadly defined, *technology* is the process firms use to turn inputs into goods and services. At any given time, firms in different countries do not all have access to the same technologies. In part, this difference is a result of past investments countries have made in higher education or in supporting research and development. Some countries are strong in *product technologies*, which involve the ability to develop new products. For example, firms in the United States have pioneered the development of such products as radios, televisions, digital computers, airliners, medical equipment, and many prescription drugs. Other countries are strong in *process technologies*, which involve the ability to improve the processes used to make existing products. For example, Japanese-based firms, such as Toyota and Honda, have succeeded by greatly improving the processes for designing and manufacturing automobiles.

- **External economies.** It is difficult to explain the location of some industries on the basis of climate, natural resources, the relative abundance of labor and capital, or technology. For example, why does southern California have a comparative advantage in making movies or Switzerland in making watches or New York in providing financial services? The answer is that once an industry becomes established in an area, firms located in that area gain advantages over firms located elsewhere.

The advantages include the availability of skilled workers, the opportunity to interact with other firms in the same industry, and proximity to suppliers. These advantages result in lower costs to firms located in the area. Because these lower costs result from increases in the size of the industry in an area, economists refer to them as **external economies**.   MyEconLab Concept Check

External economies Reductions in a firm's costs that result from an increase in the size of an industry.

Comparative Advantage over Time: The Rise and Fall—and Rise—of the U.S. Consumer Electronics Industry

A country may develop a comparative advantage in the production of a good, and then, as time passes and circumstances change, the country may lose its comparative advantage in producing that good and develop a comparative advantage in producing other goods. For several decades, the United States had a comparative advantage in the production of consumer electronic goods, such as televisions, radios, and stereos. The comparative advantage of the United States in these products was based on having developed most of the underlying technology, having the most modern factories, and having a skilled and experienced workforce. Gradually, however, other countries, particularly Japan, gained access to the technology, built modern factories, and developed skilled workforces. As mentioned earlier, Japanese firms have excelled in process technologies, which involve the ability to improve the processes used to make existing products. By the 1970s and 1980s, Japanese firms were able to produce many consumer electronic goods more cheaply and with higher quality than could U.S. firms. Japanese firms Sony, Panasonic, and Pioneer replaced U.S. firms Magnavox, Zenith, and RCA as world leaders in consumer electronics.

By the mid-2000s, however, as the technology underlying consumer electronics had evolved, comparative advantage had shifted again, and several U.S. firms had surged ahead of their Japanese competitors. For example, Apple had developed the iPod, iPhone, iPad, and Apple Watch; Linksys, a division of Cisco Systems, took the lead in home wireless networking technology; and TiVo pioneered the digital video recorder (DVR). As pictures and music converted to digital data, process technologies became less important than the ability to design and develop new products. These new consumer electronic products required skills similar to those in computer design and software writing, where the United States had long maintained a comparative advantage. Although for the most part these firms did not manufacture within the United States the products they designed and marketed, even that may be changing. Apple has begun assembling its Mac Pro computer in the United States. Foxconn, a Taiwanese electronics manufacturer, also announced plans to build factories in the United States that will produce robots and displays for electronic devices.

Once a country has lost its comparative advantage in producing a good, its income will be higher and its economy will be more efficient if it switches from producing the good to importing it, as the United States did when it switched from producing televisions to importing them. As we will see in the next section, however, there is often political pressure on governments to attempt to preserve industries that have lost their comparative advantage.   MyEconLab Concept Check

MyEconLab Study Plan

7.4 Government Policies That Restrict International Trade

LEARNING OBJECTIVE: Analyze the economic effects of government policies that restrict international trade.

Free trade, or trade between countries without government restrictions, makes consumers better off. We can expand on this idea by using the concepts of consumer surplus and producer surplus (see Chapter 4, Section 4.1). Figure 7.4 shows the market in the United States for the biofuel ethanol, which can be used as a substitute for gasoline. The figure shows the situation of autarky, where the United States does not trade with other countries. The equilibrium price of ethanol is $2.00 per gallon, and the

Free trade Trade between countries that is without government restrictions.

MyEconLab Animation

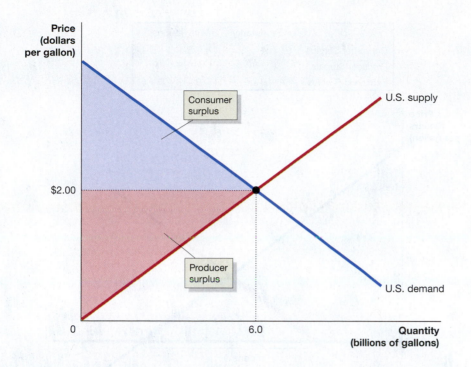

Figure 7.4

The U.S. Market for Ethanol under Autarky

This figure shows the market for ethanol in the United States, assuming autarky, where the United States does not trade with other countries. The equilibrium price of ethanol is $2.00 per gallon, and the equilibrium quantity is 6.0 billion gallons per year. The blue area represents consumer surplus, and the red area represents producer surplus.

equilibrium quantity is 6.0 billion gallons per year. The blue area represents consumer surplus, and the red area represents producer surplus.

Now suppose that the United States begins importing ethanol from Brazil and other countries that produce ethanol for $1.00 per gallon. Because the world market for ethanol is large, we will assume that the United States can buy as much ethanol as it wants without causing the *world price* of $1.00 per gallon to rise. Therefore, once imports of ethanol are allowed into the United States, U.S. firms will not be able to sell ethanol at prices higher than the world price of $1.00, and the U.S. price will become equal to the world price.

Figure 7.5 shows the result of allowing imports of ethanol into the United States. With the price lowered from $2.00 to $1.00, U.S. consumers increase their purchases from 6.0 billion gallons to 9.0 billion gallons. Equilibrium moves from point *F* to point *G*. In the new equilibrium, U.S. producers have reduced the quantity of ethanol they supply from 6.0 billion gallons to 3.0 billion gallons. Imports will equal 6.0 billion gallons, which is the difference between U.S. consumption and U.S. production.

Under autarky, consumer surplus would be area *A* in Figure 7.5. With imports, the reduction in price increases consumer surplus, so it is now equal to the sum of areas *A*, *B*, *C*, and *D*. Although the lower price increases consumer surplus, it reduces producer surplus. Under autarky, producer surplus was equal to the sum of areas *B* and *E*. With imports, it is equal to only area *E*. Recall that economic surplus equals the sum of consumer surplus and producer surplus. Moving from autarky to allowing imports increases economic surplus in the United States by an amount equal to the sum of areas *C* and *D*.

We can conclude that international trade helps consumers but hurts firms that are less efficient than foreign competitors. As a result, these firms and their workers are often strong supporters of government policies that restrict trade. These policies usually take one of two forms: (1) *tariffs*, and (2) *quotas* and *voluntary export restraints*.

Tariffs

The most common interferences with trade are *tariffs*, which are taxes imposed by a government on goods imported into the country. Like any other tax, a tariff increases the cost of selling a good. Figure 7.6 shows the effect of a tariff of $0.50 per gallon on ethanol imports into the United States. The $0.50 tariff raises the price of ethanol in the United States from the world price of $1.00 per gallon to $1.50 per gallon. At this

Figure 7.5

The Effect of Imports on the U.S. Ethanol Market

When imports are allowed into the United States, the price of ethanol falls from $2.00 to $1.00. U.S. consumers increase their purchases from 6.0 billion gallons to 9.0 billion gallons. Equilibrium moves from point *F* to point *G*. U.S. producers reduce the quantity of ethanol they supply from 6.0 billion gallons to 3.0 billion gallons. Imports equal 6.0 billion gallons, which is the difference between U.S. consumption and U.S. production. Consumer surplus equals the sum of areas *A*, *B*, *C*, and *D*. Producer surplus equals the area *E*.

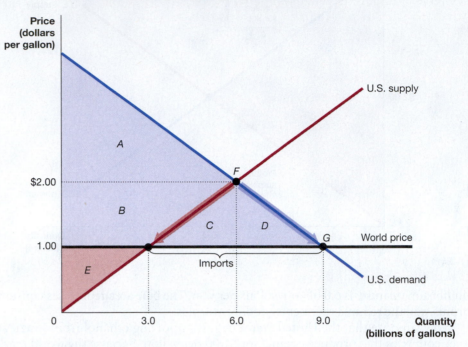

	Under Autarky	With Imports
Consumer Surplus	A	A + B + C + D
Producer Surplus	B + E	E
Economic Surplus	A + B + E	A + B + C + D + E

higher price, U.S. ethanol producers increase the quantity they supply from 3.0 billion gallons to 4.5 billion gallons. U.S. consumers, though, cut back their purchases of ethanol from 9.0 billion gallons to 7.5 billion gallons. Imports decline from 6.0 billion gallons (9.0 billion − 3.0 billion) to 3.0 billion gallons (7.5 billion − 4.5 billion). Equilibrium moves from point *G* to point *H*.

Figure 7.6

The Effects of a Tariff on Ethanol

Without a tariff on ethanol, U.S. producers will sell 3.0 billion gallons of ethanol, U.S. consumers will purchase 9.0 billion gallons, and imports will be 6.0 billion gallons. The U.S. price will equal the world price of $1.00 per gallon. The $0.50-per-gallon tariff raises the price of ethanol in the United States to $1.50 per gallon, and U.S. producers increase the quantity they supply to 4.5 billion gallons. U.S. consumers reduce their purchases to 7.5 billion gallons. Equilibrium moves from point *G* to point *H*. The ethanol tariff causes a loss of consumer surplus equal to the area *A* + *C* + *T* + *D*. The area *A* is the increase in producer surplus due to the higher price. The area *T* is the government's tariff revenue. The areas *C* and *D* represent deadweight loss.

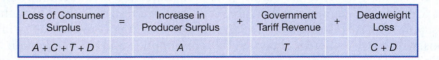

Loss of Consumer Surplus	=	Increase in Producer Surplus	+	Government Tariff Revenue	+	Deadweight Loss
A + C + T + D		A		T		C + D

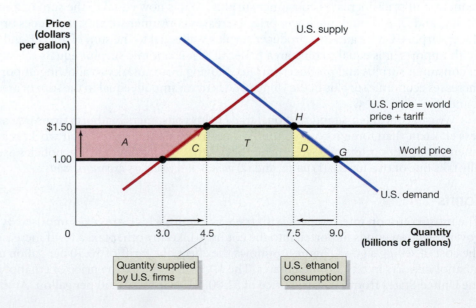

By raising the price of ethanol from $1.00 to $1.50, the tariff reduces consumer surplus by the sum of areas *A, T, C,* and *D.* Area *A* is the increase in producer surplus from the higher price. The government collects tariff revenue equal to the tariff of $0.50 per gallon multiplied by the 3.0 billion gallons imported. Area *T* represents the government's tariff revenue. Areas *C* and *D* represent losses to U.S. consumers that are not captured by anyone. These areas are deadweight loss and represent the decline in economic efficiency resulting from the ethanol tariff. Area *C* shows the effect of U.S. consumers being forced to buy from U.S. producers that are less efficient than foreign producers, and area *D* shows the effect of U.S. consumers buying less ethanol than they would have at the world price. As a result of the tariff, economic surplus has been reduced by the sum of areas *C* and *D.*

We can conclude that the tariff succeeds in helping U.S. ethanol producers but hurts U.S. consumers and the efficiency of the U.S. economy.   MyEconLab Concept Check

Quotas and Voluntary Export Restraints

A **quota** is a numerical limit on the quantity of a good that can be imported, and it has an effect similar to that of a tariff. A quota is imposed by the government of the importing country. A **voluntary export restraint (VER)** is an agreement negotiated between two countries that places a numerical limit on the quantity of a good that can be imported by one country from the other country. In the 1980s, the United States and Japan negotiated a VER that limited the quantity of automobiles the United States would import from Japan. The Japanese government agreed to the VER primarily because it was afraid that if it did not, the United States would impose a tariff or quota on imports of Japanese automobiles. Quotas and VERs have similar economic effects.

The main purpose of most tariffs and quotas is to reduce the foreign competition that domestic firms face. For many years, Congress has imposed a quota on sugar imports to protect U.S. sugar producers. Figure 7.7 shows the actual statistics for the

Quota A numerical limit a government imposes on the quantity of a good that can be imported into the country.

Voluntary export restraint (VER) An agreement negotiated between two countries that places a numerical limit on the quantity of a good that can be imported by one country from the other country.

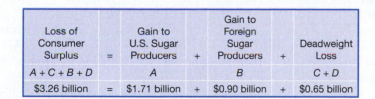

		Loss of Consumer Surplus	=	Gain to U.S. Sugar Producers	+	Gain to Foreign Sugar Producers	+	Deadweight Loss
		A + C + B + D		*A*		*B*		*C + D*
		$3.26 billion	=	$1.71 billion	+	$0.90 billion	+	$0.65 billion

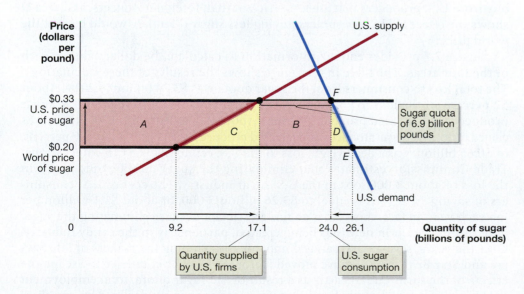

MyEconLab Animation

Figure 7.7

The Economic Effect of the U.S. Sugar Quota

Without a sugar quota, U.S. sugar producers would have sold 9.2 billion pounds of sugar, U.S. consumers would have purchased 26.1 billion pounds of sugar, and imports would have been 16.9 billion pounds. The U.S. price would have equaled the world price of $0.20 per pound. Because the sugar quota limits imports to 6.9 billion pounds (the bracket in the graph), the price of sugar in the United States rises to $0.33 per pound, and U.S. producers supply 17.1 billion pounds. U.S. consumers purchase 24.0 billion pounds rather than the 26.1 billion pounds they would purchase at the world price. Without the import quota, equilibrium would be at point *E*; with the quota, equilibrium is at point *F*. The sugar quota causes a loss of consumer surplus equal to the area *A + B + C + D*. The area *A* is the gain to U.S. sugar producers. The area *B* is the gain to foreign sugar producers. The areas *C* and *D* represent deadweight loss. The total loss to U.S. consumers in 2014 was $3.26 billion.

U.S. sugar market in 2014. The effect of a quota is very similar to the effect of a tariff. By limiting imports, a quota forces the domestic price of a good above the world price. In this case, the sugar quota limits sugar imports to 6.9 billion pounds per year (shown by the bracket in Figure 7.7), forcing the U.S. price of sugar up to $0.33 per pound, or $0.13 higher than the world price of $0.20 per pound. The U.S. price is above the world price because the quota keeps foreign sugar producers from selling the additional sugar in the United States that would drive the U.S. price down to the world price. At a price of $0.33 per pound, U.S. producers increase the quantity of sugar they supply from the 9.2 billion pounds they would supply at the world price to 17.1 billion pounds, and U.S. consumers cut back their purchases of sugar from the 26.1 billion pounds they would purchase at the world price to the 24.0 billion pounds they are willing to purchase at the higher U.S. price. If there were no import quota, equilibrium would be at the world price (point E), but with the quota, equilibrium is at the U.S. price (point F).

MyEconLab Concept Check

Measuring the Economic Effect of the Sugar Quota

We can use the concepts of consumer surplus, producer surplus, and deadweight loss to measure the economic impact of the sugar quota. Without a sugar quota, the world price of $0.20 per pound would also be the U.S. price. In Figure 7.7, without a sugar quota, consumer surplus would equal the area above the $0.20 price line and below the demand curve. The sugar quota causes the U.S. price to rise to $0.33 and reduces consumer surplus by the area $A + B + C + D$. Without a sugar quota, producer surplus received by U.S. sugar producers would be equal to the area below the $0.20 price line and above the supply curve. The higher U.S. price resulting from the sugar quota increases the producer surplus of U.S. sugar producers by an amount equal to area A.

A foreign producer must have a license from the U.S. government to import sugar under the quota system. Therefore, a foreign sugar producer that is lucky enough to have an import license also benefits from the quota because it is able to sell sugar in the U.S. market at $0.33 per pound instead of $0.20 per pound. Area B is the gain to foreign sugar producers. Areas A and B represent transfers from U.S. consumers of sugar to U.S. and foreign producers of sugar. Areas C and D represent losses to U.S. consumers that are not captured by anyone. These areas are deadweight loss and represent the decline in economic efficiency resulting from the sugar quota. Area C shows the effect of U.S. consumers being forced to buy from U.S. producers that are less efficient than foreign producers, and area D shows the effect of U.S. consumers buying less sugar than they would have at the world price.

Figure 7.7 provides enough information to calculate the dollar value of each of the four areas. The table in the figure shows the results of these calculations. The total loss to consumers from the sugar quota was $3.26 billion in 2014. About 52 percent of the loss to consumers, or $1.71 billion, was gained by U.S. sugar producers as increased producer surplus. About 28 percent, or $0.90 billion, was gained by foreign sugar producers as increased producer surplus, and about 20 percent, or $0.65 billion, was a deadweight loss to the U.S. economy. The U.S. International Trade Commission estimates that eliminating the sugar quota would result in the loss of about 3,000 jobs in the U.S. sugar industry. The cost to U.S. consumers of saving these jobs is equal to $3.26 billion/3,000, or about $1.1 million per job each year. In fact, this cost is an underestimate because eliminating the sugar quota would result in new jobs being created, particularly in the candy industry. Over the years, several U.S. candy companies—including the makers of Life Savers and Star Brite mints—have moved factories to other countries to escape the effects of the sugar quota. Partly as a result of the sugar quota, total employment in U.S. chocolate and candy firms that use sugar as an input declined by one-third between 1996 and 2014.

MyEconLab Concept Check

Solved Problem 7.4

MyEconLab Interactive Animation

Measuring the Economic Effect of a Quota

Suppose that the United States currently both produces and imports apples. The U.S. government then decides to restrict international trade in apples by imposing a quota that allows imports of only 4 million boxes of apples into the United States each year. The figure shows the results of imposing the quota.

Fill in the following table, using the prices, quantities, and letters in the figure:

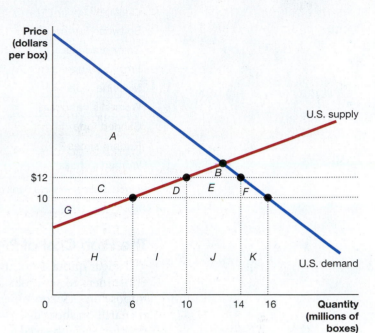

	Without Quota	With Quota
World price of apples		
U.S. price of apples		
Quantity supplied by U.S. firms		
Quantity demanded by U.S. consumers		
Quantity imported		
Area of consumer surplus		
Area of domestic producer surplus		
Area of deadweight loss		

Solving the Problem

Step 1: Review the chapter material. This problem is about measuring the economic effects of a quota, so you may want to review the sections "Quotas and Voluntary Export Restraints," which begins on page 229, and "Measuring the Economic Effect of the Sugar Quota," which begins on page 230.

Step 2: Fill in the table. After studying Figure 7.7, you should be able to fill in the table. Remember that consumer surplus is the area below the demand curve and above the market price.

	Without Quota	With Quota
World price of apples	$10	$10
U.S. price of apples	$10	$12
Quantity supplied by U.S. firms	6 million boxes	10 million boxes
Quantity demanded by U.S. consumers	16 million boxes	14 million boxes
Quantity imported	10 million boxes	4 million boxes
Area of consumer surplus	A + B + C + D + E + F	A + B
Area of domestic producer surplus	G	G + C
Area of deadweight loss	No deadweight loss	D + F

Your Turn: For more practice, do related problem 4.12 on pages 244–245 at the end of this chapter.   MyEconLab Study Plan

Table 7.5

Preserving U.S. Jobs with Tariffs and Quotas Is Expensive

Product	Number of Jobs Saved	Cost to Consumers per Year for Each Job Saved
Benzenoid chemicals	216	$1,376,435
Luggage	226	1,285,078
Softwood lumber	605	1,044,271
Dairy products	2,378	685,323
Frozen orange juice	609	635,103
Machine tools	1,556	479,452
Women's handbags	773	263,535
Canned tuna	390	257,640
Rubber shoes	1,701	168,312
Women's shoes	3,702	132,870

Source: Federal Reserve Bank of Dallas, 2002 *Annual Report*, Exhibit 11.

The High Cost of Preserving Jobs with Tariffs and Quotas

The sugar quota is not the only government policy that imposes a high cost on U.S. consumers to save jobs at U.S. firms. Table 7.5 shows the costs tariffs and quotas impose on U.S. consumers per year for each job saved in several industries. Note that the tariff on shoes discussed in the chapter opener costs U.S. consumers $300,000 per year for each job saved for just the two types of shoes listed.

Just as the sugar quota costs jobs in the candy industry, other tariffs and quotas cost jobs outside the industries immediately affected. For example, in 1991, the United States imposed tariffs on flat-panel displays used in laptop computers. The tariff was good news for U.S. producers of these displays but bad news for companies producing laptop computers. Toshiba, Sharp, and Apple all closed their U.S. laptop production facilities and moved production overseas. In fact, whenever one industry receives tariff or quota protection, other domestic industries lose jobs.   MyEconLab Concept Check

How does the Smoot-Hawley Tariff Act of 1930 affect what you pay for your shoes today?

Making the Connection
MyEconLab Video

Smoot-Hawley, the Politics of Tariffs, and the Cost of Protecting a Vanishing Industry

In the 1920s, U.S. farmers faced severe financial hardship. Congress and the president responded to that hardship. As a result of that response, in 2015 many U.S. businesses that import foreign-made shoes into the United States paid tariffs of 35 percent or more on the value of the shoes. Sound illogical? The politics of tariffs can certainly seem to be.

Here is the connection between farmers in the 1920s and shoes today: The 1920s were a period of rapid economic progress in the United States, with the mass production of automobiles, the expansion of electricity use in homes and businesses, improvements in public health, a boom in housing construction, and the development of network radio and talking films. But the incomes of many farmers declined, partly because of increasing agricultural production from foreign competitors. During the 1928 presidential election, Herbert Hoover, the Republican Party candidate, promised that if elected, he would aid farmers by raising tariffs on agriculture goods imported into the United States.

After Hoover won the election, Congress in 1929 considered a new tariff bill. During Congressional negotiations, the number of products on which tariffs would be raised quickly expanded beyond agricultural products, in a process known as *logrolling*.

Logrolling refers to members of Congress promising to support each other's legislation. In this case, a member of Congress from a district with a lot of dairy farms who wanted the tariff on milk increased would seek out a member of Congress from a district with shoe factories and negotiate along these lines: "If you vote to increase tariffs on milk, I'll vote to increase tariffs on shoes." The law Congress finally passed in 1930 is called the *Smoot-Hawley Tariff Act* and raised tariffs to the highest level in U.S. history. As a percentage of the value of imports covered by the law, tariffs reached nearly 60 percent.

The process of logrolling can lead to very detailed and complex tariffs as members of Congress attempt to protect specific firms in their districts from competition from foreign producers. For example, the 2015 tariff on shoes contains hundreds of entries, many aimed at very specific types of shoes. Here are *just a few* of those entries:

Type of Shoe	Tariff
Footwear designed to be worn over, or in lieu of, other footwear as a protection against water, oil, grease, or chemicals or cold or inclement weather	37.5%
Parts of footwear (including uppers whether or not attached to soles other than outer soles); removable insoles, heel cushions and similar articles; gaiters, leggings and similar articles, and parts thereof: Valued not over $3/pair	33.6%
Parts of footwear (including uppers whether or not attached to soles other than outer soles); removable insoles, heel cushions and similar articles; gaiters, leggings and similar articles, and parts thereof: Valued over $3/pair but not over $6.50	63 cents per pair plus 26.2%
Tennis shoes, basketball shoes, gym shoes, training shoes and the like, costing more than $12 per pair	20.0%
Footwear having uppers of which over 90 percent of the external surface area (including any accessories or reinforcements such as those mentioned in note 4(a) to this chapter) is rubber or plastics (except footwear having a foxing or a foxing-like band applied or made on a base or platform of cork)	12.5%
Footwear with open toes or open heels; footwear of the slip-on type, that is held to the foot without the use of laces or buckles or other fasteners, the foregoing except footwear of subheading 6402.99.20 and except footwear having a foxing or a foxing-having outer sole with textile materials having the greatest surface area in contact with the ground, but not taken into account under the terms of additional U.S. note 5 to this chapter	12.5%
House slippers valued not over $3 per pair having outer soles with textile materials having the greatest surface area in contact with the ground, but not taken into account under the terms of additional U.S. note 5 to this chapter	12.5%
Footwear having uppers of which over 90 percent of the external surface area (including any accessories or reinforcements such as those mentioned in note 4(a) to this chapter) is rubber or plastics (except footwear having a foxing or a foxing-like band applied or made on a base or platform of wood)	8.0%
Footwear with outer soles of rubber, plastics, leather or composition leather and uppers of textile materials: Having soles (or mid-soles, if any) of rubber or plastics which are affixed to the upper exclusively with an adhesive (any mid-soles also being affixed exclusively to one another and to the sole with an adhesive); the foregoing except footwear having uppers of vegetable fibers and having outer soles with textile materials having the greatest surface area in contact with the ground, but not taken into account under the terms of additional U.S. note 5 to this chapter	7.5%
Sandals and similar footwear of plastics, produced in one piece by molding	3.0%

Are you having trouble understanding the entries in the table? Imagine being the owner of a small business in 2015 who wants to import shoes. You will have a lot of difficulty just determining what tariff to pay, given the complexity of the law.

Canada, the largest trading partner of the United States, reacted to passage of the Smoot-Hawley Tariff by enacting large increases in tariffs on U.S. imports. Other countries raised tariffs as well, resulting in a *trade war* that led to a sharp decrease in global trade and helped increase the severity of the Great Depression of the 1930s.

Since the end of World War II in 1945, the United States and most other countries have engaged in rounds of negotiations that have greatly reduced tariffs on most goods. But the United States continues to impose high tariffs on shoes 85 years after the passage of Smoot-Hawley. During that time, employment in the U.S. shoe industry has fallen from 275,000 workers to fewer than 15,000, as more than 98 percent of the shoes sold in the United States are imported. As Table 7.5 on page 232 shows, the cost to U.S. consumers of preserving those remaining jobs is very high. The total cost to U.S. consumers from higher shoe prices due to the tariff is more than $2 billion per year. The fact that high tariffs on shoes have survived despite few shoes being manufactured in the United States anymore demonstrates how difficult it can sometimes be to remove government protection for an industry once the protection has been enacted.

One way to avoid logrolling when passing tariff laws is for Congress to give the president *fast-track authority* when negotiating trade agreements with other countries. Under fast-track authority, once the president has finished negotiating an agreement with other countries, Congress can either pass or reject the agreement but cannot change any of its provisions. With fast-track authority, the vote trading that occurred during the Congressional deliberations over Smoot-Hawley would not be possible. In 2015, only after a long political struggle was President Obama able to get Congress to grant him the fast-track authority he needed to finish negotiating the Trans-Pacific Partnership trade agreement.

Sources: U.S. International Trade Commission, *Harmonized Tariff Schedule of the United States (2015)*, http://hts.usitc.gov; Carl Hulse and Gardiner Harris, "House Republicans and White House Try to Revive Trade Bill Stalled by Democrats," *New York Times*, June 15, 2015; and Blake W. Krueger, "A Shoe Tariff With a Big Footprint," *Wall Street Journal*, November 22, 2012.

MyEconLab Study Plan   **Your Turn:** Test your understanding by doing related problems 4.14 and 4.15 on page 245 at the end of this chapter.

Gains from Unilateral Elimination of Tariffs and Quotas

Some politicians argue that eliminating U.S. tariffs and quotas would help the U.S. economy only if other countries eliminated their tariffs and quotas in exchange. It is easier to gain political support for reducing or eliminating tariffs or quotas if it is done as part of an agreement with other countries that involves their eliminating some of their tariffs or quotas. But as the example of the sugar quota shows, *the U.S. economy would experience a gain in economic surplus from the elimination of tariffs and quotas even if other countries did not reduce their tariffs and quotas.*   MyEconLab Concept Check

Other Barriers to Trade

In addition to tariffs and quotas, governments sometimes erect other barriers to trade. For example, all governments require that imports meet certain health and safety requirements. Sometimes, however, governments use these requirements to shield domestic firms from foreign competition. For example, a government may impose stricter health and safety requirements on imported goods than on goods produced by domestic firms.

Many governments also restrict imports of certain products on national security grounds. The argument is that in time of war, a country should not be dependent on imports of critical war materials. Once again, these restrictions are sometimes used more to protect domestic companies from competition than to protect national security. For example, for years, the U.S. government would buy military uniforms only from U.S. manufacturers, even though uniforms are not a critical war material. The Defense Department gives each army recruit a voucher to purchase a pair of athletic shoes for training. New Balance has attempted to force the Defense Department to require the vouchers be used only to purchase U.S.-made shoes. Many officials in the Defense Department didn't see soldiers training in foreign-made running shoes as a threat to national security.

MyEconLab Concept Check   MyEconLab Study Plan

 ## 7.5 The Arguments over Trade Policies and Globalization

LEARNING OBJECTIVE: Evaluate the arguments over trade policies and globalization.

The argument over whether the U.S. government should regulate international trade has continued since the founding of the country. One particularly controversial attempt to restrict trade took place during the Great Depression of the 1930s. At that time, the United States and other countries attempted to help domestic firms by raising tariffs on imports. The United States started the process by passing the Smoot-Hawley Tariff in 1930, which raised average tariff rates to nearly 60 percent. As other countries retaliated by raising their tariffs, international trade collapsed.

By the end of World War II in 1945, government officials in the United States and Europe were looking for a way to reduce tariffs and revive international trade. To help achieve this goal, they set up the General Agreement on Tariffs and Trade (GATT) in 1948. Countries that joined the GATT agreed not to impose new tariffs or import quotas. In addition, a series of *multilateral negotiations*, called *trade rounds*, took place, in which countries agreed to reduce tariffs from the very high levels of the 1930s.

In the 1940s, most international trade was in goods, and the GATT agreement covered only goods. In the following decades, trade in services and products incorporating *intellectual property*, such as software programs and movies, grew in importance. Many GATT members pressed for a new agreement that would cover services and intellectual property, as well as goods. A new agreement was negotiated, and in January 1995, the GATT was replaced by the **World Trade Organization (WTO)**, headquartered in Geneva, Switzerland. More than 150 countries are currently members of the WTO.

World Trade Organization (WTO) An international organization that oversees international trade agreements.

Why Do Some People Oppose the World Trade Organization?

During the years immediately after World War II, many low-income, or developing, countries enacted high tariffs and restricted investment by foreign companies. When these policies failed to produce much economic growth, many of these countries decided during the 1980s to become more open to foreign trade and investment. This process became known as **globalization**. Most developing countries joined the WTO and began to follow its policies.

During the 1990s, opposition to globalization began to increase. Over the years, protests, which have sometimes turned violent, have occurred in cities hosting WTO meetings. Why would attempts to reduce trade barriers with the objective of increasing income around the world cause such a furious reaction? The opposition to the WTO comes from three sources. First, some opponents are specifically against the globalization process that began in the 1980s and became widespread in the 1990s. Second, other opponents have the same motivation as the supporters of tariffs in the 1930s—to erect trade barriers to protect domestic firms from foreign competition. Third, some critics of the WTO support globalization in principle but believe that the WTO favors the interests of the high-income countries at the expense of the low-income countries. Let's look more closely at the sources of opposition to the WTO.

Globalization The process of countries becoming more open to foreign trade and investment.

Anti-Globalization Many of those who protest at WTO meetings distrust globalization. Some believe that free trade and foreign investment destroy the distinctive cultures of many countries. As developing countries began to open their economies to imports from the United States and other high-income countries, the imports of food, clothing, movies, and other goods began to replace the equivalent local products. So, a teenager in Thailand might be sitting in a McDonald's restaurant, wearing Levi's jeans and a Ralph Lauren shirt, listening to a song by Lady Gaga on his iPhone, before downloading *Star Wars: The Force Awakens* to his iPad. Globalization has increased the variety of products available to consumers in developing countries, but some people argue that this is too high a price to pay for what they see as damage to local cultures.

Globalization has also allowed multinational corporations to relocate factories from high-income countries to low-income countries. These new factories in Indonesia, Malaysia, Pakistan, and other countries pay much lower wages than are paid in the United States, Europe, and Japan and often do not meet the environmental or safety regulations that are imposed in high-income countries. Some factories use child labor, which is illegal in high-income countries. Some people have argued that firms with factories in developing countries should pay workers wages as high as those paid in high-income countries. They also believe these firms should abide by the health, safety, and environmental regulations that exist in the high-income countries.

The governments of most developing countries have resisted these proposals. They argue that when the currently rich countries were poor, they also lacked environmental or safety standards, and their workers were paid low wages. They argue that it is easier for rich countries to afford high wages and environmental and safety regulations than it is for poor countries. They also point out that many jobs that seem to have very low wages based on the standards of high-income countries are often better than the alternatives available to workers in low-income countries.

"Old-Fashioned" Protectionism

Protectionism The use of trade barriers to shield domestic firms from foreign competition.

The anti-globalization argument against free trade and the WTO is relatively new. Another argument against free trade, called *protectionism*, has been around for centuries. **Protectionism** is the use of trade barriers to shield domestic firms from foreign competition. For as long as international trade has existed, governments have attempted to restrict it to protect domestic firms. As we saw with the analysis of the sugar quota, protectionism causes losses to consumers and eliminates jobs in the domestic industries that buy the protected product. In addition, by reducing the ability of countries to produce according to comparative advantage, protectionism reduces incomes.

Why, then, does protectionism attract support? Protectionism is usually justified on the basis of one of the following arguments:

- **Saving jobs.** Supporters of protectionism argue that free trade reduces employment by driving domestic firms out of business. It is true that when more-efficient foreign firms drive less-efficient domestic firms out of business, jobs are lost, but jobs are also lost when more-efficient domestic firms drive less-efficient domestic firms out of business. These job losses are rarely permanent. In the U.S. economy, jobs are lost and new jobs are created continually. No economic study has ever found a long-term connection between the total number of jobs available and the level of tariff protection for domestic industries. In addition, trade restrictions destroy jobs in some industries at the same time that they preserve jobs in others. The U.S. sugar quota may have saved jobs in the U.S. sugar industry, but it has also destroyed jobs in the U.S. candy industry.

- **Protecting high wages.** Some people worry that firms in high-income countries will have to start paying much lower wages to compete with firms in developing countries. This fear is misplaced, however, because free trade actually raises living standards by increasing economic efficiency. When a country practices protectionism and produces goods and services it could obtain more inexpensively from other countries, it reduces its standard of living. The United States could ban imports of coffee and begin growing it domestically. But doing so would entail a very high opportunity cost because coffee could only be grown in the continental United States in greenhouses and would require large amounts of labor and equipment. The coffee would have to sell for a very high price to cover these costs. Suppose the United States did ban coffee imports: Eliminating the ban at some future time would eliminate the jobs of U.S. coffee workers, but the standard of living in the United States would rise as coffee prices declined and labor, machinery, and other resources were moved out of coffee production and into production of goods and services for which the United States has a comparative advantage.

- **Protecting infant industries.** It is possible that firms in a country may have a comparative advantage in producing a good, but because the country begins production of the good later than other countries, its firms initially have higher costs. In producing some goods and services, substantial "learning by doing" occurs. As workers and firms produce more of the good or service, they gain experience and become more productive. Over time, these firms will have lower costs and can charge lower prices. As the firms in the "infant industry" gain experience, they will be able to compete successfully with foreign producers. Under free trade, however, they may not get a chance. The established foreign producers can sell the product at a lower price and drive domestic producers out of business before they gain enough experience to compete. To economists, the infant industry argument is the most persuasive of the protectionist arguments. It has a significant drawback, however. Tariffs eliminate the need for firms in an infant industry to become productive enough to compete with foreign firms. After World War II, the governments of many developing countries used the infant industry argument to justify high tariff rates. Unfortunately, most of their infant industries never grew up, and they continued for years as inefficient drains on their economies.

- **Protecting national security.** A country will typically not want to rely on other countries for goods that are critical to its military defense. For example, the United States would probably not want to import all its jet fighter engines from China. The definition of which goods are critical to military defense is a slippery one, however. In fact, it is rare for an industry to ask for protection without raising the issue of national security, even if its products have mainly nonmilitary uses.

MyEconLab Concept Check

Making the Connection
MyEconLab Video

Protecting Consumer Health or Protecting U.S. Firms from Competition?

The World Trade Organization and other international agreements limit the use of tariffs and quotas. So to protect firms from foreign competition, governments sometimes regulate imports by claiming that they pose a threat to consumer health or safety.

Is imported catfish safe for U.S. consumers to eat, or does it contain bacteria and dangerous chemicals? The U.S. states that produce the most catfish are Alabama, Arkansas, Mississippi, and Texas. In 2008, members of Congress from those states pushed through legislation setting up a catfish inspection office in the U.S. Department of Agriculture. By 2014, the office had spent $20 million but had not actually inspected any imported catfish. The money had been spent on just setting up offices and paying administrators' salaries. That year, Congress set a deadline for the inspection program to begin.

Vietnam and other countries that export catfish to the United States objected that the real purpose of the inspections was to erect a barrier to trade. Those governments argued that the inspections would violate the commitments of the United States under the World Trade Organization not to erect barriers to trade. Further complicating the situation for the U.S. government was the fact that these countries were in talks with the United States about the Trans-Pacific Partnership, an agreement to reduce trade barriers among countries in the Pacific that we discussed earlier in this chapter. A trade war over catfish could interfere with completing those talks.

A study by the U.S. Government Accountability Office indicated that the health risk to U.S. consumers from imported catfish was very low, even without the proposed inspections. Some members of Congress from states that do not produce catfish also

Are restrictions on catfish imports protecting the health of U.S. consumers or the interests of U.S. producers?

argued that new inspections of imported catfish were unnecessary and would result in U.S. consumers paying higher prices.

Congress and the president are often caught in a policy dilemma over imports. Firms want to reduce or eliminate sales lost to imports, but imposing trade barriers reduces economic efficiency, lowers incomes, and invites retaliation from foreign governments. Although some imported goods can, in fact, pose threats to the health and safety of U.S. consumers, some health and safety regulations are intended to protect the U.S. firms involved rather than U.S. consumers.

Sources: Ron Nixon, "U.S. Catfish Program Could Stymie Pacific Trade Pact, 10 Nations Say," *New York Times*, June 27, 2014; Bruce Einhorn and Chau Mai, "The Catfish Wars Could Derail U.S.–Asia Trade," businessweek.com, June 30, 2014; and U.S. Government Accountability Office, *Seafood Safety: Responsibility for Inspecting Catfish Should Not Be Assigned to USDA*, GAO 12-411, May 2012.

MyEconLab Study Plan

Your Turn: Test your understanding by doing related problem 5.10 on page 247 at the end of this chapter.

Dumping

In recent years, the United States has extended protection to some domestic industries by using a provision in the WTO agreement that allows governments to impose tariffs in the case of *dumping*. **Dumping** is selling a product for a price below its cost of production. Using tariffs to offset the effects of dumping is controversial despite being allowed under the WTO agreement.

Dumping Selling a product for a price below its cost of production.

In practice, it is difficult to determine whether foreign companies are dumping goods because the true production costs of a good are not easy for governments to calculate. As a result, the WTO allows countries to determine that dumping has occurred if a product is exported for a lower price than it sells for on the home market. There is a problem with this approach, however. Often there are good business reasons for a firm to sell a product for different prices to different consumers. For example, the airlines charge business travelers higher ticket prices than leisure travelers. Firms also use "loss leaders"—products that are sold below cost, or even given away free—when introducing a new product or, in the case of retailing, to attract customers who will also buy full-price products. For example, during the holiday season, Walmart sometimes offers toys at prices below what it pays to buy them from manufacturers. It's unclear why these normal business practices should be unacceptable when used in international trade.

MyEconLab Concept Check

Positive versus Normative Analysis (Once Again)

Economists emphasize the burden on the economy imposed by tariffs, quotas, and other government restrictions on free trade. Does it follow that these interferences are bad? Remember that positive analysis concerns what *is*, while normative analysis concerns what *ought to be*. Measuring the effect of the sugar quota on the U.S. economy is an example of positive analysis. Asserting that the sugar quota is bad public policy and should be eliminated is normative analysis. The sugar quota—like all other interferences with trade—makes some people better off and some people worse off, and it reduces total income and consumption. Whether increasing the profits of U.S. sugar companies and the number of workers they employ justifies the costs imposed on consumers and the reduction in economic efficiency is a normative question.

Most economists do not support interferences with trade, such as the sugar quota. Few people become economists if they don't believe that markets should be as free as possible. But the opposite view is certainly intellectually respectable. It is possible for someone to understand the costs of tariffs and quotas but still believe that tariffs and quotas are a good idea, perhaps because he or she believes unrestricted free trade would cause too much disruption to the economy.

The success of industries in getting the government to erect barriers to foreign competition depends partly on some members of the public knowing the costs of trade barriers but supporting them anyway. However, two other factors are also at work:

1. The costs tariffs and quotas impose on consumers are large in total but relatively small per person. For example, the sugar quota imposes a total burden of $3.26 billion per year on consumers. Spread across 320 million Americans, the burden is only about $10 per person—too little for most people to worry about, even if they know the burden exists.

2. The jobs lost to foreign competition are easy to identify, but the jobs created by foreign trade are less easy to identify.

In other words, the industries that benefit from tariffs and quotas benefit a lot—for example, the sugar quota increases the profits of U.S. sugar producers by $1.71 billion per year—while each consumer loses relatively little. This concentration of benefits and widely spread burdens makes it easy to understand why members of Congress receive strong pressure from some industries to enact tariffs and quotas and relatively little pressure from the general public to reduce them.   MyEconLab Concept Check   MyEconLab Study Plan

Continued from page 215

Economics in Your Life

Did You Know There Is a Tariff on Running Shoes?

At the beginning of the chapter, we asked you to consider why the federal government has imposed a tariff on shoes, even though there are very few shoe factories remaining in the United States. We also asked why relatively few people have heard of this tariff. In the chapter, we saw that trade restrictions tend to preserve relatively few jobs in the protected industries, while they lead to job losses in other industries and cost consumers billions of dollars per year in higher prices. However, we have also seen that *per person*, the burden of specific trade restrictions can be small. For example, the tariff on shoes might cause you to pay $20 dollars more for a $100 pair of running shoes. The average person buys only one pair of running shoes per year, and few people will take the trouble of writing a letter to their member of Congress or otherwise express their views to try to save $20 per year. In fact, few people will even spend the time to become aware that a specific trade restriction exists. So, if you had never heard of the shoe tariff before you read this chapter, you are certainly not alone.

Conclusion

There are few issues economists agree upon more than the economic benefits of free trade. However, there are few political issues as controversial as government policy toward trade. Many people who would be reluctant to see the government interfere with domestic trade are quite willing to see it interfere with international trade. The damage high tariffs inflicted on the world economy during the 1930s shows what can happen when governments around the world abandon free trade. Whether future episodes of that type can be avoided is by no means certain.

Visit MyEconLab for a news article and analysis related to the concepts in this chapter.

CHAPTER SUMMARY AND PROBLEMS

Key Terms

Absolute advantage, p. 220

Autarky, p. 221

Comparative advantage, p. 219

Dumping, p. 238

Exports, p. 216

External economies, p. 226

Free trade, p. 226

Globalization, p. 235

Imports, p. 216

Opportunity cost, p. 219

Protectionism, p. 236

Quota, p. 229

Tariff, p. 216

Terms of trade, p. 221

Voluntary export restraint (VER), p. 229

World Trade Organization (WTO), p. 235

7.1 **The United States in the International Economy, pages 216–219**
LEARNING OBJECTIVE: Discuss the role of international trade in the U.S. economy.

Summary

International trade has been increasing in recent decades, in part because of reductions in *tariffs* and other barriers to trade. A **tariff** is a tax imposed by a government on imports. The quantity of goods and services the United States imports and exports has been continually increasing. **Imports** are goods and services bought domestically but produced in other countries. **Exports** are goods and services produced domestically and sold to other countries. Today, the United States is the second-leading exporting country in the world behind China, and about 20 percent of U.S. manufacturing jobs depend on exports.

 Visit **www.myeconlab.com** to complete these exercises online and get instant feedback.

Review Questions

1.1 Briefly explain whether the value of U.S. exports is typically larger or smaller than the value of U.S. imports.

1.2 Are imports and exports now a smaller or larger fraction of GDP than they were 40 years ago?

1.3 Briefly explain whether you agree with the following statement: "International trade is more important to the U.S. economy than it is to most other economies."

Problems and Applications

1.4 If the United States were to stop trading goods and services with other countries, which U.S. industries would be likely to see their sales decline the most? Briefly explain.

1.5 Briefly explain whether you agree with the following statement: "Japan has always been much more heavily involved in international trade than are most other nations. In fact, today Japan exports a larger fraction of its GDP than Germany, Great Britain, or the United States."

1.6 Why might a smaller country, such as the Netherlands, be more likely to import and export larger fractions of its GDP than would a larger country, such as China or the United States?

1.7 (Related to the Chapter Opener on page 215 and the Making the Connection on page 217) New Balance manufactures shoes in the United States, so you might expect that the firm would benefit from a tariff on shoes. Yet New Balance did not actively oppose the Obama administration's attempts to eliminate the shoe tariff imposed on countries that would be part of the Trans-Pacific Partnership. Briefly explain New Balance's position.

7.2 **Comparative Advantage in International Trade, pages 219–221**
LEARNING OBJECTIVE: Explain the difference between comparative advantage and absolute advantage in international trade.

Summary

Comparative advantage is the ability of an individual, a firm, or a country to produce a good or service at the lowest **opportunity cost**. **Absolute advantage** is the ability to produce more of a good or service than competitors when using the same amount of resources. Countries trade on the basis of comparative advantage, not on the basis of absolute advantage.

 Visit **www.myeconlab.com** to complete these exercises online and get instant feedback.

Review Questions

2.1 What is the difference between absolute advantage and comparative advantage? Will a country always be an exporter of a good in the production of which it has an absolute advantage? Briefly explain.

2.2 A World Trade Organization (WTO) publication calls comparative advantage "arguably the single most powerful insight in economics." What is comparative advantage? What makes it such a powerful insight?

Source: World Trade Organization, "Understanding the WTO," www.wto.org/english/thewto_e/whatis_e/tif_e/fact3_e.htm.

Problems and Applications

2.3 In the 2012 Summer Olympic Games, Ashton Eaton (from the United States) won a gold medal in the decathlon, which requires athletes to compete in 10 different track and field events. In one of these events Eaton ran a 100-meter race in 10.35 seconds. In a separate event, Usain Bolt (from Jamaica) won a gold medal and set a world record by running 100 meters in 9.58 seconds.

    a. Which performance—Eaton's or Bolt's—is better explained by the concept of comparative advantage? Briefly explain.

    b. Based on their performance at the 2012 Olympic Games, can we say whether Eaton or Bolt was the better athlete? Briefly explain.

2.4 An article in the *New York Times* quoted an economist as arguing that "global free trade and the European single market … encourage countries to specialize in sectors where they enjoy comparative advantage. Germany's [comparative advantage] is in cars and machine tools." For the author's observation to be correct, must Germany be able to produce more cars and machine tools per hour worked than do France, Italy, the United Kingdom, and Germany's other trading partners? Briefly explain.

Source: Anatole Kaletsky, "In Disguise, a Budget That Britain Needs," *New York Times*, March 24, 2014.

2.5 Briefly explain whether you agree with the following argument: "Unfortunately, Bolivia does not have a comparative advantage with respect to the United States in the production of any good or service." (*Hint:* You do not need any specific information about the economies of Bolivia or the United States to be able to answer this question.)

2.6 The following table shows the hourly output per worker for Greece and Italy measured as quarts of olive oil and pounds of pasta.

	Output per Hour of Work	
	Olive Oil	**Pasta**
Greece	4	2
Italy	4	8

Calculate the opportunity cost of producing olive oil and pasta in both Greece and Italy.

2.7 Using the numbers in the table, explain which country has a comparative advantage in producing smartwatches.

	Output per Hour of Work	
	Smartwatches	**Fitness Bracelets**
Switzerland	8	10
Canada	5	3

2.8 Patrick J. Buchanan, a former presidential candidate, argued in his book on the global economy that there is a flaw in David Ricardo's theory of comparative advantage:

> Classical free trade theory fails the test of common sense. According to Ricardo's law of comparative advantage … if America makes better computers and textiles than China does, but our advantage in computers is greater than our advantage in textiles, we should (1) focus on computers, (2) let China make textiles, and (3) trade U.S. computers for Chinese textiles…. The doctrine begs a question. If Americans are more efficient than Chinese in making clothes … why surrender the more efficient American industry? Why shift to a reliance on a Chinese textile industry that will take years to catch up to where American factories are today?

Do you agree with Buchanan's argument? Briefly explain.

Source: Patrick J. Buchanan, *The Great Betrayal: How American Sovereignty and Social Justice Are Being Sacrificed to the Gods of the Global Economy*, Boston: Little, Brown & Company, 1998, p. 66.

2.9 While running for president, Barack Obama made the following statement: "Well, look, people don't want a cheaper T-shirt if they're losing a job in the process." What did Obama mean by the phrase "losing a job in the process"? Using the economic concept of comparative advantage, explain under what circumstances it would make sense for the United States to produce all of the T-shirts purchased in the United States. Do you agree with President Obama's statement? Briefly explain.

Source: James Pethokoukis, "Democratic Debate Spawns Weird Economics," *U.S. News & World Report*, August 8, 2007.

7.3   How Countries Gain from International Trade, pages 221–226

LEARNING OBJECTIVE: Explain how countries gain from international trade.

Summary

Autarky is a situation in which a country does not trade with other countries. The **terms of trade** is the ratio at which a country can trade its exports for imports from other countries. When a country specializes in producing goods for which it has a comparative advantage and trades for the other goods it needs, the country will have a higher level of income and consumption. We do not see complete specialization in production for three reasons: (1) Not all goods and services are traded internationally, (2) production of most goods involves increasing opportunity costs, and (3) tastes for products differ across countries. Although the population of a country as a whole benefits from trade, firms—and their workers—that are unable to compete with lower-cost foreign producers lose. Among the main sources of comparative advantage are climate and natural resources, relative abundance of labor and capital, technology, and external economies. **External economies** are reductions in a firm's costs that result from an increase in the size of an industry. A country may develop a comparative advantage in the production of a good, and then as time passes and circumstances change, the country may lose its comparative advantage in producing that good and develop a comparative advantage in producing other goods.

MyEconLab Visit **www.myeconlab.com** to complete these exercises online and get instant feedback.

Review Questions

3.1 Briefly explain how international trade increases a country's consumption.

3.2 What is meant by a country specializing in the production of a good? Is it typical for countries to be completely specialized? Briefly explain.

3.3 What are the main sources of comparative advantage?

3.4 Does everyone gain from international trade? If not, explain which groups lose.

Problems and Applications

3.5 **(Related to** Solved Problem 7.3 **on page 222)** The following table shows the hourly output per worker in two industries in Chile and Argentina.

	Output per Hour of Work	
	Hats	**Beer**
Chile	8	6
Argentina	1	2

a. Explain which country has an absolute advantage in the production of hats and which country has an absolute advantage in the production of beer.

b. Explain which country has a comparative advantage in the production of hats and which country has a comparative advantage in the production of beer.

c. Suppose that Chile and Argentina currently do not trade with each other. Each has 1,000 hours of labor to use producing hats and beer, and the countries are currently producing the amounts of each good shown in the following table.

	Hats	**Beer**
Chile	7,200	600
Argentina	600	800

Using this information, give a numerical example of how Chile and Argentina can both gain from trade. Assume that after trading begins, one hat can be exchanged for one barrel of beer.

3.6 **(Related to** Solved Problem 7.3 **on page 222)** A political commentator makes the following statement:

> The idea that international trade should be based on the comparative advantage of each

country is fine for rich countries like the United States and Japan. Rich countries have educated workers and large quantities of machinery and equipment. These advantages allow them to produce every product more efficiently than poor countries can. Poor countries like Kenya and Bolivia have nothing to gain from international trade based on comparative advantage.

Do you agree with this argument? Briefly explain.

3.7 The following data summarize the trade between Canada and the United States in 2013 and 2014.

	Exports from the United States to Canada (billions of U.S. dollars)	**Exports from Canada to the United States (billions of U.S. dollars)**
2013	$300.8	$332.6
2014	312.4	347.8

In each year, the value of Canada's exports to the United States exceeded the value of U.S. exports to Canada. Can we conclude that foreign trade between the two countries benefited Canada more than it benefited the United States? Briefly explain.

Source: U.S. Department of Commerce, Census Bureau, Economic Indicators Division.

3.8 Is free trade likely to benefit a large, populous country more than a small country with fewer people? Briefly explain.

3.9 An article in the *New Yorker* states, "the main burden of trade-related job losses and wage declines has fallen on middle- and lower-income Americans. But … the very people who suffer most from free trade are often, paradoxically, among its biggest beneficiaries." Explain how it is possible that middle- and lower-income Americans are both the biggest losers and at the same time the biggest winners from free trade.

Source: James Surowiecki, "The Free-Trade Paradox," *New Yorker*, May 26, 2008.

3.10 Hal Varian, chief economist at Google, has made the following two observations about international trade.

a. Trade allows a country "to produce more with less."

b. "There is little doubt who wins [from trade] in the long run: consumers."

Briefly explain whether you agree with either or both of these observations.

Source: Hal R. Varian, "The Mixed Bag of Productivity," *New York Times*, October 23, 2003.

3.11 Suppose the graph on the next page shows Tanzania's production possibilities frontier for cashew nuts and mangoes. Assume that the output per hour of work is 8 bushels of cashew nuts or 2 bushels of mangoes and that Tanzania has 1,000 hours of labor. Without trade, Tanzania evenly splits its labor hours between cashews and mangoes and produces and consumes at point A.

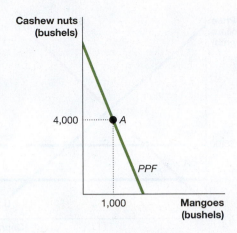

a. Suppose Tanzania opens trade with Kenya, and Kenya's output per hour of work is 1 bushel of cashew nuts or 1 bushel of mangoes. Having the comparative advantage, Tanzania completely specializes in cashew nuts. How many bushels of cashew nuts can Tanzania produce? Denote this point on the graph as point B.

b. Suppose Tanzania keeps 5,000 bushels of cashew nuts and exports the remaining 3,000 bushels. If the terms of trade are 1 bushel of mangoes for 2 bushels of cashew nuts, how many bushels of mangoes will Tanzania get in exchange? Denote on the graph the quantity of cashew nuts and mangoes that Tanzania consumes with trade and label this point as point C. How does point C with trade compare to point A without trade?

c. With trade, is Tanzania producing on its production possibilities frontier? With trade, is Tanzania consuming on its production possibilities frontier?

3.12 **(Related to the** Don't Let This Happen to You **on page 225)** President Barack Obama described a trade agreement reached with the government of Colombia as a "'win–win' for both our countries." Is everyone in both countries likely to win from the agreement? Briefly explain.

Source: Kent Klein, "Obama: Free Trade Agreement a 'Win–Win' for US, Colombia," voanews.com.

3.13 Instagram is a smartphone app that Facebook now owns. According to an article that discusses the climate for software firms in the San Francisco Bay Area, the success of Instagram "is a tale about the culture of the Bay Area tech scene, driven by a tightly woven web of entrepreneurs and investors who nurture one another's projects with money, advice and introductions to the right people." What advantages does being located in the Bay Area give to startup software firms? In what circumstances can software firms located elsewhere overcome these advantages? Are the advantages the Bay Area has likely to persist over time?

Source: Somini Sengupta, Nicole Perlroth, and Jenna Wortham, "Behind Instagram's Success, Networking the Old Way," *New York Times*, April 13, 2012.

7.4 **Government Policies That Restrict International Trade, pages 226–235**

LEARNING OBJECTIVE: Analyze the economic effects of government policies that restrict international trade.

Summary

Free trade is trade between countries without government restrictions. Government policies that interfere with trade usually take the form of *tariffs, quotas,* or *voluntary export restraints.* A tariff is a tax imposed by a government on imports. A **quota** is a numerical limit imposed by a government on the quantity of a good that can be imported into the country. A **voluntary export restraint (VER)** is an agreement negotiated between two countries that places a numerical limit on the quantity of a good that can be imported by one country from the other country. The federal government's sugar quota costs U.S. consumers $3.26 billion per year, or about $1.1 million per year for each job saved in the sugar industry. Saving jobs by using tariffs and quotas is often very expensive.

 Visit **www.myeconlab.com** to complete these exercises online and get instant feedback.

Review Questions

4.1 What is a tariff? What is a quota? Give an example, other than a quota, of a nontariff barrier to trade.

4.2 Who gains and who loses when a country imposes a tariff or a quota on imports of a good?

Problems and Applications

4.3 Political commentator B. Bruce-Briggs once wrote the following in the *Wall Street Journal*: "This is not to say that the case for international free trade is invalid; it is just irrelevant. It is an 'if only everybody … argument…. In the real world almost everybody sees benefits in economic nationalism." What do you think he means by "economic nationalism"? Do you agree that a country benefits from free trade only if every other country also practices free trade? Briefly explain.

Source: B. Bruce-Biggs, "The Coming Overthrow of Free Trade," *Wall Street Journal*, February 24, 1983.

4.4 **(Related to the** Chapter Opener **on page 215)** While running for the 2016 Democratic nomination for president, Vermont Senator Bernie Sanders opposed the Trans-Pacific Partnership in part because he believed that as a result of the agreement, "the U.S. will lose more than 130,000 jobs to Vietnam and Japan alone." Do you agree that reducing barriers to trade reduces the number of jobs available to workers in the United States? Briefly explain.

Source: Bernie Sanders, "Senator Bernie Sanders: The Trans-Pacific Trade (TPP) Agreement Must Be Defeated," http://www.sanders.senate.gov/download/the-trans-pacific-trade-tpp-agreement-must-be-defeated?inline=file.

4.5 The United States produces beef and also imports beef from other countries.
  a. Draw a graph showing the demand and supply of beef in the United States. Assume that the United States can import as much as it wants at the world price of beef without causing the world price of beef to increase. Be sure to indicate on your graph the quantity of beef imported.
  b. Now show on your graph the effect of the United States imposing a tariff on beef. Be sure to indicate on your graph the quantity of beef sold by U.S. producers before and after the tariff is imposed, the quantity of beef imported before and after the tariff, and the price of beef in the United States before and after the tariff.
  c. Discuss who benefits and who loses when the United States imposes a tariff on beef.

4.6 When Congress was considering a bill to impose quotas on imports of textiles, shoes, and other products, the late Milton Friedman, a Nobel Prize–winning economist, made the following comment: "The consumer will be forced to spend several extra dollars to subsidize the producers [of these goods] by one dollar. A straight handout would be far cheaper."
  a. Why would a quota result in consumers paying much more than domestic producers receive? Where do the other dollars go?
  b. What does Friedman mean by a "straight handout"? Why would a straight handout be cheaper than a quota?

Source: Milton Friedman, "Free Trade," *Newsweek Magazine*, August 27, 1970.

4.7 A student makes the following argument:

> Tariffs on imports of foreign goods into the United States will cause the foreign companies to add the amount of the tariff to the prices they charge in the United States for those goods. Instead of putting a tariff on imported goods, we should ban importing them. Banning imported goods is better than putting tariffs on them because U.S. producers benefit from the reduced competition, and U.S. consumers don't have to pay the higher prices caused by tariffs.

Briefly explain whether you agree with the student's reasoning.

4.8 Suppose China decides to pay large subsidies to any Chinese company that exports goods or services to the United States. As a result, these companies are able to sell products in the United States at far below their cost of production. In addition, China decides to bar all imports from the United States. The dollars that the United States pays to import Chinese goods are left in banks in China. Will this strategy raise or lower the standard of living in China? Will it raise or lower the standard of living in the United States? Briefly explain. Be sure to provide a definition of "standard of living" in your answer.

4.9 The following graph shows the effect on consumer surplus, producer surplus, government tariff revenue, and economic surplus of a tariff of $1 per unit on imports of plastic combs into the United States. Use the areas denoted in the graph to answer the following questions.

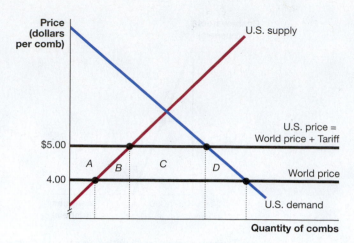

  a. Which area shows the losses to U.S. consumers of buying a smaller quantity of combs than they would have if they could have purchased them at the world price?
  b. Which area shows the losses to U.S. consumers of having to buy combs from U.S. producers who are less efficient than foreign producers?
  c. Which areas show the deadweight loss to the U.S. economy as a result of the tariff on combs?

4.10 The following graph shows the situation after the U.S. government removes a tariff on imports of canned tuna.

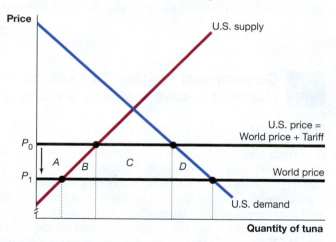

  a. Which areas show the gain in consumer surplus?
  b. Which area shows the loss in producer surplus?
  c. Which area shows the loss in government tariff revenue?
  d. Which areas show the gain in economic surplus?

4.11 According to an editorial in the *Washington Post*, "Sugar protectionism is a burden on consumers and a job-killer."
  a. In what sense does the United States practice "sugar protectionism"?
  b. In what way is sugar protectionism a burden on consumers? In what way is it a job-killer?
  c. If sugar protectionism has the bad effects stated in the editorial, why don't Congress and the president eliminate it?

Source: "Sourball," *Washington Post*, March 22, 2010.

4.12 **(Related to Solved Problem 7.4 on page 231)** Suppose that the United States currently both produces kumquats and imports them. The U.S. government then decides to restrict international trade in kumquats by imposing a quota that allows imports of only 6 million pounds of kumquats into the United States each year. The figure shows the results of imposing the quota.

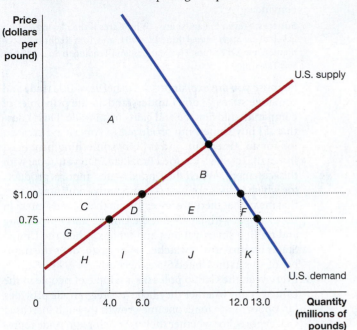

Fill in the table below using the letters in the figure:

	Without Quota	With Quota
World price of kumquats		
U.S. price of kumquats		
Quantity supplied by U.S. firms		
Quantity demanded		
Quantity imported		
Area of consumer surplus		
Area of domestic producer surplus		
Area of deadweight loss		

4.13 Suppose the government is considering imposing either a tariff or a quota on canned peaches. Assume that the proposed quota has the same effect on the U.S. price of canned peaches as the proposed tariff. Use the graph to answer the following questions.

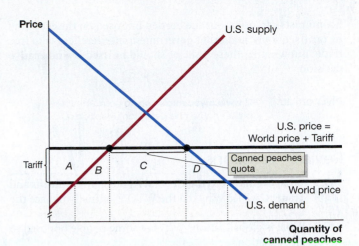

a. If the government imposes a tariff, which area shows the government tariff revenue?

b. If the government imposes a quota, which area shows the gain to foreign producers of canned peaches?

c. As a consumer of peaches, would you prefer the government impose the tariff or the quota? Briefly explain.

4.14 (Related to the Making the Connection on page 232) An economic analysis of a proposal to impose a quota on steel imports into the United States indicated that the quota would save 3,700 jobs in the steel industry but cost about 35,000 jobs in other U.S. industries. Why would a quota on steel imports cause employment to decline in other industries? Which other industries is a steel quota likely to affect?

Source: Douglas A. Irwin, *Free Trade Under Fire*, Princeton, NJ: Princeton University Press, 2002, p. 82.

4.15 (Related to the Making the Connection on page 232) For several years, the United States imposed a tariff on tire imports. According to an analysis by economists Gary Clyde Hufbauer and Sean Lowry of the Petersen Institute, of the additional $1.1 billion consumers spent on tires as a result of the tariff on Chinese tires, the workers whose jobs were saved in the U.S. tire industry received only about $48 million in wages. Wouldn't it have been cheaper for the federal government to have raised taxes on U.S. consumers and given the money to tire workers rather than to have imposed a tariff? If so, why didn't the federal government adopt this alternative policy?

Source: Gary Clyde Hufbauer and Sean Lowry, "US Tire Tariffs: Saving Few Jobs at High Cost," Peterson Institute for International Economics, Policy Brief Number PB12-9, April 2012.

7.5 | ## The Arguments over Trade Policies and Globalization, pages 235–239
LEARNING OBJECTIVE: Evaluate the arguments over trade policies and globalization.

Summary

The **World Trade Organization (WTO)** is an international organization that enforces trade agreements among members. The WTO has promoted **globalization**, the process of countries becoming more open to foreign trade and investment. Some critics of the WTO argue that globalization has damaged local cultures around the world. Other critics oppose the WTO because they believe in **protectionism**, which is the use of trade barriers to shield domestic firms from foreign competition. The WTO allows countries to use tariffs in cases of **dumping**, when an imported product is sold for a price below its cost of production.

Economists can point out the burden imposed on the economy by tariffs, quotas, and other government interferences with free trade. But whether these policies should be used is a normative decision.

MyEconLab Visit **www.myeconlab.com** to complete these exercises online and get instant feedback.

Review Questions

5.1 What events led to the General Agreement on Tariffs and Trade (GATT)? Why did the WTO eventually replace the GATT?

5.2 What is globalization? Why are some people opposed to globalization?

5.3 What is protectionism? Who benefits and who loses from protectionist policies? What are the main arguments people use to justify protectionism?

5.4 What is dumping? Who benefits and who loses from dumping? What problems arise when anti-dumping laws are implemented?

Problems and Applications

5.5 In 2015, several U.S. paper manufacturers asked the federal government to impose tariffs on paper imported from China, Indonesia, Brazil, Portugal, and Australia. According to an article in the *Wall Street Journal*, firms in these countries were accused of "dumping certain types of uncoated paper on the U.S. market, including that used for such things as computer printers, book publishing, junk mail and envelopes." What is "dumping"? If the U.S. firms succeed in having tariffs imposed on imports of paper, briefly explain who will gain and who will lose.

Source: James R. Hagerty, "The Next Trade Fight: Office Paper," *Wall Street Journal*, January 21, 2015.

5.6 Steven Landsburg, an economist at the University of Rochester, wrote the following in an article in the *Wall Street Journal*:

> Free trade is not only about the right of American consumers to buy at the cheapest possible price; it's also about the right of foreign producers to earn a living. Steelworkers in West Virginia struggle hard to make ends meet. So do steelworkers in South Korea. To protect one at the expense of the other, solely because of where they happened to be born, is a moral outrage.

How does the U.S. government protect steelworkers in West Virginia at the expense of steelworkers in South Korea? Is Landsburg making a positive statement or a normative statement? A few days later, Tom Redburn published an article disagreeing with Landsburg. Redburn argued that caring about the welfare of people in the United States more than about the welfare of people in other countries isn't "some evil character flaw." According to Redburn, "A society that ignores the consequences of economic disruption on those among its citizens who come out at the short end of the stick is not only

heartless,it also undermines its own cohesion and adaptability."

Which of the two arguments do you find most convincing?

Sources: Steven E. Landsburg, "Who Cares if the Playing Field Is Level?" *Wall Street Journal*, June 13, 2001; and Tom Redburn, "Economic View: Of Politics, Free Markets, and Tending to Society," *New York Times*, June 17, 2001.

5.7 Suppose you are explaining the benefits of free trade and someone states, "I don't understand all the principles of comparative advantage and gains from trade. I just know that if I buy something produced in America, I create a job for an American, and if I buy something produced in Brazil, I create a job for a Brazilian." Do you agree with this statement? When the United States imports products for which it does not have a comparative advantage, does that mean that there are fewer jobs in the United States? In the example with Japan and the United States producing and trading smartwatches and tablets, when the United States imports smartwatches from Japan, does the number of jobs in the United States decline?

5.8 Every year, the Gallup poll asks a sample of people in the United States whether they believe foreign trade provides "an opportunity for economic growth through increased U.S. exports," or whether they believe foreign trade represents "a threat to the economy from foreign imports." The table shows the responses for two years:

| | View of Foreign Trade | | |
Year	Favorable to Foreign Trade	Unfavorable	State of the U.S. Economy
2008	41%	52%	Deep economic recession
2015	58%	33%	Economic expansion

a. Do you believe that foreign trade helps or hurts the economy? (Be sure to define what you mean by "helps" or "hurts.")

b. Why might the general public's opinion of foreign trade be substantially different during an economic recession, when production and employment are falling, than during an economic expansion, when production and employment are increasing?

c. Typically polls show that people in the United States under 30 years of age have a more favorable opinion of foreign trade than do people age 65 and over. Why might younger people have a more favorable view of foreign trade than older people?

Source: Gallup Poll, February 8–11, 2015, http://www.gallup.com/poll/181886/majority-opportunity-foreign-trade.aspx.

5.9 At one time, Eastman Kodak was the world's largest producer of photographic film, employing nearly 145,000 workers worldwide, including thousands at its headquarters in Rochester, New York. The firm eventually laid off most of those workers because its sales declined as it failed to adjust to digital photography as quickly as many of its foreign competitors. A member of Congress from Rochester described the many new firms that were now located in buildings that were formerly owned by Kodak.

A *New York Times* columnist concluded, "Which, of course, is precisely the way globalization is supposed to work." Briefly explain what the columnist meant. Do you agree with his conclusion? Does the outcome in Rochester show that globalization is good? Briefly explain.

Source: Joe Nocera, "Don't Blame Nafta," *New York Times*, January 23, 2015.

5.10 **(Related to the** Making the Connection **on page 237)** According to an opinion column in the *New York Times*, because of attempts to make it more difficult to import catfish into the United States, during 2015 many Vietnamese businesses that export catfish shifted from exporting to the United States to exporting to China. Briefly explain who gained and who lost as a result of this adjustment by Vietnamese businesses resulting from U.S. trade restrictions.

Source: Roger Cohen, "Of Catfish Wars and Shooting Wars," *New York Times*, March 26, 2015.

GDP: Measuring Total Production and Income

Chapter Outline and Learning Objectives

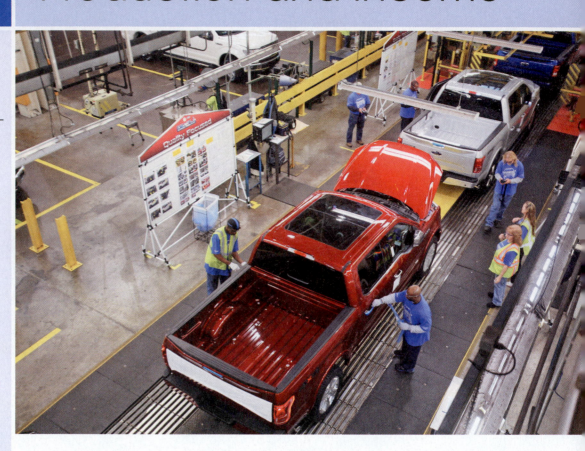

Ford Motor Company Rides the Business Cycle

In the more than 100 years that the Ford Motor Company has been in business, its experiences have often mirrored those of the U.S. economy. So, it was no surprise that in 2008, with the U.S. economy suffering from its worst downturn since the 1930s, sales of Ford cars and trucks plummeted. Overall, the automobile industry, which sold 16.1 million new vehicles in 2007, saw sales tumble to 10.4 million in 2009. Although Ford was hit hard, General Motors and Chrysler, Ford's two great American rivals, were even worse off, and both declared bankruptcy. Those firms survived largely because the federal government invested more than $62 billion in them. Ford suffered heavy losses but did not require direct government aid.

In 2015, the economy was several years into its recovery from the downturn, and Ford's sales had risen by more than one-third since their low point in 2009. With these fluctuations in sales, Ford and the automobile industry as a whole were experiencing the effects of the *business cycle*, which refers to alternating periods of economic expansion and recession. Production and employment increase during expansions and decrease during recessions.

Whether the general level of economic activity is increasing is important not just to firms such as Ford but also to workers wondering whether they will be able to keep their jobs and to college students wondering whether they will be able to find jobs when they graduate. One study found that during the slow recovery from the 2007–2009 recession, only 56 percent of those students who graduated from college in the spring of 2010 had found a job a year later. The average salary of graduates who did find a job was $27,000, down from an average of $30,000 for the classes of 2006 to 2008. What's more, students who graduate during recessions will continue to earn less for as long as 15 years after they graduate. The overall state of the economy is clearly important!

Sources: Vehicle sales data are from the U.S. Bureau of Economic Analysis and the Ford Motor Company; Catherine Rampell, "Many with New College Degrees Find the Job Market Humbling," *New York Times*, May 18, 2011; and Lisa B. Kahn, "The Long-Term Labor Market Consequences of Graduating from College in a Bad Economy," *Labour Economics*, Vol. 17, No. 2, April 2010, pp. 233–246.

Economics in Your Life

What's the Best Country for You to Work In?

Suppose that Ford offers you a job after graduation in 2016. The firm has vacancies in Canada and China, and because you are fluent in Mandarin, you get to choose the country where you will work and live. Gross domestic product (GDP) is a measure of an economy's total production of goods and services, so one factor in your decision is likely to be the growth rate of GDP in each country. Based on the International Monetary Fund's forecasts for 2016, GDP would increase by 2.4 percent in Canada but by 6.8 percent in China. What effect do these two very different growth rates have on your decision to work and live in one country or the other? If China's much higher growth rate does not necessarily lead you to decide to work and live in China, why not? As you read this chapter, try to answer these questions. You can check your answers against those we provide on **page 267** at the end of this chapter.

Microeconomics The study of how households and firms make choices, how they interact in markets, and how the government attempts to influence their choices.

Macroeconomics The study of the economy as a whole, including topics such as inflation, unemployment, and economic growth.

Business cycle Alternating periods of economic expansion and economic recession.

Expansion The period of a business cycle during which total production and total employment are increasing.

Recession The period of a business cycle during which total production and total employment are decreasing.

Economic growth The ability of an economy to produce increasing quantities of goods and services.

Inflation rate The percentage increase in the price level from one year to the next.

As we saw in Chapter 1, we can divide economics into the subfields of microeconomics and macroeconomics. **Microeconomics** is the study of how households and firms make choices, how they interact in markets, and how the government attempts to influence their choices. **Macroeconomics** is the study of the economy as a whole, including topics such as inflation, unemployment, and economic growth. In microeconomic analysis, economists generally study individual markets, such as the market for smartphones. In macroeconomic analysis, economists study factors that affect many markets at the same time.

In the following chapters, we will deal with many key macroeconomic issues, including:

- The **business cycle**, which refers to the alternating periods of expansion and recession that the U.S. economy has experienced since at least the early nineteenth century. A business cycle **expansion** is a period during which total production and total employment are increasing. A business cycle **recession** is a period during which total production and total employment are decreasing. We will discuss the factors that influence the business cycle and policies the government may use to reduce its effects.

- **Economic growth**, which refers to the ability of an economy to produce increasing quantities of goods and services. Economic growth is important because an economy that grows too slowly fails to raise living standards. In some countries in Africa, little economic growth has occurred in the past 50 years, and many people remain in severe poverty. Macroeconomics analyzes both what determines a country's rate of economic growth and the reasons growth rates differ so greatly across countries.

- Fluctuations in the total level of employment in an economy. In the short run, the level of employment is significantly affected by the business cycle, but in the long run, the effects of the business cycle disappear, and other factors determine the level of employment. A related question is why some economies are more successful than others at maintaining high levels of employment over time.

- Fluctuations in the **inflation rate**, which is the percentage increase in the average level of prices from one year to the next. Like employment, inflation is affected both by the business cycle and by long-run factors.

- Linkages among economies in the form of international trade and international finance.

Macroeconomic analysis provides information that consumers and firms need in order to understand current economic conditions and to help predict future conditions. A family may be reluctant to buy a house if employment in the economy is declining because some family members may be at risk of losing their jobs. Similarly, firms may be willing to invest in building new factories or to undertake major new expenditures on information technology only if they expect future sales to be strong. For example, in 2015, Ford opened two new factories in China and announced that it would spend more than $1 billion to expand an existing factory. Ford was relying on macroeconomic forecasts indicating that the Chinese economy would continue to grow rapidly and that sales of cars in the country would increase from 24 million in 2014 to 32 million in 2020. Macroeconomic analysis can also assist the federal government design policies that help the U.S. economy perform more efficiently.

In this and the following chapters, we begin our study of macroeconomics by considering how best to measure key macroeconomic variables. We start by considering measures of total production and total income in an economy.

8.1 Gross Domestic Product Measures Total Production

LEARNING OBJECTIVE: Explain how total production is measured.

"U.S. GDP Swings to Contraction in First Quarter"

"Canada GDP Posts Surprise Drop in April"

"Brazil GDP Shrinks in First Quarter"

"5 Things You Need to Know about India's GDP Growth"

"China Maintains 7% GDP Growth in Second Quarter"

These headlines are from articles that appeared in the *Wall Street Journal* during 2015. Why is GDP so often the focus of news stories? In this section, we explore what GDP is and how it is measured. We also explore why understanding GDP is important to consumers, firms, and government policymakers.

Measuring Total Production: Gross Domestic Product

Economists use **gross domestic product (GDP)** to measure total production. GDP is the market *value* of all *final* goods and services produced in a country during a period of time, typically one year. In the United States, the Bureau of Economic Analysis (BEA) in the Department of Commerce compiles the data needed to calculate GDP. The BEA issues reports on the GDP every three months. GDP is a central concept in macroeconomics, so we need to consider its definition carefully.

Gross domestic product (GDP) The market value of all final goods and services produced in a country during a period of time, typically one year.

GDP Is Measured Using Market Values, Not Quantities The word *value* is important in the definition of GDP. In microeconomics, we measure production in quantity terms: the number of cars Ford produces, the tons of wheat U.S. farmers grow, or the number of burritos Chipotle sells. When we measure total production in the economy, we can't just add together the quantities of every good and service because the result would be a meaningless jumble. Tons of wheat would be added to gallons of milk, numbers of burritos, and so on. Instead, we measure production by taking the *value*, in dollar terms, of all the goods and services produced.

GDP Includes Only the Market Value of Final Goods In measuring GDP, we include only the value of *final goods and services*. A **final good or service** is one that is purchased by its final user and is not included in the production of any other good or service. Examples of final goods are a hamburger purchased by a consumer and a computer purchased by a business. In contrast, **intermediate goods and services** become part of other goods and services. For example, Ford does not produce tires for its cars and trucks; it buys them from tire companies, such as Goodyear and Michelin. The tires are an *intermediate good*, while a Ford truck is a *final good*. In calculating GDP, we include the value of the Ford truck but not the value of the tire. If we included the value of the tire, we would be *double counting*: The value of the tire would be counted once when the tire company sold it to Ford and a second time when Ford sold the truck, with the tire installed, to a consumer.

Final good or service A good or service purchased by a final user.

Intermediate good or service A good or service that is an input into another good or service, such as a tire on a truck.

GDP Includes Only Current Production GDP includes only production that takes place during the indicated time period. For example, GDP in 2016 includes only the goods and services produced during that year. In particular, GDP does *not* include the value of used goods. If you buy a Blu-ray of *Star Wars: The Force Awakens* from Amazon.com, the purchase is included in GDP. If six months later you resell the Blu-ray on eBay, that transaction is not included in GDP. *MyEconLab* Concept Check

Solved Problem 8.1

Calculating GDP

MyEconLab Interactive Animation

Suppose that a very simple economy produces only four goods and services: eye examinations, pizzas, shoes, and cheese. Assume that all the cheese in this economy is used in the production of pizzas. Use the information in the following table to compute GDP for the year 2017.

Production and Price Statistics for 2017		
Product	(1) Quantity	(2) Price per Unit
Eye examinations	100	$50.00
Pizzas	80	10.00
Shoes	20	100.00
Cheese	80	2.00

Solving the Problem

Step 1: Review the chapter material. This problem is about GDP, so you may want to review the section "Measuring Total Production: Gross Domestic Product," which begins on page 251.

Step 2: Determine which goods and services listed in the table should be included in the calculation of GDP. GDP is the value of all final goods and services. Therefore, we need to calculate the value of the final goods and services listed in the table. Eye examinations, pizzas, and shoes are final goods. Cheese would also be a final good if, for instance, a consumer bought it to use in a meal. However, here we are assuming that restaurants buy all the cheese to use in making pizzas, so the cheese is an intermediate good, and its value is not included in GDP.

Step 3: Calculate the value of the three final goods and services listed in the table. Value is equal to the quantity produced multiplied by the price per unit, so we multiply the numbers in column (1) by the numbers in column (2) to calculate the numbers in column (3).

Product	(1) Quantity	(2) Price per Unit	(3) Value
Eye examinations	100	$50	$5,000
Pizzas	80	10	800
Shoes	20	100	2,000

Step 4: Add the value for each of the three final goods and services to find GDP. GDP = Value of eye examinations produced + Value of pizzas produced + Value of shoes produced = $5,000 + $800 + $2,000 = $7,800.

MyEconLab Study Plan

Your Turn: For more practice, do related problem 1.11 on page 269 at the end of this chapter.

Production, Income, and the Circular-Flow Diagram

When we measure the value of total production in the economy by calculating GDP, we are at the same time measuring the value of total income. To see why the value of total production is equal to the value of total income, consider what happens to the money you spend on a single product. Suppose you buy a pair of New Balance running shoes for $149 at a Foot Locker store. *All* of that $149 must end up as someone's income. New Balance and Foot Locker will receive some of the $149 as profits, workers at New Balance will receive some as wages, the salesperson who sold you the shoes will receive some as salary, the firms that sell components to New Balance will receive some as profits, the workers for those firms will receive some as wages, and so on. Every penny must end up as someone's income. (Note, though, that any sales tax on the shoes will be collected by the store and sent to the government, without ending up as anyone's income.) Therefore, if we add up the values of every good and service sold in the economy, we must get a total that is exactly equal to the value of all the income in the economy.

The circular-flow diagram in Figure 8.1 was introduced in Chapter 2 to illustrate the interaction of firms and households in markets. We use it here to illustrate the flow of spending and money in the economy. Firms sell goods and services to three groups: domestic households, foreign firms and households, and the government. Expenditures by foreign firms and households (shown as "Rest of the World" in the diagram) on domestically produced goods and services are called *exports*. For example, American Airlines sells many tickets to passengers in Europe and Asia. As noted at the bottom of Figure 8.1, we can measure GDP by adding up the total expenditures of these groups on goods and services.

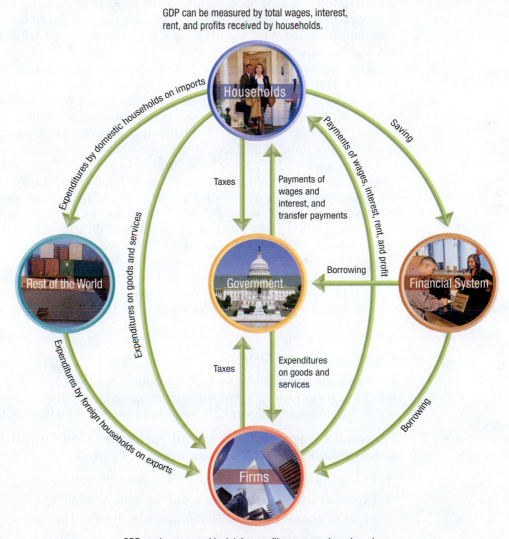

GDP can be measured by total wages, interest, rent, and profits received by households.

GDP can be measured by total expenditures on goods and services by households, firms, government, and the rest of the world.

MyEconLab Animation

Figure 8.1   The Circular Flow and the Measurement of GDP

The circular-flow diagram illustrates the flow of spending and money in the economy. Firms sell goods and services to three groups: domestic households, foreign firms and households, and the government. To produce goods and services, firms use factors of production: labor, capital, natural resources, and entrepreneurship. Households supply the factors of production to firms in exchange for income in the form of wages, interest, profit, and rent. Firms make payments of wages and interest to households in exchange for hiring workers and other factors of production. The sum of wages, interest, rent, and profit is total income in the economy. We can measure GDP as the total income received by households. The diagram also shows that households use their income to purchase goods and services, pay taxes, and save for the future. Firms and the government borrow the funds that flow from households into the financial system. We can measure GDP either by calculating the total value of expenditures on final goods and services or by calculating the value of total income.

Firms use the *factors of production*—labor, capital, natural resources, and entrepreneurial ability—to produce goods and services. Households supply the factors of production to firms in exchange for income. We divide income into four categories: wages, interest, rent, and profit. Firms pay wages to households in exchange for labor services, interest for the use of capital, and rent for natural resources such as land. Profit is the income that remains after a firm has paid wages, interest, and rent. Profit is the return to entrepreneurs and other business owners for bearing the risk of producing and selling goods and services. As Figure 8.1 shows, federal, state, and local governments make payments of wages and interest to households in exchange for hiring workers and other factors of production. Governments also make *transfer payments* to households. **Transfer payments** include Social Security payments to retired and disabled people and unemployment insurance payments to unemployed workers. These payments are not included in GDP because they are not received in exchange for production of a new good or service. The sum of wages, interest, rent, and profit is total income in the economy. As noted at the top of Figure 8.1, we can measure GDP as the total income received by households.

The diagram also allows us to trace the ways that households use their income. Households spend some of their income on goods and services. Some of this spending is on domestically produced goods and services, and some is on *imports*, which are foreign-produced goods and services. Households use some of their income to pay taxes to the government. (Note that firms also pay taxes to the government.) Households also use some of the income they earn to save by making deposits in checking or savings accounts in banks or by buying stocks or bonds. Banks and stock and bond markets make up the *financial system*. The flow of funds from households into the financial system makes it possible for the government and firms to borrow. As we will see, the health of the financial system is vital to an economy. Without the ability to borrow funds through the financial system, firms will have difficulty expanding and adopting new technologies. In fact, no country without a well-developed financial system has been able to sustain high levels of economic growth.

The circular-flow diagram shows that we can measure GDP either by calculating the total value of expenditures on final goods and services or by calculating the value of total income. We get the same dollar amount of GDP with either approach.

> **Transfer payments** Payments by the government to households for which the government does not receive a new good or service in return.

MyEconLab Concept Check

Components of GDP

The BEA divides its statistics on GDP into four major categories of expenditures: consumption, investment, government purchases, and net exports. Economists use these categories to understand why GDP fluctuates and to forecast future GDP.

Personal Consumption Expenditures, or "Consumption" Consumption expenditures are made by households and are divided into three categories:

1. Expenditures on *services*, such as medical care, education, and haircuts
2. Expenditures on *nondurable goods*, such as food and clothing
3. Expenditures on *durable goods*, such as automobiles and furniture

> **Consumption** Spending by households on goods and services, not including spending on new houses.

The spending by households on new houses is not included in consumption. Instead, spending on new houses is included in the investment category, which we discuss next.

Gross Private Domestic Investment, or "Investment" Spending on *gross private domestic investment*, or simply **investment**, is also divided into three categories.

1. *Business fixed investment* is spending by firms on new factories, office buildings, and machinery used to produce other goods. Since 2013, this category of investment has included business spending on research and development. The BEA had previously considered such spending to be an intermediate good.

> **Investment** Spending by firms on new factories, office buildings, machinery, and additions to inventories, plus spending by households and firms on new houses.

Don't Let This Happen to You

Remember What Economists Mean by *Investment*

Notice that the definition of *investment* in this chapter is narrower than in everyday use. For example, people often say they are investing in the stock market or in rare coins. As we have seen, economists reserve the word *investment* for purchases of machinery, factories, and houses. Economists don't include purchases of shares of stock or rare coins or deposits in savings accounts in the definition of investment because these activities don't result in the production of new goods. For example, a share of Twitter's stock represents part ownership of that company. When you buy a share of Twitter's stock, nothing new is produced; there is just a transfer from the seller to you of that small piece of ownership of Twitter. Similarly, buying a rare coin or putting $1,000 into a savings account does not result in an increase in production. GDP is not affected by any of these activities, so they are not included in the economic definition of investment.

MyEconLab Study Plan

Your Turn: Test your understanding by doing related problem 1.12 on page 269 at the end of this chapter.

---

2. *Residential investment* is spending by households and firms on new single-family and multi-unit houses.

3. *Changes in business inventories* are changes in the stocks of goods that have been produced but not yet sold. If Ford has $200 million worth of unsold cars at the beginning of the year and $350 million worth of unsold cars at the end of the year, then the firm has spent $150 million on inventory investment during the year.

Government Consumption and Gross Investment, or "Government Purchases" **Government purchases** are spending by federal, state, and local governments on goods and services, such as teachers' salaries, highways, and aircraft carriers. Again, government spending on transfer payments is not included in government purchases because it does not result in the production of new goods and services.

> **Government purchases** Spending by federal, state, and local governments on goods and services.

Net Exports of Goods and Services, or "Net Exports" **Net exports** are equal to *exports* minus *imports*. Exports are goods and services produced in the United States and purchased by foreign firms, households, and governments. We add exports to our other categories of expenditures because otherwise we would not be including all spending on new goods and services produced in the United States. For example, if a farmer in South Dakota sells wheat to China, the value of the wheat is included in GDP because it represents production in the United States. Imports are goods and services produced in foreign countries and purchased by U.S. firms, households, and governments. We subtract imports from total expenditures because otherwise we would be including spending that does not result in production of new goods and services in the United States. For example, if U.S. consumers buy $1 billion worth of furniture manufactured in China, that spending is included in consumption expenditures. But the value of those imports is subtracted from GDP because the imports do not represent production in the United States.

> **Net exports** Exports minus imports.

MyEconLab Concept Check

An Equation for GDP and Some Actual Values

A simple equation sums up the components of GDP:

$$Y = C + I + G + NX.$$

The equation tells us that GDP (denoted as Y) equals consumption (C) plus investment (I) plus government purchases (G) plus net exports (NX). Figure 8.2 shows the values of the components of GDP for the year 2014. The graph in the figure highlights the fact

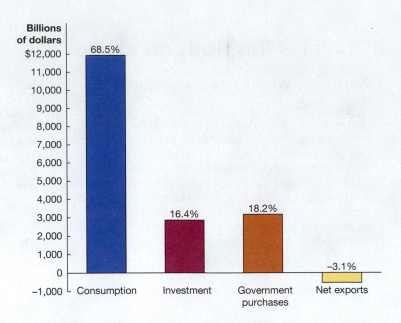

COMPONENTS OF GDP (billions of dollars)		
Consumption		$11,930
Durable goods	$1,303	
Nondurable goods	2,666	
Services	7,962	
Investment		2,852
Business fixed investment	2,211	
Residential investment	559	
Change in business inventories	82	
Government purchases		3,175
Federal	1,219	
State and local	1,956	
Net Exports		−538
Exports	2,337	
Imports	2,875	
Total GDP		$17,419

Figure 8.2   **Components of GDP in 2014**

Consumption accounts for a much larger percentage of GDP than any of the other components. In recent years, net exports have typically been negative, which reduces GDP. Note that the subtotals may not sum to the totals for each category because of rounding.

Source: U.S. Bureau of Economic Analysis.

that consumption is by far the largest component of GDP. The table provides a more detailed breakdown and shows several interesting points:

- Consumer spending on services is greater than the sum of spending on durable and nondurable goods. There has been a continuing trend in the United States and other high-income countries away from the production of goods and toward the production of services. As the populations of these countries have become, on average, both older and wealthier, their demand for services such as medical care and financial advice has increased faster than their demand for goods.

- Business fixed investment is the largest component of investment. As we will see in later chapters, spending by firms on new factories, computers, and machinery can fluctuate. For example, a decline in business fixed investment played an important role in the 2007–2009 recession.

- Purchases made by state and local governments are greater than purchases made by the federal government. Because basic government activities, such as education and law enforcement, occur largely at the state and local levels, state and local government spending is greater than federal government spending.

- Imports are greater than exports, so net exports are negative. We will discuss in Chapter 18 why imports have typically been larger than exports for the U.S. economy.   MyEconLab Concept Check

Making the Connection   MyEconLab Video

Adding More of Lady Gaga to GDP

The Bureau of Economic Analysis (BEA) is always researching to improve its measurement of GDP. A few years ago, the BEA changed how it accounts for spending on research and development (R&D). Prior to 2013, the BEA considered R&D by firms or the government to be an intermediate good, just as tires or batteries are considered intermediate goods in automobile manufacturing. But spending on R&D is similar to investment spending. For example, when Ford buys new machine tools—which are included in investment spending—it does so to help manufacture automobiles now and in the future. Similarly, when Ford spends on R&D to improve the battery in its Ford Focus electric car, it does so to help improve the car now and in the future. The BEA now counts spending on R&D as investment. In other words, the BEA shifted from not counting spending on R&D as part of GDP to counting it.

The term *research and development* brings to mind scientists working in laboratories, trying to develop new pharmaceutical drugs or improved computer chips. But just as firms and the government devote resources to R&D, movie and television studios, book authors, and musicians devote time and resources to producing new movies, television programs, books, and recordings. In past years, the BEA counted spending by firms and individuals on developing entertainment products as part of the cost of producing those products, in the same way that it

The cost to Lady Gaga and her record company of writing and recording her songs is now part of GDP.

counted the cost of labor and materials. So the cost of developing entertainment products was *not* included in GDP. But in 2013, the BEA changed its procedures to include those costs as part of investment and began including it in GDP. For example, prior to 2013, sales of Lady Gaga's songs on iTunes and on CDs as well as ticket sales for her concerts were included in GDP, but the cost to Lady Gaga and her record company of writing and recording her songs was not included. Now both types of spending are included in GDP.

By broadening the definition of investment spending, the BEA increased measured GDP in 2013 by about 3 percent. The BEA adjusted its historical data on GDP back to 1929, so while the levels of GDP increased, the changes in GDP from one year to the next were not greatly affected. The BEA makes changes to its calculations of GDP after consulting with government statistical agencies in other countries. The objective is to allow economists, firms, and policymakers to more accurately compare GDP in different countries. The broadening of the definition of investment was meant to increase the importance of *intellectual property* (IP), such as software, movies, and books, in GDP. A study by the U.S. Patent and Trademark Office estimated that in the United States, IP-intensive industries, including pharmaceuticals, computers and software, telecommunications, book publishing, and radio and television broadcasting, account for about 40 million jobs and more than one-third of GDP.

As the economy changes over time, the BEA evaluates whether to adjust the way it measures GDP.

Sources: David Kestenbaum, "Lady Gaga Writing a New Song Is Like a Factory Investing in a New Machine," www.npr.org, April 25, 2013; Osagie Imasogie and Thaddeus J. Kobylarz, "Yes, Lady Gaga's Songs Contribute to GDP," *Wall Street Journal*, May 27, 2013; U.S. Bureau of Economic Analysis, "Preview of the 2013 Comprehensive Revision of the National Income and Product Accounts," *Survey of Current Business*, Vol. 93, No. 3, March 2013; and U.S. Department of Commerce, *Intellectual Property and the U.S. Economy: Industries in Focus*, March 2012.

Your Turn: Test your understanding by doing related problem 1.13 on page 269 at the end of this chapter.

MyEconLab Study Plan

Measuring GDP Using the Value-Added Method

We have seen that GDP can be calculated by adding together all expenditures on final goods and services. An alternative way of calculating GDP is the *value-added method*. **Value added** refers to the additional market value a firm gives to a product and is equal to the difference between the price for which the firm sells a good and the price it paid other firms for intermediate goods. Table 8.1 gives a hypothetical example of the value added by each firm involved in the production of a shirt offered for sale on L.L.Bean's Web site.

Suppose a cotton farmer sells $1 of raw cotton to a textile mill. If, for simplicity, we ignore any inputs the farmer may have purchased from other firms—such as cottonseed

Value added The market value a firm adds to a product.

Table 8.1

Calculating Value Added

Firm	Value of Product	Value Added		
Cotton farmer	Value of raw cotton = $1	Value added by cotton farmer	=	$1
Textile mill	Value of raw cotton woven into cotton fabric = $3	Value added by textile mill = ($3 − $1)	=	$2
Shirt company	Value of cotton fabric made into a shirt = $15	Value added by shirt company = ($15 − $3)	=	$12
L.L.Bean	Value of shirt for sale on L.L.Bean's Web site = $35	Value added by L.L.Bean = ($35 − $15)	=	$20
	Total Value Added		=	**$35**

or fertilizer—then the farmer's value added is $1. The textile mill then weaves the raw cotton into cotton fabric, which it sells to a shirt company for $3. The textile mill's value added ($2) is the difference between the price it paid for the raw cotton ($1) and the price for which it can sell the cotton fabric ($3). Similarly, the shirt company's value added is the difference between the price it paid for the cotton fabric ($3) and the price it receives for the shirt from L.L.Bean ($15). L.L.Bean's value added is the difference between the price it pays for the shirt ($15) and the price for which it can sell the shirt on its Web site ($35). Notice that *the price of the shirt on L.L.Bean's Web site is exactly equal to the sum of the value added by each firm involved in the production of the shirt*. We can calculate GDP by adding up the market value of every final good and service produced during a particular period. Or, we can arrive at the same value for GDP by adding up the value added by every firm involved in producing those final goods and services.

 MyEconLab Study Plan

MyEconLab Concept Check

8.2 Does GDP Measure What We Want It to Measure?

LEARNING OBJECTIVE: Discuss whether GDP is a good measure of well-being.

Economists use GDP to measure total production in the economy. For that purpose, we would like GDP to be as comprehensive as possible, not overlooking any significant production that takes place in the economy. Most economists believe that GDP does a good— but not flawless—job of measuring production. GDP is also sometimes used as a measure of well-being. Although it is generally true that the more goods and services people have, the better off they are, we will see that GDP provides only a rough measure of well-being.

Shortcomings in GDP as a Measure of Total Production

When the BEA calculates GDP, it does not include two types of production: production in the home and production in the underground economy.

Household Production With few exceptions, the BEA does not attempt to estimate the value of goods and services that are not bought and sold in markets. If a carpenter makes and sells bookcases, the value of those bookcases will be counted in GDP. If the carpenter makes a bookcase for personal use, it will not be counted in GDP. *Household production* refers to goods and services people produce for themselves. The most important type of household production is the services a homemaker provides to the homemaker's family. If a person has been caring for children, cleaning the house, and preparing the family meals, the value of such services is not included in GDP. If the person then decides to work outside the home, enrolls the children in day care, hires a cleaning service, and begins buying the family's meals in restaurants, the value of GDP will rise by the amount paid for day care, cleaning services, and restaurant meals, even though production of these services has not actually increased.

The Underground Economy Individuals and firms sometimes conceal the buying and selling of goods and services, in which case their production isn't counted in GDP. Individuals and firms conceal what they buy and sell for three main reasons: They are dealing in illegal goods and services, such as drugs or prostitution; they want to avoid paying taxes on the income they earn; or they want to avoid government regulations. This concealed buying and selling is called the **underground economy**. Estimates of the size of the underground economy in the United States vary widely, but

Underground economy Buying and selling of goods and services that is concealed from the government to avoid taxes or regulations or because the goods and services are illegal.

it is probably at most 10 percent of measured GDP, or about $1.8 trillion. The underground economy in some low-income countries, such as Zimbabwe or Peru, may be more than 50 percent of measured GDP. Recently, countries in Western Europe have decided to include estimates of spending on illegal drugs and prostitution in their measures of GDP. To this point, the BEA has decided not to follow this approach. If it did, estimates are that measured U.S. GDP would increase by about 3 percent.

Is not counting household production or production in the underground economy a serious shortcoming of GDP? Most economists would answer "no" because the most important use of GDP is to measure changes in how the economy is performing over short periods of time, such as from one year to the next. For this purpose, omitting household production and production in the underground economy doesn't matter because there is not likely to be much change in household production or the size of the underground economy from one year to the next.

We also use GDP to measure how production of goods and services grows over fairly long periods of a decade or more. For this purpose, omitting household production and production in the underground economy may be more important. For example, beginning in the 1970s, the number of women working outside the home increased dramatically. Some of the goods and services—such as childcare and restaurant meals—produced in the following years were not true additions to total production; rather, they were replacing what had been household production.   MyEconLab Concept Check

Making the Connection
MyEconLab Video

Why Do Many Developing Countries Have Such Large Underground Economies?

Recent estimates put the size of the underground economy at 8 percent of measured GDP in the United States and 13 percent in Western Europe. The underground economy is much larger in many developing countries—perhaps 50 percent or more of measured GDP. In developing countries, the underground economy is often referred to as the *informal sector*, as opposed to the *formal sector*, in which output of goods and services is measured. Although it might not seem to matter whether production of goods and services is measured and included in GDP or unmeasured, a large informal sector can be a sign of government policies that are retarding economic growth.

In some developing countries, more than half the workers may be in the underground economy.

Because firms in the informal sector are operating illegally, they tend to be smaller and have less capital than firms operating legally. The entrepreneurs who start firms in the informal sector may be afraid the government could someday close or confiscate their firms. Therefore, the entrepreneurs limit their investments in these firms. As a consequence, workers in these firms have less machinery and equipment to work with and so can produce fewer goods and services. Entrepreneurs in the informal sector also have to pay the costs of avoiding government authorities. For example, construction firms operating in the informal sector in Brazil have to employ lookouts who can warn workers to hide when government inspectors come around. In many countries, firms in the informal sector have to pay substantial bribes to government officials to remain in business. The informal sector is large in some developing economies because taxes are high and government regulations are extensive. For example, firms in Brazil pay 85 percent of all taxes collected, as compared with 40 percent in the United States. Not surprisingly, about half of all Brazilian workers are employed in the informal sector. According to one estimate, firms in the informal sector in Brazil can earn three times the profit of similar-sized firms in the formal sector. In Zimbabwe and Peru, the fraction of workers in the informal sector may be as high as 60 or 70 percent. One estimate puts the size of the informal sector in India at nearly 50 percent.

Many economists believe taxes in developing countries are so high because these countries are attempting to pay for government sectors that are as large relative to their economies as the government sectors of industrial economies. Including transfer payments, government spending in Brazil, for example, is 41 percent of measured GDP, compared to 36 percent in the United States. In the early twentieth century, when the United States was much poorer than it is today, government spending was only about 8 percent of GDP, so the tax burden on U.S. firms was much lower. In countries such as Brazil, bringing firms into the formal sector from the informal sector may require reductions in government spending and taxes. In most developing countries, however, voters are reluctant to see government services reduced.

Sources: "The Price Is Wrong," *Economist*, September 28, 2013; "Dynamic but Dirty," *Economist*, December 2, 2010; "Notes from the Underground," *Economist*, April 2, 2009; Mary Anastasia O'Grady, "Why Brazil's Underground Economy Grows and Grows," *Wall Street Journal*, September 10, 2004; and the International Monetary Fund.

MyEconLab Study Plan

Your Turn: Test your understanding by doing related problems 2.8 and 2.9 on page 270 at the end of this chapter.

Shortcomings of GDP as a Measure of Well-Being

The main purpose of GDP is to measure a country's total production. GDP is also frequently used, though, as a measure of well-being. For example, news stories often include tables that show for different countries the levels of GDP per person, which is usually called *GDP per capita*. GDP per capita is calculated by dividing the value of GDP for a country by the country's population. These articles imply that people in the countries with higher levels of GDP per capita are better off. Although increases in GDP often do lead to increases in the well-being of the population, it is important to be aware that GDP is not a perfect measure of well-being for several reasons.

The Value of Leisure Is Not Included in GDP
If an economic consultant decides to retire, GDP will decline even though the consultant may value increased leisure more than the income he or she was earning from running a consulting firm. The consultant's well-being has increased, but GDP has decreased. In 1890, the typical American worked 60 hours per week. Today, the typical American works fewer than 40 hours per week. If Americans still worked 60-hour weeks, GDP would be much higher than it is now, but the well-being of a typical person would be lower because less time would be available for leisure activities.

GDP Is Not Adjusted for Pollution or Other Negative Effects of Production
When a dry cleaner cleans and presses clothes, the value of this service is included in GDP. If the chemicals the dry cleaner uses pollute the air or water, GDP is not adjusted to compensate for the cost of the pollution. Similarly, the value of cigarettes produced is included in GDP, with no adjustment made for the cost of the lung cancer that some smokers develop.

We should note, though, that increasing GDP often leads countries to devote more resources to pollution reduction. For example, in the United States between 1970 and 2013, as GDP was steadily increasing, emissions of the six main air pollutants declined by more than 50 percent. Developing countries often have higher levels of pollution than high-income countries because the lower GDPs of the developing countries make them more reluctant to spend resources on pollution reduction. Levels of pollution in China are much higher than those in the United States, Japan, or the countries of Western Europe. According to the World Health Organization, 7 of the 10 most polluted cities in the world are in China, but as Chinese GDP continues to rise, the country is likely to devote more resources to reducing pollution.

GDP Is Not Adjusted for Changes in Crime and Other Social Problems
An increase in crime reduces well-being but may actually increase GDP if it leads to greater spending on police, security guards, and alarm systems. GDP is also not adjusted for changes in divorce rates, drug addiction, or other factors that may affect people's well-being.

GDP Measures the Size of the Pie but Not How the Pie Is Divided
When a country's GDP increases, the country has more goods and services, but those goods and services may be very unequally distributed. Therefore, GDP may not provide good information about the goods and services consumed by a typical person.

To summarize, we can say that a person's well-being depends on many factors that are not considered in calculating GDP. Because GDP is designed to measure total production, it should not be surprising that it does an imperfect job of measuring well-being.

MyEconLab Concept Check

8.3 Real GDP versus Nominal GDP

LEARNING OBJECTIVE: Discuss the difference between real GDP and nominal GDP.

Because GDP is measured in value terms, we have to be careful about interpreting changes over time. To see why, consider interpreting an increase in the total value of pickup truck production from $40 billion in 2016 to $44 billion in 2017. Because $44 billion is 10 percent greater than $40 billion, were 10 percent more trucks produced in 2017 than in 2016? We can draw this conclusion only if the average price of trucks did not change between 2016 and 2017. In fact, when GDP increases from one year to the next, the increase is due partly to increases in production of goods and services and partly to increases in prices. Because we are mainly interested in GDP as a measure of production, we need a way of separating the price changes from the quantity changes.

Calculating Real GDP

The BEA separates price changes from quantity changes by calculating a measure of production called *real GDP*. **Nominal GDP** is calculated by summing the current values of final goods and services. **Real GDP** is calculated by designating a particular year as the *base year* and then using the prices of goods and services in the base year to calculate the value of goods and services in all other years. For instance, if the base year is 2009, real GDP for 2017 would be calculated by using prices of goods and services from 2009. By keeping prices constant, we know that changes in real GDP represent changes in the quantity of goods and services produced in the economy.

Nominal GDP The value of final goods and services evaluated at current-year prices.

Real GDP The value of final goods and services evaluated at base-year prices.

Solved Problem 8.3

MyEconLab Interactive Animation

Calculating Real GDP

Suppose that a very simple economy produces only the following three final goods and services: eye examinations, pizzas, and shoes. Use the information in the table on the right to compute real GDP for the year 2017. Assume that the base year is 2009.

Product	2009 Quantity	2009 Price	2017 Quantity	2017 Price
Eye examinations	80	$40	100	$50
Pizzas	90	11	80	10
Shoes	15	90	20	100

Solving the Problem

Step 1: **Review the chapter material.** This problem is about calculating real GDP, so you may want to review the section, "Calculating Real GDP," which begins on this page.

Step 2: **Calculate the value of the three goods and services listed in the table, using the quantities for 2017 and the prices for 2009.** Real GDP is the value of all final goods and services, evaluated at base-year prices. In this case, the base year is 2009, and we have the price of each product in that year:

Product	2017 Quantity	2009 Price	Value
Eye examinations	100	$40	$4,000
Pizzas	80	11	880
Shoes	20	90	1,800

Step 3:   **Add up the values of the three products to find real GDP.** Real GDP for 2017 equals the sum of:

Quantity of eye examinations in 2017 $\times$ Price of eye examinations in 2009 = $4,000
Quantity of pizzas produced in 2017 $\times$ Price of pizzas in 2009 = $880
Quantity of shoes produced in 2017 $\times$ Price of shoes in 2009 = $1,800
or, $6,680

Extra Credit: Notice that the quantities of each good produced in 2009 were irrelevant for calculating real GDP in 2017. Notice also that the value of $6,680 for real GDP in 2017 is lower than the value of $7,800 for nominal GDP in 2017 that we calculated in Solved Problem 8.1 on page 252.

MyEconLab Study Plan   **Your Turn:** For more practice, do related problem 3.4 on page 271 at the end of this chapter.

One drawback to calculating real GDP using base-year prices is that, over time, prices may change relative to each other. For example, the price of smartphones may fall relative to the price of milk. Because this change is not reflected in the fixed prices from the base year, the estimate of real GDP is somewhat distorted. The further away the current year is from the base year, the worse the problem becomes. To make the calculation of real GDP more accurate, in 1996, the BEA switched to using *chain-weighted prices*, and it now publishes statistics on real GDP in "chained (2009) dollars."

The details of calculating real GDP using chain-weighted prices are more complicated than we need to discuss here, but the basic idea is straightforward: Starting with the base year, the BEA takes an average of prices in that year and prices in the following year. It then uses this average to calculate real GDP in the year following the base year (currently the year 2009). For the next year—in other words, the year that is two years after the base year—the BEA calculates real GDP by taking an average of prices in that year and the previous year. In this way, prices in each year are "chained" to prices from the previous year, and the distortion from changes in relative prices is minimized.

Holding prices constant means that the *purchasing power* of a dollar remains the same from one year to the next. Ordinarily, the purchasing power of the dollar falls every year as price increases reduce the amount of goods and services that a dollar can buy.   MyEconLab Concept Check

Comparing Real GDP and Nominal GDP

Real GDP holds prices constant, which makes it a better measure than nominal GDP of changes in the production of goods and services from one year to the next. In fact, growth in the economy is almost always measured as growth in real GDP. If a headline in the *Wall Street Journal* states "U.S. Economy Grew 2.3% Last Year," the article will report that real GDP increased by 2.3 percent during the previous year.

We describe real GDP as being measured in "base-year dollars." For example, nominal GDP in 2014 was $17,419 billion, and, with a base year of 2009, real GDP in 2014 was $16,086 billion in 2009 dollars. Because, on average, prices rise from one year to the next, real GDP is greater than nominal GDP in years before the base year and less than nominal GDP for years after the base year. In the base year, real GDP and nominal GDP are the same because both are calculated for the base year using the same prices and quantities. Figure 8.3 shows movements in nominal GDP and real GDP between 1990 and 2014. In the years before 2009, prices were, on average, lower than in 2009, so nominal GDP was lower than real GDP. In 2009, nominal and real GDP were equal. Since 2009, prices have been, on average, higher than in 2009, so nominal GDP is higher than real GDP.   MyEconLab Concept Check

The GDP Deflator

Price level A measure of the average prices of goods and services in the economy.

Economists and policymakers are interested not just in the level of total production, as measured by real GDP, but also in the *price level*. The **price level** measures the average prices of goods and services in the economy. One of the goals of economic policy is to maintain a

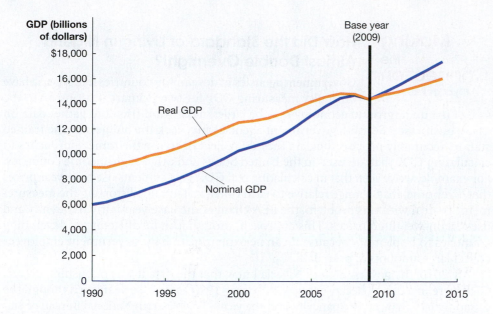

MyEconLab Real-time data

Figure 8.3

Nominal GDP and Real GDP, 1990–2014

Currently, the base year for calculating GDP is 2009. In the years before 2009, prices were, on average, lower than in 2009, so nominal GDP was lower than real GDP. In 2009, nominal and real GDP were equal. Since 2009, prices have been, on average, higher than in 2009, so nominal GDP is higher than real GDP.

Source: U.S. Bureau of Economic Analysis.

stable price level. We can use values for nominal GDP and real GDP to compute a measure of the price level called the *GDP deflator*. We calculate the **GDP deflator** using this formula:

$$\text{GDP deflator} = \frac{\text{Nominal GDP}}{\text{Real GDP}} \times 100.$$

GDP deflator A measure of the price level, calculated by dividing nominal GDP by real GDP and multiplying by 100.

To see why the GDP deflator is a measure of the price level, think about what would happen if prices of goods and services rose while production remained the same. In that case, nominal GDP would increase, but real GDP would remain constant, so the GDP deflator would increase. In reality, both prices and production usually increase each year, but the more prices increase relative to the increase in production, the more nominal GDP increases relative to real GDP, and the higher the value for the GDP deflator. Increases in the GDP deflator allow economists and policymakers to track increases in the price level over time.

Remember that in the base year (currently 2009), nominal GDP is equal to real GDP, so the value of the GDP price deflator will always be 100 in the base year. The following table gives the values for nominal and real GDP for 2013 and 2014:

	2013	**2014**
Nominal GDP	$16,768 billion	$17,419 billion
Real GDP	$15,710 billion	$16,086 billion

We can use the information from this table to calculate values for the GDP price deflator for 2013 and 2014:

Formula	Applied to 2013	Applied to 2014
$\text{GDP deflator} = \left(\dfrac{\text{Nominal GDP}}{\text{Real GDP}}\right) \times 100$	$\left(\dfrac{\$16,768 \text{ billion}}{\$15,710 \text{ billion}}\right) \times 100 = 106.7$	$\left(\dfrac{\$17,419 \text{ billion}}{\$16,086 \text{ billion}}\right) \times 100 = 108.3$

From these values for the deflator, we can calculate that the price level increased by 1.5 percent between 2013 and 2014:

$$\left(\frac{108.3 - 106.7}{106.7}\right) \times 100 = 1.5\%.$$

In the next chapter, we will see that economists and policymakers also rely on another measure of the price level, known as the consumer price index. In addition, we will discuss the strengths and weaknesses of different measures of the price level.

MyEconLab Concept Check

Making the Connection
MyEconLab Video

How Did the Standard of Living in Nigeria Almost Double Overnight?

Government agencies in developing countries like Nigeria have difficulty measuring GDP for two primary reasons: First, the size of the underground economy may be large, making it difficult to gather data on many businesses. Second, government agencies may lack the budgets or the trained staff to accurately process the data they do collect or to use the same approaches to calculating GDP that are used in the United States and other high-income countries. For example, we've seen that in calculating real GDP, governments use base-year prices that, over time, may change relative to each other, potentially distorting the measurement. To deal with this problem, the BEA changes the base year fairly frequently and uses chain-weighted prices. This approach, though, can be difficult for developing countries to implement because it can be expensive to have government employees collect large amounts of price data.

By 2010, the government of Nigeria knew that the data it was publishing on real GDP were inaccurate because it was still using 1990 as its base year, even though the economy had changed dramatically over the years. The Nigerian National Bureau of Statistics was given a larger budget and the task of both changing the real GDP base year to 2010 and gathering data on previously unrecorded output in the underground economy. As an article in the *Wall Street Journal* put it, "Nigerian number crunchers traversed the West African nation by motorcycle and speedboat, visiting Internet cafe owners, movie producers and other businesspeople to record previously uncaptured commercial activity." The number of businesses being surveyed for data increased from 85,000 to 850,000.

When the new data on GDP were released in 2014, the results were dramatic. The estimate for real GDP for 2013 was changed from $270 billion to $510 billion, an 89 percent increase. The increase was large enough for Nigeria to pass South Africa as the largest economy in Africa. As the figure below shows, the new data also gave a more accurate picture of the structure of the Nigerian economy. For instance, where previously the service sector was believed to make up less than one-third of the economy, it was shown to actually be more than half the economy. In addition, although not shown in the figure, the telecommunications sector actually makes up 9 percent of the economy, rather than the 1 percent in previous estimates, and the oil industry is only 14 percent of the economy rather than 33 percent.

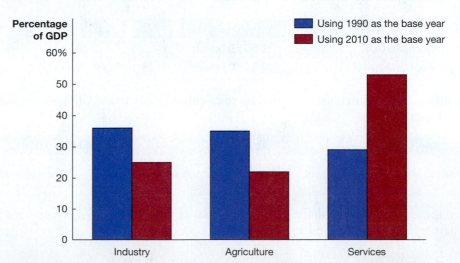

But had the standard of living of the typical Nigerian actually increased? The new estimates made it appear so, with real GDP per person increasing from $1,500 to $2,688. Of course, all that had really changed was how accurately the government was measuring real GDP. The country was producing no more goods and services on April 6, 2014, when the new GDP data were announced, than it had been the day before.

Nigeria's experience with measuring its GDP demonstrates the problems governments have in accurately constructing these statistics and how misleading it can be to rely on them as measures of a country's standard of living.

Sources: Drew Hinshaw and Patrick McGroarty, "Nigeria's Economy Surpasses South Africa's in Size," *Wall Street Journal,* April 6, 2014; Javier Blas and William Wallis, "Nigeria Almost Doubles GDP in Recalculation," *Financial Times,* April 7, 2014; and "How Nigeria's Economy Grew by 89% Overnight," *Economist,* April 7, 2014.

Your Turn: Test your understanding by doing related problem 3.10 on page 271 at the end of this chapter.

MyEconLab Study Plan

Other Measures of Total Production and Total Income

MyEconLab Study Plan

LEARNING OBJECTIVE: Describe other measures of total production and total income.

National income accounting refers to the methods the BEA uses to track total production and total income in the economy. The statistical tables containing this information are called the *National Income and Product Accounts (NIPA)* tables. Every quarter, the BEA releases NIPA tables containing data on several measures of total production and total income. We have already discussed GDP, which is the most important measure of total production and total income. In addition to computing GDP, the BEA computes the following four measures of production and income: gross national product, national income, personal income, and disposable personal income.

Gross National Product

We have seen that GDP is the value of final goods and services produced within the United States. *Gross national product (GNP)* is the value of final goods and services produced by residents of the United States, even if the production takes place *outside* the United States. U.S. firms have facilities in foreign countries, and foreign firms have facilities in the United States. Ford, for example, has assembly plants in the United Kingdom, and Toyota has assembly plants in the United States. GNP includes foreign production by U.S. firms but excludes U.S. production by foreign firms. For the United States, GNP is almost the same as GDP. For example, in 2014, GDP was $17,419 billion, and GNP was $17,631 billion, or only about 1.2 percent more than GDP.

For many years, GNP was the main measure of total production compiled by the federal government and used by economists and policymakers in the United States. However, in many countries other than the United States, a significant percentage of domestic production takes place in foreign-owned facilities. For those countries, GDP is much larger than GNP and is a more accurate measure of the level of production within the country's borders. As a result, many countries and international agencies had long preferred using GDP to using GNP. In 1991, the United States joined those countries in using GDP as its main measure of total production.   MyEconLab Concept Check

National Income

In the production of goods and services, some machinery, equipment, and buildings wear out and have to be replaced. The value of this worn-out machinery, equipment, and buildings is called *depreciation*. In the NIPA tables, depreciation is called the *consumption of fixed capital*. If we subtract this value from GDP, we are left with *national income*.

Earlier in this chapter, we stressed that the value of total production is equal to the value of total income. This point is not strictly true if by "value of total production" we mean GDP and by "value of total income" we mean national income because national income will always be smaller than GDP by an amount equal to depreciation. In practice, though, the difference between the value of GDP and value of national income does not matter for most macroeconomic issues.   MyEconLab Concept Check

Personal Income

Personal income is income received by households. To calculate personal income, we subtract the earnings that corporations retain rather than pay to shareholders in the form of dividends. We also add in the payments received by households from the government in the form of *transfer payments* or interest on government bonds.   MyEconLab Concept Check

Disposable Personal Income

Disposable personal income is equal to personal income minus personal tax payments, such as the federal personal income tax. It is the best measure of the income households actually have available to spend.

Figure 8.4 shows the values of these measures of total production and total income for 2014 in a table and a graph.   MyEconLab Concept Check

The Division of Income

Figure 8.1 on page 253 illustrates the important fact that we can measure GDP in terms of total expenditure or as the total income received by households. GDP calculated as the sum of income payments to households is sometimes called *gross domestic income*. Figure 8.5 shows the division of total income among wages, interest, rent, profit, and certain non-income items. The non-income items are included in gross domestic income because sales taxes, depreciation, and a few other items are included in the value of goods and services produced but are not directly received by households as income. *Wages* include all compensation received by employees, including fringe benefits such as health insurance. *Interest* is net interest received by households, or the difference between the interest received on savings accounts, government bonds, and other investments and the interest paid on car loans, home mortgages, and other debts. *Rent* is rent received by households. *Profits* include the profits of sole proprietorships, which are usually small businesses, and the profits of corporations. Figure 8.5 shows that the largest component of gross domestic income is wages, which are about three times as large as profits.   MyEconLab Concept Check

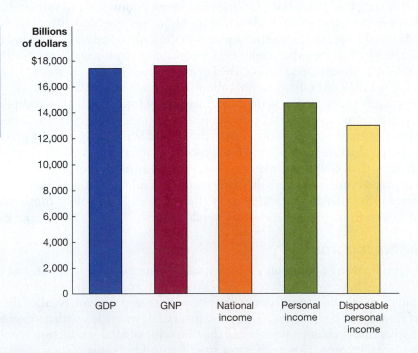

Measure	Billions of dollars
GDP	$17,419
GNP	17,631
National income	15,077
Personal income	14,734
Disposable personal income	12,990

MyEconLab Real-time data

Figure 8.4   **Measures of Total Production and Total Income, 2014**

The most important measure of total production and total income is gross domestic product (GDP). As we will see in later chapters, for some purposes, the other measures of total production and total income shown in the figure turn out to be more useful than GDP.
Source: U.S. Bureau of Economic Analysis.

	Billions of dollars
Wages	$9,237
Interest	660
Rent	640
Profit	3,076
Profits of sole proprietors	1,380
Profits of corporations	1,696
Taxes, depreciation, and statistical discrepancy	3,989

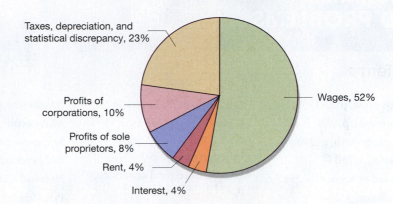

MyEconLab Animation

Figure 8.5   The Division of Income, 2014

We can measure GDP in terms of total expenditure or as the total income received by households. The largest component of income received by households is wages, which are more than three times as large as the profits received by sole proprietors and the profits received by corporations combined.

Note: The components in the figure do not sum to 100 percent because of rounding.
Source: U.S. Bureau of Economic Analysis.

Continued from page 249

Economics in Your Life

What's the Best Country for You to Work In?

At the beginning of the chapter, we posed two questions: What effect should Canada's and China's two very different growth rates have on your decision to work and live in one country or the other? And if China's much higher growth rate does not necessarily lead you to decide to work and live there, why not? This chapter has shown that although it is *generally* true that the more goods and services people have, the better off they are, GDP provides only a rough measure of well-being. GDP does not include the value of leisure; nor is it adjusted for pollution and other negative effects of production or crime and other social problems. So, in deciding where to live and work, you would need to balance China's much higher growth rate of GDP against these other considerations. You would also need to take into account that although China's *growth rate* is higher than Canada's, Canada's current *level* of real GDP is higher than China's.

Conclusion

In this chapter, we have begun the study of macroeconomics by examining an important concept: how a country's total production and income can be measured. Understanding GDP is important for understanding the business cycle and the process of long-run economic growth. In the next chapter, we discuss the issues involved in measuring two other key economic variables: the unemployment rate and the inflation rate.

Visit MyEconLab for a news article and analysis related to the concepts in this chapter.

Key Terms

Business cycle, p. 250

Consumption, p. 254

Economic growth, p. 250

Expansion, p. 250

Final good or service, p. 251

GDP deflator, p. 263

Government purchases, p. 255

Gross domestic product (GDP), p. 251

Inflation rate, p. 250

Intermediate good or service, p. 251

Investment, p. 254

Macroeconomics, p. 250

Microeconomics, p. 250

Net exports, p. 255

Nominal GDP, p. 261

Price level, p. 262

Real GDP, p. 261

Recession, p. 250

Transfer payments, p. 254

Underground economy, p. 258

Value added, p. 257

8.1 **Gross Domestic Product Measures Total Production, pages 251–258**
LEARNING OBJECTIVE: Explain how total production is measured.

Summary

Economics is divided into the subfields of **microeconomics**—which studies how households and firms make choices—and **macroeconomics**—which studies the economy as a whole. An important macroeconomic topic is the **business cycle**, which refers to alternating periods of economic expansion and economic recession. An **expansion** is a period during which production and employment are increasing. A **recession** is a period during which production and employment are decreasing. Another important macroeconomic topic is **economic growth**, which refers to the ability of the economy to produce increasing quantities of goods and services. Macroeconomics also studies the **inflation rate**, or the percentage increase in the price level from one year to the next. Economists measure total production by **gross domestic product (GDP)**, which is the value of all *final goods and services* produced in an economy during a period of time. A **final good or service** is purchased by a final user. An **intermediate good or service** is an input into another good or service and is not included in GDP. When we measure the value of total production in the economy by calculating GDP, we are simultaneously measuring the value of total income. GDP is divided into four major categories of expenditures: consumption, investment, government purchases, and net exports. **Consumption** is spending by households on goods and services, not including spending on new houses. **Investment** is spending by firms on new factories, office buildings, machinery, research and development, and additions to inventories, plus spending by households and firms on new houses. **Government purchases** is spending by federal, state, and local governments on goods and services. **Net exports** are equal to exports minus imports. Government **transfer payments** are not included in GDP because they are payments to individuals for which the government does not receive a good or service in return. We can also calculate GDP by adding up the **value added** by every firm involved in producing final goods and services.

MyEconLab Visit **www.myeconlab.com** to complete these exercises online and get instant feedback.

Review Questions

1.1 Why in microeconomics do we measure production in terms of quantity, but in macroeconomics we measure production in terms of market value?

1.2 If the U.S. Bureau of Economic Analysis added up the values of every good and service sold during the year, would the total be larger, smaller, or equal to GDP? Briefly explain.

1.3 In the circular flow of income, why must the value of total production in an economy equal the value of total income?

1.4 Describe the four major components of expenditures in GDP and write the equation that represents the relationship between GDP and the four expenditure components.

1.5 What is meant by a firm's "value added"?

Problems and Applications

1.6 A student remarks, "It doesn't make sense that intermediate goods are not counted in GDP. A computer chip is an intermediate good, and without it, a laptop won't work. So, why don't we count the computer chip in GDP?" Provide an answer to the student's question.

1.7 Briefly explain whether each of the following transactions represents the purchase of a final good.
   a. The purchase of flour by a bakery
   b. The purchase of an aircraft carrier by the federal government
   c. The purchase of French wine by a U.S. consumer
   d. The purchase of a new airliner by American Airlines

1.8 An article in the *Wall Street Journal* states that a "change in … inventories subtracted 0.57 percentage point from" what would have been the increase in GDP. For this result to occur, must there have been an increase or a decrease in inventories? Briefly explain.

   Source: Eric Morath and Ben Leubsdorf, "GDP Slows to Crawl in First Quarter, up 0.1%," *Wall Street Journal*, April 30, 2014.

1.9 (Related to the Chapter Opener on page 249) Which component of GDP will be affected by each of the following transactions involving Ford Motor Company? If you believe that none of the components of GDP will be affected by a transaction, briefly explain why.
   a. You purchase a new Ford Escape hybrid from a Ford dealer.
   b. You purchase a 2011 Ford Escape hybrid from a friend.
   c. Ford purchases door handles for the Escape from an auto parts manufacturer in Indiana.
   d. Ford produces 1,000 Escapes in a factory in Missouri and ships them to a car dealer in Shanghai, China.

e. Ford purchases new machine tools to use in its Missouri Escape factory.

f. The state of Missouri builds a new highway to help improve access to the Ford Escape plant.

1.10 Is the value of a house built in 2006 and resold in 2017 included in the GDP of 2017? Briefly explain. Would the services of the real estate agent who helped sell (or buy) the house in 2017 be counted in GDP for 2017? Briefly explain.

1.11 (Related to Solved Problem 8.1 on page 252) Suppose that a simple economy produces only four goods: shoes, hamburgers, shirts, and cotton. Assume that all the cotton is used in the production of shirts. Use the information in the following table to calculate nominal GDP for 2017.

Production and Price Statistics for 2017		
Product	Quantity	Price
Shoes	100	$60.00
Hamburgers	100	2.00
Shirts	50	25.00
Cotton	80	0.60

1.12 (Related to the Don't Let This Happen to You on page 255) Briefly explain whether you agree with the following statement: "In years when people buy many shares of stock, investment will be high and, therefore, so will GDP."

1.13 (Related to the Making the Connection on page 256) According to Dan Sichel, an economist at Wellesley College, the amount of time a singer spends working on a record album in a recording studio is "quite analogous to a factory investing in a new machine." Do you agree? Briefly explain.

Source: David Kestenbaum, "Lady Gaga Writing a New Song Is Like a Factory Investing in a New Machine," www.npr.org, April 25, 2013.

1.14 An artist buys scrap metal from a local steel mill as a raw material for her metal sculptures. Last year, she bought $5,000 worth of the scrap metal. During the year, she produced 10 metal sculptures that she sold for $800 each to a local art store. The local art store sold all of the sculptures to local art collectors, at an average price of $1,000 each. For the 10 metal sculptures, what was the total value added by the artist, and what was the total value added by the local art store?

<table>
<tr><td>**8.2**</td><td>**Does GDP Measure What We Want It to Measure? pages 258–261**
LEARNING OBJECTIVE: Discuss whether GDP is a good measure of well-being.</td></tr>
</table>

Summary

GDP does not include household production, which refers to goods and services people produce for themselves, nor does it include production in the **underground economy**, which consists of concealed buying and selling. The underground economy in some developing countries may be more than half of measured GDP. GDP is not a perfect measure of well-being because it does not include the value of leisure, it is not adjusted for pollution or other negative effects of production, and it is not adjusted for changes in crime and other social problems.

MyEconLab Visit **www.myeconlab.com** to complete these exercises online and get instant feedback.

Review Questions

2.1 Why does the size of a country's GDP matter? How does it affect the quality of life of the country's people?

2.2 What is the underground economy? Why do some countries have larger underground economies than other countries?

2.3 Why is GDP an imperfect measure of economic well-being? What types of production does GDP not measure? If GDP included these types of production, would it still be an imperfect measure of economic well-being?

Problems and Applications

2.4 Which of the following are likely to increase measured GDP, and which are likely to reduce it?

a. The fraction of women working outside the home increases.

b. There is a sharp increase in the crime rate.

c. Higher tax rates cause some people to hide more of the income they earn.

2.5 Michael Burda of Humboldt University in Germany and Daniel Hamermesh of the University of Texas examined how workers in the United States who lost their jobs spent their time. They discovered that during the period when the workers were unemployed, the decline in the number of hours of paid work these workers did was almost the same as the increase in the number of hours these workers devoted to household production. Do Burda and Hamermesh's findings allow us to draw any conclusions about whether total production in the economy—whether that production is included in GDP or not—decreased when these workers became unemployed? Does your answer depend on whether the household production they carried out while unemployed were activities, such as childcare, that the workers had been paying other people to perform before they lost their jobs? Briefly explain.

Source: Michael Burda and Daniel S. Hamermesh, "Unemployment, Market Work, and Household Production," *Economic Letters*, Vol. 107, May 2010, pp. 131–133.

2.6 A typical U.S. worker today works fewer than 40 hours per week, while in 1890, he or she worked 60 hours per week. Does this difference in the length of work weeks matter in comparing the economic well-being of U.S. workers today with that of 1890? Or can we use the difference between real GDP per capita today and in 1890 to measure differences in economic well-being while ignoring differences in the number of hours worked per week? Briefly explain.

2.7 Economic historians Roger Ransom and Richard Sutch have estimated that African-American farmers in the U.S. South worked about 30 percent fewer hours per year after the Civil War than they had as slaves before the Civil War. If after the Civil War, African-American farmers had continued to work these additional hours, their production and income would have been higher, and U.S. GDP would have been higher. Would the farmers' well-being also have been higher as a result of working these additional hours? Does your answer affect how we should interpret changes in U.S. GDP from before the Civil War to after it? Briefly explain.

Source: Roger L. Ransom and Richard Sutch, *One Kind of Freedom: The Economic Consequences of Emancipation*, 2nd edition, New York: Cambridge University Press, 2001.

2.8 **(Related to the** Making the Connection **on page 259)** An article in the *New York Times* describes the much greater use of cash, as opposed to checks and credit cards, in buying and selling in China. The article describes someone bringing several bags of cash containing the equivalent of $130,000 into a car dealership to buy a new BMW. Another article notes, "Many economists believe that the rise in [use of] cash is strongly related to growth in the so-called underground economy."
a. What is the underground economy?
b. Why might buyers and sellers in the underground economy prefer to use cash?

Sources: David Barboza, "Chinese Way of Doing Business: In Cash We Trust," *New York Times*, April 30, 2013; and Bruce Bartlett, "America's Most Profitable Export Is Cash," *New York Times*, April 9, 2013.

2.9 **(Related to the** Making the Connection **on page 259)** An article in the *Wall Street Journal* notes that many economists believe that GDP data for India are unreliable because "the average firm employs just a handful of people and the overwhelming majority of the adult population works off the books and far from major cities."
a. What does the article mean by working "off the books"?
b. Why would the problems listed make it difficult for the Indian government to accurately measure GDP?

c. What problems can be caused for a government or for businesses in a country if the government cannot accurately measure GDP?

Source: Raymond Zhong, "Just How Bad Are India's Official GDP Numbers?" *Wall Street Journal*, August 27, 2014.

2.10 The following table shows data from the Organization for Economic Co-operation and Development (OECD) on the average number of hours employed people worked per week and on real GDP per capita for seven countries.

	Average Hours Worked	Real per Capita GDP
Germany	26.2	$41,007
Canada	32.8	$41,475
Japan	33.3	$34,929
OECD average (34 nations)	34.0	$36,074
United States	34.4	$50,429
Greece	39.6	$23,919
Korea	41.6	$32,711
Mexico	43.0	$16,022

The average German worker worked 8 fewer hours but earned $9,000 less per year than did the average worker in the United States. Can we conclude anything about the well-being of the average German worker versus the well-being of the average worker in the United States from these data? What measures besides average number of hours worked and real per capita GDP would you like to see in evaluating the well-being of workers in OECD countries?

Sources: Eric Morath, "Are Americans Working Less Than the Rest of the World?" *Wall Street Journal*, July 10, 2015; and OECD Data, https://data.oecd.org/emp/hours-worked.htm#indicator-chart.

8.3 | ## Real GDP versus Nominal GDP, pages 261–265
LEARNING OBJECTIVE: Discuss the difference between real GDP and nominal GDP.

Summary

Nominal GDP is the value of final goods and services evaluated at current-year prices. **Real GDP** is the value of final goods and services evaluated at *base-year* prices. By keeping prices constant, we know that changes in real GDP represent changes in the quantity of goods and services produced in the economy. When the **price level**, the average prices of goods and services in the economy, is increasing, real GDP is greater than nominal GDP in years before the base year and less than nominal GDP for years after the base year. The **GDP deflator** is a measure of the price level and is calculated by dividing nominal GDP by real GDP and multiplying by 100.

Review Questions

3.1 Why does inflation make nominal GDP a poor measure of the increase in total production from one year to the next? How does the U.S. Bureau of Economic Analysis deal with this drawback?

3.2 What is the GDP deflator, and how is it calculated?

3.3 Assuming that inflation has occurred over time, what is the relationship between nominal GDP and real GDP in each of the following situations?
a. In the years after the base year
b. In the base year
c. In the years before the base year

 MyEconLab Visit **www.myeconlab.com** to complete these exercises online and get instant feedback.

Problems and Applications

3.4 **(Related to** Solved Problem 8.3 **on page 261)** Suppose the information in the following table is for a simple economy that produces only four goods and services: shoes, hamburgers, shirts, and cotton. Assume that all the cotton is used in the production of shirts.

	2009		2016		2017	
Product	**Quantity**	**Price**	**Quantity**	**Price**	**Quantity**	**Price**
Shoes	90	$50.00	100	$60.00	100	$65.00
Hamburgers	75	2.00	100	2.00	120	2.25
Shirts	50	30.00	50	25.00	65	25.00
Cotton	100	0.80	800	0.60	120	0.70

    a. Use the information in the table to calculate real GDP for 2016 and 2017, assuming that the base year is 2009.

    b. What is the growth rate of real GDP during 2017?

3.5 Briefly explain whether you agree with the following statements.

    a. "If nominal GDP is less than real GDP, then the price level must have fallen during the year."

    b. "Whenever real GDP declines, nominal GDP must also decline."

    c. "If a recession is so severe that the price level declines, then we know that both real GDP and nominal GDP must decline."

    d. "Nominal GDP declined between 2008 and 2009; therefore, the GDP deflator must also have declined."

3.6 An article in the *Wall Street Journal* discussed the views of Canadian Minister of Finance Joe Oliver on the effect of falling oil prices on the Canadian economy. According to the article, Oliver argued that "lower oil prices would have a broadly neutral impact on real … gross domestic product, but have a negative effect on nominal GDP." Given this view, can we tell what Oliver must be expecting the effect of lower oil prices to be on the inflation rate? Briefly explain.

Source: Scott Hagget, "Canada Pushes Back Budget to April Due to Market Instability," *New York Times*, January 15, 2015.

3.7 The following table lists hypothetical values.

(1) Year	(2) Nominal GDP	(3) GDP Deflator (base year = 2014)	(4) Real GDP (base year = 2014)	(5) Percentage Change in Real GDP	(6) GDP Deflator (base year = 2016)	(7) Real GDP (base year = 2016)	(8) Percentage Change in Real GDP
2012	$980.00	90			81.8		
2013	1,020.00	92			83.6		
2014	1,050.00	100			90.9		
2015	1,200.00	105			95.5		
2016	1,400.00	110			100.0		

    a. Fill in column (4) by calculating real GDP using the GDP deflator with a base year of 2014 from column (3). Fill in column (7) by calculating real GDP using the GDP deflator with a base year of 2016 from column (6).

    b. Fill in column (5) by calculating the annual percentage change in real GDP for each year, using the values from column (4), and fill in column (8) by calculating the annual percentage change in real GDP by using the values from column (7).

    c. What effect does the change in the base year used to compute real GDP have on your calculations of the percentage changes in real GDP?

3.8 According to an article in the *Economist*, "China's GDP grew by 7% in the second quarter, which was higher than had been expected." Is it likely that the article is referring to the change in nominal GDP or the change in real GDP? Briefly explain.

Source: "World This Week," *Economist*, July 15, 2015.

3.9 Use the data in the following table to calculate the GDP deflator for each year (values are in billions of dollars):

Year	Nominal GDP	Real GDP
2010	$14,964	$14,784
2011	15,518	15,021
2012	16,163	15,369
2013	16,768	15,710
2014	16,245	16,086

Which year from 2011 to 2014 saw the largest percentage increase in the price level, as measured by changes in the GDP deflator? Briefly explain.

3.10 **(Related to the** Making the Connection **on page 264)** An article in the *Economist* on the revisions to Nigeria's GDP commented, "The GDP revision is not mere trickery. It provides a truer picture of Nigeria's size by giving due weight to the bits of the economy, such as telecoms, banking and the Nollywood film industry, that have been growing fast in recent years."

    a. What does the article mean by "giving due weight" to the sectors of the economy that have been growing quickly?

    b. How did the Nigerian National Bureau of Statistics accomplish the task of giving these sectors their due weight?

    c. Why does making this change in calculating GDP provide a truer picture of the size of Nigeria's economy?

Source: "Africa's New Number One," *Economist*, April 12, 2014.

8.4 Other Measures of Total Production and Total Income, pages 265–267

LEARNING OBJECTIVE: Describe other measures of total production and total income.

Summary

The most important measure of total production and total income is gross domestic product (GDP). As we will see in later chapters, for some purposes, other measures of total production and total income are actually more useful than GDP. These measures are gross national product (GNP), national income, personal income, and disposable personal income.

MyEconLab   Visit www.myeconlab.com to complete these exercises online and get instant feedback.

Review Questions

4.1 What is the difference between GDP and GNP? Briefly explain whether the difference is important for the United States.

4.2 What are the differences between national income, personal income, and disposable personal income?

4.3 What is gross domestic income? Which component of gross domestic income is the largest?

Problems and Applications

4.4 Suppose Turkey has many of its citizens temporarily working in other countries, and many of its firms have facilities in other countries. Furthermore, relatively few citizens of foreign countries are working in Turkey, and relatively few foreign firms have facilities in Turkey. In these circumstances, which would you expect to be larger for Turkey, GDP or GNP? Briefly explain.

4.5 An article in the *Economist* on the Irish economy argues, "Irish progress, both economic and fiscal, is typically measured using GDP…. But for an economy where foreign firms are so dominant, GNP … is more relevant." Briefly explain the writer's reasoning.

Source: "Fitter, yet Fragile," *Economist*, January 5, 2013.

4.6 Suppose the amount the federal government collects in personal income taxes increases, while the level of GDP remains the same. What will happen to the values of national income, personal income, and disposable personal income?

4.7 If you were attempting to forecast the level of consumption spending by households, which measure of total production or total income might be most helpful to you in making your forecast? Briefly explain.

4.8 Briefly discuss the accuracy of the following statement: "Corporate profits are much too high: Most corporations make profits equal to 50 percent of the price of the products they sell."

Real-Time Data Exercises

D8.1 (Analyzing the components of personal consumption expenditures) Go to the Web site of the Federal Reserve Bank of St. Louis (FRED) (research.stlouisfed.org/fred2/).

  a. Find the values for the most recent quarter for these four variables: (1) Personal Consumption Expenditures (PCEC); (2) Personal Consumption Expenditures: Durable Goods (PCDG): (3) Personal Consumption Expenditures: Nondurable Goods (PCND); and (4) Personal Consumption Expenditures: Services (PCESV).

  b. What percentage of total household expenditures is devoted to the consumption of goods (both durable and nondurable goods)?

D8.2 (Analyzing the components of investment) Go to the Web site of the Federal Reserve Bank of St. Louis (FRED) (research.stlouisfed.org/fred2/).

  a. Find the values for the most recent quarter for these three variables: (1) Gross Private Domestic Investment (GPDI); (2) Private Nonresidential Fixed Investment (PNFI); and (3) Private Residential Fixed Investment (PRFI).

  b. Use these values to calculate the difference between private domestic investment and residential and nonresidential fixed private investment. What component of GDP does the value calculated represent?

D8.3 (Calculating net exports) Go to the Web site of the Federal Reserve Bank of St. Louis (FRED) (research.stlouisfed.org/fred2/).

  a. Find the values for the most recent two years for Real Exports of Goods and Services (EXPGSCA) and Real Imports of Goods and Services (IMPGSCA).

  b. Compute the value of net exports for each of the two most recent years.

D8.4 (Comparing GDP and GNP) Go to the Web site of the Federal Reserve Bank of St. Louis (FRED) (research.stlouisfed.org/fred2/).

  a. Find the values for the most recent quarter for Gross Domestic Product (GDP) and Gross National Product (GNP).

  b. Given these values, explain whether foreign production by U.S. firms exceeded U.S. production by foreign firms.

D8.5 (Analyzing the components of personal income) Go to the Web site of the Federal Reserve Bank of St. Louis (FRED) (research.stlouisfed.org/fred2/).

  a. Find the values for the most recent quarter for these three variables: (1) Personal Income (PINCOME); (2) Disposable Personal Income (DPI); and (3) Personal Consumption Expenditures (PCEC).

  b. Use these values to calculate the difference between personal income and disposable personal income. What does this value represent?

D8.6 **(Calculating the GDP deflator and the inflation rate)** Go to the Web site of the Federal Reserve Bank of St. Louis (FRED) (research.stlouisfed.org/fred2/).

   a. Find the values for the most recent quarter and the values for the same quarter one year ago for nominal Gross Domestic Product (GDP) and Real Gross Domestic Product (GDPC1).

   b. Use these values to calculate the GDP price deflator for the most recent quarter and the GDP price deflator for the quarter one year ago.

   c. Using the two GDP price deflators, calculate the inflation rate during this year.

   d. Look again at Figure 8.3 on page 263. Briefly explain why the nominal and real GDP lines intersect at the base year. What is the value of the GDP deflator in the year when the nominal and real GDP lines intersect?

D8.7 **(Calculating real GDP and the real growth rate)** Go to the Web site of the Federal Reserve Bank of St. Louis (FRED) (research.stlouisfed.org/fred2/).

   a. Find the values for the most recent quarter and the same quarter one year ago for nominal Gross Domestic Product (GDP) and the GDP Implicit Price Deflator (GDPDEF)

   b. Use these values to calculate real GDP for the most recent quarter and for the quarter one year ago.

   c. Use the two real GDP values to calculate the real growth rate of the economy during this year.

Unemployment and Inflation

Why Is JPMorgan Chase Laying Off Workers?

When we study macroeconomics, we are looking at the big picture: total production, total employment, and the price level. But the big picture is made up of millions of individual consumers, workers, and firms. Many workers lost their jobs during the severe 2007–2009 recession, and many firms suffered sharp declines in sales. The banking industry was hit particularly hard by the recession. JPMorgan Chase, headquartered in New York City, is the largest bank in the United States and employs more than 240,000 people. The bank was founded in the early twentieth century by legendary financier J.P. Morgan. The bank saw its profit decline by two-thirds from 2007 to 2008 as the U.S. financial system experienced its worst crisis since the Great Depression of the 1930s. By 2009, the U.S. unemployment rate had risen to 10 percent for only the second time since the 1930s.

By 2015, both the U.S. economy and JPMorgan were well into a recovery from the recession. But banks were still struggling for three key reasons: First, interest rates throughout the economy remained at very low levels, reducing banks' profits by narrowing the difference between the interest rates banks paid customers on checking and saving deposits and the interest rates that banks were able to charge on loans to households and firms. Second, large banks were also dealing with increased federal regulation that caused some to stop certain activities, which in the case of JPMorgan included making student loans. Finally, banks were dealing with technological change as more banking activity, including depositing checks and applying for loans, was taking place online. In May 2015, JPMorgan announced that it would lay off 5,000 employees, with each bank branch losing an average of two tellers. The three other largest U.S. banks—Bank of America, Citigroup, and Wells Fargo—were also laying off workers for similar reasons.

The national unemployment rate, which had remained stubbornly high for several years after the 2007–2009 recession ended, had finally reached more normal levels by 2015. Many economists, though, were concerned that wages were increasing only slowly and that the fraction of people who either had jobs or were actively looking for them was at the lowest level in many years.

In this chapter, we will focus on measuring changes in unemployment as well as changes in the price level, or inflation. Because both unemployment and inflation are major macroeconomic problems, it is important to understand how these variables are measured.

Sources: Emily Glazer, "J.P. Morgan Aims to Cut 5,000 Jobs," *Wall Street Journal*, May 28, 2015; Ryan Tracy, Victoria McGrane, and Justin Baer, "Fed Lifts Capital Requirements for Banks," *Wall Street Journal*, July 20, 2015; Eric Morath, "Jobs at a Crossroads: Hiring Up, Pay Flat," *Wall Street Journal*, July 2, 2015; and Rachel Louise Ensign and Lisa Beilfuss, "U.S. Bancorp Says Pressure from Low Rates Looks to Ease," *Wall Street Journal*, July 15, 2015.

Economics in Your Life

Should You Change Your Career Plans if You Graduate during a Recession?

Suppose that you are a sophomore majoring in either economics or finance. You plan to find a job in the banking industry after graduation. The economy is now in a deep recession, and the unemployment rate is the highest in your lifetime, at more than 10 percent. Sizable layoffs have occurred in the banking industry. Should you change your major? Should you still consider a job in the banking industry? As you read this chapter, try to answer these questions. You can check your answers against those we provide on **page 301** at the end of this chapter.

Unemployment and inflation are the macroeconomic problems that are most often discussed in the media and during political campaigns. For many people, the state of the economy can be summarized in just two measures: the unemployment rate and the inflation rate. In the 1960s, Arthur Okun, who was chairman of the Council of Economic Advisers during President Lyndon Johnson's administration, coined the term *misery index*, which adds together the inflation rate and the unemployment rate to give a rough measure of the state of the economy. As we will see in later chapters, although unemployment and inflation are important problems in the short run, the long-run success of an economy is best judged by its ability to generate high levels of real GDP per person. We devote this chapter to discussing how the government measures the unemployment and inflation rates. In particular, we will look closely at the statistics on unemployment and inflation that the federal government issues each month.

9.1 Measuring the Unemployment Rate, the Labor Force Participation Rate, and the Employment–Population Ratio

LEARNING OBJECTIVE: Define the unemployment rate, the labor force participation rate, and the employment–population ratio and understand how they are computed.

At 8:30 A.M. on a Friday early in each month, the U.S. Department of Labor reports its estimate of the previous month's unemployment rate. If the unemployment rate is higher or lower than expected, investors are likely to change their views on the health of the economy. The result is seen an hour later, when trading begins on the New York Stock Exchange. Good news about unemployment usually causes stock prices to rise, and bad news causes stock prices to fall. The unemployment rate can also have important political implications. In most presidential elections, the incumbent president is reelected if the unemployment rate is falling early in the election year but is defeated if the unemployment rate is rising. This relationship held true in 2012, when the unemployment rate was lower during the first six months of 2012 than it had been during the last six months of 2011, and incumbent Barack Obama was reelected.

The unemployment rate is a key macroeconomic statistic. But how does the Department of Labor prepare its estimates of the unemployment rate, and how accurate are these estimates? We will explore the answers to these questions in this section.

The Household Survey

Each month, the U.S. Bureau of the Census conducts the *Current Population Survey* (often called the *household survey*) to collect data needed to compute the unemployment rate. The bureau interviews adults in a sample of 60,000 households, chosen to represent the U.S. population, about the employment status of everyone in the household 16 years of age and older. The Department of Labor's Bureau of Labor Statistics (BLS) uses these data to calculate the monthly unemployment rate. People are considered:

Employed In government statistics, someone who currently has a job or who is temporarily away from his or her job.

Unemployed In government statistics, someone who is not currently at work but who is available for work and who has actively looked for work during the previous month.

Labor force The sum of employed and unemployed workers in the economy.

Unemployment rate The percentage of the labor force that is unemployed.

- **Employed** if they worked during the week before the survey or if they were temporarily away from their jobs because they were ill, on vacation, on strike, or for other reasons.

- **Unemployed** if they did not work in the previous week but were available for work and had actively looked for work at some time during the previous four weeks.

The **labor force** is the sum of the *employed* and the *unemployed*. The **unemployment rate** is the percentage of the labor force that is unemployed.

The BLS classifies the following groups of people who do not have a job and who are not actively looking for a job as *not in the labor force*:

- Retirees, homemakers, full-time students, and those on active military service, in prison, or in hospitals.

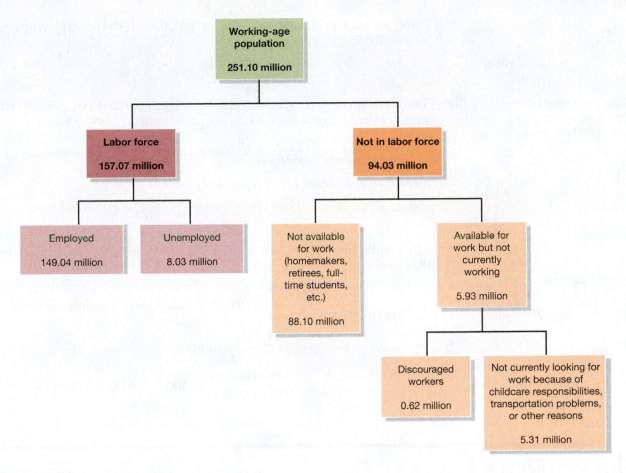

MyEconLab Animation

Figure 9.1   The Employment Status of the Civilian Working-Age Population, August 2015

In August 2015, the working-age population of the United States was 251.10 million. The working-age population is divided into those in the labor force (157.07 million) and those not in the labor force (94.03 million). The labor force is divided into the employed (149.04 million) and the unemployed (8.03 million). Those not in the labor force are divided into those not available for work (88.10 million) and those available for work but not currently working (5.93 million). Finally, those available for work but not in the labor force are divided into discouraged workers (0.62 million) and those not currently looking for work for other reasons (5.31 million).

Source: U.S. Department of Labor, Bureau of Labor Statistics, *The Employment Situation—August 2015*, September 4, 2015.

- People who are available for work and who have actively looked for a job at some point during the previous 12 months but have not looked during the previous 4 weeks. Some people are not actively looking for work for reasons such as transportation difficulties or childcare responsibilities.

- People who are available for work but have *not* actively looked for a job during the previous four weeks because they believe no jobs are available for them. These people are labeled **discouraged workers**.

Figure 9.1 shows the employment status of the civilian working-age population in August 2015.

We can use the information in the figure to calculate three important macroeconomic indicators:

- **The unemployment rate.**   The unemployment rate measures the percentage of the labor force that is unemployed:

$$\frac{\text{Number of unemployed}}{\text{Labor force}} \times 100 = \text{Unemployment rate}.$$

Discouraged workers People who are available for work but have not looked for a job during the previous four weeks because they believe no jobs are available for them.

Using the numbers from Figure 9.1, we can calculate the unemployment rate for August 2015:

$$\frac{8.03 \text{ million}}{157.07 \text{ million}} \times 100 = 5.1\%.$$

Labor force participation rate The percentage of the working-age population in the labor force.

- **The labor force participation rate.** The **labor force participation rate** measures the percentage of the working-age population in the labor force:

$$\frac{\text{Labor force}}{\text{Working-age population}} \times 100 = \text{Labor force participation rate}.$$

For August 2015, the labor force participation rate was:

$$\frac{157.07 \text{ million}}{251.10 \text{ million}} \times 100 = 62.6\%.$$

- **The employment–population ratio.** The *employment–population ratio* measures the percentage of the working-age population that is employed:

$$\frac{\text{Employment}}{\text{Working-age population}} \times 100 = \text{Employment} - \text{population ratio}.$$

For August 2015, the employment–population ratio was:

$$\frac{149.04 \text{ million}}{251.10 \text{ million}} \times 100 = 59.3\%. \quad \text{MyEconLab Concept Check}$$

Solved Problem 9.1

MyEconLab Interactive Animation

What Happens if the BLS Includes the Military?

In the BLS household survey, people on active military service are not included in the totals for employment, the labor force, or the working-age population. Suppose the BLS included the military in these categories. How would the unemployment rate, the labor force participation rate, and the employment–population ratio change?

Solving the Problem

Step 1: **Review the chapter material.** This problem is about calculating the unemployment rate, the labor force participation rate, and the employment–population ratio, so you may want to review the section "Measuring the Unemployment Rate, the Labor Force Participation Rate, and the Employment–Population Ratio," which begins on page 276.

Step 2: **Show that including people in the military decreases the measured unemployment rate.** The unemployment rate is calculated as:

$$\frac{\text{Number of unemployed}}{\text{Labor force}} \times 100.$$

Including people in the military would increase the number of people counted as being in the labor force but would leave unchanged the number of people counted as unemployed. Therefore, the unemployment rate would decrease.

Step 3: **Show how including people in the military would affect the measured labor force participation rate and the measured employment–population ratio.** The labor force participation rate is calculated as:

$$\frac{\text{Labor force}}{\text{Working-age population}} \times 100,$$

and the employment–population ratio is calculated as:

$$\frac{\text{Employment}}{\text{Working-age population}} \times 100.$$

Including people in the military would increase the number of people in the labor force, the number of people employed, and the number of people in the working-age population, all by the same amount. The labor force participation rate and the employment–population ratio would both increase because adding the same number to both the numerator and the denominator of a fraction that is less than one increases the value of the fraction.

To help see this point, consider the following simple example. Suppose that 100,000,000 people are in the working-age population and 50,000,000 are in the labor force, not counting people in the military. Suppose that 1,000,000 people are in the military. Then, the labor force participation rate excluding the military is:

$$\frac{50,000,000}{100,000,000} \times 100 = 50\%,$$

and the labor force participation rate including the military is:

$$\frac{51,000,000}{101,000,000} \times 100 = 50.5\%.$$

A similar calculation shows that including the military would also increase the employment–population ratio.

Your Turn: For more practice, do related problem 1.8 on page 302 at the end of this chapter.   MyEconLab Study Plan

Problems with Measuring the Unemployment Rate

Although the BLS reports the unemployment rate measured to the tenth of a percentage point, it is not a perfect measure of the actual state of joblessness in the economy. One problem that the BLS confronts is distinguishing between the unemployed and people who are not in the labor force. During an economic recession, for example, an increase in discouraged workers usually occurs, as people who have had trouble finding a job stop actively looking. Because these workers are not counted as unemployed, the unemployment rate as measured by the BLS may understate the true degree of joblessness in the economy. The BLS also counts people as being employed if they hold part-time jobs even though they would prefer to hold full-time jobs. In a recession, counting as "employed" a part-time worker who wants to work full time understates the degree of joblessness in the economy and makes the employment situation appear better than it is.

Not counting discouraged workers as unemployed and counting people as employed who are working part time, although they would prefer to be working full time, has a substantial effect on the measured unemployment rate. In Figure 9.2, the red line shows the official measure of the unemployment rate. The blue line shows what the unemployment rate would be if the BLS had counted as unemployed (1) all people who were available for work but not actively looking for jobs, and (2) all people who were in part-time jobs but wanted full-time jobs. The difference between the two measures of the unemployment rate is substantial and was particularly large during the slow recovery following the 2007–2009 recession. For example, in August 2015, using the broader definition of unemployment would have increased the measured unemployment rate from 5.1 percent to 10.3 percent.

There are other measurement problems, however, that cause the measured unemployment rate to *overstate* the true extent of joblessness. These problems arise because the BLS does not verify the responses of people included in the survey. Some people who claim to be unemployed and actively looking for work may not really be actively looking. A person might claim to be actively looking for a job in order to remain eligible for government payments to the unemployed. In this case, a person who is actually not in the labor force is counted as unemployed. Other people might be employed but

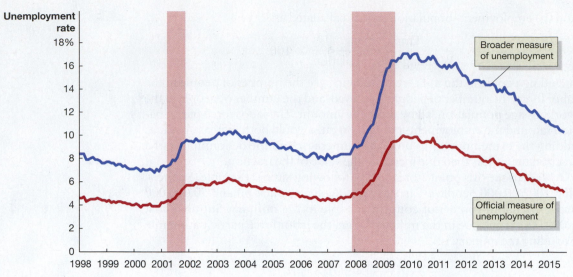

Figure 9.2 **The Official Unemployment Rate and a Broad Measure of the Unemployment Rate, 1998–2015**

The red line shows the official measure of the unemployment rate. The blue line shows what the unemployment rate would be if the BLS had counted as unemployed (1) all people who were available for work but not actively looking for jobs, and (2) all people who were in part-time jobs but wanted full-time jobs. The difference between the measures was particularly large during the 2007–2009 recession and the weak recovery that followed. Shaded areas indicate months of recession.

Note: The official measure (red line) is BLS series U-3, and the broader measure (blue line) is BLS series U-6.
Source: U.S. Bureau of Labor Statistics.

engaged in illegal activity—such as drug dealing—or might want to conceal a legitimate job to avoid paying taxes. In these cases, individuals who are actually employed are counted as unemployed. These inaccurate responses to the survey bias the unemployment rate as measured by the BLS toward overstating the true extent of joblessness. We can conclude that, although the unemployment rate provides some useful information about the employment situation in the country, it is far from an exact measure of joblessness in the economy.

Trends in Labor Force Participation

The labor force participation rate is important because it determines the amount of labor that will be available to the economy from a given population. The higher the labor force participation rate, the more labor that will be available and the higher a country's levels of GDP and GDP per person. Figure 9.3 highlights two important trends in the

Figure 9.3

Trends in the Labor Force: Participation Rates of Adult Men and Women since 1948

The labor force participation rate of adult men has declined gradually since 1948, but the labor force participation rate of adult women has increased significantly, making the overall labor force participation rate higher today than it was in 1948.
Source: U.S. Bureau of Labor Statistics.

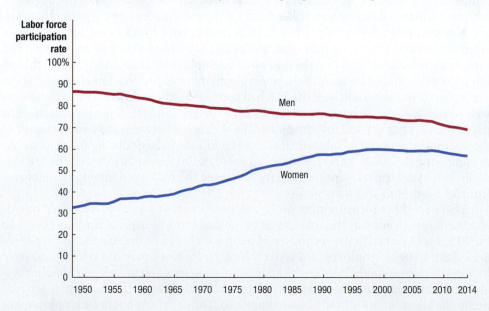

labor force participation rates of adults aged 16 years and over in the United States since 1948: the falling labor force participation rate of adult men and the rising labor force participation rate of adult women. (Note, though, that by 2014, the labor force participation rate of women had not yet fully recovered from the effects of the recession.)

The labor force participation rate of adult males fell from 87 percent in 1948 to 69 percent in 2014. Most of this decline is due to older men retiring earlier and younger men remaining in school longer. There has also been a decline in labor force participation among males who are not in school but who are too young to retire. Over the longer term, this decline in labor force participation among prime-age males appears to be partly due to Congress having made it easier for people to receive cash payments under the Social Security Disability Insurance program. In the shorter term, the decline is due to the severity of the 2007–2009 recession and the weak recovery that followed the recession.

The decline in the labor force participation rate of adult men has been more than offset by a sharp increase in the labor force participation rate of adult women, which rose from 33 percent in 1948 to 57 percent in 2014. As a result, the overall labor force participation rate rose from 59 percent in 1948 to 63 percent in 2014. The increase in the labor force participation rate of women has several causes, including changing social attitudes due in part to the women's movement, federal legislation outlawing discrimination, increasing wages for women, the typical family having fewer children, and an increase in female-headed households.   MyEconLab Concept Check

Unemployment Rates for Different Groups

Different groups in the population can have very different unemployment rates. Figure 9.4 shows unemployment rates in August 2015 for different ethnic groups and for groups with different levels of education. While the overall unemployment rate was 5.1 percent, Asians had an unemployment rate of 3.5 percent, and African Americans had an unemployment rate of 9.5 percent. The unemployment rate for people over age 25 without a high school degree was 7.7 percent, while the unemployment rate for college graduates was only 2.5 percent.   MyEconLab Concept Check

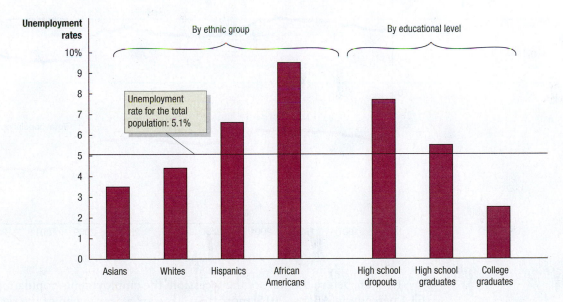

MyEconLab Real-time data

Figure 9.4   **Unemployment Rates in the United States, August 2015**

The unemployment rate of African Americans is the highest of the four ethnic groups shown, while the unemployment rate of Asians is the lowest. High school dropouts have an unemployment rate that is triple the unemployment rate for college graduates.

Notes: The unemployment rates for ethnic groups apply to people 16 years and older; the unemployment rates by educational attainment apply to people 25 years and older. People identified as Hispanic may be of any race.

Source: U.S. Department of Labor, Bureau of Labor Statistics, *The Employment Situation—August 2015*, September 4, 2015.

How Long Are People Typically Unemployed?

The longer a person is unemployed, the greater the hardship. During the Great Depression of the 1930s, some people were unemployed for years at a time. In the modern U.S. economy, a typical unemployed person stays unemployed for a relatively brief period of time, although that time lengthens significantly during a severe recession. For example, when the economy was expanding in early 2007, fewer than 20 percent of the unemployed had been jobless for more than six months. By the end of the 2007–2009 recession, though, half of the unemployed had been jobless for more than six months. The average period of unemployment had more than doubled from about 4 months to about 10 months. The severity of unemployment during and after the 2007–2009 recession was a sharp break with the normal U.S. experience in which the typical person who loses a job will find another one or be recalled to a previous job within a few months.

MyEconLab Concept Check

Making the Connection

Eight Million Workers Are Missing!

Although the unemployment rate is the most widely followed measure of the state of the labor market, during the recovery from the 2007–2009 recession, many economists and policy-makers became concerned about the employment–population ratio. As we saw earlier, the employment–population ratio measures the percentage of the working-age population that is employed. Figure 9.2 on page 280 shows that by mid-2015, the unemployment rate had fallen from its high of 10 percent in 2009 to 5.1 percent, or to roughly normal levels. But the red line in the figure below shows that the employment–population ratio did not recover completely from its decline during the 2007–2009 recession.

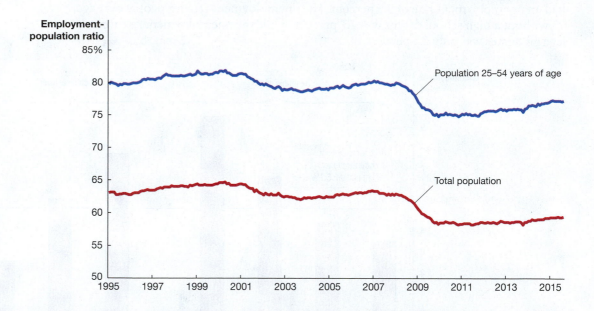

In 2006, before the start of the recession, the employment–population ratio was 63.4 percent. In August 2015, more than six years after the end of the recession, the ratio was still only 59.4 percent. If the employment–population had regained its pre-recession level, an additional 8 million people would have been working in 2015 than actually were. With 8 million additional workers, GDP would have been significantly larger than it was.

Why hasn't the employment–population ratio returned to its pre-recession levels? Part of the explanation is that as the baby boom generation—people born between the years 1946 and 1964—has gotten older, the average age of the population has increased. People in their late 50s and early 60s are less likely to have jobs than are younger people. This fact is illustrated by the blue line, which shows the employment–population ratio just for people aged 25 to 54—the age range in which people are most likely to be working. The employment–population ratio for this age range declined by about 3 percentage points between 2006 and 2015, or about one-fourth less than the decline in employment–population ratio for the whole working-age population. Economists have not reached a consensus in explaining the remainder of the decline in the employment–population ratio. Some economists note that not only did many people lose their jobs during the recession, but the slow recovery from the recession meant that some people were out of work for years. Often people who have not held a job for a long period have difficulty finding a new one because their skills deteriorate and employers therefore become more reluctant to hire them. This "labor-market scarring" may help explain some of the decline in the employment–population ratio. Other economists point to the increased number of people who receive Social Security Disability Insurance. Under this program, people with disabilities receive cash payments from the federal government and receive medical benefits under the Medicaid program. Some people who might otherwise be working are being supported by disability payments instead.

Economists at the Congressional Budget Office (CBO) estimate that the Affordable Care Act, which provides subsidies to buy medical insurance and expands Medicare coverage (see Chapter 5), has resulted in a decline in employment. According to a CBO report, as a result of the act, "some people will decide not to work or to work fewer hours than would otherwise be the case—including some people who will choose to retire earlier than they would have otherwise, and some people who will work less themselves and rely more on a spouse's earnings."

Economists Jeffrey Clemens and Michael Wither of the University of California, San Diego, have analyzed the effects of the increase in the federal minimum wage from $5.15 an hour in 2007 to $7.25 an hour in 2009. They find that by making it more difficult for low-skilled workers to find jobs, the increase in the minimum wage reduced the employment–population ratio. They estimate that this effect accounts for about 14 percent of the total decline in the ratio.

Finally, as we saw in Chapter 6, new businesses are being started at lower rates than in past years and barriers to entering certain occupations have increased as some states have imposed additional licensing requirements. Difficulties in starting new businesses mean that some people who would otherwise be self-employed as small business owners may have left the labor force instead.

As we will see in later chapters, economic growth in the United States has slowed in recent years. Many economists believe that one key to increasing growth and living standards is for the government to develop policies that will help to reverse the decline in the employment–population ratio.

Sources: Josh Zumbrun, "Labor-Market Dropouts Stay on the Sidelines," *Wall Street Journal*, December 28, 2014; Doug Elmendorf, "Frequently Asked Questions about CBO's Estimates of the Labor Market Effects of the Affordable Care Act," cbo.gov, February 10, 2014; Jeffrey Clemens and Michael Wither, "The Minimum Wage and the Great Recession: Evidence of Effects on the Employment and Income Trajectories of Low-Skilled Workers," Working Paper, University of California, San Diego, November 24, 2014; Janet L. Yellen, "Labor Market Dynamics and Monetary Policy," Speech at the Federal Reserve Bank of Kansas City Economic Symposium, Jackson Hole, Wyoming, August 22, 2014; Samuel Kapon and Joseph Tracy, "A Mis-Leading Labor Market Indicator," libertystreeteconomics.nyfed.org, February 3, 2014; and U.S. Bureau of Labor Statistics.

Your Turn: Test your understanding by doing related problem 1.10 on page 303 at the end of this chapter.

MyEconLab Study Plan

The Establishment Survey: Another Measure of Employment

In addition to the household survey, the BLS uses the *establishment survey*, sometimes called the *payroll survey*, to measure total employment in the economy. This monthly survey samples about 300,000 business establishments (such as factories, stores, and offices). A small company typically operates only one establishment, but a large company may operate many establishments. The establishment survey provides

TABLE 9.1   Household and Establishment Survey Data for July and August 2015   MyEconLab Real-time data

	Household Survey			Establishment Survey		
	July	August	Change	July	August	Change
Employed	148,840,000	149,036,000	196,000	142,115,000	142,288,000	173,000
Unemployed	8,266,000	8,029,000	−237,000			
Labor force	157,106,000	157,065,000	−41,000			
Unemployment rate	5.3%	5.1%	−0.2%			

Source: U.S. Department of Labor, Bureau of Labor Statistics, *The Employment Situation—August 2015*, September 4, 2015.

information on the total number of persons who are employed and *on a company payroll*. The establishment survey has four drawbacks:

1. The survey does not provide information on the number of self-employed persons because they are not on a company payroll.
2. The survey may fail to count some persons employed at newly opened firms that are not included in the survey.
3. The survey provides no information on unemployment.
4. The values for employment that the BLS initially announces can be significantly revised as data from additional establishments become available.

Despite these drawbacks, the establishment survey has the advantage of being determined by actual payrolls rather than by unverified answers, as is the case with the household survey. As a result, many economists rely more on establishment survey data than on household survey data in analyzing current labor market conditions. Some financial analysts who forecast the future state of the economy to help forecast stock prices also rely more on establishment survey data than on household survey data.

Table 9.1 shows household survey and establishment survey data for the months of July and August 2015. Notice that the household survey, because it includes the self-employed, gives a larger total for employment than does the establishment survey. The household survey provides information on the number of persons unemployed and on the number of persons in the labor force. This information is not available in the establishment survey. Between July and August 2015, employment rose by 196,000 in the household survey, but rose by only 173,000 in the establishment survey. This discrepancy is due partly to the slightly different groups covered by the two surveys and partly to inaccuracies in the surveys.   MyEconLab Concept Check

Revisions in the Establishment Survey Employment Data: How Bad Was the 2007–2009 Recession?

Economists and policymakers rely on government economic data, such as the employment data from the establishment survey, to understand the current state of the economy. Given the size of the U.S. economy, though, government agencies, such as the Bureau of Economic Analysis, the Bureau of Labor Statistics, and the Census Bureau, need considerable time to gather complete and accurate data on GDP, employment, and other macroeconomic variables. To avoid long waits in supplying data to policymakers and the general public, government agencies typically issue preliminary estimates that they revise as additional information becomes available. As we noted earlier, the data on employment from the establishment survey can be subject to particularly large revisions over time.

Figure 9.5 shows for each month from December 2007 to December 2010 the difference between the value for the change in employment as initially reported in the establishment survey and the revised value available in September 2015. The green bars show months for which the BLS revised its preliminary estimates to show that fewer jobs were lost (or more jobs were created) than originally reported, and the red bars show months for which the BLS revised its preliminary estimates to show that more jobs were lost (or fewer jobs were created). For example, the BLS initially reported that

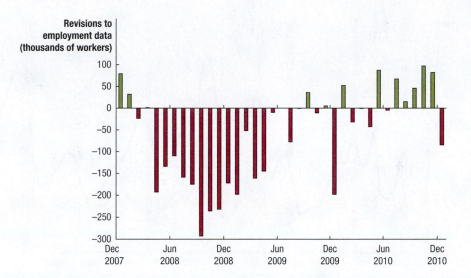

MyEconLab Animation

Figure 9.5

Revisions to Employment Changes, as Reported in the Establishment Survey, 2007–2010

Over time, the BLS revises its preliminary estimates of changes in employment. During the 2007–2009 recession, many more jobs were lost than the preliminary estimates showed. The green bars show months for which the BLS revised its preliminary estimates to show fewer jobs were lost (or more jobs were created), and the red bars show months for which the BLS revised its preliminary estimates to show more jobs were lost (or fewer jobs were created).

Source: U.S. Bureau of Labor Statistics.

employment declined by 159,000 jobs during September 2008. In fact, after additional data became available, the BLS revised its estimate to show that employment had declined by 452,000 jobs during the month—a difference of nearly 300,000 more jobs lost. As the recession deepened between April 2008 and April 2009, the BLS's initial reports underestimated the number of jobs lost by 2.3 million. In other words, the recession of 2007–2009 turned out to be much more severe than economists and policymakers realized at the time.   MyEconLab Concept Check

Job Creation and Job Destruction over Time

One important fact about employment is not very well known: The U.S. economy creates and destroys millions of jobs every year. In 2014, for example, about 29.1 million jobs were created, and about 26.1 million jobs were destroyed. This degree of job creation and destruction is not surprising in a vibrant market system where new firms are constantly being started, some existing firms are expanding, some existing firms are contracting, and some firms are going out of business. The creation and destruction of jobs results from changes in consumer tastes, technological progress, and the successes and failures of entrepreneurs in responding to the opportunities and challenges of shifting consumer tastes and technological change. The large volume of job creation and job destruction helps explain why during most years, the typical person who loses a job is unemployed for a relatively brief period of time.

When the BLS announces each month the increases or decreases in the number of persons employed and unemployed, these are net figures. That is, the change in the number of persons employed is equal to the total number of jobs created minus the number of jobs eliminated. Take, for example, the months from September to December 2014. During that period, 7,635,000 jobs were created, and 6,526,000 jobs were eliminated, for a net increase of 1,109,000 jobs. Because the net change is so much smaller than the total job increases and decreases, the net change doesn't fully represent how dynamic the U.S. job market really is.   MyEconLab Concept Check

MyEconLab Study Plan

9.2 ## Types of Unemployment
LEARNING OBJECTIVE: Identify the three types of unemployment.

Figure 9.6 illustrates that the unemployment rate follows the business cycle, rising during recessions and falling during expansions. Notice, though, that the unemployment rate never falls to zero. To understand why, we need to discuss the three types of unemployment:

1. Frictional unemployment
2. Structural unemployment
3. Cyclical unemployment

MyEconLab Real-time data

Figure 9.6

The Annual Unemployment Rate in the United States, 1950–2014

The unemployment rate rises during recessions and falls during expansions. Shaded areas indicate recessions.
Source: U.S. Bureau of Labor Statistics.

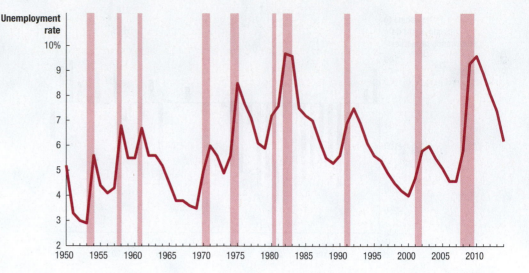

Frictional unemployment Short-term unemployment that arises from the process of matching workers with jobs.

Frictional Unemployment and Job Search

Workers have different skills, interests, and abilities, and jobs have different skill requirements, working conditions, and pay levels. As a result, a new worker entering the labor force or a worker who has lost a job probably will not find an acceptable job right away. Most workers spend at least some time in *job search*, just as most firms spend time searching for a new person to fill a job opening. **Frictional unemployment** is short-term unemployment that arises from the process of matching workers with jobs. Some frictional unemployment is unavoidable. As we have seen, the U.S. economy creates and destroys millions of jobs each year. The process of job search takes time, so there will always be some workers who are frictionally unemployed because they are between jobs and in the process of searching for new ones.

Some frictional unemployment is due to seasonal factors, such as weather or fluctuations in demand for some products or services during different times of the year. For example, stores located in beach resort areas reduce their hiring during the winter, and ski resorts reduce their hiring during the summer. Department stores increase their hiring in November and December and reduce their hiring after New Year's Day. In agricultural areas, employment increases during harvest season and declines thereafter. Construction workers in many parts of the United States experience greater unemployment during the winter than during the summer. *Seasonal unemployment* refers to unemployment due to factors such as weather, variations in tourism, and other calendar-related events. Because seasonal unemployment can make the unemployment rate seem artificially high during some months and artificially low during other months, the BLS reports two unemployment rates each month—one that is *seasonally adjusted* and one that is not seasonally adjusted. The seasonally adjusted data eliminate the effects of seasonal unemployment. Economists and policymakers rely on the seasonally adjusted data as a more accurate measure of the current state of the labor market.

Would eliminating all frictional unemployment be good for the economy? No, because some frictional unemployment actually increases economic efficiency. Frictional unemployment occurs because workers and firms take the time necessary to ensure a good match between the attributes of workers and the characteristics of jobs. By devoting time to job search, workers end up with jobs they find satisfying and in which they can be productive. Of course, having workers who are satisfied and productive is also in the best interest of firms. MyEconLab Concept Check

Structural Unemployment

Computer-generated three-dimensional animation, which has been used in movies such as *Inside Out* and *Minions*, has become much more popular than traditional hand-drawn two-dimensional animation. As a result, many people who are highly skilled in hand-drawn animation lost their jobs at movie studios such as Walt Disney Pictures and DreamWorks. To become employed again, many of these people either became skilled in computer-generated animation or found new occupations. In the meantime, they were unemployed. Economists consider these animators *structurally unemployed*. **Structural unemployment** arises from a persistent mismatch between the job skills or attributes of workers and the requirements of jobs. While frictional unemployment is short term, structural unemployment can last for longer periods because workers need time to learn new skills. For example, employment by U.S. steel firms fell by more than half between the early 1980s and the early 2000s as a result of competition from foreign producers and technological change that substituted machines for workers. Many steelworkers found new jobs in other industries only after lengthy periods of retraining.

Some workers lack even basic skills, such as literacy, or have addictions to alcohol or other drugs that make it difficult for them to perform adequately the duties of almost any job. These workers may remain structurally unemployed for long periods.   MyEconLab Concept Check

Structural unemployment
Unemployment that arises from a persistent mismatch between the skills or attributes of workers and the requirements of jobs.

Cyclical Unemployment

When the economy moves into recession, many firms find their sales falling and cut back on production. As production falls, firms start laying off workers. Workers who lose their jobs because of a recession are experiencing **cyclical unemployment**. For example, Ford Motor Company laid off workers during the recession of 2007–2009. As the economy slowly recovered from the recession, Ford began rehiring those workers. The Ford workers who had been laid off from their jobs during the recession and then rehired during the following expansion had experienced cyclical unemployment.   MyEconLab Concept Check

Cyclical unemployment
Unemployment caused by a business cycle recession.

Full Employment

As the economy moves through the expansion phase of the business cycle, cyclical unemployment eventually drops to zero. The unemployment rate will not be zero, however, because of frictional and structural unemployment. As Figure 9.6 shows, the unemployment rate in the United States is rarely less than 4 percent. The fluctuations that we see in Figure 9.6 are mainly due to the changes in the level of cyclical unemployment. When the only remaining unemployment is structural and frictional unemployment, the economy is said to be at *full employment*.

Economists consider the sum of frictional and structural unemployment to be the normal underlying level of unemployment in the economy, or the **natural rate of unemployment**. Economists disagree on the exact value of the natural rate of unemployment, and there is good reason to believe that it doesn't remain constant over long periods of a decade or more. Currently, most economists estimate the natural rate to be between 5.0 percent and 5.5 percent. The natural rate of unemployment is also sometimes called the *full-employment rate of unemployment*.   MyEconLab Concept Check

Natural rate of unemployment
The normal rate of unemployment, consisting of frictional unemployment and structural unemployment.

Making the Connection
MyEconLab Video

How Should We Categorize Unemployment at JPMorgan Chase?

We saw at the beginning of the chapter that JPMorgan Chase announced in 2015 that it was laying off 5,000 employees, with each bank branch losing on average two tellers. In addition, the bank was exiting certain lines of business, including making student loans. Did the layoffs at JPMorgan result in an increase in frictional unemployment, structural unemployment, or cyclical unemployment? In answering this question, we should acknowledge that dividing unemployment into these three categories is useful in understanding the sources of unemployment, but it can be difficult to apply these categories in a particular case.

Which category of unemployment do the workers laid off at JPMorgan Chase fit into?

The BLS, for instance, provides estimates of total unemployment but does not classify it as frictional, structural, or cyclical.

Despite these difficulties, we can roughly categorize the unemployment resulting from the layoffs at JPMorgan. At the time of the layoffs, the U.S. economy was expanding, and the demand for loans and other services the bank offered was increasing, so the unemployment at JPMorgan was not cyclical, and the firm was unlikely to rehire the workers it was laying off, even if the economic recovery became even stronger.

The decision to lay off bank tellers was the result of technological change. As more people deposit checks and make their loan payments online using smartphone apps, fewer people visit bank branches, so JPMorgan doesn't need as many bank tellers. Because other banks are affected by the same changes in technology, the laid-off bank tellers were likely to need to retrain for other jobs to find employment again. So, these workers were structurally unemployed.

As the largest U.S. bank, JPMorgan is subject to federal regulations that do not affect smaller banks. The bank was dropping some types of services, including making student loans, because new federal regulations had increased the costs facing the largest U.S. banks. So, if JPMorgan's employees who were providing these services were able to find employment with smaller banks not subject to the new regulations, during the time the employees were out of work they would have been frictionally unemployed.

It therefore seems likely that some of the unemployment at JPMorgan Chase in 2015 was structural and some was frictional. Given the state of the economy, none of it was likely cyclical.

Sources: Emily Glazer, "J.P. Morgan Aims to Cut 5,000 Jobs," *Wall Street Journal*, May 28, 2015; and Ryan Tracy, Victoria McGrane, and Justin Baer, "Fed Lifts Capital Requirements for Banks," *Wall Street Journal*, July 20, 2015.

 MyEconLab Study Plan

Your Turn: Test your understanding by doing related problems 2.6, 2.7, and 2.8 on pages 303–304 at the end of this chapter.

9.3 | Explaining Unemployment

LEARNING OBJECTIVE: Explain what factors determine the unemployment rate.

We have seen that some unemployment is a result of the business cycle. In later chapters, we will explore the causes of the business cycle, which will help us understand cyclical unemployment. In this section, we look at the factors that determine the levels of frictional and structural unemployment.

Government Policies and the Unemployment Rate

Workers search for jobs by sending out résumés, registering with Internet job sites such as Monster.com, and getting job referrals from friends and relatives. Firms fill job openings by advertising in newspapers, listing openings online, participating in job fairs, and recruiting on college campuses. Here's how government policies can aid these private employment efforts:

- Governments can help reduce the level of frictional unemployment by pursuing policies that help speed up the process of matching unemployed workers with unfilled jobs.

- Governments can help reduce structural unemployment by implementing policies that aid worker retraining. For example, the federal government's Trade Adjustment Assistance program offers training to workers who lose their jobs as a result of competition from foreign firms.

Some government policies, however, can add to the level of frictional and structural unemployment. These government policies increase the unemployment rate either by increasing the time workers devote to searching for jobs, by providing disincentives for firms to hire workers, or by keeping wages above their market level.

Unemployment Insurance and Other Payments to the Unemployed

Suppose you have been in the labor force for a few years but have just lost your job. You could probably find a low-wage job immediately if you needed to—perhaps at Walmart or McDonald's. But you might decide to search for a better, higher-paying job by sending out résumés and responding to want ads and Internet job postings. Remember that the *opportunity cost* of any activity is the highest-valued alternative that you must give up to engage in that activity. In this case, the opportunity cost of continuing to search for a job is the salary you are giving up at the job you could have taken. The longer you search, the greater your chances of finding a better, higher-paying job, but the longer you search, the more salary you have given up by not working, so the greater the opportunity cost.

In the United States and most other high-income countries, the unemployed are eligible for *unemployment insurance payments* from the government. In the United States, these payments vary by state but are generally equal to about half the average wage. The unemployed spend more time searching for jobs because they receive these payments. This additional time spent searching raises the unemployment rate. Can we conclude that the unemployment insurance program is a bad idea? Most economists would say "no." Before Congress established the unemployment insurance program at the end of the 1930s, unemployed workers suffered very large declines in their incomes, which led them to greatly reduce their spending. This reduced spending contributed to the severity of recessions. Unemployment insurance helps the unemployed maintain their income and spending, which lessens the personal hardship of being unemployed and also helps reduce the severity of recessions.

In the United States, unemployed workers are generally eligible to receive unemployment insurance payments for only six months, although this period is typically extended during recessions, as happened during and after the recession of 2007–2009. After that, the opportunity cost of continuing to search for a job rises. In many other high-income countries, such as Canada and most of the countries of Western Europe, workers are eligible to receive unemployment payments for a year or more, and the payments may equal as much as 70 percent of their previous wage. In addition, many of these countries have generous *social insurance programs* that allow unemployed adults to receive some government payments even after their eligibility for unemployment insurance has ended. In the United States, very few government programs make payments to healthy adults, with the exception of the Temporary Assistance for Needy Families program, which allows single parents to receive payments for up to five years. Although there are many reasons unemployment rates may differ across countries, most economists believe that because the opportunity cost of job search is lower in Canada and the countries of Western Europe, unemployed workers in those countries search longer for jobs and, therefore, the unemployment rates in those countries tend to be higher than in the United States. During the 2007–2009 recession, however, unemployment rates were lower in Canada and Germany than in the United States.

Minimum Wage Laws   In 1938, the federal government enacted a national minimum wage law. At first, the lowest legal wage firms could pay workers was $0.25 per hour. Over the years, Congress has gradually raised the minimum wage; in 2015, it was $7.25 per hour. Some states and cities also have minimum wage laws. For example, in 2015, the minimum wage in California was $9.00 per hour, and the minimum wage in San Francisco was $12.25 per hour. If the minimum wage is set above the market wage determined by the demand and supply of labor, the quantity of labor supplied will be greater than the quantity of labor demanded. Some workers will become unemployed who would have been employed if there was no minimum wage. As a result, the unemployment rate will be higher than it would be without a minimum wage. Economists agree that the current minimum wage is above the market wage for some workers, but they disagree on the amount of unemployment that has resulted. Because teenagers generally have relatively few job-related skills, they are the group most likely to receive the minimum wage. Studies estimate that a 10 percent increase in the minimum wage reduces teenage employment by about 2 percent. Because teenagers and others receiving the minimum wage are a relatively small part of the labor force, most economists believe that, at the minimum wage's current level, it has a fairly small effect on the unemployment rate in the United States.   MyEconLab Concept Check

Labor Unions

Labor unions are organizations of workers that bargain with employers for higher wages and better working conditions for their members. In unionized industries, the wage is usually above what otherwise would be the market wage. This above-market wage results in employers in unionized industries hiring fewer workers, but does it also significantly increase the overall unemployment rate in the economy? Most economists would say the answer is "no" because in the United States only about 9 percent of workers outside the government sector are unionized. Although unions remain strong in a few industries, such as airlines, automobiles, steel, and telecommunications, most industries are not unionized. The result is that most workers who can't find jobs in unionized industries because the wage is above its market level can find jobs in other industries.   MyEconLab Concept Check

Efficiency Wages

Efficiency wage An above-market wage that a firm pays to increase workers' productivity.

Some firms pay above-market wages not because the government requires them to or because they are unionized but because they believe doing so will increase their profits. Because wages are the largest cost for many employers, so paying higher wages seems like a good way for firms to *lower* profits rather than to increase them. The key to understanding this wage policy is that the level of wages can affect the level of workers' productivity. Many studies have shown that workers are motivated by higher wages to work harder. An **efficiency wage** is an above-market wage that a firm pays to motivate workers to be more productive. Can't firms ensure that workers work hard by supervising them? In some cases, they can. For example, a telemarketing firm can monitor workers electronically to ensure that they make the required number of phone calls per hour. In many business situations, however, it is much more difficult to monitor workers. Many firms must rely on workers being motivated enough to work hard. By paying an above-market wage, a firm raises the cost to workers of losing their jobs because many alternative jobs will pay only the market wage. The increase in productivity that results from paying the high wage can more than offset the extra cost of the wage, thereby lowering the firm's costs of production.

Because the efficiency wage is above the market wage, it results in the quantity of labor supplied being greater than the quantity of labor demanded, just as do minimum wage laws and labor unions. So, efficiency wages also contribute to economies experiencing some unemployment even when cyclical unemployment is zero.   MyEconLab Concept Check

MyEconLab Study Plan

Measuring Inflation

9.4

LEARNING OBJECTIVE: Define the price level and the inflation rate and understand how they are computed.

One of the facts of economic life is that the prices of most goods and services rise over time. As a result, the cost of living continually rises. In 1914, Henry Ford began paying his workers a wage of $5 per day, which was more than twice as much as other automobile manufacturers were paying. Ford's $5-a-day wage provided his workers with a middle-class income because prices were so low. In 1914, Ford's Model T, the best-selling car in the country, sold for less than $600, the price of a man's suit was $15, the price of a ticket to a movie theater was $0.15, and the price of a box of Kellogg's Corn Flakes was $0.08. In 2015, with the cost of living being much higher than it was in 1914, the federal minimum wage law required firms to pay a wage of at least $7.25 per *hour*, more than Ford's highly paid workers earned in a day.

Knowing how the government compiles the employment and unemployment statistics is important in interpreting them. The same is true of the government's statistics on the cost of living. The **price level** measures the average prices of goods and services in the economy (see Chapter 8). The **inflation rate** is the percentage increase in the price level from one year to the next. In the last chapter, we introduced the *GDP deflator* as a measure of the price level. The GDP deflator is the broadest measure we have of the price level because it includes the price of every final good and service. But for some purposes, it is too broad. For example, if we want to know how inflation affects a typical household, the GDP price deflator may be misleading because it includes the prices of products such as large electric generators and machine tools that are part of the investment component of GDP but are not purchased by a typical household. In this chapter, we will focus on measuring the inflation rate by changes in the *consumer price index* because changes in this index come closest to measuring changes in the cost of living as experienced by a typical household. We will also briefly discuss a third measure of inflation: the *producer price index*.

Price level A measure of the average prices of goods and services in the economy.

Inflation rate The percentage increase in the price level from one year to the next.

The Consumer Price Index

To obtain prices of a representative group of goods and services, the BLS surveys 14,000 households nationwide on their spending habits. It uses the results of this survey to construct a *market basket* of 211 types of goods and services purchased by a typical urban family of four. Figure 9.7 shows the goods and services in the market basket, grouped into eight broad categories. Almost three-quarters of the market basket falls into just three categories: housing, transportation, and food. Each month, hundreds of BLS employees visit 23,000 stores in 87 cities and record prices of the goods and services in the market basket. Each price in the consumer price index is given a weight equal to the fraction of a typical family's budget spent on that good or service.

The **consumer price index (CPI)** is a measure of the average change over time in the prices a typical urban family of four pays for the goods and services they purchase. One year is chosen as the base year, and the value of the CPI is set equal to 100 for that year. In any year other than the base year, the CPI is equal to the ratio of the dollar amount necessary to buy the market basket of goods in that year divided by the dollar amount necessary to buy the market basket of goods in the base year,

Consumer price index (CPI) A measure of the average change over time in the prices a typical urban family of four pays for the goods and services they purchase.

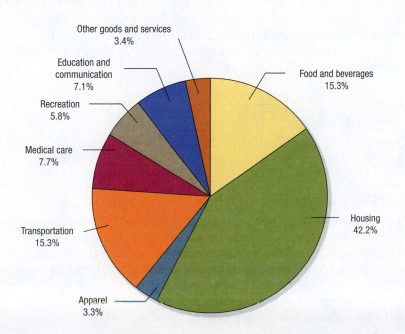

MyEconLab Animation

Figure 9.7

The CPI Market Basket, December 2014

The Bureau of Labor Statistics surveys 14,000 households on their spending habits. The results are used to construct a *market basket* of goods and services purchased by a typical urban family of four. The chart shows these goods and services, grouped into eight broad categories. The percentages represent the expenditure shares of the categories within the market basket. The categories housing, transportation, and food make up about three-quarters of the market basket.

Source: U.S. Bureau of Labor Statistics.

multiplied by 100. Because the CPI measures the cost to a typical family of buying a representative basket of goods and services, it is sometimes called the *cost-of-living index*.

A simple example can clarify how the CPI is constructed. For purposes of this example, we assume that the market basket has only three products: eye examinations, pizzas, and books:

Product	Base Year (1999)			2016		2017	
	Quantity	Price	Expenditures	Price	Expenditures (on base-year quantities)	Price	Expenditures (on base-year quantities)
Eye examinations	1	$50.00	$50.00	$100.00	$100.00	$85.00	$85.00
Pizzas	20	10.00	200.00	15.00	300.00	14.00	280.00
Books	20	25.00	500.00	25.00	500.00	27.50	550.00
TOTAL			$750.00		$900.00		$915.00

Suppose that during the base year, 1999, a survey determines that each month, a typical family purchases 1 eye examination, 20 pizzas, and 20 books. At 1999 prices, a family must spend $750.00 to purchase this market basket of goods and services. The CPI for every year after the base year is determined by dividing the amount necessary to purchase the market basket in that year by the amount required in the base year, then multiplying by 100. Notice that the quantities of the products purchased in 2016 and 2017 are irrelevant in calculating the CPI because *we are assuming that households buy the same market basket of products each month*. Using the numbers in the table, we can calculate the CPI for 2016 and 2017:

Formula	Applied to 2016	Applied to 2017
$\text{CPI} = \dfrac{\text{Expenditures in the current year}}{\text{Expenditures in the base year}} \times 100$	$\left(\dfrac{\$900}{\$750}\right) \times 100 = 120$	$\left(\dfrac{\$915}{\$750}\right) \times 100 = 122$

How do we interpret values such as 120 and 122? First, recognize that they are *index numbers*, which means they are not measured in dollars or any other units. *The CPI is intended to measure changes in the price level over time.* We can't use the CPI to tell us in an absolute sense how high the price level is—only how much it has changed over time. We measure the inflation rate as the percentage increase in the CPI from one year to the next. For our simple example, the inflation rate in 2017 would be the percentage change in the CPI from 2016 to 2017:

$$\left(\frac{122 - 120}{120}\right) \times 100 = 1.7\%.$$

Because the CPI is designed to measure the cost of living, we can also say that the cost of living increased by 1.7 percent during 2017.   MyEconLab Concept Check

Is the CPI Accurate?

The CPI is the most widely used measure of inflation. Policymakers use the CPI to track the state of the economy. Businesses use it to help set the prices of their products and the wages and salaries of their employees. Each year, the federal government increases the Social Security payments made to retired workers by an amount equal to the percentage increase in the CPI during the previous year. In setting alimony and child support payments in divorce cases, judges often order that the payments increase each year by the inflation rate, as measured by the CPI.

Don't Let This Happen to You

Don't Miscalculate the Inflation Rate

Suppose you are given the data in the following table and are asked to calculate the inflation rate for 2014:

Year	CPI
2013	233
2014	237

It is tempting to avoid any calculations and simply report that the inflation rate in 2014 was 137 percent because 237 is a 137 percent increase from 100. But 137 percent would be the wrong answer. A value for the CPI of 237 in 2014

tells us that the price level in 2014 was 137 percent higher than in the *base year*, but the inflation rate is the percentage increase in the price level from the *previous year*, *not* the percentage increase from the base year. The correct calculation of the inflation rate for 2014 is:

$$\left(\frac{237 - 233}{233}\right) \times 100 = 1.7\%.$$

MyEconLab Study Plan

Your Turn: Test your understanding by doing related problem 4.5 and 4.6 on page 305 at the end of this chapter.

It is important that the CPI be as accurate as possible, but four biases cause changes in the CPI to overstate the true inflation rate:

1. **Substitution bias.** In constructing the CPI, the BLS assumes that each month, consumers purchase the same amount of each product in the market basket. In fact, consumers are likely to buy fewer of those products that increase most in price and more of those products that increase least in price (or fall the most in price). For instance, if apple prices rise rapidly during a particular month while orange prices fall, consumers will reduce their apple purchases and increase their orange purchases. Therefore, the prices of the market basket consumers actually buy will rise less than the prices of the market basket the BLS uses to compute the CPI.

2. **Increase in quality bias.** Over time, most products included in the CPI improve in quality: Automobiles become more durable and side air bags become standard equipment, smartphones have better processors and more memory, dishwashers use less water while getting dishes cleaner, and so on. Increases in the prices of these products partly reflect their improved quality and partly are pure inflation. The BLS attempts to make adjustments so that only the pure inflation part of price increases is included in the CPI. These adjustments are difficult to make, however, so the recorded price increases overstate the pure inflation in some products.

3. **New product bias.** For many years, the BLS updated the market basket of goods used in computing the CPI only every 10 years. So, new products introduced between updates were not included in the market basket. For example, the 1987 update took place before cellphones were introduced. Although millions of U.S. households used cellphones by the mid-1990s, they were not included in the CPI until the 1997 update. The prices of many products, such as cellphones, Blu-ray players, and 4K televisions, decrease in the years immediately after they are introduced. If the market basket is not updated frequently, these price decreases are not included in the CPI.

4. **Outlet bias.** During the mid-1990s, many consumers began to increase their purchases from discount stores such as Sam's Club and Costco. By the late 1990s, the Internet began to account for a significant fraction of sales of some products. Because the BLS continued to collect price statistics from traditional full-price retail stores, the CPI did not reflect the prices some consumers actually paid.

Most economists believe these biases cause changes in the CPI to overstate the true inflation rate by 0.5 percentage point to 1 percentage point. That is, if the CPI indicates that the inflation rate is 3 percent, it is probably between 2 percent and 2.5 percent. The BLS continues to take steps to reduce the size of the bias. For example, the BLS has reduced the size of the substitution and new product biases by updating the market basket every 2 years rather than every 10 years. The BLS has reduced the size of the outlet bias by conducting a point-of-purchase survey to track where consumers actually make their purchases. Finally, the BLS has used statistical methods to reduce the size of the quality bias. Prior to these changes, the size of the total bias in the CPI was probably greater than 1 percentage point. MyEconLab Concept Check

The Producer Price Index

Producer price index (PPI)
An average of the prices received by producers of goods and services at all stages of the production process.

In addition to the GDP deflator and the CPI, the government also computes the **producer price index (PPI)**. Like the CPI, the PPI tracks the prices of a market basket of goods. But while the CPI tracks the prices of goods and services purchased by a typical household, the PPI tracks the prices firms receive for goods and services at all stages of production. The PPI includes the prices of intermediate goods, such as flour, yarn, steel, and lumber; and raw materials, such as raw cotton, coal, and crude petroleum. If the prices of these goods rise, the cost to firms of producing final goods and services will rise, which may lead firms to increase the prices of goods and services purchased by consumers. Changes in the PPI therefore can give an early warning of future movements in the CPI. MyEconLab Concept Check

MyEconLab Study Plan

9.5 | Using Price Indexes to Adjust for the Effects of Inflation

LEARNING OBJECTIVE: Use price indexes to adjust for the effects of inflation.

You are likely to receive a much higher salary after graduation than your parents did 25 or more years ago, but prices 25 years ago were, on average, much lower than prices today. In other words, the purchasing power of a dollar was much higher 25 years ago because the prices of most goods and services were much lower. Price indexes such as the CPI give us a way of adjusting for the effects of inflation so that we can compare dollar values from different years.

For example, suppose your mother received a salary of $25,000 in 1989. By using the CPI, we can calculate what $25,000 in 1989 was equivalent to in 2014. The CPI is 124 for 1989 and 237 for 2014. Because 237/124 = 1.9, we know that, on average, prices were almost twice as high in 2014 as in 1989. We can use this result to inflate a salary of $25,000 received in 1989 to its value in terms of 2014 purchasing power:

$$\text{Value in 2014 dollars} = \text{Value in 1989 dollars} \times \left(\frac{\text{CPI in 2014}}{\text{CPI in 1989}} \right)$$

$$= \$25,000 \times \left(\frac{237}{124} \right) = \$47,782.$$

Our calculation shows that if you were paid a salary of $47,782 in 2014, you would be able to purchase roughly the same amount of goods and services that your mother could have purchased with a salary of $25,000 in 1989. Economic variables that are calculated in current-year prices are referred to as *nominal variables*. The calculation we have just made uses a price index to adjust a nominal variable—your mother's salary—for the effects of inflation.

For some purposes, we are interested in tracking changes in an economic variable over time rather than in seeing what its value would be in today's dollars. In that case, to correct for the effects of inflation, we can divide the nominal variable by a price index and multiply by 100 to obtain a *real variable*. The real variable will be measured in dollars of the base year for the price index. Currently, the base year for the CPI is the average of prices in the years 1982 to 1984. MyEconLab Concept Check

Solved Problem 9.5

MyEconLab Interactive Animation

What Has Been Happening with Real Wages in the United States?

In addition to data on employment, the BLS establishment survey gathers data on average hourly earnings of production workers. Production workers are all workers, except for managers and professionals. Average hourly earnings are the wages or salaries earned by these workers per hour. Economists and policymakers closely follow changes in average hourly earnings because they are a broad measure of a typical worker's income. Note, though, that in order to measure changes in the purchasing power of these wages, we have to convert the nominal values reported by the BLS to real values. Use the information in the following table to compute real average hourly earnings

for each year. Compare the percentage change in nominal average hourly earnings between 2013 and 2014 with the percentage change in real average hourly earnings. Be sure to explain what the values you calculate for real average hourly earnings represent.

Year	Nominal Average Hourly Earnings	CPI (1982–1984 = 100)
2012	$19.73	230
2013	$20.14	233
2014	$20.60	237

Solving the Problem

Step 1: **Review the chapter material.** This problem is about using price indexes to correct for the effects of inflation, so you may want to review the section "Using Price Indexes to Adjust for the Effects of Inflation," which begins on page 294.

Step 2: **Begin by defining real average hourly earnings, calculating the value of real average hourly earnings for each year, and explaining what the values you calculated represent.** Nominal average hourly earnings are the number of dollars a worker receives. To calculate real average hourly earnings, we have to divide the nominal average earnings by the CPI for that year and multiply by 100. For example, real average hourly earnings for 2012 equal:

$$\left(\frac{\$19.73}{230}\right) \times 100 = \$8.59$$

The results for all three years are:

Year	Nominal Average Hourly Earnings	CPI (1982–1984 = 100)	Real Average Hourly Earnings (1982–1984 dollars)
2012	$19.73	230	$8.59
2013	$20.14	233	$8.65
2014	$20.60	237	$8.70

The base year for the CPI is the average of prices during the period 1982–1984. So, the values for the real average hourly earnings we calculated are in 1982–1984 dollars. In other words, these values for the real wage tell us that in 2013, $20.14 would buy what $8.65 would have bought in 1982–1984 and that in 2014, $20.60 would buy what $8.70 would have bought in 1982–1984.

Step 3: **Complete your answer by calculating the percentage change in nominal average hourly earnings and in real average hourly earnings between 2013 and 2014.** The percentage change in nominal average hourly earnings equals:

$$\left(\frac{\$20.60 - \$20.14}{\$20.14}\right) \times 100 = 2.3\%.$$

And the percentage change real average hourly earnings equals:

$$\left(\frac{\$8.70 - \$8.65}{\$8.65}\right) \times 100 = 0.6\%.$$

We can conclude that although nominal average hourly earnings increased by more than 2 percent, real average hourly earnings increased by less than 1 percent.

Extra Credit: The values we computed for the real average hourly earnings are measured in 1982–1984 dollars. Because this period is more than 30 years ago, the values are somewhat difficult to interpret. We can convert the earnings to 2014 dollars by using the method we used on page 294 to calculate your mother's salary. But for purposes of calculating the *change* in the value of real average hourly earnings over time, converting the earnings to 2014 dollars doesn't matter. The change from 2013 to 2014 would still be 0.6 percent. You can check this point by using the "mother's salary" method to calculate the real average hourly earnings for 2013 and 2014 in 2014 dollars. Then calculate the percentage change. Unless you make an arithmetic error, you should find that the answer is still 0.6 percent. Finally, keep in mind that average hourly earnings do not include employee benefits, such as employer contributions to retirement programs or the value of employer provided medical insurance. Because benefits have increased over the years relative to wages and salaries, changes in average hourly earnings can be a misleading measure of changes in the typical worker's standard of living.

MyEconLab Study Plan

Your Turn: For more practice, do related problems 5.4, 5.5, 5.6, and 5.7 on pages 306–307 at the end of this chapter.

Nominal Interest Rates versus Real Interest Rates

9.6 LEARNING OBJECTIVE: Distinguish between the nominal interest rate and the real interest rate.

The difference between nominal and real values is important when money is being borrowed and lent. The *interest rate* is the cost of borrowing funds, expressed as a percentage of the amount borrowed (see Chapter 6). If you lend someone $1,000 for one year and charge an interest rate of 6 percent, the borrower will pay back $1,060, or 6 percent more than the amount you lent. But is $1,060 received one year from now really 6 percent more than $1,000 today? If prices rise during the year, you will not be able to buy as much with $1,060 one year from now as you could with that amount today. Your true return from lending the $1,000 is equal to the percentage change in your purchasing power after taking into account the effects of inflation.

> **Nominal interest rate** The stated interest rate on a loan.
>
> **Real interest rate** The nominal interest rate minus the inflation rate.

The stated interest rate on a loan is the **nominal interest rate**. The **real interest rate** corrects the nominal interest rate for the effect of inflation on purchasing power. As a simple example, suppose that the only good you purchase is DVDs, and at the beginning of the year the price of DVDs is $10.00. With $1,000, you can purchase 100 DVDs. If you lend the $1,000 out for one year at an interest rate of 6 percent, you will receive $1,060 at the end of the year. Suppose the inflation rate during the year is 2 percent, so that the price of DVDs has risen to $10.20 by the end of the year. How has your purchasing power increased as a result of making the loan? At the beginning of the year, your $1,000 could purchase 100 DVDs. At the end of the year, your $1,060 can purchase $1,060/$10.20 = 103.92 DVDs. In other words, you can purchase almost 4 percent more DVDs. So, in this case, the real interest rate you received from lending was a little less than 4 percent (actually, 3.92 percent). For low rates of inflation, a convenient approximation for the real interest rate is:

Real interest rate = Nominal interest rate − Inflation rate.

We can calculate the real interest rate in our example using this formula as 6 percent − 2 percent = 4 percent, which is close to the actual value of 3.92 percent.

If the inflation rate during the year was 5 percent, the real interest rate would be only 1 percent. Holding the nominal interest rate constant, the higher the inflation rate, the lower the real interest rate. Notice that if the inflation rate turns out to be higher than expected, borrowers pay and lenders receive a lower real interest rate than either of them expected. For example, if both you and the person to whom you lent the $1,000 to expected the inflation rate to be 2 percent, you both expected the real interest rate on the loan to be 4 percent. If the inflation rate turns out actually to be 4 percent, the real interest rate on the loan will be 2 percent: That's bad news for you but good news for your borrower.

For the economy as a whole, we can measure the nominal interest rate as the interest rate on three-month U.S. Treasury bills. U.S. Treasury bills are short-term loans investors make to the federal government. We can use the inflation rate as measured by changes in the CPI to calculate the real interest rate on Treasury bills. Figure 9.8 shows the nominal and real interest rates for the period from 1970 through the beginning of 2015. Notice that when the inflation rate is low, as it has been during most years since the early 1990s, the gap between the nominal and real interest rates is small. When the inflation rate is high, as it was during the mid- to late 1970s, the gap between the nominal and real interest rates becomes large. In fact, a particular nominal interest rate can be associated in different periods with very different real interest rates. For example, during late 1975, the nominal interest rate was about 5.5 percent, but because the inflation rate was 7 percent, the real interest rate was −1.5 percent. In early 1987, the nominal interest rate was also 5.5 percent, but because the inflation rate was only 2 percent, the real interest rate was 3.5 percent.

This example shows that it is impossible to know whether a particular nominal interest rate is "high" or "low." It all depends on the inflation rate. *The real interest rate*

Figure 9.8   Nominal and Real Interest Rates, 1970–2015

The real interest rate is equal to the nominal interest rate minus the inflation rate. The real interest rate provides a better measure of the true cost of borrowing and the true return to lending than does the nominal interest rate. The nominal interest rate in the figure is the interest rate on three-month U.S. Treasury bills. The inflation rate is measured by the percentage change in the CPI from the same quarter during the previous year.

Source: Federal Reserve Bank of St. Louis.

provides a better measure of the true cost of borrowing and the true return from lending than does the nominal interest rate. When firms are deciding whether to borrow the funds to buy an investment good, such as a new factory, they will look at the real interest rate because it measures the true cost to the firm of borrowing.

Is it possible for the nominal interest rate to be less than the real interest rate? Yes, but only when the inflation rate is negative. A negative inflation rate is referred to as **deflation** and occurs on the rare occasions when the price level falls. During the years shown in Figure 9.8, the inflation rate as measured by changes in the CPI was negative only during the first nine months of 2009 and three months in early 2015.

Deflation A decline in the price level.

MyEconLab Study Plan

MyEconLab Concept Check

9.7 | Does Inflation Impose Costs on the Economy?

LEARNING OBJECTIVE: Discuss the problems that inflation causes.

Imagine waking up tomorrow morning and finding that every price in the economy has doubled. The prices of food, gasoline, clothing, laptops, houses, and haircuts have all doubled. But suppose that all wages and salaries have also doubled. Will this doubling of prices and wages matter? Think about walking into McDonald's, expecting to find a Big Mac selling for $4.50. Instead, you find it selling for $9.00. Will you turn around and walk out? Probably not, because your salary has also increased overnight from $45,000 per year to $90,000 per year. So, the purchasing power of your salary has remained the same, and you are just as likely to buy the Big Mac today as you were yesterday.

This hypothetical situation makes an important point: Nominal incomes generally increase with inflation. Remember that we can think of the $4.50 price of a Big Mac as representing either the value of the product or the value of all the income generated in producing the product (see Chapter 8). The two amounts are the same, whether the Big Mac sells for $4.50 or $9.00. When the price of the Big Mac rises from $4.50 to $9.00, that extra $4.50 ends up as income that goes to the workers at McDonald's, the firms selling supplies to McDonald's, or the stockholders of McDonald's, just as the first $4.50 did.

It's tempting to think that the problem with inflation is that, as prices rise, consumers can no longer afford to buy as many goods and services, but our example shows that this conclusion is a fallacy. An expected inflation rate of 10 percent will raise the average price of goods and services by 10 percent, but it will also raise average incomes by 10 percent. Goods and services will be as affordable to an average consumer as they would be if there were no inflation.

Inflation Affects the Distribution of Income

If inflation will not reduce the affordability of goods and services to an average consumer, why do people dislike inflation? One reason is that the argument in the previous section applies to the *average* person but not to every person. Some people will find their incomes rising faster than the rate of inflation, and so their purchasing power will rise. Other people will find their incomes rising more slowly than the rate of inflation—or not at all—and their purchasing power will fall. People on fixed incomes are particularly likely to be hurt by inflation. If a retired worker receives a pension fixed at $3,000 per month, over time, inflation will reduce the purchasing power of that payment. In that way, inflation can change the distribution of income in a manner that seems unfair to many people.

The extent to which inflation redistributes income depends in part on whether the inflation is *anticipated*—in which case consumers, workers, and firms can see it coming and can prepare for it—or *unanticipated*—in which case they do not see it coming and do not prepare for it.

MyEconLab Concept Check

The Problem with Anticipated Inflation

Like many of life's problems, inflation is easier to manage if you see it coming. Suppose that everyone knows that the inflation rate for the next 10 years will be 10 percent per year. Workers know that unless their wages go up by at least 10 percent per year, the real purchasing power of their wages will fall. Businesses will be willing to increase workers' wages enough to compensate for inflation because they know that the prices of the products they sell will increase. Lenders will realize that the loans they make will be paid back with dollars that are losing 10 percent of their value each year, so they will charge higher interest rates to compensate. Borrowers will be willing to pay the higher interest rates because they also know they are paying back these loans with dollars that are losing value. So far, there don't seem to be costs to anticipated inflation.

Even when inflation is perfectly anticipated, however, some individuals and firms will experience a cost:

1. Inevitably, there will be a redistribution of income, as some people's incomes fall behind even an anticipated level of inflation.

2. Firms and consumers have to hold some paper money to facilitate their buying and selling. Anyone holding paper money will find its purchasing power decreasing each year by the rate of inflation. To avoid this cost, workers and firms will try to hold as little paper money as possible, but they will have to hold some.

3. Firms that have catalogs listing the prices of their products will have to update them more frequently. Supermarkets and other stores that mark prices on packages or on store shelves will have to devote more time and labor to changing the marked prices. The costs to firms of changing prices are called **menu costs**. At moderate rates of anticipated inflation, menu costs are relatively small, but at high rates of inflation, such as those experienced in some developing countries, menu costs can become substantial.

> **Menu costs** The costs to firms of changing prices.

4. Taxes paid by investors will increase because investors are taxed on the nominal payments they receive from owning stocks and bonds or from making loans, rather than on the real payments—the nominal payments corrected for inflation. Because investors are interested in the real, after-tax return they receive when investing in firms, the higher taxes that investors pay as a result of inflation mean that firms must pay more for the funds they need to expand. **MyEconLab** Concept Check

The Problem with Unanticipated Inflation

In any high-income economy—such as the United States—households, workers, and firms routinely enter into contracts that commit them to make or receive certain payments for years in the future. For example, when firms sign wage contracts, they commit to paying a specified wage for the duration of the contract. When people buy homes, they usually borrow most of the amount they need from banks. These loans, called *mortgage loans*, commit a borrower to make a fixed monthly payment for the length of the loan. Most mortgage loans are for long periods, often as long as 30 years.

To make these long-term commitments, households, workers, and firms must forecast the rate of inflation. If a firm believes the inflation rate over the next three years will be 6 percent per year, signing a three-year contract with a union that calls for wage increases of 8 percent per year may seem reasonable because the firm may be able to raise its prices by at least the rate of inflation each year. If the firm believes that the inflation rate will be only 2 percent over the next three years, paying wage increases of 8 percent may significantly reduce its profit or even force it out of business.

When people borrow money or a bank like JPMorgan Chase lends money, they must forecast the inflation rate so they can calculate the real rate of interest on a loan. In 1980, banks were charging interest rates of 18 percent or more on mortgage loans. This rate seems very high compared to the less than 5 percent charged on such loans in 2015, but the inflation rate in 1980 was more than 13 percent and was expected to remain high. In fact, the inflation rate *declined* unexpectedly, and by 1983 it was only about 3 percent. People who borrowed money for 30 years at the high interest rates of 1980 soon found that the real interest rate on their loans was much higher than they had expected.

When the actual inflation rate turns out to be very different from the expected inflation rate, some people gain, and other people lose. This outcome seems unfair to most people because they are either winning or losing only because something unanticipated has happened. This apparently unfair redistribution is a key reason people dislike unanticipated inflation. **MyEconLab** Concept Check

What's So Bad about Falling Prices?

We have just discussed how inflation being higher than expected can cause problems for consumers, workers, and firms. But what if an economy begins to experience falling prices—*deflation*, rather than inflation? A falling price level might seem like good news for the economy. After all, falling prices should encourage consumers to increase their spending as goods and services become less expensive. In fact, though, deflation tends to have the opposite effect on consumers. Episodes of deflation are relatively rare, but we can draw some lessons from two important deflationary episodes: the United States during the 1930s and Japan during the 1990s. In both cases, many consumers reduced their spending in the face of falling prices, apparently because they were waiting for prices to go even lower. Waiting for prices to fall even lower was also a problem for the U.S. housing market in the late 2000s. A large run-up in housing prices took place from 2002 to 2006. When prices began to decline, many potential buyers postponed purchases in the expectation that prices would continue to fall.

The following figure shows changes in the CPI in the United States during the years between 1925 and 1940. The beginning of the Great Depression in 1929 caused the country to experience severe deflation.

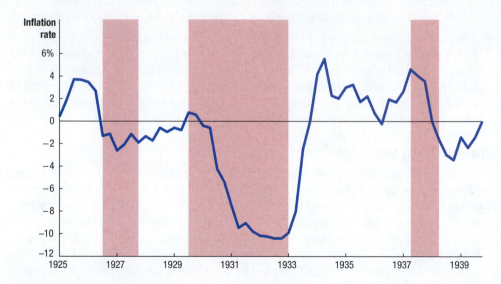

The deflation of the 1930s hurt the U.S. economy not just because it may have led some consumers to postpone purchases but also because it increased the burden on borrowers. Suppose that in 1929 you had borrowed money for five years at a nominal interest rate of 5 percent. What real interest rate would you have paid during those years? We have seen that to calculate the real interest rate, we need to subtract the inflation rate from the nominal interest rate. With deflation, the change in the price level is negative, so to calculate the real interest rate, we are in effect *adding* the change in the price level to the nominal interest rate. The following table uses the actual deflation rate in each year to calculate the resulting real interest rates on your loan:

	1929	1930	1931	1932	1933
Nominal interest rate	5%	5%	5%	5%	5%
Change in the consumer price index	0	−2.3	−9.0	−9.9	−5.1
Real interest rate	5.0	7.3	14.0	14.9	10.1

The bottom row of the table shows that although the nominal interest rate on your loan is only 5 percent, in three of the five years the real interest rate you pay is greater than 10 percent. In fact, high real interest rates inflicted serious losses on both household and business borrowers during the early 1930s and contributed to the severity of the Great Depression.

During the 2001 and 2007–2009 recessions, some policymakers and economists feared that the U.S. economy would experience deflation. Fortunately, significant deflation did not occur. If it had, those recessions would likely have been more severe than they were.   MyEconLab **Concept Check**

Your Turn: Test your understanding by doing related problems 7.9 and 7.10 on page 308 at the end of this chapter.   MyEconLab Study Plan

Continued from page 275

Economics in Your Life

Should You Change Your Career Plans if You Graduate during a Recession?

At the beginning of this chapter, we asked whether layoffs in the banking industry should cause you to change your major and give up your plans to pursue a career in banking. We have seen in this chapter that unemployment rates are higher and layoffs are more common in a recession than in an economic expansion. Because you are a sophomore, you will graduate a few years later, when the recession will likely have ended and the unemployment rate will have declined. You might also want to investigate whether the layoffs in the banking industry represent a permanent contraction in the size of the industry or a temporary decline caused by the recession. If the reduction of banking jobs is more likely to be permanent, then you might consider a career in another industry. If the layoffs appear to be related to the current recession, then you probably do not need to change your career plans.

Conclusion

Inflation and unemployment are key macroeconomic problems. Presidential elections are often won and lost on the basis of which candidate is able to convince the public that he or she can best deal with these problems. Many economists, however, would argue that, in the long run, maintaining high rates of growth of real GDP per person is the most important macroeconomic concern. Only when real GDP per person is increasing will a country's standard of living increase. In the next chapter, we look more closely at the important topic of economic growth.

Visit MyEconLab for a news article and analysis related to the concepts in this chapter.

Key Terms

Consumer price index (CPI), p. 291

Cyclical unemployment, p. 287

Deflation, p. 298

Discouraged workers, p. 277

Efficiency wage, p. 290

Employed, p. 276

Frictional unemployment, p. 286

Inflation rate, p. 291

Labor force, p. 276

Labor force participation rate, p. 278

Menu costs, p. 299

Natural rate of unemployment, p. 287

Nominal interest rate, p. 296

Price level, p. 291

Producer price index (PPI), p. 294

Real interest rate, p. 296

Structural unemployment, p. 287

Unemployed, p. 276

Unemployment rate, p. 276

9.1 **Measuring the Unemployment Rate, the Labor Force Participation Rate, and the Employment–Population Ratio, pages 276–285**

LEARNING OBJECTIVE: Define the unemployment rate, the labor force participation rate, and the employment–population ratio and understand how they are computed.

Summary

The U.S. Bureau of Labor Statistics uses the results of the monthly household survey to calculate the *unemployment rate*, the *labor force participation rate*, and the *employment–population ratio*. The **labor force** is the total number of people who have jobs (the **employed**) plus the number of people who do not have jobs but are actively looking for them (the **unemployed**). The **unemployment rate** is the percentage of the labor force that is unemployed. **Discouraged workers** are people who are available for work but who are not actively looking for a job because they believe no jobs are available for them. Discouraged workers are not counted as unemployed. The **labor force participation rate** is the percentage of the working-age population in the labor force. Since 1950, the labor force participation rate of women has been rising, while the labor force participation rate of men has been falling. The employment–population ratio measures the percentage of the working-age population that is employed. Asians, whites, and college graduates have below-average unemployment rates. African Americans, Hispanics, and high school dropouts have above-average unemployment rates. Except during severe recessions, a typical unemployed person finds a new job or returns to his or her previous job within a few months. Each year, millions of jobs are created in the United States, and millions of jobs are destroyed.

MyEconLab Visit www.myeconlab.com to complete these exercises online and get instant feedback.

Review Questions

1.1 How is the unemployment rate measured? What are the three conditions someone needs to meet to be counted as unemployed?

1.2 What are the problems in measuring the unemployment rate? In what ways does the official BLS measure of the unemployment rate *understate* the true degree of unemployment? In what ways does the official BLS measure *overstate* the true degree of unemployment?

1.3 Which groups tend to have above-average unemployment rates, and which groups tend to have below-average unemployment rates?

1.4 What does the labor force participation rate measure? Since 1950, how have the labor force participation rates of men and women changed?

1.5 What does the employment–population ratio measure? How does an unemployed person dropping out of the labor force affect the unemployment rate? How does it affect the employment–population ratio?

1.6 What is the difference between the household survey and the establishment survey? Which survey do many economists prefer for measuring changes in employment? Why?

Problems and Applications

1.7 Fill in the blank cells in the following table of data collected in the household survey for June 2015:

Working-age population	
Employment	148,739,000
Unemployment	
Unemployment rate	5.3%
Labor force	
Labor force participation rate	62.6%
Employment–population ratio	

1.8 (Related to Solved Problem 9.1 on page 278) Homemakers are not included in the employment or labor force totals compiled in the BLS household survey. They are included in the working-age population totals. Suppose that homemakers were counted as employed and included in labor force statistics. How would that change affect the unemployment rate, the labor force participation rate, and the employment–population ratio?

1.9 In June 2015, the unemployment rate declined to 5.3 percent from 5.5 percent in May. The labor force participation rate also declined from May to June, from 62.9 percent to 62.6 percent. If the labor force participation rate had remained unchanged from May to June, would the unemployment rate for June have been lower than, higher than, or equal to 5.3 percent? Briefly explain.

1.10 **(Related to the** Making the Connection **on page 282)** In discussing the labor market during the recovery from the 2007–2009 recession, Federal Reserve Chair Janet Yellen noted that "the employment-to-population ratio has increased far less over the past several years than the unemployment rate alone would indicate, based on past experience."
   a. During an economic expansion, why would we normally expect the employment–population ratio to increase as the unemployment rate falls?
   b. Why didn't the employment–population ratio increase as much as might have been expected during the recovery from the 2007–2009 recession?

   Source: Janet L. Yellen, "Labor Market Dynamics and Monetary Policy," Speech at the Federal Reserve Bank of Kansas City Economic Symposium, Jackson Hole, Wyoming, August 22, 2014.

1.11 In early 2015, the employment–population ratio was increasing while the labor force participation rate remained largely unchanged. Shouldn't both of these data series move in the same direction? Briefly explain how it is possible that they didn't.

1.12 An article in the *Wall Street Journal* contained the following observation: "Every month, millions of workers leave the job market because of retirement, to care for children or aging parents, to pursue more education, or out of discouragement. Millions of others jump in after graduating."
   a. Are the millions of workers leaving the job market for the reasons given counted as unemployed in the BLS data? Briefly explain.
   b. Will the BLS count people entering the job market after graduating from high school or college as part of the labor force even if they don't find a job right away? Briefly explain.

   Source: Josh Zumbrun, "Labor-Market Dropouts Stay on the Side-lines," *Wall Street Journal*, December 28, 2014.

1.13 An article in the *Wall Street Journal* noted that over a four-month period in late 2014, employment in the state of Georgia "rose 1% even as the state's jobless rate climbed 1.2 percentage points." Briefly explain how the state's unemployment rate could have increased at the same time that employment in the state was increasing.

   Source: Cameron McWhirter and Ben Leubsdorf, "Rising Jobless Rates Are a Southern Mystery," *Wall Street Journal*, October 5, 2014.

1.14 In his 2015 State of the Union address, President Barack Obama observed that "over the past five years, our businesses have created more than 11 million new jobs." Is it likely that the U.S. economy created only 11 million jobs during this time period? If not, what was President Obama referring to?

   Source: Barack Obama, "Remarks by the President in State of the Union Address," whitehouse.gov, January 20, 2015.

9.2 **Types of Unemployment, pages 285–288**

LEARNING OBJECTIVE: Identify the three types of unemployment.

Summary

There are three types of unemployment: frictional, structural, and cyclical. **Frictional unemployment** is short-term unemployment that arises from the process of matching workers with jobs. One type of frictional unemployment is *seasonal unemployment*, which refers to unemployment due to factors such as weather, variations in tourism, and other calendar-related events. **Structural unemployment** arises from a persistent mismatch between the job skills or attributes of workers and the requirements of jobs. **Cyclical unemployment** is caused by a business cycle recession. The **natural rate of unemployment** is the normal rate of unemployment, consisting of structural unemployment and frictional unemployment. The natural rate of unemployment is also sometimes called the *full-employment rate of unemployment*.

MyEconLab   Visit **www.myeconlab.com** to complete these exercises online and get instant feedback.

Review Questions

2.1 What are the three types of unemployment? Which type of unemployment do you consider most likely to result in hardship for people who are unemployed? Briefly explain.

2.2 What is the relationship between frictional unemployment and job search?

2.3 What is the natural rate of unemployment? What is the relationship between the natural rate of unemployment and full employment?

Problems and Applications

2.4 **(Related to the** Chapter Opener **on page 275)** Ford Motor Company employed fewer people in 2015 than it did in 1980. Is this decline in employment frictional, structural, cyclical, or some combination of these factors? What information would you need to arrive at a definite answer?

2.5 A politician makes the following argument: "The economy would operate more efficiently if frictional unemployment were eliminated. Therefore, a goal of government policy should be to reduce the frictional rate of unemployment to the lowest possible level." Briefly explain whether you agree with this argument.

2.6 **(Related to the** Making the Connection **on page 287)** What advice for finding a job would you give someone who is frictionally unemployed? What advice would you give someone who is structurally unemployed? What advice would you give someone who is cyclically unemployed?

2.7 **(Related to the** Making the Connection **on page 287)** The BLS estimated that there were 2.7 million job "quits" in May 2015. The BLS defines a job quit as a "voluntary separation initiated by an employee."

   a. Economists distinguish three types of unemployment: frictional, structural, and cyclical. How would you classify unemployment caused by an increase in job quits?

   b. Would an increase in the number of job quits suggest that it was becoming easier or more difficult for people to find jobs? Briefly explain.

Source: Bureau of Labor Statistics, "Job Openings and Labor Turnover Survey," July 7, 2015.

2.8 **(Related to the** Making the Connection **on page 287)** The headline on an article in the *New York Times* was "Unemployed in Europe Stymied by Lack of Technology Skills." Are these workers likely to be cyclically, frictionally, or structurally unemployed? Briefly explain.

Source: Liz Alderman, "Unemployed in Europe Stymied by Lack of Technology Skills," *New York Times*, January 3, 2014.

9.3 **Explaining Unemployment, pages 288–290**
LEARNING OBJECTIVE: Explain what factors determine the unemployment rate.

Summary

Government policies can reduce the level of frictional and structural unemployment by aiding the search for jobs and the retraining of workers. Some government policies, however, can add to the level of frictional and structural unemployment. Unemployment insurance payments can raise the unemployment rate by extending the time that unemployed workers search for jobs. Government policies have caused the unemployment rates in most other high-income countries typically to be higher than in the United States. Wages above market levels can also increase unemployment. Wages may be above market levels because of the minimum wage, labor unions, and *efficiency wages*. An **efficiency wage** is a higher-than-market wage that a firm pays to increase workers' productivity.

 MyEconLab   Visit **www.myeconlab.com** to complete these exercises online and get instant feedback.

Review Questions

3.1 What effect does the payment of government unemployment insurance have on the unemployment rate? On the severity of recessions?

3.2 Discuss the effect of each of the following on the unemployment rate.
   a. The federal minimum wage law
   b. Labor unions
   c. Efficiency wages

3.3 Why has the unemployment rate in the United States typically been lower than the unemployment rates in Canada and the countries in Western Europe?

Problems and Applications

3.4 When Ségolène Royal was running unsuccessfully for president of France, she proposed that workers who lost their jobs would receive unemployment payments equal to 90 percent of their previous wages during their first year of unemployment. If this proposal had been enacted, what would the effect likely have been on the unemployment rate in France? Briefly explain.

Source: Alessandra Galloni and David Gauthier-Villars, "France's Royal Introduces Platform Ahead of Election," *Wall Street Journal*, February 12, 2007.

3.5 Jared Bernstein, an economist at the Center on Budget and Policy Priorities, has stated: "I want to see receipt of unemployment insurance … go up in recessions." If government unemployment insurance payments didn't go up, he explains, it "would be a sign that something's very wrong." What would be very wrong about government unemployment insurance payments failing to rise during a recession? What would be the consequences for the unemployed and for the economy?

Source: Jared Bernstein, "Lessons of the Great Recession: How the Safety Net Performed," *New York Times*, June 24, 2013.

3.6 Discuss the likely effect of each of the following on the unemployment rate.
   a. The length of time workers are eligible to receive unemployment insurance payments doubles.
   b. The minimum wage is abolished.
   c. Most U.S. workers join labor unions.
   d. More companies make information about job openings easily available on Internet job sites.

3.7 In 1914, Henry Ford increased the wage he paid workers in his car factory in Dearborn, Michigan, to $5 per day. This wage was more than twice as much as other car manufacturers were paying. Ford was quoted as saying, "The payment of five dollars a day for an eight-hour day was one of the finest cost-cutting moves we ever made." How can paying an above-market wage result in a firm cutting its costs?

3.8 In 2015, an article on bloomberg.com noted that Walmart, Starbucks, TJ Maxx, IKEA, Gap, and several other big retailers had announced increases in the wages they were paying newly hired workers. The same article also noted that "[labor] turnover in the retail sector has been steadily rising and now stands at 5 percent a month."
   a. What do the authors mean by labor turnover?
   b. Is it likely that the increase in labor turnover is connected to the increases in entry-level wages being paid by large retailers? Briefly explain.

Source: Kyle Stock and Kim Bhasin, "Why Retailers Are Suddenly Desperate to Keep Their Least-Valuable Workers," bloomberg.com, March 6, 2015.

9.4 **Measuring Inflation, pages 290–294**

LEARNING OBJECTIVE: Define the price level and the inflation rate and understand how they are computed.

Summary

The **price level** measures the average prices of goods and services. The **inflation rate** is equal to the percentage change in the price level from one year to the next. The federal government compiles statistics on three different measures of the price level: the consumer price index, the GDP price deflator, and the producer price index. The **consumer price index (CPI)** is a measure of the average change over time in the prices a typical urban family of four pays for the goods and services they purchase. Changes in the CPI are the best measure of changes in the cost of living as experienced by a typical household. Biases in the construction of the CPI cause changes in it to overstate the true inflation rate by 0.5 percentage point to 1 percentage point. The **producer price index (PPI)** is an average of prices received by producers of goods and services at all stages of production.

MyEconLab   Visit **www.myeconlab.com** to complete these exercises online and get instant feedback.

Review Questions

4.1 Briefly describe the three major measures of the price level.

4.2 Which price index does the government use to measure changes in the cost of living?

4.3 What potential biases exist in calculating the CPI? What steps has the Bureau of Labor Statistics taken to reduce the size of the biases?

4.4 What is the difference between the CPI and the PPI?

Problems and Applications

4.5 (Related to the Don't Let This Happen to You on page 293) Briefly explain whether you agree with the following statement: "I don't believe the government price statistics. The CPI for 2014 was 237, but I know that the inflation rate couldn't have been as high as 137 percent in 2014."

4.6 (Related to the Don't Let This Happen to You on page 293) An article in the *Wall Street Journal* asks the question "How can inflation be low when everything is so expensive?" The article also notes that "the CPI shows that prices are the highest they've ever been." Is there a contradiction between a low inflation rate as measured by the CPI and the observations that prices are "the highest they've ever been" and everything is "so expensive"? Briefly explain.

Source: Josh Zumbrun, "5 Things You Always Wanted to Know about Inflation Statistics," *Wall Street Journal*, May 15, 2014.

4.7 Consider a simple economy that produces only three products: haircuts, hamburgers, and Blu-rays. Use the information in the following table to calculate the inflation rate for 2016, as measured by the CPI.

Product	Base Year (1999) Quantity	Base Year (1999) Price	2015 Price	2016 Price
Haircuts	2	$10.00	$11.00	$16.20
Hamburgers	10	2.00	2.45	2.40
Blu-rays	6	15.00	15.00	14.00

4.8 The Standard & Poor's/Case-Shiller Home Price Index is one of the leading indicators of housing price trends in the United States. The base year for the index is January 2000. The following table lists index numbers for April 2014 and April 2015 for five cities.

City	April 2014	April 2015
New York	174.5	179.3
Miami	183.2	198.5
Phoenix	145.4	150.4
Dallas	136.8	148.8
San Francisco	192.5	211.5

a. In which of these five cities did housing prices increase the fastest from April 2014 to April 2015? In which did they increase the slowest? Briefly explain the basis for your answers.

b. Can you determine from these numbers which city had the highest house prices in April 2015? Briefly explain.

Source: "House Price Indices," Federal Reserve Bank of St. Louis (FRED), research.stlouisfed.org/fred2/.

4.9 Suppose the CPI of a country follows the path shown in the following figure.

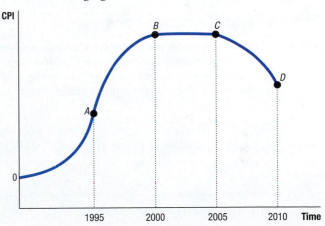

a. During which period did the country experience zero inflation?

b. During which period did the country experience an increasing rate of inflation?

c. During which period did the country experience a slowdown in inflation, although the inflation rate remained positive? (This situation is called "disinflation.")

d. During which period did the country experience deflation?

4.10 An article in the *Wall Street Journal* notes that the BLS has changed the methods it uses to calculate the CPI with the result that the measured inflation rate is lower than it would have been if the BLS had still used the old methods. The article notes, "But this is not a massive conspiracy to hide runaway inflation." What was the BLS's motivation in changing its methods of calculating the CPI?

Source: Josh Zumbrun, "5 Things You Always Wanted to Know about Inflation Statistics," *Wall Street Journal*, May 15, 2014.

4.11 In the fall of 2015, Apple introduced a new model of its iPhone. The new model had a faster processor and a better camera than the previous model but sold for the same price. How was the CPI affected by the introduction of the new model of the iPhone?

 9.5 **Using Price Indexes to Adjust for the Effects of Inflation, pages 294–296**
LEARNING OBJECTIVE: Use price indexes to adjust for the effects of inflation.

Summary

Price indexes are designed to measure changes in the price level over time, not the absolute level of prices. To correct for the effects of inflation, we can divide a *nominal variable* by a price index and multiply by 100 to obtain a *real variable*. The real variable will be measured in dollars of the base year for the price index.

MyEconLab Visit **www.myeconlab.com** to complete these exercises online and get instant feedback.

Review Questions

5.1 What is the difference between a nominal variable and a real variable?

5.2 During a period of deflation, which is likely to increase faster: nominal average hourly earnings or real average hourly earnings? Briefly explain.

Problems and Applications

5.3 The Great Depression was the worst economic disaster in U.S. history in terms of declines in real GDP and increases in the unemployment rate. Use the data in the following table to calculate the percentage decline in real GDP between 1929 and 1933:

Year	Nominal GDP (billions of dollars)	GDP Price Deflator (2009 = 100)
1929	$104.6	9.9
1933	57.2	7.3

Source: U.S. Bureau of Economic Analysis.

5.4 (Related to Solved Problem 9.5 on page 295) In 1924, the famous novelist F. Scott Fitzgerald wrote an article for the *Saturday Evening Post* titled "How to Live on $36,000 a Year," in which he wondered how he and his wife had managed to spend all of that very high income without saving any of it. The CPI in 1924 was 17, and the CPI in 2014 was 237. What income would you have needed in 2014 to have had the same purchasing power that Fitzgerald's $36,000 had in 1924? Be sure to show your calculation.
Source: F. Scott Fitzgerald, "How to Live on $36,000 a Year," *Saturday Evening Post*, April 5, 1924.

5.5 (Related to Solved Problem 9.5 on page 295) Use the information in the following table to determine the percentage changes in the U.S. and French *real* minimum wages between 1957 and 2014. Does it matter for your answer that you have not been told the base year for the U.S. CPI or the French CPI? Was the percentage increase in the price level greater in the United States or in France during these years?

	United States		France	
Year	Minimum Wage (dollars per hour)	CPI	Minimum Wage (euros per hour)	CPI
1957	$1.00	27	€0.19	8
2014	7.25	237	9.61	106

Sources: John M. Abowd, Francis Kramarz, Thomas Lemieux, and David N. Margolis, "Minimum Wages and Youth Employment in France and the United States," in D. Blanchflower and R. Freeman, eds., *Youth Employment and Joblessness in Advanced Countries*, Chicago: University of Chicago Press, 1999, pp. 427–472 (the value for the minimum wage is given in francs; it was converted to euros at a conversion rate of 1 euro = 6.55957 francs); Insee online data bank, www.insee.fr; U.S. Department of Labor; and U.S. Bureau of Labor Statistics.

5.6 (Related to Solved Problem 9.5 on page 295) In an article in the *Wall Street Journal*, a professor of financial planning noted the effect of rising prices on purchasing power: "Today, $2,000 a month seems reasonable [as an income for a retired person in addition to the person's Social Security payments], but 40 years from now that's going to be three cups of coffee and a donut." Suppose that currently three cups of coffee and a donut can be purchased for $10. The CPI in 2014 was 237. What would the CPI have to be in 2054 for $2,000 to be able to purchase only three cups of coffee and a donut? Assume that the prices of coffee and donuts increase at the same rate as the CPI during these 40 years.
Source: Matthias Rieker, "Rising Use of Immediate Annuities Raises Some Concerns," *Wall Street Journal*, December 4, 2014.

5.7 (Related to Solved Problem 9.5 on page 295) The table on the next page shows the top 10 films of all time through July 2015, measured by box office receipts in the United States, as well as several other notable films farther down the list.

The CPI in 2015 was 238. Use this information and the data in the table to calculate the box office receipts for each film in 2015 dollars. Assume that each film generated all of its box office receipts during the year it was released. Use your results to prepare a new list of the top 10 films, based on their earnings in 2015 dollars. (Some of the films, such as the first *Star Wars* film, *Gone with the Wind*, and *Snow White and the Seven Dwarfs*, were re-released to theaters several times, so their receipts were actually earned during several different years, but we will ignore that complication.)
Source: boxofficemojo.com and the U.S. Bureau of Labor Statistics.

Rank	Film	Total Box Office Receipts	Year Released	CPI
1	*Avatar*	$760,507,625	2009	215
2	*Titanic*	658,672,302	1997	161
3	*Jurassic World*	628,700,000	2015	238
4	*Marvel's The Avengers*	623,357,910	2012	230
5	*The Dark Knight*	534,858,444	2008	215
6	*Star Wars: Episode I—The Phantom Menace*	474,544,677	1999	167
7	*Star Wars*	460,998,007	1977	61
8	*Avengers: Age of Ultron*	456,774,004	2015	238
9	*The Dark Knight Rises*	448,139,099	2012	230
10	*Shrek 2*	441,226,247	2004	189
11	*ET: The Extra-Terrestrial*	435,110,554	1982	97
79	*Jaws*	260,000,000	1975	54
161	*Gone with the Wind*	198,676,459	1939	14
183	*Snow White and the Seven Dwarfs*	184,925,486	1937	14
257	*The Sound of Music*	158,671,368	1965	32
303	*101 Dalmatians*	144,880,014	1961	30

9.6 Nominal Interest Rates versus Real Interest Rates, pages 296–298

LEARNING OBJECTIVE: Distinguish between the nominal interest rate and the real interest rate.

Summary

The stated interest rate on a loan is the **nominal interest rate**. The **real interest rate** is the nominal interest rate minus the inflation rate. Because it is corrected for the effects of inflation, the real interest rate provides a better measure of the true cost of borrowing and the true return from lending than does the nominal interest rate. The nominal interest rate is always greater than the real interest rate unless the economy experiences **deflation**, which is a decline in the price level.

MyEconLab   Visit **www.myeconlab.com** to complete these exercises online and get instant feedback.

Review Questions

6.1   What is the difference between the nominal interest rate and the real interest rate?

6.2   If inflation is expected to increase, what will happen to the nominal interest rate? Briefly explain.

6.3   The chapter states that it is impossible to know whether a particular nominal interest rate is "high" or "low." Briefly explain why.

6.4   If the economy is experiencing deflation, will the nominal interest rate be higher or lower than the real interest rate?

Problems and Applications

6.5   The following appeared in a news article: "Inflation in the Lehigh Valley during the first quarter of … [the year] was less than half the national rate. … So, unlike much of the nation, the fear here is deflation—when prices sink so low

the CPI drops below zero." Do you agree with the reporter's definition of deflation? Briefly explain.

Source: Dan Shope, "Valley's Inflation Rate Slides," (Allentown, PA) *Morning Call,* July 9, 1996.

6.6   Suppose you were borrowing money to buy a car.
a. Which of these situations would you prefer: The interest rate on your car loan is 20 percent and the inflation rate is 19 percent, or the interest rate on your car loan is 5 percent and the inflation rate is 2 percent? Briefly explain.
b. Now suppose you are JPMorgan Chase, and you are making car loans. Which situation in part (a) would you now prefer? Briefly explain.

6.7   In June 2014, the nominal interest rate on a one-year Treasury bill was 0.10 percent. From June 2014 to June 2015, the consumer price index rose from 237.3 to 237.8. If you bought the one-year Treasury bill in May 2014, calculate the real interest rate you earned over the following 12-month period. Given the results of your calculation, why were investors willing to buy Treasury bills in May 2014?

6.8   Describing the situation in England in 1920, the historian Robert Skidelsky wrote the following: "Who would not borrow at 4 percent a year, with prices going up 4 percent a *month*?" What was the real interest rate paid by borrowers in this situation? (*Hint:* What is the annual inflation rate, if the monthly inflation rate is 4 percent?)

Source: Robert Skidelsky, *John Maynard Keynes: Volume 2, The Economist as Saviour 1920–1937,* New York: The Penguin Press, 1992, p. 39.

6.9   Suppose that the only good you purchase is hamburgers, and that at the beginning of the year, the price of a hamburger is $2.00. Suppose you lend $1,000 for one year at an interest rate of 5 percent. At the end of the year, a hamburger costs $2.08. What is the real rate of interest you earned on your loan?

9.7 Does Inflation Impose Costs on the Economy? pages 298–301

LEARNING OBJECTIVE: Discuss the problems that inflation causes.

Summary

Inflation does not reduce the affordability of goods and services to an average consumer, but it does impose costs on the economy. When inflation is anticipated, its main costs are that paper money loses some of its value and firms incur *menu costs*. **Menu costs** include the costs of changing prices on products and updating catalogs. When inflation is unanticipated, the actual inflation rate can turn out to be different from the expected inflation rate. As a result, income is redistributed as some people gain and some people lose.

MyEconLab Visit **www.myeconlab.com** to complete these exercises online and get instant feedback.

Review Questions

7.1 Why do nominal incomes generally increase with inflation? If nominal incomes increase with inflation, does inflation reduce the purchasing power of an average consumer? Briefly explain.

7.2 How can inflation affect the distribution of income?

7.3 Which is a greater problem: anticipated inflation or unanticipated inflation? Briefly explain.

7.4 What are menu costs? What effect has the Internet had on the size of menu costs?

7.5 What problems does deflation cause?

Problems and Applications

7.6 Suppose that the inflation rate turns out to be much higher than most people expected. In that case, would you rather have been a borrower or a lender? Briefly explain.

7.7 Suppose James and Frank both retire this year. For income during retirement, James will rely on a pension from his company that pays him a fixed $2,500 per month for as long as he lives. James hasn't saved anything for retirement. Frank has no pension but has saved a considerable amount, which he has invested in certificates of deposit (CDs) at his bank. Currently, Frank's CDs pay him interest of $2,300 per month.
   a. Ten years from now, is James or Frank likely to have a higher real income? In your answer, be sure to define *real income*.
   b. Now suppose that instead of being a constant amount, James's pension increases each year by the same percentage as the CPI. For example, if the CPI increases by 5 percent in the first year after James retires, then his pension in the second year equals $2,500 + ($2,500 × 0.05) = $2,625. In this case, 10 years from now, is James or Frank likely to have a higher real income?

7.8 Suppose that Apple and the investors buying the firm's bonds both expect a 2 percent inflation rate for the year. Given this expectation, suppose the nominal interest rate on the bonds is 6 percent and the real interest rate is 4 percent. Suppose that a year after the investors purchase the bonds, the inflation rate turns out to be 6 percent, rather than the 2 percent that had been expected. Who gains and who loses from the unexpectedly high inflation rate?

7.9 (Related to the Making the Connection on page 300) During the spring of 2015, the United Kingdom experienced a brief period of deflation. According to an article in the *Wall Street Journal*, "The U.K.'s history of sticky and hard-to-control inflation suggests that a short period of falling prices will be taken as a reprieve for consumers, not as a signal to defer purchases." Why might consumers see deflation as a "signal to defer purchases"? Shouldn't lower prices cause consumers to buy more, not less? Briefly explain.
Source: Richard Barley, "U.K. Deflation More Curiosity Than Concern," *Wall Street Journal*, May 19, 2015.

7.10 (Related to the Making the Connection on page 300) During the late nineteenth century in the United States, many farmers borrowed heavily to buy land. During most of the period between 1870 and the mid-1890s, the United States experienced mild deflation: The price level declined each year. Many farmers engaged in political protests during these years, and deflation was often a subject of their protests. Explain why farmers would have felt burdened by deflation.

Real-Time Data Exercises

D9.1 (Using the CPI to measure inflation) Go to the Web site of the Federal Reserve Bank of St. Louis (FRED) (research.stlouisfed.org/fred2/).
   a. Find values for the most recent month and for the same month one year earlier for the Consumer Price Index (CPIAUCSL).
   b. Use the values you found in part (a) to calculate the inflation rate for the past year.

D9.2 (Using CPI data and Excel to calculate the inflation rate) Go to the Web site of the Federal Reserve Bank of St. Louis (FRED) (research.stlouisfed.org/fred2/).
   a. Locate the data for the Consumer Price Index (CPI-AUCSL). Click on the "Download Data" link on the left of the page. Change the beginning date to six years prior to the most recent observation. You can leave the ending date as it is. Then click on the "Download Data" button to download the data and save it to your computer. Finally, open the Excel file that you just downloaded. (*Note:* You can also use another compatible spreadsheet program, such as OpenOffice's Calc.)
   b. Using Excel, calculate the percentage change in CPI from a year earlier for each observation, beginning with the observation one year later than the first observation. To make this calculation, click on the blank cell next to the observation corresponding to that date and then enter the following formula (note that in Excel, the symbol for multiplication is *):

$$\text{Percentage change} = \left(\frac{\text{CPI}_t - \text{CPI}_{t-1}}{\text{CPI}_{t-1}} \right) \times 100,$$

where $t-1$ is the first observation and t is the observation one year later. Repeat this process for the remaining observations. (You can use the copy and paste functions to avoid having to retype the formula.)

c. Using your calculations from part (b), create a graph of the percentage changes from a year earlier.

d. Use your calculations from part (b) to explain which period experienced the highest inflation rate. What was the inflation rate during that period?

D9.3 (Using CPI data and Excel to calculate an alternative measure of the inflation rate) In addition to the usual CPI, the BLS also calculates a CPI that does not include the prices of food and energy. Because the prices of food and energy tend to fluctuate more than other prices, some economists believe that omitting them provides a better measure of the long-run inflation rate. Go to the Web site of the Federal Reserve Bank of St. Louis (FRED) (research.stlouisfed.org/fred2/).

a. Locate the data for the Consumer Price Index (CPI-AUCSL) and the Consumer Price Index less Food and Energy (CPILFESL). Click on the "Download Data" link on the left of the page. Change the beginning date to 2006-07-01. You can leave the ending date as it is. Then click on the "Download Data" button to download the data and save it to your computer. Finally, open the Excel file that you just downloaded. (*Note:* You can also use another compatible spreadsheet program, such as OpenOffice's Calc.)

b. Using Excel, calculate the percentage change in each CPI from a year ago for each of the observations, beginning with the observation 2007-07-01. To make this calculation, click on the blank cell next to the observation corresponding to 2007-07-01, and then enter the following formula (note that in Excel, the symbol for multiplication is *):

$$\text{Percentage change} = \left(\frac{CPI_t - CPI_{t-1}}{CPI_{t-1}} \right) \times 100$$

where $t-1$ = 2007-07-01 and t = 2006-07-01. Repeat this process for the remaining observations. (You can use the copy and paste functions to avoid having to re-type the formula.)

c. Using your calculations from part (b), create a graph of the percentage changes from a year ago for both indexes. Make sure both data lines are on the same graph.

d. Discuss differences between the two measures of the inflation rate. For instance, from your calculations, what was the inflation rate in June 2009 using the two CPI measures?

D9.4 (Analyzing inflation in CPI categories) Calculating inflation rates for categories of goods and services in the CPI market basket (see page 291) can provide insight into inflation in different sectors of the economy. Go to the Web site of the Federal Reserve Bank of St. Louis (FRED) (research.stlouisfed.org/fred2/).

a. Find the most recent values and values from the same month in 2010 for the following four categories of the Consumer Price Index: (1) Food and Beverages (CPIFABSL), (2) Apparel (CPIAPPSL), (3) Transportation (CPITRNSL), and (4) Medical Care (CPIMEDSL).

b. Using the data from part (a), calculate the inflation rate over the period from 2010 to the present period for each of the four CPI categories.

c. According to your calculations, which category experienced the least amount of inflation and which category experienced the most inflation?

D9.5 (Analyzing the labor force and unemployment) Go to the Web site of the Federal Reserve Bank of St. Louis (FRED) (research.stlouisfed.org/fred2/).

a. Find the most recent values for these three variables: (1) Unemployed (UNEMPLOY), (2) Civilian Labor Force (CLF16OV), and (3) Employment Level – Part-Time for Economic Reasons, Slack Work or Business Conditions (LNS12032195). Are these data reported annually, quarterly, or monthly? What units are these values reported in?

b. Using the values you found in part (a), calculate the civilian unemployment rate and the civilian unemployment rate including persons who are underemployed (part-time for economic reasons).

D9.6 (Calculating the unemployment rate for different groups) Go to the Web site of the Federal Reserve Bank of St. Louis (FRED) (research.stlouisfed.org/fred2/).

a. Find the most recent values for these four variables: (1) Unemployment Level – Men (LNS13000001), (2) Unemployment Level – Women (LNS13000002), (3) Civilian Labor Force Level – Men (LNS11000001), and (4) Civilian Labor Force Level – Women (LNS11000002). Are these data reported annually, quarterly, or monthly? What units are these values reported in?

b. Using the values you found in part (a), calculate the unemployment rate for men and the unemployment rate for women.

c. Explain why some people are considered discouraged workers. What will happen to the unemployment rate if there is an increase in discouraged workers?

D9.7 (Calculating the employment–population ratio) Go to the Web site of the Federal Reserve Bank of St. Louis (FRED) (research.stlouisfed.org/fred2/).

a. Find the most recent values for these three variables: (1) Unemployed (UNEMPLOY), (2) Civilian Employment (CE16OV), and (3) Not in Labor Force (LNS15000000).

b. Using the values you found in part (a), calculate the working-age population (in thousands) and the employment–population ratio.

c. Holding all other factors constant, what would you expect to happen to the employment–population ratio if the economy entered a recession? Briefly explain.

D9.8 (Calculating the cyclical unemployment rate) Go to the Web site of the Federal Reserve Bank of St. Louis (FRED) (research.stlouisfed.org/fred2/).

a. Find the value for the most recent month and for the same month two years earlier for the Civilian Unemployment Rate (UNRATE) and the Natural Rate of Unemployment (NROU).

b. Using the values you found in part (a), calculate the cyclical rate of unemployment.

c. Given the change in cyclical unemployment over this two-year period, what can you conclude about the state of the economy?

D9.9 (The unemployment rate and the business cycle) Go to the Web site of the Federal Reserve Bank of St. Louis (FRED) (research.stlouisfed.org/fred2/).

a. Find the most recent values for these three variables: (1) Unemployed (UNEMPLOY), Civilian Employment

(CE16OV), (2) Employment Level – Part-Time for Economic Reasons, All Industries (LNS12032194), and (3) Not in Labor Force, Searched for Work and Available (LNU05026642).

b. Using the values you found in part (a), calculate the official unemployment rate.

c. Some economists argue that the official unemployment rate understates the degree of joblessness in the economy because it uses too narrow a definition of unemployment. The BLS also calculates a broader measure of the unemployment rate, which includes people who work part time for economic reasons and people who are available for work but not actively searching. Using the data you found in part (a), calculate this broader measure of the unemployment rate.

d. How would you expect the gap between the official rate of unemployment and the broader rate to change over the course of the business cycle?

D9.10 (Calculating the real interest rate) Go to the Web site of the Federal Reserve Bank of St. Louis (FRED) (research. stlouisfed.org/fred2/).

a. Find the most recent values for the 3-Month Treasury Bill: Secondary Market Rate (TB3MS) and the University of Michigan Inflation Expectation (MICH).

b. Using the data you found in part (a), calculate the expected real interest rate.

c. If the actual inflation rate is greater than the expected inflation rate, how are borrowers and lenders affected?

D9.11 (Calculating the effect of inflation on real wages) Go to the Web site of the Federal Reserve Bank of St. Louis (FRED) (research.stlouisfed.org/fred2/).

a. Find the values for the most recent month and for the month one year earlier for the Consumer Price Index for All Urban Consumers: All Items (CPIAUCNS) and Average Hourly Earnings of Production and Non-supervisory Employees: Total Private (AHETPI).

b. Using the data you found in part (a), calculate the average hourly real wage for each year.

c. Calculate the percentage change in the average hourly nominal wage and the average hourly real wage during this year.

d. Given your calculation in part (c), explain whether an average worker was better or worse off than a year earlier.

CHAPTER
10

Economic Growth, the Financial System, and Business Cycles

Economic Growth and the Business Cycle at Corning, Inc.

Amory Houghton founded the company that became Corning, Inc., in 1851. At first, the company manufactured basic glass products such as jars. Over time, though, the company developed a number of new products using innovative technologies. For instance, in 1921, a Corning employee invented a machine that made millions of light bulbs for Thomas Edison. In the 1970s, Corning developed fiber-optic cable that eventually became the means for carrying the electronic signals needed for modern telecommunications and the Internet. In 2007, researchers at the company developed a damage-resistant glass called Gorilla glass that is used on the screens of iPhones and many other portable electronic devices. By 2015, Corning, headquartered in Corning, New York, had more than 34,000 employees and sales of nearly $10 billion.

Corning is one of many firms responsible for the technological progress that has been the basis for the growth of the U.S. economy and the rise in U.S. living standards. Corning's experiences have mirrored two key macroeconomic facts: In the long run, the U.S. economy has experienced economic growth, and in the short run, the economy has experienced a series of business cycles. During the 2001 recession, Corning suffered a $5 billion loss as the market for fiber-optic cable collapsed as a result of the bursting of the "dot-com" stock market bubble. Similarly, the recession of 2007–2009 caused a sharp decline in the demand for durable goods, including automobiles, televisions, and computers. Because Corning supplies ceramics for automobile emissions systems, as well as display panels for televisions and computers, its sales declined and its profits fell by more than 60 percent between 2008 and 2009.

Unlike many firms, Corning did continue to earn a profit during the recession. The company managed to remain profitable due to products like Gorilla glass that continue to sell well even during recessions. The next success for Corning could be a thinner version of Gorilla glass, called Willow glass, that can be wound and shipped in rolls, which might make it possible for Apple and other firms to produce foldable smartphones and other electronic devices.

In this chapter, we provide an overview of long-run growth and the business cycle and discuss their importance for firms, consumers, and the economy as a whole.

Sources: Robin Goldwyn Blumenthal, "Corning's Latest Magic: Turning Glass into Cash," *Barron's*, June 6, 2015; Connie Guglielmo, "Working with Innovators from Thomas Edison to Steve Jobs, Corning Finds a Glass Fix," *Forbes*, September 23, 2013; and Corning, Inc., Annual Reports on corning.com.

Economics in Your Life

Do You Help the Economy More if You Spend or if You Save?

Suppose the U.S. government sends you an income tax refund. You're not sure what to do with the money, so you ask your two roommates for advice. One roommate tells you that if you want to help the economy, you should save all the money because a country's economic growth depends on the amount of saving by households. The other roommate disagrees and advises you to spend all the money because consumer spending is a major component of gross domestic product (GDP), and your spending would help increase production and create more jobs. Which of your two roommates is right? As you read this chapter, try to answer this question. You can check your answer against the one we provide on **page 340** at the end of this chapter.

A successful economy is capable of increasing production of goods and services faster than the growth in population. Attaining this level of growth is the only way that the standard of living of the average person in a country can increase. Unfortunately, some economies around the world are not growing at all or are growing very slowly. Most people in those countries live on about the same levels of income as their ancestors did decades, or even centuries, ago. In the United States and other developed countries, however, incomes and living standards are much higher today than they were 50 years ago. An important macroeconomic topic is why some countries grow much faster than others.

As we will see, one determinant of economic growth is the ability of firms to expand their operations, buy additional equipment, train workers, and adopt new technologies. To carry out these activities, firms must acquire funds from households, either directly through financial markets—such as the stock and bond markets—or indirectly through financial intermediaries—such as banks. Financial markets and financial intermediaries together comprise the *financial system*. In this chapter, we present an overview of the financial system and see how funds flow from households to firms through the *market for loanable funds*.

Since at least the early nineteenth century, the U.S. economy has experienced periods of expanding production and employment followed by periods of recession during which production and employment decline. These alternating periods of expansion and recession are called the **business cycle**. Business cycles are not uniform: Periods of expansion are not the same length, nor are periods of recession. But every period of expansion in U.S. history has been followed by a period of recession, and every period of recession has been followed by a period of expansion.

In this chapter, we begin to explore two key aspects of macroeconomics: the long-run growth that has steadily raised living standards in the United States and the short-run fluctuations of the business cycle.

Business cycle Alternating periods of economic expansion and economic recession.

10.1 Long-Run Economic Growth

LEARNING OBJECTIVE: Discuss the importance of long-run economic growth.

Most people in high-income countries such as the United States, Canada, Japan, and the countries in Western Europe expect that over time, their standard of living will improve. They expect that year after year, firms will introduce new and improved products, new prescription drugs and better surgical techniques will overcome more diseases, and their ability to afford these goods and services will increase. For most people, these are reasonable expectations.

In 1900, the United States was already enjoying the highest standard of living in the world. Yet in that year, only 3 percent of U.S. homes had electricity, only 15 percent had indoor flush toilets, and only 25 percent had running water. The lack of running water meant that before people could cook or bathe, they had to pump water from wells and haul it to their homes in buckets—on average about 10,000 gallons per year per family. Not surprisingly, water consumption averaged only about 5 gallons per person per day, compared with about 150 gallons today. The result was that people washed themselves and their clothing only infrequently. A majority of families living in cities had to use outdoor toilets, which they shared with other families. Diseases such as smallpox, typhus, dysentery, and cholera were still common. In 1900, 5,000 of the 45,000 children born in Chicago died before their first birthday. Life expectancy at birth was about 47 years, compared with 80 years in 2015. Few families had electric lights, relying instead on burning candles or burning kerosene or coal oil in lamps. Many homes were heated in the winter by burning coal, which contributed to the severe pollution that fouled the air of most large cities. In 1900, there were no modern appliances, so housework was time-consuming and physically demanding. The typical American homemaker baked a half-ton of bread per year.

The process of **long-run economic growth** brought the typical American from the standard of living of 1900 to the standard of living of today. The best measure of the standard of living is real GDP per person, which is usually called *real GDP per capita*. So, we measure long-run economic growth by increases in real GDP per capita over long periods of time, generally decades or more. We use real GDP rather than nominal GDP to adjust for changes in the price level over time. Figure 10.1 shows the growth in real GDP per capita in the United States from 1900 to 2014. The figure shows that the trend in real GDP per capita is strongly upward, although it fluctuates in the short run because of the business cycle. It is the upward trend in real GDP per capita that we focus on when discussing long-run economic growth.

The values in Figure 10.1 are measured in prices of 2009, so they represent constant amounts of purchasing power. In 1900, real GDP per capita was about $6,000. More than a century later, in 2014, it had risen to about $50,010, which means that an average American in 2014 could purchase more than eight times as many goods and services as an average American in 1900. Large as it is, this increase in real GDP per capita actually understates the true increase in the standard of living of Americans in 2014 compared with 1900. Many of today's goods and services were not available in 1900. For example, if you lived in 1900 and became ill with a serious infection, you could not purchase antibiotics to treat your illness—no matter how high your income. You might have died from an illness for which even a very poor person in today's society could receive effective medical treatment. Of course, the quantity of goods and services that a person can buy is not a perfect measure of how happy or contented that person may be. A person's happiness also depends on education, health, spiritual well-being, and many other factors ignored in calculating GDP. Nevertheless, economists rely heavily on comparisons of real GDP per capita because it is the best means of comparing the performance of one economy over time or the performance of different economies at any particular time.

MyEconLab Concept Check

Long-run economic growth The process by which rising productivity increases the average standard of living.

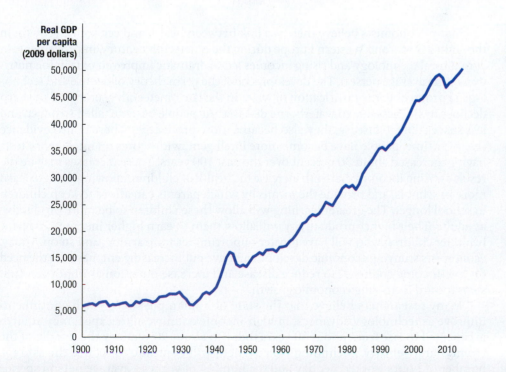

MyEconLab Real-time data

Figure 10.1

The Growth in Real GDP per Capita, 1900–2014

Measured in 2009 dollars, real GDP per capita in the United States grew from about $6,000 in 1900 to about $50,010 in 2014. An average American in 2014 could buy more than eight times as many goods and services as an average American in 1900.

Sources: Samuel H. Williamson, "What Was the U.S. GDP Then?" Measuring-Worth, July 2015; and U.S. Bureau of Economic Analysis.

Making the Connection
MyEconLab Video

The Connection between Economic Prosperity and Health

We can see the direct effect of economic growth on living standards by looking at improvements in health in high-income countries over the past 100 years. The research of the late Robert Fogel, winner of the Nobel Prize in Economics, highlights the close connection between economic growth, improvements in technology, and improvements in human physiology. One important measure of health is life expectancy at birth. As the following graph shows, in 1900, life expectancy was less than 50 years in the United States, the United Kingdom, and France. Today, life expectancy is about 80 years. Although life expectancies in the lowest-income countries remain very short, some countries that have begun to experience economic growth have seen dramatic increases in life expectancies. For example, life expectancy in India has more than doubled from 27 years in 1900 to 68 years today.

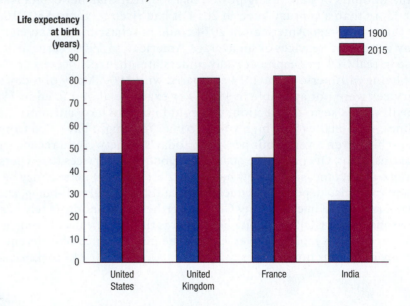

Many economists believe there is a link between health and economic growth. In the United States and Western Europe during the nineteenth century, improvements in agricultural technology and rising incomes led to dramatic improvements in the nutrition of the average person. The development of the germ theory of disease and technological progress in the purification of water in the late nineteenth century led to sharp declines in sickness due to waterborne diseases. As people became taller, stronger, and less susceptible to disease, they also became more productive. There is also evidence that over time, people have become more intelligent, with scores on intelligence tests having increased about 30 percent over the past 100 years. These increases may be the result of rising incomes that both increase the health of children, allowing them to learn more in schools, and provide the means by which parents can afford to keep children in school longer. The greater learning will allow these children to be more productive as adults. Their higher productivity will allow them to earn higher incomes and have healthier children who will have greater opportunities for learning, and so on. Today, economists studying economic development have put increasing emphasis on the need for low-income countries to reduce disease and increase nutrition as important first steps toward increasing economic growth.

Many researchers believe that the state of human physiology will continue to improve as technology advances. In high-income countries, life expectancy at birth is expected to rise from about 80 years today to about 90 years by the middle of the twenty-first century. Technological advances will continue to reduce the average number of hours worked per day and the number of years an average person spends in the paid workforce. Individuals spend about 10 hours per day sleeping, eating, and bathing. Their remaining "discretionary hours" are divided between paid work and leisure. The following graph is based on estimates by Robert Fogel that contrast how individuals in the United States will divide their time in 2040 compared with 1880 and 1995. Not only will technology and economic growth allow people in the near future to live longer lives, but a much smaller fraction of those lives will need to be spent at paid work.

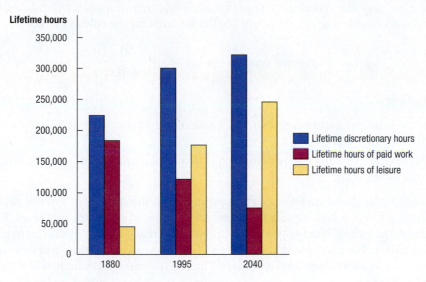

Sources: Robert William Fogel, *The Escape from Hunger and Premature Death, 1700–2100*, New York: Cambridge University Press, 2004; Alison Gopnik, "Smarter Every Year? Mystery of the Rising IQs," *Wall Street Journal*, May 27, 2015; and U.S. Central Intelligence Agency, *The 2015 World Factbook*, online version.

Your Turn: Test your understanding by doing related problem 1.7 on page 342 at the end of this chapter.

MyEconLab Study Plan

Calculating Growth Rates and the Rule of 70

The growth rate of real GDP or real GDP per capita during a particular year is equal to the percentage change from the previous year. For example, measured in 2009 prices, real GDP equaled $15,710 billion in 2013 and rose to $16,086 billion in 2014. We calculate the growth of real GDP in 2014 as:

$$\left(\frac{\$16{,}086 \text{ billion} - \$15{,}710 \text{ billion}}{\$15{,}710 \text{ billion}} \right) \times 100 = 2.4\%.$$

For longer periods of time, we can use the *average annual growth rate*. For example, real GDP in the United States was $2,184 billion in 1950 and $16,086 billion in 2014. To find the average annual growth rate during this 64-year period, we compute the annual growth rate that would result in $2,184 billion increasing to $16,086 billion over 64 years. In this case, the growth rate is 3.2 percent. That is, if $2,184 billion grows at an average rate of 3.2 percent per year, after 64 years, it will have grown to $16,086 billion.

For shorter periods of time, we get approximately the same answer by averaging the growth rate for each year. For example, real GDP in the United States grew by 2.3 percent in 2012, 2.2 percent in 2013, and 2.4 percent in 2014. So, the average annual growth rate of real GDP for the period 2012–2014 was 2.3 percent, which is the average of the three annual growth rates:

$$\frac{2.3\% + 2.2\% + 2.4\%}{3} = 2.3\%.$$

Finally, when discussing long-run economic growth, we usually shorten "average annual growth rate" to "growth rate."

We can judge how rapidly an economic variable is growing by calculating the number of years it would take to double. For example, if real GDP per capita in a country doubles, say, every 20 years, most people in the country will experience significant increases in their standard of living over the course of their lives. If real GDP per capita doubles only every 100 years, increases in the standard of living will occur too slowly to notice. One easy way to calculate approximately how many years it will take real GDP per capita to double is to use the *rule of 70*. The formula for the rule of 70 is:

$$\text{Number of years to double} = \frac{70}{\text{Growth rate}}.$$

For example:

- If real GDP per capita is growing at a rate of 5 percent per year, it will double in $70/5 = 14$ years.

- If real GDP per capita is growing at a rate of 2 percent per year, it will double in $70/2 = 35$ years.

These examples illustrate an important point: Small differences in growth rates can have large effects on how rapidly the standard of living in a country increases. Finally, notice that the rule of 70 applies not just to growth in real GDP per capita but to growth in any variable. For example, if you invest $1,000 in the stock market, and your investment grows at an average annual rate of 7 percent, your investment will double to $2,000 in 10 years.

MyEconLab Concept Check

What Determines the Rate of Long-Run Growth?

Labor productivity The quantity of goods and services that can be produced by one worker or by one hour of work.

A key point in explaining long-run growth is that *increases in real GDP per capita depend on increases in labor productivity.* **Labor productivity** is the quantity of goods and services that can be produced by one worker or by one hour of work. In analyzing long-run growth, economists usually measure labor productivity as output per hour of work to avoid the effects of fluctuations in the length of the workday and in the fraction of the population employed. If the quantity of goods and services consumed by the average person is to increase, the quantity of goods and services produced per hour of work must also increase. Why in 2014 was the average American able to consume more than eight times as many goods and services as the average American in 1900? Because the average American worker in 2014 was eight times as productive as the average American worker in 1900.

If increases in labor productivity are the key to long-run economic growth, what causes labor productivity to increase? Economists believe two key factors determine labor productivity:

1. The quantity of capital per hour worked
2. The level of technology

Therefore, economic growth occurs if the quantity of capital per hour worked increases and if there is technological change.

Increases in Capital per Hour Worked

Capital Manufactured goods that are used to produce other goods and services.

Workers today in high-income countries such as the United States have more physical capital available than workers in low-income countries or workers in the high-income countries of 100 years ago. Recall that **capital** refers to manufactured goods that are used to produce other goods and services. Examples of capital are computers, factory buildings, machine tools, warehouses, and trucks. The total amount of physical capital available in a country is known as the country's *capital stock*.

As the amount of capital per hour worked increases, worker productivity increases. An accountant who records a firm's revenues and costs using Excel is more productive than an accountant who uses only pen and paper. A worker who uses a backhoe can excavate more earth than a worker who uses only a shovel.

In explaining economic growth, economists take into account not just *physical capital*, like computers and factories, but also *human capital*, which is the accumulated knowledge and skills workers acquire from education and training or from their life experiences. For example, workers with a college education generally have more skills and are more productive than workers who have only a high school degree. Increases in human capital are particularly important in stimulating economic growth.

Technological Change   Economic growth depends more on *technological change* than on increases in capital per hour worked. *Technology* refers to the processes a firm uses to turn inputs into outputs of goods and services. Technological change is an increase in the quantity of output firms can produce, using a given quantity of inputs. Technological change can come from many sources. For example, a firm's managers may rearrange a factory floor or the layout of a retail store to increase production and sales. Most technological change, however, is embodied in new machinery, equipment, or software.

A very important point is that just accumulating more inputs—such as labor, capital, and natural resources—will not ensure that an economy experiences economic growth unless technological change also occurs. For example, the Soviet Union failed to maintain a high rate of economic growth, even though it continued to increase the quantity of capital available per hour worked, because it experienced relatively little technological change.

Entrepreneurs are critical for implementing technological change. Recall that an entrepreneur is someone who operates a business, bringing together the factors of production—labor, capital, and natural resources—to produce goods and services (see Chapter 2). In a market economy, entrepreneurs make the crucial decisions about whether to introduce new technology to produce better or lower-cost products. Entrepreneurs also decide whether to allocate a firm's resources to research and development that can result in new technologies. One of the difficulties centrally planned economies have in sustaining economic growth is that managers employed by the government are usually much slower to develop and adopt new technologies than are entrepreneurs in a market system.

Solved Problem 10.1

MyEconLab Interactive Animation

Where Does Productivity Come From?

A column in the *Wall Street Journal* argued that "productivity growth is a key ingredient to prosperity." What did the columnist mean by "prosperity"? What is the connection between productivity growth and prosperity?

Solving the Problem

Step 1:   Review the chapter material. This problem is about what determines the rate of long-run growth, so you may want to review the section "What Determines the Rate of Long-Run Growth?" which begins on page 318.

Step 2:   Answer the first question by explaining what the columnist meant by the word "prosperity" in this context. By *prosperity*, most people mean a high standard of living. In the context of economic growth, the key measure of the standard of living is real GDP per capita.

Step 3:   Answer the second question by explaining the connection between productivity growth and prosperity. *Productivity* refers to the amount of goods and services produced per worker. As we have seen, per capita real GDP increases only if productivity increases. Therefore, increases in a country's standard of living—its prosperity—are tied to increases in productivity.

Source: Jon Hilsenrath, "More Disturbing Findings Emerge on U.S. Productivity Path," *Wall Street Journal*, February 12, 2015.

Your Turn: For more practice, do related problems 1.10 and 1.11 on pages 342–343 at the end of this chapter.

MyEconLab Study Plan

Property Rights Finally, an additional requirement for economic growth is that the government must provide secure rights to private property. A market system cannot function unless rights to private property are secure (see Chapter 2). In addition, the government can aid economic growth by establishing an independent court system that enforces contracts between private individuals. Many economists would also say that the government has a role in facilitating the development of an efficient financial system, as well as systems of education, transportation, and communication. Economist Richard Sylla of New York University has argued that every country that has experienced economic growth first experienced a "financial revolution." For example, before the United States was able to experience significant economic growth in the early nineteenth century, the country's banking and monetary systems were reformed under the guidance of Alexander Hamilton, who was appointed the country's first secretary of the Treasury in 1789. Without supportive government policies, long-run economic growth is unlikely to occur.   MyEconLab Concept Check

Making the Connection
MyEconLab Video

Can India Sustain Its Rapid Growth?

When you have a computer problem and need technical support, the person who takes your call may well be in India. In addition to information technology, in recent years Indian firms have made gains in the global markets for steel, oil, and automobiles, among other goods.

To many people in the United States, the rapid economic rise of India has been unexpected. As the following figure shows, Indian real GDP per capita increased very slowly up to the time India became independent from England in 1947. As a result, in 1950, India was desperately poor. India's real GDP per capita in 1950 was less than $1,000 measured in 2015 dollars, or less than 7 percent of 1950 U.S. real GDP per capita. During the first 40 years of independence, India's growth rate increased but was still too slow to significantly reduce the country's poverty. Recent years tell a much different story, however. In 1991, the Indian government decided to scale back central planning, reduce regulations, and introduce market-based reforms. The result was that the growth rate doubled over the following decade. In the most recent period, growth has been even more rapid.

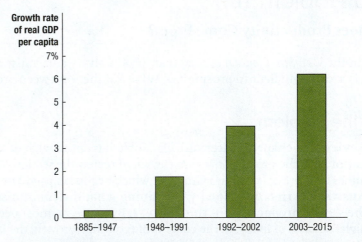

Still, India remains a very poor country. Nearly half of its population of 1.3 billion is employed in agriculture, and many can barely produce enough to feed themselves. Infant mortality rates are still at 10 times the levels in high-income countries, and about 40 percent of adult women and 20 percent of adult men are unable to read and write. The rapid economic growth that began in 1991 will have to continue in the coming decades if the average person in India is eventually to enjoy a standard of living equal to that in the United States and other high-income countries. But can India continue its rapid growth?

Some economists and policymakers worry that India's growth rates may begin to decline, leaving hundreds of millions of its people stuck in deep poverty. These economists point to several problems facing the Indian economy. The public education system has struggled to provide basic instruction, particularly in rural and poorer urban areas. India's expenditures on education rank 134th out of 173 countries, and are far below the levels in most successful developing countries. As a result, many adults lack the basic skills needed for a productive workforce. Even many high school and college graduates lack the skills to work in firms that compete in global markets. High rates of infectious disease also reduce the productivity of the workforce. Only 60 percent of urban residents have access to modern sewage systems, and fewer than one-quarter of rural residents do. In general, India has struggled to meet its infrastructure needs, as highways, bridges, and its train system—which dates from the British colonial period—have deteriorated.

India also suffers from political problems with ethnic, religious, cultural, and geographic divisions—there are 15 official languages—often making it difficult for the government to successfully implement policy reforms. Many observers believe that government corruption has increased, making it more difficult for businesses to obtain the permits necessary to operate. One estimate puts the size of the underground economy at more than 50 percent of GDP. Laws restricting the sale of agricultural land for industrial use have slowed the growth of manufacturing. Although Narendra Modi was elected prime minister in 2014 partly by promising new policies to spur economic growth, some economists and policymakers worry that the pace of market-oriented reforms has slowed over the years. They also urge the government to allow greater foreign investment in the financial and retail sectors. Greater foreign investment would allow these sectors to gain access to new technology and to increase productivity.

The economic progress India has made in the past 25 years has already lifted hundreds of millions of people out of poverty. For that progress to continue, however, many economists believe that the Indian government will need to upgrade infrastructure, improve the provision of educational and health services, and renew its commitment to the rule of law and to market-based reforms.

Sources: "Ready, Steady, Go," *Economist*, April 18, 2015; Ellen Barry, "After a Year of Outsize Expectations, Narendra Modi Adjusts His Plan for India," *New York Times*, May 25, 2015; Amartya Sen, "Why India Trails China," *New York Times*, June 19, 2013; Geeta Anand, "India Graduates Millions, but Too Few Are Fit to Hire," *Wall Street Journal*, April 5, 2011; data in graph are authors' calculations from the Maddison Project database, www.ggdc.net/maddison/maddison-project/home.htm; and International Monetary Fund, *World Economic Outlook Database*.

Your Turn: Test your understanding by doing related problems 1.13 and 1.14 on page 343 at the end of this chapter.

MyEconLab Study Plan

Potential GDP

Because economists take a long-run perspective in discussing economic growth, the concept of *potential GDP* is useful. **Potential GDP** is the level of real GDP attained when all firms are producing at *capacity*. The capacity of a firm is *not* the maximum output the firm is capable of producing. A Corning factory could operate 24 hours per day for 52 weeks per year and would be at its maximum production level. The factory's capacity, however, is measured by its production when operating on normal hours, using a normal workforce. If all firms in the economy were operating at capacity, the level of total production of final goods and services would equal potential GDP. Potential GDP increases over time as the labor force grows, new factories and office buildings are built, new machinery and equipment are installed, and technological change takes place.

From 1949 to 2015, potential GDP in the United States grew at an average annual rate of 3.2 percent. In other words, each year, on average, the capacity of the economy to produce final goods and services expanded by 3.2 percent. In any particular year, the *actual* level of real GDP increased by more or less than 3.2 percent as the economy moved through the business cycle. Figure 10.2 shows movements in actual and potential GDP for the years since 1989. The red line represents potential GDP, and the blue line represents actual real GDP. Notice that in each of the three recessions since 1989, actual real GDP has fallen below potential GDP. During the 2007–2009 recession, the

Potential GDP The level of real GDP attained when all firms are producing at capacity.

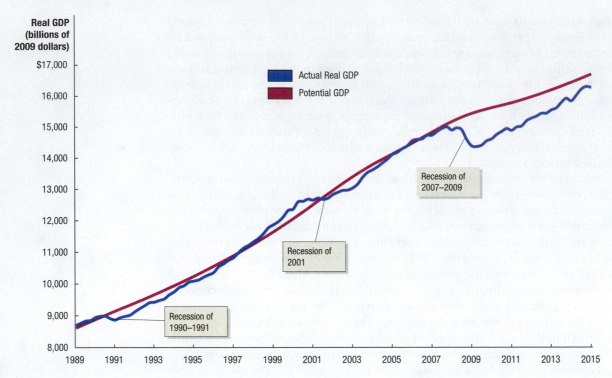

Figure 10.2 **Actual and Potential GDP**

Potential GDP increases every year as the labor force and the capital stock grow and technological change occurs. The red line represents potential GDP, and the blue line represents actual real GDP. During the three recessions since 1989, actual real GDP has been less than potential GDP.

Source: Federal Reserve Bank of St. Louis.

gap between actual real GDP and potential GDP was particularly large, which shows the severity of the recession.

 Saving, Investment, and the Financial System

LEARNING OBJECTIVE: Discuss the role of the financial system in facilitating long-run economic growth.

The process of economic growth depends on the ability of firms to expand their operations, buy additional equipment, train workers, and adopt new technologies. Firms can finance some of these activities from *retained earnings*, which are profits that are reinvested in the firm rather than paid to the firm's owners. For many firms, retained earnings are not sufficient to finance the rapid expansion required in economies experiencing high rates of economic growth. Firms can acquire funds from households, either directly through financial markets—such as the stock and bond markets—or indirectly through financial intermediaries—such as banks. Financial markets and financial intermediaries together comprise the **financial system**. Without a well-functioning financial system, economic growth is impossible because firms will be unable to expand and adopt new technologies. As we noted earlier, no country without a well-developed financial system has been able to sustain high levels of economic growth.

Financial system The system of financial markets and financial intermediaries through which firms acquire funds from households.

An Overview of the Financial System

The financial system channels funds from savers to borrowers and channels returns on the borrowed funds back to savers. In this section, we discuss the key components of the financial system and the services they provide to households and firms.

Financial Markets In **financial markets**, such as the stock market or the bond market, firms raise funds by selling financial securities directly to savers (see Chapter 6). A *financial security* is a document—sometimes in electronic form—that states the terms under which funds pass from the buyer of the security—who is providing funds—to the seller. *Stocks* are financial securities that represent partial ownership of a firm. If you buy one share of stock in Corning, you become one of millions of owners of that firm. *Bonds* are financial securities that represent promises to repay a fixed amount of funds. When Corning sells a bond, the firm promises to pay the purchaser of the bond an interest payment each year for the term of the bond, as well as a final payment of the amount of the loan.

Financial markets Markets where financial securities, such as stocks and bonds, are bought and sold.

Financial Intermediaries **Financial intermediaries**, such as banks, mutual funds, pension funds, and insurance companies, act as go-betweens for borrowers and lenders. In effect, financial intermediaries borrow funds from savers and lend them to borrowers. When you deposit funds in your checking account, you are lending your funds to the bank. The bank may lend your funds (together with the funds of other savers) to an entrepreneur who wants to start a business. Suppose Lena wants to open a laundry. Rather than your lending money directly to Lena's Laundry, the bank acts as a go-between for you and Lena. Intermediaries pool the funds of many small savers to lend to many individual borrowers. The intermediaries pay interest to savers in exchange for the use of savers' funds and earn a profit by lending money to borrowers and charging them a higher rate of interest on the loans. For example, a bank might pay you as a depositor a 2 percent rate of interest, while it lends the money to Lena's Laundry at a 6 percent rate of interest.

Financial intermediaries Firms, such as banks, mutual funds, pension funds, and insurance companies, that borrow funds from savers and lend them to borrowers.

Banks, mutual funds, pension funds, and insurance companies also make investments in stocks and bonds on behalf of savers. For example, *mutual funds* sell shares to savers and then use the funds to buy a portfolio of stocks, bonds, mortgages, and other financial securities. Large mutual fund companies, such as Fidelity, Vanguard, and Dreyfus, offer many stock and bond funds. Some funds hold a wide range of stocks or bonds; others specialize in securities issued by a particular industry or sector, such as health care; and others invest as index funds in fixed market baskets of securities, such as shares of the Standard & Poor's 500 firms. Over the past 30 years, the role of mutual funds in the financial system has increased dramatically. Today, competition among hundreds of mutual fund firms gives investors thousands of funds from which to choose.

The Services the Financial System Provides: Risk Sharing, Liquidity, and Information In addition to matching households that have excess funds with firms that want to borrow funds, the financial system provides three key services for savers and borrowers: risk sharing, liquidity, and information. *Risk* is the chance that the value of a financial security will change relative to what you expect. For example, you may buy a share of stock in Corning at a price of $25, only to have the price fall to $5. Most individual savers are not gamblers and seek a steady return on their savings rather than erratic swings between high and low earnings. The financial system provides *risk sharing* by allowing savers to spread their money among many financial investments. For example, you can divide your money among a bank certificate of deposit, individual bonds, and a stock mutual fund.

Liquidity is the ease with which a financial security can be exchanged for money. The financial system provides the service of liquidity by offering savers markets where they can sell their holdings of financial securities. For example, savers can easily sell their holdings of the stocks and bonds issued by large corporations on the major stock and bond markets.

A third service that the financial system provides savers is the collection and communication of *information*, or facts about borrowers and expectations about returns on financial securities. For example, Lena's Laundry may want to borrow $10,000 from you. Finding out what Lena intends to do with the funds and how likely she is to pay you back may be costly and time-consuming. By depositing $10,000 in the bank, you are, in effect, allowing the bank to gather this information for you. Because banks specialize in gathering information about borrowers, they are able to do it faster and at a lower cost than can individual savers. The financial system plays an important role in communicating information. If you read a news story announcing that an automobile firm has invented a car with an engine that runs on water, how would you determine the effect of that discovery on the firm's profits? Financial markets do the job for you by incorporating information into the prices of stocks, bonds, and other financial securities. In this example, the expectation of higher future profits would boost the prices of the automobile firm's stock and bonds.   MyEconLab Concept Check

The Macroeconomics of Saving and Investment

As we have seen, the funds available to firms through the financial system come from saving. When firms use funds to purchase machinery, factories, and office buildings, they are engaging in investment. In this section, we explore the macroeconomics of saving and investment. A key point we will develop is that *the total value of saving in the economy must equal the total value of investment.* National income accounting refers to the methods the Bureau of Economic Analysis uses to keep track of total production and total income in the economy (see Chapter 8). We can use some relationships from national income accounting to understand why total saving must equal total investment.

We begin with the relationship between gross domestic product, GDP (Y), and its components, consumption (C), investment (I), government purchases (G), and net exports (NX):

$$Y = C + I + G + NX.$$

Remember that GDP is a measure of both total production in the economy and total income.

In an *open economy*, there is interaction with other economies in terms of both trading of goods and services and borrowing and lending. All economies today are open economies, although they vary significantly in the extent of their openness. In a *closed economy*, there is no trading or borrowing and lending with other economies. For simplicity, we will develop the relationship between saving and investment for a closed economy, which allows us to focus on the most important points in a simpler framework. (See Chapter 18 for the case of an open economy.)

In a closed economy, net exports are zero, so we can rewrite the relationship between GDP and its components as:

$$Y = C + I + G.$$

The Savings Equals Investment Condition If we rearrange the equation showing the relationship between GDP and its components, we have an expression for investment in terms of the other variables:

$$I = Y - C - G.$$

This expression tells us that in a closed economy, investment spending is equal to total income minus consumption spending and minus government purchases.

We can also derive an expression for total saving. *Private saving* is equal to what households retain of their income after purchasing goods and services (C) and paying taxes (T). Households receive income for supplying the factors of production to firms. This portion of household income is equal to Y. Households also receive income from government in the form of *transfer payments* (TR), which include Social Security payments and unemployment insurance payments. We can write this expression for private saving (S_{Private}):

$$S_{\text{Private}} = Y + TR - C - T.$$

The government also engages in saving. *Public saving* (S_{Public}) equals the amount of tax revenue the government retains after paying for government purchases and making transfer payments to households:

$$S_{Public} = T - G - TR.$$

So, total saving in the economy (S) is equal to the sum of private saving and public saving:

$$S = S_{Private} + S_{Public},$$

or:

$$S = (Y + TR - C - T) + (T - G - TR),$$

or:

$$S = Y - C - G.$$

The right side of this expression is identical to the expression we derived earlier for investment spending. So, we can conclude that total saving must equal total investment:

$$S = I.$$

Budget Deficits and Budget Surpluses When the government spends the same amount that it collects in taxes, there is a *balanced budget*. When the government spends more than it collects in taxes, there is a *budget deficit*. In the case of a deficit, T is less than $G + TR$, which means that public saving is negative. Negative saving is also known as *dissaving*. How can public saving be negative? When the federal government runs a budget deficit, the U.S. Department of the Treasury sells Treasury bonds to borrow the money necessary to fund the gap between taxes and spending. In this case, rather than adding to the total amount of saving available to be borrowed for investment spending, the government is subtracting from it. (Notice that if households borrow more than they save, the total amount of saving will also fall.) With less saving, investment must also be lower. We can conclude that, holding constant all other factors, there is a lower level of investment spending in the economy when there is a budget deficit than when there is a balanced budget.

When the government spends less than it collects in taxes, there is a *budget surplus*. A budget surplus increases public saving and the total level of saving in the economy. A higher level of saving results in a higher level of investment spending. Therefore, holding constant all other factors, there is a higher level of investment spending in the economy when there is a budget surplus than when there is a balanced budget.

The U.S. federal government has experienced dramatic swings in the state of its budget over the past 20 years. In 1992, the federal budget deficit was $297.4 billion. The federal budget had a surplus of $189.5 billion in 2000, but a sharp decline in taxes and increase in government spending resulting from the recession of 2007–2009 led to a record budget deficit of $1.4 trillion in 2009. By 2015, the budget deficit had declined to less than $500 billion.   MyEconLab Concept Check

The Market for Loanable Funds

We have seen that the value of total saving must equal the value of total investment, but we have not yet discussed how this equality is actually brought about in the financial system. We can think of the financial system as being composed of many markets through which funds flow from lenders to borrowers: the market for certificates of deposit at banks, the market for stocks, the market for bonds, the market for mutual

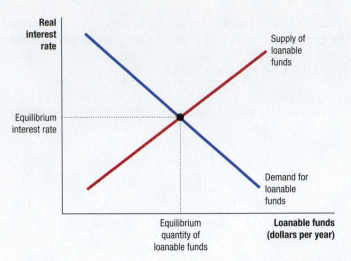

Figure 10.3 **The Market for Loanable Funds**

The demand for loanable funds is determined by the willingness of firms to borrow money to engage in new investment projects. The supply of loanable funds is determined by the willingness of households to save and by the extent of government saving or dissaving. Equilibrium in the market for loanable funds determines the real interest rate and the quantity of loanable funds exchanged.

Market for loanable funds The interaction of borrowers and lenders that determines the market interest rate and the quantity of loanable funds exchanged.

fund shares, and so on. For simplicity, we can combine these markets into a single market for *loanable funds*. In the model of the **market for loanable funds**, the interaction of borrowers and lenders determines the market interest rate and the quantity of loanable funds exchanged. As we will discuss in a later chapter, firms can also borrow from savers in other countries (see Chapter 18). For the remainder of this section, we will assume that there are no interactions between households and firms in the United States and those in other countries.

Demand and Supply in the Loanable Funds Market
The demand for loanable funds is determined by the willingness of firms to borrow money to engage in new investment projects, such as building new factories or carrying out research and development of new products. In determining whether to borrow funds, firms compare the return they expect to make on an investment with the interest rate they must pay to borrow the necessary funds. For example, if Home Depot is considering opening several new stores and expects to earn a return of 12 percent on its investment, the investment will be profitable if Home Depot can borrow the funds at an interest rate of 8 percent but will not be profitable if the interest rate is 15 percent. In Figure 10.3, the demand for loanable funds is downward sloping because the lower the interest rate, the more investment projects firms can profitably undertake, and the greater the quantity of loanable funds they will demand.

The supply of loanable funds is determined by the willingness of households to save and by the extent of government saving or dissaving. When households save, they reduce the amount of goods and services they can consume and enjoy today. The willingness of households to save rather than consume their incomes today will be determined in part by the interest rate they receive when they lend their savings. The higher the interest rate, the greater the reward for saving and the larger the amount of funds households will save. Therefore, the supply curve for loanable funds in Figure 10.3 is upward sloping because the higher the interest rate, the greater the quantity of saving supplied.

Recall the distinction between the *nominal interest rate* and the *real interest rate* (see Chapter 9). The nominal interest rate is the stated interest rate on a loan. The real interest rate corrects the nominal interest rate for the effect of inflation and is equal to the nominal interest rate minus the inflation rate. Because both borrowers and lenders are concerned about the real interest rate they will receive or pay, equilibrium in the market for loanable funds determines the real interest rate rather than the nominal interest rate.

Making the Connection
MyEconLab Video

Ebenezer Scrooge: Accidental Promoter of Economic Growth?

Ebenezer Scrooge's name has become synonymous with miserliness. Before his reform at the end of Charles Dickens's *A Christmas Carol*, Scrooge is extraordinarily reluctant to spend money. Although he earns a substantial income, he lives in a cold, dark house that he refuses to heat or light adequately, and he eats a meager diet of gruel because he refuses to buy more expensive food. Throughout most of the book, Dickens portrays Scrooge's behavior in a negative way. Only at the end of the book, when the reformed Scrooge begins to spend lavishly on himself and others, does Dickens praise his behavior.

Who was better for economic growth: Scrooge the saver or Scrooge the spender?

As economist Steven Landsburg of the University of Rochester points out, however, economically speaking, it may be the pre-reform Scrooge who is more worthy of praise:

> In this whole world, there is nobody more generous than the miser—the man who could deplete the world's resources but chooses not to. The only difference between miserliness and philanthropy is that the philanthropist serves a favored few while the miser spreads his largess far and wide.

We can extend Landsburg's discussion to consider whether the actions of the pre-reform Scrooge or the actions of the post-reform Scrooge are more helpful to economic growth. Pre-reform Scrooge spends very little, investing most of his income in the financial markets. These funds became available for firms to borrow to build new factories and to carry out research and development. Post-reform Scrooge spends much more—and saves much less. Funds that he had previously saved are now spent on food for Bob Cratchit's family and on "making merry" at Christmas. In other words, the actions of post-reform Scrooge contribute to more consumption goods being produced and fewer investment goods. We can conclude that Scrooge's reform caused economic growth to slow down—if only by a little. The larger point is, of course, that savers provide the funds that are indispensable for the investment spending that economic growth requires, and the only way to save is to not consume.

Source: Steven Landsburg, "What I Like about Scrooge," *Slate*, December 9, 2004.

Your Turn: Test your understanding by doing related problems 2.14 and 2.15 on page 345 at the end of this chapter.

MyEconLab Study Plan

Explaining Movements in Saving, Investment, and Interest Rates Equilibrium in the market for loanable funds determines the quantity of loanable funds that will flow from lenders to borrowers each period. Equilibrium also determines the real interest rate that lenders will receive and that borrowers must pay. We draw the demand curve for loanable funds by holding constant all factors, other than the interest rate, that affect the willingness of borrowers to demand funds. We draw the supply curve by holding constant all factors, other than the interest rate, that affect the willingness of lenders to supply funds. A shift in either the demand curve or the supply curve will change the equilibrium interest rate and the equilibrium quantity of loanable funds.

Figure 10.4

An Increase in the Demand for Loanable Funds

An increase in the demand for loanable funds increases the equilibrium interest rate from i_1 to i_2 and increases the equilibrium quantity of loanable funds from L_1 to L_2. As a result, saving and investment both increase.

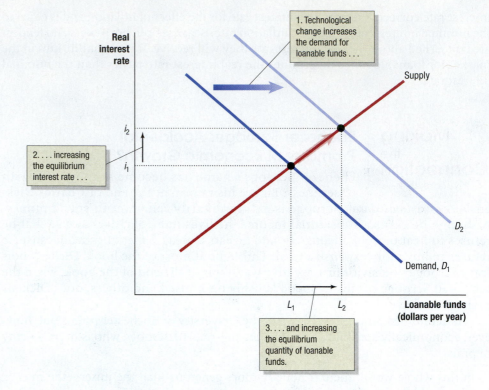

1. Technological change increases the demand for loanable funds . . .

2. . . . increasing the equilibrium interest rate . . .

3. . . . and increasing the equilibrium quantity of loanable funds.

Crowding out A decline in private expenditures as a result of an increase in government purchases.

If, for example, the profitability of new investment increases due to technological change or because the government reduces corporate taxes, firms will increase their demand for loanable funds. Figure 10.4 shows the effect of an increase in demand in the market for loanable funds. As in the markets for goods and services, an increase in demand in the market for loanable funds shifts the demand curve to the right. In the new equilibrium, the interest rate increases from i_1 to i_2, and the equilibrium quantity of loanable funds increases from L_1 to L_2. Notice that an increase in the quantity of loanable funds means that both the quantity of saving by households and the quantity of investment by firms have increased. Increasing investment increases the capital stock and the quantity of capital per hour worked, helping to increase economic growth.

We can also use the market for loanable funds to examine the effect of a government budget deficit. Putting aside the effects of foreign saving, recall that if the government begins running a budget deficit, it reduces the total amount of saving in the economy. Suppose the government increases spending, which results in a budget deficit. We illustrate the effects of the budget deficit in Figure 10.5 by shifting the supply curve for loanable funds to the left. In the new equilibrium, the interest rate is higher, and the equilibrium quantity of loanable funds is lower. Running a deficit has reduced the level of total saving in the economy and, by increasing the interest rate, has also reduced the level of investment spending by firms. By borrowing to finance its budget deficit, the government will have *crowded out* some firms that would otherwise have been able to borrow to finance investment. **Crowding out** refers to a decline in private expenditures (in this case, investment spending) as a result of an increase in government purchases. In Figure 10.5, the decline in investment spending due to crowding out is shown by the movement from L_1 to L_2 on the demand for loanable funds curve. Lower investment spending means that the capital stock and the quantity of capital per hour worked will not increase as much.

A government budget surplus has the opposite effect of a deficit: A budget surplus increases the total amount of saving in the economy, shifting the supply curve for loanable funds to the right. In the new equilibrium, the interest rate will be lower, and the quantity of loanable funds will be higher. We can conclude that a budget surplus increases the level of saving and investment.

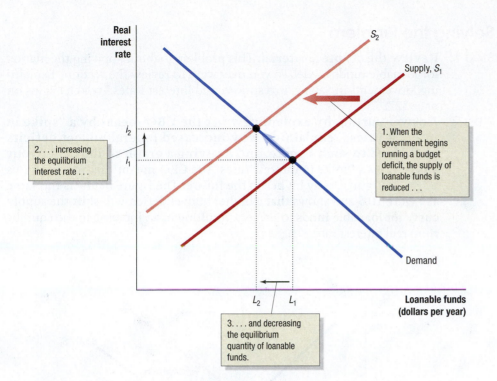

MyEconLab Animation

Figure 10.5

The Effect of a Budget Deficit on the Market for Loanable Funds

When the government begins running a budget deficit, the supply curve for loanable funds shifts to the left. The equilibrium interest rate increases from i_1 to i_2, and the equilibrium quantity of loanable funds falls from L_1 to L_2. As a result, saving and investment both decline.

(labels within figure:)

2. . . . increasing the equilibrium interest rate . . .

1. When the government begins running a budget deficit, the supply of loanable funds is reduced . . .

3. . . . and decreasing the equilibrium quantity of loanable funds.

In practice, however, the effect of government budget deficits and surpluses on the equilibrium interest rate is relatively small. (This finding reflects in part the importance of global saving in determining the interest rate.) For example, one study found that increasing government borrowing by an amount equal to 1 percent of GDP would increase the equilibrium real interest rate by only about 0.003 percentage point. However, this small effect on interest rates does not imply that we can ignore the effect of deficits on economic growth. Paying off government debt in the future may require higher taxes, which can depress economic growth. In 2015, many economists and policymakers were concerned that the large deficits projected for future years might be an obstacle to growth.

In addition to budget deficits, other government policies can affect the supply of loanable funds. The federal government gives special tax incentives for saving. For example, individuals can delay paying taxes on income they put into 401(k) retirement accounts until they actually retire. The delay in paying taxes increases the after-tax return to saving, so this policy encourages individuals to save.

Solved Problem 10.2

Are Future Budget Deficits a Threat to the Economy?

Congress gives the Congressional Budget Office (CBO) the responsibility of estimating the effects of federal spending and taxing policies on the economy. An *Associated Press* news story on a CBO report noted that federal budget deficits in the United States were likely to increase in future years. According to the CBO, these higher deficits might "pose a threat to the economy by crowding out business investment and threatening a spike in interest rates."

a. What did the CBO mean by a "spike in interest rates"? Why might increased federal budget deficits lead to a spike in interest rates? Illustrate your answer with a graph.

b. Is the spike in interest rates connected to crowding out? Why might crowding out be considered a threat to the economy?

Solving the Problem

Step 1: **Review the chapter material.** This problem is about applying the market for loanable funds model, so you may want to review the section "Explaining Movements in Saving, Investment, and Interest Rates," which begins on page 327.

Step 2: **Answer part (a) by explaining what the CBO meant by a "spike in interest rates," explaining why increased federal budget deficits could lead to such a spike, and drawing a graph to illustrate your answer.** By a "spike in interest rates" the CBO meant that interest rates might be significantly higher in the future. The figure below is the same as Figure 10.5 and shows that a higher budget deficit will shift the supply curve for loanable funds to the left, resulting in an increase in the equilibrium real interest rate.

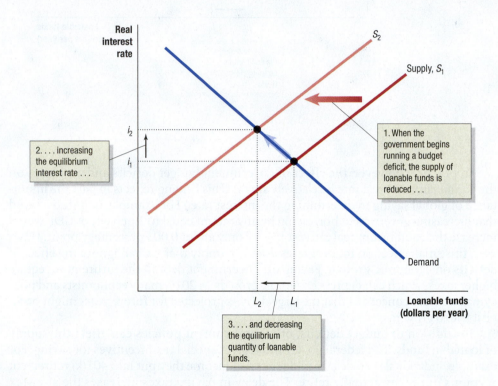

Step 3: **Answer part (b) by explaining how a spike in interest rates is connected to crowding out and why crowding out might be considered a threat to the economy.** A spike in interest rates is the way that higher budget deficits can cause crowding out. The higher interest rates will result in a decline in investment spending by firms. Lower investment spending can reduce economic growth. It is this possibility of higher deficits leading to slower economic growth that the CBO was referring to as a threat to the economy.

Source: Andrew Taylor, "CBO: Deficits to Drift Lower on Lower Health Costs," *Associated Press*, April 14, 2014.

MyEconLab Study Plan   **Your Turn:** For more practice, do related problem 2.16 on page 345 at the end of this chapter.

Table 10.1

Summary of Loanable Funds Model

An increase in ...	will shift the ...	causing ...	Graph of the effect on equilibrium in the loanable funds market
the government's budget deficit	supply of loanable funds curve to the left	the real interest rate to increase and investment to decrease.	
the desire of households to consume today	supply of loanable funds curve to the left	the real interest rate to increase and investment to decrease.	
tax benefits for saving, such as 401(k) retirement accounts, which increase the incentive to save	supply of loanable funds curve to the right	the real interest rate to decrease and investment to increase.	
expected future profits	demand for loanable funds curve to the right	the real interest rate and the level of investment to increase.	
corporate taxes	demand for loanable funds curve to the left	the real interest rate and the level of investment to decrease.	

Table 10.1 summarizes the key factors that cause shifts in the demand and supply curves for loanable funds.   MyEconLab Concept Check   MyEconLab Study Plan

10.3 The Business Cycle

LEARNING OBJECTIVE: Explain what happens during the business cycle.

Figure 10.1 on page 315 illustrates the tremendous increase during the past century in the standard of living of the average American. But close inspection of the figure reveals that real GDP per capita did not increase every year during this time. For example, during the first half of the 1930s, real GDP per capita *fell* for several years in a row. What accounts for these fluctuations in the long-run upward trend?

Some Basic Business Cycle Definitions

The fluctuations in real GDP *per capita* shown in Figure 10.1 reflect underlying fluctuations in real GDP. Since at least the early nineteenth century, the U.S. economy has

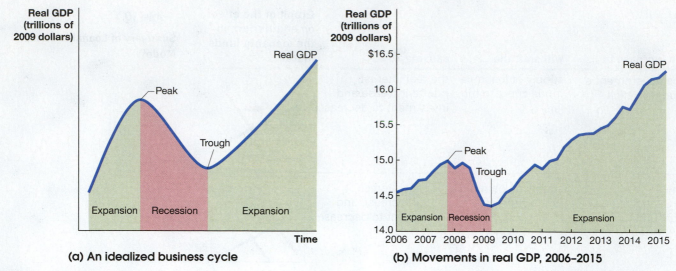

Figure 10.6   The Business Cycle

Panel (a) shows an idealized business cycle, with real GDP increasing smoothly in an expansion to a business cycle peak and then decreasing smoothly in a recession to a business cycle trough, which is followed by another expansion. The periods of expansion are shown in green, and the period of recession is shown in red. Panel (b) shows the actual movements in real GDP from 2006 to 2015. The recession that began following the business cycle peak in December 2007 was the longest and the most severe since the Great Depression of the 1930s.

experienced business cycles that consist of alternating periods of expanding and contracting economic activity. Because real GDP is our best measure of economic activity, the business cycle is usually illustrated using movements in real GDP.

During the *expansion phase* of the business cycle, production, employment, and income are increasing. The period of expansion ends with a *business cycle peak*. Following the business cycle peak, production, employment, and income decline as the economy enters the *recession phase* of the cycle. The recession comes to an end with a *business cycle trough*, after which another period of expansion begins. Figure 10.6 illustrates the phases of the business cycle. Panel (a) shows an idealized business cycle, with real GDP increasing smoothly in an expansion to a business cycle peak and then decreasing smoothly in a recession to a business cycle trough, which is followed by another expansion. Panel (b) shows the somewhat messier reality of an actual business cycle by plotting fluctuations in real GDP during the period from 2006 to 2015. The figure shows that the expansion that began in 2001 continued until a business cycle peak was reached in December 2007. The following recession was the longest and the most severe since the Great Depression of the 1930s. The severity of the recession led some economists to refer to it as the "Great Recession." The economy reached a business cycle trough in June 2009, when the next expansion began. Although real GDP grew following the business cycle trough, the growth was slower than is typical at the beginning of a business cycle expansion.

How Do We Know When the Economy Is in a Recession?

The federal government produces many statistics that make it possible to monitor the economy. But the federal government does not officially decide when a recession begins or when it ends. Instead, most economists and policymakers accept the decisions of the Business Cycle Dating Committee of the National Bureau of Economic Research (NBER), a private research group located in Cambridge, Massachusetts. Although writers for newspapers and magazines often define a recession as two consecutive quarters of declining real GDP, the NBER has a broader definition: "A recession is a significant decline in activity spread across the economy, lasting more than a few months, visible in industrial production, employment, real income, and wholesale–retail trade."

Table 10.2

The U.S. Business Cycle Since 1950

Peak	Trough	Length of Recession
July 1953	May 1954	10 months
August 1957	April 1958	8 months
April 1960	February 1961	10 months
December 1969	November 1970	11 months
November 1973	March 1975	16 months
January 1980	July 1980	6 months
July 1981	November 1982	16 months
July 1990	March 1991	8 months
March 2001	November 2001	8 months
December 2007	June 2009	18 months

Source: National Bureau of Economic Research.

The NBER is fairly slow in announcing business cycle dates because gathering and analyzing economic statistics takes time. Typically, the NBER will announce that the economy is in a recession only well after the recession has begun. For instance, it did not announce that a recession had begun in December 2007 until 11 months later, at the end of November 2008. Table 10.2 lists the business cycle peaks and troughs identified by the NBER for the years since 1950. The length of each recession is the number of months from each peak to the following trough.   MyEconLab Concept Check

Making the Connection

MyEconLab Video

Can a Recession Be a Good Time for a Business to Expand?

During a recession, business managers have to quickly make many decisions, such as whether to reduce production, cut prices, close stores or other facilities, or lay off workers. In addition to making decisions aimed at dealing with the immediate effects of the recession, managers have to consider how to prepare for the expansion that will follow the recession. Managers know that every recession, even one as severe as the recession of 2007–2009, will be followed by an expansion during which demand for their products is likely to increase. But it can be difficult to commit resources to future expansion when current conditions are bleak and when the end of the recession is difficult to predict.

The payoff to preparing for future growth can be very large, however. For example, at the end of World War II in 1945, many economists and business managers expected that the U.S. economy would enter a severe recession. Sears and Montgomery Ward were the two largest department store chains in the country. Robert Wood, CEO of Sears, expected continuing prosperity and moved to open new stores across the country. Sewell Avery, CEO of Montgomery Ward, expected falling incomes and rising unemployment and refused to authorize any new stores and closed a number of existing ones. As a result, when strong economic growth occurred during the late 1940s, Sears rapidly gained market share at Montgomery Ward's expense.

Following the September 11, 2001, terrorist attacks in the United States, the managers of many hotels expected a prolonged period of reduced travel. They responded by laying off workers and postponing or canceling new construction. Isadore Sharp, the chairman and CEO of Four Seasons Hotels, decided that although the recession would severely hurt the hotel industry, the effects would be short-lived. He decided to finish construction of 18 hotels and begin construction of 10 more. By his own account: "We maintained or enhanced our market share in most regions, contrary to the predictions of various industry experts." In a letter to his shareholders in March 2002, he wrote: "We are well positioned for the economic recovery expected later this year."

Businesses such as VF viewed the recession of 2007–2009 as an opportunity to expand operations.

During the severe recession of 2007–2009, managers had similar decisions to make. Based in Greensboro, North Carolina, VF Corporation is the largest apparel maker in the world. Among its brands are North Face, Timberland, and Wrangler. While many firms, such as J.Crew, Anne Klein, and Liz Claiborne, were closing stores or postponing opening new ones, Eric Wiseman, CEO of VF, pushed ahead, opening 89 stores in 2008 and 70 in 2009. One retail analyst was quoted as saying, "Unfortunately, many companies pull in the reins in a downturn, but these are often the best opportunities to grow." Similarly, Intel, the computer chip manufacturer, decided in early 2009 to proceed with a $7 billion expansion of its factories in the United States, while many rival firms were reducing their spending on new factories as computer sales declined. Paul Otellini, CEO of Intel, was quoted as saying, "I thought it was important for a company like Intel to stand up and say we have confidence." Heavy equipment manufacturer Caterpillar, Inc., announced that it would build several new facilities and expand some existing ones "to meet the expected increase in customer demand."

By 2015, the recovery from the 2007–2009 recession was well underway, although it was slower than a typical recovery. VF's decision to expand appeared to have been a good one as sales and profits continued to increase and its stock price was near an all-time high. The company continued to open new stores and was operating nearly 1,500 stores worldwide. The verdict for Caterpillar and Intel was more mixed, although both firms remained profitable. Intel's announcement in mid-2015 that technical problems would delay its latest generation of computer chips until late 2017 might represent a temporary setback, or it could indicate that it was beginning to fall behind rival chipmakers. Caterpillar was being hurt by declining prices for coal, iron ore, oil, and other commodities, which was reducing demand for equipment used for mining and oil exploration. Still, Caterpillar's CEO expected that sales would increase in the future as growth in the world economy caused a turnaround in commodity prices.

Over the long run, betting on the future of the U.S. economy has paid off for most firms.

Sources: Lisa Beilfuss, "VF Corp. Tops Expectations on Strength in Outdoor Sales," *Wall Street Journal*, July 24, 2015; Tiernan Ray, "Is Intel in Trouble?" *Barrons*, July 18, 2015; James R. Hagerty, "Caterpillar Resists Calls to Slash Spending," *Wall Street Journal*, July 23, 2015; Robert Sobel, *When Giants Stumble*, Paramus, NJ: Prentice Hall, 1999; Isadore Sharp, *Four Seasons: The Story of a Business Philosophy*, New York: Portfolio, 2009; Bob Tita, "Caterpillar to Expand Kansas Plant," *Wall Street Journal*, August 18, 2011; Rachel Dodes, "VF Dresses Up Its Operations, Bucking Recession," *Wall Street Journal*, March 31, 2009; and Don Clark, "Intel to Spend Heavily on U.S. Plants," *Wall Street Journal*, February 10, 2009.

MyEconLab Study Plan

Your Turn: Test your understanding by doing related problem 3.6 on page 346 at the end of this chapter.

What Happens during the Business Cycle?

Each business cycle is different. The lengths of the expansion and recession phases and the sectors of the economy that are most affected are rarely the same in any two cycles. But most business cycles share these characteristics:

1. As the economy nears the end of an expansion, interest rates are usually rising, and the wages of workers are usually increasing faster than prices. As a result of rising interest rates and wages, the profits of firms will be falling. Typically, toward the end of an expansion, both households and firms will have substantially increased their debts. These debts are the result of the borrowing that firms and households undertake to help finance their spending during the expansion. Rising debts can eventually lead households and firms to reduce their spending.

2. A recession will often begin with a decline in spending by firms on capital goods, such as machinery, equipment, new factories, and new office buildings, or by households on new houses and consumer durables, such as furniture and automobiles. As spending declines, firms that build houses and firms that sell capital goods and consumer durables will find their sales declining. As sales decline, firms cut back on production and begin to lay off workers. Rising unemployment and falling profits reduce income, which leads to further declines in spending.

3. As the recession continues, economic conditions eventually begin to improve. The declines in spending finally come to an end; households and firms begin to reduce their debts, thereby increasing their ability to spend; and interest rates decline, making it more likely that households and firms will borrow to finance new spending. Firms begin to increase their spending on capital goods as they anticipate the need for additional production during the next expansion. Increased spending by households on new houses and consumer durables and by businesses on capital goods will finally bring the recession to an end and begin the next expansion.

Corning, Technology, and the Business Cycle We have seen that long-run economic growth depends on the development of new technologies, such as those introduced over the years by firms like Corning. Often, though, these firms are exposed to the effects of the business cycle because new technologies are embodied in *durables,* which are goods that are expected to last for three or more years. Consumer durables include automobiles, laptops, and appliances. Producer durables include machine tools, electric generators, and commercial airplanes. *Nondurables* are goods that are expected to last for fewer than three years. Consumer nondurables include goods such as food and clothing. Durables are affected more by the business cycle than are nondurables. During a recession, workers reduce spending if they lose their jobs, fear losing their jobs, or suffer wage cuts. Because people can often continue using their existing automobiles, appliances, and smartphones, they are more likely to postpone spending on durables than spending on nondurables. Similarly, when firms experience declining sales and profits during a recession, they often cut back on purchases of producer durables.

We mentioned in our discussion of Corning at the beginning of this chapter that the firm has substantial sales to firms that produce automobiles, televisions, and computers. As a result, Corning's sales are significantly affected by the business cycle. Panel (a) of Figure 10.7 shows movements in real GDP for each quarter from the beginning of

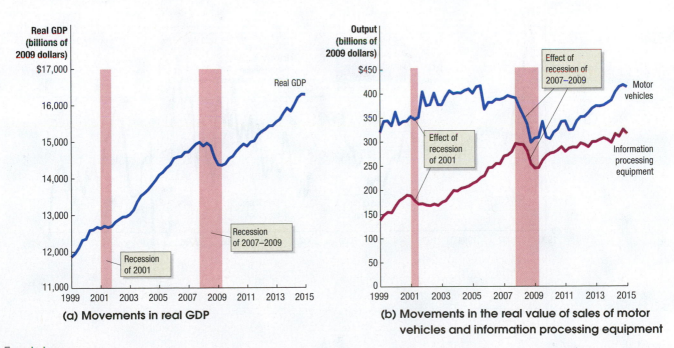

MyEconLab Real-time data

Figure 10.7   The Effect of the Business Cycle on Corning

Panel (a) shows movements in real GDP for each quarter from the beginning of 1999 through the beginning of 2015. Panel (b) shows movements in the real value of automobile production and the real value of production of information processing equipment for the same years. In panel (b), the effects of the recessions on the sales of firms that Corning sells its products to are more dramatic than the effects on the economy as a whole.

Sources: U.S. Bureau of Economic Analysis.

1999 through the beginning of 2015. We can see both the upward trend in real GDP over time and the effects of the recessions of 2001 and 2007–2009. Data for Corning's sales of individual products are not available, but panel (b) shows movements in the real value of automobile production and the real value of production of information processing equipment, such as computers. Panel (b) shows that recessions affect these industries more than they affect the economy as a whole. For example, during the 2007–2009 recession, real GDP declined by about 4 percent, while motor vehicle production declined by nearly 25 percent, and production of information processing equipment declined by 17 percent. As production declined in these industries, Corning's sales of ceramics for automobile emissions systems and display panels for computers dropped as well. As these industries recovered from the recession, so did Corning's sales.

The Effect of the Business Cycle on the Inflation Rate The *price level* measures the average prices of goods and services in the economy, and the *inflation rate* is the percentage increase in the price level from one year to the next (see Chapter 9). An important fact about the business cycle is that the inflation rate usually increases during economic expansions—particularly near the end of an expansion—and the inflation rate usually decreases during recessions. Figure 10.8 illustrates this pattern for the three recessions since 1990.

In every recession since 1950, the inflation rate has been lower during the 12 months after the recession ends than it was during the 12 months before the recession began. The average decline in the inflation rate has been about 2.5 percentage points. This result is not surprising. During a business cycle expansion, spending by businesses and

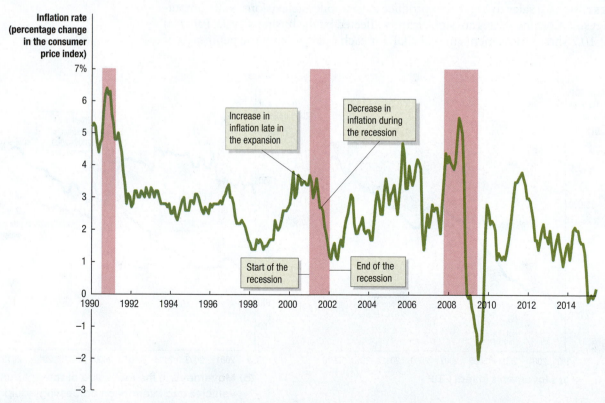

MyEconLab Real-time data

Figure 10.8   **The Effect of Recessions on the Inflation Rate**

Toward the end of a typical expansion, the inflation rate begins to rise. During recessions, marked by the shaded vertical bars, the inflation rate declines. By the end of a recession, the inflation rate is significantly below what it had been at the beginning of the recession.

Note: The points on the figure represent the annual inflation rate measured by the percentage change in the consumer price index from the same month during the previous year.

Source: U.S. Bureau of Labor Statistics.

households is strong, and producers of goods and services find it easier to raise prices. As spending declines during a recession, firms have a more difficult time selling their goods and services and are likely to increase prices less than they otherwise might have.

Don't Let This Happen to You

Don't Confuse the Price Level and the Inflation Rate

Do you agree with the following statement: "The consumer price index is a widely used measure of the inflation rate"? This statement may sound plausible, but it is incorrect. The consumer price index (CPI) tells us what a typical urban family of four pays for the goods and services they purchase relative to a base year, but values for the CPI do not directly measure the inflation rate (see Chapter 9). We can measure the inflation rate as the *percentage change* in the CPI from one year to the next. In macroeconomics, it is important not to confuse the level of a variable with the change in the variable. To give another example, real GDP does not measure economic growth. Economic growth is measured by the percentage change in real GDP from one year to the next.

MyEconLab Study Plan

Your Turn: Test your understanding by doing related problem 3.8 on page 346 at the end of this chapter.

The Effect of the Business Cycle on the Unemployment Rate Recessions cause the inflation rate to fall, but they cause the unemployment rate to increase. As firms see their sales decline, they begin to reduce production and lay off workers. Figure 10.9 illustrates this pattern for the three recessions since 1990. Notice in the

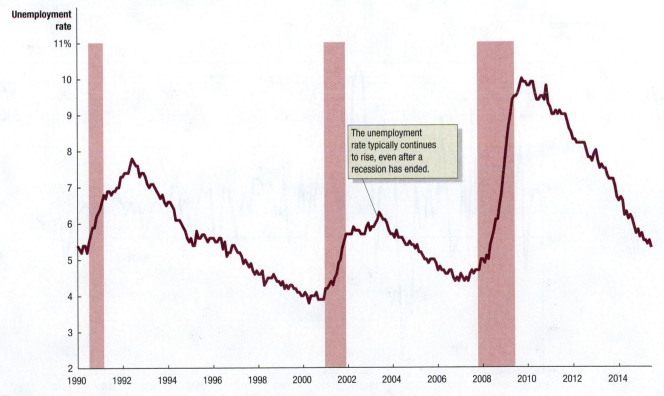

MyEconLab Real-time data

Figure 10.9 **How Recessions Affect the Unemployment Rate**

Unemployment rises during recessions and falls during expansions. The reluctance of firms to hire new employees during the early stages of a recovery usually causes the unemployment rate to continue to rise even after a recession has ended.

Source: U.S. Bureau of Labor Statistics.

figure that the unemployment rate continued to rise even after the recessions of 1990–1991, 2001, and 2007–2009 had ended. This lag before the unemployment rate begins to decline is typical and is due to two factors. First, even though employment begins to increase as a recession ends, it may be increasing more slowly than the increase in the labor force resulting from population growth. If employment increases slowly enough relative to the growth in the labor force, it is possible for the unemployment rate to rise. Second, some firms continue to operate well below their capacity even after a recession has ended and sales have begun to increase. As a result, at first, firms may not hire back all the workers they have laid off and may even continue for a while to lay off more workers.

During the recessions since 1950, the unemployment rate has risen on average by about 1.2 percentage points during the 12 months after a recession has begun. So, on average, more than 1 million more workers have been unemployed during the 12 months after a recession has begun than during the previous 12 months.

Is the "Great Moderation" Over?   Figure 10.10, which shows the year-to-year percentage changes in real GDP since 1900, illustrates a striking change in fluctuations in real GDP beginning around 1950. Before 1950, real GDP went through much greater year-to-year fluctuations than it has since that time. Fluctuations since the mid-1980s have been particularly mild. By the early twenty-first century, some economists had begun referring to the absence of severe recessions in the United States as the *Great Moderation*. However, economists began questioning this view with the recession that began in December 2007. That recession was the longest and the most severe since the Great Depression of the 1930s and has been called the *Great Recession*.

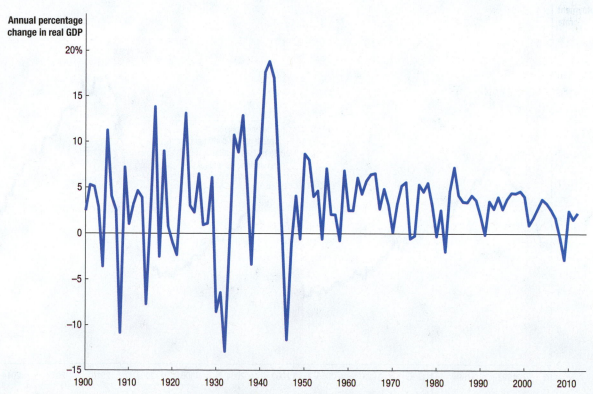

MyEconLab Real-time data

Figure 10.10   **Fluctuations in Real GDP, 1900–2014**

Fluctuations in real GDP were greater before 1950 than they have been since 1950.

Sources: Samuel H. Williamson, "What Was the U.S. GDP Then?" MeasuringWorth, July 2015; and U.S. Bureau of Economic Analysis.

Period	Average Length of Expansions	Average Length of Recessions
1870–1900	26 months	26 months
1900–1950	25 months	19 months
1950–2009	61 months	11 months

Table 10.3

Until 2007, the Business Cycle Had Become Milder

The percentage decline in real GDP during 2009 was the largest since 1932. Economists and policymakers remain unsure whether the Great Moderation will return even as the economy continued to expand more than six years after the end of the Great Recession.

The unusual severity of the 2007–2009 recession can be seen by comparing its length to those of other recessions. Table 10.3 shows that in the late nineteenth century, the average length of recessions was the same as the average length of expansions. During the first half of the twentieth century, the average length of expansions decreased slightly, and the average length of recessions decreased significantly. As a result, expansions were about six months longer than recessions during these years. The most striking change came after 1950, when the length of expansions greatly increased and the length of recessions decreased. After 1950, expansions were more than five times as long as recessions. In other words, in the late nineteenth century, the U.S. economy spent as much time in recession as it did in expansion. After 1950, the U.S. economy experienced long expansions interrupted by relatively short recessions.

The recession of 2007–2009 is an exception to this experience of relatively short, mild recessions. The recession lasted 18 months, the longest of the post-1950 period. Does the length and depth of the 2007–2009 recession indicate that the United States is returning to an era of severe fluctuations in real GDP? A full answer to this question will not be possible for at least several years. But in the next section, we provide some perspective on the question by considering why the period from 1950 to 2007 was one of relative macroeconomic stability.   MyEconLab Concept Check

Will the U.S. Economy Return to Stability?

Shorter recessions, longer expansions, and less severe fluctuations in real GDP have resulted in a significant improvement in the economic well-being of Americans. Economists have offered several explanations for why the U.S. economy experienced a period of relative stability from 1950 to 2007:

- **The increasing importance of services and the declining importance of goods.** As services such as medical care and investment advice have become a much larger fraction of GDP, there has been a corresponding relative decline in the production of goods. For example, at one time, manufacturing production accounted for about 40 percent of GDP, but in 2015, it accounted for about 12 percent. Manufacturing production, particularly of durable goods such as automobiles, fluctuates more than the production of services because during a recession, households will cut back more on purchases of durables than they will on purchases of services.

- **The establishment of unemployment insurance and other government transfer programs that provide funds to the unemployed.** Before the 1930s, programs such as unemployment insurance, which provides government payments to workers who lose their jobs, and Social Security, which provides government payments to retired and disabled workers, did not exist. These and other government programs make it possible for workers who lose their jobs during recessions to have higher incomes and, therefore, to spend more than they would otherwise. This additional spending may have helped to shorten recessions.

- **Active federal government policies to stabilize the economy.** Before the Great Depression of the 1930s, the federal government did not attempt to end recessions or prolong expansions. Because the Great Depression was so severe, with the unemployment rate rising to more than 20 percent of the labor force and real GDP declining by almost 30 percent, public opinion began favoring government attempts to stabilize the economy. In the years since World War II, the federal government has actively used macroeconomic policy measures to try to end recessions and prolong expansions. Many economists believe that these government policies have played a key role in stabilizing the economy. Other economists, however, argue that active government policy has had little effect. The debate over the role of macroeconomic policy became particularly intense during and after the 2007–2009 recession (see Chapters 15 and 16).

- **The increased stability of the financial system.** The severity of the Great Depression of the 1930s was caused in part by instability in the financial system. More than 5,000 banks failed between 1929 and 1933, reducing the savings of many households and making it difficult for households and firms to obtain the credit needed to maintain their spending. In addition, a decline of more than 80 percent in stock prices greatly reduced the wealth of many households and made it difficult for firms to raise funds by selling stock. Most economists believe that the return of financial instability during the 2007–2009 recession is a key reason the recession was so severe. If the United States is to return to macroeconomic stability, stability will first have to return to the financial system.

MyEconLab Study Plan

MyEconLab Concept Check

Continued from page 313

Economics in Your Life

Do You Help the Economy More if You Spend or if You Save?

At the beginning of this chapter, we posed a question: Which of your two roommates is right—the one who argues that you would help the economy more by saving your tax refund, or the one who argues that you should spend it? In this chapter, we have seen that consumption spending promotes the production of more consumption goods and services—such as jeans and haircuts—and fewer investment goods and services—such as physical capital and research and development. Saving (or not consuming) is necessary to fund investment expenditure. So, saving your refund will help the economy over the long run. But if the economy is in a recession, spending your refund will spur more production of consumption goods. In a sense, then, both of your roommates are correct: Spending your refund will help stimulate the economy during a recession, while saving it will help the economy grow over the long run.

Conclusion

The U.S. economy remains a remarkable engine for improving the well-being of Americans. The standard of living of Americans today is much higher than it was 100 years ago. But households and firms are still subject to the ups and downs of the business cycle. In the following chapters, we will continue our analysis of this basic fact of macroeconomics: Ever-increasing long-run prosperity is achieved in the context of short-run instability.

Visit MyEconLab for a news article and analysis related to the concepts in this chapter.

Key Terms

Business cycle, p. 314

Capital, p. 318

Crowding out, p. 328

Financial intermediaries, p. 323

Financial markets, p. 323

Financial system, p. 322

Labor productivity, p. 318

Long-run economic growth, p. 315

Market for loanable funds, p. 326

Potential GDP, p. 321

10.1 Long-Run Economic Growth, pages 314–322
LEARNING OBJECTIVE: Discuss the importance of long-run economic growth.

Summary

The U.S. economy has experienced both *long-run economic growth* and the *business cycle*. The **business cycle** refers to alternating periods of economic expansion and economic recession. **Long-run economic growth** is the process by which rising productivity increases the standard of living of the typical person. Because of economic growth, the typical American today can buy almost eight times as much as the typical American of 1900. Long-run growth is measured by increases in real GDP per capita. Increases in real GDP per capita depend on increases in labor productivity. **Labor productivity** is the quantity of goods and services that can be produced by one worker or by one hour of work. Economists believe two key factors determine labor productivity: the quantity of capital per hour worked and the level of technology. **Capital** refers to manufactured goods that are used to produce other goods and services. *Human capital* is the accumulated knowledge and skills workers acquire from education, training, or their life experiences. Economic growth occurs if the quantity of capital per hour worked increases and if technological change occurs. Economists often discuss economic growth in terms of growth in **potential GDP**, which is the level of GDP attained when all firms are producing at capacity.

MyEconLab   Visit **www.myeconlab.com** to complete these exercises online and get instant feedback.

Review Questions

1.1 By how much did real GDP per capita increase in the United States between 1900 and 2014? Discuss whether the increase in real GDP per capita is likely to be greater or smaller than the true increase in living standards.

1.2 What is the rule of 70? If real GDP per capita grows at a rate of 5 percent per year, how many years will it take to double?

1.3 What two key factors cause labor productivity to increase over time?

1.4 What is potential GDP? Does potential GDP remain constant over time?

Problems and Applications

1.5 Briefly discuss whether you would rather live in the United States of 1900 with an income of $1,000,000 per year or

the United States of 2016 with an income of $50,000 per year. Assume that the incomes for both years are measured in 2016 dollars.

1.6 Based on what you read about economic growth in this chapter, discuss the importance of growth in GDP, particularly real GDP per capita, to the quality of life of a country's citizens.

1.7 (Related to the Making the Connection on page 316) Think about the relationship between economic prosperity and life expectancy. What implications does this relationship have for the size of an economy's health care sector? In particular, is this sector of the U.S. economy likely to expand or contract in coming years?

1.8 Use the following table to answer the questions.

Year	Real GDP (billions of 2009 dollars)
1990	$8,955
1991	8,948
1992	9,267
1993	9,521
1994	9,905

a. Calculate the growth rate of real GDP for each year from 1991 to 1994.

b. Calculate the average annual growth rate of real GDP for the period from 1991 to 1994.

1.9 As discussed in this chapter, real GDP per capita in the United States grew from about $6,000 in 1900 to about $50,010 in 2014, which represents an average annual growth rate of 1.9 percent. If the U.S. economy continues to grow at this rate, how many years will it take for real GDP per capita to double? If government economic policies meant to stimulate economic growth result in the annual growth rate increasing to 2.2 percent, how many years will it take for real GDP per capita to double?

1.10 (Related to Solved Problem 10.1 on page 319) The business consulting firm McKinsey & Company released a report on world economic growth that contained the observation "productivity needs to drive growth." Is it likely that McKinsey was referring to growth in real GDP or growth in real GDP per capita? Do you agree with this observation? Briefly explain.

Source: McKinsey Global Institute, "Global Growth: Can Productivity Save the Day in an Aging World?" January 2015.

1.11 (Related to Solved Problem 10.1 on page 319) An article in the *Wall Street Journal* notes that "raising productivity in the long run is the most effective way to elevate standards of living." Do you agree? Briefly explain.

Source: Greg Ip, "Politicians Should Pay Heed to Productivity Problem," *Wall Street Journal*, July 22, 2015.

1.12 An article in the *Economist* notes, "For 60 years, from 1770 to 1830, growth in British wages, adjusted for inflation, was imperceptible because productivity growth was restricted to a few industries." Not until the late nineteenth, when productivity "gains had spread across the whole economy," did a sustained increase in real wages begin. Why would you expect there to be a close relationship between productivity gains and increases in real wages?

Source: "The Onrushing Wave," *Economist*, January 18, 2014.

1.13 (Related to the Making the Connection on page 320) Amartya Sen, a professor of economics at Harvard University and a Nobel Laureate, has argued, "For India to match China in its range of manufacturing capacity … it needs a better-educated and healthier labor force at all levels of society." What role do education and health care play in economic growth? How has India been able to experience rapid economic growth since 1991 despite poor education and health care systems?

Source: Amartya Sen, "Why India Trails China," *New York Times*, June 19, 2013.

1.14 (Related to the Making the Connection on page 320) India's labor force has been gradually shifting out of the low-productivity agricultural sector into the higher-productivity service and industrial sectors.
a. Briefly explain how this shift is affecting India's real GDP per capita.
b. Is this shift likely to result in continuing increases in India's growth rate in coming decades? Briefly explain.

10.2 Saving, Investment, and the Financial System, pages 322–331

LEARNING OBJECTIVE: Discuss the role of the financial system in facilitating long-run economic growth.

Summary

Financial markets and financial intermediaries together comprise the **financial system**. A well-functioning financial system is an important determinant of economic growth. Firms acquire funds from households, either directly through financial markets—such as the stock and bond markets—or indirectly through financial intermediaries—such as banks. The funds available to firms come from *saving*. There are two categories of saving in the economy: *private saving* by households and *public saving* by the government. The value of total saving in the economy is always equal to the value of total investment spending. In the model of the **market for loanable funds**, the interaction of borrowers and lenders determines the market interest rate and the quantity of loanable funds exchanged.

MyEconLab   Visit www.myeconlab.com to complete these exercises online and get instant feedback.

Review Questions

2.1 Why is a country's financial system important for long-run economic growth?

2.2 How does the financial system—both financial markets and financial intermediaries—provide risk sharing, liquidity, and information to savers and borrowers?

2.3 Briefly explain why the total value of saving in the economy must equal the total value of investment.

2.4 What are loanable funds? Why do businesses demand loanable funds? Why do households supply loanable funds?

Problems and Applications

2.5 Suppose you can receive an interest rate of 3 percent on a certificate of deposit at a bank that is charging borrowers 7 percent on new car loans. Why might you be unwilling to loan money directly to someone who wants to borrow from you to buy a new car, even if that person offers to pay you an interest rate higher than 3 percent?

2.6 An International Monetary Fund Factsheet makes the following observation regarding sound financial systems: "A country's financial system … provide[s] a framework … [for] supporting economic growth." Do you agree with this observation? Briefly explain.

Source: "Financial System Soundness," *International Monetary Fund Factsheet*, September 21, 2015.

2.7 Consider the following data for a closed economy:

$$Y = \$11 \text{ trillion}$$
$$C = \$8 \text{ trillion}$$
$$I = \$2 \text{ trillion}$$
$$TR = \$1 \text{ trillion}$$
$$T = \$3 \text{ trillion}$$

Use these data to calculate the following:
a. Private saving
b. Public saving
c. Government purchases
d. The government budget deficit or budget surplus

2.8 Consider the following data for a closed economy:

$$Y = \$12 \text{ trillion}$$
$$C = \$8 \text{ trillion}$$
$$G = \$2 \text{ trillion}$$
$$S_{\text{Public}} = \$-0.5 \text{ trillion}$$
$$T = \$2 \text{ trillion}$$

Use these data to calculate the following:
a. Private saving
b. Investment spending
c. Transfer payments
d. The government budget deficit or budget surplus

2.9 In problem 2.8, suppose that government purchases increase from $2 trillion to $2.5 trillion. If the values for Y and C are unchanged, what must happen to the values of S and I? Briefly explain.

2.10 Match each of the following scenarios with the appropriate graph of the market for loanable funds.

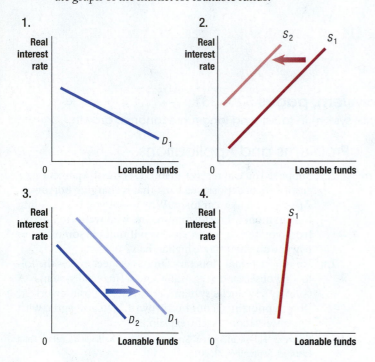

1.
2.
3.
4.

a. An increase in the real interest rate results in only a small increase in private saving by households.
b. A decrease in the real interest rate results in a substantial increase in spending on investment projects by businesses.
c. The federal government eliminates 401(k) retirement accounts.
d. The federal government reduces the tax on corporate profits. (Assume no change in the federal budget deficit or budget surplus.)

2.11 Use the following graph to answer the questions.

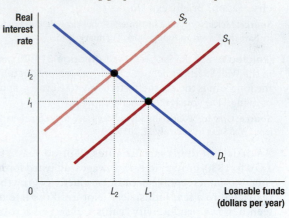

a. Does the shift from S_1 to S_2 represent an increase or a decrease in the supply of loanable funds?
b. With the shift in supply, what happens to the equilibrium quantity of loanable funds?
c. With the change in the equilibrium quantity of loanable funds, what happens to the quantity of saving? What happens to the quantity of investment?

2.12 Use the following graph to answer the questions.

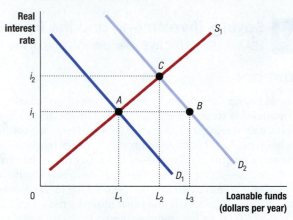

a. With the shift in the demand curve for loanable funds, what happens to the equilibrium real interest rate and the equilibrium quantity of loanable funds?
b. How can the equilibrium quantity of loanable funds increase when the real interest rate increases? Doesn't the quantity of loanable funds demanded decrease when the interest rate increases?
c. How much would the quantity of loanable funds demanded have increased if the interest rate had remained at i_1?
d. How much does the quantity of loanable funds supplied increase with the increase in the interest rate from i_1 to i_2?

2.13 Firms care about their after-tax rate of return on investment projects. In the market for loanable funds, draw a graph and explain the effect of an increase in taxes on business profits. (For simplicity, assume no change in the federal budget deficit or budget surplus.) What happens to the equilibrium real interest rate and the quantity of loanable funds? What will be the effect on the level of investment by firms and the economy's capital stock in the future?

2.14 **(Related to the** Making the Connection **on page 327)** A writer for the *Wall Street Journal* wrote a whimsical "Letter to Stingy American Consumers":

> Dear American Consumer:
>
> This is The *Wall Street Journal*. ...The sun shined in April and you didn't spend much money. ... You've been saving more too. ... This saving is not like you. ... Do you know the American economy is counting on you?

Economist Steven Landsburg praised Ebenezer Scrooge for choosing to save rather than spend his money, arguing that saving—not consumption—fuels economic growth. The *Wall Street Journal* letter pretends to chide the American consumer for saving rather than spending income, arguing that spending—not saving—fuels economic growth. Which argument is correct?

Source: John Hilsenrath, "Grand Central: A Letter to Stingy American Consumers," *Wall Street Journal*, June 2, 2015.

2.15 **(Related to the** Making the Connection **on page 327)** The *Making the Connection* claims that Ebenezer Scrooge promoted economic growth more when he was a miser and saved most of his income than when he reformed and began spending freely. Suppose, though, that after he reformed he spent most of his income buying food for the Cratchits and other poor families. Many economists believe that there is a close connection between how much very poor people eat and how much they are able to work and how productive they are while working. Does this fact affect the conclusion about whether the pre-reform or post-reform Scrooge had a more positive impact on economic growth? Briefly explain.

2.16 **(Related to** Solved Problem 10.2 **on page 329)** The federal government in the United States has been running large budget deficits. Suppose that Congress and the president take actions that turn the budget deficits into budget surpluses.

a. Use a market for loanable funds graph to illustrate the effect of the federal budget surpluses. What happens to the equilibrium real interest rate and the quantity of loanable funds? What happens to the level of saving and investment?

b. Now suppose that households believe that surpluses will result in Congress and the president cutting taxes in the near future in order to move from budget surpluses to balanced budgets. As a result, households increase their consumption spending in anticipation of paying lower taxes. Briefly explain how your analysis in part (a) will be affected.

2.17 Savers are taxed on the nominal interest payments they receive rather than the real interest payments. Suppose the federal government shifts from taxing nominal interest payments to taxing only real interest payments. (That is, savers will be allowed to subtract the inflation rate from the nominal interest rate they receive and only pay taxes on the resulting real interest rate.) Use a market for loanable funds graph to analyze the effects of this change in tax policy. What happens to the equilibrium real interest rate and the equilibrium quantity of loanable funds? What happens to the level of saving and investment?

10.3	**The Business Cycle, pages 331–340**
	LEARNING OBJECTIVE: Explain what happens during the business cycle.

Summary

During the expansion phase of the business cycle, production, employment, and income are increasing. The period of expansion ends with a business cycle peak. Following the business cycle peak, production, employment, and income decline during the recession phase of the cycle. The recession comes to an end with a business cycle trough, after which another period of expansion begins. The inflation rate usually rises near the end of a business cycle expansion and then falls during a recession. The unemployment rate declines during the latter part of an expansion and increases during a recession. The unemployment rate often continues to increase even after an expansion has begun. Until the severe recession of 2007–2009, recessions had been milder and the economy had been more stable in the period since 1950. Economists debate whether the economy will return to the stability it experienced during the period of the Great Moderation.

Review Questions

3.1 What are the names of the following events that occur during a business cycle?
a. The high point of economic activity
b. The low point of economic activity
c. The period between the high point of economic activity and the following low point
d. The period between the low point of economic activity and the following high point

3.2 Briefly describe the effect of the business cycle on the inflation rate and the unemployment rate. Why might the unemployment rate continue to rise during the early stages of an expansion?

3.3 Briefly compare the severity of recessions before and after 1950. What explanations have economists offered for the period of relative macroeconomic stability from 1950 to 2007?

Problems and Applications

3.4 **(Related to the** Chapter Opener **on page 313)** Briefly explain whether production of each of the following goods is likely to fluctuate more or less than real GDP does during the business cycle.
  a. Ford F-150 trucks
  b. McDonald's Big Macs
  c. Corning's screens for 4K televisions
  d. Huggies diapers
  e. Boeing passenger aircraft

3.5 The National Bureau of Economic Research, a private group, is responsible for declaring when recessions begin and end in the United States. Can you think of reasons the Bureau of Economic Analysis, part of the federal government, might not want to take on this responsibility?

3.6 **(Related to the** Making the Connection **on page 333)** As we have seen, some firms prosper by expanding during recessions. What risks do firms take when they pursue this strategy? Are there circumstances in particular industries that might cause firms to be more cautious during a recession? Briefly explain.

3.7 An article in the *Wall Street Journal* noted that at the end of 2014, "U.S. families' debt burdens have settled at their lowest level in over a decade." Does this information indicate that the U.S. economy was close to the end of an economic expansion in late 2014? Briefly explain.
  Source: Neil Shah, "Americans' Debt-Cutting Levels Off," *Wall Street Journal*, December 11, 2014.

3.8 **(Related to the** Don't Let This Happen to You **on page 337)** Briefly explain whether you agree with this statement: "Real GDP in 2014 was $16.1 trillion. This value is a large number. Therefore, economic growth must have been high during 2014."

3.9 **(Related to the** Chapter Opener **on page 313)** In its annual report for 2009, Corning noted declines in sales for most of its products. But it also said that these declines were "offset somewhat by an increase in sales of Gorilla glass, a protective cover glass that is optimized for portable display devices. Sales of Gorilla glass have continued to increase as the Company moves to capitalize on market opportunities for this product." Why might sales of Gorilla glass be less affected by the business cycle than sales of some of the firm's other products, such as screen for LCD televisions or ceramics used in automobile emission systems?
  Source: Corning, Inc., "Form 10-K (Annual Report), 2010, p. 34.

3.10 Robert Samuelson, a columnist for the *Washington Post*, argues that the Great Moderation actually caused the Great Recession. During the Great Moderation, "consumers could assume more debt—and lenders could lend more freely." Why might consumers have been willing to assume more debt and banks and other lenders have been willing to make loans more freely during the Great Moderation? Why might these actions have made the severe recession of 2007–2009 more likely?
  Source: Robert J. Samuelson, "Is the Economy Experiencing Another Great Moderation?" *Washington Post*, June 4, 2014.

Real-Time Data Exercises

D10.1 (Analyzing real GDP over the business cycle) Go to the Web site of the Federal Reserve Bank of St. Louis (FRED) (research.stlouisfed.org/fred2/).
  a. Find the values for the most recent quarter for the following three variables: (1) Nominal Gross Domestic Product (GDP), (2) Real Gross Domestic Product (GDPC1), and (3) Real Potential Gross Domestic Product (GDPPOT).
  b. Using the data from part (a), calculate the GDP Price Deflator for the most recent quarter.
  c. Calculate for this quarter the percentage difference between real GDP and potential GDP.
  d. Using Figure 10.2 on page 322, describe the relationship between real GDP and potential GDP over the past 10 years.

D10.2 (Analyzing saving and investment) Go to the Web site of the Federal Reserve Bank of St. Louis (FRED) (research.stlouisfed.org/fred2/).
  a. Find the most recent values and the values from the same quarter three years earlier for Gross Private Saving (GPSAVE) and Gross Government Saving (GGSAVE).
  b. Using the values found in part (a), calculate the value of total saving in the economy for these two periods.
  c. Draw a graph to show the loanable funds market in equilibrium. Explain which curve represents total saving.
  d. On the graph you drew in part (c), show the effect on the loanable funds market from the change you calculated in part (b) for total saving between the two periods.

D10.3 (Analyzing saving and investment) Go to the Web site of the Federal Reserve Bank of St. Louis (FRED) (research.stlouisfed.org/fred2/).
  a. Find the most recent value and the value from the same quarter four years earlier for Gross Government Saving (GGSAVE).
  b. Total saving in the economy is composed of private saving and government saving. What does government saving represent?
  c. Using the values found in part (a), explain whether the government budget in each of the two periods is balanced, in a surplus, or in a deficit. From the first period to the most recent period, has government saving increased, decreased, or remained constant?
  d. Draw a graph showing the loanable funds market in equilibrium. Use the graph to show the effect of the change in government saving that you calculated in part (c) on the loanable funds market. (Assume that the level of private saving is unchanged.) Explain what will happen to the level of investment in the economy.

Long-Run Economic Growth: Sources and Policies

Will Economic Reforms in Mexico Boost Growth?

Founded in 1947, Flambeau, Inc., is a family firm based in Middlefield, Ohio, that makes plastic products including Duncan yo-yos, hunting decoys, and storage containers used in homes and businesses. In recent years, the company has faced strong competition from imports and has sought ways to reduce costs. The firm considered building a factory in China but chose instead to build in Saltillo, Mexico, because it was closer, and managers from the company could more easily oversee production. Flambeau President Jason Sauey explained, "It's not just about cost; it's about speed of response and quality."

Flambeau is not alone in choosing to locate plants in Mexico rather than China. More than 18,000 U.S. companies, including many Fortune 500 firms, have operations in Mexico. As Christopher Wilson, an economist at the Woodrow Wilson International Center for Scholars in Washington, observed: "Mexico has become the most competitive place to manufacture goods for the North American market." Proximity to the United States is an advantage of doing business in Mexico, rather than China or India, but investing in Mexico can be risky. Organized crime and corruption are major concerns. Coca-Cola, for example, suspended its operations in Chilpancingo because of attacks on its employees. Some local Mexican firms have been reluctant to expand because they fear attracting the attention of criminal gangs who might demand payments or government inspectors who might demand bribes.

These problems indicate that the Mexican government has failed to fully establish the rule of law, which is critical for the long-term prospects of the Mexican economy. Without the rule of law, entrepreneurs cannot fulfill their role in the market system of bringing together the factors of production—labor, capital, and natural resources—to produce goods and services. Mexican entrepreneurs also suffer from problems in the banking system that make it difficult to obtain the funding needed to finance expansion.

Although Mexico has experienced some increases in real GDP per capita during the past 30 years, its record of economic growth has been disappointing, particularly in comparison with China and other rapidly growing countries in the developing world. Being able to attain faster rates of growth would benefit people in Mexico—particularly those with low incomes—and the wider world economy.

Sources: Damien Cave, "As Ties with China Unravel, U.S. Companies Head to Mexico," *New York Times*, May 31, 2014; Matthias Rieker, "Making Yo-Yos and More," *Wall Street Journal*, July 16, 2012; Dolia Estevez, "U.S. Warns against Rising Costs of Doing Business in Mexico Due to Criminal Activity," *Forbes*, June 5, 2014; and flambeau.com.

Economics in Your Life

Would You Be Better Off without China?

For decades, China was a very poor country whose economy was growing very slowly. The government introduced economic reforms in 1978, which spurred rapid economic growth. Suppose that you could choose to live and work in a world with the Chinese economy growing very rapidly or in a world with the Chinese economy growing as slowly as it did before 1978. In which world would you choose to live? How does the current high-growth, high-export Chinese economy affect you as a consumer? How does it affect you as someone about to start a career? As you read the chapter, try to answer these questions. You can check your answers against those we provide on **page 378** at the end of this chapter.

Economic growth is not inevitable. For most of human history, no sustained increases in output per capita occurred, and, in the words of the philosopher Thomas Hobbes, the lives of most people were "poor, nasty, brutish, and short." Sustained economic growth first began with the Industrial Revolution in England in the late eighteenth century. From there, economic growth spread to the United States, Canada, and the countries of Western Europe. Following the end of World War II in 1945, rapid economic growth also began in Japan and, eventually, in several other Asian countries, but the economies of many other countries stagnated, leaving their people trapped in poverty.

Real GDP per capita is the best measure of a country's standard of living because it represents the ability of the average person to buy goods and services. Economic growth occurs when real GDP per capita increases. In this chapter, we will develop a *model of economic growth* that will help us answer important questions like these:

- Why have countries such as the United States and the United Kingdom, which had high standards of living at the beginning of the twentieth century, continued to grow rapidly?

- Why have countries such as Argentina, which at one time had relatively high standards of living, failed to keep pace?

- Why was the Soviet Union unable to sustain the rapid growth rates of its early years?

- Why are some countries that were very poor at the beginning of the twentieth century still very poor?

- Why have some countries, such as South Korea and Japan, that once were very poor now become much richer?

- What explains China's very rapid recent growth rates?

11.1 Economic Growth over Time and around the World

LEARNING OBJECTIVE: Define economic growth, calculate economic growth rates, and describe global trends in economic growth.

You live in a world that is very different from the world when your grandparents were young. You can listen to music on an iPhone that fits in your pocket; your grandparents played vinyl records on large stereo systems. You can send a text message to someone in another city, state, or country; your grandparents mailed letters that took days or weeks to arrive. More importantly, you have access to health care and medicines that have prolonged life and improved its quality. In many poorer countries, however, people endure grinding poverty and have only the bare necessities of life, just as their parents, grandparents, and great-grandparents did.

The difference between you and people in poor countries is that you live in a country that has experienced substantial economic growth. A growing economy produces both increasing quantities of goods and services and better goods and services. It is only through economic growth that living standards can increase, but through most of human history, no economic growth took place. Even today, billions of people are living in countries where economic growth is extremely slow.

Economic Growth from 1,000,000 B.C. to the Present

In 1,000,000 B.C., our ancestors survived by hunting animals and gathering edible plants. Farming was many years in the future, and production was limited to food, clothing, shelter, and simple tools. Bradford DeLong, an economist at the University of California, Berkeley, estimates that in those primitive circumstances, GDP per capita was about $145 per year in 2015 dollars, which was the minimum amount necessary to sustain life. DeLong estimates that real GDP per capita worldwide was still $145 in the year A.D. 1300. In other words, no sustained economic growth occurred between 1,000,000 B.C. and A.D. 1300. A peasant toiling on a farm in France in the year 1300 was no better off than his ancestors thousands of years before. In fact, for most of human existence, the typical person had only the bare minimum of food, clothing, and shelter necessary to sustain life. Few people survived beyond age 40, and most people suffered from debilitating illnesses.

Sustained economic growth did not begin until the **Industrial Revolution**, which started in England around the year 1750. The production of cotton cloth in factories using machinery powered by steam engines marked the beginning of the Industrial Revolution. Before that time, production of goods had relied almost exclusively on human or animal power. The use of mechanical power spread to the production of many other goods, greatly increasing the quantity of goods each worker could produce. First England and then other countries, such as the United States, France, and Germany, experienced *long-run economic growth*, with sustained increases in real GDP per capita that eventually raised living standards in those countries to the high levels of today.

Industrial Revolution The application of mechanical power to the production of goods, beginning in England around 1750.

Making the Connection
MyEconLab Video

Why Did the Industrial Revolution Begin in England?

The Industrial Revolution was a key turning point in human history. Before it, economic growth was slow and halting. After it, economic growth became rapid and sustained in a number of countries. Although historians and economists agree on the importance of the Industrial Revolution, they have not reached a consensus on why it happened in the time and place that it did. Why the eighteenth century and not the sixteenth century or the twenty-first century? Why England and not China or India or Africa or Japan?

There is always a temptation to read history backward. We know when and where the Industrial Revolution occurred; therefore, it had to happen where it did and when it did. But what was so special about England in the eighteenth century? Nobel Laureate Douglass North of Washington University in St. Louis has argued that institutions in England differed significantly from those in other countries in ways that greatly aided economic growth. North believes that the Glorious Revolution of 1688 was a key turning point. After that date, the British Parliament, rather than the king, controlled the government. The British court system also became independent of the king. As a result, the British government was credible when it committed to upholding private property rights, protecting wealth, and eliminating arbitrary increases in taxes. These institutional changes gave entrepreneurs the confidence and the incentive to make the investments necessary to use the important technological developments of the second half of the eighteenth century—particularly the spinning jenny and the water frame, which were used in the production of cotton textiles, and the steam engine, which was used in mining and in the manufacture of textiles and other products. Without the institutional changes, entrepreneurs would have been reluctant to risk their property or their wealth by starting new businesses.

Although not all economists agree with North's specific argument about the origins of the Industrial Revolution, we will see that most economists accept the idea that economic growth is not likely to occur unless a country's government provides the type of institutional framework North describes.

The British government's guarantee of property rights set the stage for the Industrial Revolution.

Sources: Douglass C. North, *Understanding the Process of Economic Change*, Princeton, NJ: Princeton University Press, 2005; and Douglass C. North and Barry R. Weingast, "Constitutions and Commitment: The Evolution of Institutions Governing Public Choice in Seventeenth-Century England," *Journal of Economic History*, Vol. 49, No. 4, December 1989, pp. 803–832.

Your Turn: Test your understanding by doing related problem 1.3 on page 380 at the end of this chapter.

MyEconLab Study Plan

Figure 11.1

Average Annual Growth Rates for the World Economy

World economic growth was essentially zero in the years before 1300, and it was very slow—an average of only 0.2 percent per year—between 1300 and 1800. The Industrial Revolution made possible the sustained increases in real GDP per capita that have allowed some countries to attain high standards of living.

Source: J. Bradford DeLong, "Estimates World GDP, One Million B.C.–Present," Working paper, University of California, Berkeley.

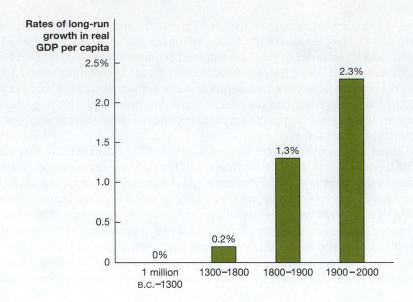

Figure 11.1 shows how growth rates of real GDP per capita for the entire world have changed over long periods. Prior to A.D. 1300, there were no sustained increases in real GDP per capita. Over the next 500 years, to 1800, there was very slow growth. Significant growth began in the nineteenth century, as a result of the Industrial Revolution. A further acceleration in growth occurred during the twentieth century, as the average growth rate increased from 1.3 percent per year to 2.3 percent per year. **MyEconLab** Concept Check

Small Differences in Growth Rates Are Important

The difference between 1.3 percent and 2.3 percent may seem trivial, but over long periods, small differences in growth rates can have a large effect. Suppose you have $100 in a savings account earning an interest rate of 1.3 percent, which means you will receive an interest payment of $1.30 this year. If the interest rate on the account is 2.3 percent, you will earn $2.30. The difference of an extra $1.00 interest payment seems insignificant. But if you leave the interest as well as the original $100 in your account for another year, the difference becomes greater because now the higher interest rate is applied to a larger amount—$102.30—and the lower interest rate is applied to a smaller amount—$101.30. This process, known as *compounding*, magnifies even small differences in interest rates over long periods of time. Over a period of 50 years, your $100 would grow to $312 at an interest rate of 2.3 percent but to only $191 at an interest rate of 1.3 percent.

The principle of compounding applies to economic growth rates as well as to interest rates. For example, in 1950, real GDP per capita in Argentina was $5,474 (measured in 2005 dollars), which was larger than Italy's real GDP per capita of $5,361. Over the next 64 years, the economic growth rate in Italy averaged 2.5 percent per year, while in Argentina, the growth rate was only 1.5 percent per year. Although this difference in growth rates of only 1 percentage point may seem small, in 2014, real GDP per capita in Italy had risen to $26,550, while real GDP per capita in Argentina was only $13,980. In other words, because of a relatively small difference in the growth rates of the two economies, the standard of living of a typical person in Italy went from being a little below that of a typical person in Argentina to being much higher. Here is the key point to keep in mind: *In the long run, small differences in economic growth rates result in big differences in living standards.* **MyEconLab** Concept Check

Why Do Growth Rates Matter?

Why should anyone care about growth rates? Growth rates matter because an economy that grows too slowly fails to raise living standards. In some countries in Africa and

Asia, very little economic growth has occurred in the past 50 years, so many people remain in severe poverty. In high-income countries, only 4 out of every 1,000 babies die before they are one year old. In the poorest countries, more than 100 out of every 1,000 babies die before they are one year old, and millions of children die annually from diseases that could be avoided by having access to clean water or that could be cured by using medicines that cost only a few dollars.

Although their problems are less dramatic, countries that experience slow growth have also missed opportunities to improve the lives of their citizens. For example, the failure of Argentina to grow as rapidly as other countries that had similar levels of GDP per capita in 1950 has left many of its people in poverty. Life expectancy in Argentina is lower than in the United States and other high-income countries, and about 50 percent more babies in Argentina die before the age of one.   MyEconLab Concept Check

---

Don't Let This Happen to You

Don't Confuse the Average Annual Percentage Change with the Total Percentage Change

When economists talk about growth rates over a period of more than one year, the numbers are always *average annual percentage changes* and *not* total percentage changes. For example, in the United States, real GDP per capita was $14,398 in 1950 and $50,398 in 2014. The percentage change in real GDP per capita between these two years is:

$$\left(\frac{\$50{,}398 \ - \ \$14{,}398}{\$14{,}398} \right) \ \times \ 100 = 250\%.$$

However, this is *not* the growth rate between the two years. The growth rate between these two years is the rate at which $14,398 in 1950 would have to grow on average *each year* to end up as $50,398 in 2014, which is 2.0 percent.

MyEconLab Study Plan

Your Turn: Test your understanding by doing related problem 1.6 on page 381 at the end of this chapter.

"The Rich Get Richer and … "

We can divide the world's economies into two groups:

1. The *high-income countries*, sometimes also referred to as the *industrial countries* or the *developed countries*, including Australia, Canada, Japan, New Zealand, the United States, and the countries of Western Europe

2. The *lower-income countries*, or *developing countries*, including most of the countries of Africa, Asia, and Latin America

In the 1980s and 1990s, a small group of countries, mostly East Asian countries such as Singapore, South Korea, and Taiwan, began to experience high rates of growth and are sometimes referred to as the *newly industrializing countries*.

Figure 11.2 shows the levels of GDP per capita around the world in 2014. GDP is measured in U.S. dollars, corrected for differences across countries in the cost of living. In 2014, GDP per capita ranged from a high of $144,400 in the Persian Gulf country of Qatar to a low of $600 in the Central African Republic. To understand why the gap between rich and poor countries exists, we need to look at what causes economies to grow.   MyEconLab Concept Check

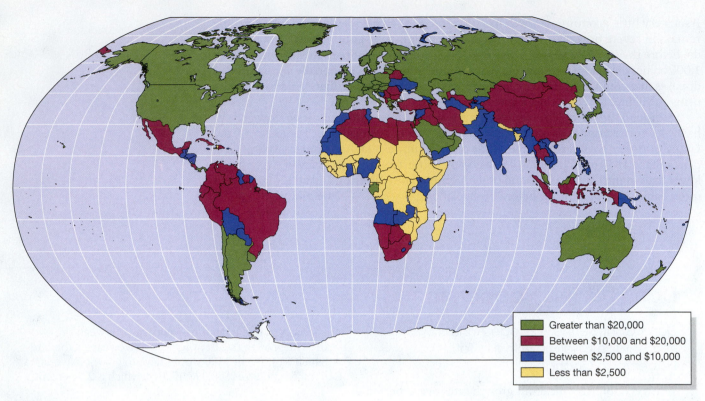

🟩	Greater than $20,000
🟥	Between $10,000 and $20,000
🟦	Between $2,500 and $10,000
🟨	Less than $2,500

MyEconLab Animation

Figure 11.2 **GDP per Capita, 2014**

GDP per capita is measured in U.S. dollars, corrected for differences across countries in the cost of living.

In sub-Saharan Africa and other parts of the world, increases in technology and knowledge are leading to improvements in health care and the standard of living.

Making the Connection
MyEconLab Video

Is Income All That Matters?

The more income you have, the more goods and services you can buy. When people are surviving on very low incomes of $2 per day or less, their ability to buy even minimal amounts of food, clothing, and housing is limited. So, most economists argue that unless the incomes of the very poor increase significantly, they will be unable to attain a higher standard of living. In some countries—primarily those colored yellow in Figure 11.2—the growth in average income has been very slow, or even negative, over a period of decades. Most economists and policymakers have concluded that the standard of living in these countries has been largely unchanged for many years.

Some economists argue, though, that if we look beyond income to other measures of the standard of living, we can see that even the poorest countries have made significant progress in recent decades. For example, Charles Kenny, an economist with the Center for Global Development, argues that "those countries with the lowest quality of life are making the fastest progress in improving it—across a range of measures including health, education, and civil and political liberties." For example, since 1960 deaths among children have declined, often by more than 50 percent, in nearly all countries, including most of those with the lowest incomes. Even in sub-Saharan Africa, where growth in incomes has been very slow, the percentage of children dying before age five has decreased by more than 30 percent over the past 50 years. Similarly, the percentage of people able to read and write has more than doubled in sub-Saharan Africa since 1970. Many more people now live in democracies where basic civil rights are respected than at any other time in world history. Although some countries, such as Somalia, the Democratic Republic of the Congo, Syria, and Afghanistan, have suffered from civil wars, improved political stability in many countries has reduced the likelihood of dying from violence.

What explains these improvements in health, education, democracy, and political stability? William Easterly, an economist at New York University, has found that although, at any given time, countries that have a higher income also have a higher standard of living, over time, increases in income *within a particular country* are typically not the main cause of improvements in its standard of living in terms of health, education, individual rights, political stability, and similar factors. Kenny's argument and Easterly's finding are connected: Some increases in living standards do not require significant increases in income. The key factors in raising living standards in low-income countries have been increases in technology and knowledge—such as the development of inexpensive vaccines that reduce epidemics or the use of mosquito-resistant netting that reduces the prevalence of malaria—that are inexpensive enough to be widely available. Changes in attitudes, such as placing a greater value on education, particularly for girls, or increasing support for political freedoms, have also played a role in improving conditions in low-income countries.

There are limits, of course, to how much living standards can increase if incomes stagnate. Ultimately, much higher rates of economic growth will be necessary for low-income countries to significantly close the gap in living standards with high-income countries.

Sources: Charles Kenny, *Getting Better*, New York: Basic Books, 2011; Ursula Casabonne and Charles Kenny, "The Best Things in Life Are (Nearly) Free: Technology, Knowledge, and Global Health," *World Development*, Vol. 40, No. 1, January 2012, pp. 21–35; and William Easterly, "Life during Growth," *Journal of Economic Growth*, Vol. 4, No. 3, September 1999, pp. 239–276.

Your Turn: Test your understanding by doing related problems 1.7 and 1.8 on page 381 at the end of this chapter.

MyEconLab Study Plan

11.2 What Determines How Fast Economies Grow?

LEARNING OBJECTIVE: Use the economic growth model to explain why growth rates differ across countries.

To explain changes in economic growth rates over time within countries and differences in growth rates among countries, we need to develop an *economic growth model*. An **economic growth model** explains growth rates in real GDP per capita over the long run. As we have seen, the average person can buy more goods and services only if the average worker produces more goods and services (see Chapter 10). Recall that **labor productivity** is the quantity of goods and services that can be produced by one worker or by one hour of work. Because of the importance of labor productivity in explaining economic growth, the economic growth model focuses on the causes of long-run increases in labor productivity.

How can a country's workers become more productive? Economists believe two key factors determine labor productivity:

1. The quantity of capital available to workers
2. The level of technology

Therefore, to explain changes in real GDP per capita, the economic growth model focuses on technological change and changes over time in the quantity of capital available to workers. Recall that **technological change** is a change in the quantity of output firms can produce using a given quantity of inputs.

There are three main sources of technological change:

1. **Better machinery and equipment.** Beginning with the steam engine during the Industrial Revolution, the invention of new machinery has been an important source of rising labor productivity. Today, continuing improvements in computers, factory machine tools, electric generators, and many other machines contribute to increases in labor productivity.

Economic growth model A model that explains growth rates in real GDP per capita over the long run.

Labor productivity The quantity of goods and services that can be produced by one worker or by one hour of work.

Technological change A change in the quantity of output a firm can produce using a given quantity of inputs.

Human capital The accumulated knowledge and skills that workers acquire from education and training or from their life experiences.

2. Increases in human capital. Capital refers to *physical capital*, including computers, factory buildings, machine tools, warehouses, and trucks. The more physical capital workers have available, the more output they can produce. **Human capital** is the accumulated knowledge and skills that workers acquire from education and training or from their life experiences. As workers increase their human capital through education or on-the-job training, their productivity also increases. The more educated workers are, the greater is their human capital.

3. Better means of organizing and managing production. Labor productivity increases if managers can do a better job of organizing production. For example, the *just-in-time system*, first developed by Toyota Motor Corporation, involves assembling goods from parts that arrive at the factory at exactly the time they are needed. With this system, firms need fewer workers to store and keep track of parts in the factory, so the quantity of goods produced per hour worked increases.

Note that technological change is *not* the same thing as more physical capital. New capital can *embody* technological change, as when a faster computer chip is embodied in a new computer. But simply adding more capital that is the same as existing capital is not technological change. To summarize: A country's standard of living will be higher the more capital workers have available on their jobs, the better the capital, the more human capital workers have, and the better the job managers do in organizing production.

The Per-Worker Production Function

Per-worker production function The relationship between real GDP per hour worked and capital per hour worked, holding the level of technology constant.

Often when analyzing economic growth, we look at increases in real GDP *per hour worked* and increases in capital *per hour worked*. We use measures of GDP per hour and capital per hour rather than per person, so we can analyze changes in the underlying ability of an economy to produce more goods with a given amount of labor without having to worry about changes in the fraction of the population working or in the length of the workday. We can illustrate the economic growth model using the **per-worker production function**, which is the relationship between real GDP per hour worked and capital per hour worked, *holding the level of technology constant*. For simplicity, from now on we will shorten "per-worker production function" to just "production function." Figure 11.3 shows the production function as a graph. We measure capital per hour worked along the horizontal axis and real GDP per hour worked along the vertical axis. Letting K stand for capital, L stand for labor, and Y stand for real GDP, real GDP per hour worked is Y/L, and capital per hour worked is K/L. The curve represents the production function. Notice that we do not explicitly show technological change in the

MyEconLab Animation

Figure 11.3

The Per-Worker Production Function

The per-worker production function shows the relationship between capital per hour worked and real GDP per hour worked, holding technology constant. Increases in capital per hour worked increase output per hour worked but at a diminishing rate. For example, an increase in capital per hour worked from $75 to $100 increases real GDP per hour worked from $48 to $53. An increase in capital per hour worked from $100 to $125 increases real GDP per hour worked by a smaller amount, from $53 to $57. Each additional $25 increase in capital per hour worked results in a progressively smaller increase in output per hour worked.

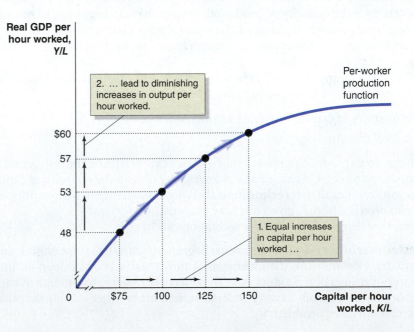

figure. We assume that as we move along the production function, the level of technology remains constant. As we will see, we can illustrate technological change using this graph by *shifting up* the curve representing the production function.

The figure shows that increases in the quantity of capital per hour worked result in movements up along the production function, increasing the quantity of output each worker produces. When *we hold technology constant*, however, equal increases in the amount of capital per hour worked lead to *diminishing* increases in output per hour worked. For example, increasing capital per hour worked from $75 to $100 increases real GDP per hour worked from $48 to $53, an increase of $5. Another $25 increase in capital per hour worked, from $100 to $125, increases real GDP per hour worked from $53 to $57, an increase of only $4. Each additional $25 increase in capital per hour worked results in progressively smaller increases in real GDP per hour worked. In fact, at very high levels of capital per hour worked, further increases in capital per hour worked will not result in any increase in real GDP per hour worked. This effect results from the *law of diminishing returns*, which states that as we add more of one input—in this case, capital—to a fixed quantity of another input—in this case, labor—output increases by smaller additional amounts.

Why are there diminishing returns to capital? Consider a simple example in which you own a copy store. At first you have 10 employees but only 1 copy machine, so each of your workers is able to produce relatively few copies per day. When you buy a second copy machine, your employees will be able to produce more copies. Adding additional copy machines will continue to increase your output—but by increasingly smaller amounts. For example, adding a twentieth copy machine to the 19 you already have will not increase the copies each worker is able to make by nearly as much as adding a second copy machine did. Eventually, adding additional copying machines will not increase your output at all.   MyEconLab Concept Check

Which Is More Important for Economic Growth: More Capital or Technological Change?

Technological change helps economies avoid diminishing returns to capital. Let's consider two simple examples of the effects of technological change. First, suppose you have 10 copy machines in your copy store. Each copy machine can produce 10 copies per minute. You don't believe that adding an eleventh machine identical to the 10 you already have will significantly increase the number of copies your employees can produce in a day. Then you find out that a new copy machine has become available that produces 20 copies per minute. If you replace your existing machines with the new machines, the productivity of your workers will increase. The replacement of existing capital with more productive capital is an example of technological change.

Or suppose you realize that the layout of your store could be improved. Maybe the paper for the machines is on shelves at the back of the store, which requires your workers to spend time walking back and forth whenever the machines run out of paper. By placing the paper closer to the copy machines, you can improve the productivity of your workers. Reorganizing how production takes place so as to increase output is also an example of technological change.   MyEconLab Concept Check

Technological Change: The Key to Sustaining Economic Growth

Figure 11.4 shows the effect of technological change on the production function. Technological change shifts up the production function and allows an economy to produce more real GDP per hour worked with the same quantity of capital per hour worked. For example, if the current level of technology puts the economy on Production function$_1$, then when capital per hour worked is $150, real GDP per hour worked is $60. Technological change that shifts the economy to Production function$_2$ makes it possible to produce $65 in goods and services per hour worked with the same level of capital per hour worked. Further increases in technology that shift the economy to higher production functions result in further increases in real GDP per hour worked. Because of diminishing returns to capital, continuing increases in real GDP per hour worked can be sustained only if there is technological change. Remember that a country will

MyEconLab Animation

Figure 11.4

Technological Change Increases Output per Hour Worked

Technological change shifts up the production function and allows more output per hour worked with the same amount of capital per hour worked. For example, along Production function₁ with $150 in capital per hour worked, the economy can produce $60 in real GDP per hour worked. However, an increase in technology that shifts the economy to Production function₂ makes it possible to produce $65 in real GDP per hour worked with the same level of capital per hour worked.

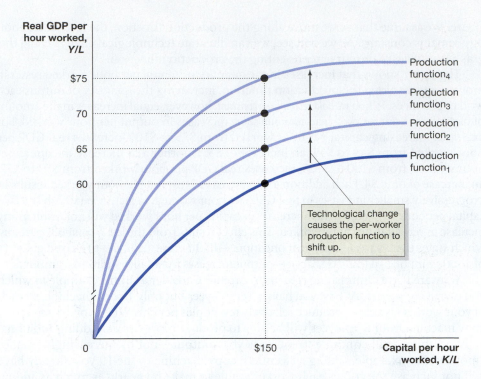

experience increases in its standard of living only if it experiences increases in real GDP per hour worked. Therefore, we can draw the following important conclusion: *In the long run, a country will experience an increasing standard of living only if it experiences continuing technological change.*

MyEconLab Concept Check

Making the Connection

MyEconLab Video

What Explains the Economic Failure of the Soviet Union?

The economic growth model can help explain one of the most striking events of the twentieth century: the economic collapse of the Soviet Union. The Soviet Union was formed from the old Russian Empire following the Russian Revolution of 1917. Under Communism, the Soviet Union was a centrally planned economy in which the government owned nearly every business and made all production and pricing decisions. In 1960, Nikita Khrushchev, the leader of the Soviet Union, addressed the United Nations in New York City. He declared to the United States and the other democracies: "We will bury you. Your grandchildren will live under Communism."

Many people at the time took Khrushchev's boast seriously. Capital per hour worked grew rapidly in the Soviet Union from 1950 through the 1980s. At first, these increases in capital per hour worked also produced rapid increases in real GDP per hour worked. Rapid increases in real GDP per hour worked during the 1950s caused some economists in the United States to predict incorrectly that the Soviet Union would someday surpass the United States economically. In fact, diminishing returns to capital meant that the additional factories the Soviet Union was building resulted in smaller and smaller increases in real GDP per hour worked.

In the former Soviet Union there were frequent shortages, and unhappy consumers often had to wait in long lines to shop for groceries and other goods.

The Soviet Union did experience some technological change—but at a rate much slower than in the United States and other high-income countries. Why did the Soviet Union fail the crucial requirement for growth: implementing new technologies? The key reason is that in a centrally planned economy, the people managing most businesses are government employees and not entrepreneurs or independent businesspeople, as is the case in market economies. Soviet managers had little incentive to adopt new ways of producing goods and services. Their pay depended on producing the quantity of output specified in the government's economic plan, not on discovering new, better, and lower-cost ways to produce goods. In addition, these managers did not have to worry about competition from either domestic or foreign firms.

Entrepreneurs and managers of firms in the United States, by contrast, are under intense competitive pressure from other firms. They must constantly search for better ways of producing the goods and services they sell. Developing and using new technologies is an important way to gain a competitive edge and earn a higher profit. The drive for profit provides an incentive for technological change that centrally planned economies are unable to duplicate. In market economies, entrepreneurs and managers who have their own money on the line make decisions about which investments to make and which technologies to adopt. Nothing concentrates the mind like having your own funds at risk.

In hindsight, it is clear that a centrally planned economy, such as the Soviet Union's, could not, over the long run, grow faster than a market economy. The Soviet Union collapsed in 1991, and contemporary Russia now has a more market-oriented system, although the government continues to play a much larger role in the economy than does the government in the United States.

Your Turn: Test your understanding by doing related problem 2.7 on page 382 at the end of this chapter.

MyEconLab Study Plan

Solved Problem 11.2

MyEconLab Interactive Animation

Using the Economic Growth Model to Analyze the Failure of the Soviet Economy

Use the economic growth model and the information in the *Making the Connection* on page 358 to analyze the economic problems the Soviet Union encountered.

Solving the Problem

Step 1:　**Review the chapter material.** This problem is about using the economic growth model to explain the failure of the Soviet economy, so you may want to review the *Making the Connection* on page 358.

Step 2:　**Draw a graph like Figure 11.3 on page 356 to illustrate the economic problems of the Soviet Union.** For simplicity, assume that the Soviet Union experienced no technological change.

　　　The Soviet Union experienced rapid increases in capital per hour worked from 1950 through the 1980s, but its failure to implement new technology meant that output per hour worked grew at a slower and slower rate.

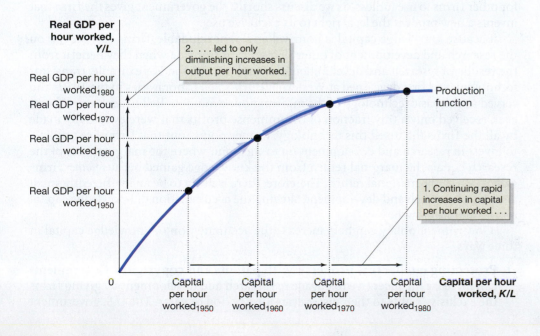

Extra Credit: The Soviet Union hoped to raise the standard of living of its citizens above that enjoyed in the United States and other high-income countries. Its strategy was to make continuous increases in the quantity of capital available to its workers. The economic growth model helps us understand the flaws in this policy for achieving economic growth.

MyEconLab Study Plan

Your Turn: For more practice, do related problems 2.8, 2.9, and 2.10 on page 382 at the end of this chapter.

New Growth Theory

New growth theory A model of long-run economic growth that emphasizes that technological change is influenced by economic incentives and so is determined by the working of the market system.

The economic growth model we have been using was first developed in the 1950s by Nobel Laureate Robert Solow of MIT. According to this model, productivity growth is the key factor in explaining long-run growth in real GDP per capita. In recent years, some economists have become dissatisfied with this model because it does not explain the factors that determine productivity growth. Paul Romer, of New York University, developed the **new growth theory** to provide a better explanation of the sources of technological change that underlie productivity growth. Romer argues that the rate of technological change is influenced by how individuals and firms respond to economic incentives. Earlier accounts of economic growth did not explain technological change or attributed it to factors such as chance scientific discoveries.

Romer argues that the accumulation of *knowledge capital* is a key determinant of economic growth. Firms add to an economy's stock of knowledge capital when they engage in research and development or otherwise contribute to technological change. We have seen that accumulation of physical capital is subject to diminishing returns: Increases in capital per hour worked lead to increases in real GDP per hour worked but at a decreasing rate. Romer argues that the same is true of knowledge capital *at the firm level*. As firms add to their stock of knowledge capital, they increase their output but at a decreasing rate. At the level of the entire economy, however, Romer argues that knowledge capital is subject to *increasing returns*. Increasing returns can exist because knowledge, once discovered, becomes available to everyone. The use of physical capital, such as a computer or machine tool, is *rival* because if one firm uses it, other firms cannot, and it is *excludable* because the firm that owns the capital can keep other firms from using it. The use of knowledge capital, such as the chemical formula for a drug that cures cancer, is nonrival, however, because one firm's using that knowledge does not prevent another firm from using it. Knowledge capital is also nonexcludable because once something like a chemical formula becomes known, it becomes widely available for other firms to use (unless, as we discuss shortly, the government gives the firm that invents a new product the legal right to its exclusive use).

Because knowledge capital is nonrival and nonexcludable, firms can *free ride* on the research and development of other firms. Firms free ride when they benefit from the results of research and development they did not pay for. For example, transistor technology was first developed at Western Electric's Bell Laboratories in the 1950s and served as the basic technology of the information revolution. Bell Laboratories, however, received only a tiny fraction of the immense profits that were eventually made by all the firms that used this technology. Romer points out that firms are unlikely to invest in research and development up to the point where the marginal cost of the research equals the marginal return from the knowledge gained because *other* firms gain much of the marginal return. Therefore, there is likely to be an inefficiently small amount of research and development, slowing the accumulation of knowledge capital and economic growth.

Government policy can help increase the accumulation of knowledge capital in three ways:

1. Protecting intellectual property with patents and copyrights. Governments can increase the incentive to engage in research and development by giving firms the exclusive rights to their discoveries for a period of years. The U.S. government grants patents to companies that develop new products or new ways of making existing products. A **patent** gives a firm the exclusive legal right to a new product for a period of 20 years from the date the patent is filed with the government. For example, a pharmaceutical firm that develops a drug that cures cancer can secure a patent on the drug, keeping other firms from manufacturing the drug without permission. The profit earned during the period the patent is in force provides firms with an incentive for undertaking research and development. The patent system has drawbacks, however. In filing for a patent, a firm must disclose information about the product or process. This information enters the public record and may help competing firms develop products or processes that are similar but that do not infringe on the patent. To avoid this problem, a firm may try to keep the results of its research a *trade secret*, without patenting it. (A famous example of a trade secret is the formula for Coca-Cola.) Tension also arises between the government's objectives of providing patent protection that gives firms the incentive to engage in research and development and making sure that the knowledge gained through the research is widely available, which increases the positive effect of the knowledge on the economy. Economists debate the features of an ideal patent system.

2. **Supporting research and development.** The government can help increase the quantity of research and development that takes place. In the United States, the federal government conducts some research directly. For example, the National Institutes of Health conducts medical research. The forerunner of the Internet—the Advanced Research Project Agency Network (ARPANET)—was developed by the U.S. Department of Defense to improve communication among defense researchers around the country. The government also subsidizes research by providing grants and other payments to researchers in universities through the National Science Foundation and other agencies. Finally, the government provides tax benefits to firms that invest in research and development.

3. **Subsidizing education.** People with technical training carry out research and development. If firms are unable to capture all the profit from research and development, they will pay lower wages and salaries to technical workers. These lower wages and salaries reduce the incentive to workers to receive this training. If the government subsidizes education, it can increase the number of workers who have technical training. In the United States, the government subsidizes education by directly providing free education from grades kindergarten through 12 and by providing support for public colleges and universities. The government also provides student loans at reduced interest rates.

These government policies can bring the accumulation of knowledge capital closer to the optimal level.

MyEconLab Concept Check

Joseph Schumpeter and Creative Destruction

The new growth theory has revived interest in the ideas of Joseph Schumpeter. Born in Austria in 1883, Schumpeter served briefly as that country's finance minister. In 1932, he became an economics professor at Harvard University. Schumpeter developed a model of growth that emphasized his view that new products unleash a "gale of creative destruction" that drives older products—and, often, the firms that produced them—out of the market. According to Schumpeter, the key to rising living standards is not small changes to existing products but, rather, new products that meet consumer wants in qualitatively better ways. For example, in the early twentieth century, the automobile displaced the horse-drawn carriage by meeting consumer demand for personal transportation in a way that was qualitatively better. In the early twenty-first century, the DVD and the DVD player displaced the VHS tape and the VCR by better meeting consumer demand for watching films at home. Downloading or streaming movies from the Internet are now in the process of displacing the DVD just as the DVD displaced the VHS tape.

To Schumpeter, the entrepreneur is central to economic growth: "The function of entrepreneurs is to reform or revolutionize the pattern of production by exploiting an

Patent The exclusive right to produce a product for a period of 20 years from the date the patent is applied for.

invention or, more generally, an untried technological possibility for producing new commodities or producing an old one in a new way."

The profit an entrepreneur hopes to earn provides the incentive for bringing together the factors of production—labor, capital, and natural resources—to start new firms and introduce new goods and services. Successful entrepreneurs can use their profits to finance the development of new products and are better able to attract funds from investors. MyEconLab Concept Check

11.3 Economic Growth in the United States

LEARNING OBJECTIVE: Discuss fluctuations in productivity growth in the United States.

The economic growth model can help us understand the record of growth in the United States. Figure 11.5 shows average annual growth rates in real GDP per hour worked since 1800. As the United States experienced the Industrial Revolution during the nineteenth century, U.S. firms increased the quantities of capital per hour worked. New technologies such as the steam engine, the railroad, and the telegraph also became available. Together, these factors resulted in an average annual growth rate of real GDP per worker of 1.3 percent from 1800 to 1900. Real GDP *per capita* grew at a slower rate of 1.1 percent during this period. At this growth rate, real GDP per capita would double about every 63 years, which means that living standards were growing steadily but relatively slowly.

By the twentieth century, technological change had been institutionalized. Many large corporations began to set up research and development facilities to improve the quality of their products and the efficiency with which they produced them. Universities also began to conduct research that had business applications. After World War II, many corporations began to provide significant funds to universities to help pay for research. In 1950, the federal government created the National Science Foundation, whose main goal is to support university researchers. The accelerating rate of technological change led to more rapid growth rates.

MyEconLab Animation

Figure 11.5

Average Annual Growth Rates in Real GDP per Hour Worked in the United States, 1800–2014

The growth rate in the United States increased from 1800 through the mid-1970s. Then, for more than 20 years, growth slowed before increasing for a 10-year period beginning in the mid-1990s. During the past 10 years, growth has slowed again.
Note: The values for 1800–1900 are real GDP per worker. The values for 1900–2014 are real GDP per hour worked; for the period 1900–2014 they are the authors' calculations, based on the methods used in Neville Francis and Valerie A. Ramey, "The Source of Historical Economic Fluctuations: An Analysis Using Long-Run Restrictions," in Jeffrey Frankel, Richard Clarida, and Francesco Giavazzi, eds., *International Seminar in Macroeconomics*, Chicago: University of Chicago Press, 2005; the authors thank Neville Francis for kindly providing some of the data used.

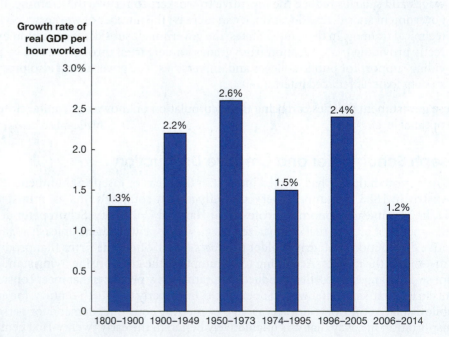

Economic Growth in the United States since 1950

Continuing technological change allowed the U.S. economy to avoid the diminishing returns to capital that stifled growth in the Soviet economy. In fact, until the 1970s, the growth rate of the U.S. economy accelerated over time. As Figure 11.5 shows, growth in the first half of the twentieth century was faster than growth during the nineteenth century, and growth in the immediate post–World War II period from 1950 to 1973 was faster yet. Then the unexpected happened: For more than 20 years, from 1974 to 1995, the growth rate of real GDP per hour worked slowed. The growth rate during these years was more than 1 percentage point per year lower than during the 1950–1973 period. Beginning in the mid-1990s, the growth rate picked up again, and many economists argued that the effects of the revolution in *information technology* (*IT*), including increased use of computers, software, cellphones, and related innovations, were causing a return to higher rates of long-run growth. But, then, beginning in 2006, growth again slowed.   MyEconLab Concept Check

Is the United States Headed for a Long Period of Slow Growth?

Economists have not reached a consensus in explaining the swings in U.S. productivity growth since the mid-1970s. Broadly speaking, economists' views fall into two camps:

- **The optimistic view.** Some economists argue that although productivity has become more difficult to measure, the United States is likely to experience high rates of productivity growth in the long run, which will significantly increase the standard of living of the average person in the decades ahead.

- **The pessimistic view.** Other economists believe that productivity growth entered a long-run decline in the mid-1970s that was overcome for only a brief period of time by the initial effects of the revolution in information technology. These economists argue that future productivity growth rates are likely to remain low and, therefore, the standard of living of the average person in the United States will increase only slowly.

We can briefly discuss some of the key issues involved in this debate.

Measurement Issues Some economists argue that recent productivity growth rates may appear worse than they are because of problems in measuring output. If growth in real GDP understates the true growth rate of output, then measured productivity growth will also understate the true growth rate of productivity. After 1970, services—such as haircuts and financial advice—became a larger fraction of GDP, and goods—such as automobiles and hamburgers—became a smaller fraction. It is more difficult to measure increases in the output of services than to measure increases in the output of goods. For example, before banks began using automated teller machines (ATMs) in the 1980s, you could withdraw money only by going to a bank before closing time—which was usually 3:00 P.M. Once ATMs became available, you could withdraw money at any time of the day or night at a variety of locations. This increased convenience from ATMs does not show up in GDP. If this and similar improvements in the quality and convenience of services were included in GDP, measured output per hour worked would have grown more rapidly.

There may also be a measurement problem in accounting for improvements in the environment and in health and safety. Beginning in 1970, new laws required firms to spend billions of dollars reducing pollution, improving workplace safety, and redesigning products to improve their safety. This spending did not result in additional output that would be included in GDP—although it may have increased overall well-being. If these increases in well-being had been included in GDP, measured output per hour worked would have grown more rapidly.

All the high-income countries have experienced roughly similar movements in productivity growth rates. Because they all began producing more services and fewer goods and enacted stricter environmental regulations at about the same time, explanations of the productivity slowdown that emphasize measurement problems become more plausible.

The Role of Information Technology Some economists argue that the development of information technology (IT) caused the higher productivity growth that began in the mid-1990s. As computers became less expensive and faster, they made it possible for people and organizations to communicate and process data more efficiently. Today, a single laptop computer has more computing power than all the mainframe computers NASA used to control the *Apollo* spacecrafts that landed on the moon in the late 1960s and early 1970s.

Faster data processing has had a major effect on nearly every firm. Business record keeping, once done laboriously by hand, is now done more quickly and accurately by computers. During the 1990s, firms used the Internet to market and sell products. Smartphones, tablets, laptop computers, and wireless Internet access allow people to work at home and while traveling. These developments in IT have significantly increased labor productivity.

Despite the wonders of IT, productivity growth since 2006 has fallen to an even lower rate than during the period of slow growth from the mid-1970s to the mid-1990s. Is IT no longer a productivity booster, or are the data not capturing some of IT's benefits? What insight do the answers to these questions give us about how rapid growth will be in the coming decades?

Some economists believe that developments in IT have improved the delivery of services to both consumers and firms in ways that the GDP statistics fail to capture. For instance, receiving detailed driving directions using TomTom or a similar app is much easier than before smartphones were developed. In recent years the widespread use of apps to arrange for car rides, make short-term room rentals, locate friends, and so on have provided benefits to consumers that are not measured or are only partially measured by GDP. Similarly, a store manager can quickly check on available warehouse inventory using a dedicated smartphone or tablet app.

Economists who believe that IT is having large, but difficult to measure, effects on the economy are usually also optimistic about future growth rates. They believe that continuing advances in semiconductor technology—which underlie progress in IT—will result in substantial gains in labor productivity. The gains will come from higher productivity in the IT sector itself and in other sectors of the economy as the result of progress made possible by advances in IT. For example, ever more rapid and inexpensive computing lowers the cost and speeds the adoption of existing products, such as 3D printers, and helps innovators develop new products, which, in turn, raise productivity growth above its current levels.

Other economists doubt that the unmeasured benefits of the IT revolution are any greater than the unmeasured benefits of earlier innovations. Robert J. Gordon of Northwestern University has argued that productivity increases from the IT revolution were in fact much smaller than increases resulting from earlier innovations, such as the railroad, electrification of homes and businesses, petroleum refining, and the automobile. Moreover, Gordon and some other economists argue that most of the gains from the IT revolution occurred in the 1990s, as a result of the development of the World Wide Web, Windows 95, and computerized inventory control systems. These innovations raised labor productivity because they changed how businesses operated. By the early 2000s, the IT revolution was having a greater effect on consumer products, such as smartphones and tablets, than on labor productivity. Gordon identifies other factors, such as an aging population, declining educational achievement, and the consequences of increased regulations and higher taxes, that will lead to lower productivity growth rates. Gordon forecasts an extended period of productivity growth rates of 0.5 percent or less.

"Secular Stagnation ... " In the late 1930s, toward the end of the Great Depression, Alvin Hansen of Harvard University predicted that the U.S. economy would experience an extended period of slow growth, or *secular stagnation*. The rapid growth rates the U.S. economy experienced beginning in 1950 indicate that Hansen's analysis was incorrect. Recently, however, Lawrence Summers of Harvard, along with some other economists, has revived the term in arguing that growth rates are likely to remain low in future years. These economists do not focus on potentially slow rates of technological progress. Instead, they believe that real GDP may grow slowly because of insufficient demand for investment spending.

In Chapter 10, we saw that in the loanable funds model, the equilibrium level of saving and investment is determined at the level of the real interest rate where the quantity of loanable funds demanded equals the quantity of loanable funds supplied. Economists who forecast a future of secular stagnation believe that the demand for loanable funds may be low in coming years for three main reasons:

1. Slowing population growth in the United States will reduce the demand for housing.

2. Modern information technology firms, such as Twitter, Google, and Facebook, require much less capital than older industrial firms, such as General Motors or Whirlpool.

3. The price of capital, particularly information technology goods such as computers, has been falling relative to the prices of other goods. Accordingly, firms can meet their needs for capital with lower levels of expenditure.

As a result of these factors, the real interest rate that brings equality to the loanable funds market may be very low—possibly even negative. So, investment spending will be very low. With this component of GDP growing slowly, GDP will itself only grow slowly.

… or a Return to Faster Growth? Critics of the secular stagnation view believe that low rates of investment in recent years have resulted from the severity of the recession of 2007–2009 and the relatively slow recovery from that recession. They argue that as the economic recovery continues, the demand for investment goods will increase. In addition, they argue that economic growth in other countries may increase the demand for U.S. goods, allowing exports to increase, thereby offsetting the effects on GDP of lower production of investment goods.

The debate over future growth rates is an important one. If the optimistic forecasts are correct, then in future decades, the U.S. standard of living will be much higher than if the pessimistic forecasts are correct. A large difference in the standard of living will have an enormous effect on nearly every aspect of life in the United States, including the extent of poverty, the ability of individuals and the government to finance increasing medical costs, and the ability of the country to deal with the effects of an aging population.

MyEconLab Concept Check   MyEconLab Study Plan

11.4 Why Isn't the Whole World Rich?

LEARNING OBJECTIVE: Explain economic catch-up and discuss why many poor countries have not experienced rapid economic growth.

The economic growth model tells us that economies grow when the quantity of capital per hour worked increases and when technological change occurs. This model seems to provide a good blueprint for developing countries to become rich:

1. Increase the quantity of capital per hour worked.

2. Use the best available technology.

There are economic incentives for both of these things to happen in poor countries. The profitability of using additional capital or better technology is generally greater in a developing country than in a high-income country. For example, replacing an existing computer with a new, faster computer will generally have a relatively small payoff for a firm in the United States. In contrast, installing a new computer in a Zambian firm where records have been kept by hand is likely to have an enormous payoff.

This observation leads to an important conclusion: *The economic growth model predicts that poor countries will grow faster than rich countries.* If this prediction is correct, we should observe poor countries catching up to rich countries in levels of GDP per capita (or income per capita). Has this **catch-up**—or *convergence*—actually occurred? Here we come to a paradox: If we look only at the countries that currently have high incomes, we see that the lower-income countries have been catching up to the higher-income

Catch-up The prediction that the level of GDP per capita (or income per capita) in poor countries will grow faster than in rich countries.

countries, but the developing countries as a group have not been catching up to the high-income countries as a group.

Catch-up: Sometimes but Not Always

We can construct a graph that makes it easier to see whether catch-up is happening. In Figure 11.6, the horizontal axis shows the initial level of real GDP per capita, and the vertical axis shows the rate at which real GDP per capita is growing. We can then plot points on the graph for rich and poor countries. Each point represents the combination of a country's initial level of real GDP per capita and its growth rate over the following years. The catch-up line in the figure shows the situation where the catch-up prediction holds exactly: Low-income countries should be on the upper-left section of the line because they would have low initial levels of real GDP per capita but fast growth rates. High-income countries should be in the lower-right section of the line because they would have high initial levels of real GDP per capita but slow growth rates. When we plot the actual observations for each country, the closer the points for each country are to the line, the more accurate the catch-up prediction is.

Catch-up among the High-Income Countries If we look at only the countries that currently have high incomes, we can see the catch-up predicted by the economic growth model. Figure 11.7 shows that the high-income countries that had the lowest incomes in 1960, such as Taiwan, Korea, and Hong Kong, grew the fastest between 1960 and 2011 (which is the most recent year for which comprehensive data are available). Countries that had the highest incomes in 1960, such as Switzerland, Australia, and the United States, grew the slowest.

Are the Developing Countries Catching Up to the High-Income Countries?
If we expand our analysis to include every country for which statistics are available, it becomes more difficult to find the catch-up predicted by the economic growth model. Figure 11.8 does not show a consistent relationship between the level of real GDP per capita in 1960 and growth from 1960 to 2011. Some countries that had low levels of real GDP per capita in 1960, such as Niger and the Democratic Republic of the Congo, actually experienced *negative* economic growth: They had *lower* levels of real GDP per capita in 2011 than in 1960. Other countries that started with low levels of real GDP per capita, such as Malaysia and China, grew rapidly. Some middle-income countries in 1960, such as Venezuela, grew slowly between 1960 and 2011, while others, such as Ireland, grew much more rapidly.   MyEconLab Concept Check

MyEconLab Animation

Figure 11.6

The Catch-up Predicted by the Economic Growth Model

According to the economic growth model, countries that start with lower levels of real GDP per capita should grow faster (points near the upper-left section of the line) than countries that start with higher levels of real GDP per capita (points near the lower-right section of the line).

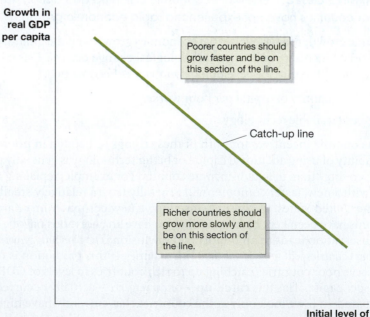

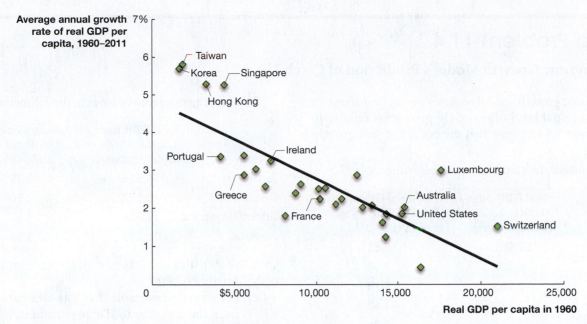

Figure 11.7   **There Has Been Catch-up among High-Income Countries**

If we look only at countries that currently have high incomes, we see that countries such as Taiwan, Korea, and Singapore that had the lowest incomes in 1960 grew the fastest between 1960 and 2011. Countries such as Switzerland and the United States that had the highest incomes in 1960 grew the slowest.

Note: Data are real GDP per capita in 2005 dollars. Each point in the figure represents one high-income country.
Source: Authors' calculations from data in *Penn World Table Version 8.1;* Robert C. Feenstra, Robert Inklaar, and Marcel P. Timmer, "The Next Generation of the Penn World Table" www.ggdc.net/pwt, April 2015.

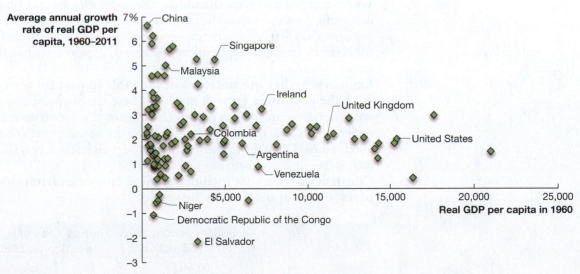

Figure 11.8   **Most of the World Hasn't Been Catching Up**

If we look at all countries for which statistics are available, we do not see the catch-up predicted by the economic growth model. Some countries that had low levels of real GDP per capita in 1960, such as Niger and the Democratic Republic of the Congo, actually experienced *negative* economic growth. Other countries that started with low levels of real GDP per capita, such as Malaysia and China, grew rapidly. Some middle-income countries in 1960, such as Venezuela, hardly grew between 1960 and 2011, while others, such as Ireland, experienced significant growth.

Note: Data are real GDP per capita in 2005 dollars. Each point in the figure represents one country.
Source: Authors' calculations from data in *Penn World Table Version 8.1;* Robert C. Feenstra, Robert Inklaar, and Marcel P. Timmer, "The Next Generation of the Penn World Table" www.ggdc.net/pwt, April 2015.

Solved Problem 11.4

The Economic Growth Model's Prediction of Catch-Up

The economic growth model makes a prediction about an economy's initial level of real GDP per capita relative to other economies and how fast the economy will grow in the future.

a. Consider the statistics in the following table:

Country	Real GDP per Capita, 1960 (2005 dollars)	Annual Growth in Real GDP per Capita, 1960–2011
Taiwan	$1,861	5.81%
Panama	2,120	3.50
Brazil	2,483	2.73
Costa Rica	4,920	1.42
Venezuela	7,015	0.91

Are these statistics consistent with the economic growth model? Briefly explain.

b. Now consider the statistics in the following table:

Country	Real GDP per Capita, 1960 (2005 dollars)	Annual Growth in Real GDP per Capita, 1960–2011
Japan	$5,586	3.39%
Belgium	10,132	2.50
United Kingdom	11,204	2.10
Australia	15,255	1.85

Are these statistics consistent with the economic growth model? Briefly explain.

c. Construct a new table that lists all nine countries, from the lowest real GDP per capita in 1960 to the highest, along with their growth rates. Are the statistics in your new table consistent with the economic growth model?

Solving the Problem

Step 1: Review the chapter material. This problem is about catch-up in the economic growth model, so you may want to review the section "Why Isn't the Whole World Rich?" which begins on page 365.

Step 2: Explain whether the statistics in the table in part (a) are consistent with the economic growth model. These statistics are consistent with the economic growth model. The countries with the lowest levels of real GDP per capita in 1960 had the fastest growth rates between 1960 and 2011, and the countries with the highest levels of real GDP per capita had the slowest growth rates.

Step 3: Explain whether the statistics in the table in part (b) are consistent with the economic growth model. These statistics are also consistent with the economic growth model. Once again, the countries with the lowest levels of real GDP per capita in 1960 had the fastest growth rates between 1960 and 2011, and the countries with the highest levels of real GDP per capita had the slowest growth rates.

Step 4: Construct a table that includes all nine countries from the tables in parts (a) and (b) and discuss the results.

Country	Real GDP per Capita, 1960 (2005 dollars)	Annual Growth in Real GDP per Capita, 1960–2011
Taiwan	$1,861	5.81%
Panama	2,120	3.50
Brazil	2,483	2.73
Costa Rica	4,920	1.42
Japan	5,586	3.39
Venezuela	7,015	0.91
Belgium	10,132	2.50
United Kingdom	11,204	2.10
Australia	15,255	1.85

The statistics in the new table are *not* consistent with the predictions of the economic growth model. For example, Australia and the United Kingdom had higher levels of real GDP per capita in 1960 than did Costa Rica and Venezuela. The economic growth model predicts that Australia and the United Kingdom should, therefore, have grown more slowly than Costa Rica and Venezuela. The data in the table show, however, that Australia and the United Kingdom grew faster. Similarly, Belgium grew faster than Costa Rica, even though its real GDP per capita was already much higher than Costa Rica's in 1960.

Extra Credit: The statistics in these tables confirm what we saw in Figures 11.7 and 11.8 on page 367: There has been catch-up among the high-income countries, but there has not been catch-up if we include in the analysis all the countries of the world.

Your Turn: For more practice, do related problems 4.4 and 4.5 on page 384 at the end of this chapter.

MyEconLab Study Plan

Why Haven't Most Western European Countries, Canada, and Japan Caught Up to the United States?

Figure 11.7 on page 367 indicates that there has been catch-up among the high-income countries over the past 50 years. If we look at the catch-up of other high-income countries to the United States during the most recent period, we discover a surprising fact: Over the past 25 years, other high-income countries have actually fallen further behind the United States rather than catching up to it. Figure 11.9 shows real GDP per capita in Canada, Japan, and the five largest economies in Western Europe relative to real GDP per capita in the United States. The blue bars show real GDP per capita in 1990 relative to the United States, and the red bars show real GDP per capita in 2014 relative to the United States. In each case, relative levels of real GDP per capita were lower in 2014 than they were in 1990. Each of these countries experienced significant catch-up to the United States between 1960 and 1990, but they have experienced no catch-up since 1990.

Why have other high-income countries had trouble completely closing the gap in real GDP per capita with the United States? Many economists believe there are two

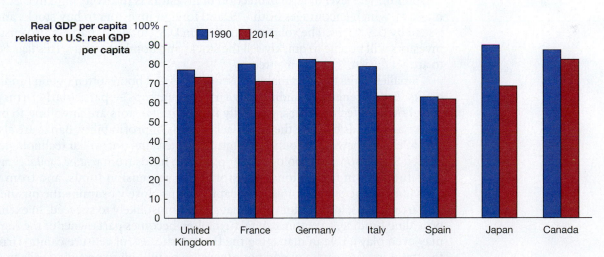

MyEconLab Real-time data

Figure 11.9   Other High-Income Countries Have Stopped Catching Up to the United States

The blue bars show real GDP per capita in 1990 relative to the United States, and the red bars show real GDP per capita in 2014 relative to the United States. In each case, relative levels of real GDP per capita are lower in 2014 than they were in 1990, which means that these countries have ceased catching up to the United States.

Source: Authors' calculations from data in Organization for Economic Co-operation and Development, stat.oecd.org.

main explanations: the greater flexibility of U.S. labor markets and the greater efficiency of the U.S. financial system. U.S. labor markets are more flexible than labor markets in other countries for several reasons. In many European countries, government regulations make it difficult for firms to fire workers and thereby make firms reluctant to hire workers in the first place. As a result, many younger workers have difficulty finding jobs, and once a job is found, a worker tends to remain in it even if his or her skills and preferences are not a good match for the characteristics of the job. In the United States, by contrast, government regulations are less restrictive, workers have an easier time finding jobs, and workers change jobs fairly frequently. This high rate of job mobility ensures a better match between workers' skills and preferences and the characteristics of jobs, which increases labor productivity. Many European countries also have restrictive work rules that limit the ability of firms to implement new technologies. These rules restrict the tasks firms can ask workers to perform and the number of hours they work. The rules reduce the ability of firms to use new technologies that may require workers to learn new skills, perform new tasks, or work during the night or early mornings.

Workers in the United States tend to enter the labor force earlier, retire later, and experience fewer long spells of unemployment than do workers in Europe. Unemployed workers in the United States typically receive smaller government payments for a shorter period of time than do unemployed workers in Canada and most of the countries of Western Europe. Because the opportunity cost of being unemployed is lower in those countries, the unemployment rate tends to be higher, and the fraction of the labor force that is unemployed for more than one year also tends to be higher. Studies have shown that workers who are employed for longer periods tend to have greater skills, greater productivity, and higher wages. Many economists believe that the design of the U.S. unemployment insurance program has contributed to the greater flexibility of U.S. labor markets and to higher rates of growth in labor productivity and real GDP per capita.

As we have seen, technological change is essential for rapid productivity growth. To obtain the funds needed to implement new technologies, firms turn to the financial system. It is important that funds for investment be not only available but also allocated efficiently. Large corporations can raise funds by selling stocks and bonds in financial markets. U.S. corporations benefit from the efficiency of U.S. financial markets (see Chapter 6). The level of legal protection of investors is relatively high in U.S. financial markets, which encourages both U.S. and foreign investors to buy stocks and bonds issued by U.S. firms. The volume of trading in U.S. financial markets also ensures that investors will be able to quickly sell the stocks and bonds they buy. This *liquidity* serves to attract investors to U.S. markets.

Smaller firms that are unable to issue stocks and bonds often obtain funding from banks. Entrepreneurs founding new firms—"startups"—particularly firms that are based on new technologies, generally find that investors are unwilling to buy their stocks and bonds because the firms lack records of profitability. Banks are also reluctant to lend to new firms founded to introduce new and unfamiliar technologies. In the United States, some technology startups obtain funds from *venture capital firms*, which raise funds from institutional investors, such as pension funds, and from wealthy individuals. The owners of venture capital firms closely examine the business plans of startup firms, looking for those that appear most likely to succeed. In exchange for providing funding, a venture capital firm often becomes part owner of the startup and may even play a role in managing the firm. A successful venture capital firm is able to attract investors who would not otherwise be willing to provide funds to startups because the investors lack enough information about the startup. A number of well-known U.S. high-technology firms, such as Google, relied on venture capital firms to fund their early expansion. The ability of venture capital firms to finance technology-driven startup firms may be giving the United States an advantage in bringing new products and new processes to market.

The U.S. financial system suffered severe problems between 2007 and 2009. But, over the long run, it has succeeded in efficiently allocating investment funds.

Why Don't More Low-Income Countries Experience Rapid Growth?

The economic growth model predicts that the countries that were very poor in 1960 should have grown rapidly over the next 50 years. As we have just seen, some did, but many did not. Why are many low-income countries growing so slowly? There is no single answer, but most economists point to four key factors:

1. Failure to enforce the rule of law
2. Wars and revolutions
3. Poor public education and health
4. Low rates of saving and investment

Failure to Enforce the Rule of Law   In the years since 1960, increasing numbers of developing countries, including China, have abandoned centrally planned economies in favor of more market-oriented economies. For entrepreneurs in a market economy to succeed, however, the government must guarantee private **property rights** and enforce contracts. Unless entrepreneurs feel secure in their property, they will not risk starting a business. Business owners also have difficulty being successful unless they can use an independent court system to enforce contracts. The **rule of law** refers to the ability of a government to enforce the laws of the country, particularly with respect to protecting private property and enforcing contracts. The failure of many developing countries to guarantee property rights and to enforce contracts has hindered their economic growth.

Consider, for example, the production of shoes. Suppose the owner of a shoe factory signs a contract with a leather tannery to deliver a specific quantity of leather on a particular date for a particular price. On the basis of this contract, the owner of the shoe factory signs a contract to deliver a specific quantity of shoes to a shoe wholesaler. This contract states the quantity of shoes to be delivered, the quality of the shoes, the delivery date, and the price. The owner of the leather tannery uses the contract with the shoe factory to enter into a contract with cattle ranchers for the delivery of hides. The shoe wholesaler enters into contracts to deliver shoes to retail stores, where they are sold to consumers. For the flow of goods from cattle ranchers to shoe customers to operate efficiently, each business must carry out the terms of the contract it has signed. In developed countries, such as the United States, businesses know that if they fail to carry out a contract, they may be sued in court and forced to compensate the other party for any economic damages.

Many developing countries do not have functioning, independent court systems. Even if a court system does exist, a case may not be heard for many years. In some countries, bribery of judges and political favoritism in court rulings are common. If firms cannot enforce contracts through the court system, they may insist on carrying out only face-to-face cash transactions. For example, the shoe manufacturer will wait until the leather producer brings the hides to the factory and will then buy the hides for cash. The wholesaler will wait until the shoes have been produced before making plans for sales to retail stores. Production still takes place, but it is carried out more slowly and inefficiently. With slow and inefficient production, firms have difficulty finding investors willing to provide them with the funds they need to expand.

Property rights The rights individuals or firms have to the exclusive use of their property, including the right to buy or sell it.

Rule of law The ability of a government to enforce the laws of the country, particularly with respect to protecting private property and enforcing contracts.

Making the Connection
MyEconLab Video

Why Hasn't Mexico Grown as Fast as China?

Many people consider China *the* great economic growth success story. The decision by Chinese government leaders in the 1970s to turn away from a centrally planned economy and toward a market system unleashed economic growth that has lifted more than a billion people in China out of poverty. As we will discuss in Section 11.5, the Chinese economy still faces significant obstacles to maintaining high growth rates, and the Chinese Communist Party has maintained its dictatorship over the country. Despite these problems, many economists and policymakers see China as an example of the rapid growth that low-income countries can attain.

As we saw in the chapter opener, some U.S. firms have chosen in recent years to locate factories and other facilities in Mexico rather than in China because Mexico is closer to the United States and because labor costs have been increasing more rapidly in China. This trend has been good news for the Mexican economy because it has increased factory employment and given the country easier access to U.S. technology. Overall, though, the growth rates of the Mexican economy have been disappointing. The graph below compares the growth rates of real GDP per capita for the Mexican and Chinese economies over the past 35 years.

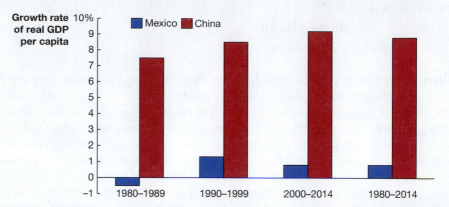

Taking the whole period between 1980 and 2014, the average annual growth rate for the Chinese economy has been 8.8 percent, while the growth rate for the Mexican economy has been a very slow 0.8 percent. In Chapter 10, we saw that if we divide a growth rate into 70, the result is approximately the number of years it will take real GDP per capita to double. When we apply that rule here, we find that it will take real GDP per capita more than 85 years to double in Mexico but only 8 years in China.

What explains the slow growth of the Mexican economy? For most of the period from the Mexican Revolution of 1910 until 2000, the Institutional Revolutionary Party (PRI) dominated the Mexican government. For decades, the party followed a policy of limiting imports and foreign investment, concentrating on building up domestic industry behind high tariff walls. The Mexican government took over, or nationalized, some businesses, including the oil industry. By the 1980s, dissatisfaction with the country's poor economic performance led the PRI, under President Miguel de la Madrid, to institute a series of reforms. The reforms, which were broadened in the 1990s, included allowing banks again to be private businesses; signing the North American Free Trade Agreement (NAFTA) with the United States and Canada, which greatly reduced tariffs on imports; and allowing foreign investment in most sectors of the economy apart from the oil industry. As the graph above shows, though, these reforms have not resulted in high rates of economic growth.

Some economic historians believe that the Spanish colonial background of the nineteenth century and earlier hobbled the Mexican economy. Unlike in the United States, in Mexico and other Spanish and Portuguese colonies, land was often concentrated in very large estates, which led to highly unequal distributions of income and may have made it difficult for a broad-based middle class capable of supporting a large manufacturing base to develop. Other countries in Latin America, though, including Chile and Uruguay, with similar colonial backgrounds have experienced much more rapid growth.

Some economists believe that the financial sector has been an important obstacle to growth. The Mexican legal system makes it difficult for banks to seize a business's assets when the business defaults on a loan. As a result, Mexican banks are reluctant to make loans to businesses. As we noted in the chapter opener, Mexico also suffers from government corruption that either makes businesses reluctant to expand or forces them to operate in the underground economy. In either case, the businesses are unable to take advantage of economies of scale and may be unwilling to make large investments in machinery or buildings. In certain areas of Mexico, criminal gangs have also disrupted business. The educational system in Mexico has failed to provide many students with the skills needed to find work at firms competing in the global marketplace. Finally, infrastructure, including poor roads and inconsistent and expensive provision of electricity—with occasional blackouts—have also hindered business expansion.

Timothy J. Kehoe of the University of Minnesota and Kim J. Ruhl of New York University note that China also suffers from institutional problems, but it has grown much faster than Mexico. China, though, began its rapid growth from very low levels of income, so that in 2014, real GDP per capita in Mexico was still more than twice the level in China. Kehoe and Ruhl argue that, as a middle-income country, Mexico has already taken advantage of many of the relatively easy ways of increasing real GDP— including moving resources out of the low-productivity agricultural sector, accumulating capital in manufacturing, and adopting modern technology. We saw in the discussion of Figure 11.9 that, probably for institutional reasons, many high-income countries have made no progress in closing the gap in real GDP per capita between themselves and the United States during the past 25 years. Mexico may now be in a similar situation of having difficulty growing fast enough to close the gap with higher-income countries. Because Mexico's institutional barriers to growth are more severe than those in European countries, the gap in real GDP per capita between the United States and Mexico may persist at a high level.

Economists and policymakers in Mexico continue to look for ways to increase growth rates. Without an increase in growth, it may be decades before millions of low-income people in Mexico are able to escape poverty.

Sources: "The 100-Year View," *Economist*, May 2, 2015; Gordon H. Hanson, "Why Isn't Mexico Rich?" *Journal of Economic Literature*, Vol. 48, No. 4, December 2010, pp. 987–1004; Timothy J. Kehoe and Kim J. Ruhl, "Why Have Economic Reforms in Mexico Not Generated Growth?" *Journal of Economic Literature*, Vol. 48, No. 4, December 2010, pp. 1004–1027; Nora Lustig, "Life Is Not Easy: Mexico's Quest for Stability and Growth," *Journal of Economic Perspectives*, Vol. 15, No. 1, Winter 2001, pp. 85–106; and Federal Reserve Bank of St. Louis.

Your Turn: Test your understanding by doing related problems 4.8 and 4.9 on page 385 at the end of this chapter.

MyEconLab Study Plan

Wars and Revolutions Many of the countries that were very poor in 1960 have experienced extended periods of war or violent changes of government during the years since. These wars have made it impossible for countries such as Afghanistan, Angola, Ethiopia, the Central African Republic, and the Democratic Republic of the Congo to accumulate capital or adopt new technologies. In fact, conducting any kind of business has been very difficult. Ending war has a positive effect on growth, as shown by the case of Mozambique, which suffered through almost two decades of civil war and declining real GDP per capita. With the end of civil war, Mozambique experienced a strong annual growth rate of 8 percent in real GDP per capita from 1990 to 2014.

Poor Public Education and Health We have seen that human capital is one of the determinants of labor productivity. Many low-income countries have weak public school systems, so many workers are unable to read and write. Few workers acquire the skills necessary to use the latest technology.

People in many low-income countries suffer from diseases that are either nonexistent or easily treated in high-income countries. For example, few people in developed countries suffer from malaria, but about 500,000 Africans die from it each year. Treatments for AIDS have greatly reduced deaths from this disease in the United States and Europe. But millions of people in low-income countries continue to die from AIDS. These countries often lack the resources, and their governments are often too ineffective, to provide even routine medical care, such as childhood vaccinations.

People who are sick work less and are less productive when they do work. Poor nutrition or exposure to certain diseases in childhood can leave people permanently weakened and can affect their intelligence as adults. Poor health has a significant negative effect on the human capital of workers in developing countries.

Low Rates of Saving and Investment To invest in factories, machinery, and computers, firms need funds. Some of the funds can come from the owners of the firm and from their friends and families, but firms in high-income countries raise most of their funds from bank loans and the sale of stocks and bonds in financial markets. In most developing countries, stock and bond markets do not exist, and often the banking system is very weak. In high-income countries, the funds that banks lend to businesses come from the savings of households. In high-income countries, many households are able to save a significant fraction of their income. In developing countries, many households barely survive on their incomes and, therefore, have little or no savings.

The low saving rates in developing countries can contribute to a *vicious cycle of poverty*. Because households have low incomes, they save very little. Because households save very little, few funds are available for firms to borrow. Lacking funds, firms do not invest in the new factories, machinery, and equipment needed for economic growth. Because the economy does not grow, household incomes remain low, as do their savings, and so on. MyEconLab Concept Check

The Benefits of Globalization

Foreign direct investment (FDI) The purchase or building by a corporation of a facility in a foreign country.

Foreign portfolio investment The purchase by an individual or a firm of stocks or bonds issued in another country.

One way for a developing country to break out of the vicious cycle of low saving and investment and low growth is through foreign investment. **Foreign direct investment (FDI)** occurs when corporations build or purchase facilities in foreign countries. **Foreign portfolio investment** occurs when an individual or a firm buys stocks or bonds issued in another country. Foreign direct investment and foreign portfolio investment can give a low-income country access to technology and funds that otherwise would not be available. Until fairly recently, many developing countries were reluctant to take advantage of this opportunity.

From the 1940s through the 1970s, many developing countries closed themselves off from the global economy. During the 1930s and early 1940s, the global trading and financial system collapsed as a result of the Great Depression and World War II. Developing countries that relied on exporting to the high-income countries were hurt economically. Also, many countries in Africa and Asia achieved independence from the colonial powers of Europe during the 1950s and 1960s and were afraid of being dominated by them economically. As a result, many developing countries imposed high tariffs on foreign imports and strongly discouraged or even prohibited foreign investment. These policies made it difficult to break out of the vicious cycle of poverty.

Globalization The process of countries becoming more open to foreign trade and investment.

MyEconLab Study Plan

The policies of erecting high tariff barriers and avoiding foreign investment failed to produce much growth, so by the 1980s, many developing countries began to change policies. The result was **globalization**, which refers to the process of countries becoming more open to foreign trade and investment. Developing countries that are more globalized have grown faster than developing countries that are less globalized. Globalization has benefited developing countries by making it easier for them to obtain technology and investment funds. MyEconLab Concept Check

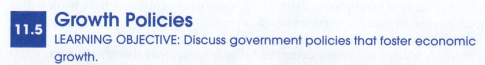

11.5 Growth Policies

LEARNING OBJECTIVE: Discuss government policies that foster economic growth.

What can governments do to promote long-run economic growth? We have seen that even small differences in growth rates compounded over the years can lead to major differences in standards of living. Therefore, there is potentially a very high payoff to government policies that increase growth rates. We have already discussed some of these policies in this chapter. In this section, we explore additional policies.

Enhancing Property Rights and the Rule of Law

A market system cannot work well unless property rights are enforced. Entrepreneurs are unlikely to risk their own funds, and investors are unlikely to lend their funds to entrepreneurs, if property is not protected from being arbitrarily seized. We have seen that in many developing countries, the rule of law and property rights are undermined by government *corruption*. In some developing countries, it is impossible for an entrepreneur to obtain a permit to start a business without paying bribes, often to several different government officials. Is it possible for a country to reform a corrupt government bureaucracy?

Although today the United States ranks among the least corrupt countries, recent research by economists Edward Glaeser and Claudia Goldin of Harvard University has shown that in the late nineteenth and early twentieth centuries, corruption was a significant problem in the United States. The fact that political reform movements and crusading newspapers helped to reduce corruption in the United States to relatively low levels by the 1920s provides some hope for reform movements that aim to reduce corruption in developing countries today.

Property rights are unlikely to be secure in countries that are afflicted by wars and civil strife. For a number of countries, increased political stability is a necessary prerequisite to economic growth. MyEconLab Concept Check

Making the Connection
MyEconLab Video

Will China's Standard of Living Ever Exceed That of the United States?

In 2014, GDP per capita in the United States was more than four times higher than GDP per capita in China. However, the growth rate of real GDP per capita in the United States has averaged only 1.7 percent per year since 1980, compared to China's average growth rate of 8.8 percent per year over the same time period. If these growth rates were to continue, China's standard of living, as measured by real GDP per capita, would exceed the U.S. standard of living in the year 2036.

Some economists argue that China may have overinvested in physical capital, such as bullet trains.

For China to maintain its high rates of growth in real GDP per capita, however, it would have to maintain high rates of productivity growth, which is unlikely for several reasons. First, the United States invests more in activities, such as research and development, that result in new technologies and increases in productivity. Although China has been successful in adopting existing technologies developed in the United States and other countries, it has been much less successful in developing new technologies. Second, a good part of China's growth is due to the transition from a centrally planned economy to a market economy, so China's growth rate is likely to decrease as the transition is completed. Third, China's economic growth has depended on moving workers from agriculture, where their productivity was low, to manufacturing jobs in cities, where their productivity is much higher. The large supply of low-wage agricultural workers helped to keep manufacturing wages low and provided China with a cost advantage in manufacturing goods compared with the United States and other high-income countries. China has exhausted much of its supply of low-wage agricultural workers, so manufacturing wages have begun to rise, eroding China's cost advantage. As we saw in the chapter opener, some U.S. firms have reacted to rising labor costs in China by moving factories to Mexico—or back to the United States.

Another looming problem is demographic. Because of China's low birth rate, the country will soon experience a decline in its labor force. Over the next two decades, the population of men and women between the ages of 15 and 29 will fall by roughly 100 million, or about 30 percent. China will also experience a large increase in older workers, a group that will on average be less productive and less healthy than younger workers. Given current trends, the U.S. Census Bureau projects fewer people under age 50 in China in 2030 than today, including fewer people in their 20s and early 30s, and many more people in their 60s and older. China still has potential sources for enhancing productivity, including the wider application of technology and the movement of workers into high-productivity industries, such as the manufacture of automobiles and household appliances, provided that domestic demand increases rapidly. These factors can fuel future growth, but at some point, China's demographic problems could slow growth.

Perhaps most troubling for China is the fact that the country remains autocratic, with the Communist Party refusing to allow meaningful elections and continuing to limit freedom of expression. The government has yet to establish secure property rights and the rule of law. Some observers believe that the lack of political freedom in China may ultimately lead to civil unrest, which could slow growth rates. Whether or not civil unrest eventually develops, the lack of democracy in China may already be resulting in problems that could slow growth in the near future. Large, state-owned firms, controlled by Communist Party members, continue to receive government subsidies. The result is that these firms, which typically have low productivity and are not globally competitive, receive funds that otherwise would have allowed high-productivity firms to expand.

Nouriel Roubini, an economist at New York University, argues that China's Communist Party may be repeating some of the mistakes the Soviet Communist Party committed decades ago. He argues that by employing policies that have resulted in investment spending being 50 percent of GDP, the government may have boosted short-term growth at the expense of the health of the economy in the long term. He notes:

> China is rife with overinvestment in physical capital, infrastructure, and property. To a visitor, this is evident in sleek but empty airports and bullet trains … highways to nowhere, thousands of colossal new central and provincial government buildings, ghost towns, and brand-new aluminum smelters kept closed to prevent global prices from plunging.

Growth in China is already showing signs of slowing. Between 2010 and 2014, real GDP per capita grew at an annual rate of 6.0 percent. While still rapid, this growth rate is well below what the Chinese economy had achieved in previous decades. In early 2015, Chinese Premier Li Keqiang noted, "The downward pressure on economic growth continues to increase."

China has been engaged in an economic experiment: Can a country maintain high rates of economic growth in the long run while denying its citizens basic political rights?

Sources: Mark Magnier, "China's First-Quarter Growth Slowest in Six Years at 7%," *Wall Street Journal*, April 15, 2015; Pranab Bardhan, "The Slowing of Two Economic Giants," *New York Times*, July 14, 2013; Alex Frangos and Eric Bellman, "China Slump Ripples Globally," *Wall Street Journal*, July 15, 2013; Nicholas Eberstadt, "The Demographic Future," *Foreign Affairs*, Vol. 89, No. 6, November/December 2010, pp. 54–64; and Nouriel Roubini, "Beijing's Empty Bullet Trains," *Slate*, April 14, 2011.

MyEconLab Study Plan

Your Turn: Test your understanding by doing related problems 5.4 and 5.5 on pages 385–386 at the end of this chapter.

Improving Health and Education

Recently, many economists have become convinced that poor health is a major impediment to growth in some countries. The research of the late Nobel Laureate Robert Fogel emphasizes the important interaction between health and economic growth (see Chapter 10). As people's health improves and they become stronger and less susceptible to diseases, they also become more productive. Recent initiatives in developing countries to increase vaccinations against infectious diseases, to improve access to treated water, and to improve sanitation have begun to reduce rates of illness and death.

We discussed earlier in this chapter Paul Romer's argument that there are increasing returns to knowledge capital. Nobel Laureate Robert Lucas of the University of Chicago similarly argues that there are increasing returns to *human* capital. Lucas argues that productivity increases as the total stock of human capital increases but that these productivity increases are not completely captured by individuals as they decide how much education to purchase. Therefore, the market may produce an inefficiently low level of education and training unless the government subsidizes education. Some researchers have been unable to find evidence of increasing returns to human capital, but many economists believe that government subsidies for education have played an important role in promoting economic growth.

The rising incomes that result from economic growth can help developing countries deal with the *brain drain*, which refers to highly educated and successful individuals leaving developing countries for high-income countries. This migration occurs when successful individuals believe that economic opportunities are very limited in the domestic economy. Rapid economic growth in India and China in recent years has resulted in more entrepreneurs, engineers, and scientists deciding to remain in those countries rather than leave for the United States or other high-income countries.   MyEconLab Concept Check

Policies That Promote Technological Change

One of the lessons of the economic growth model is that technological change is more important than increases in capital in explaining long-run growth. Government policies that facilitate access to technology are crucial for low-income countries. The easiest way for developing countries to gain access to technology is through foreign direct investment, where foreign firms are allowed to build new facilities or to buy domestic firms. Recent economic growth in India has been greatly aided by the Indian government's relaxation of regulations on foreign investment. Relaxing these regulations made it possible for India to gain access to the technology of Dell, Microsoft, and other multinational corporations.

In high-income countries, government policies can aid the growth of technology by subsidizing research and development. As we noted previously, in the United States, the federal government conducts some research and development on its own and also provides grants to researchers in universities. Tax breaks to firms undertaking research and development also facilitate technological change.   MyEconLab Concept Check

Policies That Promote Saving and Investment

Firms turn to the loanable funds market to finance expansion and research and development (see Chapter 10). Policies that increase the incentives to save and invest will increase the equilibrium level of loanable funds and may increase the level of real GDP per capita. For instance, governments can use tax incentives to increase saving. In the United States, many workers are able to save for retirement by placing funds in 401(k) or 403(b) plans or in Individual Retirement Accounts (IRAs). Income placed in these accounts is not taxed until it is withdrawn during retirement. Because the funds are allowed to accumulate tax-free, the return is increased, which raises the incentive to save.

Governments also increase incentives for firms to engage in investment in physical capital by using *investment tax credits*. Investment tax credits allow firms to deduct from their taxes some fraction of the funds they have spent on investment. Reductions in the taxes firms pay on their profits also increase the after-tax return on investments.   MyEconLab Concept Check

Is Economic Growth Good or Bad?

Although we didn't state so explicitly, in this chapter we have assumed that economic growth is desirable and that governments should undertake policies that will increase growth rates. It seems undeniable that increasing the growth rates of very low-income countries would help relieve the daily suffering that many people in those countries endure. But some people are unconvinced that, at least in the high-income countries, further economic growth is desirable.

The arguments against further economic growth reflect concern about the effects of growth on the environment or concern about the effects of the globalization process that has accompanied economic growth. In 1972, the Club of Rome published a controversial book titled *The Limits to Growth*, which predicted that economic growth would likely grind to a halt in the United States and other high-income countries because of increasing pollution and the depletion of natural resources, such as oil. Although these dire predictions have not yet come to pass, many people remain concerned that economic growth may be contributing to global warming, the destruction of rain forests, and other environmental problems.

In an earlier chapter, we discussed the opposition to globalization (see Chapter 7). We noted that some people believe that globalization has undermined the distinctive cultures of many countries, as imports of food, clothing, movies, and other goods have displaced domestically produced goods. We have seen that allowing foreign direct investment is an important way in which low-income countries can gain access to the latest technology. Some people, however, believe multinational firms behave unethically in low-income countries because they claim the firms pay very low wages and fail to follow the same safety and environmental regulations the firms are required to follow in high-income countries.

As with many other normative questions, economic analysis can contribute to the ongoing political debate over the consequences of economic growth, but it cannot settle the issue.

MyEconLab Study Plan   MyEconLab Concept Check

Continued from page 349

Economics in Your Life

Would You Be Better Off without China?

At the beginning of the chapter, we asked you to imagine that you could choose to live and work in a world with the Chinese economy growing very rapidly or in a world with the Chinese economy as it was before 1978—very poor and growing slowly. In which world would you choose to live? How does the current high-growth, high-export Chinese economy affect you as a consumer? How does it affect you as someone about to start a career?

It's impossible to walk into most stores in the United States without seeing products imported from China. Many of these products were at one time made in the United States. Imports from China replace domestically produced goods when the imports are either priced lower or have higher quality than the domestic goods they replace. Therefore, the rapid economic growth that has enabled Chinese firms to be competitive with firms in the United States has benefited you as a consumer: You have lower-priced goods and better goods available for purchase than you would if China had remained very poor. As you begin your career, there are some U.S. industries that, because of competition from Chinese firms, will have fewer jobs to offer. As we saw when discussing international trade, expanding trade changes the types of products each country makes, and, therefore, the types of jobs available, but it does not affect the total number of jobs (see Chapter 7). So, the economic rise of China will affect the mix of jobs available to you in the United States but will not make finding a job any more difficult.

Conclusion

For much of human history, most people have had to struggle to survive. Even today, a large fraction of the world's population lives in extreme poverty. The differences in living standards among countries today are a result of many decades of sharply different rates of economic growth. According to the economic growth model, increases in the quantity of capital per hour worked and increases in technology determine the growth in real GDP per hour worked and a country's standard of living. The keys to higher living standards seem straightforward:

1. Establish the rule of law.
2. Provide basic education and health care for the population.
3. Increase the amount of capital per hour worked.
4. Adopt the best technology.
5. Participate in the global economy.

However, for many countries, these policies have proved very difficult to implement.

Having discussed what determines the growth rate of economies, we will turn in the following chapters to the question of why economies experience short-run fluctuations in output, employment, and inflation.

Visit MyEconLab for a news article and analysis related to the concepts in this chapter.

CHAPTER SUMMARY AND PROBLEMS

Key Terms

Catch-up, p. 365

Economic growth model, p. 355

Foreign direct investment (FDI), p. 374

Foreign portfolio investment, p. 374

Globalization, p. 374

Human capital, p. 356

Industrial Revolution, p. 351

Labor productivity, p. 355

New growth theory, p. 360

Patent, p. 361

Per-worker production function, p. 356

Property rights, p. 371

Rule of law, p. 371

Technological change, p. 355

11.1 ## Economic Growth over Time and around the World, pages 350–355

LEARNING OBJECTIVE: Define economic growth, calculate economic growth rates, and describe global trends in economic growth.

Summary

For most of history, the average person survived with barely enough food. Living standards began to rise significantly only after the start of the **Industrial Revolution** in England in the 1700s, with the application of mechanical power to the production of goods. The best measure of a country's standard of living is its level of real GDP per capita. Economic growth occurs when real GDP per capita increases, thereby increasing the country's standard of living.

 MyEconLab Visit www.myeconlab.com to complete these exercises online and get instant feedback.

Review Questions

1.1 Why does a country's economic growth rate matter?

1.2 Explain the difference between the total percentage increase in real GDP between 2005 and 2015 and the average annual growth rate in real GDP between the same years.

Problems and Applications

1.3 **(Related to the** Making the Connection **on page 351)** Economists Carol Shiue and Wolfgang Keller of the University of Colorado published a study of "market efficiency" in the eighteenth century in England, other European countries, and China. If the markets in a country are efficient, a product should have the same price wherever in the country it is sold, allowing for the effect of transportation costs. If prices are not the same in two areas within a country, it is possible to make a profit by buying the product where its price is low and reselling it where its price is high. This trading will drive prices to equality. Trade is most likely to occur, however, if entrepreneurs feel confident that the government will not seize their gains and the courts will enforce contracts. Therefore, in the eighteenth century, the more efficient a country's markets, the more its institutions favored long-run growth. Shiue and Keller found that in 1770, the efficiency of markets in England was significantly greater than the

efficiency of markets elsewhere in Europe and in China. How does this finding relate to Douglass North's argument concerning why the Industrial Revolution occurred in England?

Source: Carol H. Shiue and Wolfgang Keller, "Markets in China and Europe on the Eve of the Industrial Revolution," *American Economic Review*, Vol. 97, No. 4, September 2007, pp. 1189–1216.

1.4 Use the data on real GDP in the following table to answer the following questions. The values are measured in each country's domestic currency. The base year for Brazil is 1995; the base year for Mexico is 2008; and the base year for Thailand is 1988.

Country	2011	2012	2013	2014
Brazil	1,192	1,213	1,247	1,248
Mexico	12,774	13,286	13,471	13,757
Thailand	4,600	4,898	5,040	5,076

a. Which country experienced the highest rate of economic growth during 2012 (that is, for which country did real GDP increase the most from 2011 to 2012)?

b. Which country experienced the highest average annual growth rate between 2012 and 2014?

c. Does it matter for your answers to parts (a) and (b) that each country's real GDP is measured in a different currency and uses a different base year? Briefly explain.

Source: International Monetary Fund, *World Economic Outlook Database*, April 2015.

1.5 Andover Bank and Lowell Bank each sell one-year certificates of deposit (CDs). The interest rates on these CDs are given in the following table for a three-year period.

Bank	2016	2017	2018
Andover Bank	5%	5%	5%
Lowell Bank	2%	6%	7%

Suppose you deposit $1,000 in a CD in each bank at the beginning of 2016. At the end of 2016, you take your $1,000 and any interest earned and invest it in a CD for the following year. You do this again at the end of 2017. At the end of 2018, will you have earned more on your Andover Bank CDs or on your Lowell Bank CDs? Briefly explain.

1.6 **(Related to the** Don't Let This Happen to You **on page 353)** Use the data for the United States in this table to answer the following questions.

Year	Real GDP per Capita (2009 prices)
2010	$47,719
2011	48,116
2012	48,822
2013	49,184
2014	50,010

a. What was the percentage change in real GDP per capita between 2010 and 2014?

b. What was the average annual growth rate in real GDP per capita between 2010 and 2014? (*Hint:* Remember that the average annual growth rate for relatively short periods can be approximated by averaging the growth rates for each year during the period [see Chapter 10].)

1.7 **(Related to the** Making the Connection **on page 354)** In his book *The White Man's Burden*, William Easterly reports:

A vaccination campaign in southern Africa virtually eliminated measles as a killer of children. Routine childhood immunization combined with measles vaccination in seven southern African nations starting in 1996 virtually eliminated measles in those countries by 2000. A national campaign in Egypt to make parents aware of the use of oral rehydration therapy from 1982 to 1989 cut childhood deaths from diarrhea by 82 percent over that period.

a. Is it likely that real GDP per capita increased significantly in southern Africa and Egypt as a result of the near elimination of measles and the large decrease in childhood deaths from diarrhea? If these events did not increase real GDP per capita, is it still possible that they increased the standard of living in southern Africa and Egypt? Briefly explain.

b. Which seems more achievable for a developing country: the elimination of measles and childhood deaths from diarrhea or sustained increases in real GDP per capita? Briefly explain.

Source: William Easterly, *The White Man's Burden: Why the West's Efforts to Aid the Rest Have Done So Much Ill and So Little Good*, New York: The Penguin Press, 2006, p. 241.

1.8 **(Related to the** Making the Connection **on page 354)** Economist Charles Kenny of the Center for Global Development has argued:

The process technologies—institutions like laws and inventory management systems—that appear central to raising incomes per capita flow less like water and more like bricks. But ideas and inventions—the importance of [education] and vaccines for DPT—really might flow more easily across borders and over distances.

If Kenny is correct, what are the implications of these facts for the ability of low-income countries to rapidly increase their rates of growth of real GDP per capita in the decades ahead? What are the implications for the ability of these countries to increase their standards of living? Briefly explain.

Source: Charles Kenny, *Getting Better*, New York: Basic Books, 2011, p. 117.

11.2 **What Determines How Fast Economies Grow? pages 355–362**

LEARNING OBJECTIVE: Use the economic growth model to explain why growth rates differ across countries.

Summary

An **economic growth model** explains changes in real GDP per capita in the long run. **Labor productivity** is the quantity of goods and services that can be produced by one worker or by one hour of work. Economic growth depends on increases in labor productivity. Labor productivity will increase if there is an increase in the amount of *capital* available to each worker or if there is an improvement in *technology*. **Technological change** is a change in the ability of a firm to produce a given level of output with a given quantity of inputs. There are three main sources of technological change: better machinery and equipment, increases in human capital, and better means of organizing and managing production. **Human capital** is the accumulated knowledge and skills that workers acquire from education and training or from their life experiences. We can say that an economy will have a higher standard of living the more capital it has per hour worked, the more human capital its workers have, the better its capital, and the better the job its business managers do in organizing production.

The **per-worker production function** shows the relationship between capital per hour worked and output per hour worked, holding technology constant. *Diminishing returns to capital* means that increases in the quantity of capital per hour worked will result in diminishing increases in output per hour worked. Technological change shifts up the per-worker production function, resulting in more output per hour worked at every level of capital per hour worked. The economic growth model stresses the importance of changes in capital per hour worked and technological change in explaining growth in output per hour worked. **New growth theory** is a model of long-run economic growth that emphasizes that technological change is influenced by how individuals and firms respond to economic incentives.

One way governments can promote technological change is by granting **patents**, which are exclusive rights to a product for a period of 20 years from the date the patent is filed with the government. To Joseph Schumpeter, the entrepreneur is central to the "creative destruction" by which the standard of living increases as qualitatively better products replace existing products.

MyEconLab   Visit **www.myeconlab.com** to complete these exercises online and get instant feedback.

Review Questions

2.1 Using the per-worker production function graph from Figures 11.3 and 11.4 on pages 356 and 358, show the effect on real GDP per hour worked of an increase in capital per hour worked, holding technology constant. Now, again using the per-worker production function graph, show the effect on real GDP per hour worked of an increase in technology, holding constant the quantity of capital per hour worked.

2.2 What are the consequences for growth of diminishing returns to capital? How are some economies able to maintain high growth rates despite diminishing returns to capital?

2.3 What is the *new growth theory*? How does the new growth theory differ from the growth theory developed by Robert Solow?

2.4 Why are firms likely to underinvest in research and development? Briefly discuss three ways in which government policy can increase the accumulation of knowledge capital.

2.5 Why does knowledge capital experience increasing returns at the economy level while physical capital experiences decreasing returns?

Problems and Applications

2.6 Which of the following will result in a movement along China's per-worker production function, and which will result in a shift of China's per-worker production function? Briefly explain.

a. Capital per hour worked increases from 200 yuan per hour worked to 250 yuan per hour worked.

b. The Chinese government doubles its spending on support for university research.

c. A reform of the Chinese school system results in more highly trained Chinese workers.

2.7 (Related to the Making the Connection **on page 358)** The *Making the Connection* emphasizes that a key difference between market economies and centrally planned economies, like that of the former Soviet Union, is as follows:

> In market economies, entrepreneurs and managers who have their own money on the line make decisions about which investments to make and which technologies to adopt. Nothing concentrates the mind like having your own funds at risk.

But in large corporations, investment decisions are often made by salaried managers who do not have their own money on the line. These managers are spending the money of the firm's shareholders rather than their own money. Why, then, do the investment decisions of salaried managers in the United States tend to be better for the long-term growth of the economy than were the decisions of salaried bureaucrats in the Soviet Union?

2.8 (Related to Solved Problem 11.2 **on page 359)** Use the following graph to answer the questions. In each case, briefly explain your answer.

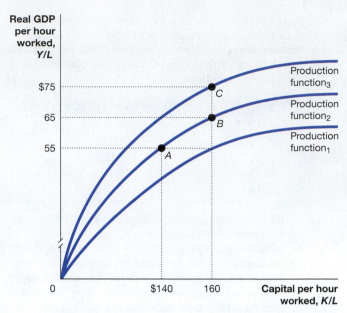

a. True or false: The movement from point A to point B shows the effects of technological change.

b. True or false: The economy can move from point B to point C only if there are no diminishing returns to capital.

c. True or false: To move from point A to point C, the economy must increase the amount of capital per hour worked *and* experience technological change.

2.9 (Related to Solved Problem 11.2 **on page 359)** If the per-worker production function were shaped as shown in the following graph, what would be the implications for economic growth of a country that was accumulating increasing quantities of capital per hour worked? Briefly explain.

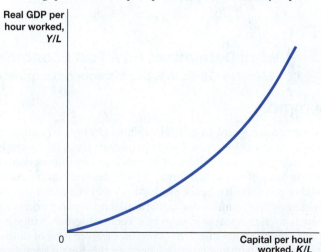

2.10 (Related to Solved Problem 11.2 **on page 359)** Shortly before the fall of the Soviet Union, the economist Gur Ofer of Hebrew University of Jerusalem wrote, "The most outstanding characteristic of Soviet growth strategy is its consistent policy of very high rates of investment, leading to a rapid growth rate of [the] capital stock." Explain why this economic growth strategy turned out to be a very poor one.

Source: Gur Ofer, "Soviet Economic Growth, 1928–1985," *Journal of Economic Literature*, Vol. 25, No. 4, December 1987, p. 1,784.

2.11 People who live in rural areas often have less access to capital and, as a result, their productivity is lower on average than the productivity of people who live in cities. An article in the *New York Times* quotes a financial analyst as arguing that "the core driver" of economic growth in China "is the simple process of urbanization."

a. What does the analyst mean by the "process of urbanization"?

b. If the analyst is correct that urbanization is the core driver of economic growth in China, would we expect that China will be able to continue to experience high rates of economic growth in the long run? Briefly explain.

Source: Neil Irwin, "China Will Keep Growing. Just Ask the Soviets," *New York Times*, October 24, 2014.

2.12 Why is the role of entrepreneurs much more important in the new growth theory than in the traditional economic growth model?

11.3 ## Economic Growth in the United States, pages 362–365

LEARNING OBJECTIVE: Discuss fluctuations in productivity growth in the United States.

Summary

Productivity in the United States grew rapidly from the end of World War II until the mid-1970s. Growth then slowed down for 20 years before increasing again for a decade after 1995. Growth has slowed again during the most recent period. Economists debate whether this growth slowdown will be long-lived or whether the U.S. economy will return to the faster growth rates of earlier years.

MyEconLab   Visit **www.myeconlab.com** to complete these exercises online and get instant feedback.

Review Questions

3.1 Describe the record of productivity growth in the United States from 1800 to the present.

3.2 Briefly describe the debate among economists over how high U.S. productivity growth rates are likely to be in the future.

Problems and Applications

3.3 Figure 11.5 on page 362 shows growth rates in real GDP per hour worked in the United States for various periods from 1800 onward. How might the growth rates in the figure be different if they were calculated for real GDP *per capita* instead of per hour worked? (*Hint:* How do you think the number of hours worked per person has changed in the United States since 1800?)

3.4 A column in the *Wall Street Journal* considers two observations about the U.S. economy: "We live in an era of accelerating technological progress. …" and "In the years since the recession … the economy has been growing very slowly." The writer concludes that "Both statements can't be completely correct." Do you agree with this conclusion? Briefly explain.

Source: Josh Zumbrun, "Goldman Sachs and J.P. Morgan Can't Agree Why the Economy's Productivity Has Slumped," *Wall Street Journal*, June 16, 2015.

3.5 Economist Robert Gordon of Northwestern University has argued:

My interpretation of the [information] revolution is that it is increasingly burdened by diminishing returns. The push to ever smaller devices runs up against the fixed size of the human finger that must enter information on the device. Most of the innovations since 2000 have been directed to consumer enjoyment rather than business productivity, including video games, DVD players, and iPods. iPhones are nice, but the ability to reschedule business meetings and look up corporate documents while on the road already existed by 2003.

If Gordon's observations about the information revolution are correct, what are the implications for future labor productivity growth rates in the United States?

Source: Robert J. Gordon, "Revisiting U.S. Productivity Growth over the Past Century with a View of the Future," National Bureau of Economic Research, Working Paper 15834, March 2010.

3.6 Some economists argue that the apparent slowdown in productivity growth in the United States in recent years is a measurement problem resulting from the failure of GDP to capture the effects of many recent innovations, such as cloud computing. James Manyika, head of technology at McKinsey & Company, argues that for many of these innovations, "we have all these benefits but we're not paying for them."

a. Before the arrival of the Internet, people looking for facts, such as the population of France or the salary of the president of the United States, had to go to the library to look them up. Now people can find that information in a few seconds with a Google search. Are the benefits to you of being able to do a Google search included in GDP? Briefly explain.

b. Does your answer to part (a) indicate that the slowdown in U.S. productivity growth in recent years is just a measurement problem? What other information would you need to arrive at a definite answer?

Source: Timothy Aeppel, "Silicon Valley Doesn't Believe U.S. Productivity Is Down," *Wall Street Journal*, July 16, 2015.

11.4 ## Why Isn't the Whole World Rich? pages 365–374

LEARNING OBJECTIVE: Explain economic catch-up and discuss why many poor countries have not experienced rapid economic growth.

Summary

The economic growth model predicts that poor countries will grow faster than rich countries, resulting in **catch-up**. In recent decades, some poor countries have grown faster than rich countries, but many have not. Some poor countries have not experienced rapid growth for four main reasons: wars and revolutions, poor public education and health, failure to enforce the rule of law, and low rates of saving and investment. The **rule of law** refers to the ability of a government to enforce the laws of the country, particularly with respect to protecting **property rights** and enforcing contracts. **Globalization** has aided countries that have opened their economies to foreign trade and investment. **Foreign direct investment (FDI)** is the purchase or building by a corporation of a facility in a foreign country. **Foreign portfolio investment** is the purchase by an individual or firm of stocks or bonds issued in another country.

MyEconLab   Visit **www.myeconlab.com** to complete these exercises online and get instant feedback.

Review Questions

4.1 Why does the economic growth model predict that poor countries should catch up to rich countries in real GDP per capita? Have poor countries been catching up to rich countries?

4.2 What are the main reasons many poor countries have experienced slow growth?

4.3 What does *globalization* mean? How have developing countries benefited from globalization?

Problems and Applications

4.4 **(Related to** Solved Problem 11.4 **on page 368)** Briefly explain whether the statistics in the following table are consistent with the economic growth model's predictions of catch-up.

Country	Real GDP per Capita, 1960 (2005 dollars)	Growth in Real GDP per Capita, 1960–2011
China	$331	6.66%
Uganda	657	1.37
Madagascar	1,051	−0.23
Ireland	7,223	3.25
United States	15,398	2.02

Source: Authors' calculations from data in *Penn World Table Version 8.1*; Robert C. Feenstra, Robert Inklaar, and Marcel P. Timmer, "The Next Generation of the Penn World Table" www.ggdc.net/pwt, April 2015.

4.5 **(Related to** Solved Problem 11.4 **on page 368)** In the following graph, each dot represents a particular country's initial level of real GDP per capita and its growth rate of real GDP per capita.

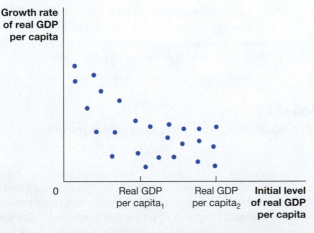

a. For the range of initial GDP per capita from 0 to Real GDP per capita$_2$, does the figure support the economic growth model's prediction of catch-up? Briefly explain.

b. For the range of initial GDP per capita from 0 to Real GDP per capita$_1$, does the figure support the catch-up prediction? Briefly explain.

c. For the range from initial Real GDP per capita$_1$ to Real GDP per capita$_2$, does the figure support the catch-up prediction? Briefly explain.

4.6 Refer to Figures 11.7–11.9 on pages 367 and 369. The lines in the following three graphs show the average relationship between the initial level of real GDP per capita and the growth rate of real GDP per capita for three groups of countries over a given time period. Match each group of countries with the graph that best depicts the relationship between the initial level of real GDP per capita and the growth rate of real GDP per capita for that group.

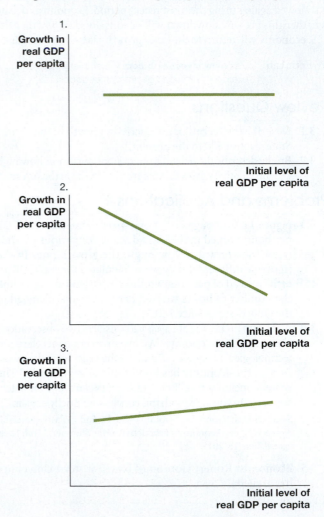

a. All countries for which statistics are available, 1960–2011

b. United States, Western Europe, Canada, and Japan, 1990–2014

c. Current high-income countries, 1960–2011

4.7 An article in the *New York Times* notes that since 2001 Italy has had the lowest rate of growth in labor productivity among European countries that use the euro common currency. The article quoted Italy's economy minister as saying, "The real tragedy for Italy is falling productivity." At the time the minister made these remarks, the unemployment rate in Italy was greater than 12 percent—more than twice the rate in Germany, the United Kingdom, or the United States. Despite the high unemployment rate, why might Italy's economy minister call low productivity growth rates "the real tragedy"?

Source: Reuters, "Italy Economy Minister Warns Deflation Would Be 'Disaster,'" *New York Times*, May 31, 2014.

4.8 (Related to the Making the Connection on page 371) A study by the McKinsey Global Institute reported that labor productivity increased at an average annual rate of 5.8 percent between 1999 and 2013 in Mexico's large companies, but it fell at an average annual rate of 6.5 percent over the same period for its smaller firms, such as family-owned stores and bakeries. Briefly explain why productivity growth would be much higher for Mexico's largest companies than for its smaller companies.

Source: Anthony Harrup, "Two Economies Explain Mexico's Productivity Quandary," *Wall Street Journal*, March 27, 2014.

4.9 (Related to the Making the Connection on page 371) In 2014, real GDP per capita in Mexico increased by 0.9 percent. A Mexican economist was quoted in an article in the *Wall Street Journal* as saying, "It's clearly insufficient if we want to significantly reduce poverty and move Mexico toward a middle-class country."

a. Given that growth rate, how long would it take the standard of living of the average person in Mexico to double?

b. Why isn't the Mexican economy growing more rapidly?

Source: Juan Montes, "Mexican Economy Expanded Modestly in 2014," *Wall Street Journal*, February 20, 2015.

4.10 In 2015, President Barack Obama was quoted in an article in the *Wall Street Journal* as warning against "rising anti-globalization sentiment," which the president called "a big mistake."

a. What did President Obama mean by "anti-globalization sentiment"?

b. Why might he have considered such sentiment to be a big mistake for the U.S. economy?

c. Is there an argument to be made that globalization hurts rather than helps the U.S. economy? Briefly explain.

Source: Gerald F. Seib, "Obama Presses Case for Asia Trade Deal, Warns Failure Would Benefit China," *Wall Street Journal*, April 27, 2015.

4.11 A columnist in the *New York Times* observes that "many analysts agree that economic reform, of which integration into the global economy was a key element, has lifted millions of people out of poverty in India." What does "integration into the global economy" mean? How might integration into the global economy reduce poverty in India?

Source: Vivek Dehejia, "Has Globalization Helped India's Poor?" *New York Times*, October 7, 2011.

4.12 The Roman Empire lasted from 27 B.C. to A.D. 476. The empire was wealthy enough to build such monuments as the Roman Coliseum. Roman engineering skill was at a level high enough that aqueducts built during the empire to carry water long distances remained in use for hundreds of years. Yet, although the empire experienced some periods of growth in real GDP per capita, these periods did not last, and there is little evidence that growth would have been sustained even if the empire had survived. Why didn't the Roman Empire experience sustained economic growth? What would the world be like today if it had? (*Note:* There are no definite answers to these questions; they are intended to get you to think about the preconditions for economic growth. Looking beyond this problem, if you are interested in the macroeconomics of the Roman economy, see Peter Temin, *The Roman Market Economy*, Princeton: Princeton University Press, 2013, Chapters 9–11.)

11.5 **Growth Policies, pages 374–379**

LEARNING OBJECTIVE: Discuss government policies that foster economic growth.

Summary

Governments can attempt to increase economic growth through policies that enhance property rights and the rule of law, improve health and education, subsidize research and development, and provide incentives for saving and investment. Whether continued economic growth is desirable is a normative question that cannot be settled by economic analysis.

MyEconLab   Visit **www.myeconlab.com** to complete these exercises online and get instant feedback.

Review Questions

5.1 Briefly describe three government policies that can increase economic growth.

5.2 Can economic analysis arrive at the conclusion that economic growth will always improve economic well-being? Briefly explain.

Problems and Applications

5.3 (Related to the Chapter Opener on page 349) An article on the Mexican economy in the *Economist* notes, "A huge, unproductive informal sector and general lawlessness also drag the economy down." If these factors were the main barriers to more rapid economic growth in Mexico, would that be good news or bad news for the Mexican government's attempts to increase its economy's growth rate? Briefly explain.

Source: "The 100-Year View," *Economist*, May 2, 2015.

5.4 (Related to the Making the Connection on page 375) In China, why may a lower birth rate lead to slower growth in real GDP per capita? Why might high levels of spending on investment in China lead to high rates of growth in the short run but not in the long run?

5.5 **(Related to the** Making the Connection **on page 375)** Pranab Bardhan, an economist at the University of California, Berkeley, argues: "China may be close to exhausting the possibilities of technological catch-up with the West, particularly in manufacturing."
   a. What does Bardhan mean by "technological catch-up"?
   b. If Bardhan is correct, what problems might the Chinese economy encounter in the future?
   c. Briefly discuss the similarities and differences between the Chinese economy today and the Soviet economy in the 1980s.

Source: Pranab Bardhan, "The Slowing of Two Economic Giants," *New York Times*, July 14, 2013.

5.6 Briefly explain which of the following policies are likely to increase the rate of economic growth in the United States.
   a. Congress passes an investment tax credit, which reduces a firm's taxes if it installs new machinery and equipment.
   b. Congress passes a law that allows taxpayers to reduce their income taxes by the amount of state sales taxes they pay.
   c. Congress provides more funds for low-interest loans to college students.

5.7 In an interview on PBS about economic development in Africa, economist George Ayettey stated that of the 54 African countries, only 8 had a free press. For Africa's economic development, Ayittey argued strongly for the establishment of a free press. Why would a free press be vital for the enhancement of property rights and the rule of law? How could a free press help reduce corruption?

Source: George Ayittey, *Border Jumpers*, Anchor Interview Transcript, WideAngle, PBS.org, July 24, 2005.

5.8 More people in high-income countries than in low-income countries tend to believe that rapid rates of economic growth are not desirable. Recall the concept of a "normal good" (see Chapter 3). Does this concept provide insight into why some people in high-income countries might be more concerned with certain consequences of rapid economic growth than are people in low-income countries?

Real-Time Data Exercises

D11.1 (Analyzing labor productivity) Using data from the St. Louis Federal Reserve (FRED) (research.stlouisfed.org/ fred2/), analyze the relationship between labor productivity in the manufacturing sector and in the non-farm business sector as a whole.
   a. Download data since 1987 on output per hour of all persons in the manufacturing sector (OPHMFG) and in the non-farm business sector (OPHNFB).
   b. Which has increased more since 1987, labor productivity in manufacturing or in the non-farm business sector?
   c. The manufacturing sector has been shrinking relative to the size of the economy in the United States and other advanced economies. What do your results imply about future labor productivity growth in advanced economies?

D11.2 (Comparing labor productivity across countries) Using data from the St. Louis Federal Reserve (FRED) (research. stlouisfed.org/fred2/), analyze differences in labor productivity among China, India, and the United States.
   a. From 1952 to the present, chart the following series on the same graph: real GDP per worker for China (RGDPL2CNA627NUPN), real GDP per worker for India (RGDPLWINA627NUPN), and real GDP per worker for the United States (RGDPLWUSA627NUPN). To chart the series on the same graph follow these steps: (1) On the page for real GDP per worker for China, click on the "Edit graph" link under the graph; (2) on the bottom of the next page, click on the "Add Data Series" link; (3) search for the other two series and click on them to add them to your graph.
   b. Calculate the relative productivity of workers in China and the United States by dividing U.S. labor productivity by China's labor productivity. Describe the change in this measure of relative productivity since 1952.
   c. Repeat part (b) for the United States and India.

D11.3 (The U.S. economy in a world context) The U.S. Central Intelligence Agency's World Factbook (https://www.cia. gov/library/publications/the-world-factbook/) offers many comparative tables of world data. Go to this site and find the following:
   a. The countries with the highest and lowest real GDPs
   b. The countries with the highest and lowest per capita real GDPs, adjusted for purchasing power
   c. The countries with the most equal and least equal income distributions
   d. The countries with the highest and lowest real GDP growth rates
   e. The rank of the United States in these categories

Aggregate Expenditure and Output in the Short Run

Chapter Outline and **Learning Objectives**

Fluctuating Demand Helps—and Hurts—Intel and Other Firms

Robert Noyce and Gordon Moore founded Intel in 1968. Today, the company is the world's largest semiconductor manufacturer and a major supplier of the microprocessors and memory chips that power desktop and laptop computers sold by Dell, Apple, Lenovo, Hewlett-Packard, and other computer manufacturers.

To this point, Intel's success has depended on the health of the computer market. As a result, the firm faces two problems: First, in the past few years, sales of computers have declined because many consumers and some businesses have switched to using tablets and smartphones to access the Internet. Second, Intel is vulnerable to the swings of the business cycle because sales of computers rise during economic expansions and fall during recessions. Intel was particularly hurt by the 2007–2009 recession. During the last quarter of 2008, Intel's revenues fell 90 percent, and the firm laid off 6,000 workers. Conditions improved for the firm beginning in 2010, as the U.S. economy recovered from the recession, although the firm was still struggling to reduce its dependence on selling chips to computer manufacturers. In 2015, Intel decided to lay off several hundred employees because businesses were only slowly increasing spending on computers and other information processing equipment.

The recovery from the 2007–2009 recession was by some measures the weakest since the end of World War II in 1945. By 2015, though, some industries were prospering. For example, sales of automobiles reached pre-recession levels. However, other industries still struggled. A weak recovery in spending by businesses on factories, office buildings, and other structures was bad news for some firms, including steelmakers. Worthington Industries, an Ohio-based steelmaker, announced that it would lay off 555 employees in 2015. Other U.S. steel companies also suffered from sluggish domestic and foreign demand. "Clearly, this is a rough patch," said Christopher Plummer, president and CEO of Metal Strategies.

These firms were dealing with changes in total spending, or *aggregate expenditure*. In this chapter, we will explore how changes in aggregate expenditure affect the level of total production in the economy.

Sources: Don Clark and Angela Chen, "Intel President Renée James to Leave as Others Also Depart," *Wall Street Journal*, July 2, 2015; Dan Gearino, "Worthington Industries to lay off 555 nationwide, including 80 in Fairfield County," *Columbus Dispatch*, March 25, 2015; John Carney, "Raising the Roof on Home Sales," *Wall Street Journal*, June 29, 2015; and Don Clark, "The Lawmaker: How Gordon Moore Predicted the Digital Revolution," *Wall Street Journal*, April 17, 2015.

Economics in Your Life

When Consumer Confidence Falls, Is Your Job at Risk?

Suppose that while attending college, you work part time at a company that manufactures door handles that it sells to automobile companies. One morning, you read in a news story online that consumer confidence in the economy has fallen, and, as a result, many households expect their future income to be well below their current income. Should you be concerned about losing your job? What factors should you consider in deciding how likely your company is to lay you off? As you read this chapter, try to answer these questions. You can check your answers against those we provide on **page 423** at the end of this chapter.

Aggregate expenditure (AE) Total spending in the economy: the sum of consumption, planned investment, government purchases, and net exports.

I n Chapter 11, we discussed the determinants of long-run growth in the economy. We now turn to exploring the causes of the business cycle. We begin by examining the effect of changes in total spending on real gross domestic product (GDP).

During some years, total spending in the economy, or **aggregate expenditure (AE)**, and total production of goods and services increase by the same amount. In this case, most firms will sell about as much as they expected to sell, and they probably will not increase or decrease production or the number of workers they hire. During other years, total spending in the economy increases more than the production of goods and services. In those years, firms will increase production and hire more workers. But there are times, such as 2008 and early 2009, when total spending does not increase as much as total production. As a result, firms cut back on production and lay off workers, and the economy moves into a recession. In this chapter, we will explore why changes in total spending play such an important role in the economy.

12.1 The Aggregate Expenditure Model

LEARNING OBJECTIVE: Understand how macroeconomic equilibrium is determined in the aggregate expenditure model.

The business cycle involves the interaction of many economic variables. A simple model called the *aggregate expenditure model* can help us understand the relationships among some of these variables. Recall that GDP is the value of all the final goods and services produced in an economy during a particular year. Real GDP corrects nominal GDP for the effects of inflation. The **aggregate expenditure model** focuses on the short-run relationship between total spending and real GDP. An important assumption of the model is that the price level is constant. In Chapter 13, we will develop a more complete model of the business cycle that relaxes the assumption of constant prices.

The key idea of the aggregate expenditure model is that *in any particular year, the level of GDP is determined mainly by the level of aggregate expenditure.* To understand the relationship between aggregate expenditure and real GDP, we need to look more closely at the components of aggregate expenditure.

Aggregate expenditure model A macroeconomic model that focuses on the short-run relationship between total spending and real GDP, assuming that the price level is constant.

Aggregate Expenditure

Economists first began to study the relationship between changes in aggregate expenditure and changes in GDP during the Great Depression of the 1930s. The United States, the United Kingdom, and other industrial countries suffered declines in real GDP of 20 percent or more during the early 1930s. In 1936, the English economist John Maynard Keynes published a book, *The General Theory of Employment, Interest, and Money*, that systematically analyzed the relationship between changes in aggregate expenditure and changes in GDP. Keynes identified four components of aggregate expenditure that together equal GDP (these are the same four components we discussed in Chapter 8):

- *Consumption (C).* Spending by households on goods and services, such as automobiles and haircuts.

- *Planned investment (I).* Planned spending by firms on capital goods, such as factories, office buildings, and machine tools, and on research and development, and spending by households and firms on new houses.

- *Government purchases (G).* Spending by local, state, and federal governments on goods and services, such as aircraft carriers, bridges, and the salaries of FBI agents.

- *Net exports (NX).* Spending by foreign firms and households on goods and services produced in the United States minus spending by U.S. firms and households on goods and services produced in other countries.

So, we can write:

$$\text{Aggregate expenditure} = \text{Consumption} + \text{Planned investment}$$
$$+ \text{Government purchases} + \text{Net exports,}$$

or:

$$AE = C + I + G + NX.$$

Governments around the world gather statistics on aggregate expenditure on the basis of these four components. And economists and business analysts usually explain changes in GDP in terms of changes in these four components of spending.   MyEconLab Concept Check

The Difference between Planned Investment and Actual Investment

Before considering further the relationship between aggregate expenditure and GDP, we need to consider an important distinction: Notice that *planned* investment spending, rather than actual investment spending, is a component of aggregate expenditure. You might wonder how the amount that businesses plan to spend on investment can be different from the amount they actually spend. We can begin resolving this puzzle by remembering that goods that have been produced but have not yet been sold are referred to as **inventories**. Changes in inventories are included as part of investment spending, along with spending on machinery, equipment, office buildings, and factories. We assume that the amount businesses plan to spend on machinery and office buildings is equal to the amount they actually spend, but the amount businesses plan to spend on inventories may be different from the amount they actually spend.

Inventories Goods that have been produced but not yet sold.

For example, Doubleday Publishing may print 1.5 million copies of the latest John Grisham novel, expecting to sell them all. If Doubleday does sell all 1.5 million, its inventories will be unchanged, but if it sells only 1.2 million, it will have an unplanned increase in inventories. In other words, changes in inventories depend on sales of goods, which firms cannot always forecast with perfect accuracy.

For the economy as a whole, we can say that actual investment spending will be greater than planned investment spending when there is an unplanned increase in inventories. Actual investment spending will be less than planned investment spending when there is an unplanned decrease in inventories. *Therefore, actual investment will equal planned investment only when there is no unplanned change in inventories.* In this chapter, we will use I to represent planned investment. We will also assume that the government data on investment spending compiled by the U.S. Bureau of Economic Analysis represents planned investment spending. This assumption is a simplification, however, because the government collects data on actual investment spending, which equals planned investment spending only when unplanned changes in inventories are zero.   MyEconLab Concept Check

Macroeconomic Equilibrium

Macroeconomic equilibrium is similar to microeconomic equilibrium. In microeconomics, equilibrium in the apple market occurs when the quantity of apples demanded equals the quantity of apples supplied. When the apple market is in equilibrium, the quantity of apples produced and sold will not change unless the demand for apples or the supply of apples changes. For the economy as a whole, macroeconomic equilibrium occurs when total spending, or aggregate expenditure, equals total production, or GDP:

$$\text{Aggregate expenditure} = \text{GDP.}$$

As we have seen, over the *long run*, real GDP in the United States increases, and the standard of living rises (see Chapter 11). In this chapter, we are interested in understanding why GDP fluctuates in the *short run*. To simplify the analysis of macroeconomic equilibrium, we assume that the economy is not growing. In Chapter 13, we will discuss the more realistic case of macroeconomic equilibrium in a growing economy. If we assume that the economy is not growing, then equilibrium GDP will not change unless aggregate expenditure changes.

MyEconLab Concept Check

Adjustments to Macroeconomic Equilibrium

The apple market isn't always in equilibrium because sometimes the quantity of apples demanded is greater than the quantity supplied, and sometimes the quantity supplied is greater than the quantity demanded. The same outcome holds for the economy as a whole. Sometimes the economy is in macroeconomic equilibrium, and sometimes it isn't. When aggregate expenditure is greater than GDP, the total amount of spending in the economy is greater than the total amount of production. With spending being greater than production, many businesses will sell more goods and services than they had expected to sell. For example, the manager of a Home Depot store might like to keep 50 refrigerators in stock to give customers the opportunity to see a variety of different sizes and models. If sales are unexpectedly high, the store may have only 20 refrigerators in stock. In that case, the store will have an unplanned decrease in inventories: Its inventory of refrigerators will decline by 30.

How will the store manager react when more refrigerators are sold than expected? The manager is likely to order more refrigerators. If other stores selling refrigerators are experiencing similar sales increases and are also increasing their orders, then Whirlpool, KitchenAid, and other refrigerator manufacturers will significantly increase their production. These manufacturers may also increase the number of workers they hire. If the increase in sales is affecting not just refrigerators but also other appliances, automobiles, furniture, and other goods and services, then GDP and total employment will begin to increase. In summary, *when aggregate expenditure is greater than GDP, inventories will decline, and GDP and total employment will increase.*

Now suppose that aggregate expenditure is less than GDP. With spending being less than production, many businesses will sell fewer goods and services than they had expected to sell, so their inventories will increase. For example, the manager of the Home Depot store who wants 50 refrigerators in stock may find that because of slow sales, the store has 75 refrigerators, so the store manager will cut back on orders for new refrigerators. If other stores also cut back on their orders, General Electric and Whirlpool will reduce production and lay off workers.

If the decrease in sales is affecting not just refrigerators but also many other goods and services, GDP and total employment will begin to decrease. Falling sales followed by reductions in production and employment occurred at many firms during 2008. In summary, *when aggregate expenditure is less than GDP, inventories will increase, and GDP and total employment will decrease.*

Only when aggregate expenditure equals GDP will firms sell what they expected to sell. In that case, their inventories will be unchanged, and they will not have an incentive to increase or decrease production. The economy will be in macroeconomic equilibrium. Table 12.1 summarizes the relationship between aggregate expenditure and GDP.

Increases and decreases in aggregate expenditure cause the year-to-year changes we see in GDP. Economists devote considerable time and energy to forecasting what will happen to each component of aggregate expenditure. If economists forecast that

Table 12.1

The Relationship between Aggregate Expenditure and GDP

If . . .	then . . .	and . . .
aggregate expenditure is *equal* to GDP	inventories are *unchanged*	the economy is in *macroeconomic equilibrium.*
aggregate expenditure is *less* than GDP	inventories *rise*	GDP and employment *decrease.*
aggregate expenditure is *greater* than GDP	inventories *fall*	GDP and employment *increase.*

aggregate expenditure will decline in the future, that is equivalent to forecasting that GDP will decline and that the economy will enter a recession. Firms, policymakers, and individuals closely watch these forecasts because changes in GDP can have dramatic consequences. When GDP is increasing, so are wages, profits, and job opportunities. Declining GDP can be bad news for workers, firms, and job seekers.

When economists forecast that aggregate expenditure is likely to decline and that the economy is headed for a recession, the federal government may implement *macroeconomic policies* in an attempt to head off the decrease in expenditure and keep the economy from falling into recession. We will discuss these macroeconomic policies in Chapters 15 and 16.   MyEconLab Concept Check   MyEconLab Study Plan

12.2 Determining the Level of Aggregate Expenditure in the Economy

LEARNING OBJECTIVE: Discuss the determinants of the four components of aggregate expenditure and define marginal propensity to consume and marginal propensity to save.

To better understand how macroeconomic equilibrium is determined in the aggregate expenditure model, we look more closely at the components of aggregate expenditure. Table 12.2 lists the four components of aggregate expenditure for 2014. The components are measured in *real* terms, which means that their values are corrected for inflation by being measured in billions of 2009 dollars. Consumption is clearly the largest component of aggregate expenditure. Investment and government purchases are of roughly similar size. Net exports was negative because in 2014, as in most years since the early 1970s, the United States imported more goods and services than it exported. Next, we consider the variables that determine each of the four components of aggregate expenditure.

Consumption

Figure 12.1 shows movements in real consumption from 1979 through the second quarter of 2015. Notice that consumption follows a smooth, upward trend. Only during periods of recession does the growth in consumption decline.

Here are the five most important variables that determine the level of consumption:

1. Current disposable income
2. Household wealth
3. Expected future income
4. The price level
5. The interest rate

Next we discuss how changes in each of these variables affect consumption.

Current Disposable Income The most important determinant of consumption is the current disposable income of households. Recall that disposable income is the income remaining to households after they have paid the personal income tax and received government *transfer payments*, such as Social Security payments (see Chapter 8). For most households, the higher their disposable income, the more they spend, and the lower their income, the less they spend. Macroeconomic consumption

MyEconLab Real-time data

Expenditure Category	Real Expenditure (billions of 2009 dollars)
Consumption	$10,876
Planned investment	2,718
Government purchases	2,838
Net exports	−443

Source: U.S. Bureau of Economic Analysis.

Table 12.2

Components of Real Aggregate Expenditure, 2014

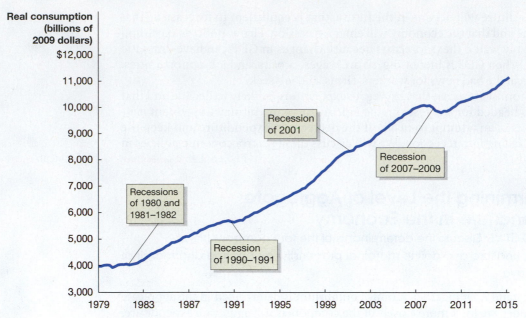

Figure 12.1 **Real Consumption, 1979–2015**

Consumption follows a smooth, upward trend, interrupted only infrequently by brief recessions.

Note: The values are quarterly data seasonally adjusted at an annual rate.

Source: U.S. Bureau of Economic Analysis.

is the total of all the consumption of U.S. households. We would expect consumption to increase when the current disposable income of households increases and to decrease when the current disposable income of households decreases. As we have seen, total income in the United States expands during most years. Only during recessions, which happen infrequently, does total income decline. The main reason for the general upward trend in consumption shown in Figure 12.1 is that disposable income has followed a similar upward trend.

Household Wealth Consumption depends in part on the wealth of households. A household's *wealth* is the value of its *assets* minus the value of its *liabilities*. Recall that an asset is anything of value owned by a person or a firm, and a liability is anything owed by a person or a firm (see Chapter 6). A household's assets include its home, stock and bond holdings, and bank accounts. A household's liabilities include any loans that it owes. A household with $10 million in wealth is likely to spend more than a household with $10,000 in wealth, even if both households have the same disposable income. Therefore, when the wealth of households increases, consumption should increase, and when the wealth of households decreases, consumption should decrease. Shares of stock are an important category of household wealth. When stock prices increase, household wealth will increase, and so should consumption. For example, a family whose stock holdings increase in value from $30,000 to $100,000 may be willing to spend a larger fraction of its income because it is less concerned with adding to its savings. A decline in stock prices should lead to a decline in consumption. Economists who have studied the determinants of consumption have concluded that permanent increases in wealth have a larger impact than temporary increases. One estimate of the effect of changes in wealth on consumption spending indicates that, for every permanent $1 increase in household wealth, consumption spending will increase by between 4 and 5 cents per year.

Expected Future Income Consumption depends in part on expected future income. Most people prefer to keep their consumption fairly stable from year to year, even if their income fluctuates significantly. Some salespeople, for example, earn most of their income from commissions, which are fixed percentages of the prices of the products they sell. A salesperson might have a high income in some years and a much lower income in other years. Most people in this situation keep their consumption steady and do not increase it during good years and then drastically cut it back during slower years. If we looked only at the current income of someone in this situation, we might have difficulty estimating the person's current consumption. Instead, we need to take into account the person's expected future income. We can conclude that current income explains current consumption well *but only when current income is not unusually high or unusually low compared with expected future income.*

The Price Level Recall that the *price level* measures the average prices of goods and services in the economy (see Chapter 9). Changes in the price level affect consumption. It is tempting to think that an increase in prices will reduce consumption by making goods and services less affordable. In fact, the effect of an increase in the price of *one* product on the quantity demanded of that product is different from the effect of an increase in the price level on *total* spending by households on goods and services. Changes in the price level affect consumption mainly through their effect on household wealth. An increase in the price level will result in a decrease in the *real* value of household wealth. For example, if you have $2,000 in a checking account, the higher the price level, the fewer goods and services you can buy with your money. Therefore, as the price level rises, the real value of your wealth declines, and so will your consumption, at least a little. Conversely, if the price level falls—which happens rarely in the United States—the real value of your $2,000 increases, and your consumption will also increase.

The Interest Rate Finally, consumption depends on the interest rate. When the interest rate is high, the reward for saving is increased, and households are likely to save more and spend less. Recall the distinction between the *nominal interest rate* and the *real interest rate* (see Chapter 9):

- The nominal interest rate is the stated interest rate on a loan or a financial investment such as a bond.
- The real interest rate corrects the nominal interest rate for the effect of inflation and is equal to the nominal interest rate minus the inflation rate.

Because households are concerned with the payments they will make or receive after the effects of inflation are taken into account, consumption spending depends on the real interest rate.

We have seen that consumption spending is divided into three categories:

1. Spending on *services*, such as medical care, education, and haircuts
2. Spending on *nondurable goods*, such as food and clothing
3. Spending on *durable goods*, such as automobiles and furniture

Spending on durable goods is most likely to be affected by changes in the interest rate because a high real interest rate increases the cost of spending financed by borrowing. The monthly payment on a four-year car loan will be higher if the real interest rate on the loan is 6 percent than if it is 4 percent.

The Consumption Function Panel (a) in Figure 12.2 illustrates the relationship between consumption and disposable income during the years 1960 to 2014. In panel (b), we draw a straight line through the points representing consumption and disposable income. The fact that most of the points lie almost on the line shows the close relationship between consumption and disposable income. Because changes in consumption depend on changes in disposable income, we can say that *consumption is a function of disposable income.* The relationship between consumption spending and disposable income illustrated in panel (b) of Figure 12.2 is called the **consumption function.**

Consumption function The relationship between consumption spending and disposable income.

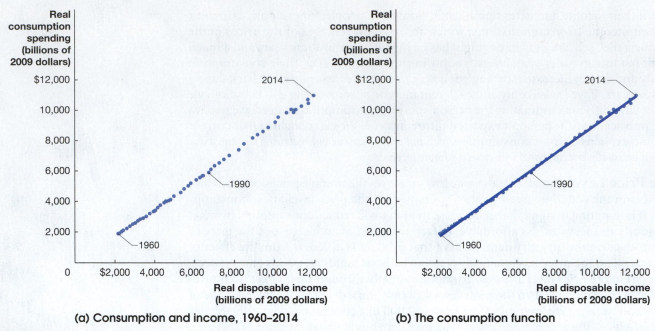

(a) Consumption and income, 1960–2014

(b) The consumption function

MyEconLab Real-time data

Figure 12.2 **The Relationship between Consumption and Income, 1960–2014**

Panel (a) shows the relationship between consumption and income. The points represent combinations of real consumption spending and real disposable income for the years 1960 to 2014. In panel (b), we draw a straight line through the points from panel (a). The line, which represents the relationship between consumption and disposable income, is called the *consumption function*. The slope of the consumption function is the marginal propensity to consume.

Source: U.S. Bureau of Economic Analysis.

Marginal propensity to consume (MPC) The slope of the consumption function: The amount by which consumption spending changes when disposable income changes.

The slope of the consumption function, which is equal to the change in consumption divided by the change in disposable income, is called the **marginal propensity to consume (MPC)**. Using the Greek letter delta, Δ, to represent "change in," C to represent consumption spending, and YD to represent disposable income, we can write the expression for the MPC as follows:

$$MPC = \frac{\text{Change in consumption}}{\text{Change in disposable income}} = \frac{\Delta C}{\Delta YD}.$$

For example, between 2013 and 2014, consumption spending increased by $285 billion, while disposable income increased by $313 billion. The marginal propensity to consume was, therefore:

$$\frac{\Delta C}{\Delta YD} = \frac{\$285 \text{ billion}}{\$313 \text{ billion}} = 0.91.$$

The value for the MPC tells us that households in 2014 spent 91 percent of the increase in their disposable income.

We can also use the MPC to determine how much consumption will change as income changes. To see this relationship, we rewrite the expression for the MPC:

$$\text{Change in consumption} = \text{Change in disposable income} \times MPC.$$

For example, with an MPC of 0.91, a $10 billion increase in disposable income will increase consumption by $10 billion $\times$ 0.91, or $9.1 billion. MyEconLab Concept Check

The Relationship between Consumption and National Income

We have seen that consumption spending by households depends on disposable income. We now shift our focus slightly to the similar relationship that exists between consumption spending and GDP. We make this shift because we are interested in using the aggregate expenditure model to explain changes in real GDP rather than changes in disposable income. The first step in examining the relationship between consumption and GDP is to recall that the differences between GDP and national income are small and can be ignored without affecting our analysis (see Chapter 8). In fact, in this and the following chapters, we will use the terms *GDP* and *national income* interchangeably. Also recall that disposable income is equal to national income plus government transfer payments minus taxes. Taxes minus government transfer payments are called *net taxes*. So, we can write the following:

Disposable income = National income − Net taxes.

We can rearrange the equation like this:

National income = GDP = Disposable income + Net taxes.

The table in Figure 12.3 shows hypothetical values for national income (or GDP), net taxes, disposable income, and consumption spending. Notice that national income and disposable income differ by a constant amount, which is equal to net taxes of $1,000 billion. In reality, net taxes are not a constant amount because they are affected by changes in income. As income rises, net taxes rise because some taxes, such as the personal income tax, increase and some government transfer payments, such as government payments to unemployed workers, fall. Nothing important is affected in our analysis, however, by our simplifying assumption that net taxes are constant.

National Income or GDP (billions of dollars)	Net Taxes (billions of dollars)	Disposable Income (billions of dollars)	Consumption (billions of dollars)	Change in National Income (billions of dollars)	Change in Disposable Income (billions of dollars)
$1,000	$1,000	$0	$750	—	—
3,000	1,000	2,000	2,250	$2,000	$2,000
5,000	1,000	4,000	3,750	2,000	2,000
7,000	1,000	6,000	5,250	2,000	2,000
9,000	1,000	8,000	6,750	2,000	2,000
11,000	1,000	10,000	8,250	2,000	2,000
13,000	1,000	12,000	9,750	2,000	2,000

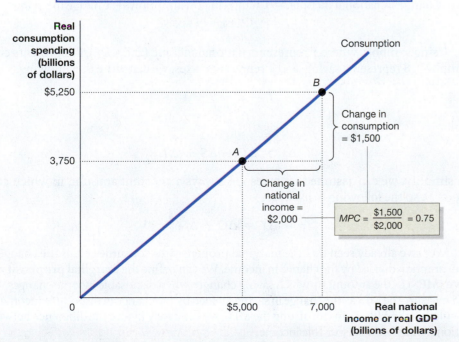

MyEconLab Animation

Figure 12.3

The Relationship between Consumption and National Income

Because national income differs from disposable income only by net taxes—which, for simplicity, we assume are constant—we can graph the consumption function using national income rather than disposable income. We can also calculate the *MPC*, which is the slope of the consumption function, using either the change in national income or the change in disposable income and always get the same value. The slope of the consumption function between points *A* and *B* is equal to the change in consumption—$1,500 billion—divided by the change in national income—$2,000 billion—or 0.75.

The graph in Figure 12.3 shows a line representing the relationship between consumption and national income. The line is very similar to the consumption function shown in panel (b) of Figure 12.2. We defined the marginal propensity to consume (*MPC*) as the change in consumption divided by the change in disposable income, which is the slope of the consumption function. In fact, notice that if we calculate the slope of the line in Figure 12.3 between points *A* and *B*, we get a result that will not change whether we use the values for national income or the values for disposable income. Using the values for national income:

$$\frac{\Delta C}{\Delta Y} = \frac{\$5,250 \text{ billion} - \$3,750 \text{ billion}}{\$7,000 \text{ billion} - \$5,000 \text{ billion}} = 0.75.$$

Using the corresponding values for disposable income from the table:

$$\frac{\Delta C}{\Delta YD} = \frac{\$5,250 \text{ billion} - \$3,750 \text{ billion}}{\$6,000 \text{ billion} - \$4,000 \text{ billion}} = 0.75.$$

It should not be surprising that we get the same result in either case. National income and disposable income differ by a constant amount, so changes in the two numbers always give us the same value, as shown in the last two columns of the table in Figure 12.3. Therefore, we can graph the consumption function using national income rather than using disposable income. We can also calculate the *MPC* using either the change in national income or the change in disposable income and always get the same value.   MyEconLab Concept Check

Income, Consumption, and Saving

To complete our discussion of consumption, we can look briefly at the relationships among income, consumption, and saving. Households spend their income, save it, or use it to pay taxes. For the economy as a whole, we can write the following:

$$\text{National income} = \text{Consumption} + \text{Saving} + \text{Taxes}.$$

When national income increases, there must be some combination of an increase in consumption, an increase in saving, and an increase in taxes:

$$\text{Change in national income} = \text{Change in consumption} + \text{Change in saving}$$
$$+ \text{ Change in taxes}.$$

Using symbols, where *Y* represents national income (and GDP), *C* represents consumption, *S* represents saving, and *T* represents taxes, we can write the following:

$$Y = C + S + T$$

and:

$$\Delta Y = \Delta C + \Delta S + \Delta T.$$

To simplify, we can assume that taxes are always a constant amount, in which case $\Delta T = 0$, so the following is also true:

$$\Delta Y = \Delta C + \Delta S.$$

Marginal propensity to save (MPS) The amount by which saving changes when disposable income changes.

We have already seen that the marginal propensity to consume equals the change in consumption divided by the change in income. We can define the **marginal propensity to save (MPS)** as the amount by which saving changes when disposable income changes. We can measure the *MPS* as the change in saving divided by the change in disposable income. In calculating the *MPS*, as in calculating the *MPC*, we can safely ignore the difference between national income and disposable income.

If we divide the previous equation by the change in income, ΔY, we get an equation that shows the relationship between the marginal propensity to consume and the marginal propensity to save:

$$\frac{\Delta Y}{\Delta Y} = \frac{\Delta C}{\Delta Y} + \frac{\Delta S}{\Delta Y},$$

or:

$$1 = MPC + MPS.$$

This equation tells us that when taxes are constant, the marginal propensity to consume plus the marginal propensity to save must always equal 1. They must add up to 1 because part of any increase in income is consumed, and whatever remains must be saved.

MyEconLab Concept Check

Solved Problem 12.2

Calculating the Marginal Propensity to Consume and the Marginal Propensity to Save

Fill in the blank cells in the following table. For simplicity, assume that taxes are zero. Show that the MPC plus the MPS equals 1.

National Income and Real GDP (Y)	Consumption (C)	Saving (S)	Marginal Propensity to Consume (MPC)	Marginal Propensity to Save (MPS)
$9,000	$8,000			
10,000	8,600			
11,000	9,200			
12,000	9,800			
13,000	10,400			

Solving the Problem

Step 1: **Review the chapter material.** This problem is about the relationship among income, consumption, and saving, so you may want to review the section "Income, Consumption, and Saving," which begins on page 398.

Step 2: **Fill in the table.** We know that $Y = C + S + T$. With taxes equal to zero, this equation becomes $Y = C + S$. We can use this equation to fill in the "Saving" column. We can use the equations for the MPC and the MPS to fill in the other two columns:

$$MPC = \frac{\Delta C}{\Delta Y}$$

$$MPS = \frac{\Delta S}{\Delta Y}$$

For example, to calculate the value of the MPC in the second row, we have:

$$MPC = \frac{\Delta C}{\Delta Y} = \frac{\$8,600 - \$8,000}{\$10,000 - \$9,000} = \frac{\$600}{\$1,000} = 0.6.$$

To calculate the value of the MPS in the second row, we have:

$$MPS = \frac{\Delta S}{\Delta Y} = \frac{\$1,400 - \$1,000}{\$10,000 - \$9,000} = \frac{\$400}{\$1,000} = 0.4.$$

National Income and Real GDP (*Y*)	Consumption (*C*)	Saving (*S*)	Marginal Propensity to Consume (*MPC*)	Marginal Propensity to Save (*MPS*)
$9,000	$8,000	$1,000	—	—
10,000	8,600	1,400	0.6	0.4
11,000	9,200	1,800	0.6	0.4
12,000	9,800	2,200	0.6	0.4
13,000	10,400	2,600	0.6	0.4

Step 3: **Show that the MPC plus the MPS equals 1.** At every level of national income, the *MPC* is 0.6 and the *MPS* is 0.4. Therefore, the *MPC* plus the *MPS* is always equal to 1.

Your Turn: For more practice, do related problem 2.10 on page 425 at the end of this chapter.

Planned Investment

Figure 12.4 shows movements in real investment spending from 1979 through the second quarter of 2015. Notice that, unlike consumption, investment does not follow a smooth, upward trend. Investment declined significantly during the recessions of 1980, 1981–1982, 1990–1991, 2001, and 2007–2009.

These are the four most important variables that determine the level of investment:

1. Expectations of future profitability
2. The interest rate
3. Taxes
4. Cash flow

Expectations of Future Profitability Investment goods, such as factories, office buildings, and machinery and equipment, are long-lived. A firm is unlikely to build a new factory unless it is optimistic that the demand for its product will remain strong for at least several years. When the economy moves into a recession, many firms postpone buying investment goods even if the demand for their own product is strong

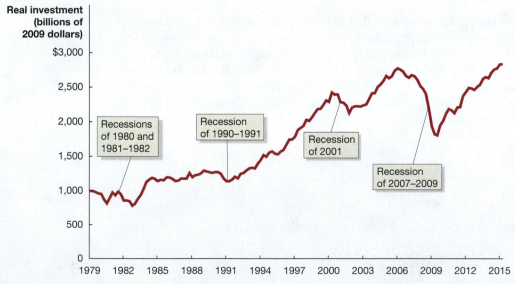

MyEconLab Real-time data

Figure 12.4 **Real Investment, 1979–2015**

Investment is subject to larger changes than is consumption. Investment declined significantly during the recessions of 1980, 1981–1982, 1990–1991, 2001, and 2007–2009.

Note: The values are quarterly data, seasonally adjusted at an annual rate.

Source: U.S. Bureau of Economic Analysis.

because they are afraid that the recession may become worse. During an expansion, some firms may become optimistic and begin to increase spending on investment goods even before the demand for their own product has increased. The key point is that *the optimism or pessimism of firms is an important determinant of investment spending.*

Residential construction is included in investment spending. Since 1990, residential construction has averaged about 30 percent of total investment spending. But the swings in residential construction have been quite substantial, ranging from a high of 36 percent of investment spending at the height of the housing boom in 2005 down to 18 percent in 2011. The sharp decline in spending on residential construction beginning in 2006 helped to cause the 2007–2009 recession and contributed to its severity.

The Interest Rate   Some business investment is financed by borrowing, as firms issue corporate bonds or receive loans from banks. Households also borrow to finance most of their spending on new homes. The higher the interest rate, the more expensive it is for firms and households to borrow. Because households and firms are interested in the cost of borrowing after taking into account the effects of inflation, investment spending depends on the real interest rate. Therefore, holding constant the other factors that affect investment spending, there is an inverse relationship between the real interest rate and investment spending: *A higher real interest rate results in less investment spending, and a lower real interest rate results in more investment spending.* The ability of households to borrow money at very low real interest rates helps explain the rapid increase in spending on residential construction from 2002 to 2006.

Taxes   Taxes affect the level of investment spending. Firms focus on the profits that remain after they have paid taxes. The federal government imposes a *corporate income tax* on the profits corporations earn, including profits from the new buildings, equipment, and other investment goods they purchase. A reduction in the corporate income tax increases the after-tax profitability of investment spending. An increase in the corporate income tax decreases the after-tax profitability of investment spending. *Investment tax incentives* increase investment spending. An investment tax incentive provides firms with a tax reduction when they buy new investment goods.

Cash Flow   Most firms do not borrow to finance spending on new factories, machinery, and equipment. Instead, they use their own funds. **Cash flow** is the difference between the cash revenues received by a firm and the cash spending by the firm. Neither noncash receipts nor noncash spending is included in cash flow. For example, tax laws allow firms to count the depreciation of worn-out or obsolete machinery and equipment as a cost, even if new machinery and equipment have not actually been purchased. Because this is noncash spending, firms do not include it when calculating cash flow. The largest contributor to cash flow is profit. The more profitable a firm is, the greater its cash flow and the greater its ability to finance investment. During periods of recession, many firms experience reduced profits, which in turn reduces their ability to finance spending on new factories or machinery and equipment.

Cash flow   The difference between the cash revenues received by a firm and the cash spending by the firm.

Making the **Connection** MyEconLab Video **Is Student Loan Debt Causing Fewer Young People to Buy Houses?**

Although our discussion in this section has concentrated on the components of investment that represent spending by businesses, household purchases of new homes are an important part of investment spending. As the graph on the next page shows, spending on residential construction rose rapidly in the period just before the recession of 2007–2009, declined dramatically during the recession, and recovered only slowly thereafter. The slow recovery in spending on residential construction is one reason the recovery from the recession was weaker than most recoveries.

Some economists believe that one factor holding back recovery in the housing market was low home-buying rates among younger households. In 2014, homeownership rates among people younger than 35 were the lowest they have been in the United States in at least 25 years. Do high levels of student debt explain why young people are buying fewer homes? If you have a college degree, you are likely to earn more than

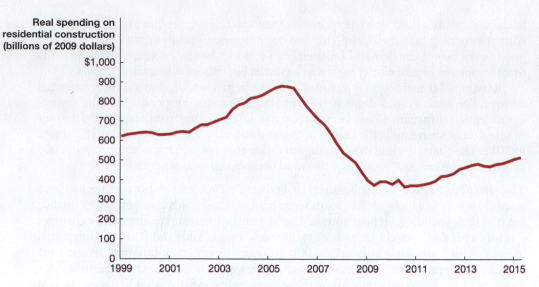

people without a college degree. So, many people consider student debt taken on to earn a degree to be a good investment. For the class of 2014, the average student debt per borrower was a record $33,000. Total student debt in 2014 was $1.1 trillion, more than the amount that all Americans owe on credit cards or automobile loans, and twice the level of student debt in 2007. Does increasing student debt explain the decline in home purchases among younger households? Economists differ in their answers to this question because other factors may be affecting homeownership rates.

Harvard economist and former Obama administration economic adviser Larry Summers argues that many college graduates have trouble accumulating the funds for a down payment on a house because they are making student loan payments. He also argues that these payments have led young college graduates to delay forming families, thereby reducing their need to move from an apartment to a house. One survey indicates that 45 percent of college graduates under age 24 are living at home or with another family member. Some economists point to rising delinquency rates on student loans as a factor that makes it difficult for some young college graduates to qualify for a mortgage loan necessary to buy a house.

Other economists are skeptical of a link between student debt and a reduced demand for housing by young college graduates. Economists who have carried out statistical studies of the link have arrived at mixed results. In testifying before Congress, Federal Reserve Chair Janet Yellen remarked of the connection between students' debt and the demand for housing that "I don't know of clear evidence of it."

Some economists believe that new government lending guidelines may be playing a role. When deciding whether to grant a mortgage loan, banks and other lenders have interpreted the guidelines to mean that they must give greater consideration to how much debt graduates have. As a result, fewer young college graduates qualify for mortgage loans. Finally, some economists argue that the weak recovery of the U.S. labor market from the recession of 2007–2009 is the key reason that young college graduates have been buying fewer houses. With unemployment rates remaining high and wages growing slowly, many young people have difficulty affording homes, even if they have limited or no student debt. As the recovery became stronger in 2015, these economists expected that younger people would be increasing their demand for housing.

Sources: Mitchell E. Daniels, "How Student Debt Harms the Economy," *Wall Street Journal*, January 27, 2015; Zeppo Mitchell, "Larry Summers: Student Debt Is Slowing the U.S. Housing Recovery," *Wall Street Journal*, May 21, 2014; Josh Mitchell, "Student Debt Takes a Toll on Some Home Buyers," *Wall Street Journal*, June 20, 2014; Susan Dynarski, "Remember the Problems with Mortgage Defaults? They're Coming Back with Student Loans," *New York Times*, June 12, 2014; Meta Brown, et al., "Measuring Student Debt and Its Performance," Federal Reserve Bank of New York, Staff Report No. 668, April 2014; and U.S. Bureau of Economic Analysis.

MyEconLab Study Plan

Your Turn: Test your understanding by doing related problem 2.11 on page 425 at the end of this chapter.

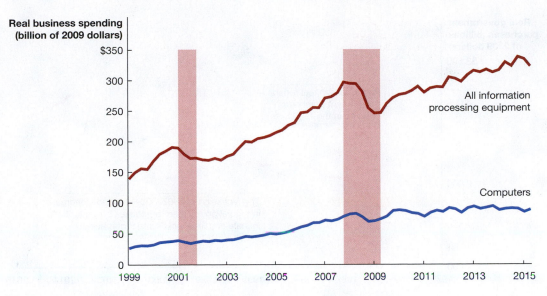

MyEconLab Animation

Figure 12.5   Spending on Information Processing Equipment, 1999–2015

Business spending on information processing equipment, particularly computers, has grown only slowly since the end of the recession of 2007–2009.

Source: U.S. Bureau of Economic Analysis.

The Surprisingly Slow Growth of Business Spending on Information Processing Equipment

In recent years, most businesses have increased their use of information technology in a variety of ways, including expanding their presence on the Internet, especially by using social networking apps such as Twitter, Instagram, and Facebook; designing company apps; and providing employees with tablets and smartphones. As Figure 12.5 shows, though, the focus of many businesses on information technology is not reflected in spending on information processing equipment. The blue line shows spending on computers, printers, and related equipment, while the red line shows spending on all information processing equipment, which in addition to computers, includes photocopiers, fax machines, and other office equipment. In 2015, total spending on information processing equipment had grown by less than 10 percent from its levels at the beginning of the recession in 2007. Spending on computers was also growing slowly and in 2015 was barely above 2010 levels.

A key reason for this slow growth in spending on information technology equipment is that over time, the frontier of developments in information technology has shifted away from equipment—particularly computers and servers—and toward software, such as apps used on smartphones and tablets. This shift has been bad news for firms like Intel, whose sales of processors are heavily dependent on sales of computers. Intel has had only mixed success in reducing its dependence on sales to computer manufacturers by shifting toward making components for tablets, smartwatches, and smartphones, including a modem chip for Apple's iPhone.

Government Purchases

Total government purchases include all spending by federal, local, and state governments for goods and services. Recall that government purchases do not include transfer payments, such as Social Security payments by the federal government or pension payments by local governments to retired police officers and firefighters, because the government does not receive a good or service in return (see Chapter 8).

Figure 12.6 shows levels of real government purchases from 1979 through the second quarter of 2015. Government purchases grew steadily for most of this period,

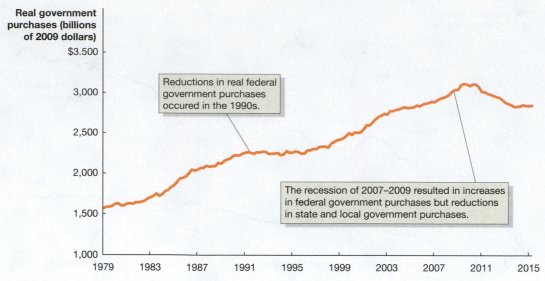

Real government purchases (billions of 2009 dollars)

Reductions in real federal government purchases occured in the 1990s.

The recession of 2007–2009 resulted in increases in federal government purchases but reductions in state and local government purchases.

Figure 12.6 **Real Government Purchases, 1979–2015**

Government purchases grew steadily for most of the 1979–2015 period, with the exception of the early 1990s, when concern about the federal budget deficit caused real government purchases to fall for three years, beginning in 1992, and the period following the recession of 2007–2009 when many state and local governments reduced spending.

Note: The values are quarterly data, seasonally adjusted at an annual rate.

Source: U.S. Bureau of Economic Analysis.

with the exception of the early 1990s and the period following the end of the recession of 2007–2009. During the early 1990s, Congress and Presidents George H. W. Bush and Bill Clinton enacted a series of spending reductions after they became concerned that spending by the federal government was growing much faster than tax receipts. As a result, real government purchases declined for three years beginning in 1992. Contributing to the slow growth of government purchases during the 1990s was the end of the Cold War between the United States and the Soviet Union in 1989. Real federal government spending on national defense declined by 24 percent from 1990 to 1998, before rising by 60 percent between 1998 and 2010 in response to the war on terrorism and the wars in Iraq and Afghanistan. As those wars wound down, defense spending declined by 18 percent between 2010 and 2015. Total federal government purchases increased in 2009 and 2010, as President Barack Obama and Congress attempted to offset declining consumption and investment spending during the recession. Federal government purchases then declined beginning in 2011 and continuing through 2015. The recession and the slow recovery resulted in declining tax revenues to state and local governments. As a result, real state and local government purchases declined between 2009 and 2013, before increasing, along with tax revenues, beginning in 2014.

MyEconLab Concept Check

Net Exports

Net exports equal exports minus imports. We can calculate net exports by taking the value of spending by foreign firms and households on goods and services produced in the United States and *subtracting* the value of spending by U.S. firms and households on goods and services produced in other countries. Figure 12.7 illustrates movements in real net exports from 1979 through the second quarter of 2015. During nearly all these years, the United States imported more goods and services than it exported, so net exports were negative. Net exports usually increase when the U.S. economy is in a recession—although they fell during the 2001 recession—and fall when the U.S. economy is in an expansion.

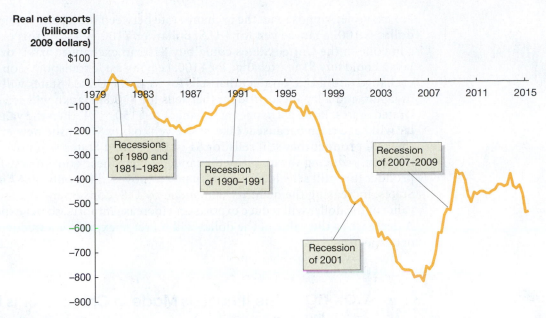

Figure 12.7   Real Net Exports, 1979–2015

Net exports were negative in most years between 1979 and 2015. Net exports have usually increased when the U.S. economy is in a recession and decreased when the U.S. economy is in an expansion, although they fell during the 2001 recession.

Note: The values are quarterly data, seasonally adjusted at an annual rate.

Source: U.S. Bureau of Economic Analysis.

The following are the three most important variables that determine the level of net exports:

1. The price level in the United States relative to the price levels in other countries
2. The growth rate of GDP in the United States relative to the growth rates of GDP in other countries
3. The exchange rate between the dollar and other currencies

The Price Level in the United States Relative to the Price Levels in Other Countries
If inflation in the United States is lower than inflation in other countries, prices of U.S. products increase more slowly than the prices of products in other countries. This slower increase in the U.S. price level increases the demand for U.S. products relative to the demand for foreign products. So, U.S. exports increase and U.S. imports decrease, which increases net exports. The reverse happens during periods when the inflation rate in the United States is higher than the inflation rates in other countries: U.S. exports decrease and U.S. imports increase, which decreases net exports.

The Growth Rate of GDP in the United States Relative to the Growth Rates of GDP in Other Countries
As GDP increases in the United States, the incomes of households rise, leading them to increase their purchases of goods and services. Some of the additional goods and services purchased with rising incomes are produced in the United States, but some are imported. When incomes rise faster in the United States than in other countries, U.S. consumers' purchases of foreign goods and services increase faster than foreign consumers' purchases of U.S. goods and services. As a result, net exports fall. When incomes in the United States rise more slowly than incomes in other countries, net exports rise.

The Exchange Rate between the Dollar and Other Currencies
As the value of the U.S. dollar rises, the foreign currency price of U.S. products sold in other countries rises, and the dollar price of foreign products sold in the United States falls.

For example, suppose that the exchange rate between the Japanese yen and the U.S. dollar is 100 Japanese yen for 1 U.S. dollar, or ¥100 = $1. At this exchange rate, someone in the United States could buy ¥100 in exchange for $1, or someone in Japan could buy $1 in exchange for ¥100. Leaving aside transportation costs, at this exchange rate, a U.S. product that sells for $1 in the United States will sell for ¥100 in Japan, and a Japanese product that sells for ¥100 in Japan will sell for $1 in the United States. If the exchange rate changes to ¥150 = $1, then the value of the dollar will have risen because it takes more yen to buy $1. At the new exchange rate, the U.S. product that still sells for $1 in the United States will now sell for ¥150 in Japan, reducing the quantity demanded by Japanese consumers. The Japanese product that still sells for ¥100 in Japan will now sell for only $0.67 in the United States, increasing the quantity demanded by U.S. consumers. An increase in the value of the dollar will reduce exports and increase imports, so net exports will fall. A decrease in the value of the dollar will increase exports and reduce imports, so net exports will rise.

MyEconLab Concept Check

Making the Connection

MyEconLab Video

The box says iPhones are made in China, but are they?

The iPhone Is Made in China … or Is It?

Designers and software engineers at Apple in Cupertino, California, designed the iPhone. However, the iPhone is sold in a box labeled "Made in China." The price of the iPhone when it is shipped from a factory in China is about $275. (The retail price is higher because Apple adds a markup, as do Best Buy and other stores that sell the iPhone.) So if you buy an iPhone, the purchase enters the GDP statistics as a $275 import to the United States from China. Recently, economists have begun to question whether the standard way of keeping track of imports and exports accurately reflects how modern businesses operate.

Recall from Chapter 2 that the iPhone contains components that are produced by a number of firms, based in several different countries, including the United States. Apple uses this *global supply chain* to take advantage of both lower production costs in other countries and the ability of different firms to use their engineering and manufacturing skills to produce the iPhone's many components. Apple arranges for these firms to ship the components to factories in China for final assembly. These Chinese factories are owned by Foxconn, a firm based in Taiwan. So, only final assembly of the iPhone takes place in China; no Chinese firm makes any of the iPhone's components.

How much of the price of the iPhone is accounted for by the value of final assembly? According to a study by economists Yuqing Xing and Neal Detert of the Asian Development Bank, less than 4 percent. In fact, they note that the value of the iPhone components China imports from U.S. firms is greater than the value of assembling the iPhones in Chinese factories. As measured in the GDP statistics, in 2015 the United States imported more than $20 billion worth of iPhones from China. In fact, most of that $20 billion represents the value of the iPhone's components, none of which are made in China.

The current system of accounting for imports and exports in the GDP statistics dates to a time when most products were produced entirely within one country. So a good the United States imported from France or Japan would have been produced completely in that country. As large firms have increasingly relied on global supply chains, the statistics on imports and exports have failed to keep up. As Pascal Lamy of the World Trade Organization put it: "The concept of country of origin for manufactured goods has gradually become obsolete." In other words, "trade statistics can mislead as much as inform," as economists Kenneth Kraemer of the University of

California, Irvine, Greg Linden of the University of California, Berkeley, and Jason Dedrick of Syracuse University put it. The U.S. Bureau of Economic Analysis and the government statistical agencies in other countries are all aware of the flaws that have developed in accounting for imports and exports. But the complexity of global supply chains makes it difficult to develop more accurate measures of imports and exports.

Sources: Izabella Kaminska, "iPhone6, the GDP Effect," ftalphaville.ft.com, September 2, 2014; Phil Izzo, "Who Gets Credit for iPhone Trade," *Wall Street Journal*, March 17, 2012; Kenneth L. Kraemer, Greg Linden, and Jason Dedrick, "Capturing Value in Global Networks: Apple's iPad and iPhone," University of California, Irvine, Working paper, July 2011; Yuqing Xing and Neal Detert, "How the iPhone Widens the United States Trade Deficit with the People's Republic of China," ADBI Working Paper Series, No. 257, May 2011; and Andrew Batson, "Not Really, 'Made in China,'" *Wall Street Journal*, December 15, 2010.

Your Turn: Test your understanding by doing related problems 2.13 and 2.14 on page 426 at the end of this chapter.

MyEconLab Study Plan

12.3 Graphing Macroeconomic Equilibrium

LEARNING OBJECTIVE: Use a 45°-line diagram to illustrate macroeconomic equilibrium.

Having examined the components of aggregate expenditure, we can now look more closely at macroeconomic equilibrium. We saw earlier in the chapter that macroeconomic equilibrium occurs when GDP is equal to aggregate expenditure. We can use a graph called the *45°-line diagram* to illustrate macroeconomic equilibrium. (The 45°-line diagram is also sometimes called the *Keynesian cross* because it is based on the analysis of John Maynard Keynes.) To become familiar with this diagram, consider Figure 12.8, which is a 45°-line diagram that shows the relationship between the quantity of Pepsi sold (on the vertical axis) and the quantity of Pepsi produced (on the horizontal axis).

The line on the diagram forms an angle of 45° with the horizontal axis. The line represents all the points that are equal distances from both axes. So, points such as

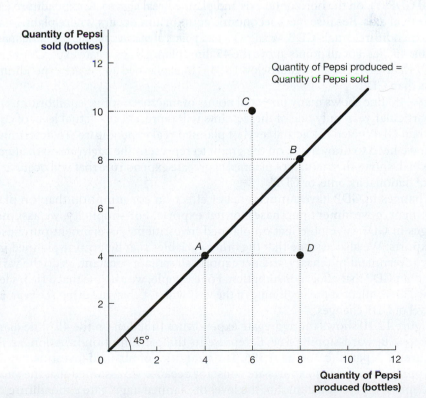

MyEconLab Animation

Figure 12.8

An Example of a 45°-Line Diagram

The 45° line shows all the points that are equal distances from both axes. Points such as *A* and *B*, at which the quantity produced equals the quantity sold, are on the 45° line. Points such as *C*, at which the quantity sold is greater than the quantity produced, lie above the line. Points such as *D*, at which the quantity sold is less than the quantity produced, lie below the line.

Figure 12.9

The Relationship between Planned Aggregate Expenditure and GDP on a 45°-Line Diagram

Every point of macroeconomic equilibrium is on the 45° line, where planned aggregate expenditure equals GDP. At points above the line, planned aggregate expenditure is greater than GDP. At points below the line, planned aggregate expenditure is less than GDP.

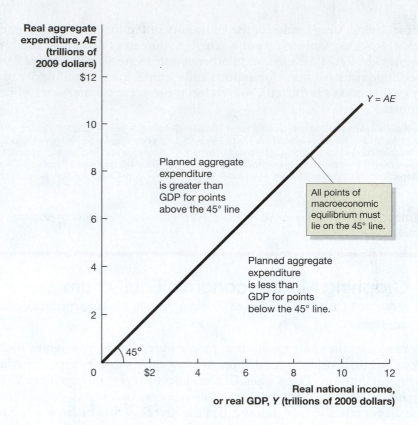

A and *B*, where the number of bottles of Pepsi produced equals the number of bottles sold, are on the 45° line. Points such as *C*, where the quantity sold is greater than the quantity produced, lie above the line. Points such as *D*, where the quantity sold is less than the quantity produced, lie below the line.

Figure 12.9 is similar to Figure 12.8 except that it measures real national income, or real GDP (*Y*), on the horizontal axis and planned real aggregate expenditure (*AE*) on the vertical axis. Because macroeconomic equilibrium occurs where planned aggregate expenditure equals GDP, *we know that all points of macroeconomic equilibrium must lie along the 45° line.* For all points above the 45° line, planned aggregate expenditure will be greater than GDP. For all points below the 45° line, planned aggregate expenditure will be less than GDP.

The 45° line shows many potential points of macroeconomic equilibrium. During any particular year, only one of these points will represent the actual level of equilibrium real GDP, given the actual level of planned real expenditure. To determine this point, we need to draw a line on the graph to represent the *aggregate expenditure function*, which shows the amount of planned aggregate expenditure that will occur at every level of national income, or GDP.

Changes in GDP have a much greater effect on consumption than on planned investment, government purchases, or net exports. For simplicity, we assume that changes in GDP have no effect on planned investment, government purchases, or net exports. We also assume that the other variables that determine planned investment, government purchases, and net exports all remain constant, as do the variables other than GDP that affect consumption. For example, we assume that a firm's level of planned investment at the beginning of the year will not change during the year, even if the level of GDP changes.

Figure 12.10 shows the aggregate expenditure function on the 45°-line diagram. The lowest upward-sloping line, *C*, represents the consumption function, as shown in Figure 12.2, panel (b), on page 396. The quantities of planned investment, government purchases, and net exports are constant because we assumed that the variables they depend on are constant. So, the level of planned aggregate expenditure at any

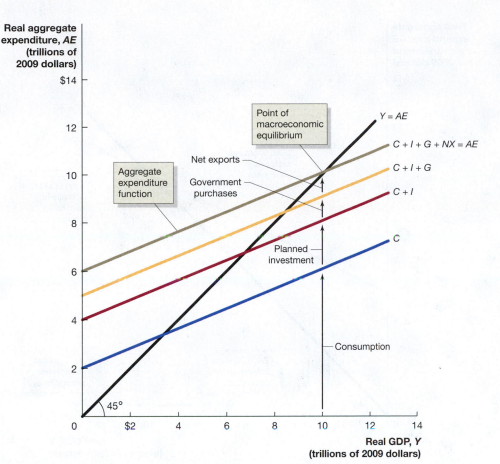

MyEconLab Animation

Figure 12.10

Macroeconomic Equilibrium on the 45°-Line Diagram

Macroeconomic equilibrium occurs where the aggregate expenditure (AE) line crosses the 45° line. The lowest upward-sloping line, C, represents the consumption function. The quantities of planned investment, government purchases, and net exports are constant because we assumed that the variables they depend on are constant. So, the total of planned aggregate expenditure at any level of GDP is the amount of consumption at that level of GDP plus the sum of the constant amounts of planned investment, government purchases, and net exports. We successively add each component of spending to the consumption function line to arrive at the gray line representing aggregate expenditure.

level of GDP is the amount of consumption spending at that level of GDP plus the sum of the constant amounts of planned investment, government purchases, and net exports. In Figure 12.10, we add each component of spending successively to the consumption function line to arrive at the line representing planned aggregate expenditure (AE). The C + I line is higher than the C line by the constant amount of planned investment; the C + I + G line is higher than the C + I line by the constant amount of government purchases; and the C + I + G + NX line is higher than the C + I + G line by the constant amount of NX. (In many years, however, NX is negative, which would cause the C + I + G + NX line to be *below* the C + I + G line.) The C + I + G + NX line shows all four components of expenditure and is the aggregate expenditure (AE) function. At the point where the AE line crosses the 45° line, planned aggregate expenditure is equal to GDP, and the economy is in macroeconomic equilibrium.

Figure 12.11 makes the relationship between planned aggregate expenditure and GDP clearer by showing only the 45° line and the AE line. The figure shows that the AE line intersects the 45° line at a level of real GDP of $10 trillion. Therefore, $10 trillion represents the equilibrium level of real GDP. To see why, consider the situation if real GDP were only $8 trillion. By moving vertically from $8 trillion on the horizontal axis up to the AE line, we see that planned aggregate expenditure will be greater than $8 trillion at this level of real GDP. Whenever total spending is greater than total production, firms' inventories will fall. The fall in inventories is equal to the vertical distance between the AE line, which shows the level of total spending, and the 45° line, which shows the $8 trillion of total production. Unplanned declines in inventories lead firms to increase their production. As real GDP increases from $8 trillion, so will total income and, therefore, consumption. The economy will move up the AE line as consumption increases. The gap between total spending and total production will fall, but as long as the AE line is above the 45° line, inventories will continue to decline, and firms will

Figure 12.11

Macroeconomic Equilibrium

Macroeconomic equilibrium occurs where the *AE* line crosses the 45° line, which occurs at GDP of $10 trillion. If GDP is less than $10 trillion, the corresponding point on the *AE* line is above the 45° line, planned aggregate expenditure is greater than total production, firms will experience an unplanned decrease in inventories, and GDP will increase. If GDP is greater than $10 trillion, the corresponding point on the *AE* line is below the 45° line, planned aggregate expenditure is less than total production, firms will experience an unplanned increase in inventories, and GDP will decrease.

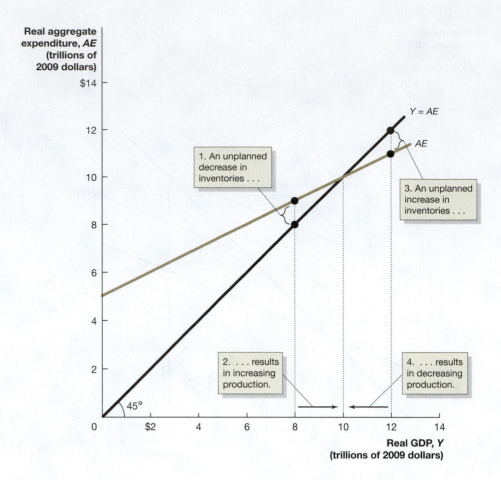

continue to expand production. When real GDP rises to $10 trillion, inventories stop falling, and the economy will be in macroeconomic equilibrium.

As Figure 12.11 shows, if GDP is initially $12 trillion, planned aggregate expenditure will be less than GDP, and firms will experience an unplanned increase in inventories. Rising inventories lead firms to decrease production. As GDP falls from $12 trillion, consumption will also fall, which causes the economy to move down the *AE* line. The gap between planned aggregate expenditure and GDP will fall, but as long as the *AE* line is below the 45° line, inventories will continue to rise, and firms will continue to cut production. When GDP falls to $10 trillion, inventories will stop rising, and the economy will be in macroeconomic equilibrium.

Showing a Recession on the 45°-Line Diagram

Notice that *macroeconomic equilibrium can occur at any point on the 45° line*. Ideally, equilibrium will occur at *potential GDP*. At potential GDP, firms will be operating at their normal level of capacity, and the economy will be at the *natural rate of unemployment*. As we have seen, at the natural rate of unemployment, the economy will be at *full employment*: Everyone in the labor force who wants a job will have one, except the structurally and frictionally unemployed (see Chapter 9). However, for equilibrium to occur at potential GDP, planned aggregate expenditure must be high enough. As Figure 12.12 shows, if there is insufficient total spending, equilibrium will occur at a lower level of real GDP. In this situation, many firms will be operating below their normal capacity, and the unemployment rate will be above the natural rate of unemployment.

Suppose that the level of potential GDP is $10 trillion. As Figure 12.12 shows, when GDP is $10 trillion, planned aggregate expenditure is below $10 trillion, perhaps because firms have become pessimistic about their future profitability and have reduced their investment spending. The shortfall in planned aggregate expenditure

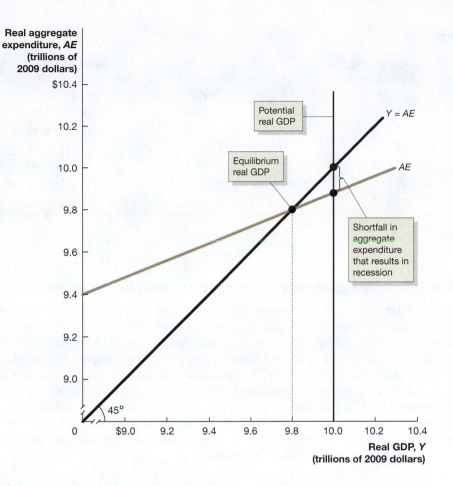

MyEconLab Animation

Figure 12.12

Showing a Recession on the 45°-Line Diagram

When the aggregate expenditure line intersects the 45° line at a level of GDP below potential GDP, the economy is in recession. The figure shows that potential GDP is $10 trillion, but because planned aggregate expenditure is too low, the equilibrium level of GDP is only $9.8 trillion, where the AE line intersects the 45° line. As a result, some firms will be operating below their normal capacity, and unemployment will be above the natural rate of unemployment. We can measure the shortfall in planned aggregate expenditure as the vertical distance between the AE line and the 45° line at the level of potential GDP.

that leads to the recession can be measured as the vertical distance between the AE line and the 45° line at the level of potential GDP. The shortfall in planned aggregate expenditure is exactly equal to the unplanned increase in inventories that would occur if the economy were initially at a level of GDP of $10 trillion. The unplanned increase in inventories measures the amount by which current planned aggregate expenditure is too low for the current level of production to be the equilibrium level. Put another way, if any of the four components of aggregate expenditure increased by this amount, the AE line would shift upward and intersect the 45° line at GDP of $10 trillion, and the economy would be in macroeconomic equilibrium at full employment.

Figure 12.12 shows that macroeconomic equilibrium will occur when real GDP is $9.8 trillion. Because real GDP is 2 percent below potential GDP of $10 trillion, many firms will be operating below their normal capacity, and the unemployment rate will be well above the natural rate of unemployment. The economy will remain at this level of real GDP until there is an increase in one or more of the components of aggregate expenditure.   MyEconLab Concept Check

The Important Role of Inventories

Whenever planned aggregate expenditure is less than real GDP, some firms will experience unplanned increases in inventories. If firms do not cut back their production promptly when spending declines, they will accumulate inventories. If firms accumulate excess inventories, then even if spending quickly returns to its normal level, firms will have to sell their excess inventories before they can return to producing at normal levels. For example, more than half of the sharp 5.4 percent annual rate of decline in real GDP during the first quarter of 2009 resulted from firms cutting production as they sold off unintended accumulations of inventories.   MyEconLab Concept Check

Table 12.3   Macroeconomic Equilibrium

Real GDP (Y)	Consumption (C)	Planned Investment (I)	Government Purchases (G)	Net Exports (NX)	Planned Aggregate Expenditure (AE)	Unplanned Change in Inventories	Real GDP Will . . .
$8,000	$6,200	$1,500	$1,500	−$500	$8,700	−$700	increase
9,000	6,850	1,500	1,500	−500	9,350	−350	increase
10,000	7,500	1,500	1,500	−500	10,000	0	be in equilibrium
11,000	8,150	1,500	1,500	−500	10,650	+350	decrease
12,000	8,800	1,500	1,500	−500	11,300	+700	decrease

Note: The values are in billions of 2009 dollars.

A Numerical Example of Macroeconomic Equilibrium

In forecasting real GDP, economists rely on quantitative models of the economy. We can increase our understanding of the causes of changes in real GDP by considering a simple numerical example of macroeconomic equilibrium. Although simplified, this example captures some of the key features contained in the quantitative models that economic forecasters use. Table 12.3 shows several hypothetical combinations of real GDP and planned aggregate expenditure. The first column lists real GDP. The next four columns list levels of the four components of planned aggregate expenditure that occur at the corresponding level of real GDP. We assume that planned investment, government purchases, and net exports do not change as GDP changes. Because consumption depends on GDP, it increases as GDP increases.

Don't Let This Happen to You

Don't Confuse Aggregate Expenditure with Consumption Spending

Macroeconomic equilibrium occurs where planned aggregate expenditure equals GDP. But remember that planned aggregate expenditure equals the sum of consumption spending, planned investment spending, government purchases, and net exports, *not* consumption spending alone. If GDP were equal to consumption, the economy would not be in equilibrium. Planned investment plus government purchases plus net exports will always be a positive number. Therefore, if consumption were equal to GDP, aggregate expenditure would have to be greater than GDP. In that case, inventories would be decreasing, and GDP would be *increasing*; GDP would not be in equilibrium.

Test your understanding of macroeconomic equilibrium with this problem:
Question: Do you agree with the following argument?

This chapter says macroeconomic equilibrium occurs where planned aggregate expenditure equals GDP. GDP is equal to national income. So, at equilibrium, planned aggregate expenditure must equal national income. But we know

that consumers do not spend all of their income: They save at least some and use some to pay taxes. Therefore, aggregate expenditure will never equal national income, and the basic macroeconomic story is incorrect.

Answer: Remember that national income equals GDP (disregarding depreciation, as we have done throughout this chapter). So, it is correct to say that in macroeconomic equilibrium, planned aggregate expenditure must equal national income. But the last sentence of the argument is incorrect because it assumes that aggregate expenditure is the same as consumption spending. Because of saving and taxes, consumption spending is always much less than national income, but in equilibrium, the sum of consumption spending, planned investment spending, government purchases, and net exports does, in fact, equal GDP and national income. So, the argument is incorrect because it confuses consumption spending with aggregate expenditure.

MyEconLab Study Plan

Your Turn: Test your understanding by doing related problem 3.11 on page 427 at the end of this chapter.

In the first row of the table, GDP of $8,000 billion (or $8 trillion) results in consumption of $6,200 billion. Adding consumption, planned investment, government purchases, and net exports across the row gives planned aggregate expenditure of $8,700 billion, which is shown in the sixth column. Because planned aggregate expenditure is greater than GDP, inventories will fall by $700 billion. This unplanned decline in inventories will lead firms to increase production, and GDP will increase. GDP will continue to increase until it reaches $10,000 billion. At that level of GDP, planned aggregate expenditure is also $10,000 billion, unplanned changes in inventories are zero, and the economy is in macroeconomic equilibrium.

In the last row, GDP of $12,000 billion results in consumption of $8,800 billion and planned aggregate expenditure of $11,300 billion. Because planned aggregate expenditure is less than GDP, inventories will increase by $700 billion. This unplanned increase in inventories will lead firms to decrease production, and GDP will decrease. GDP will continue to decrease until it reaches $10,000 billion, unplanned changes in inventories are zero, and the economy is in macroeconomic equilibrium.

Only when real GDP equals $10,000 billion will the economy be in macroeconomic equilibrium. At other levels of real GDP, planned aggregate expenditure will be higher or lower than GDP, and the economy will be expanding or contracting. MyEconLab Concept Check

Solved Problem 12.3

MyEconLab Interactive Animation

Determining Macroeconomic Equilibrium

Fill in the blank cells in the following table and determine the equilibrium level of real GDP.

Real GDP (Y)	Consumption (C)	Planned Investment (I)	Government Purchases (G)	Net Exports (NX)	Planned Aggregate Expenditure (AE)	Unplanned Change in Inventories
$8,000	$6,200	$1,675	$1,675	−$500		
9,000	6,850	1,675	1,675	−500		
10,000	7,500	1,675	1,675	−500		
11,000	8,150	1,675	1,675	−500		
12,000	8,800	1,675	1,675	−500		

Solving the Problem

Step 1: **Review the chapter material.** This problem is about determining macroeconomic equilibrium, so you may want to review the section "A Numerical Example of Macroeconomic Equilibrium," which begins on page 412.

Step 2: **Fill in the missing values in the table.** We can calculate the missing values in the last two columns by using two equations:

$$\text{Planned aggregate expenditure } (AE) = \text{Consumption } (C)$$
$$+ \text{ Planned investment } (I) + \text{ Government purchases } (G)$$
$$+ \text{ Net exports } (NX)$$

and:

$$\text{Unplanned change in inventories} = \text{Real GDP } (Y)$$
$$- \text{ Planned aggregate expenditure } (AE).$$

For example, to fill in the first row, we have AE = $6,200 billion + $1,675 billion + $1,675 billion + (−$500 billion) = $9,050 billion, and unplanned change in inventories = $8,000 billion − $9,050 billion = −$1,050 billion.

Real GDP (Y)	Consumption (C)	Planned Investment (I)	Government Purchases (G)	Net Exports (NX)	Planned Aggregate Expenditure (AE)	Unplanned Change in Inventories
$8,000	$6,200	$1,675	$1,675	−$500	$9,050	−1,050
9,000	6,850	1,675	1,675	−500	9,700	−700
10,000	7,500	1,675	1,675	−500	10,350	−350
11,000	8,150	1,675	1,675	−500	11,000	0
12,000	8,800	1,675	1,675	−500	11,650	350

Step 3: **Determine the equilibrium level of real GDP.** Once you fill in the table, you should see that equilibrium real GDP must be $11,000 billion because only at that level is real GDP equal to planned aggregate expenditure.

MyEconLab Study Plan   **Your Turn:** For more practice, do related problem 3.12 on page 427 at the end of this chapter.

12.4 The Multiplier Effect

LEARNING OBJECTIVE: Describe the multiplier effect and use the multiplier formula to calculate changes in equilibrium GDP.

So far, we have seen that aggregate expenditure determines real GDP in the short run, and we have seen how the economy adjusts if it is not in equilibrium. We have also seen that whenever aggregate expenditure changes, there will be a new level of equilibrium real GDP. In this section, we will look more closely at the effects of a change in aggregate expenditure on equilibrium real GDP. We begin the discussion with Figure 12.13, which illustrates the effect of an increase in planned investment spending. We assume that the economy starts in equilibrium at point A, at which real GDP is $9.6 trillion. Firms then become more optimistic about the future profitability of investment and increase spending on factories, machinery, and equipment by $100 billion. This increase in investment spending shifts the AE line up by

MyEconLab Animation

Figure 12.13

The Multiplier Effect

The economy begins at point A, at which equilibrium real GDP is $9.6 trillion. A $100 billion increase in planned investment shifts up aggregate expenditure from AE_1 to AE_2. The new equilibrium is at point B, where real GDP is $10.0 trillion, which is potential real GDP. Because of the multiplier effect, a $100 billion increase in investment results in a $400 billion increase in equilibrium real GDP.

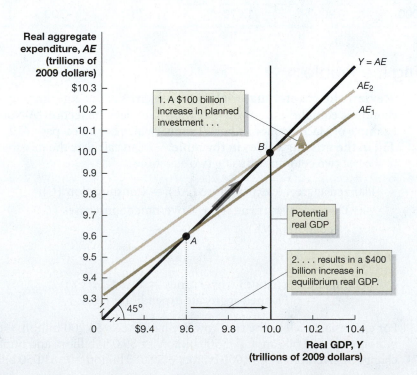

$100 billion, from AE_1 to AE_2. The new equilibrium occurs at point B, at which real GDP is $10.0 trillion, which equals potential real GDP.

Notice that the initial $100 billion increase in planned investment spending results in a $400 billion increase in equilibrium real GDP. The increase in planned investment spending has had a *multiplied effect* on equilibrium real GDP. It is not only investment spending that will have this multiplied effect; any increase in *autonomous expenditure* will shift up the aggregate expenditure function and lead to a multiplied increase in equilibrium GDP. **Autonomous expenditure** does not depend on the level of GDP. In the aggregate expenditure model we have been using, planned investment spending, government spending, and net exports are all autonomous expenditures. Consumption has both an autonomous component, which does not depend on the level of GDP, and a nonautonomous—or *induced*—component, which does depend on the level of GDP. For example, if households decide to spend more of their incomes—and save less—at every level of income, there will be an autonomous increase in consumption spending, and the aggregate expenditure function will shift up. If, however, real GDP increases and households increase their consumption spending, as indicated by the consumption function, there will be a movement up along the aggregate expenditure function, and the increase in consumption spending will be nonautonomous.

The ratio of the increase in equilibrium real GDP to the increase in autonomous expenditure is called the **multiplier**. The series of induced increases in consumption spending that results from an initial increase in autonomous expenditure is called the **multiplier effect**. The multiplier effect occurs because an initial increase in autonomous expenditure sets off a series of increases in real GDP.

We can look more closely at the multiplier effect. Suppose the whole $100 billion increase in investment spending shown in Figure 12.13 consists of firms building additional factories and office buildings. Initially, this additional spending will cause the construction of factories and office buildings to increase by $100 billion, so GDP will also increase by $100 billion. Remember that increases in production result in equal increases in national income. So, this increase in real GDP of $100 billion is also an increase in national income of $100 billion. In this example, the income is received as wages and salaries by the employees of the construction firms, as profit by the owners of the firms, and so on. After receiving this additional income, these workers, managers, and owners will increase their consumption of cars, appliances, furniture, and many other products. If the marginal propensity to consume (*MPC*) is 0.75, we know the increase in consumption spending will be $75 billion. This additional $75 billion in spending will cause the firms making the cars, appliances, and other products to increase production by $75 billion, so GDP will rise by $75 billion. This increase in GDP means national income has also increased by another $75 billion. This increased income will be received by the owners and employees of the firms producing the cars, appliances, and other products. These workers, managers, and owners in turn will increase their consumption spending, and the process of increasing production, income, and consumption will continue.

Eventually, the total increase in consumption will be $300 billion. (We will soon show how we determined this value.) The $300 billion increase in consumption combined with the initial $100 billion increase in investment spending will result in a total change in equilibrium GDP of $400 billion. Table 12.4 summarizes how changes in GDP and spending caused by the initial $100 billion increase in investment will result in equilibrium GDP rising by $400 billion. We can think of the multiplier effect occurring in rounds of spending. In round 1, there is an increase of $100 billion in autonomous expenditure—the $100 billion in planned investment spending in our example—which causes GDP to rise by $100 billion. In round 2, induced expenditure rises by $75 billion (which equals the $100 billion increase in real GDP in round 1 multiplied by the *MPC*). The $75 billion in induced expenditure in round 2 causes a $75 billion increase in real GDP, which leads to a $56 billion increase in induced expenditure in round 3, and so on. The final column adds up the total increases in expenditure, which equal the total increase in GDP. In each round, the additional induced

Table 12.4

The Multiplier Effect in Action

	Additional Autonomous Expenditure (investment)	Additional Induced Expenditure (consumption)	Total Additional Expenditure = Total Additional GDP
Round 1	$100 billion	$0	$100 billion
Round 2	0	75 billion	175 billion
Round 3	0	56 billion	231 billion
Round 4	0	42 billion	273 billion
Round 5	0	32 billion	305 billion
.	.	.	.
.	.	.	.
.	.	.	.
Round 10	0	8 billion	377 billion
.	.	.	.
.	.	.	.
Round 15	0	2 billion	395 billion
.	.	.	.
.	.	.	.
Round 19	0	1 billion	398 billion
.	.	.	.
.	.	.	.
Round *n*	0	0	400 billion

expenditure becomes smaller because the *MPC* is less than 1. By round 10, additional induced expenditure is only $8 billion, and the total increase in GDP from the beginning of the process is $377 billion. By round 19, the process is almost complete: Additional induced expenditure is only about $1 billion, and the total increase in GDP is $398 billion. Eventually, the process will be finished, although we cannot say precisely how many spending rounds it will take, so we simply label the last round *n* rather than give it a specific number.

We can calculate the value of the multiplier in our example by dividing the increase in equilibrium real GDP by the increase in autonomous expenditure:

$$\frac{\Delta Y}{\Delta I} = \frac{\text{Change in real GDP}}{\text{Change in investment spending}} = \frac{\$400 \text{ billion}}{\$100 \text{ billion}} = 4.$$

With a multiplier of 4, each increase in autonomous expenditure of $1 will result in an increase in equilibrium GDP of $4.

Making the Connection

MyEconLab Video

The Multiplier in Reverse: The Great Depression of the 1930s

An increase in autonomous expenditure causes an increase in equilibrium real GDP, but the reverse is also true: A decrease in autonomous expenditure causes a decrease in real GDP. Many Americans became aware of this fact in the 1930s, when reductions in autonomous expenditure were magnified by the multiplier into the largest decline in real GDP in U.S. history.

In August 1929, the economy reached a business cycle peak, and a downturn in production began. In October, the stock market crashed, destroying billions of dollars of wealth and increasing pessimism among households and firms. Both consumption spending and planned investment spending declined. The passage by the U.S. Congress of the Smoot-Hawley Tariff Act in June 1930 helped set off a trade war that reduced exports. A series of banking crises that began in the fall of 1930 limited the ability of households and firms to finance consumption and investment. As aggregate expenditure declined, many firms experienced declining sales and began to lay off workers. Falling levels of production and income induced further declines in consumption spending, which led to further cutbacks in production and employment, leading to further declines in income, and so on, in a downward spiral. The following table shows the severity of the economic downturn by contrasting the business cycle peak of 1929 with the business cycle trough of 1933:

The multiplier effect contributed to the very high levels of unemployment during the Great Depression.

Year	Consumption	Investment	Exports	Real GDP	Unemployment Rate
1929	$781 billion	$124 billion	$41 billion	$1,057 billion	2.9%
1933	$638 billion	$27 billion	$22 billion	$778 billion	20.9%

Note: The values are in 2009 dollars.

Sources: U.S. Bureau of Economic Analysis; and David R. Weir, "A Century of U.S. Unemployment, 1890–1990," in Roger L. Ransom, Richard Sutch, and Susan B. Carter, eds., *Research in Economic History*, Vol. 14, San Diego, CA: JAI Press, 1992, Table D3, pp. 341–343.

We can use a 45°-line diagram to illustrate the multiplier effect working in reverse during these years. The economy was at potential real GDP in 1929, before the declines in aggregate expenditure began. Declining consumption, planned investment, and net exports shifted the aggregate expenditure function down from AE_{1929} to AE_{1933}, reducing equilibrium real GDP from $1,057 billion in 1929 to $778 billion in 1933. The depth and length of this economic downturn led to its being labeled the Great Depression.

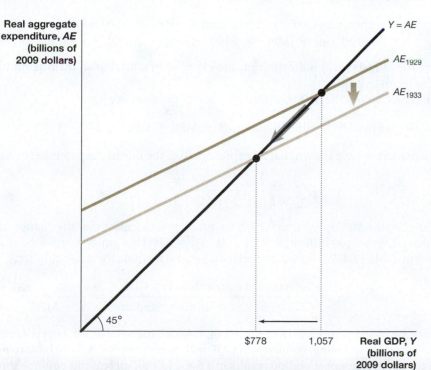

The severity of the Great Depression forced thousands of firms to declare bankruptcy. Even firms that survived experienced sharp declines in sales. By 1933, production at U.S. Steel had declined 90 percent, and production at General Motors had declined more than 75 percent. High rates of unemployment forced many families into poverty and a daily struggle for survival. Recovery from the business cycle trough in 1933 was slow. Real GDP did not regain its 1929 level until 1936, and a growing labor force meant that the unemployment rate did not return to its 1929 level until 1942, after the United States entered World War II.

MyEconLab Study Plan

Your Turn: Test your understanding by doing related problem 4.6 on page 428 at the end of this chapter.

A Formula for the Multiplier

Table 12.4 on page 416 shows that during the multiplier process, each round of increases in consumption is smaller than in the previous round, so eventually, the increases will come to an end, and we will have a new macroeconomic equilibrium. But how do we know that when we add all the increases in GDP, the total will be $400 billion? We can verify this result by first writing out the total change in equilibrium GDP:

The total change in equilibrium real GDP equals the initial increase in planned investment spending $= 100$ billion

Plus the first induced increase in consumption $= MPC \times \$100$ billion

Plus the second induced increase in consumption $= MPC \times (MPC \times \$100$ billion)
$$= MPC^2 \times \$100 \text{ billion}$$

Plus the third induced increase in consumption $= MPC \times (MPC^2 \times \$100$ billion)
$$= MPC^3 \times \$100 \text{ billion}$$

Plus the fourth induced increase in consumption $= MPC \times (MPC^3 \times \$100$ billion)
$$= MPC^4 \times \$100 \text{ billion}$$

and so on …

Or:

$$\text{Total change in GDP} = \$100 \text{ billion} + (MPC \times \$100 \text{ billion}) + (MPC^2 \times \$100 \text{ billion}) + (MPC^3 \times \$100 \text{ billion}) + (MPC^4 \times \$100 \text{ billion}) + \ldots$$

where the ellipsis (…) indicates that the expression contains an infinite number of similar terms.

If we factor out the $100 billion from each expression, we have:

$$\text{Total change in GDP} = \$100 \text{ billion} \times (1 + MPC + MPC^2 + MPC^3 + MPC^4 + \ldots)$$

Mathematicians have shown that an expression like the one in the parentheses sums to:

$$\frac{1}{1 - MPC}.$$

In this case, the MPC is equal to 0.75. So, we can now calculate that the change in equilibrium GDP $= \$100$ billion $\times [1/(1 - 0.75)] = \$100$ billion $\times 4 = \$400$ billion, as shown in Table 12.4. We have also derived a general formula for the multiplier:

$$\text{Multiplier} = \frac{\text{Change in equilibrium real GDP}}{\text{Change in autonomous expenditure}} = \frac{1}{1 - MPC}.$$

In this case, the multiplier is $1/(1 - 0.75)$, or 4, which means that for each additional $1 of autonomous spending, equilibrium GDP will increase by $4. A $100 billion increase in planned investment spending results in a $400 billion increase in equilibrium GDP.

Notice that the value of the multiplier depends on the value of the MPC. In particular, the larger the value of the MPC, the larger the value of the multiplier. For example, if the MPC were 0.9 instead of 0.75, the value of the multiplier would increase from 4 to $1/(1 - 0.9) = 10$.   MyEconLab Concept Check

Summarizing the Multiplier Effect

You should note four key points about the multiplier effect:

1. The multiplier effect occurs both when autonomous expenditure increases and when it decreases. For example, with an MPC of 0.75, a *decrease* in planned investment of $100 billion will lead to a *decrease* in equilibrium income of $400 billion.

2. The multiplier effect makes the economy more sensitive to changes in autonomous expenditure than it would otherwise be. Between the fourth quarter of 2005 and the second quarter of 2009, spending on residential construction declined by 57 percent. This decline in investment set off a series of declines in production, income, and spending so that firms such as automobile dealerships and clothing stores, which are far removed from the housing industry, also experienced declines in sales. Because of the multiplier effect, a decline in spending and production in one sector of the economy can lead to declines in spending and production in many other sectors of the economy.

3. The larger the MPC, the larger the value of the multiplier. With an MPC of 0.75, the multiplier is 4, but with an MPC of 0.50, the multiplier is only 2. This direct relationship between the value of the MPC and the value of the multiplier holds true because the larger the MPC, the larger the change in consumption that takes place after each change in income during the multiplier process.

4. The formula for the multiplier, $1/(1 - MPC)$, is oversimplified because it ignores some real-world complications, such as the effect that increases in GDP have on imports, inflation, interest rates, and individual income taxes. These effects combine to cause the simple formula to overstate the true value of the multiplier. Beginning in Chapter 13, we will start to take into account these real-world complications.   MyEconLab Concept Check

Solved Problem 12.4

MyEconLab Interactive Animation

Using the Multiplier Formula

Use the information in the table to answer the following questions:

Real GDP (Y)	Consumption (C)	Planned Investment (I)	Government Purchases (G)	Net Exports (NX)
$8,000	$6,900	$1,000	$1,000	-$500
9,000	7,700	1,000	1,000	-500
10,000	8,500	1,000	1,000	-500
11,000	9,300	1,000	1,000	-500
12,000	10,100	1,000	1,000	-500

Note: The values are in billions of 2009 dollars.

a. What is the equilibrium level of real GDP?

b. What is the MPC?

c. Suppose government purchases increase by $200 billion. What will be the new equilibrium level of real GDP? Use the multiplier formula to determine your answer.

Solving the Problem

Step 1: Review the chapter material. This problem is about the multiplier process, so you may want to review the section "The Multiplier Effect," which begins on page 414.

Step 2: Answer part (a) by determining equilibrium real GDP. Just as in Solved Problem 12.2 on page 399, we can find macroeconomic equilibrium by calculating the level of planned aggregate expenditure for each level of real GDP:

Real GDP (Y)	Consumption (C)	Planned Investment (I)	Government Purchases (G)	Net Exports (NX)	Planned Aggregate Expenditure (AE)
$8,000	$6,900	$1,000	$1,000	−$500	$8,400
9,000	7,700	1,000	1,000	−500	9,200
10,000	8,500	1,000	1,000	−500	10,000
11,000	9,300	1,000	1,000	−500	10,800
12,000	10,100	1,000	1,000	−500	11,600

We can see that macroeconomic equilibrium will occur when real GDP equals $10,000 billion.

Step 3: **Answer part (b) by calculating the MPC.**

$$MPC = \frac{\Delta C}{\Delta Y}.$$

In this case:

$$MPC = \frac{\$800 \text{ billion}}{\$1,000 \text{ billion}} = 0.8.$$

Step 4: **Answer part (c) by using the multiplier formula to calculate the new equilibrium level of real GDP.** We could find the new level of equilibrium real GDP by constructing a new table with government purchases increased from $1,000 to $1,200. But the multiplier allows us to calculate the answer directly. In this case:

$$\text{Multiplier} = \frac{1}{1 - MPC} = \frac{1}{1 - 0.8} = 5.$$

So:

Change in equilibrium real GDP = Change in autonomous expenditure × 5.

Or:

Change in equilibrium real GDP = $200 billion × 5 = $1,000 billion.

Therefore:

New level of equilibrium GDP = $10,000 billion + $1,000 billion
                            = $11,000 billion.

MyEconLab Study Plan   **Your Turn:** For more practice, do related problem 4.7 on page 428 at the end of this chapter.

The Paradox of Thrift

We have seen that an increase in saving can increase the rate of economic growth in the long run by providing funds for investment (see Chapters 9 and 10). But in the short run, if households save more of their income and spend less of it, aggregate expenditure and real GDP will decline. In discussing the aggregate expenditure model, John Maynard Keynes argued that if many households decide at the same time to increase their saving and reduce their spending, they may make themselves worse off by causing aggregate expenditure to fall, thereby pushing the economy into a recession. The lower incomes in the recession might mean that total saving does not increase, despite the attempts by many individuals to increase their own saving. Keynes called this outcome the *paradox of thrift* because what appears to be something favorable to the long-run performance of the economy might be counterproductive in the short run.

Households saved very little of their income in the mid-2000s but increased their saving markedly in late 2008 and 2009. The personal saving rate is saving by households as a percentage of disposable personal income. By mid-2009, the personal saving rate had increased to 6 percent. Some economists argued that this increase in saving contributed to the recession and weak recovery by reducing consumption spending. Other economists are skeptical of the reasoning behind the paradox of thrift. An increase in saving, by increasing the supply of loanable funds, should lower the real interest rate and increase the level of investment spending (see Chapter 10). This increase in investment spending might offset some or all of the decline in consumption spending attributable to increased saving. Economists continue to debate the short-run effects of an increase in saving.   MyEconLab Concept Check   MyEconLab Study Plan

The Aggregate Demand Curve

LEARNING OBJECTIVE: Understand the relationship between the aggregate demand curve and aggregate expenditure.

When demand for a product increases, firms usually respond by increasing production, but they are also likely to increase prices. Similarly, when demand falls, production falls, but prices may also fall. We would expect, then, that an increase or a decrease in aggregate expenditure would affect not just real GDP but also the *price level*. Will a change in the price level, in turn, affect the components of aggregate expenditure? In fact, as we will see, increases in the price level cause aggregate expenditure to fall, and decreases in the price level cause aggregate expenditure to rise. There are three main reasons for this inverse relationship between changes in the price level and changes in aggregate expenditure. We discussed the first two reasons in Section 12.2 when considering the factors that determine consumption and net exports:

1. A rising price level decreases consumption by decreasing the real value of household wealth; a falling price level has the reverse effect.

2. If the price level in the United States rises relative to the price levels in other countries, U.S. exports will become relatively more expensive, and foreign imports will become relatively less expensive, causing net exports to fall. A falling price level in the United States has the reverse effect.

3. When prices rise, firms and households need more money to finance buying and selling. If the central bank (the Federal Reserve in the United States) does not increase the money supply, the result will be an increase in the interest rate. In Chapter 14, we will analyze in more detail why the interest rate increases. As we discussed in Section 12.2, at a higher interest rate, investment spending falls as firms borrow less money to build new factories or to install new machinery and equipment and households borrow less money to buy new houses. A falling price level has the reverse effect: Other things being equal, interest rates will fall, and investment spending will rise.

We can now incorporate the effect of a change in the price level into the basic aggregate expenditure model, in which equilibrium real GDP is determined by the intersection of the aggregate expenditure (*AE*) line and the 45° line. Remember that we measure the price level as an index number with a value of 100 in the base year. If the price level rises from, say, 100 to 103, consumption, planned investment, and net exports will all fall, causing the *AE* line to shift down in the 45°-line diagram. The *AE* line shifts down because with higher prices, less spending will occur in the economy at every level of GDP. Panel (a) of Figure 12.14 shows that the downward shift of the *AE* line results in a lower level of equilibrium real GDP.

If the price level falls from, say, 100 to 97, then investment, consumption, and net exports will all rise. As panel (b) of Figure 12.14 shows, the *AE* line will shift up, which will cause equilibrium real GDP to increase.

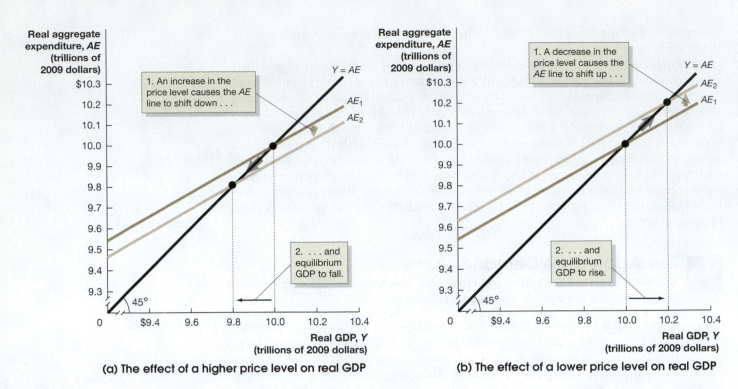

(a) The effect of a higher price level on real GDP

(b) The effect of a lower price level on real GDP

Figure 12.14 The Effect of a Change in the Price Level on Real GDP

In panel (a), an increase in the price level results in declining consumption, planned investment, and net exports and causes the aggregate expenditure line to shift down from AE_1 to AE_2. As a result, equilibrium real GDP declines from $10.0 trillion to $9.8 trillion.

In panel (b), a decrease in the price level results in rising consumption, planned investment, and net exports and causes the aggregate expenditure line to shift up from AE_1 to AE_2. As a result, equilibrium real GDP increases from $10.0 trillion to $10.2 trillion.

Aggregate demand (AD) curve
A curve that shows the relationship between the price level and the level of planned aggregate expenditure in the economy, holding constant all other factors that affect aggregate expenditure.

Figure 12.15 summarizes the effect of changes in the price level on real GDP. The table shows the combinations of price level and real GDP from Figure 12.14. The graph plots the numbers from the table. In the graph, the price level is measured on the vertical axis, and real GDP is measured on the horizontal axis. The relationship shown in Figure 12.15 between the price level and the level of planned aggregate expenditure is known as the **aggregate demand (AD) curve**.

Figure 12.15

The Aggregate Demand Curve

The aggregate demand (AD) curve shows the relationship between the price level and the level of planned aggregate expenditure in the economy. When the price level is 97, real GDP is $10.2 trillion. An increase in the price level to 100 causes consumption, investment, and net exports to fall, which reduces real GDP to $10.0 trillion.

Price level	Equilibrium real GDP
97	$10.2 trillion
100	10.0 trillion
103	9.8 trillion

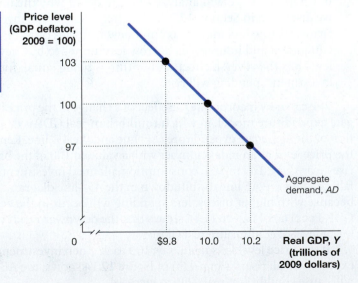

Continued from page 389

Economics in Your Life

When Consumer Confidence Falls, Is Your Job at Risk?

At the beginning of this chapter, we asked you to suppose that you work part time for a company that manufacturers door handles for automobiles. You have learned that consumer confidence in the economy has fallen and that many households expect their future income to be well below their current income. Should you be concerned about losing your job? We have seen in this chapter that if consumers expect their future income to decline, they will cut their consumption spending, and consumption spending is more than two-thirds of aggregate expenditure. So, if the decline in consumer confidence is correctly forecasting a decline in consumption spending, then aggregate expenditure and GDP will also likely decline. In deciding how likely your company is to lay you off, you should consider the following factors: If the economy moves into a recession, spending on automobiles by households and firms is likely to fall, which could reduce your firm's sales and possibly cost you a job. Before you panic, though, keep in mind that surveys of consumer confidence do not have a good track record in predicting recessions, so you may not have to move back in with your parents after all.

Conclusion

In this chapter, we examined a key macroeconomic idea: In the short run, the level of GDP is determined mainly by the level of aggregate expenditure. When economists forecast changes in GDP, they do so by forecasting changes in the four components of aggregate expenditure. We constructed an aggregate demand curve by taking into account how changes in the price level affect aggregate expenditure.

But our story is incomplete. In Chapter 13, we will analyze the *aggregate supply curve*. Then we will use the aggregate demand curve and the aggregate supply curve to show how equilibrium real GDP and the equilibrium price level are simultaneously determined.

We also need to discuss the roles that the financial system and government policy play in determining real GDP and the price level in the short run. We will cover these important topics in the following chapters.

Visit MyEconLab for a news article and analysis related to the concepts in this chapter.

Key Terms

Aggregate demand (AD) curve, p. 422

Aggregate expenditure (AE), p. 390

Aggregate expenditure model, p. 390

Autonomous expenditure, p. 415

Cash flow, p. 401

Consumption function, p. 395

Inventories, p. 391

Marginal propensity to consume (MPC), p. 396

Marginal propensity to save (MPS), p. 398

Multiplier, p. 415

Multiplier effect, p. 415

12.1 The Aggregate Expenditure Model, pages 390–393

LEARNING OBJECTIVE: Understand how macroeconomic equilibrium is determined in the aggregate expenditure model.

Summary

Aggregate expenditure (AE) is the total amount of spending in the economy. The **aggregate expenditure model** focuses on the relationship between total spending and real GDP in the short run, assuming that the price level is constant. In any particular year, the level of GDP is determined by the level of total spending, or aggregate expenditure, in the economy. The four components of aggregate expenditure are consumption (C), planned investment (I), government purchases (G), and net exports (NX). When aggregate expenditure is greater than GDP, there is an unplanned decrease in **inventories**, which are goods that have been produced but not yet sold, and GDP and total employment will increase. When aggregate expenditure is less than GDP, there is an unplanned increase in inventories, and GDP and total employment will decline. When aggregate expenditure is equal to GDP, firms will sell what they expected to sell, production and employment will be unchanged, and the economy will be in macroeconomic equilibrium.

MyEconLab   Visit **www.myeconlab.com** to complete these exercises online and get instant feedback.

Review Questions

1.1 What is the key idea in the aggregate expenditure macroeconomic model?

1.2 What are inventories? What usually happens to inventories at the beginning of a recession? At the beginning of an expansion?

1.3 Which of the following does the aggregate expenditure model seek to explain: long-run economic growth, the business cycle, inflation, or cyclical unemployment?

Problems and Applications

1.4 Into which category of aggregate expenditure would each of the following transactions fall?
   a. The Jones family buys a new car.
   b. The San Diego Unified School District buys 12 new school buses.
   c. The Jones family buys a newly constructed house from the Garcia Construction Co.
   d. Joe Jones orders a Burberry coat from an online site in the United Kingdom.
   e. Prudential insurance company purchases 250 new iPads from Apple.

1.5 Assume that Intel sells $1 billion of computer chips to Dell, Inc., for use in Dell's personal computers. How does this transaction affect aggregate expenditure?

1.6 In reporting on real GDP growth in the second quarter of 2015, an article in the *Wall Street Journal* noted that the 2.3 percent annual growth rate "would have been stronger if it hadn't been for companies drawing down inventories."
   a. If companies are "drawing down inventories," is aggregate expenditure likely to have been larger or smaller than GDP?
   b. Assume that the reduction in inventories was unplanned. What would you expect to happen to production in the future following an unplanned reduction in inventories?

Source: Justin Lahart, "Consumers Priming U.S. Pump," *Wall Street Journal*, July 30, 2015.

1.7 In the third quarter of 2015, business inventories in the United States increased by $62 billion. Can we tell from this information whether aggregate expenditure was higher or lower than GDP during the third quarter of 2015? If not, what other information do we need?

Source: Bureau of Economic Analysis.

1.8 An article in the *Wall Street Journal* stated that in China, "carmakers continue to grapple with ... rising inventories." Why might carmakers in China find that their inventories are unexpectedly rising? How are these carmakers likely to react to the increase in inventories?

Source: Colum Murphy, "China's Automobile Sales to Slow Further in 2015," *Wall Street Journal*, January 12, 2015.

1.9 According to an article in the *Wall Street Journal*, in late 2014, the Japanese economy experienced a large increase in business inventories. The article noted, "The large buildup of inventories is a reflection that the ... drop in demand was bigger than expected." Does it matter that Japanese firms didn't expect the drop in demand? Won't a decline in demand always lead to an increase in firms' holdings of inventories? Briefly explain.

Source: Eleanor Warnock, "Rising Inventories Hamper Japan Recovery," *Wall Street Journal*, September 30, 2014.

12.2   Determining the Level of Aggregate Expenditure in the Economy, pages 393–407

LEARNING OBJECTIVE: Discuss the determinants of the four components of aggregate expenditure and define marginal propensity to consume and marginal propensity to save.

Summary

The five determinants of consumption are current disposable income, household wealth, expected future income, the price level, and the interest rate. The **consumption function** is the relationship between consumption and disposable income. The **marginal propensity to consume (MPC)** is the change in consumption divided by the change in disposable income. The **marginal propensity to save (MPS)** is the change in saving divided by the change in disposable income. The determinants of planned investment are expectations of future profitability, the real interest rate, taxes, and **cash flow**, which is the difference between the cash revenues received by a firm and the cash spending by the firm. Government purchases include spending by the federal government and by local and state governments for goods and services. Government purchases do not include *transfer payments*, such as Social Security payments by the federal government or pension payments by local governments to retired police officers and firefighters. The three determinants of net exports are changes in the price level in the United States relative to changes in the price levels in other countries, the growth rate of GDP in the United States relative to the growth rates of GDP in other countries, and the exchange rate between the dollar and other currencies.

MyEconLab   Visit **www.myeconlab.com** to complete these exercises online and get instant feedback.

Review Questions

2.1 In the aggregate expenditure model, why is it important to know the factors that determine consumption spending, investment spending, government purchases, and net exports?

2.2 What are the five main determinants of consumption spending? Which of these is the most important? How would a rise in stock prices or housing prices affect consumption spending?

2.3 Compare what happened to real investment between 1979 and the second quarter of 2015 with what happened to real consumption during that period.

2.4 What are the four main determinants of investment? How would a change in interest rates affect investment?

2.5 What are the three main determinants of net exports? How would an increase in the growth rate of GDP in the BRIC nations (Brazil, Russia, India, and China) affect U.S. net exports?

Problems and Applications

2.6 (Related to the Chapter Opener on page 389) Suppose a major U.S. appliance manufacturer is forecasting demand for its products during the next year. How will the forecast be affected by each of the following?

   a. A survey shows a sharp rise in consumer confidence that income growth will be increasing.

   b. Real interest rates are expected to increase.

   c. The value of the U.S. dollar is expected to increase versus foreign currencies.

   d. Planned investment spending in the economy is expected to decrease.

2.7 Draw the consumption function and label each axis. Show the effect of an increase in income on consumption spending. Does the change in income cause a movement along the consumption function or a shift of the consumption function? How would an increase in expected future income or an increase in household wealth affect the consumption function? Would these increases cause a movement along the consumption function or a shift of the consumption function? Briefly explain.

2.8 An economics student raises the following objection: "The textbook said that a higher interest rate lowers investment, but this doesn't make sense. I know that if I can get a higher interest rate, I am certainly going to invest more in my savings account." Briefly explain whether you agree with this reasoning.

2.9 Unemployed workers receive unemployment insurance payments from the government. Does the existence of unemployment insurance make it likely that consumption will fluctuate more or less over the business cycle than it would in the absence of unemployment insurance? Briefly explain.

2.10 (Related to Solved Problem 12.2 on page 399) Fill in the blank cells in the following table. Assume for simplicity that taxes are zero. Also assume that the values represent billions of 2009 dollars.

National Income and Real GDP (Y)	Consumption (C)	Saving (S)	Marginal Propensity to Consume (MPC)	Marginal Propensity to Save (MPS)
$9,000	$8,000			
10,000	8,750			
11,000	9,500			
12,000	10,250			
13,000	11,000			

2.11 (Related to the Making the Connection on page 401) In an opinion column in the *Wall Street Journal*, Purdue University President Mitchell Daniels wrote that "today's 20- and 30-year-olds are delaying marriage and delaying childbearing, both unhelpful trends from an economic and social standpoint." Why might young people be delaying marriage and childbearing? Why would this trend be unhelpful from an economic point of view? Is the trend possibly connected with the slow recovery from the 2007–2009 recession? Briefly explain.

Source: Mitchell E, Daniels, "How Student Debt Harms the Economy," *Wall Street Journal*, January 27, 2015.

2.12 (Related to the Chapter Opener on page 381) An article in the *Wall Street Journal* on changes in Intel's sales noted, "Intel sells its chips to customers in U.S. dollars, but many PC makers that buy those chips sell their products in local currencies." In these circumstances, would an increase in the value of the dollar relative to foreign currencies be likely to help or hurt Intel's sales? Briefly explain.

Source: Tess Stynes, "Intel Earnings: What to Watch," *Wall Street Journal,* July 15, 2015.

2.13 (Related to the Making the Connection on page 406) Briefly explain which of the following statement is correct.
a. The iPhone is made in China, using Chinese-made parts.
b. The iPhone is made in the United States, using U.S.-made parts.
c. The iPhone is made in the United States, using Chinese-made parts.
d. The iPhone is made China, using parts that are all made outside China.

What relevance does your answer have to how the Bureau of Economic Analysis calculates data on U.S. imports?

2.14 (Related to the Making the Connection on page 406) In a speech to a conference of government trade officials, Angel Gurría, secretary general of the Organization for Economic Co-operation and Development, made the following observation: "As goods and services cross borders several times at different stages of processing, conventional trade statistics may not tell the whole story."
a. What does Gurría mean by "conventional trade statistics"?
b. Why might conventional trade statistics no longer be as reliable as they once were?
c. What difficulties might the problems with trade statistics cause for policymakers?

Source: Angel Gurría, "Understanding Global Value Chains," Speech delivered at the G20 trade ministers conference in Puerto Vallarta, Mexico, April 19, 2012, www.oecd.org/about/secretary-general/g20understandingglobalvaluechains.htm.

12.3 **Graphing Macroeconomic Equilibrium, pages 407–414**

LEARNING OBJECTIVE: Use a 45°-line diagram to illustrate macroeconomic equilibrium.

Summary

The 45°-line diagram shows all the points where aggregate expenditure equals real GDP. On the 45°-line diagram, macroeconomic equilibrium occurs where the line representing the aggregate expenditure function crosses the 45° line. The economy is in recession when the aggregate expenditure line intersects the 45° line at a level of GDP that is below potential GDP. Numerically, macroeconomic equilibrium occurs when:

Consumption + Planned investment + Government purchases + Net exports = GDP.

 Visit **www.myeconlab.com** to complete these exercises online and get instant feedback.

Review Questions

3.1 What is the meaning of the 45° line in the 45°-line diagram?

3.2 Use a 45°-line diagram to illustrate macroeconomic equilibrium. Make sure your diagram shows the aggregate expenditure function and the level of equilibrium real GDP and that your axes are properly labeled.

3.3 What does the slope of the aggregate expenditure line equal? How is the slope of the aggregate expenditure line related to the slope of the consumption function?

3.4 What is likely to happen if firms accumulate large amounts of unplanned inventory at the beginning of a recession?

3.5 What is the difference between aggregate expenditure and consumption spending?

Problems and Applications

3.6 At point *A* in the following graph, is planned aggregate expenditure greater than, equal to, or less than GDP? What about at point *B*? At point *C*? For points *A* and *C*, indicate the vertical distance that measures the unintended change in inventories.

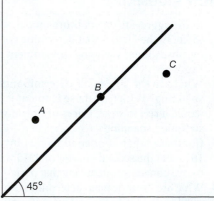

3.7 Suppose we drop the assumption that net exports do not depend on real GDP. Draw a graph with the value of net exports on the vertical axis and the value of real GDP on the horizontal axis. Now, add a line representing the relationship between net exports and real GDP. Does your net exports line have a positive or negative slope? Briefly explain.

3.8 A Federal Reserve publication notes that "the shedding of unwanted inventories often accounts for a large portion of the decline in gross domestic product (GDP) during economic recessions." What does the author mean be "shedding of unwanted inventories"? What makes the inventories unwanted? Why would shedding inventories lead to a decline in GDP?

Source: Jeremy M. Piger, "Is the Business Cycle Still an Inventory Cycle?" *Economic Synopses*, Federal Reserve Bank of St. Louis, No. 2, 2005.

3.9 An article on bloomberg.com about the Japanese economy noted, "Whether the 2.4 percent annualized gain in gross domestic product reported Wednesday can be maintained depends on consumers stepping in to buy the products that companies are piling up in warehouses."
a. Did business inventories in Japan increase or decrease during this period? Briefly explain.
b. What would happen if consumers do not buy the products that companies are piling up? Illustrate your answer with a 45°-line diagram.

Source: Keiko Ujikane and Toru Fujioka, "Japan's Economy Grows as Investment Gains, Inventories Rise," bloomberg.com, May 20, 2015.

3.10 Consider the table in the next column, which shows the change in inventories for each quarter from the first quarter of 2007 (2007:I) through the fourth quarter of 2010 (2010:IV) measured in billions of 2009 dollars. Provide a macroeconomic explanation for this pattern. (*Hint:* When did the recession during this period begin and end?)

Accompanies problem 3.10.

Year	Quarter	Change in Inventories
2007	I	$19.6
	II	49.4
	III	50.2
	IV	23.0
2008	I	−20.2
	II	−26.4
	III	−20.7
	IV	−67.4
2009	I	−144.5
	II	−190.1
	III	−206.1
	IV	−49.6
2010	I	9.8
	II	48.8
	III	116.2
	IV	58.1

3.11 **(Related to the** Don't Let This Happen to You **on page 412)** Briefly explain whether you agree with the following argument: "The equilibrium level of GDP is determined by the level of aggregate expenditure. Therefore, GDP will decline only if households decide to spend less on goods and services."

3.12 **(Related to** Solved Problem 12.3 **on page 413)** Fill in the blank cells in the table below. Assume that the value of the *MPC* does not change as real GDP changes. Also assume that the values represent billions of 2009 dollars.
a. What is the value of the *MPC*?
b. What is the value of equilibrium real GDP?

Accompanies problem 3.12.

Real GDP (Y)	Consumption (C)	Planned Investment (I)	Government Purchases (G)	Net Exports (NX)	Planned Aggregate Expenditure (AE)	Unplanned Change in Inventories
$9,000	$7,600	$1,200	$1,200	−$400		
10,000	8,400	1,200	1,200	−400		
11,000		1,200	1,200	−400		
12,000		1,200	1,200	−400		
13,000		1,200	1,200	−400		

12.4 **The Multiplier Effect, pages 414–421**

LEARNING OBJECTIVE: Describe the multiplier effect and use the multiplier formula to calculate changes in equilibrium GDP.

Summary

Autonomous expenditure is expenditure that does not depend on the level of GDP. An autonomous change is a change in expenditure not caused by a change in income. An *induced change* is a change in aggregate expenditure caused by a change in income. An autonomous change in expenditure will cause rounds of induced changes in expenditure. Therefore, an autonomous change in expenditure will have a *multiplier effect* on equilibrium GDP. The **multiplier effect** is the process by which an increase in autonomous expenditure leads to a larger increase in real GDP. The **multiplier** is the ratio of the change in equilibrium GDP to the change in autonomous expenditure. The formula for the multiplier is:

$$\frac{1}{1 - MPC}.$$

Because of the paradox of thrift, an attempt by many individuals to increase their saving may lead to a reduction in aggregate expenditure and a recession.

MyEconLab Visit www.myeconlab.com to complete these exercises online and get instant feedback.

Review Questions

4.1 The following graph contains two aggregate expenditure functions. Consider a movement from point A to point B and a movement from point B to point C. Which movement shows a change in *autonomous* expenditure? Which movement shows a change in *induced* expenditure? Briefly explain your answers.

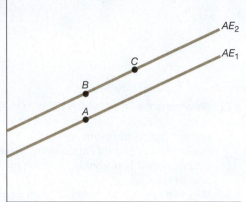

4.2 What is the multiplier effect? Use a 45°-line diagram to illustrate the multiplier effect of a decrease in government purchases.

4.3 What is the formula for the multiplier? Explain why this formula is considered to be too simple.

Problems and Applications

4.4 In Figure 12.13 on page 414, the economy is initially in equilibrium at point A. Aggregate expenditure and real GDP both equal $9.6 trillion. The increase in investment of $100 billion increases aggregate expenditure to $9.7 trillion. If real GDP increases to $9.7 trillion, will the economy be in equilibrium? Briefly explain. What happens to aggregate expenditure when real GDP increases to $9.7 trillion?

4.5 An opinion column in the *New York Times* quotes an economist's analysis of the effect of government infrastructure spending on new bridges and highways in the United States: "The investment multiplier would give a further kick to the U.S. economy."
   a. What does the economist mean by the "investment multiplier"?
   b. Briefly explain what the economist means by saying that the investment multiplier would "give a further kick to the U.S. economy."

   Source: Thomas L. Friedman, "Why 2014 Is a Big Deal," *New York Times*, December 13, 2014.

4.6 (Related to the Making the Connection on page 416) If the multiplier had a value of 4 in 1929, how large must the change in autonomous expenditure have been to have caused the decline in real GDP between 1929 and 1933 shown in the table on page 417 ? If the multiplier had a value of 2, how large must the change in autonomous expenditure have been?

4.7 (Related to Solved Problem 12.4 on page 419) Use the information in the following table to answer the questions. Assume that the values represent billions of 2009 dollars.

Real GDP (Y)	Consumption (C)	Planned Investment (I)	Government Purchases (G)	Net Exports (NX)
$8,000	$7,300	$1,000	$1,000	−$500
9,000	7,900	1,000	1,000	−500
10,000	8,500	1,000	1,000	−500
11,000	9,100	1,000	1,000	−500
12,000	9,700	1,000	1,000	−500

   a. What is the equilibrium level of real GDP?
   b. What is the *MPC*?
   c. Suppose net exports increase by $400 billion. What will be the new equilibrium level of real GDP? Use the multiplier formula to determine your answer.

4.8 An article published in an economics journal found the following: "For the poorest households, the marginal propensity to consume was close to 70%. For the richest households, the *MPC* was only 35%." Assume that the macroeconomy can be divided into three sections. Section A consists of the poorest households, Section B consists of the richest households, and Section C consists of all other households.
   a. Compute the value of the multiplier for Section A.
   b. Compute the value of the multiplier for Section B.
   c. Assume that there was an increase in planned investment of $4 billion. Compute the change in equilibrium real GDP if the *MPC* for the economy was 70 percent (or 0.70). Compute the change in equilibrium real GDP if the *MPC* for the economy was 35 percent (or 0.35).

   Source: Atif Mian and Amir Sufi, "Who Spends Extra Cash?" *House of Debt*, April 13, 2014.

4.9 Explain whether each of the following would cause the value of the multiplier to be larger or smaller.
   a. An increase in real GDP increases imports.
   b. An increase in real GDP increases interest rates.
   c. An increase in real GDP increases the marginal propensity to consume.
   d. An increase in real GDP causes the average tax rate paid by households to decrease.
   e. An increase in real GDP increases the price level.

4.10 Suppose the rate of growth of the economies in the BRIC nations (Brazil, Russia, India, and China) slows down, causing U.S. net exports to fall by $75 billion. If the *MPC* is 0.8, what will be the change in equilibrium U.S. GDP?

4.11 Would a larger multiplier lead to longer and more severe recessions or shorter and less severe recessions? Briefly explain.

4.12 A study by the management consulting company McKinsey & Company recommended that the U.S. increase spending on infrastructure, such as bridges and highways, by between $150 and $180 billion per year. The study estimated that the result would be an increase in GDP of between $270 billion and $320 billion per year. What is the implied value of the multiplier if the McKinsey study's estimate of the effect of infrastructure spending on GDP is correct?

Source: David Harrison, "Nation's Crumbling Roads Put a Dent in Drivers' Wallets," *Wall Street Journal*, July 31, 2015.

4.13 Use the following graph to answer the questions.
  a. What is the value of equilibrium real GDP?
  b. What is the value of the *MPC*?
  c. What is the value of the multiplier?
  d. What is the value of unplanned changes in inventories when real GDP has each of the following values?
    i. $10 trillion
    ii. $12 trillion
    iii. $14 trillion

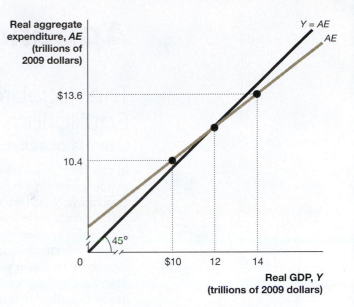

12.5 ## The Aggregate Demand Curve, pages 421–422

LEARNING OBJECTIVE: Understand the relationship between the aggregate demand curve and aggregate expenditure.

Summary

Increases in the price level cause a reduction in consumption, investment, and net exports. This causes the aggregate expenditure function to shift down on the 45°-line diagram, leading to a lower equilibrium real GDP. A decrease in the price level leads to a higher equilibrium real GDP. The **aggregate demand (AD) curve** shows the relationship between the price level and the level of aggregate expenditure, holding constant all factors other than the price level that affect aggregate expenditure.

MyEconLab   Visit **www.myeconlab.com** to complete these exercises online and get instant feedback.

Review Questions

5.1 Explain the difference between aggregate expenditure and aggregate demand.

5.2 Explain which components of aggregate expenditure are affected by a change in the price level.

5.3 Does a change in the price level cause a movement along the aggregate expenditure line or a shift of the aggregate expenditure line? Does a change in the price level cause a movement along the aggregate demand curve or a shift of the aggregate demand curve?

Problems and Applications

5.4 Explain why the aggregate expenditure line is upward sloping, while the aggregate demand curve is downward sloping.

5.5 Explain whether you agree with the following statement: "The reason the aggregate demand curve slopes downward is that when the price level is higher, people cannot afford to buy as many goods and services."

5.6 Suppose that exports become more sensitive to changes in the price level in the United States. That is, when the price level in the United States rises, exports decline by more than they previously did. Will this change make the aggregate demand curve steeper or less steep? Briefly explain.

Real-Time Data Exercises

D12.1 (Calculating the multiplier effect) Using data from the Federal Reserve Bank of St. Louis (FRED) (research.stlouisfed.org/fred2/), analyze the effect of a decline in exports on GDP.
  a. Download data since 1990 on Real Exports of Goods and Services (EXPGSC1).
  b. What was the dollar value of the decline in real exports between the second quarter of 2008 and the first quarter of 2009? If the multiplier is 2, holding everything else constant, what was the effect of this decline in exports on real GDP?

Appendix

The Algebra of Macroeconomic Equilibrium

LEARNING OBJECTIVE: Apply the algebra of macroeconomic equilibrium.

In this chapter, we relied primarily on graphs and tables to illustrate the aggregate expenditure model of short-run real GDP. Graphs help us understand economic change *qualitatively*. When we write an economic model using equations, we make it easier to make *quantitative estimates*. When economists forecast future movements in GDP, they often rely on *econometric models*. An econometric model is an economic model written in the form of equations, where each equation has been statistically estimated using methods similar to the methods used in estimating demand curves that we briefly described in Chapter 3. We can use equations to represent the aggregate expenditure model described in this chapter.

The following equations are based on the example shown in Table 12.3 on page 412. *Y* stands for real GDP, and the numbers (with the exception of the *MPC*) represent billions of dollars.

1. $C = 1{,}000 + 0.65Y$ Consumption function
2. $I = 1{,}500$ Planned investment function
3. $G = 1{,}500$ Government purchases function
4. $NX = -500$ Net export function
5. $Y = C + I + G + NX$ Equilibrium condition

The first equation is the consumption function. The *MPC* is 0.65, and 1,000 is autonomous consumption, which is the level of consumption that does not depend on income. If we think of the consumption function as a line on the 45°-line diagram, 1,000 would be the intercept, and 0.65 would be the slope. The "functions" for the other three components of planned aggregate expenditure are very simple because we have assumed that these components are not affected by GDP and, therefore, are constant. Economists who use this type of model to forecast GDP would, of course, use more realistic investment, government, and net export functions. The *parameters* of the functions—such as the value of autonomous consumption and the value of the *MPC* in the consumption function—would be estimated statistically, using data on the values of each variable over a period of years.

In this model, GDP is in equilibrium when it equals planned aggregate expenditure. Equation 5—the equilibrium condition—shows us how to calculate equilibrium in the model: We need to substitute equations 1 through 4 into equation 5. Doing so gives us the following:

$$Y = 1{,}000 + 0.65Y + 1{,}500 + 1{,}500 - 500.$$

We need to solve this expression for *Y* to find equilibrium GDP. The first step is to subtract 0.65Y from both sides of the equation:

$$Y - 0.65Y = 1{,}000 + 1{,}500 + 1{,}500 - 500.$$

Then, we solve for *Y*:

$$0.35Y = 3{,}500.$$

Or:

$$Y = \frac{3{,}500}{0.35} = 10{,}000.$$

To make this result more general, we can replace particular values with general values represented by letters:

1. $C = \bar{C} + MPC(Y)$ Consumption function
2. $I = \bar{I}$ Planned investment function
3. $G = \bar{G}$ Government purchases function
4. $NX = \overline{NX}$ Net export function
5. $Y = C + I + G + NX$ Equilibrium condition

The letters with bars over them represent fixed, or autonomous, values. So, for example, $\bar{C}$ represents autonomous consumption, which had a value of 1,000 in our original example. Now, solving for equilibrium, we get:

$$Y = \bar{C} + MPC(Y) + \bar{I} + \bar{G} + \overline{NX},$$

or:

$$Y - MPC(Y) = \bar{C} + \bar{I} + \bar{G} + \overline{NX},$$

or:

$$Y(1 - MPC) = \bar{C} + \bar{I} + \bar{G} + \overline{NX},$$

or:

$$Y = \frac{\bar{C} + \bar{I} + \bar{G} + \overline{NX}}{1 - MPC}.$$

Remember that $1/(1 - MPC)$ is the multiplier, and all four variables in the numerator of the equation represent autonomous expenditure. Therefore, an alternative expression for equilibrium GDP is:

$$\text{Equilibrium GDP} = \text{Autonomous expenditure} \times \text{Multiplier}.$$

MyEconLab Concept Check

12A   ## The Algebra of Macroeconomic Equilibrium, pages 430–431

LEARNING OBJECTIVE: Apply the algebra of macroeconomic equilibrium.

MyEconLab   Visit **www.myeconlab.com** to complete these exercises online and get instant feedback.

Review Questions

12A.1 Write a general expression for the aggregate expenditure function. If you think of the aggregate expenditure function as a line on the 45°-line diagram, what would be the intercept and what would be the slope, using the general values represented by letters?

12A.2 Find equilibrium GDP using the following macroeconomic model (where the numbers, with the exception of the *MPC*, represent billions of dollars).

1. $C = 1,500 + 0.75Y$ Consumption function
2. $I = 1,250$ Planned investment function
3. $G = 1,250$ Government purchases function
4. $NX = -250$ Net export function
5. $Y = C + I + G + NX$ Equilibrium condition

12A.3 For the macroeconomic model in problem 12A.2, write the aggregate expenditure function. For GDP of $16,000, what is the value of aggregate expenditure, and what is the value of the unintended change in inventories? For GDP of $12,000, what is the value of aggregate expenditure, and what is the value of the unintended change in inventories?

12A.4 Suppose that autonomous consumption is 500, government purchases are 1,000, planned investment spending is 1,250, net exports are −250, and the *MPC* is 0.8. What is equilibrium GDP?

CHAPTER 13

Aggregate Demand and Aggregate Supply Analysis

Chapter Outline and Learning Objectives

The Fortunes of Delta Airlines Follow the Business Cycle

An infestation of insects that threatened cotton fields in Southern states led B. R. Coad and Collett E. Woolman to form a crop-dusting business, the Huff Daland Dusters, in 1924. By 1930 the company was renamed the Delta Air Corporation and offered air-mail and passenger service. Delta Air Lines has grown into the world's largest airline, flying over 170 million passengers to more than 300 destinations worldwide in 2015 and earning revenue of more than $40 billion.

Despite Delta's long-run success, its fortunes and the fortunes of the other U.S. airlines are dependent on the ups and downs of the business cycle. As a *Wall Street Journal* article put it: "Year after year, domestic revenue came in at 0.73% of GDP." That relationship is good news during economic expansions, when GDP is increasing, but it's bad news during recessions, when GDP is falling. During the severe 2007–2009 recession, Delta both sold fewer passenger tickets and had to cut the prices of the tickets it did sell. The result was a $1.2 billion loss in 2009.

By 2015, with GDP steadily growing during the economic expansion, Delta was earning a record profit as both the number of passengers flown and ticket prices were increasing. Delta was also benefiting from falling jet fuel prices as increased output from U.S. shale oil fields led to a worldwide decline in oil prices. Many business analysts consider Delta to be the best managed of the four large U.S. airlines—the other three being Southwest, American Airlines, and United. Still, Delta management was taking steps to reduce the problems the airline would experience when—inevitably—the next recession occurred. Domestically, Delta was attempting to reduce costs by "upgauging," or adding seats to existing planes and replacing small planes with larger planes. Internationally, Delta continued a strategy of buying partial ownership of foreign airlines. In 2015, it purchased part of China Eastern Airlines. Under terms of the deal, the two airlines would list each other's flights on their reservation systems and share some facilities at Chinese airports. By expanding overseas, Delta was not only participating in rapidly growing markets but also insulating itself to some extent from the fluctuations of the U.S. business cycle.

To better understand how the business cycle affects Delta Air Lines and other firms, we need to explore the effects that recessions and expansions have on production, employment, and prices.

Sources: Susan Carey, "Delta Air Lines to Buy China Eastern Stake for $450 Million," *Wall Street Journal*, July 27, 2015; Bob McAdoo and Scott Buck, "American Airlines Shares Have Over 70% Upside," barrons.com, July 27, 2015; Susan Carey, "Airline Industry Sees Pain Extending Beyond the Recession," *Wall Street Journal*, August 17, 2009; and Delta Air Lines, "Earnings Releases," various dates.

Economics in Your Life

Is an Employer Likely to Cut Your Pay during a Recession?

Suppose that you have worked as a barista for a local coffeehouse for two years. From on-the-job training and experience, you have honed your coffee-making skills and mastered the perfect latte. Then the economy moves into a recession, and sales at the coffeehouse decline. Is the owner of the coffeehouse likely to cut the prices of lattes and other drinks? Suppose the owner asks to meet with you to discuss your wages for next year. Is the owner likely to cut your pay? As you read this chapter, try to answer these questions. You can check your answers against those we provide on **page 461** at the end of this chapter.

W
e have seen that the U.S. economy has experienced a long-run upward trend in real GDP. These increases in real GDP have raised the standard of living in the United States to a level much higher today than it was 100 years ago. In the short run, however, real GDP fluctuates around this long-run upward trend because of the business cycle. Fluctuations in GDP lead to fluctuations in employment. These fluctuations in real GDP and employment are the most visible and dramatic part of the business cycle. During recessions, we are more likely to see factories close, small businesses declare bankruptcy, and workers lose their jobs. During expansions, we are more likely to see new businesses open and new jobs created. In addition to these changes in output and employment, the business cycle causes changes in wages and prices. Some firms react to a decline in sales by cutting back on production, but they may also cut the prices they charge and the wages they pay. Other firms respond to a recession by raising prices and workers' wages by less than they otherwise would have.

In this chapter, we expand our discussion of the business cycle by developing the aggregate demand and aggregate supply model. This model will help us analyze the effects of recessions and expansions on production, employment, and prices.

13.1 Aggregate Demand

LEARNING OBJECTIVE: Identify the determinants of aggregate demand and distinguish between a movement along the aggregate demand curve and a shift of the curve.

Aggregate demand and aggregate supply model A model that explains short-run fluctuations in real GDP and the price level.

Aggregate demand (AD) curve A curve that shows the relationship between the price level and the quantity of real GDP demanded by households, firms, and the government.

Short-run aggregate supply (SRAS) curve A curve that shows the relationship in the short run between the price level and the quantity of real GDP supplied by firms.

To understand what happens during the business cycle, we need an explanation of why real GDP, the unemployment rate, and the inflation rate fluctuate. We have already seen that fluctuations in the unemployment rate are caused mainly by fluctuations in real GDP. In this chapter, we use the **aggregate demand and aggregate supply model** to explain short-run fluctuations in real GDP and the price level. As Figure 13.1 shows, real GDP and the price level in this model are determined in the short run by the intersection of the *aggregate demand curve* and the *aggregate supply curve*. Fluctuations in real GDP and the price level are caused by shifts in the aggregate demand curve or in the aggregate supply curve.

The **aggregate demand (AD) curve** shows the relationship between the price level and the quantity of real GDP demanded by households, firms, and the government. The **short-run aggregate supply (SRAS) curve** shows the relationship in the short run between the price level and the quantity of real GDP supplied by firms. The aggregate demand and short-run aggregate supply curves in Figure 13.1 look similar to the individual market demand and supply curves we studied in Chapter 3. However, because these curves apply to the whole economy, rather than to just a single market, the aggregate demand and aggregate supply model is very different from the model of demand and supply in individual markets. Because we are dealing with the economy as a whole, we need *macroeconomic* explanations of why the aggregate demand curve is downward sloping, why the short-run aggregate supply curve is upward sloping, and why the curves shift. We begin by explaining why the aggregate demand curve is downward sloping.

Why Is the Aggregate Demand Curve Downward Sloping?

We have seen that GDP has four components:

- Consumption (*C*)
- Investment (*I*)
- Government purchases (*G*)
- Net exports (*NX*)

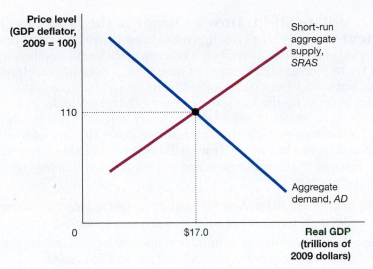

Figure 13.1   Aggregate Demand and Aggregate Supply

In the short run, real GDP and the price level are determined by the intersection of the aggregate demand curve and the short-run aggregate supply curve. In the figure, real GDP is measured on the horizontal axis, and the price level is measured on the vertical axis by the GDP deflator. In this example, the equilibrium real GDP is $17.0 trillion, and the equilibrium price level is 110.

If we let Y stand for GDP, we have the following relationship:

$$Y = C + I + G + NX.$$

The aggregate demand curve is downward sloping because a fall in the price level increases the quantity of real GDP demanded. To understand why, we need to look at how changes in the price level affect each component of aggregate demand. We begin with the assumption that government purchases are determined by the policy decisions of lawmakers and are not affected by changes in the price level. We can then consider the effect of changes in the price level on the three other components: consumption, investment, and net exports.

The Wealth Effect: How a Change in the Price Level Affects Consumption   Current income is the most important variable determining consumption by households. As income rises, consumption will rise, and as income falls, consumption will fall. But consumption also depends on household wealth, which is the difference between the value of a household's assets and the value of its debts. Consider two households, both with incomes of $80,000 per year. The first household has wealth of $5 million, and the second household has wealth of $50,000. The first household is likely to spend more of its income than the second household. So, as total household wealth rises, consumption will rise. Some household wealth is held in cash or other *nominal assets* that lose value as the price level rises and gain value as the price level falls. For instance, if you have $10,000 in cash, a 10 percent increase in the price level will reduce the purchasing power of that cash by 10 percent. When the price level rises, the *real value* of household wealth declines, and so will consumption, thereby reducing the demand for goods and services. When the price level falls, the real value of household wealth rises, and so will consumption and the demand for goods and services. The effect of the price level on consumption is called the *wealth effect*, and it is one reason the aggregate demand curve is downward sloping.

The Interest-Rate Effect: How a Change in the Price Level Affects Investment When prices rise, households and firms need more money to finance buying and selling. Therefore, when the price level rises, households and firms will try to increase the amount of money they hold by withdrawing funds from banks, borrowing from banks, or selling financial assets, such as bonds. These actions tend to drive up the interest rate banks charge on loans and the interest rate on bonds. (In Chapter 15, we analyze in more detail the relationship between money and interest rates.) A higher interest rate raises the cost of borrowing for households and firms. As a result, firms will borrow less to build new factories or install new machinery and equipment, and households will borrow less to buy new houses. To summarize:

- A higher price level will increase the interest rate and reduce investment spending, thereby reducing the quantity of goods and services demanded.
- A lower price level will decrease the interest rate and increase investment spending, thereby increasing the quantity of goods and services demanded.

To a smaller extent, consumption will also fall when the interest rate rises as households borrow less to finance spending on automobiles, furniture, and other durable goods.

The effect of the price level on investment and consumption is known as the *interest-rate effect*, and it is a second reason the aggregate demand curve is downward sloping.

The International-Trade Effect: How a Change in the Price Level Affects Net Exports *Net exports* equals spending by foreign households and firms on goods and services produced in the United States minus spending by U.S. households and firms on goods and services produced in other countries. If the price level in the United States rises relative to the price levels in other countries, U.S. exports will become relatively more expensive, and foreign imports will become relatively less expensive. Some consumers in foreign countries will shift from buying U.S. products to buying domestic products, and some U.S. consumers will also shift from buying U.S. products to buying imported products. U.S. exports will fall and U.S. imports will rise, causing net exports to fall, thereby reducing the quantity of goods and services demanded. A lower price level in the United States relative to other countries has the reverse effect, causing net exports to rise, thereby increasing the quantity of goods and services demanded. The effect of the price level on net exports is known as the *international-trade effect*, and it is a third reason the aggregate demand curve is downward sloping. MyEconLab Concept Check

Shifts of the Aggregate Demand Curve versus Movements along It

An important point to remember is that the aggregate demand curve tells us the relationship between the price level and the quantity of real GDP demanded, *holding everything else constant*. If the price level changes but other variables that affect the willingness of households, firms, and the government to spend are unchanged, the result is a movement up or down a stationary aggregate demand curve. If any variable other than the price level changes, the aggregate demand curve will shift. For example, if government purchases increase and the price level remains unchanged, the aggregate demand curve will shift to the right at every price level. Or, if firms become pessimistic about the future profitability of investment and cut back spending on factories and machinery, the aggregate demand curve will shift to the left. MyEconLab Concept Check

The Variables That Shift the Aggregate Demand Curve

The variables that cause the aggregate demand curve to shift fall into three categories:

1. Changes in government policies
2. Changes in the expectations of households and firms
3. Changes in foreign variables

Changes in Government Policies As we will discuss further in Chapters 15 and 16, the federal government uses monetary policy and fiscal policy to shift the aggregate demand curve. **Monetary policy** is the actions the Federal Reserve—the nation's central bank—takes to manage the money supply and interest rates and to ensure the flow of funds from lenders to borrowers. The Federal Reserve takes these actions to achieve macroeconomic policy objectives, such as high employment, price stability, high rates of economic growth, and stability of the financial system. For example, the Federal Reserve can lower the cost to firms and households of borrowing by taking actions that reduce interest rates. Lower borrowing costs increase consumption and investment spending, which shifts the aggregate demand curve to the right. Higher interest rates shift the aggregate demand curve to the left.

Monetary policy The actions the Federal Reserve takes to manage the money supply and interest rates to achieve macroeconomic policy objectives.

Fiscal policy is the changes in federal taxes and purchases that are intended to achieve macroeconomic policy objectives. Because government purchases are one component of aggregate demand:

Fiscal policy Changes in federal taxes and purchases that are intended to achieve macroeconomic policy objectives.

- An increase in *government purchases* shifts the aggregate demand curve to the right, and a decrease in government purchases shifts the aggregate demand curve to the left.

- An increase in *personal income taxes* reduces the amount of spendable income available to households, which reduces consumption spending and shifts the aggregate demand curve to the left. A decrease in personal income taxes shifts the aggregate demand curve to the right.

- An increase in *business taxes* reduces the profitability of investment spending and shifts the aggregate demand curve to the left. A decrease in business taxes shifts the aggregate demand curve to the right.

Changes in the Expectations of Households and Firms If households become more optimistic about their future incomes, they are likely to increase their current consumption. This increased consumption will shift the aggregate demand curve to the right. If households become more pessimistic about their future incomes, the aggregate demand curve will shift to the left. Similarly, if firms become more optimistic about the future profitability of investment spending, the aggregate demand curve will shift to the right. If firms become more pessimistic, the aggregate demand curve will shift to the left.

Don't Let This Happen to You

Understand Why the Aggregate Demand Curve Is Downward Sloping

The aggregate demand curve and the demand curve for a single product are both downward sloping—but for different reasons. When we draw a demand curve for a single product, such as apples, we know that it will slope downward because as the price of apples rises, apples become more expensive relative to other products—such as oranges—and consumers will buy fewer apples and more of the other products. In other words, consumers substitute other products for apples. When the overall price level rises, the prices of all domestically produced goods and services are rising, so consumers have no other

domestic products to which they can switch. The aggregate demand curve slopes downward because a higher price level:

- Reduces the real value of household wealth, which decreases consumption

- Raises interest rates, which decreases investment and consumption

- Makes U.S. exports more expensive and foreign imports less expensive, which decreases net exports

MyEconLab Study Plan

Your Turn: Test your understanding by doing related problem 1.8 on pages 462–463 at the end of this chapter.

Changes in Foreign Variables If households and firms in other countries buy fewer U.S. goods or if households and firms in the United States buy more foreign goods, net exports will fall, and the aggregate demand curve will shift to the left. When real GDP increases, so does the income available for consumers to spend. If real GDP in the United States increases faster than real GDP in other countries, U.S. imports will increase faster than U.S. exports, and net exports will fall. Net exports will also fall if the *exchange rate* between the dollar and foreign currencies rises because the price in foreign currency of U.S. products sold in other countries will rise, and the dollar price of foreign products sold in the United States will fall. For example, if the current exchange rate between the dollar and the euro is $1 = €1 then:

- A $20 Blu-ray disc exported from the United States to France will cost €20 in France.

- A €50 bottle of wine exported from France will cost $50 in the United States.

But if the exchange rate rises to $1 = €1.50 then:

- The disc's price will rise from €20 to €30 in France, causing its sales to decline.
- The price of the French wine will fall from $50 to $33.33 per bottle in the United States, causing its sales to increase.

As a result, U.S. exports will fall, U.S. imports will rise, and the aggregate demand curve will shift to the left.

An increase in net exports at every price level will shift the aggregate demand curve to the right. Net exports will increase if real GDP grows more slowly in the United States than in other countries or if the value of the dollar falls against other currencies. A change in net exports that results from a change in the price level in the United States will result in a movement along the aggregate demand curve, *not* a shift of the aggregate demand curve.

MyEconLab Concept Check

Solved Problem 13.1

MyEconLab Interactive Animation

Movements along the Aggregate Demand Curve versus Shifts of the Aggregate Demand Curve

Germany, along with 18 other countries in Europe, uses the euro as its currency. According to an article in the *Wall Street Journal*, in 2014 German net exports rose to "€217 billion ($246 billion), shattering the previous record of €195.3 billion set in 2007." The story quoted an economist working for a German bank as saying, "I think that due to the weaker euro we should get stronger exports."

  a. At the time this article was written, what was the exchange rate between the U.S. dollar and the euro?

  b. What does the economist mean by a "weaker euro"?
  c. Why would a weaker euro cause an increase in German net exports?
  d. Briefly explain whether a weaker euro will cause a shift in the aggregate demand curve of the German economy or a movement along the aggregate demand curve. Illustrate your answer with a graph.

Solving the Problem

Step 1: **Review the chapter material.** This problem is about understanding the difference between movements along an aggregate demand curve and shifts of an aggregate demand curve, so you may want to review the section "Shifts of the Aggregate Demand Curve versus Movements along It," and the section "The Variables that Shift the Aggregate Demand Curve," which both begin on page 436.

Step 2: **Answer part (a) by calculating the exchange rate between the euro and the U.S. dollar at the time the article was written.** If €217 billion was the equivalent of $246 billion at the time the article was written, then the exchange rate must have been $246 billion/€217 billion = $1.13 dollars per euro, or $1 = €0.88.

Step 3: **Answer part (b) by explaining what the economist meant by a "weaker euro."** A weaker euro means an exchange rate such that a dollar (or a unit of another foreign currency) would buy more euros, or, equivalently, a euro would buy fewer dollars (or units of another foreign currency).

Step 4: **Answer part (c) by explaining why a weaker euro would cause an increase in German net exports.** If it takes fewer dollars to buy German goods priced in euros, then U.S. consumers will buy more of them, increasing German exports. If it takes more euros to buy U.S. goods priced in dollars, then German consumers will buy fewer of them, decreasing German imports. We can apply similar reasoning to the products of other countries outside the eurozone. So we would expect that a weaker euro will result in an increase in German net exports.

Step 5: **Answer part (d) by explaining whether a weaker euro would cause a shift in the aggregate demand curve for the German economy or a movement along it and by drawing a graph to illustrate your answer.** Only changes in the price level in Germany will cause a movement along the aggregate demand curve for the German economy. Although a decline in the value of the euro affects the prices of exports from Germany and imports to Germany, it doesn't directly affect the price level in Germany. By increasing German net exports, the weaker euro will cause the aggregate demand curve for the German economy to shift to the right at every price level, as shown in the following graph:

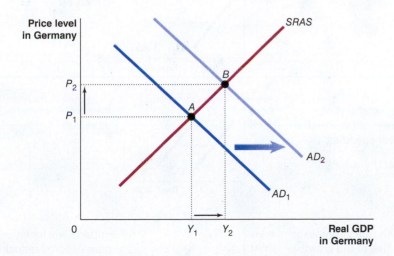

Source: Todd Buell and Bertrand Benoit, "Germany Enjoys Record Year for Trade," *Wall Street Journal*, February 9, 2015.

Your Turn: For more practice, do related problems 1.9 and 1.10 on page 463 at the end of this chapter.

MyEconLab Study Plan

Table 13.1 summarizes the most important variables that cause the aggregate demand curve to shift. The table shows the shift in the aggregate demand curve that results from an increase in each of the variables. A *decrease* in these variables will cause the aggregate demand curve to shift in the opposite direction.

Table 13.1

Variables That Shift the Aggregate Demand Curve

An increase in . . .	shifts the aggregate demand curve . . .	because . . .
interest rates	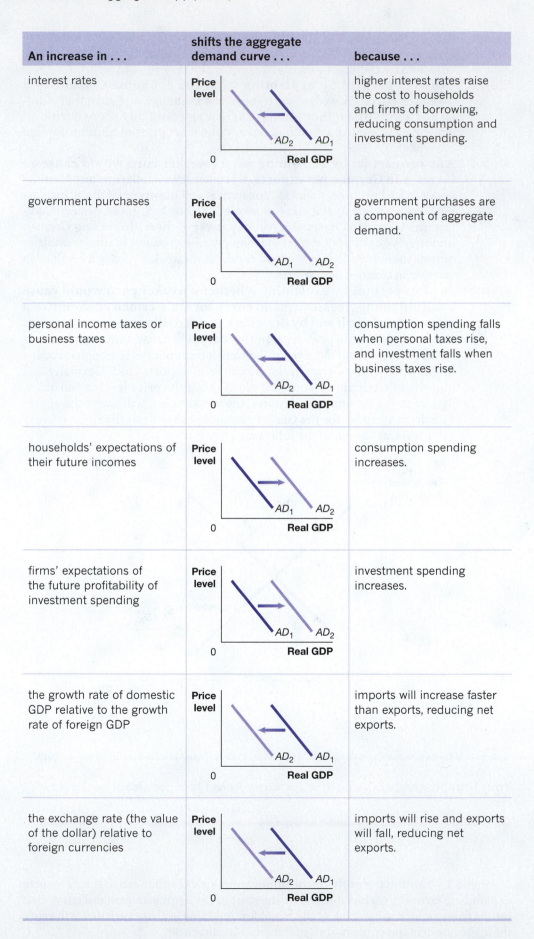	higher interest rates raise the cost to households and firms of borrowing, reducing consumption and investment spending.
government purchases		government purchases are a component of aggregate demand.
personal income taxes or business taxes		consumption spending falls when personal taxes rise, and investment falls when business taxes rise.
households' expectations of their future incomes		consumption spending increases.
firms' expectations of the future profitability of investment spending		investment spending increases.
the growth rate of domestic GDP relative to the growth rate of foreign GDP		imports will increase faster than exports, reducing net exports.
the exchange rate (the value of the dollar) relative to foreign currencies		imports will rise and exports will fall, reducing net exports.

Making
the
Connection
MyEconLab Video

Which Components of Aggregate Demand Changed the Most during the 2007–2009 Recession?

The recession of 2007–2009 was the longest and most severe since the Great Depression of the 1930s. We can better understand what happened during the 2007–2009 recession by looking at changes over time in the components of aggregate demand. In the following graphs, we show changes in the three components of aggregate demand that had the largest movements between the first quarter of 2005 and the second quarter of 2015: consumption, residential investment spending on new homes and apartments, and net exports. The shaded area represents the 2007–2009 recession. We know that potential GDP, or the level of GDP when all firms are producing at capacity, grows over time. So, economists are often interested in measuring changes in the components of aggregate demand *relative to potential GDP*, which is what we have done in these graphs.

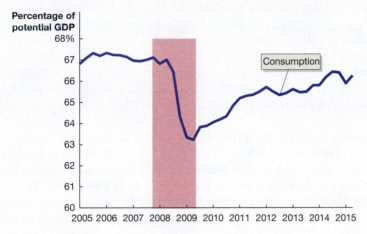

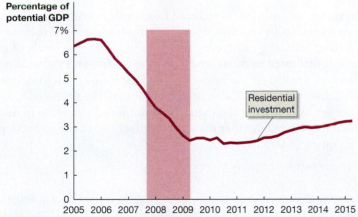

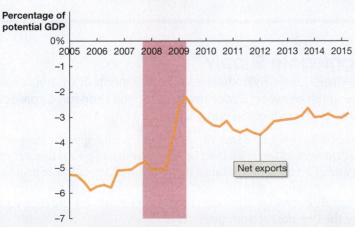

The graphs illustrate a number of facts about the 2007–2009 recession:

- In the two years before the beginning of the recession, spending on residential investment had already declined significantly relative to potential GDP.

- For the first two years following the end of the recession, spending on residential investment did not increase relative to potential GDP. Beginning in late 2011, spending on residential investment began to increase slowly, but in mid-2015, it was still far below its 2005–2006 level.

- Consumption, which usually remains relatively stable during a recession, declined significantly relative to potential GDP during the recession and had still not quite regained its 2007 level six years after the recession had ended.

- Net exports increased during the recession. (Because net exports was negative throughout this period, it increased by becoming a smaller negative number.)

Although not shown in the graphs, business fixed investment and changes in business inventories—the nonresidential construction components of investment spending—actually rose relative to potential GDP during the recession. Government purchases remained fairly stable relative to potential GDP during the recession, before declining from late 2010 through mid-2015. Federal government purchases surged during the recession but declined in later years as temporary spending programs intended to fight the recession ended and Congress and the president cut spending further to address concerns over the federal budget deficit.

We can briefly account for the four facts listed above. The housing sector underwent a boom from 2002 to 2005, with rapid increases in both housing prices and spending on new housing. But the housing boom turned into a housing bust beginning in 2006, which explains the sharp decline in residential investment. The continued low levels of residential investment help explain why the recession was the longest since the Great Depression and why the economic expansion that began in June 2009 was relatively weak.

High levels of unemployment reduced household incomes and led to declines in consumption spending. In addition, many households increased their saving and paid off debts, further reducing consumption spending. The low levels of consumption spending also contributed to the severity of the recession and the weakness of the following expansion. Finally, efforts by the Federal Reserve to reduce interest rates helped to lower the value of the U.S. dollar, thereby reducing the prices of U.S. exports and increasing the prices of foreign imports. The result was an increase in net exports during the recession. (We will further discuss the effect of Federal Reserve policy on net exports in Chapters 15 and 18.)

Sources: U.S. Bureau of Economic Analysis and Congressional Budget Office.

MyEconLab Study Plan

Your Turn: Test your understanding by doing related problem 1.11 on page 463 at the end of this chapter.

13.2 Aggregate Supply

LEARNING OBJECTIVE: Identify the determinants of aggregate supply and distinguish between a movement along the short-run aggregate supply curve and a shift of the curve.

Having discussed aggregate demand, we now turn to aggregate supply, which shows the effect of changes in the price level on the quantity of goods and services that firms are willing and able to supply. Because the effect of changes in the price level on aggregate supply is very different in the short run from what it is in the long run, we use two aggregate supply curves: one for the short run and one for the long run. We start by considering the *long-run aggregate supply curve*.

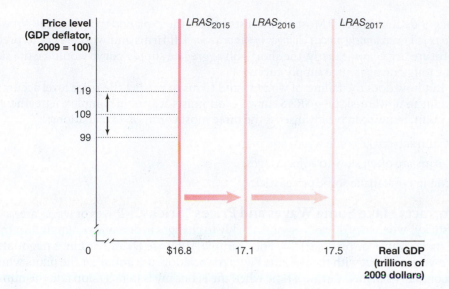

MyEconLab Animation

Figure 13.2

The Long-Run Aggregate Supply Curve

Changes in the price level do not affect the level of aggregate supply in the long run. Therefore, the long-run aggregate supply (*LRAS*) curve is a vertical line at the potential level of real GDP. For instance, the price level was 109 in 2015, and potential GDP was $16.8 trillion. If the price level had been 119, or if it had been 99, long-run aggregate supply would still have been a constant $16.8 trillion. Each year, the long-run aggregate supply curve shifts to the right, as the number of workers in the economy increases, more machinery and equipment are accumulated, and technological change occurs.

The Long-Run Aggregate Supply Curve

In the long run, the level of real GDP is determined by the number of workers, the *capital stock*—including factories, office buildings, and machinery and equipment—and the available technology (see Chapter 11). Because changes in the price level do not affect the number of workers, the capital stock, or technology, *in the long run, changes in the price level do not affect the level of real GDP.* Remember that the level of real GDP in the long run is called *potential GDP*, or *full-employment GDP*. At potential GDP, firms will operate at their normal level of capacity, and everyone who wants a job will have one, except the structurally and frictionally unemployed. There is no reason for this normal level of capacity to change just because the price level has changed. The **long-run aggregate supply (LRAS) curve** shows the relationship in the long run between the price level and the quantity of real GDP supplied. As Figure 13.2 shows, in 2015, the price level was 109, and potential GDP was $16.8 trillion. If the price level had been 119, or if it had been 99, long-run aggregate supply would still have been a constant $16.8 trillion. Therefore, the *LRAS* curve is a vertical line.

Figure 13.2 also shows that the long-run aggregate supply curve shifts to the right each year. This shift occurs because potential GDP increases each year, as (1) the number of workers in the economy increases, (2) the economy accumulates more machinery and equipment, and (3) technological change occurs. Figure 13.2 shows potential GDP increasing from $16.8 trillion in 2015 to $17.1 trillion in 2016 and to $17.5 trillion in 2017.

MyEconLab *Concept Check*

Long-run aggregate supply (LRAS) curve A curve that shows the relationship in the long run between the price level and the quantity of real GDP supplied.

The Short-Run Aggregate Supply Curve

While the *LRAS* curve is vertical, the *SRAS* curve is upward sloping because, over the short run, as the price level increases, the quantity of goods and services firms are willing to supply will increase. Firms supply more goods and services as the price level increases for two key reasons:

1. As prices of final goods and services rise, prices of inputs—such as the wages of workers or the price of natural resources—rise more slowly. Profits rise when the prices of goods and services firms sell rise more rapidly than the prices they pay for inputs. Therefore, a higher price level leads to higher profits and increases the willingness of firms to supply more goods and services.

2. As the price level rises, some firms are slow to adjust their prices. A firm that is slow to raise its prices when the price level is increasing may find its sales increasing and, therefore, will increase production.

Why do some firms adjust prices more slowly than others, and why might the wages of workers and the prices of other inputs change more slowly than the prices of final goods and services? Most economists believe the explanation is that *some firms and workers fail to accurately predict changes in the price level*. If firms and workers could predict the future price level exactly, the short-run aggregate supply curve would be the same as the long-run aggregate supply curve.

But how does the failure of workers and firms to predict the price level accurately result in an upward-sloping *SRAS* curve? Economists are not in complete agreement on this point, but we can briefly discuss the three most common explanations:

1. Contracts make some wages and prices "sticky."
2. Firms are often slow to adjust wages.
3. Menu costs make some prices sticky.

Contracts Make Some Wages and Prices "Sticky" Prices or wages are said to be "sticky" when they do not respond quickly to changes in demand or supply. Contracts can make wages or prices sticky. For example, suppose Delta Air Lines negotiates a three-year contract with the Air Line Pilots Association, the union for the pilots who fly the company's planes, during a time when the economy is in recession and the number of passenger tickets being sold is falling. Suppose that after the union signs the contract, the economy begins to expand rapidly, and the number of tickets sold increases, so that Delta can raise ticket prices. Delta will find that flying more passengers will be profitable because the prices it charges are rising, while the wages it pays its pilots are fixed by contract. Or a steel mill might sign a multiyear contract to buy coal, which is used in making steel, at a time when the demand for steel is falling. If demand for steel and steel prices begin to rise rapidly, producing additional steel will be profitable because coal prices will remain fixed by contract. In both of these cases, rising prices lead to higher output. If these examples are representative of enough firms in the economy, a rising price level should lead to a greater quantity of goods and services supplied. In other words, the short-run aggregate supply curve will be upward sloping.

Notice, though, that if the pilots working for Delta or the managers of the coal companies had accurately predicted what would happen to prices, this prediction would have been reflected in the contracts, and Delta and the steel mill would not have earned greater profits when prices rose. In that case, rising prices would not have led to higher output.

Firms Are Often Slow to Adjust Wages We just noted that the wages of many union workers remain fixed by contract for several years. Many nonunion workers have their wages or salaries adjusted only once a year. Suppose you accept a job at a management consulting firm in June, at a salary of $45,000 per year. The firm probably will not adjust your salary until the following June, even if the prices it can charge for its services later in the year are higher or lower than the firm had expected them to be when it hired you. If firms are slow to adjust wages, a rise in the price level will increase the profitability of hiring more workers and producing more output. A fall in the price level will decrease the profitability of hiring more workers and producing more output. Once again, we have an explanation for why the short-run aggregate supply curve slopes upward.

Firms are often slower to *cut* wages than to increase them. Cutting wages can have a negative effect on the morale and productivity of workers and can also cause some of a firm's best workers to quit and look for jobs elsewhere.

Making the Connection

MyEconLab Video

How Sticky Are Wages?

When we discussed the model of demand and supply in Chapter 3, we assumed that if the demand curve or supply curve for a product shifted, the price would adjust quickly from the old equilibrium to the new equilibrium. As we have just discussed, though, many economists argue that at least some wages and prices are sticky and do *not* adjust quickly to changes in demand or supply. Other economists argue that stickiness in wages and prices is not widespread enough to be important in macroeconomic analysis. In other words, these economists believe that the aggregate supply curve may be vertical in the short run, as well as in the long run.

Recently, a number of economists have examined the evidence for wage stickiness. Each month, the Bureau of Labor Statistics (BLS) collects data on average hourly earnings for all workers and for various subcategories of workers, such as workers in manufacturing. Using these data is not the best way to measure wage stickiness, though, because each of the BLS categories contains many workers. As a result, the average hourly earnings data the BLS reports represent the average change in wages but do not show how many workers received wage increases, wage decreases, or unchanged wages or how large those changes may have been. To better understand how frequently employers change wages, economists have looked instead at data on individual workers.

Separate studies of data on individual workers have arrived at similar results. One important result from these studies is that during a recession, firms are much more likely to reduce wages offered to newly hired workers than to reduce wages paid to current workers in the same job. For example, Mary C. Daly, Bart Hobijn, and Timothy Ni of the Federal Reserve Bank of San Francisco have shown that rather than cut wages during a recession, many firms reduce the *raises* they give workers, with more workers having their wages frozen, sometimes for long periods. Recall that the nominal wage is the number of dollars a firm pays a worker, while the real wage is the nominal wage divided by a price index. If a firm freezes a worker's nominal wage, the worker's real wage will gradually decline over time because of inflation. Most workers appear to be less upset if their real wage falls because of inflation than if it falls because of a cut in their nominal wage.

Daly, Hobijn, and Ni have used census data on individual workers to calculate the percentage of workers who each month were paid the same wage as they received in the same month during the previous year. The following figure shows these data for the years from 1997 through 2014. (The shaded areas are periods of recession.) Note that the percentage of workers with unchanged wages increases dramatically during recessions and the following months as the unemployment rate rises. The persistence of high rates of workers with frozen wages several years after the end of the 2007–2009 recession is an indication of how slowly the labor market recovered and how low the inflation rate has been since the recession. Other researchers using data for other countries have also found that firms are reluctant to cut nominal wages during recessions but instead freeze workers' nominal wages and allow inflation to gradually reduce real wages.

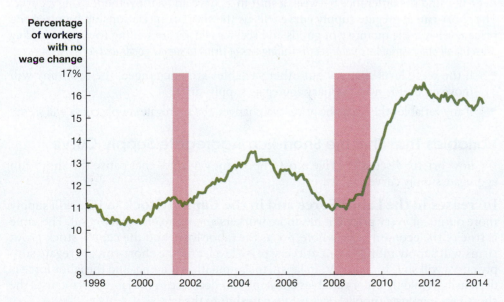

During recessions, why do firms often freeze nominal wages—frequently for extended periods—while they also lay off workers? Many economists believe that the main reason is that wage cuts upset workers. As a consequence, the productivity of workers who receive wage cuts may fall, and some workers may quit to find new jobs, either immediately or once the economy improves and the unemployment rate falls.

As Truman Bewley, an economist at Yale, puts it, "The advantage of layoffs over pay reductions was that they 'get misery out of the door.'"

Sources: Mary C. Daly, Bart Hobijn, and Timothy Ni, "The Path of Wage Growth and Unemployment," *Federal Reserve Bank of San Francisco Economic Letter,* July 15, 2013; Anabela Carneiro, Paulo Guimarães, and Pedro Portugal, "Real Wages and the Business Cycle: Accounting for Worker, Firm, and Job Title Heterogeneity," *American Economic Review: Macroeconomics,* Vol. 4, No. 2, April 2012, pp. 133–152; Hervé Le Bihan, Jérémi Montornès, and Thomas Heckel, "Sticky Wages: Evidence from Quarterly Microeconomic Data," *American Economic Review: Macroeconomics,* Vol. 4, No. 3, July 2012, pp. 1–32; Alessando Barattieri, Susanto Basu, and Peter Gottschalk, "Some Evidence on the Importance of Sticky Wages," National Bureau of Economic Research, Working Paper 16130, June 2010; William T. Dickens et al., "How Wages Change: Micro Evidence from the International Wage Flexibility Project," *Journal of Economic Perspectives,* Vol. 21, No. 2, Spring 2007, pp. 195–214; and data from Federal Reserve Bank of San Francisco, "Nominal Wage Rigidity Data Releases."

MyEconLab Study Plan

Your Turn: Test your understanding by doing related problems 2.12 and 2.13 on pages 464–465 at the end of this chapter.

Menu Costs Make Some Prices Sticky Firms base their prices today partly on what they expect future prices to be. For instance, if you own a restaurant, you will determine the prices printed on your menu based on what you expect the demand to be for the meals you sell and what you expect to pay for labor, rent, ingredients, and other inputs. Similarly, many firms list the prices of their products on their Web sites. If demand for their products or their production costs are higher or lower than the firms had expected, they may want to charge prices that are different from the ones in their menus or on their Web sites. Changing prices would be costly, however, because it would require printing new menus or entering new prices on their Web sites. The costs to firms of changing prices are called **menu costs**. To see why menu costs can lead to an upward-sloping short-run aggregate supply curve, consider the effect of an unexpected increase in the price level. In this case, firms will want to increase the prices they charge. Some firms, however, may not be willing to increase prices because of menu costs. Because their prices are now lower relative to competitors, these firms will find their sales increasing, which will cause them to increase output. Once again, a higher price level leads to a larger quantity of goods and services supplied.

Menu costs The costs to firms of changing prices.

MyEconLab Concept Check

Shifts of the Short-Run Aggregate Supply Curve versus Movements along It

Keep in mind the difference between a shift in a curve and a movement along a curve. The short-run aggregate supply curve tells us the short-run relationship between the price level and the quantity of goods and services firms are willing to supply, *holding constant all other variables that affect the willingness of firms to supply goods and services:*

- If the price level changes but other variables are unchanged, the economy will move up or down a stationary aggregate supply curve.

- If any variable other than the price level changes, the aggregate supply curve will shift.

MyEconLab Concept Check

Variables That Shift the Short-Run Aggregate Supply Curve

We now briefly discuss the five most important variables that cause the short-run aggregate supply curve to shift.

Increases in the Labor Force and in the Capital Stock A firm will supply more output at every price if it has more workers and more physical capital. The same is true of the economy as a whole. So, as the labor force and the capital stock grow, firms will supply more output at every price level, and the short-run aggregate supply curve will shift to the right. In Japan, the population is aging, and the labor force is decreasing. Holding other variables constant, this decrease in the labor force causes the short-run aggregate supply curve in Japan to shift to the left.

Technological Change As positive technological change takes place, the productivity of workers and machinery increases, which means firms can produce more goods and services with the same amount of labor and machinery. This increase in productivity reduces the firms' costs of production and allows them to produce more output at every price level. As a result, the short-run aggregate supply curve shifts to the right.

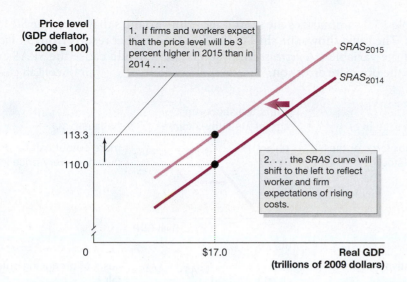

MyEconLab Animation

Figure 13.3

How Expectations of the Future Price Level Affect the Short-Run Aggregate Supply Curve

The *SRAS* curve shifts to reflect worker and firm expectations of future prices.

1. If workers and firms expect that the price level will rise by 3 percent, from 110.0 to 113.3, they will adjust their wages and prices by that amount.
2. Holding constant all other variables that affect aggregate supply, the short-run aggregate supply curve will shift to the left.

If workers and firms expect that the price level will be lower in the future, the short-run aggregate supply curve will shift to the right.

Expected Changes in the Future Price Level If workers and firms believe that the price level is going to increase by 3 percent during the next year, they will try to adjust their wages and prices accordingly. For instance, if a labor union believes there will be 3 percent inflation next year, it knows that wages must rise 3 percent to preserve the purchasing power of those wages. Similar adjustments by other workers and firms will result in costs increasing throughout the economy by 3 percent. The result, shown in Figure 13.3, is that the short-run aggregate supply curve will shift to the left, so that any level of real GDP is now associated with a price level that is 3 percent higher. In general, *if workers and firms expect the price level to increase by a certain percentage, the SRAS curve will shift by an equivalent amount*, holding constant all other variables that affect the *SRAS* curve.

Adjustments of Workers and Firms to Errors in Past Expectations about the Price Level Workers and firms sometimes make incorrect predictions about the price level. As time passes, they will attempt to compensate for these errors. Suppose that the Air Line Pilots Association signs a contract with Delta that provides for only small wage increases because the company and the union both expect only small increases in the price level. If increases in the price level turn out to be unexpectedly large, the union will take this into account when negotiating the next contract. The higher wages Delta pilots receive under the new contract will increase the company's costs and result in its needing to receive higher prices to produce the same level of output. If workers and firms across the economy are adjusting to the price level being higher than expected, the *SRAS* curve will shift to the left. If they are adjusting to the price level being lower than expected, the *SRAS* curve will shift to the right.

Unexpected Changes in the Price of an Important Natural Resource An unexpected event that causes the short-run aggregate supply curve to shift is called a **supply shock**. Supply shocks are often caused by unexpected increases or decreases in the prices of important natural resources that cause firms' costs to be different from what they had expected. Oil prices can be particularly volatile. Some firms use oil in the production process. Other firms use products, such as plastics, that are made from oil. If oil prices rise unexpectedly, the costs of production will rise for these firms. Some utilities also burn oil to generate electricity, so electricity prices will rise. Rising oil prices lead to rising gasoline prices, which raise transportation costs for many firms. Because firms face rising costs, they will supply the same level of output only if they receive higher prices, and the short-run aggregate supply curve will shift to the left.

The U.S. economy has experienced at least some inflation every year since the 1930s, so workers and firms always expect next year's price level to be higher than this year's price level. Holding everything else constant, expectations of a higher price level will cause the *SRAS* curve to shift to the left. But everything else is not constant because every year, the U.S. labor force and the U.S. capital stock expand and changes in technology occur, and these factors cause the *SRAS* curve to shift to the right. Whether in any particular year the *SRAS* curve shifts to the left or to the right depends on how large an effect these variables have during that year.

Supply shock An unexpected event that causes the short-run aggregate supply curve to shift.

Table 13.2 summarizes the most important variables that cause the *SRAS* curve to shift. The table shows the shift in the *SRAS* curve that results from an *increase* in each of the variables. A *decrease* in these variables would cause the *SRAS* curve to shift in the opposite direction.

Table 13.2

Variables That Shift the Short-Run Aggregate Supply Curve

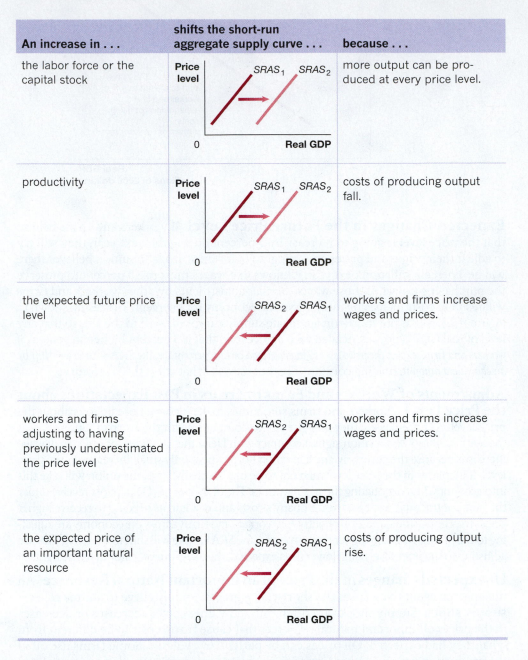

An increase in . . .	shifts the short-run aggregate supply curve . . .	because . . .
the labor force or the capital stock		more output can be produced at every price level.
productivity		costs of producing output fall.
the expected future price level		workers and firms increase wages and prices.
workers and firms adjusting to having previously underestimated the price level		workers and firms increase wages and prices.
the expected price of an important natural resource		costs of producing output rise.

13.3 Macroeconomic Equilibrium in the Long Run and the Short Run

LEARNING OBJECTIVE: Use the aggregate demand and aggregate supply model to illustrate the difference between short-run and long-run macroeconomic equilibrium.

Now that we have discussed the components of the aggregate demand and aggregate supply model, we can use it to analyze changes in real GDP and the price level. In Figure 13.4, we bring the aggregate demand curve, the short-run aggregate supply curve, and the long-run aggregate supply curve together in one graph, to show the *long-run macroeconomic equilibrium* for the economy. In the figure, equilibrium occurs at real GDP of $17.0 trillion

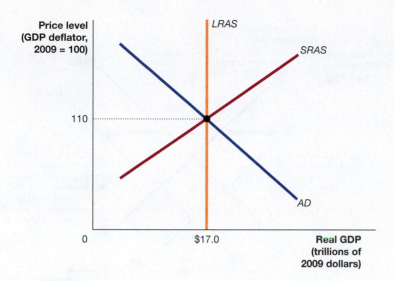

MyEconLab Animation

Figure 13.4

Long-Run Macroeconomic Equilibrium

In long-run macroeconomic equilibrium, the *AD* and *SRAS* curves intersect at a point on the *LRAS* curve. In this case, equilibrium occurs at real GDP of $17.0 trillion and a price level of 110.

and a price level of 110. Notice that in long-run equilibrium, the short-run aggregate supply curve and the aggregate demand curve intersect at a point on the long-run aggregate supply curve. Because equilibrium occurs at a point along the long-run aggregate supply curve, we know the economy is at potential GDP: Firms will be operating at their normal level of capacity, and everyone who wants a job will have one, except the structurally and frictionally unemployed. We know, however, that the economy is often not in long-run macroeconomic equilibrium. In the following section, we discuss the economic forces that can push the economy away from long-run equilibrium.

Recessions, Expansions, and Supply Shocks

Because the full analysis of the aggregate demand and aggregate supply model can be complicated, we begin with a simplified case, using two assumptions:

1. **The economy has not been experiencing any inflation.** The price level is currently 110, and workers and firms expect it to remain at 110 in the future.

2. **The economy is not experiencing any long-run growth.** Potential GDP is $17.0 trillion and will remain at that level in the future.

These assumptions are simplifications because in reality, the U.S. economy has experienced at least some inflation every year since the 1930s, and potential GDP also increases every year. However, the assumptions allow us to understand more easily the key ideas of the aggregate demand and aggregate supply model. In this section, we examine the short-run and long-run effects of recessions, expansions, and supply shocks.

Recession

The Short-Run Effect of a Decline in Aggregate Demand
Suppose that rising interest rates cause firms to reduce spending on factories and equipment and cause households to reduce spending on new homes. The decline in investment that results will shift the aggregate demand curve to the left, from AD_1 to AD_2, as shown in Figure 13.5. The economy moves from point A to a new *short-run macroeconomic equilibrium*, where the AD_2 curve intersects the $SRAS_1$ curve at point B. In the new short-run equilibrium, real GDP has declined from $17.0 trillion to $16.8 trillion and is below its potential level. This lower level of GDP will result in declining profits for many firms and layoffs for some workers: The economy will be in recession.

Adjustment Back to Potential GDP in the Long Run
We know that a recession will eventually end because there are forces at work that push the economy back to potential GDP in the long run. Figure 13.5 shows how the economy moves from recession back to potential GDP. The shift from AD_1 to AD_2 initially leads to a short-run equilibrium, with the price level having fallen from 110 to 108 (point B). Workers and firms will begin to adjust to the price level being lower than they had expected it to be. Workers will be

Figure 13.5

The Short-Run and Long-Run Effects of a Decrease in Aggregate Demand

In the short run, a decrease in aggregate demand causes a recession. In the long run, it causes only a decline in the price level.

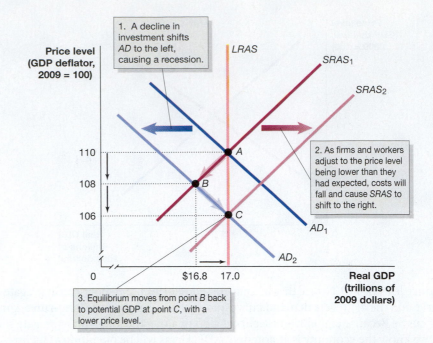

1. A decline in investment shifts *AD* to the left, causing a recession.

2. As firms and workers adjust to the price level being lower than they had expected, costs will fall and cause *SRAS* to shift to the right.

3. Equilibrium moves from point *B* back to potential GDP at point *C*, with a lower price level.

willing to accept lower wages—because each dollar of wages is able to buy more goods and services—and firms will be willing to accept lower prices. In addition, the unemployment resulting from the recession will make workers more willing to accept lower wages, and the decline in demand will make firms more willing to accept lower prices. As a result, the *SRAS* curve will shift to the right, from $SRAS_1$ to $SRAS_2$. At this point, the economy will be back in long-run equilibrium (point *C*). The shift from $SRAS_1$ to $SRAS_2$ will not happen instantly. It may take the economy several years to return to potential GDP. The important conclusion is that a decline in aggregate demand causes a recession in the short run, but in the long run it causes only a decline in the price level.

Economists refer to the process of adjustment back to potential GDP just described as an *automatic mechanism* because it occurs without any actions by the government. An alternative to waiting for the automatic mechanism to end a recession is for the government to use monetary policy or fiscal policy to shift the *AD* curve to the right and restore potential GDP more quickly. We will discuss monetary policy and fiscal policy in Chapters 15 and 16. Economists debate whether it is better to wait for the automatic mechanism to end recessions or to use monetary policy and fiscal policy.

Making the Connection

MyEconLab Video

Does It Matter What Causes a Decline in Aggregate Demand?

We have seen that GDP has four components and that a decrease in any of them can cause the aggregate demand curve to shift to the left, leading to a recession. In practice, most recessions in the United States since World War II have begun with a decline in residential construction. Edward Leamer of the University of California, Los Angeles, has gone so far as to argue that "housing *is* the business cycle," meaning that declines in residential construction are the most important reason for the declines in aggregate demand that lead to recessions. The shaded periods in the graph on the next page represent recessions. The graph shows that spending on residential construction has declined prior to every recession since 1955.

The graph also highlights a fact that we noted earlier in this chapter: The decline in residential construction during the 2007–2009 recession was particularly severe. Spending on residential construction declined by almost 60

The collapse in spending on housing added to the severity of the 2007–2009 recession.

percent from the fourth quarter of 2005 to the third quarter of 2010. Largely because of these problems in the housing sector, the decline in real GDP during the recession of 2007–2009 was larger than during any other recession since the Great Depression of the 1930s.

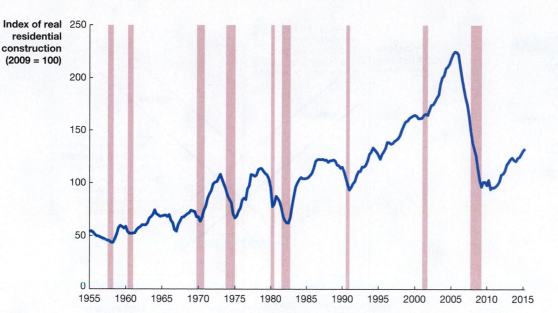

Index of real residential construction (2009 = 100)

What typically causes declines in spending on residential construction? Late in a business cycle expansion, the inflation rate and interest rates start to increase (see Chapter 10). Higher interest rates often result from monetary policy actions as the Federal Reserve tries to slow down the economy and reduce the rate of inflation (see Chapter 15). Higher interest rates reduce consumer demand for new houses by increasing the cost of loans.

But the collapse in residential construction prior to and during the recession of 2007–2009 was due more to the deflating of the "housing bubble" of 2002–2005 and to the financial crisis that began in 2007 than to higher interest rates. We will discuss both the housing bubble and the financial crisis later in this chapter. At this point, we can note that research by Carmen M. Reinhart and Kenneth S. Rogoff of Harvard University shows that declines in aggregate demand that result from financial crises tend to be larger and longer-lasting than declines due to other factors. So, the experience of 2007–2009 indicates that, in fact, the source of the decline in aggregate demand can be important in determining the severity of a recession.

Sources: Edward E. Leamer, "Housing *Is* the Business Cycle," in *Housing, Housing Finance, and Monetary Policy*, Federal Reserve Bank of Kansas City, August 2007; Carmen M. Reinhart and Kenneth S. Rogoff, "The Aftermath of Financial Crises," *American Economic Review*, Vol. 99, No. 2, May 2009, pp. 466–472; and U.S. Bureau of Economic Analysis.

Your Turn: Test your understanding by doing related problem 3.6 on page 466 at the end of this chapter.

MyEconLab Study Plan

Expansion

The Short-Run Effect of an Increase in Aggregate Demand

Suppose that instead of becoming pessimistic, many firms become optimistic about the future profitability of new investment, as happened during the information technology and telecommunications booms of the late 1990s. The resulting increase in investment will shift the *AD* curve to the right, as shown in Figure 13.6. Equilibrium moves from point *A* to point *B*. Real GDP rises from $17.0 trillion to $17.3 trillion, and the price level rises from 110 to 113. Real GDP will be above potential GDP: Firms are operating beyond their normal level of capacity, and some workers who would ordinarily be structurally or frictionally unemployed or who would not be in the labor force are employed.

Figure 13.6

The Short-Run and Long-Run Effects of an Increase in Aggregate Demand

In the short run, an increase in aggregate demand causes an increase in real GDP. In the long run, it causes only an increase in the price level.

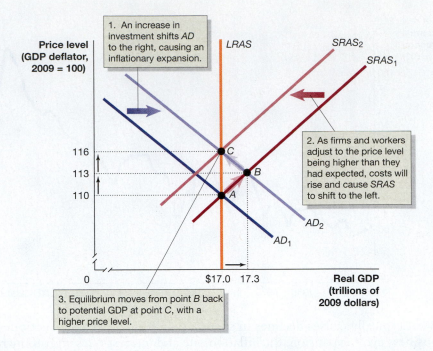

1. An increase in investment shifts *AD* to the right, causing an inflationary expansion.

2. As firms and workers adjust to the price level being higher than they had expected, costs will rise and cause *SRAS* to shift to the left.

3. Equilibrium moves from point *B* back to potential GDP at point *C*, with a higher price level.

Adjustment Back to Potential GDP in the Long Run Just as an automatic mechanism brings the economy back to potential GDP from a recession, an automatic mechanism brings the economy back from a short-run equilibrium beyond potential GDP. Figure 13.6 illustrates this mechanism. The shift from AD_1 to AD_2 initially leads to a short-run equilibrium, with the price level rising from 110 to 113 (point *B*). Workers and firms will begin to adjust to the price level being higher than they had expected. Workers will push for higher wages—because each dollar of wages is able to buy fewer goods and services—and firms will charge higher prices. In addition, the low levels of unemployment resulting from the expansion will make it easier for workers to negotiate for higher wages, and the increase in demand will make it easier for firms to receive higher prices. As a result, the *SRAS* curve will shift to the left, from $SRAS_1$ to $SRAS_2$. At this point, the economy will be back in long-run equilibrium. Once again, the shift from $SRAS_1$ to $SRAS_2$ will not happen instantly. The process of returning to potential GDP may stretch out for more than a year.

Supply Shock

The Short-Run Effect of a Supply Shock Suppose oil prices increase substantially. This supply shock will increase many firms' costs and cause the *SRAS* curve to shift to the left, as shown in panel (a) of Figure 13.7. Notice that the price level is higher in the new short-run equilibrium (112 rather than 110), but real GDP is lower ($16.7 trillion rather than $17.0 trillion). This unpleasant combination of inflation and recession is called **stagflation**.

Stagflation A combination of inflation and recession, usually resulting from a supply shock.

Adjustment Back to Potential GDP in the Long Run A recession caused by a supply shock increases unemployment and reduces output. Workers will eventually be willing to accept lower wages, and firms will be willing to accept lower prices. In panel (b) of Figure 13.7, the short-run aggregate supply curve shifts from $SRAS_2$ to $SRAS_1$, moving equilibrium from point *B* back to point *A*. Real GDP is back to potential GDP at the original price level. It may take several years for this process to be completed. An alternative would be to use monetary and fiscal policy to shift the aggregate demand curve to the right. Using policy in this way would bring real GDP back to potential GDP more quickly but would result in a permanently higher price level.

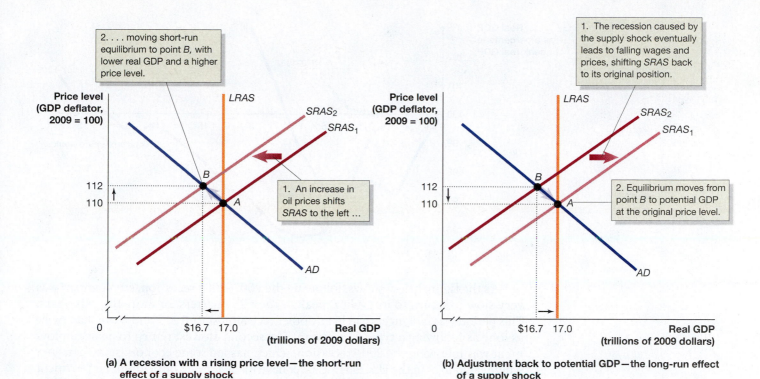

(a) A recession with a rising price level—the short-run effect of a supply shock

(b) Adjustment back to potential GDP—the long-run effect of a supply shock

MyEconLab Animation

Figure 13.7   **The Short-Run and Long-Run Effects of a Supply Shock**

Panel (a) shows that a supply shock, such as a large increase in oil prices, will cause a recession and a higher price level in the short run. The recession caused by the supply shock increases unemployment and reduces output. Panel (b) shows that rising unemployment and falling output result in workers being willing to accept lower wages and firms being willing to accept lower prices. The short-run aggregate supply curve shifts from $SRAS_2$ to $SRAS_1$. Equilibrium moves from point B back to potential GDP and the original price level at point A.

How Long Is the Long Run in Macroeconomics?

Once a recession starts, how long does it take for real GDP and employment to return to the levels they had achieved at the business cycle peak? On average, in the recessions since 1950, it has taken six quarters, or about a year and a half, for real GDP to return to its cyclical peak. During the same period, it has taken employment on average about 9.5 quarters, or nearly two and a half years, to return to its cycle peak. But these averages disguise great variation across recessions.

The figure at the top of the next page shows the recessions of 1981–1982, 1990–1991, 2001, and 2007–2009. The value of real GDP at the business cycle peak is set equal to 100. Therefore, values less than 100 represent levels of real GDP below the level at the business cycle peak. The horizontal axis shows the number of quarters since the business cycle peak. The severity of the 2007–2009 recession can be seen clearly in the figure. Real GDP reached a cyclical peak in the fourth quarter of 2007. Real GDP didn't return to this level until the second quarter of 2011, which was 14 quarters, or *three and a half years*, after the recession began. That was far longer than in any other recession since 1950. Some economists describe the 1981–1982 recession as a V-shaped recession because although the decline in real GDP was large, real GDP returned to its cyclical peak relatively quickly. The 2007–2009 recession, in contrast, was a U-shaped recession because it took an extended period for real GDP to return to its cyclical peak.

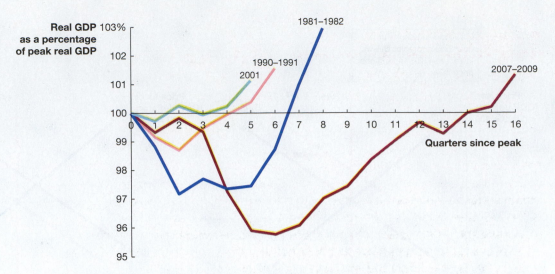

As the figure below shows, following the 2007–2009 recession, employment was very slow to return to its cyclical peak: It took 25 quarters, or more than six years. This period was far longer than in any other recession since 1950, and more than twice as long as following a typical recession. The second-slowest return to peak employment was following the 2001 recession, which has led some economists to consider whether changes in the U.S. labor market have made it more difficult for employment to return to normal levels following a recession.

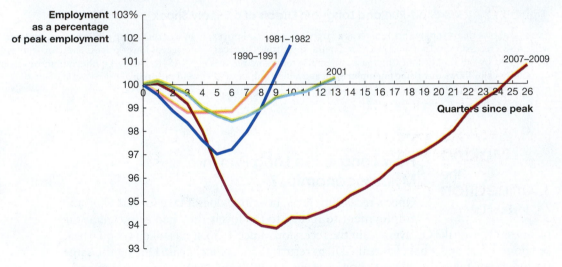

The severity of the 2007–2009 recession took most economists and policymakers by surprise because they did not predict that the decline in housing prices that began in 2006 would eventually lead to a major financial crisis in 2008. Even as the recession was ending in 2009, members of President Obama's economic staff, economists at the Federal Reserve, and economists at the Congressional Budget Office all expected that the economy would return to normal levels of real GDP and employment far sooner than it did.

In Chapters 15 and 16, we will discuss the disagreements among economists and policymakers over why the U.S. economy took so long to return to potential GDP and full employment following the 2007–2009 recession.

Sources: Board of Governors of the Federal Reserve System, "Economic Projections of Federal Reserve Board Members and Federal Reserve Bank Presidents," various dates; Congressional Budget Office, "Data Underlying Selected Economic Figures, Real Gross Domestic Product," various dates; Christina Romer and Jared Bernstein, "The Job Impact of the American Recovery and Reinvestment Plan," January 9, 2009; U.S. Bureau of Economic Analysis; U.S. Bureau of Labor Statistics; and National Bureau of Economic Research.

MyEconLab Study Plan   **Your Turn:** Test your understanding by doing related problem 3.9 on page 466 at the end of this chapter.

13.4 A Dynamic Aggregate Demand and Aggregate Supply Model*

LEARNING OBJECTIVE: Use the dynamic aggregate demand and aggregate supply model to analyze macroeconomic conditions.

The basic aggregate demand and aggregate supply model used so far in this chapter provides important insights into how short-run macroeconomic equilibrium is determined. Unfortunately, the model also provides some misleading results. For instance, it incorrectly predicts that a recession caused by the aggregate demand curve shifting to the left will result in a lower price level, which has not happened over an entire year since the 1930s. The difficulty with the basic model arises because we assumed that (1) the economy does not experience continuing inflation and (2) the economy does not experience long-run growth. We can develop a more useful aggregate demand and aggregate supply model by dropping these assumptions. The result will be a model that takes into account that the economy is not *static*, with an unchanging level of potential GDP and no continuing inflation, but *dynamic*, with potential GDP that grows over time and inflation that continues every year. We can create a *dynamic aggregate demand and aggregate supply model* by making changes to the basic model that incorporate the following important macroeconomic facts:

- Potential GDP increases continually, shifting the long-run aggregate supply curve to the right.

- During most years, the aggregate demand curve shifts to the right.

- Except during periods when workers and firms expect high rates of inflation, the short-run aggregate supply curve shifts to the right.

Figure 13.8 illustrates how incorporating these macroeconomic facts changes the basic aggregate demand and aggregate supply model. We start with $SRAS_1$ and AD_1 intersecting at point A, at a price level of 110 and real GDP of $17.0 trillion. Because this intersection occurs at a point on $LRAS_1$, we know the economy is in long-run equilibrium. We show the long-run aggregate supply curve shifting to the right, from $LRAS_1$ to $LRAS_2$, because during the year, potential GDP increases as the U.S. labor force and the U.S. capital stock increase and technological progress occurs. The short-run aggregate supply curve shifts from $SRAS_1$ to $SRAS_2$ because the same variables that cause the long-run aggregate supply curve to shift to the right will also increase the quantity of goods and services that firms are willing to supply in the short run. Finally, the aggregate demand curve shifts to the right, from AD_1 to AD_2. The aggregate demand curve shifts for several reasons: As the population grows and incomes rise, consumption will increase over time. As the economy grows, firms will expand capacity, and new firms will be formed, increasing investment. An expanding population and an expanding economy require increased government services, such as more police officers and teachers, so government purchases will increase.

The new equilibrium in Figure 13.8 occurs at point B, where AD_2 intersects $SRAS_2$ on $LRAS_2$. In the new equilibrium, the price level remains at 110, while real GDP increases to $17.4 trillion. Notice that there has been no inflation because the price level is unchanged, at 110. There has been no inflation because aggregate demand and aggregate supply shifted to the right by exactly as much as long-run aggregate supply. In fact, though, we wouldn't expect that all three curves will typically shift by the same amount. For instance, the $SRAS$ curve is also affected by workers' and firms' expectations of future changes in the price level and by supply shocks. These variables can partially or completely offset the normal tendency of the $SRAS$ curve to shift to the right over the course of a year. We also know that changes in the expenditures of consumers, firms, and the government may result in the AD curve shifting to the right by more or less than the $SRAS$ and $LRAS$ curves. In fact, as we will see shortly, *changes in the price level and in real GDP in the short run are determined by how much the SRAS and AD curves shift*.

---

*This section may be omitted without loss of continuity.

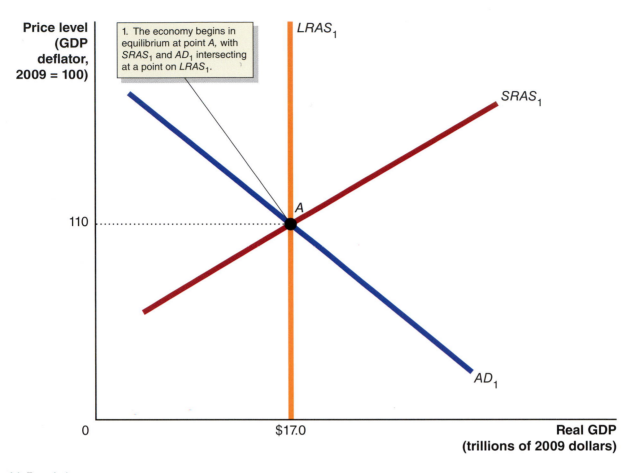

Figure 13.8 A Dynamic Aggregate Demand and Aggregate Supply Model

We start with the basic aggregate demand and aggregate supply model.

What Is the Usual Cause of Inflation?

The dynamic aggregate demand and aggregate supply model provides a more accurate explanation of the source of most inflation. If total spending in the economy grows faster than total production, prices rise. Figure 13.9 illustrates this point by showing that if the *AD* curve shifts to the right by more than the *LRAS* curve, inflation results because equilibrium occurs at a higher price level, point *B*. In the new equilibrium, the *SRAS* curve has shifted to the right by less than the *LRAS* curve because the anticipated increase in prices offsets some of the effect of the technological change and increases in the labor force and capital stock that occur during the year. Although inflation generally results from total spending growing faster than total production, a shift to the left of the short-run aggregate supply curve can also cause an increase in the price level, as we noted in Section 13.3 when discussing supply shocks.

As we saw in Figure 13.8, if aggregate demand increases by the same amount as short-run and long-run aggregate supply, the price level will not change. In this case, the economy experiences economic growth without inflation.

The Recession of 2007–2009

We can use the dynamic aggregate demand and aggregate supply model to analyze the recession of 2007–2009. The recession began in December 2007, with the end of the

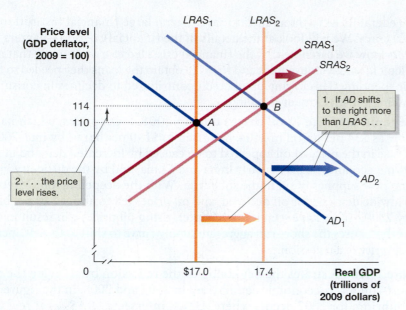

MyEconLab Animation

Figure 13.9 Using Dynamic Aggregate Demand and Aggregate Supply to Understand Inflation

The most common cause of inflation is total spending increasing faster than total production.

1. The economy begins at point *A*, with real GDP of $17.0 trillion and a price level of 110. An increase in full-employment real GDP from $17.0 trillion to $17.4 trillion causes long-run aggregate supply to

shift to the right from *LRAS*₁ to *LRAS*₂. Aggregate demand shifts to the right from *AD*₁ to *AD*₂.

2. Because *AD* shifts to the right by more than the *LRAS* curve, the price level in the new equilibrium rises from 110 to 114.

---

economic expansion that started in November 2001. Several factors combined to cause the recession:

- **The end of the housing bubble.** The figure in the *Making the Connection* on page 451 shows that spending on residential construction increased rapidly from 2002 to 2005, before declining more than 60 percent between the end of 2005 and the beginning of 2010. The increase in spending on housing through 2005 was partly the result of actions the Federal Reserve had taken to lower interest rates during and after the recession of 2001. As interest rates on mortgage loans declined, more consumers began to buy new homes. But by 2005, it was clear that a speculative bubble was partly responsible for the rapidly rising prices of both newly built and existing homes. A bubble occurs when people become less concerned with the underlying value of an asset—either a physical asset, such as a house, or a financial asset, such as a stock—and focus instead on expectations of the price of the asset increasing. In some areas of the country, such as California, Arizona, and Florida, many homes were purchased by investors who intended to resell them for higher prices than they paid for them and did not intend to live in them. Some popular television programs explored ways that people could "flip" houses by buying and quickly reselling them. Speculative bubbles eventually end, and the housing bubble started to deflate in 2006. Both new home sales and housing prices began to decline. The growth of aggregate demand slowed as spending on residential construction—a component of investment spending—fell.

- **The financial crisis.** Problems in the housing market were bad news for workers and firms involved with residential construction. In addition, falling housing prices led to an increased number of borrowers defaulting on their mortgage loans. These defaults caused banks and some other financial institutions to suffer heavy losses. Beginning in the spring of 2008, the U.S. Department of the Treasury and the Federal Reserve intervened to save several large financial institutions from bankruptcy. We will look at the details of the financial crisis in Chapters 14 and 15. For now we can note that the financial crisis led to a *credit crunch* that made it difficult for many households and firms to obtain the loans they needed to finance their spending. This drying up of credit contributed to declines in consumption spending and investment spending.

- **The rapid increase in oil prices during 2008.** Oil prices, which had been as low as $34 per barrel in 2004, had risen to $140 per barrel by mid-2008. The increase in the price of oil appeared to be caused by increased demand in rapidly growing economies, particularly India and China, and by the difficulty in developing new supplies of oil in the short run. With the deepening of the recession, worldwide demand for oil declined, and oil prices fell to about $40 per barrel in early 2009. As we have seen in this chapter, rising oil prices can result in a *supply shock* that causes the short-run aggregate supply curve to shift to the left, increasing the severity of a recession.

Figure 13.10 illustrates the beginning of the recession by showing the economy's short-run macroeconomic equilibrium in 2007 and 2008. In the figure, short-run equilibrium for 2007 occurs where AD_{2007} intersects $SRAS_{2007}$ at real GDP of $14.87 trillion and a price level of 97.3. Real GDP in 2007 was below potential GDP of $14.95 trillion, shown by $LRAS_{2007}$. During 2008, aggregate demand shifted to the

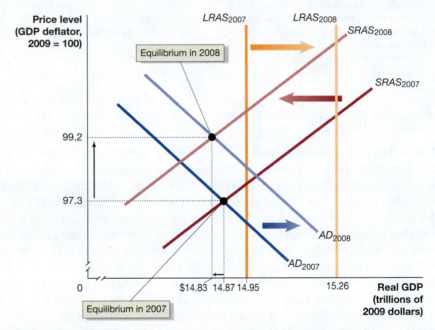

MyEconLab Animation

Figure 13.10   **The Beginning of the Recession of 2007–2009**

Between 2007 and 2008, the *AD* curve shifted to the right but not by nearly enough to offset the shift to the right of the *LRAS* curve, which represented the increase in potential GDP from $14.95 trillion to $15.26 trillion. Because of a sharp increase in oil prices, short-run aggregate supply shifted to the left, from $SRAS_{2007}$ to $SRAS_{2008}$.

Real GDP decreased from $14.87 trillion in 2007 to $14.83 trillion in 2008, which was far below the potential GDP, shown by $LRAS_{2008}$. Because the increase in aggregate demand was small, the price level increased only from 97.3 in 2007 to 99.2 in 2008, so the inflation rate for 2008 was only 2.0 percent.

right, from AD_{2007} to AD_{2008}. Aggregate demand increased by less than potential GDP because of the negative effects of the bursting of the housing bubble and the financial crisis on consumption spending and investment spending. The supply shock from higher oil prices caused short-run aggregate supply to shift to the left, from $SRAS_{2007}$ to $SRAS_{2008}$.

Short-run equilibrium for 2008 occurred at real GDP of $14.83 trillion and a price level of 99.2. A large gap opened between short-run equilibrium real GDP and potential GDP. Not surprisingly, unemployment rose from 4.6 percent in 2007 to 5.8 percent in 2008. The price level increased only from 97.3 to 99.2, so the inflation rate was a low 2.0 percent.

The recession persisted into 2009, as potential GDP increased to $15.50 trillion, while real GDP fell to $14.42 trillion. (The situation in 2009 is not shown in Figure 13.10.) The increased gap between real GDP and potential GDP caused the unemployment rate to soar to 9.3 percent—the highest unemployment rate since the recession of 1981–1982 and the second highest since the Great Depression of the 1930s. Although the recession ended in June 2009, real GDP grew only slowly during 2010 and 2011, leaving the unemployment rate above 8.5 percent.

The severity of the recession of 2007–2009 resulted in some of the most dramatic changes in government economic policy since the Great Depression. We will explore these new policies in Chapters 15 and 16.   **MyEconLab** Concept Check

---

Solved Problem 13.4

MyEconLab Interactive Animation

Showing the Oil Shock of 1974–1975 on a Dynamic Aggregate Demand and Aggregate Supply Graph

The 1974–1975 recession clearly illustrates how a supply shock affects the economy. Following the Arab–Israeli War of 1973, the Organization of the Petroleum Exporting Countries (OPEC) took actions that increased the price of a barrel of oil from less than $3 to more than $10. Use this information and the statistics in the following table to draw a dynamic aggregate demand and aggregate supply graph showing macroeconomic equilibrium for 1974 and 1975. Assume that the aggregate demand curve did not shift

between 1974 and 1975. Provide a brief explanation of your graph.

	Actual Real GDP	Potential GDP	Price Level
1974	$5.40 trillion	$5.43 trillion	28.7
1975	$5.39 trillion	$5.63 trillion	31.4

Sources: U.S. Bureau of Economic Analysis; and Federal Reserve Bank of St. Louis.

Solving the Problem

Step 1: **Review the chapter material.** This problem is about applying the dynamic aggregate demand and aggregate supply model, so you may want to review the section "A Dynamic Aggregate Demand and Aggregate Supply Model," which begins on page 455.

Step 2: **Use the information in the table to draw the graph.** You need to draw five curves: *SRAS* and *LRAS* for both 1974 and 1975 and *AD*, which is the same for both years. You know that the two *LRAS* curves will be vertical lines at the values given for potential GDP in the table. Because of the large supply shock, you know that the *SRAS* curve shifted to the left. The problem asks you to assume that the *AD* curve did not shift. Your graph should look like the following:

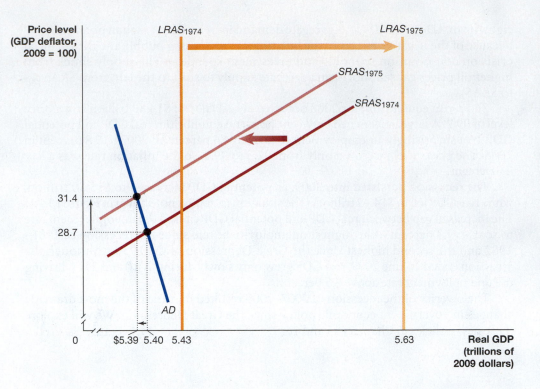

Step 3: **Explain your graph.** $LRAS_{1974}$ and $LRAS_{1975}$ are at the levels of potential GDP for each year. Macroeconomic equilibrium for 1974 occurs where the AD curve intersects the $SRAS_{1974}$ curve, with real GDP of $5.40 trillion and a price level of 28.7. Macroeconomic equilibrium for 1975 occurs where the AD curve intersects the $SRAS_{1975}$ curve, with real GDP of $5.39 trillion and a price level of 31.4.

Extra Credit: As a result of the supply shock, equilibrium real GDP moved from just below potential GDP in 1974 (the recession actually began right at the end of 1973) to well below potential GDP in 1975. With real GDP in 1975 about 4.3 percent below its potential level, the unemployment rate soared from 5.6 percent in 1974 to 8.5 percent in 1975.

MyEconLab Study Plan

Your Turn: For more practice, do related problems 4.5 and 4.6 on page 467 at the end of this chapter.

Continued from page 433

Economics in Your Life

Is an Employer Likely to Cut Your Pay during a Recession?

At the beginning of this chapter, we asked you to consider whether during a recession your employer is likely to reduce your pay and cut the prices of the products he or she sells. We have seen that even during a recession, the price level rarely falls. In fact, in the United States, the GDP deflator has not fallen for an entire year since the 1930s. Although some firms reduced prices during the recession of 2007–2009, most firms did not. So, the owner of the coffeehouse where you work will probably not cut the price of lattes unless sales have declined drastically. We also saw that most firms are more reluctant to cut wages than to increase them because wage cuts can lower worker morale and productivity. Because the recession of 2007–2009 was particularly severe, some firms did cut wages. But given that you are a highly skilled barista, your employer is unlikely to cut your wages for fear that you might quit and work for a competitor.

Conclusion

Chapter 3 demonstrated the power of the microeconomic model of demand and supply in explaining how the prices and quantities of individual products are determined. This chapter showed that we need a different model to explain the behavior of the whole economy. We saw that the macroeconomic model of aggregate demand and aggregate supply explains fluctuations in real GDP and the price level.

Fluctuations in real GDP, employment, and the price level have led the federal government to implement macroeconomic policies. We will explore these policies in later chapters after first considering the role money plays in the economy.

Visit MyEconLab for a news article and analysis related to the concepts in this chapter.

CHAPTER SUMMARY AND PROBLEMS

Key Terms

Aggregate demand (AD) curve, p. 434

Aggregate demand and aggregate supply model, p. 434

Fiscal policy, p. 437

Long-run aggregate supply (LRAS) curve, p. 443

Menu costs, p. 446

Monetary policy, p. 437

Short-run aggregate supply (SRAS) curve, p. 434

Stagflation, p. 452

Supply shock, p. 447

13.1 ## Aggregate Demand, pages 434–442

LEARNING OBJECTIVE: Identify the determinants of aggregate demand and distinguish between a movement along the aggregate demand curve and a shift of the curve.

Summary

The **aggregate demand and aggregate supply model** enables us to explain short-run fluctuations in real GDP and the price level. The **aggregate demand (AD) curve** shows the relationship between the price level and the level of planned aggregate expenditures by households, firms, and the government. The **short-run aggregate supply (SRAS) curve** shows the relationship in the short run between the price level and the quantity of real GDP supplied by firms. The long-run aggregate supply curve shows the relationship in the long run between the price level and the quantity of real GDP supplied. The four components of aggregate demand are consumption (C), investment (I), government purchases (G), and net exports (NX). The aggregate demand curve is downward sloping because a decline in the price level causes consumption, investment, and net exports to increase. If the price level changes but all else remains constant, the result is a movement up or down a stationary aggregate demand curve. If any variable other than the price level changes, the aggregate demand curve will shift. The variables that cause the aggregate demand curve to shift are divided into three categories: changes in government policies, changes in the expectations of households and firms, and changes in foreign variables. For example, **monetary policy** involves the actions the Federal Reserve takes to manage the money supply and interest rates to pursue macroeconomic policy objectives. When the Federal Reserve takes actions to change interest rates, consumption and investment spending will change, shifting the aggregate demand curve. **Fiscal policy** involves changes in the federal government's taxes and purchases that are intended to achieve macroeconomic policy objectives. Changes in federal taxes and purchases shift the aggregate demand curve.

Review Questions

1.1 What relationship does the aggregate demand curve show? What relationship does the aggregate supply curve show?

1.2 Explain the three reasons the aggregate demand curve slopes downward.

1.3 What are the differences between the AD curve and the demand curve for an individual product, such as apples?

1.4 What variables cause the AD curve to shift? For each variable, identify whether an increase in that variable will cause the AD curve to shift to the right or to the left and also indicate which component(s) of GDP—consumption, investment, government purchases, or net exports—will change.

Problems and Applications

1.5 Explain how each of the following events would affect the aggregate demand curve.
   a. An increase in the price level
   b. An increase in government purchases
   c. Higher state income taxes
   d. Higher interest rates
   e. Faster income growth in other countries
   f. A higher exchange rate between the dollar and foreign currencies

1.6 From August 2009 to August 2015, the Standard & Poor's Index of 500 stock prices more than doubled, while the consumer price index increased by just over 10 percent. Briefly explain what effect, if any, these changes had on the aggregate demand curve.

1.7 Consider the two aggregate demand curves in the following graph. What would cause a movement from point A to point B on AD_1? What would cause a movement from point A to point C?

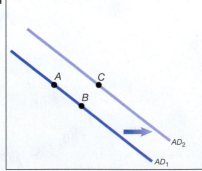

1.8 (Related to the Don't Let This Happen to You on page 437) An economics student makes the following statement: "It's easy to understand why the aggregate demand curve is downward sloping: When the price level increases, consumers substitute into less expensive products, which decreases total spending in the economy." Briefly explain whether you agree.

1.9 (Related to Solved Problem 13.1 on page 438) Explain whether each of the following will cause a shift of the *AD* curve or a movement along the *AD* curve.
   a. Firms become more optimistic and increase their spending on machinery and equipment.
   b. The federal government increases taxes in an attempt to reduce a budget deficit.
   c. The U.S. economy experiences 4 percent inflation.

1.10 (Related to Solved Problem 13.1 on page 438) A reporter for the *Wall Street Journal* wrote, "A strong dollar and weak growth overseas portend downward pressure on U.S. exports."
   a. What does the reporter mean by a "strong dollar"?
   b. What does the reporter mean by "weak growth overseas"?

   c. Briefly explain why the combination of a strong dollar and weak growth overseas might result in lower U.S. exports.
   d. Will the result of a strong dollar be a movement along the U.S. aggregate demand curve or a shift of the aggregate demand curve? Briefly explain.

Source: Jon Hilsenrath, "Rising Dollar and Falling Oil Could Be Recipe for a U.S. Asset Boom," *Wall Street Journal*, December 11, 2014.

1.11 (Related to the Making the Connection on page 441) If real GDP in the United States declined by more during the 2007–2009 recession than did real GDP in Canada, China, and other trading partners of the United States, would the effect be to increase or decrease U.S. net exports? Briefly explain.

13.2   Aggregate Supply, pages 442–448

LEARNING OBJECTIVE: Identify the determinants of aggregate supply and distinguish between a movement along the short-run aggregate supply curve and a shift of the curve.

Summary

The **long-run aggregate supply (LRAS) curve** is a vertical line because in the long run, real GDP is always at its potential level and is unaffected by the price level. The short-run aggregate supply curve slopes upward because workers and firms fail to predict accurately the future price level. The three main explanations of why this failure results in an upward-sloping aggregate supply curve are that (1) contracts make wages and prices "sticky," (2) businesses often adjust wages slowly, and (3) menu costs make some prices sticky. **Menu costs** are the costs to firms of changing prices. If the price level changes but all else remains constant, the result is a movement up or down a stationary aggregate supply curve. If any other variable that affects the willingness of firms to supply goods and services changes, the aggregate supply curve will shift. The aggregate supply curve shifts as a result of increases in the labor force and capital stock, technological change, expected increases or decreases in the future price level, adjustments of workers and firms to errors in past expectations about the price level, and unexpected increases or decreases in the price of an important raw material. A **supply shock** is an unexpected event that causes the short-run aggregate supply curve to shift.

 Visit **www.myeconlab.com** to complete these exercises online and get instant feedback.

Review Questions

2.1 Explain why the long-run aggregate supply curve is vertical.

2.2 What variables cause the long-run aggregate supply curve to shift? For each variable, identify whether an increase in that variable will cause the long-run aggregate supply curve to shift to the right or to the left.

2.3 Why does the short-run aggregate supply curve slope upward?

2.4 What variables cause the short-run aggregate supply curve to shift? For each variable, identify whether an increase in that variable will cause the short-run aggregate supply curve to shift to the right or to the left.

Problems and Applications

2.5 Explain how each of the following events would affect the long-run aggregate supply curve.
   a. A higher price level
   b. An increase in the labor force
   c. An increase in the quantity of capital goods
   d. Technological change

2.6 A student was asked to draw an aggregate demand and aggregate supply graph to illustrate the effect of an increase in aggregate supply. The student drew the following graph:

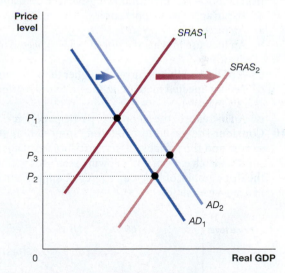

The student explains the graph as follows:

An increase in aggregate supply causes a shift from $SRAS_1$ to $SRAS_2$. Because this shift in the aggregate supply curve results in a lower price level, consumption, investment, and net exports will increase. This change causes the aggregate demand curve to shift to the right, from AD_1 to AD_2. We know that real GDP will increase, but we can't be sure whether the price level will rise or fall because that depends on whether the aggregate supply curve or the aggregate demand curve has shifted farther to the right. I assume that aggregate supply shifts out farther than aggregate demand, so I show the final price level, P_3, as being lower than the initial price level, P_1.

Explain whether you agree with the student's analysis. Be careful to explain exactly what—if anything—you find wrong with this analysis.

2.7 Consider the short-run aggregate supply curves in the following graph. What would cause a movement from point A to point B on $SRAS_1$? What would cause a movement from point A to point C?

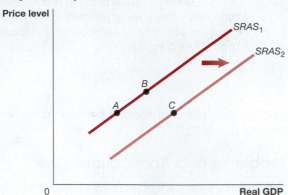

2.8 An article in the *Economist* noted that "the economy's potential to supply goods and services [is] determined by such things as the labour force and capital stock, as well as inflation expectations." Do you agree with this list of the determinants of potential GDP? Briefly explain.

Source: "Money's Muddled Message," *Economist*, March 19, 2009.

2.9 Explain how each of the following events would affect the short-run aggregate supply curve.
   a. An increase in the price level
   b. An increase in what the price level is expected to be in the future
   c. A price level that is currently higher than expected
   d. An unexpected increase in the price of an important raw material
   e. An increase in the labor force participation rate

2.10 Consider the variables that shift long-run aggregate supply and the variables that shift short-run aggregate supply. Match each of the following scenarios with one of the three graphs of long-run aggregate supply and short-run aggregate supply.

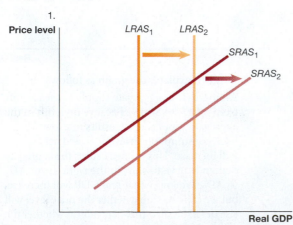

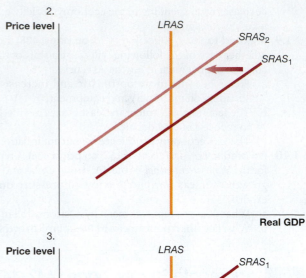

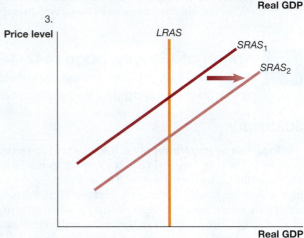

   a. The expected future price level decreases.
   b. Workers and firms adjust to having previously underestimated the price level
   c. A positive technological change occurs.

2.11 The American Trucking Association anticipates a shortage of truck drivers in coming years as the number of retirees exceeds the number of new drivers who enter the profession. The number of train boxcars is also expected to fall by over 40 percent in coming years because federal regulations limit boxcars to 50 years of service and many currently in use will reach that limit by 2020. Lumber and paper producers that depend on boxcars for their shipments fear that they will have to depend more on trucks for transportation, which will cost as much as 20 percent more than shipping by rail. Is the reduction in the number of trucks and boxcars likely to affect the short-run aggregate supply curve? Is it likely to affect the long-run aggregate supply curve? Briefly explain.

Sources: Lindsay Ellis and Laura Stevens, "International Paper Focuses on Improving Shipment Planning," *Wall Street Journal*, July 30, 2015; and Bob Tita, "Why Railroads Can't Keep Enough Boxcars in Service," *Wall Street Journal*, June 21, 2015.

2.12 (Related to the Making the Connection on page 444) Economists Mary Daly, Bart Hobijn, and Timothy Ni of the Federal Reserve Bank of San Francisco argue that "employers hesitate to reduce wages and workers are reluctant to accept wage cuts, even during recessions." If a firm faces declining sales during a recession, why might the firm's managers decide to lay off some workers and freeze the wages of other workers rather than cut workers' nominal wages?

Source: Mary C. Daly, Bart Hobijn, and Timothy Ni, "The Path of Wage Growth and Unemployment," *Federal Reserve Bank of San Francisco Economic Letter*, July 15, 2013.

2.13 **(Related to the** Making the Connection **on page 444)** An article in the *Economist* discussing the 2007–2009 recession states that "employers found it difficult to reduce the cash value of the wages paid to their staff. (Foisting a pay cut on your entire workforce hardly boosts morale.)"

  a. During a recession, couldn't firms reduce their labor costs by the same, or possibly more, if they laid off

fewer workers while cutting wages? Why did few firms use this approach?

  b. What does the article mean by firms reducing the "cash value" of workers' wages? Is it possible for firms to reduce workers' wages over time without reducing their cash value? Briefly explain.

Source: "Careful Now," *Economist*, April 11, 2015.

2.14 What are menu costs? If menu costs were eliminated, would the short-run aggregate supply curve be a vertical line? Briefly explain.

Macroeconomic Equilibrium in the Long Run and the Short Run, pages 448–454

LEARNING OBJECTIVE: Use the aggregate demand and aggregate supply model to illustrate the difference between short-run and long-run macroeconomic equilibrium.

Summary

In long-run macroeconomic equilibrium, the aggregate demand and short-run aggregate supply curves intersect at a point *on* the long-run aggregate supply curve. In short-run macroeconomic equilibrium, the aggregate demand and short-run aggregate supply curves often intersect at a point *off* the long-run aggregate supply curve. An automatic mechanism drives the economy to long-run equilibrium. If short-run equilibrium occurs at a point below potential GDP, wages and prices will fall, and the short-run aggregate supply curve will shift to the right until potential GDP is restored. If short-run equilibrium occurs at a point beyond potential GDP, wages and prices will rise, and the short-run aggregate supply curve will shift to the left until potential GDP is restored. Real GDP can be temporarily above or below its potential level, either because of shifts in the aggregate demand curve or because supply shocks lead to shifts in the short-run aggregate supply curve. **Stagflation** is a combination of inflation and recession, usually resulting from a supply shock.

MyEconLab   Visit **www.myeconlab.com** to complete these exercises online and get instant feedback.

Review Questions

3.1 Describe the relationship of the *AD*, *SRAS*, and *LRAS* curves when the economy is in long-run macroeconomic equilibrium.

3.2 Why might a supply shock lead to stagflation?

3.3 Suppose the economy enters a recession. If government policymakers—Congress, the president, and members of the Federal Reserve—do not take any policy actions in response to the recession, which of the alternatives listed below is the likely result? Be sure to carefully explain why you chose the answer you did.

  1. The unemployment rate will rise and remain higher even in the long run, and real GDP will drop below potential GDP and remain lower than potential GDP in the long run.

  2. The unemployment rate will rise in the short run but return to the natural rate of unemployment in the long run, and real GDP will drop below potential GDP in the short run but return to potential GDP in the long run.

  3. The unemployment rate will rise and remain higher even in the long run, and real GDP will drop below potential GDP in the short run but return to potential GDP in the long run.

  4. The unemployment rate will rise in the short run but return to the natural rate of unemployment in the long run, and real GDP will drop below potential GDP in the short run and remain lower than potential GDP in the long run.

Problems and Applications

3.4 An article in the *Economist* noted that in the first half of 2015, the value of Canadian oil exports declined and that "energy firms, which account for around a third of capital spending, are expected to slash investment by nearly 40% this year." As a result, real GDP in Canada declined during the first six months of 2015.

  a. Use a basic aggregate demand and aggregate supply graph (with *LRAS* constant) to illustrate this situation.

  b. On your graph show the adjustment back to long-run equilibrium.

Source: "A Rough Ride," *Economist*, July 11, 2015.

3.5 Draw a basic aggregate demand and aggregate supply graph (with *LRAS* constant) that shows the economy in long-run equilibrium.

  a. Assume that there is a large increase in demand for U.S. exports. Show the resulting short-run equilibrium on your graph. In this short-run equilibrium, is the unemployment rate likely to be higher or lower than it was before the increase in exports? Briefly explain. Explain how the economy adjusts back to long-run equilibrium. When the economy has adjusted back to long-run equilibrium, how have the values of each of the following changed relative to what they were before the increase in exports:

    i.   Real GDP

    ii.   The price level

    iii. The unemployment rate

  b. Assume that there is an unexpected increase in the price of oil. Show the resulting short-run equilibrium on your graph. Explain how the economy adjusts back to long-run equilibrium. In this short-run equilibrium, is the unemployment rate likely to be higher or lower than it was before the unexpected increase in the price of oil? Briefly explain. When the economy has adjusted back to long-run equilibrium, how have the values of each of the following changed relative to what they were before the unexpected increase in the price of oil:

i. Real GDP
ii. The price level
iii. The unemployment rate

3.6 (Related to the Making the Connection on page 450) Edward Leamer of the University of California, Los Angeles, has argued that "housing *is* the business cycle." Why would spending on housing be likely to fluctuate more than spending by households on consumer durables, such as automobiles or furniture, or spending by firms on plant and equipment?

Source: Edward E. Leamer, "Housing *Is* the Business Cycle," in *Housing, Housing Finance, and Monetary Policy*, Federal Reserve Bank of Kansas City, August 2007.

3.7 Consider the data in the following table for 1969 and 1970 (where the values for real GDP and potential GDP are in 2009 dollars):

Year	Actual Real GDP	Potential GDP	Unemployment Rate
1969	$4.71 trillion	$4.57 trillion	3.5%
1970	$4.72 trillion	$4.74 trillion	4.9%

Sources: U.S. Bureau of Labor Statistics; and Federal Reserve Bank of St. Louis.

a. In 1969, actual real GDP was greater than potential GDP. Briefly explain how this is possible.
b. Even though real GDP in 1970 was slightly greater than real GDP in 1969, the unemployment rate increased substantially from 1969 to 1970. Why did this increase in unemployment occur?
c. Was the inflation rate in 1970 likely to have been higher or lower than the inflation rate in 1969? Does your answer depend on whether the recession that began in December 1969 was caused by a change in a component of aggregate demand or by a supply shock?

3.8 Use the graph below to answer the following questions.

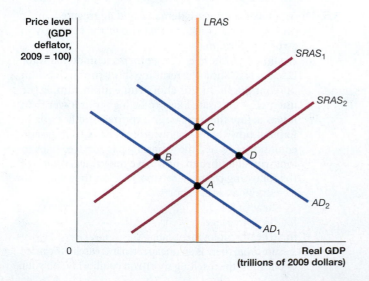

a. Which of the points *A*, *B*, *C*, or *D* can represent a long-run equilibrium?
b. Suppose that initially the economy is at point *A*. If aggregate demand increases from AD_1 to AD_2, which point represents short-run equilibrium? Which point represents the eventual long-run equilibrium? Briefly explain how the economy adjusts from the short-run equilibrium to the long-run equilibrium.

3.9 (Related to the Making the Connection on page 453) In early 2009, Christina Romer, who was then the chair of the Council of Economic Advisers, and Jared Bernstein, who was then an economic adviser to Vice President Joseph Biden, forecast how long they expected it would take for real GDP to return to potential GDP, assuming that Congress passed fiscal policy legislation proposed by President Obama:

It should be understood that all of the estimates presented in this memo are subject to significant margins of error. There is the obvious uncertainty that comes from modeling a hypothetical package rather than the final legislation passed by the Congress. But there is the more fundamental uncertainty that comes with any estimate of the effects of a program. Our estimates of economic relationships ... are derived from historical experience and so will not apply exactly in any given episode. Furthermore, the uncertainty is surely higher than normal now because the current recession is unusual both in its fundamental causes and its severity.

Why would the causes of a recession and its severity affect the accuracy of forecasts of when the economy would return to potential GDP?

Source: Christina Romer and Jared Bernstein, *The Job Impact of the American Recovery and Reinvestment Plan*, January 9, 2009, p. 2.

3.10 The following graphs show either aggregate demand or short-run aggregate supply shifting to the right or to the left.

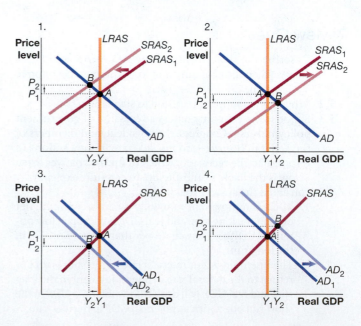

a. Match the following scenarios to the appropriate graph.
   i.   An increase in the expected price level
   ii. An increase in households' expectations of their future income
   iii. A decrease in the price of an important natural resource
   iv. A decrease in firms' expectations of the future profitability of investment spending

b. Match one or more of the four graphs to each of the following scenarios:
   i.   The economy experiences a recession
   ii. The economy experiences short-term inflation
   iii. The economy experiences stagflation

A Dynamic Aggregate Demand and Aggregate Supply Model, pages 455–460

LEARNING OBJECTIVE: Use the dynamic aggregate demand and aggregate supply model to analyze macroeconomic conditions.

Summary

To make the aggregate demand and aggregate supply model more realistic, we need to make it *dynamic* by incorporating three facts that were left out of the basic model: (1) Potential GDP increases continually, shifting the long-run aggregate supply curve to the right; (2) during most years, aggregate demand shifts to the right; and (3) except during periods when workers and firms expect high rates of inflation, the aggregate supply curve shifts to the right. The dynamic aggregate demand and aggregate supply model allows us to analyze macroeconomic conditions, including the beginning of the 2007–2009 recession.

MyEconLab   Visit **www.myeconlab.com** to complete these exercises online and get instant feedback.

Review Questions

4.1 What are the key differences between the basic aggregate demand and aggregate supply model and the dynamic aggregate demand and aggregate supply model?

4.2 In the dynamic aggregate demand and aggregate supply model, what is the result of aggregate demand increasing more than potential GDP increases? What is the result of aggregate demand increasing less than potential GDP increases?

4.3 Briefly discuss the factors that caused the recession of 2007–2009.

Problems and Applications

4.4 Draw a dynamic aggregate demand and aggregate supply graph showing the economy moving from potential GDP in 2017 to potential GDP in 2018, with no inflation. Your graph should contain the *AD*, *SRAS*, and *LRAS* curves for both 2017 and 2018 and should indicate the short-run macroeconomic equilibrium for each year and the directions in which the curves have shifted. Identify what must happen to have growth during 2018 without inflation.

4.5 (Related to Solved Problem 13.4 on page 459) Consider the information in the following table for the first two years of the Great Depression (where the values for real GDP and potential GDP are in 2009 dollars):

Year	Actual Real GDP	Potential GDP	Price Level
1929	$1,056.6 billion	$1,006.3 billion	10.6
1930	$966.7 billion	$1,094.1 billion	10.2

Sources: U.S. Bureau of Labor Statistics; and Federal Reserve Bank of St. Louis.

a. The table shows that something happened during 1929–1930 that has not happened during the recessions of the past 50 years. What is it?

b. Draw a dynamic aggregate demand and aggregate supply graph to illustrate what happened during these years. Your graph should contain the *AD*, *SRAS*, and *LRAS* curves for both 1929 and 1930 and should indicate the short-run macroeconomic equilibrium for each year and the directions in which the curves shifted.

4.6 (Related to Solved Problem 13.4 on page 459) An article in the *New York Times* in early 2015 stated that economists at the Federal Reserve were forecasting that "real GDP would expand at a faster pace than potential output in 2015" and that the inflation rate during 2015 would be about 1 percent.

a. Fill in the blank cells in the table with estimates that are consistent with these forecasts.

	2015	**2016**
Real GDP	$16.5 trillion	
Potential GDP	$16.8 trillion	$17.1 trillion
GDP deflator	119.2	

b. Draw a dynamic aggregate demand and aggregate supply graph to illustrate your answer to part a.

Source: Reuters, "Factbox: Fed Staff Forecasts from FOMC Minutes," *New York Times*, April 8, 2015.

4.7 In the following graph, suppose that the economy moves from point A in year 1 to point B in year 2. Using the graph, briefly explain your answer to each of the questions.

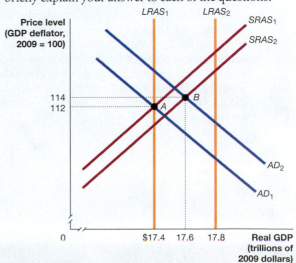

a. What is the growth rate in potential GDP from year 1 to year 2?

b. Is the unemployment rate in year 2 higher or lower than in year 1?

c. What is the inflation rate in year 2?

d. What is the growth rate of real GDP in year 2?

4.8 Explain whether you agree with the following statement:

The dynamic aggregate demand and aggregate supply model predicts that a recession caused by a decline in *AD* will cause the inflation rate to fall. I know that the 2007–2009 recession was caused by a fall in *AD*, but the inflation rate was not lower as a result of the recession. The prices of most products were definitely higher in 2008 than they were in 2007, so the inflation rate could not have fallen.

4.9 In a speech in late 2011, President Barack Obama argued, "Probably the single greatest cause of the financial crisis and this brutal recession has been the housing bubble that burst four years ago." What did the president mean by the "housing bubble"? How can a housing bubble bring on a recession?

Source: Laura Meckler, "Obama Says Plan Will Cut Mortgage Payments for Millions," *Wall Street Journal*, October 24, 2011.

4.10 (Related to the Chapter Opener on page 433) Jet fuel is the largest operating cost for Delta Air Lines. In 2015, Delta's CEO Richard Anderson announced that the firm was likely to save more than $2 billion during the year because of lower fuel prices. Are firms like airlines that have costs that are dependent on raw material prices likely to be more or less affected by the business cycle than firms like automobile companies whose costs are not as dependent on raw material prices? Briefly explain.

Source: Paul R. La Monica, "Delta Air Lines Is Saving $2 Billion on Fuel," money.cnn.com, January 20, 2015.

Real-Time Data Exercises

D13.1 (Showing movements in equilibrium real GDP and the price level) Go to the Web site of the Federal Reserve Bank of St. Louis (FRED) (research.stlouisfed.org/fred2/) and find data on real GDP (GDPCA) and the GDP price deflator (USAGDPDEFAISMEI) for 1960, 1973, 1975, and 2007.

a. In an *AD–AS* graph, using the actual values for real GDP and the GDP price deflator, show equilibrium for 1960 and for 2007. Assume that the economy was at equilibrium at potential GDP in both years. From 1960 to 2007, what happened to long-run aggregate supply? Given the change in the GDP implicit price deflator, did aggregate demand grow more or less than long-run aggregate supply?

b. In an *AD–AS* graph, using the actual values for real GDP and the GDP price deflator, show equilibrium for 1973 and for 1975. Assume that the economy was in equilibrium at potential GDP in 1973 but in only a short-run equilibrium in 1975. Given the changes in real GDP and the GDP implicit price deflator, briefly explain what happened to short-run aggregate supply from 1973 to 1975.

D13.2 (The effects of a positive supply shock) Using data from the St. Louis Federal Reserve (research.stlouisfed.org/fred2/) FRED database, examine the experience of the U.S. economy during the 1990s. The U.S. economy experienced a positive supply shock with the spread of information communication technology and the Internet after 1995.

a. Download monthly data on the Personal Consumption Expenditure Price Index (PCEPI) from 1981 to the present. Calculate the inflation rate from 1982 to 2007 as the percentage change in the PCEPI from the same month in the previous year.

b. Calculate the average inflation rate from 1982 through 1994 and the average inflation rate from 1995 through 2007.

c. Are your calculations consistent with a positive supply shock after 1994? Briefly explain.

D13.3 (Comparing business cycles across countries) During the 2007–2009 period, the economies of the United Kingdom and the United States experienced similar problems. High oil prices and a housing bubble affected both economies. The financial crisis in the United States also affected investment in the United Kingdom, both by limiting credit and by increasing risk premiums. Using data from the St. Louis Federal Reserve (research.stlouisfed.org/fred2/) FRED database, examine the behavior of the U.K. economy since 2007.

a. Download quarterly data for real GDP (GBRRGDPQDSNAQ) and the GDP deflator (GBRGDPDEFQISMEI) for the United Kingdom from 2006 to the present. Calculate the growth rate of real GDP as the percentage change from the same quarter in the previous year and calculate the inflation rate as the percentage change in the GDP deflator from the same quarter in the previous year. Download data on the unemployment rate (GBRURHARMMDSMEI) for the same time period. For the frequency of the unemployment rate data, select quarterly, to match the frequency of the real GDP and GDP deflator data.

b. Download the three data series from 2007 to the present in the same graph. What do the data indicate about how similar the experience of the United Kingdom was to that of the United States during those years?

Appendix

Macroeconomic Schools of Thought

LEARNING OBJECTIVE: Compare macroeconomic schools of thought.

Macroeconomics became a separate field of economics in 1936, with the publication of John Maynard Keynes's book *The General Theory of Employment, Interest, and Money*. Keynes, an economist at the University of Cambridge in England, was attempting to explain the devastating Great Depression of the 1930s. Real GDP in the United States declined more than 25 percent between 1929 and 1933 and did not return to its potential level until the United States entered World War II in 1941 (see Chapter 12). The unemployment rate soared above 20 percent by 1933 and did not return to its 1929 level until 1942. Keynes developed a version of the aggregate demand and aggregate supply model to explain these facts. The widespread acceptance of Keynes's model during the 1930s and 1940s became known as the **Keynesian revolution**.

In fact, using the aggregate demand and aggregate supply model remains the most widely accepted approach to analyzing macroeconomic issues. Because the model has been modified significantly from Keynes's day, many economists who use the model today refer to themselves as *new Keynesians*. The new Keynesians emphasize the importance of the stickiness of wages and prices in explaining fluctuations in real GDP. A significant number of economists, however, dispute whether using the aggregate demand and aggregate supply model, as we have discussed it in this chapter, is the best way to analyze macroeconomic issues. These alternative *schools of thought* use models that differ significantly from the standard aggregate demand and aggregate supply model. We can briefly consider four major alternative models:

1. The monetarist model
2. The new classical model
3. The real business cycle model
4. The Austrian model

Keynesian revolution The name given to the widespread acceptance during the 1930s and 1940s of John Maynard Keynes's macroeconomic model.

The Monetarist Model

The monetarist model—also known as the neo-quantity theory of money model—was developed beginning in the 1940s by Milton Friedman, an economist at the University of Chicago who was awarded the Nobel Prize in Economics in 1976. Friedman argued that the Keynesian approach overstates the amount of macroeconomic instability in the economy. In particular, he argued that the economy will ordinarily be at potential GDP. In the book *A Monetary History of the United States: 1867–1960*, written with Anna Jacobson Schwartz, Friedman argued that most fluctuations in real output are caused by fluctuations in the money supply rather than by fluctuations in consumption spending or investment spending. Friedman and Schwartz argued that the severity of the Great Depression was caused by the Federal Reserve allowing the quantity of money in the economy to fall by more than 25 percent between 1929 and 1933.

In the United States, the Federal Reserve is responsible for managing the quantity of money. As we will discuss further in Chapter 15, the Federal Reserve has typically focused more on controlling interest rates than on controlling the money supply. Friedman argued that the Federal Reserve should change its practices and adopt a **monetary growth rule**, which is a plan for increasing the quantity of money at a fixed rate. He believed that adopting a monetary growth rule would reduce fluctuations in real GDP, employment, and inflation.

Friedman's ideas, which are referred to as **monetarism**, attracted significant support during the 1970s and early 1980s, when the U.S. economy experienced high rates of unemployment and inflation. The support for monetarism declined during the late 1980s and 1990s, when the unemployment and inflation rates were relatively low. In Chapter 14, we will discuss the *quantity theory of money*, which underlies the monetarist model.

Monetary growth rule A plan for increasing the quantity of money at a fixed rate that does not respond to changes in economic conditions.

Monetarism The macroeconomic theories of Milton Friedman and his followers, particularly the idea that the quantity of money should be increased at a constant rate.

The New Classical Model

The new classical model was developed in the mid-1970s by a group of economists including Nobel Laureate Robert Lucas of the University of Chicago, Nobel Laureate Thomas Sargent of New York University, and Robert Barro of Harvard University. Some of the views held by the new classical macroeconomists are similar to those held by economists before the Great Depression. Keynes referred to the economists before the Great Depression as *classical economists*. Like the classical economists, the new classical macroeconomists believe that the economy normally will be at potential GDP. They also believe that wages and prices adjust quickly to changes in demand and supply. Put another way, they believe the stickiness in wages and prices emphasized by the new Keynesians is unimportant.

New classical macroeconomics
The macroeconomic theories of Robert Lucas and others, particularly the idea that workers and firms have rational expectations.

Lucas argues that workers and firms have *rational expectations*, meaning that they form their expectations of the future values of economic variables, such as the inflation rate, by making use of all available information, including information on changes in the quantity of money and other factors that might affect aggregate demand. Fluctuations in output and employment occur if households and firms form incorrect expectations of the inflation rate. If the actual inflation rate is lower than the expected inflation rate, the actual real wage will be higher than the expected real wage. Higher real wages will lead to a recession because firms will hire fewer workers and cut back on production. As workers and firms adjust their expectations to the lower inflation rate, the real wage will decline, and employment and production will expand, bringing the economy out of recession. The ideas of Lucas and his followers are referred to as the **new classical macroeconomics**. Supporters of the new classical model agree with supporters of the monetarist model that the Federal Reserve should adopt a monetary growth rule. They argue that a monetary growth rule will make it easier for workers and firms to accurately forecast the price level, thereby reducing fluctuations in real GDP.   MyEconLab Concept Check

The Real Business Cycle Model

In the 1980s, some economists, including Nobel Laureates Finn Kydland of the University of California, Santa Barbara, and Edward Prescott of Arizona State University, argued that Lucas was correct in assuming that workers and firms formed their expectations rationally and that wages and prices adjust quickly to supply and demand but was wrong about the source of fluctuations in real GDP. They argued that fluctuations in real GDP are caused by temporary shocks to productivity and not by inaccurate forecasts of the price level. These shocks can be negative, such as a decline in the availability of oil or other raw materials, or positive, such as technological change that makes it possible to produce more output with the same quantity of inputs.

Real business cycle model
A macroeconomic model that focuses on real, rather than monetary, causes of the business cycle.

According to this school of thought, shifts in the aggregate demand curve have no effect on real GDP because the short-run aggregate supply curve is vertical. (Other schools of thought believe that the short-run aggregate supply curve is upward sloping and that only the *long-run* aggregate supply curve is vertical.) Fluctuations in real GDP occur when a negative productivity shock causes the short-run aggregate supply curve to shift to the left—reducing real GDP—or a positive productivity shock causes the short-run aggregate supply curve to shift to the right—increasing real GDP. Because this model focuses on "real" factors—productivity shocks—rather than changes in the quantity of money to explain fluctuations in real GDP, it is known as the **real business cycle model**.   MyEconLab Concept Check

The Austrian Model

The *Austrian school* of economics began in the late nineteenth century with the writings of Carl Menger, an economist at the University of Vienna. Important later contributors to this school of thought were Ludwig von Mises, who spent the later years of his career at New York University, and Friedrich von Hayek, who spent most of his career at the London School of Economics. The Austrian school is best known for arguing the superiority of the market system over government economic planning. Hayek, in particular, emphasized that only the price system operating through markets could make use of the dispersed information available to households and firms to bring about an efficient allocation of resources.

During the 1930s, Hayek developed a theory of the business cycle that emphasized the problems arising from central banks forcing interest rates to very low levels. Low interest rates cause businesses to spend more on factories, machinery, office buildings, and other types of capital. Initially, the surge in investment spending will produce an economic expansion, but the additional capital goods eventually produce more output than firms can sell for a profit. Businesses suffer losses, reduce output, and lay off workers, resulting in a recession. The lower the central bank drives interest rates, the greater the increase in investment spending, the larger the economic expansion, and the deeper the eventual recession.

For a time in the early 1930s, Hayek's theory of the business cycle attracted significant interest from economists, particularly in the United Kingdom. After the publication of Keynes's *General Theory* in 1936, interest in Hayek's theory declined, and today only a relatively few economists belong to the Austrian school. In the past few years, however, Austrian economists have argued that the events of the 2007–2009 recession fit their model well: The Federal Reserve lowered interest rates to fight the 2001 recession, and the low interest rates sparked a surge in capital spending—in this case, spending on houses rather than on factories or office buildings. Eventually, the excessive investment in housing ended with a housing bust and a severe recession.   MyEconLab Concept Check

Making the Connection

Karl Marx: Capitalism's Severest Critic

The schools of macroeconomic thought we have discussed in this appendix are considered part of mainstream economic theory because of their acceptance of the market system as the best means of raising living standards in the long run. One quite influential critic of mainstream economic theory was Karl Marx. Marx was born in Trier, Germany, in 1818. After graduating from the University of Berlin in 1841, he began a career as a political journalist and agitator. His political activities caused him to be expelled first from Germany and then from France and Belgium. In 1849, he moved to London, where he spent the remainder of his life.

In 1867, Marx published the first volume of his greatest work, *Das Kapital*. Marx read closely the most prominent mainstream economists, including Adam Smith, David Ricardo, and John Stuart Mill. But Marx believed that he understood how market systems would evolve in the long run much better than those earlier authors. He argued that the market system would eventually be replaced by a Communist economy, in which the workers would control production. He believed in the *labor theory of value*, which attributed all the value of a good or service to the labor embodied in it. According to Marx, the owners of businesses—capitalists—did not earn profits by contributing anything of value to the production of goods or services. Instead, they earned profits because their "monopoly of the means of production"—their ownership of factories and machinery—allowed them to exploit workers by paying them wages that were much lower than the value of workers' contributions to production.

Marx argued that the wages of workers would be driven to levels that allowed only bare survival. He also argued that small firms would eventually be driven out of business by larger firms, forcing owners of small firms into the working class. Control of production would ultimately be concentrated in the hands of a few firms, which would have difficulty selling the goods they produced to the impoverished masses. A final economic crisis would lead the working classes to rise up, seize control of the economy, and establish Communism. Marx died in 1883, without having provided a detailed explanation of how the Communist economy would operate.

Marx had relatively little influence on mainstream thinking in the United States, but several political parties in Europe were guided by his ideas. In 1917, the Bolshevik

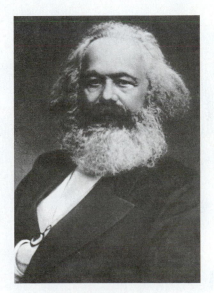

Karl Marx predicted that a final economic crisis would lead to the collapse of the market system.

Party seized control of Russia and established the Soviet Union, the first Communist state. Although the Soviet Union was a vicious dictatorship under Vladimir Lenin and his successor, Joseph Stalin, its prestige rose when it avoided the macroeconomic difficulties that plagued the market economies during the 1930s. By the late 1940s, Communist parties had also come to power in China and the countries of Eastern Europe. Poor economic performance contributed to the eventual collapse of the Soviet Union and its replacement by a market system, although one with significant government intervention in the economy. The Communist Party remains in power in China, but the economy is evolving toward a market system. Today, only North Korea and Cuba have economies that claim to be based on the ideas of Karl Marx.

Key Terms

Keynesian revolution, p. 469

Monetarism, p. 469

Monetary growth rule, p. 469

New classical macroeconomics, p. 470

Real business cycle model, p. 470

CHAPTER 4

Money, Banks, and the Federal Reserve System

Can Greece Function without Banks?

How often do you use a bank? If you are like most people, you withdraw cash from an ATM a couple of times per week and occasionally deposit checks. You may have visited a bank to apply for a student loan or a car loan. If you own your own business, you will have had many more interactions with banks. For example, you may have taken out a long-term loan to finance expanding your business.

Individuals and businesses in most countries would consider it difficult to function without banks. But that's the situation people in Greece faced in 2015. In 2001, Greece and most other European countries abandoned their individual currencies in favor of the euro. (Greece's currency had been the drachma.) Following the 2007–2009 financial crisis, the Greek government had trouble paying interest on the bonds it had issued. Many people feared that Greece might leave the euro and resume using the drachma. If that happened, the drachma might be worth less than the euro, which gave people in Greece an incentive to hold as many euros as they could. In 2015, Greece appeared to be in danger of defaulting on its debts. People responded by withdrawing large amounts of euros from Greek banks. To keep the banks from losing all their funds, the Greek government decided to close the banks for three weeks and limit withdrawals from ATM machines to 60 euros (about $66) per day.

Closing the banks dealt a heavy blow to the Greek economy. With the banks closed, many businesses insisted on being paid in cash. Consumers had trouble finding cash, though, because many ATMs had been emptied of currency. Some stores began accepting promises to pay later from customers who had no cash. Nikos Manisoitis & Son is a Greek firm that imports spices, pasta, and other products. The owner complained: "We feel like hostages. We can't move our money from the banks, and we fear that we are about to lose everything." Some importers loaded suitcases with euros and flew to other countries to pay their suppliers.

As we saw in Chapter 10, a country needs a well-functioning financial system if its economy is to prosper and grow. Greece's situation in the summer of 2015 shows what can happen when a country's banking system breaks down. In this chapter, we will study the role banks play in the financial system. We will also discuss the link between changes in the money supply and the inflation rate, as well as provide an overview of the operations of the Federal Reserve, which is the central bank of the United States.

Sources: Suzanne Daley, "Greeks Spend in Droves, Afraid of Losing Savings to a Bailout," *New York Times*, July 8, 2015; Liz Alderman, "Greek Economy under Siege, with Fears That the Worst Is Coming," *New York Times*, July 9, 2015; and "When Banks Die," *Economist*, July 5, 2015.

Economics in Your Life

What if Money Became Increasingly Valuable?

Most people are used to the fact that as prices rise each year, the purchasing power of money falls. You will be able to buy fewer goods and services with $1,000 one year from now, and you will be able to buy even fewer goods and services the year after that. In fact, with an inflation rate of just 3 percent, in 25 years, $1,000 will buy only what $475 can buy today. Suppose that you could live in an economy where the purchasing power of money *rose* each year? What would be the advantages and disadvantages of living in such an economy? As you read this chapter, try to answer these questions. You can check your answers against those we provide **on page 503** at the end of this chapter.

In this chapter, we will explore the role of money in the economy. We will see how the banking system creates money and what policy tools the Federal Reserve uses to manage the quantity of money in the United States. We will also examine the crisis in the banking system during and after the 2007–2009 recession. At the end of this chapter, we will explore the link between changes in the quantity of money and changes in the price level. What you learn in this chapter will serve as an important foundation for understanding monetary policy and fiscal policy, which we study in Chapters 15 through 17.

14.1 What Is Money, and Why Do We Need It?

LEARNING OBJECTIVE: Define money and discuss the four functions of money.

Could an economy function without money? There are historical examples of economies in which people traded goods for other goods rather than use money. For example, on the American frontier during colonial times, very little money was available, so a farmer might have traded a plow for a cow. Most economies, though, use money. The economic definition of **money** is any asset that people are generally willing to accept in exchange for goods and services or for payment of debts. Recall that an **asset** is anything of value owned by a person or a firm (see Chapter 6). There are many possible kinds of money: In West Africa, at one time, cowrie shells served as money. During World War II, prisoners of war used cigarettes as money.

Barter and the Invention of Money

To understand the importance of money, let's consider further the situation in economies that do not use money. Economies where goods and services are traded directly for other goods and services are called *barter economies*. Barter economies have a major shortcoming. To illustrate this shortcoming, consider a farmer on the American frontier in colonial days. Suppose the farmer needed a cow and proposed trading a spare plow to a neighbor for one of the neighbor's cows. If the neighbor did not want the plow, the trade would not happen. For a barter trade to take place between two people, each person must want what the other one has. Economists refer to this requirement as a *double coincidence of wants*. The farmer who wants the cow might eventually be able to obtain one if he first trades with some other neighbor for something the neighbor with the cow wants. However, it may take several trades before the farmer is ultimately able to trade for what the neighbor with the cow wants. Locating several trading partners and making several intermediate trades can take considerable time and energy.

To avoid the problems with barter, societies have an incentive to identify a product that most people will accept in exchange for what they have to trade. For example, in colonial times, animal skins were very useful in making clothing. The first governor of Tennessee actually received a salary of 1,000 deerskins per year, and the state's secretary of the Treasury received 450 otter skins per year. A good used as money that also has value independent of its use as money is called a **commodity money**. Historically, once a good became widely accepted as money, even people who did not have an immediate use for it would be willing to accept it. A colonial farmer—or the governor of Tennessee—might not want a deerskin, but as long as he knew he could use the deerskin to buy other goods and services, he would be willing to accept it in exchange for what he had to sell.

Trading goods and services is much easier when money becomes available. People only need to sell what they have for money and then use the money to buy what they want. If the colonial family could find someone to buy their plow, they could use the money to buy the cow they wanted. The family with the cow would accept the money because they knew they could use it to buy what they wanted. When money is available, families are more likely to specialize and less likely to produce everything or nearly everything they need themselves.

Money Assets that people are generally willing to accept in exchange for goods and services or for payment of debts.

Asset Anything of value owned by a person or a firm.

Commodity money A good used as money that also has value independent of its use as money.

Most people in modern economies are highly specialized. They do only one thing—work as a nurse, an accountant, or an engineer—and use the money they earn to buy everything else they need. As we discussed in Chapter 2, people become much more productive by specializing because they can pursue their *comparative advantage*. The high income levels in modern economies are based on the specialization that money makes possible. We can now answer the question, "Why do we need money?" *By making exchange easier, money allows people to specialize and become more productive.*   MyEconLab Concept Check

The Functions of Money

Anything used as money—whether a deerskin, a cowrie seashell, cigarettes, or a dollar bill—must serve four key functions in the economy:

1. It must act as a medium of exchange.
2. It must serve as a unit of account.
3. It must serve as a store of value.
4. It must offer a standard of deferred payment.

Medium of Exchange   Money serves as a medium of exchange when sellers are willing to accept it in exchange for goods or services. When the local supermarket accepts your $5 bill in exchange for bread and milk, the $5 bill is serving as a medium of exchange. With a medium of exchange, people can sell goods and services for money and use the money to buy what they want. An economy is more efficient when people accept a single good as a medium of exchange.

Unit of Account   In a barter system, each good has many prices. A cow may be worth 2 plows, 20 bushels of wheat, or 6 axes. Once a single good is used as money, each good has a single price rather than many prices. This function of money gives buyers and sellers a *unit of account*, a way of measuring value in the economy in terms of money. Because the U.S. economy uses dollars as money, each good has a price in terms of dollars.

Store of Value   Money allows people to easily store value: If you do not use all your dollars to buy goods and services today, you can hold the rest to use in the future. Money is not the only store of value, however. Any asset—shares of Facebook stock, Treasury bonds, real estate, or Renoir paintings, for example—represents a store of value. Financial assets, such as stocks and bonds, offer an important benefit relative to holding money because they pay a higher rate of interest or may increase in value in the future. Other assets also have advantages relative to money because they provide services. A house, for example, offers you a place to sleep.

Why, then, do people hold any money? The answer has to do with *liquidity*, or the ease with which people can convert an asset into the medium of exchange. Because money is the medium of exchange, it is the most liquid asset. If you want to buy something and you need to sell an asset to do so, you are likely to incur a cost. For example, if you want to buy a car and need to sell bonds or stocks to do so, you will need to pay a commission to your broker. To avoid such costs, people are willing to hold some of their wealth in the form of money, even though other assets offer a greater return as stores of value.

Standard of Deferred Payment   Money is useful because it can serve as a standard of deferred payment in borrowing and lending. It can facilitate exchange at a *given point in time* by providing a medium of exchange and unit of account. Money can facilitate exchange *over time* by providing a store of value and a standard of deferred payment. For example, a computer manufacturer may buy hard drives from another firm in exchange for the promise of making payment in 60 days.

How important is it that money be a reliable store of value and standard of deferred payment? People care about how much food, clothing, and other goods and services their dollars will buy. The value of money depends on its *purchasing power*, which refers to its ability to buy goods and services. Inflation causes a decline in purchasing power because with rising prices, a given amount of money can purchase fewer goods and services. When inflation reaches very high levels, money is no longer a reliable store of value or standard of deferred payment. MyEconLab Concept Check

What Can Serve as Money?

Having a medium of exchange helps to make transactions easier, which allows the economy to work more efficiently. The next question to consider is: What can serve as money? That is, which assets can be used as the medium of exchange? We saw earlier that an asset must, at a minimum, be generally accepted as payment to serve as money. In practical terms, however, it must be even more.

These five criteria make an asset suitable for use as a medium of exchange:

1. The asset must be *acceptable* to (that is, usable by) most people.
2. It should be of *standardized quality* so that any two units are identical.
3. It should be *durable* so that value is not lost by its quickly wearing out.
4. It should be *valuable* relative to its weight so that amounts large enough to be useful in trade can be easily transported.
5. It should be *divisible* so that it can be used in purchases of both low-priced and high-priced goods.

Dollar bills meet all these criteria. What determines the acceptability of dollar bills as a medium of exchange? Basically, it is through self-fulfilling expectations: You value something as money only if you believe that others will accept it from you as payment. A society's willingness to use paper dollars as money is what makes them an acceptable medium of exchange.

Commodity Money Commodity money has value independent of its use as money. Gold, for example, was a common form of money in the nineteenth and early twentieth centuries because it was a medium of exchange, a unit of account, a store of value, and a standard of deferred payment. But commodity money has a significant problem: Its value depends on its purity. Therefore, someone who wanted to cheat could mix a low-value metal, like iron, with a precious metal, like gold or silver. Another problem with using gold as money was that the money supply was difficult to control because it depended partly on unpredictable discoveries of new gold fields.

Fiat Money It can be inefficient for an economy to rely on only gold or other precious metals for its money supply. What if you had to transport bars of gold to settle your transactions? Not only would doing so be difficult and costly, but you would run the risk of being robbed. To get around this problem, private institutions or governments began to store gold and issue paper certificates that could be redeemed for gold. In modern economies, paper currency is generally issued by a *central bank*, which is an agency of the government that regulates the money supply. The **Federal Reserve** is the central bank of the United States. Today, no government in the world issues paper currency that can be redeemed for gold. Paper currency has no value unless it is used as money, and it is therefore not a commodity money. Instead, paper currency is a **fiat money**, which has no value except as money. If paper currency has no value except as money, why do consumers and firms use it?

If you look at the top of a U.S. dollar bill, you will see the words "Federal Reserve Note" because it is issued by the Federal Reserve. Because U.S. dollars are fiat money, the Federal Reserve is not required to give you gold or silver for your dollar bills. Federal Reserve currency is *legal tender* in the United States, which means the federal government requires that it be accepted in payment of debts and requires that cash or checks denominated in dollars be used in payment of taxes. Despite being legal tender, dollar bills would not be a good medium of exchange and could not serve as money if people didn't usually accept them. The key to this acceptance is that *households and firms have confidence that if they accept paper dollars in exchange for goods and services, the dollars will not lose much value during the time they hold them.* Without this confidence, dollar bills would not serve as a medium of exchange. MyEconLab Concept Check

Federal Reserve The central bank of the United States.

Fiat money Money, such as paper currency, that is authorized by a central bank or governmental body and that does not have to be exchanged by the central bank for gold or some other commodity money.

Making the Connection
MyEconLab Video

Apple Didn't Want My Cash!

If Federal Reserve Notes are legal tender, doesn't that mean that everyone in the United States, including every business, has to accept paper money? The answer to this question is "no," as a woman in California found out when she went to an Apple store in Palo Alto and tried to buy an iPad using $600 in currency. The store refused to sell her the iPad for cash. At that time, the iPad had just been released, and Apple did not want to sell large numbers to people who were buying them to resell on eBay, Craigslist, or elsewhere. So, a customer wanting to buy an iPad had to pay with either a credit card or a debit card, which would make it easier for Apple to keep track of anyone attempting to buy more than the limit of two per customer.

The law doesn't stop Apple from requiring customers to use a credit card rather than cash, but the company decided to lift its ban on paying for iPads with cash after bad publicity.

Because Federal Reserve Notes are legal tender, creditors must accept them in payment of debts, and the government will accept them in payment of taxes. However, as this incident demonstrates, firms do not have to accept cash as payment for goods and services. As the U.S. Treasury Department explains on its Web site:

> There is … no Federal statute mandating that a private business, a person or an organization must accept currency or coins as payment for goods and/or services. … For example, a bus line may prohibit payment of fares in pennies or dollar bills. In addition, movie theaters, convenience stores and gas stations may refuse to accept large denomination currency (usually notes above $20) as a matter of policy.

The woman who tried to buy an iPad for cash was disabled and on a limited income, so the incident led to negative publicity for Apple. As a result, Apple decided to lift its ban on paying for iPads with cash, provided that the customer was willing to set up an Apple account at the time of purchase. In addition, Apple presented a free iPad to the customer who was originally turned down when she tried to pay with cash.

Sources: Michael Winter, "Apple Ends No-Cash Policy and California Woman Gets Free iPad," www.usatoday.com, May 20, 2010; and U.S. Treasury, "FAQs: Currency," www.treasury.gov/resource-center/faqs/Currency/Pages/edu_faq_currency_index2.aspx.

Your Turn: Test your understanding by doing related problem 1.9 on page 505 at the end of this chapter.

MyEconLab Study Plan

14.2 How Is Money Measured in the United States Today?

LEARNING OBJECTIVE: Discuss the definitions of the money supply used in the United States today.

People are interested in the money supply because, as we will see, changes in the money supply can affect other economic variables, including employment, gross domestic product (GDP), and inflation. If the only function of money was to serve as a medium of exchange, then a narrow definition of the money supply should include only currency, checking account deposits, and traveler's checks because households and firms can easily use these assets to buy goods and services. A broader definition of the money supply would include other assets that can be used as a medium of exchange even though they are not as liquid as currency or checking account deposits. For example, you can't directly buy goods or services with funds in a bank savings account, but it is easy to withdraw funds from your savings account and then use these funds to buy goods and services.

Congress gave the Federal Reserve the responsibility of regulating the money supply and the task of determining how to measure it. The Federal Reserve's measures of the money supply have changed several times over the decades. Currently, the Federal Reserve publishes data on two measures of the money supply: *M1* and *M2*. These measures, sometimes called *monetary aggregates*, are important to understand, so we devote the following sections to discussing them.

M1: A Narrow Definition of the Money Supply

Figure 14.1 illustrates the definitions of the money supply. The narrow definition of the money supply, **M1**, includes the following:

M1 The narrow definition of the money supply: the sum of currency in circulation, checking account deposits in banks, and holdings of traveler's checks.

1. *Currency*, which is all the paper money and coins held by households and firms (not including currency held by banks)
2. The value of all checking account deposits in banks
3. The value of traveler's checks (Because this last category is so small—typically less than $4 billion—relative to the other two categories, we will ignore it in our discussion of the money supply.)

Although currency has almost as large a value as checking account deposits, checking account deposits are used much more often than currency to make payments. More than 80 percent of all expenditures on goods and services are made with checks rather than with currency. In fact, the total amount of currency in circulation—$1.3 trillion in July 2015—is a misleading number. This amount is more than $4,000 per person—adult or child—in the United States. If this sounds like an unrealistically large amount of currency to be held per person, it is. Economists estimate that more than 60 percent of U.S. currency is actually outside the borders of the United States. More than three-quarters of U.S. paper currency is in denominations of $100 or larger—too large to be used for routine buying and selling within the United States.

Who holds these dollars outside the United States? Foreign banks and foreign governments hold some U.S. currency, but most is held by households and firms in countries where there is not much confidence in the local currency or where the underground economy is large. When inflation rates are very high, many households and firms do not want to hold their domestic currency because it is losing its value too rapidly. The value of the U.S. dollar will be much more stable than their domestic currency. If enough people are willing to accept dollars as well as—or instead of—domestic currency, dollars become a second currency for the country. When inflation soared in the African country of Zimbabwe to the point where it took 15 *billion* Zimbabwean dollars

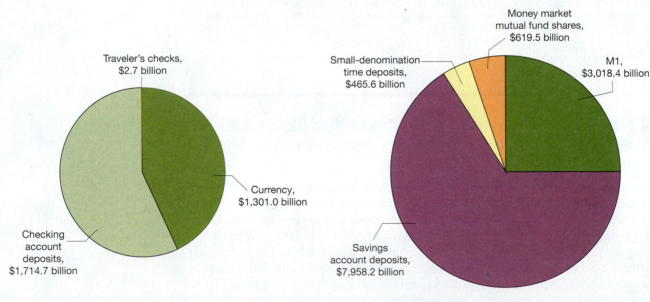

(a) M1 = $3,018.4 billion

(b) M2 = $12,061.7 billion

Figure 14.1 **Measuring the Money Supply**

The Federal Reserve uses two different measures of the money supply: M1 and M2. Panel (a) shows the assets in M1. Panel (b) shows M2, which includes the assets in M1, as well as money market mutual fund shares, small-denomination time deposits, and savings account deposits.

Source: Board of Governors of the Federal Reserve System, "Federal Reserve Statistical Release, H.6," July 30, 2015.

to buy a can of Coca-Cola, the government went so far as to adopt the U.S. dollar as the country's official currency.   MyEconLab Concept Check

M2: A Broad Definition of Money

Before 1980, U.S. law prohibited banks from paying interest on checking account deposits. Households and firms held checking account deposits primarily to buy goods and services. M1 was, therefore, very close to the function of money as a medium of exchange. Almost all currency, checking account deposits, and traveler's checks were held with the intention of buying and selling, not with the intention of storing value. In 1980, the law was changed to allow banks to pay interest on certain types of checking accounts. This change reduced the difference between checking accounts and savings accounts, although people are still not allowed to write checks against their savings account balances.

After 1980, economists began to pay closer attention to a broader definition of the money supply, **M2**. As panel (b) of Figure 14.1 shows, M2 includes everything that is in M1, plus savings account deposits, small-denomination time deposits—such as certificates of deposit (CDs)—balances in money market deposit accounts in banks, and noninstitutional money market fund shares. Small-denomination time deposits are similar to savings accounts, but the deposits are for a fixed period of time—usually from six months to several years—and withdrawals before that time are subject to a penalty. Mutual fund companies sell shares to investors and use the funds raised to buy financial assets such as stocks and bonds. Some of these mutual funds, such as Vanguard's Treasury Money Market Fund or Fidelity's Cash Reserves Fund, are called *money market mutual funds* because they invest in very short-term bonds, such as U.S. Treasury bills. The balances individual investors hold in these funds are included in M2. Each week, the Federal Reserve publishes statistics on M1 and M2. In the discussion that follows, we will use the M1 definition of the money supply because it corresponds most closely to money as a medium of exchange.

There are two key points to keep in mind about the money supply:

1. The narrowest definition of the money supply consists of *both* currency and checking account deposits.

2. Because balances in checking account deposits are included in the money supply, banks play an important role in the way the money supply increases and decreases. We will discuss this second point further in the next section.   MyEconLab Concept Check

M2 A broader definition of the money supply: It includes M1 plus savings account deposits, small-denomination time deposits, balances in money market deposit accounts in banks, and noninstitutional money market fund shares.

Don't Let This Happen to You

Don't Confuse Money with Income or Wealth

According to *Forbes*, in 2015, Bill Gates's wealth of $79 billion made him the richest person in the world. He also has a very large income, but how much money does he have? Your *wealth* is equal to the value of your assets minus the value of any debts you have. Your *income* is equal to your earnings during the year. Bill Gates's earnings as chairman of Microsoft and from his investments are very large. But his *money* is just equal to what he has in currency and checking accounts. Only a small proportion of Gates's $79 billion in wealth is likely to be in currency or checking accounts. Most of his wealth is invested in stocks and bonds and other financial assets that are not included in the definition of money.

In everyday conversation, we often describe someone who is wealthy or who has a high income as "having a lot of money." But when economists use the word *money*, they are usually referring to currency plus checking account deposits. It is important to keep straight the differences between wealth, income, and money.

Just as money and income are not the same for a person, they are not the same for the whole economy. National income in the United States was equal to $15.1 trillion in 2014. The money supply in 2014 was $2.8 trillion (using the M1 measure). There is no reason why national income in a country should be equal to the country's money supply, nor will an increase in a country's money supply necessarily increase the country's national income.

Source: "The World's Billionaires," *Forbes*, March 2, 2015.

MyEconLab Study Plan

Your Turn: Test your understanding by doing related problems 2.5 and 2.6 on page 505 at the end of this chapter.

Solved Problem 14.2

The Definitions of M1 and M2

Suppose you decide to withdraw $2,000 from your checking account and put the money into a bank certification of deposit (CD). Briefly explain how this action will affect M1 and M2.

Solving the Problem

Step 1: **Review the chapter material.** This problem is about the definitions of the money supply, so you may want to review the section "How Is Money Measured in the United States Today?" which begins on page 479.

Step 2: **Use the definitions of M1 and M2 to answer the problem.** Funds in checking accounts are included in both M1 and M2. Funds in CDs are included only in M2. It is tempting to answer this problem by saying that shifting $2,000 from a checking account to a CD reduces M1 by $2,000 and increases M2 by $2,000, but the $2,000 in your checking account was already counted in M2. So, the correct answer is that your action reduces M1 by $2,000 but leaves M2 unchanged.

MyEconLab Study Plan

Your Turn: For more practice, do related problems 2.7 and 2.8 on page 505 at the end of this chapter.

What about Credit Cards and Debit Cards?

Many people buy goods and services with credit cards, yet credit cards are not included in either definition of the money supply. The reason is that when you buy something with a credit card, you are in effect taking out a loan from the bank that issued the credit card. The transaction is complete only when you pay your credit card bill at the end of the month—often with a check or an electronic transfer from your checking account. In contrast, with a debit card, the funds to make the purchase are taken directly from your checking account. In either case, the cards themselves do not represent money.   MyEconLab Concept Check

Making the Connection
MyEconLab Video

Are Bitcoins Money?

Typically, when we think of "money," we think of currency issued by a government. But we have just seen that currency represents only a small part of the money supply of the United States, whether measured as M1 or M2. The non-currency components of M1 or M2, although not issued by the government, are familiar financial assets such as checking or savings accounts. Some households and firms have shifted away from M1 or M2 to finance their buying and selling of goods and services and are instead using e-money, or digital funds. The best-known form of e-money is PayPal, which until 2015 was owned by eBay, the online auction site. An individual or a firm can set up a PayPal account by transferring funds from a checking account or credit card. As long as a seller is willing to accept funds from a buyer's PayPal (or other e-money) account, e-money functions like conventional government-issued money.

Recently, journalists, economists, and policymakers have been debating the merits of bitcoin, a new form of e-money. Unlike PayPal and other similar services for transferring money electronically, bitcoin is not owned by a firm but is instead the product of a decentralized system of linked computers. Bitcoin was founded in 2009 by "Satoshi Nakamoto," which is likely an assumed name taken by bitcoin's founder or founders. Bitcoins are produced by people performing the complicated calculations necessary to ensure that online purchases made with bitcoins are legitimate—that is, that someone doesn't try to spend the same bitcoin multiple times. People who successfully complete these calculations are awarded a fixed amount of bitcoins—typically 14. This process of bitcoin "mining" will continue until a maximum of 21 million bitcoins has been produced—a total expected to be reached in 2030.

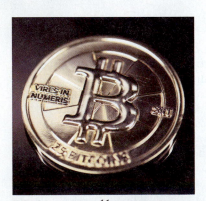

Bitcoins are created by computer calculations, not by central banks.

Because people can buy and sell bitcoins in exchange for dollars and other currencies on Web sites, some people refer to it as a "cryptocurrency." You can buy bitcoins and store them in a "digital wallet" on a smartphone. You can then buy something in a store that accepts bitcoins by scanning a bar code with your phone. A number of Web sites, such as BitPay, which is based in Atlanta, allow merchants to process purchases made with bitcoins in a manner similar to the way they process credit card payments.

Why would buyers and sellers prefer to use bitcoins rather than cash or a credit card? The popularity of bitcoins with some buyers may be due to its being a new and fashionable way to make purchases, and because of the convenience of using a smartphone to make a purchase. In addition, some people are afraid that because central banks in most countries greatly increased the money supply during and after the recession of 2007–2009, the result will eventually be high rates of inflation. These people hope that because the total amount of bitcoins is limited, inflation will not undermine their value. Finally, when you buy something with a credit card, the credit card company has a permanent record of your transaction. Bitcoin transactions are more private because no such record of your transaction exists.

Some retailers prefer bitcoins to credit card purchases because the retailers pay only about 1 percent of the sale in processing costs, as opposed to about 3 percent for a credit card purchase. In addition, a bitcoin sale is final, just as if the purchase were made with cash, unlike credit card sales, where the buyer can dispute the purchase even months after it was made.

Despite these possible benefits to using bitcoin, by 2015, it had not yet been widely adopted. The introduction of Apple Pay and Google Wallet provided consumers with a way to use their smartphones linked to a credit card to make payments, which undercut one of bitcoin's advantages. Some firms also questioned whether the software underlying bitcoin was capable of dealing with a large number of transactions, which would be a barrier to the cryptocurrency being widely used. The most popular online bitcoin exchange, Japan-based Mt. Gox, collapsed, further reducing confidence in the cryptocurrency. At the time of the firm's collapse, the CEO said that software problems had allowed hackers to withdraw more than $500 million worth of bitcoins investors had stored on the exchange. The Japanese police later arrested the CEO.

Some policymakers are concerned that investors on exchanges might manipulate the prices of bitcoins and other virtual currencies. The value of bitcoins in exchange for dollars rose from $5 per bitcoin in June 2012 to $266 per bitcoin in April 2013, before falling to $94 per bitcoin in July 2013 and then rising to $287 in July 2015. Whether these swings in value represented underlying movements in demand and supply for bitcoins or manipulation of their values was not clear.

Should the Federal Reserve include bitcoins and other virtual or cryptocurrencies in its measures of the money supply? So far, the volume of transactions in these currencies has been small, which makes the question of little practical importance. At this point, the Federal Reserve treats virtual currencies as being the equivalent of credit or debit cards, rather than currency or checking account balances, and does not include them in M1 or M2.

Sources: Paul Vigna, "Bitcoiners Decamp to Bretton Woods, Assess the Future of Bitcoin," *Wall Street Journal*, July 30, 2015; Takashi Mochizuki, "Japanese Police Arrest Mark Karpelès of Collapsed Bitcoin Exchange Mt. Gox," *Wall Street Journal*, August 1, 2015; Lingling Wei, "Fed Studying Risks at Online Payment Providers," *Wall Street Journal*, June 3, 2013; and "How Does Bitcoin Work?" *Economist*, April 11, 2013.

Your Turn: Test your understanding by doing related problem 2.11 on page 506 at the end of this chapter.

MyEconLab Study Plan

14.3 How Do Banks Create Money?

LEARNING OBJECTIVE: Explain how banks create money.

We have seen that the most important component of the money supply is checking accounts in banks. To understand the role money plays in the economy, we need to look more closely at how banks operate. Banks are profit-making private businesses, just like department stores and supermarkets. Some banks are quite small, with just a few branches, and do business in a limited area. Others are among the largest corporations in the United States, with thousands of branches spread across many states. Banks play an important role in the economy by accepting deposits and making loans. By taking these actions, banks fulfill a key function in the *money supply process* by which central banks control the money supply.

Bank Balance Sheets

To understand how banks create money, we need to briefly examine a typical bank balance sheet. On a balance sheet, a firm's assets are listed on the left, and its liabilities and stockholders' equity are listed on the right (see Chapter 6). Assets are the value of anything owned by the firm, liabilities are the value of anything the firm owes, and stockholders' equity is the difference between the total value of assets and the total value of liabilities. Stockholders' equity represents the value of the firm if it were closed, all its assets were sold, and all its liabilities were paid off. A corporation's stockholders' equity is also called its *net worth*. A bank's stockholders' equity or net worth is also called its *capital*.

Figure 14.2 shows a typical balance sheet for a large bank. The key assets on a bank's balance sheet are its *reserves*, loans, and holdings of securities, such as U.S. Treasury bills. **Reserves** are deposits that a bank has retained rather than loaned out or invested. Banks keep reserves either physically within the bank, as *vault cash*, or on deposit with the Federal Reserve. Banks are required by law to keep as reserves 10 percent of their checking account deposits above a threshold level, which in 2015 was $103.6 million. These reserves are called **required reserves**. The minimum fraction of deposits that banks are required to keep as reserves is called the **required reserve ratio**. We can abbreviate the required reserve ratio as *RR*. Any reserves that banks hold above the legal requirement are called **excess reserves**. The balance sheet in Figure 14.2 shows that loans are a typical bank's largest asset.

Banks make *consumer loans* to households and *commercial loans* to firms. A loan is an asset to a bank because it represents a promise by the person taking out the loan to make certain specified payments to the bank. A bank's reserves and its holdings of securities are also assets because they are things of value the bank owns.

Reserves Deposits that a bank keeps as cash in its vault or on deposit with the Federal Reserve.

Required reserves Reserves that a bank is legally required to hold, based on its checking account deposits.

Required reserve ratio The minimum fraction of deposits banks are required by law to keep as reserves.

Excess reserves Reserves that banks hold over the legal requirement.

Figure 14.2

The Balance Sheet of a Typical Large Bank

The entries on a bank's balance sheet of greatest economic importance are its reserves, loans, and deposits. Notice that the difference between the value of this bank's total assets and its total liabilities is equal to its stockholders' equity. As a consequence, the left side of the balance sheet always equals the right side. *Note:* Some entries have been combined to simplify the balance sheet.

Assets (in billions)		Liabilities and Stockholders' Equity (in billions)	
Reserves	$135	Deposits	$1,000
Loans	900	Short-term borrowing	400
Securities	700	Long-term debt	360
Buildings and equipment	15	Other liabilities	275
Other assets	550	Total liabilities	$2,035
		Stockholders' equity	265
Total assets	$2,300	Total liabilities and stockholders' equity	$2,300

Making the Connection MyEconLab Video

Would You Borrow from an Online Peer-to-Peer Lender?

The basic business of banks is taking in deposits from savers and using those funds to make loans to households and firms. Banks often require *collateral* before making a loan, which means that if the borrower stops making payments on the loan, the bank can seize the asset the borrower pledged as collateral. For example, if you take out a loan to buy a car and stop making payments on the loan, the bank can repossess your car and sell it to get its money back.

In addition to collateral, banks rely on a borrower's *credit score* in deciding whether to make a loan. The best-known credit score is compiled by the FICO company, which rates borrowers on a scale of 350 to 850, with higher scores meaning the borrower is less likely to default. Credit scores are determined by a variety of factors, including whether the borrower has been on time with payments on other loans and on credit cards; how long the borrower has lived at his current residence; how long the borrower has held her current job; and how much other debt the borrower has. Borrowers with high scores are called *prime borrowers*, and borrowers with low scores are called *subprime borrowers*. A bank will typically charge a prime borrower a lower interest rate than it will charge a subprime borrower. The higher interest rate on a *subprime loan* compensates the bank for the greater risk that the borrower will default. Lenders differ in the minimum score they use to consider someone a prime borrower, but it is typically around 650.

Some people with low credit scores who can't get a bank loan turn to peer-to-peer lending to borrow the funds to meet needs such as buying furniture.

During the housing bubble of the early 2000s, many banks and other lenders made mortgage loans to subprime borrowers buying houses. High default rates on these mortgages following the bursting of the housing bubble in 2006 contributed to the 2007–2009 financial crisis and led policymakers to tighten regulations on banks granting subprime loans. Some consumer advocates also criticize these loans because they believe that the high interest rates exploit borrowers. To avoid both the new regulations and the criticism, many banks have cut back on subprime loans, particularly subprime *personal loans*, which are made to individuals who do not provide collateral for the loan. In past years, after getting a job, many new college graduates would take out a personal loan from a bank to buy the furniture or small appliances needed to set up an apartment. You may have a low credit score if you were late with a couple of credit card payments, have only a short work history, and have just moved into a new apartment. A bank may then consider you a subprime borrower and be unwilling to lend you money.

You could borrow on your credit card by taking a cash advance, but the interest rate is likely to be high—typically more than 20 percent. When banks cut back on subprime personal loans, it left a hole in the financial system. In the past few years, some new businesses have developed to fill that hole. For example, Lending Club and FreedomPlus facilitate peer-to-peer lending on the Internet. These businesses gather information about a borrower, determine the interest rate on the loan, and then post the loan online. Individual investors can then choose to fund the loan. Some loans are funded by a single investor, while others are funded by several investors. The loans can be as short as a few weeks or as long as several years and can have interest rates from 7 percent to more than 20 percent, with the typical interest rate being around 14 percent. Peer-to-peer lending firms are part of the "sharing economy," which also includes the car ride firm Uber and short-term apartment rental firm Airbnb. In the case of peer-to-peer lending, it's money that is being shared.

By 2015, peer-to-peer lending sites were making $10 billion worth of loans. While this amount has been growing rapidly, it still far less than the trillions of dollars in loans of all types made by banks. It remains to be seen whether the peer-to-peer lending sites will end up becoming a major source of credit to households and firms.

Sources: Ianthe Jeanne Dugan and Telis Demos, "New Lenders Spring Up to Cater to Subprime Sector," *Wall Street Journal*, March 5, 2014; and "From the People, for the People," *Economist*, May 9, 2015.

Your Turn: Test your understanding by doing related problems 3.7 and 3.8 on pages 506–507 at the end of this chapter.

Deposits are a typical bank's largest liability. Deposits include checking accounts, savings accounts, and CDs. Deposits are liabilities to banks because they are owed to the households or firms that have deposited the funds. If you deposit $100 in your checking account, the bank owes you the $100, and you can ask for it back at any time. So, your checking account is an asset to you, and it is a liability to the bank. Banks also borrow short term from other banks and from the Federal Reserve and borrow long term by selling bonds to investors. These *borrowings* are also liabilities.   MyEconLab Concept Check

Using T-Accounts to Show How a Bank Can Create Money

It is easier to show how banks create money by using a T-account than by using a balance sheet. A T-account is a stripped-down version of a balance sheet that shows only how a transaction *changes* a bank's balance sheet. Suppose you deposit $1,000 in currency into an account at Bank of America. This transaction raises the total deposits at Bank of America by $1,000 and also raises its reserves by $1,000. We show this result on the following T-account:

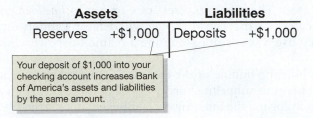

Remember that because the total value of all the entries on the right side of a balance sheet must always be equal to the total value of all the entries on the left side of a balance sheet, any transaction that increases (or decreases) one side of the balance sheet must also increase (or decrease) the other side of the balance sheet. In this case, the T-account shows that we increased both sides of the balance sheet by $1,000.

Initially, this transaction does not increase the money supply. The currency component of the money supply declines by $1,000 because the $1,000 you deposited is no longer in circulation and, therefore, is not counted in the money supply. But the decrease in currency is offset by a $1,000 increase in the checking account deposit component of the money supply.

This initial change is not the end of the story, however. Banks are required to keep 10 percent of deposits as reserves. Because the Federal Reserve pays banks only a low rate of interest on their reserves, banks have an incentive to loan out or buy securities with the other 90 percent. Suppose, for simplicity, that initially Bank of America holds no excess reserves. In that case, Bank of America can keep $100 of your deposit as required reserves and loan out the other $900, which represents its excess reserves. Assume that Bank of America loans out the $900 to someone to buy a very inexpensive used car. Bank of America could give the $900 to the borrower in currency, but usually banks make loans by increasing the borrower's checking account. We can show this transaction with another T-account:

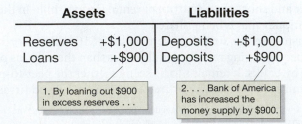

Notice that *by making this $900 loan, Bank of America has increased the money supply by $900.* The initial $1,000 in currency you deposited into your checking account has been turned into $1,900 in checking account deposits—a net increase in the money supply of $900.

But the story does not end here. The person who took out the $900 loan did so to buy a used car. To keep things simple, let's suppose he buys the car for exactly $900 and pays by writing a check on his account at Bank of America. The seller of the used car will now deposit the check in her bank. That bank may also be a branch of Bank of America, but in most cities, there are many banks, so let's assume that the seller of the car has her account at a branch of PNC Bank. Once she deposits the check, PNC Bank will send it to Bank of America to *clear* the check and collect the $900. We show the result in the following T-accounts:

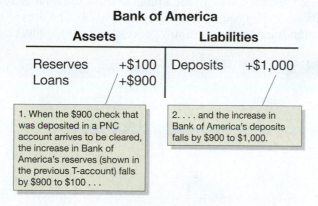

Bank of America

Assets		Liabilities	
Reserves	+$100	Deposits	+$1,000
Loans	+$900		

1. When the $900 check that was deposited in a PNC account arrives to be cleared, the increase in Bank of America's reserves (shown in the previous T-account) falls by $900 to $100 . . .

2. . . . and the increase in Bank of America's deposits falls by $900 to $1,000.

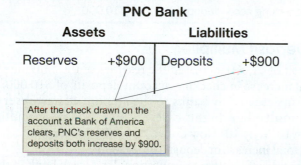

PNC Bank

Assets		Liabilities	
Reserves	+$900	Deposits	+$900

After the check drawn on the account at Bank of America clears, PNC's reserves and deposits both increase by $900.

After the car buyer's check clears, Bank of America has lost $900 in deposits—the amount loaned to the car buyer—and $900 in reserves—the amount it had to pay PNC when PNC sent Bank of America the car buyer's check. PNC has an increase in checking account deposits of $900—the deposit of the car seller—and an increase in reserves of $900—the amount it received from Bank of America.

PNC has 100 percent reserves against this new $900 deposit, but it needs only 10 percent reserves. The bank has an incentive to keep $90 as reserves and to loan out the other $810, which are excess reserves. If PNC does this, we can show the change in its balance sheet by using another T-account:

PNC Bank

Assets		Liabilities	
Reserves	+$900	Deposits	+$900
Loans	+$810	Deposits	+$810

By making an $810 loan, PNC has increased both its loans and its deposits by $810.

In loaning out the $810 in excess reserves, PNC creates a new checking account deposit of $810. The initial deposit of $1,000 in currency into Bank of America has now resulted in the creation of $1,000 + $900 + $810 = $2,710 in checking account deposits. The money supply has increased by $2,710 − $1,000 = $1,710.

The process is still not finished. The person who borrows the $810 will spend it by writing a check against his account. Whoever receives the $810 will deposit it in her bank, which could be a Bank of America branch or a PNC branch or a branch of some other bank. That new bank—if it's not PNC—will send the check to PNC and will receive $810 in new reserves. That new bank will have an incentive to loan out 90 percent of these reserves—keeping 10 percent to meet the legal requirement—and the process will go on. At each stage, the additional loans being made and the additional deposits being created are shrinking by 10 percent, because each bank has to keep that amount as required reserves. We can use a table to show the total increase in checking account deposits started by your initial deposit of $1,000. The dots in the table represent additional rounds in the money supply process: **MyEconLab** Concept Check

Bank	Increase in Checking Account Deposits
Bank of America	$1,000
PNC	+900 (= 0.9 × $1,000)
Third Bank	+810 (= 0.9 × $900)
Fourth Bank	+729 (= 0.9 × $810)
.	+ ·
.	+ ·
.	+ ·
Total change in checking account deposits	= $10,000

The Simple Deposit Multiplier

Your initial deposit of $1,000 increased the reserves of the banking system by $1,000 and led to a total increase in checking account deposits of $10,000. The ratio of the amount of deposits created by banks to the amount of new reserves is called the **simple deposit multiplier**. In this case, the simple deposit multiplier is equal to $10,000/$1,000 = 10. Why 10? How do we know that your initial $1,000 deposit ultimately leads to a total increase in deposits of $10,000?

Simple deposit multiplier The ratio of the amount of deposits created by banks to the amount of new reserves.

There are two ways to answer this question. First, each bank in the money supply process is keeping reserves equal to 10 percent of its deposits. For the banking system as a whole, the total increase in reserves is $1,000—the amount of your original currency deposit. Therefore, the system as a whole will end up with $10,000 in deposits because $1,000 is 10 percent of $10,000.

A second way to answer the question is by deriving an expression for the simple deposit multiplier. The total increase in deposits equals:

$$\$1,000 + [0.9 \times \$1,000] + [(0.9 \times 0.9) \times \$1,000] + [(0.9 \times 0.9 \times 0.9) \times \$1,000] + \ldots$$

or:

$$\$1,000 + [0.9 \times \$1,000] + [0.9^2 \times \$1,000] + [0.9^3 \times \$1,000] + \ldots$$

or:

$$\$1,000 \times (1 + 0.9 + 0.9^2 + 0.9^3 + \ldots).$$

The rules of algebra tell us that an expression like the one in the parentheses sums to:

$$\frac{1}{1 - 0.9}.$$

Simplifying further, we have:

$$\frac{1}{0.10} = 10.$$

So:

$$\text{Total increase in deposits} = \$1,000 \times 10 = \$10,000.$$

Don't Let This Happen to You

Don't Confuse Assets and Liabilities

Consider the following reasoning: "How can checking account deposits be a liability to a bank? After all, they are something of value that is in the bank. Therefore, checking account deposits should be counted as a bank *asset* rather than as a bank liability."

This statement is incorrect. The balance in a checking account represents something the bank *owes* to the owner of the account. Therefore, it is a liability to the bank, although it is an asset to the owner of the account. Similarly, your car loan is a liability to you—because it is a debt you owe to the bank—but it is an asset to the bank.

MyEconLab Study Plan

Your Turn: Test your understanding by doing related problem 3.11 on page 507 at the end of this chapter.

Note that 10 is equal to 1 divided by the required reserve ratio, *RR*, which in this case is 10 percent, or 0.10. So, we have another way of expressing the simple deposit multiplier:

$$\text{Simple deposit multiplier} = \frac{1}{RR}.$$

This formula makes it clear that the higher the required reserve ratio, the smaller the simple deposit multiplier. With a required reserve ratio of 10 percent, the simple deposit multiplier is 10. If the required reserve ratio were 20 percent, the simple deposit multiplier would fall to 1/0.20, or 5.

We can use this formula to calculate the total increase in checking account deposits from an increase in bank reserves due to, for instance, currency being deposited in a bank:

$$\text{Change in checking account deposits} = \text{Change in bank reserves} \times \frac{1}{RR}.$$

For example, if $100,000 in currency is deposited in a bank and the required reserve ratio is 10 percent, then:

$$\text{Change in checking account deposits} = \$100,000 \times \frac{1}{0.10}$$

$$= \$100,000 \times 10 = \$1,000,000.$$

MyEconLab Concept Check

Solved Problem 14.3

MyEconLab Interactive Animation

Showing How Banks Create Money

Suppose you deposit $5,000 in currency into your checking account at a branch of PNC Bank, which we will assume has no excess reserves at the time you make your deposit. Also assume that the required reserve ratio is 0.10.

a. Use a T-account to show the initial effect of this transaction on PNC's balance sheet.

b. Suppose that PNC makes the maximum loan it can from the funds you deposited. Use a T-account to show the initial effect on PNC's balance sheet from granting the loan. Also include in this T-account the transaction from part (a).

c. Now suppose that whoever took out the loan in part (b) writes a check for this amount and that the person receiving the check deposits it in Bank of America. Show the effect of these transactions on the balance sheets of PNC Bank and Bank of America *after the check has cleared*. On the T-account for PNC Bank, include the transactions from parts (a) and (b).

d. What is the maximum increase in checking account deposits that can result from your $5,000 deposit? What is the maximum increase in the money supply that can result from your deposit? Explain.

Solving the Problem

Step 1: **Review the chapter material.** This problem is about how banks create checking account deposits, so you may want to review the section "Using T-Accounts to Show How a Bank Can Create Money," which begins on page 486.

Step 2: **Answer part (a) by using a T-account to show the effect of the deposit.** Keeping in mind that T-accounts show only the changes in a balance sheet that result from the relevant transaction and that assets are on the left side of the account and liabilities are on the right side, we have:

PNC Bank

Assets		Liabilities	
Reserves	+$5,000	Deposits	+$5,000

Because the bank now has your $5,000 in currency in its vault, its reserves (and, therefore, its assets) have risen by $5,000. This transaction also increases your checking account balance by $5,000. Because the bank owes you this money, the bank's liabilities have also risen by $5,000.

Step 3: **Answer part (b) by using a T-account to show the effect of the loan.** The problem tells you to assume that PNC Bank currently has no excess reserves and that the required reserve ratio is 10 percent. This requirement means that if the bank's checking account deposits go up by $5,000, the bank must keep $500 as reserves and can loan out the remaining $4,500. Remembering that new loans usually take the form of setting up or increasing a checking account for the borrower, we have:

PNC Bank

Assets		Liabilities	
Reserves	+$5,000	Deposits	+$5,000
Loans	+$4,500	Deposits	+$4,500

The first line of the T-account shows the transaction from part (a). The second line shows that PNC has loaned out $4,500 by increasing the checking account of the borrower by $4,500. The loan is an asset to PNC because it represents the borrower's promise to make certain payments spelled out in the loan agreement.

Step 4: **Answer part (c) by using T-accounts for PNC and Bank of America to show the effect of the check clearing.** We now show the effect of the borrower having spent the $4,500 he received as a loan from PNC. The person who received the $4,500 check deposits it in her account at Bank of America. We need two T-accounts to show this activity:

PNC Bank

Assets		Liabilities	
Reserves	+$500	Deposits	+$5,000
Loans	+$4,500		

Bank of America

Assets		Liabilities	
Reserves	+$4,500	Deposits	+$4,500

Look first at the T-account for PNC. Once Bank of America sends the check written by the borrower to PNC, PNC loses $4,500 in reserves, and Bank of America gains $4,500 in reserves. The $4,500 is also deducted from the account of the borrower. PNC is now satisfied with the result. It received a $5,000 deposit in currency from you. When that money was sitting in the bank vault, it wasn't earning any interest for PNC. Now $4,500 of the $5,000 has been loaned out and is earning interest. These interest payments allow PNC to cover its costs, which it has to do to remain in business.

Bank of America now has an increase in deposits of $4,500, resulting from the check being deposited, and an increase in reserves of $4,500. Bank of America is in the same situation as PNC was in part (a): It has excess reserves as a result of this transaction and a strong incentive to lend them out.

Step 5: **Answer part (d) by using the simple deposit multiplier formula to calculate the maximum increase in checking account deposits and the maximum increase in the money supply.** The simple deposit multiplier expression is (remember that RR is the required reserve ratio):

$$\text{Change in checking account deposits} = \text{Change in bank reserves} \times \frac{1}{RR}.$$

In this case, bank reserves rose by $5,000 as a result of your initial deposit, and the required reserve ratio is 0.10, so:

$$\text{Change in checking account deposits} = \$5,000 \times \frac{1}{0.10}$$

$$= \$5,000 \times 10 = \$50,000.$$

Because checking account deposits are part of the money supply, it is tempting to say that the money supply has also increased by $50,000. Remember, though, that your $5,000 in currency was counted as part of the money supply while you had it, but it is not counted when it is sitting in a bank vault. Therefore:

$$\text{Increase in checking account deposits} - \text{Decline in currency in}$$

$$\text{circulation} = \text{Change in the money supply.}$$

Or,

$$\$50,000 - \$5,000 = \$45,000.$$

Your Turn: For more practice, do related problem 3.12 on page 507 at the end of the chapter.   MyEconLab Study Plan

The Simple Deposit Multiplier versus the Real-World Deposit Multiplier

The story we have just told of the money supply process has been simplified in two ways. First, we assumed that banks do not keep any excess reserves. That is, we assumed that when you deposited $1,000 in currency into your checking account at Bank of America, it loaned out $900, keeping only the $100 in required reserves. In fact, banks often keep some excess reserves to guard against the possibility that many depositors may simultaneously make withdrawals from their accounts. Since the financial crisis that began in 2007, banks have kept substantial excess reserves. The more excess reserves banks keep, the smaller the deposit multiplier. Imagine an extreme case in which Bank of America kept your entire $1,000 as reserves, loaning out none of it. In this case, the process we described earlier—loans leading to the creation of new deposits, leading to the making of additional loans, and so on—will not take place. The $1,000 increase in reserves will lead to just a $1,000 increase in deposits, and the deposit multiplier will be $1,000/$1,000 = 1, not 10.

Second, we assumed that the whole amount of every check is deposited in a bank; no one takes any of it out as currency. In reality, households and firms keep roughly constant the amount of currency they hold relative to the value of their checking account balances. So, we would expect to see people increasing the amount of currency they hold as the balances in their checking accounts rise. Once again, think of the extreme case. Suppose that when Bank of America makes the initial $900 loan to the borrower who wants to buy a used car, the seller of the car cashes the check instead of depositing it. In that case, PNC does not receive any new reserves and does not make any new loans. Once again, the $1,000 increase in your checking account at Bank of America is the only increase in deposits, and the deposit multiplier is 1.

The effect of these two simplifications is to reduce the real-world deposit multiplier to about 1.6 during normal times. So, a $1 increase in the reserves of the banking system typically results in about a $1.60 increase in deposits. Following the financial crisis of 2007–2009, the surge in bank holdings of excess reserves reduced the multiplier to less than 1.

Although the story of the deposit multiplier can be complicated, the key point to bear in mind is that the most important part of the money supply is the checking account balance component. When banks make loans, they increase checking account balances, and the money supply expands. Banks make new loans whenever they gain reserves. The whole process can also work in reverse: If banks lose reserves, they reduce their outstanding loans and deposits, and the money supply contracts.

We can summarize these important conclusions:

1. When banks gain reserves, they make new loans, and the money supply expands.
2. When banks lose reserves, they reduce their loans, and the money supply contracts.

MyEconLab Study Plan

MyEconLab Concept Check

 ## 14.4 The Federal Reserve System

LEARNING OBJECTIVE: Compare the three policy tools the Federal Reserve uses to manage the money supply.

Many people are surprised to learn that banks do not keep locked away in their vaults all the funds that are deposited in checking accounts. The United States, like nearly all other countries, has a **fractional reserve banking system**, which means that banks keep less than 100 percent of deposits as reserves. When people deposit money in a bank, the bank loans most of the money to someone else. What happens if depositors want their money back? Depositors withdrawing money would seem to be a problem because banks have loaned out most of the money and can't easily get it back.

In practice, withdrawals are usually not a problem for banks. On a typical day, about as much money is deposited as is withdrawn. If a small amount more is withdrawn than deposited, banks can cover the difference from their excess reserves or by borrowing from other banks. Sometimes depositors lose confidence in a bank when they question the value of the bank's underlying assets, particularly its loans. Often, the reason for a loss of confidence is bad news about the loans the bank has made, whether the news is accurate or not. When many depositors simultaneously decide to withdraw their money from a bank, there is a **bank run**. If many banks experience runs at the same time, the result is a **bank panic**. It is possible for one bank to handle a run by borrowing from other banks, but if many banks simultaneously experience runs, the banking system may be in trouble.

A central bank, like the Federal Reserve in the United States, can help stop a bank panic by acting as a *lender of last resort*. In acting as a lender of last resort, a central bank makes loans to banks that cannot borrow funds elsewhere. The banks can use these loans to pay off depositors. When the panic ends and the depositors put their money back in their accounts, the banks can repay the loans to the central bank.

The Establishment of the Federal Reserve System

Bank panics lead to severe disruptions in business activity because households and firms have trouble gaining access to their accounts and may be unable to borrow money. As we saw in the chapter opener, in 2015, bank runs in Greece prompted the

Fractional reserve banking system A banking system in which banks keep less than 100 percent of deposits as reserves.

Bank run A situation in which many depositors simultaneously decide to withdraw money from a bank.

Bank panic A situation in which many banks experience runs at the same time.

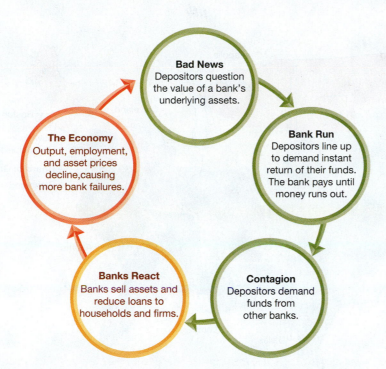

MyEconLab Animation

Figure 14.3

The Feedback Loop during a Bank Panic

Bank runs can cause good banks, as well as bad banks, to fail. Bank failures are costly because they reduce the ability of households and firms to get loans. Once a panic starts, falling incomes, employment, and asset prices can cause more bank failures. This feedback loop means that a panic can continue unless the government intervenes.

government to order banks closed for three weeks, which led to disruptions in the Greek economy, with declines in output and employment. In the United States, each bank panic in the late nineteenth and early twentieth centuries was accompanied by a recession. Figure 14.3 shows how a feedback loop during a bank run can lead to a recession. With the intention of putting an end to bank panics, in 1913, Congress passed the Federal Reserve Act, which set up the Federal Reserve System—often referred to as "the Fed." The system began operation in 1914, with the authority to make loans to banks. The loans the Fed makes to banks are called **discount loans**, and the interest rate it charges on the loans is called the **discount rate**. When a bank receives a loan from the Fed, its reserves increase by the amount of the loan.

The Fed's first test as a lender of last resort came in the early years of the Great Depression of the 1930s, when many banks were hit by bank runs as depositors pulled funds out of checking and savings accounts. Although the Fed had been established to act as a lender of last resort, Fed officials declined to make loans to many banks because the officials were worried that banks experiencing runs had made bad loans and other investments. The Fed believed that making loans to banks that were in financial trouble because of bad investments might reduce the incentive bank managers had to be careful in their investment decisions. Partly due to the Fed's unwillingness to act as a lender of last resort, more than 5,000 banks failed during the early 1930s. Today, many economists are critical of the Fed's decisions in the early 1930s because they believe these decisions increased the severity of the Great Depression. In 1934, Congress established the Federal Deposit Insurance Corporation (FDIC) to insure deposits in most banks up to a limit, which is currently $250,000 per deposit. If the bank you have your checking account in goes out of business, the FDIC will refund your money after a wait of at most two days. Deposit insurance has greatly reduced bank runs because it has reassured all but the largest depositors that their deposits are safe, even if their bank goes out of business. During the financial crisis of 2007–2009, some banks experienced runs when depositors with funds exceeding the deposit insurance limit feared that they would suffer losses if their banks failed.

In setting up the Federal Reserve System, Congress divided the country into 12 Federal Reserve districts, as shown in Figure 14.4. Each district has its own Federal Reserve Bank, which provides services to banks in that district. The real power of the Fed, however, lies in Washington, DC, with the Board of Governors. The seven members of the Board of Governors are appointed by the president of the United States to 14-year,

Discount loans Loans the Federal Reserve makes to banks.

Discount rate The interest rate the Federal Reserve charges on discount loans.

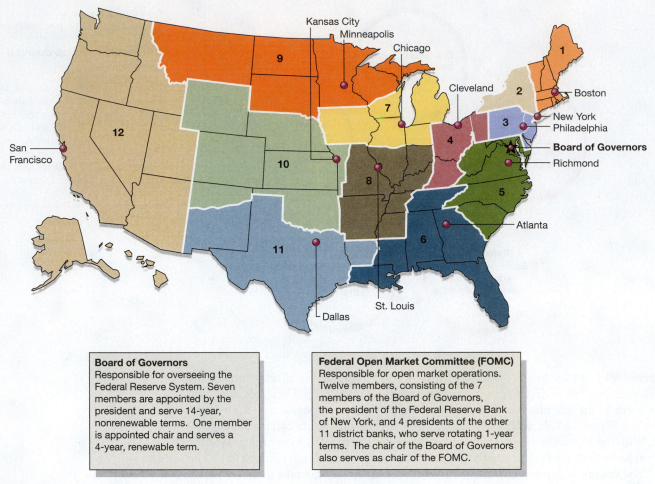

Figure 14.4 **The Federal Reserve System**

The United States is divided into 12 Federal Reserve districts, each of which has a Federal Reserve Bank. The real power within the Federal Reserve System, however, lies in Washington, DC, with the Board of Governors, which consists of 7 members appointed by the president.

The 12-member Federal Open Market Committee carries out monetary policy.

Source: Board of Governors of the Federal Reserve System.

---

nonrenewable terms. One member of the Board of Governors is appointed chair and serves a 4-year, renewable term. In addition to acting as a lender of last resort to banks, the Fed acts as a bankers' bank, providing services such as check clearing to banks, and has the responsibility of managing the U.S. money supply.   MyEconLab Concept Check

How the Federal Reserve Manages the Money Supply

Although Congress established the Fed primarily to stop bank panics by acting as a lender of last resort, today the Fed is also responsible for managing the money supply. As we will discuss in more detail in Chapter 15, managing the money supply is part of **monetary policy**, which the Fed undertakes to pursue macroeconomic policy objectives. To manage the money supply, the Fed uses three *monetary policy tools:*

Monetary policy The actions the Federal Reserve takes to manage the money supply and interest rates to pursue macroeconomic policy objectives.

1. Open market operations

2. Discount policy

3. Reserve requirements

Remember that the most important component of the money supply is checking account deposits. Not surprisingly, all three of the Fed's policy tools are aimed at affecting the reserves of banks as a means of changing the volume of checking account deposits.

Open Market Operations Eight times per year, the **Federal Open Market Committee (FOMC)** meets in Washington, DC, to discuss monetary policy. The committee has 12 voting members:

- The 7 members of the Federal Reserve's Board of Governors.
- The president of the Federal Reserve Bank of New York.
- The presidents of 4 of the other 11 Federal Reserve Banks. These 4 presidents serve one-year rotating terms as voting members of the FOMC.

All 12 Federal Reserve Bank presidents attend meetings and participate in discussions. The chair of the Board of Governors also serves as the chair of the FOMC.

The U.S. Treasury borrows money by selling bills, notes, and bonds. Remember that the *maturity* of a financial asset is the period of time until the purchaser receives payment of the face value or principal. Usually, bonds have face values of $1,000. Treasury bills have maturities of 1 year or less, Treasury notes have maturities of 2 years to 10 years, and Treasury bonds have maturities of 30 years. To control the size of the money supply, the Fed buys and sells Treasury securities in a process called **open market operations**.

To increase the money supply, the FOMC directs the *trading desk*, located at the Federal Reserve Bank of New York, to carry out an *open market purchase* by buying U.S. Treasury securities—most frequently bills, but sometimes notes or bonds—from banks. The Fed pays for the Treasury bills by depositing the funds in the reserve accounts banks maintain with the Fed.

Suppose that the Fed engages in an open market purchase of $10 million. We can illustrate the results with two T-accounts: one for the Fed and one for the banking system. The banking system's T-account is based on the banking system's balance sheet, which simply adds together all the assets and liabilities of all the commercial banks in the United States. As a result of the open market purchase, the banking system's holdings of Treasury bills fall by $10 million and its reserves increase by $10 million:

Banking System

Assets		Liabilities
Treasury bills	−$10 million	
Reserves	+$10 million	

The Fed's holdings of Treasury bills increase by $10 million, and the value of the banking system's reserve balances—which are a liability to the Fed—also increase by $10 million:

Federal Reserve

Assets		Liabilities	
Treasury bills	+$10 million	Reserves	+$10 million

This increase in reserves starts the process of expanding loans and checking account deposits that increases the money supply.

To decrease the money supply, the FOMC directs the trading desk to carry out an *open market sale* by selling Treasury securities. When the buyers of the Treasury securities pay for them with checks, the banking system's reserves fall. This decrease in reserves starts a contraction of loans and checking account deposits that reduces the money supply.

There are three reasons the Fed conducts monetary policy principally through open market operations:

1. Because the Fed initiates open market operations, it completely controls their volume, which means the Fed can carry out both large and small open market operations.

Federal Open Market Committee (FOMC) The Federal Reserve committee responsible for open market operations and managing the money supply in the United States.

Open market operations The buying and selling of Treasury securities by the Federal Reserve in order to control the money supply.

2. Open market operations are easily reversible. For example, if the Fed believes that previous open market purchases have caused the money supply to increase too rapidly, it can engage in open market sales.

3. The Fed can implement its open market operations quickly, with no administrative delay or required changes in regulations.

Many other central banks, including the European Central Bank and the Bank of Japan, also use open market operations to conduct monetary policy.

The Federal Reserve is responsible for putting the paper currency of the United States into circulation. (The currency is actually printed by the U.S. Treasury.) Recall that if you look at the top of a dollar bill, you see the words "Federal Reserve Note." When the Fed takes actions to increase the money supply, commentators sometimes say that it is "printing more money." The main way the Fed increases the money supply, however, is not by printing more currency but by buying Treasury securities. Similarly, to reduce the money supply, the Fed doesn't set fire to stacks of paper currency. Instead, it sells Treasury securities. We will spend more time discussing the Fed's management of the money supply in Chapter 15 when we discuss monetary policy.

Discount Policy As we have seen, when a bank borrows money from the Fed by taking out a discount loan, the interest rate the bank pays is called the discount rate. By lowering the discount rate, the Fed can encourage banks to take additional loans and thereby increase their reserves. With more reserves, banks will make more loans to households and firms, which will increase checking account deposits and the money supply. Raising the discount rate will have the reverse effect.

Reserve Requirements When the Fed reduces the required reserve ratio, it converts required reserves into excess reserves. For example, suppose a bank has $100 million in checking account deposits, and the required reserve ratio is 10 percent. The bank will be required to hold $10 million as reserves. If the Fed reduces the required reserve ratio to 8 percent, the bank will need to hold only $8 million as reserves. The Fed can thereby convert $2 million worth of reserves from required reserves to excess reserves. This $2 million is then available for the bank to lend out. If the Fed *raises* the required reserve ratio from 10 percent to 12 percent, it will have the reverse effect.

The Fed rarely changes reserve requirements because doing so can disrupt banks' operations by forcing them to significantly change their holdings of loans, bonds, and other securities. Also, because the Fed pays banks only a low interest rate on reserves, the use of reserve requirements to manage the money supply effectively places a tax on banks' deposit-taking and lending activities, which can be costly for the economy. The Fed relies instead on open market operations as its main tool for managing the money supply.

MyEconLab Concept Check

The "Shadow Banking System" and the Financial Crisis of 2007–2009

The banks we have been discussing in this chapter are *commercial banks*, whose most important economic role is to accept funds from depositors and lend those funds to borrowers. Large firms can sell stocks and bonds on financial markets, but investors are typically unwilling to buy stocks and bonds from small and medium-sized firms because they lack sufficient information about the financial health of smaller firms (see Chapter 6). So, smaller firms—and households—have traditionally relied on bank loans for their credit needs. In the past 25 years, however, two important developments have occurred in the financial system: (1) Banks have begun to resell many of their loans rather than keeping them until borrowers pay them off, and (2) financial firms other than commercial banks have become important sources of credit to businesses.

Securitization Comes to Banking Traditionally, when a bank made a *residential mortgage loan* to a household to buy a home or made a commercial loan to a business, the bank would keep the loan and collect the payments until the borrower paid off the loan. A financial asset—such as a loan or a stock or a bond—is considered

1. Banks grant loans to households.

2. The loans are bundled into securities.

3. And investors purchase the securities.

(a) Securitizing a loan

1. Banks collect loan payments from households.

2. Banks receive a fee for processing the payments.

3. Banks send payments to investors in the securities.

(b) The flow of payments on a securitized loan

MyEconLab Animation

Figure 14.5   **The Process of Securitization**

Panel (a) shows how in the securitization process banks grant loans to households and bundle the loans into securities that are then sold to investors.

Panel (b) shows that banks collect payments on the original loans and, after taking a fee, send the payments to the investors who bought the securities.

a **security** if it can be bought and sold in a *financial market*. Shares of stock issued by the Coca-Cola Company are an example of a security because they can be bought and sold on the New York Stock Exchange. When a financial asset is first sold, the sale takes place in the *primary market*. If an investor resells the asset, the sale takes place in the *secondary market*. Prior to 1970, most loans were not securities because they could not be resold—there was no secondary market for them. After 1970, residential mortgages and then other loans, including car loans and commercial loans, began to be *securitized*. The process of **securitization** creates a secondary market in which loans that have been bundled together can be bought and sold in financial markets, just as corporate or government bonds are. Figure 14.5 outlines the securitization process. We will discuss the process of securitization further in Chapter 15 when we consider monetary policy.

The Shadow Banking System

In addition to the changes resulting from securitization, the financial system was transformed in the 1990s and 2000s by the increasing importance of *nonbank financial firms*. Investment banks, such as Goldman Sachs and Morgan Stanley, differ from commercial banks in that they do not accept deposits, and they rarely lend directly to households. Instead, investment banks traditionally concentrated on providing advice to firms issuing stocks and bonds or considering mergers with other firms. In the late 1990s, investment banks expanded their buying of mortgages, bundling large numbers of them together as bonds known as *mortgage-backed securities*, and reselling them to investors. Mortgage-backed securities proved very popular with investors because they often paid higher interest rates than other securities that seemed to have comparable default risk.

Money market mutual funds have also increased their importance in the financial system over time. These funds sell shares to investors and use the money to buy short-term securities such as Treasury bills and commercial paper issued by corporations. Commercial paper represents short-term borrowing corporations use to fund their day-to-day operations. Many corporations that previously met such needs by borrowing from banks began instead to sell commercial paper to money market mutual funds.

Hedge funds raise money from wealthy investors and use sophisticated investment strategies that often involve significant risk. By the mid-2000s, hedge funds had become an important source of demand for securitized loans and an important source of loans to other financial firms.

Security A financial asset—such as a stock or a bond—that can be bought and sold in a financial market.

Securitization The process of transforming loans or other financial assets into securities.

In 2008, Timothy Geithner, who became Treasury secretary in the Obama administration, used the term the *shadow banking system* to refer to investment banks, money market mutual funds, hedge funds, and other nonbank financial firms engaged in similar activities. By raising money from investors and lending it directly or indirectly to firms and households, these firms were carrying out a function that at one time was almost exclusively carried out by commercial banks.

The Financial Crisis of 2007–2009 The firms in the shadow banking system differed from commercial banks in two important ways: First, the government agencies—including the Federal Reserve—that regulated the commercial banking system did not regulate these firms. Second, these firms were more highly *leveraged*—that is, they relied more heavily on borrowed money to finance their operations—than were commercial banks. If a firm uses a small amount of its own money and a lot of borrowed money to make an investment, both the firm's potential profits and its potential losses are increased. Suppose a firm invests $100 of its own money. If the investment earns a return of $3, the firm has earned 3 percent ($3/$100) on its funds. But if the firm's investment consists of $10 of its own money and $90 it has borrowed, a profit of $3 becomes a return of 30 percent ($3/$10) on the firm's $10 investment. If the investment loses $2, however, the firm's return is −20 percent (−$2/$10). Leveraged investments have a potential for both large gains and large losses.

As mentioned earlier, commercial banks rarely experienced runs after Congress established federal deposit insurance in the 1930s. However, beginning in 2007, some firms in the shadow banking system experienced runs. As we will discuss further in Chapter 15, the underlying cause of the financial crisis of 2007–2009 was problems in the U.S. housing market. As housing prices began to fall, a significant number of borrowers defaulted on their mortgages, which caused mortgage-backed securities to lose value. Financial firms that had invested in these securities, including both commercial banks and many firms in the shadow banking system, suffered losses. The more leveraged the firm, the larger the losses. Although deposit insurance helped commercial banks avoid runs, investment banks and other financial firms that had borrowed short term and invested the funds long term were in trouble. As lenders refused to renew their short-term loans, many of these firms had to sell their holdings of securities in an attempt to raise cash. But as the prices of the securities continued to fall, the losses to these firms increased.

In the spring of 2008, the investment bank Bear Stearns was saved from bankruptcy only when the Federal Reserve arranged for it to be acquired by JPMorgan Chase. In the fall of 2008, the Federal Reserve and the U.S. Treasury decided not to take action to save the investment bank Lehman Brothers, which failed. The failure of Lehman Brothers echoed throughout the financial system, setting off a panic. The process of securitization—apart from government-guaranteed residential mortgages—ground to a halt. The well-publicized difficulties of a money market mutual fund that had suffered losses on loans to Lehman Brothers led to a wave of withdrawals from these funds. In turn, the funds were no longer able to fulfill their role as buyers of corporate commercial paper. As banks and other financial firms sold assets and cut back on lending to shore up their financial positions, the flow of funds from savers to borrowers was disrupted. The resulting *credit crunch* significantly worsened the recession that had begun in December 2007.

The Fed's Response The Fed, in combination with the U.S. Treasury, took vigorous action to deal with the financial crisis. We will discuss the Fed's actions further in Chapter 15, but for now, we can mention several particularly important policy actions:

- In the fall of 2008, under the Troubled Asset Relief Program (TARP), the Fed and Treasury began attempting to stabilize the commercial banking system by providing funds to banks in exchange for stock. Taking partial ownership of private commercial banks was an unprecedented move by the federal government.

- The Fed also modified its discount policy by setting up several new "lending facilities." These lending facilities made it possible for the Fed to grant discount loans to financial firms—such as investment banks—that had not previously been eligible.

- The Fed addressed problems in the commercial paper market by directly buying commercial paper for the first time since the 1930s.

Although the recession continued into 2009, the extraordinary actions of the Treasury and Fed stabilized the financial system. It took several years, however, for the flow of funds from savers to borrowers to return to normal levels, and economists and policymakers continue to debate the wisdom of some of the Fed's actions. MyEconLab Concept Check

14.5 The Quantity Theory of Money

LEARNING OBJECTIVE: Explain the quantity theory of money and use it to explain how high rates of inflation occur.

People have been aware of the connection between increases in the money supply and inflation for centuries. In the sixteenth century, the Spanish conquered Mexico and Peru and shipped large quantities of gold and silver from those countries back to Spain. The gold and silver were minted into coins and spent across Europe to further the political ambitions of the Spanish kings. Prices in Europe rose steadily during these years, and many observers discussed the relationship between this inflation and the flow of gold and silver into Europe from the Americas.

Connecting Money and Prices: The Quantity Equation

In the early twentieth century, Irving Fisher, an economist at Yale University, formalized the connection between money and prices by using the *quantity equation*:

$$M \times V = P \times Y.$$

The quantity equation states that the money supply (M) multiplied by the *velocity of money* (V) equals the price level (P) multiplied by real output (Y). Fisher defined the **velocity of money**, often called simply "velocity," as the average number of times each dollar of the money supply is used to purchase goods and services included in GDP. Rewriting the original equation by dividing both sides by M, we have the equation for velocity:

Velocity of money The average number of times each dollar in the money supply is used to purchase goods and services included in GDP.

$$V = \frac{P \times Y}{M}.$$

If we use M1 to measure the money supply, the GDP price deflator to measure the price level, and real GDP to measure real output, the value for velocity for 2014 was:

$$V = \frac{1.09 \times \$16.0 \text{ trillion}}{\$2.8 \text{ trillion}} = 6.2.$$

This result tells us that, during 2014, each dollar of M1 was on average spent about six times on goods or services included in GDP.

Because velocity is defined to be equal to $(P \times Y)/M$, we know that the quantity equation must always hold true: The left side of the equation *must* be equal to the right side. A theory is a statement about the world that might possibly be false. Therefore, the quantity equation is not a theory. Irving Fisher turned the quantity equation into the **quantity theory of money** by arguing that velocity was constant. He argued that the average number of times a dollar is spent depends on factors that do not change often, such as how often people get paid, how often they do their grocery shopping, and how often businesses mail bills. Because this assertion may be true or false, the quantity theory of money is, in fact, a theory. MyEconLab Concept Check

Quantity theory of money A theory about the connection between money and prices that assumes that the velocity of money is constant.

The Quantity Theory Explanation of Inflation

The quantity equation gives us a way of showing the relationship between changes in the money supply and changes in the price level, or inflation. To see this relationship more clearly, we can use a handy mathematical rule that states that an equation in which variables are multiplied together is equal to an equation in which the *growth rates* of these variables are *added* together. So, we can transform the quantity equation from:

$$M \times V = P \times Y$$

to:

Growth rate of the money supply + Growth rate of velocity =
Growth rate of the price level (or the inflation rate) + Growth rate of real output.

This way of writing the quantity equation is more useful for investigating the effect of changes in the money supply on the inflation rate. Remember that the growth rate for any variable is the percentage change in the variable from one year to the next. The growth rate of the price level is the inflation rate, so we can rewrite the quantity equation to help understand the factors that determine inflation:

Inflation rate = Growth rate of the money supply +
Growth rate of velocity − Growth rate of real output.

If Irving Fisher was correct that velocity is constant, then the growth rate of velocity will be zero. For example, if velocity is always equal to six, then its percentage change from one year to the next will always be zero. This assumption allows us to rewrite the equation one last time:

Inflation rate = Growth rate of the money supply − Growth rate of real output.

This equation leads to the following predictions:

1. If the money supply grows at a faster rate than real GDP, there will be inflation.
2. If the money supply grows at a slower rate than real GDP, there will be deflation. (Recall that *deflation* is a decline in the price level.)
3. If the money supply grows at the same rate as real GDP, the price level will be stable, and there will be neither inflation nor deflation.

It turns out that Irving Fisher was wrong in asserting that the velocity of money is constant. From year to year, there can be significant fluctuations in velocity. As a result, the predictions of inflation based on the quantity theory of money do not hold every year, but most economists agree that the quantity theory provides useful insight into the long-run relationship between the money supply and inflation: *In the long run, inflation results from the money supply growing at a faster rate than real GDP.* MyEconLab Concept Check

How Accurate Are Forecasts of Inflation Based on the Quantity Theory?

Note that the accuracy of the quantity theory depends on whether the key assumption that velocity is constant is correct. If velocity is not constant, there may not be a tight link between increases in the money supply and increases in the price level. For example, an increase in the quantity of money might be offset by a decline in velocity, leaving the price level unaffected. Because velocity can move erratically in the short run, we would not expect the quantity equation to provide good forecasts of inflation in the short run. Over the long run, however, there is a strong link between changes in the money supply and inflation. Panel (a) of Figure 14.6 shows by decade the relationship in the United States between the growth of the M2 measure of the money supply and the inflation rate. (We use M2 here because data on M2 are available for a longer period of time than are data for M1.) Because of variations in the rate of growth of real GDP and in velocity, there is not an exact relationship between the growth rate of M2 and the inflation rate. But there is a clear pattern that decades with higher growth rates in the money supply were also decades with higher inflation rates. In other words, most of the variation in inflation rates across decades can be explained by variation in the rates of growth of the money supply.

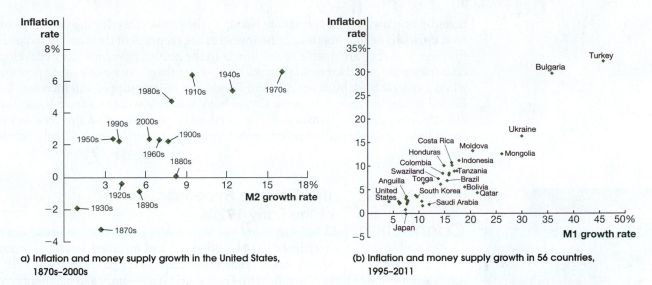

a) Inflation and money supply growth in the United States, 1870s–2000s

(b) Inflation and money supply growth in 56 countries, 1995–2011

MyEconLab Animation

Figure 14.6   **The Relationship between Money Growth and Inflation over Time and around the World**

Panel (a) shows that, by and large, the rate of inflation in the United States has been highest during the decades in which the money supply has increased most rapidly, and the rate of inflation has been lowest during the decades in which the money supply has increased least rapidly. Panel (b) shows the relationship between money supply growth and inflation for 56 countries between 1995 and 2011. There is not an exact relationship between money supply growth and inflation, but countries such as Bulgaria, Turkey, and Ukraine that had high rates of money supply growth had high inflation rates, and countries such as the United

States and Japan had low rates of money supply growth and low inflation rates.

Sources: Panel (a): For the 1870s to the 1960s, Milton Friedman and Anna J. Schwartz, *Monetary Trends in the United States and United Kingdom: Their Relation to Income, Prices, and Interest Rates, 1867–1975*, Chicago: University of Chicago Press, 1982, Table 4.8; and for the 1970s to the 2000s, Federal Reserve Board of Governors and U.S. Bureau of Economic Analysis; Panel (b): International Monetary Fund, *International Monetary Statistics*.

Panel (b) provides further evidence consistent with the quantity theory by looking at rates of growth of the money supply and rates of inflation across 56 countries for the years 1995–2011. Although there is not an exact relationship between rates of growth of the money supply and rates of inflation across countries, panel (b) shows that countries where the money supply grew rapidly tended to have high inflation rates, while countries where the money supply grew more slowly tended to have much lower inflation rates. Not included in panel (b) are data for Zimbabwe, which may be the most extreme case of inflation in recent years. In some years since 1995, the money supply in Zimbabwe grew by more than 7,500 percent. The result was an accelerating rate of inflation that eventually reached 15 billion percent during 2008. Zimbabwe was suffering from *hyperinflation*—that is, a rate of inflation that exceeds 50 percent per month.   MyEconLab Concept Check

High Rates of Inflation

The quantity theory can help us understand the reasons for very high rates of inflation. Hyperinflation is caused by central banks increasing the money supply at a rate far in excess of the growth rate of real GDP. A high rate of inflation causes money to lose its value so rapidly that households and firms avoid holding it. If, as happened in Zimbabwe, the inflation rate becomes high enough, people stop using paper currency, so it no longer serves the important functions of money discussed earlier in this chapter. Economies suffering from high inflation usually also suffer from very slow growth, if not severe recession.

Given the dire consequences that follow from high inflation, why do governments cause it by expanding the money supply so rapidly? The main reason is that governments often want to spend more than they are able to raise through taxes. Developed countries, such as the United States, can usually bridge gaps between spending and taxes by borrowing through selling bonds to the public. Developing countries often have difficulty selling bonds because investors are skeptical of their ability to pay back the money. If they are unable to sell bonds to the public, governments in developing countries will force their central banks to purchase them. As we discussed previously, when a central bank buys government bonds, the money supply will increase. In the United States, the Federal Reserve always buys Treasury securities from banks, never directly from the U.S. Treasury. This procedure helps ensure that the Treasury only issues bonds in amounts that private investors—rather than the central bank—are willing to buy.

MyEconLab Concept Check

During the German hyperinflation of the 1920s, paper currency became so worthless that people used it to light their stoves.

Making the Connection
MyEconLab Video

The German Hyperinflation of the Early 1920s

When Germany lost World War I, a revolution broke out that overthrew Kaiser Wilhelm II and installed a new government known as the Weimar Republic. In the peace treaty of 1919, the Allies—the United States, Great Britain, France, and Italy—imposed payments called *reparations* on the new German government. The reparations were meant as compensation to the Allies for the damage Germany had caused during the war. It was very difficult for the German government to use tax revenue to cover both its normal spending and the reparations.

The German government decided to pay for the difference between its spending and its tax revenues by selling bonds to the central bank, the Reichsbank. After a few years, the German government fell far behind in its reparations payments. In January 1923, the French government sent troops into the German industrial area known as the Ruhr to try to collect the payments directly. German workers in the Ruhr went on strike, and the German government decided to support them by paying their salaries. The government raised the funds by selling additional bonds to the Reichsbank, thereby further increasing the money supply.

The inflationary increase in the money supply was very large: The total number of marks—the German currency—in circulation rose from 115 million in January 1922 to 1.3 billion in January 1923 and then to 497 billion *billion*, or 497,000,000,000,000,000,000, in December 1923. Just as the quantity theory predicts, the result was a staggeringly high rate of inflation. The German price index that stood at 100 in 1914 and 1,440 in January 1922 had risen to 126,160,000,000,000 in December 1923. The German mark became worthless. The German government ended the hyperinflation by (1) negotiating a new agreement with the Allies that reduced its reparations payments, (2) reducing other government expenditures and raising taxes to balance its budget, and (3) replacing the existing mark with a new mark. Each new mark was worth 1 trillion old marks. The German central bank was also limited to issuing a total of 3.2 billion new marks.

These steps were enough to bring the hyperinflation to an end—but not before the savings of anyone holding the old marks had been wiped out. Most middle-income Germans were extremely resentful of this outcome. Many historians believe that the hyperinflation greatly reduced the allegiance of many Germans to the Weimar Republic and may have helped pave the way for Adolph Hitler and the Nazis to seize power 10 years later.

Sources: Thomas Sargent, "The Ends of Four Big Inflations," *Rational Expectations and Inflation*, 3rd ed., Princeton, NJ: Princeton University Press, 2013; and John Parke Young, *European Currency and Finance*, Washington, DC: Government Printing Office, 1925.

MyEconLab Study Plan

Your Turn: Test your understanding by doing related problem 5.10 on page 509 at the end of this chapter.

Continued from page 475

Economics in Your Life

What if Money Became Increasingly Valuable?

At the beginning of this chapter, we asked you to consider whether you would like to live in an economy in which the purchasing power of money rises every year. The first thing to consider when thinking about the advantages and disadvantages of this situation is that the only way for the purchasing power of money to increase is for the price level to fall; in other words, *deflation* must occur. Because the price level in the United States hasn't fallen for an entire year since the 1930s, most people alive today have experienced only rising price levels—and declining purchasing power of money. Would replacing rising prices with falling prices necessarily be a good thing? It might be tempting to say "yes," because if you have a job, your salary will buy more goods and services each year. But, in fact, just as a rising price level results in most wages and salaries rising each year, a falling price level is likely to mean falling wages and salaries each year. So, it is likely that, on average, people would not see the purchasing power of their incomes increase, even if the purchasing power of any currency they held increased. There can also be a significant downside to deflation, particularly if the transition from inflation to deflation happens suddenly. Recall that the real interest rate is equal to the nominal interest rate minus the inflation rate. If an economy experiences deflation, then the real interest rate will be greater than the nominal interest rate. A rising real interest rate can be bad news for anyone who has borrowed, including homeowners who may have substantial mortgage loans. So, you are probably better off living in an economy experiencing mild inflation than one experiencing deflation.

Conclusion

Money plays a key role in the functioning of an economy by facilitating trade in goods and services and by making specialization possible. Without specialization, no advanced economy can prosper. Households and firms, banks, and the central bank (the Federal Reserve in the United States) are participants in the process of creating the money supply. In Chapter 15, we will discuss how the Federal Reserve uses monetary policy to promote its economic objectives.

Visit MyEconLab for a news article and analysis related to the concepts of this chapter.

Key Terms

14.1 What Is Money, and Why Do We Need It? pages 476–479

LEARNING OBJECTIVE: Define money and discuss the four functions of money.

Summary

A *barter economy* is an economy that does not use money and in which people trade goods and services directly for other goods and services. Barter trade occurs only if there is a *double coincidence of wants*, where both parties to the trade want what the other one has. Because barter is inefficient, there is strong incentive to use **money**, which is any **asset** that people are generally willing to accept in exchange for goods or services or in payment of debts. An *asset* is anything of value owned by a person or a firm. A **commodity money** is a good used as money that also has value independent of its use as money. Money has four functions: It is a medium of exchange, a unit of account, a store of value, and a standard of deferred payment. At one time, governments issued gold coins and paper currency that were convertible into gold. Today, no government in the world issues paper currency that can be redeemed for gold. Instead, paper currency is **fiat money**, which has no value except as money.

 Visit **www.myeconlab.com** to complete these exercises online and get instant feedback.

Review Questions

1.1 A baseball fan with a Mike Trout baseball card wants to trade it for a Miguel Cabrera baseball card, but everyone the fan knows who has a Cabrera card doesn't want a Trout card. What do economists call the problem this fan is having?

1.2 What is the difference between commodity money and fiat money?

1.3 What are the four functions of money? Can something be considered money if it does not fulfill all four functions?

1.4 Why do businesses accept paper currency when they know that, unlike a gold coin, the paper the currency is printed on is worth very little?

Problems and Applications

1.5 The English economist William Stanley Jevons described a world tour during the 1880s by a French singer, Mademoiselle Zélie. One stop on the tour was a theater in the Society Islands, part of French Polynesia in the South Pacific. She performed for her usual fee, which was one-third of the receipts. This turned out to be 3 pigs, 23 turkeys, 44 chickens, 5,000 coconuts, and "considerable quantities of bananas, lemons, and oranges." She estimated that all of this would have had a value in France of 4,000 francs. According to Jevons, "as Mademoiselle could not consume any considerable portion of the receipts herself, it became necessary in the meantime to feed the pigs and poultry with the fruit." Do the goods Mademoiselle Zélie received as payment fulfill the four functions of money described in this chapter? Briefly explain.

Source: W. Stanley Jevons, *Money and the Mechanism of Exchange*, New York: D. Appleton and Company, 1889, pp. 1–2.

1.6 (Related to the Chapter Opener on page 475) An article in the *New York Times* in 2015 noted, "A rising number of Greeks in rural areas are swapping goods and services in cashless transactions since the government shut down banks on June 28 for three weeks." If Greeks were able to swap goods and services for other goods and services, did it matter that currency was not available because the banks had been closed? Briefly explain.

Source: Lefteris Karagiannopoulos, "Hay for Cheese? Barter Booms in Cash-Squeezed Rural Greece," *New York Times*, July 29, 2015.

1.7 In the late 1940s, the Communists under Mao Zedong were defeating the government of China in a civil war. The paper currency issued by the Chinese government was losing much of its value, and most businesses refused to accept it. At the same time, there was a paper shortage in Japan. During these years, Japan was still under military occupation by the United States, following its defeat in World War II. Some of the U.S. troops in Japan realized that they could use dollars to buy up vast amounts of paper currency in China, ship it to Japan to be recycled into paper, and make a substantial profit. Under these circumstances, was the Chinese paper currency a commodity money or a fiat money? Briefly explain.

1.8 According to Peter Heather, a historian at King's College London, during the time of the Roman Empire, the German tribes east of the Rhine River (the area the Romans called Germania) produced no coins of their own but used Roman coins instead:

Although no coinage was produced in Germania, Roman coins were in plentiful circulation and could easily have provided a medium of exchange (already in the first century, Tacitus tells us, Germani of the Rhine region were using good-quality Roman silver coins for this purpose).

a. What is a medium of exchange?

b. What does the author mean when he writes that Roman coins could have provided the German tribes with a medium of exchange?

c. Why would any member of a German tribe have been willing to accept a Roman coin from another member of the tribe in exchange for goods or services when the tribes were not part of the Roman Empire and were not governed by Roman law?

Source: Peter Heather, *The Fall of the Roman Empire: A New History of Rome and the Barbarians*, New York: Oxford University Press, 2006, p. 89.

1.9 (Related to the Making the Connection **on page 479)** Suppose that Congress passes a new law that requires all firms to accept paper currency in exchange for whatever they are selling. Briefly discuss who would gain and who would lose from this legislation.

1.10 On January 1, 2002, Germany officially adopted the euro as its currency, and the deutsche mark stopped being legal tender. According to an article in the *Wall Street Journal*, even 10 years later many Germans continued using the deutsche mark, and many stores in Germany continued to accept it. Briefly explain how it is possible for people to continue to use a currency when the government that issued it has replaced it with another currency.

Source: Vanessa Fuhrmans, "Who Needs the Euro When You Can Pay with Deutsche Marks?" *Wall Street Journal*, July 18, 2012.

14.2 How Is Money Measured in the United States Today? pages 479–483

LEARNING OBJECTIVE: Discuss the definitions of the money supply used in the United States today.

Summary

The narrowest definition of the money supply in the United States today is **M1**, which includes currency, checking account balances, and traveler's checks. A broader definition of the money supply is **M2**, which includes everything that is in M1, plus savings accounts, small-denomination time deposits (such as certificates of deposit [CDs]), money market deposit accounts in banks, and noninstitutional money market fund shares.

 Visit **www.myeconlab.com** to complete these exercises online and get instant feedback.

Review Questions

2.1 What is the main difference between the M1 and M2 definitions of the money supply?

2.2 Why does the Federal Reserve use two definitions of the money supply rather than one?

2.3 Distinguish among money, income, and wealth. Which one of the three does the central bank of a country control?

Problems and Applications

2.4 Briefly explain whether each of the following is counted in M1.

a. The coins in your pocket

b. The funds in your checking account

c. The funds in your savings account

d. The traveler's checks that you have left over from a trip

e. Your Citibank Platinum MasterCard

2.5 (Related to the Don't Let This Happen to You **on page 481)** Briefly explain whether you agree with the following statement: "I recently read that more than half of the money the government prints is actually held by people in foreign

countries. If that's true, then the United States is less than half as wealthy as government statistics indicate."

2.6 (Related to the Don't Let This Happen to You **on page 481)** An article in the *New York Times* contains the statement: "Income is only one way of measuring wealth." Do you agree that income is a way of measuring wealth?

Source: Sam Roberts, "As the Data Show, There's a Reason the Wall Street Protesters Chose New York," *New York Times*, October 25, 2011.

2.7 (Related to Solved Problem 14.2 **on page 482)** Suppose you decide to withdraw $100 in currency from your checking account. What is the effect on M1? Ignore any actions the bank may take as a result of your having withdrawn the $100.

2.8 (Related to Solved Problem 14.2 **on page 482)** Suppose you withdraw $1,000 from a money market mutual fund and deposit the funds in your bank checking account. Briefly explain how this action will affect M1 and M2.

2.9 Based on a Survey of Consumer Payment Choice, researchers from the Federal Reserve Bank of Boston estimated that the average consumer, 18 years of age and older, held about $340 in currency. However, as noted in the chapter, there is actually about $4,000 of currency for every person in the United States.

a. How can the amount of U.S. currency in circulation be so much higher than the amount held by the U.S. population?

b. What does the difference in part (a) imply about the measures of the money supply of the United States?

Source: Kevin Foster, Scott Schuh, and Hanbing Zhang, "The 2010 Survey of Consumer Payment Choice," Federal Reserve Bank of Boston Research Data Report, No. 13-2, November 2013.

2.10 Friedrich Schneider, an economist at the Johannes Kepler University of Linz in Austria, made the following observation about China: "The average Chinese trusts neither the Chinese banks nor the Communist Party."

a. If Schneider is correct, how might businesses and consumers prefer to carry out transactions?

b. The Chinese government has refused to print currency in denominations higher than the 100-renminbi note, which is the equivalent of about $16. The United States prints $100 bills, and all other countries print currency in denominations that are at least that high. Given your answer to part (a), why might the Chinese government be reluctant to print currency in high denominations?

Source: David Barboza, "Chinese Way of Doing Business: In Cash We Trust," *New York Times*, April 30, 2013.

2.11 (Related to the Making the Connection **on page 482)** In 2015, some business startups were offering the service of transferring money in the form of bitcoins among individuals and businesses in developing countries. At the same time, an article in the *Wall Street Journal* noted that in the United States, "Most ordinary consumers remain wary of using an unproven, six-year-old digital currency that many associate with illicit drugs, extreme price fluctuations and security risks." Why might using bitcoins be more attractive to individuals and firms in developing countries than to individuals and firms in the United States?

Source: Michael J. Casey and Paul Vigna, "Interest in Bitcoin Grows on Wall Street," *Wall Street Journal*, March 29, 2015.

2.12 The U.S. penny is made primarily of zinc. There have been several times in recent years when zinc prices have been high, and it has cost the U.S. Treasury more than one cent to manufacture a penny. There are currently about 1.4 billion pennies in circulation. Economist François Velde of the Federal Reserve Bank of Chicago has proposed making the current penny worth 5 cents. If the U.S. Treasury adopted Velde's proposal, what would be the effect on the value of M1? Is this change likely to have much effect on the economy? (*Hint:* According to the information given in this chapter, what is the current value of M1?)

Source: Austan Goolsbee, "Now That a Penny Isn't Worth Much, It's Time to Make It Worth 5 Cents," *New York Times*, February 1, 2007.

14.3 ## How Do Banks Create Money? pages 483–492
LEARNING OBJECTIVE: Explain how banks create money.

Summary

On a bank's balance sheet, *reserves* and loans are assets, and deposits are liabilities. **Reserves** are deposits that the bank has retained rather than loaned out or invested. **Required reserves** are reserves that banks are legally required to hold. The fraction of deposits that banks are required to keep as reserves is called the **required reserve ratio**. Any reserves banks hold over the legal requirement are called **excess reserves**. When a bank accepts a deposit, it keeps only a fraction of the funds as reserves and loans out the remainder. In making a loan, a bank increases the checking account balance of the borrower. When the borrower uses a check to buy something with the funds the bank has loaned, the seller deposits the check in his or her bank. The seller's bank keeps part of the deposit as reserves and loans out the remainder. This process continues until no banks have excess reserves. In this way, the process of banks making new loans increases the volume of checking account balances and the money supply. This money creation process can be illustrated with T-accounts, which are stripped-down versions of balance sheets that show only how a transaction changes a bank's balance sheet. The **simple deposit multiplier** is the ratio of the change in deposits to the change in reserves. An expression for the simple deposit multiplier is $1/RR$.

 Visit **www.myeconlab.com** to complete these exercises online and get instant feedback.

Review Questions

3.1 What are the largest asset and the largest liability of a typical bank?

3.2 Suppose you decide to withdraw $100 in cash from your checking account. Draw a T-account showing the effect of this transaction on your bank's balance sheet.

3.3 What does it mean to say that banks "create money"?

3.4 Give the formula for the simple deposit multiplier. If the required reserve ratio is 20 percent, what is the maximum increase in checking account deposits that will result from an increase in bank reserves of $20,000? Is this maximum increase likely to occur? Briefly explain.

Problems and Applications

3.5 Following the financial crisis of 2007–2009, Congress passed the Wall Street Reform and Consumer Protection Act, also known as the Dodd-Frank Act. The act increased regulation of the banking system, and from 2010 to 2015 only one new bank opened in the United States. According to an article in the *Wall Street Journal*, "Lawmakers are concerned about the dearth of new banks because small banks make the majority of farm and small-business loans." Why might farms and small-businesses be more likely to rely on banks for funding than would large corporations?

Source: Ryan Tracy, "A Local Bank in Amish Country Flourishes amid Dearth of Small Lenders," *Wall Street Journal*, March 29, 2015.

3.6 The following is from an article on community banks: "Their commercial-lending businesses, funded by their stable deposit bases, make them steady earners." What is commercial lending? In what sense are loans "funded" by deposits?

Source: Karen Richardson, "Clean Books Bolster Traditional Lenders," *Wall Street Journal*, April 30, 2007.

3.7 (Related to the Making the Connection **on page 484)** In a newspaper column, author Delia Ephron described a conversation with a friend who had a large balance on her credit card with an interest rate of 18 percent per year. The friend was worried about paying off the debt. Ephron was earning only 0.4 percent interest on her bank certificate of deposit (CD). She considered withdrawing the money from her CD and loaning it to her friend so her friend could pay off her credit card balance: "So I was thinking that all of us earning 0.4 percent could instead loan money to our friends at 0.5 percent. ... [M]y friend would get out of debt [and] I would earn $5 a month instead of $4." Why don't more people use their savings to make loans rather than keeping the funds in bank accounts that earn very low rates of interest?

Source: Delia Ephron, "Banks Taketh, but Don't Giveth," *New York Times*, January 27, 2012.

3.8 **(Related to the** Making the Connection **on page 484)** An economist commented on the situation a bank faces when making personal loans to subprime borrowers: "You have to be alert to the trade-off between serving consumers and being viewed as taking advantage of them." If banks charge subprime borrowers a higher interest on loans than they charge prime borrowers, are the banks taking advantage of the subprime borrowers? Briefly explain.

Source: Ianthe Jeanne Dugan and Telis Demos, "New Lenders Spring Up to Cater to Subprime Sector," *Wall Street Journal*, March 5, 2014.

3.9 Suppose that Deja owns a McDonald's franchise. She decides to move her restaurant's checking account to Wells Fargo, which causes the changes shown on the following T-account. If the required reserve ratio is 0.10, or 10 percent, and Wells Fargo currently has no excess reserves, what is the maximum loan Wells Fargo can make as result of this transaction?

Wells Fargo

Assets		Liabilities	
Reserves	+$100,000	Deposits	+$100,000

3.10 Consider the following simplified balance sheet for a bank:

Assets		Liabilities	
Reserves	$10,000	Deposits	$70,000
Loans	$66,000	Stockholders' equity	$6,000

a. If the required reserve ratio is 0.10, or 10 percent, how much in excess reserves does the bank hold?

b. What is the maximum amount by which the bank can expand its loans?

c. If the bank makes the loans in part (b), show the *immediate* effect on the bank's balance sheet.

3.11 **(Related to the** Don't Let This Happen to You **on page 489)** Briefly explain whether you agree with the following statement: "Assets are things of value that people own. Liabilities are debts. Therefore, a bank will always consider a checking account deposit to be an asset and a car loan to be a liability."

3.12 **(Related to** Solved Problem 14.3 **on page 489)** Suppose you deposit $2,000 in currency into your checking account at a branch of Bank of America, which we will assume has no excess reserves at the time you make your deposit. Also assume that the required reserve ratio is 0.20, or 20 percent.

a. Use a T-account to show the initial effect of this transaction on Bank of America's balance sheet.

b. Suppose that Bank of America makes the maximum loan it can from the funds you deposited. Using a T-account, show the initial effect of granting the loan on Bank of America's balance sheet. Also include on this T-account the transaction from part (a).

c. Now suppose that whoever took out the loan in part (b) writes a check for this amount and that the person receiving the check deposits it in a branch of Citibank. Show the effect of these transactions on the balance sheets of Bank of America and Citibank after the check has been cleared. (On the T-account for Bank of America, include the transactions from parts (a) and (b).)

d. What is the maximum increase in checking account deposits that can result from your $2,000 deposit? What is the maximum increase in the money supply? Briefly explain.

14.4 ### The Federal Reserve System, pages 492–499

LEARNING OBJECTIVE: Compare the three policy tools the Federal Reserve uses to manage the money supply.

Summary

The United States has a **fractional reserve banking system** in which banks keep less than 100 percent of deposits as reserves. In a **bank run**, many depositors decide simultaneously to withdraw money from a bank. In a **bank panic**, many banks experience runs at the same time. The **Federal Reserve System** ("the Fed") is the central bank of the United States. It was originally established in 1913 to stop bank panics. The recession of 2007–2009 put renewed emphasis on the Fed's goal of financial market stability. **Monetary policy** refers to the actions the Federal Reserve takes to manage the money supply and interest rates to pursue macroeconomic policy objectives. The Fed's three monetary policy tools are open market operations, discount policy, and reserve requirements. **Open market operations** are the buying and selling of Treasury securities by

the Federal Reserve. The loans the Fed makes to banks are called **discount loans**, and the interest rate the Fed charges on discount loans is the **discount rate**. The **Federal Open Market Committee (FOMC)** meets in Washington, DC, eight times per year to discuss monetary policy. In the past 20 years, a "shadow banking system" has developed. During the financial crisis of 2007–2009, the existence of the shadow banking system complicated the Fed's policy response. A **security** is a financial asset—such as a stock or a bond—that can be bought and sold in a financial market. The process of **securitization** creates a secondary market in which loans that have been bundled together can be bought and sold in financial markets just as corporate or government bonds are.

MyEconLab   Visit **www.myeconlab.com** to complete these exercises online and get instant feedback.

Review Questions

4.1 Why did Congress decide to establish the Federal Reserve System in 1913?

4.2 What policy tools does the Fed use to control the money supply? Which tool is the most important?

4.3 Why does an open market purchase of Treasury securities by the Federal Reserve increase bank reserves? Why does an open market sale of Treasury securities by the Federal Reserve decrease bank reserves?

4.4 What is the "shadow banking system"? Why were the financial firms of the shadow banking system more vulnerable than commercial banks to bank runs?

Problems and Applications

4.5 In an article in the *Wall Street Journal*, Kevin Brady, a member of Congress from Texas, stated, "To get Congress to pass the Federal Reserve Act [in 1913, President Woodrow] Wilson had to retain the support of … northeastern lawmakers while convincing southern and western Democrats that legislation would not … create a [single] central bank. Wilson's ingenious solution was federalism." Explain what Congressman Brady meant when he stated that Woodrow Wilson used "federalism" to convince Congress to pass the Federal Reserve Act.

Source: Kevin Brady, "How the Fed's East Coast Tilt Warps Monetary Policy," *Wall Street Journal*, June 4, 2015.

4.6 Suppose that the Federal Reserve makes a $10 million discount loan to First National Bank (FNB) by increasing FNB's account at the Fed.

   a. Use a T-account to show the effect of this transaction on FNB's balance sheet. Remember that the funds a bank has on deposit at the Fed count as part of its reserves.

   b. Assume that before receiving the discount loan, FNB has no excess reserves. What is the maximum amount of this $10 million that FNB can lend out?

   c. What is the maximum total increase in the money supply that can result from the Fed's discount loan? Assume that the required reserve ratio is 10 percent.

4.7 An article in the *New York Times* states that "the Bank of Japan, the central bank … is creating money on a vast scale by buying government bonds." How can a central bank "create money" by buying bonds? Doesn't the government create money by printing currency? Briefly explain.

Source: Jonathan Soble, "Japan's Economy Expands, but Less Than Expected," *New York Times*, February 15, 2015.

4.8 Suppose that the Federal Reserve engages in an open market sale of $25 million in U.S. Treasury bills to banks. In the T-accounts for the Fed and for the banking system shown here, fill in the missing information.

Federal Reserve

Assets		Liabilities	
_____	−$25 million	Reserves	−$25 million

Banking System

Assets		Liabilities
Treasury bills	+$25 million	
_____	−$25 million	

4.9 In a speech delivered in June 2008, Timothy Geithner, then president of the Federal Reserve Bank of New York and later U.S. Treasury secretary, said:

> The structure of the financial system changed fundamentally during the boom. … [The] non-bank financial system grew to be very large. … [The] institutions in this parallel financial system [are] vulnerable to a classic type of run, but without the protections such as deposit insurance that the banking system has in place to reduce such risks.

   a. What did Geithner mean by the "nonbank financial system"?

   b. What is a "classic type of run," and why were institutions in the nonbank financial system vulnerable to such a run?

   c. Why would deposit insurance provide the banking system with protection against runs?

Source: Timothy F. Geithner, "Reducing Systemic Risk in a Dynamic Financial System," Remarks at the Economic Club of New York, June 9, 2008.

4.10 An article in the *Wall Street Journal* on the shadow banking system contained the following observation: "If investors rush to the exits en masse, acting as a herd, asset prices could plummet and markets could face funding problems." Why might people who have invested in a money market mutual fund, for example, be more likely to "rush to the exits" if they heard bad news about the fund's investments than would bank depositors if they received bad news about their bank's investments?

Source: Ian Talley, "IMF Warns (Again) of Growing Shadow-Banking Risks," *Wall Street Journal*, April 8, 2015.

4.11 An article in the *Wall Street Journal* reported in 2015 that the People's Bank of China, which is the central bank of China, "is freeing up cash by reducing the amount that banks must keep in reserve." What monetary policy tool was the People's Bank of China using? In what sense did this policy change "free up cash"? What was the People's Bank of China hoping the result of this policy action would be?

Source: Lingling Wei, "China Central Bank Checks Europe Playbook on Credit," *Wall Street Journal*, April 19, 2015.

The Quantity Theory of Money, pages 499–502

LEARNING OBJECTIVE: Explain the quantity theory of money and use it to explain how high rates of inflation occur.

Summary

The *quantity equation*, which relates the money supply to the price level, is $M \times V = P \times Y$, where M is the money supply, V is the *velocity of money*, P is the price level, and Y is real output. The **velocity of money** is the average number of times each dollar in the money supply is spent during the year. Economist Irving Fisher developed the **quantity theory of money**, which assumes that the velocity of money is constant. If the quantity theory of money is correct, the inflation rate should equal the rate of growth of the money supply minus the rate of growth of real output. Although the quantity theory of money is not literally correct because the velocity of money is not constant, it is true that in the long run, inflation results from the money supply growing faster than real GDP. When governments attempt to raise revenue by selling large quantities of bonds to the central bank, the money supply will increase rapidly, resulting in high rates of inflation.

MyEconLab   Visit **www.myeconlab.com** to complete these exercises online and get instant feedback.

Review Questions

5.1 What is the quantity theory of money? What explanation does the quantity theory provide for inflation?

5.2 Is the quantity theory of money better able to explain the inflation rate in the long run or in the short run? Briefly explain.

5.3 What is hyperinflation? Why do governments sometimes allow it to occur?

Problems and Applications

5.4 If the money supply is growing at a rate of 6 percent per year, real GDP is growing at a rate of 3 percent per year, and velocity is constant, what will the inflation rate be? If velocity is increasing 1 percent per year instead of remaining constant, what will the inflation rate be?

5.5 If velocity does not change when the money supply of a country increases, will nominal GDP definitely increase? Will real GDP definitely increase? Briefly explain.

5.6 During the years from 2010 to 2014, the average annual growth rate of M1 was 12.7 percent, while the inflation rate as measured by the GDP deflator averaged 1.8 percent. Are these values consistent with the quantity equation? If you would need additional information to answer, state what the information is. Are the values consistent with the quantity theory of money? Briefly explain.

Source: Data from the Federal Reserve Bank of St. Louis.

5.7 In an article in the *American Free Press*, Professor Peter Spencer of York University in England is quoted as saying: "This printing of money 'will keep the [deflation] wolf from the door.'" In the same article, Ambrose Evans-Pritchard, a writer for the London-based newspaper *The Telegraph*, is quoted as saying, "Deflation has … insidious traits. It causes shoppers to hold back. Once this psychology gains

a grip, it can gradually set off a self-feeding spiral that is hard to stop."
a. What is price deflation?
b. What does Professor Spencer mean by the statement, "This printing of money 'will keep the [deflation] wolf from the door'"?
c. Why would deflation cause "shoppers to hold back," and what does Evans-Pritchard mean when he says, "Once this psychology gains a grip, it can gradually set off a self-feeding spiral that is hard to stop"?

Source: Doug French, "We Should Celebrate Price Deflation," *American Free Press*, November 17, 2008.

5.8 During the Civil War, the Confederate States of America printed large amounts of its own currency—Confederate dollars—to fund the war. By the end of the war, the Confederate government had printed nearly 1.5 billion paper dollars. How would such a large quantity of Confederate dollars have affected the value of the Confederate currency? With the war drawing to an end, would Southerners have been as willing to use and accept Confederate dollars? How else could they have bought and sold goods?

Source: Federal Reserve Bank of Richmond, "Textual Transcript of Confederate Currency."

5.9 An article in the *Economist* notes that the government of Venezuela running a large budget deficit "caused the money supply almost to quadruple in two years and led to the world's highest inflation rate, of over 60% a year."
a. Why would running a large budget deficit cause the money supply in Venezuela to increase so rapidly?
b. If the money supply increased by 150 percent per year (or 300 percent over two years) while the inflation rate was 60 percent, what must have happened to velocity in Venezuela during this period?

Source: "Of Oil and Coconut Water," *Economist*, September 20, 2014.

5.10 **(Related to the** Making the Connection **on page 502)** During the German hyperinflation of the 1920s, many households and firms in Germany were hurt economically. Do you think any groups in Germany benefited from the hyperinflation? Briefly explain.

Real-Time Data Exercises

D14.1 (The components of M1) Go to the Web site of the Federal Reserve Bank of St. Louis (FRED) (research.stlouisfed.org/fred2/) and find the most recent values for the following four variables: (1) M1 Money Stock (M1), (2) the Currency Component of M1 (CURRENCY), (3) Total Checkable Deposits (TCD), and (4) Travelers Checks Outstanding (WTCSL). Which of the components of M1 is the largest? Which is the smallest?

D14.2 (Calculating M1 from data on M2) Go to the Web site of the Federal Reserve Bank of St. Louis (FRED) (research.stlouisfed.org/fred2/) and find the most recent values for the following four variables: (1) M2 Money Stock (M2), (2) the Total Savings Deposits at all Depository Institutions (SAVINGS), (3) Retail Money Funds (WRMFSL), and (4) Small Time Deposits – Total (WSMTIME).

a. Using these data, calculate the value of M1.
b. What are Retail Money Funds? What percentage of M2 are they?
c. If households were to shift funds from savings accounts to checking accounts, what would happen to the values of M1 and M2?

D14.3 (The relationship between M1 and M2) Go to the Web site of the Federal Reserve Bank of St. Louis (FRED) (research. stlouisfed.org/fred2/) and find the most recent monthly values and values from the same month 5 years and 10 years earlier for the M1 Money Stock (M1SL) and the M2 Money Stock (M2SL).

a. Using these data, calculate M1 as a proportion of M2 for each of the years.
b. Explain whether this proportion has increased, decreased, or remained the same over time. Can you think of an explanation for any changes you observe?

D14.4 (The equation of exchange) Go to the Web site of the Federal Reserve Bank of St. Louis (FRED) (research.stlouisfed. org/fred2/) and find the most recent values and values for the same quarter in 1985 for the following three variables: (1) Nominal Gross Domestic Product (GDP), (2) the Velocity of M1 Money Stock (M1V), and (3) the Velocity of M2 Money Stock (M2V).

a. Using these data, calculate M1 and M2 for both periods.
b. Describe how M1 velocity and M2 velocity differ in the two quarters.

D14.5 (Applying the equation of exchange) Go to the Web site of the Federal Reserve Bank of St. Louis (FRED) (research. stlouisfed.org/fred2/) and find the most recent values and values from the same quarter 10 years earlier for the following three variables: (1) Real Gross Domestic Product (GDPC1), (2) the GDP Price Deflator (GDPDEF), and (3) the M2 Money Stock (M2SL).

a. Using these data, calculate the average annual rate of change in both real GDP and M2 over this 10-year period.
b. If we assume that velocity was constant during this period, what was the average annual inflation rate?
c. Using the GDP Price Deflator data, calculate the average annual inflation rate over this 10-year period.
d. Use your answers to parts (b) and (c) to discuss what must have happened to velocity during this period.

D14.6 (Applying the equation of exchange) Go to the Web site of the Federal Reserve Bank of St. Louis (FRED) (research. stlouisfed.org/fred2/) and find the most recent value for Real Gross Domestic Product (GDPC1) and the value from the same quarter eight years in the future for Real Potential Gross Domestic Product (GDPPOT).

a. Using these data, calculate the average annual rate of growth in real GDP over this eight-year period, assuming that real GDP equals potential GDP in the quarter that is eight years in the future.
b. If the velocity of money is constant during this eight-year period, what will the growth rate of M1 have to be if the annual inflation rate averages 2 percent? Briefly explain.
c. Suppose that M1 grows at this rate, but the actual inflation over this period averages more than 2 percent. What can you conclude about velocity during this period?

Monetary Policy

Why Would a Bank Pay a Negative Interest Rate?

In 2015, some banks in Europe were in an unusual—and unwelcome—situation: They were receiving negative nominal interest rates on loans. That is, the banks had to make interest payments to borrowers rather than receive interest payments from borrowers. One borrower in Spain boasted, "I'm going to frame my bank statement, which shows that Bankinter is paying me interest on my mortgage. That's financial history." Why would a bank pay someone to borrow money? The answer is that the interest rates on these loans were not fixed but were instead adjusted based on changes in short-term interest rates that depend on the actions of central banks in Europe. When some of these interest rates became negative, banks had to automatically make the interest rates on some of their mortgage loans negative as well.

Central banks, including the U.S. Federal Reserve, had driven interest rates to historically low levels as they tried to pull their economies out of the severe worldwide recession of 2007–2009. In conducting monetary policy, the Fed often concentrates on the federal funds rate, which is the interest rate that banks charge each other on short-term loans. In December 2008, the Fed reduced its target for the federal funds rate to almost zero, and kept it there for nearly seven years.

In the fall of 2015, many businesspeople, policymakers, and economists were focused on predicting when Fed Chair Janet Yellen would raise the target for the federal funds rate and by how much. Does this focus indicate that the Fed chair is more important to the U.S. economy than the president of the United States? Most economists would answer "yes." The president can take actions that affect the economy, but needs the approval of Congress before enacting most polices. In contrast, the structure of the Fed gives the chair substantial control over monetary policy. As a result, the Fed chair can often have greater influence over the economy than the president.

European banks paying negative interest rates on loans is a striking example of how central bank policy can affect businesses. Homebuilders like Toll Brothers and car dealers like Ford that sell durable goods are also directly affected by changes in interest rates because their customers frequently borrow money to buy these goods. Other businesses will be affected indirectly because changes in interest rates cause changes in aggregate demand. Not surprisingly, many businesses watch the Fed carefully for signs of whether interest rates are likely to rise or fall.

In this chapter, we will study the Federal Reserve and how monetary policy affects GDP, employment, and inflation.

Sources: Patricia Kowsmann and Jeannette Neumann, "Tumbling Interest Rates in Europe Leave Some Banks Owing Money on Loans to Borrowers," *Wall Street Journal*, April 13, 2015; and Min Zeng, "Government Bond Yields Turn Negative," *Wall Street Journal*, January 14, 2015.

Economics in Your Life

Should You Buy a House during a Recession?

Think ahead a few years to when you might be married and maybe even (gasp!) have children. You decide to leave behind years of renting apartments and buy a house, but then you read a *Wall Street Journal* article that states that a majority of economists predict a recession is likely to begin soon. What should you do? Would it be a good time or a bad time to buy a house? As you read this chapter, try to answer these questions. You can check your answers against those we provide on **page 547** at the end of this chapter.

I n Chapter 14, we saw that banks play an important role in providing credit to house-holds and firms and in creating money in the form of checking account deposits. We also saw that Congress established the Federal Reserve to stabilize the financial system and that the Fed is responsible for managing the money supply. In this chapter, we will discuss the Fed's main policy goals. We will also explore how the Federal Reserve decides which *monetary policy* actions to take to achieve its goals.

15.1 What Is Monetary Policy?

LEARNING OBJECTIVE: Define monetary policy and describe the Federal Reserve's monetary policy goals.

In 1913, Congress passed the Federal Reserve Act, creating the Federal Reserve System (the Fed). The main responsibility of the Fed was to make discount loans to banks to prevent the bank panics we discussed in Chapter 14. As a result of the Great Depression of the 1930s, Congress amended the Federal Reserve Act to give the Federal Reserve's Board of Governors broader responsibility to act "so as to promote effectively the goals of maximum employment, stable prices, and moderate long-term interest rates."

Since World War II, the Federal Reserve has carried out an active *monetary policy*. **Monetary policy** is the actions the Fed takes to manage the money supply and interest rates to achieve its macroeconomic policy goals.

Monetary policy The actions the Federal Reserve takes to manage the money supply and interest rates to achieve macroeconomic policy goals.

The Goals of Monetary Policy

The Fed has four main *monetary policy goals* that are intended to promote a well-functioning economy:

1. Price stability
2. High employment
3. Stability of financial markets and institutions
4. Economic growth

We briefly consider each of these goals.

Price Stability Rising prices reduce the usefulness of money as a medium of exchange and a store of value. Especially after inflation rose dramatically and unexpectedly during the 1970s, policymakers in most industrial countries have had price stability as a key policy goal. Figure 15.1 shows that from the early 1950s until 1968, the inflation rate in the United States remained below 4 percent per year. Inflation rose above 10 percent for several years in the late 1970s and early 1980s. After 1992, the inflation rate has usually been below 4 percent. The 2007–2009 recession caused several months of deflation—a falling price level—during early 2009, and the slowness of the recovery from the recession resulted in three months of deflation during early 2015.

The inflation rates during the years 1979–1981 were the highest the United States has ever experienced during peacetime. When Paul Volcker became chairman of the Federal Reserve's Board of Governors in August 1979, he made fighting inflation his top policy goal. Later Fed chairs continued to focus on inflation, arguing that if inflation is low over the long run, the price system will do a better job of efficiently allocating resources, and the Fed will have the flexibility it needs to increase aggregate demand to fight recessions. Although the severity of the 2007–2009 recession led the Fed to adopt extraordinary policy measures that we will discuss later in this chapter, price stability remains a key policy goal of the Fed.

High Employment In addition to price stability, high employment (or a low rate of unemployment) is an important monetary policy goal. Unemployed workers and

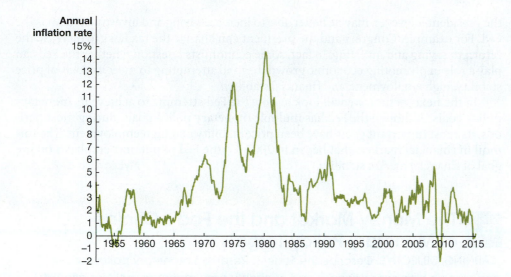

MyEconLab Real-time data

Figure 15.1

The Inflation Rate, January 1952–June 2015

For most of the 1950s and 1960s, the inflation rate in the United States was 4 percent or less. During the 1970s, the inflation rate increased, peaking during 1979–1981, when it averaged more than 10 percent. After 1992, the inflation rate was usually less than 4 percent, until increases in oil prices pushed it above 5 percent during the summer of 2008. The effects of the recession caused several months of deflation—a falling price level—during early 2009, and the slowness of the recovery caused three months of deflation in early 2015.

Note: The inflation rate is measured as the percentage change in the consumer price index from the same month in the previous year.

Source: Federal Reserve Bank of St. Louis.

underused factories and office buildings reduce GDP below its potential level. Unemployment can cause workers who lack jobs to suffer financial distress and lower self-esteem. The goal of high employment extends beyond the Fed to other branches of the federal government. At the end of World War II, Congress passed the Employment Act of 1946, which stated that it was the "responsibility of the Federal Government … to foster and promote … conditions under which there will be afforded useful employment, for those able, willing, and seeking to work, and to promote maximum employment, production, and purchasing power." Because price stability and high employment are explicitly mentioned in the Employment Act, it is sometimes said that the Fed has a *dual mandate* to attain these two goals.

Stability of Financial Markets and Institutions Firms often need to borrow funds as they design, develop, produce, and market their products. Savers look to financial investments to increase the value of their savings as they prepare to buy homes, pay for the educations of their children, and provide for their retirement. The Fed promotes the stability of financial markets and institutions so that an efficient flow of funds from savers to borrowers will occur. As we saw in Chapter 14, the financial crisis of 2007–2009 brought the issue of stability in financial markets to the forefront.

The financial crisis was similar to the banking crises that led Congress to create the Federal Reserve System in 1913. A key difference is that while earlier banking crises affected commercial banks, the events of 2007–2009 also affected investment banks and other financial firms in the *shadow banking system*. Investment banks, money market mutual funds, and other financial firms can be subject to *liquidity problems* because they often borrow short term—sometimes as short as overnight—and invest the funds in long-term securities. Just as commercial banks can experience a crisis if depositors begin to withdraw funds, investment banks and other financial firms can experience a crisis if investors stop providing them with short-term loans. In 2008, the Fed took several steps to ease the liquidity problems of these financial firms because the Fed believed these problems were increasing the severity of the recession. In Section 15.6, we will discuss in more detail the new policies the Fed enacted to help deal with the financial crisis.

Economic Growth We discussed in Chapters 10 and 11 the importance of economic growth to raising living standards. Policymakers aim to encourage *stable* economic growth, which allows households and firms to plan accurately and encourages firms to engage in the investment that is needed to sustain growth. Policy can spur economic growth by providing incentives for saving to ensure a large pool of investment funds, as well as by providing direct incentives for business investment. Congress and the president, however, may be better able to increase saving and investment than is the Fed. For example, Congress and the president can change the tax laws to increase the return to saving and investing. In fact, some economists question whether the Fed can play a role in promoting economic growth beyond attempting to meet its goals of price stability, high employment, and financial stability.

In the next section, we will look at how the Fed attempts to achieve its monetary policy goals. Although the Fed has multiple monetary policy goals, during most periods, its most important goals have been price stability and high employment. The turmoil in financial markets that began in 2007 led the Fed to put new emphasis on the goal of financial market stability.

MyEconLab Study Plan

MyEconLab Concept Check

15.2 The Money Market and the Fed's Choice of Monetary Policy Targets

LEARNING OBJECTIVE: Describe the Federal Reserve's monetary policy targets and explain how expansionary and contractionary monetary policies affect the interest rate.

The Fed uses its policy tools to achieve its monetary policy goals. Recall that the Fed's policy tools are open market operations, discount policy—making discount loans to banks and changing the discount rate it charges on those loans—and changes in reserve requirements. At times, the Fed encounters conflicts among its policy goals. For example, as we will discuss later in this chapter, the Fed can raise interest rates to reduce the inflation rate. But higher interest rates typically reduce household and firm spending, which may result in slower growth and higher unemployment. So, a policy that is intended to achieve one monetary policy goal, such as reducing inflation, may make it more difficult to achieve another policy goal, such as high employment.

Monetary Policy Targets

The Fed tries to keep both the unemployment and inflation rates low, but it can't affect either of these economic variables directly. The Fed cannot tell firms how many people to employ or what prices to charge for their products. Instead, the Fed uses variables, called *monetary policy targets*, that it can affect directly and that, in turn, affect variables, such as real GDP, employment, and the price level, that are closely related to the Fed's policy goals. The two main monetary policy targets are the money supply and the interest rate. As we will see, the Fed typically uses the interest rate as its policy target.

Bear in mind that while the Fed has typically used the money supply and the interest rate as its targets, these targets were not central to the Fed's policy decisions during the recession of 2007–2009. As we will discuss in Section 15.6, because U.S. financial markets suffered a degree of disruption not seen since the Great Depression of the 1930s, the Fed was forced to develop new policy tools. However, it is still important to have a good grasp of how the Fed carries out policy during normal times.

MyEconLab Concept Check

The Demand for Money

The Fed's two monetary policy targets are related. To understand this relationship, we first need to examine the *money market*, which brings together the demand and supply for money. Figure 15.2 shows the demand curve for money. The interest rate is on the vertical axis, and the quantity of money is on the horizontal axis. Here we are using the M1 definition of money, which equals currency plus checking account deposits. Notice that the demand curve for money is downward sloping.

To understand why the demand curve for money is downward sloping, consider that households and firms have a choice between holding money and holding other

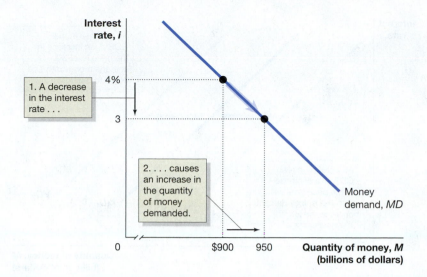

MyEconLab Animation

Figure 15.2

The Demand for Money

The money demand curve slopes downward because a lower interest rate causes households and firms to switch from financial assets such as U.S. Treasury bills to money. All other things being equal, a fall in the interest rate from 4 percent to 3 percent will increase the quantity of money demanded from $900 billion to $950 billion. An increase in the interest rate will decrease the quantity of money demanded.

financial assets, such as U.S. Treasury bills. In making the choice, households and firms take into account that:

- Money has one particularly desirable characteristic: You can use it to buy goods, services, or financial assets.

- Money also has one undesirable characteristic: It earns either a zero interest rate or a very low interest rate.

The currency in your wallet earns no interest, and the money in your checking account earns either no interest or very little interest. Alternatives to money, such as U.S. Treasury bills, pay interest but have to be sold if you want to use the funds to buy something. When interest rates rise on financial assets such as U.S. Treasury bills, the amount of interest that households and firms lose by holding money increases. When interest rates fall, the amount of interest households and firms lose by holding money decreases. Remember that *opportunity cost* is what you have to forgo to engage in an activity. The interest rate is the opportunity cost of holding money.

We now have an explanation for why the demand curve for money slopes downward: When interest rates on Treasury bills and other financial assets are low, the opportunity cost of holding money is low, so the quantity of money demanded by households and firms will be high; when interest rates are high, the opportunity cost of holding money will be high, so the quantity of money demanded will be low. In Figure 15.2, a decrease in the interest rate from 4 percent to 3 percent causes the quantity of money demanded by households and firms to rise from $900 billion to $950 billion.

MyEconLab Concept Check

Shifts in the Money Demand Curve

We saw in Chapter 3 that the demand curve for a good is drawn holding constant all variables, other than the price, that affect the willingness of consumers to buy the good. Changes in variables other than the price cause the demand curve to shift. Similarly, the demand curve for money is drawn holding constant all variables, other than the interest rate, that affect the willingness of households and firms to hold money. Changes in variables other than the interest rate cause the demand curve to shift. The two most important variables that cause the money demand curve to shift are real GDP and the price level.

Figure 15.3 illustrates shifts in the money demand curve. An increase in real GDP means that the amount of buying and selling of goods and services will increase. This additional buying and selling increases the demand for money as a medium of exchange, so the quantity of money households and firms want to hold increases at each interest rate, shifting the money demand curve to the right. A decrease in real GDP

Figure 15.3

Shifts in the Money Demand Curve

Changes in real GDP or the price level cause the money demand curve to shift. An increase in real GDP or an increase in the price level will cause the money demand curve to shift to the right from MD_1 to MD_2. A decrease in real GDP or a decrease in the price level will cause the money demand curve to shift to the left from MD_1 to MD_3.

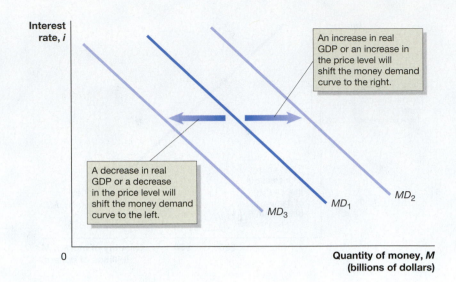

An increase in real GDP or an increase in the price level will shift the money demand curve to the right.

A decrease in real GDP or a decrease in the price level will shift the money demand curve to the left.

decreases the quantity of money demanded at each interest rate, shifting the money demand curve to the left. A higher price level increases the quantity of money required for a given amount of buying and selling. Eighty years ago, for example, when the price level was much lower and someone could purchase a new car for $500 and a salary of $30 per week was typical for someone in the middle class, the quantity of money demanded by households and firms was much lower than today, even adjusting for the effect of the lower real GDP and smaller population of those years. An increase in the price level increases the quantity of money demanded at each interest rate, shifting the money demand curve to the right. A decrease in the price level decreases the quantity of money demanded at each interest rate, shifting the money demand curve to the left.

How the Fed Manages the Money Supply: A Quick Review

Having discussed money demand, we now turn to money supply. In Chapter 14, we saw how the Federal Reserve manages the money supply. Eight times per year, the Federal Open Market Committee (FOMC) meets in Washington, DC. If the FOMC decides to increase the money supply, it orders the trading desk at the Federal Reserve Bank of New York to purchase U.S. Treasury securities. The sellers of these Treasury securities deposit the funds they receive from the Fed in banks, which increases bank reserves. Typically, banks loan out most of these reserves, which creates new checking account deposits and expands the money supply. If the FOMC decides to decrease the money supply, it orders the trading desk to sell Treasury securities, which decreases bank reserves and contracts the money supply.

Equilibrium in the Money Market

In Figure 15.4, we include both the money demand and money supply curves. We can use this figure to see how the Fed affects both the money supply and the interest rate. For simplicity, we assume that the Federal Reserve is able to completely control the money supply. With this assumption, the money supply curve is a vertical line, and changes in the interest rate have no effect on the quantity of money supplied. Just as with other markets, equilibrium in the *money market* occurs where the money demand curve crosses the money supply curve. If the Fed increases the money supply, the money supply curve will shift to the right, and the equilibrium interest rate will fall. In Figure 15.4, when the Fed increases the money supply from $900 billion to $950 billion, the money supply curve shifts to the right from MS_1 to MS_2, and the equilibrium interest rate falls from 4 percent to 3 percent.

In the money market, the adjustment from one equilibrium to another equilibrium is different from the adjustment in the market for a good. In Figure 15.4, the money

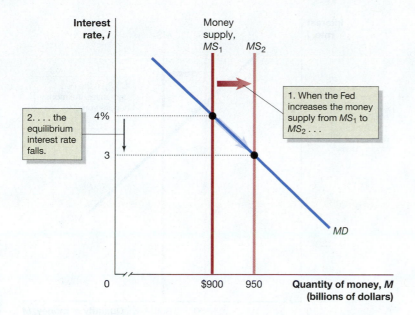

MyEconLab Animation

Figure 15.4

The Effect on the Interest Rate When the Fed Increases the Money Supply

When the Fed increases the money supply, households and firms will initially hold more money than they want, relative to other financial assets. Households and firms use the money they don't want to hold to buy Treasury bills and make deposits in interest-paying bank accounts. This increase in demand allows banks and sellers of Treasury bills and similar securities to offer lower interest rates. Eventually, interest rates will fall enough that households and firms will be willing to hold the additional money the Fed has created. In the figure, an increase in the money supply from $900 billion to $950 billion causes the money supply curve to shift to the right, from MS_1 to MS_2, and causes the equilibrium interest rate to fall from 4 percent to 3 percent.

market is initially in equilibrium, with an interest rate of 4 percent and a money supply of $900 billion. When the Fed increases the money supply by $50 billion, households and firms have more money than they want to hold at an interest rate of 4 percent. What do households and firms do with the extra $50 billion? They are most likely to use the money to buy short-term financial assets, such as Treasury bills, or to deposit the money in interest-paying bank accounts, such as certificates of deposit. This increase in demand for interest-paying bank accounts and short-term financial assets allows banks to offer lower interest rates on certificates of deposit, and it allows sellers of Treasury bills and similar assets to also offer lower interest rates. As the interest rates on certificates of deposit, Treasury bills, and other short-term assets fall, the opportunity cost of holding money also falls. The result is a movement down the money demand curve. Eventually the interest rate falls enough that households and firms are willing to hold the additional $50 billion worth of money the Fed has created, and the money market will be back in equilibrium. To summarize: *When the Fed increases the money supply, the short-term interest rate must fall until it reaches a level at which households and firms are willing to hold the additional money.*

Figure 15.5 shows what happens when the Fed decreases the money supply. The money market is initially in equilibrium, at an interest rate of 4 percent and a money supply of $900 billion. If the Fed decreases the money supply to $850 billion, households and firms will be holding less money than they would like, relative to other financial assets, at an interest rate of 4 percent. To increase their money holdings, they will sell Treasury bills and other short-term financial assets and withdraw funds from certificates of deposit and other interest-paying bank accounts. Banks will have to offer higher interest rates to retain depositors, and sellers of Treasury bills and similar securities will have to offer higher interest rates to find buyers. Rising short-term interest rates increase the opportunity cost of holding money, causing a movement up the money demand curve. Equilibrium is restored at an interest rate of 5 percent.

MyEconLab Concept Check

A Tale of Two Interest Rates

In Chapter 10, we discussed the loanable funds model of the interest rate. In that model, the equilibrium interest rate is determined by the demand and supply for loanable funds. So, we have two models of the interest rate:

1. The loanable funds model is concerned with the *long-term real rate of interest*, which is the interest rate that is most relevant when savers consider purchasing a long-term financial security such as a corporate bond. It is also the rate of interest that is most

Figure 15.5

The Effect on the Interest Rate When the Fed Decreases the Money Supply

When the Fed decreases the money supply, households and firms will initially hold less money than they want, relative to other financial assets. Households and firms will sell Treasury bills and other financial assets and withdraw money from interest-paying bank accounts. These actions will increase interest rates. Interest rates will rise to the point at which households and firms will be willing to hold the smaller amount of money that results from the Fed's actions. In the figure, a reduction in the money supply from $900 billion to $850 billion causes the money supply curve to shift to the left, from MS_1 to MS_2, and causes the equilibrium interest rate to rise from 4 percent to 5 percent.

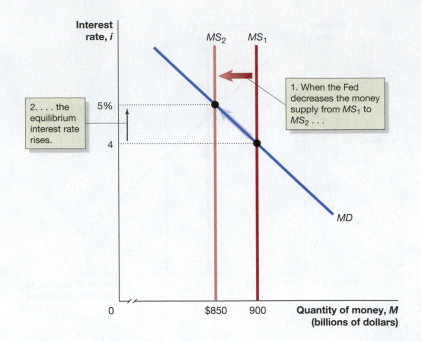

relevant to firms that are borrowing to finance long-term investment projects such as new factories or office buildings, or to households that are taking out mortgage loans to buy new homes.

2. The money market model is concerned with the *short-term nominal rate of interest*. When analyzing monetary policy, economists focus on the short-term nominal interest rate because it is the interest rate most affected by increases and decreases in the money supply.

Often—but not always—there is a close connection between movements in the short-term nominal interest rate and movements in the long-term real interest rate. So, when the Fed takes actions to increase the short-term nominal interest rate, usually the long-term real interest rate also increases. In other words, as we will discuss in the next section, when the interest rate on Treasury bills rises, the real interest rate on mortgage loans usually also rises, although sometimes only after a delay.   MyEconLab Concept Check

Choosing a Monetary Policy Target

As we have seen, the Fed uses monetary policy targets to affect economic variables, such as real GDP or the price level, that are closely related to the Fed's policy goals. The Fed can use either the money supply or the interest rate as its monetary policy target. As Figure 15.5 shows, the Fed is capable of affecting both. The Fed has generally focused on the interest rate rather than on the money supply. In 1980, Congress began allowing banks to pay interest on checking accounts. At the same time, money market mutual funds were becoming more popular with small savers as a way to earn higher interest rates than banks offered. As a result of these developments, some economists argued that the Fed should focus less on M1 than on M2. They argued that the relationship between M2 and inflation and changes in GDP was more stable than the relationship between M1 and these variables. But even the relationship between M2 and other key economic variables broke down in the early 1990s. In July 1993, then Fed Chairman Alan Greenspan informed the U.S. Congress that the Fed would cease using M1 or M2 targets to guide the conduct of monetary policy. The Fed has correspondingly increased its reliance on interest rate targets.

There are many different interest rates in the economy. For purposes of monetary policy, the Fed has targeted the interest rate known as the *federal funds rate*. In the next section, we will discuss the federal funds rate before examining how targeting the interest rate can help the Fed achieve its monetary policy goals.   MyEconLab Concept Check

The Importance of the Federal Funds Rate

Recall that every bank must keep 10 percent of its checking account deposits above a certain threshold amount as reserves, either as currency held in the bank or as deposits with the Fed (see Chapter 14). The Fed pays banks only a low interest rate on their reserve deposits, so banks normally have an incentive to invest reserves above the 10 percent minimum rather than leave these funds with the Fed. During the financial crisis, bank reserves soared as banks attempted to meet an increase in deposit withdrawals and as they became reluctant to lend to any borrowers except those with flawless credit histories. Banks continued to hold large reserve deposits for several years following the end of the financial crisis. These conditions were very unusual, however. In normal times, banks keep few excess reserves, and when they need additional reserves, they borrow in the *federal funds market* from banks that have reserves available. The **federal funds rate** is the interest rate banks charge each other on loans in the federal funds market. The loans are usually very short term, often just overnight.

Federal funds rate The interest rate banks charge each other for overnight loans.

Despite the name, the Fed does not actually set the federal funds rate. Instead, the rate is determined by the demand for and supply of reserves. Because the Fed can increase and decrease the supply of bank reserves through open market operations, it can set a *target* for the federal funds rate and usually come very close to hitting it. The FOMC announces a target for the federal funds rate after each meeting. In Figure 15.6, the orange line shows the Fed's targets for the federal funds rate since 2000. The jagged green line represents the actual federal funds rate on a weekly basis. The figure shows the rapid declines in the target for the federal funds rate beginning in September 2007, as the Fed responded to the start of the financial crisis. In December 2008, the Fed announced a range of 0 to 0.25 percent as its target. The actual federal funds rate fluctuated between 0.06 and 0.23 percent. These very low federal funds rates reflect the severity of the financial crisis.

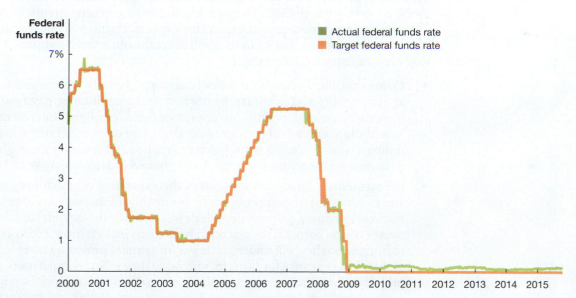

MyEconLab Real-time data

Figure 15.6   **Federal Funds Rate Targeting, January 2000–October 2015**

The Fed does not set the federal funds rate. However, the Fed's ability to increase or decrease bank reserves quickly through open market operations keeps the actual federal funds rate close to the Fed's target rate. The orange line is the Fed's target for the federal funds rate, and the jagged green line represents the actual value for the federal funds rate on a weekly basis.

Note: The federal funds target for the period after December 2008 was 0 to 0.25 percent through October 2015.

Source: Board of Governors of the Federal Reserve System.

Because only banks can borrow or lend in the federal funds market, the federal funds rate is not directly relevant for households and firms. However, changes in the federal funds rate usually result in changes in interest rates on both short-term financial assets, such as Treasury bills, and long-term financial assets, such as corporate bonds and mortgages. A change in the federal funds rate has a greater effect on short-term interest rates than on long-term interest rates, and its effect on long-term interest rates may occur only after a lag in time. Although a majority of economists support the Fed's choice of the interest rate as its monetary policy target, some economists believe the Fed should concentrate on the money supply instead. We will discuss these views in Section 15.5.

MyEconLab Study Plan   MyEconLab Concept Check

15.3 Monetary Policy and Economic Activity

LEARNING OBJECTIVE: Use aggregate demand and aggregate supply graphs to show the effects of monetary policy on real GDP and the price level.

The Fed uses the federal funds rate as a monetary policy target because it controls this interest rate through open market operations and because it believes that changes in the federal funds rate will ultimately affect economic variables that are related to its monetary policy goals. It is important to consider again the distinction between the nominal interest rate and the real interest rate. Recall that we calculate the real interest rate by subtracting the inflation rate from the nominal interest rate. Ultimately, the ability of the Fed to use monetary policy to affect economic variables such as real GDP depends on its ability to affect long-term real interest rates, such as the real interest rates on mortgages and corporate bonds. Because the federal funds rate is a short-term nominal interest rate, the Fed sometimes has difficulty affecting long-term real interest rates. Nevertheless, for purposes of the following discussion, we will assume that the Fed is able to use open market operations to affect long-term real interest rates.

How Interest Rates Affect Aggregate Demand

Changes in interest rates affect *aggregate demand*, which is the total level of spending in the economy. Recall that aggregate demand has four components: consumption, investment, government purchases, and net exports. Changes in interest rates will not affect government purchases, but they will affect the other three components of aggregate demand in the following ways:

- **Consumption.** Many households finance purchases of consumer durables, such as automobiles and furniture, by borrowing. Lower interest payments on loans increase household spending on consumer durables. Higher interest rates reduce household spending on consumer durables. Lower interest rates also reduce the return to saving, leading households to save less and spend more. Higher interest rates increase the return to saving, leading households to save more and spend less.

- **Investment.** Firms finance most of their spending on machinery, equipment, and factories out of their profits or by borrowing. Firms borrow either in financial markets by issuing corporate bonds or by obtaining loans from banks. Higher interest rates on corporate bonds or on bank loans make it more expensive for firms to borrow, so they will undertake fewer investment projects. Lower interest rates make it less expensive for firms to borrow, so they will undertake more investment projects. Lower interest rates can also have an effect on stock prices, which can increase firms' investment spending. As interest rates decline, stocks become a more attractive investment relative to bonds. The increase in demand for stocks raises their prices. By issuing additional shares of stock, firms can acquire the funds they need to buy new factories and equipment, so investment increases.

  Spending by households on new homes is also part of investment. When interest rates on mortgage loans rise, the cost of buying new homes rises, and fewer new homes will be purchased. When interest rates on mortgage loans fall, more new homes will be purchased.

- **Net exports.** Recall that net exports is equal to spending by foreign households and firms on goods and services produced in the United States minus spending by U.S. households and firms on goods and services produced in other countries. The value of net exports depends partly on the exchange rate between the U.S. dollar and foreign currencies. When the value of the dollar rises, households and firms in other countries will pay more for goods and services produced in the United States, but U.S. households and firms will pay less for goods and services produced in other countries. As a result, the United States will export less and import more, so net exports will fall. When the value of the dollar falls, net exports will rise. If interest rates in the United States rise relative to interest rates in other countries, investing in U.S. financial assets will become more desirable, causing foreign investors to increase their demand for dollars, which will increase the value of the dollar. As the value of the dollar increases, net exports will fall. If interest rates in the United States decline relative to interest rates in other countries, the value of the dollar will fall, and net exports will rise.   MyEconLab Concept Check

The Effects of Monetary Policy on Real GDP and the Price Level

In Chapter 13, we developed the *aggregate demand and aggregate supply model* to explain fluctuations in real GDP and the price level. In the basic version of the model, we assume that there is no economic growth, so the long-run aggregate supply curve does not shift. In panel (a) of Figure 15.7, we assume that short-run equilibrium is at point A, where the aggregate demand (AD_1) curve intersects the short-run aggregate supply ($SRAS$) curve. Real GDP is below potential GDP, as shown by the $LRAS$ curve, so the economy is in a recession, with some firms operating below normal capacity and some workers having been laid off. To reach its goal of high employment, the Fed carries out

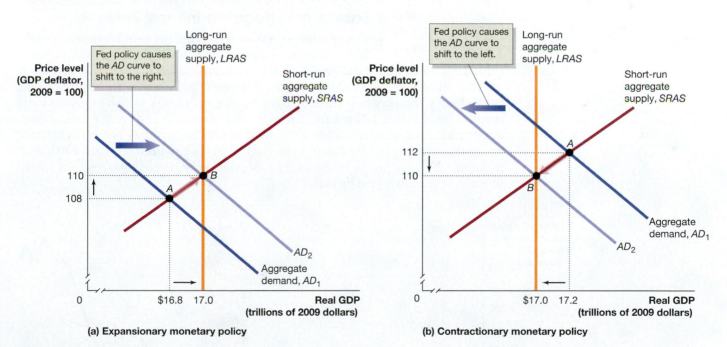

MyEconLab Animation

Figure 15.7   **Monetary Policy**

In panel (a), short-run equilibrium is at point A, with real GDP of $16.8 trillion and a price level of 108. An expansionary monetary policy causes aggregate demand to shift to the right, from AD_1 to AD_2, increasing real GDP from $16.8 trillion to $17.0 trillion and the price level from 108 to 110 (point B). With real GDP back at its potential level, the Fed can meet its goal of high employment. In panel (b), short-run equilibrium is at point A, with real GDP at $17.2 trillion and the price level at 112. Because real GDP is greater than potential GDP, the economy experiences rising wages and prices. A contractionary monetary policy causes aggregate demand to shift to the left, from AD_1 to AD_2, causing real GDP to decrease from $17.2 trillion to $17.0 trillion and the price level to decrease from 112 to 110 (point B). With real GDP back at its potential level, the Fed can meet its goal of price stability.

Expansionary monetary policy The Federal Reserve's policy of decreasing interest rates to increase real GDP.

Contractionary monetary policy The Federal Reserve's policy of increasing interest rates to reduce inflation.

an **expansionary monetary policy** by increasing the money supply and decreasing interest rates. Lower interest rates cause an increase in consumption, investment, and net exports, which shifts the aggregate demand curve to the right, from AD_1 to AD_2. Real GDP increases from $16.8 trillion to potential GDP of $17.0 trillion, and the price level rises from 108 to 110 (point B). The policy successfully returns real GDP to its potential level. Rising production leads to increasing employment, allowing the Fed to achieve its goal of high employment.

In panel (b) of Figure 15.7, short-run equilibrium is at point A, with real GDP of $17.2 trillion, which is above potential GDP of $17.0 trillion. With some firms producing beyond their normal capacity and the unemployment rate being very low, wages and prices are increasing. To reach its goal of price stability, the Fed needs to carry out a **contractionary monetary policy** by decreasing the money supply and increasing interest rates. Higher interest rates cause a decrease in consumption, investment, and net exports, which shifts the aggregate demand curve from AD_1 to AD_2. Real GDP decreases from $17.2 trillion to $17.0 trillion, and the price level falls from 112 to 110 (point B). Why would the Fed want to intentionally cause real GDP to decline? Because in the long run, real GDP cannot continue to remain above potential GDP. Attempting to keep real GDP above potential GDP would result in rising inflation. As aggregate demand declines and real GDP returns to its potential level, upward pressure on wages and prices will be reduced, allowing the Fed to achieve its goal of price stability.

We can conclude that the Fed can use monetary policy to affect the price level and, in the short run, the level of real GDP, allowing it to attain its policy goals of high employment and price stability.

MyEconLab Concept Check

Making the Connection
MyEconLab Video

Too Low for Zero: Central Banks, Quantitative Easing, and Negative Interest Rates

The Fed and central banks around the world responded to the 2007–2009 recession by pushing overnight lending rates—the federal funds rate in the United States—to nearly zero. But these very low interest rates failed to result in rapid economic recovery. To lower the federal funds rate, the Fed buys Treasury bills through open market purchases, which increases bank reserves. Banks then lend out these reserves to households and firm. As the following graph shows, however, in late 2008, many banks began piling up excess reserves rather than lending out the funds. Total bank reserves had been less than $50 billion in August 2008, but as the financial crisis became more severe, total reserves soared to more than $900 billion by May 2009.

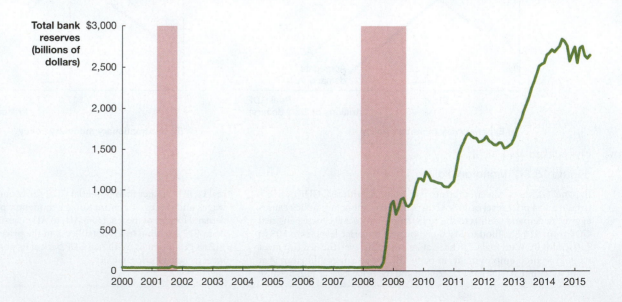

The increase in bank reserves was partly due to the Fed having received authorization from Congress in October 2008 to start paying interest of 0.25 percent on bank reserves held as deposits at the Fed. Primarily, though, the increase in reserves occurred because banks were reluctant to make loans at low interest rates to households and firms whose financial positions had been damaged by the recession. Some economists argued that the Fed was facing a situation known as a *liquidity trap*, in which short-term interest rates are pushed to zero, leaving the central bank unable to lower them further. Liquidity traps may also have occurred in the United States during the 1930s and in Japan during the 1990s.

To try to spur economic recovery, the Fed, the European Central Bank, the Bank of Japan, and other central banks turned to a policy of *quantitative easing* (QE), which involves buying securities beyond the short-term government securities that are usually involved in open market operations. The Fed began purchasing 10-year U.S. Treasury notes to push their interest rates lower. Interest rates on home mortgage loans typically move closely with interest rates on 10-year Treasury notes. The Fed also purchased certain *mortgage-backed securities*. The Fed's objective was to keep interest rates on mortgages low and to keep funds flowing into the mortgage market to help stimulate demand for housing.

The Fed's first round of QE began in November 2008. Because the U.S. economy recovered more slowly than expected, the Fed engaged in two additional rounds of QE before ending the program in October 2014. The use of QE by the Fed and other central banks, combined with very low inflation rates and the slow recovery from the 2007–2009 recession, led to historically low interest rates in most countries. The graph below shows interest rates on 10-year U.S. Treasury notes and on the corresponding German government bonds.

Nominal interest rates on government bonds were so low that real interest rates were nearly zero or even negative. For example, in April 2015, the nominal interest rate on 10-year German government bonds was 0.12%, while the inflation rate in Germany was 0.5%. Even more remarkable, in early 2015, the German government sold 5-year bonds with a *nominal* interest rate of −0.08%. This negative interest rate meant that investors were willing to pay the German government to keep their money for five years. Why would an investor accept a negative interest rate? With interest rates on many corporate bonds and on bank deposits being at very low levels, investors did not believe that the interest rates were sufficiently high to compensate for the default risk on those bonds and deposits. So, investors were willing to receive a negative nominal interest rate from the German government because they believed there was no chance that the government would default. As we saw in the chapter opener, some banks tie the interest rates they charge on loans to the interest rates on government bonds. The result of determining loan interest rates in this way was that banks like the Spanish bank Bankinter had to make interest payments *to* borrowers.

Economists remain divided over whether central banks had succeeded in using QE to expand the growth of employment and output. Economists who were skeptical of QE pointed to negative nominal interest rates as an example of the distortions in the financial system that had resulted from these policies. Later in this chapter, we will consider other new programs the Fed put in place to deal with the recession of 2007–2009 and the slow recovery that followed, as its traditional focus on lowering the federal funds rate to stimulate the economy proved ineffective.

Sources: Emese Bartha and Ben Edwards, "Germany Sells Five-Year Debt at Negative Yield for First Time on Record," *Wall Street Journal*, February 25, 2015; and data from the Federal Reserve Bank of St. Louis and the Organization for Economic Co-operation and Development.

MyEconLab Study Plan

Your Turn: Test your understanding by doing related problems 3.9 and 3.10 on page 550 at the end of this chapter.

Can the Fed Eliminate Recessions?

Panel (a) of Figure 15.7 on page 523 shows a completely successful expansionary monetary policy that shifts the *AD* curve to bring real GDP back to potential GDP. In practice, this ideal is very difficult for the Fed to achieve, as the length and severity of the 2007–2009 recession illustrates. In practice, the best the Fed can do is keep recessions shorter and milder than they would otherwise be.

If the Fed is to succeed in offsetting the effects of the business cycle, it needs to quickly recognize the need for a change in monetary policy. If the Fed is late in recognizing that a recession has begun or that the inflation rate is increasing, it may not be able to implement a new policy quickly enough to do much good. There is typically a *lag*, or delay, between a policy change and its effect on real GDP, employment, inflation, and other economic variables. Nobel Laureate Milton Friedman famously described the lags for monetary policy as "long and variable," which means that it can take months or years for changes in monetary policy to affect real GDP and inflation and that the lags vary based on economic circumstances. Once the Fed reduces the target federal funds rate, it takes time for the interest rates that affect firm and household behavior to also decline. Then it takes time for firms to identify newly profitable investment projects, obtain loans from banks or arrange to sell bonds, and start spending the borrowed funds. Similarly, it takes time for families to respond to lower mortgage interest rates by buying houses and for homebuilders to begin building the houses. As a result, the full effect of a change in monetary policy is typically spread out over several years.

Implementing a policy too late may actually destabilize the economy. To see why, consider Figure 15.8. The straight line represents the long-run growth trend in real GDP in the United States. On average, real GDP grows about 3 percent per year. The actual path of real GDP differs from the underlying trend because of the business cycle, which is shown by the red curved line. As we saw in Chapter 10, the actual business cycle is more irregular than the stylized cycle shown here.

Suppose that a recession begins in August 2018. Because it takes months for economic statistics to be gathered by the Commerce Department, the Census Bureau, the Bureau of Labor Statistics, and the Fed itself, there is a lag before the Fed recognizes that a recession has begun. Finally, in June 2019, the FOMC concludes that the economy is in recession and begins an expansionary monetary policy. As it turns out, June 2019 is actually the trough of the recession, meaning that the recession has already ended, and an expansion has begun. In these circumstances, the Fed's expansionary policy is not needed to end the recession. The increase in aggregate demand caused by the Fed's lowering interest rates is likely to push the economy beyond potential GDP and cause

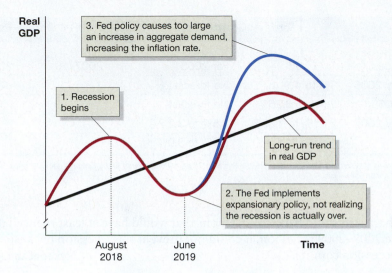

MyEconLab Animation

Figure 15.8

The Effect of a Poorly Timed Monetary Policy on the Economy

The upward-sloping straight line represents the long-run growth trend in real GDP. The curved red line represents the path real GDP takes because of the business cycle. If the Fed is too late in implementing a change in monetary policy, real GDP will follow the curved blue line. The Fed's expansionary monetary policy results in too great an increase in aggregate demand during the next expansion, which causes an increase in the inflation rate.

a significant acceleration in inflation. Real GDP ends up following the path indicated by the blue curved line. The Fed has inadvertently engaged in a *procyclical policy*, which increases the severity of the business cycle, as opposed to a *countercyclical policy*, which is meant to reduce the severity of the business cycle and which is what the Fed intends to use. As we saw in Chapter 10, the typical recession since 1950 has lasted less than one year, which increases the likelihood that the Fed may accidentally engage in a procyclical policy. Making this mistake is, of course, less likely in a long and severe recession such as the recession of 2007–2009.   MyEconLab Concept Check

Fed Forecasts

Because it can take a long time for a change in monetary policy to affect real GDP, the Fed tries to set policy according to what it forecasts the state of the economy will be in the future, when the policy change actually affects the economy. For example, when the Fed considered raising its target for the federal funds rate in 2015, the lag associated with monetary policy meant that the full effect of the rate increase on the economy would be spread out over several years. In making that increase, the Fed was thinking about the economy's future performance.

For the Fed to succeed in reducing the severity of business cycles, it must often act before a recession or an acceleration of inflation shows up in the economic data. So, good policy requires good economic forecasts based on models that describe accurately how the economy functions. Unfortunately, economic forecasts and models can be unreliable because changes in aggregate demand and short-run aggregate supply can be unpredictable. For example, the forecasts of most economists at the end of 2006 and the beginning of 2007 did not anticipate the severity of the recession that began in December 2007. Only after financial market conditions began to deteriorate rapidly did economists significantly reduce their forecasts of GDP growth in 2008 and 2009.

Table 15.1 summarizes the Fed's estimates for the growth rate of real GDP for 2007 and 2008 given in its *Monetary Policy Report to Congress*. To keep a recession from starting in 2007, the Fed would have had to change policy before 2007. However, in February 2006, the Fed expected the economy to grow by 3 percent to 4 percent in 2007, so it had little reason to change policy. Similarly, the Fed could have changed policy in an attempt to keep the economy growing in 2008, but it would have had to change policy before 2008, and as late as July 2007, the Fed still expected the economy to grow by 2.5 percent to 3.0 percent in 2008. In fact, real GDP increased by only 1.8 percent in 2007, and it declined by 0.3 percent in 2008. We can conclude that,

Table 15.1

Fed Forecasts of Real GDP Growth during 2007 and 2008

	Forecast Growth Rate		Actual Growth Rate	
Date forecast was made	For 2007	For 2008	2007	2008
February 2006	3% to 4%	No forecast	1.8%	−0.3%
May 2006	2.5% to 3.25%	No forecast		
February 2007	2.25% to 3.25%	2.5% to 3.25%		
July 2007	No forecast	2.5% to 3.0%		

Sources: Board of Governors of the Federal Reserve System, *Monetary Policy Report to the Congress*, various dates; and U.S. Bureau of Economic Analysis.

although the Fed could have taken actions that would have at least reduced the severity of the 2007–2009 recession, it could not prevent the recession because it did not see the recession coming.

MyEconLab Concept Check

Making the Connection
MyEconLab Video

Trying to Hit a Moving Target: Making Policy with "Real-Time Data"

The Fed relies on macroeconomic data to formulate monetary policy. One key piece of economic data is GDP, which is calculated quarterly by the Bureau of Economic Analysis (BEA). Unfortunately for Fed policymakers, the GDP data the BEA provides are frequently revised, and the revisions can be large enough that the actual state of the economy can be different from what it at first appeared to be.

The BEA's *advance estimate* of a quarter's GDP is not released until about a month after the quarter has ended. This delay can be a problem for policymakers because it means that they will not receive an estimate of GDP for the period from January through March, for instance, until the end of April. Presenting even more difficulty is the fact that the advance estimate will be subject to a number of revisions. The second estimate of a quarter's GDP is released about two months after the end of the quarter. The third estimate is released about three months after the end of the quarter. Although the BEA used to refer to the third estimate as the "final estimate," in fact, it continues to revise its estimates through the years. The BEA releases its first annual, second annual, and third annual estimates one, two, and three years after the third estimate. And that is not the end: Benchmark revisions occur in later years.

Why are there so many estimates? Because GDP is such a comprehensive measure of output in the economy, it is very time-consuming to collect the necessary data. To provide the advance estimate, the BEA relies on surveys conducted by the Commerce Department of retail sales and manufacturing shipments, as well as data from trade organizations, estimates of government spending, and so on. As time passes, these organizations gather additional data, and the BEA is able to refine its estimates.

Do these revisions to the GDP estimates matter? Sometimes they do, as the following example indicates. At the beginning of 2008, some economists believed that the U.S. economy might be in a recession. The effects of the continuing decline in housing prices were being felt in the financial system, and the unemployment rate was increasing. Members of the Fed's Open Market Committee remained cautiously optimistic, however, forecasting that real GDP would increase about 1.7 percent during the year. The BEA's advance estimate of the first quarter's GDP seemed to confirm that this forecast of slow growth might be accurate by showing an increase in real GDP of 0.6 percent at an annual rate. As the following graph shows, though, that estimate of real GDP growth was revised a number of times over the years, mostly downward.

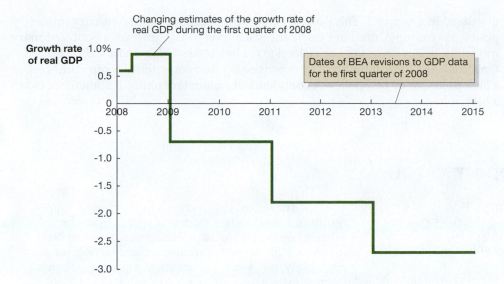

Currently, BEA data indicate that real GDP actually declined by 2.7 percent at an annual rate during the first quarter of 2008. This swing of more than 3 percentage points is a large difference, which changes the picture of what happened during the first quarter of 2008 from one of an economy experiencing slow growth to one of an economy suffering a sharp downturn as it fell into the worst recession since the Great Depression of the 1930s. The National Bureau of Economic Research has since determined that December 2007 was the beginning of the recession of 2007–2009.

This example shows that in addition to the other problems the Federal Reserve encounters in successfully conducting monetary policy, it must make decisions using data that may be subject to substantial revisions.

Sources: Federal Reserve Bank of Philadelphia, "Historical Data Files for the Real-Time Data Set," August 7, 2015; Board of Governors of the Federal Reserve System, "Minutes of the Federal Open Market Committee January 29–30, 2008," February 20, 2008; and Bruce T. Grimm and Teresa Weadock, "Gross Domestic Product: Revisions and Source Data," *Survey of Current Business*, Vol. 86, No. 2, February 2006, pp. 11–15.

Your Turn: Test your understanding by doing related problems 3.11 and 3.12 on page 550 at the end of this chapter.

MyEconLab Study Plan

A Summary of How Monetary Policy Works

Table 15.2 compares the steps involved in expansionary and contractionary monetary policies. We need to note an important qualification to this summary. At every point, we should add the phrase "relative to what would have happened without the policy." The table isolates the effect of monetary policy, *holding constant all other factors affecting the variables involved.* In other words, we are invoking the *ceteris paribus* condition,

Table 15.2   Expansionary and Contractionary Monetary Policies

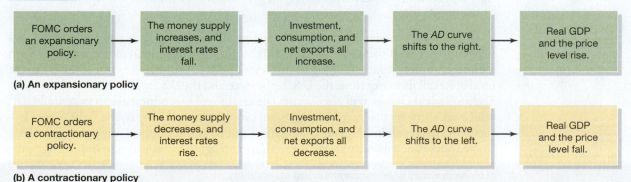

(a) An expansionary policy

(b) A contractionary policy

discussed in Chapter 3. This point is important because a contractionary monetary policy, for example, does not cause the price level to fall; instead, a contractionary monetary policy causes the price level *to rise by less than it would have without the policy*. One final note on terminology: An expansionary monetary policy is sometimes called a *loose* policy, or an *easy* policy. A contractionary monetary policy is sometimes called a *tight* policy.

MyEconLab Concept Check

Don't Let This Happen to You

Remember That with Monetary Policy, It's the Interest Rates—Not the Money—That Counts

It is tempting to think of monetary policy as working like this: If the Fed wants more spending in the economy, it increases the money supply, and people spend more because they now have more money. If the Fed wants less spending in the economy, it decreases the money supply, and people spend less because they now have less money. In fact, that is *not* how monetary policy works. Remember the important difference between money and income: The Fed increases the money supply by buying Treasury bills. The sellers of the Treasury bills have just exchanged one asset—Treasury bills—for another asset—a check from the Fed; the sellers have *not* increased their income. Even though the money supply is now larger, no one's income has increased, so no one's spending should be affected.

It is only when this increase in the money supply results in lower interest rates that spending is affected. When interest rates are lower, households are more likely to buy new homes and automobiles, and businesses are more likely to buy new factories and warehouses. Lower interest rates also lead to a lower value of the dollar, which lowers the prices of exports and raises the prices of imports, thereby increasing net exports. It isn't the increase in the money supply that has brought about this additional spending, *it's the lower interest rates*. To understand how monetary policy works, and to interpret news reports about the Fed's actions, remember that it is the change in interest rates, not the change in the money supply, that is most important.

MyEconLab Study Plan

Your Turn: Test your understanding by doing related problem 3.13 on page 551 at the end of this chapter.

MyEconLab Study Plan

15.4 ## Monetary Policy in the Dynamic Aggregate Demand and Aggregate Supply Model*

LEARNING OBJECTIVE: Use the dynamic aggregate demand and aggregate supply model to analyze monetary policy.

The overview of monetary policy we just finished contains a key idea: The Fed can use monetary policy to affect aggregate demand, thereby changing the price level and the level of real GDP. The discussion of monetary policy illustrated by Figure 15.7 on page 523 is simplified, however, because it ignores two important facts about the economy:

1. The economy experiences continuing inflation, with the price level rising every year.

2. The economy experiences long-run growth, with the *LRAS* curve shifting to the right every year.

In Chapter 13, we developed a *dynamic aggregate demand and aggregate supply model* that takes into account these two facts. In this section, we use the dynamic model to gain a more complete understanding of monetary policy. Let's briefly review the dynamic model. Recall that over time, the U.S. labor force and the U.S. capital stock will increase. Technological change will also occur. The result will be an increase in potential GDP, which we show by the long-run aggregate supply curve shifting to the right. These factors will also result in firms supplying more goods and services at any given price level in the short run, which we show by the short-run aggregate supply curve shifting to the

*This section may be omitted without loss of continuity.

right. During most years, the aggregate demand curve will also shift to the right, indicating that aggregate expenditure will be higher at every price level. Aggregate expenditure usually increases for these key reasons:

- As population grows and incomes rise, consumption will increase over time.
- As the economy grows, firms expand capacity, and new firms are established, increasing investment spending.
- An expanding population and an expanding economy require increased government services, such as more police officers and teachers, so government purchases will expand.

The Effects of Monetary Policy on Real GDP and the Price Level: A More Complete Account

During certain periods, *AD* does not increase enough during the year to keep real GDP at potential GDP. This slow growth in aggregate demand may be due to households and firms becoming pessimistic about the future state of the economy, leading them to cut back their spending on consumer durables, houses, and factories. As we have seen, the collapse of the housing bubble and the resulting financial crisis had a negative effect on aggregate demand during the 2007–2009 recession. There are other reasons why aggregate demand might grow slowly: The federal government could decide to balance the budget by cutting back its purchases and raising taxes, or recessions in other countries might cause a decline in U.S. exports. In the hypothetical situation shown in Figure 15.9, in the first year, equilibrium is at point A, with potential GDP of $17.0 trillion and a price level of 110. In the second year, *LRAS* increases to $17.4 trillion, but *AD* increases only to $AD_{2(\text{without policy})}$, which is not enough to keep real GDP at potential GDP. If the Fed does not intervene, the new short-run equilibrium will occur at $17.3 trillion (point B). The $100 billion gap between this level of real GDP and potential GDP at $LRAS_2$ means that some firms are operating at less than their normal capacity. Incomes and profits will fall, firms will begin to lay off workers, and the unemployment rate will rise.

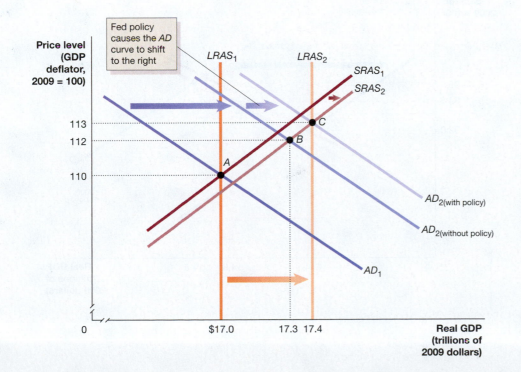

MyEconLab Animation

Figure 15.9

An Expansionary Monetary Policy

Initially, equilibrium is at point A, with real GDP of $17.0 trillion and a price level of 110. Without monetary policy, aggregate demand will shift from AD_1 to $AD_{2(\text{without policy})}$, which is not enough to keep the economy at full employment because long-run aggregate supply has shifted from $LRAS_1$ to $LRAS_2$. Short-run equilibrium is at point B, with real GDP of $17.3 trillion and a price level of 112. By lowering interest rates, the Fed increases investment, consumption, and net exports sufficiently to shift aggregate demand to $AD_{2(\text{with policy})}$. Equilibrium will be at point C, with real GDP of $17.4 trillion, which is its full employment level, and a price level of 113. The price level is higher than it would have been if the Fed had not acted to increase spending in the economy.

Economists at the Federal Reserve closely monitor the economy and continually update forecasts of future levels of real GDP and prices. When these economists anticipate that aggregate demand is not growing fast enough to allow the economy to remain at full employment, they present their findings to the FOMC, which decides whether circumstances require a change in monetary policy. For example, suppose that the FOMC meets and considers a forecast from the staff indicating that during the following year, a gap of $100 billion will open between equilibrium real GDP and potential GDP. In other words, the macroeconomic equilibrium illustrated by point B in Figure 15.9 will occur. The FOMC may then decide to carry out an expansionary monetary policy to lower interest rates to stimulate aggregate demand. The figure shows the results of a successful attempt to do this: AD has shifted to the right, and equilibrium occurs at potential GDP (point C). The Fed will have successfully headed off the falling incomes and rising unemployment that otherwise would have occurred. Bear in mind that we are illustrating a perfectly executed monetary policy that keeps the economy at potential GDP, which is difficult to achieve in practice for reasons discussed in the previous section.

Notice in Figure 15.9 that the expansionary monetary policy caused the inflation rate to be higher than it would have been. Without the expansionary policy, the price level would have risen from 110 to 112, so the inflation rate for the year would have been 1.8 percent. By shifting the aggregate demand curve, the expansionary policy caused the price level to increase from 112 to 113, raising the inflation rate from 1.8 percent to 2.7 percent.

MyEconLab Concept Check

Using Monetary Policy to Fight Inflation

In addition to using an expansionary monetary policy to reduce the severity of recessions, the Fed can use a contractionary monetary policy to keep aggregate demand from expanding so rapidly that the inflation rate begins to increase. Figure 15.10 shows the situation during 2005 and 2006, when the Fed faced this possibility. During 2005,

MyEconLab Animation

Figure 15.10

A Contractionary Monetary Policy in 2006

In 2005, equilibrium is at point A, with real GDP equal to potential GDP of $14.2 trillion and a price level of 92.0. From 2005 to 2006, potential GDP increased from $14.2 trillion to $14.6 trillion, as long-run aggregate supply increased from $LRAS_{2005}$ to $LRAS_{2006}$. The Fed raised interest rates because it believed the housing boom was causing aggregate demand to increase too rapidly. Without the increase in interest rates, aggregate demand would have shifted from AD_{2005} to $AD_{2006(without policy)}$, and the new short-run equilibrium would have occurred at point B. Real GDP would have been $14.8 trillion—$200 billion greater than potential GDP—and the price level would have been 96.1. The increase in interest rates resulted in aggregate demand increasing only to $AD_{2006(with policy)}$. Equilibrium occurred at point C, with real GDP of $14.6 trillion, which was equal to potential GDP, and the price level rose only to 94.8.

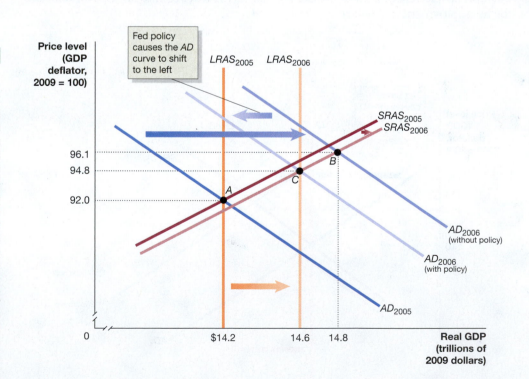

real GDP was equal to potential GDP, but Fed Chair Alan Greenspan and other members of the FOMC were concerned that the continuing boom in the housing market might lead aggregate demand to increase so rapidly that the inflation rate would begin to accelerate. The Fed had been gradually increasing the target for the federal funds rate since mid-2004.

When Ben Bernanke was appointed Fed chair in early 2006, he advocated continued increases in the target for the federal funds rate to slow the growth in aggregate demand. By June 2006, the target for the federal funds rate had been raised to 5.25 percent, from the low target rate of 1 percent that had prevailed from June 2003 to May 2004. The FOMC issues a statement after each meeting that summarizes the committee's views on the current state of the economy and gives some indication of how monetary policy might change in the near future. After its meeting on June 29, 2006, the FOMC included the following remarks in its statement:

> The Federal Open Market Committee decided today to raise its target for the federal funds rate … to 5-1/4 percent. Recent indicators suggest that economic growth is moderating from its quite strong pace earlier this year, partly reflecting a gradual cooling of the housing market and the lagged effects of increases in … interest rates. … Although the moderation in the growth of aggregate demand should help to limit inflation pressures over time, the Committee judges that some inflation risks remain.

The committee kept the target for the federal funds rate constant at 5.25 percent until September 2007, when concern about problems in financial markets led it to cut the target to 4.75 percent. Although it is impossible to know exactly what would have happened during 2006 without the Fed's policy change, Figure 15.10 presents a plausible scenario. The figure shows that without the Fed's actions to increase interest rates, aggregate demand would have shifted farther to the right, and equilibrium would have occurred at a level of real GDP that was beyond the potential level. The price level would have risen from 92.0 in 2005 to 96.1 in 2006, meaning that the inflation rate would have been 4.5 percent. Because the Fed kept aggregate demand from increasing as much as it otherwise would have, short-run equilibrium occurred at potential GDP, and the price level in 2006 rose to only 94.8, keeping the inflation rate at 3.0 percent.

MyEconLab Concept Check

Solved Problem 15.4

MyEconLab Interactive Animation

The Effects of Monetary Policy

The hypothetical information in the following table shows what the values for real GDP and the price level will be in 2019 if the Fed does *not* use monetary policy:

Year	Potential GDP	Real GDP	Price Level
2018	$17.9 trillion	$17.9 trillion	114
2019	18.3 trillion	18.1 trillion	116

a. If the Fed wants to keep real GDP at its potential level in 2019, should it use an expansionary policy or a contractionary policy? Should the trading desk buy Treasury bills or sell them?

b. Suppose the Fed's policy is successful in keeping real GDP at its potential level in 2019. State whether each of the following will be higher or lower than if the Fed had taken no action:

  i. Real GDP

  ii. Potential GDP

  iii. The inflation rate

  iv. The unemployment rate

c. Draw an aggregate demand and aggregate supply graph to illustrate your answer. Be sure that your graph contains LRAS curves for 2018 and 2019; SRAS curves for 2018 and 2019; AD curves for 2018 and for 2019, with and without monetary policy action; and equilibrium real GDP and the price level in 2019, with and without policy.

534   CHAPTER 15 Monetary Policy

Solving the Problem

Step 1: **Review the chapter material.** This problem is about the effects of monetary policy on real GDP and the price level, so you may want to review the section "The Effects of Monetary Policy on Real GDP and the Price Level: A More Complete Account," which begins on page 531.

Step 2: **Answer the questions in part (a) by explaining how the Fed can keep real GDP at its potential level.** The information in the table tells us that without monetary policy, the economy will be below potential GDP in 2019. To keep real GDP at its potential level, the Fed must undertake an expansionary policy. To carry out an expansionary policy, the trading desk needs to buy Treasury bills. Buying Treasury bills will increase reserves in the banking system. Banks will increase their loans, which will increase the money supply and lower the interest rate.

Step 3: **Answer part (b) by explaining the effect of the Fed's policy.** If the Fed's policy is successful, real GDP in 2019 will increase from $18.1 trillion, as given in the table, to its potential level of $18.3 trillion. Potential GDP is not affected by monetary policy, so its value will not change. Because the level of real GDP will be higher, the unemployment rate will be lower than it would have been without policy. The expansionary monetary policy shifts the *AD* curve to the right, so short-run equilibrium will move up the short-run aggregate supply (*SRAS*) curve, and the price level will be higher.

Step 4: **Answer part (c) by drawing the graph.** Your graph should look similar to Figure 15.9.

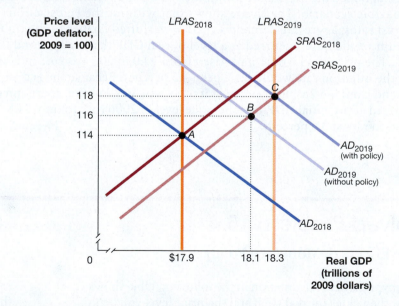

Equilibrium in 2018 is at point *A*, with the *AD* and *SRAS* curves intersecting along the *LRAS* curve. Real GDP is at its potential level of $17.9 trillion, and the price level is 114. Without monetary policy, the *AD* curve shifts to $AD_{2019(\text{without policy})}$, and short-run equilibrium is at point *B*. Because potential GDP has increased from $17.9 trillion to $18.3 trillion, real GDP of $18.1 trillion is below the potential level. The price level has increased from 114 to 116. With policy, the *AD* curve shifts to $AD_{2019(\text{with policy})}$, and equilibrium is at point *C*. Real GDP is at its potential level of $18.3 trillion. We don't have enough information to be sure of the new equilibrium price level. We do know that it will be higher than 116. The graph shows the price level rising to 118. Therefore, without the Fed's expansionary policy, the inflation rate in 2019 would have been about 1.8 percent. With policy, it will be about 3.5 percent.

Extra Credit: Bear in mind that, in reality, the Fed is unable to use monetary policy to keep real GDP exactly at its potential level, as this problem suggests.

Your Turn: For more practice, do related problems 4.4 and 4.5 on pages 551–552 at the end of this chapter.

MyEconLab Study Plan

A Closer Look at the Fed's Setting of Monetary Policy Targets

LEARNING OBJECTIVE: Describe the Fed's setting of monetary policy targets.

We have seen that in carrying out monetary policy, the Fed changes its target for the federal funds rate depending on the state of the economy. Is the Fed's approach correct? During times when the economy is not experiencing a financial crisis, is using the federal funds rate as a target the best way to conduct monetary policy? If the Fed targets the federal funds rate, how should it decide what the target level should be? In this section, we consider these important issues concerning the Fed's targeting policy.

Should the Fed Target the Money Supply?

Some economists have argued that rather than use an interest rate as its monetary policy target, the Fed should use the money supply. Many of the economists who make this argument belong to a school of thought known as *monetarism*. The leader of the monetarist school was Milton Friedman, who was skeptical that the Fed would be able to correctly time changes in monetary policy.

Friedman and his followers favored replacing *monetary policy* with a *monetary growth rule*. Ordinarily, we expect monetary policy to respond to changing economic conditions: When the economy is in recession, the Fed reduces interest rates, and when inflation is increasing, the Fed raises interest rates. A monetary growth rule, in contrast, is a plan for increasing the money supply at a constant rate that does not change in response to economic conditions. Friedman and his followers proposed a monetary growth rule of increasing the money supply every year at a rate equal to the long-run annual growth rate of real GDP, which has been about 3 percent since 1950. If the Fed adopted this monetary growth rule, it would stick to it through changing economic conditions.

But what happens under a monetary growth rule if the economy moves into recession? Shouldn't the Fed abandon the rule to drive down interest rates? Friedman argued that the Fed should stick to the rule even during recessions because he believed that active monetary policy destabilizes the economy by increasing the number of recessions and their severity. By keeping the money supply growing at a constant rate, Friedman argued, the Fed would greatly increase economic stability.

During the 1970s, some economists and politicians pressured the Federal Reserve to adopt a monetary growth rule. Most of that pressure has disappeared in recent years because the fairly close relationship between movements in the money supply and movements in real GDP and the price level that existed before 1980 has become much weaker. Since 1980, the growth rate of M1 has been unstable. In some years, M1 has grown more than 10 percent, while in other years, it has actually fallen. Yet despite these wide fluctuations in the growth of M1, growth in real GDP has been fairly stable, and inflation has remained low during most years.   MyEconLab Concept Check

Why Doesn't the Fed Target Both the Money Supply and the Interest Rate?

Most economists believe that the interest rate is the best monetary policy target. But as we have just seen, other economists believe the Fed should target the money supply. Why doesn't the Fed satisfy both groups by targeting both the money supply and the interest rate? The simple answer is that the Fed can't target both at the same time. To see why, look at Figure 15.11, which shows the money market.

Figure 15.11

The Fed Can't Target Both the Money Supply and the Interest Rate

The Fed is forced to choose between using either the interest rate or the money supply as its monetary policy target. In this figure, the Fed can set a target of $900 billion for the money supply or a target of 5 percent for the interest rate, but the Fed can't hit both targets because it can achieve only combinations of the interest rate and the money supply that represent equilibrium in the money market.

Source: Federal Reserve Bank of St. Louis.

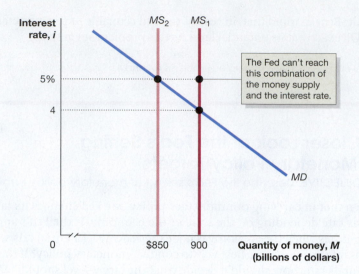

The Fed can't reach this combination of the money supply and the interest rate.

Remember that the Fed controls the money supply, but it does not control money demand. Money demand is determined by decisions of households and firms as they weigh the trade-off between the convenience of money and its low interest rate compared with other financial assets. Suppose the Fed is targeting the interest rate and decides, given conditions in the economy, that the interest rate should be 5 percent. Or, suppose the Fed is targeting the money supply and decides that the money supply should be $900 billion. Figure 15.11 shows that the Fed can bring about an interest rate of 5 percent or a money supply of $900 billion, but it can't bring about both. The point representing an interest rate of 5 percent and a money supply of $900 billion is not on the money demand curve, so it can't represent an equilibrium in the money market. The Fed can only attain combinations of the interest rate and the money supply that represent equilibrium. Therefore, the Fed has to choose between targeting an interest rate and targeting the money supply. For most of the period since World War II, the Fed has chosen the federal funds rate as its target.   MyEconLab Concept Check

The Taylor Rule

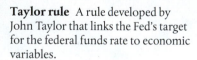

Taylor rule A rule developed by John Taylor that links the Fed's target for the federal funds rate to economic variables.

How does the Fed choose a target for the federal funds rate? The discussions at the meetings of the FOMC can be complex, and they take into account many economic variables. John Taylor of Stanford University has analyzed Fed decision making and developed the **Taylor rule** to explain federal funds rate targeting. The Taylor rule begins with an estimate of the value of the equilibrium real federal funds rate, which is the federal funds rate—adjusted for inflation—that would be consistent with real GDP being equal to potential GDP in the long run. Taylor believes this rate to be 2 percent. According to the Taylor rule, the Fed should set the target for the federal funds rate so that it is equal to the sum of the inflation rate, the equilibrium real federal funds rate, and two additional terms. The first of these additional terms is the *inflation gap*—the difference between current inflation and a target rate; the second is the *output gap*—the percentage difference between real GDP and potential GDP. The inflation gap and output gap are each given "weights" that reflect their influence on the federal funds target rate. With weights of 1/2 for both gaps, we have the following Taylor rule:

Federal funds target rate = Current inflation rate + Equilibrium real federal funds rate
$$+ [(1/2) \times \text{Inflation gap}] + [(1/2) \times \text{Output gap}].$$

The Taylor rule includes expressions for the inflation gap and the output gap because the Fed is concerned about both inflation and fluctuations in real GDP. Taylor demonstrated that if the equilibrium real federal funds rate is 2 percent and the target rate of inflation is 2 percent, the preceding equation does a good job of explaining changes in the Fed's target for the federal funds rate during most years. Consider an example in which the current inflation rate is 1 percent, and real GDP is 1 percent below potential GDP. In that case, the inflation gap equals 1 percent − 2 percent = −1 percent, and the output gap is also −1 percent. Inserting these values in the Taylor rule, we can calculate the predicted value for the federal funds target rate:

$$\text{Federal funds target rate} = 1\% + 2\% + [(1/2) \times -1\%] + [(1/2) \times -1\%] = 2\%$$

The Taylor rule accurately predicted changes in the federal funds target during the period of Alan Greenspan's leadership of the Federal Reserve from 1987 to 2006. For the period of the late 1970s and early 1980s, when Paul Volcker was chairman of the Federal Reserve, the Taylor rule predicts a federal funds rate target *lower* than the actual target the Fed used. In other words, Chairman Volcker kept the federal funds rate at an unusually high level to bring down the very high inflation rates of the late 1970s and early 1980s. In contrast, using data from the chairmanship of Arthur Burns from 1970 to 1978, the Taylor rule predicts a federal funds rate target *higher* than the actual target. Chairman Burns kept the federal funds rate at an unusually low level during these years, which helps to explain why the inflation rate grew worse. During the mid-2000s, the actual federal funds rate was also lower than the predicted federal funds rate. Some economists, including Taylor, argue that these low targets for the federal funds rate contributed to the excessive increase in spending on housing that we will discuss in the next section.

Taylor has proposed that the Fed adopt an explicit rule to guide its monetary policy actions. The Fed would not be constrained to mechanically following the exact Taylor rule given earlier, but whatever rule the Fed adopted, it would have to publically justify deviating from the rule, if a majority of the FOMC came to believe that was necessary. Representative Kevin Brady, Chairman of the Congressional Joint Economic Committee, has introduced the Sound Dollar Act, one provision of which incorporates Taylor's proposal. Former Fed Chair Ben Bernanke and most current members of the FOMC are against the proposal because they believe it might limit the Fed's ability to pursue innovative policies in a financial crisis. They also note that the Taylor rule does not account for changes over time in the equilibrium real interest rate, or for changes the FOMC might want to make in the target inflation rate.   MyEconLab **Concept Check**

Solved Problem 15.5

MyEconLab **Interactive Animation**

Applying the Taylor Rule

An article in the *Wall Street Journal* discussed the views of John Williams, the president of the Federal Reserve Bank of San Francisco, about the Taylor rule. According to the article, Williams argued that if the Fed had attempted to follow the Taylor rule during the recession of 2007–2009, it would have had to do "something not easily done, and that would have been for the Fed to have pushed short-term rates deeply into negative territory."

a. What does it mean for an interest rate to be negative?
b. Use the equation for the Taylor rule to show how the federal funds rate target might be negative. Assume that the equilibrium real federal funds rate and the target rate of inflation are both 2 percent and the current inflation rate is 0 percent.

Solving the Problem

Step 1: **Review the chapter material.** This problem is about using the Taylor rule to evaluate monetary policy, so you may want to review the section "The Taylor Rule," which begins on page 536.

Step 2: **Answer part (a) by explaining what it means for an interest rate to be negative.** We expect interest rates to be positive, which results in the borrower paying the lender back more than the amount of the funds borrowed. As we saw in the chapter opener and discussed further in the *Making the*

Connection on page 524, with a negative interest rate, the borrower would pay the lender back less than the amount of the funds borrowed. Note that Williams is referring to a negative *nominal* interest rate, which is very rare. A negative *real* interest rate that results from the inflation rate being higher than the nominal interest rate occurs more frequently.

Step 3: **Answer part (b) by constructing an example where the target federal funds rate might be negative.** This is the equation for the Taylor rule:

$$\text{Federal funds target rate} = \text{Current inflation rate}$$
$$+ \text{Equilibrium real federal funds rate}$$
$$+ [(1/2) \times \text{Inflation gap}]$$
$$+ [(1/2) \times \text{Output gap}].$$

If we substitute the values given in the problem, we have:

$$\text{Federal funds rate target} = 0\% + 2\% + [(1/2) \times (0\% - 2)]$$
$$+ [(1/2) \times \text{output gap}],$$

or:

$$\text{Federal funds taget rate target} = 1\% + [(1/2) \times \text{output gap}].$$

So, for the federal funds rate target to be negative, the output gap will have to be larger (in absolute value) than -2%. For example, if the output gap is -4%, then:

$$\text{Federal funds rate target} = 1\% + [(1/2) \times (-4)] = -1\%$$

In fact, the output gap rose above -6 percent during the recession. So, Williams is correct that following the Taylor rule exactly would have required the federal funds rate to be negative, which means that banks would have to have been willing to pay interest when lending to other banks in the federal funds market rather than receive interest. This outcome is very unlikely.

Extra Credit: The inability of the Fed to push the federal funds rate to negative values is sometimes called the *zero lower bound* to monetary policy.

Source: Michael S. Derby and Benjamin Fritz, "Fed's Williams Says Summer Rate Rise Possible if Data Supports Action," *Wall Street Journal*, May 1, 2015.

Your Turn: For more practice, do related problems 5.5, 5.6, and 5.7 on pages 552–553 at the end of this chapter.

Inflation Targeting

Inflation targeting A framework for conducting monetary policy that involves the central bank announcing its target level of inflation.

Many economists and central bankers believe that *inflation targeting* provides a useful framework for carrying out monetary policy. With **inflation targeting**, a central bank publicly sets an explicit target for the inflation rate over a period of time, and the government and the public then judge the performance of the central bank on the basis of its success in hitting the target.

Beginning in the 1980s, inflation targeting was adopted by a number of central banks around the world, including the Bank of England and, after its founding in the late 1990s, the European Central Bank. After many years of not having an explicit inflation target, the Fed announced in 2012 that it would attempt to maintain an average inflation rate of 2 percent per year.

With inflation targeting, the Fed can still respond to periods of recession or other economic problems without following an inflexible rule. An inflation target allows monetary policy to focus on inflation and inflation forecasts except during times of severe recession. Arguments supporting the Fed's use of an explicit inflation target focus on the following points. First, announcing explicit targets for inflation draws the public's attention to what the Fed can actually achieve in practice. Most economists believe that over the long run, monetary policy has a greater effect on inflation than on the growth of real GDP. Second, announcing an inflation target provides an anchor for inflationary expectations. If households, firms, and participants in financial markets believe that the Fed will hit an annual inflation target of 2 percent, then they will expect that if inflation is temporarily lower or higher, it will eventually return to the target rate. Third, inflation targets promote accountability for the Fed by providing a yardstick against which its performance can be measured.

Some economists and policymakers were critical of the Fed's decision to adopt an explicit inflation target. Opponents make several arguments. First, rigid numerical targets for inflation diminish the flexibility of monetary policy to address other policy goals. Second, because monetary policy affects inflation with a lag, inflation targeting requires that the Fed use forecasts of future inflation, which may turn out to be inaccurate. Third, holding the Fed accountable only for a goal of low inflation may make it more difficult for elected officials to monitor the Fed's support for good economic policy overall. Finally, inflation targets may increase uncertainty over whether the Fed will take prompt action to return the economy to full employment following a recession.

Economists and policymakers continue to debate whether inflation targets improve economic policy.
MyEconLab Concept Check

Making the Connection
MyEconLab Video

Should the Fed Worry about the Prices of Food and Gasoline?

Surveys show that many people in the United States are skeptical about whether changes in the consumer price index (CPI) are a good measure of inflation. The CPI measures the price level based on a market basket that contains 211 goods and services, including shirts, refrigerators, textbooks, and doctor visits. But many people think of inflation in terms of increases in the prices of the goods they buy most frequently—particularly food and gasoline.

Not only does the Fed not concentrate on changes in the prices of food and gasoline, it actually prefers to *exclude* food and gasoline prices when measuring inflation. Fed policymakers refer to these adjusted measures of inflation as "core" inflation. Why does the Fed ignore the prices that many people think are the most important? The key reason is that monetary policy affects the economy with a lag of many months. As a result, Fed policymakers don't want to react to every movement—up or down—in prices. The green line in the graph shows the CPI calculated using prices for all 211 goods and services in the consumer market basket. The red line shows the CPI calculated by leaving out the prices of food and energy, such as gasoline and natural gas used in heating homes.

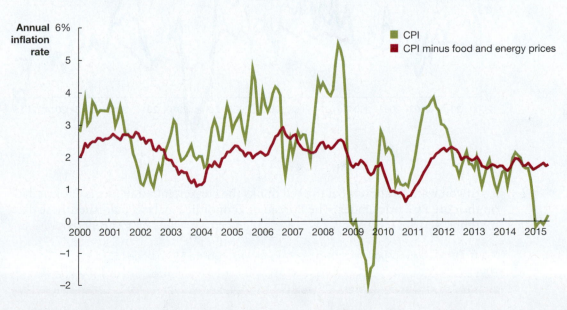

As the graph shows, food and energy prices are much more volatile than are the prices of all the goods in the CPI. For instance, during the recession of 2007–2009, the inflation rate measured by the CPI was negative—deflation occurred—during nine months. When changes in food and energy prices are excluded, by contrast, the inflation rate is positive in every month. This pattern repeated in early 2015, when falling energy prices caused the CPI to decline for several months.

Why are food and energy prices so volatile? Food prices can be volatile because weather-related problems such as too little or too much rain can lead to large fluctuations in supply. Energy prices can fluctuate when political unrest in the Middle East or other energy-producing regions disrupts supply or when the Organization of the Petroleum Exporting Countries (OPEC) oil cartel attempts to increase prices. Because the factors that cause volatility in food and energy prices tend not to persist for more than a few months, they don't have a long-lasting effect on the overall rate of inflation. As Fed Chair Janet Yellen has put it, Fed policymakers "pay attention to core inflation and similar measures because, in light of the volatility of food and energy prices, core inflation has been a better forecaster of overall inflation." In other words, to reach its goal of price stability, the Fed has to concentrate on the underlying inflation rate and avoid being distracted by temporary increases in food or energy prices—however painful the typical consumer may find those increases to be.

The Fed's preferred measure of inflation is the core *personal consumption expenditures (PCE) price index*, which excludes food and energy prices. The PCE price index is a measure of the price level that is similar to the GDP deflator, except it includes only the prices of goods from the consumption category of GDP. The PCE price index includes the prices of more goods and services than the CPI, so it is a broader measure of inflation.

The following graph shows movements in the CPI, the PCE price index, and the core PCE price index from January 2000 through July 2015. Although the three measures of inflation move roughly together, the core PCE price index has been more stable than the other two. Note in particular that in early 2009, when the CPI and the PCE price index were indicating that the economy was experiencing deflation, the core PCE price index was still showing inflation rates above 1 percent. The core PCE price index also showed more stability in late 2014 and early 2015, a period of rapid declines in oil prices.

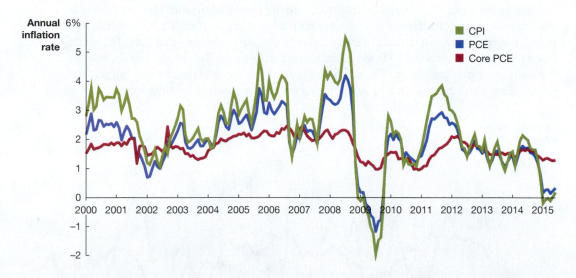

If you want to know what the Fed thinks the current inflation rate is, look at data on the core PCE price index. The Bureau of Economic Analysis publishes these data monthly. MyEconLab Real-time data

15.6 Fed Policies during the 2007-2009 Recession

LEARNING OBJECTIVE: Describe the policies the Federal Reserve used during the 2007-2009 recession.

As we have seen, the Fed's traditional response to a recession is to lower the target for the federal funds rate. The severity of the recession of 2007-2009, particularly the problems in financial markets during those years, complicated the Fed's job. By December 2008, the Fed had effectively lowered the target for the federal funds rate to zero, but the zero interest rate alone did not result in a sufficient increase in aggregate demand to end the recession. In this section, we will discuss some of the additional policy measures the Fed took during the 2007-2009 recession. Some of these measures were used for the first time in the Fed's history.

The Inflation and Deflation of the Housing Market Bubble

To understand the 2007-2009 recession and the financial crisis that accompanied it, we need to start by considering the housing market. The Fed lowered the target for the federal funds rate during the 2001 recession to stimulate demand for housing. The policy was successful, and most builders, such as Toll Brothers, experienced several years of high demand. By 2005, however, many economists argued that a "bubble" had formed in the housing market. As we discussed in Chapter 6, the price of any asset reflects the returns the owner of the asset expects to receive. For example, the price of a share of stock reflects the profitability of the firm issuing the stock because the owner of a share of stock has a claim on the firm's profits.

Many economists believe, however, that sometimes a *stock market bubble* can form when the prices of stocks rise above levels that can be justified by the profitability of the firms issuing the stocks. Stock market bubbles end when enough investors decide stocks are overvalued and begin to sell. Why would an investor be willing to pay more for stocks than would be justified by their underlying value? There are two main explanations:

1. The investor may be caught up in the enthusiasm of the moment and, by failing to gather sufficient information, may overestimate the true value of the stocks.

2. The investor may expect to profit from buying stocks at inflated prices if the investor can sell them at even higher prices before the bubble bursts.

The price of a house should reflect the value of the housing services it provides. We can use the rents charged for comparable houses in an area to measure the value of housing services. We would expect, then, that housing prices and rents would increase at roughly the same rate. If prices of single-family homes rise significantly relative to rents for single-family homes, it is likely that the housing market is experiencing a bubble. As Figure 15.12 shows, housing prices and housing rents generally

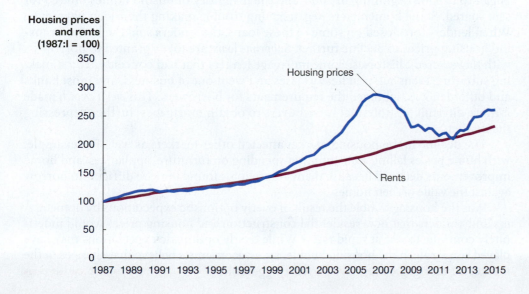

MyEconLab Real-time data

Figure 15.12

Housing Prices and Housing Rents, 1987-2015

Typically, housing prices increase at about the same rate as housing rents. But during the housing bubble, housing prices increased far more than did rents.

Note: For both series, the values for the first quarter of 1987 (1987:I) are set equal to 100.

Source: Federal Reserve Bank of St. Louis.

New home sales
(thousands of homes)

Figure 15.13 **The Housing Bubble**

Sales of new homes in the United States went on a roller-coaster ride, rising by 60 percent between January 2000 and July 2005 before falling by 80 percent between July 2005 and May 2010.

Note: The data are seasonally adjusted at an annual rate.
Source: U.S. Bureau of the Census.

increase at about the same rate, but between January 2000 and May 2006, housing prices nearly doubled, while rents increased by less than 25 percent. This large divergence between housing prices and rents is evidence of a bubble. In addition, in some cities, there was an increase in the number of buyers who did not intend to live in the houses they purchased but were using them as investments. Like stock investors during a stock market bubble, these housing investors were expecting to make a profit by selling houses at higher prices than they had paid for them, and they were not concerned about whether the prices of the houses were above the value of the housing services provided.

During 2006 and 2007, the air was rapidly escaping from the housing bubble. Figure 15.13 shows new home sales for each month from January 2000 through June 2015. New home sales rose by 60 percent between January 2000 and July 2005 and then fell by 80 percent between July 2005 and May 2010. Sales then began to gradually increase but were still at low levels well into 2015. Sales of existing homes followed a similar pattern. Prices of new and existing homes in most markets also began to decline beginning in 2006, and the inventory of unsold homes offered for sale soared. Some homebuyers began having trouble making their loan payments. When lenders foreclosed on some of these loans, the lenders sold the homes, causing housing prices to decline further. *Subprime loans* are loans granted to borrowers with flawed credit histories. Some mortgage lenders that had concentrated on making subprime loans suffered heavy losses and went out of business, and most banks and other lenders tightened the requirements for borrowers. This *credit crunch* made it more difficult for potential homebuyers to obtain mortgages, further depressing the market.

The decline in the housing market affected other markets as well. For example, with home prices falling, consumption spending on furniture, appliances, and home improvements declined because many households found it more difficult to borrow against the value of their homes.

Was the housing bubble the result of overly optimistic expectations by homebuyers and builders that new residential construction and housing prices would indefinitely continue to rise at rapid rates? While overly optimistic expectations may have played some role in the housing bubble, many economists believe that changes in the market for mortgages may have played a bigger role.

MyEconLab Concept Check

The Changing Mortgage Market

Until the 1970s, the commercial banks and savings and loans that granted mortgages kept the loans until the borrowers paid them off. As we saw in Chapter 14, a financial asset such as a mortgage is a security only if it can be resold in a secondary market. Many members of Congress believed that home ownership could be increased by creating a secondary market in mortgages. If banks and savings and loans could resell mortgages, then individual investors would in effect be able to provide funds for mortgages. The process would work like this: If a bank or savings and loan granted a mortgage and then resold the mortgage to an investor, the bank could use the funds received from the investor to grant another mortgage. In this way, banks and savings and loans could grant more mortgage loans because they would no longer depend only on deposits for the funds needed to make the loans. One barrier to creating a secondary market in mortgages was that most investors were unwilling to buy mortgages because they were afraid of losing money if the borrower stopped making payments, or *defaulted*, on the loan.

To reassure investors, Congress used two *government-sponsored enterprises (GSEs)*: the Federal National Mortgage Association ("Fannie Mae") and the Federal Home Loan Mortgage Corporation ("Freddie Mac"). These two institutions stand between investors and banks that grant mortgages. Fannie Mae and Freddie Mac sell bonds to investors and use the funds to purchase mortgages from banks. By the 1990s, a large secondary market existed in mortgages, with funds flowing from investors through Fannie Mae and Freddie Mac to banks and, ultimately, to individuals and families borrowing money to buy houses.   MyEconLab Concept Check

The Role of Investment Banks

By the 2000s, further changes had taken place in the mortgage market. First, investment banks became significant participants in the secondary market for mortgages. As we have seen, investment banks, such as Goldman Sachs and Morgan Stanley, differ from commercial banks in that they do not take in deposits and rarely lend directly to households. Instead, investment banks concentrate on providing advice to firms issuing stocks and bonds or considering mergers with other firms. Investment banks began buying mortgages, bundling large numbers of them together as bonds called *mortgage-backed securities*, and reselling them to investors. Mortgage-backed securities proved very popular with investors because they often paid higher interest rates than other securities that investors believed had comparable default risk.

Second, by the height of the housing bubble in 2005 and early 2006, lenders had greatly loosened the standards for obtaining a mortgage loan. Traditionally, only borrowers with good credit histories and who were willing to make a down payment equal to at least 20 percent of the value of the house they were buying would be able to receive a mortgage. By 2005, however, lenders were issuing many mortgages to subprime borrowers with flawed credit histories. In addition, "Alt-A" borrowers—who stated but did not document their incomes—and borrowers who made very small down payments found it easier to get loans. Lenders also created new types of *adjustable-rate mortgages* that allowed borrowers to pay a very low interest rate for the first few years of the mortgage and then pay a higher rate in later years. The chance that the borrowers using these nontraditional mortgages would default was higher than for borrowers using traditional mortgages. Why would borrowers take out mortgages if it might be difficult for them to make the payments, and why would lenders grant these mortgages? Both borrowers and lenders were anticipating that housing prices would continue to rise, which would reduce the chance that borrowers would default on the mortgages and would also make it easier for borrowers to convert to more traditional mortgages in the future.

Unfortunately, the decline in housing prices led to rising defaults among subprime and Alt-A borrowers, borrowers with adjustable-rate mortgages, and borrowers who had made only small down payments. When borrowers began defaulting on mortgages, the values of many mortgage-backed securities declined sharply. Investors feared that if they purchased these securities, they would not receive the promised payments because the payments on the securities depended on borrowers making their mortgage payments, which an increasing number of borrowers were failing to do. Many commercial and investment banks owned these mortgage-backed securities, so the decline in the value of the securities caused these banks to suffer heavy losses. By mid-2007, the decline in the value of mortgage-backed securities and the large losses suffered by commercial and investment banks began to concern investors and policymakers. Many investors refused to buy mortgage-backed securities, and some investors would buy only bonds issued by the U.S. Treasury.   MyEconLab Concept Check

Making the Connection
MyEconLab Video

The Wonderful World of Leverage

Traditionally, most people taking out a mortgage made a down payment equal to 20 percent of the price of the house and borrowed the remaining 80 percent. During the housing boom, however, many people purchased houses with down payments of 5 percent or less. These borrowers were highly *leveraged*, which means that their investment in their house was made mostly with borrowed money.

To see how leverage works in the housing market, consider the following example: Suppose you buy a $200,000 house on January 1, 2018. On January 1, 2019, the price of the house—if you decide to sell it—has risen to $220,000. What return have you earned on your investment in the house? The answer depends on how much you invested when you bought the house. For example, if you paid $200,000 in cash for the house, your return on that $200,000 investment is the $20,000 increase in the price of the house divided by your $200,000 investment, or 10 percent. Suppose that rather than paying cash, you made a down payment of 20 percent, or $40,000, and borrowed the rest by taking out a mortgage loan of $160,000. Now the return on your investment in the house is the $20,000 increase in the price of the house divided by your $40,000 investment, or 50 percent. If the down payment is less than 20 percent, your return on investment will be higher. The second column in the following table shows how the return on your investment increases as your down payment decreases:

Making a very small down payment on a home mortgage leaves a buyer vulnerable to falling house prices.

	Return on your investment as a result of . . .	
Down Payment	**a 10 percent increase in the price of your house.**	**a 10 percent decrease in the price of your house.**
100%	10%	−10%
20	50	−50
10	100	−100
5	200	−200

An investment financed at least partly by borrowing is called a *leveraged investment*. As this example shows, the larger the fraction of an investment financed by borrowing, the greater the degree of leverage in the investment, and the greater the potential return. But as the third column in the table shows, the reverse is also true: The greater the leverage, the greater the potential loss. To see why, suppose once again that you buy a house for $200,000, except that in this case, after one year, the price of the house falls to $180,000. If you paid $200,000 in cash for the house—so your leverage was zero—the $20,000 decline in the price of the house represents a loss of 10 percent of your investment. But if you made a down payment of only $10,000 and borrowed the remaining $190,000, then the $20,000 decline in the price of the house represents a loss of 200 percent of your investment. In fact, the house is now worth $10,000 less than the amount of your mortgage loan. The *equity* in your house is the difference between the market price of the house and the amount you owe on a loan. If the amount you owe is greater than the price of the house, you have *negative equity*. A homeowner who has negative equity is also said to be "upside down" or "underwater" on his or her mortgage.

When the housing bubble burst and housing prices started to fall, many people found that they had negative equity. In that situation, some people defaulted on their loans, sometimes by simply moving out and abandoning their homes. Leverage had contributed to the housing boom and bust and the severity of the 2007–2009 recession.

Your Turn: Test your understanding by doing related problem 6.9 on page 554 at the end of this chapter.

MyEconLab Study Plan

The Fed and the Treasury Department Respond

Because the problems in financial markets resulting from the bursting of the housing bubble were so severe, the Fed entered into an unusual partnership with the U.S. Treasury Department to develop suitable policies. Fed Chairman Ben Bernanke and U.S. Treasury Secretaries Henry Paulson (in the Bush administration) and Timothy Geithner (in the Obama administration) responded to the crisis by intervening in financial markets in unprecedented ways.

Initial Fed and Treasury Actions The financial crisis significantly worsened following the bankruptcy of the investment bank Lehman Brothers on September 15, 2008. So it is useful to look at the actions taken by the Fed and the Treasury before and after that date. Table 15.3 shows four key actions the Fed and Treasury took to deal with problems in the financial system before the bankruptcy of Lehman Brothers.

Date	Action	Goal
March 2008	Although the Fed traditionally made discount loans only to commercial banks, the Fed announced it would temporarily make discount loans to *primary dealers*—firms that participate in regular open market transactions with the Fed.	Provide short-term funds to these dealers, some of which are investment banks, so they would not have to raise funds by selling securities, which might further reduce the prices of these securities.
March 2008	The Fed announced that it would loan up to $200 billion of Treasury securities in exchange for mortgage-backed securities.	Make it possible for primary dealers that owned mortgage-backed securities that were difficult or impossible to sell to have access to Treasury securities that they could use as collateral for short-term loans.
March 2008	The Fed and the Treasury helped JPMorgan Chase acquire the investment bank Bear Stearns, which was close to failing.	Avoid a financial panic that the Fed and the Treasury believed would result from Bear Stearns's failure. Its failure might have caused many investors and financial firms to stop making loans to other investment banks.
September 2008	The Treasury moved to have the federal government take control of Fannie Mae and Freddie Mac. Although the federal government sponsored Fannie Mae and Freddie Mac, they were actually private businesses. The firms were placed under the supervision of the Federal Housing Finance Agency.	Avoid further devastating a weak housing market. The Treasury believed that the bankruptcy of Fannie Mae and Freddie Mac would have caused a collapse in confidence in mortgage-backed securities.

Table 15.3

Treasury and Fed Actions at the Beginning of the Financial Crisis

Responses to the Failure of Lehman Brothers Some economists and policymakers criticized the decision by the Fed and the Treasury to help arrange the sale of Bear Stearns to JPMorgan Chase. Their main concern was with the *moral hazard problem*, which is the possibility that managers of financial firms such as Bear Stearns might make riskier investments if they believe that the federal government will save them from bankruptcy. The Treasury and the Fed acted to save Bear Stearns because they believed that the failure of a large financial firm could have wider economic repercussions. As we discussed in Chapter 14, when a financial firm sells off its holdings of bonds and other assets, it causes their prices to fall, which in turn can undermine the financial position of other firms that also own these assets. In September 2008, when the investment bank Lehman Brothers was near bankruptcy, the Fed and the Treasury had to weigh the moral hazard problem against the possibility that the failure of Lehman Brothers would lead to further declines in asset prices and endanger the financial positions of other firms. Chairman Ben Bernanke and other Fed officials were also concerned that they lacked the legal authority to make loans to Lehman Brothers. They believed that the Federal Reserve Act prohibited making loans to a firm that was insolvent, meaning that the value of the firm's assets—such as its holdings of mortgage securities—was less than the value of its liabilities—such as the loans it had received from other financial firms.

The Fed and the Treasury decided to allow Lehman Brothers to go bankrupt, which it did on September 15. The adverse reaction in financial markets was stronger than the Fed and the Treasury had expected, and just two days later, the Fed agreed to provide an \$85 billion loan to the American International Group (AIG)—the largest insurance company in the United States—in exchange for the federal government receiving an 80 percent ownership stake, effectively giving the government control of the company.

One important result of the failure of Lehman Brothers was the heavy losses suffered by Reserve Primary Fund, a money market mutual fund that had made short-term loans to Lehman Brothers. The problems at Reserve led many investors to withdraw their funds from it and other money market funds. These withdrawals reduced the ability of the money market funds to purchase commercial paper from corporations. Because in recent years corporations had become dependent on selling commercial paper to finance their operations, the Treasury and the Fed moved to stabilize this market and ensure that the flow of funds from investors to corporations continued. The Treasury announced a plan to temporarily provide insurance for deposits in money market mutual funds, similar to the existing insurance on bank deposits. The Fed announced that for a limited time, it would lend directly to corporations by purchasing three-month commercial paper issued by nonfinancial corporations.

Finally, in October 2008, Congress passed the *Troubled Asset Relief Program* (*TARP*), under which the Treasury attempted to stabilize the commercial banking system by providing funds to banks in exchange for stock. Taking partial ownership positions in private commercial banks was an unprecedented action for the federal government.

Many of the Treasury's and the Fed's new approaches to policy were controversial because they involved partial government ownership of financial firms, implicit guarantees to large financial firms that they would not be allowed to go bankrupt, and unprecedented intervention in financial markets. Although the approaches were new, they were intended to achieve the traditional macroeconomic policy goals of high employment, price stability, and stability of financial markets. What remains to be seen is whether these new approaches represent a permanent increase in federal government involvement in U.S. financial markets or whether policy will eventually return to more traditional approaches.

Continued from page 513

Economics in Your Life

Should You Buy a House during a Recession?

At the beginning of this chapter, we asked whether it is a good idea to buy a house during a recession. Buying a house is the largest purchase you are likely to make in your lifetime, so you need to carefully consider a number of factors, including the price of the house relative to comparable houses in the neighborhood; whether house prices in the neighborhood have been rising or falling; and the location of the house relative to stores, work, and good schools. Also important is the interest rate you will have to pay on the mortgage loan you would need in order to buy the house. As we have seen in this chapter, during a recession, the Fed often takes actions to lower interest rates. So, mortgage rates are typically lower during a recession than at other times. You may want to take advantage of low interest rates to buy a house during a recession. But recessions are also times of rising unemployment, and you would not want to make a commitment to borrow a lot of money for 15 or more years if you were in danger of losing your job. We can conclude that if your job seems secure, buying a house during a recession may be a good idea.

Conclusion

Monetary policy is one way governments pursue goals for inflation, employment, and financial stability. The chair of the Federal Reserve may have a greater ability than the president of the United States to affect the U.S. economy. Congress and the president, however, also use their power over spending and taxes to try to stabilize the economy. In Chapter 16, we will discuss how *fiscal policy*—changes in government spending and taxes—affect the economy.

Visit MyEconLab for a news article and analysis related to the concepts of this chapter.

CHAPTER SUMMARY AND PROBLEMS

Key Terms

Contractionary monetary policy, p. 524

Expansionary monetary policy, p. 524

Federal funds rate, p. 521

Inflation targeting, p. 538

Monetary policy, p. 514

Taylor rule, p. 536

15.1 ## What Is Monetary Policy? pages 514–516

LEARNING OBJECTIVE: Define monetary policy and describe the Federal Reserve's monetary policy goals.

Summary

Monetary policy is the actions the Fed takes to manage the money supply and interest rates to achieve its macroeconomic policy goals. The Fed has four *monetary policy goals* that are intended to promote a well-functioning economy: price stability, high employment, stability of financial markets and institutions, and economic growth.

 MyEconLab Visit www.myeconlab.com to complete these exercises online and get instant feedback.

Review Questions

1.1 When Congress established the Federal Reserve in 1913, what was its main responsibility? When did Congress broaden the Fed's responsibilities?

1.2 What are the Fed's four monetary policy goals?

1.3 In what sense does the Fed have a "dual mandate"?

1.4 How can investment banks be subject to liquidity problems?

Problems and Applications

1.5 What is a bank panic? Why are policymakers more concerned about bank failures than failures of restaurants or clothing stores?

1.6 An article in the *Wall Street Journal* quoted a Federal Reserve economist as referring to "the Fed's existing dual mandate to achieve maximum sustainable employment in the context of price stability."

a. Does "maximum sustainable employment" mean a zero percent unemployment rate? Briefly explain.

b. Does "price stability" mean a zero percent inflation rate? Briefly explain.

Source: Pedro Nicolaci Da Costa, "Fed Should Make Bond Buys a Regular Policy Tool, a Boston Fed Paper Finds," *Wall Street Journal*, April 23, 2015.

1.7 A former Federal Reserve official argued that at the Fed, "the objectives of price stability and low long-term interest rates are essentially the same objective." Briefly explain his reasoning.

Source: William Poole, "Understanding the Fed," *Federal Reserve Bank of St. Louis Review*, Vol. 89, No. 1, January/February 2007, p. 4.

1.8 In the summer of 2015, many economists and policymakers expected that the Federal Reserve would increase its target for the federal funds rate by the end of the year. Some economists argued, though, that it would be better for the Fed to leave its target unchanged. At the time, the unemployment rate was 5.3 percent, close to full employment, but the inflation rate was below the Fed's target of 2 percent. What policy goal would the Fed promote if it did *not* increase its target for the federal funds rate? Briefly explain.

Source: Min Zeng, "Inflation Expectations Fall, Making Rate Hike 'More Difficult to Justify,'" *Wall Street Journal*, August 6, 2015.

15.2 ## The Money Market and the Fed's Choice of Monetary Policy Targets, pages 516–522

LEARNING OBJECTIVE: Describe the Federal Reserve's monetary policy targets and explain how expansionary and contractionary monetary policies affect the interest rate.

Summary

The Fed's *monetary policy targets* are economic variables that it can affect directly and that in turn affect variables such as real GDP and the price level that are closely related to the Fed's policy goals. The two main monetary policy targets are the money supply and the interest rate. The Fed has most often chosen to use the interest rate as its monetary policy target. The Federal Open Market Committee announces a target for the **federal funds rate** after each meeting. The federal funds rate is the interest rate banks charge each other for overnight loans. To lower the interest rate, the Fed increases the money supply. To raise the interest rate, the Fed decreases the money supply. In a graphical analysis of the money market, when the money supply curve shifts to the right, the result is a movement down the money demand curve and a new equilibrium at a lower interest rate. When the money supply curve shifts to the left, the result is a movement up the money demand curve and a new equilibrium at a higher interest rate.

 MyEconLab Visit www.myeconlab.com to complete these exercises online and get instant feedback.

Review Questions

2.1 What is a monetary policy target? Why does the Fed use policy targets?

2.2 What do economists mean by the *demand for money*? What is the advantage of holding money? What is the disadvantage? Why does an increase in the interest rate decrease the quantity of money demanded?

2.3 Draw a demand and supply graph showing equilibrium in the money market. Suppose the Fed wants to lower the equilibrium interest rate. Show on the graph how the Fed would accomplish this objective.

2.4 What is the federal funds rate? What role does it play in monetary policy?

Problems and Applications

2.5 In the following graph of the money market, what could cause the money supply curve to shift from MS_1 to MS_2? What could cause the money demand curve to shift from MD_1 to MD_2?

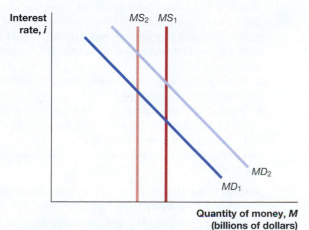

2.6 In 2015, one article in the *Wall Street Journal* discussed the possibility of "a September quarter-point increase in the Fed's range for overnight target rates," while another article noted, "the U.S. central bank's discount rate … has been set at 0.75% since February 2010."
a. What is the name of the Fed's "target rate"?
b. Briefly explain who borrows money and who lends money at this "target rate."
c. What is the discount rate, and how is it different from the "target rate"?

Sources: Justin Lahart, "Jobs Give Fed Green Light; Inflation Sets Speed Limit," *Wall Street Journal*, August 7, 2015; and Ben Leubsdorf, "Five Regional Fed Banks Asked to Raise Discount Rate," *Wall Street Journal*, July 14, 2015.

2.7 In response to problems in financial markets and a slowing economy, the Federal Open Market Committee (FOMC) began lowering its target for the federal funds rate from 5.25 percent in September 2007. Over the next year, the FOMC cut its federal funds rate target in a series of steps. Economist Price Fishback of the University of Arizona observed, "The Fed has been pouring more money into the banking system by cutting the target federal funds rate to 0 to 0.25 percent in December 2008." What is the relationship between the federal funds rate falling and the money supply increasing? How does lowering the target for the federal funds rate "pour money" into the banking system?

Source: Price Fishback, "The Financial Meltdown Now and Then," freakonomics.com, May 12, 2009.

2.8 An article in the *New York Times* in 1993 stated the following about Fed Chairman Alan Greenspan's decision to no longer announce targets for the money supply: "Since the late 1970's, the Federal Reserve has made many of its most important decisions by setting a specific target for growth in the money supply … and often adjusted interest rates to meet them." If the Fed would no longer have a specific target for the money supply, what was it targeting? Why did the Fed give up targeting the money supply?

Source: Steven Greenhouse, "Fed Abandons Policy Tied to Money Supply," *New York Times*, July 23, 1993.

15.3 ## Monetary Policy and Economic Activity, pages 522–530

LEARNING OBJECTIVE: Use aggregate demand and aggregate supply graphs to show the effects of monetary policy on real GDP and the price level.

Summary

An **expansionary monetary policy** lowers interest rates to increase consumption, investment, and net exports. This increase in aggregate demand increases real GDP and the price level. An expansionary monetary policy can help the Fed achieve its goal of high employment. A **contractionary monetary policy** raises interest rates to decrease consumption, investment, and net exports. This decrease in aggregate demand reduces both real GDP and the inflation rate below what they would be in the absence of policy. A contractionary monetary policy can help the Fed achieve its goal of price stability.

Review Questions

3.1 Briefly discuss how an increase in interest rates affects each component of aggregate demand.

3.2 If the Fed believes the economy is headed for a recession, what actions should it take? If the Fed believes the inflation rate is about to sharply increase, what actions should it take?

3.3 What is quantitative easing? Why have central banks used this policy?

Problems and Applications

3.4 A student says the following: "I understand why the Fed uses expansionary policy, but I don't understand why it would ever use contractionary policy. Why would the government ever want the economy to contract?" Briefly answer the student's question.

3.5 In explaining why monetary policy did not pull Japan out of a recession in the early 2000s, an official at the Bank of Japan was quoted as saying that despite "major increases in the money supply," the money "stay[ed] in banks." Explain what the official meant by saying that the money stayed in banks. Why would that be a problem? Where does the money go if an expansionary monetary policy is successful?

Source: James Brooke, "Critics Say Koizumi's Economic Medicine Is a Weak Tea," *New York Times*, February 27, 2002.

3.6 An article in the *Wall Street Journal* discussing the Federal Reserve's monetary policy included the following observation: "Fed officials have been signaling since last year that they expected to raise rates in 2015 … pushing up the value of the currency and contributing to the economic slowdown officials now confront."

a. What does "pushing up the value of the currency" mean?

b. Why would the Fed's increasing U.S. interest rates cause the value of the currency to increase?

c. Why would an increase in the value of the currency contribute to a slowdown in the growth of the U.S. economy?

Source: Jon Hilsenrath, "Fed's Rate Decisions Hang on Dollar, Growth Concerns," *Wall Street Journal*, April 22, 2015.

3.7 According to an article in the *Wall Street Journal*, "Brazil's economy grew just 2.3% in 2013, compared with 7.5% in 2010. The country also has struggled with persistently high inflation, which has forced its central bank to raise interest rates."

a. Why would the Brazilian central bank have been "forced" to raise interest rates because of rising inflation?

b. Could the increase in interest rates be connected to the slowing rate of economic growth? Briefly explain.

Source: Emese Glazer and Luciana Magalhaes, "Brazil's Debt-Laden Firms Try to Stay Afloat," *Wall Street Journal*, March 18, 2014.

3.8 William McChesney Martin, who was Federal Reserve chairman from 1951 to 1970, was once quoted as saying, "The role of the Federal Reserve is to remove the punchbowl just as the party gets going." What did he mean?

3.9 (Related to the Making the Connection on page 526) An article in the *Wall Street Journal* in 2015 reported that the interest rate on five-year German government bonds had become negative: "The negative yield means investors are effectively paying the German state for holding its debt." The article quoted an investment analyst as saying: "The negative yield is not scaring investors away."

a. What caused the interest rate on German government bonds to become negative?

b. Why are investors willing to buy bonds with a negative interest rate?

Source: Emese Bartha and Ben Edwards, "Germany Sells Five-Year Debt at Negative Yield for First Time on Record," *Wall Street Journal*, February 25, 2015.

3.10 (Related to the Making the Connection on page 526) An article in the *Wall Street Journal* notes that before the financial crisis of 2007–2009, the Fed "managed just one short-term interest rate and expected that to be enough to meet its goals for inflation and unemployment."

a. What short-term interest rate is the article referring to? How would the Fed expect controlling that one interest rate would allow it to meet its goals for inflation and unemployment?

b. The article also notes that after the financial crisis, "the Fed is working through a broader spectrum of interest rates." What does "a broader spectrum of interest rates" mean? How is the Fed able to affect a broader spectrum of interest rates?

Source: Jon Hilsenrath, "Easy-Money Era a Long Game for Fed," *Wall Street Journal*, March 17, 2013.

3.11 (Related to the Making the Connection on page 528) Each year, the president's Council of Economic Advisers prepares and sends to Congress *The Economic Report of the President*. The report published in February 2008 contained the following summary of the economic situation: "Economic growth is expected to continue in 2008. Most market forecasts suggest a slower pace in the first half of 2008, followed by strengthened growth in the second half of the year."

a. What in fact happened to economic growth during 2008?

b. What conclusion can you draw from your answer to part (a) with respect to economic forecasting and the formulation of economic policy?

Source: Executive Office of the President, *Economic Report of the President*, 2008, Washington, DC: USGPO, 2008, p. 17.

3.12 (Related to the Making the Connection on page 528) The following is from a Federal Reserve publication:

In practice, monetary policymakers do not have up-to-the-minute, reliable information about the state of the economy and prices. Information is limited because of lags in the publication of data. Also, policymakers have less-than-perfect understanding of the way the economy works, including the knowledge of when and to what extent policy actions will affect aggregate demand. The operation of the economy changes over time, and with it the response of the economy to policy measures. These limitations add to uncertainties in the policy process and make determining the appropriate setting of monetary policy … more difficult.

If the Fed itself admits that there are many obstacles in the way of effective monetary policy, why does it still engage in active monetary policy rather than use a monetary growth rule, as suggested by Milton Friedman and his followers?

Source: Board of Governors of the Federal Reserve System, *The Federal Reserve System: Purposes and Functions*, Washington, DC, 1994.

3.13 (Related to the Don't Let This Happen to You **on page 530)** Briefly explain whether you agree with the following statement: "The Fed has an easy job. Say it wants to increase real GDP by $200 billion. All it has to do is increase the money supply by that amount."

3.14 (Related to the Chapter Opener **on page 513)** An investment blog said about Fed Chair Janet Yellen, "She is arguably the world's most powerful woman, and perhaps the most powerful person in the world. Can you name anybody with more might?" Do you agree with this assessment? Briefly explain.

Source: Barbara Friedberg, "Fed Chief Janet Yellen: The Most Powerful Woman in the World," blog.personalcapital.com, September 17, 2014.

15.4 Monetary Policy in the Dynamic Aggregate Demand and Aggregate Supply Model, pages 530–535

LEARNING OBJECTIVE: Use the dynamic aggregate demand and aggregate supply model to analyze monetary policy.

Summary

We can use the *dynamic aggregate demand and aggregate supply model* introduced in Chapter 13 to look more closely at expansionary and contractionary monetary policies. The dynamic aggregate demand and aggregate supply model takes into account that (1) the economy experiences continuing inflation, with the price level rising every year, and (2) the economy experiences long-run growth, with the *LRAS* curve shifting to the right every year. In the dynamic model, an expansionary monetary policy tries to ensure that the aggregate demand curve will shift far enough to the right to bring about macroeconomic equilibrium with real GDP equal to potential GDP. A contractionary monetary policy attempts to offset movements in aggregate demand that would cause macroeconomic equilibrium to occur at a level of real GDP that is greater than potential GDP.

MyEconLab Visit **www.myeconlab.com** to complete these exercises online and get instant feedback.

Review Questions

4.1 What are the key differences between how we illustrate an expansionary monetary policy in the basic aggregate demand and aggregate supply model and in the dynamic aggregate demand and aggregate supply model?

4.2 What are the key differences between how we illustrate a contractionary monetary policy in the basic aggregate demand and aggregate supply model and in the dynamic aggregate demand and aggregate supply model?

Problems and Applications

4.3 Explain whether you agree with this argument:

> If the Fed actually ever carried out a contractionary monetary policy, the price level would fall. Because the price level has not fallen in the United States over an entire year since the 1930s, we can conclude that the Fed has not carried out a contractionary policy since the 1930s.

4.4 (Related to Solved Problem 15.4 **on page 533)** Use the graph to answer the following questions.

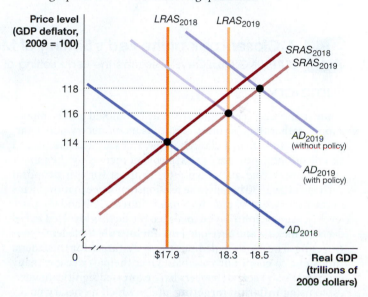

a. If the Fed does not take any policy action, what will be the level of real GDP and the price level in 2019?

b. If the Fed wants to keep real GDP at its potential level in 2019, should it use an expansionary policy or a contractionary policy? Should the trading desk be buying Treasury bills or selling them?

c. If the Fed takes no policy action, what will be the inflation rate in 2019? If the Fed uses monetary policy to keep real GDP at its potential level, what will be the inflation rate in 2019?

4.5 (Related to Solved Problem 15.4 **on page 533)** The hypothetical information in the following table shows what the situation will be in 2019 if the Fed does *not* use monetary policy.

Year	Potential GDP	Real GDP	Price Level
2018	$17.9 trillion	$17.9 trillion	110.0
2019	18.3 trillion	18.2 trillion	112.0

a. If the Fed wants to keep real GDP at its potential level in 2019, should it use an expansionary policy or a contractionary policy? Should the trading desk be buying T-bills or selling them?

b. If the Fed's policy is successful in keeping real GDP at its potential level in 2019, state whether each of the following will be higher, lower, or the same as it would have been if the Fed had taken no action:
   i.   Real GDP
   ii. Potential GDP
   iii. The inflation rate
   iv. The unemployment rate

c. Draw an aggregate demand and aggregate supply graph to illustrate the effects of the Fed's policy. Be sure that your graph contains *LRAS* curves for 2018 and 2019; *SRAS* curves for 2018 and 2019; *AD* curves for 2018 and 2019, with and without monetary policy action; and equilibrium real GDP and the price level in 2019, with and without policy.

4.6 According to an article in the *Wall Street Journal*, the Reserve Bank of India lowered its key policy interest rate in 2015, "citing weakness in parts of the economy as well as favorable inflation figures." The article notes that the central bank lists constraints to further interest rate cuts, including the "risk that inflation could flare again."

a. Use the dynamic aggregate demand and aggregate supply model to show where the Reserve Bank of India expected real GDP to be in 2015 without the interest rate cut, and indicate what the central bank is trying to achieve with the interest rate cut. Assume, for simplicity, that real GDP in India in 2014 equaled potential GDP.

b. Is there a connection between India experiencing slow growth in output at the same time that it experienced a lower inflation rate? Briefly explain.

Source: Gabriele Parussini, "India Cuts Key Interest Rate for Second Time This Year," *Wall Street Journal*, March 4, 2015.

15.5 | ## A Closer Look at the Fed's Setting of Monetary Policy Targets, pages 535–540
LEARNING OBJECTIVE: Describe the Fed's setting of monetary policy targets.

Summary

Some economists have argued that the Fed should use the money supply, rather than an interest rate, as its monetary policy target. Milton Friedman and other monetarists argued that the Fed should adopt a monetary growth rule of increasing the money supply every year at a fixed rate. Support for this proposal declined after 1980 because the relationship between movements in the money supply and movements in real GDP and the price level weakened. John Taylor analyzed the factors involved in Fed decision making and developed the **Taylor rule** for federal funds targeting. The Taylor rule links the Fed's target for the federal funds rate to economic variables. Over the past decade, many economists and central bankers have expressed significant interest in using **inflation targeting**, under which monetary policy is conducted to commit the central bank to achieving a publicly announced inflation target. In 2012, the Fed joined a number of foreign central banks in adopting inflation targeting. The Fed's performance in the 1980s, 1990s, and early 2000s generally received high marks from economists.

MyEconLab   Visit **www.myeconlab.com** to complete these exercises online and get instant feedback.

Review Questions

5.1 What is a *monetary rule*, as opposed to a *monetary policy*? What monetary rule would Milton Friedman have liked the Fed to follow? Why has support for a monetary rule of the kind Friedman advocated declined since 1980?

5.2 For more than 20 years, the Fed has used the federal funds rate as its monetary policy target. Why doesn't the Fed target the money supply at the same time?

5.3 What is the Taylor rule? What is its purpose?

Problems and Applications

5.4 In an interview, Paul Volcker, chairman of the Federal Reserve's Board of Governors from 1979 to 1987, was asked about the Fed's use of monetary policy to reduce the rate of inflation. Volcker replied:

> The Federal Reserve had been attempting to deal with ... inflation for some time. ... By the time I became chairman ... we adopted an approach of ... saying, We'll take the emphasis off of interest rates and put the emphasis on the growth in the money supply, which is at the root cause of inflation ... we will stop the money supply from increasing as rapidly as it was ... and interest rates went up a lot. ... We said ... we'll take whatever consequences that means for the interest rate because that will enable us to get inflation under control.

Explain why the Fed, while Paul Volcker was chairman, did not target both the growth of the money supply and interest rates.

Source: "Paul Volcker Interview," http://www.pbs.org/fmc/interviews/volcker.htm.

5.5 **(Related to Solved Problem 15.5 on page 537)** Suppose that the equilibrium real federal funds rate is 2 percent and the target rate of inflation is 2 percent. Use the following information and the Taylor rule to calculate the federal funds rate target:

   Current inflation rate = 4 percent
   Potential GDP = 17.0 trillion
   Real GDP = 17.17 trillion

5.6 **(Related to Solved Problem 15.5 on page 537)** In discussing the Taylor rule, John Taylor wrote, "I realize that there are differences of opinion about what is the best rule to guide policy and that some at the Fed (including Janet Yellen) now prefer a rule with a higher coefficient [on the output gap]."

a. If Fed policy were guided by a Taylor rule with a coefficient of 1, rather than 0.5, on the output gap, would the federal funds rate be higher or lower during a recession? Briefly explain.

b. Why might economists and policymakers disagree over the best rule to guide monetary policy?

Source: John Taylor, "Cross-Checking 'Checking in on the Taylor Rule,'" www.economicsone.com, July 16, 2013.

5.7 **(Related to** Solved Problem 15.5 **on page 537)** Two economists at the Federal Reserve Bank of Cleveland note that "estimates of potential GDP are very fluid, [which] suggests there is considerable error in our current measure." They conclude that "this lack of precision should be recognized when policy recommendations are made using a Taylor-type rule." Briefly explain their reasoning.

Source: Charles Carlstrom and Timothy Stehulak, "Mutable Economic Laws and Calculating Unemployment and Output Gaps—An Application to Taylor Rules," Federal Reserve Bank of Cleveland, June 6, 2015.

5.8 While serving as the president of the Federal Reserve Bank of St. Louis, William Poole stated, "Although my own preference is for zero inflation properly managed, I believe that a central bank consensus on some other numerical goal of reasonably low inflation is more important than the exact number." Briefly explain why the economy might benefit from an explicit inflation target even if the target chosen is not a zero rate of inflation.

Source: William Poole, "Understanding the Fed," *Federal Reserve Bank of St. Louis Review*, Vol. 89, No. 1, January/February 2007, p. 4.

5.9 **(Related to the** Making the Connection **on page 539)** October 2015 was the forty-second consecutive month that the rate of inflation as measured by the personal consumption expenditures (PCE) price index was below the Federal Reserve's target of 2 percent.

a. Briefly explain why using the consumer price index (CPI) might yield a rate of inflation different from that found using the PCE price index.

b. Explain how the choice of the price index the Federal Reserve uses to measure inflation can affect monetary policy.

Source: Zeppo Mitchell, "Inflation Misses Fed 2% Target for 38th Straight Month," *Wall Street Journal*, August 3, 2015.

15.6	**Fed Policies during the 2007–2009 Recession, pages 541–546**
	LEARNING OBJECTIVE: Describe the policies the Federal Reserve used during the 2007–2009 recession.

Summary

A housing bubble that began to deflate in 2006 helped cause the recession of 2007–2009 and an accompanying financial crisis. In response, the Federal Reserve instituted a variety of policy actions. In a series of steps, it cut the target for the federal funds rate from 5.25 percent in September 2007 to effectively zero in December 2008. The decline in the housing market caused wider problems in the financial system, as defaults on home mortgages rose and the value of mortgage-backed securities declined. The Fed and the U.S. Treasury Department implemented a series of new policies to provide liquidity and restore confidence. The Fed expanded the types of firms eligible for discount loans and began lending directly to corporations by purchasing commercial paper. Under the *Troubled Asset Relief Program*, the Treasury provided financial support to banks and other financial firms in exchange for part ownership. The Treasury also moved to have the federal government take control of Fannie Mae and Freddie Mac, government-sponsored firms that play a key role in the mortgage market. The failure of the investment bank Lehman Brothers in September 2008 led to a deepening of the financial crisis and provided the motivation for some of the new policies. Ultimately, the new policies stabilized the financial system, but their long-term effects remain the subject of debate.

 MyEconLab Visit **www.myeconlab.com** to complete these exercises online and get instant feedback.

Review Questions

6.1 What is a mortgage? What were the important developments in the mortgage market during the years after 1970?

6.2 Beginning in 2008, the Federal Reserve and the U.S. Treasury Department responded to the financial crisis by intervening in financial markets in unprecedented ways. Briefly summarize the actions of the Fed and the Treasury.

Problems and Applications

6.3 A newspaper article in the fall of 2007 stated, "The luxury-home builder Hovnanian Enterprises reported its fourth consecutive quarterly loss on Thursday, citing continuing problems of credit availability and high inventory." Why was Hovnanian suffering losses? What does the article mean by "credit availability"? How would problems of credit availability affect a homebuilder such as Hovnanian Enterprises?

Source: "New Loss for Home Builder," Associated Press, September 7, 2007.

6.4 An article in a Federal Reserve publication observes that "20 or 30 years ago, local financial institutions were the only option for some borrowers. Today, borrowers have access to national (and even international) sources of mortgage finance." What caused this change in the sources of mortgage finance? What would be the likely consequence of this change for the interest rates borrowers have to pay on mortgages? Briefly explain.

Source: Daniel J. McDonald and Daniel L. Thornton, "A Primer on the Mortgage Market and Mortgage Finance," *Federal Reserve Bank of St. Louis Review*, January/February 2008, pp. 31–45.

6.5 The Federal Reserve releases transcripts of its Federal Open Market Committee (FOMC) meetings only after a five-year lag in order to preserve the confidentiality of the discussions. When the transcripts of the FOMC's 2008 meetings were released, one member of the Board of Governors was quoted as saying in an April 2008 meeting, "I think it is very possible that we will look back and say, particularly after the Bear Stearns episode, that we have turned the corner in terms of the financial disruption." Did this member's analysis turn out to be correct? Briefly explain why his prediction may have seemed reasonable at the time.

Source: Jon Hilsenrath, "New View into Fed's Response to Crisis," *Wall Street Journal*, February 21, 2014.

6.6 In late 2012, the U.S. Treasury sold the last of the stock it had purchased in the insurance company AIG. The Treasury earned a profit on the $22.7 billion it had invested in AIG in 2008. An article in *Wall Street Journal* noted, "This step in AIG's turnaround, which essentially closes the book on one of the most controversial bailouts of the financial crisis, seemed nearly unattainable in 2008, when the insurer's imminent collapse sent shockwaves through the global economy."
a. Why did the federal government bail out AIG?
b. Why was the government bailout controversial?
c. Does the fact the federal government earned a profit on its investment in AIG mean that economists and policymakers who opposed the bailout were necessarily wrong? Briefly explain.

Source: Jeffrey Sparshott and Erik Holm, "End of a Bailout: U.S. Sells Last AIG Shares," *Wall Street Journal*, December 11, 2012.

6.7 Recall that *securitization* is the process of turning a loan, such as a mortgage, into a bond that can be bought and sold in secondary markets. An article in the *Economist* notes:

> That securitization caused more subprime mortgages to be written is not in doubt. By offering access to a much deeper pool of capital, securitization helped to bring down the cost of mortgages and made home-ownership more affordable for borrowers with poor credit histories.

What is a "subprime mortgage"? What is a "deeper pool of capital"? Why would securitization give mortgage borrowers access to a deeper pool of capital? Would a subprime borrower be likely to pay a higher or a lower interest rate than a borrower with a better credit history? Under what circumstances might a lender prefer to loan money to a borrower with a poor credit history rather than to a borrower with a good credit history? Briefly explain.

Source: "Ruptured Credit," *Economist*, May 15, 2008.

6.8 In 2015, Richard Fuld, the last CEO of Lehman Brothers, gave a talk in which, according to an article in the *Wall Street Journal*, "He outlined what he called the 'perfect storm' of events that led to the financial crisis, saying 'it all started with the government' and policies that subsidized cheap loans for people to buy homes in order to help them chase the American dream."
a. Briefly outline the events that led to the financial crisis. Do you agree with Fuld that the events constitute a "perfect storm"—that is, a series of unfortunate events happening at the same time in a way that would have been difficult to anticipate?
b. Which government policies mentioned in the chapter could be said to be subsidizing cheap loans? What does Fuld mean by saying that these policies were intended to help people "chase the American dream"?

Source: Maureen Farrell, "Lehman's Fuld Says It Wasn't His Fault," *Wall Street Journal*, May 28, 2015.

6.9 (Related to the Making the Connection on page 544) Suppose you buy a house for $150,000. One year later, the market price of the house has risen to $165,000. What is the return on your investment in the house if you made a down payment of 20 percent and took out a mortgage loan for the other 80 percent? What if you made a down payment of 5 percent and borrowed the other 95 percent? Be sure to show your calculations in your answer.

Real-Time Data Exercises

D15.1 (Following news of FOMC meetings) Go to www.federalreserve.gov, the Web site for the Federal Reserve Board of Governors, and read the most recent Federal Open Market Committee (FOMC) press release. At the Web site, select "Monetary Policy" at the top of the screen and then select "Federal Open Market Committee" on the far left of the screen. Select "Meeting calendars and information." Finally, scroll down and select Statement for the date of the most recent FOMC meeting. Answer the following questions on the basis of the FOMC press release.
a. Did the FOMC change the target for the federal funds rate? If so, what was the change?
b. On balance, in its statement, does the FOMC appear to be more concerned about slow economic growth or high inflation?
c. Did the FOMC change the interest rate paid on bank reserves?
d. Did the Fed announce any other monetary policy actions?

D15.2 (Movements in the federal funds rate relative to the target) Go to the Web site of the Federal Reserve Bank of St. Louis (FRED) (research.stlouisfed.org/fred2) and download and graph the data series for the effective federal funds rate (DFF), the upper limit of the target range for the federal funds rate (DFEDTARU), and the lower limit for the target range (DFEDTARL). Plot on the same graph values for all three data series from December 16, 2008, to the most recent day available. Over this period, has the Fed been able to keep the effective federal funds rate within the target range? Briefly explain.

D15.3 (Comparing different measures of the inflation rate) Go to the Web site of the Federal Reserve Bank of St. Louis (FRED) (research.stlouisfed.org/fred2/) and find the most recent values and values from the same month one year before for the following three measures of the price level: (1) the Consumer Price Index for All Urban Consumers: All Items (CPIAUCSL), (2) the Personal Consumption Expenditures: Chain-type Price Index (PCEPI), and (3) the

Personal Consumption Expenditures excluding food and energy (chain-type price index) (DPCCRG3A086NBEA).

a. Using these data, calculate the inflation rate over this year as measured by each of the three price indexes.

b. Which of the three measures of inflation was highest during this year? Which measure was lowest? Why do the measures of inflation differ?

CHAPTER

16

Fiscal Policy

Chapter Outline and Learning Objectives

Does Government Spending Create Jobs?

The Golden Gate Bridge is an international symbol of San Francisco. The bridge spans the entrance to San Francisco Bay from the Pacific Ocean. Construction of the bridge began in 1933, and the bridge was open to traffic in 1937. Doyle Drive is a 1.6-mile stretch of U.S. Highway 101 and the main approach to the bridge from the San Francisco side. Doyle Drive was in desperate need of reconstruction, but for many years the city of San Francisco and the state of California had failed to provide the funding. In early 2009, President Barack Obama and Congress enacted the American Recovery and Reinvestment Act (ARRA, often referred to as the "stimulus bill") in an attempt to increase aggregate demand during the recession of 2007–2009. The ARRA is an example of *discretionary fiscal policy* aimed at increasing real GDP and employment. Some of the funds from the act were allocated to the Doyle Drive project. San Francisco Mayor Gavin Newsom welcomed the news: "This project is shovel ready and a signature example of how the federal stimulus can close the funding gap, stimulate the economy, improve transportation, and create jobs in San Francisco."

The Doyle Drive project was designed by the Flatiron Corporation, and construction was carried out by Kiewit Construction, headquartered in Omaha, Nebraska. Kiewit hired hundreds of workers for the project, which was completed in July 2015. The project to rebuild Doyle Drive is an example of increased government spending resulting in increased employment. Or is it? A majority of economists agree that a temporary increase in government spending can lead to increased employment during a recession. But some economists argue that fiscal policy actions like ARRA shift employment from one group of workers to another but do not increase total employment. The argument over the effect of government spending on employment continued years after the end of the recession of 2007–2009.

When the federal government spends more than it collects in taxes, the result is a federal budget deficit. Following the recession, the federal government ran the largest peacetime deficits in history. During 2011 and 2012, Congress and President Obama enacted cuts in federal spending, increases in taxes, and limits on future spending increases to try to reduce the budget deficit. In 2015, Congress and the president somewhat loosened the limits on federal spending while continuing to debate whether additional spending was necessary to help the economy finally make it back to potential GDP.

In this chapter, we will examine discretionary fiscal policy, the federal budget deficit, and the debate over their effects.

Sources: David R. Baker, "Presidio Parkway, the New Doyle Drive, Is Now Open," sfgate.com, July 13, 2015; Metropolitan Transit Commission, "Speaker Pelosi and Mayor Newsom Announce Doyle Drive Project Is Shovel Ready," February 28, 2009; Jonathan Weisman, "Republicans Aim to Hamper Obama's Policies with Spending Bills," *New York Times*, July 7, 2015; and http://goldengatebridge.org.

Economics in Your Life

What Would You Do with an Extra $500?

Suppose that the federal government announces that it will immediately mail you, and everyone else in the economy, a $500 tax rebate. In addition, you expect that in future years, your taxes will also decrease by $500. How will you respond to this increase in your disposable income? What effect will this tax rebate likely have on equilibrium real GDP in the short run? As you read this chapter, try to answer these questions. You can check your answers against those we provide on **page 589** at the end of this chapter.

I n Chapter 15, we discussed how the Federal Reserve uses monetary policy to pursue macroeconomic policy goals, including price stability and high employment. In this chapter, we will explore how the government uses *fiscal policy*, which involves changes in taxes and government purchases, to achieve similar policy goals. As we have seen, in the short run, the price level and the levels of real GDP and total employment in the economy depend on aggregate demand and short-run aggregate supply. In the long run, the levels of real GDP and employment depend on long-run aggregate supply. The government can affect the levels of both aggregate demand and aggregate supply through fiscal policy. We will discuss how Congress and the president decide which fiscal policy actions to take to achieve their goals. We will also discuss the debates among economists and policymakers over the effectiveness of fiscal policy.

16.1 What Is Fiscal Policy?

LEARNING OBJECTIVE: Define fiscal policy.

Since the end of World War II, the federal government has been committed under the Employment Act of 1946 to intervening in the economy "to promote maximum employment, production, and purchasing power." As we saw in Chapter 15, the Federal Reserve's Federal Open Market Committee meets eight times per year to decide whether to change monetary policy. Less frequently, Congress and the president also make changes in taxes and government purchases to achieve macroeconomic policy goals, such as high employment, price stability, and high rates of economic growth. Changes in federal taxes and purchases that are intended to achieve macroeconomic policy goals are called **fiscal policy**.

Fiscal policy Changes in federal taxes and purchases that are intended to achieve macroeconomic policy goals.

What Fiscal Policy Is and What It Isn't

In the United States, federal, state, and local governments all have responsibility for taxing and spending. Economists typically use the term *fiscal policy* to refer only to the actions of the federal government. State and local governments sometimes change their taxing and spending policies to aid their local economies, but these are not fiscal policy actions because they are not intended to affect the national economy. The federal government makes many decisions about taxes and spending, but not all of these decisions are fiscal policy actions because they are not intended to achieve macroeconomic policy goals. For example, a decision to cut the taxes of people who buy hybrid cars is an environmental policy action, not a fiscal policy action. Similarly, the spending increases to fund the war on terrorism and the wars in Iraq and Afghanistan were part of defense and homeland security policy, not fiscal policy. MyEconLab Concept Check

Automatic Stabilizers versus Discretionary Fiscal Policy

There is an important distinction between *automatic stabilizers* and *discretionary fiscal policy*. Government spending and taxes that automatically increase or decrease along with the business cycle are called **automatic stabilizers**. The word *automatic* in this case refers to the fact that changes in these types of spending and taxes happen without actions by the government. For example, when the economy is expanding and employment is increasing, government spending on unemployment insurance payments to workers who have lost their jobs will automatically decrease. During a recession, as employment declines, this type of spending will automatically increase. Similarly, when the economy is expanding and incomes are rising, the amount the government collects in taxes will increase as people pay additional taxes on their higher incomes. When the economy is in a recession, the amount the government collects in taxes will fall.

Automatic stabilizers Government spending and taxes that automatically increase or decrease along with the business cycle.

With discretionary fiscal policy, the government takes actions to change spending or taxes. The tax cuts and spending increases in the American Recovery and Reinvestment Act (ARRA) that Congress and the president enacted in 2009, as mentioned in the chapter opener, are examples of discretionary fiscal policy actions. MyEconLab Concept Check

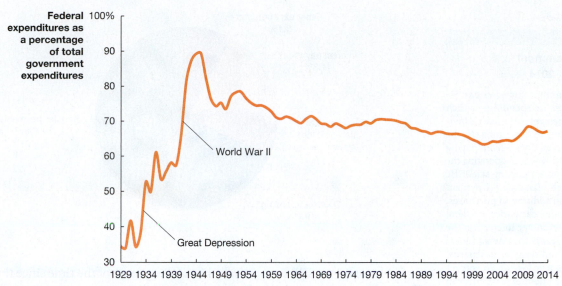

MyEconLab Real-time data

Figure 16.1   The Federal Government's Share of Total Government Expenditures, 1929–2014

Until the Great Depression of the 1930s, the majority of government spending in the United States occurred at the state and local levels.

Since World War II, the federal government's share of total government expenditures has been between two-thirds and three-quarters.

Source: U.S. Bureau of Economic Analysis.

An Overview of Government Spending and Taxes

To provide a context for discussing fiscal policy, it is important to understand the big picture of government taxing and spending. Before the Great Depression of the 1930s, the majority of government spending in the United States took place at the state and local levels. As Figure 16.1 shows, the size of the federal government expanded significantly during the crisis of the Great Depression. Since World War II, the federal government's share of total government expenditures has been between two-thirds and three-quarters.

Economists often measure government spending relative to the size of the economy by calculating government spending as a percentage of GDP. Remember that there is a difference between federal government *purchases* and federal government *expenditures*. When the federal government purchases an aircraft carrier or the services of an FBI agent, it receives a good or service in return. Federal government expenditures include purchases plus federal government spending—such as Social Security payments— that does not involve purchases. As Figure 16.2 shows, federal government *purchases*

MyEconLab Real-time data

Figure 16.2

Federal Purchases and Federal Expenditures as a Percentage of GDP, 1950–2014

As a fraction of GDP, the federal government's *purchases* of goods and services have been declining since the Korean War in the early 1950s. Total *expenditures* by the federal government—including transfer payments—as a fraction of GDP slowly rose from 1950 through the early 1990s and fell from 1992 to 2001, before rising again. The recession of 2007–2009 and the slow recovery that followed led to a surge in federal government expenditures, causing them to rise to their highest level as a percentage of GDP since the end of World War II in 1945.

Source: U.S. Bureau of Economic Analysis.

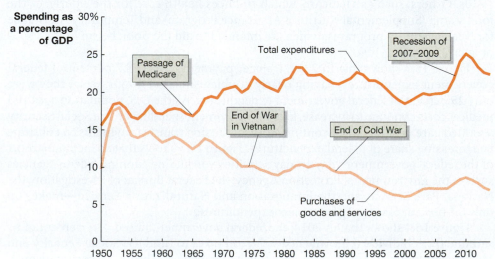

MyEconLab Real-time data

Figure 16.3

Federal Government Expenditures, 2014

Federal government *purchases* can be divided into defense spending—which makes up 19.2 percent of the federal budget—and spending on everything else the federal government does—from paying the salaries of FBI agents, to operating the national parks, to supporting scientific research—which makes up 8.1 percent of the budget. In addition to purchases, there are three other categories of federal government *expenditures*: interest on the national debt, grants to state and local governments, and transfer payments. Transfer payments rose from 25 percent of federal government expenditures in the 1960s to 48.7 percent in 2014.

Source: U.S. Bureau of Economic Analysis.

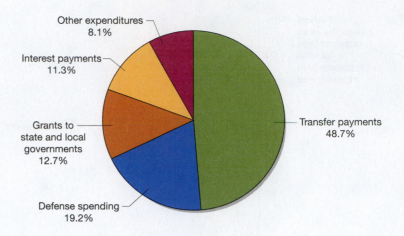

as a percentage of GDP have actually been falling most of the time since the end of the Korean War in the early 1950s. Total federal *expenditures* as a percentage of GDP rose from 1950 to the early 1990s and then fell from 1992 to 2000, before rising again. The decline in expenditures between 1992 and 2001 was partly the result of the end of the Cold War between the Soviet Union and the United States, which allowed for a substantial reduction in defense spending. Real federal government spending on national defense declined by almost 25 percent between 1990 and 1998, before rising by more than 60 percent between 1998 and 2010 in response to the war on terrorism and the wars in Iraq and Afghanistan and then declining more than 15 percent by 2014 as those wars wound down. The recession of 2007–2009 and the slow recovery that followed led to a surge in federal government expenditures, which in 2011 rose to their highest level as a percentage of GDP since the end of World War II in 1945 before declining again in the following years as a result of limits on spending enacted by Congress and the president.

In addition to purchases, there are three other categories of federal government expenditures: *interest on the national debt, grants to state and local governments,* and *transfer payments*. Interest on the national debt represents payments to holders of the bonds the federal government has issued to borrow money. Grants to state and local governments are payments made by the federal government to support government activity at the state and local levels. For example, to help reduce crime, Congress implemented a program of grants to local governments to hire more police officers. The largest and fastest-growing category of federal expenditures is transfer payments. Some of these programs, such as Social Security and unemployment insurance, began in the 1930s. Others, such as Medicare, which finances health care for the elderly, or the food stamp (Supplemental Nutrition Assistance Program) and Temporary Assistance for Needy Families programs, which are intended to aid the poor, began in the 1960s or later.

Figure 16.3 shows that in 2014, transfer payments were 48.7 percent of federal government expenditures, having nearly doubled since the 1960s, when they were only 25 percent of federal government expenditures. As the U.S. population ages and medical costs continue to increase, federal government spending on the Social Security and Medicare programs will continue to rise, causing transfer payments to consume an increasing share of federal expenditures. Figure 16.3 shows that spending on most of the federal government's day-to-day activities—including running federal agencies such as the Environmental Protection Agency, the Federal Bureau of Investigation, the National Park Service, and the Immigration and Naturalization Service—makes up only 8.1 percent of federal government expenditures.

Figure 16.4 shows that in 2014, the federal government raised 42.8 percent of its revenue from individual income taxes. Payroll taxes to fund the Social Security and Medicare programs raised 35.1 percent of federal revenues. The tax on corporate profits raised 12.8 percent of federal revenues. The remaining 9.3 percent of federal revenues were raised from excise taxes on certain products, such as cigarettes and gasoline,

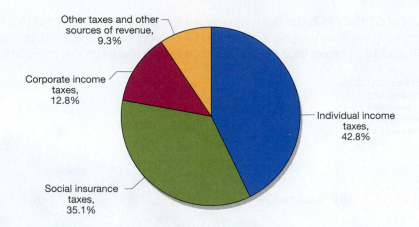

MyEconLab Real-time data

Figure 16.4

Federal Government Revenue, 2014

In 2014, individual income taxes raised 42.8 percent of the federal government's revenues. Corporate income taxes raised 12.8 percent of revenue. Payroll taxes to fund the Social Security and Medicare programs raised 35.1 percent of revenue. The remaining 9.3 percent of revenues were raised from excise taxes, tariffs on imports, and other sources.

Source: U.S. Bureau of Economic Analysis.

from tariffs on goods imported from other countries, from payments by the Federal Reserve from its profits on its security holdings, and from other sources, such as payments by companies that cut timber on federal lands.   MyEconLab Concept Check

Making the Connection
MyEconLab Video

Is Spending on Social Security and Medicare a Fiscal Time Bomb?

The federal government established Social Security in 1935 to provide payments to retired workers. The program began as a "pay-as-you-go" system, meaning that payments to current retirees were made with taxes collected from current workers. In the early years of the program, many workers were paying into the system, and there were relatively few retirees. For example, in 1940, more than 35 million workers were paying into the system, and only 222,000 people were receiving benefits—a ratio of more than 150 workers to each retiree. In those early years, most retirees received far more in benefits than they had paid in taxes. The first beneficiary was a legal secretary named Ida May Fuller. She worked for three years after the program began and paid total taxes of only $24.75. During her retirement, she collected $22,888.92 in benefits.

The Social Security and Medicare programs have been very successful in reducing poverty among older Americans, but in recent years, the ability of the federal government to finance current promises has been called into doubt. After World War II, the United States experienced a "baby boom," as birthrates rose and remained high through the early 1960s. Falling birthrates after 1965 have caused long-run problems for the Social Security system because the number of workers per retiree has continually declined. Currently, there are only 2.8 workers per retiree, and that ratio could decline to 2 workers per retiree by 2035. Congress has attempted to deal with this problem by gradually raising the age to receive full benefits from 65 to 67 and by increasing payroll taxes. Social Security and Medicare are financed from a payroll tax on individuals' wages and self-employment income. Workers and firms are each liable for half the tax. In 1940, the payroll tax rate was 2 percent; in 2015, it was 15.3 percent. Beginning in 2013, individuals earning more than $200,000 in either wages or self-employment income have paid two additional Medicare taxes: an additional 0.9 percent tax on their wages and an additional 3.8 percent tax on their investment income.

The federal government established the Medicare program in 1965 to provide health care coverage to people age 65 and over. The long-term financial situation for Medicare is an even greater cause for concern than is Social Security. As Americans live longer and as new—and expensive—medical procedures are developed, the projected expenditures under the Medicare program will eventually far outstrip projected tax revenues. The federal government also faces increasing expenditures under the Medicaid program, which is administered by state governments and provides health care coverage to low-income people. In 2015, federal spending on Social Security, Medicare, and Medicaid equaled 10.1 percent of GDP. Spending on these three programs was less than

3 percent of GDP in 1962. The Congressional Budget Office (CBO) forecasts that federal spending on these three programs will rise to 14.2 percent of GDP in 2040, 16.2 percent by 2060, and 19.8 percent by 2090. The following graph illustrates these forecasts.

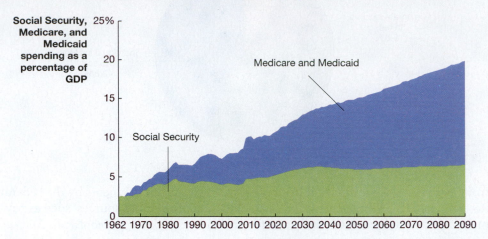

Note: The area labeled "Medicare and Medicaid" also includes federal spending on the Children's Health Insurance Program (CHIP) and federal subsidies to health care exchanges.

Over the past 40 years, the federal government has spent an average of about 21.5 percent of GDP on *all programs* combined—from buying aircraft carriers to paying the salaries of FBI agents to making Social Security and Medicare payments. So, if current trends continue, the federal government will eventually be spending, as a fraction of GDP, nearly as much on these three programs as it currently does on all programs combined.

The Board of Trustees of the Social Security Administration forecasts that through 2090, the gap between the benefits projected to be paid under the Social Security and Medicare programs and projected tax revenues is a staggering $49 *trillion,* or more than two and half times the value of GDP in 2015. If current projections are accurate, policymakers are faced with the choice of significantly restraining spending on these programs, greatly increasing taxes on households and firms, or implementing some combination of spending restraints and tax increases. The alternatives are all unpleasant. A report from the CBO concluded: "Even if taxation reached levels that were unprecedented in the United States, current spending policies could become financially unsustainable."

A lively political debate has taken place over the future of the Social Security and Medicare programs. Some policymakers have proposed increasing taxes to fund future benefit payments. The tax increases needed, however, could be as much as 50 percent higher than current rates, and tax increases of that magnitude could discourage work effort, entrepreneurship, and investment, thereby slowing economic growth. There have also been proposals to slow the rate of growth of future benefits, while guaranteeing benefits to current recipients. While this strategy would avoid the need to raise taxes significantly, it would also require younger workers to save more for their retirements. Some economists and policymakers have argued for slower benefit growth for higher-income workers while leaving future benefits unchanged for lower-income workers. Whatever changes are ultimately made in the Medicare and Social Security programs, the outcome of this policy debate will have important effects on the futures of today's college students.

Sources: Congressional Budget Office, "Supplemental Data for CBO's 2015 Long-Term Budget Outlook," June 2015; Congressional Budget Office, "Baseline Projections of Mandatory Outlays," January 2015; Board of Trustees, Federal Old-Age and Survivors Insurance and Federal Disability Insurance Trust Funds, "The 2015 Annual Report of the Board of Trustees of the Federal Old-Age and Survivors Insurance and Disability Insurance Trust Funds," July 22, 2015; and the Social Security Administration Web site (www.ssa.gov).

MyEconLab Study Plan   **Your Turn:** Test your understanding by doing related problem 1.7 on page 590 at the end of this chapter.

16.2 The Effects of Fiscal Policy on Real GDP and the Price Level

LEARNING OBJECTIVE: Explain how fiscal policy affects aggregate demand and how the government can use fiscal policy to stabilize the economy.

The federal government uses macroeconomic policies to offset the effects of the business cycle on the economy. We saw in Chapter 15 that the Federal Reserve carries out monetary policy through changes in interest rates and the money supply. Congress and the president carry out fiscal policy through changes in government purchases and taxes. Because changes in government purchases and taxes lead to changes in aggregate demand, they can affect the level of real GDP, employment, and the price level. When the economy is in a recession, *increases* in government purchases or *decreases* in taxes will increase aggregate demand. As we saw in Chapter 13, the inflation rate may increase when real GDP is beyond potential GDP. Decreases in government purchases or increase in taxes can slow the growth of aggregate demand and reduce the inflation rate.

Expansionary and Contractionary Fiscal Policy

Expansionary fiscal policy involves increasing government purchases or decreasing taxes. An increase in government purchases will increase aggregate demand directly because government purchases are a component of aggregate demand. A cut in taxes has an indirect effect on aggregate demand. Remember that the income households have available to spend after they have paid their taxes is called *disposable income* (see Chapter 8). Cutting the individual income tax will increase household disposable income and consumption spending. Cutting taxes on business income can increase aggregate demand by increasing investment spending.

Figure 16.5 shows the results of an expansionary fiscal policy, using the basic aggregate demand and aggregate supply model. In this model, there is no economic

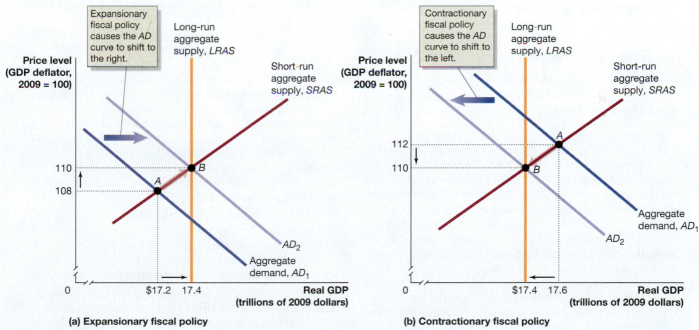

(a) Expansionary fiscal policy

(b) Contractionary fiscal policy

MyEconLab Animation

Figure 16.5 **Fiscal Policy**

In panel (a), short-run equilibrium is at point A, with real GDP of $17.2 trillion and a price level of 108. Real GDP is below potential GDP, so the economy is in a recession. An expansionary fiscal policy will cause aggregate demand to shift to the right, from AD_1 to AD_2, increasing real GDP from $17.2 trillion to $17.4 trillion and the price level from 108 to 110 (point B).

In panel (b), the economy begins at point A, with real GDP at $17.6 trillion and the price level at 112. Because real GDP is greater than potential GDP, the economy will experience rising wages and prices. A contractionary fiscal policy will cause aggregate demand to shift to the left, from AD_1 to AD_2, decreasing real GDP from $17.6 trillion to $17.4 trillion and the price level from 112 to 110 (point B).

growth, so the long-run aggregate supply (*LRAS*) curve does not shift. Notice that this figure is very similar to Figure 15.7 on page 523, which shows the effects of an expansionary monetary policy. The goal of both expansionary monetary policy and expansionary fiscal policy is to increase aggregate demand relative to what it would have been without the policy.

In panel (a) of Figure 16.5, we assume that short-run equilibrium occurs at point *A*, where the aggregate demand (AD_1) curve intersects the short-run aggregate supply (*SRAS*) curve. Real GDP is below potential GDP, so the economy is in a recession, with some firms operating below normal capacity and some workers having been laid off. To bring real GDP back to potential GDP, Congress and the president increase government purchases or cut taxes, which will shift the aggregate demand curve to the right, from AD_1 to AD_2. Real GDP increases from $17.2 trillion to potential GDP of $17.4 trillion, and the price level rises from 108 to 110 (point *B*). The policy has successfully returned real GDP to its potential level. Rising production will lead to increasing employment, reducing the unemployment rate.

Contractionary fiscal policy involves decreasing government purchases or increasing taxes. Policymakers use contractionary fiscal policy to reduce increases in aggregate demand that seem likely to lead to inflation. In panel (b) of Figure 16.5, short-run equilibrium occurs at point *A*, with real GDP of $17.6 trillion, which is above potential GDP of $17.4 trillion. With some firms producing beyond their normal capacity and the unemployment rate very low, wages and prices will be increasing. To bring real GDP back to potential GDP, Congress and the president decrease government purchases or increase taxes, which will shift the aggregate demand curve to the left, from AD_1 to AD_2. Real GDP falls from $17.6 trillion to $17.4 trillion, and the price level falls from 112 to 110 (point *B*).

We can conclude that Congress and the president can attempt to stabilize the economy by using fiscal policy to affect the price level and the level of real GDP. Of course, in practice it is extremely difficult for Congress and the president to use fiscal policy to eliminate the effects of the business cycle and keep real GDP always equal to potential GDP.

MyEconLab Concept Check

Don't Let This Happen to You

Don't Confuse Fiscal Policy and Monetary Policy

If you keep in mind the definitions of *money*, *income*, and *spending*, the difference between monetary policy and fiscal policy will be clearer. Students often make these two related mistakes: (1) They think of monetary policy as the Federal Reserve fighting recessions by increasing the money supply so people will have more money to spend; and (2) they think of fiscal policy as Congress and the president fighting recessions by spending more money. In this view, the only difference between fiscal policy and monetary policy is the source of the money.

To understand what's wrong with the descriptions of fiscal policy and monetary policy just given, first remember that the problem during a recession is not that there is too little *money*—currency plus checking account deposits—but too little *spending*. There may be too little spending for a number of reasons. For example, households may cut back on their spending on cars and houses because they are pessimistic about the future. Firms may reduce their spending because they have lowered their estimates of the future profitability of new machinery and factories. Or major trading partners of the United States—such as Japan and Canada—may be suffering from recessions,

which cause households and firms in those countries to reduce their spending on U.S. products.

The purpose of expansionary monetary policy is to lower interest rates, which in turn increases aggregate demand. When interest rates fall, households and firms are willing to borrow more to buy cars, houses, and factories. The purpose of expansionary fiscal policy is to increase aggregate demand by:

1. Having the government directly increase its own purchases, or
2. Cutting income taxes to increase household disposable income and, therefore, consumption spending, or
3. Cutting business taxes to increase investment spending

Just as increasing or decreasing the money supply does not have a direct effect on government spending or taxes, increasing or decreasing government spending or taxes does not have a direct effect on the money supply. Fiscal policy and monetary policy have the same goals, but they attempt to reach those goals in different ways.

MyEconLab Study Plan

Your Turn: Test your understanding by doing related problem 2.6 on page 591 at the end of this chapter.

Problem	Type of Policy Required	Actions by Congress and the President	Result
Recession	Expansionary	Increase government purchases or cut taxes	Real GDP and the price level rise.
Rising inflation	Contractionary	Decrease government purchases or raise taxes	Real GDP and the price level fall.

Table 16.1

Countercyclical Fiscal Policy

A Summary of How Fiscal Policy Affects Aggregate Demand

Table 16.1 summarizes how fiscal policy affects aggregate demand. Just as we did with monetary policy, we must add a very important qualification to this summary of fiscal policy: The table isolates the effect of fiscal policy *by holding constant monetary policy and all other factors affecting the variables involved.* In other words, we are again invoking the *ceteris paribus* condition we discussed in Chapter 3. This point is important because, for example, in the actual economy, a contractionary fiscal policy does not cause the price level to fall. A contractionary fiscal policy causes the price level *to rise by less than it would have without the policy.*

MyEconLab Concept Check   MyEconLab Study Plan

16.3 Fiscal Policy in the Dynamic Aggregate Demand and Aggregate Supply Model*

LEARNING OBJECTIVE: Use the dynamic aggregate demand and aggregate supply model to analyze fiscal policy.

The overview of fiscal policy we just finished contains a key idea: Congress and the president can use fiscal policy to affect aggregate demand, thereby changing the price level and the level of real GDP. The discussion of expansionary and contractionary fiscal policy illustrated by Figure 16.5 on page 563 is simplified, however, because it ignores two important facts about the economy: (1) The economy experiences continuing inflation, with the price level rising every year, and (2) the economy experiences long-run growth, with the *LRAS* curve shifting to the right every year. In Chapter 13, we developed a *dynamic aggregate demand and aggregate supply model* that took these two facts into account. In this section, we use the dynamic model to gain a more complete understanding of fiscal policy.

To briefly review the dynamic model, recall that over time, potential GDP increases, which we show by shifting the *LRAS* curve to the right. The factors that cause the *LRAS* curve to shift also cause firms to supply more goods and services at any given price level in the short run, which we show by shifting the *SRAS* curve to the right. Finally, during most years, the aggregate demand curve also shifts to the right, indicating that aggregate expenditure is higher at every price level.

Figure 16.6 shows the results of an expansionary fiscal policy using the dynamic aggregate demand and aggregate supply model. Notice that this figure is very similar to Figure 15.9 on page 531, which showed the effects of an expansionary monetary policy. The goal of both expansionary monetary policy and expansionary fiscal policy is to increase aggregate demand relative to what it would have been without the policy.

In the hypothetical situation shown in Figure 16.6, equilibrium is initially at point A, with real GDP equal to potential GDP of $17.0 trillion and the price level equal to 110. In the second year, *LRAS* increases to $17.4 trillion, but aggregate demand increases only from AD_1 to $AD_{2(\text{without policy})}$, which is not enough to keep real GDP equal to potential GDP. Let's assume that the Fed does not react to the situation with an expansionary monetary policy. In that case, short-run equilibrium will occur at point B, with real GDP of $17.3 trillion and a price level of 113. The $100 billion gap between real GDP and potential GDP means that some firms are operating at less than their full capacity. Incomes and profits will be falling, firms will begin to lay off workers, and the unemployment rate will increase.

*This section may be omitted without loss of continuity.

MyEconLab Animation

Figure 16.6

An Expansionary Fiscal Policy in the Dynamic Model

Equilibrium is initially at point *A*, with real GDP equal to potential GDP of \$17.0 trillion and the price level equal to 110. Without an expansionary policy, aggregate demand will shift from AD_1 to $AD_{2(\text{without policy})}$, which is not enough to keep real GDP equal to potential GDP because long-run aggregate supply has shifted from $LRAS_1$ to $LRAS_2$. The new short-run equilibrium is at point *B*, with real GDP of \$17.3 trillion and a price level of 113. Increasing government purchases or cutting taxes will shift aggregate demand to $AD_{2(\text{with policy})}$. Equilibrium will be at point *C*, with real GDP of \$17.4 trillion, which is its potential level, and a price level of 115. The price level is higher than it would have been without an expansionary fiscal policy.

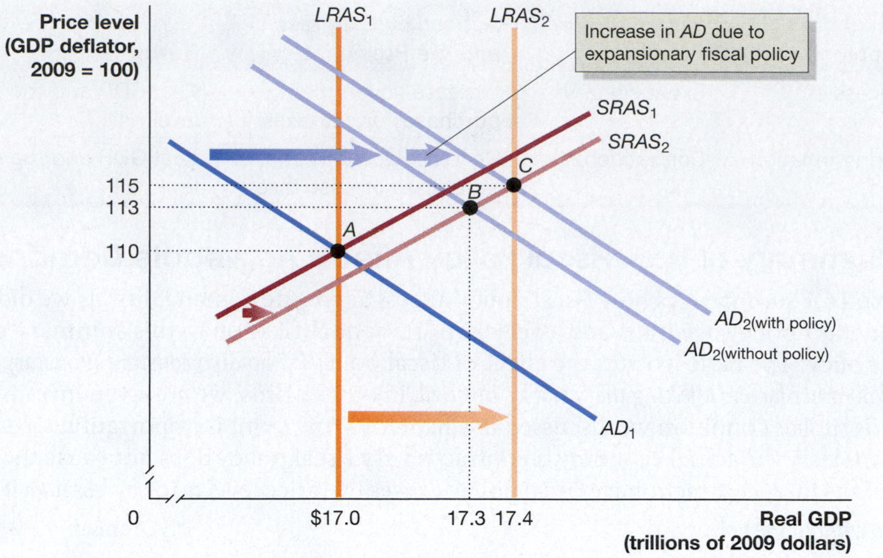

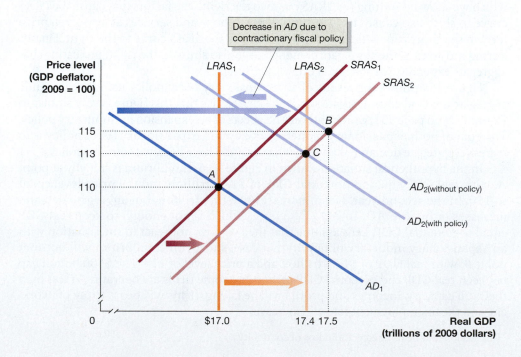

Increasing government purchases or cutting taxes can shift aggregate demand to $AD_{2(\text{with policy})}$. Equilibrium will be at point *C*, with real GDP of \$17.4 trillion, which is its potential level, and a price level of 115. The price level is higher than it would have been without an expansionary fiscal policy.

Contractionary fiscal policy involves decreasing government purchases or increasing taxes. Policymakers use contractionary fiscal policy to reduce increases in aggregate demand that seem likely to lead to inflation. In Figure 16.7, equilibrium is initially at point *A*, with real GDP equal to potential GDP of \$17.0 trillion and the price level equal to 110. Once again, *LRAS* increases to \$17.4 trillion in the second year. In this scenario, the shift in aggregate demand to $AD_{2(\text{without policy})}$ results in a short-run macroeconomic equilibrium at point *B*, with real GDP of \$17.5 trillion, which is greater than potential GDP. If we assume that the Fed does not respond to the situation with a contractionary monetary policy, the economy will experience a rising inflation rate. Decreasing government purchases or increasing taxes can keep real GDP from moving beyond its potential level. The result, shown in Figure 16.7, is that in the new equilibrium at point *C*, the inflation rate is 2.7 percent rather than 4.5 percent. MyEconLab Concept Check

MyEconLab Study Plan

MyEconLab Animation

Figure 16.7

A Contractionary Fiscal Policy in the Dynamic Model

Equilibrium is initially at point *A*, with real GDP equal to potential GDP of \$17.0 trillion and the price level equal to 110. Without a contractionary policy, aggregate demand will shift from AD_1 to $AD_{2(\text{without policy})}$, which results in a short-run equilibrium at point *B*, with real GDP of \$17.5 trillion, which is greater than potential GDP, and a price level of 115. Decreasing government purchases or increasing taxes can shift aggregate demand to $AD_{2(\text{with policy})}$. Equilibrium will be at point *C*, with real GDP of \$17.4 trillion, which is its potential level, and a price level of 113. The inflation rate will be 2.7 percent, as opposed to the 4.5 percent it would have been without the contractionary fiscal policy.

16.4 The Government Purchases and Tax Multipliers

LEARNING OBJECTIVE: Explain how the government purchases and tax multipliers work.

We saw in the chapter opener that Congress and the president authorized spending to rebuild Doyle Drive in San Francisco in order to increase aggregate demand during the recession of 2007–2009. Suppose that Congress and the president decide to spend $100 billion on rebuilding Doyle Drive and similar projects. (The total increase in federal spending under the American Recovery and Reinvestment Act (ARRA) of 2009 was actually about $500 *billion*, including the $83 million in ARRA funds contributed to the project to reconstruct Doyle Drive.) How much will equilibrium real GDP increase as a result of this increase in government purchases? We might expect real GDP to increase by more than $100 billion because the initial increase in aggregate demand should lead to additional increases in income and spending. For example, to reconstruct Doyle Drive, the California Department of Transportation hired Kiewit, a private construction firm. Kiewit and its subcontractors, in turn, hired workers for the project. The firms that carried out the many other projects authorized under the ARRA also hired new workers. Workers who were formerly unemployed are likely to increase their spending on cars, furniture, appliances, and other products. Sellers of these products will increase their production and hire more workers, and so on. At each step, real GDP and income will rise, thereby increasing consumption spending and aggregate demand.

Economists refer to the initial increase in government purchases as *autonomous* because it is a result of a decision by the government and is not directly caused by changes in the level of real GDP. The increases in consumption spending that result from the initial autonomous increase in government purchases are *induced* because they are caused by the initial increase in autonomous spending. Economists call the series of induced increases in consumption spending that results from an initial increase in autonomous expenditures the **multiplier effect**.

Figure 16.8 illustrates how an increase in government purchases affects the aggregate demand curve. The initial increase causes the aggregate demand curve to shift to the right because total spending in the economy is now higher at every price level. The shift to the right from AD_1 to the dashed AD curve represents the effect of the initial increase of $100 billion in government purchases. Because this initial increase in government purchases raises incomes and leads to further increases in consumption spending, the aggregate demand curve will ultimately shift from AD_1 all the way to AD_2.

To better understand the multiplier effect, let's start with a simplified analysis in which we assume that the price level is constant. In other words, initially we will ignore

Multiplier effect The series of induced increases in consumption spending that results from an initial increase in autonomous expenditures.

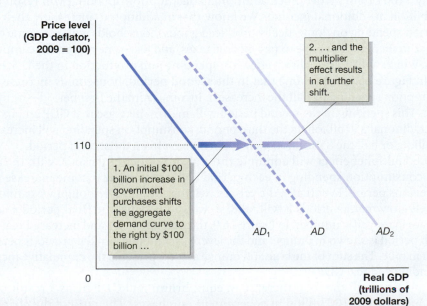

MyEconLab Animation

Figure 16.8

The Multiplier Effect and Aggregate Demand

An initial increase in government purchases of $100 billion causes the aggregate demand curve to shift to the right, from AD_1 to the dashed AD curve, and represents the effect of the initial increase of $100 billion in government purchases. Because this initial increase raises incomes and leads to further increases in consumption spending, the aggregate demand curve will ultimately shift further to the right, to AD_2.

Period	Additional Spending This Period	Cumulative Increase in Spending and Real GDP
1	$100 billion in government purchases	$100 billion
2	$50 billion in consumption spending	$150 billion
3	$25 billion in consumption spending	$175 billion
4	$12.5 billion in consumption spending	$187.5 billion
.	.	.
.	.	.
.	.	.
n	0	$200 billion

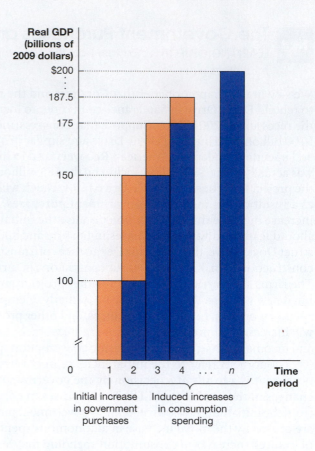

MyEconLab Animation

Figure 16.9 **The Multiplier Effect of an Increase in Government Purchases**

Following an initial increase in government purchases, spending and real GDP increase over a number of periods due to the multiplier effect. The new spending and increased real GDP in each period is shown in orange, and the level of spending from the previous period is shown in blue. The sum of the blue and orange areas represents the cumulative increase in spending and real GDP. In total, equilibrium real GDP will increase by $200 billion as a result of an initial increase of $100 billion in government purchases.

the effect of an upward-sloping *SRAS* curve. Figure 16.9 shows how spending and real GDP increase over a number of periods, beginning with the initial increase in government purchases in the first period, which raises real GDP and total income in the economy by $100 billion. How much additional consumption spending will result from $100 billion in additional income? We know that in addition to increasing their consumption spending on domestically produced goods, households will save some of the increase in income, use some to pay income taxes, and use some to purchase imported goods, which will have no direct effect on spending and production in the U.S. economy. In Figure 16.9, we assume that in the second period, households increase their consumption spending by half the increase in income from the first period—or by $50 billion. This spending in the second period will, in turn, increase real GDP and income by an additional $50 billion. In the third period, consumption spending will increase by $25 billion, or half the $50 billion increase in income from the second period.

The multiplier effect will continue through a number of periods, with the additional consumption spending in each period being half of the income increase from the previous period. Eventually, the process will be complete, although we cannot say precisely how many periods it will take, so we simply label the final period *n* rather than give it a specific number. In Figure 16.9, the new spending and increased real GDP in each period is shown in orange, and the level of spending from the previous period is shown in blue. The sum of the blue and orange areas represents the cumulative increase in spending and real GDP.

How large will the total increase in equilibrium real GDP be as a result of the initial increase of $100 billion in government purchases? The ratio of the change in equilibrium real GDP to the initial change in government purchases is called the *government purchases multiplier*:

$$\text{Government purchases multiplier} = \frac{\text{Change in equilibrium real GDP}}{\text{Change in government purchases}}.$$

If, for example, the government purchases multiplier has a value of 2, an increase in government purchases of $100 billion should increase equilibrium real GDP by $2 \times \$100$ billion = $200 billion. We show this result in Figure 16.9 by having the cumulative increase in real GDP equal $200 billion.

Tax cuts also have a multiplier effect because they increase the disposable income of households. When household disposable income rises, so will consumption spending. These increases in consumption spending will set off further increases in real GDP and income, just as increases in government purchases do. Suppose we consider a change in taxes of a specific amount—say, a tax cut of $100 billion—with the tax *rate* remaining unchanged. The expression for this tax multiplier is:

$$\text{Tax multiplier} = \frac{\text{Change in equilibrium real GDP}}{\text{Change in taxes}}.$$

The tax multiplier is a negative number because changes in taxes and changes in real GDP move in opposite directions: An increase in taxes reduces disposable income, consumption, and real GDP, and a decrease in taxes raises disposable income, consumption, and real GDP. For example, if the tax multiplier is -1.6, a $100 billion *cut* in taxes will increase real GDP by $-1.6 \times (-\$100$ billion) = $160 billion. We would expect the tax multiplier to be smaller in absolute value than the government purchases multiplier. To see why, think about the difference between a $100 billion increase in government purchases and a $100 billion decrease in taxes. The whole of the $100 billion in government purchases results in an increase in aggregate demand. But households will save rather than spend some portion of a $100 billion decrease in taxes, and they will spend some portion on imported goods. The fraction of the tax cut that households save or spend on imports will not increase aggregate demand. Therefore, the first period of the multiplier process will involve a smaller increase in aggregate demand than occurs when there is an increase in government purchases, and the total increase in equilibrium real GDP will be smaller.

The Effect of Changes in the Tax Rate

A change in the tax *rate* has a more complicated effect on equilibrium real GDP than does a tax cut of a fixed amount. To begin with, the value of the tax rate affects the size of the multiplier effect. The higher the tax rate, the smaller the multiplier effect. To see why, think about the size of the additional spending increases that take place in each period following an increase in government purchases. The higher the tax rate, the smaller the amount of any increase in income that households have available to spend, which reduces the size of the multiplier effect. So, a cut in the tax rate affects equilibrium real GDP through two channels: (1) A cut in the tax rate increases the disposable income of households, which leads them to increase their consumption spending, and (2) a cut in the tax rate increases the size of the multiplier effect.   MyEconLab Concept Check

Taking into Account the Effects of Aggregate Supply

To this point, as we discussed the multiplier effect, we assumed that the price level was constant. We know, though, that because the *SRAS* curve is upward sloping, when the *AD* curve shifts to the right, the price level will rise. As a result of the rise in the price level, equilibrium real GDP will not increase by the full amount that the multiplier effect indicates. Figure 16.10 illustrates how an upward-sloping *SRAS* curve affects the size of the multiplier. To keep the graph relatively simple, we assume that the *SRAS* and *LRAS* curves do not shift. Short-run equilibrium is initially at point *A*, with real GDP

Figure 16.10

The Multiplier Effect and Aggregate Supply

Short-run equilibrium is initially at point A. An increase in government purchases causes the aggregate demand curve to shift to the right, from AD_1 to the dashed AD curve. The multiplier effect results in the aggregate demand curve shifting further to the right, to AD_2 (point B). Because of the upward-sloping supply curve, the shift in aggregate demand results in a higher price level. In the new equilibrium at point C, both real GDP and the price level have increased. The increase in real GDP is less than that indicated by the multiplier effect with a constant price level.

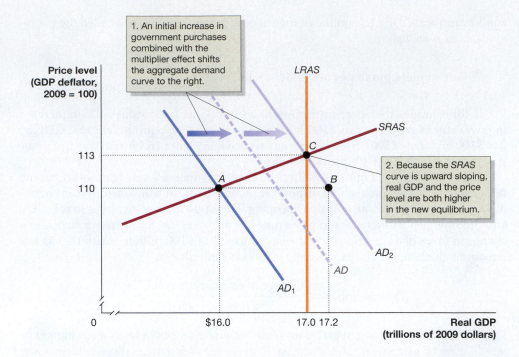

1. An initial increase in government purchases combined with the multiplier effect shifts the aggregate demand curve to the right.

2. Because the SRAS curve is upward sloping, real GDP and the price level are both higher in the new equilibrium.

below its potential level. An increase in government purchases shifts the aggregate demand curve from AD_1 to the dashed AD curve. Just as in Figure 16.8, the multiplier effect causes a further shift in the aggregate demand curve to AD_2. If the price level remained constant, real GDP would increase from $16.0 trillion at point A to $17.2 trillion at point B. However, because the SRAS curve is upward sloping, the price level rises from 110 to 113, reducing the total quantity of goods and services demanded in the economy. The new equilibrium occurs at point C, with real GDP having risen to $17.0 trillion, or by $200 billion less than if the price level had remained unchanged. We can conclude that the actual change in real GDP resulting from an increase in government purchases or a cut in taxes will be less than that indicated by the simple multiplier effect with a constant price level.   MyEconLab Concept Check

The Multipliers Work in Both Directions

Increases in government purchases and cuts in taxes have a positive multiplier effect on equilibrium real GDP. Decreases in government purchases and increases in taxes also have a multiplier effect on equilibrium real GDP, but in this case, the effect is negative. An increase in taxes will reduce household disposable income and consumption. As households buy fewer cars, furniture, refrigerators, and other goods, the firms that sell these goods will cut back their production and begin laying off workers. Falling incomes will lead to further reductions in consumption. A reduction in government spending on defense would set off a similar process of decreases in real GDP and income. The reduction would affect defense contractors first because they sell directly to the government, and then it would spread to other firms.

We look more closely at the government purchases multiplier and the tax multiplier in the appendix to this chapter.   MyEconLab Concept Check

Solved Problem 16.4

Fiscal Policy Multipliers

Briefly explain whether you agree with the following statement: "Real GDP is currently $17.2 trillion, and potential GDP is $17.4 trillion. If Congress and the president would increase government purchases by $200 billion or cut taxes by $200 billion, the economy could be brought to equilibrium at potential GDP."

Solving the Problem

Step 1: **Review the chapter material.** This problem is about the multiplier process, so you may want to review the section "The Government Purchases and Tax Multipliers," which begins on page 567.

Step 2: **Explain how the necessary increase in purchases or cut in taxes is less than $200 billion because of the multiplier effect.** The statement is incorrect because it does not consider the multiplier effect. Because of the multiplier effect, an increase in government purchases or a decrease in taxes of less than $200 billion is necessary to increase equilibrium real GDP by $200 billion. For instance, assume that the government purchases multiplier is 2 and the tax multiplier is −1.6. We can then calculate the necessary increase in government purchases as follows:

$$\text{Government puchases multipiler} = \frac{\text{Change in equilibrium real GDP}}{\text{Change in government purchases}}$$

$$2 = \frac{\$200 \text{ billon}}{\text{Change in government purchases}}$$

$$\text{Change in government purchases} = \frac{\$200 \text{ billon}}{2} = \$100 \text{ billon}.$$

And the necessary change in taxes:

$$\text{Tax multipler} = \frac{\text{Change in equilibrium real GDP}}{\text{Change in taxes}}$$

$$-1.6 = \frac{\$200 \text{ billon}}{\text{Change in taxes}}$$

$$\text{Change in taxes} = \frac{\$200 \text{ billion}}{-1.6} = -\$125 \text{ billion}.$$

Your Turn: For more practice, do related problems 4.6 and 4.7 on page 593 at the end of this chapter.  MyEconLab Study Plan

---

16.5 The Limits to Using Fiscal Policy to Stabilize the Economy

LEARNING OBJECTIVE: Discuss the difficulties that can arise in implementing fiscal policy.

Poorly timed fiscal policy, like poorly timed monetary policy, can do more harm than good. As we discussed in Chapter 15, it takes time for policymakers to collect statistics and identify changes in the economy. If the government decides to increase spending or cut taxes to fight a recession that is about to end, the effect may be to increase the inflation rate. Similarly, cutting spending or raising taxes to slow down an economy that has actually already moved into a recession can increase the length and depth of the recession.

Getting the timing right can be more difficult with fiscal policy than with monetary policy for two main reasons. Control over monetary policy is concentrated in the hands of the Federal Open Market Committee, which can change monetary policy at any of its meetings. By contrast, the president and a majority of the 535 members of Congress have to agree on changes in fiscal policy. The delays caused by the legislative process can be very long. For example, in 1962, President John F. Kennedy concluded that the U.S. economy was operating below potential GDP and proposed a tax cut to stimulate aggregate demand. Congress eventually agreed to the tax cut—but not until 1964. The events of 2001 and 2009 show, though, that it is sometimes possible to authorize changes in fiscal policy relatively quickly. When George W. Bush came into office in January 2001, the economy was on the verge of a recession, and he immediately proposed a tax cut. Congress passed the tax cut, and the president signed it into law in early June 2001. Similarly, Barack Obama proposed a stimulus package as soon as he came into office in January 2009, and Congress had passed the proposal by February.

Even after a change in fiscal policy has been approved, it takes time to implement it. Suppose Congress and the president agree to increase aggregate demand by spending $30 billion more on constructing subway systems in several cities. It will probably take at least several months to prepare detailed plans for the construction. Local governments will then ask for bids from private construction companies. Once the winning bidders have been selected, they will usually need several months to begin the project. Only then will significant amounts of spending actually take place. This delay may push the spending beyond the end of the recession that the spending was intended to fight. Delays of this type are less of a concern during long and severe recessions, such as that of 2007–2009.

Making the Connection

MyEconLab Video

As this stock trader knows, the financial crisis made the recession of 2007–2009 more severe and long-lasting than many other recessions.

Why Was the Recession of 2007–2009 So Severe?

Even some economists who are normally skeptical of fiscal policy believed that the severity of the 2007–2009 recession required Congress and the president to increase spending and cut taxes to increase aggregate demand. As we saw in Chapters 14 and 15, the recession was accompanied by a financial crisis. The U.S. economy had not experienced a significant financial crisis since the Great Depression of the 1930s. Both the Great Depression and the recession of 2007–2009 were severe. Do recessions accompanied by financial crises tend to be more severe than recessions that do not involve financial crises?

In an attempt to answer this question, Carmen Reinhart and Kenneth Rogoff of Harvard University have gathered data on recessions and financial crises in a number of countries. The table at the top of the next page shows the average change in key economic variables during the period following a financial crisis for a number of countries, including the United States during the Great Depression and European and Asian countries in the post–World War II era. The table shows that for these countries, on average, the recessions following financial crises were quite severe:

- Unemployment rates increased by 7 percentage points—for example, from 5 percent to 12 percent—and continued increasing for nearly five years after a crisis had begun.

- Real GDP per capita also declined sharply, and the average length of a recession following a financial crisis has been nearly two years.

- Adjusted for inflation, stock prices declined by more than half, and housing prices declined by more than one-third.

- Government debt soared by 86 percent. The increased government debt was partly the result of increased government spending, including spending to bail out failed financial institutions. But most of the increased debt was due to government budget deficits resulting from sharp declines in tax revenues as wages and profits fell during the recession. (We discuss government budget deficits and government debt in Section 16.6.)

Economic Variable	Average Change	Average Duration of Change	Number of Countries
Unemployment rate	+7 percentage points	4.8 years	14
Real GDP per capita	−9.3%	1.9 years	14
Real stock prices	−55.9%	3.4 years	22
Real house prices	−35.5%	6 years	21
Real government debt	+86%	3 years	13

The following table shows some key indicators for the 2007–2009 U.S. recession compared with other U.S. recessions of the post–World War II period:

	Duration	Decline in Real GDP	Peak Unemployment Rate
Average for postwar recessions	10.4 months	−1.7%	7.6%
Recession of 2007–2009	18 months	−4.2%	10.0%

Consistent with Reinhart and Rogoff's findings that recessions following financial panics tend to be unusually severe, the 2007–2009 recession was the worst in the United States since the Great Depression of the 1930s. The recession lasted nearly twice as long as the average of earlier postwar recessions, GDP declined by more than twice the average, and the peak unemployment rate was about one-third higher than the average.

While some economists argue that better monetary or fiscal policies might have shortened the recession and made it less severe, most economists agree that the financial panic plays a key role in explaining the severity of the 2007–2009 recession.

Note: In the second table, the duration of recessions is based on National Bureau of Economic Research business cycle dates, the decline in real GDP is measured as the simple percentage change from the quarter of the cyclical peak to the quarter of the cyclical trough, and the peak unemployment rate is the highest unemployment rate in any month following the cyclical peak.

Sources: The first table is adapted from data in Carmen M. Reinhart and Kenneth S. Rogoff, *This Time Is Different: Eight Centuries of Financial Folly*, Princeton, NJ: Princeton University Press, 2009, Figures 14.1–14.5; and the second table uses data from the U.S. Bureau of Economic Analysis and National Bureau of Economic Research.

Your Turn: Test your understanding by doing related problem 5.6 on page 594 at the end of this chapter.

MyEconLab Study Plan

Does Government Spending Reduce Private Spending?

In addition to the timing issue, using increases in government purchases to increase aggregate demand presents another potential problem. We have been assuming that when the federal government increases its purchases by $30 billion, the multiplier effect will cause the increase in aggregate demand to be greater than $30 billion. However, the size of the multiplier effect may be limited if the increase in government purchases causes one of the nongovernment, or private, components of aggregate expenditures—consumption, investment, or net exports—to fall. A decline in private expenditures as a result of an increase in government purchases is called **crowding out**.

MyEconLab Concept Check

Crowding out A decline in private expenditures as a result of an increase in government purchases.

Crowding Out in the Short Run

Consider the case of a temporary increase in government purchases. Suppose the federal government decides to fight a recession by spending $30 billion more this year on subway construction. When the $30 billion has been spent, the program will end, and government purchases will drop back to their previous level. As the spending takes place, income and real GDP will increase. These increases in income and real GDP will cause households and firms to increase their demand for currency and checking

Figure 16.11

An Expansionary Fiscal Policy Increases Interest Rates

An increase in government purchases will increase the demand for money from Money demand₁ to Money demand₂ as real GDP and income rise. With the supply of money constant, at $950 billion, the result is an increase in the equilibrium interest rate from 3 percent to 5 percent, which crowds out some consumption, investment, and net exports.

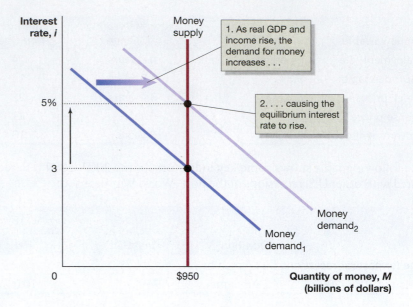

1. As real GDP and income rise, the demand for money increases . . .

2. . . . causing the equilibrium interest rate to rise.

account balances to accommodate the increased buying and selling. Figure 16.11 shows the result, using the money market graph introduced in Chapter 15.

At higher levels of real GDP and income, households and firms demand more money at every interest rate. When the demand for money increases, the equilibrium interest rate will rise. Higher interest rates will result in a decline in each component of private expenditures. Consumption spending and investment spending will decline because households will borrow less to buy houses, cars, furniture, and appliances, and firms will borrow less to buy factories, warehouses, and machine tools. Net exports will also decline because higher interest rates in the United States will attract foreign investors. German, Japanese, and Canadian investors will want to exchange the currencies of their countries for U.S. dollars to invest in U.S. Treasury bills and other U.S. financial assets. This increased demand for U.S. dollars will cause an increase in the exchange rate between the dollar and other currencies. When the dollar increases in value, the prices of U.S. products in foreign countries rise—causing a reduction in U.S. exports—and the prices of foreign products in the United States fall—causing an increase in U.S. imports. Falling exports and rising imports mean that net exports are falling.

The greater the sensitivity of consumption, investment, and net exports to changes in interest rates, the more crowding out will occur. In a deep recession, many firms may be pessimistic about the future and have so much excess capacity that investment spending will fall to very low levels and will be unlikely to fall much further, even if interest rates rise. In this case, crowding out is unlikely to be a problem. If the economy is close to potential GDP, however, and firms are optimistic about the future, an increase in interest rates may result in a significant decline in investment spending.

Figure 16.12 shows that crowding out may reduce the effectiveness of an expansionary fiscal policy. Short-run equilibrium is initially at point A, with real GDP at $17.2 trillion. Real GDP is below potential GDP, so the economy is in a recession. Suppose that Congress and the president decide to increase government purchases to increase real GDP to potential GDP. In the absence of crowding out, the increase in government purchases will shift the aggregate demand curve to $AD_{2(\text{no crowding out})}$, and equilibrium will be at point B, with real GDP equal to potential GDP of $17.4 trillion. But the higher interest rate resulting from the increased government purchases will reduce consumption, investment, and net exports, causing the aggregate demand curve to shift back to $AD_{2(\text{crowding out})}$. The result is a new short-run equilibrium at point C, with real GDP of $17.3 trillion, which is $100 billion short of potential GDP. (Note that the price level increase shown in Figure 16.10 on page 570 also contributes to reducing the effect of an increase in government purchases on equilibrium real GDP.) MyEconLab Concept Check

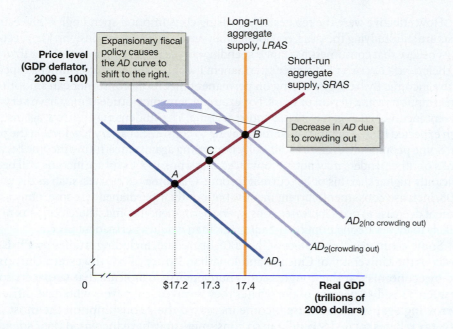

MyEconLab Animation

Figure 16.12

The Effect of Crowding Out in the Short Run

Equilibrium is initially at point *A*, with real GDP of $17.2 trillion below potential GDP, so the economy is in a recession. In the absence of crowding out, an increase in government purchases will shift aggregate demand to $AD_{2(\text{no crowding out})}$, and equilibrium is at potential GDP of $17.4 trillion (point *B*). But the higher interest rate resulting from the increased government purchases will reduce consumption, investment, and net exports, causing aggregate demand to shift to $AD_{2(\text{no crowding out})}$. The result is a new short-run equilibrium at point *C*, with real GDP of $17.3 trillion, which is $100 billion short of potential GDP.

Crowding Out in the Long Run

Most economists agree that in the short run, an increase in government purchases results in partial, but not complete, crowding out. What is the long-run effect of a *permanent* increase in government spending? In this case, most economists agree that the result is complete crowding out. In the long run, the decline in investment, consumption, and net exports exactly offsets the increase in government purchases, and aggregate demand remains unchanged. Recall that *in the long run, real GDP returns to potential GDP* (see Chapter 13). Suppose that real GDP currently equals potential GDP and that government spending is 35 percent of GDP. In that case, private expenditures—the sum of consumption, investment, and net exports—will make up the other 65 percent of GDP. If government spending is increased permanently to 37 percent of GDP, in the long run, private expenditures must fall to 63 percent of GDP. There has been complete crowding out: Private expenditures have fallen by the same amount that government spending has increased. If government spending is taking a larger share of GDP, then private spending must take a smaller share.

An expansionary fiscal policy does not have to cause complete crowding out in the short run. If real GDP is below potential GDP, it is possible for both government purchases and private expenditures to increase. But in the long run, any permanent increase in government spending must come at the expense of private expenditures. Keep in mind, however, that it may take several—possibly many—years to arrive at this long-run outcome.

MyEconLab Concept Check

Fiscal Policy in Action: Did the Stimulus Package of 2009 Succeed?

As we have seen, Congress and the president can increase government purchases and cut taxes to increase aggregate demand either to avoid a recession or to shorten the length or severity of a recession that is already under way. The recession of 2007–2009 occurred during the end of the presidency of George W. Bush and the beginning of the presidency of Barack Obama. Both presidents used fiscal policy to fight the recession.

In 2008, economists advising President Bush believed that the housing crisis, the resulting credit crunch, and rising oil prices were pushing the economy into a recession. (As we now know, a recession had actually already begun in December 2007.) These economists proposed cutting taxes to increase household disposable income, which would increase consumption spending and aggregate demand. Congress enacted a tax cut that took the form of *rebates* of taxes that households had already paid. Rebate checks totaling $95 billion were sent to taxpayers between April and July 2008.

How effective were the rebates in increasing consumption spending? While economists are still studying the issue, economic analysis can give us some insight. Many economists believe that consumers base their spending on their *permanent income* rather than just on their *current income*. A consumer's permanent income reflects the consumer's expected future income. By basing spending on permanent income, a consumer can smooth out consumption over a period of years. For example, a medical student may have very low current income but a high expected future income. The student may borrow against this high expected future income rather than having to consume at a very low level in the present. Some people, however, have difficulty borrowing against their future income because banks or other lenders may not be convinced that a borrower's future income will be significantly higher than his or her current income. One-time tax rebates, such as the one in 2008, increase consumers' current income but not their permanent income. Only a permanent decrease in taxes increases consumers' permanent income. Therefore, a tax rebate is likely to increase consumption spending less than would a permanent tax cut.

Some estimates of the effect of the 2008 tax rebate, including studies by Christian Broda of the University of Chicago and Jonathan Parker of Northwestern University, and by economists at the Congressional Budget Office, indicate that taxpayers spent between 33 and 40 percent of the rebates they received. Taxpayers who have difficulty borrowing against their future income increased their consumption the most. The 2008 tax rebates totaled $95 billion, so consumers may have increased their spending by about $35 billion.

American Recovery and Reinvestment Act of 2009 Although the tax rebates helped to increase aggregate demand, we saw in Chapter 15 that the recession worsened in September 2008, following the bankruptcy of the Lehman Brothers investment bank and the deepening of the financial crisis. President Obama took office in January 2009, pledging to pursue an expansionary fiscal policy. Congress responded in February by passing the American Recovery and Reinvestment Act of 2009, an $840 billion package of spending increases and tax cuts that was by far the largest fiscal policy action in U.S. history. The "stimulus package," as it came to be known, is difficult to summarize, but Figure 16.13 provides some highlights.

About two-thirds of the stimulus package took the form of increases in government expenditures, and one-third took the form of tax cuts. Panel (a) shows the major

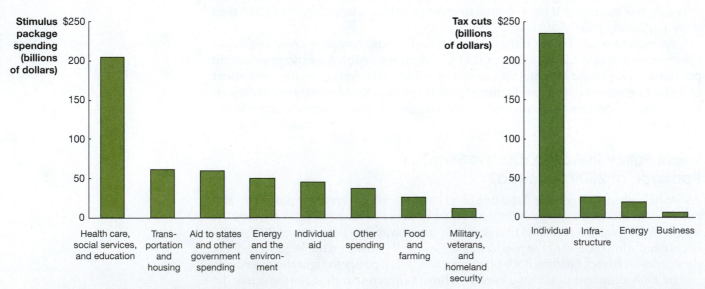

(a) Spending increases in the 2009 stimulus package

(b) Tax cuts in the 2009 stimulus package

MyEconLab Animation

Figure 16.13 The 2009 Stimulus Package

Congress and President Obama intended the spending increases and tax cuts in the stimulus package to increase aggregate demand and help pull the economy out of the 2007–2009 recession. Panel (a) shows how the increases in spending were distributed, and panel (b) shows how the tax cuts were distributed.

Source: Congressional Budget Office.

categories of spending increases. The largest category—health care, social services, and education—included funds for biomedical research and grants to state governments to help fund Medicare spending, as well as funds for many other programs. The energy category included funds for research into alternative energy sources as well as modernization of the electric grid. Transportation and housing included substantial spending on infrastructure projects, such as repairing and expanding highways, bridges, and airports. The spending to reconstruct Doyle Drive in San Francisco, as mentioned in the chapter opener, is an example of the infrastructure spending included in the act. Individual aid included spending on extended unemployment insurance payments. Panel (b) shows the major categories of tax cuts. The largest category was individual tax cuts, which included a $400 reduction in payroll taxes for workers earning up to $75,000 per year and a tax credit of up to $2,500 for tuition and other college expenses.

Congress and the president intended the changes to federal expenditures and taxes from the stimulus package to be temporary. Figure 16.14 shows the effect of the stimulus package on federal government expenditures and revenue over time. Panel (a) shows that the effect on federal government expenditures was greatest during 2010 and declined sharply during 2011. Panel (b) shows that the effect on federal government revenue was greatest during 2010 and had declined to almost zero by early 2011.

How Can We Measure the Effectiveness of the Stimulus Package? At the time the stimulus package was passed, economists working for the Obama administration estimated that the increase in aggregate demand resulting from the package would increase real GDP by 3.5 percent by the end of 2010 and increase employment by 3.5 million. In fact, between the beginning of 2009 and the end of 2010, real GDP increased by 4.0 percent, while employment declined by 3.3 million. Do these results indicate that the stimulus package was successful in increasing GDP but not employment? We have to be careful in drawing that conclusion. To judge the effectiveness of the stimulus package, we have to measure its effects on real GDP and employment, *holding constant all other factors affecting real GDP and employment.* In other words, the actual movements in real GDP and employment are a mixture of the effects of the stimulus package and the effects of other factors, such as the Federal Reserve's monetary policy

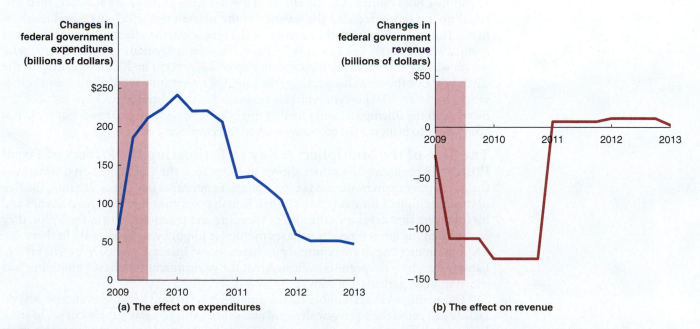

Figure 16.14   **The Effect of the Stimulus Package on Federal Expenditures and Revenue**

Congress and President Obama intended the spending increases and tax cuts in the stimulus package to be temporary. Panel (a) shows that the effect of the stimulus package on federal expenditures was greatest during 2010 and declined in the following years. Panel (b) shows that the effect on federal government revenue was greatest during 2010 and had declined to almost zero by early 2011.
Source: Federal Reserve Bank of St. Louis.

Table 16.2

CBO Estimates of the Effects of the Stimulus Package

Year	Change in Real GDP	Change in the Unemployment Rate	Change in Employment (millions of people)
2009	0.4% to 1.8%	−0.1% to −0.5%	0.3 to 1.3
2010	0.7% to 4.1%	−0.4% to −1.8%	0.9 to 4.7
2011	0.4% to 2.3%	−0.2% to −1.4%	0.6 to 3.6
2012	0.1% to 0.8%	−0.1% to −0.6%	0.2 to 1.3
2013	0.1% to 0.4%	0% to −0.3%	0.1 to 0.5
2014	0% to 0.2%	0% to −0.2%	0.1 to 0.3

Source: Congressional Budget Office, "Estimated Impact of the American Recovery and Reinvestment Act on Employment and Economic Output in 2014," February 20, 2015.

and the typical changes in real GDP and employment during a business cycle that occur independently of government policy. Isolating the effects of the stimulus package from the effects of these other factors is very difficult and explains why economists differ in their views on the effectiveness of the stimulus package.

Table 16.2 shows estimates from economists at the CBO of the effectiveness of the stimulus package. The CBO is a nonpartisan organization, and many economists believe its estimates are reasonable. But because the estimates depend on particular assumptions about the size of the government purchases and tax multipliers, some economists believe that the CBO estimates are too high, while other economists believe the estimates are too low. To reflect the uncertainty in its calculation, the CBO provides a range of estimates. For example, in the absence of the stimulus package, the CBO estimates that in 2010 between 0.9 million and 4.7 million *fewer* people would have been employed than actually were, and the unemployment rate would have been between 0.4 percent and 1.8 percentage points *higher* than it actually was. By 2014, the effects of the stimulus package were small because several years had passed since most of the temporary spending increases and tax cuts had ended and because the economy had gradually moved back toward potential GDP.

If the CBO's estimates of the effects of the stimulus package are accurate, then this fiscal policy action reduced the severity of the recession of 2007–2009 and its aftermath. However, relative to the severity of the recession, the effect of the package was comparatively small. For example, in 2010, the unemployment rate was 9.6 percent, which was far above the unemployment rate of 4.6 percent in 2007. According to the CBO, without the stimulus package, the unemployment rate would have been somewhere between 10.0 percent and 11.4 percent. So, the stimulus package reduced the increase in the unemployment rate that might otherwise have occurred, but it did not come close to bringing the economy back to full employment.

The Size of the Multiplier: A Key to Estimating the Effects of Fiscal Policy In preparing the values shown in Table 16.2, the CBO relied on estimates of the government purchases and tax multipliers. Economists have been debating the size of these multipliers for many years. When British economist John Maynard Keynes and his followers first developed the idea of spending and tax multipliers in the 1930s, they argued that the government purchases multiplier might be as large as 10. In that case, a $1 billion increase in government purchases would increase real GDP by $10 billion. Later research by economists indicated that the government purchases multiplier was much smaller, perhaps less than 2.

Estimating an exact number for the multiplier is difficult because over time, several factors can cause the aggregate demand and short-run aggregate supply curves to shift, leading to a change in equilibrium real GDP. It can be challenging to isolate the effect of an increase in government purchases on equilibrium GDP. Before the stimulus package was proposed to Congress in 2009, economists in the Obama administration estimated the package's effect on GDP by using an average of multiplier estimates from the Federal Reserve and from a private macroeconomic forecasting firm. Their estimate that the government purchases multiplier was 1.57 means that a $1 billion increase in government purchases would increase equilibrium real GDP by $1.57 billion.

Because of the difficulty of estimating the size of the multiplier, some economists argue that the value economists in the Obama administration used was too high, while others argue that it was too low. Robert Barro of Harvard University maintains that increases in government spending during wartime are so large relative to other changes in aggregate demand that data from periods of war are best suited to estimating the size of the multiplier. Using such data, Barro estimated that the government purchases multiplier is only 0.8. Lawrence Christiano, Martin Eichenbaum, and Sergio Rebelo of Northwestern University argue, on the other hand, that the multiplier is likely to be larger when, as during 2009, short-term interest rates are near zero. They estimate that for these periods, the government purchases multiplier could be as large as 3.7.

As Table 16.3 shows, economists' estimates of the size of the multiplier vary widely. The uncertainty about the size of the multiplier indicates the difficulty that economists have in arriving at a firm estimate of the effects of fiscal policy.   MyEconLab Concept Check

Table 16.3

Estimates of the Size of the Multiplier

Economist Making the Estimate	Type of Multiplier	Size of Multiplier
Congressional Budget Office	Government purchases	0.5–2.5
Lawrence Christiano, Martin Eichenbaum, and Sergio Rebelo, Northwestern University	Government purchases	1.05 when short-term interest rates are not zero; 3.7 when short-term interest rates are expected to be zero for at least five quarters
Tommaso Monacelli, Roberto Perotti, and Antonella Trigari, Universita Bocconi	Government purchases	1.2 after one year; 1.5 after two years
Ethan Ilzetzki, London School of Economics, Enrique G. Mendoza, University of Pennsylvania, and Carlos A. Vegh, University of Maryland	Government purchases	0.8
Valerie Ramey, University of California, San Diego	Military expenditure	0.6–1.1
Robert J. Barro, Harvard University, and Charles J. Redlick, Bain Capital, LLC	Military expenditure	0.4–0.5 after one year; 0.6–0.7 after two years
John Cogan and John Taylor, Stanford University, and Tobias Cwik and Volker Wieland, Goethe University	A permanent increase in government expenditures	0.4
Christina Romer, University of California, Berkeley, and Jared Bernstein, chief economist and economic policy adviser to Vice President Joseph Biden	A permanent increase in government expenditures	1.6
Christina Romer (prior to serving as chair of the Council of Economic Advisers) and David Romer, University of California, Berkeley	Tax	2–3
Congressional Budget Office	Tax	0.3–1.5 for a two-year tax cut for lower- and middle-income people; 0.1–0.6 for a one-year tax cut for higher-income people
Robert J. Barro, Harvard University, and Charles J. Redlick, Bain Capital, LLC	Tax	1.1

Note: The sources of these estimates are given on the Credits page in the back of the book.

Making the Connection

MyEconLab Video

Should macroeconomic policy rely less on Fed Chair Yellen and her colleagues?

Do We Depend Too Much on the Fed?

We have seen that the recovery from the Great Recession of 2007–2009 was slower than many economists had expected. As Fed Chair Janet Yellen noted in a speech in 2014, "Five years after the end of the recession, the labor market has yet to fully recover." The $840 billion American Recovery and Reinvestment Act (ARRA) of 2009 was by far the largest fiscal policy action in U.S. history. However, the figure below shows that in 2015, real GDP had not yet returned to potential GDP. The gap between potential GDP and real GDP, which had been as large as 7 percent during the worst of the recession, was still nearly 3 percent—unusually high so far into an economic recovery. The U.S. economy was still operating well below capacity, producing fewer goods and services and creating fewer jobs than it would have at potential GDP.

As Table 16.2 on page 578 showed, by 2011, most of the effects of ARRA on real GDP and employment had already occurred. If macroeconomic policy were to help bring the economy back to potential GDP, it appeared that it would therefore be up to the Federal Reserve. As we saw in Chapter 15, the Fed used innovative policies, including multiple rounds of quantitative easing (QE), in an attempt to increase aggregate demand. With the Fed having ended the last round of QE in October 2014, some economists and policymakers argued that fiscal policy actions were necessary to expand production and employment. Reports of crumbling bridges and railroad accidents led some policymakers to argue that increased infrastructure spending on highways, bridges, and railroad lines would provide both a short-term boost to aggregate demand and longer-term gains to productivity and economic growth. In 2015, President Obama proposed $478 billion in additional infrastructure spending to be paid for by a new tax on the foreign earnings of U.S. corporations. However, not all economists are convinced of the effectiveness of infrastructure spending, particularly if members of Congress direct the spending to projects in their states or districts that might not produce large benefits relative to their costs.

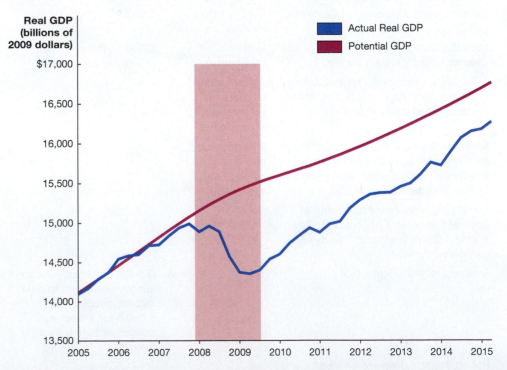

Supporters of infrastructure projects argue that long-term spending might convince businesses that aggregate demand increases would be maintained over a period of years, providing them with the confidence to expand production and employment. Supporters of tax reform to increase economic growth propose lowering tax rates on businesses to spur investment in new innovations and shifting toward consumption-based taxes to spur saving. Some economists argue that trade policy, although not traditionally fiscal policy, could be used to increase the efficiency of the economy and spur exports, while immigration policy could attract high-skilled immigrants, which would increase long-run growth.

The slow recovery from the Great Recession inspired a wide-ranging debate over the use of monetary and fiscal policies to manage the economy.

Sources: Michael D. Shear, "Obama Proposes Tax for Upgrade of Infrastructure," *New York Times*, February 2, 2015; R. Glenn Hubbard, "Stop Depending on the Fed," politico.com, August 20, 2014; Martin S. Feldstein, "Saving the Fed from Itself," *New York Times*, December 8, 2013; Mark Magnier, "Benefits of Infrastructure Spending Not So Clear-Cut, Economists Say," *Wall Street Journal*, February 1, 2015; and Janet L. Yellen, "Labor Market Dynamics and Monetary Policy," Talk delivered at the Federal Reserve Bank of Kansas City Economic Symposium, Jackson Hole, Wyoming, August 22, 2014.

Your Turn: Test your understanding by doing related problem 5.8 on page 594 at the end of this chapter.

MyEconLab Study Plan

Deficits, Surpluses, and Federal Government Debt

LEARNING OBJECTIVE: Define federal budget deficit and federal government debt and explain how the federal budget can serve as an automatic stabilizer.

The federal government's budget shows the relationship between its expenditures and its tax revenue. If the federal government's expenditures are greater than its tax revenue, a **budget deficit** results. If the federal government's expenditures are less than its tax revenue, a **budget surplus** results. As with many other macroeconomic variables, it is useful to consider the size of the surplus or deficit relative to the size of the overall economy. Figure 16.15 shows that, as a percentage of GDP, the largest deficits of the twentieth century came during World Wars I and II. During major wars, higher taxes only partially offset massive increases in government expenditures, leaving large budget deficits. Figure 16.15 also shows that during recessions, government spending increases and tax revenues fall, increasing the budget deficit. In 1970, the federal government entered a long period of continuous budget deficits. From 1970 through 1997, the federal government's budget was in deficit every year. From 1998 through 2001, there were four years of budget surpluses. The recessions of 2001 and 2007–2009, tax cuts, and increased government spending on homeland security and the wars in Iraq and Afghanistan helped keep the budget in deficit in the years after 2001.

Figure 16.15 also shows the effects on the federal budget deficit of the Obama administration's $840 billion stimulus package and the severity of the 2007–2009 recession.

Budget deficit The situation in which the government's expenditures are greater than its tax revenue.

Budget surplus The situation in which the government's expenditures are less than its tax revenue.

MyEconLab Real-time data

Figure 16.15

The Federal Budget Deficit, 1901–2015

During wars, government spending increases far more than tax revenues, increasing the budget deficit. The budget deficit also increases during recessions, as government spending increases and tax revenues fall.

Note: The value for 2015 is an estimate prepared by the Congressional Budget Office in March 2015.

Sources: *Budget of the United States Government, Fiscal Year 2003, Historical Tables,* Washington, DC: U.S. Government Printing Office, 2002; U.S. Bureau of Economic Analysis; and Congressional Budget Office.

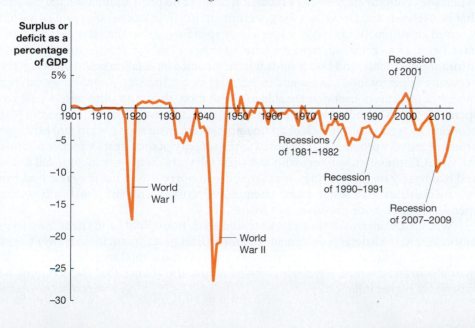

From 2009 through 2011, the federal budget deficit was greater than 8 percent of GDP, which was the first time in the history of the country that the deficit had been this large except during major wars. The economic recovery combined with tax increases and reductions in federal spending lowered the deficit to less than 3 percent of GDP in 2015.

How the Federal Budget Can Serve as an Automatic Stabilizer

Discretionary fiscal policy can increase the federal budget deficit during recessions by increasing spending or cutting taxes to increase aggregate demand. For example, as we have just seen, the Obama administration's spending increases and tax cuts significantly increased the federal budget deficit during 2009 and 2010. In many milder recessions, though, no significant fiscal policy actions are taken. In fact, most of the increase in the federal budget deficit during a typical recession takes place without Congress and the president taking any action but is instead due to the effects of the *automatic stabilizers* we mentioned earlier in this chapter.

Deficits occur automatically during recessions for two reasons: First, during a recession, wages and profits fall, causing government tax revenues to fall. Second, the government automatically increases its spending on transfer payments when the economy moves into a recession. The federal government's contributions to the unemployment insurance program will increase as unemployment rises. Spending will also increase on programs to aid low-income people, such as the food stamp, Temporary Assistance for Needy Families, and Medicaid programs. These spending increases take place without Congress and the president taking any action. Existing laws already specify who is eligible for unemployment insurance and these other programs. As the number of eligible persons increases during a recession, so does government spending on these programs.

Because budget deficits automatically increase during recessions and decrease during expansions, economists often look at the *cyclically adjusted budget deficit or surplus*, which can provide a more accurate measure of the effects on the economy of the government's spending and tax policies than can the actual budget deficit or surplus. The **cyclically adjusted budget deficit or surplus** measures what the deficit or surplus would be if real GDP were at potential GDP. For example, the federal budget deficit in 2014 was 2.7 percent of GDP. The CBO estimates that if real GDP had been at its potential level, the deficit would have been about 1.6 percent of GDP, with the remaining 1.1 percent representing the increase in the deficit due to the effects of automatic stabilizers. When the federal government runs an expansionary fiscal policy, the result is a cyclically adjusted budget deficit. When the federal government runs a contractionary fiscal policy, the result is a cyclically adjusted budget surplus.

Automatic budget surpluses and deficits can help to stabilize the economy. When the economy moves into a recession, wages and profits fall, reducing the taxes that households and firms owe the government. In effect, households and firms have received an automatic tax cut that keeps their spending higher than it otherwise would have been. In a recession, workers who have been laid off receive unemployment insurance payments, and households whose incomes have fallen below a certain level become eligible for food stamps and other government transfer programs. By receiving this extra income, households are able to spend more than they otherwise would have spent. The extra spending helps reduce the length and severity of the recession. Many economists argue that the lack of an unemployment insurance system and other government transfer programs contributed to the severity of the Great Depression. During the Great Depression, workers who lost their jobs saw their wage income fall to zero and had to rely on their savings, what they could borrow, or what they received from private charities. As a result, many unemployed workers cut back drastically on their spending, which made the downturn worse.

When GDP increases above its potential level, households and firms have to pay more taxes to the federal government, and the federal government makes fewer transfer payments. Higher taxes and lower transfer payments cause total spending to rise by less than it otherwise would have, which helps reduce the chance that the economy will experience higher inflation.

Cyclically adjusted budget deficit or surplus The deficit or surplus in the federal government's budget if the economy were at potential GDP.

MyEconLab Concept Check

Making the Connection

MyEconLab Video

Did Fiscal Policy Fail during the Great Depression?

Modern macroeconomic analysis began during the 1930s, with the publication of *The General Theory of Employment, Interest, and Money* by John Maynard Keynes. One conclusion many economists drew from Keynes's book was that an expansionary fiscal policy would be necessary to pull the United States out of the Great Depression. When Franklin D. Roosevelt became president in 1933, federal government expenditures increased as part of his New Deal program, and there was a federal budget deficit during each remaining year of the decade, except for 1937. The U.S. economy recovered very slowly, however, and did not reach potential GDP again until the outbreak of World War II in 1941.

Some economists and policymakers at the time argued that because the economy recovered slowly despite increases in government spending, fiscal policy had been ineffective. During the debate over President Obama's stimulus package, the argument that fiscal policy had failed during the New Deal was raised again. Economic historians have noted, however, that despite the increases in government spending, Congress and the president had not, in fact, implemented an expansionary fiscal policy during the 1930s. In separate studies, economists E. Cary Brown of MIT and Larry Peppers of Washington and Lee University argued that there was a cyclically adjusted budget deficit during only one year of the 1930s, and that one deficit was small. The following table provides data supporting their arguments. (All variables in the table are nominal rather than real.) The second column shows federal government expenditures increasing from 1933 to 1936, falling in 1937, and then increasing in 1938 and 1939. The third column shows a similar pattern, with the federal budget being in deficit each year after 1933 except for 1937. The fourth column, however, shows that in each year after 1933, the federal government ran a cyclically adjusted budget *surplus*. Because the level of income was so low and the unemployment rate was so high during these years, tax collections were far below what they would have been if the economy had been at potential GDP. As the fifth column shows, in 1933 and again from 1937 to 1939, the cyclically adjusted surpluses were large relative to GDP.

Although government spending increased during the Great Depression, the cyclically adjusted budget was in surplus most years.

Year	Federal Government Expenditures (billions of dollars)	Actual Federal Budget Deficit or Surplus (billions of dollars)	Cyclically Adjusted Budget Deficit or Surplus (billions of dollars)	Cyclically Adjusted Budget Deficit or Surplus as a Percentage of GDP
1929	$2.6	$1.0	$1.24	1.20%
1930	2.7	0.2	0.81	0.89
1931	4.0	−2.1	−0.41	−0.54
1932	3.0	−1.3	0.50	0.85
1933	3.4	−0.9	1.06	1.88
1934	5.5	−2.2	0.09	0.14
1935	5.6	−1.9	0.54	0.74
1936	7.8	−3.2	0.47	0.56
1937	6.4	0.2	2.55	2.77
1938	7.3	−1.3	2.47	2.87
1939	8.4	−2.1	2.00	2.17

Although President Roosevelt proposed many new government spending programs, he had also promised during the 1932 presidential election campaign to balance the federal budget. He achieved a balanced budget only in 1937, but his reluctance to allow the actual budget deficit to grow too large helps explain why the cyclically adjusted budget remained in surplus. Many economists today would agree with

E. Cary Brown's conclusion: "Fiscal policy, then, seems to have been an unsuccessful recovery device in the 'thirties—not because it did not work, but because it was not tried."

Sources: E. Cary Brown, "Fiscal Policy in the 'Thirties: A Reappraisal," *American Economic Review*, Vol. 46, No. 5, December 1956, pp. 475–497; Larry Peppers, "Full Employment Surplus Analysis and Structural Changes," *Explorations in Economic History*, Vol. 10, Winter 1973, pp. 197–210; and U.S. Bureau of Economic Analysis.

MyEconLab Study Plan   **Your Turn:** Test your understanding by doing related problem 6.7 on page 595 at the end of this chapter.

Should the Federal Budget Always Be Balanced?

Although many economists believe that it is a good idea for the federal government to have a balanced budget when real GDP is at potential GDP, few economists believe that the federal government should attempt to balance its budget every year. To see why economists take this view, consider what the federal government would have to do to keep the budget balanced during a recession, when the budget automatically moves into deficit. To bring the budget back into balance, the government would have to raise taxes or cut spending, but these actions would reduce aggregate demand, thereby making the recession worse. Similarly, when GDP increases above its potential level, the budget automatically moves into surplus. To eliminate this surplus, the government would have to cut taxes or increase government spending. But these actions would increase aggregate demand, thereby pushing GDP further beyond potential GDP and increasing the risk of higher inflation. To balance the budget every year, the government might have to take actions that would destabilize the economy.

Solved Problem 16.6

MyEconLab Interactive Animation

The Greek Government Confronts a Budget Deficit

According to an article in the *Wall Street Journal*, in 2015, some economists believed that the Greek economy might be about to enter a recession. The article noted, "Renewed recession in Greece … could force the government to impose further spending cuts and tax hikes to avoid a renewed budget deficit."

a. Why would the Greek economy entering a recession lead to the Greek government having a budget deficit?

b. If the Greek government, in reaction to the budget deficit, takes the steps the article indicates, what would be the likely effect on the Greek economy?

Solving the Problem

Step 1: **Review the chapter material.** This problem is about the effects of a government attempting to balance its budget during a recession, so you may want to review the sections "How the Federal Budget Can Serve as an Automatic Stabilizer" and "Should the Federal Budget Always Be Balanced?" which are on pages 582 and 584.

Step 2: **Answer part (a) by explaining why a government's budget will automatically run a deficit during a recession.** Deficits occur automatically during recessions because falling wages and profits cause government tax revenues to fall and because government spending on transfer payments, such as unemployment insurance payments, increases.

Step 3: **Answer part (b) by explaining the likely effect on the Greek economy if the Greek government were to cut spending and increase taxes.** We have seen that reductions in government spending and increases in taxes will reduce aggregate demand. A reduction in aggregate demand will likely reduce real GDP and employment, making the recession in Greece worse.

Source: Nektaria Stamouli and Stelios Bouras, "Greek Economy Risks Slipping Back Into Recession, Say Analysts," *Wall Street Journal*, April 6, 2015.

MyEconLab Study Plan   **Your Turn:** For more practice, do related problem 6.9 on page 595 at the end of this chapter.

Some economists argue that the federal government should normally run a deficit, even at potential GDP. When the federal budget is in deficit, the U.S. Treasury sells bonds to investors to raise the funds necessary to pay the government's bills. Borrowing to pay the bills is a bad policy for a household, a firm, or the government when the bills are for current expenses, but it is not a bad policy if the bills are for long-lived capital goods. For instance, most families pay for a new home by taking out a 15- to 30-year mortgage. Because houses last many years, it makes sense to pay for a house out of the income the family makes over a long period of time rather than out of the income they receive in the year they bought the house. Businesses often borrow the funds to buy machinery, equipment, and factories by selling 30-year corporate bonds. Because these capital goods generate profits for the businesses over many years, it makes sense to pay for them over a period of years as well. By similar reasoning, when the federal government contributes to the building of a new highway, bridge, or subway, it may want to borrow funds by selling Treasury bonds. The alternative is to pay for these long-lived capital goods out of the tax revenues received in the year the goods were purchased. But that means that the taxpayers in that year have to bear the whole burden of paying for the projects, even though taxpayers for many years in the future will be enjoying the benefits.   MyEconLab Concept Check

The Federal Government Debt

Every time the federal government runs a budget deficit, the Treasury must borrow funds from investors by selling Treasury securities. For simplicity, we will refer to all Treasury securities as "bonds." When the federal government runs a budget surplus, the Treasury pays off some existing bonds. Figure 16.15 on page 581 shows that there are many more years of federal budget deficits than years of federal budget surpluses. As a result, the total number of Treasury bonds outstanding has grown over the years. The total value of U.S. Treasury bonds outstanding is called the *federal government debt* or, sometimes, the *national debt*. Each year the federal budget is in deficit, the federal government debt grows. Each year the federal budget is in surplus, the debt shrinks.

   Figure 16.16 shows federal government debt as a percentage of GDP in the years from 1901 to 2015. The ratio of debt to GDP increased during World Wars I and II and the Great Depression, reflecting the large government budget deficits of those years. After the end of World War II, GDP grew faster than the debt until the early 1980s, which caused the ratio of debt to GDP to fall. The large budget deficits of the 1980s and early 1990s sent the debt-to-GDP ratio climbing. The budget surpluses of 1998 to 2001 caused the debt-to-GDP ratio to fall, but it rose again with the return of deficits beginning in 2002. The large deficits beginning in 2008 caused the ratio to rise above 100 percent of GDP for the first time since 1947.   MyEconLab Concept Check

Is Government Debt a Problem?

Debt can be a problem for a government for the same reasons it can be a problem for a household or a business. If a family has difficulty making the monthly mortgage payment, it will have to cut back spending on other goods and services. If the family is unable to make the payments, it will have to *default* on the loan and will probably lose its house. The federal government is not in danger of defaulting on its debt. Ultimately, the government can raise the funds it needs through taxes to make the interest payments on the debt. If the debt becomes very large relative to the economy, however, the government may have to raise taxes to high levels or cut back on other types of spending to make the interest payments on the debt. Interest payments are currently about 11 percent of total federal expenditures. At this level, tax increases or significant cutbacks in other types of federal spending are not required.

   In the long run, a debt that increases in size relative to GDP, as happened after 2008, can pose a problem. As we discussed previously, crowding out of investment spending may occur if increasing debt drives up interest rates. Lower investment spending means a lower capital stock in the long run and a reduced capacity of the economy to produce goods and services. This effect is somewhat offset if some of the government debt was incurred to finance improvements in *infrastructure*, such as bridges, highways, and ports; to finance education; or to finance research and development. Improvements in infrastructure, a better-educated labor force, and additional research and development can add to the productive capacity of the economy.   MyEconLab Concept Check   MyEconLab Study Plan

MyEconLab Real-time data

Figure 16.16

The Federal Government Debt, 1901–2015

The federal government debt increases whenever the federal government runs a budget deficit. The large deficits incurred during World Wars I and II, the Great Depression, and the 1980s and early 1990s increased the ratio of debt to GDP. The large deficits after 2008 caused the ratio to spike up to its highest level since 1947.

Note: The value for 2015 is an estimate prepared by the Congressional Budget Office in March 2015.

Sources: U.S. Bureau of the Census, *Historical Statistics of the United States, Colonial Times to 1970,* Washington, DC: U.S. Government Printing Office, 1975; *Budget of the United States Government, Fiscal Year 2003,* Historical Printing Office, 2002; Federal Reserve Bank of St. Louis; and Congressional Budget Office.

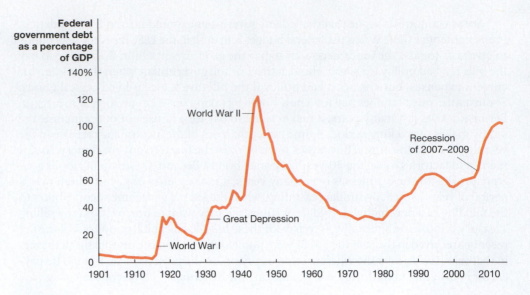

Tax wedge The difference between the pretax and posttax return to an economic activity.

16.7 The Effects of Fiscal Policy in the Long Run

LEARNING OBJECTIVE: Discuss the effects of fiscal policy in the long run.

Some fiscal policy actions are intended to meet the short-run goal of stabilizing the economy. Other fiscal policy actions are intended to have long-run effects by expanding the productive capacity of the economy and increasing the rate of economic growth. Because these policy actions primarily affect aggregate supply rather than aggregate demand, they are sometimes called *supply-side economics.* Most fiscal policy actions that attempt to increase aggregate supply do so by changing taxes to increase the incentives to work, save, invest, and start a business.

The Long-Run Effects of Tax Policy

The difference between the pretax and posttax return to an economic activity is called the **tax wedge**. It is determined by the *marginal tax rate,* which is the fraction of each additional dollar of income that must be paid in taxes. For example, the U.S. federal income tax has several tax brackets, which are the income ranges within which a tax rate applies. In 2015, for a single taxpayer, the tax rate was 10 percent on the first $9,225 earned during a year. The tax rate rose for higher income brackets, until it reached 39.6 percent on income earned above $413,200. Suppose you are paid a wage of $20 per hour. If your marginal income tax rate is 25 percent, then your posttax wage is $15, and the tax wedge is $5. When discussing the model of demand and supply in Chapter 3, we saw that increasing the price of a good or service increases the quantity supplied. So, we would expect that reducing the tax wedge by cutting the marginal tax rate on income would result in a larger quantity of labor supplied because the posttax wage would be higher. Similarly, we saw in Chapter 10 that a reduction in the income tax rate would increase the posttax return to saving, causing an increase in the supply of loanable funds, a lower equilibrium interest rate, and an increase in investment spending. In general, economists believe that the smaller the tax wedge for any economic activity—such as working, saving, investing, or starting a business—the more of that economic activity that will occur. When workers, savers, investors, or entrepreneurs change their actions as a result of a tax change, economists say that there has been a *behavioral response* to the tax change.

We can look briefly at the effects on aggregate supply of cutting each of the following taxes:

- **Individual income tax.** As we have seen, reducing the marginal tax rates on individual income will reduce the tax wedge workers face, thereby increasing the quantity of labor supplied. Many small businesses are *sole proprietorships,* whose profits are taxed at the individual income tax rates. Therefore, cutting the individual income tax rates also raises the return to entrepreneurship, encouraging the opening of new businesses. Most households are taxed on their returns from saving at the individual income tax rates. Reducing marginal income tax rates, therefore, also increases the return to saving.

- **Corporate income tax.**   The federal government taxes the profits corporations earn under the corporate income tax. In 2015, most corporations faced a marginal corporate tax rate of 35 percent. Cutting the marginal corporate income tax rate would encourage investment spending by increasing the return corporations receive from new investments in equipment, factories, and office buildings. Because innovations are often embodied in new investment goods, cutting the corporate income tax can potentially increase the pace of technological change.

- **Taxes on dividends and capital gains.**   Corporations distribute some of their profits to shareholders in the form of payments known as *dividends*. Shareholders also may benefit from higher corporate profits by receiving *capital gains*. A capital gain is the increase in the price of an asset, such as a share of stock. Rising profits usually result in rising stock prices and capital gains to shareholders. Individuals pay taxes on both dividends and capital gains (although the tax on capital gains can be postponed if the stock is not sold). As a result, the same earnings are, in effect, taxed twice: once when a corporation pays the corporate income tax on its profits and a second time when individual investors receive the profits in the form of dividends or capital gains. Economists debate the costs and benefits of a separate tax on corporate profits. With the corporate income tax remaining in place, one way to reduce the "double taxation" problem is to reduce the tax rates on dividends and capital gains. These rates were reduced in 2003 before being increased in 2013. Generally, the marginal tax rates on dividends and capital gains are still below the top marginal tax rate on individual income. Lowering the tax rates on dividends and capital gains increases the supply of loanable funds from households to firms, increasing saving and investment and lowering the equilibrium real interest rate.

Tax Simplification

In addition to the potential gains from cutting individual taxes, there are also gains from tax simplification. The complexity of the tax code, which is 3,000 pages long, has created a whole industry of tax preparation services, such as H&R Block. The Internal Revenue Service estimates that taxpayers spend more than 6.4 billion hours each year filling out their tax forms, or about 45 hours per tax return. Households and firms have to deal with more than 480 tax forms to file their federal taxes and spend more than $10 billion per year to hire accountants to help fill out the forms. It is not surprising that there are more H&R Block offices around the country than Starbucks coffeehouses.

If the tax code were greatly simplified, the economic resources currently used by the tax preparation industry would be available to produce other goods and services. In addition to wasting resources, the complexity of the tax code may also distort the decisions households and firms make. For example, the tax rate on dividends has clearly affected whether corporations pay dividends. When Congress passed a reduction in the tax on dividends in 2003, many firms—including Microsoft—began paying dividends for the first time. A simplified tax code would increase economic efficiency by reducing the number of decisions households and firms make solely to reduce their tax payments.

MyEconLab Concept Check

The Economic Effect of Tax Reform

We can analyze the economic effects of tax reduction and simplification by using the aggregate demand and aggregate supply model. Figure 16.17 shows that without tax changes, the long-run aggregate supply curve will shift from $LRAS_1$ to $LRAS_2$. This shift represents the increases in the labor force and the capital stock and the technological change that would occur even without tax reduction and simplification. To focus on the effect of tax changes on aggregate supply, we will ignore any shifts in the short-run aggregate supply curve, and we will assume that the aggregate demand curve remains unchanged, at AD_1. In this case, equilibrium moves from point A to point B, with real GDP increasing from Y_1 to Y_2 and the price level decreasing from P_1 to P_2.

MyEconLab Animation

Figure 16.17

The Supply-Side Effects of a Tax Change

The initial equilibrium is at point A. With no tax change, the long-run aggregate supply curve shifts to the right, from $LRAS_1$ to $LRAS_2$. Equilibrium moves to point B, with the price level falling from P_1 to P_2 and real GDP increasing from Y_1 to Y_2. With tax reductions and simplifications, the long-run aggregate supply curve shifts further to the right, to $LRAS_3$, and equilibrium moves to point C, with the price level falling to P_3 and real GDP increasing to Y_3.

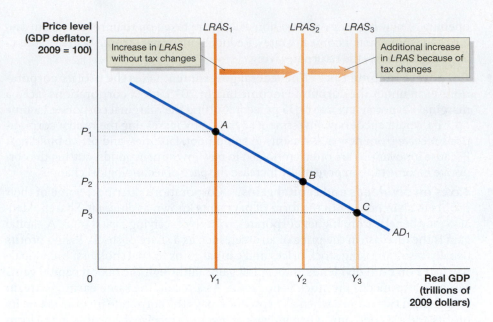

MyEconLab Concept Check

If tax reduction and simplification are effective, the economy will experience increases in labor supply, saving, investment, and the formation of new firms. Economic efficiency will also be improved. Together these factors will result in an increase in the quantity of real GDP supplied at every price level. We show the effects of the tax changes in Figure 16.17 by a shift in the long-run aggregate supply curve to $LRAS_3$. With aggregate demand remaining unchanged, equilibrium moves from point A to point C (rather than to point B, which is the equilibrium without tax changes), with real GDP increasing from Y_1 to Y_3 and the price level decreasing from P_1 to P_3. Notice that compared with the equilibrium without tax changes (point B), the equilibrium with tax changes (point C) occurs at a lower price level and a higher level of real GDP. We can conclude that the tax changes have benefited the economy by increasing output and employment while at the same time reducing the price level.

Clearly, our analysis is unrealistic because we have ignored the changes that will occur in aggregate demand and short-run aggregate supply. How would a more realistic analysis differ from the simplified one in Figure 16.17? The change in real GDP would be the same because in the long run, real GDP is equal to its potential level, which is represented by the *long-run aggregate supply* curve. The outcome for the price level would be different, however, because we would expect both the aggregate demand curve and the short-run aggregate supply curve to shift to the right. The most likely outcome is that the price level would end up higher in the new equilibrium than in the original equilibrium. However, because the position of the long-run aggregate supply curve is further to the right as a result of the tax changes, the increase in the price level will be smaller; that is, the price level at point C is likely to be lower than P_2, even if it is higher than P_3, although—as we will discuss in the next section—not all economists would agree. We can conclude that a successful policy of tax reductions and simplifications will benefit the economy by increasing output and employment and, at the same time, may result in smaller increases in the price level.

How Large Are Supply-Side Effects?

Most economists would agree that there are supply-side effects to reducing taxes: Decreasing marginal income tax rates will increase the quantity of labor supplied, cutting the corporate income tax will increase investment spending, and so on. The magnitude of the effects is the subject of considerable debate, however. For example, some economists argue that the increase in the quantity of labor supplied following a tax cut will be limited because many people work a number of hours set by their employers and lack the opportunity to work additional hours. Similarly, some economists believe that tax changes have only a small effect on saving and investment. In this view, saving and investment are affected much more by changes in income or changes in expectations of the future profitability of new investment due to technological change or improving macroeconomic conditions than they are by changes in taxes.

Economists who are skeptical of the magnitude of supply-side effects believe that tax cuts have their greatest effect on aggregate demand rather than on aggregate supply. In their view, focusing on the effect of tax cuts on aggregate demand, while ignoring any effect on aggregate supply, yields accurate forecasts of future movements in real GDP and the price level, which indicates that the supply-side effects must be small. If tax changes have only small effects on aggregate supply, they are unlikely to reduce the size of price increases to the extent shown in Figure 16.17.

Ultimately, the debate over the size of the supply-side effects of tax policy can be resolved only through careful study of the effects of differences in tax rates on labor supply and on saving and investment decisions. Some recent studies have arrived at conflicting conclusions, however. For example, a study by Nobel Laureate Edward Prescott of Arizona State University concludes that the differences between the United States and Europe with respect to the average number of hours worked per week and the average number of weeks worked per year are due to differences in tax rates. The lower marginal tax rates in the United States compared with Europe increase the return to working for U.S. workers and result in a larger quantity of labor supplied. But another study by Alberto Alesina and Edward Glaeser of Harvard University and Bruce Sacerdote of Dartmouth College argues that the more restrictive labor market regulations in Europe explain the shorter work weeks and longer vacations of European workers and that differences in tax rates have only a small effect.

As in other areas of economics, differences among economists in their estimates of the supply-side effects of tax changes may narrow over time as they conduct more studies.   MyEconLab Concept Check   MyEconLab Study Plan

Continued from page 557

Economics in Your Life

What Would You Do with an Extra $500?

At the beginning of the chapter, we asked how you would respond to a $500 tax rebate and what effect this tax rebate would likely have on equilibrium real GDP in the short run. This chapter has shown that tax cuts increase disposable income and, therefore, consumption spending. So, you will likely respond to a permanent $500 increase in your disposable income by increasing your spending. How much your spending increases depends in part on your overall financial situation. As mentioned in the chapter, people who are able to borrow usually try to smooth out their spending over time and don't increase spending much in response to a one-time increase in their income. But if you are a student struggling to get by on a low income and you are unable to borrow against the higher income you expect to earn in the future, you may well spend most of the rebate. This chapter has also shown that tax cuts have a multiplier effect on the economy. That is, an increase in consumption spending sets off further increases in real GDP and income. So, if the economy is not already at potential GDP, this tax rebate will likely increase equilibrium real GDP in the short run.

Conclusion

In this chapter, we have seen how the federal government uses changes in government purchases and taxes to achieve its economic policy goals. We have seen that economists debate the effectiveness of discretionary fiscal policy actions intended to stabilize the economy. Congress and the president share responsibility for economic policy with the Federal Reserve. In the next chapter, we will discuss further some of the challenges that the Federal Reserve faces as it carries out monetary policy. In the following chapters, we will look more closely at the international economy, including how monetary and fiscal policy are affected by the linkages between economies.

Visit MyEconLab for a news article and analysis related to the concepts in this chapter.

Key Terms

Automatic stabilizers, p. 558

Budget deficit, p. 581

Budget surplus, p. 581

Crowding out, p. 573

Cyclically adjusted budget deficit or surplus, p. 582

Fiscal policy, p. 558

Multiplier effect, p. 567

Tax wedge, p. 586

16.1 What Is Fiscal Policy? pages 558–562

LEARNING OBJECTIVE: Define fiscal policy.

Summary

Fiscal policy involves changes in federal taxes and purchases that are intended to achieve macroeconomic policy goals. **Automatic stabilizers** are government spending and taxes that automatically increase or decrease along with the business cycle. Since World War II, the federal government's share of total government expenditures has been between two-thirds and three-quarters. Federal government *expenditures* as a percentage of GDP rose from 1950 to the early 1990s, fell between 1992 and 2001, and then rose once again. Federal government *purchases* have declined as a percentage of GDP since the end of the Korean War in the early 1950s. The largest component of federal expenditures is transfer payments. The largest sources of federal government revenue are individual income taxes, followed by social insurance taxes, which are used to fund the Social Security and Medicare systems.

MyEconLab   Visit www.myeconlab.com to complete these exercises online and get instant feedback.

Review Questions

1.1 What is fiscal policy? Who is responsible for fiscal policy?

1.2 Economist Mark Thoma wrote, "One of the difficulties in using fiscal policy to combat recessions is getting Congress to agree on what measures to implement. … Automatic stabilizers bypass this difficulty by doing exactly what their name implies." What are automatic stabilizers? Name two examples of automatic stabilizers and explain how they can reduce the severity of a recession.

Source: Mark Thoma, "The Importance of Automatic Stabilizers to the Economy," cbsnews.com, January 25, 2010.

1.3 What is the difference between federal purchases and federal expenditures? Are federal purchases higher today as a percentage of GDP than they were in 1960? Are federal expenditures as a percentage of GDP higher?

Problems and Applications

1.4 In 2009, Congress and the president enacted "cash for clunkers" legislation that paid up to $4,500 to people buying new cars if they traded in an older, low-gas-mileage car. Was this legislation an example of fiscal policy? Does your answer depend on what goals Congress and the president had in mind when they enacted the legislation?

Source: Justin Lahart, "Trade-in Program Tunes Up Economic Engine," *Wall Street Journal*, August 4, 2009.

1.5 Briefly explain whether each of the following is (1) an example of a discretionary fiscal policy, (2) an example of an automatic stabilizer, or (3) not an example of fiscal policy.
   a. The federal government increases spending on rebuilding the New Jersey shore following a hurricane.
   b. The Federal Reserve sells Treasury securities.
   c. The total amount the federal government spends on unemployment insurance decreases during an expansion.
   d. The revenue the federal government collects from the individual income tax declines during a recession.
   e. The federal government changes the required fuel efficiency for new cars.
   f. Congress and the president enact a temporary cut in payroll taxes.
   g. During a recession, California voters approve additional spending on a statewide high-speed rail system.

1.6 The federal government collected less in total individual income taxes in 1983 than in 1982. Can we conclude that Congress and the president cut individual income tax rates in 1983? Briefly explain.

1.7 (Related to the Making the Connection on page 561) According to a Congressional Budget Office (CBO) report:

> During the next decade alone, the number of people age 65 or older is expected to rise by more than one-third, and the share of the population age 65 or older is projected to grow from the current 15 percent to 21 percent in 2040.

Why is the over-65 population increasing so rapidly? What are the implications of this increase for future federal spending on Social Security and Medicare as a percentage of GDP? What choices do policymakers face in dealing with this issue?

Source: Congressional Budget Office, "The 2015 Long-Term Budget Outlook," June 2015, p. 21.

16.2 The Effects of Fiscal Policy on Real GDP and the Price Level, pages 563–565

LEARNING OBJECTIVE: Explain how fiscal policy affects aggregate demand and how the government can use fiscal policy to stabilize the economy.

Summary

To fight recessions, Congress and the president can increase government purchases or cut taxes. This expansionary policy increases aggregate demand, raising the level of real GDP and the price level. To fight rising inflation, Congress and the president can decrease government purchases or raise taxes. This contractionary policy reduces aggregate demand relative to what it would otherwise be, thereby reducing the inflation rate.

MyEconLab Visit www.myeconlab.com to complete these exercises online and get instant feedback.

Review Questions

2.1 What is an expansionary fiscal policy? What is a contractionary fiscal policy?

2.2 If Congress and the president decide that an expansionary fiscal policy is necessary, what changes should they make in government spending or taxes? What changes should they make if they decide that a contractionary fiscal policy is necessary?

Problems and Applications

2.3 Briefly explain whether you agree with the following statements: "An expansionary fiscal policy involves an increase in government purchases or an increase in taxes. A contractionary fiscal policy involves a decrease in government purchases or a decrease in taxes."

2.4 Identify each of the following as (1) part of an expansionary fiscal policy, (2) part of a contractionary fiscal policy, or (3) not part of fiscal policy.
   a. The corporate income tax rate is increased.
   b. Defense spending is increased.

   c. The Federal Reserve lowers the target for the federal funds rate.
   d. Families are allowed to deduct all their expenses for day care from their federal income taxes.
   e. The individual income tax rate is decreased.

2.5 Use an aggregate demand and aggregate supply graph to illustrate the situation where equilibrium initially occurs with real GDP equal to potential GDP and then the aggregate demand curve shifts to the left. What actions can Congress and the president take to move real GDP back to potential GDP? Show the results of these actions on your graph. Assume that the *LRAS* curve doesn't shift.

2.6 (Related to the Don't Let This Happen to You on page 564) Is it possible for Congress and the president to carry out an expansionary fiscal policy if the money supply does not increase? Briefly explain.

2.7 A political commentator argues: "Congress and the president are more likely to enact an expansionary fiscal policy than a contractionary fiscal policy because expansionary policies are popular and contractionary policies are unpopular." Briefly explain whether you agree.

2.8 (Related to the Chapter Opener on page 557) In 2015, in proposing a $478 billion increase in federal spending on infrastructure, President Obama argued that the spending would increase total employment in the United States.
   a. Will increases in federal spending always increase real GDP and employment in the short run? Briefly explain.
   b. Are there circumstances in which the federal government would not want to increase its spending even if the result was to increase real GDP and employment in the short run? What was President Obama assuming about the state of the economy in 2015?

Source: Michael D. Shear, "Obama Proposes Tax for Upgrade of Infrastructure," *New York Times*, February 2, 2015.

16.3 Fiscal Policy in the Dynamic Aggregate Demand and Aggregate Supply Model, pages 565–566

LEARNING OBJECTIVE: Use the dynamic aggregate demand and aggregate supply model to analyze fiscal policy.

Summary

We can use the *dynamic aggregate demand and aggregate supply model* to look more closely at expansionary and contractionary fiscal policies. This model takes into account that (1) the economy experiences continuing inflation, with the price level rising every year, and (2) the economy experiences long-run growth, with the *LRAS* curve shifting to the right every year. In the dynamic model, an expansionary fiscal policy tries to ensure that the aggregate demand curve will shift far enough to the right to bring about macroeconomic equilibrium with real GDP equal to potential GDP. A contractionary fiscal policy attempts to offset movements in aggregate demand that would cause macroeconomic

equilibrium to occur at a level of real GDP that is greater than potential GDP.

MyEconLab Visit www.myeconlab.com to complete these exercises online and get instant feedback.

Review Questions

3.1 What are the key differences between how we illustrate an expansionary fiscal policy in the basic aggregate demand and aggregate supply model and in the dynamic aggregate demand and aggregate supply model?

3.2 What are the key differences between how we illustrate a contractionary fiscal policy in the basic aggregate demand and aggregate supply model and in the dynamic aggregate demand and aggregate supply model?

Problems and Applications

3.3 A report from the Congressional Budget Office (CBO) notes, "Potential GDP is CBO's estimate of the maximum sustainable output of the economy." In early 2015, the CBO estimated that the gap between real GDP and potential GDP would fall from 2.9 percent in 2014 to zero in 2017. In 2014, real GDP was $16.3 trillion, and the CBO's estimate of potential GDP was $16.8 trillion. The CBO forecast that potential GDP would increase to $17.5 trillion.

    a. Why does the CBO include the word "sustainable" in its definition of potential GDP?

    b. Draw an aggregate demand and aggregate supply graph to illustrate the macroeconomic situation in 2014 and in 2017 (you do not have to show on your graph the situation in 2015 or 2016). Be sure that your graph contains *LRAS* curves for 2014 and 2017, *SRAS* curves for 2014 and 2017, and *AD* curves for 2014 and 2017, and that it shows equilibrium real GDP and the price levels for both years.

    Sources: Congressional Budget Office, "The 2015 Long-Term Budget Outlook," June 2015, p. 36; and Congressional Budget Office, "The Budget and Economic Outlook: 2015 to 2025," January 2015.

3.4 Use the graph to answer the following questions.

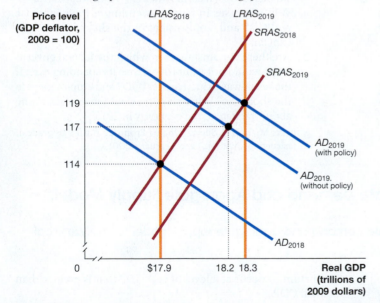

    a. If the government takes no policy actions, what will be the values of real GDP and the price level in 2019?

    b. What actions can the government take to bring real GDP to its potential level in 2019?

    c. If the government takes no policy actions, what will the inflation rate be in 2019? If the government uses fiscal policy to keep real GDP at its potential level, what will the inflation rate be in 2019?

3.5 The hypothetical information in the following table shows what the situation will be in 2019 if Congress and the president do *not* use fiscal policy:

Year	Potential GDP	Real GDP	Price Level
2018	$17.9 trillion	$17.9 trillion	113.7
2019	$18.3 trillion	$17.9 trillion	115.9

    a. If Congress and the president want to keep real GDP at its potential level in 2019, should they use an expansionary policy or a contractionary policy? In your answer, be sure to explain whether Congress and the president should increase or decrease government purchases and taxes.

    b. If Congress and the president are successful in keeping real GDP at its potential level in 2019, state whether each of the following will be higher, lower, or the same as it would have been if they had taken no action:

       i. Real GDP

       ii. Potential GDP

       iii. The inflation rate

       iv. The unemployment rate

    c. Draw an aggregate demand and aggregate supply graph to illustrate your answer. Be sure that your graph contains *LRAS* curves for 2018 and 2019; *SRAS* curves for 2018 and 2019; *AD* curves for 2018 and 2019, with and without fiscal policy action; and equilibrium real GDP and the price level in 2019, with and without fiscal policy.

3.6 Use a dynamic aggregate demand and aggregate supply graph to illustrate the change in macroeconomic equilibrium from 2019 to 2020, assuming that the economy experiences deflation during 2020. In order for deflation to take place in 2020, does the economy also have to be experiencing a recession? Briefly explain.

16.4 **The Government Purchases and Tax Multipliers, pages 567–571**
    LEARNING OBJECTIVE: Explain how the government purchases and tax multipliers work.

Summary

Because of the **multiplier effect**, an increase in government purchases or a cut in taxes will have a multiplied effect on equilibrium real GDP. The *government purchases multiplier* is equal to the change in equilibrium real GDP divided by the change in government purchases. The *tax multiplier* is equal to the change in equilibrium real GDP divided by the change in taxes. Increases in government purchases and cuts in taxes have a positive multiplier effect on equilibrium real GDP. Decreases in government purchases and increases in taxes have a negative multiplier effect on equilibrium real GDP.

MyEconLab   Visit **www.myeconlab.com** to complete these exercises online and get instant feedback.

Review Questions

4.1 Why can a $1 increase in government purchases lead to more than a $1 increase in income and spending?

4.2 Define *government purchases multiplier* and *tax multiplier*.

4.3 Why does a higher income tax rate reduce the multiplier effect?

Problems and Applications

4.4 **(Related to the** Chapter Opener **on page 557)** Another infrastructure project in northern California funded in part by ARRA funds involved expanding the Caldecott Tunnel between the cities of Oakland and Orinda. A spokesperson for the California state agency in charge of the project mentioned that the Caldecott Tunnel project would have a "ripple effect" on employment. What did the spokesperson mean by a ripple effect?

Source: Zusha Elinson, "Caldecott Tunnel Edges Forward, Tribute to Stimulus Bill," *New York Times*, September 10, 2011.

4.5 In *The General Theory of Employment, Interest, and Money*, John Maynard Keynes wrote:

> If the Treasury were to fill old bottles with banknotes, bury them at suitable depths in disused coal mines which are then filled up to the surface with town rubbish, and leave it to private enterprise ... to dig the notes up again ... there need be no more unemployment and, with the help of the repercussions, the real income of the community ... would probably become a good deal greater than it is.

Which important macroeconomic effect is Keynes discussing here? What does he mean by "repercussions"? Why does he appear unconcerned about whether government spending is wasteful?

Source: John Maynard Keynes, *The General Theory of Employment, Interest and Money*, New York: Harcourt Brace, 1936, p. 128.

4.6 **(Related to** Solved Problem 16.4 **on page 570)** Suppose that real GDP is currently $17.1 trillion, potential GDP is $17.4 trillion, the government purchases multiplier is 2, and the tax multiplier is -1.6.

a. Holding other factors constant, by how much will government purchases need to be increased to bring the economy to equilibrium at potential GDP?

b. Holding other factors constant, by how much will taxes have to be cut to bring the economy to equilibrium at potential GDP?

c. Construct an example of a *combination* of increased government spending and tax cuts that will bring the economy to equilibrium at potential GDP.

4.7 **(Related to** Solved Problem 16.4 **on page 570)** Briefly explain whether you agree with the following statement:

> Real GDP is currently $17.7 trillion, and potential GDP is $17.4 trillion. If Congress and the president would decrease government purchases by $300 billion or increase taxes by $300 billion, the economy could be brought to equilibrium at potential GDP.

4.8 A Federal Reserve publication argues that the size of the multiplier "depends on the type of fiscal policy changes in question and the environment in which they are implemented."

a. What does the author mean by "the type of fiscal policy changes in question"? Why does the type of policy matter for the size of the multiplier?

b. What does the author mean by "the environment in which they are implemented"? Would the size of the multiplier be affected by how close real GDP is to potential GDP? Briefly explain.

Source: Daniel J. Wilson, "Government Spending: An Economic Boost?" *Federal Reserve Bank of San Francisco Economic Letter*, February 6, 2012.

4.9 If the short-run aggregate supply (*SRAS*) curve were a horizontal line at the current price level, what would be the effect on the size of the government purchases and tax multipliers? Briefly explain.

16.5 | # The Limits to Using Fiscal Policy to Stabilize the Economy, pages 571–581
LEARNING OBJECTIVE: Discuss the difficulties that can arise in implementing fiscal policy.

Summary

Poorly timed fiscal policy can do more harm than good. Getting the timing right with fiscal policy can be difficult because a president obtaining approval from Congress for a new fiscal policy can be a very long process, and it can take months for an increase in authorized spending to actually take place. Because an increase in government purchases may lead to a higher interest rate, it may result in a decline in consumption, investment, and net exports. A decline in private expenditures as a result of an increase in government purchases is called **crowding out**. Crowding out may cause an expansionary fiscal policy to fail to meet its goal of keeping real GDP at potential GDP.

Review Questions

5.1 Which can be changed more quickly: monetary policy or fiscal policy? Briefly explain.

5.2 What is meant by "crowding out"? Explain the difference between crowding out in the short run and in the long run.

Problems and Applications

5.3 Some economists argue that because increases in government spending crowd out private spending, increased government spending will reduce the long-run growth rate of real GDP.

a. Is this outcome most likely to occur if the private spending being crowded out is consumption spending, investment spending, or net exports? Briefly explain.

b. In terms of its effect on the long-run growth rate of real GDP, would it matter if the additional government spending involves (i) increased spending on highways and bridges or (ii) increased spending on national parks? Briefly explain.

5.4 According to a study by Kanishka Misra of the University of Michigan and Paolo Surico of the London Business School, "Almost half of American families did not adjust their consumption following receipt of the ... 2008 tax rebate." Don't we expect that people will increase their consumption if their disposable income increases? Was there anything about the form of the 2008 tax cut that made it more likely that people would not respond by increasing their consumption spending? Briefly explain.

Source: Kanishka Misra and Paolo Surico, "Consumption, Income Changes, and Heterogeneity: Evidence from Two Fiscal Stimulus Programs," *American Economic Journal: Macroeconomics*, Vol. 6, No. 4, October 2014, pp. 84–106.

5.5 We saw that in calculating the stimulus package's effect on real GDP, economists in the Obama administration estimated that the government purchases multiplier has a value of 1.57. John F. Cogan, Tobias Cwik, John B. Taylor, and Volker Wieland argue that the value is only 0.4.
a. Briefly explain how the government purchases multiplier can have a value of less than 1.
b. Why does an estimate of the size of the multiplier matter in evaluating the effects of an expansionary fiscal policy?

Source: John Cogan, Tobias Cwik, John Taylor, and Volker Wieland, "New Keynesian versus Old Keynesian Government Spending Multipliers," *Journal of Economic Dynamics and Control*, Vol. 34, No. 3, March 2010, pp. 281–295.

5.6 (Related to the Making the Connection **on page 572**) Why would a recession accompanied by a financial crisis be more severe than a recession that did not involve a financial crisis? Were the large budget deficits in 2009 and 2010 primarily the result of the stimulus package of 2009? Briefly explain.

5.7 Suppose that at the same time Congress and the president pursue an expansionary fiscal policy, the Federal Reserve pursues an expansionary monetary policy. How might an expansionary monetary policy affect the extent of crowding out in the short run?

5.8 (Related to the Making the Connection **on page 580**) A report from the International Monetary Fund in late 2014 contained the following observations: "Five years after the global financial crisis, the economic recovery continues but remains weak. ... Given ... the current environment of low government borrowing costs ... might this be a good time to increase public infrastructure investment?"
a. What does the report mean by "low government borrowing costs"? Why would low government borrowing costs be relevant to whether a government increases infrastructure investment?
b. The report also notes, "In advanced economies an increase in infrastructure investment ... is one of the few remaining policy levers available to support growth." What does the report mean by a "policy lever"? Why would the authors of the report consider infrastructure one of the few remaining policy levers?

Source: International Monetary Fund, "World Economic Outlook: Legacies, Clouds, Uncertainties," October 2014, pp. 75–76.

16.6 Deficits, Surpluses, and Federal Government Debt, pages 581–586

LEARNING OBJECTIVE: Define federal budget deficit and federal government debt and explain how the federal budget can serve as an automatic stabilizer.

Summary

A **budget deficit** occurs when the federal government's expenditures are greater than its tax revenues. A **budget surplus** occurs when the federal government's expenditures are less than its tax revenues. A budget deficit automatically increases during recessions and decreases during expansions. The automatic movements in the federal budget help to stabilize the economy by cushioning the fall in spending during recessions and restraining the increase in spending during expansions. The **cyclically adjusted budget deficit or surplus** measures what the deficit or surplus would be if the economy were at potential GDP. The federal government debt (or national debt) is the value of outstanding bonds issued by the U.S. Treasury. The national debt is a problem if interest payments on it require taxes to be raised substantially or require other federal expenditures to be cut.

Review Questions

6.1 In what ways does the federal budget serve as an automatic stabilizer for the economy?

6.2 What is the cyclically adjusted budget deficit or surplus? Suppose that real GDP is currently at potential GDP, and the federal budget is balanced. If the economy moves into a recession, what will happen to the federal budget?

6.3 Why do few economists believe it would be a good idea to balance the federal budget every year?

6.4 What is the difference between the federal budget deficit and federal government debt?

Problems and Applications

6.5 *Wall Street Journal* writers Josh Zumbrun and Nick Timiraos published answers to several of their readers' questions regarding the federal government's debt. Two of the questions were:
a. Why is government debt different from mine?

b. How important is it to pay off this debt?

Write a brief response to each of these questions.

Source: Josh Zumbrun and Nick Timiraos, "Q&A: What the $18 Trillion National Debt Means for the U.S. Economy," *Wall Street Journal*, February 1, 2015.

6.6 In a column in the *Financial Times*, the prime minister and the finance minister of the Netherlands argue that the European Union, an organization of 28 countries in Europe, should appoint "a commissioner for budgetary discipline." They believe that "the new commissioner should be given clear powers to set requirements for the budgetary policy of countries that run excessive deficits." What is an "excessive" budget deficit? Does judging whether a deficit is excessive depend in part on whether the country is in a recession? How can budgetary policies be used to reduce a budget deficit?

Source: Mark Rutte and Jan Kees de Jager, "Expulsion from the Eurozone Has to Be the Final Penalty," *Financial Times*, September 7, 2011.

6.7 **(Related to the** Making the Connection **on page 583)** The following is from a message by President Herbert Hoover to Congress, dated May 5, 1932:

> I need not recount that the revenues of the Government as estimated for the next fiscal year show a decrease of about $1,700,000,000 below the fiscal year 1929, and inexorably require a broader basis of taxation and a drastic reduction of expenditures in order to balance the Budget. Nothing is more necessary at this time than balancing the Budget.

Do you think President Hoover was correct in saying that, in 1932, nothing was more necessary than balancing the federal government's budget? Explain.

Source: Herbert Hoover, "Special Message to the Congress on Budgetary Legislation," in *Public Papers of the Presidents of the United States: Herbert Hoover, 1932–1933*, 1977, p. 194.

6.8 In February 2013, the Congressional Budget Office (CBO) forecast that the federal budget deficit for fiscal year 2013 would be approximately $850 billion. In May 2013, the CBO revised down its forecast of the budget deficit to $642 billion. The CBO stated that a major reason for the downward revision was "factors related mainly to the strengthening economy."

a. Why would a "strengthening economy" lead to a downward revision of the projected budget deficit?

b. Suppose that Congress and the president were committed to balancing the budget each year. Does what happened during 2013 provide any insight into difficulties they might run into in trying to balance the budget every year?

Source: Susan Davis, "CBO Drops 2013 Deficit Estimate to $642 Billion," usatoday.com, May 15, 2013.

6.9 **(Related to** Solved Problem 16.6 **on page 584)** An article in the *Wall Street Journal* in 2015 noted that an official of the European Union was forecasting that "Greece faces two years of recession amid sharp budget cuts." What typically happens to a government's budget deficit during a recession? Do governments typical respond with budget cuts as the Greek government did? Briefly explain.

Source: Gabriele Steinhauser and Andrea Thomas, "Greece Faces Two-Year Recession amid Bailout Cuts," *Wall Street Journal*, August 12, 2015.

6.10 In 2015, an article in the *Wall Street Journal* noted that "Prime Minister Shinzo Abe is expected to unveil a plan to balance Japan's budget in five years … as a step toward reducing the country's debt burden, according to government officials." What is the connection between the government's budget deficit and its debt? If the debt is a "burden," briefly explain what it is a burden on.

Source: Tatsuo Ito, "Japan Government Takes On Its Deficit-Ridden Finances," *Wall Street Journal*, June 17, 2015.

6.11 A political columnist wrote the following:

> Today … the main purpose [of governments issuing bonds] is to let craven politicians launch projects they know the public, at the moment, would rather not fully finance. The tab for these projects will not come due, probably, until after the politicians have long since departed for greener (excuse the expression) pastures.

Do you agree with this commentator's explanation for why some government spending is financed through tax receipts and other government spending is financed through borrowing, by issuing bonds? Briefly explain.

Source: Paul Carpenter, "The Bond Issue Won't Be Repaid by Park Tolls," (Allentown, PA) *Morning Call*, May 26, 2002.

16.7 ## The Effects of Fiscal Policy in the Long Run, pages 586–589

LEARNING OBJECTIVE: Discuss the effects of fiscal policy in the long run.

Summary

Some fiscal policy actions are intended to have long-run effects by expanding the productive capacity of the economy and increasing the rate of economic growth. Because these policy actions primarily affect aggregate supply rather than aggregate demand, they are sometimes called *supply-side economics*. The difference between the pretax and posttax return to an economic activity is called the **tax wedge**. Economists believe that the smaller the tax wedge for any economic activity—such as working, saving, investing, or starting a business—the more of that economic activity will occur. Economists debate the size of the supply-side effects of tax changes.

MyEconLab Visit **www.myeconlab.com** to complete these exercises online and get instant feedback.

Review Questions

7.1 What is meant by "supply-side economics"?

7.2 What is the "tax wedge"?

Problems and Applications

7.3 It seems that both households and businesses would benefit if the federal income tax were simpler and tax forms were easier to fill out. Why then have the tax laws become increasingly complicated?

7.4 Some economists and policymakers have argued in favor of a "flat tax." A flat tax would replace the current individual income tax system, with its many tax brackets, exemptions, and deductions, with a new system containing a single tax rate and few, or perhaps no, deductions and exemptions. Suppose a political candidate hired you to develop two arguments in favor of a flat tax. What two arguments would you advance? Alternatively, if you were hired to develop two arguments against a flat tax, what two arguments would you advance?

7.5 Suppose that an increase in marginal tax rates on individual income affects both aggregate demand and aggregate supply. Briefly describe the effect of the tax increase on equilibrium real GDP and the equilibrium price level. Will the changes in equilibrium real GDP and the price level be larger or smaller than they would be if the tax increase affected only aggregate demand? Briefly explain.

7.6 Writing in the *Wall Street Journal*, Martin Feldstein, an economist at Harvard University, argues that "behavioral responses" of taxpayers to the cuts in marginal tax rates enacted in 1986 resulted in "an enormous rise in the taxes paid, particularly by those who experienced the greatest reductions in marginal tax rates." How is it possible for cuts in marginal tax rates to result in an increase in total taxes collected? What does Feldstein mean by a "behavioral response" to tax cuts?

Source: Martin Feldstein, "The Tax Reform Evidence from 1986," *Wall Street Journal*, October 24, 2011.

Real-Time Data Exercises

D16.1 (Comparing macroeconomic conditions in different countries) The International Monetary Fund (IMF) publishes *The World Economic Outlook*. Go to www.imf.org and look at the most recent version available. The IMF measures the output gap as the difference between real GDP and potential GDP as a percentage of potential GDP. A negative value for the output gap means that real GDP is below potential GDP. Look at the data on the output gap for Japan, the United Kingdom, and the United States for 2013 to 2018 (the values for the later years will be forecasts).

    a. Which country had the largest output gap (in absolute value) in 2013? Which country had the smallest output gap?

    b. Discuss what fiscal policies the governments of these countries could use to bring the output gaps to zero.

    c. Describe at least two problems that these countries would have in implementing your suggested policies.

D16.2 (Comparing the actual and cyclically adjusted budget deficits in the United States) The Congressional Budget Office (CBO) provides data on the actual and cyclically adjusted budget deficits. You can find data for the years 1965–2014 at https://www.cbo.gov/sites/default/files/114th-congress-2015-2016/reports/49892/49892-breakout-AppendixD.pdf.

    a. The CBO calls the budget deficit or surplus "Deficit or Surplus with Automatic Stabilizers," and calls the cyclically adjusted deficit or surplus the "Deficit or Surplus without Automatic Stabilizers." Briefly explain why the CBO uses these labels.

    b. For the years 2000-2014, enter the data from the columns "Deficit or Surplus with Automatic Stabilizers," and "Deficit or Surplus without Automatic Stabilizers" into an Excel spreadsheet. Use the data to graph the budget deficit or surplus and the cyclically adjusted deficit or surplus for these years.

    c. Calculate the average surplus or deficit and the average cyclically adjusted surplus or deficit for these years. Which was larger? Briefly explain your result.

D16.3 (Comparing budget deficits in different countries) The International Monetary Fund (IMF) publishes *The World Economic Outlook*. Go to www.imf.org and find the IMF data for the cyclically adjusted budget deficit as a percentage of potential GDP (which the IMF calls "General Government Structural Balance") for Brazil, China, France, and Germany from 2000 to 2018 (the values for the later years will be forecasts). Use the series for the cyclically adjusted budget deficit that is measured as a percentage of potential GDP.

    a. Download the data and plot them in a graph. Which country relied the most on discretionary fiscal policy in response to the financial crisis of 2008 and 2009? Briefly explain how you are able to tell.

    b. From 2013 to 2018, which of these four countries is expected to have the most expansionary fiscal policy? Briefly explain.

Appendix

A Closer Look at the Multiplier

LEARNING OBJECTIVE: Apply the multiplier formula.

In this chapter, we saw that changes in government purchases and changes in taxes have a multiplied effect on equilibrium real GDP. In this appendix, we will build a simple economic model of the multiplier effect. When economists forecast the effect of a change in spending or taxes, they often rely on *econometric models*. These are economic models written in the form of equations, where each equation has been statistically estimated, using methods similar to those used in estimating demand curves, as briefly described in Chapter 3.

An Expression for Equilibrium Real GDP

We can write a set of equations that includes the key macroeconomic relationships we have studied in this and previous chapters. It is important to note that in this model, we will be assuming that the price level is constant. We know that this assumption is unrealistic because an upward-sloping *SRAS* curve means that when the aggregate demand curve shifts, the price level will change. Nevertheless, our model will be approximately correct when changes in the price level are small. It also serves as an introduction to more complicated models that take into account changes in the price level. For simplicity, we start with three assumptions: (1) Taxes, T, do not depend on the level of real GDP, Y; (2) there are no government transfer payments to households; and (3) we have a closed economy, with no imports or exports. The numbers (with the exception of the *MPC*) represent billions of dollars:

(1) $C = 1,000 + 0.75(Y - T)$	Consumption function
(2) $I = 1,500$	Planned investment function
(3) $G = 1,500$	Government purchases function
(4) $T = 1,000$	Tax function
(5) $Y = C + I + G$	Equilibrium condition

The first equation is the consumption function. The marginal propensity to consume, or *MPC*, is 0.75, and 1,000 is the level of autonomous consumption, which is the level of consumption that does not depend on income. We assume that consumption depends on disposable income, which is $Y - T$. The functions for planned investment spending, government spending, and taxes are very simple because we have assumed that these variables are not affected by GDP and, therefore, are constant. Economists who use this type of model to forecast GDP would, of course, use more realistic planned investment, government purchases, and tax functions.

Equation (5)—the equilibrium condition—states that equilibrium GDP equals the sum of consumption, planned investment spending, and government purchases. To calculate a value for equilibrium real GDP, we need to substitute equations (1) through (4) into equation (5). This substitution gives us the following:

$$Y = 1,000 + 0.75(Y - 1,000) + 1,500 + 1,500$$

$$= 1,000 + 0.75Y - 750 + 1,500 + 1,500.$$

We need to solve this equation for Y to find equilibrium GDP. The first step is to subtract $0.75Y$ from both sides of the equation:

$$Y - 0.75Y = 1,000 - 750 + 1,500 + 1,500.$$

Then, we solve for Y:

$$0.25Y = 3,250,$$

or:

$$Y = \frac{3,250}{0.25} = 13,000.$$

To make this result more general, we can replace particular values with general values represented by letters:

$C = \overline{C} + MPC(Y - T)$	Consumption function
$I = \overline{I}$	Planned investment function
$G = \overline{G}$	Government purchases function
$T = \overline{T}$	Tax function
$Y = C + T + G$	Equilibrium condition

The letters with bars above them represent fixed, or *autonomous*, values that do not depend on the values of other variables. So, $\overline{C}$ represents autonomous consumption, which had a value of 1,000 in our original example. Now, solving for equilibrium, we get:

$$Y = \overline{C} + MPC(Y - \overline{T}) + \overline{I} + \overline{G}$$

or:

$$Y - MPC(Y) = \overline{C} - (MPC \times \overline{T}) + \overline{I} + \overline{G}$$

or:

$$Y(1 - MPC) = \overline{C} - (MPC \times \overline{T}) + \overline{I} + \overline{G}$$

or:

MyEconLab Concept Check

$$Y = \frac{\overline{C} - (MPC \times \overline{T}) + \overline{I} + \overline{G}}{1 - MPC}.$$

A Formula for the Government Purchases Multiplier

To find a formula for the government purchases multiplier, we need to rewrite the last equation for changes in each variable rather than levels. Letting Δ stand for the change in a variable, we have:

$$\Delta Y = \frac{\Delta\overline{C} - (MPC \times \Delta\overline{T}) + \Delta\overline{I} + \Delta\overline{G}}{1 - MPC}.$$

We can find a formula for the government purchases multiplier, which is the ratio of the change in equilibrium real GDP to the change in government purchases. If we hold constant changes in autonomous consumption spending, planned investment spending, and taxes, then from the previous equation we have the following:

$$\Delta Y = \frac{\Delta G}{1 - MPC}.$$

So, we have:

$$\text{Government purchases multiplier} = \frac{\Delta Y}{\Delta G} = \frac{1}{1 - MPC}.$$

For an MPC of 0.75, the government purchases multiplier will be:

$$\frac{1}{1 - 0.75} = 4.$$

MyEconLab Concept Check
A government purchases multiplier of 4 means that an increase in government spending of \$10 billion will increase equilibrium real GDP by $4 \times \$10$ billion $= \$40$ billion.

A Formula for the Tax Multiplier

We can also find a formula for the tax multiplier. We start again with this equation:

$$\Delta Y = \frac{\Delta \bar{C} - (MPC \times \Delta \bar{T}) + \Delta \bar{I} + \Delta \bar{G}}{1 - MPC}.$$

Now we hold constant the values of autonomous consumption spending, planned investment spending, and government purchases, but we allow the value of taxes to change:

$$\Delta Y = \frac{-MPC \times \Delta T}{1 - MPC}.$$

So, we have:

$$\text{The tax multiplier} = \frac{\Delta Y}{\Delta T} = \frac{-MPC}{1 - MPC}.$$

For an MPC of 0.75, the tax multiplier will be:

$$\frac{-0.75}{1 - 0.75} = -3.$$

The tax multiplier is a negative number because an increase in taxes causes a decrease in equilibrium real GDP, and a decrease in taxes causes an increase in equilibrium real GDP. A tax multiplier of −3 means that a decrease in taxes of $10 billion will increase equilibrium real GDP by −3 × −$10 billion = $30 billion. Earlier in this chapter, we discussed the economic reasons for the tax multiplier being smaller than the government spending multiplier. MyEconLab Concept Check

The "Balanced Budget" Multiplier

What will be the effect of equal increases (or decreases) in government purchases and taxes on equilibrium real GDP? At first, it might appear that the tax increase would exactly offset the government purchases increase, leaving real GDP unchanged. But we have just seen that the government purchases multiplier is larger (in absolute value) than the tax multiplier. We can use our formulas for the government purchases multiplier and the tax multiplier to calculate the net effect of increasing government purchases by $10 billion at the same time that taxes are increased by $10 billion:

Increase in real GDP from the increase in government purchases

$$= \$10 \text{ billion} \times \frac{1}{1 - MPC}.$$

Decrease in real GDP from the increase in taxes $= \$10 \text{ billion} \times \dfrac{-MPC}{1 - MPC}.$

So, the combined effect equals:

$$\$10 \text{ billion} \times \left[\left(\frac{1}{1 - MPC} \right) + \left(\frac{-MPC}{1 - MPC} \right) \right],$$

or:

$$\$10 \text{ billion} \times \left(\frac{1 - MPC}{1 - MPC} \right) = \$10 \text{ billion}.$$

The balanced budget multiplier is, therefore, equal to $(1 - MPC)/(1 - MPC)$, or 1. Equal dollar increases and decreases in government purchases and in taxes lead to the same dollar increase in real GDP in the short run. MyEconLab Concept Check

The Effects of Changes in Tax Rates on the Multiplier

We now consider the effect of a change in the tax *rate*, as opposed to a change in a fixed amount of taxes. Changing the tax rate actually changes the value of the multiplier. To see this, suppose that the tax rate is 20 percent, or 0.2. In that case, an increase in household income of $10 billion will increase *disposable income* by only $8 billion [or 10 billion $\times$ (1 − 0.2) In general, an increase in income can be multiplied by (1 − *t*) to find the increase in disposable income, where *t* is the tax rate. So, we can rewrite the consumption function as:

$$C = \overline{C} + MPC(1 - t)Y.$$

We can use this expression for the consumption function to find an expression for the government purchases multiplier, using the same method we used previously:

$$\text{Government purchases multiplier} = \frac{\Delta Y}{\Delta G} = \frac{1}{1 - MPC(1 - t)}.$$

We can see the effect of changing the tax rate on the size of the multiplier by trying some values. First, assume that $MPC = 0.75$ and $t = 0.2$. Then:

$$\text{Government purchases multiplier} = \frac{\Delta Y}{\Delta G} = \frac{1}{1 - 0.75(1 - 0.2)} = \frac{1}{1 - 0.6} = 2.5$$

This value is smaller than the multiplier of 4 that we calculated by assuming that there was only a fixed amount of taxes (which is the same as assuming that the marginal tax *rate* was zero). This multiplier is smaller because spending in each period is now reduced by the amount of taxes households must pay on any additional income they earn. We can calculate the multiplier for an *MPC* of 0.75 and a lower tax rate of 0.1:

$$\text{Government purchases multiplier} = \frac{\Delta Y}{\Delta G} = \frac{1}{1 - 0.75(1 - 0.1)} = \frac{1}{1 - 0.675} = 3.1.$$

Cutting the tax rate from 20 percent to 10 percent increased the value of the multiplier from 2.5 to 3.1. **MyEconLab** Concept Check

The Multiplier in an Open Economy

Up to now, we have assumed that the economy is closed, with no imports or exports. We can consider the case of an open economy by including net exports in our analysis. Recall that net exports equal exports minus imports. Exports are determined primarily by factors—such as the exchange value of the dollar and the levels of real GDP in other countries—that we do not include in our model. So, we will assume that exports are fixed, or autonomous:

$$\text{Exports} = \overline{\text{Exports}}.$$

Imports will increase as real GDP increases because households will spend some portion of an increase in income on imports. We can define the *marginal propensity to import* (*MPI*) as the fraction of an increase in income that is spent on imports. So, our expression for imports is:

$$\text{Imports} = MPI \times Y.$$

We can substitute our expressions for exports and imports into the expression we derived earlier for equilibrium real GDP:

$$Y = \overline{C} + MPC(1 - t)Y + \overline{I} + \overline{G} + [\overline{\text{Exports}} - (MPI \times Y)],$$

where the expression $[\overline{\text{Exports}} - (MPI \times Y)]$ represents net exports. We can now find an expression for the government purchases multiplier by using the same method we used previously:

$$\text{Government purchases multiplier} = \frac{\Delta Y}{\Delta G} = \frac{1}{1 - [MPC(1 - t) - MPI]}.$$

We can see the effect of changing the value of the marginal propensity to import on the size of the multiplier by trying some values of key variables. First, assume that $MPC = 0.75$, $t = 0.2$, and $MPI = 0.1$. Then:

$$\text{Government purchases multiplier} = \frac{\Delta Y}{\Delta G} = \frac{1}{1 - (0.75(1 - 0.2) - 0.1)} = \frac{1}{1 - 0.5}$$
$$= 2.$$

This value is smaller than the multiplier of 2.5 that we calculated by assuming that there were no exports or imports (which is the same as assuming that the marginal propensity to import is zero). This multiplier is smaller because spending in each period is now reduced by the amount of imports households buy with any additional income they earn. We can calculate the multiplier with $MPC = 0.75$, $t = 0.2$, and a higher MPI of 0.2:

$$\text{Government purchases multiplier} = \frac{\Delta Y}{\Delta G} = \frac{1}{1 - (0.75(1 - 0.2) - 0.2)} = \frac{1}{1 - 0.4}$$
$$= 1.7.$$

Increasing the marginal propensity to import from 0.1 to 0.2 decreases the value of the multiplier from 2 to 1.7. We can conclude that countries with a higher marginal propensity to import will have smaller multipliers than countries with a lower marginal propensity to import.

Bear in mind that the multiplier is a short-run effect that assumes that real GDP is less than potential GDP. In the long run, real GDP equals potential GDP, so an increase in government purchases causes a decline in the nongovernment components of real GDP but leaves the level of real GDP unchanged.

The analysis in this appendix is simplified compared to what would be carried out by an economist forecasting the effects of changes in government purchases or changes in taxes on equilibrium real GDP in the short run. In particular, our assumption that the price level is constant is unrealistic. However, looking more closely at the determinants of the multiplier has helped us see some important macroeconomic relationships more clearly.   MyEconLab Concept Check

---

16A	**A Closer Look at the Multiplier, pages 597–601**

LEARNING OBJECTIVE: Apply the multiplier formula.

MyEconLab   Visit **www.myeconlab.com** to complete these exercises online and get instant feedback.

Problem and Applications

16A.1 Assuming a fixed amount of taxes and a closed economy, calculate the value of the government purchases multiplier, the tax multiplier, and the balanced budget multiplier if the marginal propensity to consume equals 0.6.

16A.2 Calculate the value of the government purchases multiplier if the marginal propensity to consume equals 0.8, the tax rate equals 0.25, and the marginal propensity to import equals 0.2.

16A.3 Use a graph to show the change in the aggregate demand curve resulting from an increase in government

purchases if the government purchases multiplier equals 2. On the same graph, show the change in the aggregate demand curve resulting from an increase in government purchases if the government purchases multiplier equals 4.

16A.4 Using your understanding of multipliers, explain why an increase in the tax rate would decrease the size of the government purchases multiplier. Similarly, explain why a decrease in the marginal propensity to import would increase the size of the government purchases multiplier.

16A.5 In 2012, the ratio of imports to GDP was 14 percent in Japan and 83 percent in Belgium. On the basis of this information, can you draw any conclusions about the relative sizes of the government purchases multiplier in each country?

Inflation, Unemployment, and Federal Reserve Policy

Why Does Goodyear Worry about Monetary Policy?

The Federal Reserve's dual mandate of price stability and high employment can present the Federal Open Market Committee (FOMC) with difficult decisions. For example, in mid-2015, although the unemployment rate had fallen from a high of 10.0 percent in October 2009 to 5.1 percent, the inflation rate had been well below the Fed's target of 2 percent for more than three years. Investors, as well as many households and firms, anticipated that Federal Reserve Chair Janet Yellen and her colleagues on the FOMC would finally increase the target for the federal funds rate. The federal funds rate had remained effectively at zero since December 2008, which represented a period of very low interest rates longer than any other in U.S. history. The labor market seemed healthy enough to withstand higher interest rates, but higher rates could slow growth and move inflation further below the Fed's target. The Fed was also concerned that higher interest rates would increase the exchange rate between the U.S. dollar and other currencies, making U.S. exports more expensive.

Many businesses—especially those that depend on sales of durable goods that are typically purchased with borrowed funds—closely follow monetary policy because the Fed's actions to increase and decrease interest rates affect their sales. Among these businesses is the Goodyear Tire & Rubber Company. Founded in 1898 in Akron, Ohio, Goodyear employs more than 65,000 people and had sales of more than $18 billion in 2015.

As the recession of 2007–2009 devastated the U.S. automobile market, sales of Goodyear tires plummeted, and the firm laid off thousands of workers. As the economy began to recover, in part because of the Fed's monetary policies, car and truck sales expanded, and Goodyear's fortunes improved. After a combined loss of $668 million from 2008 to 2010, Goodyear's profits in 2014 were $2.4 billion.

Interest rates affect Goodyear through their effect on car and truck sales but also through their effect on the exchange rate. As investors anticipated the Fed's raising the target for the federal funds rate, other U.S. interest rates rose, making financial investments in the United State more attractive to foreign investors. The result was a rising exchange rate and a decline in the dollar value of Goodyear's foreign sales.

The strong dollar also meant that the dollar prices of imports to the United States were falling, which would likely contribute to the inflation rate remaining below the Fed's target rate of 2 percent. In 2015, as the Fed prepared to increase its target for the federal funds rate, Yellen and her colleagues were attempting to achieve their dual mandate by reaching their targets for both the unemployment rate and the inflation rate.

Sources: Jeff Bennett, "Goodyear's Profit Drops on Currency Fluctuations," *Wall Street Journal*, July 29, 2015; Jon Hilsenrath, "Grand Central: Fed Doesn't Demand Wage Growth Before Increasing Interest Rate," *Wall Street Journal*, August 3, 2015; and Goodyear Tire & Rubber Company, *Annual Reports*, various years.

Economics in Your Life

Are There Benefits to Delaying a Job Search?

During a recession, your friend is laid off from her entry-level job as a computer analyst. You call her, but she does not seem very upset. "Our state offers workers up to 99 weeks of unemployment compensation. I have almost two years before I have to find a new job. With my education and job experience, I should be able to find a new job by then without much trouble." Your friend did well in school, but you are not sure that waiting to find a new job is a good idea. What advice would you give someone who has decided to wait so long to look for a new job? As you read the chapter, try to answer this question. You can check your answer against the one we provide on **page 627** at the end of this chapter.

A n important consideration for the Federal Reserve as it carries out monetary policy is that in the short run, there can be a trade-off between unemployment and inflation: Lower unemployment rates can result in higher inflation rates. In the long run, however, this trade-off disappears, and the unemployment rate is independent of the inflation rate. In this chapter, we will explore the relationship between inflation and unemployment in both the short run and the long run, and we will discuss what this relationship means for monetary policy. We will also provide an overview of how monetary policy has evolved over the years and conclude with a discussion of the debate over Fed policy during and after the 2007–2009 recession.

17.1 The Discovery of the Short-Run Trade-Off between Unemployment and Inflation

LEARNING OBJECTIVE: Describe the Phillips curve and the nature of the short-run trade-off between unemployment and inflation.

During most of the Fed's history, unemployment and inflation have been the two great macroeconomic problems it has contended with. When aggregate demand increases, unemployment usually falls, and inflation rises. When aggregate demand decreases, unemployment usually rises, and inflation falls. As a result, there is a *short-run trade-off* between unemployment and inflation: Higher unemployment is usually accompanied by lower inflation, and lower unemployment is usually accompanied by higher inflation. As we will see later in this chapter, this trade-off exists in the short run—a period that may be as long as several years—but disappears in the long run.

Although today the short-run trade-off between unemployment and inflation plays a role in the Fed's monetary policy decisions, this trade-off was not widely recognized until the late 1950s. In 1957, New Zealand economist A. W. Phillips plotted data on the unemployment rate and the inflation rate in Great Britain and drew a curve showing their average relationship. Since that time, a graph showing the short-run relationship between the unemployment rate and the inflation rate has been called a **Phillips curve**. (Phillips actually measured inflation by the percentage change in wages rather than by the percentage change in prices. Because wages and prices usually move together, this difference is not important to our discussion.) Figure 17.1 shows a graph similar to the one Phillips prepared. Each point on the Phillips curve represents a possible combination of the unemployment rate and the inflation rate that might be observed in a given year. Point A represents a year in which the inflation rate is 4 percent and the unemployment rate is 5 percent, and point B represents a year in which the inflation rate

Phillips curve A graph showing the short-run relationship between the unemployment rate and the inflation rate.

MyEconLab Animation

Figure 17.1

The Phillips Curve

A. W. Phillips was the first economist to show that there is usually an inverse relationship between unemployment and inflation. Here we can see this relationship at work: In the year represented by point A, the inflation rate is 4 percent and the unemployment rate is 5 percent. In the year represented by point B, the inflation rate is 2 percent and the unemployment rate is 6 percent.

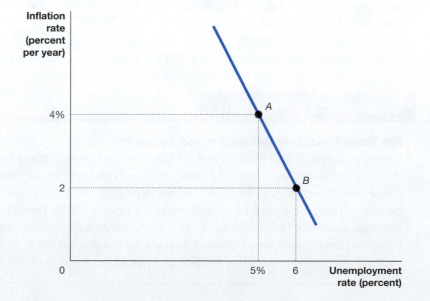

is 2 percent and the unemployment rate is 6 percent. Phillips documented that there is usually an *inverse relationship* between unemployment and inflation. During years when the unemployment rate is low, the inflation rate tends to be high, and during years when the unemployment rate is high, the inflation rate tends to be low.

Explaining the Phillips Curve with Aggregate Demand and Aggregate Supply Curves

The inverse relationship between unemployment and inflation that Phillips discovered is consistent with the aggregate demand and aggregate supply analysis we developed in Chapter 13. Figure 17.2 shows why this inverse relationship exists.

Panel (a) shows the aggregate demand and aggregate supply (*AD–AS*) model, and panel (b) shows the Phillips curve. For simplicity, in panel (a), we are using the basic *AD–AS* model, and we are assuming that the long-run aggregate supply curve and the short-run aggregate supply curve do not shift. To take a hypothetical example, assume that the economy in 2017 is at point *A*, with real GDP of $17.0 trillion and a price level of 110.0. If there is weak growth in aggregate demand during 2018, short-run equilibrium is at point *B*, with real GDP of $17.3 trillion and a price level of 112.2. The inflation rate is 2 percent, and the unemployment rate is 6 percent, which corresponds to point *B* on the Phillips curve in panel (b). If there is strong growth in aggregate demand during 2018, short-run equilibrium is at point *C*, with real GDP of $17.6 trillion and a price level of 114.4. Strong aggregate demand growth results in a higher inflation rate of 4 percent but a lower unemployment rate of 5 percent. This combination of higher inflation and lower unemployment is shown as point *C* on the Phillips curve in panel (b).

To summarize, the *AD–AS* model indicates that slow growth in aggregate demand leads to both higher unemployment and lower inflation. This result explains why

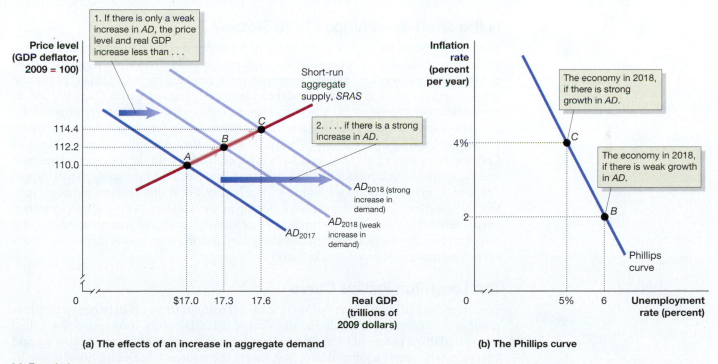

(a) The effects of an increase in aggregate demand   (b) The Phillips curve

MyEconLab Animation

Figure 17.2   **Using Aggregate Demand and Aggregate Supply to Explain the Phillips Curve**

In panel (a), short-run equilibrium in 2017 is at point *A*, with real GDP of $17.0 trillion and a price level of 110.0. If there is weak growth in aggregate demand during 2016, short-run equilibrium is at point *B*, with real GDP of $17.3 trillion and a price level of 112.2. The inflation rate is 2 percent, and the unemployment rate is 6 percent, which corresponds to point *B* on the Phillips curve in panel (b). If there is strong growth in aggregate demand during 2018, short-run equilibrium is at point *C*, with real GDP of $17.6 trillion and a price level of 114.4. Strong aggregate demand growth results in a higher inflation rate of 4 percent but a lower unemployment rate of 5 percent. This combination of higher inflation and lower unemployment is shown as point *C* on the Phillips curve in panel (b).

there is a short-run trade-off between unemployment and inflation, as shown by the downward-sloping Phillips curve. The *AD–AS* model and the Phillips curve provide different ways of illustrating the same macroeconomic events. The Phillips curve has an advantage over the *AD–AS* model, however, when we want to explicitly analyze *changes* in the inflation and unemployment rates.   MyEconLab Concept Check

Is the Phillips Curve a Policy Menu?

During the 1960s, some economists argued that the Phillips curve represented a *structural relationship* in the economy. A **structural relationship** depends on the basic behavior of consumers and firms and that remains unchanged over long periods. Structural relationships are useful in formulating economic policy because policymakers can anticipate that these relationships are constant—that is, the relationships will not change as a result of changes in policy.

    If the Phillips curve were a structural relationship, it would present policymakers with a reliable menu of combinations of unemployment and inflation. Potentially, policymakers could use expansionary monetary and fiscal policies to choose a point on the curve that had lower unemployment and higher inflation. They could also use contractionary monetary and fiscal policies to choose a point that had lower inflation and higher unemployment. Because many economists and policymakers in the 1960s viewed the Phillips curve as a structural relationship, they believed it represented a *permanent trade-off between unemployment and inflation*. As long as policymakers were willing to accept a permanently higher inflation rate, they would be able to keep the unemployment rate permanently lower. Similarly, a permanently lower inflation rate could be achieved at the cost of a permanently higher unemployment rate. As we discuss in the next section, however, economists came to realize that the Phillips curve did *not*, in fact, represent a permanent trade-off between unemployment and inflation.

Is the Short-Run Phillips Curve Stable?

During the 1960s, the basic Phillips curve relationship seemed to hold because a stable trade-off appeared to exist between unemployment and inflation. In the early 1960s, the inflation rate was low, and the unemployment rate was high. In the late 1960s, the unemployment rate had declined, and the inflation rate had increased. Then, in 1968, in his presidential address to the American Economic Association, Milton Friedman of the University of Chicago argued that the Phillips curve did *not* represent a *permanent* trade-off between unemployment and inflation. At almost the same time, Edmund Phelps of Columbia University published an academic paper making a similar argument. Friedman and Phelps noted that economists had come to agree that the long-run aggregate supply curve was vertical (a point we discussed in Chapter 13). If this observation is correct, the Phillips curve cannot be downward sloping in the long run. A critical inconsistency exists between a vertical long-run aggregate supply curve and a downward-sloping long-run Phillips curve. Friedman and Phelps argued, in essence, that there is no trade-off between unemployment and inflation in the long run.

The Long-Run Phillips Curve

To understand the argument that there is no permanent trade-off between unemployment and inflation, first recall that the level of real GDP in the long run is also called *potential GDP*. At potential GDP, firms will operate at their normal level of capacity, and everyone who wants a job will have one, except the structurally and frictionally unemployed. Friedman defined the **natural rate of unemployment** as the unemployment rate that exists when the economy is at potential GDP. The actual unemployment rate will fluctuate in the short run but will always come back to the natural rate in the long run. In the same way, the actual level of real GDP will fluctuate in the short run but will always come back to potential GDP in the long run.

    In the long run, a higher or lower price level has no effect on real GDP because real GDP is always at potential GDP in the long run. In the same way, in the long run, a higher or lower inflation rate will have no effect on the unemployment rate because

Structural relationship A relationship that depends on the basic behavior of consumers and firms and that remains unchanged over long periods.

MyEconLab Concept Check

MyEconLab Concept Check

Natural rate of unemployment The unemployment rate that exists when the economy is at potential GDP.

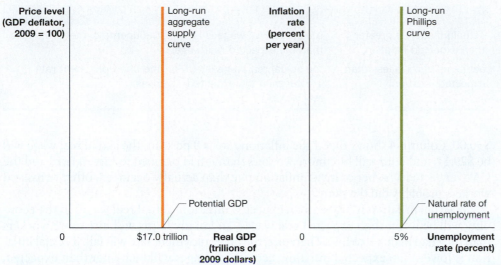

MyEconLab Animation

Figure 17.3

A Vertical Long-Run Aggregate Supply Curve Means a Vertical Long-Run Phillips Curve

Milton Friedman and Edmund Phelps argued that there is no trade-off between unemployment and inflation in the long run. If real GDP automatically returns to its potential level in the long run, the unemployment rate must return to the natural rate of unemployment in the long run. In this figure, we assume that potential GDP is $17.0 trillion and the natural rate of unemployment is 5 percent.

the unemployment rate is always equal to the natural rate in the long run. Figure 17.3 illustrates Friedman's conclusion that the long-run aggregate supply curve is a vertical line at the potential real GDP, and *the long-run Phillips curve is a vertical line at the natural rate of unemployment.*

MyEconLab Concept Check

The Role of Expectations of Future Inflation

If the long-run Phillips curve is a vertical line, *no trade-off exists between unemployment and inflation in the long run.* This conclusion seemed to contradict the experience of the 1950s and 1960s, which showed a stable trade-off between unemployment and inflation. Friedman argued that the statistics from those years actually showed only a short-run trade-off between inflation and unemployment.

Friedman argued that the short-run trade-off existed only because workers and firms sometimes expected the inflation rate to be either higher or lower than it turned out to be. Differences between the expected inflation rate and the actual inflation rate could lead the unemployment rate to rise above or fall below the natural rate. To see why, consider a simple case of Ford negotiating a wage contract with the United Auto Workers (UAW) union. Remember that both Ford and the UAW are interested in the real wage, which is the nominal wage corrected for inflation. Column 1 of Table 17.1 shows Ford and the UAW agreeing on a wage of $34.65 per hour to be paid during 2018. Column 2 shows the situation if both Ford and the UAW expect that the price level will increase from 110.0 in 2017 to 115.5 in 2018, so the inflation rate will be 5 percent. We can calculate the real wage Ford expects to pay and the UAW expects to receive as follows:

$$\text{Real wage} = \frac{\text{Nominal wage}}{\text{Price level}} \times 100 = \frac{\$34.65}{115.5} \times 100 = \$30.00.$$

But suppose that the actual inflation rate turns out to be higher or lower than the expected inflation rate of 5 percent. Column 3 shows that if the price level (*P*) rises only to 112.2 in 2018, the inflation rate will be 2 percent, and the actual real wage will be $30.88, which is higher than Ford and the UAW had expected. With a higher real wage, Ford will hire fewer workers than it had planned to at the expected real wage of

Nominal Wage	Expected Real Wage	Actual Real Wage With 2% Inflation	Actual Real Wage With 8% Inflation
	Expected $P_{2018} = 115.5$	Actual $P_{2018} = 112.2$	Actual $P_{2018} = 118.8$
	Expected inflation = 5%	Actual inflation = 2%	Actual inflation = 8%
$34.65	$\frac{\$34.65}{115.5} \times 100 = \$30.00$	$\frac{\$34.65}{112.2} \times 100 = \$30.88$	$\frac{\$34.65}{118.8} \times 100 = \$29.17$

Table 17.1

The Effect of Unexpected Price Level Changes on the Real Wage

Table 17.2

The Basis for the Short-Run Phillips Curve

If . . .	then . . .	and . . .
actual inflation is greater than expected inflation,	the actual real wage is less than the expected real wage,	the unemployment rate falls.
actual inflation is less than expected inflation,	the actual real wage is greater than the expected real wage,	the unemployment rate rises.

$30.00. Column 4 shows that if the inflation rate is 8 percent, the actual real wage will be $29.17, and Ford will hire more workers than it had planned to hire. If Ford and the UAW expected a higher or lower inflation rate than actually occurred, other firms and workers probably did the same.

If actual inflation is higher than expected inflation, actual real wages in the economy will be lower than expected real wages, and many firms will hire more workers than they had planned to hire. Therefore, the unemployment rate will fall. If actual inflation is lower than expected inflation, actual real wages will be higher than expected, many firms will hire fewer workers than they had planned to hire, and the unemployment rate will rise. Table 17.2 summarizes this argument.

Friedman and Phelps concluded that *an increase in the inflation rate increases employment (and decreases unemployment) only if the increase in the inflation rate is unexpected.* Friedman argued that in 1968, the unemployment rate was 3.6 percent rather than 5 percent only because the inflation rate of 4 percent was above the 1 percent to 2 percent inflation that workers and firms had expected: "There is always a temporary trade-off between inflation and unemployment; there is no permanent trade-off. The temporary trade-off comes not from inflation per se, but from unanticipated inflation." **MyEconLab** Concept Check

Making the Connection
MyEconLab Video

Do Workers Understand Inflation?

A higher inflation rate can lead to lower unemployment if *both* workers and firms mistakenly expect the inflation rate to be lower than it turns out to be. But this same result might be due to firms forecasting inflation more accurately than workers do or because firms understand better the effects of inflation. Some large firms employ economists to help them gather and analyze information that is useful in forecasting inflation. Many firms also have human resources or employee compensation departments that gather data on wages competing firms pay and analyze trends in compensation. Workers generally rely on much less systematic information about wages and prices. Workers also often fail to realize a fact we discussed in Chapter 9: *Expected inflation increases the value of total production and the value of total income by the same amount.* Therefore, although not all wages will rise as prices rise, inflation will increase average wages in the economy at the same time that it increases average prices.

Nobel Laureate Robert Shiller of Yale University conducted a survey on inflation and discovered that, although most economists believe an increase in inflation will lead quickly to an increase in wages, a majority of the general public thinks otherwise. As part of the survey, Shiller asked how "the effect of general inflation on wages or salary relates to your own experience and your own job." The most popular response was: "The price increase will create extra profits for my employer, who can now sell output for more; there will be no effect on my pay. My employer will see no reason to raise my pay."

Shiller also asked the following question:

> Imagine that next year the inflation rate unexpectedly doubles. How long would it probably take, in these times, before your income is increased enough so that you can afford the same things as you do today? In other words, how long will it be before a full inflation correction in your income has taken place?

Will prices rise faster than his wage?

Eighty-one percent of the public answered either that it would take several years for the purchasing power of their income to be restored or that it would never be restored.

If workers fail to understand that rising inflation leads over time to comparable increases in wages, then when inflation increases, firms, in the short run, can increase wages by less than inflation without needing to worry about workers quitting or their morale falling. As a result, a higher inflation rate will lead in the short run to lower real wages and lower unemployment. In other words, we have an explanation for a downward-sloping short-run Phillips curve.

Source: Robert J. Shiller, "Why Do People Dislike Inflation?" in *Reducing Inflation: Motivation and Strategy* by Christina D. Romer and David H. Romer, eds., Chicago: University of Chicago Press, 1997.

Your Turn: Test your understanding by doing related problems 1.11 and 1.12 on page 629 at the end of this chapter.

MyEconLab Study Plan

 17.2 **The Short-Run and Long-Run Phillips Curves**
LEARNING OBJECTIVE: Explain the relationship between the short-run and long-run Phillips curves.

If there is both a short-run Phillips curve and a long-run Phillips curve, how are the two curves related? We can begin answering this question with the help of Figure 17.4, which represents macroeconomic conditions in the United States during the 1960s. In the late 1960s, workers and firms were still expecting the inflation rate to be about 1.5 percent, as it had been from 1960 to 1965. Expansionary monetary and fiscal policies, however, had moved the short-run equilibrium up the short-run Phillips curve to an inflation rate of 4.5 percent and an unemployment rate of 3.5 percent. This very low unemployment rate was possible only because the real wage rate was unexpectedly low.

Once workers and firms began to expect that the inflation rate would continue to be about 4.5 percent, they changed their behavior. Firms knew that only nominal wage increases of more than 4.5 percent would increase real wages. Workers realized that unless they received a nominal wage increase of at least 4.5 percent, their real wage would be falling. Higher expected inflation rates had an effect throughout the economy. For example, when banks make loans, they are interested in the *real interest rate* on the loan (see Chapter 14). The real interest rate is the nominal interest rate minus the expected inflation rate. Banks will charge a nominal interest rate of 4.5 percent to receive a real interest rate of 3 percent on home mortgage loans when they expect the inflation rate to be 1.5 percent. If banks revise their expectations of the inflation rate to 4.5 percent, they will increase the nominal interest rate they charge on mortgage loans to 7.5 percent.

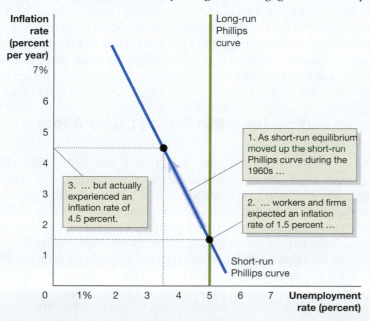

MyEconLab Animation

Figure 17.4

The Short-Run Phillips Curve of the 1960s and the Long-Run Phillips Curve

In the late 1960s, U.S. workers and firms were expecting the 1.5 percent inflation rates of the recent past to continue. However, expansionary monetary and fiscal policies moved short-run equilibrium up the short-run Phillips curve to an inflation rate of 4.5 percent and an unemployment rate of 3.5 percent.

Figure 17.5

Expectations and the Short-Run Phillips Curve

By the end of the 1960s, workers and firms had revised their expectations of inflation from 1.5 percent to 4.5 percent. As a result, the short-run Phillips curve shifted up, which made the short-run trade-off between unemployment and inflation worse.

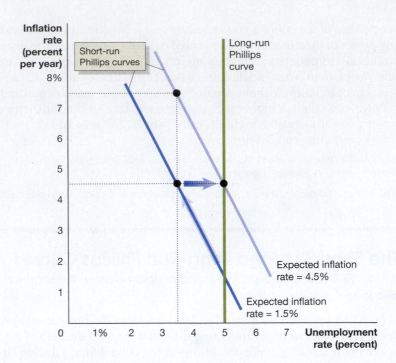

Shifts in the Short-Run Phillips Curve

A new, higher expected inflation rate can become *embedded* in the economy, meaning that workers, firms, consumers, and the government all take the inflation rate into account when making decisions. The short-run trade-off between unemployment and inflation now takes place from this higher, less favorable level, as shown in Figure 17.5.

As long as workers and firms expected the inflation rate to be 1.5 percent, the short-run trade-off between unemployment and inflation was the more favorable one shown by the lower Phillips curve. Along this Phillips curve, an inflation rate of 4.5 percent was enough to drive down the unemployment rate to 3.5 percent. Once workers and firms adjusted their expectations to an inflation rate of 4.5 percent, the short-run trade-off deteriorated to the one shown by the higher Phillips curve. At this higher expected inflation rate, the real wage rose, causing some workers to lose their jobs, and equilibrium returned to the natural rate of unemployment of 5 percent—but now with an inflation rate of 4.5 percent rather than 1.5 percent. On the higher short-run Phillips curve, an inflation rate of 7.5 percent would be necessary to reduce the unemployment rate to 3.5 percent. An inflation rate of 7.5 percent would keep the unemployment rate at 3.5 percent only until workers and firms revised their expectations of inflation up to 7.5 percent. In the long run, equilibrium would return to the 5 percent natural rate of unemployment.

As Figure 17.6 shows, there is a short-run Phillips curve for every level of expected inflation. Each short-run Phillips curve intersects the long-run Phillips curve at the expected inflation rate.   MyEconLab Concept Check

How Does a Vertical Long-Run Phillips Curve Affect Monetary Policy?

By the 1970s, most economists accepted the argument that the long-run Phillips curve is vertical. In other words, economists realized that the common view of the 1960s had been wrong: It was *not* possible to buy a permanently lower unemployment rate at the cost of a permanently higher inflation rate. The conclusion is that *in the long run, there is no trade-off between unemployment and inflation.* In the long run, the unemployment rate always returns to the natural rate, no matter what the inflation rate is.

Figure 17.7 shows that the inflation rate is stable only when the unemployment rate is equal to the natural rate. If the Federal Reserve were to attempt to use expansionary monetary policy to push short-run equilibrium to a point such as A, where the unemployment rate is below the natural rate, the result would be a movement up the short-run Phillips curve with increasing inflation. If short-run equilibrium remained below

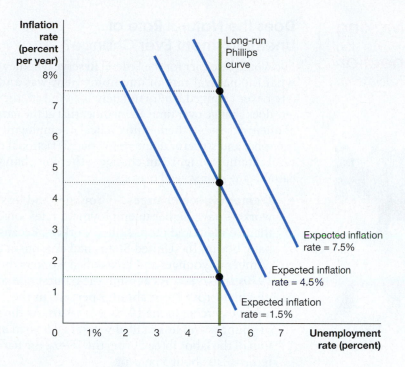

MyEconLab Animation

Figure 17.6

A Short-Run Phillips Curve for Every Expected Inflation Rate

There is a different short-run Phillips curve for every expected inflation rate. Each short-run Phillips curve intersects the long-run Phillips curve at the expected inflation rate.

the natural rate long enough, the short-run Phillips curve would shift up as workers and firms adjusted to the new, higher inflation rate. During the 1960s and 1970s, the short-run Phillips curve did shift up, presenting policymakers with a more unfavorable short-run trade-off between unemployment and inflation.

If the Federal Reserve used contractionary policy to push short-run equilibrium to a point such as B, where the unemployment rate is above the natural rate, the inflation rate would decrease. If short-run equilibrium remained above the natural rate long enough, the short-run Phillips curve would shift down as workers and firms adjusted to the new, lower inflation rate. Only at a point such as C, where the unemployment rate is equal to the natural rate, will the inflation rate be stable. Because the inflation rate has no tendency to increase or decrease when the unemployment rate equals the natural rate, the natural rate of unemployment is sometimes called the **nonaccelerating inflation rate of unemployment (NAIRU)**. We can conclude that *in the long run, the Federal Reserve can affect the inflation rate but not the unemployment rate.*   MyEconLab Concept Check

Nonaccelerating inflation rate of unemployment (NAIRU) The unemployment rate at which the inflation rate has no tendency to increase or decrease.

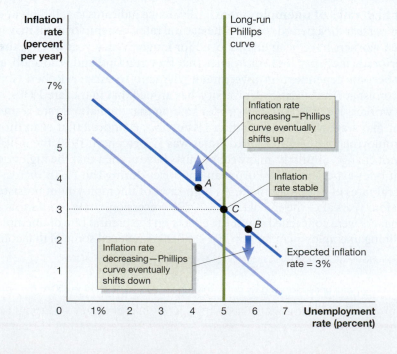

MyEconLab Animation

Figure 17.7

The Inflation Rate and the Natural Rate of Unemployment in the Long Run

The inflation rate is stable only if the unemployment rate equals the natural rate of unemployment (point C). If the unemployment rate is below the natural rate (point A), the inflation rate increases, and, eventually, the short-run Phillips curve shifts up. If the unemployment rate is above the natural rate (point B), the inflation rate decreases, and, eventually, the short-run Phillips curve shifts down.

Making
the
Connection
MyEconLab Video

An increase in the number of younger and less-skilled workers in an economy can make the natural rate of unemployment increase.

Does the Natural Rate of Unemployment Ever Change?

Life would be easier for the Federal Reserve if it knew exactly what the natural rate of unemployment was and if that rate never changed. Unfortunately for the Fed, the natural rate does change over time. Remember that at the natural rate of unemployment, there is no cyclical unemployment, only frictional and structural unemployment. Frictional or structural unemployment can change—thereby changing the natural rate—for several reasons:

- **Demographic changes.** Younger and less-skilled workers have higher unemployment rates, on average, than do older and more-skilled workers. Because of the baby boom, the United States had an unusually large number of younger and less-skilled workers during the 1970s and 1980s. As a result, the natural rate of unemployment rose from about 5 percent in the 1960s to about 6 percent in the 1970s and 1980s. As the number of younger and less-skilled workers declined as a fraction of the labor force during the 1990s, the natural rate returned to about 5 percent.

- **Labor market institutions.** Labor market institutions such as the unemployment insurance system, unions, and legal barriers to firing workers can increase the unemployment rate (see Chapter 9). Because many European countries have generous unemployment insurance systems, strong unions, and restrictive policies on firing workers, the natural rate of unemployment in most of these countries has been well above the rate in the United States. During and after the recession of 2007–2009, some economists believed that many workers in the United States had become less mobile because of the bursting of the housing bubble. These economists argued that because workers either were unable to sell their homes or were unwilling to do so because they did not want to sell for a low price, they were less likely to move from a geographic area of high unemployment to one of lower unemployment. Economists at JPMorgan Chase estimated that this lack of mobility might have temporarily increased the natural rate of unemployment from about 5 percent to about 6 percent. Economists at the Congressional Budget Office estimated that the increase in the natural rate had been somewhat smaller—from 5.0 percent to 5.5 percent.

- **Past high rates of unemployment.** Evidence indicates that if high unemployment persists for a period of years, the natural rate of unemployment may increase. When workers have been unemployed for longer than a year or two, their skills deteriorate, they may lose confidence that they can find and hold a job, and they may become dependent on government payments to survive. Robert Gordon, an economist at Northwestern University, has argued that in the late 1930s, so many U.S. workers had been out of work for so long that the natural rate of unemployment may have risen to more than 15 percent. He noted that even though the unemployment rate in the United States was 17 percent in 1939, the inflation rate did not change. Similarly, many economists have argued that the high unemployment rates experienced by European countries during the 1970s increased their natural rates of unemployment. As high rates of unemployment persisted more than four years after the end of the 2007–2009 recession, some economists and policymakers were concerned about the effects on the natural rate of unemployment. Declining unemployment rates in 2014 and 2015 reduced some of that concern.

Sources: Federal Reserve Bank of St. Louis; and "Damage Assessment," *Economist*, May 14, 2009.

MyEconLab Study Plan

Your Turn: Test your understanding by doing related problem 2.8 on page 630 at the end of this chapter.

Solved Problem 17.2

Changing Views of the Phillips Curve

Writing in a Federal Reserve publication, Bennett McCallum, an economist at Carnegie Mellon University, argues that during the 1970s, the Fed was "acting under the influence of 1960s academic ideas that posited the existence of a long-run and exploitable Phillips-type tradeoff between inflation and unemployment rates." What does McCallum mean by a "long-run and exploitable Phillips-type tradeoff"? How would the Fed have attempted to exploit this long-run trade-off? What would be the consequences for the inflation rate?

Solving the Problem

Step 1: **Review the chapter material.** This problem is about the relationship between the short-run and long-run Phillips curves, so you may want to review the section "The Short-Run and Long-Run Phillips Curves," which begins on page 609.

Step 2: **Explain what a "long-run exploitable Phillips-type tradeoff" means.** A "long-run exploitable Phillips-type tradeoff" means a Phillips curve that in the long run is downward sloping rather than vertical. An "exploitable" trade-off is one that the Fed could take advantage of to *permanently* reduce unemployment, at the expense of higher inflation, or to permanently reduce inflation, at the expense of higher unemployment.

Step 3: **Explain how the inflation rate will accelerate if the Fed tries to exploit a long-run trade-off between unemployment and inflation.** As we have seen, during the 1960s, the Fed conducted expansionary monetary policies to move up what it thought was a stationary short-run Phillips curve. By the late 1960s, these policies resulted in very low unemployment rates. In the long run, there is no stable trade-off between unemployment and inflation. Attempting to permanently keep the unemployment rate at very low levels leads to a rising inflation rate, which is what happened in the late 1960s and early 1970s.

Source: Bennett T. McCallum, "Recent Developments in Monetary Policy Analysis: The Roles of Theory and Evidence," *Federal Reserve Bank of Richmond Economic Quarterly*, Winter 2002, p. 73.

Your Turn: For more practice, do related problem 2.12 on page 631 at the end of this chapter.

17.3 Expectations of the Inflation Rate and Monetary Policy

LEARNING OBJECTIVE: Discuss how expectations of the inflation rate affect monetary policy.

How quickly does short-run equilibrium adjust from a point that is on the short-run Phillips curve but not on the long-run Phillips curve back to a point that is on the long-run Phillips curve? It depends on how quickly workers and firms adjust their expectations of future inflation to changes in current inflation. The experience in the United States over the past 60 years indicates that how quickly workers and firms adjust their expectations of inflation depends on how high the inflation rate is. There are three possibilities:

- **Low inflation.** When the inflation rate is low, as it was during most of the 1950s, the early 1960s, the 1990s, and the 2000s, workers and firms tend to ignore it. For example, if the inflation rate is low, a restaurant may not want to pay for printing new menus that would show slightly higher prices.

- **Moderate but stable inflation.** For the four-year period from 1968 to 1971, the inflation rate in the United States stayed in the narrow range between 4 percent and 5 percent. This rate was high enough that workers and firms could not ignore it without seeing their real wages and profits decline. It was also likely that the next year's inflation rate would be very close to the current year's inflation rate. In fact, workers and firms during the 1960s acted as if they expected changes in the inflation rate during one year to continue into the following year. People are said to have *adaptive expectations* of inflation if they assume that future rates of inflation will follow the pattern of rates of inflation in the recent past.

- **High and unstable inflation.** Inflation rates above 5 percent during peacetime have been rare in U.S. history, but the inflation rate was above 5 percent every year from 1973 through 1982. Not only was the inflation rate high during those years, it was also unstable—rising from 6 percent in 1973 to 11 percent in 1974, before falling below 6 percent in 1976 and rising again to 13.5 percent in 1980. In the mid-1970s, Nobel Laureates Robert Lucas of the University of Chicago and Thomas Sargent of New York University argued that the gains to accurately forecast inflation had dramatically increased. Workers and firms that failed to correctly anticipate the fluctuations in inflation during these years could experience substantial declines in real wages and profits. Therefore, Lucas and Sargent argued, people should use all available information when forming their expectations of future inflation. Expectations formed by using all available information about an economic variable are called **rational expectations**.

Rational expectations Expectations formed by using all available information about an economic variable.

The Implications of Rational Expectations for Monetary Policy

Lucas and Sargent pointed out an important consequence of rational expectations: An expansionary monetary policy would not work. In other words, there might not be a trade-off between unemployment and inflation, even in the short run. By the mid-1970s, most economists had accepted the idea that an expansionary monetary policy could cause the actual inflation rate to be higher than the expected inflation rate. This gap between actual and expected inflation would cause the actual real wage to fall below the expected real wage, pushing the unemployment rate below the natural rate. Short-run equilibrium would move up the short-run Phillips curve.

Lucas and Sargent argued that this explanation of the Phillips curve assumed that workers and firms either ignored inflation or used adaptive expectations in making their forecasts of inflation. If workers and firms have rational expectations, they will use all available information, *including knowledge of the effects of Federal Reserve policy*. If workers and firms know that an expansionary monetary policy will raise the inflation rate, they should use this information in their forecasts of inflation. If they do, an expansionary monetary policy will not cause the actual inflation rate to be above the expected inflation rate. Instead, the actual inflation rate will equal the expected inflation rate, the actual real wage will equal the expected real wage, and the unemployment rate will not fall below the natural rate.

Figure 17.8 illustrates this argument. Suppose that equilibrium is initially at point A, where the short-run Phillips curve intersects the long-run Phillips curve. The actual and expected inflation rates are both equal to 1.5 percent, and the unemployment rate equals the natural rate of 5 percent. Now suppose the Fed engages in an expansionary monetary policy. If workers ignore inflation or if they form their expectations adaptively, the expansionary monetary policy will cause the actual inflation rate to be higher than the expected inflation rate, and short-run equilibrium will move from point A on the short-run Phillips curve to point B. The inflation rate will rise to 4.5 percent, and the unemployment rate will fall to 3.5 percent. The decline in unemployment will be only temporary because workers and firms will eventually adjust to the fact that the actual inflation rate is 4.5 percent, not the 1.5 percent they had expected. The short-run Phillips curve will shift up, and the unemployment rate will return to 5 percent at point C.

Lucas and Sargent argued that if workers and firms have rational expectations, they will realize that the Fed's expansionary policy will result in an inflation rate of 4.5 percent. Therefore, as soon as the Fed announces its new policy, workers and firms

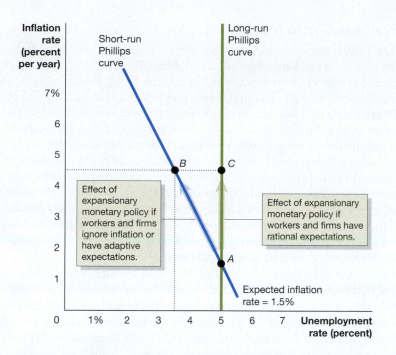

MyEconLab Animation

Figure 17.8

Rational Expectations and the Phillips Curve

If workers and firms ignore inflation, or if they have adaptive expectations, an expansionary monetary policy will cause short-run equilibrium to move from point A on the short-run Phillips curve to point B; inflation will rise, and unemployment will fall. If workers and firms have rational expectations, an expansionary monetary policy will cause the short-run equilibrium to move up the long-run Phillips curve from point A to point C. Inflation will still rise, but there will be no change in unemployment.

should adjust their expectations of inflation from 1.5 percent to 4.5 percent. There will be no temporary decrease in the real wage, leading to a temporary increase in employment and real GDP. Instead, short-run equilibrium will move immediately from point A to point C on the long-run Phillips curve. The unemployment rate will never drop below 5 percent, and the *short-run* Phillips curve will be vertical. MyEconLab Concept Check

Is the Short-Run Phillips Curve Really Vertical?

The claim by Lucas and Sargent that the short-run Phillips curve is vertical and that an expansionary monetary policy cannot reduce the unemployment rate below the natural rate surprised many economists. An obvious objection to the argument of Lucas and Sargent was that the 1950s and 1960s seemed to show that there was a short-run trade-off between unemployment and inflation and that, therefore, the short-run Phillips curve was downward sloping and not vertical. Lucas and Sargent argued that the apparent short-run trade-off was actually the result of *unexpected* changes in monetary policy. During those years, the Fed did not announce changes in policy, so workers, firms, and financial markets had to *guess* when the Fed had begun using a new policy. In that case, an expansionary monetary policy might cause the unemployment rate to fall because workers and firms would be taken by surprise, and their expectations of inflation would be too low. Lucas and Sargent argued that a policy that was announced ahead of time would not cause a change in unemployment.

Many economists have remained skeptical of the argument that the short-run Phillips curve is vertical. The two main objections raised are that (1) workers and firms may not have rational expectations, and (2) the rapid adjustment of wages and prices needed for the short-run Phillips curve to be vertical will not actually take place. Many economists doubt that people are able to use information about the Fed's monetary policy to make reliable forecasts of the inflation rate. If workers and firms do not know what effect an expansionary monetary policy will have on the inflation rate, the actual real wage may still end up being lower than the expected real wage. Also, firms may have contracts with their workers and suppliers that keep wages and prices from adjusting quickly. If wages and prices adjust slowly, then even if workers and firms have rational expectations, an expansionary monetary policy may still be able to reduce the unemployment rate in the short run. MyEconLab Concept Check

Real Business Cycle Models

During the 1980s, some economists, including Nobel Laureates Finn Kydland of the University of California, Santa Barbara, and Edward Prescott of Arizona State University, argued that Robert Lucas was correct in assuming that workers and firms formed their expectations rationally and that wages and prices adjust quickly, but that he was wrong in assuming that fluctuations in real GDP are caused by unexpected changes in monetary policy. Instead, Kydland and Prescott argued that fluctuations in "real" factors, particularly *technology shocks*, explain deviations of real GDP from its potential level. Technology shocks are changes to the economy that make it possible to produce either more output (a positive shock) or less output (a negative shock) with the same number of workers, machines, and other inputs. Real GDP will be above its previous potential level following a positive technology shock and below its previous potential level following a negative technology shock. Because these models focus on real factors—rather than on changes in the money supply—to explain fluctuations in real GDP, they are known as **real business cycle models**.

> **Real business cycle models** Models that focus on real rather than monetary explanations of fluctuations in real GDP.

The approach of Lucas and Sargent and the real business cycle models are sometimes grouped together under the label *the new classical macroeconomics* because they share the assumptions that people have rational expectations and that wages and prices adjust rapidly. Some of the assumptions of the new classical macroeconomics are similar to those held by economists before the Great Depression of the 1930s. John Maynard Keynes, in his 1936 book *The General Theory of Employment, Interest, and Money*, referred to these earlier economists as "classical economists." Like the classical economists, the new classical macroeconomists believe that the economy will normally be at its potential level.

Economists who find the assumptions of rational expectations and rapid adjustment of wages and prices appealing are likely to accept the real business cycle model approach. Other economists are skeptical of these models because the models explain recessions as being caused by negative technology shocks. Negative technology shocks are uncommon and, apart from the oil price increases of the 1970s, real business cycle theorists have had difficulty identifying shocks that would have been large enough to cause recessions. Some economists have begun to develop real business cycle models that allow for the possibility that changes in monetary policy may affect the level of real GDP. If real business cycle models continue to develop along these lines, they may eventually converge with the models the Fed uses.

MyEconLab Study Plan   MyEconLab Concept Check

17.4 Federal Reserve Policy from the 1970s to the Present

LEARNING OBJECTIVE: Use a Phillips curve graph to show how the Federal Reserve can permanently lower the inflation rate.

We have already seen that the high inflation rates of the late 1960s and early 1970s were due in part to the Federal Reserve's attempts to keep the unemployment rate below the natural rate. By the mid-1970s, the Fed also had to deal with the inflationary effect of oil price increases resulting from actions by the Organization of the Petroleum Exporting Countries (OPEC). By the late 1970s, as the Fed attempted to deal with the problem of high and worsening inflation rates, it received conflicting policy advice. Many economists argued that the inflation rate could be reduced only at the cost of a temporary increase in the unemployment rate. Followers of the Lucas–Sargent rational expectations approach, however, argued that a painless reduction in the inflation rate was possible. Before analyzing the actual policies the Fed used, we can look at why the oil price increases of the mid-1970s made the inflation rate worse.

The Effect of a Supply Shock on the Phillips Curve

As we saw in Chapter 13, the increases in oil prices in 1974 caused the short-run aggregate supply curve to shift to the left. This shift is shown in panel (a) of Figure 17.9. (For simplicity, in this panel, we use the basic rather than the dynamic AD–AS model.)

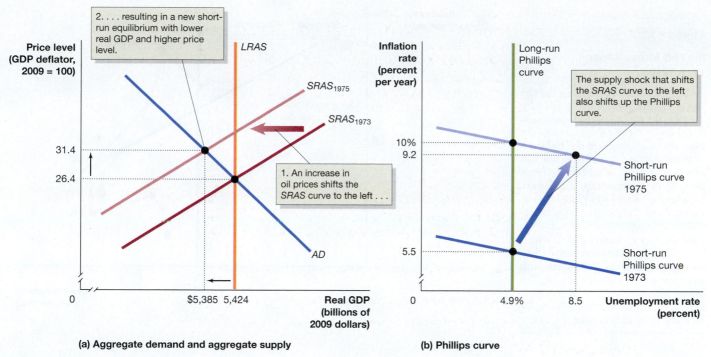

(a) Aggregate demand and aggregate supply

(b) Phillips curve

MyEconLab Animation

Figure 17.9   A Supply Shock Shifts the *SRAS* Curve and the Short-Run Phillips Curve

When actions by OPEC increased the price of a barrel of oil from less than $3 to more than $10, panel (a) shows that the *SRAS* curve shifted to the left. Between 1973 and 1975, real GDP declined from $5,424 billion to $5,385 billion, and the price level rose from 26.4 to 31.4. Panel (b) shows that the supply shock shifted up the Phillips curve. In 1973, the U.S. economy had an inflation rate of 5.5 percent and an unemployment rate of 4.9 percent. By 1975, the inflation rate had risen to about 9.2 percent and the unemployment rate to about 8.5 percent.

The result was an increase in the price level from 26.4 to 31.4 and a decrease in real GDP from $5,424 billion to $5,385 billion. On a Phillips curve graph—panel (b) of Figure 17.9—we can shift the short-run Phillips curve up to show that the inflation rate and unemployment rate both increased: from an unemployment rate of 4.9 percent and an inflation rate of about 5.5 percent in 1973 to an unemployment rate of 8.5 percent and an inflation rate of about 9.2 percent in 1975.

This combination of rising unemployment and rising inflation placed the Federal Reserve in a difficult position. If the Fed used an expansionary monetary policy to fight the high unemployment rate, the *AD* curve would shift to the right, and short-run equilibrium would move up the short-run Phillips curve. Real GDP would increase, and the unemployment rate would fall—but at the cost of higher inflation. If the Fed used a contractionary monetary policy to fight the high inflation rate, the *AD* curve would shift to the left, and short-run equilibrium would move down the short-run Phillips curve. As a result, real GDP would fall, and the inflation rate would be reduced—but at the cost of higher unemployment. In the end, the Fed chose to fight high unemployment with an expansionary monetary policy, even though that decision worsened the inflation rate.

MyEconLab Concept Check

Paul Volcker and Disinflation

By the late 1970s, the Federal Reserve had gone through two decades of continually increasing the rate of growth of the money supply. In August 1979, President Jimmy Carter appointed Paul Volcker as chairman of the Federal Reserve. Along with most other economists, Volcker was convinced that high inflation rates were damaging the economy. To reduce inflation, Volcker began reducing the annual growth rate of the money supply. This contractionary monetary policy raised interest rates, causing a

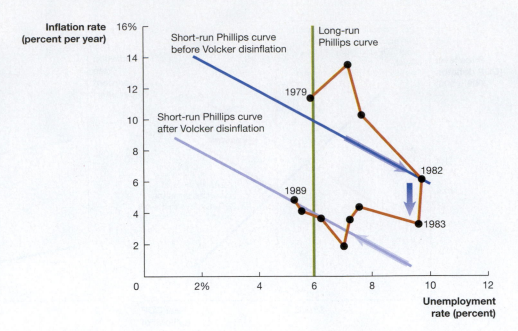

Figure 17.10

The Fed Tames Inflation, 1979–1989

Under Chairman Paul Volcker, the Fed began fighting inflation in 1979 by reducing the growth of the money supply, thereby raising interest rates. By 1982, the unemployment rate had risen to 10 percent, and the inflation rate had fallen to 6 percent. As workers and firms lowered their expectations of future inflation, the short-run Phillips curve shifted down. This adjustment in expectations allowed the Fed to switch to an expansionary monetary policy, which by 1987 brought unemployment back to the natural rate of unemployment, with an inflation rate of about 4 percent. The orange line shows the actual combinations of unemployment and inflation for each year from 1979 to 1989.

Disinflation A significant reduction in the inflation rate.

decline in aggregate demand. Figure 17.10 uses the Phillips curve model to analyze the movements in unemployment and inflation from 1979 to 1989.

The Fed's contractionary monetary policy moved short-run equilibrium down the short-run Phillips curve, lowering the inflation rate from 11 percent in 1979 to 6 percent in 1982—but at a cost of raising the unemployment rate from 6 percent to 10 percent. As workers and firms lowered their expectations of future inflation, the short-run Phillips curve shifted down, improving the short-run trade-off between unemployment and inflation. This adjustment in expectations allowed the Fed to switch to an expansionary monetary policy. By 1987, equilibrium was back to the natural rate of unemployment, which during these years was about 6 percent. The orange line in Figure 17.10 shows the actual combinations of unemployment and inflation for each year from 1979 to 1989.

Under Volcker's leadership, the Fed had reduced the inflation rate from more than 10 percent to less than 5 percent. The inflation rate has generally remained below 5 percent ever since. A significant reduction in the inflation rate is called **disinflation**. In fact, this episode is often called the "Volcker disinflation." The disinflation had come at a very high price, however. From September 1982 through June 1983, the unemployment rate was above 10 percent for the first time since the end of the Great Depression of the 1930s.

Some economists argue that the Volcker disinflation provides evidence against the view that workers and firms have rational expectations. Newspapers and television widely publicized Volcker's announcement in October 1979 that he planned to use a contractionary monetary policy to bring down the inflation rate. If workers and firms had rational expectations, we might expect that they would have quickly reduced their expectations of future inflation. There should have been a smooth movement down the long-run Phillips curve. As we have seen, however, there was a movement down the existing short-run Phillips curve, and only after several years of high unemployment did the short-run Phillips curve shift down. Apparently, workers and firms had adaptive expectations—changing their expectations of future inflation only after the current inflation rate had fallen.

Robert Lucas and Thomas Sargent argue, however, that a less painful disinflation would have occurred if workers and firms had *believed* Volcker's announcement that he was fighting inflation. The problem was that previous Fed chairmen had made similar

Don't Let This Happen to You

Don't Confuse Disinflation with Deflation

Disinflation refers to a decline in the *inflation rate*. *Deflation* refers to a decline in the *price level*. Paul Volcker and the Federal Reserve brought about a substantial disinflation in the United States during the years between 1979 and 1983. The inflation rate fell from more than 11 percent in 1979 to less than 5 percent in 1984. Yet even in 1984, there was no deflation: The price level was still rising—but at a slower rate.

The last period of significant deflation in the United States was in the early 1930s, during the Great Depression. The following table shows the consumer price index for each of those years.

Because the price level fell each year from 1929 to 1933, there was deflation.

Year	Consumer Price Index	Deflation Rate
1929	17.1	—
1930	16.7	−2.3%
1931	15.2	−9.0
1932	13.7	−9.9
1933	13.0	−5.1

MyEconLab Study Plan

Your Turn: Test your understanding by doing related problem 4.5 on page 632 at the end of this chapter.

promises throughout the 1970s, but the inflation rate had continued to increase. By 1979, the credibility of the Fed was at a low point. Some support for Lucas's and Sargent's argument comes from surveys of business economists at the time, which showed that they also reduced their forecasts of future inflation only slowly, even though they were well aware of Volcker's announcement of a new policy.   MyEconLab Concept Check

Solved Problem 17.4

MyEconLab Interactive Animation

Using Monetary Policy to Lower the Inflation Rate

Consider the following hypothetical situation: The unemployment rate is currently at the natural rate of 5 percent, the actual inflation rate is 6 percent, and, because it has remained at 6 percent for several years, workers and firms expect the inflation rate to remain at 6 percent in the future.

The Federal Reserve decides to reduce the inflation rate permanently to 2 percent. How can the Fed use monetary policy to achieve this objective? Be sure to use a Phillips curve graph in your answer.

Solving the Problem

Step 1:   Review the chapter material.   This problem is about using a Phillips curve graph to show how the Fed can fight inflation, so you may want to review the section "Paul Volcker and Disinflation," which begins on page 617.

Step 2:   Explain how the Fed can use monetary policy to reduce the inflation rate.   To reduce the inflation rate significantly, the Fed will have to raise the target for the federal funds rate. Higher interest rates will reduce aggregate demand, raise unemployment, and move equilibrium down the short-run Phillips curve.

Step 3:   Illustrate your argument with a Phillips curve graph.   How much the unemployment rate would have to rise to drive the inflation rate down from 6 percent to 2 percent depends on the steepness of the short-run Phillips curve. In drawing this graph, we have assumed that the unemployment rate would have to rise from 5 percent to 7 percent.

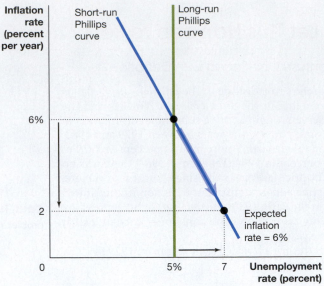

Step 4: **Show on your graph how the Fed can achieve a permanent reduction in the inflation rate from 6 percent to 2 percent.** For the decline in the inflation rate to be permanent, the expected inflation rate has to decline from 6 percent to 2 percent. We can show this decline on the graph:

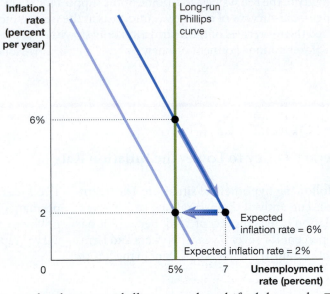

Once the short-run Phillips curve has shifted down, the Fed can use an expansionary monetary policy to push equilibrium back to the natural rate of unemployment. This policy is similar to the one carried out by the Fed after Paul Volcker became chairman in 1979. The downside to these policies of disinflation is that they lead to significant short-term increases in unemployment.

Extra Credit: A follower of the new classical macroeconomics approach would have a more optimistic view of the consequences of using monetary policy to lower the inflation rate from 6 percent to 2 percent. According to new classical approach, the Fed's policy announcement should cause people to immediately revise downward their expectations of future inflation from 6 percent to 2 percent. Short-run equilibrium would move directly down the long-run Phillips curve from an inflation rate of 6 percent to an inflation rate of 2 percent, while keeping the unemployment rate constant at 5 percent. For the reasons discussed in this chapter, many economists are skeptical that disinflation can be brought about so painlessly.

MyEconLab Study Plan   **Your Turn:** For more practice, do related problem 4.7 on page 632 at the end of this chapter.

Alan Greenspan, Ben Bernanke, Janet Yellen, and the Crisis in Monetary Policy

President Ronald Reagan appointed Alan Greenspan to succeed Paul Volcker as Fed chairman in 1987. Greenspan served for more than 18 years. When he stepped down in January 2006, President George W. Bush appointed Ben Bernanke to take his place. In January 2013, President Barack Obama appointed Janet Yellen to take Bernanke's place. Greenspan, Bernanke, and Yellen shared Volcker's determination to keep the inflation rate low. Table 17.3 shows that the average annual inflation rate was lower during Greenspan's and Bernanke's terms, and the initial months of Yellen's term, than it had been during the terms of their three most immediate predecessors. Under Greenspan's leadership of the Fed, inflation was reduced nearly to the low levels experienced during the term of Chairman William McChesney Martin in the 1950s and 1960s. Greenspan's term was marked by only two short and mild recessions, in 1990–1991 and 2001. When Greenspan left office in 2006, he was widely applauded by economists, policymakers, and the media.

Following the severe recession of 2007-2009, some critics questioned whether decisions the Fed made under Greenspan's leadership might have played a role in bringing on the financial crisis that led to the recession. We will discuss those arguments after briefly reviewing two other developments in monetary policy during the past 20 years:

- **Deemphasizing the money supply.**   Greenspan's term was notable for the Fed's continued movement away from using the money supply as a monetary policy target. We saw in Chapter 14 that during the 1980s and 1990s, the close relationship between growth in the money supply and inflation broke down. Before 1987, the Fed would announce annual targets for the growth rates of M1 and M2. In February 1987, near the end of Paul Volcker's term, the Fed announced that it would no longer set targets for M1. In July 1993, Alan Greenspan announced that the Fed also would no longer set targets for M2. Instead, the Federal Open Market Committee (FOMC) has relied on setting targets for the federal funds rate to meet its dual mandate of price stability and high employment.

- **Emphasizing Fed credibility.**   The Fed learned an important lesson during the 1970s: Workers, firms, and investors in stock and bond markets have to view Fed announcements as credible if monetary policy is to be effective. As inflation worsened throughout the late 1960s and the 1970s, the Fed announced repeatedly that it would take actions to reduce inflation. In fact, policies either were not implemented or were ineffective, and inflation rose. These repeated failures to follow through on announced policies had greatly reduced the Fed's credibility by the time Paul Volcker took office in August 1979. The contractionary monetary policy that the Fed announced in October 1979 had less effect on the expectations of workers, firms, and investors than it would have had if the Fed's credibility had been greater. It took a severe recession to convince people that this time, the inflation rate really was coming down. Only then were workers willing to accept lower nominal wage increases, banks willing to accept lower interest rates on mortgage loans, and investors willing to accept lower interest rates on bonds.

Table 17.3

The Record of Fed Chairs and Inflation

Federal Reserve Chairman	Term	Average Annual Inflation Rate during Term
William McChesney Martin	April 1951 to January 1970	2.2%
Arthur Burns	February 1970 to March 1978	6.5
G. William Miller	March 1978 to August 1979	9.1
Paul Volcker	August 1979 to August 1987	6.2
Alan Greenspan	August 1987 to January 2006	3.1
Ben Bernanke	January 2006 to January 2014	2.2
Janet Yellen	January 2014 to October 2015*	0.9

* The value for Janet Yellen is computed for just these initial months of her term.

Sources: U.S. Bureau of Labor Statistics; and Federal Reserve Board of Governors.

Over the past 25 years, the Fed has taken steps to enhance its credibility. Most importantly, whenever a change in Fed policy has been announced, the change has actually taken place. In addition, Greenspan revised the previous Fed policy of keeping secret the target for the federal funds rate. Since February 1994, any change in the target rate has been announced at the conclusion of the FOMC meeting at which the change is made. In addition, the minutes of the FOMC meetings are now made public after a brief delay. In February 2000, the Fed began making its intentions for future policy clearer by stating at the end of each FOMC meeting whether it considered the economy in the future to be at greater risk of higher inflation or of recession. In 2011, Ben Bernanke began holding press conferences following some FOMC meetings, which was the first time a Fed chair had done so.

The Decision to Intervene in the Failure of Long-Term Capital Management Greenspan's ability to help guide the economy through a long period of economic stability and his moves to enhance Fed credibility were widely applauded. However, two actions by the Fed during Greenspan's term have been identified as possibly contributing to the financial crisis that increased the length and severity of the 2007–2009 recession. One was the decision during 1998 to help save the hedge fund Long-Term Capital Management (LTCM). Hedge funds raise money, typically from wealthy investors, and use sophisticated investment strategies that often involve significant risk. Hedge funds generally rely heavily on borrowing in order to leverage their investments, thereby increasing potential returns. LTCM included as partners Robert Merton and Myron Scholes, who had both been awarded the Nobel Prize in Economics.

In the spring of 1998, LTCM suffered heavy losses on several of its investments, partly because the Russian government announced it would no longer make payments on some of its bonds, causing their value to sharply decline. Other financial firms that had loaned money to LTCM feared that the hedge fund would go bankrupt and began to push for repayment of their loans. We have seen that a run on a financial firm can cause widespread problems in the financial system. If LTCM had been forced to quickly sell all of its investments, the prices of the securities it owned would have declined, causing problems for other financial firms that held the same securities (see Chapter 14). The Fed was concerned that a sudden failure of LTCM might lead to failures of other financial firms. With the support of Alan Greenspan, William McDonough, president of the Federal Reserve Bank of New York, held a meeting between the management of LTCM and the financial firms to which LTCM owed money. The firms were persuaded to give LTCM enough time to slowly sell off—or "unwind"—its investments to keep the prices of those investments from falling too rapidly and to avoid a financial panic.

The Fed's actions succeeded in avoiding wider damage from LTCM's failure, but some critics argued that the Fed's intervention had negative consequences in the long run because it allowed the owners of LTCM and the firms that had loaned LTCM money to avoid the full consequences of LTCM's failed investments. These critics argued that the Fed's intervention set the stage for other firms—particularly highly leveraged investment banks and hedge funds—to take on excessive risk, with the expectation that the Fed would intervene on their behalf should they suffer heavy losses on the investments.

Although some critics see the Fed's actions in the case of LTCM as encouraging the excessive risk taking that helped result in the financial crisis of 2007–2009, other observers doubt that the Fed's actions had much effect on the behavior of managers of financial firms.

The Decision to Keep the Target for the Federal Funds Rate at 1 Percent from June 2003 to June 2004 In response to the popping of the dot-com stock bubble in the spring of 2000, the beginning of a recession in March 2001, and the terrorist attacks of September 11, 2001, the Fed successively lowered the target for the federal funds rate. The target rate was cut in a series of steps from 6.5 percent in May 2000 to 1 percent in June 2003. The target remained at 1 percent until the Fed raised it to 1.25 percent in June 2004. Some economists and policymakers have criticized the Fed's decision to continue cutting the target for the federal funds rate for more than 18 months after the end of the recession in November 2001 and to keep the rate at 1 percent for another year. At the time, the FOMC argued that although the recession of 2001 was mild, the very low inflation rates of late 2001 and 2002 raised the possibility that the U.S. economy could slip into a period of deflation. As we have seen, deflation can damage the economy by raising real interest rates and by causing consumers to postpone purchases, based on the expectation that future prices will be lower than current prices (see Chapter 15).

Critics argued, though, that by keeping interest rates low for an extended period, the Fed helped to fuel the housing bubble that eventually deflated beginning in 2006, with disastrous results for the economy. We have seen that the origins of the housing bubble are complex and that contributing factors included the increase in securitization of mortgages, the willingness of banks and other lenders to give loans to subprime and Alt-A borrowers, and the widespread use of adjustable-rate mortgages that allowed borrowers to qualify for larger loans than would have been possible using conventional mortgages. Economists will continue to debate whether the Fed's policy of keeping the target for the federal funds rate very low for an extended period caused the housing bubble. MyEconLab Concept Check

Making the Connection
MyEconLab Video

Should the Fed Attempt to Guide the Expectations of Investors?

In testifying before Congress in 2015, Federal Reserve Chair Janet Yellen discussed how the Fed has been using "forward guidance" as a monetary policy tool since 2008. Forward guidance refers to central banks telling the public what future monetary policy will be. As Yellen put it, "The FOMC is . . . providing forward guidance that offers information about our policy outlook and expectations for the future path of the federal funds rate."

The Fed targets the federal funds rate and can control its value. But the Fed has less control over long-term interest rates, such as the interest rates on mortgage loans or corporate bonds, that have a direct effect on household and firm spending. The level of long-term interest rates depends partly on the expectations of households, firms, and investors of future short-term interest rates. For example, when investors believe that the federal funds rate will be low in future years, the interest rate on 10-year U.S. Treasury notes will usually also be low. The interest rate on 10-year Treasury notes plays an important role in the financial system because changes in it are typically reflected in other long-term interest rates, particularly the interest rate on mortgage loans. Beginning in 2008, the Fed used forward guidance to help keep the interest rate on 10-year Treasury notes low. As the figure below shows, this key interest rate generally remained at very low levels during and following the recession.

Federal Reserve Chair Janet Yellen testified before Congress in 2015 and explained the monetary policy tool of "forward guidance."

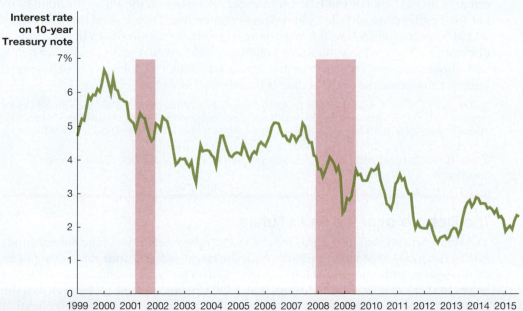

After becoming Fed chair in 2013, Yellen quickly learned how sensitive investors are to any hint from the Fed that interest rate policy might change. At a press conference after her first FOMC meeting, some of her remarks seemed to indicate that the Fed might raise its target for the federal funds rate earlier than investors had anticipated. The result shown in the graph below was a quick upward spike in the interest rate on the 10-year Treasury note.

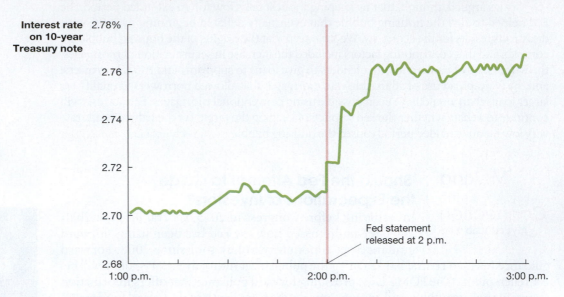

Eventually, Yellen and other Fed officials were able to reassure investors that Fed policy had not abruptly changed, and the interest rate on the 10-year Treasury declined. Still, as Yellen put it, "We will try as hard as we can not to be a source of instability here."

Many economists credited the Fed's policy of forward guidance, in combination with its policy of quantitative easing (discussed in Chapter 15), with aiding the recovery from the 2007–2009 recession by keeping long-term interest rates low. Some economists, though, were concerned that forward guidance was contributing to a prolonged period of abnormally low interest rates. Such low interest rates could lead to distortions in the financial system and the wider economy by, for instance, leading to speculative bubbles in stocks or other financial assets as investors borrowed at low interest rates to buy these assets. Some economists were also troubled by the effect that stray remarks by Fed officials can have on financial markets—as shown by the bond market's strong reaction to Yellen's initial press conference. They argued that Fed policy would be more transparent if it were constrained by a rule similar to the Taylor rule discussed in Chapter 15. A rules-based monetary policy would make it easier for firms, households, and investors to accurately anticipate future Fed policy without having to interpret sometimes unclear statements from Fed officials.

Sources: Janet L. Yellen, *Semiannual Monetary Policy Report to the Congress,* February 25, 2015; Jon Hilsenrath and Victoria McGrane, "Yellen Debut Rattles Markets," *Wall Street Journal,* March 19, 2014; David Wessel, "Ahead of Janet Yellen's Testimony, Fed's Forward Guidance Is Working," *Wall Street Journal,* February 10, 2014; and Federal Reserve Bank of St. Louis.

MyEconLab Study Plan **Your Turn:** Test your understanding by doing related problem 4.9 on page 633 at the end of this chapter.

The Debate over the Fed's Future

The financial crisis of 2007–2009 led the Fed to move well beyond the federal funds rate as the focus of monetary policy. With the target federal funds rate having been driven to zero without sufficient expansionary effect on the economy, some observers began to speak of a "crisis in monetary policy." In Chapters 14 and 15, we reviewed the new policies the Fed used during and after the financial crisis. Like many policies that represent a sharp break with the past, the Fed's actions had both supporters and critics. While most economists and policymakers gave the Fed credit for keeping the financial crisis from leading to a downturn as severe as the Great Depression of the 1930s, some argued that the Fed had overstepped its authority as determined by the Federal Reserve Act. In this section, we review some of the changes to Fed operations contained in the Wall Street Reform and Consumer Protection Act (Dodd-Frank Act), which Congress passed in 2010, and also discuss current proposals in Congress for additional changes.

Changes under the Dodd-Frank Act Traditionally, the Fed had made discount loans only to commercial banks. Under Section 13(3) of the Federal Reserve Act, though, the Fed had the legal authority in "unusual and exigent circumstances" to make loans to "any individual, partnership, or corporation." During the financial crisis, the Fed invoked this authority to make loans to investment banks, provide funds for JPMorgan Chase's purchase of the failing investment bank Bear Stearns, provide funds to the AIG insurance company, and buy commercial paper issued by nonfinancial firms.

Some members of Congress were critical of these actions because they saw them as going too far beyond the Fed's mandate and were concerned that the Fed would make similar loans as a routine part of monetary policy. As a result, a provision of the Dodd-Frank Act revised Section 13(3) of the Federal Reserve Act to restrict the Fed's ability to make loans except to commercial banks. In particular, the Fed is no longer allowed to make loans "for the purpose of assisting a single and specific company avoid bankruptcy." During the crisis, the Fed took action to save Bear Stearns and AIG under what is called the **too-big-to-fail policy**, which holds that the federal government should not allow large financial firms to fail, for fear of damaging the financial system. As we saw in Chapter 15, however, some economists believe that this policy increases moral hazard because managers of financial firms may make riskier investments if they believe that the federal government will save them from bankruptcy. These provisions of the Dodd-Frank Act make it much more difficult for the Fed to use a too-big-to-fail policy.

Some economists are critical of these restrictions on the Fed's ability to lend freely in a crisis. They argue that the failure of the Lehman Brothers investment bank in September 2008 shows the damage to the financial system that can occur as the result of the failure of a single large financial firm.

Too-big-to-fail policy A policy under which the federal government does not allow large financial firms to fail, for fear of damaging the financial system.

Proposals for Further Changes to the Fed In 2015, several proposals in Congress were intended to change the Fed's operations or structure. There were competing bills, and it was unclear which, if any, of them might be enacted into law, but these were the key changes being considered:

- **Require the Fed to adopt a formal policy rule.** As we noted in Chapter 15, the Sound Dollar Act incorporated a provision that would require the Fed to adopt a policy rule like the Taylor rule. Although the FOMC would be able to deviate from the rule in a crisis, it would be required to state the reasons for the deviation. The purpose of the rule is to reduce the discretion of the FOMC to pursue policies, such as those pursued prior to Paul Volcker becoming Fed chair in 1979, that might result in high inflation rates. It would also avoid prolonged periods of very low targets for the federal funds rate, such as occurred in 2003–2004 and again after 2011. In both these cases, the Taylor rule indicated a higher target for the federal funds rate than the Fed actually implemented. A rules-based policy also makes it easier for businesses, households, and investors to anticipate future Fed actions. Critics of this proposal argued that it would further reduce the ability of the Fed to respond rapidly to a financial crisis.

- **Make price stability the Fed's sole policy goal.** For many years, the Fed has interpreted the Federal Reserve Act as giving it a *dual mandate* of price stability and high employment. Because, as we have seen, in the long run the Fed can affect the price level but not the level of real GDP or employment, some policymakers and economists believe that the Fed should have the single goal of price stability. Critics of this proposal believe it would handicap the Fed in responding to declines in output and employment during recessions.

- **Changes to the Fed's structure.** Members of Congress proposed various changes to the Fed's structure. One relatively minor change would make all 12 Federal Reserve District Bank presidents voting members of the FOMC. Recall from Chapter 14 that under the current procedure, the president of the Federal Reserve Bank of New York is always a voting member of the FOMC, while 4 of the other 11 District Bank presidents rotate through one-year terms as voting members. Another proposal was to add two new Federal Reserve Districts and realign the boundaries of the current districts to reflect the changes in the distribution of the U.S. population since the Fed's founding in 1914. Finally, some members of Congress proposed that the president of the United States directly appoint the presidents of the Federal Reserve District Banks. Currently, the presidents are elected by the boards of directors of the District Banks, subject to the approval of the Fed's Board of Governors.

- **Audit the Fed's monetary policy actions.** The General Accountability Office (GAO) audits—or reviews—the Fed's finances, as it does the finances of other federal agencies. Congress has not given the GAO the authority to audit the Fed's monetary policy actions, although the Dodd-Frank Act changed the law to allow the GAO to audit other Fed activities, such as loans made to a single firm—like the loans provided to Bear Stearns during the financial crisis. Senator Rand Paul of Kentucky proposed that the GAO's authority be extended so that it can audit and provide public evaluations of the Fed's monetary policy actions. Fed officials and many economists were critical of this proposal because they believed the audits might be used by Congress to pressure the Fed into avoiding monetary policy actions that were in the best interest of the economy, but that might be politically unpopular.

A key point in the debate over changes to the Fed's structure and operations is concern over undermining the Fed's ability to carry out monetary policy without regard to possible political pressure from Congress or the president. The main reason to keep the Fed—or any country's central bank—independent of the rest of the government is to avoid inflation. Whenever a government is spending more than it is collecting in taxes, it must borrow the difference by selling bonds. The governments of many developing countries have difficulty finding anyone other than their central bank to buy their bonds. The more bonds the central bank buys, the faster the money supply grows, and the higher the inflation rate will be. Even in developed countries, governments that control their central banks may be tempted to sell bonds to the central bank rather than to the public.

Another fear is that a government that controls the central bank may use that control to further its political interests. It is difficult in any democratic country for a government to be reelected at a time of high unemployment. In the United States, for example, a president who had control over the Fed might be tempted to increase the money supply and drive down interest rates to increase production and employment just before running for reelection, even if doing so led in the long run to higher inflation and accompanying economic costs.

We might expect that the more independent a country's central bank is, the lower the inflation rate in the country, and the less independent a country's central bank, the higher the inflation rate. In a classic study, Alberto Alesina and Lawrence Summers, who were both economists at Harvard University at the time, tested this idea by comparing the degree of central bank independence and the inflation rate for 16 high-income countries during the years 1955–1988. Figure 17.11 shows the results.

Countries with highly independent central banks, such as the United States, Switzerland, and Germany, had lower inflation rates than countries whose central banks had little independence, such as New Zealand, Italy, and Spain. In the following

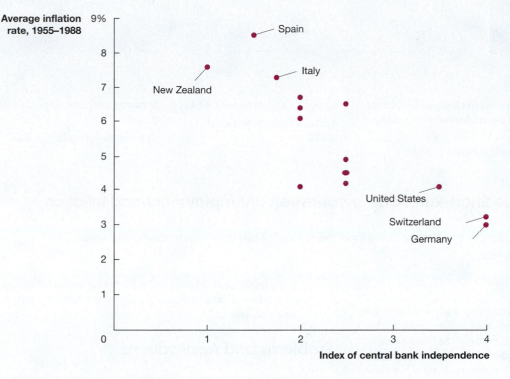

MyEconLab Animation

Figure 17.11

The More Independent the Central Bank, the Lower the Inflation Rate

For 16 high-income countries, the greater the degree of central bank independence from the rest of the government, the lower the inflation rate. Central bank independence is measured by an index ranging from 1 (minimum independence) to 4 (maximum independence). During these years, Germany had a high index of independence of 4 and a low average inflation rate of just over 3 percent. New Zealand had a low index of independence of 1 and a high average inflation rate of over 7 percent.
Source: "Central Bank Independence and Macroeconomic Performance: Some Comparative Evidence" by Alberto Alesina and Lawrence H. Summer from the Journal of Money, Credit and Banking, Vol. 25, No. 2, May 1993. Copyright © 1993 by the Ohio State University. Reprinted by permission.

years, New Zealand and Canada granted their banks more independence, at least partly to better fight inflation.

It remains to be seen which, if any, of the proposals for changing the Fed's structure and operations will be enacted by Congress and whether such changes will have a significant effect on the Fed's ability to carry out monetary policy free of political pressure.   MyEconLab Concept Check

MyEconLab Study Plan

Continued from page 603

Economics in Your Life

Are There Benefits to Delaying a Job Search?

At the beginning of the chapter, we posed this question: What advice would you give someone who has decided to wait a considerable time to look for a new job? As we discussed in the chapter, evidence shows that many of those who are unemployed for longer than a year or two find it more difficult to find new employment than if they searched for a new job soon after they were laid off. The longer workers are unemployed, especially in a high-technology field, the more their skills deteriorate. By delaying her job search, your friend risks being unemployed for longer than she expects if her skills deteriorate. Eventually, she may have to be retrained or take additional courses in a different field in order to find a job. Tell your friend to start her job search right away!

Conclusion

The workings of the economy are complex. The attempts by the Federal Reserve to keep unemployment near the natural rate while also keeping the inflation rate low have not always been successful. Economists continue to debate the best approaches for the Fed to use.

Visit MyEconLab for a news article and analysis related to the concepts in this chapter.

Key Terms

Disinflation, p. 618

Natural rate of unemployment, p. 606

Nonaccelerating inflation rate of unemployment (NAIRU), p. 611

Phillips curve, p. 604

Rational expectations, p. 614

Real business cycle models, p. 616

Structural relationship, p. 606

Too-big-to-fail policy, p. 625

17.1 **The Discovery of the Short-Run Trade-off between Unemployment and Inflation, pages 604–609**
LEARNING OBJECTIVE: Describe the Phillips curve and the nature of the short-run trade-off between unemployment and inflation.

Summary

The **Phillips curve** illustrates the short-run trade-off between the unemployment rate and the inflation rate. The inverse relationship between unemployment and inflation the Phillips curve shows is consistent with the aggregate demand and aggregate supply (*AD–AS*) model. The *AD–AS* model indicates that slow growth in aggregate demand leads to both higher unemployment and lower inflation, and rapid growth in aggregate demand leads to both lower unemployment and higher inflation. This relationship explains why there is a short-run trade-off between unemployment and inflation. Many economists initially believed that the Phillips curve was a **structural relationship** that depended on the basic behavior of consumers and firms and that remained unchanged over time. If the Phillips curve were a stable relationship, it would present policymakers with a menu of combinations of unemployment and inflation from which they could choose. Milton Friedman argued that there is a **natural rate of unemployment**, which is the unemployment rate that exists when real GDP equals potential GDP. Because in the long run unemployment always returns to the natural rate, there is no trade-off between unemployment and inflation in the long run, and the long-run Phillips curve is a vertical line at the natural rate of unemployment.

MyEconLab Visit **www.myeconlab.com** to complete these exercises online and get instant feedback.

Review Questions

1.1 What is the Phillips curve? Draw a graph of a short-run Phillips curve.

1.2 What actions should the Fed take if it wants to move from a point on the short-run Phillips curve representing high unemployment and low inflation to a point representing lower unemployment and higher inflation?

1.3 Why did economists during the early 1960s think of the Phillips curve as a "policy menu"? Were they correct to think of it in this way? Briefly explain.

1.4 Why did Milton Friedman argue that the Phillips curve did not represent a permanent trade-off between unemployment and inflation? In your answer, be sure to explain what Friedman meant by the "natural rate of unemployment."

Problems and Applications

1.5 Use these two graphs to answer the following questions.

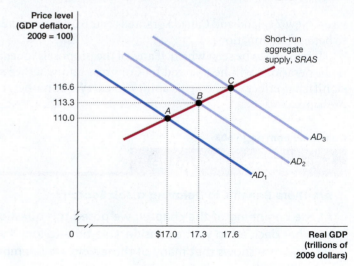

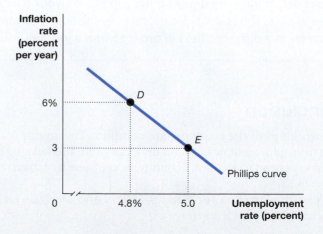

a. Briefly explain which point on the Phillips curve graph best represents the same economic situation as point *B* on the aggregate demand and aggregate supply graph.

b. Briefly explain which point on the Phillips curve graph best represents the same economic situation as point *C* on the aggregate demand and aggregate supply graph.

1.6 Given that the Phillips curve is derived from the aggregate demand and aggregate supply model, why do we use the Phillips curve analysis? What benefits does the Phillips curve analysis offer compared to the aggregate demand and aggregate supply model?

1.7 In macroeconomics courses in the 1960s and early 1970s, some economists argued that one of the U.S. political parties was willing to have higher unemployment in order to achieve lower inflation and that the other major political party was willing to have higher inflation in order to achieve lower unemployment. Why might such views of the trade-off between inflation and unemployment have existed in the 1960s? Why are such views rare today?

1.8 The text discussed how if Ford and the UAW fail to accurately forecast the inflation rate, the real wage will be different than the company and the union expected. Why, then, do the company and the union sign long-term contracts rather than negotiate a new contract each year?

1.9 General Juan Perón, the former dictator of Argentina, once said of the labor market in his country: "Prices have gone up the elevator, and wages have had to use the stairs." In this situation, what was happening to real wages in Argentina? Was unemployment likely to have been relatively high or relatively low?

Source: Robert J. Shiller, "Why Do People Dislike Inflation?" in Christina D. Romer and David H. Romer, eds., *Reducing Inflation: Motivation and Strategy*, Chicago: University of Chicago Press, 1997.

1.10 An article in the *Wall Street Journal* has the headline "Don't Look Now, but Market Inflation Expectations Are Falling."

If inflation turns out to be lower than households and firms had previously expected, will the actual real wage end up being higher or lower than the expected real wage? Will employment in the short run end up being higher or lower? Briefly explain.

Source: Jon Hilsenrath, "Don't Look Now, but Market Inflation Expectations Are Falling," *Wall Street Journal*, August 10, 2015.

1.11 **(Related to the** Making the Connection **on page 608)** Robert Shiller asked a sample of the general public and a sample of economists the following question: "Do you agree that preventing high inflation is an important national priority, as important as preventing drug abuse or preventing deterioration in the quality of our schools?" Fifty-two percent of the general public, but only 18 percent of economists, fully agreed. Why does the general public believe inflation is a bigger problem than economists do?

1.12 **(Related to the** Making the Connection **on page 608)** When Robert Shiller asked a sample of the general public what they thought caused inflation, the most frequent answer he received was "corporate greed." Do you agree that greed causes inflation? Briefly explain.

1.13 **(Related to the** Chapter Opener **on page 603)** In its 2014 *Annual Report*, Goodyear noted, "The increasing strength of the U.S. dollar created unfavorable foreign currency translation for many of our businesses around the world."

a. What did the company mean by the "increasing strength of the U.S. dollar"?

b. What did it mean by an "unfavorable foreign currency translation"?

c. During this period was Fed policy attempting to reach a point on the short-run Phillips curve representing higher unemployment and lower inflation, or a point representing higher inflation and lower unemployment? Briefly explain.

d. What connection is there between Fed policy and this statement in Goodyear's annual report?

Source: Goodyear Tire & Rubber Company, *2014 Annual Report*, p. 3.

17.2 The Short-Run and Long-Run Phillips Curves, pages 609–613

LEARNING OBJECTIVE: Explain the relationship between the short-run and long-run Phillips curves.

Summary

There is a short-run trade-off between unemployment and inflation only if the actual inflation rate differs from the inflation rate that workers and firms had expected. There is a different short-run Phillips curve for every expected inflation rate. Each short-run Phillips curve intersects the long-run Phillips curve at the expected inflation rate. With a vertical long-run Phillips curve, it is not possible for policymakers to buy a permanently lower unemployment rate at the cost of a permanently higher inflation rate. If the Federal Reserve attempts to keep the unemployment rate below the natural rate, the inflation rate will

increase. Eventually, the expected inflation rate will also increase, which causes the short-run Phillips curve to shift up and pushes the unemployment rate back to the natural rate. The reverse happens if the Fed attempts to keep the unemployment rate above the natural rate. In the long run, the Federal Reserve can affect the inflation rate but not the unemployment rate. The **nonaccelerating inflation rate of unemployment (NAIRU)** is the unemployment rate at which the inflation rate has no tendency to increase or decrease.

MyEconLab   Visit **www.myeconlab.com** to complete these exercises online and get instant feedback.

Review Questions

2.1 Suppose that the expected inflation rate increases from 4 percent to 6 percent. What will happen to the short-run Phillips curve?

2.2 What is the relationship between the short-run Phillips curve and the long-run Phillips curve?

2.3 Why is it inconsistent to believe that the long-run aggregate supply curve is vertical and the long-run Phillips curve is downward sloping?

Problems and Applications

2.4 Use the following information to draw a graph showing the short-run and long-run Phillips curves:

> Natural rate of unemployment = 5 percent
>
> Current rate of unemployment = 4 percent
>
> Expected inflation rate = 4 percent
>
> Current inflation rate = 6 percent

Be sure your graph shows the point where the short-run and long-run Phillips curves intersect.

2.5 Consider the long-run Phillips curve and the short-run Phillips curve in this graph. What would cause a movement from point *A* to point *B*? What would cause a movement from point *A* to point *C*?

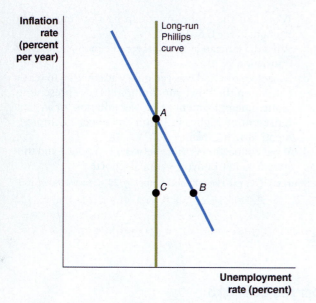

2.6 In 1968, Herbert Stein, who would later serve on President Nixon's Council of Economic Advisers, wrote: "Some who would opt for avoiding inflation would say that in the long run such a policy would cost little, if any, additional unemployment." Was Stein correct? Did most economists in 1968 agree with him? Briefly explain.

Source: Herbert Stein, *The Fiscal Revolution in America*, Chicago: University of Chicago Press, 1969, p. 382.

2.7 In the next column are four graphs and four economic scenarios, each of which would cause either a movement along the short-run or long-run Phillips curve or a shift in the short-run or long-run Phillips curve. Match each scenario with the appropriate graph.

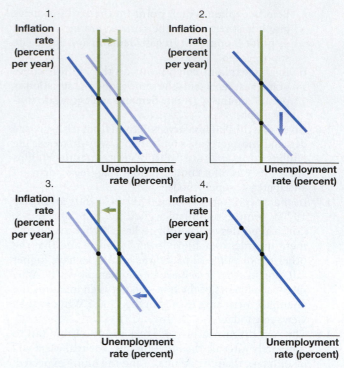

a. The proportion of younger and less-skilled workers in the labor force decreases.

b. The Fed carries out an expansionary monetary policy.

c. Congress enacts significant new legal barriers to firing workers.

d. Workers and firms lower the inflation rate they expect.

2.8 **(Related to the** Making the Connection **on page 612)** In 2015, an article in a publication of the Federal Reserve Bank of San Francisco noted, "FOMC participants have steadily lowered their estimates of the natural rate of unemployment . . . over the past several years." The article also noted that "a lower natural rate of unemployment also implies a lower target policy rate."

a. Why might members of the FOMC have believed that the natural rate of unemployment was lower in 2015 than it had been several years earlier?

b. What does the article mean by the Fed's "target policy rate"?

c. Why would a lower estimate of the natural rate of unemployment lead the Fed to lower its target policy rate?

Source: Mary C. Daly, Fernanda Nechio, and Benjamin Pyle, "Finding Normal: Natural Rates and Policy Prescriptions," *FRBSF Economic Letter,* July 6, 2015.

2.9 Over time, the Federal Reserve Board of Governors has changed its estimate of the nonaccelerating inflation rate of unemployment (NAIRU). The following are the board's NAIRU estimates for selected years.

Year	NAIRU (percent)
1970	6.0
1980	6.4
1990	5.6
2000	5.1
2008	4.8

a. Why would the board change its estimate of the NAIRU over time?

b. Suppose that the board simply kept its estimate fixed at 5.5 percent. What would have been the consequences for monetary policy during a period when the actual NAIRU was higher? What would have been the consequences for monetary policy during a period when the actual NAIRU was lower?

Source: Board of Governors of the Federal Reserve System.

2.10 In congressional testimony, former Federal Reserve Chairman Ben Bernanke said:

> Another significant factor influencing medium-term trends in inflation is the public's expectations of inflation. These expectations have an important bearing on whether transitory influences on prices, such as changes in energy costs, become embedded in wage and price decisions and so leave a lasting imprint on the rate of inflation.

What did Bernanke mean when he said that the public's expectations of inflation could "become embedded in wage and price decisions"? What would be the effect on the short-run Phillips curve of the public coming to expect a higher inflation rate?

Source: "Testimony of Chairman Ben S. Bernanke before the Joint Economic Committee, U.S. Congress," March 28, 2007.

2.11 In early 2015, an article in the *Economist* noted that it was possible that in the United States, "the NAIRU may already have been reached and inflation will start accelerating; the Fed should act soon."

a. What is the NAIRU?

b. If this evaluation of the economic situation is correct, what action should the Fed take?

c. If the Fed fails to act, what is likely to happen to the short-run Phillips curve over time? Briefly explain.

Source: "Jobs Matter, Not the Dollar," *Economist*, March 25, 2015.

2.12 **(Related to Solved Problem 17.2 on page 613)** In a speech in September 1975, Fed Chairman Arthur Burns said the following:

> There is no longer a meaningful trade-off between unemployment and inflation. In the current environment, a rapidly rising level of consumer prices will not lead to the creation of new jobs. . . . Highly expansionary monetary and fiscal policies might, for a short time, provide some additional thrust to economic activity. But inflation would inevitably accelerate—a development that would create even more difficult economic problems than we have encountered over the past year.

How do Burns's views in this speech compare with the views at the Fed in the late 1960s? Why do you think he specifically says that "in the current environment" there is no trade-off between unemployment and inflation?

Source: Arthur F. Burns, "The Real Issues of Inflation and Unemployment," in Federal Reserve Bank of New York, *Federal Reserve Readings on Inflation*, February 1975.

17.3 **Expectations of the Inflation Rate and Monetary Policy, pages 613–616**
LEARNING OBJECTIVE: Discuss how expectations of the inflation rate affect monetary policy.

Summary

When the inflation rate is moderate and stable, workers and firms tend to have *adaptive expectations*. That is, they form their expectations under the assumption that future inflation rates will follow the pattern of inflation rates in the recent past. Robert Lucas and Thomas Sargent argued that during the high and unstable inflation rates of the mid- to late 1970s, workers and firms would have *rational expectations*. **Rational expectations** are formed by using all the available information about an economic variable, including the effect of the policy being used by the Federal Reserve. Lucas and Sargent argued that if people have rational expectations, expansionary monetary policy will not work if workers and firms anticipate the policy. If workers and firms know that an expansionary monetary policy is going to raise the inflation rate, the actual inflation rate will be the same as the expected inflation rate. Therefore, the unemployment rate won't fall. Many economists remain skeptical of Lucas's and Sargent's argument. **Real business cycle models** focus on "real" factors—technology shocks—rather than changes in monetary policy to explain fluctuations in real GDP.

Review Questions

3.1 Why do workers, firms, banks, and investors in financial markets care about the future rate of inflation? How do they form their expectations of future inflation? Do current conditions in the economy have any effect on how they form their expectations? Briefly explain.

3.2 What does it mean to say that workers and firms have rational expectations?

3.3 Why did Robert Lucas and Thomas Sargent argue that the Phillips curve might be vertical in the short run? What difference would it make for monetary policy if they were right?

Problems and Applications

3.4 During a time when the inflation rate is increasing each year for a number of years, are adaptive expectations or rational expectations likely to give the more accurate forecasts? Briefly explain.

3.5 An article in the *Economist* states that, "Robert Lucas . . . showed how incorporating expectations into macroeconomic models muddled the framework economists prior to the 'rational expectations revolution' thought they saw so clearly." What economic framework did economists change as a result of Lucas's arguments? Do all economists agree with Lucas's main conclusions about whether monetary policy is effective? Briefly explain.

Source: "How to Know What Causes What," *Economist*, October 10, 2011.

3.6 In an article in *Forbes*, Paul Roderick Gregory, an economist at the University of Houston, commented on the use of monetary policy to fight a recession: "Those who devise stimulus programs must know in advance the extent to which households and businesses will correctly anticipate the policy. A policy that has been used x times in the past is unlikely to have a stimulative effect because it will be easily anticipated." Does Gregory believe that households and businesses have adaptive expectations or rational expectations regarding monetary policy? Briefly explain.

Source: Paul Roderick Gregory, "Thomas Sargent, Rational Expectations And The Keynesian Consensus," *Forbes*, October 11, 2011.

3.7 If both the short-run and long-run Phillips curves are vertical, what will be the effect on the inflation rate and the unemployment rate of an expansionary monetary policy? Use a Phillips curve graph to illustrate your answer.

3.8 An article in the *Economist* observes that "a sudden unanticipated spurt of inflation could lead to rapid economic growth."
a. Briefly explain the reasoning behind this statement.
b. Does it matter whether a spurt of inflation is unanticipated? Might different economists provide different answers to this question? Briefly explain.

Source: "How We Got Here," *Economist*, January 21, 2013.

<table><tr><td>**17.4**</td><td>**Federal Reserve Policy from the 1970s to the Present, pages 616–627**</td></tr></table>

LEARNING OBJECTIVE: Use a Phillips curve graph to show how the Federal Reserve can permanently lower the inflation rate.

Summary

Inflation worsened through the 1970s. Paul Volcker became Fed chairman in 1979, and, under his leadership, the Fed used contractionary monetary policy to reduce inflation. A significant reduction in the inflation rate is called **disinflation**. This contractionary monetary policy pushed short-run equilibrium down the short-run Phillips curve. As workers and firms lowered their expectations of future inflation, the short-run Phillips curve shifted down, improving the short-run trade-off between unemployment and inflation. This change in expectations allowed the Fed to switch to an expansionary monetary policy to bring the unemployment rate back to the natural rate. During Alan Greenspan's term as Fed chairman, inflation remained low, and the credibility of the Fed increased. In recent years, some economists have argued that monetary policy decisions during Greenspan's term may have contributed to the problems the financial system experienced during the 2007–2009 recession. The Fed's actions during and after the financial crisis, including its use of a **too-big-to-fail policy**, led some economists and policymakers to believe that reforms were needed in the Fed's structure and operations. However, other economists and policymakers fear that reducing the Fed's independence may undermine good policy.

 Visit **www.myeconlab.com** to complete these exercises online and get instant feedback.

Review Questions

4.1 What was the "Volcker disinflation"? What happened to the unemployment rate during the period of the Volcker disinflation?

4.2 What changes did the Dodd-Frank Act make in the Fed's operations? List three key proposals for changes in the Fed's operations or structure.

4.3 Why do most economists believe that it is important for a country's central bank to be independent of the rest of the country's central government?

Problems and Applications

4.4 An article in the *New York Times* in 2015 quoted Minneapolis Fed President Narayana Kocherlakota as stating that "disinflation is worrisome." Most economists applaud the "Volcker disinflation" of the 1980s. Why might disinflation have been a good thing in the 1980s but worrisome in 2015?

Source: Reuters, "Fed's Kocherlakota Sees Risk of U.S. Disinflation," *New York Times*, April 14, 2015.

4.5 **(Related to the** Don't Let This Happen to You **on page 619)** Look again at the table on prices during the early 1930s on page 619. Was there disinflation during 1933? Briefly explain.

4.6 Suppose the current inflation rate and the expected inflation rate are both 4 percent. The current unemployment rate and the natural rate of unemployment are both 5 percent. Use a Phillips curve graph to show the effect of a supply shock. If the Federal Reserve keeps monetary policy unchanged, what will happen eventually to the unemployment rate? Show this change on your Phillips curve graph.

4.7 **(Related to** Solved Problem 17.4 **on page 619)** Suppose the inflation rate has been 15 percent for the past four years. The unemployment rate is currently at the natural rate of unemployment of 5 percent. The Federal Reserve decides that it wants to permanently reduce the inflation rate to 5 percent. How can the Fed use monetary policy to achieve this objective? Be sure to use a Phillips curve graph in your answer.

4.8 While many economists and policymakers supported the Fed's decision to maintain the federal funds rate at a near-zero level for over six years, Charles Schwab, the founder and chairman of a discount brokerage firm that bears his name, argued that the economy was harmed by keeping interest rates low for an extended period of time:

> U.S. households lost billions in interest income during the Fed's near-zero interest rate experiment. . . . Because they are often

reliant on income from savings, seniors were hit the hardest.... Seniors make up 13% of the U.S. population and spend about $1.2 trillion annually.... This makes for a potent multiplier effect.

a. What type of spending was Schwab expecting would have increased if the Fed had raised interest rate earlier than it did?

b. Would higher interest rates have had an effect on other types of spending? Briefly explain.

c. Which of the types of spending that you discussed in answering parts (a) and (b) does the Fed appear to believe has the more "potent multiplier effect"? Briefly explain.

Source: Charles R. Schwab, "Raise Interest Rates, Make Grandma Smile," *Wall Street Journal*, November 19, 2014.

4.9 (Related to the Making the Connection **on page 623)** In an opinion column in the *New York Times*, economist Justin Wolfers of the University of Michigan noted, "Over recent years, policy makers have also worked to lower long-term interest rates by shaping expectations about future monetary policy decisions."

a. What does the Fed call such an attempt to shape expectations of future policy decisions?

b. Briefly explain how this approach works.

Source: Justin Wolfers, "The Fed Has Not Stopped Trying to Stimulate the Economy," *New York Times*, October 29, 2014.

4.10 Robert Lucas said, "In practice, it is much more painful to put a modern economy through a deflation than the monetary theory we have would lead us to expect. I take this to mean that we have 'price stickiness.'"

a. What does Lucas mean by "the monetary theory we have"?

b. What events may have led Lucas to conclude that it is more painful to reduce the inflation rate than theory would predict?

c. Why does he conclude that the U.S. economy apparently has "price stickiness"?

Source: Paul A. Samuelson and William A. Barnett, eds., *Inside the Economist's Mind: Conversations with Eminent Economists*, Malden, MA: Blackwell Publishing, 2007.

4.11 An opinion column in the *Wall Street Journal* notes, "In a democracy, the tradeoff for a central bank's independence is accountability to the nation's elected leadership."

a. Why would a country want to grant its central bank more independence than it grants, say, its department of agriculture or department of education?

b. In the United States, how is the Fed held accountable to the nation's elected leadership?

Source: David Wessel, "Explaining 'Audit the Fed,'" *Wall Street Journal*, February 17, 2015.

4.12 In an opinion column in the *Wall Street Journal*, Stanford University economist John Taylor, originator of the Taylor rule, argued, "As I see it, the broader evidence in the United States and in many other countries ... is that a rules-based policy has worked and that discretion—constrained or otherwise—has not."

a. What does Taylor mean by a "rules-based policy"?

b. How can we tell whether a monetary policy has worked?

c. Why have many Fed officials been opposed to adopting a rules-based policy?

Source: John B. Taylor, "Taylor on Bernanke: Monetary Rules Work Better Than 'Constrained Discretion,'" *Wall Street Journal*, May 2, 2015.

Real-Time Data Exercises

D17.1 (Testing the Phillips curve) Go to the Web site of the Federal Reserve Bank of St. Louis (FRED) (research.stlouisfed.org/fred2) and download annual unemployment data (UNRATE) for 1962 to the present. (To convert the data from a monthly frequency to an annual frequency, click on "Graph" and "Frequency.") Next, download the annual inflation rate measured using the consumer price index, or CPI (CPIAUCSL). (Once you have converted the data from a monthly frequency to an annual frequency, you can find the inflation rate by clicking on "Units" and selecting "Percent Change from Year Ago.") Plot both series on the same graph. Briefly explain whether for each of the following periods, the relationship between the annual unemployment rate and the annual inflation rate is consistent with a movement along the short-run Phillips curve or with a shift in the Phillips curve.

a. 1966–1969

b. 1973–1975

c. 1992–1994

d. 2000–2002

D17.2 (Comparing actual inflation and expected inflation) Go to the Web site of the Federal Reserve Bank of St. Louis (FRED) (research.stlouisfed.org/fred2) and download monthly data on the inflation rate expected by consumers as measured by the University of Michigan's survey (MICH) for 1978 to the present. Next, download the monthly inflation rate measured using the consumer price index, or CPI (CPIAUCSL), for the same period. (You can find the inflation rate by clicking on "Units" and selecting "Percent Change from Year Ago.") Plot both series on the same graph. During which periods did consumers do a good job of forecasting the inflation rate? During which periods did they do a poor job? Do consumers' expectations of the inflation rate tend to be more volatile or less volatile than the actual inflation rate?

CHAPTER
18

Macroeconomics in an Open Economy

Chapter Outline and **Learning Objectives**

IBM Sings the Dollar Blues

The company that became the International Business Machines Corporation (IBM) was founded in New York City in 1911. For decades, under the leadership of CEOs Tom Watson, Sr., and his son Tom Watson, Jr., IBM was best known for manufacturing large computer systems used by corporations. As business computing made the transition from mainframes to desktop computers, IBM established a new standard with its personal computers powered by Intel chips and using an operating system developed by Microsoft. In 2015, IBM was well into another transition, away from manufacturing hardware and toward selling cloud-based computing software services. As CEO Virginia Rometty put it, "We've reinvented this company one more time." Today, IBM has more than 375,000 employees, $90 billion in revenue, and $20 billion in profits.

Most people think of IBM as a giant of U.S. business. However, as the company name indicates, IBM is an international company with offices throughout Europe, Latin America, Africa, and Asia. In 2014, more than two-thirds of IBM's revenue was earned outside the United States. As a result, the company's profits are affected by fluctuations in the value of the dollar in exchange for other currencies. In some years, converting revenue from foreign currencies yields fewer dollars than in other years. For example, in 2014, IBM's global revenue was nearly $2 billion lower when measured in terms of dollars than when measured in local currencies—pounds in Great Britain, euros in Germany, yen in Japan. Why the discrepancy? The value of the dollar had increased relative to most other currencies. So, converting pounds, euros, and yen into dollars yielded fewer dollars for IBM. As an article in the *Wall Street Journal* put it, "The company . . . has run into a stiff headwind from the rising value of the dollar."

As we saw in Chapter 15, one reason for the increasing value of the U.S. dollar in 2015 was rising U.S. interest rates. Higher interest rates made financial investments in the United States more attractive to foreign investors, which increased the demand for U.S. dollars and the exchange rate between the dollar and other currencies. In this chapter and the next, we will look more closely at how exchange rates are determined and at other important issues involving the international financial system.

Sources: Don Clark, "IBM Pumps $4 Billion into Cloud and Mobile Initiatives," *Wall Street Journal*, February 26, 2015; Steve Lohr, "IBM Revenue Falls 13% Despite Big Gains in New Fields," *New York Times*, July 20, 2015; and International Business Machines Corporation, *2014 IBM Annual Report*, February 24, 2015.

Economics in Your Life

The South Korean Central Bank and Your Car Loan

Suppose that you are shopping for a new car, which you plan to finance with a loan from a local bank. While reading an article in the *Wall Street Journal* on your smartphone one morning, you see this headline: "The Bank of Korea, South Korea's central bank, announces it will sell its large holdings of U.S. Treasury bonds." Will the Bank of Korea's decision to sell its U.S. Treasury bonds affect the interest rate you pay on your car loan? As you read this chapter, try to answer this question. You can check your answer against the one we provide on **page 655** at the end of this chapter.

I n Chapter 7, we looked at the basics of international trade. In this chapter, we look more closely at the linkages among countries at the macroeconomic level. Countries are linked by trade in goods and services and by flows of financial investment. We will see how policymakers in all countries take these linkages into account when conducting monetary policy and fiscal policy.

18.1 The Balance of Payments: Linking the United States to the International Economy

LEARNING OBJECTIVE: Explain how the balance of payments is calculated.

Today, consumers, firms, and investors routinely interact with consumers, firms, and investors in other economies. A consumer in France may use computer software produced in the United States, watch a television manufactured in South Korea, and wear a sweater made in Italy. A U.S. firm like IBM may sell its products in dozens of countries around the world. An investor in London may sell a U.S. Treasury bill to an investor in Mexico City. Nearly all economies are **open economies** and have extensive interactions in trade or finance with other countries. Open economies interact by trading goods and services and by making investments in each other's economies. A **closed economy** has no interactions in trade or finance with other countries. No economy today is completely closed, although a few countries, such as North Korea, have very limited economic interactions with other countries.

A good way to understand the interactions between one economy and other economies is through the **balance of payments**, which is a record of a country's trade with other countries in goods, services, and assets. Just as the U.S. Bureau of Economic Analysis is responsible for collecting data on the gross domestic product (GDP), it is also responsible for collecting data on the balance of payments. Table 18.1 shows the balance of payments for the United States in 2014. Notice that the table contains three "accounts": the *current account*, the *financial account*, and the *capital account*.

The Current Account

The **current account** records *current*, or short-term, flows of funds into and out of a country. The current account for the United States includes: (1) exports and imports of goods and services (recall that the difference between exports and imports of goods and services is called *net exports*); (2) income received by U.S. residents from investments in other countries and income paid on investments in the United States owned by residents of other countries (the difference between investment income received and investment income paid is called *net income on investments*); and (3) the difference between transfers made to residents of other countries and transfers received by U.S. residents from other countries (called *net transfers*). If you make a donation to a charity caring for orphans in Afghanistan, it will be included in net transfers. Any payments received by U.S. residents are positive numbers in the current account, and any payments made by U.S. residents are negative numbers in the current account.

The Balance of Trade Part of the current account is the **balance of trade**, which is the difference between the value of the goods a country exports and the value of the goods the country imports. The balance of trade is the largest item in the current account and is a topic that politicians and the media often discuss. If a country exports more goods than it imports, it has a *trade surplus*. If a country exports less than it imports, it has a *trade deficit*. In 2014, the United States had a trade deficit of $741 billion. In the same year, Japan had a trade deficit of $121 billion, and China had a trade surplus of $369 billion. Figure 18.1 on page 638 shows imports and exports of goods between the United States and its trading partners and between Japan and its trading partners. The data show that the United States ran a trade deficit in 2014 with all its major trading partners and with every region of the world apart from Latin America (except Mexico) and Africa. Japan ran trade surpluses with the United States, Asia (except China), and Latin America, and it ran trade deficits with the other regions. (Note that exports from

Open economy An economy that has interactions in trade or finance with other countries.

Closed economy An economy that has no interactions in trade or finance with other countries.

Balance of payments The record of a country's trade with other countries in goods, services, and assets.

Current account The part of the balance of payments that records a country's net exports, net income on investments, and net transfers.

Balance of trade The difference between the value of the goods a country exports and the value of the goods a country imports.

Current Account

Exports of goods	$1,633	
Imports of goods	−2,374	
Balance of trade		−741
Exports of services	711	
Imports of services	−477	
Balance of services		234
Income received on investments	823	
Income payments on investments	−585	
Net income on investments		238
Net transfers		−120
Balance on current account		**−389**

Financial Account

Increase in foreign holdings of assets in the United States	1,031	
Increase in U.S. holdings of assets in foreign countries	−792	
Balance on financial account		239

Balance on Capital Account

	0
Statistical discrepancy	150
Balance of payments	0

Note: Subtotals may not sum to totals because of rounding.

Source: U.S. Bureau of Economic Analysis, "U.S. International Transactions," June 18, 2015.

MyEconLab Real-time data

Table 18.1

The U.S. Balance of Payments, 2014 (billions of dollars)

The sum of the balance of trade and the balance of services equals net exports.

the United States to Japan in panel (a) of Figure 18.1 should equal imports by Japan from the United States in panel (b). These two numbers are different because international trade statistics are not measured exactly.)

Net Exports Equals the Sum of the Balance of Trade and the Balance of Services Recall that *net exports* is a component of aggregate expenditure. Net exports is not explicitly shown in Table 18.1, but we can calculate it by adding the balance of trade and the balance of services. The *balance of services* is the difference between the value of the services a country exports and the value of the services the country imports. Notice that, technically, net exports is *not* equal to the current account balance because this account also includes net income on investments and net transfers. Because these other two items are relatively small, though, it is often a convenient simplification to think of net exports as being equal to the current account balance. MyEconLab Concept Check

The Financial Account

The **financial account** records purchases of assets a country has made abroad and foreign purchases of assets in the country. The financial account records long-term flows of funds into and out of a country. There is a *capital outflow* from the United States when an investor in the United States buys a bond issued by a foreign company or government or when a U.S. firm builds a factory in another country. There is a *capital inflow* into the United States when a foreign investor buys a bond issued by a U.S. firm or by the government or when a foreign firm builds a factory in the United States. Notice that we are using the word *capital* here to apply not just to physical assets, such as factories, but also to financial assets, such as shares of stock. When firms build or buy facilities in

Financial account The part of the balance of payments that records purchases of assets a country has made abroad and foreign purchases of assets in the country.

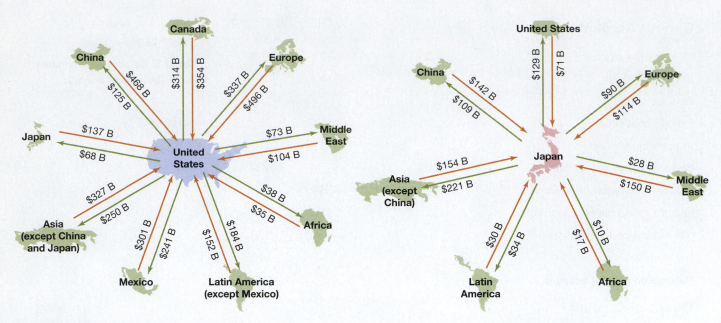

(a) Trade flows for the United States (in billions of dollars)

(b) Trade flows for Japan (in billions of dollars)

MyEconLab Animation

Figure 18.1 **Trade Flows for the United States and Japan, 2014**

Panel (a) shows that in 2014, the United States ran a trade deficit with all its major trading partners and with every region of the world except for Latin America and Africa. Panel (b) shows that Japan ran trade deficits with China, Latin America, Europe, Africa, and the Middle East, and it ran trade surpluses with the United States and Asia. In each panel, the green arrows represent exports from the United States or Japan, and the red arrows represent imports.

Note: Japanese data are converted from yen to dollars at the average 2014 exchange rate of 105.7 yen per dollar.
Sources: U.S. Bureau of Economic Analysis, "U.S. International Transactions," June 18, 2015; and Japanese Ministry of Finance, *Trade Statistics of Japan.*

---

foreign countries, they are engaging in *foreign direct investment*. When investors buy stock or bonds issued in another country, they are engaging in *foreign portfolio investment*.

Another way of thinking of the balance on the financial account is as a measure of *net capital flows*, or the difference between capital inflows and capital outflows. (Here we are omitting a few transactions included in the capital account, as discussed in the next section.) A concept closely related to net capital flows is **net foreign investment**, which is equal to capital outflows minus capital inflows. Net capital flows and net foreign investment are always equal but have opposite signs: When net capital flows are positive, net foreign investment is negative, and when net capital flows are negative, net foreign investment is positive. Net foreign investment is also equal to net foreign direct investment plus net foreign portfolio investment. In Section 18.3, we will use the relationship between the balance on the financial account and net foreign investment to understand an important aspect of the international economic system.   MyEconLab Concept Check

Net foreign investment The difference between capital outflows from a country and capital inflows, also equal to net foreign direct investment plus net foreign portfolio investment.

The Capital Account

A third, less important, part of the balance of payments is called the *capital account*. The **capital account** records relatively minor transactions, such as migrants' transfers— which consist of goods and financial assets people take with them when they leave or enter a country—and sales and purchases of nonproduced, nonfinancial assets. A nonproduced, nonfinancial asset is a copyright, patent, trademark, or right to natural resources. The definitions of the financial account and the capital account are often misunderstood because the capital account prior to 1999 recorded all the transactions now included in both the financial account and the capital account. In other words, capital account transactions went from being a very important part of the balance of payments to being a relatively unimportant part. Because the balance on what is now called the capital account is so small—only $45 million in 2014, which we

Capital account The part of the balance of payments that records relatively minor transactions, such as migrants' transfers and sales and purchases of nonproduced, nonfinancial assets.

rounded to zero in Table 18.1—for simplicity we will ignore it in the remainder of this chapter.   MyEconLab Concept Check

Why Is the Balance of Payments Always Zero?

The sum of the current account balance, the financial account balance, and the capital account balance equals the balance of payments. Table 18.1 on page 637 shows that the balance of payments for the United States in 2014 was zero. It's not just by chance that this balance was zero; *the balance of payments is always zero*. Notice that the current account balance in 2014 was –$389 billion. The balance on the financial account (which has the opposite sign to the balance on the current account) was $239 billion. To make the balance on the current account equal to the balance on the financial account, the balance of payments includes an entry called the *statistical discrepancy*. (Remember that we are ignoring the balance on the capital account. If we included it, we would say that the statistical discrepancy takes on a value equal to the difference between the current account balance and the sum of the balance on the financial account and the balance on the capital account.)

Why does the U.S. Department of Commerce include the statistical discrepancy entry to force the balance of payments to equal zero? If the sum of the current account balance and the financial account balance does not equal zero, some imports or exports of goods and services or some capital inflows or capital outflows were not measured accurately.

To better understand why the balance of payments must equal zero every year, consider the following: In 2014, the United States spent $389 billion more on goods, services, and other items in the current account than it received. What happened to that $389 billion? We know that every dollar of that $389 billion was used by foreign individuals or firms to invest in the United States or was added to foreign holdings of dollars. We know this because logically there is nowhere else for the dollars to go: If the dollars weren't spent on U.S. goods and services—and we know they weren't because if they had been, they would have shown up in the current account—they must have been spent on investments in the United States or not spent at all. Dollars that aren't spent are added to foreign holdings of dollars. Changes in foreign holdings of dollars are called *official reserve transactions*. Foreign investment in the United States and additions to foreign holdings of dollars both show up as positive entries in the U.S. financial

Don't Let This Happen to You

Don't Confuse the Balance of Trade, the Current Account Balance, and the Balance of Payments

The terminology of international economics can be tricky. Remember that the *balance of trade* includes only trade in goods; it does not include services. This observation is important because the United States, for example, usually imports more *goods* than it exports, but it usually exports more *services* than it imports. As a result, the U.S. trade deficit is almost always larger than the current account deficit. The *current account balance* includes the balance of trade, the balance of services, net investment income, and net transfers. Net investment income and net transfers are much smaller than the balance of trade and the balance of services.

Even though the *balance of payments* is equal to the sum of the current account balance and the financial account balance—and must equal zero—you may sometimes see references to a balance of payments "surplus" or "deficit."

These references have two explanations. The first is that the person making the reference has confused the balance of payments with either the balance of trade or the current account balance. This mistake is very common. The second explanation is that the person is not including official reserve transactions in the financial account. If we separate changes in U.S. holdings of foreign currencies and changes in foreign holdings of U.S. dollars from other financial account entries, the current account balance and the financial account balance do not have to sum to zero, and there can be a balance of payments surplus or deficit. These distinctions may sound complicated—and they are! But don't worry. Knowing how official reserve transactions are accounted for is not crucial to understanding the basic ideas behind the balance of payments.

MyEconLab Study Plan

Your Turn: Test your understanding by doing related problem 1.6 on pages 656–657 at the end of this chapter.

account. Therefore, a current account deficit must be exactly offset by a financial account surplus, leaving the balance of payments equal to zero. Similarly, a country that runs a current account surplus, such as China, must run a financial account deficit of exactly the same size. If a country's current account surplus is not exactly equal to its financial account deficit, or if a country's current account deficit is not exactly equal to its financial account surplus, some transactions must not have been accounted for. The statistical discrepancy is included in the balance of payments to compensate for these uncounted transactions.   MyEconLab Concept Check

---

Solved Problem 18.1

MyEconLab Interactive Animation

Understanding the Arithmetic of the Balance of Payments

Test your understanding of the relationship between the current account and the financial account by evaluating the following assertion by a political commentator:

The industrial countries are committing economic suicide. Every year, they invest more and more in emerging countries, such as South Korea. Every year, more U.S., Japanese, and European manufacturing firms move their factories to emerging countries. With extensive new factories and low wages, emerging countries now export far more to the industrial countries than they import.

Solving the Problem

Step 1: **Review the chapter material.** This problem is about the relationship between the current account and the financial account, so you may want to review the section "Why Is the Balance of Payments Always Zero?" which begins on page 639.

Step 2: **Explain the errors in the commentator's argument.** The argument sounds plausible. It would be easy to find statements similar to this one in recent books and articles by well-known political commentators. But the argument contains an important error: The commentator has failed to understand the relationship between the current account and the financial account. The commentator asserts that emerging countries are receiving large capital inflows from industrial countries. In other words, emerging countries are running financial account surpluses. The commentator also asserts that emerging countries are exporting more than they are importing. In other words, they are running current account surpluses. As we have seen in this section, it is impossible to run a current account surplus *and* a financial account surplus simultaneously. A country that runs a current account surplus *must* run a financial account deficit and vice versa.

Extra Credit: Most emerging economies that have received large inflows of foreign investment during the past two decades, such as South Korea, Thailand, and Malaysia, have run current account deficits: They import more goods and services than they export. Emerging economies that run current account surpluses, such as Singapore, also run financial account deficits: They invest more abroad than other countries invest in them.

The point here is not obvious; if it was, it wouldn't confuse so many intelligent politicians, journalists, and political commentators. Unless you understand the relationship between the current account and the financial account, you won't be able to understand a key aspect of the international economy.

MyEconLab Study Plan

Your Turn: For more practice, do related problems 1.7, 1.8, and 1.9 on page 657 at the end of this chapter.

18.2 The Foreign Exchange Market and Exchange Rates

LEARNING OBJECTIVE: Explain how exchange rates are determined and how changes in exchange rates affect the prices of imports and exports.

A firm that operates entirely within the United States will price its products in dollars and will use dollars to pay its suppliers' bills, wages and salaries to its workers, interest to its bondholders, and dividends to its shareholders. A multinational corporation such as IBM, in contrast, may sell its products in many different countries and receive payments in many different currencies. Its suppliers and workers may also be spread around the world and may have to be paid in local currencies. In addition to exchanging currencies, corporations may also use the international financial system to borrow in a foreign currency. For example, during a period of rapid expansion in East Asian countries such as Thailand and South Korea during the late 1990s, many large firms received dollar loans from foreign banks. When firms make extensive use of foreign currencies, they must deal with fluctuations in the exchange rate.

The **nominal exchange rate** is the value of one country's currency in terms of another country's currency. Economists also calculate the *real exchange rate*, which corrects the nominal exchange rate for changes in prices of goods and services. We discuss the real exchange rate later in this section. The nominal exchange rate determines how many units of a foreign currency you can purchase with $1. For example, the exchange rate between the U.S. dollar and the Japanese yen can be expressed as ¥100 = $1. (This exchange rate can also be expressed as how many U.S. dollars are required to buy 1 Japanese yen: $0.01 = ¥1.) The market for foreign exchange is very active, with the equivalent of more than $4 trillion worth of currency being traded each day. The exchange rates that result from this trading are reported on a number of online sites devoted to economic news and in the business or financial sections of most newspapers.

Banks and other financial institutions around the world employ currency traders, who are linked together by computer. Rather than exchange large amounts of paper currency, they buy and sell deposits in banks. For example, a bank buying or selling dollars will actually be buying or selling dollar bank deposits. Dollar bank deposits exist not just in banks in the United States but also in banks around the world. Suppose that the Crédit Agricole bank in France wants to sell U.S. dollars and buy Japanese yen. The bank may exchange U.S. dollar deposits that it owns for Japanese yen deposits owned by the Deutsche Bank in Germany. Businesses and individuals usually obtain foreign currency from banks in their own country.

> **Nominal exchange rate** The value of one country's currency in terms of another country's currency.

Making the Connection MyEconLab Video

Exchange Rate Listings

You can find the exchange rates between the dollar and other major currencies on many online sites, such as wsj.com, Bloomberg.com, or finance.yahoo.com, as well as in the financial pages of most newspapers. The exchange rates in the following table are for August 14, 2015. The euro is the common currency used by 19 European countries, including France, Germany, and Italy, but not the United Kingdom.

	Exchange Rate between the U.S. Dollar and the Indicated Currency	
Currency	**Units of Foreign Currency per U.S. Dollar**	**U.S. Dollars per Unit of Foreign Currency**
Canadian dollar	1.31	0.763
Japanese yen	124.32	0.008
Mexican peso	16.37	0.061
British pound	0.64	1.56
Euro	0.90	1.11

Notice that the expression for the exchange rate stated as units of foreign currency per U.S. dollar is the *reciprocal* of the exchange rate stated as U.S. dollars per unit of foreign currency. So, the exchange rate between the U.S. dollar and the British pound can be stated as either 0.64 British pounds per U.S. dollar or 1/0.64 = 1.56 U.S. dollars per British pound.

Banks are the most active participants in the market for foreign exchange. Typically, banks buy currency for slightly less than the amount for which they sell it. This spread between the buying and selling prices allows banks to cover their costs from currency trading. Therefore, when most businesses and individuals buy foreign currency from a bank, they receive fewer units of foreign currency per dollar than would be indicated by the exchange rate shown on online business sites or printed in the newspaper.

Source: *Wall Street Journal*, August 14, 2015.

MyEconLab Study Plan

Your Turn: Test your understanding by doing related problem 2.5 on pages 657–658 at the end of this chapter.

The market exchange rate is determined by the interaction of demand and supply, just as other prices are. There are three sources of foreign currency demand for the U.S. dollar:

1. Foreign firms and households that want to buy goods and services produced in the United States.

2. Foreign firms and households that want to invest in the United States either through foreign direct investment—buying or building factories or other facilities in the United States—or through foreign portfolio investment—buying stocks and bonds issued in the United States.

3. Currency traders who believe that the value of the dollar in the future will be greater than its value today.

Equilibrium in the Market for Foreign Exchange

Figure 18.2 shows the demand and supply of U.S. dollars for Japanese yen. Notice that as we move up the vertical axis, the value of the dollar increases relative to the value of the yen. When the exchange rate is ¥150 = $1, the dollar is worth 1.5 times as much relative to the yen as when the exchange rate is ¥100 = $1. Consider, first, the demand curve for dollars in exchange for yen. The demand curve has the normal downward slope. When the value of the dollar is high, the quantity of dollars demanded will be low. A Japanese investor will be more likely to buy a $1,000 bond issued by the U.S.

MyEconLab Animation

Figure 18.2

Equilibrium in the Foreign Exchange Market

When the exchange rate is ¥150 to the dollar, the exchange rate is above its equilibrium level, and there will be a surplus of dollars. When the exchange rate is ¥100 to the dollar, it is below its equilibrium level, and there will be a shortage of dollars. At an exchange rate of ¥120 to the dollar, the foreign exchange market is in equilibrium.

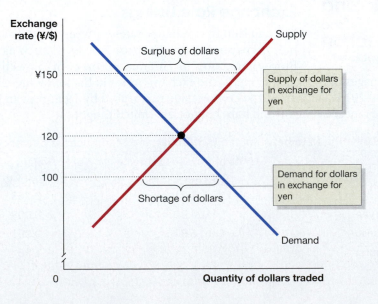

Treasury when the exchange rate is ¥100 = $1 and the investor pays only ¥100,000 to buy $1,000 than when the exchange rate is ¥150 = $1 and the investor must pay ¥150,000. Similarly, a Japanese firm is more likely to buy $150 million worth of microchips from Intel Corporation when the exchange rate is ¥100 = $1 and the microchips can be purchased for ¥15 billion than when the exchange rate is ¥150 = $1 and the microchips cost ¥22.5 billion.

Now consider the supply curve for dollars in exchange for yen. The supply curve has the normal upward slope. When the value of the dollar is high, the quantity of dollars supplied in exchange for yen will be high. A U.S. investor will be more likely to buy a ¥200,000 bond issued by the Japanese government when the exchange rate is ¥200 = $1 and he needs to pay only $1,000 to buy ¥200,000 than when the exchange rate is ¥100 = $1 and he must pay $2,000. The owner of a U.S. electronics store is more likely to buy ¥20 million worth of television sets from the Sony Corporation when the exchange rate is ¥200 = $1 and she needs to pay only $100,000 to purchase the televisions than when the exchange rate is ¥100 = $1 and she must pay $200,000.

As in any other market, equilibrium occurs in the foreign exchange market where the quantity supplied equals the quantity demanded. In Figure 18.2, ¥120 = $1 is the equilibrium exchange rate. At exchange rates above ¥120 = $1, there will be a surplus of dollars and downward pressure on the exchange rate. The surplus and the downward pressure will not be eliminated until the exchange rate falls to ¥120 = $1. If the exchange rate is below ¥120 = $1, there will be a shortage of dollars and upward pressure on the exchange rate. The shortage and the upward pressure will not be eliminated until the exchange rate rises to ¥120 = $1. Surpluses and shortages in the foreign exchange market are eliminated very quickly because the volume of trading in major currencies such as the dollar and the yen is large, and currency traders are linked together by computer.

Currency appreciation occurs when the market value of a country's currency increases relative to the value of another country's currency. **Currency depreciation** occurs when the market value of a country's currency decreases relative to the value of another country's currency. **MyEconLab** Concept Check

Currency appreciation An increase in the market value of one currency relative to another currency.

Currency depreciation A decrease in the market value of one currency relative to another currency.

How Do Shifts in Demand and Supply Affect the Exchange Rate?

Shifts in the demand and supply curves cause the equilibrium exchange rate to change. Three main factors cause the demand and supply curves in the foreign exchange market to shift:

1. Changes in the demand for U.S.-produced goods and services and changes in the demand for foreign-produced goods and services

2. Changes in the desire to invest in the United States and changes in the desire to invest in foreign countries

3. Changes in the expectations of currency traders about the likely future value of the dollar and the likely future value of foreign currencies

Shifts in the Demand for Foreign Exchange Consider how the three factors just listed will affect the demand for U.S. dollars in exchange for Japanese yen. During an economic expansion in Japan, the incomes of Japanese households will rise, and the demand by Japanese consumers and firms for U.S. goods will increase. At any given exchange rate, the demand for U.S. dollars will increase, and the demand curve will shift to the right. Similarly, if interest rates in the United States rise, the desirability of investing in U.S. financial assets will increase, and the demand curve for dollars will also shift to the right. **Speculators** are currency traders who buy and sell foreign exchange in an attempt to profit from changes in exchange rates. If a speculator becomes convinced that the value of the dollar is going to rise relative to the value of the yen, the speculator will sell yen and buy dollars. If the current exchange rate is ¥120 = $1, and the speculator is convinced that it will soon rise to ¥140 = $1, the speculator could sell

Speculators Currency traders who buy and sell foreign exchange in an attempt to profit from changes in exchange rates.

¥600,000,000 and receive $5,000,000 (= ¥600,000,000/¥120) in return. If the speculator is correct and the value of the dollar rises against the yen to ¥140 = $1, the speculator will be able to exchange $5,000,000 for ¥700,000,000 (= $5,000,000 × ¥140) for a profit of ¥100,000,000.

To summarize, the demand curve for dollars shifts to the right when incomes in Japan rise, when interest rates in the United States rise, or when speculators decide that the value of the dollar will rise relative to the value of the yen.

During a recession in Japan, Japanese incomes will fall, reducing the demand for U.S.-produced goods and services and shifting the demand curve for dollars to the left. Similarly, if interest rates in the United States fall, the desirability of investing in U.S. financial assets will decrease, and the demand curve for dollars will shift to the left. Finally, if speculators become convinced that the future value of the dollar will be lower than its current value, the demand for dollars will fall, and the demand curve will shift to the left.

Shifts in the Supply of Foreign Exchange The factors that affect the supply curve for dollars are similar to those that affect the demand curve for dollars. An economic expansion in the United States increases the incomes of Americans and increases their demand for goods and services, including goods and services made in Japan. As U.S. consumers and firms increase their spending on Japanese products, they must supply dollars in exchange for yen, which causes the supply curve for dollars to shift to the right. Similarly, an increase in interest rates in Japan will make financial investments in Japan more attractive to U.S. investors. These higher Japanese interest rates will cause the supply curve for dollars to shift to the right, as U.S. investors exchange dollars for yen. Finally, if speculators become convinced that the future value of the yen will be higher relative to the dollar than it is today, the supply curve for dollars will shift to the right as traders attempt to exchange dollars for yen.

A recession in the United States will decrease the demand for Japanese products and cause the supply curve for dollars to shift to the left. Similarly, a decrease in interest rates in Japan will make financial investments in Japan less attractive and cause the supply curve for dollars to shift to the left. If traders become convinced that the future value of the yen will be lower relative to the dollar, the supply curve will also shift to the left.

Adjustment to a New Equilibrium The factors that affect the demand and supply for currencies are constantly changing. Whether the exchange rate increases or decreases depends on the direction and size of the shifts in the demand curve and supply curve. For example, as Figure 18.3 shows, if the demand curve for dollars in

MyEconLab Animation

Figure 18.3

Shifts in the Demand and Supply Curve Resulting in a Higher Exchange Rate

Holding other factors constant, an increase in the supply of dollars will decrease the equilibrium exchange rate. An increase in the demand for dollars will increase the equilibrium exchange rate. In the case shown in this figure, both the demand curve and the supply curve have shifted to the right. Because the demand curve has shifted to the right by more than the supply curve, the equilibrium exchange rate has increased from ¥120 to $1 at point A to ¥130 to $1 at point B.

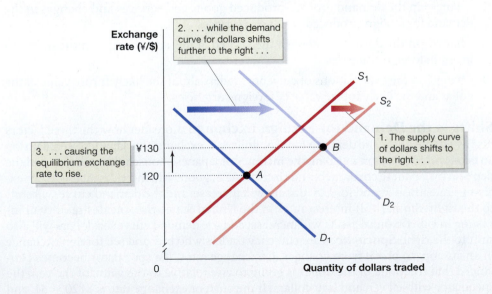

exchange for Japanese yen shifts to the right by more than the supply curve shifts, the equilibrium exchange rate will increase.   MyEconLab Concept Check

Some Exchange Rates Are Not Determined by the Market

To this point, we have assumed that exchange rates are determined by the market. This assumption is a good one for many currencies, including the U.S. dollar, the euro, the Japanese yen, and the British pound. Some currencies, however, have *fixed exchange rates* that do not change over long periods. For example, for more than 10 years, the value of the Chinese yuan was fixed against the U.S. dollar at a rate of 8.28 yuan to the dollar. As we will discuss in more detail in Chapter 19, a country's central bank has to intervene in the foreign exchange market to buy and sell its currency if it wishes to keep the exchange rate fixed.   MyEconLab Concept Check

How Movements in the Exchange Rate Affect Exports and Imports

When the market value of the dollar increases, the foreign currency price of U.S. exports rises, and the dollar price of foreign imports falls. Suppose that initially the market exchange rate between the U.S. dollar and the euro is $1 = €1. In that case, a Blu-ray disc that has a price of $20 in the United States will have a price of €20 in France. A bottle of French wine that has a price of €50 in France will have a price of $50 in the United States. Now suppose the market exchange rate between the U.S. dollar and the euro changes to $1.20 = €1. Because it now takes more dollars to buy a euro, the dollar has *depreciated* against the euro, and the euro has *appreciated* against the dollar. The depreciation of the dollar has decreased the euro price of the Blu-ray disc from €20 to $20/(1.20 dollars/euro) = €16.67. The dollar price of the French wine has risen from $50 to €50 ×1.20 dollars/euro = $60. As a result, we would expect more Blu-ray discs to be sold in France and less French wine to be sold in the United States.

   To generalize, we can conclude:

1. A depreciation in the domestic currency will increase exports and decrease imports, thereby increasing net exports. If real GDP is currently below potential GDP, then, holding all other factors constant, a depreciation in the domestic currency should increase net exports, aggregate demand, and real GDP.

2. An appreciation in the domestic currency should have the opposite effect: Exports should fall, and imports should rise, which will reduce net exports, aggregate demand, and real GDP.   MyEconLab Concept Check

Making the Connection

MyEconLab Video

Is a Strong Currency Good for a Country?

News stories often refer to a country as having a "strong" currency when the currency's value has been rising relative to other countries' currencies. Should a country want a strong currency? "Strong" certainly seems better than "weak," so most people would answer "yes" to that question. During late 2014 and 2015, as investors anticipated that the Federal Reserve would take action to increase U.S. interest rates, the value of the dollar increased, as shown in the graph on the next page. The graph shows the *trade-weighted exchange rate* for the U.S. dollar, which is an index number similar to the consumer price index (CPI). Just as the CPI weights individual prices by the share the product takes up in a household's budget, the trade-weighted exchange rate for the U.S. dollar weights each individual exchange rate by the share of that country's trade with the United States.

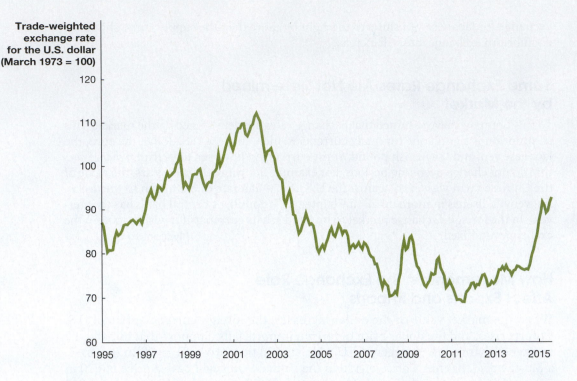

Trade-weighted
exchange rate
for the U.S. dollar
(March 1973 = 100)

In June 2015, President Barack Obama attended a meeting of the Group of 7, an organization of high-income countries. He was initially quoted as saying at that meeting that a strong dollar was a problem for the United States. There was a public outcry, and the president later denied he had made the statement. But clearly, not everyone in a country benefits from a strong currency. Firms that are exporters generally don't benefit. As one headline in the *Wall Street Journal* put it, "Strong Dollar Squeezes U.S. Firms." The CEO of Caterpillar, the U.S.-based heavy equipment manufacturer, was quoted as saying, "The rising dollar will not be good for U.S. manufacturing and the U.S. economy." A strong dollar increases the foreign currency price of U.S. exports, so to buy U.S.-produced goods, European consumers have to pay more euros, Canadian consumers have to pay more Canadian dollars, and Japanese consumers have to pay more yen. The result is a decline in profits for U.S. exporters. As we saw in the chapter opener, IBM experienced a lower profit in 2014 due to the strong dollar. U.S. firms facing competition from foreign imports can also be hurt by a strong dollar as the dollar prices of foreign imports are reduced.

Although a strong dollar can be bad news for U.S. exporters like Caterpillar and IBM, it can actually be *good* news for U.S. consumers. Between the beginning of 2014 and the middle of 2015, the average price of goods imported into the United States dropped by over 9 percent. U.S. consumers benefited from lower prices of imported goods from cars to clothing to electronics.

If many U.S. firms were hurt by the strong value of the dollar in 2014 and 2015, while U.S. consumers were helped, the reverse was true in Japan, where the value of the yen was falling. The Bank of Japan was pursuing an expansionary monetary policy that had driven Japanese interest rates to low levels. Investors reacted by selling yen and buying U.S. dollars and other currencies, driving down the value of the yen. The value of the yen declined by more than 30 percent in exchange for the U.S. dollar. Five Japanese automobile companies were able to report record profits as the prices of the cars they were exporting fell in terms of dollars and other foreign currencies. But because Japan relies heavily on imports of food, oil, and other important goods, consumers suffered as yen prices of foreign imports soared. As one Japanese politician put it, the Japanese government, by allowing the value of the yen to decline, had shown "little concern for . . . ordinary households."

We can conclude that neither a "strong" currency nor a "weak" currency is all good or all bad for a country's businesses and households. Swings in exchange rates create both winners and losers.

Sources: James Ramage, "Dollar Retreats as Investors Cash in on Jobs-Report Gains," *Wall Street Journal*, June 8, 2015; Paul Ziobro, Josh Mitchell, and Theo Francis, "Strong Dollar Squeezes U.S. Firms," *Wall Street Journal*, January 27, 2015; Mitsuru Obe, "Falling Yen Stirs Debate in Japan," *Wall Street Journal*, December 7, 2014; and data from the Federal Reserve Bank of St. Louis and the U.S. Bureau of Economic Analysis.

Your Turn: Test your understanding by doing related problem 2.6 on page 658 at the end of this chapter.

MyEconLab Study Plan

Don't Let This Happen to You

Don't Confuse What Happens When a Currency Appreciates with What Happens When It Depreciates

One of the most confusing aspects of exchange rates is that they can be expressed in two ways. We can express the exchange rate between the dollar and the yen either as how many yen can be purchased with $1 or as how many dollars can be purchased with ¥1. That is, we can express the exchange rate as ¥100 = $1 or as $0.01 = ¥1.

When a currency appreciates, it increases in value relative to another currency. When it depreciates, it decreases in value relative to another currency. If the exchange rate changes from ¥100 = $1 to ¥120 = $1, the dollar has appreciated and the yen has depreciated because it now takes more yen to buy $1. If the exchange rate changes from $0.010 = ¥1 to $0.015 = ¥1, however, the dollar has depreciated and the yen has appreciated because it now takes more dollars to buy ¥1. This situation can appear somewhat confusing because the exchange rate seems to have "increased" in both cases. To determine which currency has appreciated and which has depreciated, it is important to remember that an appreciation of the domestic currency means that it now takes *more* units of the foreign currency to buy one unit of the domestic currency. A depreciation of the domestic currency means it takes *fewer* units of the foreign currency to buy one unit of the domestic currency. This observation holds no matter which way we express the exchange rate.

MyEconLab Study Plan

Your Turn: Test your understanding by doing related problem 2.7 on page 658 at the end of the chapter.

Solved Problem 18.2

MyEconLab Interactive Animation

Subaru Benefits from a Weak Yen

Today, most Japanese automobile companies have manufacturing plants in the United States. Honda, for example, exports from Japan only 21 percent of the cars it sells in the United States. Fuji Heavy Industries, whose main car brand is Subaru, is an exception in still producing most of its cars in Japan. An article in the *Wall Street Journal* observed that for Fuji Heavy Industries, "the plunging yen has turned a problem—a shortage of production in the U.S.—into an unexpected boon."

a. What does the article mean by a "plunging yen"?

b. Why would a plunging yen be a boon for Fuji Heavy Industries?

c. Briefly explain whether a plunging yen would help or hurt Honda.

Solving the Problem

Step 1: **Review the chapter material.** This problem is about changes in the value of a currency, so you may want to review the section "How Movements in the Exchange Rate Affect Exports and Imports" on page 645.

Step 2: **Answer part (a) by explaining what the article means by a "plunging yen."** In this case, a plunging yen means a yen that is worth less in exchange for the U.S. dollar. With a plunging yen, a larger number of yen would be needed to exchange for one U.S. dollar.

Step 3: **Answer part (b) by explaining how a plunging yen will affect Fuji Heavy Industries.** When Fuji Heavy Industries manufactures cars in Japan, it pays its production costs—including the salaries of its assembly-line workers and payments to its suppliers—with yen. With a falling value of the yen, the dollar price of cars Fuji sells in the United States decreases. As a result,

Fuji will gain sales from other companies, particularly those that produce their cars in the United States. If Fuji produced its cars in the United States, it would *not* have gained this advantage.

Step 4: **Answer part (c) by explaining whether a plunging yen will help or hurt Honda.** Because most of the cars Honda sells in the United States are also produced here, most of the company's production costs and also most of the revenue it earns are in dollars. So, Honda will not be directly affected by fluctuations in the yen–dollar exchange rate. Honda will, though, likely lose some sales to Fuji as the dollar prices of Subarus declines.

Extra Credit: Managers at Honda, Toyota, and Nissan are aware that when the value of the yen declines against the dollar, they would be better off producing in Japan the cars they planned to sell in the United States. But, unlike the managers of Fuji, the managers of these firms decided that moving production to the United States would allow them to plan better and to stabilize their profits because their sales would no longer be affected as much by fluctuations in the exchange rate.

Source: Yoko Kubota, "Subaru Rides a Weaker Yen into the U.S.," *Wall Street Journal*, November 15, 2014.

MyEconLab Study Plan   **Your Turn:** For more practice, do related problem 2.10 on page 658 at the end of this chapter.

The Real Exchange Rate

Real exchange rate The price of domestic goods in terms of foreign goods.

We have seen that an important factor in determining the level of a country's exports to and imports from another country is the relative prices of each country's goods. The relative prices of two countries' goods are determined by two factors: the relative price levels in the two countries and the nominal exchange rate between the two countries' currencies. Economists combine these two factors in the **real exchange rate**, which is the price of domestic goods in terms of foreign goods. Recall that the price level is a measure of the average prices of goods and services in an economy. We can calculate the real exchange rate between two currencies as:

$$\text{Real exchange rate} = \text{Norminal exchange rate} \times \left(\frac{\text{Domestic price level}}{\text{Foreign price level}} \right).$$

Notice that both changes in the nominal exchange rate and changes in the relative price levels cause movements in the real exchange rate. Suppose that the exchange rate between the U.S. dollar and the British pound is $1 = £1, the price level in the United States is 100, and the price level in the United Kingdom is also 100. Then the real exchange rate between the dollar and the pound is:

$$\text{Real exchange rate} = 1 \text{ pound/dollar} \times \left(\frac{100}{100} \right) = 1.00.$$

Now suppose that the nominal exchange rate increases to 1.1 pounds per dollar, while the price level in the United States rises to 105 and the price level in the United Kingdom remains 100. In this case, the real exchange rate will be:

$$\text{Real exchange rate} = 1.1 \text{ pound/dollar} \times \left(\frac{105}{100} \right) = 1.15.$$

The increase in the real exchange rate from 1.00 to 1.15 tells us that the prices of U.S. goods and services are now 15 percent higher relative to British goods and services.

Real exchange rates are reported as index numbers, with one year chosen as the base year. As with the consumer price index, the main value of the real exchange rate is in tracking changes over time—in this case, changes in the relative prices of domestic goods in terms of foreign goods.

MyEconLab Study Plan   MyEconLab Concept Check

18.3 The International Sector and National Saving and Investment

LEARNING OBJECTIVE: Define and apply the saving and investment equation.

Having studied what determines the exchange rate, we are now ready to explore further the linkages between the U.S. economy and foreign economies. Until 1970, U.S. imports and exports were usually 4 percent to 5 percent of GDP (see Figure 7.1 in Chapter 7). Imports and exports are now three times as large a fraction of U.S. GDP. Imports have also consistently been larger than exports, meaning that net exports have been negative.

Net Exports Equal Net Foreign Investment

If your spending is greater than your income, what can you do? You can sell some assets—maybe those 20 shares of stock in IBM your grandparents gave you—or you can borrow money. A firm can be in the same situation: If a firm's costs are greater than its revenues, it has to make up the difference by selling assets or by borrowing. A country is in the same situation when it imports more than it exports: The country must finance the difference by selling assets—such as land, office buildings, or factories—to foreigners or by borrowing from foreigners.

In other words, for any country, a current account deficit must be exactly offset by a financial account surplus. When a country sells more assets to foreigners than it buys from foreigners, or when it borrows more from foreigners than it lends to foreigners—as it must if it is running a current account deficit—the country experiences a net capital inflow and a financial account surplus. Remember that net exports is roughly equal to the current account balance. Remember also that the financial account balance is roughly equal to net capital flows, which are in turn equal to net foreign investment but with the opposite sign. To review these two points, look again at Table 18.1 on page 637, which shows that the current account balance is determined mainly by the balance of trade and the balance of services, and the financial account is equal to net capital flows. Also, remember the definition of net foreign investment.

When imports are greater than exports, net exports are negative, and there will be a net capital inflow as people in the United States sell assets and borrow to pay for the surplus of imports over exports. Therefore, net capital flows will be equal to net exports (but with the opposite sign), and net foreign investment will also be equal to net exports (with the same sign). Because net exports are usually negative for the United States, in most years, the United States must be a net borrower from abroad, and U.S. net foreign investment will be negative.

We can summarize this discussion with the following equations:

$$\text{Current account balance} + \text{Financial account balance} = 0$$

or:

$$\text{Current account balance} = -\text{Financial account balance}$$

or:

$$\text{Net exports} = \text{Net foreign investment.}$$

The last equation tells us, once again, that countries such as the United States that import more than they export must borrow more from abroad than they lend abroad: If net exports are negative, net foreign investment will also be negative by the same amount. Countries such as China that export more than they import must lend abroad more than they borrow from abroad: If net exports are positive, net foreign investment will also be positive by the same amount.   MyEconLab Concept Check

Domestic Saving, Domestic Investment, and Net Foreign Investment

We can think of the total saving in any economy as equal to saving by the private sector plus saving by the government sector, which we call *public saving* (see Chapter 10, Section 10.2). When the government runs a budget surplus by spending less than it receives in taxes, public saving is positive. When the government runs a budget deficit, public saving is negative. Negative saving is also known as *dissaving*. We can write the following expression for the level of saving in the economy:

$$\text{National saving} = \text{Private saving} + \text{Public saving}$$

or:

$$S = S_{\text{private}} + S_{\text{public}}.$$

Private saving is equal to what households have left of their income after spending on consumption goods and paying taxes (for simplicity, we assume that transfer payments are zero):

$$\text{Private saving} = \text{National income} - \text{Consumption} - \text{Taxes}$$

or:

$$S_{\text{private}} = Y - C - T.$$

Public saving is equal to the difference between government spending and taxes:

$$\text{Government saving} = \text{Taxes} - \text{Government spending}$$

or:

$$S_{\text{public}} = T - G.$$

Finally, remember the basic macroeconomic equation for GDP or national income:

$$Y = C + I + G + NX.$$

We can use this last equation, our definitions of private and public saving, and the fact that net exports equal net foreign investment to arrive at an important relationship, called the **saving and investment equation**:

$$\text{National saving} = \text{Domestic investment} + \text{Net foreign investment}$$

or:

$$S = I + NFI.$$

Saving and investment equation An equation that shows that national saving is equal to domestic investment plus net foreign investment.

This equation is an *identity* because it must always be true, given the definitions we have used.

The saving and investment equation tells us that a country's saving will be invested either domestically or overseas. If you save $1,000 and use the funds to buy a bond issued by IBM, IBM may use the $1,000 to partially pay for a cloud computing facility in the United States (*I*) or for a software consulting office in China (*NFI*).

Solved Problem 18.3

MyEconLab Interactive Animation

Arriving at the Saving and Investment Equation

Use the definitions of private and public saving, the equation for GDP or national income, and the fact that net exports (*NX*) must equal net foreign investment (*NFI*) to arrive at the saving and investment equation.

Solving the Problem

Step 1: **Review the chapter material.** This problem is about the saving and investment equation, so you may want to review the section "Domestic Saving, Domestic Investment, and Net Foreign Investment," which begins on page 649.

Step 2: **Derive an expression for national saving (*S*) in terms of national income (*Y*), consumption (*C*), and government purchases (*G*).** We can bring together the four equations we need:

1. $S_{\text{private}} = Y - C - T$
2. $S_{\text{public}} = T - G$

3. $Y = C + I + G + NX$

4. $NX = NFI$

Because national saving (S) appears in the saving and investment equation, we need to find an equation for it in terms of the other variables. Adding equation (1) plus equation (2) yields national saving:

$$S = S_{\text{private}} + S_{\text{public}} = (Y - C - T) + (T - G) = Y - C - G.$$

Step 3: **Use the result from step 2 to derive an expression for national saving in terms of investment (I) and net exports (NX).** Because GDP (Y) does not appear in the saving and investment equation, we need to substitute the expression for it given in equation (3):

$$S = (C + I + G + NX) - C - G$$

and simplify:

$$S = I + NX.$$

Step 4: **Use the results of steps 2 and 3 to derive the saving and investment equation.** Finally, substitute net foreign investment for net exports:

$$S = I + NFI.$$

Your Turn: For more practice, do related problem 3.8 on page 659 at the end of this chapter.   MyEconLab Study Plan

---

A country such as the United States that has negative net foreign investment must be saving less than it is investing domestically. To understand why, rewrite the saving and investment equation by moving domestic investment to the left side:

$$S - I = NFI.$$

If net foreign investment is negative—as it is for the United States nearly every year—domestic investment (I) must be greater than national saving (S).

In most years, the level of saving in Japan has been well above domestic investment. The result has been high levels of Japanese net foreign investment. For example, Japanese automobile companies Toyota, Honda, and Nissan have all constructed factories in the United States. Sony purchased the Columbia Pictures film studio. Japan has made many similar investments in countries around the world, which has sometimes caused resentment in those countries. There were some protests in the United States in the 1980s, for example, when Japanese investors purchased the Pebble Beach golf course in California and the Rockefeller Center complex in New York City. (Both were eventually purchased by U.S. investors.)

Japan typically needs a high level of net exports to help offset a low level of domestic investment. When exports of a product begin to decline and imports begin to increase, governments are often tempted to impose tariffs or quotas to reduce imports. (See Chapter 7 to review tariffs and quotas and their negative effects on the economy.) In fact, some Japanese firms have been urging the Japanese government to impose trade restrictions on imports from China.   MyEconLab Concept Check   MyEconLab Study Plan

18.4 The Effect of a Government Budget Deficit on Investment

LEARNING OBJECTIVE: Explain the effect of a government budget deficit on investment in an open economy.

The link we have just developed among saving, investment, and net foreign investment can help us understand some of the effects of changes in a government's budget deficit. When the government runs a budget deficit, national saving will decline unless private saving increases by the amount of the budget deficit, which is unlikely. As the saving and investment equation ($S = I + NFI$) shows, the result of a decline in national saving must be a decline in either domestic investment or net foreign investment. The algebra is clear, but why, economically, does an increase in the government budget deficit cause a fall in domestic investment or net foreign investment?

To understand the answer to this question, remember that if the federal government runs a budget deficit, the U.S. Treasury must raise an amount equal to the deficit by selling bonds. To attract investors, the Treasury may have to raise the interest rates on its bonds. As interest rates on Treasury bonds rise, other interest rates, including those on corporate bonds and bank loans, will also rise. Higher interest rates will discourage some firms from borrowing funds to build new factories or to buy new equipment or computers. Higher interest rates on financial assets in the United States will attract foreign investors. Investors in Canada, Japan, or China will have to buy U.S. dollars to be able to purchase bonds in the United States. This greater demand for dollars will increase their value relative to foreign currencies. As the value of the dollar rises, exports from the United States will fall, and imports to the United States will rise. Net exports and, therefore, net foreign investment will fall.

When a government budget deficit leads to a decline in net exports, the result is sometimes called the *twin deficits*, which refers to the possibility that a government budget deficit will also lead to a current account deficit. The twin deficits idea first became widely discussed in the United States during the early 1980s, when the federal government ran a large budget deficit that resulted in high interest rates, a high exchange value of the dollar, and a large current account deficit.

Figure 18.4 shows that in the early 1980s, the United States had large federal budget deficits and large current account deficits. The figure also shows, however, that the twin deficits idea does not consistently match the experience of the United States after 1990. The large federal budget deficits of the early 1990s occurred at a time of relatively small current account deficits, and the budget surpluses of the late 1990s occurred at a time of then-record current account deficits. Both the current account deficit and the federal budget deficit increased in the early 2000s, but the federal budget deficit declined in the mid-2000s much more than did the current account deficit. Beginning in 2008, the federal budget deficit soared and then sharply declined, while the current account deficit declined.

The experience of other countries also shows only mixed support for the twin deficits idea. Germany ran large budget deficits and large current account deficits during the early 1990s, but both Canada and Italy ran large budget deficits during the 1980s

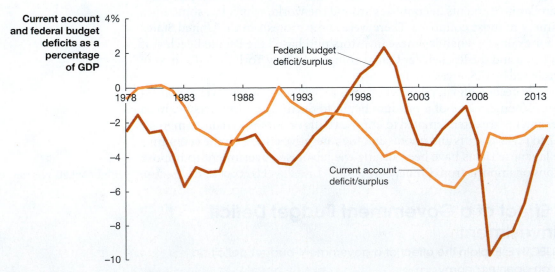

Figure 18.4 **The Twin Deficits, 1978–2014**

During the early 1980s, large federal budget deficits occurred at the same time as large current account deficits, but twin deficits did not occur in most other periods during these years.
Source: U.S. Bureau of Economic Analysis.

without running current account deficits. The saving and investment equation shows that an increase in the government budget deficit will not lead to an increase in the current account deficit, provided that either private saving increases or domestic investment declines. According to the twin deficits idea, when the federal government ran budget surpluses in the late 1990s, the current account should also have been in surplus, or at least the current account deficit should have been small. In fact, the increase in national saving due to the budget surpluses was more than offset by a sharp decline in private saving, and the United States ran very large current account deficits.   MyEconLab Concept Check

Making the Connection
MyEconLab Video

Why Is the United States Called the "World's Largest Debtor"?

The following graph shows the current account balance as a percentage of GDP for the United States for the period 1960–2014. The United States has had a current account deficit every year since 1982, with the exception of 1991. Between 1960 and 1975, the United States ran a current account deficit in only five years. Many economists believe that the current account deficits of the 1980s were closely related to the federal budget deficits of those years. High interest rates attracted foreign investors to U.S. bonds, which raised the exchange rate between the dollar and foreign currencies. The high exchange rate reduced U.S. exports and increased imports, leading to current account deficits.

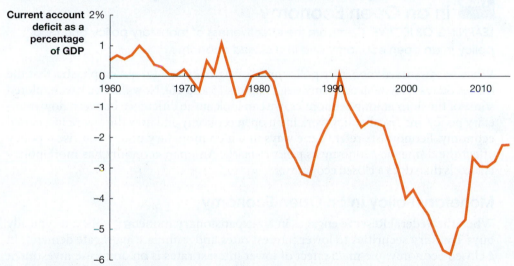

MyEconLab Real-time data

Source: Federal Reserve Bank of St Louis.

As the federal budget deficit narrowed in the mid-1990s and disappeared in the late 1990s, the foreign exchange value of the dollar remained high—and large current account deficits continued—because foreign investors persisted in investing in the United States, despite low interest rates. In the late 1990s, a number of countries around the world, such as South Korea, Indonesia, Brazil, and Russia, suffered severe economic problems. In a process known as *flight to quality*, many investors sold their investments in those countries and bought investments in the United States. In addition, the strong performance of the U.S. stock market through the spring of 2000 attracted many investors. Finally, the sharp decline in private saving in the United States that began during the late 1990s also contributed to the U.S. current account deficit. The fall in the value of the dollar after 2008 helped reduce the size of the current account deficit. In late 2014 and 2015, though, the deficit was increasing along with the value of the dollar.

Are persistent current account deficits a problem for the United States? Current account deficits result in U.S. net foreign investment being negative. Each year, foreign investors accumulate many more U.S. assets—such as stocks, bonds, and factories—than U.S. investors accumulate foreign assets. In 1986, for the first time since the nineteenth century, the value of foreign-owned assets in the United States became larger than the value of U.S.-owned assets abroad. At the end of 2014, foreign investors owned about $7 trillion more of U.S. assets than U.S. investors owned of foreign assets, which is why the United States is sometimes called "the world's largest debtor." But the continued willingness of foreign investors to buy U.S. stocks and bonds and of foreign companies to build factories in the United States can be seen as a vote of confidence in the strength of the U.S. economy and the buying power of U.S. consumers. When private saving rates declined in the United States to historically low levels in the mid-2000s, only the continued flow of funds from foreign investors made it possible for the United States to maintain the high levels of domestic investment required for economic growth. Beginning in 2009, private saving rates increased, but public saving turned sharply negative between 2009 and 2012 as the federal budget deficit soared. Even though public saving has been less negative in the past few years, domestic investment in the United States remains reliant on funds from foreign investors.

Source: Elena L. Nguyen, "The U.S. Net International Investment Position at the End of the First Quarter of 2015, Year 2014, and Annual Revisions," *Survey of Current Business*, July 2015, pp. 1–10.

MyEconLab Study Plan   **Your Turn:** Test your understanding by doing related problem 4.7 on page 660 at the end of this chapter.

18.5 Monetary Policy and Fiscal Policy in an Open Economy

LEARNING OBJECTIVE: Compare the effectiveness of monetary policy and fiscal policy in an open economy and in a closed economy.

When we discussed monetary policy and fiscal policy, we did not emphasize that the United States is an open economy (see Chapters 15 and 16). Now that we have explored some of the links among economies, we can look at the difference between how monetary policy and fiscal policy work in an open economy and how they work in a closed economy. Economists refer to the ways in which monetary policy and fiscal policy affect the domestic economy as *policy channels*. An open economy has more policy channels than does a closed economy.

Monetary Policy in an Open Economy

When the Federal Reserve engages in an expansionary monetary policy, it typically buys Treasury securities to lower interest rates and stimulate aggregate demand. In a closed economy, the main effect of lower interest rates is on domestic investment spending and purchases of consumer durables. In an open economy, lower interest rates will also affect the exchange rate between the dollar and foreign currencies. Lower interest rates will cause some investors in the United States and abroad to switch from investing in U.S. financial assets to investing in foreign financial assets. The result is a lower demand for the dollar relative to foreign currencies and a decline in the dollar's value. A lower exchange rate will decrease the prices of U.S. products in foreign markets and increase the prices of foreign products in the United States. As a result, net exports will increase. This additional policy channel will increase the ability of an expansionary monetary policy to affect aggregate demand.

When the Fed wants to reduce aggregate demand to reduce inflation, it engages in a contractionary monetary policy. The Fed sells Treasury securities to increase interest rates and reduce aggregate demand. In a closed economy, the main effect is once again on domestic investment spending and purchases of consumer durables. In an open economy, higher interest rates will lead to a higher foreign exchange value of the dollar. The prices of U.S. products in foreign markets will increase, and the prices of foreign products in the United States will fall. As a result, net exports will fall. The contractionary policy will have a larger effect on aggregate demand, and therefore it will be more effective in slowing the growth in economic activity. To summarize: *Monetary policy has a greater effect on aggregate demand in an open economy than in a closed economy.*   MyEconLab Concept Check

Fiscal Policy in an Open Economy

To engage in an expansionary fiscal policy, the federal government increases its purchases or cuts taxes. Increases in government purchases directly increase aggregate demand. Tax cuts increase aggregate demand by increasing household disposable income and business income, which results in increased consumption spending and investment spending. An expansionary fiscal policy may result in higher interest rates. In a closed economy, the main effect of higher interest rates is to reduce domestic investment spending and purchases of consumer durables. In an open economy, higher interest rates will also lead to an increase in the foreign exchange value of the dollar and a decrease in net exports. Therefore, in an open economy, an expansionary fiscal policy may be less effective because the *crowding out effect* may be larger. In a closed economy, only consumption and investment are crowded out by an expansionary fiscal policy. In an open economy, net exports may also be crowded out.

The government can fight inflation by using a contractionary fiscal policy to slow the growth of aggregate demand. A contractionary fiscal policy cuts government purchases or raises taxes to reduce household disposable income and consumption spending. It also reduces the federal budget deficit (or increases the budget surplus), which may lower interest rates. Lower interest rates will increase domestic investment and purchases of consumer durables, thereby offsetting some of the reduction in government spending and increases in taxes. In an open economy, lower interest rates will also reduce the foreign exchange value of the dollar and increase net exports. Therefore, in an open economy, a contractionary fiscal policy will have a smaller effect on aggregate demand and therefore will be less effective in slowing an economy. In summary: *Fiscal policy has a smaller effect on aggregate demand in an open economy than in a closed economy.*   MyEconLab Concept Check   MyEconLab Study Plan

Continued from page 635

Economics in Your Life

The South Korean Central Bank and Your Car Loan

At the beginning of this chapter, we posed this question: Will the Bank of Korea's decision to sell its U.S. Treasury bonds affect the interest rate you pay on your car loan? To sell its holdings of Treasury bonds, South Korea's central bank may have to offer them at a lower price. When the prices of bonds fall, the interest rates on them rise. As the interest rates on U.S. Treasury bonds increase, the interest rates on corporate bonds and bank loans, including car loans, may also increase. So, the decision of the Bank of Korea has the potential to increase the interest rate you pay on your car loan. In practice, the interest rate on your car loan is likely to be affected only if the Bank of Korea sells a very large number of bonds and if investors consider it likely that other foreign central banks may soon do the same thing. The basic point is important, however: Economies are interdependent, and interest rates in the United States are not determined entirely by the actions of people in the United States.

Conclusion

At one time, U.S. policymakers—and economics textbooks—ignored the linkages between the United States and other economies. In the modern world, these linkages have become increasingly important, and economists and policymakers must take them into account when analyzing the economy. In Chapter 19, we will discuss further how the international financial system operates.

Visit MyEconLab for a news article and analysis related to the concepts in this chapter.

Key Terms

18.1 The Balance of Payments: Linking the United States to the International Economy, pages 636–640

LEARNING OBJECTIVE: Explain how the balance of payments is calculated.

Summary

Nearly all economies are **open economies** that trade with and invest in other economies. A **closed economy** has no transactions in trade or finance with other economies. The **balance of payments** is the record of a country's trade with other countries in goods, services, and assets. The **current account** records a country's net exports, net investment income, and net transfers. The **financial account** shows investments a country has made abroad and foreign investments received by the country. The **balance of trade** is the difference between the value of the goods a country exports and the value of the goods a country imports. **Net foreign investment** is the difference between capital outflows from a country and capital inflows. The **capital account** is a part of the balance of payments that records relatively minor transactions. Apart from measurement errors, the sum of the current account and the financial account must equal zero. Therefore, the balance of payments must also equal zero.

 Visit **www.myeconlab.com** to complete these exercises online and get instant feedback.

Review Questions

1.1 What is the relationship among the current account, the financial account, and the balance of payments?

1.2 What is the difference between net exports and the current account balance?

1.3 The late economist Herbert Stein described the accounts that comprise a country's balance of payments:

> A country is more likely to have a deficit in its current account the higher its price level, the higher its gross [domestic] product, the higher its interest rates, the lower its barriers to imports, and the more attractive its investment opportunities—all compared with conditions in other countries—and the higher its exchange rate. The effects of a change in one of these factors on the current account balance cannot be predicted without considering the effect on the other causal factors.

a. Briefly describe the transactions included in a country's current account.

b. Briefly explain why, compared to other countries, a country is more likely to have a deficit in its current account, holding other factors constant, if it has each of the following:
i. A higher price level
ii. An increase in interest rates
iii. Lower barriers to imports
iv. More attractive investment opportunities

Source: Herbert Stein, "Balance of Payments," *Library of Economics and Liberty,* http://www.econlib.org.

Problems and Applications

1.4 In 2014, France had a current account deficit of €19.5 billion (approximately $25.9 billion). Did France experience a net capital outflow or a net capital inflow during 2014? Briefly explain.

Source: Banque de France, "France's Balance of Payments," https://www.banque-france.fr/en/economics-statistics/stats-infos/frances-balance-of-payments.html.

1.5 Use the information in the following table to solve for the value of the statistical discrepancy and prepare a balance of payments account, like the one shown in Table 18.1 on page 637. Assume that the balance on the capital account is zero.

Increase in foreign holdings of assets in the United States	$1,181
Exports of goods	856
Imports of services	−256
Statistical discrepancy	?
Net transfers	−60
Exports of services	325
Income received on investments	392
Imports of goods	−1,108
Increase in U.S. holdings of assets in foreign countries	−1,040
Income payments on investments	−315

1.6 (Related to the Don't Let This Happen to You on page 639) In 2014, Germany had a balance of trade surplus of €217 billion and a current account surplus of €215 billion.

Explain how Germany's current account surplus could be smaller than its trade surplus. In 2014, what would we expect Germany's balance on the financial account to have been? Briefly explain.

Source: Statistisches Bundesamt.

1.7 **(Related to** Solved Problem 18.1 **on page 640)** A news article notes, "China recorded a current-account surplus of $76.6 billion in the second quarter but that was offset by a deficit of the same amount on its capital and financial account." Is this outcome surprising? Briefly explain.

Source: Grace Zhu, "China's Current-Account Surplus at $76.6 bln: SAFE," marketwatch.com, August 7, 2015.

1.8 **(Related to** Solved Problem 18.1 **on page 640)** An article in the *Wall Street Journal* about China's balance of payments contained the following observations: "A country's balance of payments still has to add up to zero. If foreign investors wish to acquire assets denominated in yuan, the necessary implication is that China will have to run a trade deficit."

a. Do you agree that the balance of payments must add up to zero?

b. If China were to have a deficit in its balance of trade of −100 billion yuan, must it have a surplus in its financial account of +100 billion yuan? Briefly explain.

Source: Andrew Colquhoun, "The Yuan Isn't Ready to Be a Global Reserve Currency," *Wall Street Journal*, August 12, 2015.

1.9 **(Related to** Solved Problem 18.1 **on page 640)** An article in the *New York Times* has the headline "U.S. Trade Deficit Widened Over Summer." The first sentence in the article is, "The current-account trade deficit widened slightly in the July–September quarter." The statement that the "trade deficit for goods and services" declined during this period appears later in the article. Is this article's headline consistent with the two statements in the article? Briefly explain.

Source: Associated Press, "U.S. Trade Deficit Widened Over Summer," *New York Times*, December 17, 2014.

1.10 An article in the *Wall Street Journal* refers to "debt-strapped emerging markets already struggling with current-account deficits." Why might we expect that countries running current account deficits might also have substantial foreign debts?

Source: Anjani Trivedi, "Emerging Markets Suffer Largest Outflow in Seven Years," *Wall Street Journal*, June 12, 2015.

18.2 | ## The Foreign Exchange Market and Exchange Rates, pages 640–648

LEARNING OBJECTIVE: Explain how exchange rates are determined and how changes in exchange rates affect the prices of imports and exports.

Summary

The **nominal exchange rate** is the value of one country's currency in terms of another country's currency. The exchange rate is determined in the foreign exchange market by the demand and supply of a country's currency. Changes in the exchange rate are caused by shifts in demand or supply. The three main sets of factors that cause the demand and supply curves in the foreign exchange market to shift are: (1) changes in the demand for U.S.-produced goods and services and changes in the demand for foreign-produced goods and services; (2) changes in the desire to invest in the United States and changes in the desire to invest in foreign countries; and (3) changes in the expectations of currency traders—particularly **speculators**—concerning the likely future value of the dollar and the likely future values of foreign currencies. **Currency appreciation** occurs when a currency's market value increases relative to another currency. **Currency depreciation** occurs when a currency's market value decreases relative to another currency. The **real exchange rate** is the price of domestic goods in terms of foreign goods. The real exchange rate is calculated by multiplying the nominal exchange rate by the ratio of the domestic price level to the foreign price level.

MyEconLab   Visit **www.myeconlab.com** to complete these exercises online and get instant feedback.

Review Questions

2.1 If the exchange rate between the Japanese yen and the U.S. dollar expressed in terms of yen per dollar is ¥125 = $1, what is the exchange rate when expressed in terms of dollars per yen?

2.2 Suppose that the current exchange rate between the dollar and the euro is €0.80 = $1. If the exchange rate changes to €0.85 = $1, has the euro appreciated or depreciated against the dollar? Briefly explain.

2.3 Why do foreign households and foreign firms demand U.S. dollars in exchange for foreign currency? Why do U.S. households and firms supply U.S. dollars in exchange for foreign currency?

2.4 What are the three main sets of factors that cause the supply and demand curves in the foreign exchange market to shift?

Problems and Applications

2.5 **(Related to the** Making the Connection **on page 641)** On January 1, 2002, there were 15 member countries in the European Union. Twelve of those countries eliminated their own individual currencies and began using a new common currency, the euro. For a three-year period from January 1, 1999, through December 31, 2001, these 12 countries priced goods and services in terms of both their own currencies and the euro. During that period, the values of their currencies were fixed against each other and against the euro. So during that time, the dollar had an exchange rate against each of these currencies and against the euro. The following table shows the fixed exchange rates of four European currencies against the euro and their exchange rates against the U.S. dollar on March 2, 2001. Use the information in the table on the next page to calculate the exchange rate between the dollar and the euro (in euros per dollar) on March 2, 2001.

Currency	Units per Euro (fixed)	Units per U.S. Dollar (as of March 2, 2001)
German mark	1.9558	2.0938
French franc	6.5596	7.0223
Italian lira	1,936.2700	2,072.8700
Portuguese escudo	200.4820	214.6300

2.6 **(Related to the** Making the Connection **on page 645)** Paul De Grauwe, an economist at the London School of Economics, wrote in the *Economist* that the quantitative easing policies of the European Central Bank "will contribute to a further weakening of the euro vis-à-vis other currencies such as the dollar, the pound and the yuan, thereby increasing exports and boosting inflation."
  a. What does De Grauwe mean by "a weakening of the euro"?
  b. What is quantitative easing, and why should it lead to a weakening of the euro?
  c. If you ran a business in France that exports to the United States and Japan, would this development help you? If you were a consumer in France, would this development help you? Briefly explain.

Source: Paul De Grauwe, "The Sad Consequences of the Fear of QE," *Economist*, January 21, 2015.

2.7 **(Related to the** Don't Let This Happen to You **on page 647)** If we know the exchange rate between Country A's currency and Country B's currency and we know the exchange rate between Country B's currency and Country C's currency, then we can compute the exchange rate between Country A's currency and Country C's currency.
  a. Suppose the exchange rate between the Japanese yen and the U.S. dollar is currently ¥95 = $1 and the exchange rate between the British pound and the U.S. dollar is £0.64 = $1. What is the exchange rate between the yen and the pound?
  b. Suppose the exchange rate between the yen and the dollar changes to ¥100 = $1 and the exchange rate between the pound and the dollar changes to £0.55 = $1. Has the dollar appreciated or depreciated against the yen? Has the dollar appreciated or depreciated against the pound? Has the yen appreciated or depreciated against the pound?

2.8 Graph the demand and supply of U.S. dollars for euros and label each axis. Show graphically and explain the effect on the demand and supply of dollars and the resulting change in the exchange rate of euros for U.S. dollars if the European Central Bank takes action to increase interest rates.

Source: Jon Hilsenrath, "Rising Dollar and Falling Oil Could Be Recipe for a U.S. Asset Boom," *Wall Street Journal*, December 11, 2014.

2.9 Use the graph to answer the following questions.

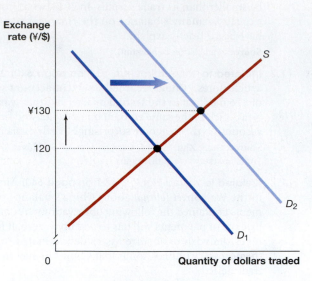

  a. Briefly explain whether the dollar appreciated or depreciated against the yen.
  b. Which of the following events could have caused the shift in demand shown in the graph?
    i. Interest rates in the United States declined.
    ii. Income rose in Japan.
    iii. Speculators began to believe the value of the dollar would be higher in the future.

2.10 **(Related to** Solved Problem 18.2 **on page 647)** An article in the *Wall Street Journal* notes, "For every one yen rise in the value of the dollar, Fuji Heavy's full-year operating profit increases by ¥9.7 billion, the company says." Would Honda's profits be likely to increase as much as a result of a rise in the value of the dollar versus the yen? Briefly explain.

Source: Yoko Kubota, "Subaru Rides a Weaker Yen into the U.S.," *Wall Street Journal*, November 15, 2014.

2.11 According to an article in the *Wall Street Journal*, in 2014, "The Australian dollar tumbled after muted inflation data scotched investors' expectations that the central bank would raise interest rates."
  a. Why would the inflation rate being lower than expected make it less likely that the Australian central bank would raise interest rates?
  b. Why would the fact that it was less likely that the Australian central bank was going to raise interest rates cause the value of the Australian dollar to fall?

Source: James Ramage, "Australian Dollar Tumbles after Data Scotches Rate-Increase Expectations," *Wall Street Journal*, April 23, 2014.

2.12 **(Related to the** Chapter Opener **on page 635)** In preparing their financial statements, U.S. firms with sales in foreign currencies have to engage in "foreign currency translations"; that is, they have to convert foreign currency values into U.S. dollars. In its *2014 Annual Report*, IBM made the following statement: "As with all companies with a similar global business profile, with the dollar strengthening, the company also expects that currency will have a significant translation impact on its profit growth."

a. What does the report mean by "the dollar strengthening"?

b. As a U.S.-based company, doesn't IBM benefit when the U.S. dollar is stronger? Briefly explain.

Source: International Business Machines Corporation, *2014 IBM Annual Report*, February 24, 2015, p. 64.

2.13 In the summer of 2015, the exchange rate of China's currency, the yuan, declined against other currencies. The lower value for the yuan was expected to have a negative effect on firms such as Apple and Yum Brands (owners of KFC and Pizza Hut) that have stores or restaurants in China. But the lower value of the yuan was expected to benefit Foxconn, a firm based in Taiwan that assembles iPhones in China. Briefly explain how the decline in the value of the yuan would have a negative effect on firms, such as Apple and Yum, but would benefit other firms, such as Foxconn, that also operate in China.

Source: Lorraine Luk and Eva Dou, "Devalued Yuan Set to Take Bite Out of Apple, Give Boost to Chinese Rivals," *Wall Street Journal*, August 11, 2015.

18.3 The International Sector and National Saving and Investment, pages 649–651

LEARNING OBJECTIVE: Define and apply the saving and investment equation.

Summary

A current account deficit must be exactly offset by a financial account surplus. The financial account is equal to net capital flows, which is equal to net foreign investment but with the opposite sign. Because the current account balance is roughly equal to net exports, we can conclude that net exports will equal net foreign investment. National saving is equal to private saving plus government saving. Private saving is equal to national income minus consumption and minus taxes. Government saving is the difference between taxes and government spending. GDP (or national income) is equal to the sum of investment, consumption, government spending, and net exports. We can use this fact, our definitions of private and government saving, and the fact that net exports equal net foreign investment to arrive at an important relationship known as the **saving and investment equation**: $S = I + NFI$.

 Visit **www.myeconlab.com** to complete these exercises online and get instant feedback.

Review Questions

3.1 Explain the relationship between net exports and net foreign investment.

3.2 What is the saving and investment equation? If national saving declines, what will happen to domestic investment and net foreign investment?

3.3 If a country saves more than it invests domestically, what must be true of its net foreign investment?

Problems and Applications

3.4 Writing in the *New York Times*, Simon Johnson, an economist at MIT, makes the argument that people outside the United States may at some point decide to "save less (in which case they may hold onto their existing United States government debt but not want to buy so much of new issues)." What does saving by people outside the United States have to do with sales of U.S. government debt? Does the level of domestic investment occurring in foreign countries matter for your answer? Briefly explain.

Source: Simon Johnson, "The Real Fiscal Risks in the United States," *New York Times*, December 6, 2012.

3.5 In 2014, domestic investment in Japan was 21.7 percent of GDP, and Japanese national saving was 22.4 percent of GDP. What percentage of GDP was Japanese net foreign investment?

3.6 In 2014, France's net foreign investment was negative. Which was larger in France in 2014: national saving or domestic investment? Briefly explain.

3.7 Briefly explain whether you agree with the following statement: "Because in 2014 national saving was a larger percentage of GDP in the United States than in the United Kingdom, domestic investment must also have been a larger percentage of GDP in the United States than in the United Kingdom."

3.8 **(Related to Solved Problem 18.3 on page 650)** Look again at Solved Problem 18.3, where the saving and investment equation $S = I + NX$ is derived. In deriving this equation, we assumed that national income was equal to Y. But Y only includes income *earned* by households. In the modern U.S. economy, households receive substantial transfer payments—such as Social Security payments and unemployment insurance payments—from the government. Suppose that we define national income as being equal to $Y + TR$, where TR equals government transfer payments, and we also define government spending as being equal to $G + TR$. Show that after making these adjustments, we end up with the same saving and investment equation.

3.9 Use the saving and investment equation to explain why the United States experienced large current account deficits in the late 1990s.

3.10 Former congressman and presidential candidate Richard Gephardt once proposed that tariffs be imposed on imports from countries with which the United States has a trade deficit. If this proposal were enacted and if it were to succeed in reducing the U.S. current account deficit to zero, what would be the likely effect on domestic investment spending within the United States? Assume that no other federal government economic policy is changed. (*Hint:* Use the saving and investment equation to answer this question.)

18.4 **The Effect of a Government Budget Deficit on Investment, pages 651–654**
LEARNING OBJECTIVE: Explain the effect of a government budget deficit on investment in an open economy.

Summary

When the government runs a budget deficit, national saving will decline unless private saving increases by the full amount of the budget deficit, which is unlikely. As the saving and investment equation ($S = I + NFI$) shows, the result of a decline in national saving must be a decline in either domestic investment or net foreign investment.

 Visit **www.myeconlab.com** to complete these exercises online and get instant feedback.

Review Questions

4.1 What happens to national saving when the government runs a budget surplus? What is the twin deficits idea? Did it hold for the United States in the 1990s? Briefly explain.

4.2 Why were the early and mid-1980s particularly difficult times for U.S. exporters?

4.3 Why is the United States sometimes called the "world's largest debtor"?

Problems and Applications

4.4 An investment analyst recommended that investors "gravitate toward the stronger currencies and countries that are running current-account and fiscal surpluses," such as South Korea and Taiwan.
   a. Holding all other factors constant, would we expect a country that is running a government budget surplus to have a currency that is increasing in value or decreasing in value? Briefly explain.
   b. Holding all other factors constant, would we expect a country that has a currency that is increasing in value to have an increasing or decreasing current account surplus? Briefly explain.
   c. Is the combination of economic characteristics this analyst has identified likely to be commonly found among countries? Briefly explain.
   Source: Paul J. Lim, "Suddenly, BRIC Markets Are on a Shakier Foundation," *New York Times*, January 9, 2015.

4.5 According to an article in the *Economist*, "countries with persistent current-account deficits tend to have higher real interest rates than surplus countries." What do high interest rates have to do with current account deficits?
   Source: "Carry on Trading," *Economist*, August 10, 2013.

4.6 Section 18.4 states: "The budget surpluses of the late 1990s occurred at a time of then-record current account deficits." Holding everything else constant, what would the likely effect have been on domestic investment in the United States during those years if the current account had been balanced instead of being in deficit?

4.7 **(Related to the** Making the Connection **on page 653)** Why might "the continued willingness of foreign investors to buy U.S. stocks and bonds and foreign companies to build factories in the United States" result in the United States running a current account deficit?

4.8 An article in GulfNews.com noted that in September 2012, the Indian government of Prime Minister Manmohan Singh made "urgently needed reforms to reduce the fiscal deficit and attract foreign investment to help the current account deficit and growth."
   a. Could there be a connection between India's fiscal (budget) deficit and its current account deficit? Briefly explain.
   b. How would attracting foreign investment help the current account deficit and (economic) growth?
   c. The article further notes that the Reserve Bank of India (the central bank) stated. "Financing the CAD [current account deficit] with increasingly risky and volatile flows increases the economy's vulnerability to sudden shifts in risk appetite and liquidity preference, potentially threatening macroeconomic and exchange rate stability." What does India's central bank mean by "risky and volatile flows" that finance the current account deficit? How could those flows threaten India's macroeconomic stability?
   Source: "India's Central Bank Lowers Interest Rate," gulfnews.com, January 29, 2013.

18.5 **Monetary Policy and Fiscal Policy in an Open Economy, pages 654–655**
LEARNING OBJECTIVE: Compare the effectiveness of monetary policy and fiscal policy in an open economy and in a closed economy.

Summary

When the Federal Reserve engages in an expansionary monetary policy, it buys government bonds to lower interest rates and increase aggregate demand. In a closed economy, the main effect of lower interest rates is on domestic investment spending and purchases of consumer durables. In an open economy, lower interest rates will also cause an increase in net exports. When the Fed wants to slow the rate of economic growth to reduce inflation, it engages in a contractionary monetary policy by selling government bonds to increase interest rates and reduce aggregate demand. In a closed economy, the main effect is once again on domestic investment and purchases of consumer durables. In an open economy, higher interest rates will also reduce net exports. We can conclude that monetary policy has a greater impact on aggregate demand in an open economy than in a closed economy. To engage in an expansionary fiscal policy, the government increases government spending or cuts taxes. An expansionary fiscal policy can lead to higher interest rates. In a closed economy, the main effect of higher interest rates is on domestic investment spending and spending on consumer durables. In an open economy, higher interest rates will also reduce net exports. A contractionary fiscal policy will reduce the budget deficit and may lower interest rates. In a closed economy, lower interest rates increase domestic investment and spending on consumer durables. In an open economy, lower interest rates also increase net exports. We can conclude that fiscal policy has a smaller effect on aggregate demand in an open economy than in a closed economy.

MyEconLab Visit **www.myeconlab.com** to complete these exercises online and get instant feedback.

Review Questions

5.1 What is meant by a *policy channel*?

5.2 Why does monetary policy have a greater effect on aggregate demand in an open economy than in a closed economy?

5.3 Why does fiscal policy have a smaller effect on aggregate demand in an open economy than in a closed economy?

Problems and Applications

5.4 An article in the *Economist* quotes the finance minister of Peru as saying, "We are one of the most open economies of Latin America." What did he mean by Peru being an "open economy"? Is fiscal policy in Peru likely to be more or less effective than it would be in a less open economy? Briefly explain.

Source: "Hold on Tight," *Economist*, February 2, 2013.

5.5 Suppose that Federal Reserve policy leads to higher interest rates in the United States.

a. How will this policy affect real GDP in the short run if the United States is a closed economy?

b. How will this policy affect real GDP in the short run if the United States is an open economy?

c. How will your answer to part (b) change if interest rates also rise in the countries that are the major trading partners of the United States?

5.6 An economist remarks, "In the 1960s, using fiscal policy would have been a better way to stabilize the economy, but I believe that monetary policy is better today." What has changed about the U.S. economy that might have led the economist to this conclusion?

5.7 Suppose the federal government increases spending without also increasing taxes. In the short run, how will this action affect real GDP and the price level in a closed economy? How will the effects of this action differ in an open economy?

Real-Time Data Exercises

D18.1 **(Exchange rate movements)** Go to the Web site of the Federal Reserve Bank of St. Louis (FRED) (research.stlouisfed.org/fred2/) and download the most recent value and the value from the same month one year earlier from FRED for the U.S./Euro Foreign Exchange Rate (EXUSEU).

a. Using these values, compute the percentage change in the euro's value.

b. Explain whether the dollar appreciated or depreciated against the euro.

D18.2 **(Exchange rate movements)** Go to the Web site of the Federal Reserve Bank of St. Louis (FRED) (research.stlouisfed.org/fred2/) and download and plot the U.S. dollar–euro exchange rate (EXUSEU), the U.S. dollar–yen exchange rate (EXJPUS), and the U.S. dollar–Canadian dollar exchange rate (EXCAUS) for the period from 2001 to the present. Answer the following questions on the basis of your graphs.

a. In what year did the euro reach its highest value?

b. During the financial crisis of 2007–2009, did the yen appreciate or depreciate against the dollar? Briefly explain.

c. Against which currency did the U.S. dollar depreciate the most during this period?

D18.3 **(Exchange rate movements)** One way to gauge the general value of one currency relative to other currencies is to calculate the *trade-weighted exchange rate*, which is an index number similar to the consumer price index. The trade-weighted exchange rate for the U.S. dollar weights each individual exchange rate by the share of that country's trade with the United States. Go to the Web site of the Federal Reserve Bank of St. Louis (FRED) (research.stlouisfed.org/fred2/) and download monthly data on the trade-weighted exchange rate for the U.S. dollar against major currencies (TWEXMMTH) from 1973 to the present.

a. What has been the long-term trend in the exchange value of the dollar? What effect should changes in the exchange rate during this period have had on U.S. net exports? Briefly explain.

b. What has been the trend in the exchange value of the dollar over the past year? What effect should changes in the exchange rate during the past year have had on U.S. net exports? Briefly explain.

D18.4 **(Exchange rates and exports)** Go to the Web site of the Federal Reserve Bank of St. Louis (FRED) (research.stlouisfed.org/fred2/) and find the most recent values for the Japan/U.S. Foreign Exchange Rate (DEXJPUS) and the U.S. Exports of Goods to Japan (EXPJP) and the values for one year earlier. Given the change in the exchange rate between the two periods, is the change in U.S. exports to Japan consistent with what the analysis in this chapter would predict? Briefly explain.

D18.5 **(Exchange rates and imports)** Go to the Web site of the Federal Reserve Bank of St. Louis (FRED) (research.stlouisfed.org/fred2/) and find the most recent values from FRED for the Japan/U.S. Foreign Exchange Rate (DEXJPUS) and the U.S. Imports of Goods from Japan (IMPJP) and the values for one year earlier. Given the change in the exchange rate between the two periods, is the change in U.S. imports from Japan consistent with what the analysis in this chapter would predict? Briefly explain.

CHAPTER 19

The International Financial System

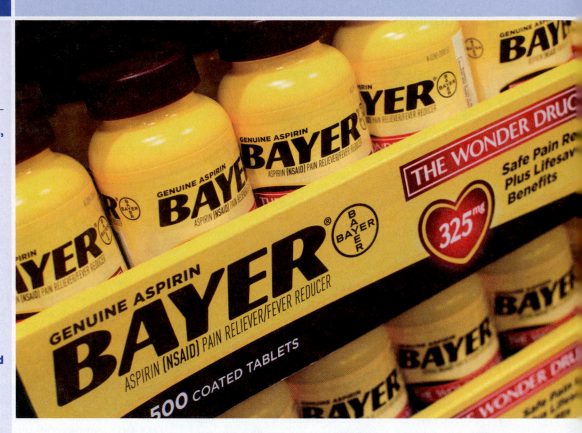

Bayer Uses a Weak Euro to Increase Sales

Most people in the United States know the German firm Bayer mainly from its aspirin, which is sold in bottles with labels that display the firm's name in a distinctive cross. Although the chemical formula for aspirin had been known for decades, it was only in 1899 that Bayer began marketing aspirin as a pain reliever. Because no other effective over-the-counter pain relievers were available until the 1950s, Bayer aspirin was probably the most profitable medication ever sold.

Today, Bayer sells a variety of products, including prescription and over-the-counter pharmaceuticals and agricultural products. Bayer's acquisition of Merck & Company's over-the-counter unit in 2014 added brand names such as Coppertone, Dr. Scholl's, and Claritin to its product line. In addition to exports, Bayer has affiliates in North America, Latin and South America, Europe and Asia that manufacture and sell its products. As a result, it receives revenue in many different currencies. As the exchange rate of each of the currencies changes relative to the euro, the value of Bayer's sales and profits change.

German manufacturers benefited from the introduction of the euro, the common currency of 19 members of the European Union. Because of the euro, Bayer and other German firms don't have to worry about fluctuations in exchange rates within most of Europe. Before the adoption of the euro, countries such as France, Italy, and Spain were able to bring about declines in the exchange values of their currencies, which made the output of their companies' products more competitive with those of Germany. These countries can no longer pursue this strategy in competing with Germany. When Bayer and other German companies export outside Europe, they still must deal with fluctuations in the value of the euro. When the value of the euro increases, as it did during 2012 and 2013, the prices of goods exported from Germany increase, and Bayer's sales can be hurt. But when the value of the euro falls, as it did during 2014 and 2015, it's good news for Bayer and other German exporters. For example, in the second quarter of 2015, Bayer's profits rose nearly 20 percent as a result of the lower value of the euro.

In this chapter, we will look more closely at the international financial system and at what determines fluctuations in exchange rates.

Sources: Bryce Hoffman, "Bayer CEO Focuses On Company's Strengths," *Forbes*, April 4, 2015; Christopher Alessi, "Bayer Profit Rises on Healthy Currency Effects," *Wall Street Journal*, July 29, 2015; Peter Loftus, "Bayer Bulks Up Its Medicine Chest With Merck Brands," *Wall Street Journal*, May 7, 2014; and American Chemical Society, "Molecule of the Week: Aspirin," June 4, 2012.

Economics in Your Life

Exchange Rate Risk Can Affect Your Savings

Suppose that you decide to accept a job in Japan. You plan to work there for the next 10 years, build up some savings, and then return to the United States. As you prepare for your move, you read that economists expect the average productivity of Japanese firms to grow faster than the average productivity of U.S. firms over the next 10 years. If economists are correct, all else being equal, will the savings that you accumulate (in yen) be worth more or less in U.S. dollars than it would have been worth without the relative gains in Japanese productivity? As you read this chapter, try to answer this question. You can check your answer against the one we provide on **page 679** at the end of this chapter.

A key fact about the international economy is that exchange rates among the major currencies fluctuate. These fluctuations have important consequences for firms, consumers, and governments. In Chapter 18, we discussed the basics of how exchange rates are determined. We also looked at the relationship between a country's imports and exports, and at capital flows into and out of a country. In this chapter, we will look further at the international financial system and at the role central banks play in the system.

19.1 Exchange Rate Systems

LEARNING OBJECTIVE: Describe how different exchange rate systems operate.

Floating currency The outcome of a country allowing its currency's exchange rate to be determined by demand and supply.

A country's exchange rate can be determined in several ways. Some countries simply allow the exchange rate to be determined by demand and supply, just as other prices are. A country that allows demand and supply to determine the value of its currency is said to have a **floating currency**. Some countries attempt to keep the exchange rate between their currency and another currency constant. For example, China kept the exchange rate constant between its currency, the yuan, and the U.S. dollar, from 1994 until 2005, when it began allowing greater exchange rate flexibility. When countries can agree on how exchange rates should be determined, economists say that there is an **exchange rate system**. Currently, many countries, including the United States, allow their currencies to float most of the time, although they occasionally intervene to buy and sell their currency or other currencies to affect exchange rates. In other words, many countries attempt to *manage* the float of their currencies. As a result, the current exchange rate system is a **managed float exchange rate system**.

Exchange rate system An agreement among countries about how exchange rates should be determined.

Managed float exchange rate system The current exchange rate system, under which the value of most currencies is determined by demand and supply, with occasional government intervention.

Fixed exchange rate system A system under which countries agree to keep the exchange rates among their currencies fixed for long periods.

Historically, the two most important alternatives to the managed float exchange rate system were the *gold standard* and the *Bretton Woods system*. These were both **fixed exchange rate systems**, in which exchange rates remained constant for long periods. Under the gold standard, a country's currency consisted of gold coins and paper currency that the government was committed to redeem for gold. The gold standard was a fixed exchange rate system that lasted from the nineteenth century until the 1930s.

Under the gold standard, exchange rates were determined by the relative amounts of gold in each country's currency, and the size of a country's money supply was determined by the amount of gold available. To rapidly expand its money supply during a war or an economic depression, a country would need to leave the gold standard. By the mid-1930s, in response to the Great Depression, the United States and most other countries had abandoned the gold standard. Although during the following decades there were occasional discussions about restoring the gold standard, there was no serious attempt to do so.

A conference held in Bretton Woods, New Hampshire, in 1944 set up an exchange rate system in which the United States pledged to buy or sell gold at a fixed price of $35 per ounce. The central banks of all other members of the new Bretton Woods system pledged to buy and sell their currencies at a fixed rate against the dollar. By fixing their exchange rates against the dollar, these countries were fixing the exchange rates among their currencies as well. Unlike under the gold standard, neither the United States nor any other country was willing to redeem its paper currency for gold domestically. The United States would redeem dollars for gold only if they were presented by a foreign central bank. Fixed exchange rate regimes can run into difficulties because exchange rates are not free to adjust quickly to changes in demand and supply for currencies. As we will see in the next section, central banks often encounter problems if they are required to keep an exchange rate fixed over a period of years. By the early 1970s, the difficulty of keeping exchange rates fixed led to the end of the Bretton Woods system. The appendix to this chapter contains additional discussion of the gold standard and the Bretton Woods system.

Don't Let This Happen to You

Remember That Modern Currencies Are Fiat Money

Although the United States has not been on the gold standard since 1933, many people still believe that somehow gold continues to "back" U.S. currency. The U.S. Department of the Treasury still owns billions of dollars' worth of gold bars, most of which are stored at the Fort Knox Bullion Depository in Kentucky. (Even more gold is stored in a basement of the Federal Reserve Bank of New York, which holds about one-quarter of the world's monetary gold supply—almost 10 percent of all the gold ever mined.

This gold, however, is entirely owned by foreign governments and international agencies.) The gold in Fort Knox no longer has any connection to the amount of paper money issued by the Federal Reserve. U.S. currency—like the currencies of other countries—is *fiat money*, which means it has no value except as money (see Chapter 14). The link between gold and money that existed for centuries has been broken in modern economies.

MyEconLab Study Plan

Your Turn: Test your understanding by doing related problem 1.3 on page 680 at the end of this chapter.

19.2 **The Current Exchange Rate System**

LEARNING OBJECTIVE: Discuss the three key features of the current exchange rate system.

The current exchange rate system has three important features:

1. The United States allows the dollar to float against other major currencies.
2. Nineteen countries in Europe have adopted a single currency, the **euro**.
3. Some developing countries have attempted to keep their currencies' exchange rates fixed against the dollar or another major currency.

Euro The common currency of many European countries.

We begin our discussion of the current exchange rate system by looking at the changing value of the dollar over time. In discussing the value of the dollar, we can look further at what determines exchange rates in the short run and in the long run.

The Floating Dollar

Since 1973, the value of the U.S. dollar has fluctuated widely against other major currencies. Panel (a) of Figure 19.1 shows the exchange rate between the U.S.

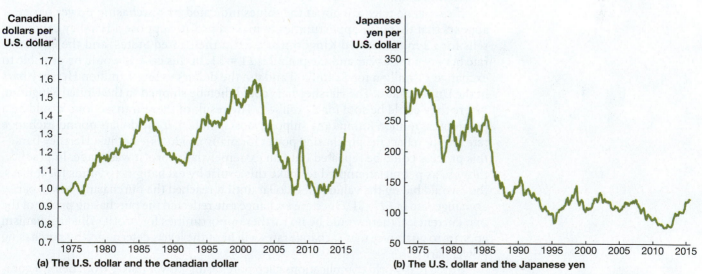

(a) The U.S. dollar and the Canadian dollar

(b) The U.S. dollar and the Japanese yen

MyEconLab Real-time data

Figure 19.1 **Canadian Dollar–U.S. Dollar and Yen–U.S. Dollar Exchange Rates, 1973–2015**

Panel (a) shows that from the end of the Bretton Woods system in 1973 through August 2015, the U.S. dollar gained more than 30 percent in value against the Canadian dollar. Panel (b) shows that during the same period, the U.S. dollar lost almost 60 percent of its value against the Japanese yen.

Source: Federal Reserve Bank of St Louis.

dollar and the Canadian dollar between January 1973 and August 2015, and panel (b) shows the exchange rate between the U.S. dollar and the Japanese yen for the same period. Remember that the dollar increases in value when it takes more units of foreign currency to buy $1, and it falls in value when it takes fewer units of foreign currency to buy $1. From January 1973 to August 2015, the U.S. dollar lost nearly 60 percent in value against the yen, while it gained more than 30 percent in value against the Canadian dollar. Both exchange rates fluctuated substantially during those years. MyEconLab Concept Check

What Determines Exchange Rates in the Long Run?

Over the past 40 years, why has the value of the U.S. dollar fallen substantially against the Japanese yen but risen against the Canadian dollar? In the short run, the two most important causes of exchange rate movements are changes in interest rates—which cause investors to change their views of which countries' financial investments will yield the highest returns—and changes in investors' expectations about the future values of currencies. Over the long run, other factors are also important in explaining movements in exchange rates.

Purchasing power parity The theory that in the long run exchange rates move to equalize the purchasing powers of different currencies.

The Theory of Purchasing Power Parity

It seems reasonable that, in the long run, exchange rates should be at a level that makes it possible to buy the same amount of goods and services with the equivalent amount of any country's currency. In other words, the purchasing power of every country's currency should be the same. The idea that in the long run exchange rates move to equalize the purchasing power of different currencies is called the theory of **purchasing power parity**.

Consider a simple example: Suppose that a Hershey candy bar has a price of $1 in the United States and £1 in the United Kingdom and that the exchange rate is £1 = $1. In that case, at least with respect to candy bars, the dollar and the pound have equivalent purchasing power. If the price of a Hershey bar increases to £2 in the United Kingdom but stays at $1 in the United States, the exchange rate will have to change to £2 per $1 in order for the pound to maintain its relative purchasing power. As long as the exchange rate adjusts to reflect purchasing power, it will be possible to buy a Hershey bar for $1 in the United States or to exchange $1 for £2 and buy the candy bar in the United Kingdom.

If exchange rates are not at the values indicated by purchasing power parity, it appears that there are opportunities to make a profit. Suppose a Hershey candy bar sells for £2 in the United Kingdom and $1 in the United States, and the exchange rate between the dollar and the pound is £1 = $1. In this case, it would be possible to exchange £1 million for $1 million and use the dollars to buy 1 million Hershey bars in the United States. The Hershey bars could then be shipped to the United Kingdom, where they could be sold for £2 million. The result of these transactions would be a profit of £1 million (minus any shipping costs). In fact, if the dollar–pound exchange rate fails to reflect the purchasing power for many products—not just Hershey bars—this process could be repeated until an extremely large profit was made. In practice, though, as people attempted to make this profit by exchanging pounds for dollars, they would bid up the value of the dollar until it reached the purchasing power parity exchange rate of £2 = $1. Once the exchange rate reflected the purchasing power of the two currencies, there would be no further opportunities for profit. This mechanism appears to guarantee that exchange rates will be at the levels determined by purchasing power parity.

Three real-world complications keep purchasing power parity from being a complete explanation of exchange rates, even in the long run:

1. **Not all products can be traded internationally.** Where goods are traded internationally, profits can be made whenever exchange rates do not reflect their purchasing power parity values. However, more than half of all goods and services produced in the United States and most other countries are not traded

internationally. When goods are not traded internationally, their prices will not be the same in every country. Suppose that the exchange rate is £1 for $1, but the price for having a cavity filled by a dentist is twice as high in the United States as it is in the United Kingdom. In this case, there is no way to buy up the low-priced British service and resell it in the United States. Because many goods and services are not traded internationally, exchange rates will not reflect exactly the relative purchasing powers of currencies.

2. **Products and consumer preferences are different across countries.** We expect the same product to sell for the same price around the world, but if a product is similar but not identical to another product, their prices might be different. For example, a 3-ounce Hershey candy bar may sell for a different price in the United States than does a 3-ounce Cadbury candy bar in the United Kingdom. Prices of the same product may also differ across countries if consumer preferences differ. If consumers in the United Kingdom like candy bars more than do consumers in the United States, a Hershey candy bar may sell for more in the United Kingdom than in the United States.

3. **Countries impose barriers to trade.** Most countries, including the United States, impose *tariffs* and *quotas* on imported goods. A **tariff** is a tax imposed by a government on imports. A **quota** is a government-imposed numerical limit on the quantity of a good that can be imported. For example, the United States has a quota on imports of sugar. As a result, the price of sugar in the United States is much higher than the price of sugar in other countries. Because of the quota, there is no legal way to buy up the cheap foreign sugar and resell it in the United States.

Tariff A tax imposed by a government on imports.

Quota A numerical limit that a government imposes on the quantity of a good that can be imported into the country.

Making the Connection
MyEconLab Video

The Big Mac Theory of Exchange Rates

In a lighthearted attempt to test the accuracy of the theory of purchasing power parity, the *Economist* regularly compares the prices of Big Macs in different countries. If purchasing power parity holds, you should be able to take the dollars required to buy a Big Mac in the United States and exchange it for the amount of foreign currency needed to buy a Big Mac in any other country. The following table is from July 2015, when Big Macs were selling for an average price of $4.79 in the United States. The "implied exchange rate" shows what the exchange rate would be if purchasing power parity held for Big Macs. For example, a Big Mac sold for 49 pesos in Mexico and $4.79 in the United States, so for purchasing power parity to hold, the exchange rate should have been 49 pesos/$4.79, or 10.23 pesos = $1. The actual exchange rate in July 2015 was 15.74 pesos = $1. So, on Big Mac purchasing power parity grounds, the Mexican peso was *undervalued* against the dollar by 35 percent: ([10.23 − 15.74]/15.74) × 100 = −35%). That is, if Big Mac purchasing power parity held, it would have taken 35 percent fewer Mexican pesos to buy a dollar than it actually did.

Is the price of a Big Mac in Mexico City the same as the price of a Big Mac in New York?

Could you take advantage of this difference between the purchasing power parity exchange rate and the actual exchange rate to become fabulously wealthy by buying up low-priced Big Macs in Mexico City and reselling them at a higher price in New York? Unfortunately, the low-priced Mexican Big Macs would be a soggy mess by the time you got them to New York. The fact that Big Mac prices are not the same around the world illustrates one reason purchasing power parity does not hold exactly: Many goods are not traded internationally.

Country	Big Mac Price	Implied Exchange Rate	Actual Exchange Rate
Mexico	49 pesos	10.23 pesos per dollar	15.74 pesos per dollar
Japan	370 yen	77.24 yen per dollar	123.94 yen per dollar
United Kingdom	2.89 pounds	0.60 pound per dollar	0.64 pound per dollar
Switzerland	6.5 Swiss francs	1.36 Swiss francs per dollar	0.95 Swiss francs per dollar
Indonesia	30,500 rupiahs	6,367 rupiahs per dollar	13,345 rupiahs per dollar
Canada	5.85 Canadian dollars	1.22 Canadian dollars per U.S. dollar	1.29 Canadian dollars per U.S. dollar
China	17 yuan	3.55 yuan per dollar	6.21 yuan per dollar

Source: "The Big Mac Index," *Economist*, July 16, 2015.

MyEconLab Study Plan

Your Turn: Test your understanding by doing related problem 2.10 on page 681 at the end of this chapter.

Solved Problem 19.2

MyEconLab Interactive Animation

Calculating Purchasing Power Parity Exchange Rates Using Big Macs

Fill in the missing cells in the following table. Remember that the implied exchange rate shows what the exchange rate would be if purchasing power parity held for Big Macs. Assume that the Big Mac is selling for $4.79 in the United States. Explain whether the U.S. dollar is overvalued or undervalued relative to each currency and predict what will happen in the future to each exchange rate if the actual exchange rate moves toward the purchasing power parity exchange rate. Finally, calculate the implied exchange rate between the Polish zloty and the Brazilian real (the plural of *real* is *reais*) and explain which currency is undervalued in terms of Big Mac purchasing power parity.

Country	Big Mac Price	Implied Exchange Rate	Actual Exchange Rate
Brazil	13.5 reais		3.15 reais per dollar
Poland	9.6 zlotys		3.77 zlotys per dollar
South Korea	4,300 won		1,143.5 won per dollar
Sweden	43.7 kronor		8.52 kronor per dollar

Solving the Problem

Step 1: **Review the chapter material.** This problem is about the theory of purchasing power parity as illustrated by prices of Big Macs, so you may want to review the section "The Theory of Purchasing Power Parity," which begins on page 666, and the *Making the Connection,* "The Big Mac Theory of Exchange Rates" on page 667.

Step 2: **Fill in the table.** To calculate the purchasing power parity exchange rate, divide the foreign currency price of a Big Mac by the U.S. price. For example, the implied exchange rate between the Brazilian real and the U.S. dollar is 13.5 reais/$4.79, or 2.82 reais per dollar.

Country	Big Mac Price	Implied Exchange Rate	Actual Exchange Rate
Brazil	13.5 reais	2.82 reais per dollar	3.15 reais per dollar
Poland	9.6 zlotys	2.00 zlotys per dollar	3.77 zlotys per dollar
South Korea	4,300 won	897.7 won per dollar	1,143.5 won per dollar
Sweden	43.7 kronor	9.12 kronor per dollar	8.52 kronor per dollar

Step 3: **Explain whether the U.S. dollar is overvalued or undervalued against the other currencies.** The dollar is overvalued if the actual exchange rate is greater than the implied exchange rate, and it is undervalued if the actual exchange rate is less than the implied exchange rate. In this case, the dollar is overvalued against the real, the zloty, and the won, but it is undervalued against the krona. So, we would predict that in the future the value of the dollar should rise against the krona but fall against the real, the zloty, and the won.

Step 4: **Calculate the implied exchange rate between the zloty and the real.** The implied exchange rate between the zloty and the real is 9.6 zlotys/13.5 reais, or 0.71 zlotys per real. We can calculate the actual exchange rate by taking the ratio of zlotys per dollar to reais per dollar: 3.77 zlotys/3.15 reais, or 1.20 zlotys per real. Therefore, the zloty is undervalued relative to the real because our Big Mac purchasing power parity calculation tells us that it should take fewer zlotys to buy a real than it actually does.

Source: "The Big Mac Index," *Economist*, July 16, 2015.

Your Turn: For more practice, do related problem 2.11 on page 681 at the end of this chapter.   MyEconLab Study Plan

The Four Determinants of Exchange Rates in the Long Run We can take into account the shortcomings of the theory of purchasing power parity to develop a more complete explanation of how exchange rates are determined in the long run. There are four main determinants of exchange rates in the long run:

1. **Relative price levels.** The purchasing power parity theory is correct in arguing that, in the long run, the most important determinant of exchange rates between two countries' currencies is their relative price levels. If prices of goods and services rise faster in Canada than in the United States, the value of the Canadian dollar has to decline to maintain demand for Canadian products. Over the past 40 years, the price level in Canada has risen somewhat faster than the price level in the United States, while the price level in Japan has risen more slowly. These facts help explain why the U.S. dollar has increased in value against the Canadian dollar while losing value against the Japanese yen.

2. **Relative rates of productivity growth.** When the productivity of a firm increases, the firm is able to produce more goods and services using fewer workers, machines, or other inputs. The firm's costs of production fall, and usually so do the prices of its products. If the average productivity of Japanese firms increases faster than the average productivity of U.S. firms, Japanese products will have relatively lower prices than U.S. products, which increases the quantity demanded of Japanese products relative to U.S. products. As a result, the value of the yen should rise against the dollar. For most of the period from the early 1970s to the early 1990s, Japanese productivity increased faster than U.S. productivity, which contributed to the fall in the value of the dollar versus the yen. However, between 1992 and 2015, U.S. productivity increased faster than Japanese productivity, which explains why the value of the dollar stopped its rapid decline against the yen in the early 1990s.

3. **Preferences for domestic and foreign goods.** If consumers in Canada increase their preferences for U.S. products, the demand for U.S. dollars will increase relative to the demand for Canadian dollars, and the U.S. dollar will increase in value relative to the Canadian dollar. During the 1970s and 1980s, many U.S. consumers increased their preferences for Japanese products, particularly automobiles and consumer electronics. This greater preference for Japanese products helped to increase the value of the yen relative to the dollar.

4. **Tariffs and quotas.** The U.S. sugar quota forces firms such as Hershey Foods Corporation to buy expensive U.S. sugar rather than less expensive foreign sugar. The quota increases the demand for dollars relative to the currencies of foreign sugar

producers and, therefore, leads to a higher exchange rate. Changes in tariffs and quotas have not been a significant factor, though, in explaining trends in the U.S. dollar–Canadian dollar or U.S. dollar–yen exchange rates.

Because these four factors change over time, the value of one country's currency can increase or decrease by substantial amounts in the long run. These changes in exchange rates can create uncertainty for firms. A decline in the value of a country's currency lowers the foreign currency prices of the country's exports and increases the prices of imports. An increase in the value of a country's currency has the reverse effect. Firms can be both helped and hurt by exchange rate fluctuations. MyEconLab Concept Check

The Euro

A second key aspect of the current exchange rate system is that most countries in Western Europe have adopted a single currency. After World War II, many of these countries wanted to more closely integrate their economies. In 1957, Belgium, France, West Germany, Italy, Luxembourg, and the Netherlands signed the Treaty of Rome, which established the European Economic Community, often called the European Common Market. Tariffs and quotas on products being shipped within the European Common Market were greatly reduced. Over the years, Britain, Sweden, Denmark, Finland, Austria, Greece, Ireland, Spain, and Portugal joined the European Economic Community, which was renamed the European Union (EU) in 1991. By 2015, 28 countries were members of the EU.

EU members decided to move to a common currency beginning in 1999. Three of the 15 countries that were then members of the EU—the United Kingdom, Denmark, and Sweden—decided to retain their domestic currencies. The move to a common currency took place in several stages. On January 1, 1999, the exchange rates of the 12 participating countries were permanently fixed against each other and against the common currency, the *euro*. At first, the euro was a pure *unit of account*. No euro currency was actually in circulation, although firms began quoting prices in both domestic currency

MyEconLab Animation

Figure 19.2

Countries Adopting the Euro

The 19 member countries of the European Union (EU) that have adopted the euro as their common currency as of the end of 2015 are shaded with red hash marks. The members of the EU that have not adopted the euro are colored tan. Countries in white are not members of the EU.

and in euros. On January 1, 2002, euro coins and paper currency were introduced, and on June 1, 2002, the old domestic currencies were withdrawn from circulation. Figure 19.2 shows the 19 countries in the EU that had adopted the euro as of the end of 2015. These countries are sometimes called the *eurozone*.

A new European Central Bank (ECB) was also established. Although the central banks of the member countries continue to exist, the ECB has assumed responsibility for monetary policy and for issuing currency. The ECB is run by a governing council that consists of a six-member executive board—appointed by the participating governments—and the governors of the central banks of the 19 member countries that have adopted the euro. The ECB represents a unique experiment in allowing a multinational organization to control the domestic monetary policies of independent countries.

MyEconLab Concept Check

Making the Connection
MyEconLab Video

Greece and Germany: Diverse Economies, Common Currency

Most of Europe experienced relative economic stability from the introduction of the euro in 2002 to the beginning of the global economic downturn in 2007. With low interest rates, low inflation rates, and expanding employment and production, the advantages of having a common currency seemed obvious. Firms no longer had to worry about exchange rate instability when selling within Europe, and the cost of doing business was reduced because, for example, it was no longer necessary for a French firm to exchange francs for marks to do business in Germany.

By 2008, however, some economists and policymakers questioned whether the euro was making the effects of the global recession worse. The countries using the euro cannot pursue independent monetary policies because the ECB determines those policies from its headquarters in Frankfurt, Germany. Countries that were particularly hard hit by the recession—for example, Spain, where the unemployment rate had more than doubled to 18 percent by 2009 and was 22 percent in mid-2015—were unable to pursue a more expansionary policy than the ECB was willing to implement for the eurozone as a whole. Similarly, countries could not attempt to revive their exports by allowing their currencies to depreciate because (1) many of their exports were to other eurozone countries, and (2) the value of the euro was determined by factors affecting the eurozone as a whole.

In 2010, a *sovereign debt* crisis developed when investors began to believe that a number of European governments, particularly those of Greece, Ireland, Spain, Portugal, and Italy, would have difficulty making interest payments on their bonds—or sovereign debt. The International Monetary Fund and the European Union put together aid packages to keep the countries from defaulting. In exchange for the aid, these countries were required to adopt *austerity programs*—cutting government spending and raising taxes—even though doing so sparked protests from unions, students, and other groups. The controversy was greatest over Greece, which had large debts and a high unemployment rate, and where political resistance to multiple rounds of austerity made it uncertain whether the country would remain in the eurozone.

Did the euro contribute to the slow recovery from the 2007–2009 financial crisis? The figure below shows the average unemployment rate for the eurozone countries for the period 2007–2014 compared with the unemployment rates for the United States, the United Kingdom, and Iceland. The eurozone was still suffering from high unemployment rates more than seven years after the beginning of the financial crisis. The German economy, however, performed very well during and after the financial crisis, with its unemployment rate in 2014 being below what it had been in 2007. In fact, German firms, including Bayer, benefited from the euro because if the country had retained the deutsche mark as its currency, the deutsche mark would likely have increased in value during 2014 and 2015. The euro decreased in value during that period, thereby increasing German exports more than would have happened without the common currency. As the blue line shows, the unemployment rate in the eurozone looks significantly worse if Germany is left out.

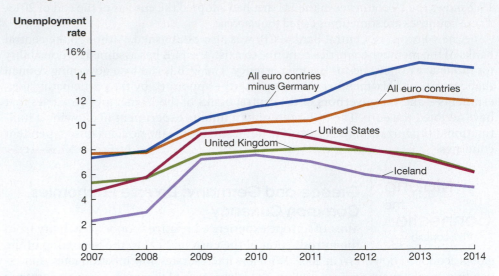

The United Kingdom, Iceland, and the United States all use their own currencies and all recovered more quickly from the financial crisis and recession than did most of the countries using the euro. The United Kingdom is a member of the European Union but continues to use the pound as its currency. Iceland is not a member of the European Union and does not use the euro. The situation in Iceland is particularly interesting because no country was more severely affected by the global financial crisis. Although it is a small country, its banks aggressively made loans around the world in the years leading up to the crisis. By 2007, Icelandic banks had made loans equal to nine times the country's GDP. When many borrowers defaulted on those loans, the government of Iceland took over the banks and assumed their debt of about $100 billion—or more than $300,000 for each citizen of Iceland. Iceland's krona, the British pound, and the U.S. dollar all depreciated against the euro in the period immediately following the financial crisis, which was good news for these countries because it helped them increase exports, but it was bad news for countries using the euro, many of which faced declining exports outside Europe.

The crisis over Greece highlighted another key problem facing the euro: the lack of coordinated government spending policies. The eurozone is a *monetary union*—the member countries all use the same currency and follow a joint monetary policy—but not a *fiscal union*—the member countries pursue independent fiscal policies. Although we don't usually think of countries in these terms, the states of the United States, the provinces of Canada, and the prefectures of Japan represent both monetary unions and fiscal unions. If during a recession Nevada suffers a particularly sharp decline in production and employment, the federal government provides support to the economy of Nevada through unemployment insurance and other transfer programs. Greece, by contrast, must fund such payments largely from its own revenues. The resulting large government budget deficits contributed to the sovereign debt crisis discussed earlier.

Some economists and policymakers wonder whether a monetary union of such diverse economies can survive in the absence of further fiscal integration. However, the political support for further fiscal integration of the eurozone countries seemed lacking. In 2015, the ultimate fate of Europe's great economic experiment of having independent countries use a single currency was very much in doubt.

Note: Data for the figure are from the International Monetary Fund. The unemployment rate for the euro countries is for all members of the eurozone as of 2008, weighted by their shares in total employment in 2007.
Sources: Nektaria Stamouli, "Greece Wants European Parliament Involved in Overseeing Bailout," *Wall Street Journal*, August 19, 2015; "A Third Bail-out Gets the Green Light," *Economist*, August 15, 2015; and Terence Roth, "Everything You Need to Know about European Political Union," *Economist*, July 27, 2015.

MyEconLab Study Plan   **Your Turn:** Test your understanding by doing related problems 2.12 and 2.13 on page 682 at the end of this chapter.

Pegging against the Dollar

A final key feature of the current exchange rate system is that some developing countries have attempted to keep their exchange rates fixed against the dollar or another major currency. Having a fixed exchange rate can provide important advantages for a country that has extensive trade with another country. When the exchange rate is fixed, business planning becomes much easier. For instance, if the South Korean won increases in value relative to the dollar, Korean car manufacturer Hyundai may have to raise the dollar price of cars it exports to the United States, thereby reducing sales. If the exchange rate between the Korean won and the dollar is fixed, Hyundai's planning is much easier.

In the 1980s and 1990s, an additional reason developed for having fixed exchange rates. During those decades, the flow of foreign investment funds to developing countries, particularly those in East Asia, increased substantially. It became possible for firms in countries such as Korea, Thailand, Malaysia, and Indonesia to borrow dollars directly from foreign investors or indirectly from foreign banks. For example, a Thai firm might borrow U.S. dollars from a Japanese bank. If the Thai firm wants to build a new factory in Thailand with the borrowed dollars, it has to exchange the dollars for the equivalent amount of Thai currency, the baht. When the factory opens and production begins, the Thai firm will be earning the additional baht it needs to exchange for dollars to make the interest payments on the loan. A problem arises if the value of the baht falls against the dollar. Suppose that the exchange rate is 25 baht per dollar when the firm takes out the loan. A Thai firm making an interest payment of $100,000 per month on a dollar loan could buy the necessary dollars for 2.5 million baht. But if the value of the baht declines to 50 baht to the dollar, it would take 5 million baht to buy the dollars necessary to make the interest payment. These increased payments might be a crushing burden for the Thai firm. The government of Thailand would have a strong incentive to avoid this problem by keeping the exchange rate between the baht and the dollar fixed.

Finally, in the 1980s and 1990s, some countries feared the inflationary consequences of a floating exchange rate. When the value of a currency falls, the prices of imports rise. If imports are a significant fraction of the goods consumers buy, a fall in the value of the currency may significantly increase the inflation rate. During the 1990s, an important part of Brazil's and Argentina's anti-inflation policies was a fixed exchange rate against the dollar. (As we will see, there are difficulties with following a fixed exchange rate policy, and ultimately, both Brazil and Argentina abandoned fixed exchange rates.)

The East Asian Exchange Rate Crisis of the Late 1990s
When a country keeps its currency's exchange rate fixed against another country's currency, it is **pegging** its currency. It is not necessary for both countries involved in a peg to agree to it. When a developing country has pegged the value of its currency against the dollar, the responsibility for maintaining the peg has been entirely with the developing country.

Pegging A policy by which a country keeps fixed the exchange rate between its currency and another country's currency.

Countries attempting to maintain a peg can run into problems, however. When the government fixes the price of a good or service, the result can be persistent surpluses or shortages (see Chapter 4). Figure 19.3 shows the exchange rate between the dollar and the Thai baht. The figure is drawn from the Thai point of view, so we measure the exchange rate on the vertical axis as dollars per baht. The figure represents the situation in the 1990s, when the government of Thailand pegged the exchange rate between the dollar and the baht above the equilibrium exchange rate, as determined by demand and supply. A currency pegged at a value above the market equilibrium exchange rate is said to be *overvalued*. A currency pegged at a value below the market equilibrium exchange rate is said to be *undervalued*.

Pegging both made it easier for Thai firms to export products to the United States and protected Thai firms that had taken out dollar loans. The pegged exchange rate was 25.19 baht to the dollar, or about $0.04 to the baht. By 1997, this exchange rate was well above the market equilibrium exchange rate of 35 baht to the dollar, or about $0.03

Figure 19.3

By 1997, the Thai Baht Was Overvalued against the Dollar

The government of Thailand pegged the value of the baht against the dollar to make it easier for Thai firms to export to the United States and to protect Thai firms that had taken out dollar loans. The pegged exchange rate of $0.04 per baht was well above the equilibrium exchange rate of $0.03 per baht. In the example in this figure, the overvalued exchange rate created a surplus of 70 million baht, which the Thai central bank had to purchase with dollars.

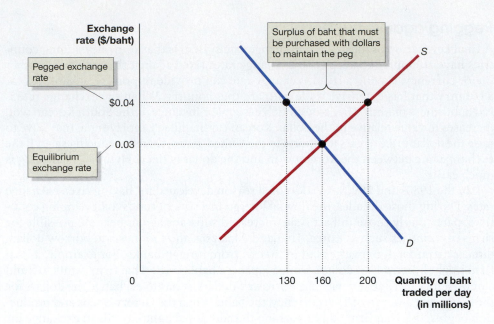

to the baht. The result was a surplus of baht on the foreign exchange market. To keep the exchange rate at the pegged level, the Thai central bank, the Bank of Thailand, had to buy these baht with dollars. In doing so, the Bank gradually used up its holdings of dollars, or its *dollar reserves*. To continue supporting the pegged exchange rate, the Bank borrowed additional dollar reserves from the International Monetary Fund (IMF). The Bank of Thailand also raised interest rates to attract more foreign investors to investments in Thailand, thereby increasing the demand for the baht. The Bank of Thailand took these actions even though allowing the value of the baht to decline against the dollar would have helped Thai firms exporting to the United States by reducing the dollar prices of their goods. The Thai government was afraid of the negative consequences of abandoning the peg even though the peg had led to the baht being overvalued.

Although higher domestic interest rates helped attract foreign investors, they made it more difficult for Thai firms and households to borrow the funds they needed to finance their spending. As a consequence, domestic investment and consumption declined, pushing the Thai economy into recession. International investors realized that there were limits to how high the Bank of Thailand would be willing to push interest rates and how many dollar loans the IMF would be willing to extend to Thailand. These investors began to speculate against the baht by exchanging baht for dollars at the official, pegged exchange rate. If, as they expected, Thailand were forced to abandon the peg, they would be able to buy back the baht at a much lower exchange rate, making a substantial profit. Because these actions by investors make it more difficult to maintain a fixed exchange rate, they are called *destabilizing speculation*. Figure 19.4 shows the results of this destabilizing speculation. The decreased demand for baht shifted the demand curve for baht from D_1 to D_2, increasing the quantity of baht the Bank of Thailand needed to buy in exchange for dollars.

Foreign investors also began to sell off their investments in Thailand and exchange their holdings of baht for dollars. This *capital flight* forced the Bank of Thailand to run through its dollar reserves. Dollar loans from the IMF temporarily allowed Thailand to defend the pegged exchange rate. Finally, on July 2, 1997, Thailand abandoned its pegged exchange rate against the dollar and allowed the baht to float. Thai firms that had borrowed dollars were now faced with interest payments that were much higher than they had planned. Many firms were forced into bankruptcy, and the Thai economy plunged into a deep recession.

Many currency traders became convinced that other East Asian countries, such as South Korea, Indonesia, and Malaysia, would have to follow Thailand and abandon their pegged exchange rates. The result was a wave of speculative selling of these countries'

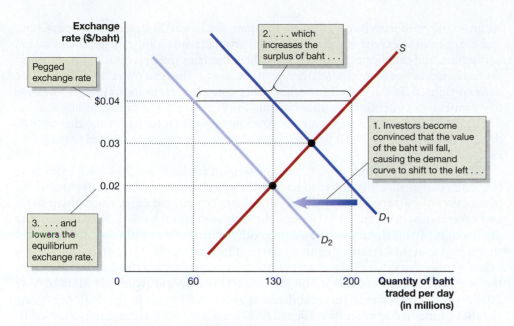

Exchange rate ($/baht)

Pegged exchange rate

$0.04

0.03

0.02

2. . . . which increases the surplus of baht . . .

S

1. Investors become convinced that the value of the baht will fall, causing the demand curve to shift to the left . . .

D_1

D_2

3. . . . and lowers the equilibrium exchange rate.

0   60   130   200   Quantity of baht traded per day (in millions)

MyEconLab Animation

Figure 19.4

Destabilizing Speculation against the Thai Baht

In 1997, the pegged exchange rate of $0.04 = 1 baht was above the equilibrium exchange rate of $0.03 = 1 baht. As investors became convinced that Thailand would have to abandon its pegged exchange rate against the dollar and allow the value of the baht to fall, they decreased their demand for baht, causing the demand curve to shift from D_1 to D_2. The new equilibrium exchange rate became $0.02 = 1 baht. To defend the pegged exchange rate, the Bank of Thailand had to increase the quantity of baht it purchased in exchange for dollars from 70 million to 140 million per day. The *destabilizing speculation* by investors caused Thailand to abandon its pegged exchange rate in July 1997.

currencies. These waves of selling—sometimes called *speculative attacks*—were difficult for countries to fight off. Even if a country's currency was not initially overvalued at the pegged exchange rate, the speculative attacks would cause a large reduction in the demand for the country's currency. The demand curve for the currency would shift to the left, which would force the country's central bank to quickly exhaust its dollar reserves. Within a few months, South Korea, Indonesia, the Philippines, and Malaysia abandoned their pegged currencies. All these countries also plunged into recession.

The Decline in Pegging   Following the disastrous events experienced by the East Asian countries, the number of countries with pegged exchange rates declined sharply. Most countries that continue to use pegged exchange rates are small and trade primarily with a single, much larger, country. For instance, several Caribbean countries continue to peg against the dollar, and several former French colonies in Africa that formerly pegged against the French franc now peg against the euro. Overall, the trend has been toward replacing pegged exchange rates with managed floating exchange rates.   MyEconLab Concept Check

Making the Connection

MyEconLab Video

The Chinese Yuan: The World's Most Controversial Currency

In 1978, China began to move away from central planning and toward a market system. The result was a sharp acceleration in economic growth. Real GDP per capita grew at a rate of 6.5 percent per year between 1979 and 1995 and at the even more rapid rate of 8.8 percent per year between 1996 and 2014. An important part of Chinese economic policy was the decision in 1994 to peg the value of the Chinese currency, the yuan, to the dollar at a fixed rate of 8.28 yuan to the dollar. Pegging against the dollar ensured that Chinese exporters would face stable dollar prices for the goods they sold in the United States. By the early 2000s, many economists and policymakers argued that the yuan was undervalued against the dollar—possibly significantly undervalued. Some policymakers claimed that the undervaluation of the yuan gave Chinese firms an unfair advantage in competing with U.S. firms.

To support the undervalued exchange rate, the Chinese central bank had to buy large amounts of dollars with yuan. By 2005, the Chinese government had accumulated more than $700 billion, a good portion of which it had used to buy U.S. Treasury bonds. By this time, China was coming under pressure from its trading partners to allow the yuan to increase in value. Chinese exports of textile products were driving some textile producers out of business in Japan, the United States, and Europe. China had also begun to export more sophisticated products, including televisions, personal computers, and cellphones. Politicians in other countries were anxious to protect their domestic industries from Chinese competition, even if the result was higher prices for their consumers. In the United States and other countries, accusations that the Chinese government was intentionally undervaluing the yuan became a heated political issue. The Chinese government was reluctant to allow the market to determine the value of the yuan, however, because it believed high levels of exports were needed to maintain rapid economic growth.

In July 2005, the Chinese government announced that it would switch from pegging the yuan against the dollar to linking the value of the yuan to the average value of a basket of currencies—the dollar, the Japanese yen, the euro, the Korean won, and several other currencies. Although the Chinese central bank did not explain the details of how this linking of the yuan to other currencies would work, it declared that it had switched from a peg to a managed floating exchange rate. As the figure below shows, the value of the yuan gradually increased versus the dollar for most of the period from 2005 to 2015. The exception is the period from July 2008 to May 2010, when the exchange rate stabilized at about 6.83 yuan to the dollar, indicating that China had apparently returned to a "hard peg." This change in policy led to renewed criticism from policymakers in the United States. In mid-2010, President Barack Obama argued that "market-determined exchange rates are essential to global economic activity." In the face of this criticism, the Chinese central bank allowed the yuan to resume its slow increase in value versus the dollar. (Note that the figure shows the number of yuan per dollar, so an increase represents a *depreciation* of the yuan relative to the dollar and a decrease represents an *appreciation* of the yuan relative to the dollar.)

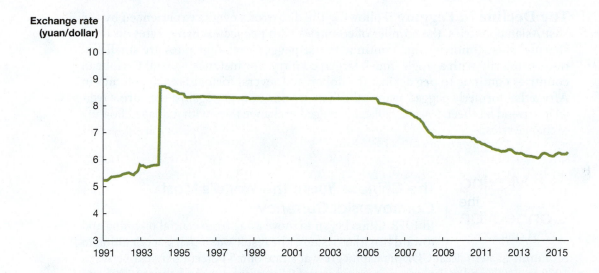

In 2015, the Chinese government was concerned that the growth rate of real GDP had slowed to about 7 percent, the lowest rate in more than 6 years. On August 11 of that year, the yuan was once again in the news when the Chinese central bank made a surprise announcement that it would buy dollars with yuan in order to reduce its value by about 3 percent, the largest one-day decline in the currency since 1994. The Chinese central bank again stated that it would allow the market to play a greater role in determining the value of the yuan. Many policymakers and economists were skeptical that the central bank truly intended to relax its control over the currency. And once again, politicians in the United States and elsewhere were critical of what they considered to be an attempt by the Chinese government to manipulate the value of yuan to gain an unfair advantage over its trading partners.

As long as the Chinese central bank continues to override the market to control the value of the yuan, controversy over Chinese exchange rate policies is likely to continue.

Sources: "Yuan Thing after Another," *Economist*, August 15, 2015; Lingling Wei, "China Moves to Devalue Yuan," *Wall Street Journal*, August 11, 2015; Greg Ip, "Why China's Yuan 'Reform' Merits Skepticism," *Wall Street Journal*, August 19, 2015; and Federal Reserve Bank of St. Louis.

Your Turn: Test your understanding by doing related problems 2.19 and 2.20 on page 682 at the end of this chapter.

MyEconLab Study Plan

International Capital Markets

LEARNING OBJECTIVE: Discuss the growth of international capital markets.

One important reason exchange rates fluctuate is that investors seek out the best investments they can find anywhere in the world. For instance, if Chinese investors increase their demand for U.S. Treasury bills, the demand for dollars will increase, and the value of the dollar will rise. But if interest rates in the United States decline, foreign investors may sell U.S. investments, and the value of the dollar will fall.

Shares of stock and long-term debt, including corporate and government bonds and bank loans, are bought and sold on *capital markets*. Before 1980, most U.S. corporations raised funds only in U.S. stock and bond markets or from U.S. banks. And U.S. investors rarely invested in foreign capital markets. In the 1980s and 1990s, European governments removed many restrictions on foreign investments in their financial markets. It became possible for U.S. and other foreign investors to freely invest in Europe and for European investors to freely invest in foreign markets. Improvements in communications and computer technology made it possible for U.S. investors to receive better and more timely information about foreign firms and for foreign investors to receive better information about U.S. firms. The growth in economies around the world also increased the savings available to be invested.

Although at one time the U.S. capital market was larger than all other capital markets combined, that is no longer the case. Today, there are large capital markets in Europe and Japan, and there are smaller markets in Latin America and East Asia. The three most important international financial centers today are New York, London, and Tokyo. Each day, the *Wall Street Journal* provides data not just on the Dow Jones Industrial Average and the Standard & Poor's 500 stock indexes of U.S. stocks, but also on foreign stock indexes such as the Nikkei 225 average of Japanese stocks, the FTSE 100 index of stocks on the London Stock Exchange, and the Hang Seng Index of stocks traded on the Hong Kong stock exchange. By 2015, corporations, banks, and governments were raising more than $1 trillion in funds on global financial markets each year.

Beginning in the 1990s, the flow of foreign funds into U.S. stocks and bonds—or *portfolio investments*—increased substantially. As Figure 19.5 shows, foreign purchases of stocks and bonds issued by corporations and bonds issued by the federal government increased dramatically between 1995 and 2007. In 2014, foreign purchases of U.S. corporate stocks and bonds, while still substantial, had declined, partly because of low interest rates in the United States. Growth in China, India, and some European countries also attracted both U.S. and foreign investors to securities issued in those countries. The fact that the United States continued to run large current account deficits resulted in a continuing foreign demand for U.S. government bonds. The current account deficits led to an accumulation of dollars by foreign central banks and foreign investors who used the dollars to purchase U.S. government bonds.

Figure 19.6 shows the distribution in June 2015 of foreign holdings of U.S. stocks and bonds by country. Japan and China together hold almost one-quarter of foreign-owned U.S. securities. The large holdings in the Cayman Islands and Luxembourg are the result of investors taking advantage of the favorable tax treatment of investment income available in those countries.

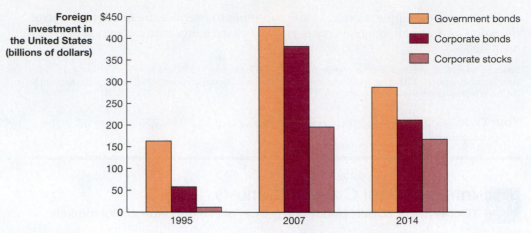

MyEconLab Animation

Figure 19.5 **Growth of Foreign Portfolio Investment in the United States**

Between 1995 and 2007, there was a large increase in foreign purchases of stocks and bonds issued by U.S. corporations and of bonds issued by the federal government. In 2014, partly because of low interest rates in the United States, foreign purchases of U.S. corporate stocks and bonds had declined. Foreign purchases of U.S. government bonds remained high.

Sources: International Monetary Fund, *International Capital Markets*, August 2001; and Board of Governors of the Federal Reserve System.

The globalization of financial markets has helped increase growth and efficiency in the world economy. It is now possible for the savings of households around the world to be channeled to the best investments available. It is also possible for firms in nearly every country to tap the savings of foreign households to gain the funds needed for expansion. No longer are firms forced to rely only on the savings of domestic households to finance investment.

But the globalization of financial markets also has a downside, as the events of 2007–2009 showed. Because financial securities issued in one country are held by investors and firms in many other countries, if those securities decline in value, the financial pain will be widely distributed. For example, the sharp decline in the value of mortgage-backed securities issued in the United States hurt not only U.S. investors and financial firms but investors and financial firms in many other countries as well.

MyEconLab Study Plan

MyEconLab Concept Check

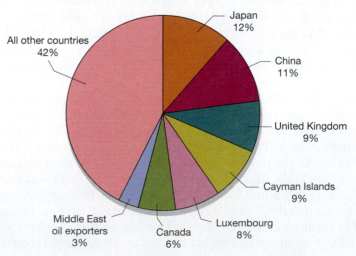

MyEconLab Animation

Figure 19.6 **The Distribution of Foreign Holdings of U.S. Stocks and Bonds by Country, June 2015**

Investors in China and Japan own almost one-quarter of foreign-owned U.S. stocks and bonds.

Source: U.S. Department of the Treasury.

Continued from page 663

Economics in Your Life

Exchange Rate Risk Can Affect Your Savings

At the beginning of this chapter, we posed this question: If economists are correct about the relative rates of average productivity growth between Japan and the United States in the next decade, then, all else being equal, will the savings that you accumulate (in yen) be worth more or less in U.S. dollars than the savings would have been worth without the relative gains in Japanese productivity? We saw in this chapter that when the average productivity of firms in one country increases faster than the average productivity of firms in another country, the value of the faster-growing country's currency should—all else being equal—rise against the slower-growing country's currency. But the savings that you accumulate in yen while you are in Japan are likely to be worth more in U.S. dollars than they would have been worth without the gains in Japanese productivity.

Conclusion

Fluctuations in exchange rates continue to cause difficulties for firms and governments. From the gold standard to the Bretton Woods system to currency pegging, governments have attempted to find a workable system of fixed exchange rates. Fixing exchange rates runs into the same problems as fixing any other price: As demand and supply shift, surpluses and shortages will occur unless the price adjusts. Nineteen countries in Europe are attempting to avoid this problem by using a single currency. Economists are looking closely at the results of that experiment.

Visit MyEconLab for a news article and analysis related to the concepts in this chapter.

Key Terms

Euro, p. 665

Exchange rate system, p. 664

Fixed exchange rate system, p. 664

Floating currency, p. 664

Managed float exchange rate system, p. 664

Pegging, p. 673

Purchasing power parity, p. 666

Quota, p. 667

Tariff, p. 667

19.1 Exchange Rate Systems, pages 664–665

LEARNING OBJECTIVE: Describe how different exchange rate systems operate.

Summary

When countries agree on how exchange rates should be determined, economists say that there is an **exchange rate system**. A **floating currency** is the outcome of a country allowing its currency's exchange rate to be determined by demand and supply. The current exchange rate system is a **managed float exchange rate system**, under which the value of most currencies is determined by demand and supply, with occasional government intervention. A **fixed exchange rate system** is a system under which countries agree to keep the exchange rates among their currencies fixed. Under the gold standard, the exchange rate between two currencies was automatically determined by the quantity of gold in each currency. By the end of the Great Depression of the 1930s, every country had abandoned the gold standard. Under the Bretton Woods system, which was in place between 1944 and the early 1970s, the United States agreed to exchange dollars for gold at a price of $35 per ounce. The central banks of all other members of the system pledged to buy and sell their currencies at a fixed rate against the dollar.

MyEconLab Visit **www.myeconlab.com** to complete these exercises online and get instant feedback.

Review Questions

1.1 What is an exchange rate system? What is the difference between a fixed exchange rate system and a managed float exchange rate system?

1.2 How were exchange rates determined under the gold standard? How did the Bretton Woods system differ from the gold standard?

Problems and Applications

1.3 (Related to the Don't Let This Happen to You **on page 665**) Briefly explain whether you agree with the following statement: "The Federal Reserve is limited in its ability to issue paper currency by the amount of gold the federal government has in Fort Knox. To issue more paper currency, the government first has to buy more gold."

1.4 An article in the *Atlantic* referred to a poll of economists that found no support for the United States to readopt the gold standard:

> It prevents the central bank from fighting recessions by outsourcing monetary policy decisions to how much gold we have—which, in turn, depends on our trade balance and on how much of the shiny rock we can dig up. When we peg the dollar to gold we have to raise interest rates when gold is scarce, regardless of the state of the economy.

Why does the writer state that a gold standard would prevent "the central bank from fighting recessions"?

Source: Matthew O'Brien, "Why the Gold Standard Is the World's Worst Economic Idea, in 2 Charts," *Atlantic*, August 26, 2012.

1.5 The United States and most other countries abandoned the gold standard during the 1930s. Why would the 1930s have been a particularly difficult time for countries to have remained on the gold standard? (*Hint:* Think about the macroeconomic events of the 1930s and about the possible problems with carrying out an expansionary monetary policy while remaining on the gold standard.)

1.6 After World War II, why might countries have preferred the Bretton Woods system to reestablishing the gold standard? In your answer, be sure to note the important ways in which the Bretton Woods system differed from the gold standard.

19.2 The Current Exchange Rate System, pages 665–677

LEARNING OBJECTIVE: Discuss the three key features of the current exchange rate system.

Summary

The current exchange rate system has three key features: (1) The U.S. dollar floats against other major currencies, (2) most countries in Western Europe have adopted a common currency, and (3) some developing countries have fixed their currencies' exchange rates against the dollar or against another major currency. Since 1973, the value of the U.S. dollar has fluctuated widely against other major currencies. The theory of **purchasing power parity** states that in the long run, exchange rates move to equalize the purchasing power of different currencies. This theory helps to explain some of the long-run movements in the value of the U.S. dollar relative to other currencies. Purchasing power parity does not provide a complete explanation of movements in exchange rates for several reasons, including the existence of *tariffs* and *quotas*. A **tariff** is a tax imposed by a government on imports. A **quota** is a government-imposed limit on the quantity of a good that can be imported. Currently, 19 European Union member countries use a common currency known as the **euro**. The experience of the countries using the euro will provide economists with information about the costs and benefits to countries of using the same currency.

When a country keeps its currency's exchange rate fixed against another country's currency, it is **pegging** its currency. Pegging can result in problems similar to the difficulties countries encountered with fixed exchange rates under the Bretton Woods system. If investors become convinced that a country pegging its exchange rate will eventually allow the exchange rate to decline to a lower level, the demand curve for the currency will shift to the left. This destabilizing speculation makes it difficult for a central bank to maintain a fixed exchange rate.

MyEconLab Visit www.myeconlab.com to complete these exercises online and get instant feedback.

Review Questions

2.1 What is the theory of purchasing power parity? Does the theory give a complete explanation for movements in exchange rates in the long run? Briefly explain.

2.2 Briefly describe the four determinants of exchange rates in the long run.

2.3 Which European countries currently use the euro as their currency? Why did these countries agree to replace their previous currencies with the euro?

2.4 What does it mean when one currency is "pegged" against another currency? Why do countries peg their currencies? What problems can result from pegging?

Problems and Applications

2.5 An article in the *Toronto Star* discussed the Canadian teams that play in the National Hockey League, the National Basketball Association, Major League Baseball, and Major League Soccer. The article noted, "Under their collective agreements players get paid in U.S. dollars. The majority of [team] revenue, however, is in Canadian currency." Are Canadian professional sports teams better off when the Canadian dollar increases in value relative to the U.S. dollar or when it decreases in value? Briefly explain.

Source: Josh Rubin, "MLSE, Blue Jays Deal with Dollar Dive," thestar.com, January 25, 2015.

2.6 An article in the *Economist* discussed the situation facing the U.S. economy in mid-2015: "The combination of weaker-than-expected CPI inflation and some dovish comments in the minutes of the Federal Reserve's July meeting have caused the dollar … to fall. Inflation continues to languish close to zero due to cheap oil and the effect of a strengthening dollar." By "dovish comments,"

the article meant that some members of the Fed's Federal Open Market Committee did not believe that the target for the federal funds rate should be raised in the coming months.

a. If investors come to believe that the Fed might not be increasing interest rates, why would the value of the dollar decline?

b. What does "the strengthening of the dollar" mean? Why would a strengthening of the dollar reduce the inflation rate in the United States?

Source: "Fed Leaders Begin to Recognise that September Is Too Soon to Hike Rates," *Economist*, August 20, 2015.

2.7 Consider this statement:

> It takes more than 120 yen to buy 1 U.S. dollar and more than 1.5 dollars to buy 1 British pound. These values show that the United States must be a much wealthier country than Japan and that the United Kingdom must be wealthier than the United States.

Do you agree with this reasoning? Briefly explain.

2.8 According to the theory of purchasing power parity, if the inflation rate in Australia is higher than the inflation rate in New Zealand, what should happen to the exchange rate between the Australian dollar and the New Zealand dollar? Briefly explain.

2.9 In December 2014, you needed 30 percent more pesos to buy one U.S. dollar than you had needed in December 2004. Over the same time period, the consumer price index in Mexico increased 49.5 percent, and the consumer price index in the United States increased 23.3 percent. Are these data consistent with the theory of purchasing power parity? Briefly explain.

2.10 **(Related to the Making the Connection on page 667)** Look again at the table on page 668 that shows the prices of Big Macs and the implied and actual exchange rates. Indicate whether the U.S. dollar is overvalued or undervalued against each currency.

2.11 **(Related to Solved Problem 19.2 on page 668)** Fill in the missing values in the following table. Assume that the Big Mac is selling for $4.79 in the United States. Explain whether the U.S. dollar is overvalued or undervalued relative to each of the other currencies and predict what will happen in the future to each exchange rate if the actual exchange rate moves toward the purchasing power parity exchange rate. Finally, calculate the implied exchange rate between the Russian ruble and the New Zealand dollar and explain which currency is overvalued in terms of Big Mac purchasing power parity.

Country	Big Mac Price	Implied Exchange Rate	Actual Exchange Rate
Chile	2,100 pesos		642.45 pesos per dollar
Israel	17.5 shekels		3.78 shekels per dollar
Russia	107 rubles		56.82 rubles per dollar
New Zealand	5.9 New Zealand dollars		1.51 New Zealand dollars per U.S. dollar

Source: "The Big Mac Index," *Economist*, July 16, 2015.

2.12 (Related to the Making the Connection on page 671) Britain decided not to join other European Union countries in using the euro as its currency. One British opponent of adopting the euro argued, "It comes down to economics. We just don't believe that it's possible to manage the entire economy of Europe with just one interest rate policy. How do you alleviate recession in Germany and curb inflation in Ireland?"

a. What interest rate policy would be used to alleviate recession in Germany?

b. What interest rate policy would be used to curb inflation in Ireland?

c. What does adopting the euro have to do with interest rate policy?

Source: Alan Cowell, "Nuanced Conflict over Euro in Britain," *New York Times*, June 22, 2001.

2.13 (Related to the Making the Connection on page 671) An article in *USA Today* argues, "Ironically, the euro's fall—and the benefit for German exports—is largely the result of eurozone policies that Germany has taken the lead in opposing . . . [including] easier money policies by the European Central Bank."

a. How does the "euro's fall" benefit German exports?

b. How is the euro's fall related to policies of the European Central Bank?

Source: Mihret Yohannes, "Germany Benefits from Weak Euro Policies It Deplores," usatoday.com, March 4, 2015.

2.14 In January 2007, before the financial crisis, the exchange rate was $1.30 per euro. In July 2008, during the financial crisis, the exchange rate was $1.58 per euro. Was this change in the dollar–euro exchange rate good news or bad news for U.S. firms exporting goods and services to Europe? Was it good news or bad news for European consumers buying goods and services imported from the United States? Briefly explain.

2.15 Although it is a member of the European Community, Denmark is not part of the eurozone; it has its own currency, the krone. Because the krone is pegged to the euro, Denmark's central bank is obliged to maintain the value of the krone within 2.25 percent either above or below the value of the euro. To maintain the peg with the euro, in 2015 the Danish central bank was forced to offer negative interest rates on deposits of krone that it held. Was the Danish central bank's action in response to an increase or a decrease in the value of the euro? Briefly explain.

Source: Charles Duxbury and Josie Cox, "Denmark Cuts Rates Again to Protect Currency Peg," *Wall Street Journal*, February 5, 2015.

2.16 (Related to the Chapter Opener on page 663) The German firm Bayer reported that its pharmaceutical group experienced a 21 percent increase in profit for the second quarter of 2015. The firm stated that the increase was partly the result of "favorable currency effects."

a. Briefly explain what the firm means by "favorable currency effects."

b. How would favorable currency effects increase Bayer's profit?

c. Would these effects still have raised Bayer's profit if all of the firm's production and all of its sales were within Europe? Briefly explain.

Source: Christopher Alessi, "Bayer Profit Rises on Healthy Currency Effects," *Wall Street Journal*, July 29, 2015.

2.17 Use the graph to answer the following questions.

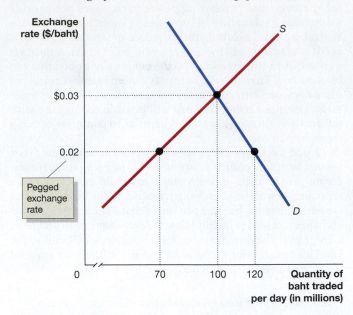

a. According to the graph, is there a surplus or a shortage of baht in exchange for U.S. dollars? Briefly explain.

b. To maintain the pegged exchange rate, will the Thai central bank need to buy baht in exchange for dollars or sell baht in exchange for dollars? How many baht will the Thai central bank need to buy or sell?

2.18 The *Economist* observed, "In Argentina, many loans were taken out in dollars: this had catastrophic consequences for borrowers once the peg collapsed." What does the article mean when it says that Argentina's "peg collapsed"? Why was this collapse catastrophic for borrowers in Argentina who had taken out dollar loans?

Source: "Spoilt for Choice," *Economist*, June 3, 2002.

2.19 (Related to the Making the Connection on page 675) Graph the demand and supply of Chinese yuan for U.S. dollars and label each axis. To maintain a pegged exchange rate, the Chinese central bank can use yuan to buy U.S. dollars. Indicate whether the Chinese central bank would typically be interested in pegging the exchange rate above or below the market equilibrium exchange rate, and show on the graph the quantity of yuan the Chinese central bank would have to supply each trading period.

2.20 (Related to the Making the Connection on page 675) In August 2015, after the Chinese central bank moved to decrease the value of the yuan in exchange for the dollar, a column in the *Wall Street Journal* offered this opinion: "China's trading partners are right to suspect that the real purpose of the so-called reform is a competitive devaluation that boosts exports and growth at the rest of the world's expense."

a. What does the writer mean by a "competitive devaluation"?

b. How would such a devaluation boost Chinese exports and growth?

c. Why would a boost in Chinese exports and growth come at the rest of the world's expense?

Source: Greg Ip, "Why China's Yuan 'Reform' Merits Skepticism," *Wall Street Journal*, August 19, 2015.

19.3 International Capital Markets, pages 677–678

LEARNING OBJECTIVE: Discuss the growth of international capital markets.

Summary

A key reason exchange rates fluctuate is that investors seek out the best investments they can find anywhere in the world. Since 1980, the markets for stocks and bonds have become global. Foreign purchases of U.S. corporate bonds and stocks and U.S. government bonds have increased greatly in the period since 1995. As a result of the globalization of capital markets, firms around the world are no longer forced to rely only on the savings of domestic households for funds.

MyEconLab Visit **www.myeconlab.com** to complete these exercises online and get instant feedback.

Review Questions

3.1 What were the main factors behind the globalization of capital markets in the 1980s and 1990s?

3.2 Briefly describe the pattern of foreign investments in U.S. securities between 1995 and 2014.

Problems and Applications

3.3 Why are foreign investors more likely to invest in U.S. government bonds than in U.S. corporate stocks and bonds?

3.4 The text states that "the globalization of financial markets has helped increase growth and efficiency in the world economy." Briefly explain which aspects of globalization help to increase growth in the world economy.

3.5 The global financial crisis of 2007–2009 led some economists and policymakers to suggest the reinstitution of capital controls—or limits on the flow of foreign exchange and financial investments across countries—which existed in many European countries prior to the 1960s. Why would a financial crisis lead policymakers to reconsider using capital controls? What problems might result from reinstituting capital controls?

Real-Time Data Exercises

D19.1 (Big Mac prices and purchasing power parity) Go to the Web site of the Federal Reserve Bank of St. Louis Federal Reserve (FRED) (research.stlouisfed.org/fred2/) and find the most recent values for the Japan/U.S. Foreign Exchange Rate (DEXJPUS), China/U.S. Foreign Exchange Rate (DEXCHUS), and the Mexico/U.S. Foreign Exchange Rate (DEXMXUS).

a. Explain whether the exchange rates are quoted as U.S. dollars per unit of foreign currency or units of foreign currency per U.S. dollar.

b. Suppose a Big Mac sells for 300 yen in Japan, 14 yuan in China, and 34 pesos in Mexico. What is the price of a Big Mac in each country in terms of U.S. dollars?

c. Are your results from part (b) consistent with the theory of purchasing power parity? Briefly explain.

d. Assuming no transportation costs and a no-cost means of preserving Big Macs while they are being transported, explain in which county you would want to purchase a Big Mac and in which country you would want to sell the same Big Mac in order to make the highest profit possible.

D19.2 (Explaining movements in the yuan-dollar exchange rate) Go to the Web site of the Federal Reserve Bank of St. Louis (FRED) (research.stlouisfed.org/fred2/) and find the values for the China/U.S. Foreign Exchange Rate (DEXCHUS) from 1981 to the most recent date available.

a. Compared with its value in 1981, has the yuan appreciated or depreciated against the U.S. dollar? Briefly explain.

b. Summarize the movements in the yuan–dollar exchange rate during these years and explain why the pattern occurred.

D19.3 (Analyzing global capital flows) The U.S. Treasury publishes data on capital flows. Treasury International Capital Flows can be found at www.treasury.gov/resource-center/data-chart-center/tic/Pages/index.aspx. Go to "Monthly Transactions in Long-Term Securities."

a. Look at recent net purchases of long-term securities. How has the volume of purchases changed over the past five years?

b. Now look at gross purchases of long-term securities. Which countries hold the most U.S. securities? How have foreign holdings of U.S. securities changed over time?

Appendix

The Gold Standard and the Bretton Woods System

LEARNING OBJECTIVE: Explain the gold standard and the Bretton Woods system.

It is easier to understand the current exchange rate system by considering further two earlier systems—the gold standard and the Bretton Woods system—that together lasted from the early nineteenth century through the early 1970s.

The Gold Standard

As we saw in this chapter, under the gold standard, the currency of a country consisted of gold coins and paper currency that people could redeem for gold. Great Britain adopted the gold standard in 1816, but as late as 1870, only a few nations had followed. In the late nineteenth century, however, Great Britain's share of world trade had increased, as had its overseas investments. The dominant position of Great Britain in the world economy motivated other countries to adopt the gold standard. By 1913, every country in Europe, except Spain and Bulgaria, and most countries in the Western Hemisphere had adopted the gold standard.

Under the gold standard, the exchange rate between two currencies was automatically determined by the quantity of gold in each currency. If there was 1/5 ounce of gold in a U.S. dollar and 1 ounce of gold in a British pound, the price of gold in the United States would be $5 per ounce, and the price of gold in Britain would be £1 per ounce. The exchange rate would therefore be $5 = £1.   MyEconLab Concept Check

The End of the Gold Standard

From a modern point of view, the greatest drawback to the gold standard was that the central bank lacked control of the money supply. The size of a country's money supply depended on its gold supply, which could be greatly affected by chance discoveries of gold or by technological change in gold mining. For example, the gold discoveries in California in 1849 and Alaska in the 1890s caused rapid increases in the U.S. money supply. Because the central bank cannot determine how much gold will be discovered, it lacks the control of the money supply necessary to pursue an active monetary policy. During wartime, countries usually went off the gold standard to allow their central banks to expand the money supply as rapidly as was necessary to pay for the war. Britain left the gold standard at the beginning of World War I in 1914 and did not resume redeeming its paper currency for gold until 1925.

When the Great Depression began in 1929, governments came under pressure to leave the gold standard to allow their central banks to pursue active monetary policies. In 1931, Great Britain became the first major country to abandon the gold standard. A number of other countries also went off the gold standard that year. The United States remained on the gold standard until 1933, and a few countries, including France, Italy, and Belgium, stayed on even longer. By the late 1930s, the gold standard had collapsed.

The earlier a country abandoned the gold standard, the easier time it had fighting the Depression with expansionary monetary policies. The countries that abandoned the gold standard by 1932 suffered an average decline in production of only 3 percent between 1929 and 1934. The countries that stayed on the gold standard until 1933 or later suffered an average decline of more than 30 percent. The devastating economic performance of the countries that stayed on the gold standard the longest during the 1930s is the key reason no attempt was made to bring back the gold standard in later years.   MyEconLab Concept Check

The Bretton Woods System

In addition to the collapse of the gold standard, the global economy suffered during the 1930s from tariff wars. The United States had started the tariff wars in June 1930 by enacting the Smoot-Hawley Tariff Act, which raised the average U.S. tariff rate to more than 50 percent. Many other countries raised tariffs during the next few years, leading to a collapse in world trade.

As World War II was coming to an end, economists and government officials in the United States and Europe concluded that they needed to restore the international economic system to avoid another depression. In 1947, the United States and most other major countries, apart from the Soviet Union, began participating in the General Agreement on Tariffs and Trade (GATT), under which they worked to reduce trade barriers. The GATT was very successful in sponsoring rounds of negotiations among countries, which led to sharp declines in tariffs. U.S. tariffs dropped from an average rate of more than 50 percent in the early 1930s to an average rate of less than 2 percent in 2015. In 1995, the GATT was replaced by the World Trade Organization (WTO), which has similar objectives.

The effort to develop a new exchange rate system to replace the gold standard was more complicated than establishing the GATT. A conference held in Bretton Woods, New Hampshire, in 1944 set up a system in which the United States pledged to buy or sell gold at a fixed price of $35 per ounce. The central banks of all other members of the new **Bretton Woods system** pledged to buy and sell their currencies at a fixed rate against the dollar. By fixing their exchange rates against the dollar, these countries were fixing the exchange rates among their currencies as well. Unlike under the gold standard, neither the United States nor any other country was willing to redeem its paper currency for gold domestically. The United States would redeem dollars for gold only if they were presented by a foreign central bank. The United States continued the prohibition, first enacted in the early 1930s, against private citizens owning gold, except in the form of jewelry or rare coins. The prohibition was not lifted until the 1970s, when it again became possible for Americans to own gold as an investment.

Under the Bretton Woods system, central banks were committed to selling dollars in exchange for their own currencies. This commitment required them to hold *dollar reserves*. If a central bank ran out of dollar reserves, it could borrow them from the newly created **International Monetary Fund (IMF)**. In addition to providing loans to central banks that were short of dollar reserves, the IMF would oversee the operation of the system and approve adjustments to the agreed-on fixed exchange rates.

Under the Bretton Woods system, a fixed exchange rate was called a *par exchange rate*. If the par exchange rate was not the same as the exchange rate that would have been determined in the market, the result would be a surplus or a shortage. For example, Figure 19A.1 shows the exchange rate between the dollar and the British pound. The figure is drawn from the British point of view, so we measure the exchange rate on the vertical axis as dollars per pound. In this case, the par exchange rate between the dollar and the pound is above the equilibrium exchange rate, as determined by demand and supply.

At the par exchange rate of $4 per pound, the quantity of pounds demanded by people who want to buy British goods and services or who want to invest in British assets is smaller than the quantity of pounds supplied by people who would like to exchange them for dollars. As a result, the Bank of England must use dollars to buy the surplus of £1 million per day. Only at an exchange rate of $2.80 per pound would the surplus be eliminated. If the par exchange rate was below the equilibrium exchange rate, there would be a shortage of domestic currency in the foreign exchange market.

A persistent shortage or surplus of a currency under the Bretton Woods system was seen as evidence of a *fundamental disequilibrium* in a country's exchange rate. After consulting with the IMF, countries in this position were allowed to adjust their exchange rates. In the early years of the Bretton Woods system, many countries found that their currencies were *overvalued* versus the dollar, meaning that their par exchange rates were too high. A reduction in a fixed exchange rate is a **devaluation**. An increase in a fixed exchange rate is a **revaluation**. In 1949, there was a devaluation of several currencies,

Bretton Woods system An exchange rate system that lasted from 1944 to 1973, under which countries pledged to buy and sell their currencies at a fixed rate against the dollar.

International Monetary Fund (IMF) An international organization that provides foreign currency loans to central banks and oversees the operation of the international monetary system.

Devaluation A reduction in a fixed exchange rate.

Revaluation An increase in a fixed exchange rate.

Figure 19A.1

A Fixed Exchange Rate above Equilibrium Results in a Surplus of Pounds

Under the Bretton Woods system, if the par exchange rate was above equilibrium, the result would be a surplus of domestic currency in the foreign exchange market. If the par exchange rate was below equilibrium, the result would be a shortage of domestic currency. In the figure, the par exchange rate between the pound and the dollar is $4 = £1$, while the equilibrium exchange rate is $2.80 = £1$. This gap forces the Bank of England to buy £1 million per day in exchange for dollars.

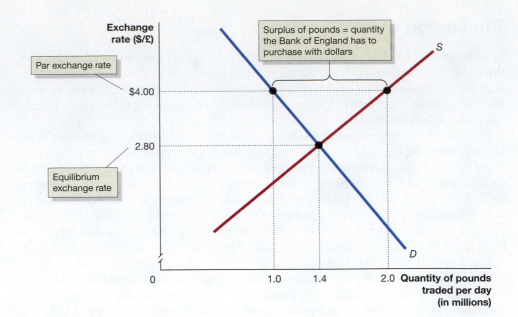

including the British pound, reflecting the fact that those currencies had been overvalued against the dollar.

The Collapse of the Bretton Woods System

By the late 1960s, the Bretton Woods system faced two severe problems. The first was that after 1963, the total number of dollars held by foreign central banks was larger than the gold reserves of the United States. In practice, most central banks—with the Bank of France being the main exception—rarely redeemed dollars for gold. But the basis of the system was a credible promise by the United States to redeem dollars for gold if called upon to do so. By the late 1960s, as the gap between the dollars held by foreign central banks and the gold reserves of the United States grew larger and larger, other countries began to doubt the U.S. promise to redeem dollars for gold.

The second problem the Bretton Woods system faced was that some countries with undervalued currencies, particularly West Germany, were unwilling to revalue their currencies. Governments resisted revaluation because it would have increased the prices of their countries' exports. Many German firms put pressure on the government not to endanger their sales in the U.S. market by raising the exchange rate of the deutsche mark against the dollar. Figure 19A.2 shows the situation the German government faced in 1971. The figure takes the German point of view, so the exchange rate is expressed in terms of dollars per deutsche mark.

Under the Bretton Woods system, the Bundesbank, the German central bank, was required to buy and sell deutsche marks for dollars at a rate of $0.27 per deutsche mark. The equilibrium that would have prevailed in the foreign exchange market if the Bundesbank had not intervened was about $0.35 per deutsche mark. Because the par exchange rate was below the equilibrium exchange rate, the quantity of deutsche marks demanded by people wanting to buy German goods and services or wanting to invest in German assets was greater than the quantity of deutsche marks supplied by people who wanted to exchange them for dollars. To maintain the exchange rate at $0.27 per deutsche mark, the Bundesbank had to buy dollars and sell deutsche marks. The number of deutsche marks supplied by the Bundesbank was equal to the shortage of deutsche marks at the par exchange rate.

By selling deutsche marks and buying dollars to defend the par exchange rate, the Bundesbank was increasing the West German money supply, risking an increase in the inflation rate. Because Germany had suffered a devastating hyperinflation during the 1920s, the fear of inflation was greater in Germany than in any other industrial country. No German government could survive politically if it allowed a significant increase in

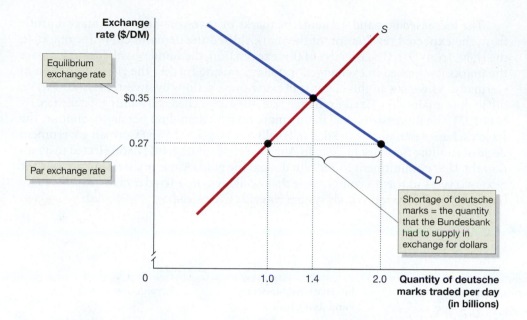

MyEconLab Animation

Figure 19A.2

West Germany's Undervalued Exchange Rate

The Bundesbank, the German central bank, was committed under the Bretton Woods system to defending a par exchange rate of $0.27 per deutsche mark (DM). Because this exchange rate was lower than what the equilibrium market exchange rate would have been, there was a shortage of DMs in the foreign exchange market. The Bundesbank had to supply DMs equal to the shortage in exchange for dollars. The shortage in the figure is equal to 1 billion DMs per day.

inflation. Knowing this fact, many investors in Germany and elsewhere became convinced that, eventually, the German government would have to allow a revaluation of the mark.

During the 1960s, most European countries, including Germany, relaxed their **capital controls**, which are limits on the flow of foreign exchange and financial investment across countries. The loosening of capital controls made it easier for investors to speculate on changes in exchange rates. For instance, an investor in the United States could sell $1 million and receive about 3.7 million deutsche marks at the par exchange rate of $0.27 per deutsche mark. If the exchange rate rose to $0.35 per deutsche mark, the investor could then exchange deutsche marks for dollars, receiving $1.3 million at the new exchange rate: a return of 30 percent on an initial $1 million investment. The more convinced investors became that Germany would have to allow a revaluation, the more dollars they exchanged for deutsche marks. Figure 19A.3 shows the results.

Capital controls Limits on the flow of foreign exchange and financial investment across countries.

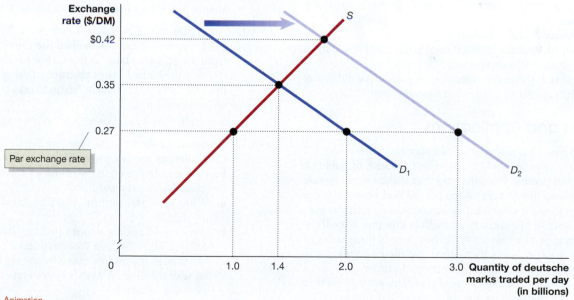

MyEconLab Animation

Figure 19A.3 **Destabilizing Speculation against the Deutsche Mark, 1971**

In 1971, the par exchange rate of $0.27 = 1 deutsche mark was below the equilibrium exchange rate of $0.35 = 1 deutsche mark. As investors became convinced that West Germany would have to revalue the deutsche mark, they increased their demand for marks, shifting the demand curve from D_1 to D_2. The new equilibrium exchange rate became $0.42 = 1 deutsche mark. This increase in demand raised the quantity of marks the Bundesbank had to supply in exchange for dollars to defend the par exchange rate from 1 billion deutsche marks to 2 billion deutsche marks per day.

The increased demand for deutsche marks by investors hoping to make a profit from the expected revaluation of the mark shifted the demand curve for marks to the right, from D_1 to D_2. Because of this expectation, the Bundesbank had to increase the marks it supplied in exchange for dollars, raising further the risk of inflation in Germany. As we saw in this chapter, because these actions by investors make it more difficult to maintain a fixed exchange rate, they are called *destabilizing speculation*. By May 1971, the Bundesbank had to buy more than $250 million per day to support the fixed exchange rate against the dollar. Finally, on May 5, the West German government decided to allow the mark to float. In August, President Richard Nixon elected to abandon the U.S. commitment to redeem dollars for gold. Attempts were made over the next two years to reach a compromise that would restore a fixed exchange rate system, but by 1973, the Bretton Woods system was effectively dead.   MyEconLab Concept Check

MyEconLab Study Plan

Key Terms

Bretton Woods system, p. 685

Capital controls, p. 687

Devaluation, p. 685

International Monetary Fund (IMF), p. 685

Revaluation, p. 685

19.A

The Gold Standard and the Bretton Woods System, pages 684–688

LEARNING OBJECTIVE: Explain the gold standard and the Bretton Woods system.

 MyEconLab   Visit **www.myeconlab.com** to complete these exercises online and get instant feedback.

Review Questions

19A.1 What determined the exchange rates among currencies under the gold standard? Why did the gold standard collapse?

19A.2 Briefly describe how the Bretton Woods system operated.

19A.3 What is the difference between a devaluation and a revaluation?

19A.4 What are capital controls?

19A.5 What role did the International Monetary Fund play in the Bretton Woods system?

19A.6 What is destabilizing speculation? What role did it play in the collapse of the Bretton Woods system?

Problems and Applications

19A.7 Suppose that under the gold standard, there was 1/5 ounce of gold in a U.S. dollar and 1 ounce of gold in a British pound. Demonstrate that if the exchange rate between the dollar and the pound was $4 = £1 rather than $5 = £1, you could make unlimited profits by buying gold in one country and selling it in the other. If the exchange rate was $6 = £1, how would your strategy change? For simplicity, assume that there was no cost to shipping gold from one country to the other.

19A.8 If a country is using the gold standard, what is likely to happen to its money supply if new gold deposits are discovered in the country, as happened in the United States with the gold discoveries in California in 1849? Is this change in the money supply desirable? Briefly explain.

19A.9 An article in the *Economist* observes, "When the Depression [of the 1930s] struck, this gold standard became a noose around the necks of struggling economies." In

what sense was the gold standard a "noose around the necks of struggling economies" during the 1930s?

Source: "A Brief Post on Competitive Devaluation," *Economist*, October 31, 2011.

19A.10 An article in the *Economist* observed that there were "some perturbing parallels between the gold standard and the euro." What parallels are there between the gold standard and the euro? What would make these parallels perturbing?

Source: "Perturbing Parallels," *Economist*, July 5, 2013.

19A.11 An article in the *New York Times* states, "On Aug. 15, 1971, President Nixon unhitched the value of the dollar from the gold standard." Is the author of this article correct that the United States abandoned the gold standard in 1971? What led President Nixon to take the action described in the article?

Source: "Bretton Woods System" *New York Times*, August 20, 2015.

19A.12 An opinion column in the *New York Times* offers the view that "zealous money printing in the 1960s led to the inevitable collapse of the Bretton Woods system (and complete fiat money was born)."
  a. What does the author mean by "zealous money printing"?
  b. Why would zealous money printing have led to the collapse of the Bretton Woods system?
  c. What does the author mean by saying that the collapse of the Bretton Woods system resulted in "complete fiat money"?

Source: Mark Spitznagel, "The Myth of Black Swan Market Events," *New York Times*, February 13, 2015.

19A.13 One economist has argued that the East Asian exchange rate crisis of the late 1990s was due to "the simple failure of governments to remember the lessons from the breakdown of the Bretton Woods System." What are these lessons? In what sense did the East Asian governments fail to learn these lessons?

Source: Thomas D. Willett, "Crying for Argentina," *Milken Institute Review*, Second Quarter 2002.

19A.14 Economists Michael Bordo of Rutgers University and Angela Redish of the University of British Columbia have argued that the "Bretton Woods system functioned for a number of years but beginning in the late 1960s, in the face of inflationary US monetary policy it became a slow moving train wreck." Why would inflationary U.S. monetary policy cause problems for the Bretton Woods system?

Source: Michael Bordo and Angela Redish, "Putting the 'System' in the International Monetary System," www.voxeu.org, June 20, 2013.

19A.15 An article in the *Economist* notes that after the end of the Bretton Woods system, "the Europeans did not like leaving their currencies to the whims of the markets." What does it mean for a country to leave its currency to the "whims of the markets"? What problems might a country experience as a result? What exchange rate system did most European countries ultimately adopt?

Source: "Forty Years On," *Economist*, August 13, 2011.

Real-Time Data Exercise

D19A.1 (Gold prices and the gold standard) Go to the Web site of the Federal Reserve Bank of St. Louis (FRED) (research.stlouisfed.org/fred2/) and find the Gold Fixing Price 10:30 A.M. (London time) in the London Bullion Market in U.S. Dollars (GOLDAMGBD228NLBM) from 1968 to the most recent available date.

   a. What explains the relative stability of the price of gold from 1968 to 1971?

   b. What implications do the movements in gold prices since 1971 have for an attempt by the United States and other countries to reestablish a gold standard?

GLOSSARY

A

Absolute advantage The ability of an individual, a firm, or a country to produce more of a good or service than competitors, using the same amount of resources.

Accounting profit A firm's net income, measured as revenue minus operating expenses and taxes paid.

Adverse selection The situation in which one party to a transaction takes advantage of knowing more than the other party to the transaction.

Aggregate demand (AD) curve A curve that shows the relationship between the price level and the level of planned aggregate expenditure in the economy, holding constant all other factors that affect aggregate expenditure.

Aggregate demand and aggregate supply model A model that explains short-run fluctuations in real GDP and the price level.

Aggregate expenditure (AE) Total spending in the economy: the sum of consumption, planned investment, government purchases, and net exports.

Aggregate expenditure model A macroeconomic model that focuses on the short-run relationship between total spending and real GDP, assuming that the price level is constant.

Allocative efficiency A state of the economy in which production is in accordance with consumer preferences; in particular, every good or service is produced up to the point where the last unit provides a marginal benefit to society equal to the marginal cost of producing it.

Asset Anything of value owned by a person or a firm.

Asymmetric information A situation in which one party to an economic transaction has less information than the other party.

Autarky A situation in which a country does not trade with other countries.

Automatic stabilizers Government spending and taxes that automatically increase or decrease along with the business cycle.

Autonomous expenditure An expenditure that does not depend on the level of GDP.

B

Balance of payments The record of a country's trade with other countries in goods, services, and assets.

Balance of trade The difference between the value of the goods a country exports and the value of the goods a country imports.

Balance sheet A financial statement that sums up a firm's financial position on a particular day, usually the end of a quarter or year.

Bank panic A situation in which many banks experience runs at the same time.

Bank run A situation in which many depositors simultaneously decide to withdraw money from a bank.

Black market A market in which buying and selling take place at prices that violate government price regulations.

Bond A financial security that represents a promise to repay a fixed amount of funds.

Bretton Woods system An exchange rate system that lasted from 1944 to 1973, under which countries pledged to buy and sell their currencies at a fixed rate against the dollar.

Budget deficit The situation in which the government's expenditures are greater than its tax revenue.

Budget surplus The situation in which the government's expenditures are less than its tax revenue.

Business cycle Alternating periods of economic expansion and economic recession.

C

Capital account The part of the balance of payments that records relatively minor transactions, such as migrants' transfers and sales and purchases of nonproduced, nonfinancial assets.

Capital controls Limits on the flow of foreign exchange and financial investment across countries.

Capital Manufactured goods that are used to produce other goods and services.

Cash flow The difference between the cash revenues received by a firm and the cash spending by the firm.

Catch-up The prediction that the level of GDP per capita (or income per capita) in poor countries will grow faster than in rich countries.

Centrally planned economy An economy in which the government decides how economic resources will be allocated.

Ceteris paribus ("all else equal") condition The requirement that when analyzing the relationship between two variables—such as price and quantity demanded—other variables must be held constant.

Circular-flow diagram A model that illustrates how participants in markets are linked.

Closed economy An economy that has no interactions in trade or finance with other countries.

Commodity money A good used as money that also has value independent of its use as money.

Comparative advantage The ability of an individual, a firm, or a country to produce a good or service at a lower opportunity cost than competitors.

Competitive market equilibrium A market equilibrium with many buyers and sellers.

Complements Goods and services that are used together.

Consumer price index (CPI) A measure of the average change over time in the prices a typical urban family of four pays for the goods and services they purchase.

Consumer surplus The difference between the highest price a consumer is willing to pay for a good or service and the actual price the consumer pays.

Consumption Spending by households on goods and services, not including spending on new houses.

Consumption function The relationship between consumption spending and disposable income.

Contractionary monetary policy The Federal Reserve's policy of increasing interest rates to reduce inflation.

Corporate governance The way in which a corporation is structured and the effect that structure has on the corporation's behavior.

Corporation A legal form of business that provides owners with protection from losing more than their investment should the business fail.

Coupon payment An interest payment on a bond.

Crowding out A decline in private expenditures as a result of an increase in government purchases.

Currency appreciation An increase in the market value of one currency relative to another currency.

Currency depreciation A decrease in the market value of one currency relative to another currency.

Current account The part of the balance of payments that records a country's net exports, net income on investments, and net transfers.

Cyclically adjusted budget deficit or surplus The deficit or surplus in the federal government's budget if the economy were at potential GDP.

Cyclical unemployment Unemployment caused by a business cycle recession.

D

Deadweight loss The reduction in economic surplus resulting from a market not being in competitive equilibrium.

Deflation A decline in the price level.

Demand curve A curve that shows the relationship between the price of a product and the quantity of the product demanded.

Demand schedule A table that shows the relationship between the price of a product and the quantity of the product demanded.

Demographics The characteristics of a population with respect to age, race, and gender.

Devaluation A reduction in a fixed exchange rate.

Direct finance A flow of funds from savers to firms through financial markets, such as the New York Stock Exchange.

Discount loans Loans the Federal Reserve makes to banks.

Discount rate The interest rate the Federal Reserve charges on discount loans.

Discouraged workers People who are available for work but have not looked for a job during the previous four weeks because they believe no jobs are available for them.

Disinflation A significant reduction in the inflation rate.

Dividends Payments by a corporation to its shareholders.

Dumping Selling a product for a price below its cost of production.

E

Economic efficiency A market outcome in which the marginal benefit to consumers of the last unit produced is equal to its marginal cost of production and in which the sum of consumer surplus and producer surplus is at a maximum.

Economic growth model A model that explains growth rates in real GDP per capita over the long run.

Economic growth The ability of an economy to produce increasing quantities of goods and services.

Economic model A simplified version of reality used to analyze real-world economic situations.

Economic profit A firm's revenues minus all of its implicit and explicit costs.

Economics The study of the choices people make to attain their goals, given their scarce resources.

Economic surplus The sum of consumer surplus and producer surplus.

Economic variable Something measurable that can have different values, such as the incomes of doctors.

Efficiency wage An above-market wage that a firm pays to increase workers' productivity.

Employed In government statistics, someone who currently has a job or who is temporarily away from his or her job.

Entrepreneur Someone who operates a business, bringing together the factors of production—labor, capital, and natural resources—to produce goods and services.

Equity The fair distribution of economic benefits.

Euro The common currency of many European countries.

Excess reserves Reserves that banks hold over the legal requirement.

Exchange rate system An agreement among countries about how exchange rates should be determined.

Excludability The situation in which anyone who does not pay for a good cannot consume it.

Expansion The period of a business cycle during which total production and total employment are increasing.

Expansionary monetary policy The Federal Reserve's policy of decreasing interest rates to increase real GDP.

Explicit cost A cost that involves spending money.

Exports Goods and services produced domestically but sold in other countries.

External economies Reductions in a firm's costs that result from an increase in the size of an industry.

F

Factor market A market for the factors of production, such as labor, capital, natural resources, and entrepreneurial ability.

Factors of production Labor, capital, natural resources, and other inputs used to make goods and services.

Federal funds rate The interest rate banks charge each other for overnight loans.

Federal Open Market Committee (FOMC) The Federal Reserve committee responsible for open market operations and managing the money supply in the United States.

Federal Reserve The central bank of the United States.

Fee-for-service A system under which doctors and hospitals receive a payment for each service they provide.

Fiat money Money, such as paper currency, that is authorized by a central bank or governmental body and that

does not have to be exchanged by the central bank for gold or some other commodity money.

Final good or service A good or service purchased by a final user.

Financial account The part of the balance of payments that records purchases of assets a country has made abroad and foreign purchases of assets in the country.

Financial intermediaries Firms, such as banks, mutual funds, pension funds, and insurance companies, that borrow funds from savers and lend them to borrowers.

Financial markets Markets where financial securities, such as stocks and bonds, are bought and sold.

Financial system The system of financial markets and financial intermediaries through which firms acquire funds from households.

Fiscal policy Changes in federal taxes and purchases that are intended to achieve macroeconomic policy goals.

Fiscal policy Changes in federal taxes and purchases that are intended to achieve macroeconomic policy objectives.

Fixed exchange rate system A system under which countries agree to keep the exchange rates among their currencies fixed for long periods.

Floating currency The outcome of a country allowing its currency's exchange rate to be determined by demand and supply.

Foreign direct investment (FDI) The purchase or building by a corporation of a facility in a foreign country.

Foreign portfolio investment The purchase by an individual or a firm of stocks or bonds issued in another country.

Fractional reserve banking system A banking system in which banks keep less than

100 percent of deposits as reserves.

Free market A market with few government restrictions on how a good or service can be produced or sold or on how a factor of production can be employed.

Free trade Trade between countries that is without government restrictions.

Frictional unemployment Short-term unemployment that arises from the process of matching workers with jobs.

G

GDP deflator A measure of the price level, calculated by dividing nominal GDP by real GDP and multiplying by 100.

Globalization The process of countries becoming more open to foreign trade and investment.

Government purchases Spending by federal, state, and local governments on goods and services.

Gross domestic product (GDP) The market value of all final goods and services produced in a country during a period of time, typically one year.

H

Health care Goods and services, such as prescription drugs, consultations with a doctor, and surgeries, that are intended to maintain or improve a person's health.

Health insurance A contract under which a buyer agrees to make payments, or *premiums*, in exchange for the provider's agreeing to pay some or all of the buyer's medical bills.

Human capital The accumulated knowledge and skills that workers acquire from formal training and education or from life experiences.

I

Implicit cost A nonmonetary opportunity cost.

Imports Goods and services bought domestically but produced in other countries.

Income effect The change in the quantity demanded of a good that results from the effect of a change in the good's price on consumers' purchasing power.

Income statement A financial statement that shows a firm's revenues, costs, and profit over a period of time.

Indirect finance A flow of funds from savers to borrowers through financial intermediaries such as banks. Intermediaries raise funds from savers to lend to firms (and other borrowers).

Industrial Revolution The application of mechanical power to the production of goods, beginning in England around 1750.

Inferior good A good for which the demand increases as income falls and decreases as income rises.

Inflation rate The percentage increase in the price level from one year to the next.

Inflation targeting A framework for conducting monetary policy that involves the central bank announcing its target level of inflation.

Interest rate The cost of borrowing funds, usually expressed as a percentage of the amount borrowed.

Intermediate good or service A good or service that is an input into another good or service, such as a tire on a truck.

International Monetary Fund (IMF) An international organization that provides foreign currency loans to central banks and oversees the operation of the international monetary system.

Inventories Goods that have been produced but not yet sold.

Investment Spending by firms on new factories, office buildings, machinery, and additions to inventories, plus spending by households and firms on new houses.

Isocost line All the combinations of two inputs, such as capital and labor, that have the same total cost.

K

Keynesian revolution The name given to the widespread acceptance during the 1930s and 1940s of John Maynard Keynes's macroeconomic model.

L

Labor force participation rate The percentage of the working-age population in the labor force.

Labor force The sum of employed and unemployed workers in the economy.

Labor productivity The quantity of goods and services that can be produced by one worker or by one hour of work.

Law of demand A rule that states that, holding everything else constant, when the price of a product falls, the quantity demanded of the product will increase, and when the price of a product rises, the quantity demanded of the product will decrease.

Law of supply A rule that states that, holding everything else constant, increases in price cause increases in the quantity supplied, and decreases in price cause decreases in the quantity supplied.

Liability Anything owed by a person or a firm.

Limited liability A legal provision that shields owners of a corporation from losing more than they have invested in the firm.

Long-run economic growth The process by which rising productivity increases the average standard of living.

M

M1 The narrow definition of the money supply: the sum of currency in circulation, checking account deposits in banks, and holdings of traveler's checks.

M2 A broader definition of the money supply: It includes M1 plus savings account deposits, small-denomination time deposits, balances in money market deposit accounts in banks, and noninstitutional money market fund shares.

Macroeconomics The study of the economy as a whole, including topics such as inflation, unemployment, and economic growth.

Managed float exchange rate system The current exchange rate system, under which the value of most currencies is determined by demand and supply, with occasional government intervention.

Marginal analysis Analysis that involves comparing marginal benefits and marginal costs.

Marginal benefit The additional benefit to a consumer from consuming one more unit of a good or service.

Marginal cost The additional cost to a firm of producing one more unit of a good or service.

Marginal product of labor The additional output a firm produces as a result of hiring one more worker.

Marginal propensity to consume (MPC) The slope of the consumption function: The amount by which consumption spending changes when disposable income changes.

Marginal propensity to save (MPS) The amount by which saving changes when disposable income changes.

Market A group of buyers and sellers of a good or service and the institution or arrangement by which they come together to trade.

Market-based reforms Changes in the market for health care that would make it more like the markets for other goods and services.

Market demand The demand by all the consumers of a given good or service.

Market economy An economy in which the decisions of households and firms interacting in markets allocate economic resources.

Market equilibrium A situation in which quantity demanded equals quantity supplied.

Market for loanable funds The interaction of borrowers and lenders that determines the market interest rate and the quantity of loanable funds exchanged.

Menu costs The costs to firms of changing prices.

Microeconomics The study of how households and firms make choices, how they interact in markets, and how the government attempts to influence their choices.

Mixed economy An economy in which most economic decisions result from the interaction of buyers and sellers in markets but in which the government plays a significant role in the allocation of resources.

Monetarism The macroeconomic theories of Milton Friedman and his followers, particularly the idea that the quantity of money should be increased at a constant rate.

Monetary growth rule A plan for increasing the quantity of money at a fixed rate that does not respond to changes in economic conditions.

Monetary policy The actions the Federal Reserve takes to manage the money supply and interest rates to achieve macroeconomic policy goals.

Money Assets that people are generally willing to accept in exchange for goods and services or for payment of debts.

Moral hazard The actions people take after they have entered into a transaction that make the other party to the transaction worse off.

Multiplier effect The process by which an increase in autonomous expenditure leads to a larger increase in real GDP.

Multiplier The increase in equilibrium real GDP divided

by the increase in autonomous expenditure.

N

Natural rate of unemployment The normal rate of unemployment, consisting of frictional unemployment and structural unemployment.

Net exports Exports minus imports.

Net foreign investment The difference between capital outflows from a country and capital inflows, also equal to net foreign direct investment plus net foreign portfolio investment.

New classical macroeconomics The macroeconomic theories of Robert Lucas and others, particularly the idea that workers and firms have rational expectations.

New growth theory A model of long-run economic growth that emphasizes that technological change is influenced by economic incentives and so is determined by the working of the market system.

Nominal exchange rate The value of one country's currency in terms of another country's currency.

Nominal GDP The value of final goods and services evaluated at current-year prices.

Nominal interest rate The stated interest rate on a loan.

Nonaccelerating inflation rate of unemployment (NAIRU) The unemployment rate at which the inflation rate has no tendency to increase or decrease.

Normal good A good for which the demand increases as income rises and decreases as income falls.

Normative analysis Analysis concerned with what ought to be.

O

Open economy An economy that has interactions in trade or finance with other countries.

Open market operations The buying and selling of Treasury securities by the Federal Reserve in order to control the money supply.

Opportunity cost The highest-valued alternative that must be given up to engage in an activity.

P

Partnership A firm owned jointly by two or more persons and not organized as a corporation.

Patent The exclusive right to produce a product for a period of 20 years from the date the patent is applied for.

Patient Protection and Affordable Care Act (ACA) Health care reform legislation passed by Congress and signed by President Barack Obama in 2010.

Pegging A policy by which a country keeps fixed the exchange rate between its currency and another country's currency.

Per-worker production function The relationship between real GDP per hour worked and capital per hour worked, holding the level of technology constant.

Perfectly competitive market A market that meets the conditions of having (1) many buyers and sellers, (2) all firms selling identical products, and (3) no barriers to new firms entering the market.

Phillips curve A graph showing the short-run relationship between the unemployment rate and the inflation rate.

Positive analysis Analysis concerned with what is.

Potential GDP The level of real GDP attained when all firms are producing at capacity.

Present value The value in today's dollars of funds to be paid or received in the future.

Price ceiling A legally determined maximum price that sellers may charge.

Price floor A legally determined minimum price that sellers may receive.

Price level A measure of the average prices of goods and services in the economy.

Principal–agent problem A problem caused by agents pursuing their own interests rather than the interests of the principals who hired them.

Producer price index (PPI) An average of the prices received by producers of goods and services at all stages of the production process.

Producer surplus The difference between the lowest price a firm would be willing to accept for a good or service and the price it actually receives.

Production possibilities frontier (PPF) A curve showing the maximum attainable combinations of two goods that can be produced with available resources and current technology.

Product market A market for goods—such as computers—or services—such as medical treatment.

Productive efficiency A situation in which a good or service is produced at the lowest possible cost.

Property rights The rights individuals or firms have to the exclusive use of their property, including the right to buy or sell it.

Protectionism The use of trade barriers to shield domestic firms from foreign competition.

Purchasing power parity The theory that in the long run exchange rates move to equalize the purchasing powers of different currencies.

Q

Quantity demanded The amount of a good or service that a consumer is willing and able to purchase at a given price.

Quantity supplied The amount of a good or service that a firm is willing and able to supply at a given price.

Quantity theory of money A theory about the connection between money and prices that assumes that the velocity of money is constant.

Quota A numerical limit a government imposes on the quantity of a good that can be imported into the country.

R

Rational expectations Expectations formed by using all available information about an economic variable.

Real business cycle model A macroeconomic model that focuses on real, rather than monetary, causes of the business cycle.

Real business cycle models Models that focus on real rather than monetary explanations of fluctuations in real GDP.

Real exchange rate The price of domestic goods in terms of foreign goods.

Real GDP The value of final goods and services evaluated at base-year prices.

Real interest rate The nominal interest rate minus the inflation rate.

Recession The period of a business cycle during which total production and total employment are decreasing.

Required reserve ratio The minimum fraction of deposits banks are required by law to keep as reserves.

Required reserves Reserves that a bank is legally required to hold, based on its checking account deposits.

Reserves Deposits that a bank keeps as cash in its vault or on deposit with the Federal Reserve.

Revaluation An increase in a fixed exchange rate.

Rule of law The ability of a government to enforce the laws of the country, particularly with respect to protecting private property and enforcing contracts.

S

Saving and investment equation An equation that shows that national saving is equal to domestic investment plus net foreign investment.

Scarcity A situation in which unlimited wants exceed the limited resources available to fulfill those wants.

Securitization The process of transforming loans or other financial assets into securities.

Security A financial asset—such as a stock or a bond—that can be bought and sold in a financial market.

Separation of ownership from control A situation in a corporation in which the top management, rather than the shareholders, controls day-to-day operations.

Short-run aggregate supply (SRAS) curve A curve that shows the relationship in the short run between the price level and the quantity of real GDP supplied by firms.

Shortage A situation in which the quantity demanded is greater than the quantity supplied.

Simple deposit multiplier The ratio of the amount of deposits created by banks to the amount of new reserves.

Single-payer health care system A system, such as the one in Canada, in which the government provides health insurance to all of the country's residents.

Socialized medicine A health care system under which the government owns most of the hospitals and employs most of the doctors.

Sole proprietorship A firm owned by a single individual and not organized as a corporation.

Speculators Currency traders who buy and sell foreign exchange in an attempt to profit from changes in exchange rates.

Stagflation A combination of inflation and recession, usually resulting from a supply shock.

Stock A financial security that represents partial ownership of a firm.

Stockholders' equity The difference between the value of a corporation's assets and the value of its liabilities; also known as *net worth.*

Structural relationship A relationship that depends on the basic behavior of consumers and firms and that remains unchanged over long periods.

Structural unemployment Unemployment that arises from a persistent mismatch between the skills or attributes of workers and the requirements of jobs.

Substitutes Goods and services that can be used for the same purpose.

Substitution effect The change in the quantity demanded of a good that results from a change in price, making the good more or less expensive relative to other goods that are substitutes.

Supply curve A curve that shows the relationship between the price of a product and the quantity of the product supplied.

Supply schedule A table that shows the relationship between the price of a product and the quantity of the product supplied.

Supply shock An unexpected event that causes the short-run aggregate supply curve to shift.

Surplus A situation in which the quantity supplied is greater than the quantity demanded.

T

Tariff A tax imposed by a government on imports.

Tax incidence The actual division of the burden of a tax between buyers and sellers in a market.

Tax wedge The difference between the pretax and posttax return to an economic activity.

Taylor rule A rule developed by John Taylor that links the Fed's target for the federal funds rate to economic variables.

Technological change A positive or negative change in the ability of a firm to produce a given level of output with a given quantity of inputs.

Terms of trade The ratio at which a country can trade its exports for imports from other countries.

Too-big-to-fail policy A policy under which the federal government does not allow large financial firms to fail, for fear of damaging the financial system.

Trade The act of buying and selling.

Trade-off The idea that, because of scarcity, producing more of one good or service means producing less of another good or service.

Transfer payments Payments by the government to households for which the government does not receive a new good or service in return.

U

Underground economy Buying and selling of goods and services that is concealed from the government to avoid taxes or regulations or because the goods and services are illegal.

Unemployed In government statistics, someone who is not currently at work but who is available for work and who has actively looked for work during the previous month.

Unemployment rate The percentage of the labor force that is unemployed.

V

Value added The market value a firm adds to a product.

Velocity of money The average number of times each dollar in the money supply is used to purchase goods and services included in GDP.

Voluntary exchange A situation that occurs in markets when both the buyer and the seller of a product are made better off by the transaction.

Voluntary export restraint (VER) An agreement negotiated between two countries that places a numerical limit on the quantity of a good that can be imported by one country from the other country.

W

Wall Street Reform and Consumer Protection Act (Dodd-Frank Act) Legislation passed during 2010 that was intended to reform regulation of the financial system.

World Trade Organization (WTO) An international organization that oversees international trade agreements.

COMPANY INDEX

Key terms and the page on which they are defined appear in **boldface**.

CREDITS

Photo

Front matter, *page vii(t),* Courtesy of Glenn Hubbard; *page vii(b),* Courtesy of Tony O'Brien

Chapter 1, *page 2,* Phanie/ Alamy Stock Photo; *page 9,* Chris Grosser/Southcreek Global/ ZUMApress.com/Alamy Stock Photo; *page 16,* Paul Bradbur/ Caiaimage/OJO+/Getty Images

Chapter 2, *page 40,* Michael Short/Bloomberg/Getty Images; *page 53,* Rolf Bruderer/ Glow Images; *page 55B,* Mikael Damkier/Shutterstock; *page 55L,* Elena Elisseeva/Shutterstock; *page 55R,* Stockbroker/MBI/ Alamy Stock Photo; *page 55T,* JupiterImages/Getty Images; *page 58,* Qilai Shen/Bloomberg/ Getty Images; *page 61,* Photos 12/ Alamy Stock Photo

Chapter 3, *page 72,* Xinhua/ Alamy Stock Photo; *page 77,* Maxim Shemetov/Reuters; *page 78,* Tim Boyle/Getty Images; *page 81,* Peter Horree/ Alamy Stock Photo

Chapter 4, *page 108,* Symphonie/ The Image Bank/Getty Images; *page 124,* Silke Woweries/Corbis

Chapter 5, *page 146,* Bill Aron/ PhotoEdit, Inc.

Chapter 6, *page 180,* Anil Kumar/Alamy Stock Photo; *page 191,* Wang Lei/CHINE NOUVELLE/SIPA/Newscom

Chapter 7, *page 214,* Pablo Martinez Monsivais/AP Images; *page 218,* Boston Globe/Getty Images; *page 232,* i4images rm/ Alamy Stock Photo; *page 237,* Lucenet Patrice/Oredia/Alamy Stock Photo

Chapter 8, *page 248,* Regina H. Boone/Detroit Free Press/ TNS/Tribune Content Agency LLC/Alamy Stock Photo; *page 253B,* Mikael Damkier/ Shutterstock; *page 253C,* Yoshio Tomii/SuperStock; *page 253L,* Eric Gevaert/Shutterstock; *page 253R,* Bill Aron/PhotoEdit, Inc.; *page 253T,* JupiterImages/ Getty Images; *page 257,* Herve Coste/MAXPPP/Newscom; *page 259,* Nureldin Abdallah Mohamed/Reuters

Chapter 9, *page 274,* Eduardo Munoz/Reuters; *page 287,* Andrew Burton/Reuters/Landov

Chapter 10, *page 312,* Steve Marcus/Reuters/Landov; *page 327,* Everett Collection; *page 333,* Bradley C. Bower/ Bloomberg/Getty Images

Chapter 11, *page 348,* Sollina Images/Blend Images/Getty Images; *page 351,* Franck Iren/ Author's Image Ltd/Alamy Stock Photo; *page 354,* Grant Neuenburg/Corbis; *page 358,* Peter Turnley/Corbis; *page 375,* Claro Cortes IV/Corbis

Chapter 12, *page 388,* Hon Siu Keung/EyePress/Newscom; *page 406,* Kin Cheung/AP Images; *page 417,* Everett Collection/SuperStock

Chapter 13, *page 432,* Steve Allen/Allen Creative/Alamy Stock Photo; *page 450,* Kimberly White/Corbis; *page 471,* Lebrecht Music and Arts Photo Library/ Alamy Stock Photo

Chapter 14, *page 474,* Laurence Geai/SIPA/Newscom; *page 479,* Bloomberg/Getty Images; *page 482,* Bloomberg/Getty Images; *page 485,* Air Images/ Shutterstock; *page 497,* Lynne Sladky/AP Images; *page 497,* Ezio Petersen/UPI/Landov; *page 497,* Eightfish/Alamy; *page 497,* Dietmar Plewka/imagebroker/ Alamy; *page 502,* Bettmann/Corbis

Chapter 15, *page 512,* PHILIPPE DESMAZES/AFP/Getty Images; *page 544,* Rebecca Cook/Reuters/ Corbis

Chapter 16, *page 556,* Bob Kreisel/ Alamy Stock Photo; *page 572,* Richard Drew/AP Images; *page 580,* Bao Dandan/Xinhua/Alamy Stock Photo; *page 583,* AP Images

Chapter 17, *page 602,* Bloomberg/Getty Images; *page 608,* Paul Bradbury/OJO+/ Getty Images; *page 612,* Lynne Sladky/AP Images; *page 623,* Ron Sachs/ZUMA Press/Newscom

Chapter 18, *page 634,* Du Gang/ ZUMA Press/Newscom

Chapter 19, *page 662,* Kristoffer Tripplaar/Alamy Stock Photo; *page 667,* Bloomberg/Getty Images

Text

Chapter 1 *page 22,* John Hechinger, "FBI Presses Banks to Boost Security as Robberies Rise," *Wall Street Journal,* October 8, 2002.

page 27, © 2011 City Maps Inc.

Chapter 6 *pages 197–198,* Michael Lewis, "The End," *Portfolio,* December 2008.

Chapter 8 *page 250,* Christina Rogers, "Ford Trims Production in China on Select Models to Avoid Price Cuts," *Wall Street Journal,* May 21, 2015.

Chapter 10 *page 320,* Richard Sylla, "Financial Systems and Economic Modernization," *Journal of Economic History,* Vol. 62. No. 2, June 2002.

Chapter 11 *pages 361–362,* Joseph Schumpeter, *Socialism, and Democracy,* New York: Harper, 1962 (originally published 1942), p. 13.

page 364, Robert J. Gordon, "Is U.S. Economic Growth Over? Innovation Confronts Six Headwinds," NBER Working Paper 18315, August 2012.

page 375, Edward Glaeser and Claudia Goldin, eds., *Corruption and Reform: Lessons from America's History,* Chicago, IL: University of Chicago Press, 2006.

Chapter 17 *pages 606–607,* Milton Friedman, "The Role of Monetary Policy," *American Economic Review,* Vol. 58, No. 1, March 1968, 1–17.